Principles *of*
Corporate Finance

.....

THE MCGRAW HILL SERIES IN FINANCE, INSURANCE, AND REAL ESTATE

Financial Management

Block, Hirt, and Danielsen
Foundations of Financial Management
Eighteenth Edition

Brealey, Myers, Allen, and Edmans
Principles of Corporate Finance
Fourteenth Edition

Brealey, Myers, and Allen
Principles of Corporate Finance, Concise
Second Edition

Brealey, Myers, and Marcus
Fundamentals of Corporate Finance
Eleventh Edition

Brooks
FinGame Online 5.0

Bruner
Case Studies in Finance: Managing for Corporate Value Creation
Eighth Edition

Cornett, Adair, and Nofsinger
Finance: Applications and Theory
Sixth Edition

Cornett, Adair, and Nofsinger
M: Finance
Fifth Edition

DeMello
Cases in Finance
Third Edition

Grinblatt (editor)
Stephen A. Ross, Mentor: Influence through Generations

Grinblatt and Titman
Financial Markets and Corporate Strategy
Second Edition

Higgins
Analysis for Financial Management
Thirteenth Edition

Ross, Westerfield, Jaffe, and Jordan
Corporate Finance
Thirteenth Edition

Ross, Westerfield, Jaffe, and Jordan
Corporate Finance: Core Principles and Applications
Sixth Edition

Ross, Westerfield, and Jordan
Essentials of Corporate Finance
Eleventh Edition

Ross, Westerfield, and Jordan
Fundamentals of Corporate Finance
Thirteenth Edition

Shefrin
Behavioral Corporate Finance: Decisions That Create Value
Second Edition

Investments

Bodie, Kane, and Marcus
Essentials of Investments
Twelfth Edition

Bodie, Kane, and Marcus
Investments
Twelfth Edition

Hirt and Block
Fundamentals of Investment Management
Tenth Edition

Jordan and Miller
Fundamentals of Investments: Valuation and Management
Ninth Edition

Stewart, Piros, and Heisler
Running Money: Professional Portfolio Management

Sundaram and Das
Derivatives: Principles and Practice
Second Edition

Financial Institutions and Markets

Rose and Hudgins
Bank Management and Financial Services
Ninth Edition

Rose and Marquis
Financial Institutions and Markets
Eleventh Edition

Saunders and Cornett
Financial Institutions Management: A Risk Management Approach
Tenth Edition

Saunders and Cornett
Financial Markets and Institutions
Eighth Edition

International Finance

Eun and Resnick
International Financial Management
Ninth Edition

Real Estate

Brueggeman and Fisher
Real Estate Finance and Investments
Seventeenth Edition

Ling and Archer
Real Estate Principles: A Value Approach
Sixth Edition

Financial Planning and Insurance

Allen, Melone, Rosenbloom, and Mahoney
Retirement Plans: 401(k)s, IRAs, and Other Deferred Compensation Approaches
Thirteenth Edition

Altfest
Personal Financial Planning
Second Edition

Kapoor, Dlabay, and Hughes
Focus on Personal Finance: An Active Approach to Help You Develop Successful Financial Skills
Seventh Edition

Kapoor, Dlabay, and Hughes
Personal Finance
Fourteenth Edition

Walker and Walker
Personal Finance: Building Your Future
Second Edition

Principles *of*
Corporate Finance

FOURTEENTH EDITION

Richard A. Brealey
Emeritus Professor of Finance
London Business School

Stewart C. Myers
Emeritus Professor of Financial Economics
Sloan School of Management
Massachusetts Institute of Technology

Franklin Allen
Professor of Finance and Economics
Imperial College London

Alex Edmans
Professor of Finance
London Business School

PRINCIPLES OF CORPORATE FINANCE

Published by McGraw Hill LLC, 1325 Avenue of the Americas, New York, NY 10019. Copyright ©2023 by McGraw Hill LLC. All rights reserved. Printed in the United States of America. No part of this publication may be reproduced or distributed in any form or by any means, or stored in a database or retrieval system, without the prior written consent of McGraw Hill LLC, including, but not limited to, in any network or other electronic storage or transmission, or broadcast for distance learning.

Some ancillaries, including electronic and print components, may not be available to customers outside the United States.

This book is printed on acid-free paper.

1 2 3 4 5 6 7 8 9 LWI 27 26 25 24 23 22

ISBN 978-1-265-07415-9
MHID 1-265-07415-1

Cover Image:

Dedication

To our parents.

About the Authors

❯Richard A. Brealey

Emeritus Professor of Finance at London Business School. He is the former president of the European Finance Association and a former director of the American Finance Association. He is a fellow of the British Academy and has served as a special adviser to the Governor of the Bank of England and director of a number of financial institutions. Other books written by Professor Brealey include *Introduction to Risk and Return from Common Stocks*.

❯Stewart C. Myers

Emeritus Professor of Financial Economics at MIT's Sloan School of Management. He is past president of the American Finance Association, a research associate at the National Bureau of Economic Research, a principal of the Brattle Group Inc., and a retired director of Entergy Corporation. His research is primarily concerned with the valuation of real and financial assets, corporate financial policy, and financial aspects of government regulation of business. He is the author of influential research papers on many topics, including adjusted present value, rate of return regulation, pricing and capital allocation in insurance, real options, and moral hazard and information issues in capital structure decisions.

❯Franklin Allen

Professor of Finance and Economics, Imperial College London, and Emeritus Nippon Life Professor of Finance at the Wharton School of the University of Pennsylvania. He is past president of the American Finance Association, Western Finance Association, Society for Financial Studies, Financial Intermediation Research Society, and Financial Management Association. His research has focused on financial innovation, asset price bubbles, comparing financial systems, and financial crises. He is Director of the Brevan Howard Centre for Financial Analysis at Imperial College Business School.

❯Alex Edmans

Professor of Finance at London Business School and Mercers School Memorial Professor of Business at Gresham College. He is Managing Editor of the *Review of Finance* and was previously a tenured professor at Wharton, where he won 14 teaching awards in six years. His research focuses on corporate finance, responsible business, and behavioral finance. He has spoken at the World Economic Forum in Davos and given the TED talk "What to Trust in a Post-Truth World" and the TEDx talk "The Social Responsibility of Business"; he is also advisor to several asset managers. He is the author of *Grow the Pie: How Great Companies Deliver Both Purpose and Profit*. Poets & Quants named him MBA Professor of the Year for 2021.

This book describes the theory and practice of corporate finance. We hardly need to explain why financial managers have to master the practical aspects of their job, but we should spell out why down-to-earth managers need to bother with theory.

Managers learn from experience how to cope with routine problems. But the best managers are also able to respond to change. To do so you need more than time-honored rules of thumb; you must understand why companies and financial markets behave the way they do. In other words, you need a *theory* of finance.

That should not sound intimidating. Good theory helps you to grasp what is going on in the world around you. It helps you to ask the right questions when times change and new problems need to be analyzed. It also tells you which things you do *not* need to worry about. Throughout this book, we show how managers use financial theory to solve practical problems.

Of course, the theory presented in this book is not perfect and complete—no theory is. There are some famous controversies where financial economists cannot agree. We have not glossed over these disagreements. We set out the arguments for each side and tell you where we stand.

Much of this book is concerned with understanding what financial managers do and why. But we also say what financial managers *should* do to increase company value. Where theory suggests that financial managers are making mistakes, we say so, while admitting that there may be hidden reasons for their actions. In brief, we have tried to be fair but to pull no punches.

This book may be your first view of the world of modern finance. If so, you will read first for new ideas, and for an understanding of how finance theory translates into practice. But eventually you will be in a position to make financial decisions, not just study them. At that point, you can turn to this book as a reference and guide.

Changes in the Fourteenth Edition

What has changed in this edition? You will have seen the first change on the cover: Alex Edmans has joined the author team. Alex is a global authority in corporate finance, with particular expertise in corporate governance, responsible business, and behavioral finance—three areas we have significantly bolstered as we will shortly describe. In addition to being a leading researcher, he has substantial practitioner expertise. He has also won a multitude of teaching awards at MIT, Wharton, and London Business School and is particularly noted for the ability to explain complex finance concepts in simple language. He recently gave a year-long Gresham College public lecture series on the principles of finance attended by a diverse audience, from schoolchildren to retirees.

This expansion of the author team has led to a number of important changes. For example, in recent years many observers have questioned companies' focus on profits and have suggested that managers should promote the interests of *all* stakeholders rather than simply seeking to maximize shareholder value. The issue is an important one and we have, therefore, added a new chapter, Chapter 20, that discusses these different corporate objectives, how far they conflict, and how a responsible business should behave.

The structure of a firm's governance is closely related to its objectives. We have therefore moved the material on corporate governance and agency issues to Chapter 19, where it now sits next to the chapter on corporate objectives. This chapter has also been substantially rewritten.

Other chapters with major changes include the two chapters on the pricing of risky assets (Chapters 7 and 8). Chapter 7 now focuses on portfolio choice and a stock's effect on portfolio risk, while Chapter 8 concentrates on asset pricing. This is a clearer separation of topics than in previous editions; we think that it is more logical and helps understanding.

The discussion of market efficiency (Chapter 12) has also undergone substantial revision with additional and updated sections on empirical evidence. The chapter also contains an expanded discussion of behavioral finance and the evidence for behavioral biases.

Financial innovation today is being driven by technological developments such as artificial intelligence, big data, and cloud computing. Chapter 13 now includes a new section that reviews seven ways in which financial technology is changing financial practice.

U.S. financial managers work in a global environment and need to understand the financial systems of other countries. Also, many of the text's readers come from countries other than the United States. Therefore, in recent editions, we have progressively introduced more international material, including information about the major developing economies, such as China and India. Material on international differences in financing is now integrated in Chapter 14, while Chapter 19 includes a discussion of governance systems around the world.

PEDAGOGICAL CHANGES

Throughout, we have tried to explain the material much more clearly--importantly, without dumbing it down. The style of this edition is more direct and less whimsical, with terms being precisely defined and key concepts made explicit rather than having to be inferred from the narrative. In many cases, the changes consist of some updated data here and a new example there. Often, these additions reflect some recent development in the financial markets or company practice.

We have also changed the introduction to each chapter to include summaries of the content of each of the chapter's sections. We think that this will make it easier for the reader to understand the organization of the chapter and to jump forward to a particular topic of interest. Chapters now also conclude with key takeaway bullet points summarizing the chapter's principal lessons.

Within each chapter we have interspersed a number of new self-test questions that provide an opportunity for readers to pause and check their understanding. Answers to these self-tests are located at the end of the chapter.

The Beyond the Page digital extensions and applications provide additional examples, anecdotes, spreadsheet programs, and more detailed explanations and practice examples of some topics. This extra material makes it possible to escape from the constraints of the printed page by providing more explanation for readers who need it and additional material for those who would like to dig deeper. There are now more than 150 of these apps. They are seamlessly available with a click on the e-version of the book, but they are also readily accessible in the traditional hard copy of the text using the shortcut URLs provided in the margins of relevant pages. Check out **mhhe.com/brealey14e** to learn more.

Examples of these applications include:

- **Chapter 2** Would you like to learn more about how to use Excel spreadsheets to solve time value of money problems? A Beyond the Page application shows how to do so.
- **Chapter 3** Do you need to calculate a bond's duration, see how it predicts the effect of small interest rate changes on bond price, calculate the duration of a common stock, or learn how to measure convexity? The duration app allows you to do so.
- **Chapter 5** Want more practice in valuing annuities? There is an application that provides worked examples and hands-on practice.

- **Chapter 7** Ever wondered how COVID-19 has affected the risk of stocks in the travel industry? An app provides the answer.
- **Chapter 12** Want an example of how speculative trading can swamp the actions of arbitrageurs? The app on the explosion in the price of GameStop shares provides one.
- **Chapter 18** The text briefly describes the flow-to-equity method for valuing businesses, but using the method can be tricky. We provide an application that guides you step by step.
- **Chapter 22** The Black–Scholes Beyond the Page application provides an option calculator. It also shows how to estimate the option's sensitivity to changes in the inputs and how to measure an option's risk.

❯ Chapter Structure

Each chapter of the book includes an introductory preview, a list of key takeaways, and suggested further reading. The list of candidates for further reading is now voluminous. Rather than trying to include every important article, we largely list survey articles or general books. We give more specific references in footnotes.

In addition to the self-test questions within the chapter, each chapter is followed by a set of problems on both numerical and conceptual topics, together with a few challenge problems.

We include a Finance on the Web section in chapters where it makes sense to do so. This section now houses a number of Web Projects, along with new Data Analysis problems. These exercises seek to familiarize the reader with some useful websites and to explain how to download and process data from the web.

The book also contains 12 end-of-chapter Mini-Cases. These include specific questions to guide the case analyses. Answers to the mini-cases are available to instructors on the book's website.

Spreadsheet programs such as Excel are tailor-made for many financial calculations. Several chapters include boxes that introduce the most useful financial functions and provide some short practice questions. We show how to use the Excel function key to locate the function and then enter the data. We think that this approach is much simpler than trying to remember the formula for each function.

We conclude the book with a glossary of financial terms.

The 34 chapters in this book are divided into 12 parts. Parts 1, 2, and 3 cover valuation and capital investment decisions, including portfolio theory, asset pricing models, and the cost of capital. Parts 4 through 9 cover financing decisions, payout policy and capital structure, corporate objectives and governance, options, debt financing, and risk management. Part 10 covers financial analysis, planning, and working-capital management. Part 11 covers mergers and acquisitions, and corporate restructuring. Part 12 concludes.

We realize that instructors will wish to select topics and may prefer a different sequence. We have therefore written chapters so that topics can be introduced in several logical orders. For example, there should be no difficulty in reading the chapters on financial analysis and planning before the chapters on valuation and capital investment.

❯ Acknowledgments

We have a long list of people to thank for their helpful criticism of earlier editions and for assistance in preparing this one. They include Faiza Arshad, Aleijda de Cazenove Balsan, Donna Cheung, Kedran Garrison, Robert Pindyck, and Gretchen Slemmons at MIT; Elroy Dimson, Paul Marsh, Mike Staunton, and Stefania Uccheddu at London Business School; Lynda Borucki, Marjorie Fischer, Larry Kolbe, Michael Vilbert, Bente Villadsen, and Fiona Wang at The Brattle Group Inc.; Alex Triantis at Johns Hopkins University; Adam Kolasinski at Texas A&M University; Simon Gervais at Duke University; Michael Chui at Bank for International Settlements; Pedro Matos at the University of Virginia; Yupana Wiwattanakantang at National University of Singapore; Nickolay Gantchev at Warwick University; Tina Horowitz at the University of Pennsylvania; Lin Shen at INSEAD; Darien Huang at Tudor Investment; Julie Wulf at Harvard University; Jinghua Yan at SAC Capital; Bennett Stewart at EVA Dimensions; and Mobeen Iqbal, Antoine Uettwiller and Tong Yu at Imperial College London.

We would also like to thank the dedicated experts who have helped with updates to the instructor materials and online content in Connect and LearnSmart, including Nicholas Racculia.

We want to express our appreciation to those instructors whose insightful comments and suggestions were invaluable to us during the revision process:

Ibrahim Affaneh *Indiana University of Pennsylvania*
Neyaz Ahmed *University of Maryland*
Alexander Amati *University of Connecticut*
Anne Anderson *Middle Tennessee State University*
Noyan Arsen *Koc University*
Anders Axvarn *Gothenburg University*
John Banko *University of Florida, Gainesville*
Michael Barry *Boston College*
Jan Bartholdy *Aarhus University*
Penny Belk *Loughborough University*
Omar Benkato *Ball State University*
Erik Benrud *Indiana University*
Ronald Benson *University of Maryland, University College*
Peter Berman *University of British Columbia*
Kevin Boeh *University of Washington*
Tom Boulton *Miami University of Ohio*
Edward Boyer *Temple University*
Alon Brav *Duke University*
Jean Canil *University of Adelaide*
Robert Carlson *Bethany College*
Chuck Chahyadi *Eastern Illinois University*
Chongyang Chen *Pacific Lutheran University*
Fan Chen *University of Mississippi*
Bill Christie *Vanderbilt University*
Celtin Ciner *University of North Carolina, Wilmington*
John Cooney *Texas Tech University*
Charles Cuny *Washington University, St. Louis*
John Davenport *Regent University*
Ray DeGennaro *University of Tennessee, Knoxville*
Adri DeRidder *Uppsala University*
William Dimovski *Deakin University, Melbourne*
David Ding *Nanyang Technological University*
Robert Duvic *University of Texas at Austin*
Susan Edwards *Grand Valley State University*
Riza Emekter *Robert Morris University*
Robert Everett *Millersville University*
Dave Fehr *Southern New Hampshire University*
Donald Flagg *University of Tampa*
Frank Flanegin *Robert Morris University*
Zsuzanna Fluck *Michigan State University*
Connel Fullenkamp *Duke University*
Mark Garmaise *University of California, Los Angeles*
Sharon Garrison *University of Arizona*
Christopher Geczy *University of Pennsylvania*
George Geis *University of Virginia*
Bradford Gibbs *Brown University*
Stuart Gillan *University of North Texas*
Felix Goltz *Edhec Business School*
Ning Gong *Deakin Business School*
Levon Goukasian *Pepperdine University*
Gary Gray *Pennsylvania State University*
C. J. Green *Loughborough University*
Mark Griffiths *Miami University*
Anthony Gu *SUNY Geneseo*
Re-Jin Guo *University of Illinois, Chicago*
Pia Gupta *California State University, Long Beach*
Ann Hackert *Idaho State University*
Winfried Hallerbach *Robeco Asset Management*
Milton Harris *University of Chicago*
Mary Hartman *Bentley College*
Glenn Henderson *University of Cincinnati*
Donna Hitscherich *Columbia University*
Ronald Hoffmeister *Arizona State University*
James Howard *University of Maryland, College Park*
George Jabbour *George Washington University*
Ravi Jagannathan *Northwestern University*

Abu Jalal *Suffolk University*
Nancy Jay *Mercer University*
Thadavillil Jithendranathan *University of Saint Thomas*
Travis Jones *Florida Gulf Coast University*
Kathleen Kahle *University of Arizona*
Jarl Kallberg *NYU, Stern School of Business*
Ron Kaniel *University of Rochester*
Steve Kaplan *University of Chicago*
Eric Kelley *University of Tennessee, Knoxville*
Arif Khurshed *Manchester Business School*
Ken Kim *University at Buffalo School of Management, SUNY*
Jiro Kondo *McGill University*
C. R. Krishnaswamy *Western Michigan University*
George Kutner *Marquette University*
Dirk Laschanzky *University of Iowa*
Scott Lee *University of Nevada, Las Vegas*
Becky Lafrancois *Colorado School of Mines*
Bob Lightner *San Diego Christian College*
David Lins *University of Illinois, Urbana*
Brandon Lockhart *University of Nebraska, Lincoln*
David Lovatt *University of East Anglia*
Greg Lucado *University of the Sciences in Philadelphia*
Debbie Lucas *Massachusetts Institute of Technology*
Brian Lucey *Trinity College, Dublin*
Suren Mansinghka *University of California, Irvine*
Ernst Maug *University of Mannheim*
George McCabe *University of Nebraska*
Eric McLaughlin *California State University, Pomona*
Joe Messina *San Francisco State University*
Tim Michael *University of Houston, Clear Lake*
Dag Michalsen *BI Norwegian Business School*
Franklin Michello *Middle Tennessee State University*
Peter Moles *University of Edinburgh*
Katherine Morgan *Columbia University*
James Nelson *East Carolina University*
James Owens *West Texas A&M University*
Darshana Palkar *Minnesota State University, Mankato*
Claus Parum *Copenhagen Business School*
Dilip Patro *Federal Deposit Insurance Corporation (FDIC)*
John Percival *Minerva University*
Birsel Pirim *The Ohio State University*
Latha Ramchand *University of Houston*
Narendar V. Rao *Northeastern University*
Rathin Rathinasamy *Ball State University*
Raghavendra Rau *University of Cambridge*
Joshua Rauh *Stanford University*
Charu Reheja *TriageLogic Group*
Thomas Rhee *California State University, Long Beach*
Tom Rietz *University of Iowa*
Robert Ritchey *Texas Tech University*
Michael Roberts *University of Pennsylvania*
Mo Rodriguez *Texas Christian University*
John Rozycki *Drake University*
Frank Ryan *San Diego State University*
Patricia Ryan *Colorado State University*
George Sarraf *University of California, Irvine*
Eric Sartell *Whitworth University*
Marc Schauten *Vrije Universiteit Amsterdam*
Anjolein Schmeits *NYU Stern School of Business*
Brad Scott *Webster University*
Nejat Seyhun *University of Michigan*

Jay Shanken *Emory University*
Chander Shekhar *University of Melbourne*
Hamid Shomali *Golden Gate University*
Richard Simonds *Michigan State University*
Bernell Stone *Brigham Young University*
John Strong *College of William & Mary*
Avanidhar Subrahmanyam *University of California, Los Angeles*
Tim Sullivan *UKG (Ultimate Kronos Group)*
Shrinivasan Sundaram *Ball State University*
Chu-Sheng Tai *Texas Southern University*
Tom Tallerico *Dowling College*
Stephen Todd *Loyola University, Chicago*
Walter Torous *University of California, Los Angeles*
Emery Trahan *Northeastern University*
Gary Tripp *Southern New Hampshire University*
Ilias Tsiakas *University of Guelph*
David Vang *St. Thomas University*
Nikhil Varaiya, *San Diego State University*
Steve Venti *Dartmouth College*
Joseph Vu *DePaul University*
John Wald *University of Texas, San Antonio*
Chong Wang *Naval Postgraduate School*
Faye Wang *University of Illinois, Chicago*
Kelly Welch *University of Kansas*
Jill Wetmore *Saginaw Valley State University*
John Wheeler *University of Michigan*
Patrick Wilkie *University of Virginia*
Matt Will *University of Indianapolis*
David Williams *Texas A&M University, Commerce*
Kalman Vadasz *Stevens Institute of Technology*
Art Wilson *George Washington University*
Albert Wang *Auburn University*
Shee Wong *University of Minnesota, Duluth*
Bob Wood *Tennessee Tech University*
Fei Xie *University of Delaware*
Minhua Yang *University of Central Florida*
David Zalewski *Providence College*
Chenying Zhang *University of Pennsylvania*

This list is surely incomplete. We know how much we owe to our colleagues at London Business School, MIT's Sloan School of Management, Imperial College London, and the University of Pennsylvania's Wharton School. In many cases, the ideas that appear in this book are as much their ideas as ours.

We would also like to thank all those at McGraw Hill Education who worked on the book, including Chuck Synovec, Executive Brand Manager; Allison McCabe-Carroll, Senior Product Developer; Trina Mauer, Executive Marketing Manager; Fran Simon, Project Manager; and Matt Diamond, Designer.

Richard A. Brealey
Stewart C. Myers
Franklin Allen
Alex Edmans

Pedagogical Features

❯ Chapter Overview

Each chapter begins with a brief narrative and outline to explain the concepts that will be covered in more depth. Useful websites related to material for each part are provided in the Connect library.

❯ Finance in Practice Boxes

Relevant news articles, often from financial publications, appear in various chapters throughout the text. Aimed at bringing real-world flavor into the classroom, these boxes provide insight into the business world today.

❯ Numbered Examples

Numbered and titled examples are called out within chapters to further illustrate concepts. Students can learn how to solve specific problems step-by-step and apply key principles to answer concrete questions and scenarios.

❯ Self-Test Questions

Each chapter includes a number of self-test questions that allow students to check their understanding. Answers to these questions are given at the end of the chapter.

❯ Numbered Equations

Where a result can be stated formally, we do so in the form of a numbered equation. However, we are also careful to explain the intuition behind a financial theory, so that readers without a quantitative background should be able to read with understanding.

❯ Beyond the Page Interactive Content and Applications

Additional resources and hands-on applications are just a click away. Students can use the web address or click on the icon in the eBook to learn more about key concepts and try out calculations, tables, and figures when they go Beyond the Page.

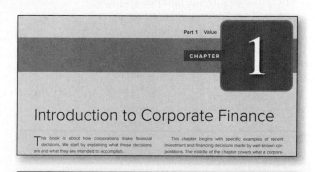

FINANCE IN PRACTICE

Arithmetic Averages and Compound Annual Returns

EXAMPLE 9.1 • A Railroad Industry Cost of Capital for Berkshire Hathaway

6.4 Self-Test

The following simple formula[5] shows how DOL is related to the business's fixed costs (including depreciation) as a proportion of pretax profits:

$$DOL = 1 + \frac{fixed\ costs\ including\ depreciation}{pretax\ profits} \qquad (10.1)$$

BEYOND THE PAGE

Try It! Figure 10.3: Decision tree for the pharmaceutical project

mhhe.com/brealey14e

Excel

▶ Spreadsheet Functions Boxes

These boxes provide detailed examples of how to use Excel spreadsheets when applying financial concepts. Questions that apply to the spreadsheet follow for additional practice.

▶ Excel Exhibits

Select tables are set as spreadsheets, and the corresponding Excel files are also available in Connect and through the Beyond the Page features.

		Year 0	1	2	3	4	5	6	7
1	Capital investment	12,000							−1,949[a]
2	Accumulated depreciation		2,000	4,000	6,000	8,000	10,000	12,000	0
3	Year-end book value	12,000	10,000	8,000	6,000	4,000	2,000	0	0
4	Working capital		550	1,289	3,261	4,890	3,583	2,002	0
5	Revenues		523	12,887	32,610	48,901	35,834	19,717	
6	Expenses	4,000	3,037	8,939	20,883	30,809	23,103	13,602	
7	Depreciation[a]		2,000	2,000	2,000	2,000	2,000	2,000	0
8	Pretax profit (5 − 6 − 7 − 1)	−4,000	−4,514	1,948	9,727	16,092	10,731	4,115	1,949[a]
9	Tax at 21%	−840[c]	−948	409	2,043	3,379	2,254	864	409
10	Profit after tax (8 − 9)	−3,160	−3,566	1,539	7,684	12,713	8,477	3,251	1,540

▶**TABLE 6.2** Initial forecast data for guano project.

[a] In the income statement, the initial investment of $12 million is depreciated straight-line over the six years.
[b] Gain on sale of assets. The asset has been entirely depreciated for tax purposes and the entire sales price is, therefore, subject to tax.
[c] A negative tax payment means a cash inflow, assuming that IM&C can use the tax loss on the guano project to shield income from the rest of its operations.

End-of-Chapter Features

❯ Problem Sets

Beside each end-of-chapter problem we note the
section of the chapter to which the question relates.
This helps instructors create assignments and makes
it simpler for students to look back for help. These
end-of-chapter problems give students hands-on
practice with key concepts and applications.

PROBLEM SETS Mc Graw Hill **connect**   Select problems are available in McGraw-Hill's *Connect*. Please see the preface for more information.

1. **Behavioral biases (S11.1)** Explain why setting a higher discount rate is not a cure for upward-biased cash-flow forecasts.

2. **Behavioral biases (S11.1)** Look back to the cash flows for projects F and G in Section 5-3. The cost of capital was assumed to be 10%. Assume that the forecasted cash flows for projects of this type are overstated by 8% on average. That is, the forecast for each cash flow from each project should be reduced by 8%. But a lazy financial manager, unwilling to take the time to argue with the projects' sponsors, instructs them to use a discount rate of 18%.
   a. What are the projects' true NPVs?
   b. What are the NPVs at the 18% discount rate?
   c. Are there any circumstances in which the 18% discount rate would give the correct NPVs? (*Hint:* Could upward bias be more severe for more-distant cash flows?)

3. **Market values (S11.2)** Your brother-in-law wants you to join him in purchasing a building on the outskirts of town. You and he would then develop and run a Taco Palace restaurant. Both of you are extremely optimistic about future real estate prices in this area, and your brother-in-law has prepared a cash-flow forecast that implies a large positive NPV. This calculation assumes sale of the property after 10 years. What further calculations should you do before going ahead?

CHALLENGE PROBLEMS

20. **Economic rents (S11.3)** Accidental setbacks can result in negative rents in any year. But can a project have *expected* positive rents in some years and negative expected rents in other years? Explain.

21. **Economic rents (S11.3)** The manufacture of polysyllabic acid is a competitive industry. Most plants have an annual output of 100,000 tons. Operating costs are $0.90 a ton, and the sales price is $1 a ton. A 100,000-ton plant costs $100,000 and has an indefinite life. Its current scrap value of $60,000 is expected to decline to $57,900 over the next two years.

    Phlogiston Inc. proposes to invest $100,000 in a plant that employs a new low-cost process to manufacture polysyllabic acid. The plant has the same capacity as existing units, but operating costs are $0.85 a ton. Phlogiston estimates that it has two years' lead over each of its rivals in use of the process but is unable to build any more plants itself before year 2. Also it believes that demand over the next two years is likely to be sluggish and that its new plant will therefore cause temporary overcapacity.

    You can assume that there are no taxes and that the cost of capital is 10%.

❯ Excel Problems

Most chapters contain problems, denoted by an icon,
specifically linked to Excel spreadsheets that are
available in Connect and through the Beyond the
Page features.

BEYOND THE PAGE
Try it! The Black-Scholes model
mhhe.com/brealey14e

3. **Expansion options (S23.1)** You own a one-year call option to buy one acre of Los Angeles real estate. The exercise price is $2 million, and the current, appraised market value of the land is $1.7 million. The land is currently used as a parking lot, generating just enough money to cover real estate taxes. The annual standard deviation is 15% and the interest rate 12%. How much is your call worth? Use the Black–Scholes formula. You may find it helpful to go to the spreadsheet for Chapter 22, which calculates Black–Scholes values (see the Beyond the Page feature).

❯ Finance on the Web

These web exercises give students the opportunity to explore financial websites on their own. The web exercises make it easy to include current, real-world data in the classroom.

❯ Mini-Cases

Mini-cases are included in select chapters so students can apply their knowledge to real-world scenarios.

MINI-CASE • • •

Waldo County

Waldo County, the well-known real estate developer, worked long hours, and he expected his staff to do the same. So George Chavez was not surprised to receive a call from the boss just as George was about to leave for a long summer's weekend.

Mr. County's success had been built on a remarkable instinct for a good site. He would exclaim "Location! Location! Location!" at some point in every planning meeting. Yet finance was not his strong suit. On this occasion, he wanted George to go over the figures for a new $90 million outlet mall designed to intercept tourists heading downeast from Bar Harbor through southern Maine. "First thing Monday will do just fine," he said as he handed George the file. "I'll be in my house in Bar Harbor if you need me."

George's first task was to draw up a summary of the projected revenues and costs. The results are shown in Table 10.6. Note that the mall's revenues would come from two sources: The company would charge retailers an annual rent for the space they occupied and, in addition, it would receive 5% of each store's gross sales.

Construction of the mall was likely to take three years. The construction costs could be depreciated straight-line over 15 years starting in year 3. As in the case of the company's other developments, the mall would be built to the highest specifications and would not need to be rebuilt until year 17. The land was expected to retain its value, but could not be depreciated for tax purposes.

Construction costs, revenues, operating and maintenance costs, and local real estate taxes were all likely to rise in line with inflation, which was forecasted at 2% a year. Local real estate taxes are deductible for corporate tax. The company's corporate tax rate was 25% and the cost of capital was 9% in nominal terms.

George decided first to check that the project made financial sense. He then proposed to look at some of the things that might go wrong. His boss certainly had a nose for a good retail project, but he was not infallible. The Salome project had been a disaster because store sales had turned out to be 40% below forecast. What if that happened here? George wondered just how far sales could fall short of forecast before the project would be underwater.

> In this edition, we have gone to great lengths to ensure that our supplements are equal in quality and authority to the text itself.

MCGRAW HILL'S *CONNECT*

Less Managing. More Teaching. Greater Learning.

McGraw Hill's *Connect* is an online assignment and assessment solution that connects students with the tools and resources they'll need to achieve success.

McGraw Hill's *Connect* helps prepare students for their future by enabling faster learning, more efficient studying, and higher retention of knowledge.

McGraw Hill's *Connect* Features

 *Connect* offers a number of powerful tools and features to make managing assignments easier, so faculty can spend more time teaching. With *Connect,* students can engage with their coursework anytime and anywhere, making the learning process more accessible and efficient. *Connect* offers the features described here.

Simple Assignment Management

With *Connect,* creating assignments is easier than ever, so instructors can spend more time teaching and less time managing. The assignment management function enables the instructor to:

- Create and deliver assignments easily from end-of-chapter questions and test bank items.
- Streamline lesson planning, student progress reporting, and assignment grading to make classroom management more efficient than ever.
- Go paperless with the eBook and online submission and grading of student assignments.

Automatic Grading

When it comes to studying, time is precious. *Connect* helps students learn more efficiently by providing feedback and practice material when they need it, where they need it. When it comes to teaching, the instructor's time is also precious. The grading function enables the instructor to:

- Score assignments automatically, giving students immediate feedback on their work and side-by-side comparisons with correct answers.
- Access and review each response, manually change grades, or leave comments for students to review.
- Reinforce classroom concepts with practice tests and instant quizzes.

Test Builder Within Connect

Available within Connect, Test Builder is a cloud-based tool that enables instructors to format tests that can be printed or administered within an LMS. Test Builder offers a modern, streamlined interface for easy content configuration that matches course needs, without requiring a download.

Test Builder allows you to:

- Access all test bank content from a particular title.
- Easily pinpoint the most relevant content through robust filtering options.
- Manipulate the order of questions or scramble questions and/or answers.
- Pin questions to a specific location within a test.
- Determine your preferred treatment of algorithmic questions.
- Choose the layout and spacing.
- Add instructions and configure default settings.

Test Builder provides a secure interface for better protection of content and allows for just-in-time updates to flow directly into assessments.

Instructor Library

The *Connect* Instructor Library provides additional resources to improve student engagement in and out of class. This library contains information about the book and the authors, as well as all of the instructor supplements, many of which were carefully updated for this edition by Nicholas Racculia, St. Vincent College.

- **Instructor's Manual** The Instructor's Manual contains an overview of each chapter, teaching tips, learning objectives, challenge areas, key terms, and an annotated outline that provides references to the PowerPoint slides.

- **Solutions Manual** The Solutions Manual contains solutions to all basic, intermediate, and challenge problems found at the end of each chapter.
- **Test Bank** The Test Bank contains hundreds of multiple-choice and short answer/discussion questions, updated based on the revisions of the authors. The level of difficulty varies, as indicated by the easy, medium, or difficult labels.
- **PowerPoint Presentations** The PowerPoint presentations contain exhibits, outlines, key points, and summaries in a visually stimulating collection of slides. The instructor can edit, print, or rearrange the slides to fit the needs of his or her course.
- **Beyond the Page** The authors have created a wealth of additional examples, explanations, and applications, available for quick access by instructors and students. Each Beyond the Page feature is called out in the text with an icon that links directly to the content.
- **Excel Solutions and Templates** There are templates for select exhibits, as well as various end-of-chapter problems that have been set as Excel spreadsheets—all denoted by an icon. They correlate with specific concepts in the text and allow students to work through financial problems and gain experience using spreadsheets. Useful Spreadsheet Functions Boxes are sprinkled throughout the text to provide helpful prompts on working in Excel.

SmartBook: Diagnostic and Adaptive Learning of Concepts

SMARTBOOK® SmartBook®, powered by LearnSmart, is the first and only adaptive reading experience designed to change the way students read and learn. It creates a personalized reading experience by highlighting the most important concepts a student needs to learn at each moment in time. As a student engages with Smart-Book, the reading experience continuously adapts by highlighting content based on what the student knows and doesn't know. This ensures that the focus is on the content he or she needs to learn, while simultaneously promoting long-term retention of material. Use SmartBook's real-time reports to quickly identify the concepts that require more attention from individual students—or the entire class. The end result? Students are more engaged with course content, can better prioritize their time, and come to class ready to participate.

Student Study Center

The Connect Student Study Center is the place for students to access additional resources. The Student Study Center:

- Offers students quick access to the Beyond the Page features, Excel files and templates, lectures, practice materials, eBooks, and more.
- Provides instant practice material and study questions, easily accessible on the go.

Student Progress Tracking

Connect keeps instructors informed about how each student, section, and class is performing, allowing for more productive use of lecture and office hours. The progress-tracking function enables you to

- View scored work immediately and track individual or group performance with assignment and grade reports.
- Access an instant view of student or class performance relative to learning objectives.

TEGRITY CAMPUS: LECTURES 24/7

 Tegrity in Connect is a tool that makes class time available 24/7 by automatically capturing every lecture. With a simple one-click start-and-stop process, you capture all computer screens and corresponding audio in a format that is easy to search, frame by frame. Students can replay any part of any class with easy-to-use, browser-based viewing on a PC, Mac, iPad, or other mobile devices.

Educators know that the more students can see, hear, and experience class resources, the better they learn. In fact, studies prove it. Tegrity's unique search feature helps students efficiently find what they need, when they need it, across an entire semester of class recordings. Help turn your students' study time into learning moments immediately supported by your lecture. With Tegrity, you also increase intent listening and class participation by easing students' concerns about note-taking. Using Tegrity in Connect will make it more likely you will see students' faces, not the tops of their heads.

MCGRAW HILL CUSTOMER CARE CONTACT INFORMATION

At McGraw Hill, we understand that getting the most from new technology can be challenging. That's why our services don't stop after you purchase our products. You can e-mail our Product Specialists 24 hours a day to get product training online. Or you can search our knowledge bank of Frequently Asked Questions on our support website.

For Customer Support, call 800-331-5094 or visit **www.mhhe.com/support**. One of our Technical Support Analysts will be able to assist you in a timely fashion.

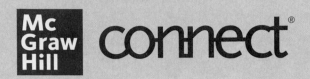

Instructors: Student Success Starts with You

Tools to enhance your unique voice

Want to build your own course? No problem. Prefer to use an OLC-aligned, prebuilt course? Easy. Want to make changes throughout the semester? Sure. And you'll save time with Connect's auto-grading too.

65%
Less Time Grading

Laptop: McGraw Hill; Woman/dog: George Doyle/Getty Images

Study made personal

Incorporate adaptive study resources like SmartBook® 2.0 into your course and help your students be better prepared in less time. Learn more about the powerful personalized learning experience available in SmartBook 2.0 at **www.mheducation.com/highered/connect/smartbook**

Affordable solutions, added value

Make technology work for you with LMS integration for single sign-on access, mobile access to the digital textbook, and reports to quickly show you how each of your students is doing. And with our Inclusive Access program you can provide all these tools at a discount to your students. Ask your McGraw Hill representative for more information.

Padlock: Jobalou/Getty Images

Solutions for your challenges

A product isn't a solution. Real solutions are affordable, reliable, and come with training and ongoing support when you need it and how you want it. Visit **www.supportateverystep.com** for videos and resources both you and your students can use throughout the semester.

Checkmark: Jobalou/Getty images

Students: Get Learning that Fits You

Effective tools for efficient studying

Connect is designed to help you be more productive with simple, flexible, intuitive tools that maximize your study time and meet your individual learning needs. Get learning that works for you with Connect.

Study anytime, anywhere

Download the free ReadAnywhere app and access your online eBook, SmartBook 2.0, or Adaptive Learning Assignments when it's convenient, even if you're offline. And since the app automatically syncs with your Connect account, all of your work is available every time you open it. Find out more at **www.mheducation.com/readanywhere**

"I really liked this app—it made it easy to study when you don't have your textbook in front of you."

- Jordan Cunningham, Eastern Washington University

Everything you need in one place

Your Connect course has everything you need—whether reading on your digital eBook or completing assignments for class, Connect makes it easy to get your work done.

Calendar: owattaphotos/Getty Images

Learning for everyone

McGraw Hill works directly with Accessibility Services Departments and faculty to meet the learning needs of all students. Please contact your Accessibility Services Office and ask them to email accessibility@mheducation.com, or visit **www.mheducation.com/about/accessibility** for more information.

Top: Jenner Images/Getty Images, Left: Hero Images/Getty Images, Right: Hero Images/Getty Images

Brief Contents

Contents

5   Net Present Value and Other Investment Criteria   119

6   Making Investment Decisions with the Net Present Value Rule   149

I Part Two: Risk

7   Introduction to Risk, Diversification, and Portfolio Selection   184

I Part Four: Financing Decisions and Market Efficiency

12 Efficient Markets and Behavioral Finance   327

13 An Overview of Corporate Financing   368

14 How Corporations Issue Securities   399

I Part Five: Payout Policy and Capital Structure

I Part Six: Corporate Objectives and Governance

19 Agency Problems and Corporate Governance 555

20 Stakeholder Capitalism and Responsible Business 588

Note: Present value tables are available in Connect.

CHAPTER

1

Introduction to Corporate Finance

This book is about how corporations make financial decisions. We start by explaining what these decisions are and what they are intended to accomplish.

Corporations invest in real assets, which generate income. Some of these assets, such as plant and machinery, are tangible; others, such as brand names and patents, are intangible. Corporations finance their investments through the money they earn from selling goods and services, and by raising additional cash through borrowing from banks or issuing shares to investors.

Thus, the financial manager faces two broad financial questions: First, what investments should the company make? Second, how should it pay for those investments? The investment decision involves spending money; the financing decision involves raising it.

A large corporation may have hundreds of thousands of shareholders. These shareholders differ in many ways, including their wealth, risk tolerance, and investment horizon. Yet we shall see that they usually share the same financial objective. They want the financial manager to increase the value of the corporation; in an efficient market, this will in turn increase its current stock price.

Thus, the secret of success in financial management is to increase value. That is easy to say but not very helpful. Instructing the financial manager to increase shareholder value is like advising an investor in the stock market to find stocks that will go up in the future. The problem is how to do it. That's the purpose of this book. It covers the concepts that govern good financial decisions, and it shows you how to use the tools of the trade of modern finance.

This chapter begins with specific examples of recent investment and financing decisions made by well-known corporations. The middle of the chapter covers what a corporation is and what its financial managers do. We conclude by explaining why increasing the market value of the corporation is a sensible financial goal.

Financial managers increase value whenever the corporation earns a higher return than shareholders can earn for themselves. The shareholders' investment opportunities *outside* the corporation set the standard for investments *inside* the corporation. Financial managers, therefore, refer to the *opportunity cost* of the capital contributed by shareholders.

Managers are, of course, human beings with their own interests and circumstances; they are not always the perfect servants of shareholders. Therefore, corporations must combine governance rules and procedures with appropriate incentives to make sure that all managers and employees pull together to increase value.

This chapter introduces five themes that occur again and again throughout the book:

1. Corporate finance is all about maximizing shareholder value.
2. Maximizing shareholder value involves considering the long-term consequences of all decisions, including their effects on stakeholders such as customers, employees, and the environment.
3. The opportunity cost of capital sets the standard for investment decisions.
4. A safe dollar is worth more than a risky dollar.
5. Good governance matters.

The second point is important, but frequently misunderstood. We will stress that maximizing the current stock price does *not* involve focusing on short-term profits, and increasing shareholder value does *not* involve price-gouging customers, overworking employees, or polluting the environment. In a forward-looking market, even the short-term share price takes these long-term effects into account. However, we will also highlight the arguments for managers having objectives other than shareholder value.

● ● ● ● ●

1-1   Corporate Investment and Financing Decisions

To do business, a corporation needs an almost endless variety of **real assets.** These may be tangible assets, such as oil fields, factories, and machines, or intangible assets, such as patents, brands, and corporate culture.

Real assets don't drop free from a blue sky. Corporations pay for their real assets by selling claims on them and the cash flows they will generate. These claims are called **financial assets.** One example of a financial asset is a bank loan. The bank provides the corporation with cash in exchange for a financial asset, which is the corporation's promise to repay the loan with interest. A second example is a corporate bond. The corporation sells the bond to investors in exchange for the promise to pay interest on the bond and to pay off the bond at its maturity. The main difference between a bond and a bank loan is that bonds can be sold second-hand to other investors in financial markets. Tradeable financial assets are known as **securities.** Shares of stock are also securities, as are a dizzying variety of specialized instruments such as options. We describe bonds in Chapter 3, stocks in Chapter 4, and other securities in later chapters.

The above discussion suggests the following definitions:

Investment decision = purchase of real assets

Financing decision = sale of financial assets

But these equations are too simple. The investment decision also involves managing assets already in place and deciding when to shut down and dispose of assets that are no longer profitable. The corporation also has to manage and control the risks of its investments. The financing decision includes not just raising cash today but also meeting its obligations to banks, bondholders, and shareholders that have contributed financing in the past. For example, the corporation has to repay its debts when they become due. If it cannot do so, it ends up insolvent and bankrupt. Sooner or later the corporation will also want to pay out cash to its shareholders.[1]

1.1 Self-Test

Are the following assets tangible, intangible, or financial?
- a. Unsold goods on your store shelves.
- b. Your company's reputation for customer service.
- c. The negotiation skills of your company's sales force.
- d. A 5% stake in your main supplier.

---

[1]We have referred to the corporation's owners as "shareholders" and "stockholders." The two terms mean exactly the same thing and are used interchangeably. Corporations are also referred to casually as "companies," "firms," or "businesses." We also use these terms interchangeably.

Let's go to more specific examples. Table 1.1 lists 10 well-known corporations from all over the world.

Investment Decisions

The second column of Table 1.1 shows an important recent investment decision for each corporation. Some of the investments in Table 1.1, such as Shell's new oil field or Intel's factory, involve buying or building tangible assets. Such investment decisions are often referred to as **capital expenditure (CAPEX)** or **capital budgeting** decisions. However, corporations also need to invest in intangible assets, through undertaking research and development (R&D), advertising, and developing computer software. For example, GlaxoSmithKline and other major pharmaceutical companies invest billions every year on R&D for new drugs. Similarly, consumer goods companies, such as Unilever or Procter & Gamble, invest huge sums in advertising and marketing their products. These outlays are investments because they build know-how, brand recognition, and reputation for the long run.

Today's investments generate future cash returns. Sometimes the cash inflows last for decades. For example, many U.S. nuclear power plants, which were initially licensed by the Nuclear Regulatory Commission to operate for 40 years, are now being re-licensed for 20 more years and may be able to operate efficiently for 80 years overall. Investing to develop self-driving cars or reduce greenhouse gas emissions also has long-term payoffs.

Of course, not all investments have such distant payoffs. For example, Walmart spends about $50 billion each year to stock up its stores and warehouses before the holiday season. The company's return on this investment comes within months as the inventory is drawn down and the goods are sold.

In addition, financial managers know (or quickly learn) that cash returns are not guaranteed. An investment could be a smashing success or a dismal failure. For example, Disneyland Paris opened in 1992 and became Europe's largest tourist attraction by visitor numbers. After

Company	Recent Investment Decisions	Recent Financing Decisions
Intel (U.S.)	Invests $7 billion in expanding semiconductor plant in Chandler, Arizona.	Borrows $600 million from Chandler Industrial Development Authority.
Amazon (U.S.)	Acquires self-driving start-up, Zoox, for over $1.2 billion	Reinvests $33 billion that it generates from operations
Tesla (U.S.)	Announces construction of new plant to build the electric Cybertruck	Announces plans to sell $2 billion of shares
Shell (U.K./Holland)	Starts production at a deep-water development in the Gulf of Mexico	Cuts dividend to preserve cash
GlaxoSmithKline (U.K.)	Spends $6 billion on research and development for new drugs.	Raises $1 billion by an issue 8-year bonds
Ørsted (Denmark)	Completes a 230-MW wind farm in Nebraska	Arranges a borrowing facility with 14 international banks
Unilever (U.K./Holland)	Spends $8 billion on advertising and marketing	Pays a dividend and completes $200 million program to buy back shares
Carnival Corporation (U.S./U.K.)	Launches four new cruise ships	Raises $770 million by sale of bonds; each bond can be converted into about 19 shares

❭TABLE 1.1   Examples of recent investment and financing decisions by major public corporations.

Europe's debt crisis in the early 2010s and subsequent terror attacks in Paris, attendance fell, and its huge debts led Disney to bail it out in 2014 and 2017.

Financing Decisions

The third column of Table 1.1 lists a recent financing decision by each corporation. A corporation can raise money from lenders or from shareholders. If it borrows, the lenders contribute the cash, and the corporation promises to pay back the debt plus a fixed rate of interest. If the shareholders put up the cash, they do not get a fixed return, but instead a fraction of any future dividends the company chooses to pay out. The shareholders are *equity investors,* who contribute *equity financing.* The choice between debt and equity financing is called the **capital structure** decision. *Capital* refers to the firm's sources of long-term financing.

The financing choices available to large corporations seem almost endless. Suppose the firm decides to borrow. Should it borrow from a bank or issue tradeable bonds? Should it borrow for 1 year or 20 years? If it borrows for 20 years, should it reserve the right to pay off the debt early? Should it borrow in Paris, receiving and promising to repay euros, or should it borrow dollars in New York?

Corporations raise equity financing in two ways. First, they can issue new shares of stock. The investors who buy the new shares put up cash in exchange for a fraction of the corporation's future cash flow and profits. Second, the corporation can take the cash flow generated by its existing assets and reinvest that cash in new assets. In this case the corporation is reinvesting on behalf of existing shareholders. No new shares are issued.

That last observation is important. Often, a manager may think that a corporation's money is hers, free to invest as she pleases. But whenever a manager reinvests cash, she's choosing not to pay out that cash to shareholders—she's effectively raising money from shareholders. For example, let's say you own a house and hire a property management company to rent it out for you. You receive the monthly rental payments, less the company's management fee and expenses. So if the management company uses some of the rent to pay for repairs, it's you who's financing the repairs because they come out of your monthly income.

What happens when a corporation does not reinvest all of the cash flow generated by its existing assets? It may hold the cash in reserve for future investment, or it may pay the cash back to its shareholders. Table 1.1 shows that Unilever paid back $200 million to its shareholders by repurchasing shares, in addition to paying a cash dividend. The decision to pay dividends or repurchase shares is called the *payout decision.* We cover payout decisions in Chapter 15.

Both investment and financing decisions are important, so we will consider both carefully in this book. But the real value of a company stems from its investment decisions—what makes a company great is what it does (its investment decisions) rather than how it pays for it (its financing decisions). That's why financial managers say that "value comes mainly from the asset side of the balance sheet." Take Apple as an example. Its *market capitalization* or *market cap* is about $2 trillion. Where did this market value come from? It came from Apple's best-selling products, from its brand name and worldwide customer base, from its research and development, and from its ability to make profitable future investments. The value did *not* come from sophisticated financing. Apple's financing strategy is very simple: It carries no debt to speak of and finances almost all investment by retaining and reinvesting cash flow. Indeed, the most successful corporations sometimes have the simplest financing strategies.

While investment decisions matter more on the upside, financial decisions are particularly important on the downside. Financing decisions alone can't turn a company into a success, but they can cause it to fail. For example, after a consortium of investment companies bought the energy giant TXU in 2007, the company took on an additional $50 billion of debt. This decision proved fatal. The consortium did not foresee the expansion of shale gas production and the resulting sharp fall in natural gas and electricity prices. In 2014, the company (renamed Energy Future Holdings) was no longer able to service its debts and filed for bankruptcy.

Business is inherently risky. The financial manager needs to identify the risks and make sure they are managed properly. For example, debt has its advantages, but too much debt can land the company in bankruptcy, as the buyers of TXU discovered. Companies can also be knocked off course by recessions, by changes in commodity prices, interest rates and exchange rates, or by adverse political developments. Some of these risks can be hedged or insured, however, as we explain in Chapters 27 and 28.

1.2 Self-Test

Are the following decisions investment or financing decisions?
 a. Redesigning your products' packaging to use less plastic.
 b. Launching a program to improve employee mental health.
 c. Lending to your supplier to enable them to develop a new technology.
 d. Accepting a capital injection from a venture capital firm.
 e. Selling an airplane and leasing it back.

What Is a Corporation?

We have been referring to "corporations." Before going too far or too fast, we need to offer some basic definitions. Details follow in later chapters.

A **corporation** is a legal entity. In the view of the law, it is a legal *person* that is owned by its shareholders. As a legal person, the corporation can make contracts, carry on a business, borrow or lend money, and sue or be sued. It must also pay taxes. Unlike an actual person, a corporation cannot vote, but it can buy another corporation.

In the United States, corporations are formed under state law, based on *articles of incorporation* that set out the purpose of the business and how it is to be governed and operated.[2] For example, the articles of incorporation specify the composition and role of the *board of directors*.[3] A corporation's directors are elected by the shareholders. They choose and advise top management and must sign off on important corporate actions, such as mergers and the payment of dividends to shareholders. We'll consider how a corporation is governed in more detail in Chapter 19, and the purpose of the corporation in Chapter 20.

A corporation is owned by its shareholders but is legally distinct from them. Therefore the shareholders have **limited liability,** which means that they cannot be held personally responsible for the corporation's debts. When the U.S. financial corporation Lehman Brothers failed in 2008, its shareholders did not have to put up more money to cover Lehman's massive debts. Shareholders can lose their entire investment in a corporation, but no more.

BEYOND THE PAGE

Zipcar's articles

mhhe.com/brealey14e

---

[2]In the U.S., corporations are identified by the label "Corporation," "Incorporated," or "Inc.," as in Iridium Communications Inc. The U.K. identifies public corporations by "plc" (short for "Public Limited Corporation"). French corporations have the suffix "SA" ("Société Anonyme"). The corresponding labels in Germany are "GmbH" ("Gesellschaft mit beschränkter Haftung") or "AG" ("Aktiengesellschaft").

[3]The corporation's bylaws set out in more detail the duties of the board of directors and how the firm should conduct its business.

When a corporation is first established, its shares may be privately held by a small group of investors, such as the company's managers and a few backers. In this case, the shares are not publicly traded and the company is *closely held.* Eventually, when the firm grows and new shares are issued to raise additional capital, its shares are traded in public markets such as the New York Stock Exchange or Hong Kong Stock Exchange. These corporations are known as *public companies.* Most well-known corporations in the United States are public companies with widely dispersed shareholdings. In other countries, it is more common for large corporations to remain in private hands, and many public companies may be controlled by just a handful of investors. The latter category includes such well-known names as Volkswagen (Germany), Alibaba (China), Softbank (Japan), and the Swatch Group (Switzerland).

A large public corporation may have millions of shareholders, who own the business but cannot possibly manage or control it directly. This *separation of ownership and control* gives corporations permanence. Even if managers quit or are dismissed and replaced, the corporation survives. Today's shareholders can sell all their shares to new investors without disrupting the operations of the business. Corporations can, in principle, live forever, and in practice, they may survive many human lifetimes. One of the oldest corporations is the Hudson's Bay Company, which was formed in 1670 to profit from the fur trade between northern Canada and England. Although the company still operates as one of Canada's leading retail chains, its shareholders voted in 2020 to turn it into a private company, and it was delisted from the Toronto Stock Exchange.

The separation of ownership and control can also have a downside because it can open the door for managers and directors to act in their own interests rather than in the shareholders' interest. We return to this problem later in this chapter and again in Chapter 19.

Almost all large and medium-sized businesses are corporations, but the nearby *Finance in Practice* box describes how smaller businesses may be organized.

BEYOND THE PAGE

Zipcar's bylaws

mhhe.com/brealey14e

BEYOND THE PAGE

An Early Corporation

mhhe.com/brealey14e

1.3 Self-Test

A company is bankrupt and has outstanding debt of $100 million. Its assets can be liquidated for $80 million.

    a. How much will creditors receive?

    b. How much will shareholders receive?

    c. How much extra are shareholders obliged to pay into the company to stop it from going bankrupt?

The Role of the Financial Manager

What is the essential role of the financial manager? Figure 1.1 gives one answer. The figure traces how money flows from investors to the corporation and back to investors again. The flow starts when cash is raised from investors (arrow 1 in the figure). The cash could come from banks or from securities sold to investors in financial markets. The cash is then used to pay for the real assets needed for the corporation's business (arrow 2). Later, as the business operates, the assets produce cash inflows (arrow 3). That cash is either reinvested (arrow 4a) or returned to the investors who furnished the money in the first place (arrow 4b). Of course, the choice between arrows 4a and 4b is constrained by the promises made when cash was raised at arrow 1. For example, if the firm borrows money from a bank at arrow 1, it must repay this money plus interest at arrow 4b.

Other Forms of Business Organization

❭ Corporations do not have to be prominent, multinational businesses such as those listed in Table 1.1. You can organize a local plumbing contractor or barber shop as a corporation if you want to take the trouble. But most corporations are larger businesses or businesses that aspire to grow. Small "mom-and-pop" businesses are usually organized as sole proprietorships.

What about the middle ground? What about businesses that grow too large for sole proprietorships but don't want to reorganize as corporations? For example, suppose you wish to pool money and expertise with some friends or business associates. The solution is to form a *partnership* and enter into a partnership agreement that sets out how decisions are to be made and how profits are to be split up. Partners, like sole proprietors, face unlimited liability. If the business runs into difficulties, each partner can be held responsible for *all* the business's debts.

Partnerships have a tax advantage. Partnerships, unlike corporations, do not have to pay income taxes. The partners simply pay personal income taxes on their shares of the profits.

Some businesses are hybrids that combine the tax advantage of a partnership with the limited liability advantage of a corporation. In a *limited partnership,* partners are classified as general or limited. General partners manage the business and have unlimited personal liability for its debts. Limited partners are liable only for the money they invest and do not participate in management.

Many states allow *limited liability partnerships (LLPs)* or, equivalently, *limited liability companies (LLCs).* These are partnerships in which all partners have limited liability.

Another variation on the theme is the *professional corporation (PC)* or *professional limited liability company (PLCC),* which is commonly used by doctors, lawyers, and accountants. In this case, the business has limited liability, but the professionals can still be sued personally—for example, for malpractice.

Most large investment banks such as Morgan Stanley and Goldman Sachs started as partnerships. But eventually these companies and their financing requirements grew too large for them to continue as partnerships, and they reorganized as corporations. The partnership form of organization does not work well when ownership is widespread and separation of ownership and management is essential.

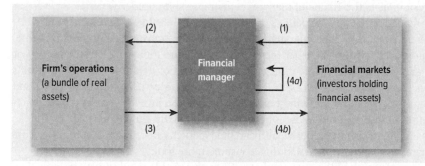

❭ **FIGURE 1.1**

Flow of cash between financial markets and the firm's operations. Key: (1) Cash raised by selling financial assets to investors; (2) cash invested in the firm's operations and used to purchase real assets; (3) cash generated by the firm's operations; (4a) cash reinvested; (4b) cash returned to investors.

You can see examples of arrows 4a and 4b in Table 1.1. Amazon financed its new projects by reinvesting earnings (arrow 4a). Unilever decided to return cash to shareholders by paying cash dividends and by buying back its stock (arrow 4b).

Notice how the financial manager stands between the firm and outside investors. On the one hand, the financial manager helps manage the firm's operations, particularly by helping to make good investment decisions. On the other hand, the financial manager deals with investors—not just with shareholders but also with financial institutions such as banks and with financial markets such as the New York Stock Exchange.

BEYOND THE PAGE

S-corporations

mhhe.com/brealey14e

BEYOND THE PAGE

The financial
managers

mhhe.com/brealey14e

Notice also that the structure of Figure 1.1 mirrors the structure of a company's balance sheet. A company's investments are on the left-hand side of the balance sheet, and the financial assets that it has issued—its *liabilities*— are on the right-hand side.[4]

<hr>

| 1-2 | The Financial Goal of the Corporation |

Shareholders Want Managers to Maximize Market Value

Major corporations may have millions of shareholders. There is no way that all of these shareholders can be actively involved in management; it would be like trying to run a city solely through local meetings where residents vote on every tax and expenditure decision. Authority has to be delegated to professional managers, just as residents delegate the running of a city to the mayor.

A mayor's job is complex. She is supposed to act in residents' interests. But residents have different views on how high taxes should be and what projects money should be spent on—and these views may change over time. It would be impractical to run every decision past the residents. Then, how does the mayor know what to do to serve their interests?

It might seem that a company manager's job is equally complex. Shareholders have different interests. Some may plan to cash in their investments next year; others may be investing for a distant old age. Some may be wary of taking much risk; others may be more venturesome. How does the manager know what to do to serve their interests? Fortunately, for managers, there is a natural financial objective on which most shareholders can agree despite their differences: Maximize the current market value of shareholders' investment in the firm.

A smart and effective manager makes decisions that increase the current market value of the company's shares. This increased market value can then be put to whatever purposes the shareholders want. They can sell their shares and give the proceeds to charity or spend them on exotic holidays; they can alternatively retain their entire investment in the firm. Whatever their personal tastes or objectives, they can all do more when their shares are worth more. Thus, *every* investor wants the financial manager to increase shareholder wealth.

Maximizing market value is a sensible goal when the shareholders have access to well-functioning financial markets.[5] Financial markets allow them to transport savings across time, by borrowing money or selling shares (if they wish to consume today) or lending money or buying more shares (if they prefer to consume in the future). For example, the corporation's roster usually includes investors with both long horizons (such as a child's trust fund) and short horizons (such as retirees). You might expect short-horizon investors to say, "Sure, maximize value, but don't invest in too many long-term projects." But they won't, because if the long-term project increases shareholder wealth and thus market value, short-horizon investors can sell their shares for a higher price and thus consume more today.

The same is true for risk. Financial markets allow shareholders to adjust the risk they bear. A corporation's roster of shareholders usually includes both risk-averse and risk-tolerant investors. You might expect the risk-averse to say, "Sure, maximize value, but don't touch too many high-risk projects." Instead, they say, "Risky projects are OK, *provided* that expected

<hr>

[4]Note that the investments on the left-hand side of a balance sheet include both real and financial assets. A company may own cash, Treasury bills, and shares in other companies.

[5]Here we use "financial markets" as shorthand for the financial sector of the economy. Strictly speaking, we should say "access to well-functioning financial markets and institutions." Many investors deal mostly with financial institutions, for example, banks, insurance companies, or mutual funds. The financial institutions in turn engage in financial markets, including the stock and bond markets. The institutions act as financial intermediaries on behalf of individual investors.

returns are more than enough to offset the risks. If this firm ends up too risky for my taste, I'll adjust my investment portfolio to make it safer." They could sell their shares in the risky firm and buy safer ones or government bonds. If the risky investments increase market value, the departing shareholders can sell at a higher price, and thus are better off, than if the risky investments were turned down. Financial markets give them the flexibility to manage their own savings and investment plans, leaving the corporation's financial managers with only one task: to increase market value and hence shareholder wealth.

Sometimes, managers say that, rather than maximizing wealth, their job is to "maximize profits." That sounds reasonable. After all, don't shareholders want their company to be profitable? But taken literally, profit maximization is not a well-defined financial objective for at least two reasons:

1. Which year's profits? A corporation may be able to increase current profits by cutting R&D, but that may result in lower profits in the future. How do we know whether "profits" are maximized if some years' profits rise and others fall?

2. What about risk? If a project will increase the company's profits but also make it riskier, it is not clear that the manager should take it. As we'll soon explain, risk is a crucial factor that affects shareholder wealth.

While profits are not defined, shareholder wealth is. As Chapter 2 will show, it considers all future profits from a company and converts them into the common currency of current shareholder wealth that takes into account whether they are short-term or long-term, risky or safe.

A Fundamental Result: Why Maximizing Shareholder Wealth Makes Sense

The goal of maximizing shareholder value is widely accepted in both theory and practice. It's important to understand why. Let's walk through the argument step by step, assuming that the financial manager should act in the interests of the firm's owners, its shareholders.

1. Each shareholder wants three things:
   a. To be as rich as possible—that is, to maximize his current wealth.
   b. To manage the timing of his consumption plan by deciding whether to consume his wealth now or invest it to spend later.
   c. To manage the risk characteristics of that consumption plan.

2. But shareholders don't need the financial manager's help to achieve the best time pattern of consumption. They can do that on their own, provided they have free access to competitive financial markets, by deciding when to sell their shares. They can also choose the risk characteristics of their consumption plan by investing in more- or less-risky securities.

3. How then can the financial manager help the firm's shareholders? There is only one way: by increasing their wealth. That means increasing the market value of the firm and the current price of its shares.

Economists have proved this value-maximization principle with great rigor and generality. It is known as the *Fisher separation theorem,* because it shows that a financial manager's investment decisions can be separated from shareholder preferences. After you have absorbed this chapter, take a look at the Appendix, which contains a simple example that illustrates how the principle of value maximization follows from formal economic reasoning.

It's important to highlight the role of well-functioning financial markets in this result. We often think that the main role of financial markets is to allow companies to raise funds for investment. *Primary financial markets* are where companies obtain new money—through selling shares, issuing bonds, or taking out a bank loan. But most activity takes place in *secondary financial markets.* On a typical day in the New York Stock Exchange, investors trade over 1 trillion shares with each other. These shares are "second hand"—they'd been issued previously. No new money flows to companies, yet secondary financial markets have an important social function. By giving shareholders freedom to do what they want with their wealth, they not only improve shareholders' welfare but also make the manager's task simple—to maximize shareholder wealth.

Should Managers Maximize Shareholder Wealth?

We earlier wrote that managers have a single objective: to "maximize the current market value of shareholders' investment in the firm." We've explained how this idea has several advantages—it gives a clear decision rule for managers and benefits almost all shareholders regardless of their preferences.

But this idea has also been heavily criticized. One challenge is that maximizing the "current" market value leads managers to be short-termist—that is, focus on short-term profits by reducing investment or cutting wages. A second criticism is that it's narrowly focused on shareholders at the expense of *stakeholders*—other parties affected by the company, such as customers, employees, suppliers, the environment, communities, and taxpayers. A single-minded focus on shareholders might cause managers to price-gouge customers, overwork employees, or pollute the environment in pursuit of shareholder wealth.

These two criticisms must be taken seriously. Indeed, they have led to capitalism becoming unpopular with many citizens and politicians. Perhaps in response, in August 2019, 181 CEOs of the largest U.S. companies signed a statement claiming their objective was no longer solely "generating long-term value for shareholders" but also "delivering value to our customers . . . investing in our employees . . . dealing fairly and ethically with our suppliers . . . supporting the communities in which we work."*

However, these criticisms are not fully warranted. Starting with the former, as we'll explain in Chapter 2, *current* shareholder wealth depends on *all future* cash flows generated by a company, not just current cash flows. A company developing renewable energy may be improving current shareholder wealth, even if the project is not profitable for 20 years. A company failing to train its workforce may be destroying shareholder value, even though the cost savings will boost short-term profits.

Moving to the latter, it is not true that a focus on enriching the shareholders means that managers must act as greedy mercenaries riding roughshod over the weak and helpless. In most instances, little conflict arises between doing well (increasing shareholder value) and doing good (increasing stakeholder value). Investing in stakeholders often benefits shareholders, and any financial manager who fails to take these effects into account is failing at her job. Profitable firms are those with satisfied customers and loyal employees; firms with dissatisfied customers and a disgruntled workforce will probably end up with declining profits and a low stock price. Indeed, as we explain in Chapter 20, evidence shows that companies that treat customers, employees, and the environment well also generate higher longer-term returns to their shareholders.

So, when we say that the objective of the firm is to maximize shareholder wealth, we don't mean that managers should ignore everything else. The law deters managers from making blatantly exploitative decisions. But managers shouldn't be simply concerned with observing the letter of the law or with keeping to written contracts—they should go above and beyond. This is not just for "ethical" reasons; it's good business sense. In business and finance, as in other

---

*Source: Fitzgerald, Maggie. "The CEOs of nearly 200 companies just said shareholder value is no longer their main objective" CNBC, August 19, 2019.

day-to-day affairs, there are unwritten rules of behavior that can't be specified in a contract. These rules make routine transactions feasible because each party trusts the other to keep their side of the bargain. Corporations create shareholder value by building long-term relationships with their customers and establishing a reputation for fair dealing and financial integrity.

When something happens to damage that trust, the costs can be enormous. Volkswagen (VW) is a case in point. VW had installed secret software that cut emissions by up to forty times when it detected a test was being conducted. Discovery of the software in 2015 caused a tidal wave of criticism. VW's stock price dropped by 35%. Its CEO was fired. VW diesel vehicles piled up unsold in car dealers' lots. In the United States alone, the scandal may ultimately cost the company more than $35 billion in fines and compensation payments.

While we have explained how shareholder and stakeholder value are much more aligned than commonly believed, it is important to acknowledge that the two preceding criticisms may sometimes be valid. This is why we earlier said that they are "not fully warranted" rather than "unwarranted."

Starting with the short-termism critique, we've implicitly assumed that the stock market is efficient—an assumption we will later devote an entire chapter to scrutinizing (Chapter 12). In an efficient stock market, the share price indeed takes into account all future cash flows from a company. But what if the stock market is myopic and ignores cash flows far into the future? Then, market value no longer equals shareholder value. A company that undertakes a far-sighted investment might be unfairly punished with a low stock price. Knowing that, the manager may turn down the investment even if it creates shareholder value. As we'll explain in Chapter 19, a solution is to pay the manager in long-term shares, so that she is less concerned with the short-term stock price.

Let's move to the second criticism, that maximizing shareholder value means exploiting stakeholders. We've argued that, in many cases, maximizing shareholder value involves taking seriously a company's responsibility to stakeholders. But some investments in stakeholders won't fully feed back into shareholder value, even in the long term. If a company invests billions in reducing its greenhouse gas emissions, the benefits are enjoyed by many, but the company's own share of the gains may be small. The consequences that companies exert on society, but don't feed back into their profits, are known as *externalities*. A company that's focused on shareholder wealth will ignore externalities and thus may turn down certain investments in stakeholders. As a result, managers' objectives may need to be broadened for them to fully take stakeholder interests into account.

We'll revisit this issue in Chapter 20 and consider how a financial manager makes decisions under multiple objectives. This is not to sweep it under the carpet; in contrast, the idea that the purpose of the corporation may be wider than shareholder wealth should be taken sufficiently seriously that it merits its own chapter. For now, we will take the manager's objective as maximizing shareholder wealth for two main reasons. First, it does take into account most effects on stakeholders, even those that arise in the very long-term. Second, it leads to a clear framework for making decisions. Under multiple objectives, it is unclear (for example) how much to pay workers. Increasing wages will benefit employees but may hurt shareholders, and there's no clear way of evaluating this trade-off. Under shareholder wealth maximization, there is a clear rule—balance the financial costs of higher pay with the financial benefits stemming from superior worker recruitment, retention, and motivation.

1.4 Self-Test

a. Does maximizing current shareholder value lead managers to be short-termist?

b. Does maximizing current shareholder value lead to managers completely ignoring stakeholders?

The Investment Trade-Off

Taking the manager's objective as being market value, we now must ask: Why do some investments increase market value while others reduce it? The answer is given by Figure 1.2, which sets out the fundamental trade-off for corporate investment decisions. Suppose the corporation has a proposed investment in a real asset and enough cash on hand to finance it. If the corporation doesn't invest, it can instead pay out the cash to shareholders—say, as an extra dividend. How does the financial manager decide whether to go ahead with the project or to pay out the cash? (The investment and dividend arrows in Figure 1.2 are arrows 2 and 4b in Figure 1.1.)

Assume that the financial manager is acting in the interests of the corporation's owners, its shareholders. What do these shareholders want the financial manager to do? The answer depends on the project's rate of return versus the rate of return that the shareholders can earn by investing in financial markets.

To see this, let's say the investment project in Figure 1.2 is a proposal for Tesla to launch a new electric car. Suppose Tesla has set aside cash to launch the new model in 2025. It could go ahead with the launch, or it could cancel the investment and instead pay the cash out to its shareholders. If it pays out the cash, the shareholders can then invest for themselves.

Suppose that Tesla's new project is just about as risky as the U.S. stock market and that investment in the stock market offers a 10% expected rate of return. If the project offers a superior rate of return—say, 20%—then Tesla's shareholders would be happy for the company to keep the cash and invest it in the new model. If the project offers only a 5% return, then the shareholders are better off with the cash and without the new model; in that case, the financial manager should turn down the project.

As long as a corporation's proposed investments offer higher rates of return than its shareholders can earn for themselves in financial markets, its shareholders will welcome the investments, and its stock price will increase. But if the company earns an inferior return, shareholders are unhappy, the stock price falls, and shareholders demand their money back so that they can invest on their own.

In our example, the minimum acceptable rate of return on Tesla's new car is 10%. This minimum rate of return is called the **opportunity cost of capital** (or *cost of capital* for short) because it depends on the investment *opportunities* available to investors in financial markets. Whenever a corporation invests cash in a new project, its shareholders lose the opportunity to invest the cash on their own. Corporations increase value by accepting all investment projects that earn more than the opportunity cost of capital. For this reason, the cost of capital is also

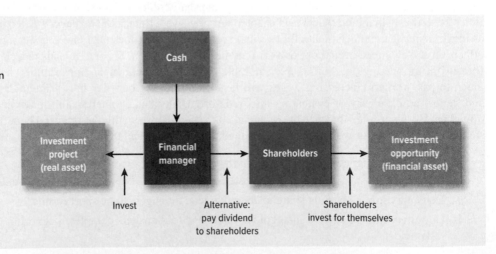

▶ **FIGURE 1.2**

The firm can either keep and reinvest cash or return it to investors. (Arrows represent possible cash flows or transfers.) If cash is reinvested, the opportunity cost is the expected rate of return that shareholders could have obtained by investing in financial assets.

known as the *hurdle rate,* because a project's return must be higher than this hurdle for it to create value for shareholders.

Notice that the opportunity cost of capital depends on the risk of the proposed investment project. The "apples-to-apples" alternative of investing in a project is to pay out the cash to shareholders and allow them to invest in financial markets *at the same level of risk.* In turn, the return that shareholders get when they invest on their own depends on the risk they take. The safest investments, such as U.S. government debt, offer low rates of return. Investments with higher expected rates of return—the stock market, for example—are riskier and sometimes deliver painful losses. (The U.S. stock market was down 38% in 2008 and fell more than 20% in March 2020, for example.) Other investments, such as high-tech growth stocks, are riskier still and thus investors demand higher returns.

That the hurdle rate is an opportunity cost of investing elsewhere should make it clear that the minimum required return for a project depends entirely on *external* factors—the rates of return that shareholders could obtain elsewhere. It does not depend on *internal* factors, such as the interest rate the company pays on a bank loan, or the return on a company's existing investments.

Managers look to the financial markets to measure the opportunity cost of capital for the firm's investment projects. They can observe the opportunity cost of capital for safe investments by looking up current interest rates on safe debt securities. For risky investments, the opportunity cost of capital has to be estimated. We start to tackle this task in Chapter 7.

1.5 Self-Test

a. Epsilon is taking out a low-interest-rate bank loan to finance construction of a number of stores in South Carolina. Upsilon is making a similar-risk investment in North Carolina, which it is financing with an issue of shares. Should Upsilon require a higher return than Epsilon on its investment?

b. Two pharmaceuticals companies are developing a cure for cancer. Company A has been successful in drug development in the past and earned a 25% rate of return on its past investments. Company B has been less successful and only yielded 15%. Should Company A require a higher, lower, or the same return on the cancer cure than Company B?

Agency Problems and Corporate Governance

We have emphasized the *separation of ownership and control* in public corporations. The owners (shareholders) cannot control what the managers do, except indirectly through the board of directors. This separation is necessary but also dangerous. You can see the risks. Managers may be tempted to buy flashy corporate jets or to schedule business meetings at luxury resorts. They may shy away from attractive but risky projects because they are worried more about the safety of their jobs than about maximizing shareholder value. They may work just to maximize their own bonuses, and therefore slash investment in employees or reducing their company's carbon footprint.

Conflicts between shareholders' and managers' objectives create *agency problems.* Agency problems arise when *agents* work for *principals.* The shareholders are the principals; the managers are their agents. **Agency costs** are incurred when (1) managers do not attempt to maximize firm value and (2) shareholders incur costs to monitor the managers and constrain their actions.

Agency problems can sometimes lead to outrageous behavior. For example, when Dennis Kozlowski, the CEO of Tyco, threw a $2 million 40th birthday bash for his wife, he charged half of the cost to the company. This, of course, was an extreme conflict of interest, as well as illegal. But more subtle and moderate agency problems arise whenever managers don't own the entirety of their firm. As we'll revisit in Chapter 20, *errors of omission* (failing to take good actions, such as launching a new product or closing down an unprofitable division) are often even more serious than *errors of commission* (undertaking bad actions).

Later in the book, and in particular in Chapter 19, we will look at how good systems of governance ensure that managers' hearts are close to shareholders' pockets. This means well-designed incentives for managers, standards for accounting and disclosure to investors, requirements for boards of directors, and legal sanctions for self-dealing by management. When scandals happen, we say that corporate governance has broken down. When corporations compete effectively and ethically to deliver value to shareholders, we conclude that governance is working properly.

1-3   Key Questions in Corporate Finance

Figure 1.2 illustrates how the financial manager can add value for the firm and its shareholders. She searches for investments that offer rates of return higher than the opportunity cost of capital. But that search opens up a treasure chest of follow-up questions.

- *How do I calculate the rate of return?* The rate of return is calculated from the cash inflows and outflows generated by the investment project (Chapters 2 and 5).

- *Is a higher rate of return on investment always better?* Not always, for two reasons. First, a lower-but-safer return can be better than a higher-but-riskier return. Second, an investment with a higher percentage return can generate less value than a lower-return investment that is larger or lasts longer. In Chapter 2, we show how to calculate the present value (PV) of the stream of cash flows from an investment. Present value is a workhorse concept of corporate finance that shows up in almost every chapter.

- *What determines value in financial markets?* We cover valuation of bonds and common stocks in Chapters 3 and 4. We will return to valuation principles again and again in later chapters. Sometimes the financial manager may be lucky and find an almost identical asset whose value is already known. The idea that identical assets must have the same value is known as the *law of one price.* But there is no identical asset to Shell's offshore oil field in the Gulf of Mexico or GlaxoSmithKline's investment in research. For most major financial decisions, the manager needs some fundamental principles to help him to determine value.

- *What are the cash flows?* The future cash flows from an investment project should be the sum of all cash inflows and outflows caused by the decision to invest. Cash flows are calculated after corporate taxes are paid. They are the free cash flows that can be paid out to shareholders or reinvested on their behalf. Chapter 6 explains how to calculate these cash flows.

- *How does the financial manager judge whether cash-flow forecasts are realistic?* As Niels Bohr, the 1922 Nobel Laureate in Physics, observed, "Prediction is difficult, especially if it's about the future." But good financial managers take care to assemble relevant information and to purge forecasts of bias and thoughtless optimism. See Chapters 6, 9, 10 and 11.

- *How do we measure risk?* We look to the risks borne by shareholders, recognizing that investors can dilute or eliminate some risks by holding diversified portfolios (Chapter 7).

- *How does risk affect the opportunity cost of capital?* Here we need a theory of risk and return in financial markets. The most widely used theory is the **capital asset pricing model** (Chapters 8 and 9).

- *Where does financing come from?* Broadly speaking, from borrowing or from cash invested or reinvested by stockholders. But financing can get complicated when you get down to specifics. Chapter 13 gives an overview of financing. Chapters 24 through 26 cover sources of debt financing, including financial leases, which are debt in disguise.

- *How do companies issue new debt or equity* Financing for young companies may be provided by venture capitalists, but larger, more mature companies typically make public issues of securities. In Chapter 14 we explain how they go about raising new funds.

- *How does the company's payout policy affect shareholder wealth?* This involves answers to two questions. First, how much cash should the corporation pay out to its shareholders? Second, should the cash be distributed by paying cash dividends or by repurchasing shares? (Chapter 15)

- *Debt or equity? Does it matter?* Not in a world of perfect financial markets. But in the real world, the choice between debt and equity does matter for many possible reasons, including taxes, the risks of bankruptcy, information differences, and incentives (Chapters 16 and 17). How the choice affects investment decisions is considered in Chapter 18.

- *How do we ensure that managers act in shareholders' interest?* Various governance mechanisms exist to ensure that managers maximize shareholder value rather than their own pay or private benefits. We consider these in Chapter 19.

- *Should managers maximize shareholder wealth or social value?* Companies do invest in their stakeholders, contrary to common belief. Chapter 20 discusses more fully whether the objective of maximizing shareholder wealth is beneficial for society.

That's enough questions to start, but you can see certain themes emerging. For example, corporate finance is "all about valuation," not only for the reasons just listed, but because value maximization is the natural financial goal of the corporation. In turn, valuation involves taking the long-term consequences of decisions into account, including any effects on stakeholders that ultimately impact shareholders. Another theme is the importance of the opportunity cost of capital, which is established in financial markets. The financial manager is an intermediary, who needs to understand financial markets as well as the operations and investments of the corporation.

● ● ● ● ●

KEY TAKEAWAYS

- Corporations face two principal financial decisions. First, what investments should the corporation make? Second, how should it pay for the investments? The first decision is the investment decision; the second is the financing decision.

- The shareholders who own the corporation want its managers to maximize its overall value and the current price of its shares. The stockholders can all agree on the goal of value maximization, so long as financial markets give them the flexibility to manage their own savings and investment plans.

- Maximizing shareholder wealth does not imply ignoring the interests of other stakeholders. Successful companies consider the welfare of customers, suppliers, employees, and local communities. However, companies may fail to undertake some expenditures that may be good for society as a whole but do not benefit these stakeholders. These effects are called *externalities*.

- Investment decisions involve a trade-off. The firm can either invest cash or return it to shareholders, for example, as an extra dividend. When the firm invests cash rather than paying it out, shareholders forgo the opportunity to invest it for themselves in financial markets. The return that they are giving up is called the opportunity cost of capital. If the firm's investments can earn a higher return than the opportunity cost of capital, the stock price increases. If the firm invests at a return lower than the opportunity cost of capital, the stock price falls.

- Managers are not endowed with a special value-maximizing gene. They will be tempted to consider their own personal interests, which may create a conflict of interest with outside shareholders. This conflict is called an agency problem. Any loss of value that results is called an agency cost. Investors will not entrust the firm with their savings unless they are confident that management will act ethically on their behalf. Successful firms have governance systems that help to align managers' and shareholders' interests.

- Remember the following five themes, for you will see them again and again throughout this book:

  1. Corporate finance is all about maximizing shareholder value.

  2. Maximizing shareholder value involves considering the long-term consequences of all decisions, including their effects on stakeholders such as customers, employees, and the environment.

  3. The opportunity cost of capital sets the standard for investment decisions.

  4. A safe dollar is worth more than a risky dollar.

  5. Good governance matters.

• • • • •

PROBLEM SETS

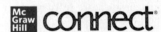   **Select problems are available in McGraw-Hill's *Connect*.**

1. **Investment and financing decisions (S1.1)** Read the following passage: "Companies usually buy (a) assets. These include both tangible assets such as (b) and intangible assets such as (c). To pay for these assets, they sell (d) assets such as (e). The decision about which assets to buy is usually termed the (f) or (g) decision. The decision about how to raise the money is usually termed the (h) decision."

   Now fit each of the following terms into the most appropriate space: *financing, real, bonds, investment, executive airplanes, financial, capital expenditure, brand names.*

2. **Investment and financing decisions (S1.1)** Which of the following are real assets, and which are financial?

   a. A share of stock.

   b. A personal IOU.

   c. A trademark.

   d. A factory.

   e. Undeveloped land.

   f. The balance in the firm's checking account.

   g. An experienced and hardworking sales force.

   h. A corporate bond.

3. **Investment and financing decisions (S1.1)** Vocabulary test. Explain the differences between:

   a. Real and financial assets.

   b. Capital expenditure and financing decisions.

   c. Closely held and public corporations.

   d. Limited and unlimited liability.

4. **Corporations (S1.1)** Which of the following statements always apply to corporations?

    a. Unlimited liability.
    b. Limited life.
    c. Ownership can be transferred without affecting operations.
    d. Managers can be fired with no effect on ownership.

5. **Separation of ownership (S1.1)** In most large corporations, ownership and management are separated. What are the main implications of this separation?

6. **Corporate goals (S1.2)** We can imagine the financial manager doing several things on behalf of the firm's shareholders. For example, the manager might:

    a. Make shareholders as wealthy as possible by investing in real assets.
    b. Modify the firm's investment plan to help shareholders achieve a particular time pattern of consumption.
    c. Choose high- or low-risk assets to match shareholders' risk preferences.
    d. Help balance shareholders' checkbooks.

    But in well-functioning capital markets, shareholders will vote for only one of these goals. Which one? Why?

7. **Maximizing shareholder value (S1.2)** Ms. Espinoza is retired and depends on her investments for her income. Mr. Liu is a young executive who wants to save for the future. Both are shareholders in Scaled Composites LLC, which is building SpaceShipOne to take commercial passengers into space. This investment's payoff is many years away. Assume it has a positive NPV for Mr. Liu. Explain why this investment also makes sense for Ms. Espinoza.

8. **Opportunity cost of capital (S1.2)** F&H Corp. continues to invest heavily in a declining industry. Here is an excerpt from a recent speech by F&H's CFO:

    > We at F&H have of course noted the complaints of a few spineless investors and uninformed security analysts about the slow growth of profits and dividends. Unlike those confirmed doubters, we have confidence in the long-run demand for mechanical encabulators, despite competing digital products. We are therefore determined to invest to maintain our share of the overall encabulator market. F&H has a rigorous CAPEX approval process, and we are confident of returns around 8% on investment. That's a far better return than F&H earns on its cash holdings. The CFO went on to explain that F&H invested excess cash in short-term U.S. government securities, which are almost entirely risk-free but offered only a 4% rate of return.

    a. Is a forecasted 8% return in the encabulator business necessarily better than a 4% safe return on short-term U.S. government securities? Why or why not?
    b. Is F&H's opportunity cost of capital 4%? How in principle should the CFO determine the cost of capital?

9. **Agency issues (S1.2)** Why might one expect managers to act in shareholders' interests? Give some reasons.

10. **Agency issues (S1.2)** Many firms have devised defenses that make it more difficult or costly for other firms to take them over. How might such defenses affect the firm's agency problems? Are managers of firms with formidable takeover defenses more or less likely to act in the shareholders' interests rather than their own? What would you expect to happen to the share price when management proposes to institute such defenses?

● ● ● ● ●

**SOLUTIONS
TO SELF-TEST
QUESTIONS**

1.1   a. Tangible;
      b. Intangible;
      c. Intangible;
      d. Financial;

1.2   a. Investment;
      b. Investment;
      c. Investment;
      d. Financing;
      e. Financing

1.3   a. $80 million;
      b. Nothing;
      c. Nothing: they are protected by limited liability

1.4   a. No; *current* shareholder wealth depends on *all future* cash flows generated by a company, not just current cash flows.
      b. No: in order to maximize shareholder value, a company must invest in its employees, customers and other stakeholders. Such investments affect future cash flows and thus current shareholder value.

1.5   a. No. The required returns should depend on what shareholders could expect to earn for themselves by investing in shares of equal risk. Whether one company happens to be taking out a bank loan at the time is irrelevant.
      b. The same. The opportunity cost of capital depends on the risk of the project and not on the characteristics of the company undertaking it.

APPENDIX • • •

Why Maximizing Shareholder Value Makes Sense

We have suggested that well-functioning financial markets allow different investors to agree on the objective of maximizing value. This idea is sufficiently important that we need to pause and examine it more carefully.

How Financial Markets Reconcile Preferences for Current vs. Future Consumption

Suppose that there are two possible investors with entirely different preferences. Think of Y as a young girl (or her trust fund), who wishes to save for the future, and of O as an old man, who would prefer to spend all his wealth on some ephemeral frolic, taking no heed of tomorrow. Suppose that each has a nest egg of exactly $100,000 in cash. O chooses to spend all of it today, while Y prefers to invest it in the financial market. If the interest rate is 10%, Y would then have 1.10 × $100,000 = $110,000 to spend a year from now. Of course, there are many possible intermediate strategies. For example, Y or O could choose to split the difference, spending $50,000 now and putting the remaining $50,000 to work at 10% to provide 1.10 × $50,000 = $55,000 next year. The entire range of possibilities is shown by the green line in Figure 1A.1.

In our example, Y used the financial market to postpone consumption. But the market can also be used to bring consumption forward in time. Let's illustrate by assuming that instead of having cash on hand of $100,000, our two friends are due to receive $110,000 each at the end of the year. In this case, Y will be happy to wait and spend the income when it arrives. O will prefer to borrow against his future income and party it away today. With an interest rate of 10%, O can borrow and spend $110,000/1.10 = $100,000. Thus the financial market provides a kind of time machine that allows people to separate the timing of their income from that of their spending. Notice that with an interest rate of 10%, Y and O are equally happy with cash on hand of $100,000 or an income of $110,000 at the end of the year. They do not care about the timing of the cash flow; they just prefer the cash flow that has the highest value today ($100,000 in our example).

Investing in Real Assets

In practice, individuals are not limited to investing in financial markets; they may also acquire plant, machinery, and other real assets. For example, suppose that Y and O are offered the opportunity to invest their $100,000 in a new business that a friend is founding. This will produce a

BEYOND THE PAGE

Foundations of NPV

mhhe.com/brealey14e

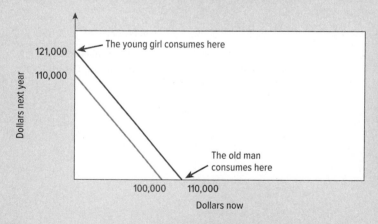

▶ **FIGURE 1A.1**

The green line shows the possible spending patterns for the young girl and old man if they invest $100,000 in the capital market. The maroon line shows the possible spending patterns if they invest in their friend's business. Both are better off by investing in the business as long as the old man can borrow against the future income.

one-off surefire payment of $121,000 next year. Y would clearly be happy to invest in the business. It will provide her with $121,000 to spend at the end of the year, rather than the $110,000 that she gets by investing her $100,000 in the financial market. But what about O, who wants money now, not in one year's time? He too is happy to invest, as long as he can borrow against the future pay-off of the investment project. At an interest rate of 10%, Y can borrow $110,000 and so will have an extra $10,000 to spend today. Both Y and O are better off investing in their friend's venture. The investment increases their wealth. It moves them up from the green to the maroon line in Figure 1A.1.

Why can both Y and O spend more by investing $100,000 in their friend's business? Because the business provides a return of $21,000, or 21%, whereas they would earn only $10,000, or 10%, by investing their money in the capital market.

A Crucial Assumption

The key condition that allows Y and O to agree to invest in the new venture is that both have access to a well-functioning, competitive financial market, in which they can borrow and lend at the same rate. Whenever the corporation's shareholders have equal access to competitive financial markets, the goal of maximizing market value makes sense.

It is easy to see how this rule would be damaged if we did *not* have such a well-functioning financial market. For example, suppose that O could not easily borrow against future income. In that case he might well prefer to spend his cash today rather than invest it in the new venture. If Y and O were shareholders in the same enterprise, Y would be happy for the firm to invest, while O would be clamoring for higher current dividends.

No one believes unreservedly that financial markets function perfectly. Later in this book we discuss several cases in which differences in taxation, transaction costs, and other imperfections must be taken into account in financial decision making. However, we also discuss research indicating that, in general, financial markets function fairly well. In this case maximizing shareholder value is a sensible corporate objective. But for now, having glimpsed the problems of imperfect markets, we shall, like an economist in a shipwreck, simply *assume* our life jacket and swim safely to shore.

QUESTIONS

1. **Maximizing shareholder value** Look back to the numerical example graphed in Figure 1A.1. Suppose the interest rate is 20%. What would the young girl (Y) and old man (O) do if they both start with $100,000? Would they invest in their friend's business? Would they borrow or lend? How much and when would each consume?

2. **Maximizing shareholder value** Answer this question by drawing graphs like Figure 1A.1. Casper Milktoast has $200,000 on hand to support consumption in periods 0 (now) and 1 (next year). He wants to consume *exactly* the same amount in each period. The interest rate is 8%. There is no risk.

   a. How much should he invest, and how much can he consume in each period?

   b. Suppose Casper is given an opportunity to invest up to $200,000 at 10% risk-free. The interest rate stays at 8%. What should he do, and how much can he consume in each period?

How to Calculate Present Values

Companies invest in lots of things. Some are *tangible assets* such as factories, machinery, and offices. Others are *intangible assets,* such as patents or trademarks. In each case, the company lays out some money now in the hope of receiving even more money later.

Individuals also make investments. For example, your college education may cost you $40,000 per year. That is an investment you hope will pay off in the form of a higher salary later in life. You are sowing now and expecting to reap later.

Companies pay for their investments by raising money and, in the process, assuming liabilities. For example, they may borrow money from a bank and promise to repay it with interest later. You also may have financed your investment in a college education by borrowing money that you plan to pay back in the future out of that higher salary.

All these financial decisions require comparisons of cash payments at different dates. Will your future salary be sufficient to justify the current expenditure on college tuition? How much will you have to repay the bank if you borrow to finance your degree? In this chapter, we take the first steps toward understanding the relationship between the value of dollars today and that of dollars in the future.

Section 2-1 How to calculate future and present values

We start in Section 2-1 by showing how money invested at a specific interest rate will grow over time. We then turn the question around to ask how much you would need to invest today to produce a specified future cash flow. This is called the **present value** of the cash flow. The difference between the present value of a project's cash flow and the project's cost is called its **net present value.** Companies help their shareholders by investing in projects that are worth more than they cost. These are the projects with positive net present values.

Section 2-2 How to value perpetuities and annuities

In Section 2-2 we introduce some shortcut formulas for working out the present value of a series of level cash payments.

Section 2-3 How to value growing perpetuities and annuities

You may often need to value a stream of cash flows that grow at a constant rate. Section 2-3 provides the necessary formulas.

Section 2-4 How interest is paid and quoted

The term *interest rate* sounds straightforward enough, but rates can be quoted in different ways. Therefore, in Section 2-4 we explain the difference between a quoted interest rate and the equivalent annually compounded interest rate.

Once you have learned how to value cash flows that occur at different points in time, we move on to look at how bonds and stocks are valued in Chapters 3 and 4. After that, we will tackle capital investment decisions at a practical level of detail.

For simplicity, every problem in this chapter is set out in dollars, but the concepts and calculations are identical in euros, Japanese yen, or Mongolian tugrik.

2-1   How to Calculate Future and Present Values

Calculating Future Values

Money can be invested to earn interest. So, if you are offered the choice between $100 today and $100 next year, you naturally take the money now to get a year's interest. Financial managers make the same point when they say that money has a *time value* or when they quote a basic principle of finance: *A dollar today is worth more than a dollar tomorrow.*

Suppose you invest $100 in a bank account that offers a return of $r = 7\%$ a year. In the first year, you will earn a return of $0.07 \times \$100 = \$7$ and the value of your investment will grow from its **present value (PV)** of $100 to $107:

Value of investment after 1 year = present value $\times (1 + r) = \$100 \times 1.07 = \$107$

By investing, you give up the opportunity to spend $100 today, but you gain the opportunity to spend $107 next year.

If you leave your money in the bank for a second year, you earn interest of $0.07 \times \$107 = \$7.49$ and your investment will grow to $114.49:

Value of investment after 2 years = $\$107 \times 1.07 = \$100 \times 1.07^2 = \$114.49$

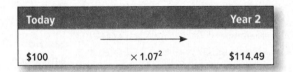

Today		Year 2
$100	$\times 1.07^2$	$114.49

Notice that in the second year you earn interest on both your initial investment ($100) and the previous year's interest ($7). Thus your wealth grows at a *compound rate* and the interest that you earn is called **compound interest**.

If you invest your $100 for t years, your investment will continue to grow at a 7% compound rate to $\$100 \times (1.07)^t$. For any interest rate r, the general formula for future value is

$$\text{Future value} = \text{present value} \times (1 + r)^t \qquad (2.1)$$

The higher the interest rate, the faster your savings will grow. Figure 2.1 shows that a few percentage points added to the interest rate can do wonders for your future wealth. For example, by the end of 20 years, $100 invested at invested at 5% will grow to $\$100 \times (1.05)^{20} = \$265.33$. If it is invested at 10%, it will grow to $\$100 \times (1.10)^{20} = \$672.75$.

EXAMPLE 2.1 • Calculating Future Values

In 1880, five aboriginal trackers were each promised the equivalent of $100 Australian dollars for helping to capture the notorious outlaw Ned Kelly. One hundred and thirteen years later, the granddaughters of two of the trackers claimed that the reward had not been paid. How much would the disputed A$100 have accumulated to by that point?

The interest rate over the period averaged about 4.5%. So to calculate the future value of the reward, we simply plug these numbers into the formula for future value:

Future value = present value $\times (1 + r)^t = \text{A}\$100 \times 1.045^{113} = \text{A}\$14,459$

• • • • •

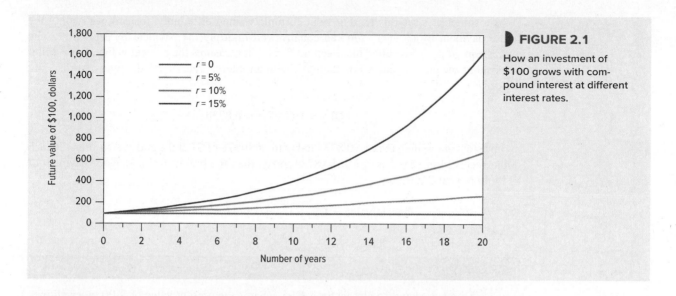

▶ **FIGURE 2.1**

How an investment of $100 grows with compound interest at different interest rates.

2.1 Self-Test

a. Janet Shih invests $3,200 at a compound interest rate of 8%. How much interest will she earn in the first year?

b. If she continues to keep her money invested, how much will her investment be worth at the end of five years?

c. If she keeps her money invested for an additional sixth year, how much interest will she earn in that final year?

Calculating Present Values

We have seen that $100 invested for two years at 7% will grow to a future value of $100 \times 1.07^2 = 114.49. Let's turn this around and ask how much you need to invest *today* to produce $114.49 at the end of the second year. In other words, what is the present value (PV) of the $114.49 payoff?

You already know that the answer is $100. But, if you didn't know, you can just run the future-value calculation in reverse and divide the future payoff by $(1.07)^2$:

$$\text{Present value} = \text{PV} = \frac{\$114.49}{(1.07)^2} = \$100$$

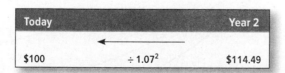

In general, suppose that you will receive a cash flow of C_t dollars at the end of year t. The present value of this future payment is

$$\text{Present value} = \text{PV} = \frac{C_t}{(1 + r)^t}$$

The rate, r, in the formula is called the discount rate, and the present value is the discounted value of the cash flow, C_t.

You sometimes see this present value formula written differently. Instead of dividing the future payment by $(1 + r)^t$, you can equally well multiply the payment by $1/(1 + r)^t$. The expression $1/(1 + r)^t$ is called the **discount factor**. It measures the present value of one dollar received at the end of year t. For example, with an interest rate of 7% the two-year discount factor is

$$DF_2 = 1/(1.07)^2 = 0.8734$$

Investors are willing to pay $0.8734 today for delivery of $1 at the end of two years. If each dollar received in year 2 is worth $0.8734 today, then the present value of your payment of $114.49 in year 2 must be

$$\text{Present value} = DF_2 \times C_2 = 0.8734 \times 114.49 = \$100$$

2.2 Self-Test

a. If the one-year discount factor is 0.95, what is the present value of $100 received in year 1?

b. If the two-year discount factor is 0.90, what is the present value of $200 received in year 2?

c. If the interest rate is 8%, what is the three-year discount factor?

The longer you have to wait for your money, the lower its present value. This is illustrated in Figure 2.2. Notice how small variations in the interest rate can have a powerful effect on the present value of distant cash flows. At an interest rate of 5%, a payment of $100 in year 20 is worth $37.69 today. If the interest rate increases to 10%, the present value of the future payment falls by about 60% to $14.86.

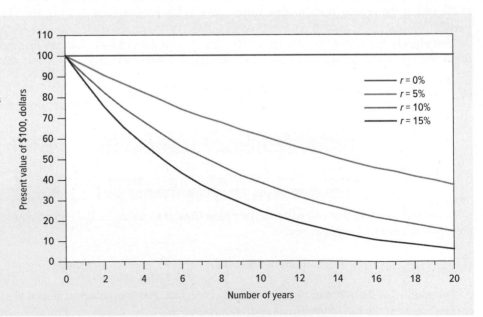

▶ **FIGURE 2.2**

Present value of a future cash flow of $100. Notice that the longer you have to wait for your money, the less it is worth today.

EXAMPLE 2.2 • Comparing Cash Flows at Different Dates

Gamma Motors is offering free credit on a $20,000 car. You pay $8,000 up front and the balance at the end of 2 years. Competitor Delta Motors does not offer free credit but will give you $1,000 off the list price. If the interest rate is 10%, which company is offering the better deal?

Notice that, although you pay $1,000 more with Gamma's offer, part of the payment is deferred. To compare the two deals, you need to calculate the *present value* of Gamma's payments. When cash flows occur at different points in time, it is often helpful to draw a timeline showing the date and value of each cash flow. Figure 2.3 shows a timeline for the payments to Gamma. The first payment, $8,000, takes place today. The second payment takes place at the end of two years. The total present value of the payments to Gamma is therefore

$$PV = \$8,000 + \$12,000/1.10^2 = \$17,917.36$$

Suppose that you start with $17,917.36. You make a down payment of $8,000 to Gamma and invest the balance of $9,917.36. At an interest rate of 10%, this will grow over two years to $9,917.36 \times 1.10^2 = \$12,000$, just enough to make the final payment. The $17,917.36 total cost is a better deal than the $19,000 charged by Delta.

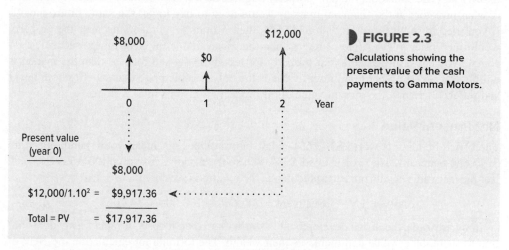

▶ **FIGURE 2.3**

Calculations showing the present value of the cash payments to Gamma Motors.

2.3 Self-Test

True or false?

a. To calculate the present value of $1 million received in year 10, you need to divide by the 10-year discount factor.

b. The present value of $1 million received in year 10 is less than $1 million.

c. Other things equal, the higher the interest rate, the greater is the present value of a future cash flow.

Valuing an Investment Opportunity

How do you decide whether an investment opportunity is worth undertaking? Suppose that you are the manager of a small company that is contemplating construction of a suburban office block. The cost of buying the land and constructing the building is $700,000. Your company has cash in the bank to finance construction. You forecast a shortage of office space in the area and predict that you will be able to sell the building next year for $800,000. For simplicity, we will assume initially that this $800,000 is a sure thing.

Figure 2.4 summarizes your choices. (Note the resemblance to Figure 1.2 in the previous chapter.) You can invest in the project or pay cash out to the shareholders, who can invest on their own. We assume that they can earn a 7% profit by investing for one year in safe assets (U.S. Treasury debt securities, for example).

What is the opportunity cost of capital for the office investment? The answer is 7%: That's the rate of return that your company's shareholders could get by investing on their own in risk-free government debt. (Remember, we are assuming for now that the future value of the office block is known with certainty.)

How much is the investment worth and how much will will it add to your shareholders' wealth? The project produces a cash flow at the end of one year. To find its present value we discount that cash flow by the opportunity cost of capital:

$$\text{Present value} = \text{PV} = \frac{C_1}{1+r} = \frac{800,000}{1.07} = \$747,664$$

Suppose that as soon as you have bought the land and paid for the construction, you decide to sell the project. How much could you sell it for? That is an easy question. If the venture will return a surefire $800,000, then the property ought to be worth its PV of $747,664 today. That is what investors in the financial markets would need to pay to get the same future payoff. If you tried to sell it for more than $747,664, there would be no takers because the property would then offer a lower rate of return than the 7% available on government securities. Of course, you could always sell your property for less, but why sell for less than the market is willing to pay? The $747,664 present value is the only feasible price that satisfies both buyer and seller. Therefore, the present value of the property is also its market price.

Net Present Value

The office building is worth $747,664 today, but that does not mean your shareholders are $747,664 better off. The project costs $700,000, so the **net present value (NPV)** is $47,664. Net present value equals present value minus the required investment:

$$\text{NPV} = \text{PV} - \text{investment} = 747,664 - 700,000 = \$47,664$$

In other words, the office development is worth more than it costs. It makes a *net* contribution to shareholder value and increases their wealth. The formula for calculating the NPV of the project is:

$$\text{NPV} = C_0 + C_1/(1+r)$$

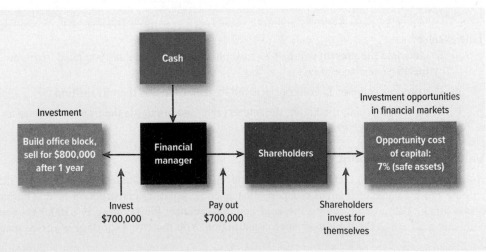

> **FIGURE 2.4**
>
> Your company can either invest $700,000 in an office block and sell it after one year for $800,000, or it can return the $700,000 to shareholders to invest in the financial markets.

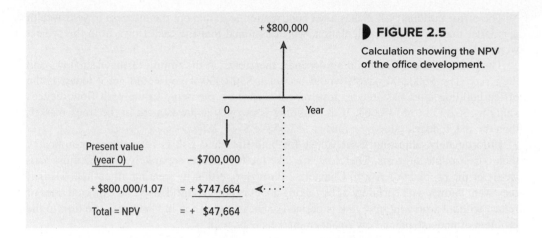

▶ FIGURE 2.5

Calculation showing the NPV
of the office development.

Remember that C_0, the cash flow at time 0 (that is, today) is usually a negative number. In other words, C_0 is an investment and therefore a cash outflow. In our example, $C_0 = -\$700,000$.

Figure 2.5 shows a timeline for your office development. It sets out the net present value calculation assuming that the discount rate r is 7%.[1]

Risk and Present Value

We made one unrealistic assumption in our discussion of the office development: We assumed that you could sell it next year for $800,000 with certainty. In reality, you can't be certain about the resale value. $800,000 represents your best guess, but it's not a sure thing.

If the cash flows are uncertain, your calculation of NPV is wrong. Investors could achieve a *certain* $800,000 next year by buying $747,664 worth of U.S. government securities. So they won't pay $747,664 for a building that's worth an *uncertain* $800,000 next year. You would have to cut your asking price to attract investors' interest.

Here we can invoke a second basic financial principle: *A safe dollar is worth more than a risky dollar.* Most investors dislike risky ventures and won't invest in them unless they see the prospect of a higher return. The riskier the venture, the less that they will be prepared to pay and the higher the return that they will demand.

The concepts of present value and the opportunity cost of capital still hold for risky investments: You still need to discount the payoff by the opportunity cost of capital. But now the cash flow that you discount is the *expected* cash flow and the opportunity cost of capital is now the rate of return available in financial markets on investments *of similar risk* to your project.[2]

Not all investments are equally risky. The office development is more risky than a government security but less risky than a start-up biotech venture. Suppose you believe that investing in the office building is as risky as investment in the stock market and that stocks are expected to provide a 12% return. Then 12% is the opportunity cost of capital for your project. That's what you are giving up by investing in the office building and not investing in equally risky securities.

Now recompute NPV with $r = 0.12$:

$$PV = \frac{800,000}{1.12} = \$714,286$$

$$NPV = PV - 700,000 = \$14,286$$

[1]You sometimes hear lay people refer to "net present value" when they mean "present value," and vice versa. Just remember, *present value* is the value of the investment today; *net present value* is the addition that the investment makes to your wealth.
[2]We define "expected" more carefully in Chapter 9. For now think of expected payoff as a realistic forecast, neither optimistic nor pessimistic. Forecasts of expected payoffs are correct on average.

The office building still makes a net contribution to value, but the increase in your wealth is smaller than in our first calculation, which assumed that the cash flows from the project were risk-free.

The value of the office building depends, therefore, on the timing of the cash flows and their risk. The $800,000 payoff would be worth $800,000 if you could get it today. If the office building is as risk-free as government securities, the delay in the cash flow reduces value by $52,336 to $747,664. If the building is as risky as investment in the stock market, then the risk reduces value by a further $33,378 to $714,286.

Unfortunately, adjusting asset values for both time and risk is often more complicated than our example suggests. Therefore, we take the two effects separately. For the most part, we defer the problem of risk in Chapters 2 through 6, either by treating all cash flows as if they were known with certainty or by talking about expected cash flows and expected rates of return without worrying how risk is defined or measured. Then in Chapter 7, we turn to the problem of understanding how financial markets cope with risk.

2.4 Self-Test

As the risk of a project increases, does the discount factor rise or fall?

Present Values and Rates of Return

We have decided that constructing the office building is a smart thing to do since it is worth more than it costs. To discover how much it is worth, we asked how much your shareholders would need to invest in equally risky securities to achieve the same payoff. That is why we discounted the project's future payoff by the rate of return offered by these equivalent-risk securities—the overall stock market in our example.

We can state our decision rule in another way: Your real estate venture is worth undertaking because its rate of return exceeds the opportunity cost of capital. The rate of return is simply the profit as a proportion of the initial outlay:

$$\text{Return} = \frac{\text{profit}}{\text{investment}} = \frac{800,000 - 700,000}{700,000} = 0.143, \text{ or } 14.3\%$$

The cost of capital is once again the return foregone by *not* investing in financial markets. If the office building is as risky as investing in the stock market, the return foregone is 12%. Since the 14.3% return on the office building exceeds the 12% opportunity cost, you should go ahead with the project.

We can justify the investment in the office building by either one of the following two rules:[3]

- *Net present value rule.* Accept investments that have positive net present values.
- *Rate of return rule.* Accept investments that offer rates of return in excess of their opportunity costs of capital.

Properly applied, both rules give the same answer, although we will encounter some cases in Chapter 5 where the rate of return rule is easily misused. In those cases, it is safest to use the net present value rule.

Calculating Present Values When There Are Multiple Cash Flows

One of the nice things about present values is that they are all expressed in current dollars—so you can add them up. In other words, the present value of cash flow (A + B) is equal to the present value of cash flow A plus the present value of cash flow B.

---

[3]You might check for yourself that these are equivalent rules. In other words, if the return of $100,000/$700,000 is greater than r, then the net present value −$700,000 + [$800,000/(1 + r)] *must* be greater than 0.

Suppose that you wish to value a stream of cash flows extending over a number of years. Our rule for adding present values tells us that the *total* present value is:

$$PV = \frac{C_1}{(1+r)} + \frac{C_2}{(1+r)^2} + \frac{C_3}{(1+r)^3} + \ldots + \frac{C_T}{(1+r)^T}$$

This is called the **discounted cash flow** (or **DCF**) formula. A shorthand way to write it is

$$PV = \sum_{t=1}^{T} \frac{C_t}{(1+r)^t} \tag{2.2}$$

where Σ refers to the sum of the series of discounted cash flows. To find the *net* present value (NPV) we add the (usually negative) initial cash flow:

$$NPV = C_0 + PV = C_0 + \sum_{t=1}^{T} \frac{C_t}{(1+r)^t} \tag{2.3}$$

Your two-period calculations in Example 2.3 required just a few keystrokes on a calculator. Real problems can be much more complicated, so financial managers usually turn to financial calculators especially programmed for present value calculations or to computer spreadsheet programs. A box near the end of the chapter introduces you to some useful Excel functions that can be used to solve discounting problems.

EXAMPLE 2.3 • Present Values with Multiple Cash Flows

You have thought of an alternative to selling the office building at the end of the year. Instead of selling, you believe that you could rent it out for two years at $30,000 a year. You forecast that at the end of that time you will be able to sell the building for $840,000. Thus, there are now two future cash flows—a cash flow of $C_1 = \$30,000$ at the end of one year and a further cash flow of $C_2 = (30,000 + 840,000) = \$870,000$ at the end of the second year.

The present value of your property development is equal to the present value of C_1 plus the present value of C_2. Figure 2.6 shows that the value of the first year's cash flow is $C_1/(1 + r) = 30,000/1.12 = \$26,786$ and the value of the second year's flow is $C_2/(1 + r)^2 = 870,000/1.12^2 = \$693,559$. Therefore, our rule for adding present values tells us that the *total* present value of your investment is:

$$PV = \frac{C_1}{1+r} + \frac{C_2}{(1+r)^2} = \frac{30,000}{1.12} + \frac{870,000}{1.12^2} = 26,786 + 693,559 = \$720,344$$

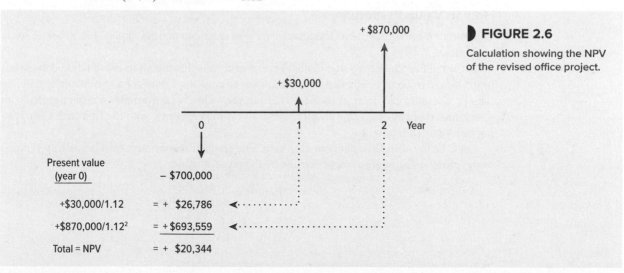

FIGURE 2.6

Calculation showing the NPV of the revised office project.

It looks as if you should adopt this alternative idea. NPV is higher than if you were to sell in year 1:

$$\text{NPV} = \$720,344 - \$700,000 = \$20,344$$

• • • • •

The Opportunity Cost of Capital

If investment in the office building is uncertain, your shareholders would be giving up the opportunity to earn an expected return of 12% from an equally risky investment in the stock market. The opportunity cost of capital is therefore 12%. When you discount the expected cash flows by the opportunity cost of capital, you are asking how much investors in the financial markets are prepared to pay for a security that produces a similar stream of future cash flows. Your calculations in Example 2.3 showed that these investors would need to pay $720,344 for an investment that produces cash flows of $30,000 at year 1 and $870,000 at year 2. Therefore, that is what they would be prepared to pay for your office building.

Confusion sometimes sneaks into discussions of the cost of capital. Suppose a banker approaches. "Your company is a fine and safe business with few debts," she says. "My bank will lend you the $700,000 that you need for the office block at 8%." Does this mean that the cost of capital is 8%? If so, the project would be even more worthwhile. At an 8% cost of capital, PV would be $30,000/1.08 + 870,000/1.08^2 = \$773,663$ and NPV $= \$773,663 - \$700,000 = +\$73,663$.

But that can't be right. First, the interest rate on the loan has nothing to do with the risk of the project: It reflects the good health of your existing business. Thus, you'd be able to borrow at 8% regardless of whether you bought the office block—it's not a consequence of taking the project. Second, whether you take the loan or not, you still face the choice between the office building and an equally risky investment in the stock market. A financial manager who borrows $700,000 at 8% and invests in an office building is not smart, but foolish, if the company or its shareholders can borrow at 8% and make an equally risky investment in the stock market offering an even higher return. That is why the 12% expected return on the stock market is the opportunity cost of capital for your project.

2-2   How to Value Perpetuities and Annuities

How to Value Perpetuities

Sometimes there are shortcuts that make it easy to calculate present values. Let's look at some examples.

In the eighteenth century, the British government consolidated all its outstanding debt issues into a single issue of bonds that became known as consols. Consols had no maturity date, so they promised to pay interest to the owner forever.[4] This is an example of a **perpetuity**—an investment that pays the same cash flow every year in perpetuity, with the first cash flow arising one year from now.

Let C be the cash flow paid out each year. The annual rate of return on a perpetuity is equal to the promised annual payment divided by the present value:

$$\text{Return} = \frac{\text{cash flow}}{\text{present value}}$$

$$r = \frac{C}{\text{PV}}$$

---

[4]However, the government had the option to redeem Consols, and it finally did so in 2015.

If we twist this around, we find the present value of a perpetuity given the discount rate r and the cash payment C:[5]

$$\text{PV of perpetuity} = \frac{C}{r} \qquad\qquad (2.4)$$

EXAMPLE 2.4 • Valuing a Perpetuity

The year is 2030. You have been fabulously successful and have decided to follow in the footsteps of two of your philanthropic heroes, Bill Gates and Warren Buffett. Malaria is still a scourge, and you want to endow a foundation to combat the disease. You aim to provide $1 billion a year in perpetuity, starting in one year's time. So, if the interest rate is 10%, you need to write a check today for

$$\text{PV of perpetuity} = \frac{C}{r} = \frac{\$1\text{ billion}}{0.1} = \$10\text{ billion}$$

• • • • •

Two warnings about the perpetuity formula. First, at a quick glance, you can easily confuse the formula with the present value of a single payment. A payment of $1 at the end of one year has a present value of $1/(1 + r)$. The perpetuity has a value of $1/r$. These are quite different.

Second, the perpetuity formula tells us the value of a regular stream of payments *starting one period from now*. If the cash flow starts in year $t + 1$, then the formula gives you a present value as of year t. In other words, the formula gives you the value of the perpetuity one year before the first cash flow arises. In Example 2.4, a $10 billion endowment today is enough to provide $1 billion each year as long as the first payment arises in one year's time. If you want the payments to start immediately, you'll need an extra $1 billion to cover the first payment, for a total of $11 billion.

Such a perpetuity—one that starts immediately—is known as a **perpetuity due**. In general, to find the present value of a perpetuity due, we simply add on the first year's cash flow to a regular perpetuity—that is,

$$\text{PV} = C + \frac{C}{\text{r}} = \frac{C}{r}(1 + r)$$

So, a perpetuity due is worth $(1 + r)$ times as much as a regular perpetuity. If the first payment in Example 2.4 starts now, you need to provide $10(1 + 0.10) = \$11$ billion.

Sometimes you may need to calculate the value of a perpetuity that does not start to make payments for several years. The following example shows how to do so.

---

[5]You can check this by writing down the present value formula

$$\text{PV} = \frac{C}{1 + r} + \frac{C}{(1 + r)^2} + \frac{C}{(1 + r)^3} + \cdots$$

Now let $C/(1 + r) = a$ and $1/(1 + r) = x$. Then we have (1) $\text{PV} = a(1 + x + x^2 + \cdots)$. Multiplying both sides by x, we have (2) $\text{PV}x = a(x + x^2 + \cdots)$. Subtracting (2) from (1) gives us $\text{PV}(1 - x) = a$. Therefore, substituting for a and x,

$$\text{PV}\left(1 - \frac{1}{1 + r}\right) = \frac{C}{1 + r}$$

Multiplying both sides by $(1 + r)$ and rearranging gives

$$\text{PV} = \frac{C}{r}$$

EXAMPLE 2.5 • Valuing a Delayed Perpetuity

Suppose that your lawyers have warned that it will take several years to set up your foundation, so that you now propose to provide $1 billion a year in perpetuity with the first payment four years from now. Figure 2.7 provides a timeline of these payments. Think first about how much they will be worth in year 3. (Remember that the perpetuity formula gives a valuation one year before the first payment). At that point, the endowment will be an ordinary perpetuity. So our perpetuity formula tells us that in year 3, the endowment will be worth $1/r = $1/0.1 = $10 billion. But it is not worth that much now. To find *today's* value, we need to discount that figure by $(1 + r)^3$. Thus, the "delayed" perpetuity is worth $10 billion × $1/(1.10)^3$ = $7.51 billion. The full calculation is:

$$PV = C \times \frac{1}{r} \times \frac{1}{(1 + r)^3} = \$1 \text{ billion} \times \frac{1}{0.10} \times \frac{1}{(1.10)^3} = \$7.51 \text{ billion}$$

▶ **FIGURE 2.7**

This perpetuity makes a series of payments of $1 billion a year starting in year 4.

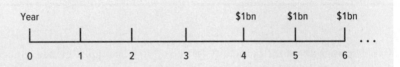

2.5 Self-Test

a. You have planted a money tree that is expected to produce $8,000 at the end of each year in perpetuity starting one year from now. If the interest rate is 7%, what is the present value of the money tree?

b. Now you realize that the tree will not start to bear fruit until the end of year 3. How does this change your calculation of the tree's value?

How to Value Annuities

Unlike a perpetuity which goes on forever, an **annuity** is an asset that pays a fixed sum each year for a specified number of years. The equal-payment house mortgage or installment credit agreement are common examples of annuities. So are interest payments on most bonds, as we shall see in the next chapter.

You can always value an annuity by calculating the value of each cash flow and finding the total. However, it is often quicker to use a simple formula which states that if the interest rate is *r*, then the present value of an annuity that pays $C a period for each of *t* periods starting one period from now is:

$$PV \text{ of } t\text{-year annuity} = C\left[\frac{1}{r} - \frac{1}{r(1 + r)^t}\right] \tag{2.5}$$

The expression in brackets is the *t*-year **annuity factor**. It shows the present value of $1 a year for each of *t* years. Recall that a perpetuity is worth *C/r*. The annuity is worth less because the cash flows are finite—hence the subtraction term at the end of the annuity formula. As the value of *t* increases, the subtraction term declines. When *t* is infinite, the annuity and perpetuity formulas are identical.

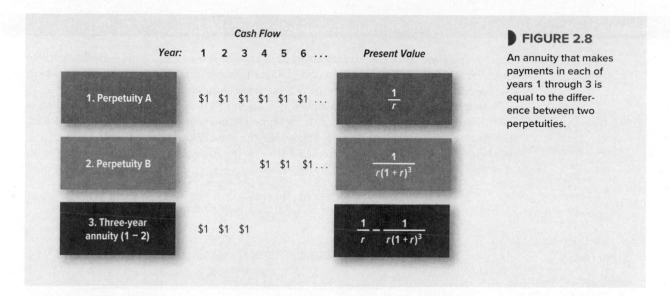

Cash Flow

FIGURE 2.8

An annuity that makes payments in each of years 1 through 3 is equal to the difference between two perpetuities.

If you're wondering where this formula comes from, look at Figure 2.8. It shows the payments and values of three investments.

Row 1   The investment in the first row provides a perpetual stream of $1 starting at the end of the first year. We have already seen that this perpetuity has a present value of $1/r$.

Row 2   Now look at the investment shown in the second row of Figure 2.8. It also provides a perpetual stream of $1 payments, but these payments don't start until year 4. This stream of payments is identical to the payments in row 1, except that they are delayed for an additional three years. In year 3, the investment will be an ordinary perpetuity with payments starting in one year and will therefore be worth $1/r$ in year 3. To find the value *today,* we simply multiply this figure by the three-year discount factor. Thus, as we saw earlier

$$PV = \frac{1}{r} \times \frac{1}{(1+r)^3}$$

Row 3   Finally, look at the investment shown in the third row of Figure 2.8. This provides a level payment of $1 a year for each of three years. In other words, it's a three-year annuity. You can also see that, taken together, the investments in rows 2 and 3 provide exactly the same cash payments as the investment in row 1. Thus the value of our annuity (row 3) must be equal to the value of the row 1 perpetuity less the value of the delayed row 2 perpetuity:

$$\text{Present value of a 3-year annuity of \$1 a year} = \frac{1}{r} - \frac{1}{r(1+r)^3}$$

Remembering formulas is about as difficult as remembering other people's birthdays. But as long as you bear in mind that an annuity is equivalent to the difference between an immediate and a delayed perpetuity, you shouldn't have any difficulty.[6]

---

[6]Some people find the following equivalent formula more intuitive:

$$\text{Present value of annuity} = \underset{\substack{\uparrow \\ \text{Perpetuity} \\ \text{formula}}}{\frac{1}{r}} \times \underset{\substack{\uparrow \qquad\quad \uparrow \\ \$1 \\ \text{Starting} \quad \text{Minus \$1} \\ \text{next year} \;\; \text{starting at } t+1}}{\left[1 - \frac{1}{(1+r)^1}\right]}$$

EXAMPLE 2.6 • Using the Annuity Formula to Value an Aircraft Lease

Most leasing plans call for a level stream of payments. Suppose that Omega Airlines wishes to lease a new airliner for five years at a cost of $5 million a year, payable at the end of each year, starting one year from now. What is the present value of these payments?

First, let's do the calculations the slow way to show that if the discount rate is 7%, the present value of these payments is $20,501. The timeline in Figure 2.9 shows the value of each cash flow and the total present value. The annuity formula, however, is generally quicker; you simply need to multiply the $5 million cash flow by the five-year annuity factor:

$$PV = 5\left[\frac{1}{0.07} - \frac{1}{0.07(1.07)^5}\right] = 5 \times 4.1002 = \$20.501 \text{ million}$$

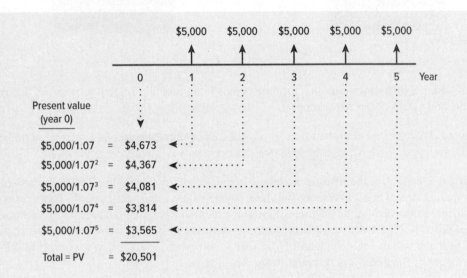

▶ FIGURE 2.9

Calculations showing the year-by-year present value of the lease payments (figures in $ millions). [*Note:* Divide all $ figures by 1,000—e.g., $5.0/1.07 not $5,000/1.07.]

2.6 Self-Test

A kindly uncle has promised to pay you $6,000 at the end of each of the next six years. If the interest rate is 5%, what is the present value of this gift?

Valuing Annuities Due

When we costed the aircraft lease in Example 2.6, we assumed that the first payment was made at the end of the year. Suppose instead that the first of the five yearly payments is due immediately. How does this change the cost?

If we discount each cash flow by one less year, the present value is increased by the multiple $(1 + r)$. In the case of the lease, the present value of the payments becomes 20.501 × $(1 + r) = 20.501 \times 1.07 = \$21.94$ million.

A level stream of payments starting immediately is called an **annuity due**. Just as a perpetuity due is worth $(1 + r)$ times the value of an ordinary perpetuity, so an annuity due is worth $(1 + r)$ times the value of an ordinary annuity.

BEYOND THE PAGE

Try It! More on annuities

mhhe.com/brealey14e

Calculating Annual Payments

Annuity problems can be confusing at first, but you'll find that with practice they are generally straightforward. For example, here is a case where you need to use the annuity formula to find the amount of the payment *given* the present value.

EXAMPLE 2.7 • Using the Annuity Formula to Calculate the Payments on a Bank Loan

Loans that involve a series of level payments are known as *amortizing loans.* "Amortizing" means that part of the regular payment is used to pay interest on the loan and part is used to pay off or *amortize* the loan. Suppose that you take out a four-year loan of $1,000. The bank requires you to repay the loan evenly over the four years. It must therefore set the four annual payments so that they have a present value of $1,000. Thus,

$$PV = \text{annual loan payment} \times \text{4-year annuity factor} = \$1,000$$
$$\text{Annual loan payment} = \$1,000/\text{4-year annuity factor}$$

Suppose that the interest rate is 10% a year. Then

$$\text{4-year annuity factor} = \left[\frac{1}{0.10} - \frac{1}{0.10(1.10)^4}\right] = 3.170$$

and

$$\text{Annual loan payment} = 1,000/3.170 = \$315.47$$

Let's check that this annual payment is sufficient to repay the loan. Table 2.1 provides the calculations. At the end of the first year, the interest charge is 10% of $1,000, or $100. So $100 of the first payment is absorbed by interest, and the remaining $215.47 is used to reduce the loan balance to $784.53.

Year	Beginning-of-Year Balance	Year-End Interest on Balance	Total Year-End Payment	Amortization of Loan	End-of-Year Balance
1	$1,000.00	$100.00	$315.47	$215.47	$784.53
2	784.53	78.45	315.47	237.02	547.51
3	547.51	54.75	315.47	260.72	286.79
4	286.79	28.68	315.47	286.79	0

〉TABLE 2.1   An example of an amortizing loan. If you borrow $1,000 at an interest rate of 10%, you would need to make an annual payment of $315.47 over four years to repay that loan with interest.

Next year, the outstanding balance is lower, so the interest charge is only $78.45. Therefore $315.47 − $78.45 = $237.02 can be applied to paying off the loan. Because the loan is progressively paid off, the fraction of each payment devoted to interest steadily falls over time, while the fraction used to reduce the loan increases. By the end of year 4, the amortization is just enough to reduce the balance of the loan to zero.

EXAMPLE 2.8 • Using the Annuity Formula to Calculate Mortgage Payments

Most mortgages are amortizing loans. For example, suppose that you take out a $250,000 house mortgage from your local savings bank when the interest rate is 12%. The bank requires you to repay the mortgage in equal annual installments over the next 30 years.

Thus,

$$\text{Annual mortgage payment} = \$250{,}000/\text{30-year annuity factor}$$

$$\text{30-year annuity factor} = \left[\frac{1}{0.12} - \frac{1}{0.12(1.12)^{30}}\right] = 8.055$$

and

$$\text{Annual mortgage payment} = 250{,}000/8.055 = \$31{,}036$$

Figure 2.10 shows that in the early years, almost all of the mortgage payment is eaten up by interest and only a small fraction is used to reduce the amount of the loan. Even after 15 years, the bulk of the annual payment goes to pay the interest on the loan. From then on, the amount of the loan begins to decline rapidly.

▶ FIGURE 2.10

Mortgage amortization. This figure shows the breakdown of mortgage payments between interest and amortization.

BEYOND THE PAGE

Try It! Figure 2.10: The amortization schedule

mhhe.com/brealey14e

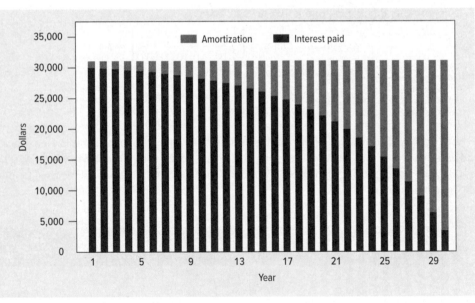

2.7 Self-Test

a. What will be the monthly payment if you take out a $240,000 20-year mortgage at an interest rate of 1% per month?

b. How much of the first monthly payment is interest and how much is amortization?

Future Value of an Annuity

Sometimes you need to calculate the *future* value of a level stream of payments. We know how to calculate its present value. So to calculate the future value we just need to multiply the present value by $(1 + r)^t$. The general formula for the future value of a level stream of cash flows of $1 a year for t years is, therefore,

$$\text{Future value of annuity} = \text{present value of annuity of \$1 a year} \times (1 + r)^t$$

$$= \left[\frac{1}{r} - \frac{1}{r(1+r)^t}\right] \times (1+r)^t = \frac{(1+r)^t - 1}{r}$$

There is a general point here. If you can find the present value of *any* series of cash flows, you can always calculate its future value by multiplying by $(1 + r)^t$:

$$\text{Future value at the end of year } t = \text{present value} \times (1 + r)^t$$

EXAMPLE 2.9 • Calculating the Future Value of an Annuity

Perhaps your ambition is to buy a sailboat. You estimate that you could save $20,000 a year out of your income starting at the end of this year, and earn a return of 8% on these savings. How much will you be able to spend after five years?

Think first how much your savings are worth today. You will set aside $20,000 at the end of each of the next five years. The present value of this five-year annuity is therefore equal to

$$\text{PV} = \$20,000 \times 5\text{-year annuity factor}$$

$$= \$20,000 \times \left[\frac{1}{0.08} - \frac{1}{0.08(1.08)^5} \right] = \$79,854$$

Once you know today's value of the stream of cash flows, it is easy to work out its value in the future. Just multiply by $(1.08)^5$:

$$\text{Value at end of year } 5 = \$79,854 \times 1.08^5 = \$117,332$$

You should be able to buy yourself a nice boat for $117,000.

• • • • •

2-3   How to Value Growing Perpetuities and Annuities

Growing Perpetuities

You now know how to value level streams of cash flows, but you often need to value a stream of cash flows that grow at a constant rate. For example, think back to your plans to donate $10 billion to fight malaria and other infectious diseases. Unfortunately, you made no allowance for the growth in salaries and other costs, which will probably average about 4% a year starting in year 1. Therefore, instead of providing $1 billion a year in perpetuity, you need to provide $1 billion in year 1, $1.04 \times \$1$ billion in year 2, and so on. If we call the growth rate in costs g, we can write down the present value of this stream of cash flows as follows:

$$\text{PV} = \frac{C_1}{1 + r} + \frac{C_2}{(1 + r)^2} + \frac{C_3}{(1 + r)^3} + \cdots$$

$$= \frac{C_1}{1 + r} + \frac{C_1(1 + g)}{(1 + r)^2} + \frac{C_1(1 + g)^2}{(1 + r)^3} + \cdots$$

Fortunately, there is a simple formula for the sum of this geometric series.[7] If we assume that r is greater than g,[8] our clumsy-looking calculation simplifies to

$$\text{PV of growing perpetuity} = \frac{C_1}{r - g} \tag{2.7}$$

---

[7] We need to calculate the sum of an infinite geometric series $\text{PV} = a(1 + x + x^2 + \ldots)$ where $a = C_1/(1 + r)$ and $x = (1 + g)/(1 + r)$. In footnote 4 we showed that the sum of such a series is $a/(1 - x)$. Substituting for a and x in this formula,

$$\text{PV} = \frac{C_1}{(r - g)}$$

[8] The asset has a finite value only if r is less than g.

Therefore, if you want to provide a perpetual stream of income that keeps pace with the growth rate in costs, the amount that you must set aside today is

$$PV = \frac{C_1}{r-g} = \frac{\$1 \text{ billion}}{0.10 - 0.04} = \$16.667 \text{ billion}$$

You will meet this perpetual-growth formula again in Chapter 4, where we use it to value the stocks of mature, slowly growing companies.

2.8 Self-Test

a. At the end of the next year, General Supplies is expected to pay a dividend of $4 a share. You expect the dividend to grow thereafter by 4% a year in perpetuity. If investors demand a return of 8% on the stock, what is its present value?

b. Could you use the same formula to calculate the value of General Supplies' stock if the expected growth rate was 10% rather than 4%?

Growing Annuities

EXAMPLE 2.10 • Valuing a Growing Annuity

In October 2018, a South Carolina woman won a record $1.54 billion in the Mega Millions lottery. We suspect she received unsolicited congratulations and requests for money from dozens of more or less worthy charities, relations, and newly devoted friends. In response, she could fairly point out that the prize wasn't really worth $1.54 billion. That sum was to be paid in 30 annual installments. The payment in the first year was $23.18 million, but it then increased each year by 5% so that the final payment was $95.41 million. The total amount paid out was $1.54 billion, but the winner had to wait to get it.

If the interest rate was 3.4%, what was that $1.54 billion prize really worth? Suppose that the first payment occurs at the end of year 1, so that $C_1 = \$23.18$ million. If the payments then grow at the rate of $g = 0.05$ each year, the payment in year 2 is 23.18×1.05, and in year 3 it is 23.18×1.05^2. Of course, you could calculate each of the 30 cash flows and discount them at 3.4%. The alternative is to use the following formula for the present value of a growing annuity:[9]

$$PV \text{ of growing annuity} = C \times \frac{1}{r-g}\left[1 - \frac{(1+g)^t}{(1+r)^t}\right] \tag{2.8}$$

---

[9]We can derive the formula for a growing annuity by taking advantage of our earlier trick of finding the difference between the values of two perpetuities. Imagine three investments (A, B, and C) that make the following dollar payments:

Year	1	2	3	4	5	6	...
A	$1	$(1+g)$	$(1+g)^2$	$(1+g)^3$	$(1+g)^4$	$(1+g)^5$	etc.
B				$(1+g)^3$	$(1+g)^4$	$(1+g)^5$	etc.
C	$1	$(1+g)$	$(1+g)^2$				

Investments A and B are growing perpetuities; A makes its first payment of $1 in year 1, while B makes its first payment of $(1 + g)^3$ in year 4. C is a three-year growing annuity; its cash flows are equal to the difference between the cash flows of A and B. You know how to value growing perpetuities such as A and B. So you should be able to derive the formula for the value of growing annuities such as C:

$$PV(A) = \frac{1}{(r-g)}$$

$$PV(B) = \frac{(1+g)^3}{(r-g)} \times \frac{1}{(1+r)^3}$$

So

$$PV(C) = PV(A) - PV(B) = \frac{1}{(r-g)} - \frac{(1+g)^3}{(r-g)} \times \frac{1}{(1+r)^3} = \frac{1}{r-g}\left[1 - \frac{(1+g)^3}{(1+r)^3}\right]$$

If $r = g$, then the formula blows up. In that case, the cash flows grow at the same rate as the amount by which they are discounted. Therefore, each cash flow has a present value of $C/(1 + r)$ and the total present value of the annuity equals $t \times C/(1 + r)$. If $r < g$, then this particular formula remains valid, though still treacherous.

In the case of our lottery, the present value of the growing stream of payments is

$$PV = 23.18 \times \frac{1}{0.034 - 0.05}\left[1 - \frac{(1.05)^{30}}{(1.034)^{30}}\right] = 23.18 \times 36.57 = \$847.7 \text{ million}$$

Thus, the present value of the growing stream of payments starting at the end of the first year is $847.7 million.

In practice, the lottery winner receives the first payment immediately (in year 0) and the last one is received in year 29 rather than in year 30. Therefore, it's a growing annuity due, and we need to increase our estimate of present value by $1 + r$. So the present value of the prize is $847.7 \times 1.034 = \$876.5$ million.

If the total prize money was paid out immediately, it would be worth $1.54 billion. Paying out this money over the next 29 years reduces the value of the prize to about $876.5 million, much below the well-trumpeted prize but still not a bad day's haul.

For winners with big spending plans, lottery operators generally make arrangements so that they may take an equivalent lump sum. In our example, the winner could either take the $1.54 billion spread over 30 years or receive $876.5 million up front. Both arrangements had the same present value.

• • • • •

Too many formulas are bad for the digestion. So we will stop at this point and spare you any more of them. The formulas discussed so far appear in Table 2.2.

Year:	0	1	2 ...	... $t-1$	t	$t+1$ ...	Present Value
Perpetuity		1	1 ...	1	1	1 ...	$\frac{1}{r}$
t-period annuity		1	1 ...	1	1		$\frac{1}{r} - \frac{1}{r(1+r)^t}$
t-period annuity due	1	1	1 ...	1			$(1+r)\left(\frac{1}{r} - \frac{1}{r(1+r)^t}\right)$
Growing perpetuity		1	$1 \times (1+g)$ ...	$1 \times (1+g)^{t-2}$	$1 \times (1+g)^{t-1}$	$1 \times (1+g)^{t \cdot \cdot}$	$\frac{1}{r-g}$
t-period growing annuity		1	$1 \times (1+g)$ ...	$1 \times (1+g)^{t-2}$	$1 \times (1+g)^{t-1}$		$\frac{1}{r-g}\left[1 - \frac{(1+g)^t}{(1+r)^t}\right]$

〉**TABLE 2.2** Some useful shortcut formulas.

Note: a. The growing perpetuity formula works only if the discount rate r is greater than the growth rate g.
  b. The growing annuity formula blows up if $r = g$. In this case, the value of the growing annuity is $C \times t/(1+r)$.

2-4 How Interest Is Paid and Quoted

In our examples, we have assumed that cash flows occur only at the end of each year. This is sometimes the case. For example, in France and Germany, the government pays interest on its bonds annually. However, in the United States and Britain, government bonds pay interest semiannually. So if a U.S. government bond promises to pay interest of 10% a year, the investor in practice receives interest of 5% every six months.

If the first interest payment is made at the end of six months, you can earn an additional six months' interest on this payment. For example, if you invest $100 in a bond that pays interest of 5% every half year, your wealth will grow to $1.05 \times \$100 = \$105$ by the end of six months and to $1.05 \times \$105 = \$110.25$ by the end of the year. In other words, interest of 5% paid every half year is equivalent to 10.25% compounded annually. The extra $0.25 is due to compounding or "interest-on-interest"—the $5 interest paid at the end of six months earns the semiannual interest rate of 5% over the next six months.

The 10% in this example is known as the **annual percentage rate**, or **APR**. It tells you how much interest is paid over the course of the year, ignoring how often it's paid. But because it ignores compounding, it doesn't tell us how much interest an investor accumulates over the year. The equivalent annually compounded rate is 10.25% and is commonly known as the **effective annual rate (EAR)**. The effective annual rate takes into account how often the APR is paid—every six months in the preceding example—and the effect of compounding.

Let's take another example. Suppose a bank offers you a car loan at an APR of 12% with interest to be paid monthly. By this, the bank means that each month you need to pay one-twelfth of the annual rate—that is, 12/12 = 1% a month. Thus the bank is *quoting* a rate of 12%, but the loan's true cost is the effective annual rate of $1.01^{12} - 1 = 0.1268$ or 12.68%.[10]

Our examples show that knowing the annual percentage rate alone is insufficient. You also need to know how often the interest is paid. The effective annual rate takes both components into account—it converts the APR into an effective rate assuming compounding once a year. Thus, when interest is paid once a year, the two rates are identical. When interest is paid more frequently, the effective annual rate is higher than the APR.

In general, if you invest $1 at a rate of r per year compounded m times a year, your investment at the end of the year will be worth $[1 + (r/m)]^m$ and the effective annual rate is $[1 + (r/m)]^m - 1$. In our automobile loan example, $r = 0.12$ and $m = 12$. So the effective annual interest rate was $[1 + 0.12/12]^{12} - 1 = 0.1268$, or 12.68%.

Continuous Compounding

Instead of compounding interest monthly or semiannually, the rate could be compounded weekly ($m = 52$) or daily ($m = 365$). In fact, there is no limit to how frequently interest could be paid. One can imagine a situation where the payments are spread evenly and continuously throughout the year, so the interest rate is continuously compounded.[11] In this case m is infinite.

It turns out that there are many occasions in finance when continuous compounding is useful. For example, one important application is in option pricing models, such as the Black–Scholes model that we introduce in Chapter 22. So you will find that most computer programs for calculating option values ask for the continuously compounded interest rate.

It may seem that a lot of calculations would be needed to find a continuously compounded interest rate. However, think back to your high school algebra. You may recall that as m approaches infinity $[1 + (r/m)]^m$ approaches $(2.718)^r$. The figure 2.718—or e, as it is called—is the base for natural logarithms. Therefore, $1 invested at a continuously compounded rate of r will grow to $e^r = (2.718)^r$ by the end of the first year. By the end of t years it will grow to $e^{rt} = (2.718)^{rt}$.

If we reverse the calculation, we obtain the present value of $1 received at the end of year t when the continuously compounded rate is r

$$PV = \$1/e^{rt} \tag{2.9}$$

---

[10]In the U.S., truth-in-lending laws oblige the company to quote an APR that is calculated by multiplying the payment each period by the number of payments in the year. APRs are calculated differently in other countries. For example, in the European Union, APRs must be expressed as annually compounded rates, so consumers know the effective interest rate that they are paying.

[11]When we talk about *continuous* payments, we are pretending that money can be dispensed in a continuous stream like water out of a faucet. One can never quite do this. For example, instead of paying out $1 billion every year to combat malaria, you could pay out about $1 million every 8 3/4 hours or $10,000 every 5 1/4 minutes or $10 every 3 1/6 seconds but you could not pay it out *continuously*. Financial managers *pretend* that payments are continuous rather than hourly, daily, or weekly because (1) it simplifies the calculations and (2) it gives a very close approximation to the PV of frequent payments.

EXAMPLE 2.11 • Present Value of a One-Year Investment Using a Continuously Compounded Rate

Suppose you invest $1 at a continuously compounded rate of 11% ($r = 0.11$) for one year ($t = 1$). The end-year value is $e^{0.11}$, or $1.1163. In other words, investing at 11% a year *continuously* compounded is exactly the same as investing at 11.63% a year *annually* compounded.

If we reverse the process, we obtain the present value of $1 received at the end of the year at a continuously compounded rate or r = 0.11:

$$PV = \$1.1163/e^{0.11} = \$1.00$$

EXAMPLE 2.12 • Future Value of Investing for *t* Years at a Continuously Compounded Rate

Suppose you invest $1 at a continuously compounded rate of 11% ($r = 0.11$) for two years ($t = 2$). The final value of the investment is $e^{rt} = e^{0.22}$, or $1.2461.

Sometimes it may be more reasonable to assume that the cash flows from a project are spread evenly over the year rather than occurring at the year's end. For example, a supermarket sells goods each day, rather than only at the end of the year. It is easy to adapt our previous formulas to handle this. For example, suppose that we wish to compute the present value of a perpetuity of C dollars a year. We already know that if the payment is made at the end of the year, we divide the payment by the *annually* compounded rate of *r*:

$$PV = \frac{C}{r}$$

If the same total payment is made in an even stream throughout the year, we use the same formula but substitute the *continuously* compounded rate.

Suppose the annually compounded rate is 18.5%. The present value of a $100 perpetuity, with each cash flow received at the end of the year, is 100/0.185 = $540.54. If the cash flow is received continuously, we must divide $100 by 17%, because 17% continuously compounded is equivalent to 18.53% annually compounded ($e^{0.17} = 1.1853$). The present value of the continuous cash flow stream is 100/0.17 = $588.24. Investors are prepared to pay more for the continuous cash payments because the cash starts to flow in immediately.

EXAMPLE 2.13 • Calculating the Value of a Continuous Stream of Cash Flows

After you have retired, you plan to spend $200,000 a year for 20 years. The annually compounded interest rate is 10%. How much must you save by the time you retire to support this spending plan?

Let's first do the calculations assuming that you spend the cash at the end of each year. In this case, we can use the simple annuity formula that we derived earlier:

$$PV = C\left(\frac{1}{r} - \times \frac{1}{r(1+r)^t}\right)$$

$$= \$200,000 \left(\frac{1}{0.10} - \frac{1}{0.10(1.10)^{20}}\right) = \$200,000 \times 8.514 = \$1,702,800$$

Thus, you will need to have saved $1.7 million by the time you retire.

Instead of waiting until the end of each year before you spend any cash, it is more reasonable to assume that your expenditure will be spread evenly over the year. In this case, instead of using the annually compounded rate of 10%, we must use the continuously compounded rate of $r = 9.53\%$ ($e^{0.0953} = 1.10$). Therefore, to cover a steady stream of expenditure, you need to set aside the following sum:[12]

$$PV = C\left(\frac{1}{r} - \times \frac{1}{r}\frac{1}{e^{rt}}\right)$$

$$= \$200,000 \left(\frac{1}{.0953} - \frac{1}{.0953} \times \frac{1}{6.727}\right) = \$200,000 \times 8.932 = \$1,786,400$$

To support a steady stream of outgoings, you must save an additional $83,600.

● ● ● ● ●

Often in finance you need only a ballpark estimate of present value. An error of 5% in a present value calculation may be perfectly acceptable. In such cases, it doesn't usually matter whether you assume that cash flows occur at the end of the year or in a continuous stream. At other times precision matters, and you do need to worry about the exact frequency of the cash flows.

2.9 Self-Test

a. Suppose you invest $1 in an investment that pays interest m times a year. If the quoted interest rate is r per year, what is the value of your investment at the end of 1 year?

b. What is its value after n years?

c. Now suppose that interest is paid continuously throughout the year. What is the value of an investment of $1 at the end of the year if the annually compounded interest rate is r?

d. What is its value after n years?

---

[12]Remember that an annuity is simply the difference between a perpetuity received today and a perpetuity received in year t. A continuous stream of C dollars a year in perpetuity is worth C/r, where r is the continuously compounded rate. Our annuity, then, is worth

$$PV = \frac{C}{r} - \text{Present value of } \frac{C}{r} \text{ received in year } t$$

Since r is the continuously compounded rate, C/r received in year t is worth (C/r) × (1/e^{rt}) today. Our annuity formula is therefore

$$PV = \frac{C}{r} - \frac{C}{r} \times \frac{1}{e^{rt}}$$

sometimes written as

$$\frac{C}{r}(1 - e^{-rt})$$

Discounting Cash Flows

❯Spreadsheet programs such as Excel provide built-in functions to solve discounted cash flow (DCF) problems. You can find these functions by pressing *fx* on the Excel toolbar under the Formulas tab. If you then click on the function that you wish to use, Excel asks you for the inputs that it needs. At the bottom left of the function box there is a Help facility with an example of how the function is used.

Here is a list of useful functions for DCF problems and some points to remember when entering data:

- **FV:** Future value of single investment or annuity.
- **PV:** Present value of single future cash flow or annuity.
- **RATE:** Interest rate (or rate of return) needed to produce given future value or annuity.
- **NPER:** Number of periods (e.g., years) that it takes an investment to reach a given future value or series of future cash flows.
- **PMT:** Amount of annuity payment with a given present or future value.
- **NPV:** Calculates the value of a stream of negative and positive cash flows. (When using this function, note the warning below.)
- **EFFECT:** The effective annual interest rate, given the quoted rate (APR) and number of interest payments in a year.
- **NOMINAL:** The quoted interest rate (APR) given the effective annual interest rate.

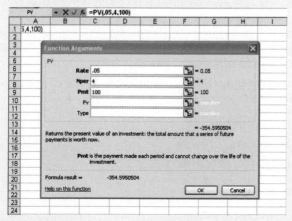

Source: Microsoft Excel

All the inputs in these functions can be entered directly as numbers or as the addresses of cells that contain the numbers.

Three warnings:

1. PV is the amount that needs to be invested today to produce a given future value. It should therefore be entered as a negative number. Entering both PV and FV with the same sign when solving for RATE results in an error message.

2. Always enter the interest or discount rate as a decimal value (e.g., 0.05 rather than 5%).

3. Use the NPV function with care. Better still, don't use it at all. It gives the value of the cash flows one period *before* the first cash flow and not the value at the date of the first cash flow.

Spreadsheet Questions

The following questions provide opportunities to practice each of the Excel functions.

1. (FV) In 1459 the Medici Bank in Florence lent the Duke of Milan 218,000 Milanese pounds at an interest rate of 15.4%. Suppose that the loan was for three years. What would have been the value of the Medici's investment by the end of that three years?

2. (PV) Your adviser has produced revised figures for your office building. It is forecasted to produce a cash flow of $40,000 in year 1 but only $850,000 in year 2, when you come to sell it. If the cost of capital is 12%, what is the value of the building?

3. (PV) Your company can lease a truck for $10,000 a year (paid at the end of the year) for six years, or it can buy the truck today for $50,000. At the end of the six years, the truck will be worthless. If the interest rate is 6%, what is the present value of the lease payments? Is the lease worthwhile?

4. (RATE) Ford Motor stock was one of the victims of the coronavirus pandemic. At the end of June 2020, Ford stock price stood at $6.08. Six months later it was $8.79. What was the *annual* rate of return over this period to an investor in Ford stock?

BEYOND THE PAGE

Try It! Using Excel to solve spreadsheet questions

mhhe.com/brealey14e

5. (NPER) An investment adviser has promised to double your money. If the interest rate is 7% a year, how many years will she take to do so?

6. (PMT) You need to take out a home mortgage for $200,000. If payments are made annually over 30 years and the interest rate is 8%, what is the amount of the annual payment?

7. (EFFECT) First National Bank pays 6.2% interest compounded annually. Second National Bank pays 6% interest compounded monthly. Which bank offers the higher effective annual interest rate?

8. (NOMINAL) What monthly compounded interest rate would Second National Bank need to pay on savings deposits to provide an effective rate of 6.2%?

• • • • •

KEY TAKEAWAYS

Financial decisions usually involve a comparison of cash flows at different points in time. In this chapter, we have shown how to convert between present and future values of a cash flow.

- **Future values** An investment of $1 earning an interest rate of r will increase in value each period by the factor $(1 + r)$. The future value after t periods is:

$$\text{Future value} = \text{present value} \times (1 + r)^t$$

- **Present values** The present value (PV) of a future cash payment is the amount that you would need to invest today to produce that future payment. To calculate present value, discount future cash flows (C_t) by an appropriate rate r, usually called the *discount rate, hurdle rate,* or *opportunity cost of capital*:

$$\text{Present value} = \text{PV} = \sum_{t=1}^{T} \frac{C_t}{(1 + r)^t}$$

Net present value is present value plus any immediate cash flow:

$$\text{Net present value (NPV)} = C_0 + \text{PV}$$

Remember that C_0 is negative if the immediate cash flow is an investment, that is, if it is a cash outflow. Firms can best help their shareholders by accepting all projects that are worth more than they cost. In other words, they need to seek out projects with positive net present values.

- **The discount rate (r)** Cash flows are discounted for two reasons: (1) A dollar today is worth more than a dollar tomorrow because the dollar today can be invested to earn interest, and (2) a safe dollar is worth more than a risky one. The discount rate r is determined by rates of return prevailing in financial markets. If the future cash flow is safe, then the discount rate is the interest rate on safe securities such as U.S. government debt. If the cash flow is uncertain, then the discount rate is the expected rate of return offered by equivalent-risk securities. (We talk more about risk and the cost of capital in Chapters 7 to 9.)

- **Perpetuities** A level stream of cash payments that continues indefinitely is known as a perpetuity. The present value of a perpetuity of C per period is

$$\text{PV of perpetuity} = \frac{C}{r}$$

- **Annuities** A level stream of payments that continues for a limited number of years is called an annuity. The present value of an annuity of C per period is

$$\text{PV of } t\text{-year annuity} = C \left[\frac{1}{r} - \frac{1}{r(1 + r)^t} \right]$$

- **Growing perpetuities** You may often need to value a stream of cash flows that grow at a constant rate, g, in perpetuity. As long as r is greater than g,

$$\text{PV of growing perpetuity} = \frac{C_1}{r - g}$$

• **How interest rates are quoted** When someone offers to lend you a dollar at a quoted interest rate, you should always check how frequently the interest is to be paid. If you invest $1 at an *annual percentage rate* (APR) of r per year compounded m times a year, your investment at the end of the year will be worth $[1 + (r/m)]^m$. The equivalent annually compounded rate, or *effective annual rate,* is $[1 + (r/m)]^m - 1$. If interest is compounded continuously at the rate r, then the *effective annual rate* is e^{rt}, where e is the base for natural logarithms.

McGraw Hill connect®   Select problems are available in McGraw-Hill's *Connect.*

PROBLEM SETS

1. **Opportunity cost of capital (S2.1)** Which of the following statements are true? The opportunity cost of capital:

   a. Equals the interest rate at which the company can borrow.

   b. Depends on the risk of the cash flows to be valued.

   c. Depends on the rates of return that shareholders can expect to earn by investing on their own.

   d. Equals zero if the firm has excess cash in its bank account and the bank account pays no interest.

2. **Compound interest (S2.1)** Old Time Savings Bank pays 4% interest on its savings account. If you deposit $1,000 in the bank and leave it there:

   a. How much interest will you earn in the first year?

   b. How much interest will you earn in the second year?

   c. How much interest will you earn in the tenth year?

3. **Compound interest (S2.1)** In 1973, Gordon Moore, one of Intel's founders, predicted that the number of transistors that could be placed on a single silicon chip would double every 18 months, equivalent to an annual growth rate of 59% (i.e., $1.59^{1.5} = 2.0$). The first microprocessor was built in 1971 and had 2,250 transistors. In 2019, the AMD Epyc chip contained 32 billion transistors, 1.42 million times the number of transistors 48 years earlier. What has been the annual compound rate of growth in processing power? How does it compare with the prediction of Moore's law?

4. **Compound interest (S2.1)** New Savings Bank pays 4% interest on deposits. If you deposit $1,000 in the bank and leave it there, will it take more or less than 25 years for your investment to double? You should be able to answer this without a calculator.

5. **Compound interest (S2.1)** In 2017, Leonardo da Vinci's painting *Salvator Mundi* sold for a record $450.3 million. In 1958, it sold for $125, equivalent in purchasing power to about $1,060 at 2017 prices. The painting was originally commissioned by King Louis XII of France in about 1500. *The Wall Street Journal* guesstimated that the king may have paid Leonardo the equivalent in purchasing power of $575,000 in 1519.[13]

   a. What was the annual rate of appreciation in the price of the painting between 1958 and 2017 adjusted for inflation?

   b. What was the annual estimated rate of appreciation in the price of the painting between 1519 and 2017 adjusted for inflation.

6. **Future values (S2.1)** If you invest $100 at an interest rate of 15%, how much will you have at the end of eight years?

---

[13]See J. Zweig, "Is Da Vinci's *Salvator Mundi* Worth $450 Million or $454,680?" *The Wall Street Journal,* November 16, 2017.

7. **Future values (S2.1)** Compute the future value of a $100 investment for the following combinations of rates and times.

   a. $r = 6\%$, $t = 10$ years.

   b. $r = 6\%$, $t = 20$ years.

   c. $r = 4\%$, $t = 10$ years.

   d. $r = 4\%$, $t = 20$ years.

8. **Discount factors (S2.1)**

   a. If the present value of $139 is $125, what is the discount factor?

   b. If that $139 is received in year 5, what is the interest rate?

9. **Present values (S2.1)** If the cost of capital is 9%, what is the PV of $374 paid in year 9?

10. **Present values (2.1)** A project produces a cash flow of $432 in year 1, $137 in year 2, and $797 in year 3. If the cost of capital is 15%, what is the project's PV? If the project requires an investment of $1,200, what is its NPV?

11. **Present values (2.1)** What is the PV of $100 received in:

    a. Year 10 (at a discount rate of 1%)?

    b. Year 10 (at a discount rate of 13%)?

    c. Year 15 (at a discount rate of 25%)?

    d. Each of years 1 through 3 (at a discount rate of 12%)?

12. **Present values (S2.1)** Lofting Snodbury is considering investing in a new boring machine. It costs $380,000 and is expected to produce the following cash flows:

Year	1	2	3	4	5	6	7	8	9	10
Cash flow ($000s)	50	57	75	80	85	92	92	80	68	50

   If the cost of capital is 12%, what is the machine's NPV?

13. **Present values (S2.1)** A factory costs $800,000. You estimate that it will produce an inflow after operating costs of $170,000 a year for 10 years. If the opportunity cost of capital is 14%, what is the net present value of the factory? What will the factory be worth at the end of five years?

14. **Present values (S2.1)** Recalculate the NPV of the office building venture in Example 2.3 at interest rates of 5, 10, and 15%. Plot the points on a graph with NPV on the vertical axis and the discount rates on the horizontal axis. At what discount rate (approximately) would the project have zero NPV? Check your answer.

15. **Present values and opportunity cost of capital (S2.1)** Halcyon Lines is considering the purchase of a new bulk carrier for $8 million. The forecasted revenues are $5 million a year and operating costs are $4 million. A major refit costing $2 million will be required after both the fifth and tenth years. After 15 years, the ship is expected to be sold for scrap at $1.5 million.

    a. What is the NPV if the opportunity cost of capital is 8%?

    b. Halcyon could finance the ship by borrowing the entire investment at an interest rate of 4.5%. How does this borrowing opportunity affect your calculation of NPV?

16. **Perpetuities (S2.2)** An investment costs $1,548 and pays $138 in perpetuity. If the interest rate is 9%, what is the NPV?

17. **Perpetuities (S2.2)** You have just read an advertisement stating, "Pay us $100 a year for 10 years and we will pay you $100 a year thereafter in perpetuity." If this is a fair deal, what is the rate of interest?

18. **Perpetuities and annuities (S2.2)** The interest rate is 10%.

    a. What is the PV of an asset that pays $1 a year in perpetuity?

    b. The value of an asset that appreciates at 10% per annum approximately doubles in seven years. What is the approximate PV of an asset that pays $1 a year in perpetuity beginning in year 8?

    c. What is the approximate PV of an asset that pays $1 a year for each of the next seven years?

    d. A piece of land produces an income that grows by 5% per annum. If the first year's income is $10,000, what is the value of the land?

19. **Discount factors and annuity factors (S2.2)**

    a. If the one-year discount factor is 0.905, what is the one-year interest rate?

    b. If the two-year interest rate is 10.5%, what is the two-year discount factor?

    c. Given these one- and two-year discount factors, calculate the two-year annuity factor.

    d. If the PV of $10 a year for three years is $24.65, what is the three-year annuity factor?

    e. From your answers to parts (c) and (d), calculate the three-year discount factor.

20. **Annuities (S2.2)** David and Helen Zhang are saving to buy a boat at the end of five years. If the boat costs $20,000 and they can earn 10% a year on their savings, how much do they need to put aside at the end of years 1 through 5?

21. **Annuities (S2.2)** Siegfried Basset is 65 years of age and has a life expectancy of 12 more years. He wishes to invest $20,000 in an annuity that will make a level payment at the end of each year until his death. If the interest rate is 8%, what income can Mr. Basset expect to receive each year?

22. **Annuities (S2.2)** Several years ago, *The Wall Street Journal* reported that the winner of the Massachusetts State Lottery prize had the misfortune to be both bankrupt and in prison for fraud. The prize was $9,420,713, to be paid in 19 equal annual installments. (There were 20 installments, but the winner had already received the first payment.) The bankruptcy court judge ruled that the prize should be sold off to the highest bidder and the proceeds used to pay off the creditors.

    a. If the interest rate was 8%, how much would you have been prepared to bid for the prize?

    b. Enhance Reinsurance Company was reported to have offered $4.2 million. Use Excel to find the return that the company was looking for.

23. **Annuities (S2.2)** The *annually* compounded discount rate is 5.5%. You are asked to calculate the present value of a 12-year annuity with payments of $50,000 per year. Calculate PV for each of the following cases.

    a. The annuity payments arrive at one-year intervals. The first payment arrives one year from now.

    b. The first payment arrives in six months. Following payments arrive at one-year intervals (i.e., at 18 months, 30 months, etc.).

24. **Annuities (S2.2)**

    Dear Financial Adviser,

    My spouse and I are each 62 and hope to retire in three years. After retirement we will receive $7,500 per month after taxes from our employers' pension plans and $1,500 per month after taxes from Social Security. Unfortunately our monthly living expenses are $15,000. Our social obligations preclude further economies.

    We have $1,000,000 invested in a high-grade, tax-free municipal-bond mutual fund. The return on the fund is 3.5% per year. We plan to make annual withdrawals from the mutual fund to cover the difference between our pension and Social Security income and our living expenses. How many years before we run out of money?

Sincerely,

Luxury Challenged

Marblehead, MA

You can assume that the withdrawals (one per year) will sit in a checking account (no interest) until spent. The couple will use the account to cover the monthly shortfalls.

25. **Perpetuities and annuities (S2.2, S2.3)** If the rate of interest is 8% rather than 10%, how much would you need to set aside to provide each of the following?

   a. $1 billion at the end of each year in perpetuity.

   b. A perpetuity that pays $1 billion at the end of the first year and that grows at 4% a year.

   c. $1 billion at the end of each year for 20 years.

   d. $1 billion a year spread evenly over 20 years.

26. **Annuities due (S2.2)** The $40 million lottery prize that you have just won actually pays out $2 million a year for 20 years. The interest rate is 8%.

   a. If the first payment comes after 1 year, what is the present value of your winnings?

   b. What is the present value if the first payment comes immediately?

27. **Annuities due (S2.2)** A store offers two payment plans. Under the installment plan, you pay 25% down and 25% of the purchase price in each of the next three years. If you pay the entire bill immediately, you can take a 10% discount from the purchase price.

   a. Which is the better deal if the interest rate is 5%?

   b. How will your answer change if the four payments on the installments do not start until the end of the year?

28. **Amortizing loans (S2.2)** A bank loan requires you to pay $70,000 at the end of each of the next eight years. The interest rate is 8%.

   a. What is the present value of these payments?

   b. For each year, calculate the loan balance that remains outstanding, the interest payment on the loan, and the reduction in the loan balance.

29. **Amortizing loans (S2.2)** Suppose that you take out a $200,000, 20-year mortgage loan to buy a condo. The interest rate on the loan is 6%, and payments on the loan are made annually at the end of each year.

   a. What is your annual payment on the loan?

   b. Construct a mortgage amortization table in Excel similar to Table 2.1, showing the interest payment, the amortization of the loan, and the loan balance for each year.

   c. What fraction of your initial loan payment is interest? What about the last payment? What fraction of the loan has been paid off after 10 years? Why is the fraction less than half?

30. **Future values and annuities (S2.2)**

   a. The cost of a new automobile is $10,000. If the interest rate is 5%, how much would you have to set aside now to provide this sum in five years?

   b. You have to pay $12,000 a year in school fees at the end of each of the next six years. If the interest rate is 8%, how much do you need to set aside today to cover these bills?

   c. You have invested $60,476 at 8%. After paying the above school fees, how much would remain at the end of the six years?

31. **Growing perpetuities (S2.3)** A common stock will pay a cash dividend of $4 next year. After that, the dividends are expected to increase indefinitely at 4% per year. If the discount rate is 14%, what is the PV of the stream of dividend payments?

32. **Growing annuities (S2.3)** You estimate that by the time you retire in 35 years, you will have accumulated savings of $2 million. If the interest rate is 8% and you live 15 years after retirement, what annual level of expenditure will those savings support?

    Unfortunately, inflation will eat into the value of your retirement income. Assume a 4% inflation rate and work out a spending program for your $2 million in retirement savings that will allow you to increase your expenditure in line with inflation.

33. **Growing annuities (S2.3)** You are contemplating membership in the St. Swithin's and Ancient Golf Club. The annual membership fee for the coming year is $5,000, but you can make a single payment today of $12,750, which will provide you with membership for the next three years. Suppose that the annual fee is payable at the end of each year and is expected to increase by 6% a year. The discount rate is 10%. Which is the better deal?

34. **Growing perpetuities and annuities (S2.3)** As winner of a breakfast cereal competition, you can choose one of the following prizes:

    a. $100,000 now.

    b. $180,000 at the end of five years.

    c. $11,400 a year forever.

    d. $19,000 for each of 10 years.

    e. $6,500 next year and increasing thereafter by 5% a year forever.

    If the interest rate is 12%, which is the most valuable prize?

35. **Growing perpetuities and annuities (S2.3)** Your firm's geologists have discovered a small oil field in New York's Westchester County. The field is forecasted to produce a cash flow of $C_1 = \$2$ million in the first year. You estimate that you could earn a return of $r = 12\%$ from investing in stocks with a similar degree of risk to your oil field. Therefore, 12% is the opportunity cost of capital. What is the present value? The answer, of course, depends on what happens to the cash flows after the first year. Calculate present value for the following cases:

    a. The cash flows are forecasted to continue forever, with no expected growth or decline.

    b. The cash flows are forecasted to continue for 20 years only, with no expected growth or decline during that period.

    c. The cash flows are forecasted to continue forever, increasing by 3% per year because of inflation.

    d. The cash flows are forecasted to continue for 20 years only, increasing by 3% per year because of inflation.

36. **Compounding intervals (S2.4)** A leasing contract calls for an immediate payment of $100,000 and nine subsequent $100,000 semiannual payments at six-month intervals. What is the PV of these payments if the *annual* discount rate is 8%?

37. **Compounding intervals (S2.4)** Which would you prefer?

    a. An investment paying interest of 12% compounded annually.

    b. An investment paying interest of 11.7% compounded semiannually.

    c. An investment paying 11.5% compounded continuously.

    Work out the value of each of these investments after 1, 5, and 20 years.

38. **Compounding intervals (S2.4)** You are quoted an interest rate of 6% on an investment of $10 million. What is the value of your investment after four years if interest is compounded:

    a. Annually?

    b. Monthly?

    c. Continuously?

39. **Perpetuities and continuous compounding (S2.4)** If the interest rate is 7% compounded annually, what is the value of the following three investments?

    a. An investment that offers you $100 a year in perpetuity with the payment at the *end* of each year.

    b. A similar investment with the payment at the *beginning* of each year.

    c. A similar investment with the payment spread evenly over each year.

40. **Continuous compounding (S2.4)** How much will you have at the end of 20 years if you invest $100 today at 15% *annually* compounded? How much will you have if you invest at 15% *continuously* compounded?

41. **Continuous compounding (S2.4)** The continuously compounded interest rate is 12%.

    a. You invest $1,000 at this rate. What is the investment worth after five years?

    b. What is the PV of $5 million to be received in eight years?

    c. What is the PV of a continuous stream of cash flows, amounting to $2,000 per year, starting immediately and continuing for 15 years?

CHALLENGE PROBLEMS

42. **Annuities (S2.2)** Use Excel to construct your own set of annuity tables showing the annuity factor for a selection of interest rates and years.

43. **Declining perpetuities and annuities (S2.3)** You own an oil pipeline that will generate a $2 million cash return over the coming year. The pipeline's operating costs are negligible, and it is expected to last for a very long time. Unfortunately, the volume of oil shipped is declining, and cash flows are expected to decline by 4% per year. The discount rate is 10%.

    a. What is the PV of the pipeline's cash flows if its cash flows are assumed to last forever?

    b. What is the PV of the cash flows if the pipeline is scrapped after 20 years?

44. **Future values and continuous compounding (S2.4)** Here are two useful rules of thumb. The "rule of 72" says that with discrete compounding the time it takes for an investment to double in value is roughly 72/interest rate (in percent). The "rule of 69" says that with continuous compounding the time that it takes to double is exactly 69.3/interest rate (in percent).

    a. If the annually compounded interest rate is 12%, use the rule of 72 to calculate roughly how long it takes before your money doubles. Now work it out exactly.

    b. Can you prove the rule of 69?

SOLUTIONS TO SELF-TEST QUESTIONS

2.1   a. $3,200 \times 0.08 = $256
       b. $3,200 \times 1.08^5 = $4,702
       c. $4,702 \times 0.08 = $376

2.2   a. $.95 \times $100 = $95
       b. $.90 \times $200 = $180
       c. $1/(1.08^3) = 0.794$

2.3 a. False (you should multiply by the discount factor)

b. True (assuming interest rates are positive)

c. False (a high interest rate reduces the discounted value)

2.4 Falls (higher risk increases the opportunity cost of capital and lowers discount factor)

2.5 a. $8,000/0.07 = \$114,286$

b. The tree will be worth (8,000/0.07) at the end of year 2, and therefore, its present value is $(8,000/0.07) \times 1/1.07^2 = \$99,822$.

2.6 $PV = 6,000 \left[\dfrac{1}{0.05} - \dfrac{1}{0.05(1.05)^6} \right] = \$30,454$

2.7 a. Monthly annuity factor $= \left[\dfrac{1}{0.01} - \dfrac{1}{0.01(1.01)^{240}} \right] = 90.82$

Monthly payment $= \$240,000/90.82 = \$2,643$

b. Interest $= 0.01 \times 240,000 = 2,400$; repayment $= 2,643 - 2,400 = \$243$

2.8 a. $PV = \dfrac{C_1}{r - g} = \dfrac{\$4}{0.08 - 0.04} = \$100$

b. The formula works only if r is greater than g.

2.9 a. Future value $= [1 + (r/m)]^m$

b. Future value $= [1 + (r/m)]^{nm}$

c. Future value $= e^r$

d. Future value $= e^{nr}$

Finance.yahoo.com is a marvelous source of stock price data. You should get used to using it. Go to **finance.yahoo.com** and look up "Analyst Estimates" for Apple (AAPL). You should find earnings per share (EPS) for the current year, the percentage annual growth rate of EPS for the past five years, and also a five-year EPS growth-rate forecast. What will be Apple's EPS after five years if EPS grows at the five-year historical average rate? What will EPS be if it grows at the analysts' forecasted rate? Try the same exercise for other stocks—for example, Microsoft (MSFT), Merck (MRK), or the railroad CSX (CSX).

FINANCE ON THE WEB

Valuing Bonds

Investment in new plant and equipment requires money—often a lot of money. Sometimes firms can retain earnings to cover the cost of investment, but often they need to raise extra cash from investors. If they choose not to sell additional shares of stock, the cash has to come from borrowing. If cash is needed for only a short while, firms may borrow from a bank. If they need cash for long-term investments, they generally issue bonds, which are simply long-term loans.

Companies are not the only bond issuers. Municipalities also raise money by selling bonds. So do national governments. We start our analysis of the bond market by looking at the valuation of government bonds and at the interest rate that the government pays when it borrows. Although companies can't borrow as cheaply as governments, the interest rates on government bonds are benchmarks for all interest rates. When government interest rates go up or down, corporate rates follow more or less proportionally. Therefore, financial managers had better understand how the government rates are determined and what happens when they change.

Do not confuse the interest rate on bonds with the cost of capital for a corporation. The projects that companies undertake are almost invariably risky, and investors demand higher prospective returns from such projects than from safe government bonds. (In Chapter 7, we start to look at the additional returns that investors demand from risky assets.)

Section 3-1 Using the present value formula to value bonds
We start by showing the relationship between the price of a government bond and the return that investors receive.

Section 3-2 How bond prices vary with the level of interest rates
When interest rates fall, bond prices rise, but the prices of long-term bonds are much more sensitive than short-term bonds to changes in interest rates. But what do we mean by long-term? It's not just about the bond's maturity, because most bonds make regular interest payments before they are finally repaid. Duration is a measure of the average time to a bond's cash payments. We explain how to measure duration and how it is related to a bond's volatility.

Section 3-3 The term structure of interest rates
The relationship between short- and long-term interest rates is called the term structure. In Section 3-3, we define the term structure and explain how it can be measured.

Section 3-4 Explaining the term structure
Why do short- and long-term interest rates often differ? We explain that it may be due to expectations about future interest rates, or it may reflect the extra risks that investors run when they buy long-term bonds.

Section 3-5 Real and nominal interest rates
Payments on most bonds are fixed in nominal terms and make no promises about what the money will buy. However, the U.S. Treasury also issues inflation-indexed bonds, known as TIPS, that promise a fixed *real* return. We describe these bonds and the relationship between the nominal and real rate of interest.

Section 3-6 The risk of default
Corporate bonds are more complex securities than government bonds. In particular, it is more likely that a company will be unable to come up with the money to pay its debts. We show how this affects the "spread" of corporate bond rates over comparable government bond rates. This chapter only introduces corporate debt. We take a more detailed look in Chapters 24 and 25.

| **3-1** | **Using the Present Value Formula to Value Bonds** |

If you own a bond, you are entitled to a fixed set of cash payoffs. Every year until the bond matures, you collect regular interest payments. At maturity, when you receive the final interest payment, you also get back the **face value** of the bond, which is sometimes called the *principal* or *par value*.

A Short Trip to Paris to Value a Government Bond

Why are we going to Paris, apart from the cafés, restaurants, and sophisticated nightlife? Because we want to start with the simplest type of bond, one that makes payments just once a year.

French government bonds, known as OATs (short for Obligations Assimilables du Trésor), pay interest and principal in euros (€). Suppose that in April 2020 you decide to buy €100 face value of the 3.50% OAT maturing in April 2026. Each year until the bond matures, you are entitled to an interest payment of $0.035 \times 100 = €3.50$. This amount is called the bond's *coupon*.[1] When the bond matures in 2026, the government makes the final €3.50 coupon payment, plus the final payment of €100. So the cash payments from the bond are as follows:

Cash Payments (€)					
2021	2022	2023	2024	2025	2026
3.50	3.50	3.50	3.50	3.50	103.50

What is the present value of these payments? It depends on the opportunity cost of capital, which in this case equals the rate of return offered by similar French government debt issues. Suppose that other government bonds maturing in 2026 offered an interest rate of 5%. That is what you would have given up if you bought the 3.50% OATs.

To value the OATs, we discount the cash flows by the 5% interest rate that we assumed were offered by similar issues. Thus the value of the 3.50% OATs is

$$PV = \frac{3.50}{1.05} + \frac{3.50}{1.05^2} + \frac{3.50}{1.05^3} + \frac{3.50}{1.05^4} + \frac{3.50}{1.05^5} + \frac{103.50}{1.05^6} = €92.39$$

Bond prices are usually expressed as a percentage of face value. So the price of your 3.50% OAT would be quoted as 92.39%.

You may have noticed a shortcut way to value this bond. It amounts to a package of two investments. The first investment gets the six annual coupon payments of €3.50 each. The second gets the €100 face value at maturity. You can use the annuity formula from Chapter 2 to value the coupon payments and then add on the present value of the final payment.

PV (bond) = PV (annuity of coupon payments) + PV (final payment of principal)

= (coupon × 6-year annuity factor) + (final payment × discount factor)

$$= 3.50 \left[\frac{1}{0.05} - \frac{1}{0.05(1.05)^6} \right] + 100 \times \frac{1}{1.05^6} = 17.76 + 74.62 = €92.39$$

Thus, the bond can be valued as a package of an annuity (the coupon payments) and a single, final payment (the repayment of principal).[2]

---

[1]Bonds used to come with a coupon attached that had to be clipped off and presented to the issuer to obtain the interest payments. This is still the case with bearer bonds, where the only evidence of ownership is the bond certificate. In many parts of the world, bearer bonds are still issued and are popular with investors who would rather remain anonymous. The alternative is registered bonds, where the identity of the bond's owner is recorded and the coupon payments are sent automatically. OATS are registered bonds.

[2]You could also value a five-year annuity of € 3.50 plus a final payment of €103.50.

We have just used a 5% interest rate to calculate the present value of the OAT. Now we turn the valuation around and ask: If the price of the OAT is 92.39%, what is the interest rate? What return do investors get if they buy the bond and hold it to maturity? To answer this question, you need to find the value of the variable y that solves the following equation:

$$92.39 = \frac{3.50}{1+y} + \frac{3.50}{(1+y)^2} + \frac{3.50}{(1+y)^3} + \frac{3.50}{(1+y)^4} + \frac{3.50}{(1+y)^5} + \frac{103.50}{(1+y)^6}$$

The interest rate y is called the bond's **yield to maturity.** In this case, we already know that the present value of the bond is 92.39% at a 5% discount rate, so the yield to maturity must be 5%. If you were to buy the bond at 92.39% and hold it to maturity, you would earn a return of 5% per year. As you can see from the equation, the higher the yield to maturity, the lower the price of the bond.

Why is the yield to maturity more than the 3.50% coupon rate? Because you are paying €92.39 for a bond with a face value of €100. So you not only receive the annual coupon payments, you also realize a capital gain of €7.61 if you hold the bond to maturity. The yield to maturity blends the return from the coupon payments with the increasing value of the bond over its remaining life.

Let's generalize. A bond that is priced below its face value is said to sell at a discount and is known as a *discount bond.* Investors who buy a discount bond receive a capital gain over the life of the bond, so the yield to maturity on these bonds is always more than the coupon rate. A bond that is priced above face value sells at a premium and is known as a *premium bond.* Investors in premium bonds face a capital *loss* over the life of the bond, so the yield to maturity on a premium bond is less than the coupon rate. A bond that is priced at face value, or at par, is known as a *par bond.* Its yield equals the coupon rate.

The only general procedure for calculating the yield to maturity is trial and error. You guess at a figure and calculate the present value of the bond's payments. If the present value is greater than the actual price, your discount rate must have been too low, and you need to try a higher rate. The more practical solution is to use a spreadsheet program or a specially programmed calculator. At the end of Section 3.2, you will find a box that lists the Excel function for calculating yield to maturity plus several other useful functions for bond analysts.

3.1 Self-Test

A government bond is priced at 105%. Is the yield to maturity higher or lower than the coupon rate?

When we valued the 3.50% OATS, we assumed that investors demanded a positive 5% rate of interest. Throughout history, positive interest rates have been the norm. In recent years, yields on short-term Treasury bonds in the United States have hovered just above zero, but in Europe and Japan yields on government bonds have been *negative;* you *paid* the government to borrow your money. In November 2020, a record $17 trillion of debt globally, including both government and corporate debt, had negative yields. The nearby box provides some background on this unusual situation.

If interest rates are negative, you still use the same procedure for calculating a bond's value, but in this case, $(1 + r)$ is less than 1, and $(1 + r)^2$ is less still. In contrast to positive rates, a cash flow in the future is worth *more* than the same cash flow today.

In April 2020, the yield on medium-term French government bonds was not 5.0%, but about –0.4%. So our calculation of the bond's value was wrong. It should have been

$$PV = \frac{3.50}{0.996} + \frac{3.50}{0.996^2} + \frac{3.50}{0.996^3} + \frac{3.50}{0.996^4} + \frac{3.50}{0.996^5} + \frac{103.50}{0.996^6} = €123.73$$

Why Interest Rates Can Be Negative

❭ Does it make sense for individuals to lend money at a negative nominal interest rate? Wouldn't they do better to keep their money in cash under the mattress and earn zero? For individuals that is risky, but for a large corporation with millions of euros or yen to invest, it is infeasible. It could place the money in a deposit account with a bank. But no bank is totally safe. This was particularly true during the eurozone crisis, when many corporations were content to buy government bonds with a negative yield or to pay a small negative interest rate to have banks look after their money.

In 2020 Switzerland's central bank, the Swiss National Bank, had the lowest policy rate in the world at –0.75%, while the European Central Bank had a rate of –0.50%. Banks that held reserves with these central banks needed to pay for the privilege.

It is not clear what is the lowest rate that a central bank could choose before inducing widespread withdrawals to cash, but it may be near –0.75%. The cash must be put somewhere, and even in a bank vault, the cash is risk-free only if it is insured against fire and theft. These insurance costs are around 0.2% to 0.25%. In addition, there are the costs of hiring a vault that can be significant—2 billion euros in 200 euro notes weigh roughly 11 tons.

EXAMPLE 3.1 • When Money can be Costly to Store

At the peak of his power, Pablo Escobar, the boss of the Medellin drug cartel, was earning $420 million a week. This was far too much for him to launder safely or to place in a bank deposit. So, rather than store it under the mattress, he stashed it in Colombian farming fields, in dilapidated warehouses, and in the walls of cartel members' homes. The problem was that up to 10% of this money was damaged by water or eaten by rats.

For Escobar, the net return on cash was not zero; it was *minus* 10%. Since he had more money than he knew what to do with, these losses to water and rodents were probably not a matter for serious concern.

Source: R. Escobar and D. Fisher, *The Accountant's Story: Inside the Violent World of the Medellin Cartel* (New York: Grand Central Publishing, 2010).

• • • • •

Back to the United States: Semiannual Coupons and Bond Prices

Just like the French government, the U.S. Treasury raises money by regular auctions of government debt. Longer-term issues of debt are known as *bonds;* issues that mature in 10 years or less at the time of issue are known as *notes.* The Treasury also issues short-term debt maturing in a year or less. These short-term securities are known as *Treasury bills.* The market for these government securities is huge. In December 2020, investors held $21.4 trillion of U.S. government debt, and the massive borrowing program brought about by the coronavirus pandemic meant that this figure was rising by the minute.

You can't buy Treasury bonds or notes on the stock exchange. They are traded by a network of bond dealers, who quote prices at which they are prepared to buy and sell. If you wish to buy a bond, you contact a broker, who checks the current price on his screen. If you are happy to go ahead with the purchase, your broker contacts a bond dealer and the trade is done.

At any moment there are about 300 different Treasury notes and bonds in issue. Table 3.1 shows the prices of just a small sample of them. All these bonds have a face value of $1,000.

Maturity	Coupon	Ask Price (%)	Yield to Maturity (%)
May 2023	1.75	104.21	0.189
May 2024	2.50	108.94	0.252
May 2025	2.125	108.26	0.331
May 2026	1.625	107.03	0.422
May 2027	2.375	113.01	0.478
May 2028	2.875	118.10	0.533
May 2030	0.625	99.28	0.638
May 2040	4.375	159.27	1.049

❭ TABLE 3.1   Treasury bond quotes, May 15, 2020.

Source: *The Wall Street Journal* website, www.wsj.com.

When the bond finally matures, the government pays the $1,000 face value in addition to the last interest payment. Each year until then, the bondholder receives a regular coupon payment, but in contrast to our French bond, coupons on Treasury bonds and notes are paid *semi-annually.*[3]

We have highlighted the entry for the 2.5% bonds maturing in 2024, commonly referred to as "the 2.5s of 2024." Anyone buying the 2.5s of 2024 would need to pay the **ask price**, which is given as 108.94%. This means that the price is 108.94% of $1,000, or $1,089.40.[4] The final column of the table is the bond's yield to maturity, which is the return to an investor who buys the bond at the asked price and holds it until maturity. Because interest is semi-annual, yields on U.S. bonds are quoted as twice the semi-annual yield. Thus, if you buy the 2.5% bond and hold it to maturity, every six months you earn a return of 0.252%/2 = 0.126%.[5]

You can now repeat the present value calculations that we did for the French government bond. You just need to recognize that bonds in the United States have a face value of $1,000, that their coupons are paid semi-annually, and that the quoted yield is a semi-annually compounded rate.

If we call the ith cash payment C_i, the annual yield to maturity y, and the number of interest payments each year n, then the general formula for a bond's present value is:

$$\text{PV} = \sum C_i / \left(1 + y/n\right)^i \tag{3.1}$$

The cash payments on the 2.5s of 2024 are:

Cash Payments (C_t)							
Nov. 2020	May 2021	Nov. 2021	May 2022	Nov. 2022	May 2023	Nov. 2023	May 2024
$12.5	$12.5	$12.5	$12.5	$12.5	$12.5	$12.5	$1,012.5

[3]The frequency of interest payments varies from country to country. For example, most bonds issued by eurozone governments pay interest annually (Italy and Malta are exceptions), while most bonds in the United States, United Kingdom, and Japan pay interest semi-annually.

[4]The quoted bond price is known as the *flat* (or *clean*) price. The price that the bond buyer actually pays (sometimes called the *full* or *dirty* price) is equal to the flat price *plus* the interest that the seller has already earned on the bond since the last interest payment. The precise method for calculating this *accrued interest* varies from one type of bond to another. Always use the flat price to calculate the yield.

[5]Notice that the quoted yield is the same as the APR that we encountered in the last chapter, but bond investors never use the term "APR."

In May 2020, the yield to maturity on similar four-year Treasury bonds was $y = 0.252\%$. That is what you were giving up when you bought the 2.5s of 2024. If interest is paid twice a year, then $n = 2$. Therefore, to calculate the value of the 2.5s of 2024, you must discount the cash payments at $y/n = 0.126\%$:

$$PV = \frac{12.50}{1.00126} + \frac{12.50}{1.00126^2} + \frac{12.50}{1.00126^3} + \frac{12.50}{1.00126^4} + \frac{12.50}{1.00126^5} + \frac{12.50}{1.00126^6} + \frac{12.50}{1.00126^7}$$

$$+ \frac{1,012.50}{1.00126^8} = \$1,089.41$$

The bond is worth $1,089.41 or 108.94% of face value.

Again we could turn the problem around: If the price of the bond is 108.94%, what is the yield to maturity? Try it, and you will find (no surprise) that the semi-annual rate of return that you can earn over the eight remaining half-year periods is 0.126%. Take care to remember that the yield is quoted as an annual rate, calculated as $2 \times 0.126 = 0.252\%$. If you read that a U.S. Treasury bond has a yield to maturity of y, you have to remember to use $y/2$ as the semi-annual rate for discounting the cash flows.

3.2 Self-Test

A one-year U.S. Treasury bond has a coupon rate of 10%. a. What are the cash flows on this bond? b. The bond's yield to maturity is 6%. What is the present value of the bond? c. If the yield to maturity is 6%, what return do you earn every 6 months? d. What is the bond's effective annual rate of return?

3-2   How Bond Prices Vary with Yields

Figure 3.1 plots the yield to maturity on 10-year U.S. Treasury bonds[6] from 1900 to 2020. Notice how much the rate fluctuates. For example, interest rates climbed sharply after 1979 when Paul Volcker, the new chairman of the Fed, instituted a policy of tight money to rein in inflation. Within two years the interest rate on 10-year government bonds rose from 9% to a midyear peak of 15.8%. Contrast this with the spring of 2020, when long-term Treasury bonds offered a measly 1.0% rate of interest.

In the last section, we valued a four-year Treasury bond with a 2.5% coupon. This coupon rate is fixed, but the bond's yield may change from day to day and minute to minute, and, as the yield changes, so does the bond price. For example, suppose that investors demand a semi-annual return of 1% on the 2.5s of 2024, rather than the 0.126% semiannual return we used previously. In this case the price would be

$$PV = \frac{12.5}{1.01} + \frac{12.5}{1.01^2} + \frac{12.5}{1.01^3} + \ldots + \frac{12.5}{1.01^6} + \frac{12.5}{1.01^7} + \frac{1,012.5}{1.01^8} = \$1,019.13$$

The higher yield results in a lower price.

Bond prices and yields *must* move in opposite directions. The yield to maturity, our measure of the interest rate on a bond, is *defined* as the discount rate that explains the bond price.

---

[6]From this point forward, we will just say "bonds" and not distinguish notes from bonds unless we are referring to a specific security. Note also that bonds with long maturities end up with short maturities when they approach the final payment date. Thus, you will encounter 30-year bonds trading 20 years later at the same prices as new 10-year notes.

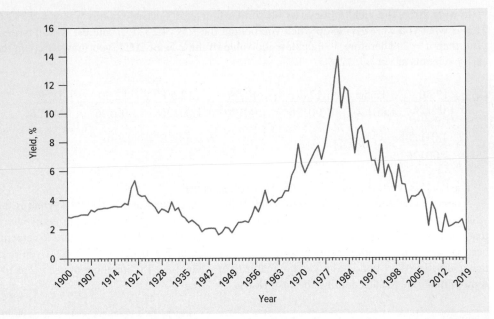

> ▶ **FIGURE 3.1**
>
> The interest rate on 10-year U.S. Treasury bonds.

When bond prices fall, interest rates (i.e., yields to maturity) must rise. When interest rates rise, bond prices must fall. We recall a hapless TV pundit who intoned, "The recent decline in long-term interest rates suggests that long-term bond prices may rise over the next week or two." Of course, the bond prices had already gone up. We are confident that you won't make the pundit's mistake.

3.3 Self-Test

    a. Which does not change during the bond's life—the coupon or the yield?

    b. If the yield rises, does the bond price rise or fall?

The brown line in Figure 3.2 shows the value of our 2.5% bond for different interest rates. As the yield to maturity rises, the bond price falls. When the annual yield is equal to the bond's coupon rate (2.5%), the bond sells for exactly its face value. When the yield is higher than 2.5%, the bond sells at a discount. When the yield is lower than 2.5%, the bond sells at a premium.

Bond investors cross their fingers that market interest rates will fall so that the price of their securities will rise. If they are unlucky and interest rates jump up, the value of their investment declines.

EXAMPLE 3.2 • Changes in Interest Rates and Bond Returns

On May 15, 2008, the U.S. Treasury sold $9 billion of 4.375% bonds maturing in February 2038. The bonds were issued at a price of 96.38% and offered a yield to maturity of 4.60%. This was the return to anyone buying at the issue price and holding the bonds to maturity. In the months following the issue, the financial crisis reached its peak. Lehman Brothers filed for bankruptcy with assets of $691 billion, and the government poured money into rescuing Fannie Mae, Freddie Mac, AIG, and a host of banks. As investors rushed to the safety of Treasury bonds, prices soared. By mid-December, the price of the 4.375s of 2038 had reached 138.05% of face value, and the yield had fallen to 2.5%. Anyone fortunate enough to have bought the bond at the issue price would have made a capital gain of $1,380.50 − $963.80 = $416.70. In addition, on August 15 the bond made its first coupon payment of $21.875 (this is the semiannual payment on the 4.375% coupon bond with a face value of $1,000). Our lucky investor would, therefore, have earned a seven-month **rate of return** of 45.5%:

$$\text{Rate of return} = \frac{\text{coupon income} + \text{price change}}{\text{investment}}$$

$$= \frac{\$21.875 + 416.70}{\$963.80} = 0.455, \text{ or } 45.5\%$$

Suddenly, government bonds did not seem quite so boring as before.

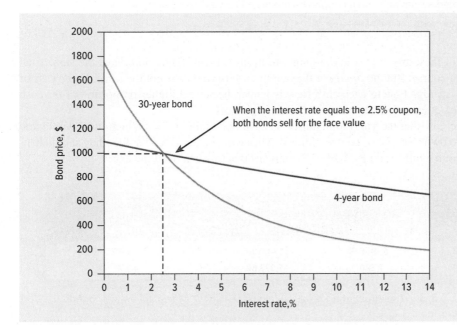

▶ **FIGURE 3.2**

Plot of bond prices as a function of the interest rate. The price of long-term bonds is more sensitive to changes in the interest rate than the price of short-term bonds.

A change in interest rates has only a modest impact on the value of near-term cash flows but a much greater impact on the value of distant cash flows. Thus the price of long-term bonds is affected more by changing interest rates than the price of short-term bonds. For example, compare the two curves in Figure 3.2. The brown line shows how the price of the four-year 2.5% bond varies with the interest rate. The blue line shows how the price of a 30-year 2.5% bond varies. You can see that the 30-year bond is much more sensitive to interest rate fluctuations than the three-year bond.

BEYOND THE PAGE

Try It! Figure 3.2: How changes in interest rates affect long- and short-term bonds

mhhe.com/brealey14e

Duration and Interest-Rate Sensitivity

Changes in interest rates have a greater impact on the prices of long-term bonds than on those of short-term bonds. But what do we mean by "long term" and "short term"? You might think that it depends only on the bond's maturity. However, a coupon bond that matures in year 30 makes payments in *each* of years 1 through 30. It's misleading to describe the bond as a 30-year bond; the *average* time to each cash payment is less than 30 years.

EXAMPLE 3.3 • Which is the Longer-Term Bond?

Table 3.2 calculates the prices of two seven-year bonds. We assume annual coupon payments and a yield to maturity of 4% per year. Take a look at the time pattern of each bond's cash payments and review how the prices are calculated:

Coupon	Price ($)	Year 1	Year 2 ...	Year 6	Year 7
		Cash Payments ($)			
3%	$ 939.98	$30	$30	$30	$1,030
9%	1,300.10	90	90	90	1,090

)TABLE 3.2   A comparison of the cash flows and prices of two bonds. Price is calculated assuming annual coupon payments and a yield to maturity of 4%.

Note: Both securities mature at the end of year 7.

Which of these two bonds is the longer-term investment? They both have the same final maturity, of course. But the *timing* of the bonds' cash payments is not the same. In the case of the 3s, the *average* time to each cash flow is longer, because a higher proportion of the cash flows occurs at maturity, when the face value is paid off.

Suppose now that the yield to maturity on each bond falls to 3%. Which bond would you most like to own? The 3s, of course. Since they have the longer effective life, they should benefit most from a fall in yields. Table 3.3 confirms that this is indeed the case:

Coupon	Yield = 4% Price ($)	Yield = 3% Price ($)	Change in Price (%)
3%	$ 939.98	$1,000.00	+6.4%
9%	1,300.10	1,373.82	+5.7

)TABLE 3.3   The effect of a 1% fall in yield on the prices of two seven-year bonds. Compare Table 3.2.

• • • • •

The 9% bonds in this example have the shorter average life, and therefore a shift in interest rates has a more muted effect on the price. That much is clear. However, it would be useful to have a precise measure of the average life, one that could be used to predict the exposure of each bond's price to fluctuations in interest rates. There is such a measure, and it is called **duration** or *Macaulay duration* after its founder.

Duration is the weighted average of the times to each of the cash payments. The weight for each year is the present value of the cash flow received at that time divided by the total present value of the bond. Thus:

$$Duration = \sum \frac{t_i PV(C_i)}{PV} \tag{3.2}$$

where t_i is the number of years to the ith payment, $PV(C_i)$ is the present value of the ith payment, and PV is the present value of the bond.

		Year (t)						
	1	2	3	4	5	6	7	
Payment at year end	$90	$90	$90	$90	$90	$90	$1,090	
PV(C_t) at 4%	$86.54	$83.21	$80.01	$76.93	$73.97	$71.13	$828.31	PV=$1,300.10
Fraction of total value [PV(C_t)/PV]	0.0666	0.0640	0.0615	0.0592	0.0569	0.0547	0.6371	
Year × fraction of total value [t × PV(C_t)/PV]	0.0666	0.1280	0.1846	0.2367	0.2845	0.3283	4.4598	Total=duration=5.69

❭**TABLE 3.4**   Calculating the duration of the 9% seven-year bonds. The yield to maturity is 4% a year. Coupon payments are assumed to be annual.

Table 3.4 shows how to compute duration for the 9% seven-year bonds, assuming annual payments.[7] First, we value each of the coupon payments of $90 and the final payment of coupon plus face value of $1,090. Of course, the present values of these payments add up to the bond price of $1,300.10. Then we calculate the fraction of the price accounted for by each cash flow and multiply each fraction by the year of the cash flow. The results sum across to a duration of 5.69 years.

We leave it to you to calculate duration for the 3% bonds in Table 3.2. You will find that duration is higher at 6.40 years.

To measure how bond prices change when interest rates change, we need to use *modified duration,* which is just duration divided by one plus the yield to maturity:

$$\text{Modified duration} = \frac{\text{duration}}{1 + \text{yield}} \tag{3.3}$$

Modified duration measures the percentage change in bond price for a 1 percentage-point change in yield. In other words, the derivative of the bond price with respect to a change in yield to maturity is $dPV/dy = -$modified duration.

Let's try out this formula for our seven-year 9% bond in Table 3.3. The bond's modified duration is duration/(1 + yield) = 5.69/1.04 = 5.47. This means that a 1% change in the yield to maturity should change the bond price by 5.47%.

We can check that prediction. Suppose the yield to maturity either increases or declines by 0.5%:

Yield to Maturity (%)	Price ($)	Change (%)
4.5%	$1265.17	−2.687%
4.0	1300.10	—
3.5	1336.30	+2.784

The total percentage difference between the price at yields of 4.5% and 3.5% is 2.687 + 2.784 = 5.47%. Thus, a 1% change in interest rates means a 5.47% change in bond price, just as predicted.

The modified duration for the 3% bond in Table 3.3 is 6.40/1.04 = 6.15%. In other words, a 1% change in yield to maturity results in a 6.15% change in the bond's price.

BEYOND THE PAGE

Try It! More on duration

mhhe.com/brealey14e

---

[7]If coupon payments were semi-annual, there would be $t_1 = 0.5$ year to the first payment, $t_2 = 1.0$ years to the second payment, and so on.

Years to Maturity	Coupon	Yield to Maturity (%)	Duration (years)
3	1.75	0.189	2.937
4	2.50	0.252	3.840
5	2.125	0.331	4.782
6	1.625	0.422	5.752
7	2.375	0.478	6.528
8	2.875	0.533	7.282
9	0.625	0.638	8.765
10	4.375	1.049	8.476

〉TABLE 3.5   The duration in May 2020 of the Treasury bonds shown in Table 3.1. These duration calculations recognize that coupon payments are semi-annual.

You can see why modified duration is a handy measure of interest-rate risk.[8] For example, the mini-case at the end of Chapter 27 looks at how financial managers can use the measure to protect the pension plan against unexpected changes in interest rates.

You may be interested to look at Table 3.5, which shows the duration in May 2020 of the sample of U.S. Treasury bonds from Table 3.1. Notice that in all cases, the duration is shorter than the number of years to maturity and the difference is most marked in the case of high coupon bonds.

3.4 Self-Test

If yields decline, which bond is likely to appreciate the most:
    a. A 20-year 8% bond or a 5-year 8% bond?

    b. A 20-year 8% bond or a 20-year 2% bond?

3-3   The Term Structure of Interest Rates

When we explained in Chapter 2 how to calculate present values, we used the same discount rate to calculate the value of each period's cash flow. Similarly, in Section 3.1, we derived a single discount rate, y, that would correctly value the 2.5s of 2024. For many purposes, using a single discount rate is a perfectly acceptable approximation, but there are also occasions when you need to recognize that short-term interest rates may be different from long-term rates. In this case, it may be worth discounting each cash flow at a different rate.

The relationship between short- and long-term interest rates is called the **term structure of interest rates**. Look, for example, at Figure 3.3, which shows the term structure in two different years. Notice that in the earlier year, the term structure sloped downward; long-term interest rates were lower than short-term rates. In the later year, the pattern was reversed and long-term bonds offered a much higher interest rate than short-term bonds.

---

[8]For simplicity, we assumed that the two Treasury bonds paid annual coupons. Calculating Macaulay duration for a bond with semiannual coupons is no different except that there are twice as many cash flows. To calculate modified duration with semiannual coupons you need to divide Macaulay duration by the semiannual yield to maturity.

Valuing Bonds

❯ Spreadsheet programs such as Excel provide built-in functions to solve for a variety of bond valuation problems. You can find these functions by pressing *fx* on the Excel toolbar. If you then click on the function that you wish to use, Excel will ask you for the inputs that it needs. At the bottom left of the function box, there is a Help facility with an example of how the function is used.

Here is a list of useful functions for valuing bonds, together with some points to remember when entering data:

- **PRICE:** The price of a bond given its yield to maturity.
- **YLD:** The yield to maturity of a bond given its price.
- **DURATION:** The duration of a bond.
- **MDURATION:** The modified duration of a bond.

Note:

- You can enter all the inputs in these functions directly as numbers or as the addresses of cells that contain the numbers.

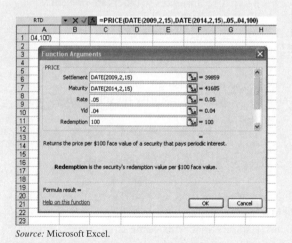

Source: Microsoft Excel.

- You must enter the yield and coupon as decimal values, for example, for 3% you would enter 0.03.
- Settlement is the date that payment for the security is made. Maturity is the maturity date. You can enter these dates directly using the Excel date function; for example, you would enter 15 Feb 2009 as DATE(2009,02,15). Alternatively, you can enter these dates in a cell and then enter the cell address in the function.
- In the functions for PRICE and YLD you need to scroll down in the function box to enter the frequency of coupon payments. Enter 1 for annual payments or 2 for semiannual.
- The functions for PRICE and YLD ask for an entry for "basis." We suggest you leave this blank. (See the Help facility for an explanation.)

Spreadsheet Questions

The following questions provide an opportunity to practice each of these functions.

1. (PRICE) In February 2009, Treasury 8.5s of 2020 yielded 3.30%. What was their price? If the yield rose to 4%, what would happen to the price?

2. (YLD) On the same day, Treasury 3.5s of 2018 were priced at 107.469%. What was their yield to maturity? Suppose that the price was 110.0%. What would happen to the yield?

3. (DURATION) What was the duration of the Treasury 8.5s? How would duration change if the yield rose to 4%? Can you explain why?

4. (MDURATION) What was the modified duration of the Treasury 8.5s? How would modified duration differ if the coupon were only 7.5%?

You need to learn how to measure the term structure and understand why long- and short-term rates often differ. Consider a simple loan that pays $1 at the end of one year. To find the present value of this loan you need to discount the cash flow by the one-year rate of interest, r_1:

$$PV = 1/(1 + r_1)$$

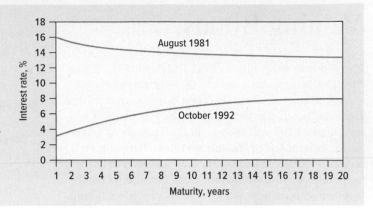

▶ FIGURE 3.3

Short- and long-term interest rates do not always move in parallel. In August 1981, U.S. short-term interest rates were higher than long-term rates. In October 1992, the term structure was upward sloping and long-term rates were higher than short-term rates.

Source: https://www.federalreserve.gov/data/nominal-yield-curve.htm.

This rate, r_1, is called the one-year **spot rate.** To find the present value of a loan that pays \$1 at the end of two years, you need to discount by the two-year spot rate, r_2:

$$PV = 1/(1 + r_2)^2$$

The first year's cash flow is discounted at today's one-year spot rate, and the second year's flow is discounted at today's two-year spot rate. So each spot rate is used to discount a single cash flow occurring at a single point in time. The series of spot rates $r_1, r_2, \ldots, r_t, \ldots$ traces out the term structure of interest rates.

Now suppose you have to value \$1 paid at the end of years 1 *and* 2. If the spot rates are different—say, $r_1 = 3\%$ and $r_2 = 4\%$—then we need two discount rates to calculate present value:

$$PV = \frac{1}{1.03} + \frac{1}{1.04^2} = 1.895$$

Once we know that PV = 1.895, we can go on to calculate a single discount rate that would give the same answer. That is, we could calculate the yield to maturity by solving for y in the following equation:

$$PV = 1.895 = \frac{1}{(1 + y)} + \frac{1}{(1 + y)^2}$$

This gives a yield to maturity of 3.66%. Once we have the yield, we could use it to value other two-year annuities. But we can't get the yield to maturity until we know the price. The price is determined by the spot interest rates for dates 1 and 2. Spot rates come first. Yields to maturity come later, after bond prices are set. That is why professionals often identify spot interest rates and discount each cash flow at the spot rate for the date when the cash flow is received.

3.5 Self-Test

Suppose that you used the 3.66% yield, calculated earlier, to value a two-year 5% bond.
  a. Would you get the correct answer? If not, why not?
  b. Do you think that you would over- or under-value the bond?

Spot Rates, Bond Prices, and the Law of One Price

The *law of one price* states that in a competitive market, two identical assets must sell for the same price. Therefore, if two assets each make a safe dollar payment on the same future date, these payments must be worth the same today, and should be discounted at the same spot interest rate.

EXAMPLE 3.4 • Spot rates and Bond Prices

Table 3.6 illustrates how this applies to government bonds. It lists three government bonds, which we assume make annual coupon payments. All the bonds have the same coupon, but they have different maturities. The shortest (bond A) matures in two years and the longest (bond C) in four.

Spot rates and discount factors are given at the top of each column. The law of one price says that investors place the same value on a risk-free dollar regardless of whether it is provided by bond A, B, or C. You can check that the law holds in the table. For example, the year 1 coupon of $80 is worth $77.67 regardless of which bond provides it.

Each bond is priced by adding the present values of each of its cash flows. Once total PV is calculated, we have the bond price. Only then can the yield to maturity be calculated.

Notice how the yield to maturity increases as bond maturity increases. The yields increase with maturity because the term structure of spot rates in this example is upward-sloping. Yields to maturity are complex averages of spot rates. For example, you can see that the yield on the four-year bond (5.81%) lies between the one- and four-year spot rates (3% and 6%). In practice the differences in spot rates are seldom as marked as in our simple example, and therefore the yields on bonds with nearby maturities do not show such large variations.

	Year (t)					
	1	**2**	**3**	**4**	**Bond Price (PV)**	**Yield to Maturity (y, %)**
Spot rates	0.03	0.04	0.05	0.06		
Discount factors	0.9709	0.9246	0.8638	0.7921		
Bond A (8% coupon)						
Payment (C_t)	$80.00	1,080.00				
PV (C_t)	$77.67	998.52			$1,076.19	3.96
Bond B (8% coupon)						
Payment (C_t)	$80.00	80.00	1,080.00			
PV (C_t)	$77.67	73.96	932.94		$1,084.58	4.90
Bond C (8% coupon)						
Payment (C_t)	$80.00	80.00	80.00	1,080.00		
PV (C_t)	$77.67	73.96	69.11	855.46	$1,076.20	5.81

❭TABLE 3.6   The law of one price applied to government bonds.

• • • • •

Financial managers who want a quick, summary measure of interest rates bypass spot interest rates and look in the financial press at yields to maturity. They may refer to the *yield curve,* which plots yields to maturity, instead of referring to the *term structure,* which plots spot rates. They may use the yield to maturity on one bond to value another bond with roughly

BEYOND THE PAGE

Try It!
Table 3.6:
Spot rates,
forward
rates, and
arbitrage

mhhe.com/brealey14e

the same coupon and maturity. They may speak with a broad brush and say, "Ampersand Bank will charge us 6% on a three-year loan," referring to a 6% yield to maturity.

Throughout this text, we too use the yield to maturity to summarize the return required by bond investors. But you also need to understand the measure's limitations when spot rates are not equal.

Measuring the Term Structure

We defined the spot rate, r_t, as the rate of interest on a bond that makes a single payment at time t. Such simple bonds do exist. They are known as **stripped bonds**, or **strips**. On request the U.S. Treasury will split a normal coupon bond into a package of mini-bonds, each of which makes just one cash payment. Our 2.5% bonds of 2024 could be exchanged for eight semiannual coupon strips, each paying $12.5, and a principal strip paying $1,000. In May 2020, this package of strips would have cost $108.98, just a little more than it cost to buy one 2.5% bond. The similarity should be no surprise. Because the two investments provide identical cash payments, they must sell for very close to the same price.

In Figure 3.4, we have plotted the term structure of spot rates from 1 to 30 years. You can see that in 2020 investors required a higher interest rate for lending for 25 years rather than for 1.

EXAMPLE 3.5 • Using Treasury Strips to Calculate Spot Rates

We can use the prices of strips to measure spot rates of interest. For example, in May 2020, a five-year strip cost $950. In return, investors could look forward to a single payment of $1,000 in May 2025. Thus, investors were prepared to pay $0.950 for the promise of $1 at the end of five years. The five-year discount factor was $DF_5 = 1/(1 + r_5)^5 = 0.950$, and the five-year spot rate was $r_5 = (1/0.950)^{0.2} - 1 = 0.0103$, or 1.03%.

Trading is much more active in Treasury bonds than in strips, and as a result, the price data are more reliable. In practice, therefore, analysts often look at Treasury bond data and calculate an estimate of strip prices and spot rates from these. For example, you can find the Fed's estimates of spot rates on https://www.federalreserve.gov/data/nominal-yield-curve.htm. By the way the estimated spot rates in Figure 3.4 are taken from the Fed.

• • • • •

3.6 Self-Test

Suppose that the 20-year discount factor is 0.3769. What is the 20-year spot rate, r_{20}?

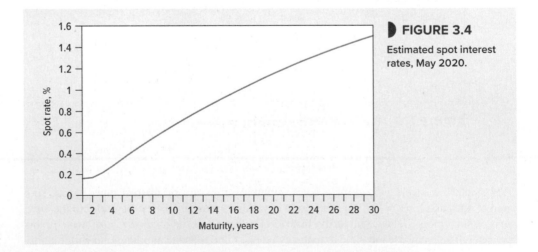

FIGURE 3.4

Estimated spot interest rates, May 2020.

Why the Discount Factor Declines as Futurity Increases

In Chapter 2, we saw that the longer you have to wait for your money, the less is its present value. In other words, the two-year discount factor $DF_2 = 1/(1 + r_2)^2$ is less than the one-year discount factor $DF_1 = 1/(1 + r_1)$. But is this *necessarily* the case when there can be a different spot interest rate for each period?

EXAMPLE 3.6 • Increasing Discount Factors and Money Machines

Suppose that the one-year spot rate of interest is $r_1 = 20\%$ and the two-year spot rate is $r_2 = 7\%$. In this case, the one-year discount factor is $DF_1 = 1/1.20 = 0.833$ and the two-year discount factor is $DF_2 = 1/1.07^2 = 0.873$. Apparently, a dollar received the day after tomorrow is not necessarily worth less than a dollar received tomorrow.

But there is something wrong with this example. Anyone who could borrow and invest at these interest rates could become a millionaire overnight. Let's see how such a "money machine" would work.

Suppose the first person to spot the opportunity is Hermione Kraft. Ms. Kraft first buys a one-year Treasury strip for $0.833 \times \$1,000 = \$833$. Now she notices that there is a way to earn an *immediate* surefire profit on this investment. She reasons as follows. Next year the strip will pay off $1,000 that can be reinvested for a further year. Although she does not know what interest rates will be at that time, she does know that she can always put the money in a checking account or under the mattress and be certain of having $1,000 at the end of year 2. Her next step, therefore, is to go to her bank and borrow the present value of this $1,000. At 7% interest the present value is $PV = 1000/(1.07)^2 = \$873$.

So Ms. Kraft borrows $873, invests $830, and walks away with a profit of $43. If that does not sound like very much, notice that by borrowing more and investing more she can make much larger profits. For example, if she borrows $21,778,584 and invests $20,778,584, she would become a millionaire.[9]

• • • • •

Of course this story is completely fanciful. Such an opportunity would not last long in well-functioning capital markets. Any bank that allowed you to borrow for two years at 7% when the one-year interest rate was 20% would soon be wiped out by a rush of small investors hoping to become millionaires and a rush of millionaires hoping to become billionaires. There are, however, two lessons to our story.

The first lesson is a general one and can be summed up by this precept: "There is no such thing as a surefire money machine." The technical term for money machine is **arbitrage**. Arbitrageurs are always on the look out for cases where two identical sets of future cash flows are selling at different prices.[10] In well-functioning markets, where the costs of buying and selling are low, arbitrage opportunities are eliminated almost instantaneously by investors who try to take advantage of them. Later in the book we invoke the *absence* of arbitrage opportunities to prove several useful properties about security prices. That is, we make statements like, "The prices of securities X and Y must be in the following relationship—otherwise there would be potential arbitrage profits. Since capital markets would not be in equilibrium, prices would change."

---

[9]We exaggerate Ms. Kraft's profits. There are always costs to financial transactions, though they may be very small. For example, Ms. Kraft could use her investment in the one-year strip as security for the bank loan, but the bank would need to charge more than 7% on the loan to cover its costs.

[10]In this case, the arbitrageur would earn a risk-free profit. In practice, arbitrageurs commonly take some risk.

The second lesson to our story is that the value of a dollar tomorrow must be less than that of a dollar the day after tomorrow *as long as you can hold cash to earn a non-negative return.*[11] In other words, a dollar received at the end of two years (DF_2) is worth less than a dollar received at the end of one year (DF_1). There must be some extra gain from lending for two periods rather than one, in which case $(1 + r_2)^2$ will be greater than $1 + r_1$.

3-4   Explaining the Term Structure

The term structure that we showed in Figure 3.4 was upward-sloping. Long-term spot rates of interest were about 1.4%; short-term rates barely registered. Why then didn't everyone rush to buy long-term bonds?

Suppose that you held a portfolio of one-year U.S. Treasuries in May 2020. Here are three possible reasons you might decide to hold on to them, despite their low rate of return:

1. You believe that short-term interest rates will be higher in the future.

2. You worry about the greater exposure of long-term bonds to changes in interest rates.

3. You worry about the risk of higher future inflation.

We review each of these reasons.

Expectations Theory of the Term Structure

Recall that you own a portfolio of one-year Treasuries. A year from now, when these Treasuries mature, you can reinvest the proceeds for another one-year period and enjoy whatever interest rate the bond market offers then. The interest rate for the second year may be high enough to offset the low return in the first year. Therefore, you often see an upward-sloping term structure when future interest rates are expected to rise.

EXAMPLE 3.7 • Expectations and the Term Structure

Suppose that the one-year interest rate, r_1, is 5%, and the two-year rate, r_2, is 7%. If you invest $100 for one year, your investment grows to $100 \times 1.05 = \$105$; if you invest for two years, it grows to $100 \times 1.07^2 = \$114.49$. The extra return that you earn for that second year is $1.07^2/1.05 - 1 = 0.090$, or 9.0%.[12]

Would you be happy to earn that extra 9% for investing for two years rather than one? The answer depends on how you expect interest rates to change over the coming year. If you are confident that in 12 months' time one-year bonds will yield more than 9.0%, you would do better to invest in a one-year bond and, when that matured, reinvest the cash for the next year at the higher rate. If you forecast that the future one-year rate is exactly 9.0%, then you will be indifferent between buying a two-year bond or investing for one year and then rolling the investment forward at next year's short-term interest rate.

If everyone is thinking as you just did, then the two-year interest rate has to adjust so that everyone is equally happy to invest for one year or two years. Thus the two-year rate will incorporate both today's one-year rate and the consensus forecast of next year's one-year rate.

• • • • •

---

[11]The qualification is important. If it becomes costly to hold cash, interest rates can become negative and the value of a dollar tomorrow would be greater than that of a dollar today.

[12]The extra return for lending for one more year is termed the *forward rate of interest.* In our example, the forward rate is 9.0%. In Ms. Kraft's arbitrage example, the forward interest rate was negative. In real life, forward interest rates are rarely negative.

We have just illustrated the **expectations theory** of the term structure. It states that in well-functioning bond markets investment in a series of short-maturity bonds must offer the same expected return as an investment in a single long-maturity bond. Only if that is the case would investors be prepared to hold both short- and long-maturity bonds.

The expectations theory implies that the *only* reason for an upward-sloping term structure is that investors expect short-term interest rates to rise; the *only* reason for a declining term structure is that they expect short-term rates to fall.

If short-term interest rates are significantly lower than long-term rates, it is tempting to borrow short term rather than long term. The expectations theory implies that such naïve strategies won't work. If short-term rates are lower than long-term rates, then investors must be expecting interest rates to rise. When the term structure is upward-sloping, you are likely to make money by borrowing short only if investors are *overestimating* future increases in interest rates.

Even at a casual glance, the expectations theory does not seem to be the complete explanation of term structure. For example, if we look back over the period 1900–2020, we find that the return on long-term U.S. Treasury bonds was on average 1.7 percentage points higher than the return on short-term Treasury bills. Perhaps short-term interest rates stayed lower than investors expected, but it seems more likely that investors wanted some extra return for holding long bonds and that on average they got it. If so, the expectations theory is only a first step.

These days, the expectations theory has few strict adherents. But, while expectations about future interest rates do not seem to be the only factor that drives the term structure, they're still an important factor. For example, you often hear market commentators remark that since the six-month interest rate is higher than the three-month rate, the market must be expecting the Federal Reserve Board to raise interest rates.

3.7 Self-Test

The one-year spot interest rate is $r_1 = 5\%$ and the 2-year rate is $r_2 = 10\%$. Does this suggest that rates are more likely to rise or fall?

Interest Rate Risk

What does the expectations theory leave out? The most obvious answer is "risk." If you are confident about the future level of interest rates, you will simply choose the strategy that offers the highest return. But, if you are not sure of your forecasts, you may well opt for a less risky strategy even if it means giving up some return.

Remember that the prices of long-duration bonds are more volatile than prices of short-duration bonds. A sharp increase in interest rates can knock 30% or 40% off the price of long-term bonds.

For some investors, this extra volatility of long-duration bonds may not be a concern. For example, pension funds and life insurance companies have fixed long-term liabilities and may prefer to lock in future returns by investing in long-term bonds. However, the volatility of long-term bonds *does* create extra risk for investors who do not have such long-term obligations. These investors will be prepared to hold long bonds only if they offer the compensation of a higher prospective return. In this case, the term structure will be upward-sloping even if interest rates are expected to remain the same.

BEYOND THE PAGE

Arbitrage models of term structure

mhhe.com/brealey14e

Inflation Risk

Suppose you are saving for your retirement 20 years from now. Which of the following strategies is more risky? Invest in a succession of one-year Treasuries, rolled over annually, or invest once in 20-year strips? The answer depends on how confident you are about future inflation.

If you buy the 20-year strips, you know exactly how much money you will have at year 20, but you don't know what that money will buy. Inflation may seem benign now, but who knows what it will be in 10 or 15 years? This uncertainty about inflation may make it uncomfortably risky for you to lock in one 20-year interest rate by buying the strips.

You can reduce exposure to inflation risk by investing short-term and rolling over the investment. You do not know future short-term interest rates, but you do know that future interest rates will adapt to inflation. If inflation takes off, you will probably be able to roll over your investment at higher interest rates.

If inflation is an important source of risk for long-term investors, borrowers must offer some extra incentive to induce investors to lend long. That is why we often see a steeply upward-sloping term structure when inflation is particularly uncertain.

3-5   Real and Nominal Interest Rates

It is now time to review more carefully the relation between inflation and interest rates. Suppose you invest $1,000 in a one-year bond that makes a single payment of $1,100 at the end of the year. Your cash flow is certain, but the government makes no promises about what that money will buy. If the prices of goods and services increase by more than 10%, you will lose ground in terms of purchasing power.

Several indexes are used to track the general level of prices. The best known is the consumer price index (CPI), which measures the number of dollars that it takes to pay for a typical family's purchases. The change in the CPI from one year to the next measures the rate of inflation.

Figure 3.5 shows the rate of inflation in the U.S. since 1900. Inflation touched a peak at the end of World War I, when it reached 21%. However, this figure pales into insignificance compared with the hyperinflation in Venezuela in 2018 when prices rose by nearly 1 million percent.

Prices can fall as well as rise. The U.S. experienced severe *deflation* in the Great Depression, when prices fell by 24% in three years. In Japan, which has experienced persistent deflation, prices in 2019 were only marginally higher than they had been 20 years earlier.

The *average* U.S. inflation rate from 1900 to 2020 was 3.0%. As you can see from Figure 3.6, among major economies, the United States has been almost top of the class in holding inflation in check. Countries torn by war have generally experienced much higher inflation. For example, in Italy and Japan, inflation since 1900 has averaged around 10% a year.

BEYOND THE PAGE

The German hyperinflation

mhhe.com/brealey14e

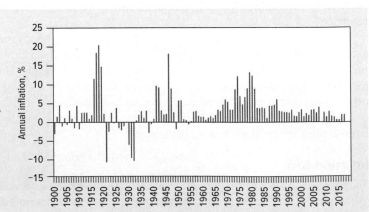

▶ **FIGURE 3.5**

Annual rates of inflation in the United States from 1900–2020.

Source: E. Dimson, P. R. Marsh, and M. Staunton, *Triumph of the Optimists: 101 Years of Investment Returns* (Princeton, NJ: Princeton University Press, 2002), with updates provided by the authors.

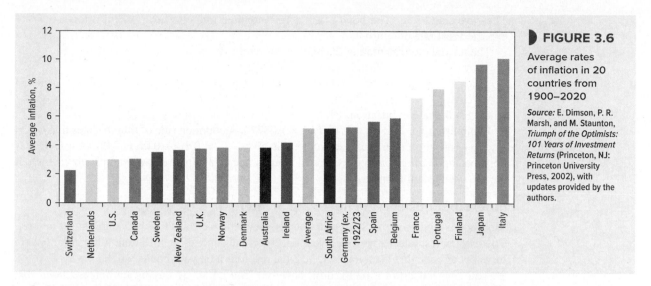

FIGURE 3.6

Average rates of inflation in 20 countries from 1900–2020

Source: E. Dimson, P. R. Marsh, and M. Staunton, *Triumph of the Optimists: 101 Years of Investment Returns* (Princeton, NJ: Princeton University Press, 2002), with updates provided by the authors.

Economists contrast *nominal* (or *current*) dollars with *real* (or *constant*) dollars. For example, the nominal cash flow from your one-year bond is $1,100. But if prices rise over the year by 6%, then each dollar will buy you 6% less next year than it does today. So at the end of the year, $1,100 has the same purchasing power as 1,100/1.06 = $1,037.74 today. The *nominal* payoff on the bond is $1,100, but the *real* payoff is only $1,037.74. Part of the 10% nominal return to your one-year bond is compensation for inflation. If there were no inflation, you'd only be offered a return of 3.8%.

The formula for converting nominal cash flows in a future period t to real cash flows today is

$$\text{Real cash flow at date } t = \frac{\text{nominal cash flow at date } t}{(1 + \text{inflation rate})^t} \qquad (3.4)$$

For example, suppose you invest in a 20-year Treasury strip, but prices over that period grow by 6% per year. The strip pays $1,000 in year 20, but the real value of that payoff is only $1,000/1.06^{20} = \$311.80$. In this example, the purchasing power of $1 today declines to just over $.31 after 20 years.

These examples show you how to get from nominal to real cash flows. The journey from nominal to real interest rates is similar. When a bond dealer says that your bond yields 10%, she is quoting a nominal interest rate. That rate tells you how rapidly your money will grow—say, over one year:

Invest Current Dollars	Receive Dollars in Year 1	Result
$1,000 →	$1,100	10% *nominal rate of return*

However, with an expected inflation rate of 6%, you are only 3.774% better off at the end of the year than at the start:

Invest Current Dollars	Expected Real Value of Dollars in Year 1	Result
$1,000 →	$1,037.74 (=1,100/1.06)	3.774% expected *real* rate of return

Thus, we could say, "The bond offers a 10% nominal rate of return," or "It offers a 3.774% expected real rate of return."

The formula for calculating the real rate of return is:

$$1 + r_{real} = (1 + r_{nominal})/(1 + i) \tag{3.5}$$

where i is the rate of inflation.

In our example, $1 + r_{real} = 1.10/1.06 = 1.03774$. A common rule of thumb states that $r_{real} = r_{nominal} - $ inflation rate. In our example, this gives $r_{real} = 0.10 - 0.06 = 0.04$, or 4%. This is not a bad approximation to the true real interest rate of 3.774%. But when inflation is high, it pays to use the full formula.[13]

Indexed Bonds and the Real Rate of Interest

Most bonds are like our U.S. Treasury bonds; they promise you a fixed *nominal* rate of interest. The *real* interest rate that you receive is uncertain and depends on inflation. If the inflation rate turns out to be higher than you expected, the real return on your bonds will be lower.

You *can* nail down a real return, however. You do so by buying an *indexed bond* that makes cash payments linked to inflation. Indexed bonds known as TIPS (Treasury Inflation-Protected Securities) were first issued in the United States in 1997.[14]

The real cash flows on TIPS are fixed, but the nominal cash flows (interest and principal) increase as the CPI increases.[15] For example, suppose that the U.S. Treasury issues 3% 20-year TIPS at a price equal to its face value of $1,000. If during the first year the CPI rises by 10%, then the coupon payment on the bond increases by 10% from $30 to $30 \times 1.10 = \$33$.[16] The amount that you will be paid at maturity also increases to $1,000 \times 1.10 = \$1,100$. The purchasing power of the coupon and face value remain constant at $33/1.10 = \$30$ and $1,100/1.10 = \$1,000$. Thus, an investor who buys the bond at the issue price earns a surefire real interest rate of 3%.

Ten-year TIPS offered a yield of –0.45% in May 2020. This is a *real* yield to maturity. It measures the extra goods and services your investment will allow you to buy. The –0.45% yield on TIPS was about 1.1% less than the nominal yield on ordinary Treasury bonds. If the annual inflation rate turns out to be higher than 1.1%, investors will earn a higher return by holding long-term TIPS; if the inflation rate turns out to be less than 1.1%, they would have been better off with nominal bonds.

What Determines the Real Rate of Interest?

The real rate of interest depends on people's willingness to save (the supply of capital)[17] and the opportunities for productive investment by governments and businesses (the demand for capital). For example, suppose that investment opportunities improve. Firms have more good projects, so they are willing to invest more than previously at the current real interest rate. Therefore, the rate has to rise to induce individuals to save the additional amount that firms want to invest.[18] Conversely, if investment opportunities deteriorate, there will be a fall in the real interest rate.

---

[13]To see this, note that from (3.5) $r_{nominal} - r_{real} = i + r_{real} \times i$. The approximation ignores the cross-product $r_{real} \times i$.

[14]Indexed bonds were not completely unknown in the United States before 1997. For example, in 1780 American Revolutionary soldiers were compensated with indexed bonds that paid the value of "five bushels of corn, 68 pounds and four-seventh parts of a pound of beef, ten pounds of sheep's wool, and sixteen pounds of sole leather."

[15]The reverse happens if there is deflation. In this case, the coupon payment and principal amount are adjusted downward. However, the U.S. government guarantees that when the bond matures, it will not pay less than its original nominal face value.

[16]Our example assumes annual coupon payments.

[17]Some of this saving is done indirectly. For example, if you hold 100 shares of IBM stock, and IBM retains and reinvests earnings of $1.00 a share, IBM is saving $100 on your behalf. The government may also oblige you to save by raising taxes to invest in roads, hospitals, etc.

[18]We assume that investors save more as interest rates rise. It doesn't have to be that way. Suppose that 20 years hence you will need $50,000 in today's dollars for your children's college tuition. How much will you have to set aside today to cover this obligation? The answer is the present value of a real expenditure of $50,000 after 20 years, or $50,000/(1 + \text{real interest rate})^{20}$. The higher the real interest rate, the lower the present value and the less you have to set aside.

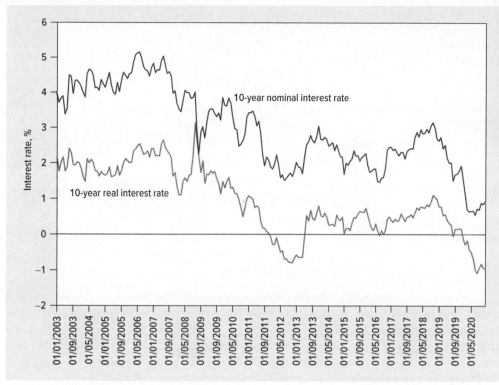

▶ **FIGURE 3.7**

The green line shows the real yield from January 2003 to December 2020 on 10-year TIPS issued by the U.S. government. The brown line shows the corresponding yield on long-term nominal bonds.

For many years, real interest rates were much more stable than nominal rates, but as you can see from Figure 3.7, both nominal and real interest rates have plummeted since the financial crash of 2007–2009.

Inflation and Nominal Interest Rates

How does the inflation outlook affect the nominal rate of interest? Here is how economist Irving Fisher answered the question. Suppose that consumers are equally happy with 100 apples today or 103 apples in a year's time. In this case, the real or "apple" interest rate is 3%. If the price of apples is constant at (say) $1 each, then we will be equally happy to receive $100 today or $103 at the end of the year. That extra $3 will allow us to buy 3% more apples at the end of the year than we could buy today.

But suppose now that the apple price is expected to increase by 5% to $1.05 each. In that case, we would *not* be happy to give up $100 today for the promise of $103 next year. To buy 103 apples in a year's time, we will need to receive 1.05 × $103 = $108.15. In other words, the nominal rate of interest must increase by the expected rate of inflation to 8.15%.

This is Fisher's theory: A change in the expected inflation rate causes the same proportionate change in the *nominal* interest rate; it has no effect on the required real interest rate.

Not all economists would agree with Fisher that the real rate of interest is unaffected by the inflation rate. For example, if changes in prices are associated with changes in the level of industrial activity, then in inflationary conditions I might want more or less than 103 apples in a year's time to compensate for the loss of 100 today.

We wish we could show you the past behavior of interest rates and *expected* inflation. Instead, we have done the next best thing and plotted in Figure 3.8 the return on Treasury bills (short-term government debt) against *actual* inflation for the United States. Notice that since 1953, the return on Treasury bills has generally been a little above the rate of inflation. Investors in each country earned an average real return of about 1% during this period.

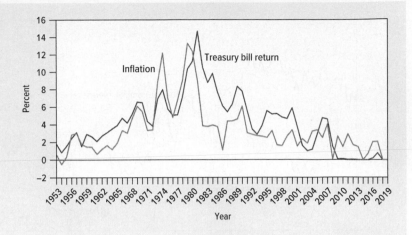

> ▶ **FIGURE 3.8**
>
> The return on Treasury bills and the rate of inflation in the United States, 1953–2020.
>
> *Source:* E. Dimson, P. R. Marsh, and M. Staunton, *Triumph of the Optimists: 101 Years of Investment Returns* (Princeton, NJ: Princeton University Press, 2002), with updates provided by the authors.

Look now at the relationship between the rate of inflation and the Treasury bill rate. Figure 3.8 shows that investors have for the most part demanded a higher rate of interest when inflation was high. So it looks as if Fisher's theory provides a useful rule of thumb for financial managers. If the expected inflation rate changes, it is a good bet that there will be a corresponding change in the nominal interest rate. In other words, a strategy of rolling over short-term investments affords some protection against uncertain inflation.

3.8 Self-Test

A booming economy leads investors to raise their forecast of inflation by 1%. What according to Fisher would be the likely effect on a. The nominal interest rate? b. The real rate?

3-6   The Risk of Default

Corporate Bonds and Default Risk

Look at Table 3.7, which shows the yields to maturity on a sample of corporate bonds. Notice that the bonds all mature in 2027, but their yields to maturity differ dramatically. With a yield of 36%, the bonds of AMC Entertainment appeared to offer a mouth-watering rate of return. However, the company had been operating at a loss and had substantial debts. Investors foresaw that there was a good chance that the company would default and that they would not get their money back. Thus, the payments promised to the bondholders represent a best-case scenario: The firm will never pay more than the promised cash flows, but in hard times, it may pay less. This risk applies in some measure to all corporate bonds, but investors were much more confident that Johnson & Johnson would be able to service its debt and this is reflected in the low yield on its bonds.

The safety of most corporate bonds can be judged from bond ratings provided by rating agencies such as Moody's, Standard & Poor's (S&P), and Fitch. Table 3.8 lists the possible bond ratings in declining order of quality. For example, the bonds that receive the highest Standard & Poor's rating are known as AAA (or "triple A") bonds. Then come AA (double A), A, BBB bonds, and so on. Bonds rated BBB and above are called *investment grade,* while those with a rating of BB or below are referred to as speculative grade, or equivalently

BEYOND THE PAGE

Bond rating definitions

mhhe.com/brealey14e

Issuer Name	Coupon (%)	Maturity	S&P Rating	Price (%)	Yield (%)
Johnson & Johnson	2.95	2027	AAA	111.58	1.12
MMM	2.875	2027	AA	109.98	1.42
Raytheon	7.2	2027	A	135.31	1.98
Champion Intl.	7.15	2027	BBB	114.00	4.94
Belo Corp.	7.75	2027	BB	102.68	7.26
Amsted	5.625	2027	BB	100.20	5.57
American Axle & Mfg.	6.5	2027	B	77.35	11.30
AMC Entertainment	6.125	2027	CCC	25.0	36.01

❯ **TABLE 3.7**
Prices and yields of a sample of corporate bonds in 2020.

Source: Bond transactions reported on FINRA's TRACE service: http://finra-markets.morningstar.com/BondCenter/Screener.jsp.

Moody's	Standard & Poor's and Fitch
Investment-grade bonds	
Aaa	AAA
Aa	AA
A	A
Baa	BBB
Junk bonds	
Ba	BB
B	B
Caa	CCC
Ca	CC
C	C

❯ **TABLE 3.8** Key to bond ratings. The higher-quality bonds rated Baa/BBB or above are investment grade.

high-yield, or junk bonds. Notice that the bonds in the first four rows of Table 3.7 are all investment-grade bonds; the rest are junk bonds. In general, we will be using S&P designations throughout.

It is rare for highly rated bonds to default. However, when an investment-grade bond does go under, the shock waves are felt in all major financial centers. For example, in May 2001, WorldCom sold $11.8 billion of bonds with an investment-grade rating. About one year later, WorldCom filed for bankruptcy, and its bondholders lost more than 80% of their investment. For these bondholders, the agencies that had assigned investment-grade ratings were not the flavor of the month.

Because of the risk of default, yields on corporate bonds are higher than those of government bonds. For example, Figure 3.9 shows the yield spread of corporate bonds against U.S. Treasuries. Notice that the spreads widen as safety falls off. Notice also how spreads vary over time. On average, the spread on BBB bonds has been just under 2%, but it increased to more than 6% during the credit crunch of 2007 to 2009.[19]

[19]Corporate bonds are also less liquid than Treasuries: They are more difficult and expensive to trade, particularly in large quantities or on short notice. Many investors value liquidity and will demand a higher interest rate on a less liquid bond. Lack of liquidity accounts for some of the spread between yields on corporate and Treasury bonds.

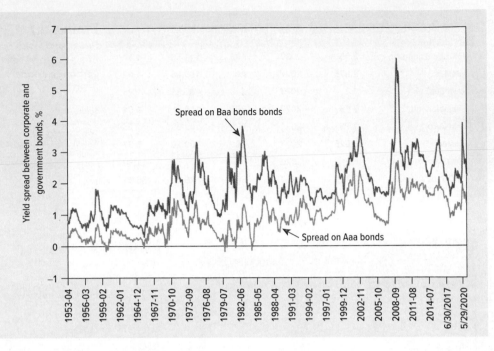

FIGURE 3.9

Yield spreads between corporate and 10-year Treasury bonds, January 1953–December 2020.

Sovereign Bonds and Default Risk

When investors buy corporate bonds or a bank lends to a company, they worry about the possibility of default and spend considerable time and effort assessing differences in credit risk. By contrast, when the U.S. government issues dollar bonds, investors can generally be confident that those bonds will be repaid in full and on time. Of course, bondholders don't know what that money will be worth. Governments have a nasty habit of reducing the real value of their debts by inflationary policies.

Although sovereign debt is generally less risky than corporate debt, we should not leave you with the impression that it is *always* safe even in money terms. Countries do occasionally default on their debts, and when they do so, the effects can be catastrophic. We will look briefly at three circumstances in which countries may default.

Foreign Currency Debt   Most government bond defaults have occurred when a foreign government borrows dollars. In these cases, investors worry that in some future crisis the government may run out of taxing capacity and may not be able to come up with enough dollars to repay the debt. This worry shows up in bond prices and yields to maturity. For example, in 2017 the Venezuelan government defaulted on $65 billion of debt. As the prospect of default loomed, the price of Venezuelan bonds slumped, and the promised yield climbed to more than 40 percentage points above the yield on U.S. Treasuries. Venezuela has plenty of company. Since 1970, there have been more than 100 occasions that sovereign governments have defaulted on their foreign currency bonds.[20]

Own Currency Debt   If a government borrows in its own currency, there is less likelihood of default. After all, the government can always print the money needed to repay the bonds. Very occasionally, governments have chosen to default on their domestic debt rather than create

---

[20]Occasionally, defaults have been a case of "won't pay" rather than "can't pay." For example, in 2008 Ecuador's president announced that his country would disavow $3.9 billion of "illegal" debts contracted by earlier regimes. In dealing with international lenders, he said, "We are up against real monsters."

the money to pay it off. That was the case in Russia in the summer of 1998, when political instability combined with a slump in oil prices, declining government revenues, and pressure on the exchange rate. By August of that year, yields on government ruble bonds had reached 200%, and it no longer made sense for Russia to create the money to service its debt. That month the government devalued the ruble and defaulted on its domestic ruble debt. The ruble lost two-thirds of its value in a few weeks, and many banks failed.

Eurozone Debt The 19 countries in the eurozone do not even have the option of printing money to service their domestic debts; they have given up control over their own money supply to the European Central Bank. This was to pose a major problem for the Greek government, which had amassed a massive €330 billion (or about $440 billion) of debt. In May 2010, other eurozone governments and the International Monetary Fund (IMF) rushed to Greece's aid, but investors were unconvinced that their assistance would be sufficient, and the yield on 10-year Greek government debt climbed to nearly 27%. In 2012, in return for a further bailout package, investors in Greek bonds were obliged to accept a write-down of some $100 billion in the value of their bonds. It was the largest ever sovereign default. However, the difficulties for Greece were by no means over. The rescue package required it to adopt an austerity policy that resulted in a sharp fall in national income and considerable hardship for the Greek people.

• • • • •

KEY TAKEAWAYS

- Bonds are simply long-term loans. If you own a bond, you are entitled to a regular interest (or *coupon*) payment. In some countries coupons are paid annually, but in the U.S. they are normally paid every six months. At maturity bondholders receive the final interest payment plus the bond's face value (or *principal*), which in the United States is usually $1,000.

- The present value of a bond is equal to the series of cash payments discounted by the yield that investors demand. The general formula for the present value of a bond is:

$$PV = \sum C_i/(1 + y/n)^i \tag{3.1}$$

where C_i is the ith payment, y is the yield to maturity, and n is the number of coupon payments in each year. Notice that, when coupon payments are semi-annual, the quoted yield to maturity is expressed as a semi-annually compounded rate.

- The yield to maturity measures the rate of return that a bondholder will earn if she holds the bond to maturity. However, the return in any single period will equal the yield only if the yield does not change during that period. If, for example, yields rise, the bond price falls, and the bondholder's return is *less* than the yield to maturity in that period.

- Prices of long-term bonds are more affected by changes in interest rates than prices of short-term bonds. The average number of years to a bond's discounted cash flows is called its duration. Duration is calculated as:

$$Duration = \sum_{i=1}^{T} \frac{t_i PV(C_i)}{PV} \tag{3.2}$$

where T is the number of payments, t_i is the year of the ith payment, $PV(C_i)$ is the present value of the ith payment, and PV is the present value of the bond.
Long-duration bonds are more volatile than short-duration bonds.

- The t-period spot rate of interest is the interest rate that investors require for an investment that makes a single payment in year t. All other safe cash payments on that date can be valued at that same spot rate. The yield to maturity discounts all cash payments on a bond at the *same* rate, even if spot rates differ. It is, therefore, rather like an average of the different spot rates.

- The term structure of interest rates is upward-sloping more often than not. This means that long-term spot rates are higher than short-term spot rates. But it does *not* mean that investing long is more profitable than investing short. The *expectations theory* of the term structure states that bonds are priced so that an investor who holds a succession of short bonds can expect the same return as another investor who holds a long bond. The expectations theory predicts an upward-sloping term structure only when future short-term interest rates are expected to rise.

- The expectations theory cannot be a complete explanation of term structure if investors are worried about risk. Long bonds may be a safe haven for investors with long-term fixed liabilities, but other investors may not like the extra volatility of long-term bonds or may be concerned that a sudden burst of inflation may largely wipe out the real value of these bonds. These investors will be prepared to hold long-term bonds only if they offer the compensation of a higher rate of interest.

- Bonds promise fixed nominal cash payments, but the *real* interest rate that they provide depends on the inflation rate, *i:*

$$1 + r_{real} = (1 + r_{nominal})/(1 + i) \tag{3.5}$$

- The best-known theory about the effect of inflation on interest rates was proposed by Irving Fisher. He argued that the nominal, or money, rate of interest is equal to the required real rate plus the expected rate of inflation, which is independent of the real rate. If the expected inflation rate increases by 1%, so too will the money rate of interest. During the past 70 years, Fisher's simple theory has not done a bad job of explaining changes in short-term interest rates.

- When you buy a U.S. Treasury bond, you can be fairly confident that you will get your money back. This is not true for some countries and the interest rate they have to pay is higher as a result. When you lend to a company, you also face the risk that it will default on its bonds. Defaults are rare for companies with investment-grade bond ratings, but companies need to compensate investors for default risk by promising to pay higher rates of interest.

- - - - -

FURTHER READING

Some good general texts on fixed income markets are:

F. J. Fabozzi and S. V. Mann, *Handbook of Fixed Income Securities,* 9th ed. (New York: McGraw-Hill, 2021).

S. Sundaresan, *Fixed Income Markets and Their Derivatives,* 4th ed. (San Diego, CA: Academic Press, 2014).

B. Tuckman and A. Serrat, *Fixed Income Securities: Tools for Today's Markets,* 3rd ed. (New York: Wiley, 2011).

P. Veronesi, *Handbook of Fixed-Income Securities—Wiley Handbooks in Financial Engineering and Econometrics* (New York: Wiley, 2016).

- - - - -

PROBLEM SETS   Mc Graw Hill **connect**®   **Select problems are available in McGraw-Hill's *Connect.***

1. **Bond prices and yields (S3.1)** A 10-year bond is issued with a face value of $1,000, paying interest of $60 a year. If interest rates increase shortly after the bond is issued, what happens to the bond's

   a. Coupon rate?

   b. Price?

   c. Yield to maturity?

2. **Bond prices and yields (S3.1) The following statements are true. Explain why.**

   a. If a bond's coupon rate is higher than its yield to maturity, then the bond will sell for more than face value.

   b. If a bond's coupon rate is lower than its yield to maturity, then the bond's price will increase over its remaining maturity.

3. **Bond prices and yields (S3.1)** Construct some simple examples to illustrate your answers to the following:

   a. If interest rates rise, do bond prices rise or fall?

   b. If the bond yield to maturity is greater than the coupon, is the price of the bond greater or less than 100?

   c. If the price of a bond exceeds 100, is the yield to maturity greater or less than the coupon?

   d. Do high-coupon bonds sell at higher or lower prices than low-coupon bonds?

   e. If interest rates change, do the prices of high-coupon bonds change proportionately more than that of low-coupon bonds?

4. **Bond prices and yields (S3.1)** A 10-year German government bond (bund) has a face value of €100 and a coupon rate of 5% paid annually. Assume that the interest rate (in euros) is equal to 6% per year. What is the bond's PV?

5. **Bond prices and yields (S3.1)** In December 2020, Treasury $4^1/_4$s of 2040 offered a semiannually compounded yield to maturity of 1.32%. Recognizing that coupons are paid semiannually, calculate the bond's price.

6. **Bond prices and yields (S3.1)** A 10-year U.S. Treasury bond with a face value of $1,000 pays a coupon of 5.5% (2.75% of face value every six months). The reported yield to maturity is 5.2% (a six-month discount rate of $5.2/2 = 2.6\%$).

   a. What is the present value of the bond?

   b. Generate a graph or table showing how the bond's present value changes for semiannually compounded interest rates between 1% and 15%.

7. **Bond prices and yields (S3.1)** Choose 10 U.S. Treasury bonds with different coupons and different maturities. Calculate how their prices would change if their yields to maturity increased by 1 percentage point. Are long- or short-term bonds most affected by the change in yields? Are high- or low-coupon bonds most affected? (For simplicity, assume annual coupon payments.)

8. **Bond returns (S3.1)** If a bond's yield to maturity does not change, the return on the bond each year will be equal to the yield to maturity. Confirm this with a simple example of a four-year bond selling at a premium to face value. Now do the same for a four-year bond selling at a discount. For convenience, assume annual coupon payments.

9. **Bond returns (S3.1)**

   a. An 8%, five-year bond yields 6%. If this yield to maturity remains unchanged, what will be its price one year hence? Assume annual coupon payments and a face value of $1,000.

   b. What is the total return to an investor who held the bond over this year?

   c. What can you deduce about the relationship between the bond return over a particular period and the yields to maturity at the start and end of that period?

10. **Bond returns (S3.1)** A six-year government bond makes annual coupon payments of 5% and offers a yield of 3% annually compounded. Suppose that one year later the bond still yields 3%. What return has the bondholder earned over the 12-month period? Now suppose that the bond yields 2% at the end of the year. What return did the bondholder earn in this case?

11. **Duration (S3.2)** True or false? Explain.

    a. Longer-maturity bonds necessarily have longer durations.

    b. The longer a bond's duration, the lower its volatility.

    c. Other things equal, the lower the bond coupon, the higher its volatility.

    d. If interest rates rise, bond durations rise also.

12. **Duration (S3.2)** Here are the prices of three bonds with 10-year maturities:

Bond Coupon (%)	Price (%)
2%	81.62%
4	98.39
8	133.42

    If coupons are paid annually, which bond offered the highest yield to maturity? Which had the lowest? Which bonds had the longest and shortest durations?

13. **Duration (S3.2)** Calculate the durations and volatilities of securities A, B, and C. Their cash flows are shown below. The interest rate is 8%.

	Period 1	Period 2	Period 3
A	40	40	40
B	20	20	120
C	10	10	110

14. **Duration (S3.2)** Calculate durations and modified durations for the 3% bonds in Table 3.2. You can follow the procedure set out in Table 3.4 for the 9% coupon bonds. Confirm that modified duration closely predicts the impact of a 1% change in interest rates on the bond prices.

15. **Duration (S3.2)** Find the spreadsheet for Table 3.4 in Connect. Show how duration and volatility change if (a) the bond's coupon is 8% of face value and (b) the bond's yield is 6%. Explain your finding.

16. **Duration (S3.2)** The formula for the duration of a perpetual bond that makes an equal payment each year in perpetuity is $(1 + yield)/yield$. If each bond yields 5%, which has the longer duration—a perpetual bond or a 15-year zero-coupon bond? What if the yield is 10%?

17. **Spot interest rates and yields (S3.3)** Which comes first in the market for U.S. Treasury bonds:

    a. Spot interest rates or yields to maturity?

    b. Bond prices or yields to maturity?

18. **Spot interest rates and yields (S3.3)** Look again at Table 3.6. Suppose that spot interest rates all change to 4%—a "flat" term structure of interest rates.

    a. What is the new yield to maturity for each bond in the table?

    b. Recalculate the price of bond A.

19. **Spot interest rates and yields (S3.3)** Look again at Table 3.6. Suppose the spot interest rates change to the following *downward-sloping* term structure: $r_1 = 4.6\%$, $r_2 = 4.4\%$, $r_3 = 4.2\%$, and $r_4 = 4.0\%$. Recalculate discount factors, bond prices, and yields to maturity for each of the bonds listed in the table.

20. **Spot interest rates and yields (S3.3)** Look at the spot interest rates shown in Problem 19. Suppose that someone told you that the five-year spot interest rate was 2.5%. Why would you doubt him? How could you make money if he was right? What is the minimum likely value for the five-year spot rate?

21. **Spot interest rates and yields (S3.3)** Assume annual coupons.

    a. What is the formula for the value of a two-year, 5% bond in terms of spot rates?

    b. What is the formula for its value in terms of yield to maturity?

    c. If the two-year spot rate is higher than the one-year rate, is the yield to maturity greater or less than the two-year spot rate?

22. **Spot interest rates and yields (S3.3)** A 6% six-year bond yields 12% and a 10% six-year bond yields 8%. Calculate the six-year spot rate. Assume annual coupon payments. (*Hint:* What would be your cash flows if you bought 1.2 10% bonds?)

23. **Spot interest rates and yields (S3.3)** Is the yield on high-coupon bonds more likely to be higher than that on low-coupon bonds when the term structure is upward-sloping or when it is downward-sloping? Explain.

24. **Spot interest rates and yields (S3.3)** You have estimated spot rates as follows:

$$r_1 = 5.00\%, r_2 = 5.40\%, r_3 = 5.70\%, r_4 = 5.90\%, r_5 = 6.00\%.$$

    a. What are the discount factors for each date (i.e., the present value of $1 paid in year t)?

    b. Calculate the PV of the following bonds assuming annual coupons and face values of $1,000: (i) 5%, two-year bond; (ii) 5%, five-year bond; and (iii) 10%, five-year bond.

25. **Spot interest rates and yields (S3.3)** Look again at the bonds in part (b) of Problem 24.

    a. Explain intuitively why the yield to maturity on the 10% bond is less than that on the 5% bond.

    b. What should be the yield to maturity on a five-year zero-coupon bond?

    c. Show that the correct yield to maturity on a five-year annuity is 5.75%.

    d. Explain intuitively why the yield on the five-year bonds described in part (b) of Problem 24 must lie between the yield on a five-year zero-coupon bond and a five-year annuity.

26. **Measuring term structure (S3.3)** The following table shows the prices of a sample of Narnian Treasury strips in December 2020. Each strip makes a single payment of $1,000 at maturity.

    a. Calculate the annually compounded, spot interest rate for each year.

    b. Is the term structure upward- or downward-sloping or flat?

    c. Would you expect the yield on a coupon bond maturing in December 2025 to be higher or lower than the yield on the 2022 strip?

Maturity	Price (%)
December 2022	90.703%
December 2023	85.892
December 2024	81.491
December 2025	77.243

27. **Term-structure theories (S3.4)** The one-year spot interest rate is $r_1 = 5\%$ and the two-year rate is $r_2 = 6\%$. If the expectations theory is correct, what is the expected one-year interest rate in one year's time?

28. **Term-structure theories (S3.4)** Look again at the spot interest rates shown in Problem 24. What can you deduce about the one-year spot interest rate in three years if:

    a. The expectations theory of term structure is right?

    b. Investing in long-term bonds carries additional risks?

29. **Real interest rates (S3.5)** The two-year interest rate is 10% and the expected annual inflation rate is 5%.

    a. What is the expected real interest rate?

    b. If the expected rate of inflation suddenly rises to 7%, what does Fisher's theory say about how the real interest rate will change? What about the nominal rate?

30. **Nominal and real returns (S3.5)** Suppose that you buy a two-year 8% bond at its face value.

    a. What will be your *total* nominal return over the two years if inflation is 3% in the first year and 5% in the second? What will be your *total* real return?

    b. Now suppose that the bond is a TIPS. What will be your *total* two-year real and nominal returns?

31. **Bond ratings (S3.6)** A bond's credit rating provides a guide to its price. In December 2020, Aaa bonds yielded 1.29% and Baa bonds yielded 3.11%. If some bad news causes a 10% five-year bond to be unexpectedly downrated from Aaa to Baa, what would be the likely effect on the bond price? (Assume annual coupons.)

CHALLENGE

32. **Bond prices and yields (S3.1)** Write a spreadsheet program to construct a series of bond tables that show the present value of a bond given the coupon rate, maturity, and yield to maturity. Assume that coupon payments are semiannual and yields are compounded semiannually.

33. **Duration (S3.2)** The duration of a bond that makes an equal payment each year in perpetuity is $(1 + \text{yield})/\text{yield}$. Prove it.

34. **Price and spot interest rates (S3.3)** Find the arbitrage opportunity(ies). Assume for simplicity that coupons are paid annually. In each case, the face value of the bond is $1,000.

Bond	Maturity (years)	Coupon ($)	Price ($)
A	3	0	751.30
B	4	50	842.30
C	4	120	1,065.28
D	4	100	980.57
E	3	140	1,120.12
F	3	70	1,001.62
G	2	0	834.00

35. **Prices and spot interest rates (S3.3)** What spot interest rates are implied by the following Treasury bonds? Assume for simplicity that the bonds pay annual coupons. The price of a one-year strip is 97.56%, and the price of a four-year strip is 87.48%.

Maturity (years)	Coupon	Price (%)
5	2	92.89
5	3	97.43
3	5	105.42

36. **Prices and spot interest rates (S3.3) Look one more time at Table 3.6.**

    a. Suppose you knew the bond prices but not the spot interest rates. Explain how you would calculate the spot rates. (*Hint:* You have four unknown spot rates, so you need four equations.)

    b. Suppose that you could buy bond C in large quantities at $1,040 rather than at its equilibrium price of $1,076.20. Show how you could make a zillion dollars without taking on any risk.

3.1 Since the bond provides a guaranteed loss over its life time, the yield must be lower than the coupon rate.

3.2 a. $50 at month 6 and $1,050 at month 12;

 b. $50/1.03 + 1,050/1.03^2 = \$1,038.27$;

 c. $6\%/2 = 3\%$; d. $1.03^2 - 1 = 0.0609$, or 6.09%.

3.3 a. The coupon;

 b. price falls.

3.4 a. A 20-year 8% bond;

 b. 2% bond (a larger proportion of the value comes from the final payment).

3.5 a. No, the 3.66% yield is only accurate for valuing an annuity.

 b. You would overvalue it (the major part of the bond's cash flow occurs in year 2 and should be discounted at the higher spot rate).

3.6 $(1/0.3769)^{(1/20)} - 1 = 0.05$, or 5%.

3.7 If this difference in rates reflects investor expectations, rates are more likely to rise.

3.8 a. Rise by 1%;

 b. no effect on real rate.

The websites of *The Wall Street Journal* (**www.wsj.com**) and the *Financial Times* (**www.ft.com**) are wonderful sources of market data. You should become familiar with them.

 1. Use **www.wsj.com** to answer the following questions:

    a. Find a long-term Treasury bond with a low coupon and calculate its duration. Now find another bond with a similar maturity and a higher coupon. Which has the longer duration?

    b. Look up the yields on 10-year nominal Treasury bonds and on TIPS. If you are confident that inflation will average 2% a year, which bond will provide the higher real return?

 2. Bond transactions are reported on FINRA's TRACE service, which was the source of the data for Table 3.7. Use the Advanced Search facility in TRACE to find bond prices for Johnson & Johnson (JNJ), Walmart (WMT), Disney (DIS), SunTrust Banks (STI), and U.S. Steel (X). If possible, exclude callable issues that the company can buy back.

Part 1 Value

CHAPTER

Valuing Stocks

On a typical day in the New York Stock Exchange, investors trade over 1 trillion shares of stock. What determines the prices at which these shares are bought and sold? In other words, what determines the values of these shares to investors? This chapter explains the fundamental tools and concepts that investors and financial analysts use to value stocks.

Why should you care about valuation fundamentals? If you want to know what a stock is worth, why can't you just look up the price on the Internet?

There are several reasons you should care:

1. The stock price may not always be right. Before the dot-com bubble burst in 2000, prices of Internet stocks were unsustainably high. On the other hand, hindsight tells us that most stock prices were abnormally low in the depths of the Great Recession of 2007–2009. Financial analysts use the tools and concepts presented in this chapter as they try to identify which stocks to buy and which to stay away from.

2. Many companies are not public. A private company may want to understand what its stock is worth or what it would be worth if it were traded.

3. Changes in the price of a public company's shares reveal how well the company is doing financially, at least in the eyes of investors, and usually determine a large fraction of top management's compensation. If your company is going to use its stock price to assess performance, you had better understand what determines the price.

4. A firm that acts in its shareholders' interest should accept capital investments that increase the value of their stake in the firm. In order to do this, the financial manager needs to understand what determines the value of the firm's shares.

Section 4-1 How stocks are traded

We begin with a brief look at how stocks are traded. Then we introduce some key statistics and valuation ratios that investors use to evaluate stocks, including dividend yields, price-earnings (P/E) ratios and market-to-book ratios.

Section 4-2 Valuation by comparables

We start our discussion of share valuation by looking at a venerable, but still widely used valuation approach, *comparable companies analysis*. That approach rests on the common-sense idea that similar stocks ought to sell at similar valuation ratios, for example, similar P/Es.

Section 4-3 Dividends and stock prices

In this section, we derive and explain *dividend discount models*. These models all start with a present value equation: the market price of a share of stock equals the present value of all future cash dividends paid to the current and future owners of that share. This fundamental PV equation can be written as:

$$P_0 = \sum_{t=1}^{\infty} \frac{DIV_t}{(1 + r)^t} \qquad (4.1A)$$

where P_0 is today's price, DIV_t the expected dividend per share at future date t, and r the discount rate, the *cost of equity*.

Section 4-4 Dividend discount model applications

If the expected growth rate of dividends is steady and perpetual, the present value formula simplifies to:

$$P_0 = \frac{DIV_1}{r - g} \qquad (4.2)$$

where DIV_1 is next year's expected dividend, g is the growth rate, and r is the cost of equity.

When the forecasted growth rate is steady and perpetual, you can also turn Equation (4.2) around to estimate the cost of equity capital. In other cases, you need to go back to the fundamental equation for the present value of a share to estimate the cost of equity capital. We also work through valuation exercises using dividend discount models with two stages of growth.

Section 4-5 Income stocks and growth stocks

Here we explain the fundamental differences between *income stocks* and *growth stocks.* Investors don't buy stocks just for dividends, but also for anticipated growth in stock price. The most exciting stocks often pay no dividends at all, and are unlikely to initiate dividends soon. Who cares about dividends if stock price grows robustly? But how much growth is needed to offset the lack of immediate dividends, and what does a company have to do to deliver that growth? This section explains.

Section 4-6 Valuation based on free cash flow

Sometimes it is easier and more practical to value all shares taken together rather than a single share. Section 4-6 explains why and how. The present-value equation is the same, except that it now determines *market capitalization*—that is,

the market value of all outstanding shares. Market capitalization equals the present value of all future *free cash flow.* Free cash flow is the after-tax cash flow generated by the company's operations after subtracting investment required for growth. Free cash flow is the amount of cash available for payout to all shareholders.

It is still early in this book, so we have deferred several important issues. For example, we treat the cost of equity r as an unexplained constant. In fact, it depends on the level of interest rates, as one would expect from Chapter 3, and also on risk (Chapters 7, 8, 9) and on the choice between debt and equity financing (Chapters 16, 17). Chapter 18 covers valuation models taking all these issues into account.

Financial experts face certain occupational hazards. One is being cornered at cocktail parties by people who are eager to explain their system for making large profits by investing in stocks. One of the few good things about a financial crisis is that these bores tend to disappear, at least temporarily.

We may exaggerate the perils of the trade. The point is that there is no easy way to ensure superior investment performance. Therefore, when in this chapter we use present value calculations to value stocks, we are not providing a key to investment success nor attempting to turn you into a cocktail-party bore. We are just explaining the fundamental reasons some stocks are more valuable than others.

• • • • •

4-1 How Stocks Are Traded

Cummins Inc., a long-established manufacturer of diesel engines and other power and industrial equipment, had 150.7 million shares outstanding at the end of February 2020. Shareholders included large pension funds and insurance companies that each owned millions of shares, as well as individuals who owned a handful. If you owned one Cummins share, you would own 0.0000006% of the company and have a claim on the same tiny fraction of its profits. Of course, the more shares you own, the larger your "share" of the company.

If Cummins wishes to raise new capital, it can sell new shares to investors. These share issues occur in the *primary market.* But most trades in Cummins take place on the stock exchange, where investors buy and sell existing Cummins shares. Stock exchanges are really markets for secondhand shares, but they prefer to describe themselves as *secondary markets,* which sounds more important.

The two principal U.S. stock exchanges are the New York Stock Exchange (NYSE) and Nasdaq. Both compete vigorously for business and just as vigorously tout the advantages of their trading systems. In addition to the NYSE and Nasdaq, there are *electronic communication networks (ECNs)* that connect traders with each other. Large U.S. companies may also arrange for their shares to be traded on foreign exchanges, such as the London exchange or the Euronext exchange which serves seven European countries. At the same time, many foreign companies are listed on the U.S. exchanges. For example, the NYSE trades shares in Sony,

BEYOND THE PAGE

Major
world stock
exchanges

mhhe.com/brealey14e

Royal Dutch Shell, Canadian Pacific, Tata Motors, Deutsche Bank, Telefonica Brasil, China Eastern Airlines, and more than 500 other companies.

Suppose that Ms. Jones, a long-time Cummins shareholder, no longer wishes to hold her shares. She can sell them via the NYSE to Mr. Brown, who wants to increase his stake in the firm. The transaction merely transfers partial ownership of the firm from one investor to another. No new shares are created, and Cummins will neither care nor know that the trade has taken place.

Ms. Jones and Mr. Brown do not show up on the floor of the NYSE to execute their sell and buy orders personally. Their stock brokers convey their orders to the NYSE, which operates a huge auction market matching up orders from thousands of investors. Most major exchanges around the world, including the Tokyo, Shanghai, and London stock exchanges and the Deutsche Börse, are also auction markets, but the auctioneer in these cases is a computer.[1] This means that there is no stock exchange floor to show on the evening news and no one needs to ring a bell to start trading.

Nasdaq is not an auction market. All trades on Nasdaq take place between the investor and one of a group of professional dealers who are prepared to buy and sell stock. Dealer markets are common for other financial instruments. For example, most bonds are traded in dealer markets.

Trading Results for Cummins

You can track trades in Cummins and other public corporations on the Internet. For example, if you go to **finance.yahoo.com** and enter the ticker symbol CMI, you will see trading results displayed as in Table 4.1.[2]

Cummins's closing price on February 27, 2020 was $154.46, down $3.51, or 2.22%, from the previous close of $157.97. Cummins stock started the trading day at $152.22 and traded in a range of $151.93 to $160.37. Trading volume was 1,784,318 shares, larger than average volume.

Cummins Inc. Common Stock (CMI) (NYSE)			
154.46 −3.51 (−2.22%) Feb. 27 4:00 pm EST			
Previous close	157.97	Market cap	23.211 B
Open	152.22	Beta	1.19
Day's range	151.93–160.37	EPS (TTM)	14.48
52-week range	141.14–186.73	P/E ratio (TTM)	10.67
Volume	1,784,318	P/E ratio (FWD)	13.39
Average volume	1,161,193	Dividend (FWD)	5.24 (3.39%)
		Price/book value	2.74

❭**TABLE 4.1** Summary of Yahoo Finance's table of trading results for Cummins Inc. on February 27, 2020.

Source: finance.yahoo.com.

---

[1] Trades are still made face to face on the floor of the NYSE, but computerized trading is taking over. In 2006, the NYSE merged with Archipelago, an electronic trading system, and transformed itself into a public corporation. The NYSE is now owned by Intercontinental Exchange Inc., a U.S.-based network of exchanges and clearing houses.

[2] This table reports a small slice of what Yahoo! Finance provides. For example, you can dig deeper into trading history, financial statements and analyst forecasts. Other good sources of trading and financial information include **moneycentral.msn.com, finance. google.com** and the online edition of the *Wall Street Journal* at **www.wsj.com** (look for the "Market" and then the "Market Data" tabs).

Cummins had 150.7 million shares outstanding, so its *market cap* (short for *market capitalization*) was $150.7 \times 154.46 = \$23.2$ billion.

Cummins's earnings per share (EPS) for 2019 were $14.48. EPS equaled net income—calculated after taxes, interest on borrowing, and all operating expenses—divided by the number of shares held by investors. "TTM" stands for "trailing 12 months." The ratio of stock price to trailing EPS was P/E = 10.67. Security analysts were forecasting a drop in EPS for 2020, however, so the *forward* (FWD) P/E at 13.39 was higher than trailing P/E at 10.67. The ratio of stock price to the book value per share was 2.74. We say more about book value below.

Cummins had announced a dividend of $5.24 per share for 2020, so its forward dividend yield (dividend divided by stock price) was 3.39%. Its beta of 1.19 indicated risk higher than the market-average risk of 1.0. We explain betas in Chapters 7, 8, and 9.

Cummins stock had not been an exceptional investment at the time of our table in February 2020. Its stock price fluctuated in the previous 52 weeks and ended up about where it started. But Cummins escaped the precipitous downsides that sometimes hit even the best and biggest companies. Take GE as an example. GE used to be one of the most powerful and admired U.S. companies. But GE stock fell by 40% over the 12 months ending on November 16, 2017—a period in which the S&P 500 market index gained 18.5%. The stock fell by 23% in the last month of that period when its new CEO cut GE's dividend in half and announced a plan for drastic restructuring. There weren't many GE stockholders piping up at cocktail parties over the 2017 holiday season; they either kept quiet or were not invited.

Most of the trading on the NYSE and Nasdaq is in ordinary "common" stocks, but other securities are traded also, including preferred stocks, which we cover in Chapter 13, and warrants, which we cover in Chapter 22. Investors can also choose from hundreds of *exchange-traded funds (ETFs),* which are portfolios of stocks that can be bought or sold in a single trade. Most ETFs are not actively managed; they simply aim to track a well-known market index such as the Dow Jones Industrial Average or the S&P 500. Others track specific industries or commodities. ETFs may also invest in bonds or other investments. We discuss ETFs more fully in Chapter 13. You can also buy shares in closed-end mutual funds[3] that invest in portfolios of securities. These include country funds, such as the Mexico and India funds, that invest in portfolios of stocks in specific countries. Unlike ETFs, most closed-end funds are actively managed and seek to "beat the market."

Market Price vs. Book Value

Cummins, like all public companies, publishes quarterly and annual financial statements, including balance sheets, which report the *book values* of all assets and liabilities—in other words, the values reported on the company's "books." At the end of 2019, the total book value of all Cummins assets—plant and machinery, inventories, accounts receivable from customers, cash, etc.—was $19.737 billion. Its total liabilities—outstanding bonds and bank loans, accounts payable to suppliers, taxes due and other obligations—was $11.272 billion. The difference of $8.465 billion was the *book value of equity.* Book value per share was $56.17.

Cummins's ratio of stock price to book value per share (P/B ratio) of 2.74 means that stock price was almost three times the book value per share reported at year-end 2019. Does that mean that investors were three times as optimistic as the accountants who prepared the financial statements? No, because accountants do not try to forecast performance. Instead they calculate the book value of equity by recording the company's cumulative past investments in its business, less an allowance for depreciation, and then subtracting debt and other liabilities.

---

[3]*Closed-end* mutual funds issue shares that are traded on stock exchanges. *Open-end* funds are not traded on exchanges. Investors in open-end funds transact directly with the fund. The fund issues new shares to investors and redeems shares from investors who want to withdraw money from the fund.

The resulting *historical cost* of investments is not a good measure of current value. Investors care much more about future earnings than historical costs.

One can go on and on about the deficiencies of book value as a measure of market value. Book values do not incorporate inflation. (Countries with high or volatile inflation often require inflation-adjusted book values, however.) Book values usually exclude intangible assets such as trademarks and patents. Also accountants simply add up the book values of individual assets, and thus do not capture *going-concern value*. Going-concern value is created when a collection of assets is organized into a healthy operating business.

Book values can nevertheless be a useful benchmark. Suppose, for example, that Holstein Oil's market cap is $900 million. Its book value of equity is $450 million. A financial analyst might say, "Holstein sells for two times book value. It has doubled shareholders' cumulative past investment in the company." He might also say, "Holstein's market value added is $900 − 450 = $450 million." (There is more on *market value added* in Chapter 29.)

Book values may also be useful clues about *liquidation value*. Liquidation value is what investors get when a failed company is shut down and its assets are sold off. Book values of "hard" assets like land, buildings, vehicles, and machinery can indicate possible liquidation values.

Intangible "soft" assets can be important even in liquidation, however. Eastman Kodak provides a good example. Kodak, which was one of the "Nifty Fifty" U.S. growth stocks of the 1960s, suffered a long decline and finally filed for bankruptcy in January 2012. What was one of its most valuable assets in bankruptcy? Its portfolio of 79,000 patents, which was subsequently sold for $525 million.

4-2   Valuation by Comparables

There are two approaches to valuing stocks. The first involves identifying a sample of similar firms as potential *comparables* and then examining how much investors in these comparable companies are prepared to pay per dollar of earnings or book value. They see what the business would be worth if it traded at the comparables' price–earnings (P/E = P/EPS) or price-to-book-value (P/B) ratios. (Other ratios are also used in practice, but for now we illustrate with these two ratios only.[4]) This valuation approach is called *valuation by comparables or comparable companies analysis*. The second approach is to forecast and then discount the business's dividends or future cash flows. In practice, both methods are widely used, and, when estimating the value of a business, an analyst will typically try both techniques.[5] We start by looking at valuation by comparables.

Valuation by comparables works best if the relevant financial ratios cluster together by industry and for similar companies in the same industry. Table 4.2 illustrates this clustering, sometimes close, sometimes imperfect. The top line of the table reports P/Es and P/Bs for Coca-Cola and PepsiCo, the two largest U.S. soft-drinks companies. The match was almost perfect. (We were probably lucky to catch the two companies on a trading day where the ratios lined up almost exactly.)

---

[4]We discuss financial ratios in Chapter 29.

[5]For an analysis of the valuation techniques that are used by practitioners, see L. Mukhlynina and K. G. Nyborg, "The Choice of Valuation Techniques in Practice: Education versus Profession," *Critical Finance Review* 9 (2020) pp. 201–265. The authors find systematic differences between professional groups in the way that the two valuation methods are applied.

Company	Stock Price	P/E	P/B	Comparable	P/E	P/B
Coca-Cola (beverages)	$ 55	24.0	12.4	PepsiCo	23.1	12.8
Union Pacific (railroad)	$ 157	17.2	6.1	Canadian Pacific	18.0	6.5
				CSX	15.2	4.5
				Kansas City Southern	18.5	3.0
				Norfolk Southern	16.5	3.1
				Average	17.1	4.3
Bank of America (bank)	$28.50	9.6	1.1	JPMorgan Chase	11.1	1.6
				Wells Fargo	10.6	1.1
				Citigroup	7.6	0.8
				Capital One	7.5	0.7
				Key Corp	9.1	1.2
				US Bancorp	10.8	1.6
				Average	9.5	1.2

❭TABLE 4.2 Stock price, price–earnings (P/E), and market-book (P/B) in March 2020 for three companies and potential comparable companies.

Source: finance.yahoo.com.

The second part of Table 4.2 compares ratios for the Union Pacific railroad (UNP) with four other railroads. UNP's P/E was almost identical to the average P/E of the other four. If you didn't know UNP's stock price, you could get an excellent estimate by multiplying UNP's forecasted earnings per share by the average P/E of 17.1. On the other hand, UNP's P/B ratio was higher than all the comparables except Canadian Pacific (CP). A stock-price estimate based on average P/B would be too low—*unless* further investigation revealed that CP was a better match to UNP than the other railroads, so that CP's P/B could be used instead of the average.

The bottom block of the table compares Bank of America (BAC) with six other U.S banks. Here again BAC's ratios are close to the average ratios.

Of course, investors did not need valuation by comparables to value any of the companies in Table 4.2. They are all public companies with actively traded shares. Valuation by comparables is most useful when you don't have a stock price. For example, suppose a European bank is investigating a sale of its U.S. operations. The bank could get a start on valuing the operations by applying the ratios for banks in Table 4.2 to the book value and projected earnings of the U.S. operations.

In practice, valuation by comparables requires much more investigation and judgment than we have deployed here. For example, the European bank would probably put more weight on ratios for Capital One, Keycorp, and U.S. Bancorp, which are more focused on U.S. banking than much larger global banks such as Citigroup and JPMorgan Chase. It might also look for smaller, regional banks that would be better matches to its own U.S. operations.

We return to valuation by comparables in Chapter 18. There, the first task is estimating *enterprise value,* defined as equity market cap plus debt—in other words, as the total value of the firm to debt and equity investors combined. In this setting, valuation ratios are often based on EBIT (earnings before interest and taxes) or EBITDA (earnings before interest, taxes, depreciation, and amortization). For example, a financial manager may calculate ratios of enterprise value to EBIT for a sample of similar companies to see what she could learn from their market values.

Note that the earnings per share, E, in the P/E ratio are calculated after deducting interest expense and, therefore, depend on the amount of debt the company has issued. EBIT and EBITDA are calculated before that deduction and depend on the firm's operating profitability, not its amount of debt financing. EBIT and EBITDA are likewise insulated from accounting differences in calculating tax expense. EBITDA is also insulated from accounting differences in how assets are depreciated or amortized. These differences are covered in Chapter 6.

Once the financial manager has a satisfactory estimate of enterprise value, stock price is only two steps away. First she subtracts debt to obtain the market cap of equity. Then she divides by the number of outstanding shares to get price per share. We work through detailed examples in Chapter 18.

Sections 4-1 and 4-2 *used* stock-market prices but did not attempt to *explain* them. We start in the next section by connecting stock prices to cash dividends.

4-3   Dividends and Stock Prices

Think back to Chapter 3, where we explained how bonds are valued. The market value of a bond equals the discounted present value (PV) of the cash flows (interest and principal payments) that the bond will pay out over its lifetime. Let's import and apply this idea to stocks. The future cash flows to the owner of a share of stock are the future dividends per share that the company will pay out. Thus, the logic of discounted cash flow suggests

PV (share of stock) = PV (expected future dividends per share)

This PV equation can be written as:

$$\text{Price} = P_0 = \sum_{t=1}^{\infty} \frac{\text{DIV}_t}{(1+r)^t} \qquad (4.1A)$$

where P_0 is today's price, DIV_t the expected dividend per share at future date t, and r the discount rate. The formula's summation sign $\sum$ says that the PVs of all future dividends are added up from date $t = 1$ to infinity (∞). Why infinity? Because a stock has no maturity date and could last forever.

The discount rate r in this valuation equation is the expected rate of return demanded by investors in the firm's stock. It is called the **cost of equity** because shareholders provide equity financing.[6] They do so in two ways: (1) when they buy newly issued shares and (2) when the firm retains and reinvests earnings that otherwise could be paid out. The cost of equity equals shareholders' *opportunity cost of capital,* defined as the expected return on other securities with the same risks as the company's stock.

This PV equation (Eq. 4.1A) is called the **DCF** (for **discounted cash flow**) or **dividend discount model** of stock prices. The equation does not require the firm to pay dividends immediately, although it is most useful for firms that do. Nor does it require investors to hold a common stock forever. All investors will sell sooner or later, and when they do, they sell the dividends still to come to the next investor.

When investors sell, they hope to get more for the stock than they paid for it and thereby realize a *capital gain.* The dividend discount model says nothing about capital gains. But there is no inconsistency, as we now demonstrate.

---

[6]The cost of equity is sometimes also called the market capitalization rate.

Dividends and Capital Gains

For now, we will assume a mature firm that pays regular cash dividends. Its fickle shareholders, however, plan to invest for one year only. Their rate of return equals the expected dividend per share DIV_1 plus the expected price appreciation per share $P_1 - P_0$, all divided by the price at the start of the year P_0:

$$\text{Expected return} = r = \frac{DIV_1 + P_1 - P_0}{P_0}$$

Suppose Establishment Electronics stock is selling for $100 a share ($P_0 = 100$). Investors expect a $5 cash dividend over the next year ($DIV_1 = 5$). They also expect the stock to sell for $110 a year, hence ($P_1 = 110$). Then the expected return to the stockholders is 15%:

$$r = \frac{5 + 110 - 100}{100} = 0.15 \text{ or } 15\%$$

Today's Price? You can instead predict today's price if you are given investors' forecasts of year-end dividend and price and the expected return offered by other equally risky stocks:

$$\text{Price} = P_0 = \frac{DIV_1 + P_1}{1 + r}$$

For Establishment Electronics, $DIV_1 = 5$ and $P_1 = 110$. If r, the expected return for Establishment is 15%, then today's price should be $100:

$$P_0 = \frac{5 + 110}{1.15} = \$100$$

Many stocks will be safer than Establishment and many riskier. But among the thousands of traded stocks, there will be a group with essentially the same risks. Call this group Establishment's *risk class.* Then all stocks in this risk class have to be priced to offer the same expected rate of return.

Let's suppose that the other stocks in Establishment's risk class all offer the same 15% expected return. Then $100 per share has to be the right price for Establishment stock. In fact, it is the only possible price. What if Establishment's price were above $P_0 = \$100$? In this case, the expected return would be less than 15%. Investors would shift their capital to the other stocks and, in the process, would force down the price of Establishment stock. If P_0 were less than $100, the process would reverse. Investors would rush to buy, forcing the price up to $100. Therefore, at each point in time, *all stocks of equivalent risk are priced to offer the same expected return.* This is a condition for equilibrium in well-functioning capital markets. It is also common sense.

If all stocks of equivalent risk offer the same expected rate of return, that rate of return becomes the cost of equity for each one of the stocks in the equivalent-risk class. Establishment's cost of equity equals the opportunity cost of capital for its shareholders, who in our example can get an expected 15% return in other stocks with risks equivalent to Establishment's.

4.1 Self-Test

a. The stock of Thor Hammer Co. offers an expected one-year rate of return of 11%. How is that possible if the company pays no cash dividends?

b. Steamtool Inc. pays a generous cash dividend, but investors regard its stock as much riskier than Thor stock. What can you conclude about the expected rate of return on Steamtool stock?

Next Year's Price?   We have managed to explain today's stock price P_0 in terms of the dividend DIV_1 and the expected price next year P_1. Future stock prices are not easy things to forecast directly. But think about what determines next year's price. If our price formula holds now, it ought to hold then as well:

$$P_1 = \frac{DIV_2 + P_2}{1 + r}$$

That is, a year from now, investors will be looking out at dividends in year 2 and price at the end of year 2. Thus, we can forecast P_1 by forecasting DIV_2 and P_2, and we can express P_0 in terms of DIV_1, DIV_2, and P_2:

$$P_0 = \frac{1}{1+r}(DIV_1 + P_1) = \frac{1}{1+r}\left(DIV_1 + \frac{DIV_2 + P_2}{1+r}\right) = \frac{DIV_1}{1+r} + \frac{DIV_2 + P_2}{(1+r)^2}$$

Consider Establishment Electronics. A plausible explanation for why investors expect its stock price to rise by the end of the first year is that they expect higher dividends and still more capital gains in the second. For example, suppose that they are looking today for dividends of \$5.50 in year 2 and a subsequent price of \$121. That implies a price at the end of year 1 of

$$P_1 = \frac{5.50 + 121}{1.15} = \$110$$

Today's price can then be computed either from our original formula

$$P_0 = \frac{DIV_1 + P_1}{1 + r} = \frac{5.00 + 110}{1.15} = \$100$$

or from our expanded formula

$$P_0 = \frac{DIV_1}{1+r} + \frac{DIV_2 + P_2}{(1+r)^2} = \frac{5.00}{1.15} + \frac{5.50 + 121}{(1.15)^2} = \$100$$

We have succeeded in relating today's price to the forecasted dividends for two years (DIV_1 and DIV_2) plus the forecasted price at the end of the *second* year (P_2). You will not be surprised to learn that we could go on to replace P_2 by $(DIV_3 + P_3)/(1 + r)$ and relate today's price to the forecasted dividends for three years (DIV_1, DIV_2, and DIV_3) plus the forecasted price at the end of the third year (P_3). In fact, we can look as far out into the future as we like, removing Ps as we go. Let us call this final period H. This gives us a general stock price formula:

$$P_0 = \frac{DIV_1}{1+r} + \frac{DIV_2}{(1+r)^2} + \cdots + \frac{DIV_H + P_H}{(1+r)^H}$$

$$= \sum_{t=1}^{H} \frac{DIV_t}{(1+r)^t} + \frac{P_H}{(1+r)^H} \qquad\qquad \textbf{(4.1B)}$$

The expression $\sum_{t=1}^{H}$ sums up the discounted dividends from year 1 to year H.

	Expected Future Values		Present Values		
Horizon Period (H)	Dividend (DIV_t)	Price (P_t)	Cumulative Dividends	Future Price	Total
0	—	100	—	—	100
1	5.00	110	4.35	95.65	100
2	5.50	121	8.51	91.49	100
3	6.05	133.10	12.48	87.52	100
4	6.66	146.41	16.29	83.71	100
10	11.79	259.37	35.89	64.11	100
20	30.58	672.75	58.89	41.11	100
50	533.59	11,739.09	89.17	10.83	100
100	62,639.15	1,378,061.23	98.83	1.17	100

❭**TABLE 4.3**   Applying the stock valuation formula Eq. (4.1B) to Establishment Electronics.

Assumptions:
1. Dividends increase at 10% per year, compounded.
2. Discount rate (cost of equity) is 15%.

Table 4.3 continues the Establishment Electronics example for various time horizons, assuming that the dividends are expected to increase at a steady 10% compound rate. The expected price P_t increases at the same rate each year. Each line in the table represents an application of our general formula for a different value of H. Figure 4.1 is a graph of the table. Each column shows the present value of the dividends up to the time horizon and the present value of the price at the horizon. As the horizon recedes, the dividend stream accounts for an increasing proportion of present value, but the *total* present value of dividends plus terminal price always equals $100.

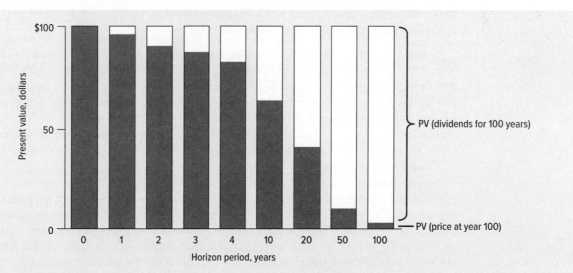

❭ **FIGURE 4.1**   As your horizon recedes, the present value of the future price (shaded area) declines, but the present value of the stream of dividends (unshaded area) increases. The total present value (future price and dividends) remains the same.

BEYOND THE PAGE

Try It! Figure
4.1: Value
and the
investor's
horizon

mhhe.com/brealey14e

How far out could we look? In principle, the horizon period H could be infinitely distant. Common stocks do not expire of old age. Barring such corporate hazards as bankruptcy or acquisition, they are immortal. As H approaches infinity, the present value of the terminal price ought to approach zero, as it does in the final column of Figure 4.1. We can, therefore, forget about the terminal price entirely and express today's price as the present value of a perpetual stream of cash dividends.

Two Versions of the Dividend Discount Model

We can write the dividend discount model in two equivalent ways:

$$P_0 = \sum_{t=1}^{\infty} \frac{\text{DIV}_t}{(1 + r)^t} \tag{4.1A}$$

and

$$P_0 = \frac{\text{DIV}_1}{1 + r} + \frac{\text{DIV}_2}{(1 + r)^2} + \ldots + \frac{\text{DIV}_H + P_H}{(1 + r)^H}$$

$$= \sum_{t=1}^{H} \frac{\text{DIV}_t}{(1 + r)^t} + \frac{P_H}{(1 + r)^H} \tag{4.1B}$$

Equation (4.1A) projects dividends to infinity. Equation (4.1B) projects dividends year-by-year to a horizon date H and then adds P_H to capture the value of dividends after the horizon date. The ending value P_H is often called a *terminal value* or *horizon value*. The two equations are consistent and in principle give exactly the same answer.

4.2 Self-Test

Kevin Devon plans to hold his position in Steamtool shares for two years. His Aunt Cleo has also purchased Steamtool shares and contributed them to a trust for her granddaughter. The trust will probably hold these shares for at least a decade. Could you apply the DCF valuation formula to both investments? Explain how briefly.

Notice that it is *not* correct to say that the value of a share is equal to the sum of the discounted stream of *earnings* per share. Earnings are generally larger than dividends because part of those earnings is not paid out but is retained and reinvested in new plant, equipment, and working capital. Discounting earnings would recognize the rewards of that investment (higher *future* earnings and dividends) but not the sacrifice (a lower dividend *today*). The correct formulation states that share value is equal to the discounted stream of dividends per share. Share price is connected to future earnings per share, but by a different formula, which we cover later in this chapter.

Although mature companies generally pay cash dividends, thousands of companies do not. For example, Amazon has never paid a dividend, yet it is a successful company with a market capitalization in December 2020 of $1.6 trillion. Why would a successful company decide *not* to pay cash dividends? There are at least two reasons. First, a growing company may maximize value by reinvesting all its earnings rather than paying out a dividend. The shareholders are better off with this policy, provided that the investments offer an expected rate of return higher than shareholders could get by investing on their own. In other words, shareholder value is maximized if the firm invests in projects that can earn more than the opportunity cost of capital. If such projects are plentiful, shareholders will be prepared to forgo immediate dividends. They will be happy to wait and receive larger dividends later.[7]

The dividend discount model is still logically correct for growth companies, but difficult to use when cash dividends are far in the future. In this case, most analysts switch to valuation by comparables, which we discussed earlier, or to earnings-based formulas, which we cover in Section 4-5.

Second, a company may pay out cash not as dividends but by repurchasing shares from stockholders. But repurchases do not invalidate the dividend discount model. The model projects dividends paid on a share that is *not* repurchased. Repurchases reduce the number of shares and may allow the company to pay higher dividends per remaining share. Repurchases can make dividends per share more difficult to forecast, but do not undermine the proposition that the price of one share of stock equals the PV of dividends that will be paid to the owners of that share.[8] We cover the choice between dividends and repurchases in Chapter 15.

The dividend discount model can be difficult to deploy if repurchases are irregular and unpredictable. In these cases, it can be better to start by calculating the present value of the total free cash flow available for dividends and repurchases. Discounting free cash flow gives the present value of the company as a whole. Dividing by the current number of shares outstanding gives present value per share. We cover this valuation approach in Section 4-6.

The next section considers simplified versions of the dividend discount model and shows how they are used to estimate the cost of equity. We will also deploy Eq. (4.1B) for that purpose and in some more detailed valuation exercises.

4-4   Dividend Discount Model Applications

In Chapter 2, we encountered some simplified versions of the basic present value formula. Let us see whether they offer any insights into stock values. Suppose, for example, that we forecast a constant growth rate for a company's dividends. This does not preclude year-to-year deviations from the forecast. It means only that *expected* dividends grow at a constant rate. Such an investment would be just another example of the growing perpetuity that we valued in Chapter 2. To find its present value, we must divide the first year's cash payment by the difference between the discount rate and the growth rate:

$$P_0 = \frac{\text{DIV}_1}{r - g} \tag{4.2}$$

This is the *constant-growth* DCF model. Remember that we can use the model only when g, the anticipated growth rate, is less than r, the discount rate. As g approaches r, the stock price becomes infinite. Obviously, r must be greater than g if growth really is perpetual.

Our growing perpetuity formula explains P_0 in terms of next year's expected dividend DIV_1, the projected growth trend g, and the expected rate of return on other securities of

---

[7]The deferred payout may come all at once if the company is taken over by another. The selling price per share is equivalent to a bumper dividend.

[8]Or we could use Eq. (4.1B). Suppose a share will be repurchased by the company at a future date $t = H$. Then the horizon value P_H equals the repurchase price. The formula would still include the PV of dividends per share up to date H, and the repurchase price would capture the PV of dividends per share from date $H + 1$ onward.

equivalent risk r. The formula can also be turned around to obtain an estimate of r from DIV_1, P_0, and g:

$$r = \frac{DIV_1}{P_0} + g \qquad (4.3)$$

The expected return equals the **dividend yield** (DIV_1/P_0) plus the expected rate of growth in dividends (g).

These two formulas are much easier to work with than the general statement that "price equals the present value of expected future dividends."[9] Here is a practical example.

Using the Constant-Growth DCF Model to Set Water, Gas, and Electricity Prices

In the United States, the prices charged by local water, electric, and gas utilities are regulated by state commissions. The regulators try to keep consumer prices down but are supposed to allow the utilities to earn a fair rate of return. But what is fair? It is usually interpreted as r, the cost of equity. In other words, the fair rate of return on equity for a public utility ought to be its cost of equity—that is, the rate offered by securities that have the same risk as the utility's stock.[10]

Small variations in estimates of this return can have large effects on the prices charged to customers and on the regulated firm's profits. So both the firms' managers and regulators work hard to estimate the cost of equity. They've noticed that most utilities are mature, stable companies that pay regular dividends. Such companies could be tailor-made for application of the constant-growth DCF formula.

EXAMPLE 4.1 • Cost of Equity for Water Companies

Suppose you wished to estimate the cost of equity for American States Water, a water distribution company. American's stock (ticker symbol AWR) was selling for $76.32 per share at mid-October 2020. Dividend payments for the next year were expected to be $1.34 a share. Thus, it was a simple matter to calculate the first half of the constant-growth DCF formula:

$$\text{Dividend yield} = \frac{DIV_1}{P_0} = \frac{1.34}{76.32} = 0.018 \ or \ 1.8\%$$

The hard part is estimating g, the expected rate of dividend growth. One option is to consult the views of security analysts who study the prospects for each company. Analysts are rarely prepared to stick their necks out by forecasting dividends far out in the future, but they often forecast growth rates of earnings and dividends over the next five years, and these estimates may provide an indication of the expected long-run growth path. In the case of American, analysts in 2020 were forecasting an annual growth of 5.6%.[11] This, together with the dividend yield, gives an estimate of the cost of equity:

$$r = \frac{DIV_1}{P_0} + g = 0.018 + 0.056 = 0.074 \ or \ 7.4\%$$

---

[9]These formulas were first developed in 1938 by Williams and were rediscovered by Gordon and Shapiro. See J. B. Williams, *The Theory of Investment Value* (Cambridge, MA: Harvard University Press, 1938); and M. J. Gordon and E. Shapiro, "Capital Equipment Analysis: The Required Rate of Profit," *Management Science* 3 (October 1956), pp. 102–110.

[10]This is the accepted interpretation of the U.S. Supreme Court's directive in 1944 that "The returns to the equity owner [of a regulated business] should be commensurate with returns on investments in other enterprises having corresponding risks." *Federal Power Commission v. Hope Natural Gas Company,* 302 U.S. 591 at 603.

[11]The growth rate was based on the average earnings growth forecasted by analysts as compiled by Bloomberg. In this calculation, we are therefore assuming that earnings and dividends are forecasted to grow forever at the same rate g. We show how to relax this assumption later in this chapter.

An alternative approach to estimating long-run growth starts with the **payout ratio**, the ratio of dividends to earnings per share (EPS). For American, this ratio has been about 60%. In other words, each year the company was plowing back into the business about 40% of earnings per share:

$$\text{Plowback ratio} = 1 - \text{payout ratio} = 1 - \frac{\text{DIV}}{\text{EPS}} = 1 - 0.60 = 0.40$$

Also, American's ratio of earnings to book equity was about 13%. This is its **return on equity**, or **ROE**:

$$\text{Return on equity} = \text{ROE} = \frac{\text{EPS}}{\text{book equity per share}} = 0.13$$

If American earns 13% on book equity and reinvests 40% of earnings, then book equity will increase by $0.40 \times 0.13 = 0.052$, or 5.2%. Earnings and dividends per share will also increase by 5.2%:

$$\text{Dividend growth rate} = g = \text{plowback ratio} \times \text{ROE} = 0.40 \times 0.13 = 0.052, \text{ or } 5.2\%$$

This formula ($g = \text{plowback rate} \times \text{ROE}$) is often called the *sustainable growth rate*. We can use that rate to get a second estimate of the cost of equity:

$$r = \frac{\text{DIV}_1}{P_0} + g = 0.018 + 0.052 = 0.07 \text{ or } 7\%$$

• • • • •

Although these estimates of American's cost of equity seem reasonable, there are obvious dangers in analyzing any single firm's stock with the constant-growth DCF formula. First, the underlying assumption of regular future growth is at best an approximation. Second, even if it is an acceptable approximation, errors can creep into the estimate of g.

Remember, American's cost of equity is not its personal property. In well-functioning capital markets, investors capitalize the dividends of all securities in American's risk class at exactly the same rate. But any estimate of r for a single common stock is "noisy" and subject to error. Good practice does not put too much weight on single-company estimates of the cost of equity. It collects samples of similar companies, estimates r for each, and takes an average. The average gives a more reliable benchmark for decision making.

The next-to-last column of Table 4.4 gives constant-growth DCF cost-of-equity estimates for American and five other water companies. These are all stable, mature companies for which the constant-growth DCF formula *ought* to work. But notice the variation in the cost-of-equity estimates. Some of the variation may reflect differences in the risk, but most is just temporary noise. The outlandishly high growth rates for California Water and SJW Group reflected recovery from the Covid-19 pandemic. These growth rates could not be maintained in perpetuity, as the constant-growth DCF formula assumes.

The last column of Table 4.4 shows results from a multistage DCF model. These results seem much more stable and reasonable than the constant-growth estimates. We will explain how the multistage models work in a moment.

Constant-Growth DCF Formulas—Summary   The constant-growth DCF formula is an extremely useful guide, but no more than that. Naive trust in the formula has led many financial analysts to silly conclusions.

	Stock Price	Dividend[a]	Dividend Yield	Long-Term Growth Rate[a]	DCF Cost of Equity[b]	Multistage DCF Cost of Equity[c]
American States Water	$76.32	$1.34	1.8%	5.6%	7.4%	6.1%
American Water Works	151.43	2.20	1.5%	7.3%	8.7%	6.0%
California Water	44.69	0.85	1.9%	17.7%	19.6%	8.7%
Middlesex Water	63.74	1.04	1.6%	3.3%	4.9%	5.7%
SJW Corp.	61.37	1.28	2.1%	14.8%	16.9%	8.3%
York Water Co.	43.43	0.75	1.7%	5.1%	6.8%	6.0%
				Average	10.7%	6.8%

❭**TABLE 4.4**   Cost-of-equity estimates for water companies in October 2020. The long-term growth rate is based on security analysts' forecasts. In the multistage DCF model, growth after five years is assumed to adjust gradually to the estimated long-term growth rate of gross domestic product (GDP).

[a]Dividend and analysts' long-term growth-rate forecasts in October 2020.
[b]Sum of dividend yield and long-term growth rate. This column contains some small rounding differences.
[c]Long-term growth rate of GDP was forecasted at 4.1% by Blue-Chip Economic Indicators.

Source: The Brattle Group, Inc.

We have stressed the difficulty of estimating r by analysis of one stock only. Try to use a large sample of equivalent-risk securities. Even that may not work, but at least it gives the analyst a fighting chance because the inevitable errors in estimating r for a single security tend to balance out across a broad sample.

Also, resist the temptation to apply the formula to firms having high current rates of growth. Such growth can rarely be sustained indefinitely, but the constant-growth DCF formula assumes it can. This erroneous assumption leads to an overestimate of r.

EXAMPLE 4.2 • The cost of equity for U.S. railroads

The U.S. Surface Transportation Board (STB) tracks the "revenue adequacy" of U.S. railroads by comparing the railroads' returns on book equity with estimates of their costs of equity. To estimate the cost of equity, the STB traditionally used the constant-growth formula. It measured g by stock analysts' forecasts of long-term earnings growth. The formula assumes that earnings and dividends grow at a constant rate forever, but the analysts' "long-term" forecasts looked out five years at most. As the railroads' profitability improved, the analysts became more and more optimistic. By 2009, their forecasts for growth averaged 12.5% per year. The average dividend yield was 2.6%, so the constant-growth model estimated the industry-average cost of capital at $2.6 + 12.5 = 15.1\%$.

So the STB said, in effect, "Wait a minute: Railroad earnings and dividends can't grow at 12.5% forever. The constant-growth formula no longer works for railroads. We've got to find a more accurate method." The STB now uses a multistage growth model.[12]

• • • • •

4.3 Self-Test

Note the double-digit cost of equity estimates for California Water and SJW Group in Table 4.4. Explain why these estimates *must* be worthless.

---

[12]The STB makes two estimates of the cost of equity. One is based on a three-stage DCF model, and the other uses the capital asset pricing model, which we describe in Chapter 8. The STB averages the two estimates.

DCF Models with Two or More Stages of Growth

We have seen how the constant-growth DCF model fails when forecast growth for the next few years cannot be sustained indefinitely. We need a DCF model with more degrees of freedom. In fact we already have one:

$$P_0 = \sum_{t=1}^{H} \frac{DIV_t}{(1+r)^t} + \frac{P_H}{(1+r)^H} \qquad (4.1B)$$

This model accommodates any pattern of year-by-year dividends from $t = 1$ to the horizon period $t = H$. Then we may be able to use the constant-growth DCF formula to capture PV of dividends from periods $H + 1$ onward.

Consider Growth-Tech Inc., a firm with $DIV_1 = \$0.50$ and $P_0 = \$50$. The firm has plowed back or, in other words, reinvested 80% of earnings and has had a return on equity (ROE) of 25%. This means that *in the past*

$$\text{Dividend growth rate} = \text{plowback ratio} \times \text{ROE} = 0.80 \times 0.25 = 0.20$$

The temptation is to assume that the future long-term growth rate g also equals 0.20. This would imply

$$r = \frac{0.50}{50.00} + g = 0.21$$

You would, of course, resist temptation. No firm can continue growing at 20% per year forever, except possibly under extreme inflationary conditions. Eventually, profitability will fall and the firm will respond by investing less.

In real life, the return on equity will probably decline gradually over time, but for simplicity, let's assume it suddenly drops to 16% at year 3 and the firm responds by plowing back only 50% of earnings. Then g drops to $0.50 \times 0.16 = 0.08$.

Table 4.5 shows what's going on. Growth-Tech starts year 1 with book equity of $10.00 per share. It earns $2.50, pays out 50 cents as dividends, and plows back $2. Thus, it starts year 2 with book equity of $10 + 2 = \$12$. After another year at the same ROE and payout, it starts year 3 with equity of $14.40. However, ROE drops to 0.16, and the firm earns only $2.30.

	Year			
	1	2	3	4
Book equity	10.00	12.00	14.40	15.55
Earnings per share (EPS)	2.50	3.00	2.30	2.48
Return on equity (ROE)	0.25	0.25	0.16	0.16
Payout ratio	0.20	0.20	0.50	0.50
Dividends per share (DIV)	0.50	0.60	1.15	1.24
Growth rate of dividends (%)	—	20	92	8

❯ TABLE 4.5   Forecast earnings and dividends for Growth-Tech. Note the changes in year 3: ROE and earnings drop, but payout ratio increases, causing a big jump in dividends. However, subsequent growth in earnings and dividends falls to 8% per year. Note that the increase in equity equals the earnings not paid out as dividends.

Dividends go up to $1.15 because the payout ratio increases, but the firm has only $1.15 to plow back. Therefore, subsequent growth in earnings and dividends drops to 8%.

Now we can use Eq. (4.1B):

$$P_0 = \sum_{t=1}^{H} \frac{DIV_t}{(1+r)^t} + \frac{P_H}{(1+r)^H}$$

BEYOND THE PAGE

Try it! Table
4.5: Valuing
Growth-Tech

mhhe.com/brealey14e

Investors in year 3 will view Growth-Tech as offering 8% per year dividend growth. So we can use the constant-growth formula to calculate P_3:

$$P_3 = \frac{DIV_4}{r - 0.08}$$

$$P_0 = \frac{DIV_1}{1+r} + \frac{DIV_2}{(1+r)^2} + \frac{DIV_3}{(1+r)^3} + \frac{1}{(1+r)^3} \times \frac{DIV_4}{r - 0.08}$$

$$= \frac{0.50}{1+r} + \frac{0.60}{(1+r)^2} + \frac{1.15}{(1+r)^3} + \frac{1}{(1+r)^3} \times \frac{1.24}{r - 0.08}$$

In this example, we know the current price $P_0 = \$50$. The cost of equity r is the unknown. We can calculate it, however, using trial and error to find the value of r that makes P_0 equal $50. It turns out that the r implicit in these more realistic forecasts is 0.099 or 9.9%, quite a difference from our "constant-growth" estimate of 0.21 or 21%.

Our present value calculations for Growth-Tech used a *two-stage* DCF valuation model. In the first stage (years 1 and 2), Growth-Tech is highly profitable (ROE = 25%), and it plows back 80% of earnings. Book equity, earnings, and dividends increase by 20% per year. In the second stage, starting in year 3, profitability and plowback decline, and earnings settle into long-term growth at 8%. Dividends jump up to $1.15 in year 3, and then also grow at 8%.

Cyclical Growth in Profitability   Growth rates can vary for many reasons. Sometimes, growth is high in the short run not because the firm is unusually profitable, but because it is recovering from an episode of *low* profitability. Table 4.6 displays projected earnings and dividends for Phoenix Corp., which is gradually regaining financial health after a near meltdown. The company's equity is growing at a moderate 4%. ROE in year 1 is only 4%, however, so Phoenix has to reinvest all its earnings, leaving no cash for dividends. As profitability increases in years 2 and 3, an increasing dividend can be paid. Finally, starting in year 4, Phoenix settles into steady-state growth, with equity, earnings, and dividends all increasing at 4% per year.

	Year			
	1	**2**	**3**	**4**
Book equity at start of year	10.00	10.40	10.82	11.25
Earnings per share (EPS)	0.40	0.73	1.08	1.12
Return on equity (ROE)	0.04	0.07	0.10	0.10
Dividends per share (DIV)	0	0.31	0.65	0.67
Growth rate of dividends (%)	—	—	110	4

❭**TABLE 4.6**   Forecast earnings and dividends per share for Phoenix Corp. The company can initiate and increase dividends as profitability (ROE) recovers. Note that the increase in book equity equals the earnings not paid out as dividends.

Assume the cost of equity is 10%. Then Phoenix shares should be worth $9.13 per share:

$$P_0 = \underbrace{\frac{0}{1.1} + \frac{0.31}{(1.1)^2} + \frac{0.65}{(1.1)^3}}_{\text{PV (first-stage dividends)}} + \underbrace{\frac{1}{(1.1)^3} \times \frac{0.67}{(0.10 - 0.04)}}_{\text{PV (second-stage dividends)}} = \$9.13$$

You could go on to valuation models with three or more stages. For example, the far right column of Table 4.4 presents multistage DCF estimates of the cost of equity for our local water companies. In this case, the long-term growth rates reported in the table do not continue forever. After five years, each company's growth rate gradually adjusts down to an estimated long-term 4.1% growth rate for U.S. gross domestic product (GDP). The reduced growth rate cuts the average cost of equity to 6.8%.

Practical Tips   When you use dividend discount models, you always end up forecasting growth. Earnings and dividends can grow for two reasons.

1. *Investment and expansion.* If the growth rate is moderate, you may be able to use the perpetual growth formula, Eq. (4.2). But if the rate of expansion and the near-term dividend-growth rate are high—greater than the growth rate of the economy overall—then the growth rate will inevitably decline. You must therefore use a DCF model with two or more growth rates, as in Table 4.5 and 4.6. Remember that the amount of cash available for payout to investors increases as the investment declines.

2. *Increasing profitability.* Earnings increase if ROE increases, even if the rate of investment is steady. But ROE will not increase forever. In this case, you need a two-stage DCF model, as in Table 4.5. The growth rate decreases when ROE reaches a stable, long-run level.

In practice, it's almost always worthwhile to lay out a simple spreadsheet, like Table 4.5 or 4.6, to ensure that your dividend projections are consistent with the company's earnings and required investments. Also, be careful about using DCF valuation formulas to test whether the market is correct in its assessment of a stock's value. If your estimate of the value is different from the market value, it is probably because you have used poor dividend forecasts. Remember what we said at the beginning of this chapter about simple ways of making money on the stock market: There aren't any.

4.4 Self-Test

What circumstances require a DCF valuation model with two or more growth stages?

4-5   Income Stocks and Growth Stocks

Investors distinguish *growth stocks* from *income stocks*. They buy growth stocks primarily for the expectation of capital gains, and they are more interested in the future growth of earnings rather than in next year's dividends. They buy income stocks primarily for their near-term earnings and dividends. Let us see whether this distinction makes sense.

Imagine first the case of a company that does not grow at all. It does not plow back any earnings and simply produces a constant stream of dividends. Its stock would resemble the perpetual bond described in Chapter 2. Remember that the return on a perpetuity is equal to the yearly cash flow divided by the present value. So the expected return on our share would be equal to the dividend divided by the share price (the dividend yield). Since all the earnings are paid out as dividends, the expected return is also equal to the earnings per share divided by the share price (the earnings–price ratio). For example, if the dividend is $10 a share and the stock price is $100, we have

Expected return with no growth = dividend yield = earnings-price ratio

$$= \frac{DIV_1}{P_0} \qquad = \frac{EPS_1}{P_0}$$

$$= \frac{10.00}{100} \qquad = 0.10$$

The price equals

$$P_0 = \frac{DIV_1}{r} = \frac{EPS_1}{r} = \frac{10.00}{0.10} = 100$$

The opportunity cost of capital for this company is the cost of equity, which in this example is 10%.

The expected return for *growing* firms can also equal the earnings–price ratio. The key is whether earnings are reinvested to provide a return equal to the cost of equity. For example, suppose our monotonous company suddenly hears of an opportunity to invest $10 a share next year. This would mean no dividend at $t = 1$. However, the company expects that in each subsequent year the project would earn $1 per share, and therefore the dividend could be increased to $11 a share starting in period $t = 2$.

Let's assume that this investment opportunity has about the same risk as the existing business. Then we can discount its cash flow at the 10% cost of equity to find its NPV at year 1:

$$\text{NPV per share at year 1} = -10 + \frac{1}{0.10} = 0$$

Thus, the investment opportunity will make no contribution to the company's value. Its prospective return is equal to the opportunity cost of capital.

What effect will the decision to undertake the project have on the company's share price? Clearly none. The reduction in value caused by the nil dividend in year 1 is exactly offset by the increase in value caused by the extra dividends in later years. Therefore, once again the cost of equity equals the earnings–price ratio:

$$r = \frac{EPS_1}{P_0} = \frac{10}{100} = 0.10$$

Table 4.7 repeats our example for different assumptions about the cash flow generated by the new project. Note that the earnings–price ratio, measured in terms of EPS_1, next year's expected earnings, equals the cost of equity (r) only when the new project's NPV = 0. This is an extremely important point—do not confuse earnings–price ratios with costs of equity.

In general, we can think of stock price as the value of average earnings under a no-growth policy, plus **PVGO,** the **net present value of growth opportunities:**

$$P_0 = \frac{EPS_1}{r} + PVGO \tag{4.4}$$

The earnings–price ratio, therefore, equals

$$\frac{EPS_1}{P_0} = r\left(1 - \frac{PVGO}{P_0}\right) \tag{4.5}$$

Project Rate of Return	Incremental Cash Flow (C)	Project NPV in Year 1[a]	Project's Impact on Share Price in Year 0[b]	Share Price in Year 0 (P_0)	$\dfrac{EPS_1}{P_0}$	r
0.05	$0.50	−$5.00	−$4.55	$ 95.45	0.105	0.10
0.10	1.00	0	0	100.00	0.10	0.10
0.15	1.50	+5.00	+4.55	104.55	0.096	0.10
0.20	2.00	+10.00	+9.09	109.09	0.092	0.10

❭ **TABLE 4.7**   Effect on stock price of investing an additional $10 in year 1 at different rates of return. Notice that the earnings–price ratio overestimates the 10% cost of equity when the project has negative NPV and underestimates it when the project has positive NPV.

[a]Project costs $10.00 (EPS$_1$). NPV $= -10 + C/r$, where $r = 0.10$.
[b]NPV is calculated at year 1. To find the impact on P_0, discount for one year at $r = 0.10$.

It will underestimate r if PVGO is positive and overestimate it if PVGO is negative. The latter case is less likely since firms are rarely forced to take projects with negative net present values.

PVGO is defined as the net value today (NPV) of all investments the company is expected to make in the future. PVGO is positive only if the company can be expected to invest at returns higher than the cost of equity.[13] If that is true, then the faster the growth rate the better. Growth stocks are stocks of companies where PVGO is positive and accounts for a substantial fraction of stock price. Investors in growth stocks are attracted by the capital gains they will get if expansion succeeds.

Income stocks are stocks of companies where PVGO accounts for a relatively small fraction of stock price. Such companies may still grow, but are not able to invest at returns substantially above the cost of equity. The price of income stocks depends mostly on future earnings and dividends from existing assets.

Some stocks are clearly growth stocks, some clearly income stocks. Of course there are also intermediate cases, stocks with attributes of both.

Calculating the Present Value of Growth Opportunities for Establishment Electronics

Now let us return to that well-known growth stock, Establishment Electronics, which is described in Table 4.4. Establishment's cost of equity is 15%. The company is expected to pay a dividend of $5 in the first year, and thereafter the dividend is predicted to increase indefinitely by 10% a year. We can use the constant-growth DCF formula to work out Establishment's price:

$$P_0 = \frac{DIV_1}{r - g} = \frac{5}{0.15 - 0.10} = \$100$$

Suppose that Establishment has earnings per share of $EPS_1 = \$8.33$. Its payout ratio is then

$$\text{Payout ratio} = \frac{DIV_1}{EPS_1} = \frac{5.00}{8.33} = 0.6$$

---

[13]Later in the book we will interpret PVGO more generally as the NPV today of the firm's *real options* to expand in the future. See Chapter 23.

In other words, the company is plowing back $1 - 0.6$, or 40% of earnings. Suppose also that Establishment's ratio of earnings to book equity is ROE $= 0.25$. This explains the growth rate of 10%:

$$\text{Growth rate} = g = \text{plowback ratio} \times \text{ROE} = 0.4 \times 0.25 = 0.10$$

The PV of Establishment's earnings per share if it had a no-growth policy would be:

$$\frac{\text{EPS}_1}{r} = \frac{8.33}{0.15} = \$55.56$$

But we know that the value of Fledgling stock is \$100. The difference of \$44.44 must be the amount that investors are paying for growth opportunities. Let's see if we can explain that figure.

Each year Fledgling plows back 40% of its earnings into new assets. In the first year, Establishment invests \$3.33 at a permanent 25% return on equity. Thus, the cash generated by this investment is $0.25 \times 3.33 = \$0.83$ per year starting at $t = 2$. The net present value of the investment as of $t = 1$ is

$$\text{NPV}_1 = -3.33 + \frac{0.83}{0.15} = \$2.22$$

Everything is the same in year 2 except that Establishment will invest \$3.67, 10% more than in year 1 (remember $g = 0.10$). Therefore, at $t = 2$, an investment is made with a net present value of

$$\text{NPV}_2 = -3.67 + \frac{0.83 \times 1.10}{0.15} = \$2.44$$

Thus, the payoff to the owners of Establishment Electronics stock can be represented as the sum of (1) a level stream of earnings, which could be paid out as cash dividends if the firm did not grow, and (2) a set of tickets, one for each future year, representing the opportunity to make investments having positive NPVs. We know that the first component of the value of the share is

$$\text{Present value of level stream of earnings} = \frac{\text{EPS}_1}{r} = \frac{8.33}{0.15} = \$55.56$$

The first ticket is worth \$2.22 in $t = 1$; the second is worth $\$2.22 \times 1.10 = \$2.44$ in $t = 2$; the third is worth $\$2.44 \times 1.10 = \$2.69$ in $t = 3$. These are the forecasted cash values of the tickets. We know how to value a stream of future cash values that grows at 10% per year: Use the constant-growth DCF formula, replacing the forecasted dividends with forecasted ticket values:

$$\text{Present value of growth opportunities} = \text{PVGO} = \frac{\text{NPV}_1}{r - g} = \frac{2.22}{0.15 - 0.10} = \$44.44$$

Now everything checks:

$$\begin{aligned}\text{Share price} &= \text{present value of level stream of earnings}\\ &\quad + \text{present value of growth opportunities}\\ &= \frac{\text{EPS}_1}{r} + \text{PVGO}\\ &= \$55.56 + \$44.44\\ &= \$100\end{aligned}$$

Why is Establishment Electronics a growth stock? Not just because it is expanding at 10% per year. It is a growth stock because PVGO, the net present value of its future investments, accounts for 44% of the stock's price. That price incorporates investors' expectations about the earning power of the firm's current and *future* assets.

We admit that calculating PVGO is more difficult in practice than for Establishment Electronics. Corporations are complex, and future investment and profitability are difficult to forecast. PVGO is nevertheless an important *practical* concept—the key to understanding the potential value of future investment and growth. Also, we can infer PVGO even when we cannot calculate it step by step as we did for Establishment.

EXAMPLE 4.4 • PVGO for Cummins and Microsoft

Table 4-1 reports statistics for Cummins stock at the close of trading on one day in February 2020. The stock closed at $154.46 per share. The forward P/E was 13.39. EPS forecasted for 2020 were about $11.55.

Suppose that Cummins grew no further and that future EPS were expected to stay constant at $11.55. Cummins could afford to pay a constant dividend of $11.55 per share. If the cost of equity is, say, 8%, the market price would have been 11.55/0.08 = $144.38, about $10 per share less than the actual price. Thus Cummins is an income stock because PVGO is a small fraction of its stock price.

Contrast Cummins with Microsoft. Its price in early 2020 was at $139, with forward EPS of $5.24 and a forward P/E of 26.53. Suppose it stopped growing and paid a constant dividend of $5.24 instead of its actual dividend of $2.04. If we use the same 8% cost of equity as for Cummins, its zero-growth stock price would be 5.24/0.08 = $65.50, less than half its actual stock price. Microsoft does pay a regular cash dividend, but it is nevertheless a growth stock because a large fraction of its market value comes from PVGO.

• • • • •

4.5 Self-Test

Wilderness Matchmakers is growing rapidly, but intense competition restricts the rate of return on new investment to its cost of equity capital. How does the company's P/E ratio depend on its future rate of growth?

BEYOND THE PAGE

Valuing Alphabet

mhhe.com/brealey14e

4-6 Valuation Based on Free Cash Flow

So far we have focused on price per share of common stock. But it's often simpler or more convenient to value shareholders' equity, the aggregate of all outstanding shares. The DCF principle is the same, except that free cash flow takes the place of dividends per share:

PV(equity) = market capitalization = PV(expected future free cash flow)

Free cash flow (FCF) equals the after-tax cash flow generated by the company's operations after subtracting investment required for growth. Free cash flow is the amount of cash available for payout to all shareholders.

Here are three examples where this valuation approach would make sense.

1. The owners of a private business ask what the company would be worth if publicly traded. The owners are less interested in price per share than in the potential total market value of their business.

2. A company has an opportunity to sell one of its manufacturing divisions. The division is wholly owned by the company and has no outside shareholders. The company wants to know what the division is worth overall.

3. A security analyst is trying to value a public company using DCF. The company is simultaneously paying dividends and paying out cash by repurchasing shares. The repurchases fluctuate year to year, which makes the number of remaining shares, and therefore earnings and dividends *per share,* hard to predict. So the analyst decides to forecast and value free cash flow. He knows that free cash flow is the *total* amount of cash that can be paid out to investors and doesn't want to worry about how payout is split between dividends and repurchases. (More on dividends vs. repurchases in Chapter 15.)

We now work through a numerical example.

Valuing the Concatenator Business

Concatenator Inc. is a privately owned business. A potential acquirer is trying to figure out how much to offer for it.

Table 4.8 gives a forecast of FCF for Concatenator. As we will see, FCF can be negative for rapidly growing businesses.

Table 4.8 is similar to Table 4.5, which forecast earnings and dividends per share for Growth-Tech, based on assumptions about Growth-Tech's equity per share, return on equity, and the growth of its business. For Concatenator, we also have assumptions about assets, profitability—in this case, after-tax operating earnings relative to assets[14]—and growth. Growth starts out at a rapid 12% per year, then falls in two steps to a moderate 6% rate for the long run. The growth rate determines the net additional investment required to expand assets, and the profitability rate determines the earnings thrown off by the business.

	1	2	3	4	5	6	7	8	9	10
Asset value, start of year	10.00	11.20	12.54	14.05	15.31	16.69	18.19	19.29	20.44	21.67
Earnings	1.20	1.34	1.51	1.69	1.84	2.00	2.18	2.31	2.45	2.60
Investment	1.20	1.34	1.51	1.26	1.38	1.50	1.09	1.16	1.23	1.30
Free cash flow (FCF)	0.00	0.00	0.00	0.42	0.46	0.50	1.09	1.16	1.23	1.30
Asset value, end of year	11.20	12.54	14.05	15.31	16.69	18.19	19.29	20.44	21.67	22.97
Return on assets (ROA)	0.12	0.12	0.12	0.12	0.12	0.12	0.12	0.12	0.12	0.12
Asset growth rate	0.12	0.12	0.12	0.09	0.09	0.09	0.06	0.06	0.06	0.06
Earnings growth rate, from previous year		0.12	0.12	0.12	0.09	0.09	0.09	0.06	0.06	0.06

⟩TABLE 4.8   Forecasts of free cash flow in $ millions for Concatenator Inc. Free cash flow is zero for periods 1 to 3 because investment absorbs all of net income. Free cash flow turns positive when growth slows down after period 3. Inputs required for the table's calculations are in bold type.

Notes:
1. Starting asset value is $10 million. Assets grow at 12% to start, then at 9%, and finally at 6% in perpetuity. Profitability is assumed constant at 12%.
2. Free cash flow equals earnings minus net investment. Net investment equals total capital outlays minus depreciation. We assume that investment for replacement of existing assets is covered by depreciation and that net investment is devoted to growth. Earnings are net of depreciation and taxes.
3. Concatenator has no debt outstanding. Therefore profitability is measured as return on assets (ROA).

---

[14]Concatenator has no debt, so the return on assets and equity are the same (ROA = ROE). We use ROA in the table because it forecasts growth in assets.

Free cash flow, the fourth line in Table 4.8, is equal to earnings less *new* investment. (We assume for simplicity that investment to maintain and replace existing assets is covered by depreciation.[15]) Free cash flow is zero in years 1 to 3, because Concatenator is investing over $4 million during this period.

Are the early zeros for free cash flow a bad sign? No: Free cash flow is zero because the business is growing rapidly, not because it is unprofitable. Rapid growth is good news, not bad, because the business is earning 12%, 2 percentage points over the 10% cost of capital. If the business could grow at 20%, Concatenator's private shareholders would be happier still, although growth at 20% would mean still higher investment, negative free cash flow and require additional financing.

Valuation Format

Concatenator's value equals the discounted value of its free cash flows out to a *valuation horizon (H),* plus the forecasted value of the business at the horizon, also discounted back to present value.

$$PV = \underbrace{\frac{FCF_1}{1 + r} + \frac{FCF_2}{(1 + r)^2} + \ldots + \frac{FCF_H}{(1 + r)^H}}_{PV(\text{free cash flow})} + \underbrace{\frac{PV_H}{(1 + r)^H}}_{PV(\text{horizon value})} \qquad (4.6)$$

This equation is exactly the same as Eq. (4.1B), except that free cash flow takes the place of expected dividends. PV_H stands in for free cash flow in periods $H + 1$, $H + 2$, and so on.

Valuation horizons are often chosen arbitrarily. Sometimes the boss tells everybody to use 10 years because that's a round number. We will try year 6, because growth of the Concatenator business seems to settle down to a long-run trend after year 7.

Estimating Horizon Value

There are two common approaches to estimating horizon value. One uses valuation by comparables, which we discussed earlier, based on P/E, market-to-book, or other ratios. The other uses DCF, which we also discussed earlier. We will start with valuation by comparables, using P/E and P/B ratios as in Section 4-2.

Horizon Value Based on P/E Ratios   Suppose you can observe stock prices for good comparables—that is, for mature manufacturing companies whose scale, risk, and growth prospects today roughly match those projected for Concatenator in year 6.[16] Suppose further that these companies tend to sell at price–earnings ratios of about 11. Then you could reasonably guess that the price–earnings ratio of a mature, public concatenator company would likewise be 11. That implies:

$$PV \text{ (horizon value)} = \frac{1}{(1.1)^6} (11 \times 2.18) = 13.5$$

---

[15]We could have built the table using after-tax operating cash flow instead of earnings. Cash flow equals earnings plus depreciation. (Depreciation is added back because it is a non-cash expense.) In this case investment would include all outlays for maintenance and replacement as well as growth. But we have focused on earnings throughout this chapter, and we keep that focus here. We cover the components of cash flow in detail in Chapter 6, including the impact of accrual accounting.

[16]We have not asked how the concatenator business would be financed if it were a stand-alone business. Table 4.8 assumes assuming 100% equity and zero debt. Therefore the comparables should also have little or no debt. If they do have debt, EBIT or EBITDA ratios would be better than P/E ratios. See the examples in Section 18-2.

The present value of free cash flow up to the horizon is $0.9 million. Therefore:

$$PV \text{ (business)} = 0.9 + 13.5 = \$14.4 \text{ million}$$

Horizon Value Based on Price–Book Ratios   Suppose also that the market–book ratios of the sample of mature manufacturing companies tend to cluster around 1.5. If Concatenator's market–book ratio is 1.5 in year 6,

$$PV \text{ (horizon value)} = \frac{1}{(1.1)^6}(1.5 \times 16.69) = 14.1$$

$$PV \text{ (business)} = 0.9 + 14.1 = \$15.0 \text{ million}$$

It's easy to poke holes in these last two calculations. Book value, for example, is often a poor measure of the true value of a company's assets. It can fall far behind actual asset values when there is rapid inflation, and it often entirely misses important intangible assets, such as patents for Concatenator design. Earnings may also be biased by inflation or arbitrary accounting choices. Finally, you never know when you have found a sample of truly similar companies to use as comparables.

But remember, the purpose of discounted cash flow is to estimate market value—to estimate what investors would pay for a stock or business. When you can *observe* what they actually pay for similar companies, that's valuable evidence. Try to figure out a way to use it. As illustrated above, one way to use it is by valuation by comparables. Simple valuation methods, artfully employed, sometimes beat a complex discounted cash flow calculation hands down.

Horizon Value Based on DCF   Now let us try the constant-growth DCF formula. This requires free cash flow for year 7, which we have at $1.09 million from Table 4.8; a long-run growth rate, which appears to be 6%; and a discount rate, which some high-priced consultant has told us is 10%. Therefore,

$$\text{Horizon value (PV looking forward from period 6)} = PV_H = \frac{1.09}{0.10 - 0.06} = \$27.3 \text{ million}$$

$$\text{Horizon value (discounted back to PV in period 0)} = \frac{27.3}{(1.1)^6} = \$15.4 \text{ million}$$

The PV of the near-term free cash flows is $0.9 million. Thus, the present value of the concatenator division is

$$\begin{aligned} PV \text{ (business)} &= PV \text{ (free cash flow)} + PV \text{ (horizon value)} \\ &= 0.9 + 15.4 \\ &= \$16.3 \text{ million} \end{aligned}$$

Now, are we done? Well, the mechanics of this calculation are perfect. But doesn't it make you just a little nervous to find that 94% of the value of the business rests on the horizon value? Moreover, a little checking shows that horizon value can change dramatically in response to small changes in the assumed long-term growth rate.

Suppose the growth rate is 7% instead of 6%. That means that asset value has to grow by an extra 1% per year, requiring extra investment of $0.18 million in period 7, which reduces FCF_7 to $0.91 million. Horizon value increases to $PV_H = \$30.3$ million in year 6 and to

$17.1 million discounted to year zero. PV increases from $16.3 million to $0.9 + 17.1 = $18.0 million.

Practical Tips: Two Warnings   *Warning 1:* When you use the constant-growth DCF formula to calculate horizon value, always remember that faster growth requires increased investment, which reduces free cash flow. Slower growth requires less investment, which increases free cash flow.

For Concatenator, 7% instead of 6% growth increases PV by $18.0 – 16.3 = $1.7 million. Why? We did not ignore warning 1: We accounted for the increased investment required for faster growth. Therefore the additional investment in periods 7 and beyond must have generated additional positive NPV. In other words, we must have assumed expanded growth opportunities and added more PVGO to the value of the business.

Notice in Table 4.8 that the return on assets (ROA) is forecasted at 12% forever, 2 percentage points higher than the assumed discount rate of 10%. Thus, every dollar invested in period 7 and beyond generates positive NPV and adds to horizon value and the PV of the business.

But is it realistic to assume that any business can keep on growing and making positive-NPV investments forever? Sooner or later you and your competitors will be on an equal footing. You may still be earning a superior return on past investments, but you will find that introductions of new products or attempts to expand profits from existing products trigger vigorous resistance from competitors who are just as smart and efficient as you are. When that time comes, the NPV of subsequent investments will average out to zero. After all, PVGO is positive only when investments can be expected to earn more than the cost of capital.

Warning 2: Always check to see whether horizon value includes post-horizon PVGO. You can check on warning 2 by changing the assumed long-term growth rate. If a higher growth rate increases horizon value—after you have taken care to respect warning 1—then you are assuming positive post-horizon PVGO. Is it realistic to assume that the firm can earn more than the cost of capital in perpetuity? If not, adjust your forecasts accordingly.

There is an easy way to calculate horizon value if post-horizon PVGO is zero. Recall that PV depends on next period's earnings plus PVGO:

$$PV_t = \frac{earnings_{t+1}}{r} + PVGO$$

If PVGO = 0 at the horizon period H, then,

$$PV_H = \frac{earnings_{H+1}}{r}$$

In other words, when the competition catches up and the firm can only earn its cost of equity on new investment, the price–earnings ratio will equal $1/r$, because PVGO disappears.

This latest formula for PV_H is still DCF. We are valuing the business *as if* assets and earnings will not grow after the horizon date.[17] (The business probably will grow, but the growth can be ignored, because it will add no net value if PVGO goes to zero.) With no growth, there is no net investment,[18] and all of earnings ends up as free cash flow.

---

[17] But what does "no growth" mean? Suppose that the concatenator business maintains its assets and earnings in real (inflation-adjusted) terms. Then nominal earnings will grow at the inflation rate. This takes us back to the constant-growth formula: Earnings in period $H + 1$ should be valued by dividing by $r - g$, where g in this case equals the inflation rate.

We have simplified the concatenator example. In real-life valuations, with big bucks involved, be careful to track growth from inflation as well as growth from investment. For guidance see M. Bradley and G. Jarrell, "Expected Inflation and the ConstantGrowth Valuation Model," *Journal of Applied Corporate Finance* 20 (Spring 2008), pp. 66–78.

[18] The business must invest enough to maintain its assets, even in the no-growth case. We have assumed that a base level of investment equal to depreciation is sufficient to maintain assets. Note that earnings are calculated after depreciation—that is, after paying for the base investment. Depreciation and this investment are not broken out in Table 4.8.

Therefore, we can calculate the horizon value at period 6 as the present value of a level stream of earnings starting in period 7 and continuing indefinitely. The resulting value for Concatenator is:

$$\text{PV (horizon value)} = \frac{1}{(1+r)^6} \left(\frac{\text{earnings in period 7}}{r} \right)$$

$$= \frac{1}{(1.1)^6} \left(\frac{2.18}{0.10} \right)$$

$$= \$12.3 \text{ million}$$

$$\text{PV (business)} = 0.9 + 12.3 = \$13.2 \text{ million}$$

A Value Range for Concatenator We now have four estimates of PV based on four different methods of estimating horizon value. There is no best method, although we like the last method, which forces managers to remember that sooner or later competition catches up.

Our calculated values for the concatenator business range from $13.2 to $16.3 million, a difference of about $3 million. The width of the range may be disquieting, but it is not unusual. Discounted cash flow formulas only estimate market value, and the estimates change as forecasts and assumptions change. Managers cannot know market value for sure until an actual transaction takes place.

4.6 Self-Test

How do you check whether horizon value in a DCF model includes post-horizon PVGO? Why is this check important in practice?

● ● ● ● ●

KEY TAKEAWAYS

In this chapter, we have used present value (PV) formulas to explain the market prices of common stocks.

- **Dividend-discount (DCF) model** The value of a share of stock equals the PV of the future cash dividends paid to the current and future owners of that share. Common stocks have no fixed maturity and may survive forever. The formula is:

$$P_0 = \sum_{t=1}^{\infty} \frac{\text{DIV}_t}{(1+r)^t} \qquad (4.1\text{A})$$

- **DCF model with horizon value** It is often convenient to calculate the PV of dividends out to some horizon date H and then add the PV of P_H, the forecasted price on that date. In this case, the PV formula is:

$$P_0 = \sum_{t=1}^{H} \frac{\text{DIV}_t}{(1+r)^t} + \frac{P_H}{(1+r)^H} \qquad (4.1\text{B})$$

The forecasted *horizon* or *terminal value* P_H stands in for the PV of dividends per share after date H.

- **Dividends and capital gains** These DCF formulas do not assume that investors purchase shares solely for dividends. The one-period PV formula values next period's dividend plus next period's price, which incorporates capital gains or losses:

$$P_0 = \frac{\text{DIV}_1 + P_1}{1+r}$$

The discount rate r (the *cost of equity*) is an opportunity cost of capital. It equals the expected rate of return on all stocks subject to the same degree of risk as the stock being valued.

The one-period PV formula is a condition of market equilibrium. If it did not hold, the stock would be over- or underpriced and investors would rush to sell or buy it. The flood of sell or buy orders would enforce the formula.

We showed how application of the one-period formula to repeated future dates leads to the long-term DCF formulas, Eq. (4.1A) and Eq. (4.1B).

- **Perpetual growth** If dividends are expected to grow forever at a constant rate g,

$$P_0 = \frac{\text{DIV}_1}{r - g} \tag{4.2}$$

where r *must* be greater than g.

- **Estimating the cost of equity** The perpetual-growth formula can be twisted around to estimate the cost of equity:

$$r = \frac{\text{DIV}_1}{P_0} + g \tag{4.3}$$

The constant-growth formula incorporates a very strict assumption: a constant dividend growth rate in perpetuity. This assumption may be acceptable for mature, low-risk firms, but for many firms, near-term growth is unsustainably high. Thus, cost-of-equity estimates are often based on two-stage DCF models. Near-term dividends are forecasted and valued, and the perpetual-growth DCF model is used to forecast horizon value.

- **Earnings and growth opportunities** Dividend-discount models are most useful for mature firms that pay regular cash dividends. They are less useful for young, rapidly growing firms that pay out no dividends. The share price of such firms is better expressed as:

$$P_0 = \frac{\text{EPS}_1}{r} + \text{PVGO} \tag{4.4}$$

The ratio EPS_1/r is the present value of earnings per share that the firm would generate if it did not grow. With zero growth, all of EPS could be paid out as dividends. PVGO is the the NPV of the *future* investments that the firm will make in order to grow. A growth firm is one with large PVGO relative to the PV of its EPS with no growth. Most growth firms are expanding rapidly, but rapid growth does not necessarily create high PVGO. Positive PVGO requires that the return on investment exceeds the cost of equity.

- **Valuation of a business based on free cash flow** Free cash flow (FCF) is the total amount of cash available for payout to investors after subtracting all investments necessary for growth. The PV formula is:

$$\text{PV}_0 = \sum_{t=1}^{H} \frac{\text{FCF}_t}{(1 + r)^t} + \frac{\text{PV}_H}{(1 + r)^H} \tag{4.1B}$$

where PV_H represents the PV of FCF for all future periods after date H. PV_H may be estimated using the perpetual-growth DCF formula or by assuming a future price-earnings or price-book ratio.

PVs based on free cash flow are useful when the firm pays out cash by repurchases or by a combination of repurchases and dividends. They are also useful for valuing privately owned businesses or operating divisions of larger companies.

• • • • •

PROBLEM SETS   **McGraw Hill connect**   Select problems are available in McGraw-Hill's *Connect*.

1. **Stock markets (S4.1)** True or false?

   a. The sale of shares by a large investor usually takes place in the primary market.

   b. Electronic Communications Network refers to the automated ticker tape on the New York Stock Exchange.

2. **Stock quotes (S4.1)** Go to **finance.yahoo.com** or another Internet source and get trading quotes for IBM.

   a. What is the latest IBM stock price and market cap?

   b. What is IBM's dividend payment and dividend yield?

   c. What is IBM's trailing P/E ratio?

   d. Calculate IBM's forward P/E ratio using the EPS forecasted by analysts for the next year.

   e. What is IBM's price–book (P/B) ratio?

3. **Valuation by comparables (S4.2)** Look up P/E and P/B ratios for Entergy (ticker symbol ETR), using Yahoo! Finance or another Internet source. Calculate the same ratios for the following potential comparables: American Electric Power (AEP), Eversource Energy (ES), and Southern Company (SO). Set out the ratios in the same format as Table 4.2. Are the ratios for these electric companies tightly grouped or scattered? If you didn't know Entergy's stock price, would the comparables give a good estimate?

4. **Dividend discount model (S4.3)** True or false?

   a. All stocks in an equivalent-risk class are priced to offer the same expected rate of return.

   b. The value of a share equals the PV of future dividends per share.

   c. The value of a share equals the PV of earnings per share assuming the firm does not grow, plus the NPV of future growth opportunities.

5. **Dividend discount model (S4.3)** Respond briefly to the following statement: "You say stock price equals the present value of future dividends? That's crazy! All the investors I know are looking for capital gains."

6. **Dividend discount model (S4.3)** Company X is expected to pay an end-of-year dividend of $5 a share. After the dividend, its stock is expected to sell at $110. If the cost of equity is 8%, what is the current stock price?

7. **Dividend discount model (S4.3)** Company Y does not plow back any earnings and is expected to produce a level dividend stream of $5 a share. If the current stock price is $40, what is the cost of equity?

8. **Constant-growth DCF model (S4.4)** Company Z's earnings and dividends per share are expected to grow indefinitely by 5% a year. If next year's dividend is $10 and the cost of equity is 8%, what is the current stock price?

9. **Constant-growth DCF model (S4.4)** Consider three investors:

   a. Mr. Single invests for one year.

   b. Ms. Double invests for two years.

   c. Mrs. Triple invests for three years.

   Assume each invests in company Z (see Problem 8). Show that each expects to earn a rate of return of 8% per year.

10. **Constant-growth DCF model (S4.4)** Pharmecology just paid an annual dividend of $1.35 per share. It's a mature company, but future EPS and dividends are expected to grow with inflation, which is forecasted at 2.75% per year.

    a. What is Pharmecology's current stock price? The nominal cost of capital is 9.5%.

    b. Redo part (a) using forecasted real dividends and a real discount rate.

11. **Constant-growth DCF model (S4.4)**

    Here are forecasts for next year for two stocks:

	Stock A	Stock B
Return on equity	15%	10%
Earnings per share	$2.00	$1.50
Dividends per share	$1.00	$1.00

    a. What are the dividend payout ratios for each firm?

    b. What are the expected sustainable dividend growth rates for each stock?

    c. If investors require a return of 15% on each stock, what are their values?

12. **Constant-growth DCF model (S4.4)** Look up General Mills (GIS), Kellogg (K), and Campbell Soup (CPB).

    a. What are the current P/E and P/B ratios for these food companies? What are the dividend and dividend yield for each company?

    b. What are the growth rates of EPS and dividends for each company over the last five years? What EPS growth rates are forecasted by analysts? Do these growth rates appear to be on a steady trend that could be projected for the long run?

    c. Would you be confident in applying the constant-growth DCF model to measure these companies' costs of equity? Why or why not?

13. **Two-stage DCF model (S4.4)** Company Z-prime is like Z in Problem 8 in all respects save one: Its growth will stop after year 4. In year 5 and afterward, it will pay out all earnings as dividends. What is Z-prime's stock price? Assume next year's EPS is $15.

14. **Two-stage DCF model (S4.4)** Consider the following three stocks:

    a. Stock A is expected to provide a dividend of $10 a share forever.

    b. Stock B is expected to pay a dividend of $5 next year. Thereafter, dividend growth is expected to be 4% a year forever.

    c. Stock C is expected to pay a dividend of $5 next year. Thereafter, dividend growth is expected to be 20% a year for five years (years 2 through 6, as C recovers from a severe recession) and zero thereafter.

    If the cost of equity for each stock is 10%, which stock is the most valuable? What if the capitalization rate is 7%?

15. **Two-stage DCF model (S4.4)** Company Q's current return on equity (ROE) is 14%. It pays out one half of earnings as cash dividends (payout ratio = 0.5). Current book value per share is $50. Book value per share will grow as Q reinvests earnings. Assume that the ROE and payout ratio stay constant for the next four years. After that, competition forces ROE down to 11.5% and the payout ratio increases to 0.8. The cost of equity is 11.5%.

    a. What are Q's EPS and dividends next year? How will EPS and dividends grow in years 2, 3, 4, 5, and subsequent years?

    b. What is Q's stock worth per share? How does that value depend on the payout ratio and growth rate after year 4?

16. **Two-stage DCF model (S4.4)** Compost Science Inc. (CSI) is in the business of converting Boston's sewage sludge into fertilizer. The business is not in itself very profitable. However, to induce CSI to remain in business, the Metropolitan District Commission (MDC) has agreed to pay whatever amount is necessary to yield CSI a 10% book return on equity. At the end of the year, CSI is expected to pay a $4 dividend. It has been reinvesting 40% of earnings and growing at 4% a year.

    a. Suppose CSI continues on this growth trend. What is the expected long-run rate of return from purchasing the stock at $100? What part of the $100 price is attributable to the present value of growth opportunities?

    b. Now the MDC announces a plan for CSI to treat Cambridge sewage. CSI's plant will, therefore, be expanded gradually over five years. This means that CSI will have to reinvest 80% of its earnings for five years. Starting in year 6, however, it will again be able to pay out 60% of earnings. What will be CSI's stock price once this announcement is made and its consequences for CSI are known?

17. **Cost of equity (S4.5)** Under what conditions does r, a stock's market capitalization rate, equal its earnings–price ratio EPS_1/P_0?

18. **Cost of equity (S4.5)** Each of the following formulas for determining shareholders' required rate of return can be right or wrong depending on the circumstances:

    a. $r = DIV_1/ P_0 + g$

    b. $r = EPS_1/ P_0$

    For each formula, construct a simple numerical example showing that the formula can give wrong answers and explain why the error occurs. Then construct another simple numerical example for which the formula gives the right answer.

19. **Growth opportunities (S4.5)** If company Z (see Problem 8) were to distribute all its earnings, it could maintain a level dividend stream of $15 a share. How much is the market actually paying per share for growth opportunities?

20. **Growth opportunities (S4.5)** Look up Intel (INTC), Oracle (ORCL), and HP (HPQ) on finance.yahoo.com or another Internet source. Rank the companies' forward P/E ratios from highest to lowest. What are the possible reasons for the different ratios? Which of these companies appears to have the most valuable growth opportunities?

21. **Growth opportunities (S4.5)** Alpha Corp's earnings and dividends are growing at 15% per year. Beta Corp's earnings and dividends are growing at 8% per year. The companies' assets, earnings, and dividends per share are now (at date 0) exactly the same. Yet PVGO accounts for a greater fraction of Beta Corp's stock price. How is this possible? (*Hint:* There is more than one possible explanation.)

22. **Growth opportunities (S4.5)** Look again at the financial forecasts for Growth-Tech given in Table 4.5. This time assume you know that the opportunity cost of capital is $r = 0.12$ (discard the 0.099 figure calculated in the text). Assume you do not know Growth-Tech's stock value. Otherwise follow the assumptions given in the text.

    a. Calculate the value of Growth-Tech stock.

    b. What part of that value reflects the discounted value of P_3, the price forecasted for year 3?

    c. What part of P_3 reflects the present value of growth opportunities (PVGO) after year 3?

    d. Suppose that competition will catch up with Growth-Tech by year 4 so that it can earn only its cost of capital on any investments made in year 4 or subsequently. What is Growth-Tech stock worth now under this assumption? (Make additional assumptions if necessary.)

23. **Free cash flow (S4.6)** What do financial managers mean by "free cash flow"? How is free cash flow calculated? Briefly explain.

24. **Horizon value (S4.6)** What is meant by the "horizon value" of a business? How can it be estimated?

25. **Horizon value (S4.6)** Suppose the horizon date is set at a time when the firm will run out of positive-NPV investment opportunities. How would you calculate the horizon value? (*Hint:* What is the *P/E* ratio when PVGO = 0?)

26. **Valuing a business (S4.6)** Permian Partners (PP) produces from aging oil fields in west Texas. Production is currently 1.8 million barrels per year, but is declining at 7% per year for the foreseeable future. Costs of production, transportation, and administration add up to $25 per barrel. The current oil price is $65 per barrel. PP has 7 million shares outstanding. The cost of equity is 9%. All of PP's net income is distributed as dividends. For simplicity, assume that the company will stay in business forever and that costs per barrel are constant at $25. Also, ignore taxes.

    a. What is the value of one PP share? Assume that oil prices are expected to fall to $60 per barrel next year, and to $55 and $50 per barrel in the two years following. After that decrease, assume a long-term trend of oil-price increases at 5% per year.

    b. What is PP's *E/P* ratio, and why is it not equal to the 9% cost of capital?

27. **Valuing a business (S4.6)** Construct a new version of Table 4.8, assuming that competition drives down profitability (on existing assets as well as new investment) to 11.5% in year 6, 11% in year 7, 10.5% in year 8, and 8% in year 9 and all later years. What is Concatenator's PV?

28. **Valuing a business (S4.6)** Mexican Motors' market cap is 200 billion pesos. Next year's free cash flow is 8.5 billion pesos. Security analysts are forecasting that free cash flow will grow by 7.5% per year for the next five years.

    a. Assume that the 7.5% growth rate is expected to continue forever. What rate of return are investors expecting?

    b. Mexican Motors has generally earned about 12% on book equity (ROE = 12%) and reinvested 50% of earnings. The remaining 50% of earnings has gone to free cash flow. Suppose the company maintains the same ROE and investment rate for the long run. What is the implication for the growth rate of earnings and free cash flow? For the cost of equity? Should you revise your answer to part (a) of this question?

29. **Valuing a business (S4.6)** Phoenix Corp. faltered during the Covid pandemic but is recovering. Free cash flow has grown rapidly. Forecasts made in 2021 are as follows:

($ millions)	2022	2023	2024	2025	2026
Net income	1.0	2.0	3.2	3.7	4.0
Investment	1.0	1.0	1.2	1.4	1.4
Free cash flow	0	1.0	2.0	2.3	2.6

Phoenix's recovery will be complete by 2026, and there will be no further growth in net income or free cash flow.

a. Calculate the PV of free cash flow, assuming a cost of equity of 9%.

b. Assume that Phoenix has 12 million shares outstanding. What is the price per share?

c. Confirm that the expected rate of return on Phoenix stock is exactly 9% in each of the years from 2022 to 2026.

CHALLENGE

30. **Constant-growth DCF formula (S4.4)** The constant-growth DCF formula:

$$P_0 = \frac{DIV_1}{r - g}$$

is sometimes written as:

$$P_0 = \frac{ROE(1 - b)BVPS}{r - bROE}$$

where BVPS is book equity value per share, b is the plowback ratio, and ROE is the ratio of earnings per share to BVPS. Use this equation to show how the price-to-book ratio varies as ROE changes. What is price-to-book when $ROE = r$?

31. **DCF valuation (S4.4)** Portfolio managers are frequently paid a proportion of the funds under management. Suppose you manage a $100 million equity portfolio offering a dividend yield (DIV_1/P_0) of 5%. Dividends and portfolio value are expected to grow at a constant rate. Your annual fee for managing this portfolio is 0.5% of portfolio value and is calculated at the end of each year. Assuming that you will continue to manage the portfolio from now to eternity, what is the PV of the management contract? How would the contract value change if you invested in stocks with a 4% yield?

32. **Valuing a business (S4.6)** Construct a new version of Table 4.8, assuming that Concatenator grows at 20%, 12%, and 6%, instead of 12%, 9%, and 6%. You will get negative early free cash flows.

    a. Recalculate the PV of free cash flow. What does your revised PV say about the Concatenator's PVGO?

    b. Suppose Concatenator has no other resources. Thus, it will have to issue stock to cover the negative free cash flows. Does the need to issue shares change your valuation? Explain. (*Hint:* Suppose first that Concatenator's existing stockholders buy all of the newly issued shares. What is the value of the company to these stockholders? Now suppose instead that all the shares are issued to new stockholders, so that existing stockholders don't have to contribute any cash. Does the value of the company to the existing stockholders change, assuming that the new shares are sold at a fair price?)

* * * * *

SOLUTIONS TO SELF-TEST QUESTIONS

4.1   a. Investors expect Thor's stock price to increase by 11%. The 11% capital gain makes up for a dividend of zero.

b. Steamtool's higher risk drives down its stock price, increasing the expected rate of return. Steamtool's higher return comes as a combination of cash dividends and capital gains.

4.2   Yes. Mr. Devon could use Eq. (4.1B) with the horizon date set at $H = 2$. Aunt Cleo's trust could use the same equation with $H = 10$.

4.3   The constant-growth DCF model requires that the expected growth rates be constant in perpetuity. The growth rate used in the model must therefore be sustainable—not much greater than the long-run growth rate for the economy as a whole. The U.S. economy's forecasted long-term growth rate is about 4%, including inflation. Growth rates of 14.8% or 17.7% cannot be perpetual.

4.4   When growth rates forecasted for the near or medium term are materially different from long-run growth rates.

4.5   It doesn't. Future investment for growth contributes no net present value when expected rates of return just equal the cost of capital. In this case, the rate of growth does not affect price *P* or the *P/E* ratio.

4.6   Increase the assumed post-horizon growth rate, taking care to increase investment when the growth rate is higher. If higher growth generates higher present value, then your model must be generating positive PVGO post-horizon.

The major stock exchanges have wonderful websites. Start with the NYSE (**www.nyse.com**) and Nasdaq (**www.nasdaq.com**). Make sure you know how trading takes place on these exchanges.

● ● ● ● ●

FINANCE ON THE WEB

MINI-CASE ● ● ● ●

Reeby Sports

Ten years ago, in 2013, George Reeby founded a small mail-order company selling high-quality sports equipment. Since those early days, Reeby Sports has grown steadily and been consistently profitable. The company has issued 2 million shares, all of which are owned by George Reeby and his five children.

For some months, George has been wondering whether the time has come to take the company public. This would allow him to cash in on part of his investment and would make it easier for the firm to raise capital should it wish to expand in the future.

But how much are the shares worth? George's first instinct is to look at the most recent year-end balance sheet, which shows that the book value of the equity was $26.34 million, or $13.17 per share. A share price of $13.17 would put the stock on a P/E ratio of 6.6. That is quite a bit lower than the 13.1 P/E ratio of Reeby's larger rival, Molly Sports.

George suspects that book value is not necessarily a good guide to a share's market value. He thinks of his daughter Jenny, who works in an investment bank. She would undoubtedly know what the shares are worth. He decides to phone her after she finishes work that evening at 9 o'clock or before she starts the next day at 6.00 a.m.

Before phoning, George jots down some basic data on the company's profitability. After recovering from its early losses, the company has earned a return that is higher than its estimated 10% cost of equity. George is fairly confident that the company could continue to grow fairly steadily for the next six to eight years. In fact, he feels that the company's growth has been somewhat held back in the last few years by the demands from two of the children for the company to make large dividend payments. Perhaps, if the company went public, it could hold back on dividends and plow more money back into the business.

There are some clouds on the horizon. Competition is increasing, and only that morning, Molly Sports announced plans to form an on-line division. George is worried that beyond the next six or so years, it might become difficult to find worthwhile investment opportunities.

George realizes that Jenny will need to know much more about the prospects for the business before she can put a final figure on the value of Reeby Sports, but he hopes that the information is sufficient for her to give a preliminary indication of the value of the shares.

	2014	2015	2016	2017	2018	2019	2020	2021	2022	2023E
Earnings per share ($)	−2.10	−0.70	0.23	0.81	1.10	1.30	1.52	1.64	2.00	2.03
Dividend ($)	0.00	0.00	0.00	0.20	0.20	0.30	0.30	0.60	0.60	0.80
Book value per share ($)	9.80	7.70	7.00	7.61	8.51	9.51	10.73	11.77	13.17	14.40
ROE (%)	−27.10	−7.1	3.0	11.6	14.5	15.3	16.0	15.3	17.0	15.4

QUESTIONS

1. Help Jenny to forecast dividend payments for Reeby Sports and to estimate the value of the stock. Of course, you will have to make some simplifying assumptions. For example, you could assume a ROE of 15% at least for the first six years, and a dividend payout ratio of 30%. Those assumptions will drive growth in assets, earnings, and dividends. What happens if ROE falls to 10% after six years?

2. How much of your estimate of the value of Reeby's stock comes from the present value of growth opportunities?

Net Present Value and Other Investment Criteria

A company's shareholders prefer to be rich rather than poor. Therefore, they want the firm to invest in projects that are worth more than they cost. The difference between a project's value and its cost is its *net present value (NPV)*. Companies can best help their shareholders by investing in projects with a positive NPV and rejecting those with a negative NPV.

Companies sometimes calculate other measures to judge a project's worth. Therefore, it is important to understand why these measures may *not* lead to correct investment decisions, or why they may be misused.

Section 5-1 A review of the net present value rule
We start the chapter with a review of the net present value rule, and we set out five key criteria for a sensible investment benchmark. When we assess other measures that companies use when making investment decisions, we will consider how they stack up against these criteria.

Section 5-2 The payback and accounting rate of return rules
We start with two rules of thumb that companies sometimes use. These measures are the project's payback period and its accounting rate of return. Both are easy to calculate and

to communicate, but we show that they are not adequate for making significant investment decisions.

Section 5-3 The internal rate of return rule
Companies often calculate the expected rate of return from investing in the project. They then compare the return on the project with the return that shareholders could earn on equivalent-risk investments in the financial markets. The company accepts those projects that provide a higher return than shareholders could earn for themselves. If used correctly, this rule should always identify projects that increase firm value. However, we shall see that it sets several traps for the unwary.

Section 5-4 Choosing capital investments when resources are limited
We conclude the chapter by showing how to cope with situations when there is a shortage of capital or other resources. There are two things to consider. One is computational. In simple cases, we just choose those projects that give the highest NPV per dollar invested, but more elaborate techniques are sometimes needed to sort through the possible alternatives. The other problem is to decide whether capital rationing really exists and whether it invalidates the net present value rule. Guess what? NPV, properly interpreted, wins out in the end.

5-1 A Review of the Net Present Value Rule

Vegetron's chief financial officer (CFO) is wondering how to analyze a proposed $1 million investment in a new venture, code-named project X. She asks what you think.

Your response should be as follows: "First, forecast the cash flows generated by project X over its economic life. Second, determine the appropriate opportunity cost of capital (r). This should reflect both the time value of money and the risk involved in project X. Third, use this opportunity cost of capital to discount the project's future cash flows. The sum of the discounted cash flows is called present value (PV). Fourth, calculate *net* present value (NPV) by subtracting the $1 million investment from PV. If we call the opportunity cost of capital r and the cash flows C_0, C_1, and so on, then

$$\text{NPV} = C_0 + \sum_{t=1}^{t=T} \frac{C_t}{(1+r)^t} \tag{5.1}$$

where $C_0 = -\$1$ million. We should invest in project X if its NPV is greater than zero."

However, Vegetron's CFO is not convinced. She asks why NPV is so important.

You: Let us look at what is best for Vegetron shareholders. They want you to make their Vegetron shares as valuable as possible.

Right now Vegetron's total market value (price per share times the number of shares outstanding) is $10 million. That includes $1 million cash, which we can invest in project X. The value of Vegetron's other assets and opportunities must therefore be $9 million. We have to decide whether it is better to keep the $1 million cash and reject project X or to spend the cash and accept the project. Let's call the value of the new project PV. Then the choice is as follows:

	Market Value ($ millions)	
Asset	Reject Project X	Accept Project X
Cash	1	0
Other assets	9	9
Project X	0	PV
	10	9 + PV

Clearly project X is worthwhile if its present value (PV) is greater than $1 million, that is, if net present value is positive.

CFO: How do I know that the PV of project X will actually show up in Vegetron's market value?

You: Suppose we set up a new, independent firm X, whose only asset is project X. What would be the market value of firm X?

Investors would forecast the dividends that firm X would pay and discount those dividends by the expected rate of return of securities having similar risks. We know that stock prices are equal to the present value of forecast dividends.

Since project X is the only asset, the dividend payments we'd expect firm X to pay are exactly the cash flows we have forecast for project X. Moreover, the rate that investors would use to discount firm X's dividends is exactly the rate we should use to discount project X's cash flows.

I agree that firm X is hypothetical. But if project X is accepted, investors holding Vegetron stock will really hold a portfolio of project X and the firm's other assets. We know the other assets are worth $9 million considered as a separate venture. Since asset values add up, we can easily figure out the portfolio value once we calculate the value of project X as a separate venture.

By calculating the present value of project X, we are replicating the process by which the common stock of firm X would be valued in the financial markets.

CFO: The one thing I don't understand is where the discount rate comes from.

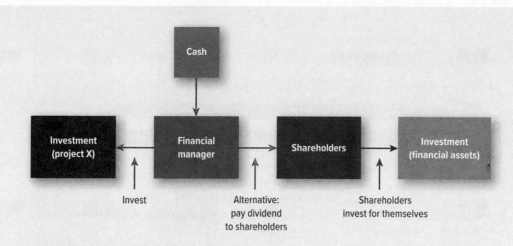

FIGURE 5.1   The firm can either keep and reinvest cash or return it to investors. (Arrows represent possible cash flows or transfers.) If cash is reinvested, the opportunity cost is the expected rate of return that shareholders could have obtained by investing in financial assets.

You: I agree that the discount rate is difficult to measure precisely. But it's easy to see what we are *trying* to measure. The discount rate is the opportunity cost of investing in the project rather than in the financial markets. In other words, instead of accepting a project, the firm can always return the cash to the shareholders and let them invest it in financial assets.

You can see the trade-off (Figure 5.1). The opportunity cost of taking the project is the return shareholders could have earned had they invested the money on their own. When we discount the project's cash flows by the expected rate of return on financial assets, we are measuring how much investors would be prepared to pay for your project.

CFO: But which financial assets? The fact that investors expect only 12% on low-risk IBM stock does not mean that we should purchase a risky start-up if it offers 13%.

You: The opportunity-cost concept makes sense only if assets of equivalent risk are compared. In general, you should identify financial assets that have the same risk as your project, estimate the expected rate of return on these assets, and use this rate as the opportunity cost.

Net Present Value's Competitors

When you advised the CFO to calculate the project's NPV, you were in good company. Most corporations calculate net present value when deciding on investment projects. However, as you can see from Figure 5.2, NPV is not the only investment criterion that companies use, and firms often look at more than one measure of a project's attractiveness.

About three-quarters of firms calculate the project's internal rate of return (or IRR); that is roughly the same proportion that use NPV. The IRR rule is a close relative of NPV and, when used properly, it will give the same answer. You therefore need to understand the IRR rule and how to take care when using it.

A large part of this chapter is concerned with explaining the IRR rule, but first we look at two other measures of a project's attractiveness—the project's payback and its accounting rate of return. As we'll explain, both measures have obvious defects. Few companies rely on them

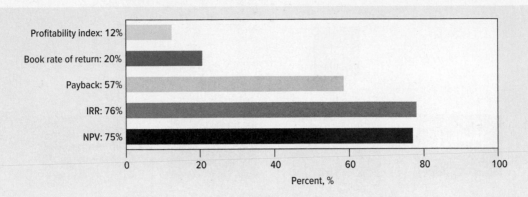

FIGURE 5.2   Survey evidence on the percentage of CFOs who always, or almost always, use a particular technique for evaluating investment projects.

Source: J. R. Graham and C. R. Harvey, "The Theory and Practice of Corporate Finance: Evidence from the Field," *Journal of Financial Economics* 60 (2001), pp. 187–243.

to make their investment decisions, but they do use them as supplementary measures that may help to distinguish the marginal project from the no-brainer.

Later in the chapter we also come across one further investment measure, the profitability index. Figure 5.2 shows that it is not often used, but you will find that there are circumstances in which this measure has some special advantages.

Five Points to Remember about NPV

As you look at these different criteria, it is worth keeping in mind five key advantages of the net present value rule.

- The NPV rule offers a clear benchmark with which to compare a project's NPV. You should accept all projects with a positive NPV and reject all projects with a negative NPV.

- NPV depends on *all* the forecast cash flows from the project. Any rule that ignores some of those cash flows will lead to poor decisions.

- The NPV rule recognizes that *a dollar today is worth more than a dollar tomorrow* because the dollar today can be invested to earn interest immediately.

- Net present value depends solely on the *forecast cash flows* from the project and the *opportunity cost of capital.* It is not affected by the profitability of the company's existing business, or the profitability of other independent projects. Nor is it affected by the company's choice of accounting method,

- If you have two dollars in your purse and one dollar in your pocket, you own in total three dollars. That is obvious. Similarly, because present values are all measured in today's dollars, you can add them up. Therefore, if you have two projects A and B, the net present value of the combined investment is

$$NPV(A + B) = NPV(A) + NPV(B)$$

This adding-up property has important implications. Suppose project B has a negative NPV. If you tack it onto project A, the joint project (A + B) will have a lower NPV than A on its own. Therefore, you will correctly reject a poor project (B) even if it is packaged with a good one (A). As we shall see, the alternative measures do not have this property. If you are not careful, you may be tricked into deciding that a package of a good and a bad project is better than the good project on its own.

| 5-2 | The Payback and Accounting Rate of Return Rules |

The Payback Rule

We suspect that you have often heard conversations that go something like this: "We are spending around $300 a year, at the laundromat. If we bought a washing machine for $800, it would pay for itself within three years. That's well worth it." You have just encountered the payback rule.

A project's **payback period** is found by counting the number of years it takes before the cumulative cash flow equals the initial investment.[1] For the washing machine the payback period was just under three years. The **payback rule** states that a project should be accepted if its payback period is less than some specified cutoff period. For example, if the cutoff period is four years, the washing machine makes the grade; if the cutoff is two years, it doesn't.

We have no quarrel with those who use payback as a descriptive statistic. It is perfectly fine to say that the washing machine has a three-year payback. But payback should never be a *rule*.

EXAMPLE 5.1 • The Payback Rule

Consider the following three projects:

	Cash Flows ($)					
Project	C_0	C_1	C_2	C_3	Payback Period (years)	NPV at 10%
A	−2,000	500	500	5,000	3	+2,624
B	−2,000	500	1,800	0	2	−58
C	−2,000	1,800	500	0	2	+50

Project A involves an initial investment of $2,000 ($C_0 = -2,000$) followed by cash inflows during the next three years. Suppose the opportunity cost of capital is 10%. Then project A has an NPV of +$2,624:

$$\text{NPV(A)} = -2,000 + \frac{500}{1.10} + \frac{500}{1.10^2} + \frac{5,000}{1.10^3} = +\$2,624$$

Project B also requires an initial investment of $2,000 but produces a cash inflow of $500 in year 1 and $1,800 in year 2. At a 10% opportunity cost of capital project B has an NPV of −$58:

$$\text{NPV(B)} = -2,000 + \frac{500}{1.10} + \frac{1,800}{1.10^2} = -\$58$$

The third project, C, involves the same initial outlay as the other two projects but its first-period cash flow is larger. It has an NPV of +$50:

$$\text{NPV(C)} = -2,000 + \frac{1,800}{1.10} + \frac{500}{1.10^2} = +\$50$$

The net present value rule tells us to accept projects A and C but to reject project B.

---

[1]Occasionally firms discount the cash flows before calculating the payback period. The discounted payback measure asks, How many years does the project have to last in order for it to make sense in terms of net present value? The discounted payback rule will never accept a negative-NPV project. On the other hand, it takes no account of cash flows after the cutoff date, so that good long-term projects risk rejection.

Now look at how rapidly each project pays back its initial investment. With project A, you take three years to recover the $2,000 investment; with projects B and C, you take only two years. If the firm used the *payback rule* with a cutoff period of two years, it would accept only projects B and C; if it used the payback rule with a cutoff period of three or more years, it would accept all three projects. Therefore, regardless of the choice of cutoff period, the payback rule gives different answers from the net present value rule.

● ● ● ● ●

You can see why payback can give misleading answers:

1. *The payback rule ignores all cash flows after the cutoff date.* If the cutoff date is two years, the payback rule rejects project A in our example regardless of the size of the cash inflow in year 3. So, payback will tend to favor many poor short-lived projects and reject many good long-lived ones.

2. *The payback rule gives equal weight to all cash flows before the cutoff date.* The payback rule says that projects B and C are equally attractive, but because C's cash inflows occur earlier, C has the higher net present value at any positive discount rate.

3. *The choice of a cutoff period is arbitrary.* The decision whether to accept or reject a project depends on the cutoff period. But there is no clear criterion for choosing this cutoff period.

5.1 Self-Test

True or false?
  a. The payback rule takes account only of cash flows after the cutoff date.
  b. The payback rule ignores the time pattern of cash flows occurring before the cutoff date.

We have had little good to say about payback. Yet 57% of companies report that they take payback into account when making investment decisions. Why is this? Senior managers don't truly believe that all cash flows after the payback period are irrelevant. We suggest three explanations, although none is fully satisfactory:

1. Payback may be used because it is the simplest way to *communicate* an idea of project profitability. Investment decisions require discussion and negotiation among people from all parts of the firm, and it is important to have a measure that everyone can understand.

2. Managers may be pursuing their own objectives, rather than shareholder value, as discussed in Chapter 1. For example, middle managers in a large corporation may prefer projects with short paybacks because they believe that quicker projects mean quicker promotion.

3. Owners of small public firms with limited access to capital may worry about their future ability to raise capital. These worries may lead them to favor rapid payback projects even though a longer-term venture may have a higher NPV. However, as we will discuss in Section 5-4, the NPV rule can be easily modified to take into account capital constraints.

Accounting Rate of Return

Net present value depends only on the project's cash flows and the opportunity cost of capital. But when companies report to shareholders, they do not simply show the cash flows. They also report accounting profits and assets—that is, the profits and assets that are carried on the firm's books.

Shareholders often calculate profitability measures, such as the company's profits divided by its assets. Knowing this, some financial managers may also evaluate a project by calculating a profitability measure such as the project's expected average profits divided by the project's average assets. This measure is known as the *accounting rate of return* or *book rate of return,* and is calculated as follows:

$$\text{Accounting rate of return} = \frac{\text{average profits}}{\text{average assets}} \qquad (5.2)$$

EXAMPLE 5.2 • Calculating the Accounting Rate of Return

Spiral Corp is considering production of a new universal twister. It involves an initial investment of $80,000 which will be depreciated straight-line over four years. The following table shows the forecast profits on the project and the depreciated asset value.

The average yearly net profit is $7,000, and the average asset value is $50,000. So the project is forecast to provide an accounting return of 7,000/50,000 = 0.14, or 14%. Since this is higher than the return that Spiral earns on its existing assets, it decides to go ahead with the investment.

Forecasts ($000s)				
Year	1	2	3	4
Revenues	271.4	285.7	342.9	312.9
Cost	264.3	277.1	328.6	302.9
Pretax profit	7.1	8.6	14.3	10.0
Tax @ 30%	2.1	2.6	4.3	3.0
Net profit	5	6	10	7

5.2 Self-Test

Suppose that Spiral in Example 5.1 reduced its forecast of net profits in year 1 by $5,000 and increased its forecast in year 4 by $5,000. Would the accounting return rise, fall, or stay the same? Do you think the project would be more, less, or equally attractive?

Shareholders must rely on accounting data to evaluate the company (as we'll explore in more detail in Chapter 29), and it is therefore natural that managers worry about how shareholders will react to the company's financial statements. However, accounting measures of profitability provide an unreliable criterion for the firm's investment decisions for at least two reasons:

1. *Accounting return ignores the time value of money.* The accounting rate of return depends on accounting profits, which are different from cash flow. For example, if a company sells goods this year which are paid for next year, it generates profits but no cash, but we know that cash is preferable as it can be invested. Moreover, accounting return depends on the average profits over the lifetime of the project, and doesn't take into account when these profits are received.

2. *No clear benchmark.* There is no natural benchmark for judging whether a project's accounting return is attractive. Managers sometimes compare the profitability of a

proposed project with the profitability of the company as a whole. But the success of the firm's past investments should not affect whether to go ahead with the current proposal. What matters are the cash flows that the proposed project is likely to generate and the opportunity cost of the capital that is tied up in the project.

Think of a firm that has been exceptionally lucky and successful. Say its average accounting return is 24%, double shareholders' 12% opportunity cost of capital. Should it demand that all *new* investments offer 24% or better? Clearly not: That would mean passing up many positive-NPV opportunities with rates of return between 12 and 24%.

5-3   The Internal Rate of Return Rule

Whereas payback and accounting rate of return are unreliable measures of a project's attractiveness, the internal rate of return (IRR) has a much more respectable ancestry and is recommended in many finance texts. If we dwell more on its deficiencies, it is not because they are more numerous, but because they are less obvious.

In Chapter 2, we noted that the net present value rule could also be expressed as a rate of return rule: "Accept investment opportunities offering rates of return in excess of their opportunity costs of capital." That statement, properly interpreted, is absolutely correct. However, interpretation is not always easy for long-lived investment projects.

There is no ambiguity in defining the true rate of return of an investment that generates a single payoff after one period:

$$\text{Rate of return} = \frac{\text{payoff}}{\text{investment}} - 1$$

Alternatively, we could write down the NPV of the investment and find the discount rate that makes NPV = 0.

$$\text{NPV} = C_0 + \frac{C_1}{1 + \text{discount rate}} = 0$$

implies

$$\text{Discount rate} = \frac{C_1}{-C_0} - 1$$

Of course, C_1 is the payoff and $-C_0$ is the required investment, so our two equations say exactly the same thing. *The discount rate that makes NPV = 0 is also the rate of return.*

How do we calculate return when the project produces cash flows in several periods? Answer: We use the same definition that we just developed for one-period projects—*the project rate of return is the discount rate that gives a zero NPV.* This discount rate is known as the **internal rate of return (IRR)**. The internal rate of return is used frequently in finance. It can be a handy measure, which we shall from time to time use. The problem, as we shall see, is that it can easily be misused. You should, therefore, know how to calculate it and how to use it properly.

Calculating the IRR

The internal rate of return is defined as the rate of discount that makes NPV = 0. So to find the IRR for an investment project lasting T years, we must solve for IRR in the following expression:

$$\text{NPV} = C_0 + \sum_{t=1}^{t=T} \frac{C_t}{(1 + \text{IRR})^t} = 0 \qquad (5.3)$$

Actual calculation of IRR usually involves trial and error. For example, consider a project that produces the following flows:

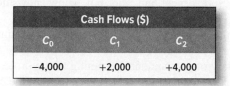

Cash Flows ($)		
C_0	C_1	C_2
−4,000	+2,000	+4,000

The internal rate of return is IRR in the equation

$$\text{NPV} = -4{,}000 + \frac{2{,}000}{1 + \text{IRR}} + \frac{4{,}000}{(1 + \text{IRR})^2} = 0$$

Let us arbitrarily try a zero discount rate. In this case, NPV is not zero but +$2,000:

$$\text{NPV} = -4{,}000 + \frac{2{,}000}{1.0} + \frac{4{,}000}{(1.0)^2} = +\$2{,}000$$

The NPV is positive; therefore, the IRR must be greater than zero. The next step might be to try a discount rate of 50%. In this case, net present value is −$889:

$$\text{NPV} = -4{,}000 + \frac{2{,}000}{1.50} + \frac{4{,}000}{(1.50)^2} = -\$889$$

The NPV is negative; therefore, the IRR must be less than 50%. In Figure 5.3, we have plotted the net present values implied by a range of discount rates. From this, we can see that a discount rate of 28.08% gives the desired net present value of zero. Therefore, IRR is 28.08%.[2] (We carry the IRR calculation to two decimal places to avoid confusion from rounding. In practice, no one would worry about the 0.08%.)

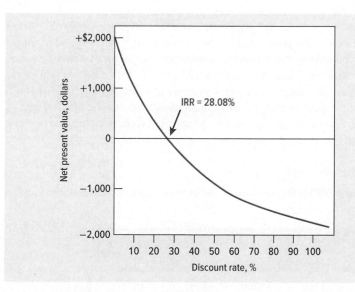

▶ FIGURE 5.3

This project costs $4,000 and then produces cash inflows of $2,000 in year 1 and $4,000 in year 2. Its internal rate of return (IRR) is 28.08%, the rate of discount at which NPV is zero.

---

[2]The IRR is a first cousin to the yield to maturity on a bond. Recall from Chapter 3 that the yield to maturity is the discount rate that makes the present value of future interest and principal payments equal to the bond's price. If you buy the bond at that market price and hold it to maturity, the yield to maturity is the IRR on your bond investment.

You can always find the IRR by plotting an NPV profile, as in Figure 5.3, but it is quicker and more accurate to let a spreadsheet or specially programmed calculator do the trial and error for you. The Useful Spreadsheet Functions box below shows how to use the Excel function to calculate an IRR.

Some people confuse the internal rate of return and the opportunity cost of capital because both appear as discount rates in the NPV formula. The internal rate of return is a *profitability measure* that depends solely on the amount and timing of the project cash flows. The opportunity cost of capital is a *benchmark* against which we compare the profitability measure. The opportunity cost of capital is established in the financial markets. It is the expected rate of return offered by other assets with the same risk as the project being evaluated.

BEYOND THE PAGE

Calculating
the IRR

mhhe.com/brealey14e

5.3 Self-Test

Suppose a project costs $200 and is forecast to produce cash flows of $110 in year 1 and $121 in year 2. Draw a figure similar to Figure 5.3. What is the project's IRR?

BEYOND THE PAGE

Interpreting
the IRR

mhhe.com/brealey14e

The IRR Rule

The internal rate of return rule states that the firm should accept an investment project if the opportunity cost of capital is less than the internal rate of return. You can see the reasoning behind this idea if you look again at Figure 5.3. If the opportunity cost of capital is less than the 28.08% IRR, then the project has a *positive* NPV when discounted at the opportunity cost of capital. If it is equal to the IRR, the project has a *zero* NPV. And if it is greater than the IRR, the project has a *negative* NPV because shareholders could earn a higher return by investing their funds in the capital market. Therefore, when we compare the opportunity cost of capital with the IRR on our project, we are effectively asking whether our project has a positive NPV. This is true not only for our example. The rule will give the same answer as the net present value rule *whenever the NPV of a project is a continuously declining function of the discount rate.*

The 28.08% internal rate of return on our project tells us how high the opportunity cost of capital would need to be before the project should be rejected. That can be good to know, for, although we might not be able to put a precise number on the project's cost of capital, we might nevertheless be confident that it was less than 28.08%. In this case, we can safely go ahead with the project. You can understand, therefore, why a manager may find it helpful to know the project's IRR. Our worries concern those managers who use the internal rate of return as a criterion *in preference to net present value.* Although, properly stated, the two criteria are formally equivalent, the internal rate of return rule contains several pitfalls.

Pitfall 1—Lending or Borrowing?

Not all cash-flow streams have NPVs that decline as the discount rate increases. Consider the following projects A and B:

	Cash Flows ($)			
Project	C_0	C_1	IRR	NPV at 10%
A	−1,000	+1,500	+50%	+364
B	+1,000	−1,500	+50%	−364

Each project has an IRR of 50%. (In other words, −1,000 + 1,500/1.50 = 0 and +1,000 − 1,500/1.50 = 0.)

Does this mean that they are equally attractive? Clearly not, for in the case of A, where we are initially paying out $1,000, we are effectively *lending* money at 50%; in the case of B, where we are initially receiving $1,000, we are *borrowing* money at 50%. When we lend money, we want a *high* rate of return; when we borrow money, we want a *low* rate of return. The sale of insurance is an activity that resembles borrowing: the insurance company receives insurance premiums up-front and pays out claims later.

If you plot a graph like Figure 5.3 for project B, you will find that NPV increases as the discount rate increases. Obviously the internal rate of return rule, as we stated it above, won't work in this case; we have to look for an IRR that is *less* than the opportunity cost of capital.

That sounds straightforward, but sometimes the sign of the cash flows may change several times. Consider Project C below:

Project	Cash Flows ($)				IRR (%)	NPV at 10%
	C_0	C_1	C_2	C_3		
C	+1,000	−3,600	+4,320	−1,728	20	+1,298

In this case, it is not clear whether we are lending or borrowing and, thus, whether the IRR of 20% should be higher or lower than the opportunity cost of capital for the project to be approved. However, the project's positive NPV makes it clear that the project is worth more than it costs.

Pitfall 2—Multiple Rates of Return

A second problem is that projects may have two or more rates of return as the following example illustrates:

EXAMPLE 5.3 • Projects May Have Multiple IRRs

Helmsley Iron is proposing to develop a new strip mine in Western Australia. The mine involves an initial investment of A$30 billion and is expected to produce a cash inflow of A$10 billion a year for the next nine years. At the end of that time, the company will incur A$65 billion of cleanup costs. Thus, the cash flows from the project are:

Cash Flows (billions of Australian dollars)				
C_0	C_1	...	C_9	C_{10}
−30	10		10	−65

Helmsley calculates the project's IRR and its NPV as follows:

IRR (%)	NPV at 10%
+3.50 *and* 19.54	$A2.53 billion

Note that there are *two* discount rates that make NPV = 0. That is, *each* of the following statements holds:

$$\text{NPV} = -30 + \frac{10}{1.035} + \frac{10}{1.035^2} + \cdots + \frac{10}{1.035^9} - \frac{65}{1.035^{10}} = 0$$

$$\text{NPV} = -30 + \frac{10}{1.1954} + \frac{10}{1.1954^2} + \cdots + \frac{10}{1.1954^9} - \frac{65}{1.1954^{10}} = 0$$

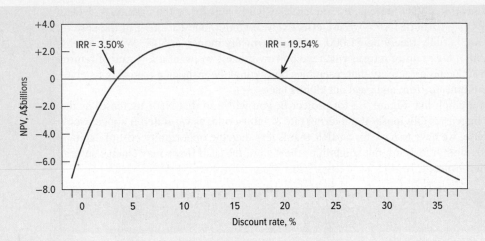

FIGURE 5.4   Helmsley Iron's mine has two internal rates of return. NPV = 0 when the discount rate is +3.50% and when it is +19.54%.

In other words, the investment has an IRR of both 3.50% *and* 19.54%. It is not clear which of the two IRRs to compare with the opportunity cost of capital. Figure 5.4 shows how this comes about. As the discount rate increases, NPV initially rises and then declines. The reason for this is the double change in the sign of the cash-flow stream. There can be as many internal rates of return for a project as there are changes in the sign of the cash flows.[3]

Decommissioning and clean-up costs can sometimes lead to huge negative cash flows at the end of a project. The cost of decommissioning oil platforms in the British North Sea has been estimated at $75 billion. It can cost more than $500 million to decommission a nuclear power plant. These are obvious instances where cash flows go from positive to negative, but you can probably think of a number of other cases where the company needs to plan for later expenditures. Ships periodically need to go into dry dock for a refit, hotels may receive a major face-lift, machine parts may need replacement, and so on. Whenever the cash-flow stream is expected to change sign more than once, the company typically sees more than one IRR.

As if this is not difficult enough, there are also cases in which *no* internal rate of return exists. For example, project C has a positive net present value at all discount rates:

| | Cash Flows ($) | | | | |
Project	C_0	C_1	C_2	IRR (%)	NPV at 10%
C	+1,000	−3,000	+2,500	None	+339

[3]By Descartes's "rule of signs" there can be as many different solutions to a polynomial as there are changes of sign.

A number of adaptations of the IRR rule have been devised to handle the problem of multiple rates of return, but the simple solution is to use net present value.[4]

BEYOND THE PAGE

Try It!
Calculate
the MIRR

mhhe.com/brealey14e

5.4 Self-Test

A project is forecast to have the following cash flows:

C_0	C_1	C_2	C_3	C_4	C_5
−420	250	250	350	350	−800

There are 2 IRRs for this project, +3.1% and +25.2%. In what circumstances would it have a positive NPV?

Pitfall 3—Mutually Exclusive Projects

Firms often have to choose between several alternative ways of doing the same job or using the same facility. In other words, they need to choose between **mutually exclusive projects**. Here, too, the IRR rule can be misleading if the projects differ in scale or in their patterns of cash flow over time.

Consider projects D and E:

	Cash Flows ($)			
Project	C_0	C_1	IRR (%)	NPV at 10%
D	−10,000	+20,000	100	+8,182
E	−20,000	+35,000	75	+11,818

Perhaps project D is a manually controlled machine tool, and project E is the same tool with the addition of computer control. Both are good investments, but E has the higher NPV and, therefore, adds more to shareholder wealth. However, the IRR rule seems to indicate that if you have to choose, you should go for D because it has the higher IRR. If you follow the IRR rule, you have the satisfaction of earning a 100% rate of return; if you follow the NPV rule, you are $11,818 richer. The problem arises because the IRR doesn't take the project's scale into account. Project D offers a high return of 100%, but only on an initial investment of $10,000. Project E offers a return of "only" 75%, but on an initial investment of double the size.

You can salvage the IRR rule in these cases by looking at the internal rate of return on the *incremental* flows. Here is how to do it: First, consider the smaller project (D in our example).

---

[4]Companies sometimes get around the problem of multiple rates of return by discounting the later cash flows back at the cost of capital until there remains only one change in the sign of the cash flows. A modified internal rate of return (MIRR) can then be calculated on this revised series. In our example, the MIRR is calculated as follows:

1. Calculate the present value in year 5 of all the subsequent cash flows:

$$\text{PV in year 5} = 10/1.1 + 10/1.1^2 + 10/1.1^3 + 10/1.1^4 - 65/1.1^5 = -8.66$$

2. Add to the year 5 cash flow the present value of subsequent cash flows:

$$C5 + \text{PV(subsequent cash flows)} = 10 - 8.66 = 1.34$$

3. Since there is now only one change in the sign of the cash flows, the revised series has a unique rate of return, which is 13.7%:

$$\text{NPV} = -30 + 10/1.137 + 10/1.137^2 + 10/1.137^3 + 10/1.137^4 + 1.34/1.137^5 = 0$$

Since the MIRR of 13.7% is greater than the cost of capital (and the initial cash flow is negative), the project has a positive NPV when valued at the cost of capital.

Of course, it would be much easier in such cases to abandon the IRR rule and just calculate project NPV.

It has an IRR of 100%, which is well in excess of the 10% opportunity cost of capital. You know, therefore, that D is acceptable. You now ask yourself whether it is worth making the *additional* $10,000 investment in E. The incremental flows from undertaking E rather than D are as follows:

Cash Flows ($)				
Project	C_0	C_1	IRR (%)	NPV at 10%
E − D	−10,000	+15,000	50	+3,636

The IRR on the incremental investment is 50%. While that is not as good as D's IRR, it is well in excess of the 10% opportunity cost of capital. So you should undertake the additional investment and take project E rather than project D.[5]

Unless you look at the incremental expenditure, IRR is unreliable in ranking projects of different scale. It is also unreliable in ranking projects with different patterns of cash flow over time. For example, sometimes it can be worth taking a project that offers a good rate of return for a long period rather than one that offers an even higher rate for just a few years. To illustrate, suppose the firm can take project F or project G but not both:

Cash Flows ($)										
Project	C_0	C_1	C_2	C_3	C_4	C_5	C_6	C_7	C_8	IRR (%)	NPV at 10%
F	−10,000	+6,000	+6,000	+6,000	0	0	0	0	0	36.3	4,921
G	−10,000	+3,000	+3,000	+3,000	+3,000	+3,000	+3,000	+3,000	+3,000	25.0	6,005

The short-lived project, F, offers the higher IRR, but at a 10% cost of capital, project G has the higher NPV and would therefore make shareholders wealthier.

Figure 5.5 shows how the choice between these two projects depends on the discount rate. Notice that if investors require a relatively low rate of return (less than 13.9%), they will pay

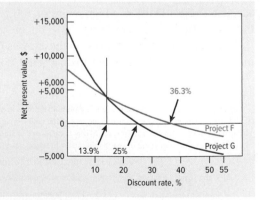

▶ FIGURE 5.5   The IRR of project F exceeds that of project G, but the NPV of project F is higher only if the discount rate is greater than 13.9%.

[5]When you examine incremental cash flows, you may find that you have jumped out of the frying pan into the fire. The series of incremental cash flows may involve several changes in sign. In this case, there are likely to be multiple IRRs, and you will be forced to use the NPV rule after all.

a higher price for project G with its longer life. The short-lived project F is superior only if investors demand a very high rate of return (greater than 13.9%) and therefore place a low value on the more distant cash flows. This is not something you could discover by comparing the project IRRs.[6]

The simplest way to choose between projects F and G is to compare their net present values. But if your heart is set on the IRR rule, you can use it as long as you look at the return on the incremental cash flows. The procedure is exactly the same as we showed earlier. First you check that project F has a satisfactory IRR. Then you look at the return on the *incremental* cash flows from G.

The IRR on the incremental cash flows from G is 13.9%. Since this is greater than the opportunity cost of capital, you should undertake G rather than F:[7]

Cash Flows ($)										
Project	C_0	C_1	C_2	C_3	C_4	C_5	C_6	C_7	C_8	IRR (%)	NPV at 10%
G – F	0	−3,000	−3,000	−3,000	+3,000	+3,000	+3,000	+3,000	+3,000	+13.9	+1,084

5.5 Self-Test

You are considering two mutually exclusive projects with the following cash flows:

Cash Flows ($000)				
Project	C_0	C_1	C_2	IRR
A	−300	+200	+200	21.53%
B	−100	+88	+75	41.14%
A-B	−200	+112	+125	11.87%

The IRR of A is 21.53% and that of B is 41.14%. You calculate the differences between the cash flows of A and those of B and find that the IRR of these extra cash flows is 11.87%. If the cost of capital is 10%, which project would you accept? What if the cost of capital is 14%?

Pitfall 4—What Happens When There Is More Than One Opportunity Cost of Capital

So far in this chapter we have assumed that the opportunity cost of capital is the same for all the cash flows, C_1, C_2, C_3, and so on. But suppose that there is a different cost of capital for each cash flow. Perhaps the long-term interest rate is higher than the short-term rate, or

---

[6]It is often suggested that the choice between the net present value rule and the internal rate of return rule should depend on the probable reinvestment rate. This is wrong. The prospective return on another independent investment should not be allowed to influence the investment decision.

[7]Because F and G had the same 10% cost of capital, we can choose between the two projects by asking whether the IRR on the incremental cash flows is greater or less than 10%. But suppose that F and G had different risks and, therefore, different costs of capital. In that case, there would be no simple yardstick for assessing whether the IRR on the incremental cash flows was adequate.

perhaps the more distant cash flows have different risks. In this case, in order to calculate NPV, each cash flow needs to be discounted at a different rate:

$$\text{NPV} = C_0 + \frac{C_1}{1 + r_1} + \frac{C_2}{(1 + r_2)^2} + \frac{C_3}{(1 + r_3)^3} + \cdots$$

In other words, we discount C_1 at the opportunity cost of capital for one year, C_2 at the opportunity cost of capital for two years, and so on. The IRR rule tells us to accept a project if the IRR is greater than the opportunity cost of capital. But what do we do when we have several opportunity costs? Do we compare IRR with r_1, r_2, r_3, . . . ? Actually we would have to compute a complex weighted average of these rates to obtain a number comparable to IRR.

The differences between short- and long-term discount rates can be important when the term structure of interest rates is not flat. Suppose a leasing company is considering what rentals to charge on a 10-year lease. If short-term interest rates are very different from long-term rates, the company might be well advised to use a different discount rate for 1-year payments than for 10-year payments.

But the extra precision from building the term structure of interest rates into discount rates for risky capital investment projects is rarely worth the trouble. The gains from accurately forecasting project cash flows far outweigh the gains from more precise discounting. Thus, the IRR usually survives, even when the term structure is not flat.

The Verdict on IRR

We have given four examples of things that can go wrong with IRR. We spent much less space on payback or accounting rate of return. Does this mean that IRR is worse than the other two measures? Quite the contrary. There is little point in dwelling on the deficiencies of payback or accounting rate of return. They are clearly ad hoc measures that often lead to silly conclusions. The IRR rule has a much more respectable ancestry. It is less easy to use than NPV, but, used properly, it gives the same answer.

Nowadays, few large corporations use the payback period or accounting rate of return as their primary measure of project attractiveness. Most use **discounted cash flow (DCF)**, and for many companies, DCF means IRR, not NPV. For "normal" investment projects with an initial cash outflow followed by a series of cash inflows, there is no difficulty in using the internal rate of return to make a simple accept/reject decision. However, we think that the financial managers who use IRRs need to worry more about pitfall 3, which threatens whenever there is a choice between competing projects. Financial managers never see all possible projects. Most projects are proposed by operating managers. A company that instructs non-financial managers to look first at project IRRs prompts a search for those projects with the highest IRRs rather than the highest NPVs. It also encourages managers to *modify* projects so that their IRRs are higher. Where do you typically find the highest IRRs? In short-lived projects requiring little up-front investment. Such projects may not add much to the value of the firm.

We don't know why managers pay such close attention to the internal rate of return. Perhaps it is because it provides a natural comparison with the opportunity cost of capital. Or perhaps it is because their estimate of the cost of capital is imprecise. If a project's IRR is much higher than the cost of capital, the company can confidently go ahead without worrying too much as to whether they have a precise estimate of the cost of capital.

Internal Rate of Return

❯ Spreadsheet programs such as Excel provide built-in functions to solve for internal rates of return. You can find these functions by pressing *fx* on the Excel toolbar. If you then click on the function that you wish to use, Excel will guide you through the inputs that are required. At the bottom left of the function box, there is a Help facility with an example of how the function is used.

Here is a list of useful functions for calculating internal rates of return, together with some points to remember when entering data:

- **IRR:** Internal rate of return on a series of regularly spaced cash flows.

- **XIRR:** The same as IRR, but for irregularly spaced flows.

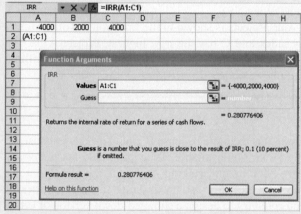

Source: Microsoft Excel.

Note the following:

- For these functions, you must enter the addresses of the cells that contain the input values.
- The IRR functions calculate (at most) only one IRR even when there are multiple IRRs.

Spreadsheet Questions

The following questions provide an opportunity to practice each of the above functions:

1. (IRR) Check the IRRs for project F in Section 5-3.

2. (IRR) Calculate the IRR of a project with the following cash flows:

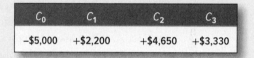

C_0	C_1	C_2	C_3
−$5,000	+$2,200	+$4,650	+$3,330

3. (XIRR) Calculate the IRR of a project with the following cash flows:

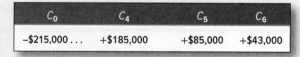

C_0	C_4	C_5	C_6
−$215,000 ...	+$185,000	+$85,000	+$43,000

(All other cash flows are 0.)

5-4 **Choosing Capital Investments When Resources Are Limited**

Our entire discussion of methods of capital budgeting has rested on the proposition that the wealth of a firm's shareholders is highest if the firm accepts *every* project that has a positive net present value. Suppose, however, that there are limitations on the amount of capital available to the firm. In this case, you need to select the package of projects that is within the company's resources yet gives the highest possible net present value. To do so, you need to focus on which projects give the biggest bang for your buck. In other words, you should pick the projects that offer the highest net present value per dollar of initial outlay. This ratio is known as the **profitability index:**[8]

$$\text{Profitability index} = \frac{\text{net present value}}{\text{investment}} \qquad (5.4)$$

EXAMPLE 5.4 • Using The Profitability Index When Capital is Rationed

Your company is presented with the following three projects:

Project	Investment ($ millions)	NPV ($ millions)	Profitability Index
A	8	18	2.3
B	5	16	3.2
C	5	12	2.4

All of them are attractive with positive NPVs, but suppose that you are limited to spending $10 million. In that case, you can invest *either* in project A *or* in projects B and C, but you cannot invest in all three. Although, individually, B and C have lower net present values than project A, when taken together, they have the higher net present value. So you cannot choose A simply because it has the highest stand-alone NPV.

The profitability index for each of your projects is shown in the final column of the table. Project B has the highest profitability index and C has the next highest. Project A has the highest NPV but the lowest profitability index. Therefore, if your budget limit is $10 million, you should accept B and C, and (regretfully) reject A.

• • • • •

The profitability index works nicely in this example because B and C exactly exhaust the budget. But suppose that you had only $9 million available. Then you could not undertake both B and C, and you would maximize NPV by undertaking A, despite the fact that it has the lowest profitability index. But you would probably also try to scrape together an extra $1 million to pay for C as well as B. Or you could try to design a slimmed-down version of C that would cost only $4 million.

If a project has a positive profitability index, it must also have a positive NPV. Therefore, firms occasionally use the profitability index to select projects when capital is *not* limited. However, like the IRR, the profitability index can be misleading when used to choose between mutually exclusive projects. For example, suppose you are forced to choose between (1) investing $100,000 in a project with a PV of $200,000 or (2) investing $1 million in a project with a PV of $1.5 million. The first investment has the higher profitability index; the second adds much more to the value of the firm.

In Example 5.4, we assumed that the firm faced a shortage of capital, but the profitability index may also be useful when some other resource, such as the supply of skilled staff, is rationed. In such cases you just need to redefine the profitability index as the NPV per unit of the resource and choose the projects with the highest values of the index.

---

[8]Sometimes the profitability index is defined as the ratio of the present value to initial outlay—that is, as PV/investment. This measure is also known as the *benefit–cost ratio*. To calculate the benefit–cost ratio, simply add 1.0 to each profitability index. Project rankings are unchanged.

5.6 Self-Test

A company has 80 skilled electroscopotic engineers. It has the opportunity to invest in the following four projects. All have positive NPVs but would need to draw on the limited pool of engineers.

Project	Engineers Required	NPV ($ millions)	NPV per Engineer
A	30	60	
B	20	25	
C	60	70	
D	50	150	

Complete the table. Which projects should the company accept?

The profitability index can cope with these simple cases of resource rationing, but it has some important limitations. One of the most serious is that it breaks down whenever there is more than one constraint on the choice of projects. For example, perhaps B and C in Example 5.4 require the same piece of land, so you cannot undertake both. In that case, you would do better to take project A despite the fact that it has the lowest profitability index.

For more complex rationing problems, the only general solutions are (1) a trial-and-error search for the package of projects that satisfies the constraints and has the highest total NPV or (2) a computer program that does the search for you. Excel's Goal Seek is a simple version of such a computer model. Linear programming models are also useful, especially when the number of decisions and constraints is large.[9]

BEYOND THE PAGE

Capital rationing models

mhhe.com/brealey14e

How Important Is Capital Rationing in Practice?

Are capital constraints widespread or rare? What creates the constraints when they do exist? Do they change the firm's objectives? In Chapter 1, we pointed out that shareholders will unanimously vote for companies to maximize NPV as long as they have access to well-functioning capital markets. But if the capital constraints arise because capital markets do *not* function well, then the very concept of NPV may be undermined.

Soft Rationing Many firms' capital constraints are "soft." By this we mean that they reflect no shortcoming in financial markets. Instead, they are provisional limits adopted by management as an aid to controlling the firm's investment expenditures.

Ambitious plant and divisional managers tend to overstate their investment opportunities. Rather than trying to distinguish which project proposals really are worthwhile, headquarters may force the plants and divisions to set their own priorities by imposing an upper limit on the amount that each can invest. In such instances, budget limits are a rough but effective way of dealing with biased cash-flow forecasts.

In other cases, management may believe that very rapid corporate growth could impose intolerable strains on management and the organization. Since it is difficult to quantify such constraints explicitly, the budget limit may be used as a proxy device to slow down growth.

Because such budget limits have nothing to do with any defect in the financial market, there is no contradiction in seeking to maximize NPV subject to the budget constraint.

---

[9]The rationing problems that we have discussed are known collectively as the knapsack problem. Solutions to the knapsack problem are widely discussed in the linear programming literature.

We believe that most instances of capital rationing are "soft," at least for healthy corporations in developed economies.

Hard Rationing   Soft rationing should never cost the firm anything. If capital constraints become tight enough to hurt—in the sense that projects with significant positive NPVs are passed up—then the firm should raise more money and loosen the constraint. But what if a constrained firm *can't* raise more money—what if it faces *hard* rationing?

Sometimes firms find it difficult to raise additional financing even when financial markets are working perfectly. Consider a company that has accumulated excessive debt and finds that further borrowing would come at painfully high interest rates and carry tough restrictions on the company's operations. A stock issue would relieve the constraint, but the CFO worries that the benefits of the stock issue would largely go to enhance the value of existing creditors' claims. (We cover these financing issues in Chapter 17.) Therefore, the CFO recoils from raising additional capital.

The difficulties facing this unfortunate CFO do not change the company's fundamental financial objective, which is to maximize value. The company may *choose* not to raise more capital, but that does not imply a market failure. The company's stock can still be priced correctly, albeit marked down because of the company's financial difficulties. Shareholders will still vote unanimously for financial decisions that increase firm value. Therefore, the CFO should seek to maximize NPV subject to the capital constraint.

EXAMPLE 5.5 • Capital Rationing and the NPV Rule

Arizona Aquaculture Inc. (AAI) borrows as much as it is prepared to, yet it still has good investment opportunities. This is not hard rationing so long as AAI can issue stock. But the founder and majority shareholder vetoes the issue from fear of losing voting control of the firm.[10]

This does not invalidate the use of NPV or of the profitability index. AAI's *outside* shareholders can borrow or lend, sell their shares, or buy more. They have free access to financial markets. The only way AAI can help them is to make them richer. Thus, AAI should invest its available cash in the package of projects having the largest aggregate net present value.

• • • • •

A barrier that prevents the firm from accessing the financial markets does not undermine the objective of maximizing shareholder value so long as the barrier is the *only* market imperfection. The important thing is that the firm's *shareholders* have free access to well-functioning financial markets.

The shareholder-value objective *is* undermined when the imperfections restrict shareholders' portfolio choice. Suppose that Nevada Aquaculture Inc. (NAI), a private company, is solely owned by its founder, Alexander Turbot. Mr. Turbot has no cash or credit remaining, but he still wants to expand. He has tried to sell stock but has found that prospective investors, skeptical of prospects for fish farming in the desert, offer him much less than he thinks his firm is worth. For Mr. Turbot, financial markets hardly exist. We can perhaps excuse him if he drifts away from a sole focus on NPV and if his personal preferences and risk tolerance influence his financial decisions.

---

[10]In some countries, such as Chile, state-owned enterprises cannot borrow unless they have Ministry of Finance permission.

- **The net present value rule (NPV)** A project's net present value is the discounted stream of the expected cash flows. The net present value *rule* states that companies should accept all projects with a positive NPV and reject others. The rule has some important features. In particular, it depends solely on the *forecast cash flows* from the project and the *opportunity cost of capital*. But, if you are going to persuade your company to use the net present value rule, you must be prepared to explain why other rules may *not* lead to correct decisions. We examined three alternative investment criteria in this chapter.

- **The payback rule** Some companies use the payback rule to help make investment decisions. In other words, they accept only those projects that recover their initial investment within a specified period. Payback is a senseless rule. It ignores the timing of cash flows within the payback period, and it ignores subsequent cash flows entirely. It therefore takes no account of the time value of money.

- **Accounting rate of return** Some firms look at the accounting rate of return on the project. In this case, the company calculates the ratio of a project's average profit to the average book value of the assets. Such accounting measures of profitability ignore the time value of money and lack a clear benchmark. Few companies nowadays base their investment decision simply on the accounting rate of return, but since shareholders rely on the company's financial statements to judge firm profitability, managers may look with a jaundiced eye on projects that would damage the company's accounting rate of return.

- **The internal rate of return rule (IRR)** The internal rate of return (IRR) is defined as the rate of discount at which a project would have zero NPV. The IRR rule states that companies should accept any investment offering an IRR in excess of the opportunity cost of capital. Like net present value, the IRR rule is a technique based on discounted cash flow (DCF). It will therefore give the correct answer if properly used, but there are four things to look out for:

  1. *Lending or borrowing?* Projects that offer positive cash flows followed by negative flows resemble borrowing. In such cases, NPV *rises* as the discount rate is increased. You should accept such projects if their IRR is *less* than the opportunity cost of capital.

  2. *Multiple rates of return.* If there is more than one change in the sign of the cash flows, the project may have several IRRs (so you don't know which one to compare with the opportunity cost of capital). Some projects may have no IRR at all.

  3. *Mutually exclusive projects.* The IRR rule may give the wrong ranking of mutually exclusive projects that differ in economic life or in the scale of required investment. If you use IRR to rank mutually exclusive projects, you must examine the IRR on each incremental investment.

  4. *The cost of capital for near-term cash flows may be different from the cost for distant cash flows.* The IRR rule requires you to compare the project's IRR with the opportunity cost of capital. But in some cases, there may be a different cost of capital for each cash flow. In these cases, there is no simple yardstick for evaluating the IRR of a project.

- **Capital rationing** The NPV rule assumes that the company can maximize shareholder wealth by accepting every project that is worth more than it costs. But that may not be possible if capital is limited. A solution is to calculate each project's profitability index, which is the project's net present value per dollar of investment. You then pick the projects with the highest profitability indexes until you have run out of capital. Sadly, this procedure fails when there are other constraints on project choice.

Where there are well-functioning capital markets, hard capital rationing is rare. Many firms do use soft capital rationing, however. That is, they set up self-imposed limits when they are concerned about the volume of proposed investments.

● ● ● ● ●

KEY TAKEAWAYS

FURTHER READING

For a survey of capital budgeting procedures, see:

J. Graham and C. Harvey, "How Do CFOs Make Capital Budgeting and Capital Structure Decisions?" *Journal of Applied Corporate Finance* 15 (Spring 2002), pp. 8–23.

PROBLEM SETS

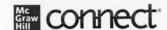   Select problems are available in McGraw-Hill's *Connect.*

1. Payback (S5.2)

   a. What is the payback period on each of the following projects?

Project	Cash Flows ($)				
	C_0	C_1	C_2	C_3	C_4
A	−5,000	+1,000	+1,000	+3,000	0
B	−1,000	0	+1,000	+2,000	+3,000
C	−5,000	+1,000	+1,000	+3,000	+5,000

   b. Given that you wish to use the payback rule with a cutoff period of two years, which projects would you accept?

   c. If you use a cutoff period of three years, which projects would you accept?

   d. If the opportunity cost of capital is 10%, which projects have positive NPVs?

   e. "If a firm uses a single cutoff period for all projects, it is likely to accept too many short-lived projects." True or false?

2. Payback (S5.2) Consider the following projects:

Project	Cash Flows ($)					
	C_0	C_1	C_2	C_3	C_4	C_5
A	−1,000	+1,000	0	0	0	0
B	−2,000	+1,000	+1,000	+4,000	+1,000	+1,000
C	−3,000	+1,000	+1,000	0	+1,000	+1,000

   a. If the opportunity cost of capital is 10%, which projects have a positive NPV?

   b. Calculate the payback period for each project.

   c. Which project(s) would a firm using the payback rule accept if the cutoff period is three years?

3. Payback and Accounting Rate of Return (S5.2) In Section 5.1, we listed five key features of the NPV rule. Which of these features characterize the payback rule? What about the accounting rate of return rule?

4. Payback and IRR rules (S5.2, S5.3) Respond to the following comments:

   a. "I like the IRR rule. I can use it to rank projects without having to specify a discount rate."

   b. "I like the payback rule. As long as the minimum payback period is short, the rule makes sure that the company takes no borderline projects. That reduces risk."

5. IRR (S5.3) Write down the equation defining a project's internal rate of return (IRR). In practice, how is IRR calculated?

6. **IRR (S5.3)**

   a. Calculate the net present value of the following project for discount rates of 0, 50, and 100%:

Cash Flows ($)		
C_0	C_1	C_2
−6,750	+4,500	+18,000

   b. What is the IRR of the project?

7. **IRR (S5.3)** Calculate the IRR (or IRRs) for the following project:

C_0	C_1	C_2	C_3
−3,000	+3,500	+4,000	−4,000

   For what range of discount rates does the project have a positive NPV?

8. **IRR rule (S5.3)** You have the chance to participate in a project that produces the following cash flows:

Cash Flows ($)		
C_0	C_1	C_2
−5,000	+4,000	−11,000

   The internal rate of return is 13%. If the opportunity cost of capital is 10%, would you accept the offer?

9. **IRR rule (S5.3)** Consider a project with the following cash flows:

Cash Flows ($)		
C_0	C_1	C_2
−100	+200	−75

   a. How many internal rates of return does this project have?

   b. Which of the following numbers is the project IRR: (i) −50%; (ii) −12%; (iii) +5%; (iv) +50%?

   c. The opportunity cost of capital is 20%. Is this an attractive project?

   d. For what range of discount rates is the project attractive?

10. **IRR rule (S5.3)** Consider projects Alpha and Beta:

	Cash Flows ($)			
Project	C_0	C_1	C_2	IRR (%)
Alpha	−400,000	+241,000	+293,000	21
Beta	−200,000	+131,000	+172,000	31

    The opportunity cost of capital is 8%. Suppose you can undertake Alpha or Beta, but not both. Use the IRR rule to make the choice. (*Hint:* What's the incremental investment in Alpha?)

11. **IRR rule (S5.3)** Consider the following two mutually exclusive projects:

	Cash flows ($)			
Project	C_0	C_1	C_2	C_3
A	−50	+60	+60	0
B	−50	0	0	+140

  a. Calculate the NPV of each project for discount rates of 0%, 10%, and 20%. Plot these on a graph with NPV on the vertical axis and discount rate on the horizontal axis.

  b. What is the approximate IRR for each project?

  c. In what circumstances should the company accept project A?

  d. Calculate the NPV of the incremental investment (B − A) for discount rates of 0%, 10%, and 20%. Plot these on your graph. Show that the circumstances in which you would accept A are also those in which the IRR on the incremental investment is less than the opportunity cost of capital.

12. **IRR rule (S5.3)** Cyrus Clops, the president of Giant Enterprises, has to make a choice between two possible investments:

	Cash Flows ($000)			
Project	C_0	C_1	C_2	IRR (%)
A	−400	+250	+300	23
B	−200	+140	+179	36

The opportunity cost of capital is 9%. Mr. Clops is tempted to take B, which has the higher IRR.

  a. Explain to Mr. Clops why this is not the correct procedure.

  b. Show him how to adapt the IRR rule to choose the best project.

  c. Show him that this project also has the higher NPV.

13. **IRR rule (S5.3)** The Titanic Shipbuilding Company has a noncancelable contract to build a small cargo vessel. Construction involves a cash outlay of $250,000 at the end of each of the next two years. At the end of the third year, the company will receive payment of $650,000. The company can speed up construction by working an extra shift. In this case, there will be a cash outlay of $550,000 at the end of the first year followed by a cash payment of $650,000 at the end of the second year. Use the IRR rule to show the (approximate) range of opportunity costs of capital at which the company should work the extra shift.

14. **IRR rule (S5.3)** Plot the NPVs for the following projects for discount rates from 0% to 30%:

Project	C_0	C_1	C_2
A	−100	20	100
B	−1,000	2,260	−1,270
C	100	−50	−80
D	−1,080	2,510	−1,500

  a. Which one of these projects has no IRR?

  b. One of the projects has two IRRs. Which is this project and what are the IRRs?

  c. What are the IRRs of the other two projects?

d. Suppose projects A and C are mutually exclusive. If the cost of capital is 6%, which one would you accept?

e. If the cost of capital is very high, would you accept project C? Why or why not?

15. **IRR rule (S5.3)** The following table shows the forecast cash flows for two projects:

	C_0	C_1	C_2	C_3	C_4	C_5
A	−1,000	20	20	20	20	1,200
B	−1,000	50	50	1,050		

Now suppose that the term structure is upward sloping and investors demand a higher return on the more distant flows as in the following table:

			t		
	1	**2**	**3**	**4**	**5**
r_t	4.0%	4.5%	5.0%	5.5%	6.0%

Calculate the IRR on the two projects and the NPV. Do the two measures give the same ranking for the two projects? Explain why or why not.

16. **Investment criteria (S5.1–S5.3)** Consider the following two projects:

Cash Flows	Project A	Project B
C_0	−$200	−$200
C_1	80	100
C_2	80	100
C_3	80	100
C_4	80	

a. If the opportunity cost of capital is 11%, which of these two projects would you accept (A, B, or both)?

b. Suppose that you can choose only one of these two projects. Which would you choose? The discount rate is still 11%.

c. Which one would you choose if the cost of capital is 16%?

d. What is the payback period of each project?

e. Is the project with the shortest payback period also the one with the highest NPV?

f. What are the internal rates of return on the two projects?

g. Does the IRR rule in this case give the same answer as NPV?

h. If the opportunity cost of capital is 11%, what is the profitability index for each project? Is the project with the highest profitability index also the one with the highest NPV? Which measure should you use to choose between the projects?

17. **Profitability index (S5.4)** Look again at projects D and E in Section 5-3. Assume that the projects are mutually exclusive and that the opportunity cost of capital is 10%.

a. Calculate the profitability index for each project.

b. Show how the profitability-index rule can be used to select the superior project.

18. **Profitability index (S5.4)** Sometimes firms use the profitability index as an investment criterion when there is no rationing of capital or other resources. Look back at the pitfalls surrounding the IRR. Do you think that these would also apply to the use of the profitability index?

19. **Capital rationing (S5.4)** Suppose you have the following investment opportunities, but only $90,000 available for investment. Which projects should you take?

Project	NPV ($)	Investment ($)
1	5,000	10,000
2	5,000	5,000
3	10,000	90,000
4	15,000	60,000
5	15,000	75,000
6	3,000	15,000

20. **Capital rationing (S5.4)** Borgia Pharmaceuticals has $1 million allocated for capital expenditures. Which of the following projects should the company accept to stay within the $1 million budget? How much does the budget limit cost the company in terms of its market value? The opportunity cost of capital for each project is 11%.

Project	Investment ($000)	NPV ($000)	IRR (%)
1	300	66	17.2
2	200	−4	10.7
3	250	43	16.6
4	100	14	12.1
5	100	7	11.8
6	350	63	18.0
7	400	48	13.0

CHALLENGE PROBLEMS

21. **NPV and IRR rules (S5.3)** Some people believe passionately that ranking projects on IRR is OK if each project's cash flows can be reinvested at the project's IRR. They also say that the IRR rule "assumes that cash flows are reinvested at the opportunity cost of capital." Think carefully about these statements. Are they true? Are they helpful?

22. **Modified IRR (S5.3)** Look again at the project cash flows in Problem 7. Calculate the modified IRR (MIRR) as defined in footnote 4 in Section 5-3. Assume the cost of capital is 12%.

Now try the following variation on the MIRR concept. Figure out the fraction x such that x times C_1 and C_2 has the same present value as (minus) C_3.

$$xC_1 + \frac{xC_2}{1.12} = -\frac{C_3}{1.12^2}$$

Define the modified project IRR as the solution of

$$C_0 + \frac{(1-x)C_1}{1 + \text{IRR}} + \frac{(1-x)C_2}{(1 + \text{IRR})^2} = 0$$

Now you have two MIRRs. Which is more meaningful? If you can't decide, what do you conclude about the usefulness of MIRRs?

23. **Capital rationing (S5.3)** Consider the following capital rationing problem:

Project	C_0	C_1	C_2	NPV
W	−10,000	−10,000	0	+6,700
X	0	−20,000	+5,000	+9,000
Y	−10,000	+5,000	+5,000	+0
Z	−15,000	+5,000	+4,000	−1,500
Financing available	20,000	20,000	20,000	

Set up this problem as a linear program and solve it.

You can allow partial investments, that is, $0 \le x \le 1$. Calculate and interpret the shadow prices[16] on the capital constraints.

5.1   a. False

b. True

5.2   Average profits and accounting return do not change, but the project is now less attractive since shareholders now have to wait longer for their cash flows.

5.3   IRR = 10%

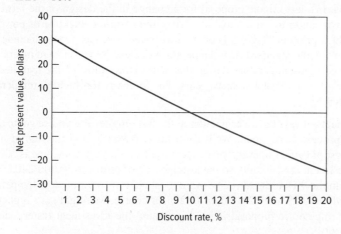

5.4   If the opportunity cost of capital was greater than 3.1% and less than 25.2% (see figure).

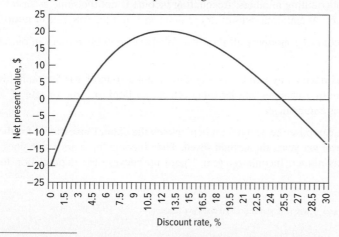

---

[16]A shadow price is the marginal change in the objective for a marginal change in the constraint.

5.5   a. A (the incremental IRR is higher than the cost of capital)

   b. B (the incremental IRR is lower than the cost of capital)

5.6

Project	Engineers Required	NPV ($ millions)	NPV per Engineer
A	30	60	2.0
B	20	25	1.25
C	60	70	1.17
D	50	150	3

Accept projects D and A.

MINI-CASE ••••

Vegetron's CFO Calls Again

(The first episode of this story was presented in Section 5-1.)

Later that afternoon, Vegetron's CFO bursts into your office in a state of anxious confusion. The problem, she explains, is a last-minute proposal for a change in the design of the fermentation tanks that Vegetron will build to extract hydrated zirconium from a stockpile of powdered ore. The CFO has brought a printout (Table 5.1) of the forecasted revenues, costs, income, and accounting rates of return for the standard, low-temperature design. Vegetron's engineers have just proposed an alternative high-temperature design that will extract most of the hydrated zirconium over a shorter period, five instead of seven years. The forecasts for the high-temperature method are given in Table 5.2.[17]

CFO: Why do these engineers always have a bright idea at the last minute? But you've got to admit the high-temperature process looks good. We'll get a faster payback, and the rate of return beats Vegetron's 9% cost of capital in every year except the first. Let's see, income is $30,000 per year. Average investment is $240,000, so the average rate of return is 30,000/240,000, or 12.5%—a lot better than the 9% hurdle rate. The average rate of return for the low-temperature process is not that good, only 28,000/229,000, or 12.2%. Of course, we might get a higher rate of return for the low-temperature proposal if we depreciated the investment faster—do you think we should try that?

You: Let's not fixate on accounting numbers. Accounting income is not the same as cash flow to Vegetron or its investors. Accounting rates of return don't measure the true rate of return.

CFO: But people use accounting numbers all the time. We have to publish them in our annual report to investors.

You: Accounting numbers have many valid uses, but they're not a sound basis for capital investment decisions. Accounting changes can have big effects on book income or rate of return, even when cash flows are unchanged.

Here's an example. Suppose the accountant depreciates the capital investment for the low-temperature process over six years rather than seven. Then income for years 1 to 6 goes down because depreciation is higher. Income for year 7 goes up because the depreciation for that

---

[17]For simplicity we have ignored taxes. There will be plenty about taxes in Chapter 6.

	Year						
	1	**2**	**3**	**4**	**5**	**6**	**7**
1. Revenue	140	140	140	140	140	140	140
2. Operating costs	55	55	55	55	55	55	55
3. Depreciation[a]	57	57	57	57	57	57	57
4. Net income	28	28	28	28	28	28	28
5. Start-of-year book value[b]	400	343	286	229	171	114	57
6.Accounting rate of return (4÷5)	7%	8.2%	9.8%	12.2%	16.4%	24.6%	49.1%

〉**TABLE 5.1**   Income statement and accounting rates of return for each year low-temperature extraction of hydrated zirconium ($ thousands)

[a] Rounded. Straight-line depreciation over seven years is 400/7 = 57.14, or $57,140 per year.
[b] Capital investment is $400,000 in year 0.

	Year				
	1	**2**	**3**	**4**	**5**
1. Revenue	180	180	180	180	180
2. Operating costs	70	70	70	70	70
3. Depreciation[a]	80	80	80	80	80
4. Net income	30	30	30	30	30
5. Start-of-year book value[b]	400	320	240	160	80
6.Accounting rate of return (4÷5)	7.5%	9.4%	12.5%	18.75%	37.5%

〉**TABLE 5.2**   Income statement and accounting rates of return for each year high-temperature extraction of hydrated zirconium ($ thousands)

[a] Straight-line depreciation over five years is 400/5 = 80, or $80,000 per year.
[b] Capital investment is $400,000 in year 0.

year becomes zero. But there is no effect on year-to-year cash flows because depreciation is not a cash outlay. It is simply the accountant's device for spreading out the "recovery" of the up-front capital outlay over the life of the project.

CFO: So how do we get cash flows?

You: In these cases, it's easy. Depreciation is the only noncash entry in your spreadsheets (Tables 5.1 and 5.2), so we can just leave it out of the calculation. Cash flow equals revenue minus operating costs. For the high-temperature process, annual cash flow is:

Cash flow = revenue − operating cost = 180 − 70 = 110, or $110,000

CFO: In effect you're adding back depreciation because depreciation is a noncash accounting expense.

You: Right. You could also do it this way:

Cash flow = net income + depreciation = 30 + 80 = 110, or $110,000

CFO: Of course. I remember all this now, but accounting returns seem important when someone shoves them in front of your nose.

You: It's not clear which project is better. The high-temperature process appears to be less efficient. It has higher operating costs and generates less total revenue over the life of the project, but of course, it generates more cash flow in years 1 to 5.

CFO: Maybe the processes are equally good from a financial point of view. If so, we'll stick with the low-temperature process rather than switching at the last minute.

You: We'll have to lay out the cash flows and calculate NPV for each process.

CFO: OK, do that. Come back in a half hour—and I also want to see each project's true, DCF rate of return.

QUESTIONS

1. Are the accounting rates of return reported in Tables 5.1 and 5.2 useful inputs for the capital investment decision?

2. Calculate NPV and IRR for each process. What is your recommendation? Be ready to explain to the CFO.

Making Investment Decisions with the Net Present Value Rule

In January 2020, the pharmaceutical company, Eli Lilly, announced plans to invest $470 million in a new facility in North Carolina to produce injectible products. How does a company decide to go ahead with such an investment? We know the answer in principle. The company needs to forecast the project's cash flows and discount them at the opportunity cost of capital to arrive at the project's NPV. If the project has a positive NPV, it increases shareholder value and should be accepted.

But those cash flow forecasts do not arrive on a silver platter. For example, Eli Lilly's managers would have needed answers to several basic questions. How soon can the new plant be brought into operation? What are the likely revenues and production costs? How long will the plant stay in production, and what happens to the plant and equipment at the end of that time? This chapter looks at some of the practical issues in forecasting cash flows.

Section 6-1 Forecasting a project's cash flows

We first discuss the difference between accounting profits and cash flows and show how to get from the former to the latter. The manager also needs to recognize and include hidden cash flows and to reject accounting entries that look like cash flows but truly are not.

Section 6-2 Corporate income taxes

Cash flow forecasts need to take account of corporate taxes. This is the first chapter in which we grapple with the complexities of taxes and recognize their impact on cash flows.

Section 6-3 A worked example of a project analysis

In this section, we work through a realistic and comprehensive example of a capital investment analysis, in which we start with profit forecasts, convert them to cash flow forecasts, and recognize the impact of taxes.

Section 6-4 How to choose between competing projects

Sometimes two projects may be mutually exclusive; it is possible to take either one but not both. If you have to choose between two such projects, the general rule is to choose the one with the higher NPV. However, complications occur when the choice affects future decisions that you might wish to make. We show how to analyze four common problems:

- The timing decision: When to commit to a positive-NPV project.

- The horizon decision: The choice between long- and short-lived equipment.

- The replacement decision: When to replace a machine.

- The capacity decision: The cost of using spare capacity.

When you are faced with such problems, a useful trick is to transform the present value of the cash flow into an *equivalent annual flow*—that is, the total cash per year from buying and operating the asset.

Many projects require a heavy initial outlay on new production facilities. But often, the largest investments involve the acquisition of intangible assets. For example, U.S. banks invest huge sums annually in new information technology (IT) projects. Much of this expenditure goes to intangibles such as system design, programming, testing, and training. Think also of the huge expenditure by big tech companies on research and development (R&D). For example, in 2020 Amazon spent $42 billion on R&D.

Expenditures on intangible assets such as IT and R&D are investments just like expenditures on new plant and equipment. In each case, the company is spending money today in the expectation that it will generate a stream of future profits. Ideally, firms should apply the same criteria to all capital investments, regardless of whether they involve a tangible or intangible asset.

We have seen that an investment in any asset creates wealth if the discounted value of the future cash flows exceeds the up-front cost. Up to this point, however, we have glossed over the problem of *what* to discount. When you are faced with this problem, you should stick to five general rules:

1. Discount cash flows, not profits.
2. Discount *incremental* cash flows and ignore non-incremental flows.
3. Treat inflation consistently.
4. Separate investment and financing decisions.
5. Forecast cash flows after taxes.

We discuss each of these rules in turn.

Rule 1: Discount Cash Flows, Not Profits

The first and most important point: Net present value depends on the expected future cash flow. Cash flow is simply the difference between cash received and cash paid out. Many people confuse cash flow with accounting profits. Accounting profit is intended to show how well the company is performing. Therefore, accountants *start* with "dollars in" and "dollars out," but to obtain accounting profit, they adjust these inputs in two principal ways.

Capital Expenditures   The accountant takes the cash expenditures and divides them into two groups—current expenditures (such as wages) and capital expenditures (such as the purchase of new machinery). When calculating profits, *current* expenditures are deducted from current revenues. However, the accountant does not deduct *capital* expenditures. There is a good reason for this. If the firm lays out $1 million on a new machine, you do not conclude that the firm is performing poorly, even though a lot of cash is going out the door. The firm hasn't "lost" $1 million nor is its performance worse by $1 million. It has simply exchanged one asset ($1 million of cash) for another (a machine worth $1 million). Therefore, rather than deducting the cost of long-lived machinery in the year it is purchased, the accountant spreads the cost over its forecasted life by making an annual charge for depreciation. For example, suppose a $1 million investment is depreciated by $100,000 a year for 10 years. In calculating accounting profits, this depreciation is treated as an annual expense, although the cash actually went out of the door when the asset was first purchased.

Depreciating capital expenditures makes sense when judging firm performance, but it will get you into trouble when working out net present value. For example, suppose you are analyzing an investment proposal. It costs $2,000 and is expected to provide a cash flow of $1,500 in the first year and $500 in the second. If the accountant depreciates the capital expenditure straight-line over the two years, accounting income is $500 in year 1 and −$500 in year 2:

	Year 1	Year 2
Cash inflow	+$1,500	+$ 500
Less depreciation	– 1,000	– 1,000
Accounting income	+$ 500	–$ 500

Suppose you were given this forecast income and naïvely discounted it at 10%. NPV would appear positive:

$$\text{Apparent NPV} = \frac{\$500}{1.10} + \frac{-\$500}{1.10^2} = \$41.32$$

This has to be nonsense. The project is obviously a loser. You are laying out $2,000 today and simply getting it back later. At any positive discount rate the project has a negative NPV.

The message is clear: When calculating NPV, state capital expenditures when they occur, not later when they show up as depreciation. Capital expenditure affects cash flow but not profits, while depreciation affects profits but not cash flow. *To go from accounting profit to cash flow, you need to add back depreciation (which is not a cash outflow) and subtract capital expenditure (which is a cash outflow).*

6.1 Self-Test

A supermarket is considering today (year 0) whether to install a tewgit machine in each of its stores. Tewgits cost $250,000 each, and projected profit per machine is as follows:

	Year				
	1	2	3	4	5
Sales	$250,000	$300,000	$300,000	$240,000	$240,000
Operating expenses	200,000	200,000	200,000	200,000	200,000
Depreciation	50,000	50,000	50,000	50,000	50,000
Accounting profit	0	50,000	50,000	–10,0000	–10,000

Why would a store continue to operate a machine in years 4 and 5 if it produces a loss? What are the cash flows from investing in a Tewgit? Assume that each machine has no salvage value. Ignore taxes.

Working Capital   Net working capital (often referred to simply as working capital) is the difference between a company's short-term assets and its short-term liabilities. The principal short-term assets are accounts receivable (customers' unpaid bills) and inventories of raw materials and finished goods. The principal short-term liabilities are accounts payable (bills that you have not yet paid) and accruals (liabilities for wages or taxes that have been incurred but not yet paid).[1]

Most projects entail an additional investment in working capital. For example, consider a company that spends $60 in period 1 to obtain raw materials. It processes these materials and sells the finished goods in period 2 for $100, but its customers do not pay their bills until period 3. The following diagram shows the firm's cash flows. In period 1, there is a cash *outflow* of $60 when the firm purchases raw materials. Then, when customers pay their bills in period 3, there is an *inflow* of $100.

---

[1]If you delay paying *your* bills, your investment in net working capital is reduced. When you finally pay up, it is increased.

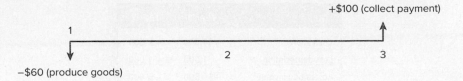

It would be misleading to say that the firm was running at a loss in period 1 (when cash flow was negative) or that it was extremely profitable in period 3 (when cash flow was positive). Therefore, the accountant looks at when the sale was made (period 2 in our example) and gathers together all the revenues and expenses associated with that sale. In the case of our company, the accountant would show for period 2.

Revenue	$100
Less cost of goods sold	– 60
Profit	$ 40

Of course, the accountant does not ignore the actual timing of the cash expenditures and payments. So the $60 cash outlay in the first period will be treated not as an expense, but as an *investment* in inventories. Subsequently, in period 2, when the goods are taken out of inventory and sold, the accountant shows a $60 *reduction* in inventories.

The accountant also does not ignore the fact that the firm has to wait to collect on its bills. When the sale is made in period 2, the accountant will record accounts receivable of $100 to show that the company's customers owe $100 in unpaid bills. Later, when the customers pay those bills in period 3, accounts receivable are reduced by that $100.

To go from the figure for accounting profit to the actual cash flows, you need to add back these changes in inventories and receivables:

	Period		
	1	**2**	**3**
Accounting profit	0	+40	0
− Investment in inventories	−60	+60	0
− Investment in receivables	0	−100	+100
= Cash flow	−60	0	+100

An increase in current assets, such as inventory or accounts receivable, represents a cash expenditure. Conversely an increase in current liabilities represents a cash inflow. For example, whenever you delay paying your bills (an increase in accounts payable), your cash flow is higher. For example, if our firm did not pay for its purchase of raw materials until period 2, there would be an increase in payables in period 1, and our cash flow calculation would change as follows:

	Period		
	1	**2**	**3**
Accounting profit	0	+40	0
− Change in inventories	−60	+60	0
− Change in receivables	0	−100	+100
+ Change in payables	+60	−60	0
= Cash flow	0	−60	+100

Most projects entail an investment in net working capital. This investment is a cash outflow, just like an investment in capital equipment. Therefore, each period's change in working capital should be recognized in your cash-flow forecasts.[2] By the same token, when the project comes to an end, you can usually recover some of the investment. This results in a cash inflow.

Working capital is a common source of confusion in capital investment calculations. Here are the most common mistakes:

1. *Forgetting about working capital entirely.* We hope that you do not fall into that trap.

2. *Forgetting that working capital may change during the life of the project.* Imagine that you sell $100,000 of goods a year and customers pay on average six months late. You therefore have $50,000 of unpaid bills. Now you increase prices by 10%, so revenues increase to $110,000. If customers continue to pay six months late, unpaid bills increase to $55,000, and so you need to make an *additional* investment in working capital of $5,000.

3. *Forgetting that working capital is recovered at the end of the project.* When the project comes to an end, inventories are run down, any unpaid bills are (you hope) paid off, and you recover your investment in working capital. This generates a cash *inflow*.

6.2 Self-Test

Assume that our company continues to produce and sell the same amount of goods with the same lags between investing in inventory and being paid by the customer. To keep life simple, assume also that in each period the company pays immediately for the raw materials (i.e., payables are zero in each period). Adapt the above table to show the accounting income and cash flow in each of years 1–4.

Rule 2: Discount Incremental Cash Flows and Ignore Non-Incremental Cash Flows

The value of a project depends on *all* the additional cash flows that follow from project acceptance. Here are four common incremental effects to look for when you are deciding which cash flows to include.

1. Include the Project's Effects on the Firm's Other Business   Many new projects have an effect on the firm's existing business. For example, suppose Sony proposes to launch PlayStation X, a new version of its videogame console. Demand for the new product will almost certainly cut into sales of Sony's existing consoles. This incidental effect needs to be factored into the incremental cash flows. Of course, Sony may reason that it needs to go ahead with the new product because its existing product line is likely to come under increasing threat from competitors. So, even if it decides not to produce the new PlayStation, there is no guarantee that sales of the existing consoles will continue at their present level. Sooner or later, they will decline.

Sometimes a new project will *help* the firm's existing business. Suppose that you are the financial manager of an airline that is considering opening a new short-haul route from Harrisburg, Pennsylvania, to Chicago's O'Hare Airport. When considered in isolation, the new route may have a negative NPV. But once you allow for the additional business that the new route brings to your other traffic out of O'Hare, it may be a very worthwhile investment.

---

[2] Holdings of cash and marketable securities are also short-term assets and debt due within a year is a short-term liability. These are *not* generally relevant to your capital budgeting calculations.

6.3 Self-Test

Electric Auto (EA) currently earns $1.5 billion a year from its popular Fuse1 model. However, the model is looking dated, and increasing competition from rivals will cause that figure to decline in the future to $1.0 billion. EA is considering the launch of Fuse2. Fuse2 would produce yearly income of $2.5 billion a year. On the other hand, it would effectively wipe out any income from Fuse1. What would be the incremental income from the new model?

2. Recognize After-Sales Cash Flows   Financial managers should forecast all incremental cash flows generated by an investment. Sometimes these incremental cash flows last for decades. When GE commits to the design and production of a new jet engine, the cash inflows come first from the sale of engines and then from service and spare parts. A jet engine will be in use for 30 years. Over that period, revenues from service and spare parts will be roughly seven times the engine's purchase price.

Many other manufacturing companies depend on the revenues that come *after* their products are sold. For example, services and parts typically account for about 25% of auto company revenues and 50% of profits.[3]

3. Remember Salvage Value   When a project comes to an end, you may be able to sell the plant and equipment or redeploy the assets elsewhere in the business. If the equipment is sold, you must pay tax on the difference between the sale price and the book value of the asset. The salvage value (net of any taxes) represents a positive cash flow to the firm. If the asset can be used elsewhere in the business, the cash saved from not having to buy a new asset is also a positive cash flow.

Some projects have significant shutdown costs, in which case the final cash flows may be *negative*. For example, the mining company, FCX, has earmarked $454 million to cover the future reclamation and closure costs of its New Mexico mines.

4. Include Opportunity Costs   The cost of a resource may be relevant to the investment decision even when no cash changes hands. For example, suppose a new manufacturing operation uses land that could otherwise be sold for $100,000. This resource is not free: It has an opportunity cost, which is the cash it could generate for the company if the project were rejected and the resource were sold or put to some other use.

To calculate opportunity costs, you need to take the difference between the cash flows with the project and those without the project. In our land example:

With	Take Project	After	Cash Flow, with Project
Firm owns land	→	Firm still owns land	0

Without	Do Not Take Project	After	Cash Flow, without Project
	→	Firm sells land for $100,000	$100,000

Comparing the "with" and the "without," we see that the firm gives up $100,000 by undertaking the project. This reasoning still holds if the land will not be sold but is worth $100,000 to the firm in some other use.

Sometimes opportunity costs may be very difficult to estimate. However, where the resource can be freely traded, its opportunity cost is simply equal to the market price. Consider a widely used aircraft such as the Boeing 737. Secondhand 737s are regularly traded, and their

---

[3] Accenture, "Refocusing on the After-Sales Market," 2010.

prices are quoted on the web. So, if an airline needs to know the opportunity cost of continuing to use one of its 737s, it just needs to look up the market price of a similar plane. The opportunity cost of using the plane is equal to the cost of buying an equivalent aircraft to replace it.

In addition to including all incremental cash flows, you also need to ignore those cash flows that are *not* incremental. Here are two examples.

1. Beware of Allocated Overhead Costs   We have already mentioned that the accountant's objective is not always the same as that of the financial manager. A case in point is the allocation of overhead costs. Overheads include such items as supervisory salaries, rent, heat, and light. These overheads may not be related to any particular project, but they have to be paid for somehow. Therefore, when the accountant assigns costs to the firm's projects, a charge for overhead is usually made.

Now our principle of incremental cash flows says that in investment appraisal we should include only the *extra* expenses that would result from the project. A project may generate extra overhead expenses; then again, it may not. If the company still pays the same supervisory salaries, rent, heat, and light as it did before, there is no incremental cash outflow.

2. Forget Sunk Costs

- A pharmaceutical company has spent $50 million on R&D into a new drug. It is now assessing whether to go ahead with clinical trials.

- A railroad is considering whether it should go ahead with the construction of a new high-speed line. It has already spent $50 million on engineering services.

- Development of new software has proved more costly than anticipated and management is considering scrapping the project.

Each of these expenditures is a sunk cost Like spilled milk, they are past and irreversible outflows. Because sunk costs are bygones, they cannot be affected by the decision to accept or reject the project, and they should be ignored.

Rule 3: Treat Inflation Consistently

As we pointed out in Chapter 3, interest rates are usually quoted in *nominal* rather than *real* terms. For example, if you buy an 8% Treasury bond, the government promises to pay you $80 interest each year, but it does not promise what that $80 will buy. Investors take inflation into account when they decide what is an acceptable rate of interest.

If the discount rate is stated in nominal terms, then consistency requires that cash flows should also be estimated in nominal terms, taking account of trends in selling price, the cost of labor and materials, and so on. This calls for more than simply applying a single assumed inflation rate to all components of cash flow. Remember that tax savings from depreciation do *not* increase with inflation; they are constant in nominal terms because tax law in most countries allows only the original cost of assets to be depreciated.

Of course, there is nothing wrong with discounting real cash flows at a real discount rate. Here is a simple example showing that real and nominal discounting, properly applied, always give the same present value.

Suppose your firm usually forecasts cash flows in nominal terms and discounts at a 15% nominal rate. In this particular case, however, you are given project cash flows in real terms, that is, current dollars:

Real Cash Flows ($000)			
C_0	C_1	C_2	C_3
−100	+35	+50	+30

It would be inconsistent to discount these real cash flows at the 15% nominal rate. You have two alternatives: Either restate the cash flows in nominal terms and discount at 15%, or restate the discount rate in real terms and use it to discount the real cash flows.

Assume that inflation is projected at 10% a year. Then for year 1 the real cash flow of $35,000, will be $35,000 \times 1.10 = \$38,500$ in year 1 dollars. Similarly, the cash flow for year 2 will be $50,000 \times (1.10)^2 = \$60,500$ in year 2 dollars, and so on. If we discount these nominal cash flows at the 15% nominal discount rate, we have

$$NPV = -100 + \frac{38.5}{1.15} + \frac{60.5}{(1.15)^2} + \frac{39.9}{(1.15)^3} = 5.5, \text{ or } \$5,500$$

Instead of converting the cash-flow forecasts into nominal terms, we could convert the discount rate into real terms by using the following relationship:

$$\text{Real discount rate} = \frac{1 + \text{ nominal discount rate}}{1 + \text{inflation rate}} - 1 \qquad \textbf{(6.1)}$$

In our example, this gives

$$\text{Real discount rate} = \frac{1.15}{1.10} - 1 = 0.045, \text{ or } 4.5\%$$

If we now discount the real cash flows by the real discount rate, we have an NPV of $5,500, just as before:

$$NPV = -100 + \frac{35}{1.045} + \frac{50}{(1.045)^2} + \frac{30}{(1.045)^3} = 5.5, \text{ or } \$5,500$$

The message of all this is quite simple. Discount nominal cash flows at a nominal discount rate. Discount real cash flows at a real rate. *Never* mix real cash flows with nominal discount rates or nominal flows with real rates.

Rule 4: Separate Investment and Financing Decisions

Suppose you finance a project partly with debt. How should you treat the proceeds from the debt issue and the interest and principal payments on the debt? Answer: You should *neither* subtract the debt proceeds from the required investment *nor* recognize the interest and principal payments on the debt as cash outflows. Regardless of the actual financing, you should view the project as if it were all-equity-financed, treating all cash outflows required for the project as coming from stockholders and all cash inflows as going to them.

This procedure focuses exclusively on the *project* cash flows, not the cash flows associated with alternative financing schemes. We explain how to recognize the effect of financing choices on project values in Chapter 18.

Rule 5: Forecast Cash Flows after Taxes

Taxes are an expense just like wages and raw materials. Therefore, cash flows should be estimated on an after-tax basis. You need to subtract tax payments from pretax cash flows and discount the net amount.

Some firms do not deduct tax payments. They try to offset this mistake by discounting the pretax cash flows at a rate that is higher than the cost of capital. Unfortunately, there is no reliable formula for making such adjustments to the discount rate.

Be careful to subtract *cash* taxes. Cash taxes paid are often different from the taxes reported on the income statement provided to shareholders. For example, shareholder accounts in the

United States typically assume straight-line depreciation instead of the accelerated depreciation allowed by the U.S. tax code. We will highlight the differences between straight-line and accelerated depreciation later in this chapter.

The next section takes a broader look at corporate income taxes.

6.4 Self-Test

A firm is considering investment in a new manufacturing plant. The site is owned by the company, but existing buildings would need to be demolished. Which of the following should be treated as incremental cash flows?

a. The market value of the site.

b. The market value of the existing buildings.

c. Demolition costs and site clearance.

d. The cost of a new access road put in last year.

e. Lost cash flows on an existing product that will be replaced by the new proposal.

f. Future depreciation of the new plant.

g. The reduction in the firm's tax bill resulting from depreciation of the new plant.

h. The initial investment in inventories of raw materials.

i. Money already spent on engineering design of the new plant.

6-2   Corporate Income Taxes

Companies pay tax on their income. Look at Table 6.1, which shows corporate income tax rates in 11 countries. These are the tax rates imposed by the national governments, but corporations may also need to pay tax to a regional government. For example, in Canada, the provincial governments levy an additional tax of between 11% and 16%. In the United States, states and some municipalities also impose an extra layer of corporate tax that averages around 4%. To complicate matters further, in many countries, the first part of income may be taxed at a lower rate, or special arrangements may apply to some types of business.

Country	Corporate Tax Rate (%)
Australia	30
Brazil	34
Canada	15
China	25
France	33
Germany	16
India	30
Ireland	13
Japan	23
United Kingdom	19
United States	21

❭**TABLE 6.1**   National corporate tax rates.

Source: PWC, Worldwide Tax Summaries: Corporate Taxes, 2018–2020, www.taxsummaries.pwc.com.

Tax rates change over time, sometimes dramatically. For example, in the United States when the U.S. Tax Cuts and Jobs Act was implemented in 2018, the corporate tax rate dropped almost overnight from 35% to 21%. By the time you read this, the U.S. tax rate may have changed again.

Depreciation Deductions

When firms calculate taxable income, they are not allowed to deduct capital expenditures, but they can deduct an allowance for depreciation. Most countries specify that this depreciation must be calculated on a straight-line basis. For example, if the firm spends $10,000 to buy equipment with a five-year useful life, it can deduct each year depreciation of 10,000/5 = $2,000. This reduces taxable profits by $2,000 each year. If the corporate tax rate is 30%, the company gains a tax saving, or depreciation tax shield, of $0.30 \times \$2,000 = \$600$.

In some countries, the tax authorities allow firms to use accelerated depreciation, which means that they can claim a higher depreciation in the early year's of an asset's life but correspondingly lower depreciation in the later years. From 1986 to 2017, U.S. companies could use a system of accelerated depreciation called the *modified accelerated cost recovery system* (MACRS). Since 2018 companies have been permitted by the Internal Revenue Service to take *bonus* depreciation that is sufficient to write off 100% of investment immediately—the ultimate in accelerated depreciation. With 100% bonus depreciation, U.S. firms can treat investments in plant and equipment as immediate expenses. This bonus depreciation is a temporary provision, however. It is scheduled to phase-out starting in 2023. By 2027, it will be gone. We will have to wait and see what depreciation schedules apply to subsequent investments—perhaps we will return to MACRS.

Not all investment expenditures qualify for bonus depreciation. Investment in real estate must be depreciated straight-line over periods of 15 years or more. Also, since 2021, R&D expenditures cannot be expensed but must be written off over five years.

Note that all large U.S. corporations keep two separate sets of books: one for shareholders and one for the IRS. Many companies use straight-line depreciation on the shareholder books and accelerated depreciation on the tax books. They prefer accelerated depreciation for the tax books because the depreciation tax shields come earlier and therefore have a higher present value. They favor straight-line depreciation on the shareholder books because it reduces depreciation charges in early years, thus making reported earnings higher in those years. While the IRS doesn't object to this, there are other countries, such as Germany, that require the tax books to be identical to the shareholder books.

Financial analysts need to be careful to remember which set of books they are looking at. In capital budgeting, only the tax books are relevant, but to an outside investor, only the shareholder books are available.

6.5 Self-Test

A company is considering the purchase of a new machine tool for $9 million. It is permitted, when calculating tax, to depreciate the purchase straight-line over years 1–6. Sales in year 1 are forecast at $4 million and operating costs at $1.5 million. If the tax rate is 30%, how much tax will the company pay in year 1?

Tax on Salvage Value

If a company is able to sell an asset at the end of a project, it must pay tax on the difference between the asset's salvage value and the *depreciated value* that is shown in the tax books. For example, suppose a company purchases a machine for $10,000. If the company can depreciate the expenditure over five years for tax purposes, the depreciated value will be zero at the end of that period. If it then sells the machine for $1,000, it must pay tax on the entire sale proceeds.

Tax Loss Carry-Forwards

When firms make profits, they pay a proportion of those profits to the tax authorities. But the process doesn't work in reverse; if the firm suffers a loss, the tax authorities do not send it a check for a proportion of the loss. However, the firm can generally carry the losses forward, and use them to offset future tax obligations.[4]

EXAMPLE 6.1 ● Tax loss carry-forwards in the United States

In the United States, losses can be carried forward indefinitely and used to offset up to 80% of future years' income. Suppose, for example, that a manufacturer of gargle blasters loses $100,000 in 2020 but earns $100,000 in 2021 and 2022. It pays no tax in 2020, but carries forward the loss. In 2021, it can use $80,000 of the loss (80% of $100,000) to offset income, and therefore pays tax that year of $4,200 (21% of $20,000). In 2022, it uses the remaining $20,000 carried forward, paying tax of $16,800 (21% of $80,000).

● ● ● ● ●

6-3   A Worked Example of a Project Analysis

We will soon walk through, step-by-step, an example of how to calculate a project's free cash flow in a world of taxes. But before we go into a specific example, here is a framework for calculating free cash flow in any situation.

The Three Components of Project Cash Flows

You can think of an investment project's cash flow as composed of three elements:

$$\text{Total cash flow} = \text{cash flow from capital investment}$$
$$+ \text{ operating cash flow} \tag{6.2}$$
$$+ \text{ cash flow from investment in working capital}$$

Cash Flow from Capital Investment

To get a project off the ground, a company typically makes an up-front investment in plant, equipment, research, start-up costs, and diverse other outlays. This expenditure is a negative cash flow—negative because cash goes out the door.

When the project comes to an end, the company can either sell the plant and equipment or redeploy it elsewhere in its business. This salvage value (net of any taxes if the plant and equipment is sold) is a positive cash flow. However, remember our earlier comment that final cash flows can be negative if there are significant shutdown costs.

Operating Cash Flow

Operating cash flow consists of the net increase in sales revenue brought about by the new project less outlays for production, marketing, and other incremental costs. Incremental taxes are likewise subtracted.

$$\text{Operating cash flow} = \text{revenues} - \text{expenses} - \text{taxes} \tag{6.3A}$$

---

[4]Some countries allow firms to carry back losses to offset against taxable profits in earlier years. Starting in 2018, carry-backs are no longer allowed in the United States.

Many investments do not produce any additional revenues; they are simply designed to reduce the costs of the company's existing operations. Such projects also contribute to the firm's operating cash flow. The after-tax cost saving is a positive addition to the cash flow.

Don't forget that the depreciation charge is not a cash flow. It affects the tax that the company pays, but the company does not send anyone a check for depreciation, and it should not be deducted when calculating operating cash flow.

Equation (6.3A) is the most direct way to calculate operating cash flow. It uses only the items from the income statement that represent actual cash flows. But two other methods are often useful and produce the same result. One adds depreciation back to accounting profits. This gives

$$\text{Operating cash flow} = \text{after-tax profit} + \text{depreciation} \qquad \textbf{(6.3B)}$$

The third method focuses on the depreciation tax shield—that is, the reduction in taxes attributable to depreciation. The tax shield equals the product of the tax rate and the depreciation charge:

$$\text{Depreciation tax shield} = \text{tax rate} \times \text{depreciation}$$

We can then calculate operating cash flow by starting with after-tax profit assuming no depreciation and then adding in the tax shield:

$$\text{Operating cash flow} = (\text{revenues} - \text{expenses}) \times (1 - \text{tax rate}) + (\text{tax rate} \times \text{depreciation}) \qquad \textbf{(6.3C)}$$

Investment in Working Capital

When a company builds up inventories of raw materials or finished products, this investment in inventories requires cash. Cash is also absorbed when customers are slow to pay their bills; in this case, the firm makes an investment in accounts receivable. On the other hand, cash is preserved when the firm delays paying its bills.

Investment in net working capital, just like investment in plant and equipment, represents a negative cash flow. Later in the project's life, as inventories are sold and accounts receivable are collected, working capital is reduced and the firm enjoys a positive cash flow.

How to Construct a Set of Cash Flow Forecasts: An Example

We will now work through a realistic example showing how to construct a set of cash flow forecasts.

As the newly appointed financial manager of International Mulch and Compost Company (IM&C), you are about to analyze a proposal for marketing guano as a garden fertilizer. You are given the forecasts shown in Table 6.2. The project requires an investment of $12 million in plant and machinery (line 1). In year 7, this machinery can be dismantled and sold for estimated net proceeds of $1,949 (line 1 column 7). This is the forecast salvage value. The figures in row 2 for accumulated depreciation assume that the machinery will be fully depreciated over six years using straight-line depreciation of $2,000 a year.[5]

Lines 5 through 10 in Table 6.2 show a simplified income statement for the guano project.[6] This will be our starting point for estimating cash flow. All the entries in the table are nominal amounts. In other words, IM&C's managers have taken into account the likely effect of inflation on revenues and costs.

---

[5]We have assumed that IM&C depreciates the investment to zero. In their financial statements, companies commonly depreciate investment to an estimated salvage value. However, when calculating the company's tax liability, the IRS always assumes a salvage value of zero.

[6]We have departed from the usual income-statement format by separating out depreciation.

					Year			
		0	1	2	3	4	5	6	7
1	Capital investment	12,000							−1,949[a]
2	Accumulated depreciation		2,000	4,000	6,000	8,000	10,000	12,000	0
3	Year-end book value	12,000	10,000	8,000	6,000	4,000	2,000	0	0
4	Working capital		550	1,289	3,261	4,890	3,583	2,002	0
5	Revenues		523	12,887	32,610	48,901	35,834	19,717	
6	Expenses	4,000	3,037	8,939	20,883	30,809	23,103	13,602	
7	Depreciation[a]		2,000	2,000	2,000	2,000	2,000	2,000	0
8	Pretax profit (5 − 6 − 7 − 1)	−4,000	−4,514	1,948	9,727	16,092	10,731	4,115	1,949[a]
9	Tax at 21%		−840[c]	−948	409	2,043	3,379	2,254	864	409
10	Profit after tax (8 − 9)	−3,160	−3,566	1,539	7,684	12,713	8,477	3,251	1,540

❭TABLE 6.2   Initial forecast data for guano project.

[a] In the income statement, the initial investment of $12 million is depreciated straight-line over the six years.
[b] Gain on sale of assets. The asset has been entirely depreciated for tax purposes and the entire sales price is, therefore, subject to tax.
[c] A negative tax payment means a cash inflow, assuming that IM&C can use the tax loss on the guano project to shield income from the rest of its operations.

Table 6.3 derives the expected cash flows from the accounting data in Table 6.2

BEYOND THE PAGE

Try It!
The guano
spreadsheets

mhhe.com/brealey14e

Capital Investment

Rows 1 through 4 of Table 6.3 show the cash flows from the investment in fixed assets. The project requires an investment of $12 million in plant and machinery. IM&C expects to sell the equipment in year 7 for $1.949 million. Any difference between this figure and the book value of the equipment is a taxable gain. By that point, IM&C has fully depreciated the equipment, so the company will be taxed on a capital gain of $1.949 million. If the tax rate is 21%, the company will pay tax of 0.21 × 1.949 = $0.409 million, and the net cash flow from the sale of equipment will be 1.949 − 0.409 = $1.540 million. This is shown in rows 2 and 3 of the table.

Operating Cash Flow

Panel B of Table 6.3 shows the calculation of the operating cash flow from the guano project. Operating cash flow consists of revenues from the sale of guano less the expenses of production and any taxes.

Table 6.3 assumes initially that for tax purposes the company also uses straight-line depreciation. In other words, when it calculates each year's taxable income, it deducts one-sixth of the initial investment, or $2 million. For example, in year 2

Pretax profit = revenues − costs − depreciation = 12.887 − 8.939 − 2.000 = $1.948 million
Tax = 0.21 × pretax profit = 0.21 × 1.948 = $0.409 million

Notice that, when calculating operating cash flow, we ignored the possibility that the project may be partly financed by debt. Following our earlier Rule 4, we did not deduct any debt proceeds from the original investment, and we did not deduct interest payments from the cash inflows. Standard practice forecasts cash flows as if the project is all-equity financed. Any additional value resulting from financing decisions is considered separately.

	Year:	0	1	2	3	4	5	6	7
Panel A Capital Investment									
1 Cash flow from investment in fixed assets		−12,000							
2 Sale of fixed assets									1,949
3 Less tax on sale									409[a]
4 Cash flow from capital investment (1 + 2 − 3)		−12,000							1,540
Panel B Operating Cash Flow									
5 Revenues			523	12,887	32,610	48,901	35,834	19,717	
6 Expenses		4,000	3,037	8,939	20,883	30,809	23,103	13,602	
7 Depreciation[b]			2,000	2,000	2,000	2,000	2,000	2,000	
8 Pretax profit (5 − 6 − 7)		−4,000	−4,514	1,948	9,727	16,092	10,731	4,115	
9 Tax (0.21 × 8)		−840[c]	−948	409	2,043	3,379	2,254	864	
10 Profit after tax (8 − 9)		−3,160	−3,566	1,539	7,684	12,713	8,477	3,251	
11 Operating cash flow (5 − 6 − 9)		−3,160	−1,566	3,539	9,684	14,713	10,477	5,251	
Panel C Investment in Working Capital									
12 Working capital			550	1,289	3,261	4,890	3,583	2,002	0
13 Change in working capital			550	739	1,972	1,629	−1,307	−1,581	−2,002
14 Cash flow from investment in working capital (−14)			−550	−739	−1,972	−1,629	1,307	1,581	2,002
Panel D Project Valuation									
15 Total project cash flow (4 + 11 + 14)		−15,160	−2,116	2,800	7,712	13,084	11,784	6,832	3,542
16 Discount factor at 20%		1.0	0.833	0.694	0.579	0.482	0.402	0.335	0.279
17 Discounted cash flows (15 × 16)		−15,160	−1,763	1,944	4,463	6,310	4,736	2,288	988
18 NPV		+3,806							

❯TABLE 6.3 Calculating the cash flows and net present value of IM&C's guano project assuming straight-line depreciation ($ thousands).

[a] The asset has been entirely depreciated for tax purposes and the entire sales price is subject to tax.
[b] Depreciation for tax purposes is calculated straight line on the initial investment of $12 million.
[c] A negative tax payment means a cash inflow, assuming that IM&C can use the tax loss on the guano project to shield income from the rest of its business.

6.6 Self-Test

The calculation of operating cash flow followed our Eq. (6.3A). Equations (6.3B) and (6.3C) gave two other ways to calculate operating cash flow. Check that these methods give the same figure for year 2 operating cash flow.

Investment in Working Capital

You can see from Table 6.3 that working capital increases in the early and middle years of the project. Why is this? There are several possible reasons:

1. Sales recorded on the income statement overstate actual cash receipts from guano shipments because sales are increasing and customers are slow to pay their bills. Therefore, accounts receivable increase.

2. It takes several months for processed guano to age properly. Thus, as projected sales increase, larger inventories have to be held in the aging sheds.

3. An offsetting effect occurs if payments for materials and services used in guano production are delayed. In this case accounts payable will increase.

Thus, the additional investment in working capital can be calculated as:

$$
\begin{array}{ccc}
\text{Additional} & & \text{increase in} & \text{increase in} \\
\text{investment in} & = \text{increase in} + \text{accounts} & - \text{accounts} \\
\text{working capital} & \text{inventory} & \text{receivable} & \text{payable}
\end{array}
$$

Project Valuation   Rows 15 to 18 of Table 6.3 show the calculation of project NPV. Row 15 shows the total cash flow from IM&C's project as the sum of the cash flow from the capital investment, the operating cash flow, and the cash flow from investment in working capital. IM&C estimates the opportunity cost of capital for projects of this type as 20%.

Remember that to calculate the present value of a cash flow in year t, you can either divide the cash flow by $(1 + r)^t$, or you can multiply by a discount factor that is equal to $1/(1 + r)^t$. Row 16 shows the discount factors for a 20% discount rate, and row 17 multiplies the discount factor by the cash flow to give each flow's present value. When all the cash flows are discounted and added up, the project is seen to offer a net present value of $3.806 million.

Accelerated Depreciation and First-Year Expensing

Depreciation is a noncash expense; it is important only because it reduces taxable income. It provides an annual *tax shield* equal to the product of depreciation and the marginal tax rate. In the case of IM&C:

Annual tax shield = depreciation × tax rate = 2,000 × 0.21 = 420.0, or $420,000

At a 20% discount rate, the present value of these tax shields ($420,000 for six years) is $1,397,000.

In Table 6.3, we assumed that IM&C was required to use straight-line depreciation, which allowed it to write off a fixed proportion of the initial investment each year. Although this is the most common method of depreciation, some countries permit firms to depreciate their investments more rapidly. For example, since 2018 companies in the United States have been permitted to write off the entire amount of their investment in plant and machinery immediately. Table 6.4 recalculates the NPV of the guano project, assuming that the full $12 million investment can be depreciated immediately.

When we assumed that the guano project could be depreciated straight-line over six years, NPV was $3.806 million. When we calculated NPV assuming the full first-year expensing introduced in the 2017 tax reform NPV increased to $4.929 million.

BEYOND THE PAGE

MACRS depreciation system

mhhe.com/brealey14e

| 6.7 Self-Test |

Accelerated depreciation results in a larger depreciation deduction in the early years of the project. So how is it that project NPV increases?

Project Analysis

Let us review. Earlier in this section, you embarked on an analysis of IM&C's guano project. You drew up a series of cash-flow forecasts assuming straight-line depreciation. Then you remembered that under the Tax Cuts and Jobs Act, IM&C could write off the capital expenditure in the year that it was incurred.

		Period							
		0	1	2	3	4	5	6	7
	Panel A Capital Investment								
1	Investment in fixed assets	−12,000							
2	Sale of fixed assets								1,949
3	Less tax on sale								409
4	Cash flow from capital investment (2 + 3 + 1)	−12,000							1,540
	Panel B Operating Cash Flow								
5	Revenues	0	523	12,887	32,610	48,901	35,834	19,717	
6	Cost of goods sold	4,000	3,037	8,939	20,883	30,809	23,103	13,602	
7	Depreciation	12,000	0	0	0	0	0	0	
8	Pretax profit (5 − 6 − 7 − 8)	−16,000	−2,514	3,948	11,727	18,092	12,731	6,115	
9	Tax (0.21 × 9)	−3,360	−528	829	2,463	3,799	2,674	1,284	
10	Profit after tax (9 − 10)	−12,640	−1,986	3,119	9,264	14,293	10,057	4,831	
11	Operating cash flow (8 + 11)	−640	−1,986	3,119	9,264	14,293	10,057	4,831	
	Panel C Investment in Working Capital								
12	Working capital		550	1,289	3,261	4,890	3,583	2,002	0
13	Change in working capital		550	739	1,972	1,629	−1,307	−1,581	−2,002
14	Cash flow from investment in working capital (−13)		−550	−739	−1,972	−1,629	1,307	1,581	2,002
	Panel D Project Valuation								
15	Total project cash flow (4 + 11 + 14)	−12,640	−2,536	2,380	7,292	12,664	11,364	6,412	3,542
16	Discount factor	1.000	0.833	0.694	0.579	0.482	0.402	0.335	0.279
17	Discounted cash flows (16 × 17)	−12,640	−2,113	1,653	4,220	6,107	4,567	2,147	988
18	NPV	4,929							

❯ **TABLE 6.4**   IM&C's guano project. Revised analysis with immediate expensing of investment expenditures.

You were lucky to get away with just two NPV calculations. In real situations, it often takes several tries to purge all inconsistencies and mistakes. Then you may want to analyze some alternatives. For example, should you go for a larger or smaller project? Would it be better to market the fertilizer through wholesalers or directly to the consumer? Should you build 90,000-square-foot aging sheds for the guano in northern South Dakota rather than the planned 100,000-square-foot sheds in southern North Dakota? In each case, your choice should be the one offering the highest NPV.

You will also want to ask some "what if" questions. How would NPV be affected if inflation rages out of control? What if technical problems delay start-up? What if gardeners prefer chemical fertilizers to your natural product? Managers employ a variety of techniques to develop a better understanding of how such unpleasant surprises could damage NPV. We will practice using these techniques in Chapter 10. You will find that project analysis is much more than one or two NPV calculations.[7]

6-4   How to Choose between Competing Projects

Almost all real-world investment decisions entail either-or choices. Such choices are said to be *mutually exclusive*. We came across an example of mutually exclusive investments in Chapter 2, where we looked at whether it was better to build an office block for immediate sale or to rent it out and sell it at the end of two years. To decide between these alternatives, we calculated the NPV of each and chose the one with the higher NPV.

That is the correct procedure as long as the choice between the two projects does not affect any future decisions that you might wish to make. But sometimes the choices that you make today *will* have an impact on future opportunities. When that is so, choosing between competing projects is trickier. Here are four important, and often challenging, problems:

· *The investment timing problem.* Should you invest now or wait and think about it again next year? (Here, today's investment is competing with possible future investments.)

· *The choice between long- and short-lived equipment.* Should the company save money today by choosing cheaper machinery that will not last as long? (Here, today's decision would accelerate a later investment in machine replacement.)

· *The replacement problem.* When should existing machinery be replaced? (Using it another year would delay investment in more modern equipment.)

· *The cost of excess capacity.* What is the cost of using equipment that is temporarily not being used? (Increasing use of the equipment may bring forward the date at which additional capacity is required.)

We will look at each of these problems in turn.

Problem 1: The Investment Timing Decision

The fact that a project has a positive NPV does not mean that it is best undertaken now. It might be even more valuable if undertaken in the future. The question of optimal timing is not difficult when the cash flows are certain. In this case, you must first examine alternative start dates for the investment and calculate the net *future* value at each of these dates. Then, to find which of the alternatives would add most to the firm's *current* value, you need to discount these net future values back to the present:

$$\text{Net present value of investment if undertaken at date } t = \frac{\text{net future value at date } t}{(1 + r)^t}$$

For example, suppose you own a large tract of inaccessible timber. To harvest it, you need to invest a substantial amount in access roads and other facilities. The longer you wait, the higher the investment required. On the other hand, lumber prices may rise as you wait, and the trees will keep growing, although at a gradually decreasing rate.

---

[7]In the meantime, you might like to get ahead of the game by viewing the spreadsheets for the guano project and seeing how NPV would change with a shortfall in sales or an unexpected rise in costs.

Let us suppose that the net present value of the harvest at different *future* dates is as follows:

	Year of Harvest					
	0	1	2	3	4	5
Net future value ($ thousands)	50	64.4	77.5	89.4	100	109.4
Change in value from previous year (%)		+28.8	+20.3	+15.4	+11.9	+9.4

The choices are mutually exclusive since you can only harvest the timber once. As you can see, the longer you defer cutting the timber, the more money you will make. However, your concern is with the date that maximizes the net *present* value of your investment, that is, its contribution to the value of your firm *today.* You therefore need to discount the net future value of the harvest back to the present. Suppose the appropriate discount rate is 10%. Then, if you harvest the timber in year 1, it has a net *present* value of $58,500:

$$\text{NPV if harvested in year } 1 = \frac{64.4}{1.10} = 58.5, \text{ or } \$58,500$$

The net present value for other harvest dates is as follows:

	Year of Harvest					
	0	1	2	3	4	5
Net present value ($ thousands)	50	58.5	64.0	67.2	68.3	67.9

The optimal point to harvest the timber is year 4 because this is the point that maximizes NPV.

Notice that before year 4, the net future value of the timber increases by more than 10% a year: The gain in value is greater than the cost of the capital tied up in the project. After year 4, the gain in value is still positive but less than the required return. So delaying the harvest further just reduces shareholder wealth.[8]

The investment timing problem is much more complicated when you are unsure about future cash flows. We return to the problem of investment timing under uncertainty in Chapters 10 and 23.

BEYOND THE PAGE

Investment timing decisions

mhhe.com/brealey14e

EXAMPLE 6.2 • When to buy a new computer

Obsolete Technologies is wondering whether to invest in a new computer, but the CFO points out that computer costs are falling and it might be better to delay purchase. The following table sets out the basic data:

---

[8]Our timber-cutting example conveys the right idea about investment timing, but it misses an important practical point: The sooner you cut the first crop of trees, the sooner the second crop can start growing. Thus, the value of the second crop depends on when you cut the first. This more complex and realistic problem can be solved in one of two ways: 1. Find the cutting dates that maximize the present value of a series of harvests, taking into account the different growth rates of young and old trees. 2. Repeat our calculations, counting the future market value of cut-over land as part of the payoff to the first harvest. The value of cut-over land includes the present value of all subsequent harvests. The second solution is far simpler if you can figure out what cut-over land will be worth.

Dollar Values ($ thousands)				
Year of Purchase	Computer Cost	PV Savings	NPV at Year of Purchase	NPV Today ($r = 10\%$)
0	$50	$70	$20	$20
1	45	$70	25	22.7
2	40	$70	30	24.8
3	36	$70	34	25.5 < optimal purchase date
4	33	$70	37	25.3
5	21	$70	39	24.2

Notice that the cost of the computer continues to fall and the gain from purchase continues to increase. However, the decision should depend on the *present value* of those future gains. This is shown in the final column assuming a 10% cost of capital. The NPV of the gain is maximized if the purchase is made in year 3.

Problem 2: The Choice between Long- and Short-Lived Equipment

An advertising agency needs to choose between two digital presses. Let's call them machines A and B. The two machines are designed differently but have identical capacity and do exactly the same job. Machine A costs $15,000 and will last three years. It costs $5,000 per year to run. Machine B is an "economy" model, costing only $10,000, but it will last only two years and costs $6,000 per year to run.

The only way to choose between these two machines is on the basis of cost. The present value of each machine's cost is as follows:

Costs ($ thousands)					
Year:	0	1	2	3	PV at 6% ($ thousands)
Machine A	15	5	5	5	$28.37
Machine B	10	6	6	—	21.00

Should the agency take machine B, the one with the lower present value of costs? Not necessarily. All we have shown is that machine B offers two years of service for a lower total cost than three years of service from machine A. But is the *annual* cost of using B lower than that of A?

Suppose that the financial manager agrees to buy machine A and pay for its operating costs out of her budget. She then charges the user a rental fee for use of the machine. The financial manager has to make sure that the present value of the rental payments equals the present value of the costs of each machine.

In the case of machine A, we need to calculate the three annual rental payments that have a present value of $28,370? Notice that these payments constitute an annuity, so we can calculate their amount using the annuity formula that we introduced in Section 2.2:

$$\text{PV of } t\text{–year annuity} = C\left[\frac{1}{r} - \frac{1}{r(1+r)^t}\right] = C \times \left[t\text{-year annuity factor}\right]$$

BEYOND THE PAGE

Equivalent annual costs

mhhe.com/brealey14e

At a 6% cost of capital, the three-year annuity factor is 2.673. So the annual rental payment (*C*) is 28,370/2.673 = $10,612. In other words, the present value of the cost of buying and operating machine A over its three-year life is the same as the present value of an annual rental charge of $10,612 a year for three years. This figure is called the *equivalent annual cost* of A.

Costs ($ thousands)					
Year:	0	1	2	3	PV at 6% ($ thousands)
Machine A	15	5	5	5	28.37
Equivalent annual cost		10.61	10.61	10.61	28.37

A similar calculation for machine B gives an equivalent annual cost of $11,454:

Costs ($ thousands)				
Year:	0	1	2	PV at 6% ($ thousands)
Machine B	10	6	6	21.00
Equivalent annual cost		11.45	11.45	21.00

Machine A is better because its equivalent annual cost is less ($10,612 versus $11,454 for machine B).

6.8 Self-Test

Now assume a third machine, C, which costs $15,000, lasts eight years, and costs $5,000 a year to run. What is its equivalent annual cost? Which machine would you now choose?

Equivalent Annual Cost, Inflation, and Technological Change   When we calculated the equivalent annual costs of machines A and B, we implicitly assumed that inflation is zero. But, in practice, the cost of buying and operating the machines is likely to rise with inflation. If so, the *nominal* costs of operating the machines will rise, while the *real* costs will be constant. Therefore, when you compare the equivalent annual costs of two machines, we strongly recommend doing the calculations in real terms. Do *not* calculate equivalent annual cash flows as level *nominal* annuities. This procedure can give incorrect rankings of true equivalent annual flows at high inflation rates. See Challenge Problem 38 at the end of this chapter for an example.[9]

There will also be circumstances in which even the real costs of buying and operating the two machines are not expected to be constant. For example, suppose that thanks to technological improvements, new machines cost 20% less each year in *real* terms to buy and operate. In this case, future owners of brand-new, lower-cost machines will be able to cut their (real) rental cost by 20%, and owners of old machines will be forced to match this reduction. Thus, we now need to ask: If the real level of rents declines by 20% a year, how much will it cost to rent each machine?

---

[9]If you actually rent out the machine to the plant manager, or anyone else, be careful to specify that the rental payments be "indexed" to inflation. If inflation runs on at 5% per year and rental payments do not increase proportionally, then the real value of the rental payments must decline and will not cover the full cost of buying and operating the machine.

If the real rent for year 1 is rent$_1$, then the real rent for year 2 is rent$_2 = 0.8 \times$ rent$_1$. Rent$_3$ is $0.8 \times$ rent$_2$, or $0.64 \times$ rent$_1$. The owner of each machine must set the real rents sufficiently high to recover the present value of the costs. If the real cost of capital is 6%:

$$\text{PV of renting machine A} = \frac{\text{rent}_1}{1.06} + \frac{\text{rent}_2}{1.06^2} + \frac{\text{rent}_3}{1.06^3} = 28.37$$

$$= \frac{\text{rent}_1}{1.06} + \frac{0.8(\text{rent}_1)}{1.06^2} + \frac{0.64(\text{rent}_1)}{1.06^3} = 28.37$$

rent$_1$ = 12.94, or $12,940

For machine B:

$$\text{PV of renting machine B} = \frac{\text{rent}_1}{1.06} + \frac{0.8(\text{rent}_1)}{1.06^2} = 21.00$$

rent$_1$ = 12.69, or $12,690

The merits of the two machines are now reversed. Once we recognize that technology is expected to reduce the real costs of new machines, then it pays to buy the shorter-lived machine B rather than become locked into an aging technology with machine A in year 3.

You can imagine other complications. Perhaps machine D will arrive in year 1 with an even lower equivalent annual cost. You would then need to consider scrapping or selling machine B at year 1 (more on this decision follows). The financial manager could not choose between machines A and B in year 0 without taking a detailed look at what each machine could be replaced with.

Comparing equivalent annual costs should never be a mechanical exercise; always think about the assumptions that are implicit in the comparison. Finally, remember why equivalent annual cash flows are necessary in the first place. It is because A and B will be replaced at different future dates. The choice between them therefore affects future investment decisions. If subsequent decisions are not affected by the initial choice (for example, because neither machine will be replaced), then we do not need to take future decisions into account.[10]

Equivalent Annual Costs and Taxes   We have not mentioned taxes. But you surely realized that machine A and B's lifetime costs should be calculated after-tax, recognizing that operating costs are tax-deductible and that capital investment generates depreciation tax shields.

EXAMPLE 6.3 • Comparing the costs of LED and incandescent bulbs

An 8.5-W LED light bulb costs about $5 compared with about $1 for an equivalent incandescent bulb. However the LED may last about 10 years compared with no more than two years for an incandescent, and the cost of electricity of using an LED is about $1.25 a year, compared with $9 for an incandescent bulb. If the interest rate is 5%, what is the gain from switching to an LED?

---

[10]However, if neither machine will be replaced, then we have to consider the extra revenue generated by machine A in its third year, when it will be operating but B will not.

Since the bulbs have different lives, we need to calculate their equivalent annual cost. The annual cost of each bulb is

Annual cost of LED = ($5 ÷ 10-year annuity factor) + $1.25 = $0.65 + $1.25 = $1.90

Annual cost of incandescent = ($1 ÷ 2-year annuity factor) + $9 = $0.54 + $9 = $9.54

The cost of the LED is $7.64 a year less than that of the incandescent.

• • • • •

Problem 3: When to Replace an Old Machine

Our earlier comparison of machines A and B took the life of each machine as fixed. In practice, the point at which equipment is replaced reflects economics, not physical collapse. Usually, *we* must decide when to replace. The machine will rarely decide for us.

Here is an example. You are operating an elderly machine that is expected to produce a net cash *inflow* of $4,000 in the coming year and $4,000 next year. After that it will stop functioning. You can replace it now with a new machine, which costs $15,000 but is much more efficient and will provide a cash inflow of $8,000 a year for three years. You want to know whether you should replace your equipment now or wait a year.

We can calculate the NPV of the new machine and also its *equivalent annual cash flow*—that is, the three-year annuity that has the same net present value:

	Cash Flows ($ thousands)				
	C_0	C_1	C_2	C_3	NPV at 6% ($ thousands)
New machine	−15	+8	+8	+8	6.38
Equivalent annual cash flow		+2.387	+2.387	+2.387	6.38

In other words, the cash flows of the new machine are equivalent to an annuity of $2,387 per year. So we can equally well ask at what point we would want to replace our old machine with a new one producing $2,387 a year. When the question is put this way, the answer is obvious. As long as your old machine can generate a cash flow of $4,000 a year, you won't want to replace it with one that generates only $2,387 a year. If you postpone replacement for a year, you gain 4,000 − 2,387 = $1,613.

Remember that the logic of such comparisons requires that the new machine be the best of the available alternatives and that, in turn, it be replaced at the optimal point.

EXAMPLE 6.4 • Replacement problems and salvage value

Suppose that the old machine can be sold currently for $8,000 but that next year its sale value will be only $7,000. Should that persuade you to replace now?

If you keep the machine for another year, you gain $7,000. However, you lose today's salvage value plus a year's return on your money. That is $8,000 × 1.06 = $8,480. So if you postpone replacement, you lose $8,480 − $7,000 = $1,480 from the delay in salvage value, which only partly offsets the $1,613 gain in operating costs.

• • • • •

Problem 4: Cost of Excess Capacity

Any firm with a centralized information system (computer servers, storage, software, and telecommunication links) encounters many proposals for using it. Recently installed systems tend to have excess capacity, and since the marginal costs of using them seem to be negligible, management often encourages new uses. Sooner or later, however, the load on a system increases to the point at which management must either terminate the uses it originally encouraged or invest in another system several years earlier than it had planned. Such problems can be avoided if a proper charge is made for the use of spare capacity.

Suppose we have a new investment project that requires heavy use of an existing information system. The effect of adopting the project is to bring the purchase date of a new, more capable system forward from year 4 to year 3. This new system has a life of five years, and at a discount rate of 6%, the present value of the cost of buying and operating it is $500,000.

We begin by converting the $500,000 present value of the cost of the new system to an equivalent annual cost of $118,700 for each of five years.[11] Of course, when the new system in turn wears out, we will replace it with another. So we face the prospect of future information-system expenses of $118,700 a year. If we undertake the new project, the series of expenses begins in year 4; if we do not undertake it, the series begins in year 5. The new project, therefore, results in an *additional* cost of $118,700 in year 4. This has a present value of $118,700/(1.06)^4$, or about $94,000. This cost is properly charged against the new project.

When we recognize it, the NPV of the project may prove to be negative. If so, we still need to check whether it is worthwhile undertaking the project now and abandoning it later, when the excess capacity of the present system disappears.

---

[11]The present value of $118,700 a year for five years discounted at 6% is $500,000.

- **Project Cash Flows** When estimating project cash flows, you need to forecast each of the three components:

$$\text{Free cash flow} = \text{cash flow from capital investment}$$
$$+ \text{ operating cash flow}$$
$$+ \text{ cash flow from changes in working capital}$$

- **Forecasting a project's cash flows** Here is a checklist of things to remember when forecasting cash flows:

1. Discount cash flows, not profits.
   a. Remember that depreciation is not a cash flow (though it affects tax payments).
   b. Remember to track investment in working capital. As sales increase, firms need to make additional investments in working capital (a cash outflow), and as the project comes to an end, they recover those investments (a cash inflow).
2. Estimate the project's *incremental* cash flows—that is, the difference between the cash flows with the project and those without the project. For example, you should include all indirect effects of the project, such as its impact on the sales of the firm's other products, and you should include *opportunity costs,* such as the value of land that you would otherwise sell. Non-incremental cash flows, such as sunk costs, should *not* be included.

3. Treat inflation consistently.

   a. If cash flows are forecast in nominal terms, use a nominal discount rate.

   b. Discount real cash flows at a real rate.

4. Forecast cash flows as if the project is all-equity-financed. Thus, project cash flows should exclude debt interest or the cost of repaying any loans. This enables you to separate the investment from the financing decision.

5. Calculate cash flows after taxes. Although depreciation is not a cash flow, it does affect the taxes that the company pays. In most countries firms are allowed to deduct each year a constant proportion of the asset's cost. Other countries allow some form of accelerated depreciation. In the United States, firms can deduct the entire cost of the asset immediately (though this provision is due to phase out starting in 2023).

6. How to choose between competing projects To decide between alternative projects, you generally need to choose the one with the highest NPV, but sometimes the choices that you make will affect subsequent decisions. We looked at four common cases:

   1. The investment timing problem. (Should you accept the project now or defer for a year?)

   2. The choice between equipment with different lives. (Should you buy an expensive but durable machine or a cheaper but less long-lasting one?)

   3. The decision whether to replace equipment. (Should you replace an aging machine now or wait until next year?)

   4. The cost of using excess capacity. (What is the cost of allowing others in the company to use excess capacity?)

   When faced with such choices, it is often useful to compare the **equivalent annual cash flows** from the two projects.

- - - - -

FURTHER READING

For a valuable summary of tax rules in different countries, see

PWC, *Worldwide Tax Summaries, Corporate Taxes 2018–2020,* www.taxsummaries.pwc.com.

- - - - -

PROBLEM SETS

 **Select problems are available in McGraw-Hill's *Connect.*** **Please see the preface for more information.**

1. **Cash flows (S6.1)** Reliable Electric, a major Ruritanian producer of electrical products, is considering a proposal to manufacture a new type of industrial electric motor that would replace most of its existing product line. A research breakthrough has given Reliable a two-year lead on its competitors. The project proposal is summarized in Table 6.5.

   a. Read the notes to the table carefully. Which entries make sense? Which do not? Why or why not?

   b. What additional information would you need to construct a version of Table 6.5 that makes sense?

   Construct such a table and recalculate NPV. Make additional assumptions as necessary.

	2021	2022	2023	2024–2031
1. Capital expenditure	−10,400			
2. Research and development	−2,000			
3. Working capital	4,000			
4. Revenue		8,000	16,000	40,000
5. Operating costs		−4,000	−8,000	−20,000
6. Overhead		−800	−1,600	−4,000
7. Depreciation		−1,040	−1,040	−1,040
8. Interest		−2,160	−2,160	−2,160
9. Income	−2,000	0	3,200	12,800
10. Tax @ 30%	0	0	360	3,840
11. Net cash flow	−16,400	0	2,840	8,960
12. Net present value =	+16,149			

〉TABLE 6.5 Cash flows and present value of Reliable Electric's proposed investment ($ thousands). See Problem 1.

Notes:
1. *Capital expenditure:* $8 million for new machinery and $2.4 million for a warehouse extension. The full cost of the extension has been charged to this project, although only about half of the space is currently needed. Since the new machinery will be housed in an existing factory building, no charge has been made for land and building.
2. *Research and development:* $1.82 million spent in 2020. This figure was corrected for 10% inflation from the time of expenditure to date. Thus, 1.82 × 1.1 = $2 million.
3. *Working capital:* Initial investment in inventories.
4. *Revenue:* These figures assume sales of 2,000 motors in 2022, 4,000 in 2023, and 10,000 per year from 2024 through 2031. The initial unit price of $4,000 is forecasted to remain constant in real terms.
5. *Operating costs:* These include all direct and indirect costs. Indirect costs (heat, light, power, fringe benefits, etc.) are assumed to be 200% of direct labor costs. Operating costs per unit are forecasted to remain constant in real terms at $2,000.
6. *Overhead:* Marketing and administrative costs, assumed equal to 10% of revenue.
7. *Depreciation:* Straight-line for 10 years.
8. *Interest:* Charged on capital expenditure and working capital at Reliable's current borrowing rate of 15%.
9. *Income:* Revenue less the sum of research and development, operating costs, overhead, depreciation, and interest.
10. *Tax:* 30% of income. However, income is negative in 2021. This loss is carried forward and deducted from taxable income in 2023.
11. *Net cash flow:* Assumed equal to income less tax.
12. *Net present value:* NPV of net cash flow at a 15% discount rate.

2. **Cash flows (S6.1)** True or false?

   a. Project cash flows should take account of interest paid on any borrowing undertaken to finance the project.

   b. Accelerated depreciation reduces near-term project cash flows and therefore reduces project NPV.

   c. The depreciation tax shields of a project depend on the rate of inflation.

3. **Cash flows (S6.1)** In 1898, Simon North announced plans to construct a funeral home on land he owned and rented out as a storage area for railway carts. (A local newspaper commended Mr. North for not putting the cart before the hearse.) Rental income from the site barely covered real estate taxes, but the site was valued at $45,000. However, Mr. North had refused several offers for the land and planned to continue renting it out if, for some reason, the funeral home was not built. Therefore, he did not include the value of the land as an outlay in his NPV analysis of the funeral home. Was this the correct procedure? Explain.

4. **Cash flows (S6.1)** Andronicus Corporation has the following jumbled information about an investment proposal:

   a. Revenues in each of years 1–3 = $20,000

   b. Year 0 initial investment = $40,000

   c. Inventory level = $10,000 in year 1, $10,500 in year 2, and $5,000 in year 3

   d. Production costs = $7,000 in each of years 1–3

   e. Salvage value = $12,000 in year 4

   f. Depreciation = 100% immediate bonus depreciation

   g. Tax rate = 21%

   h. Customers pay with a 6-month lag

   Draw up a set of cash flow forecasts as in Table 6.4. If the cost of capital is 8%, what is the project's NPV? Assume that, if the project generates losses, those losses can be used to offset profits elsewhere in the business.

5. **Operating cash flow (S6.1)** A company is considering the purchase of a universal grinding machine. The following table sets out a forecast of the annual accounting profit:

Revenues	$400,000
Costs[a]	280,000
Pretax profit	120,000
Tax at 25%	30,000
After-tax profit	$ 90,000

[a] *Note:* costs include depreciation of $80,000.

Calculate the operating cash flow using the three methods set out in Eqs. (6.3A), (6.3B), and (6.3C).

6. **Real and nominal flows (S6.1)** Mr. Art Deco will be paid $100,000 one year hence. This is a nominal flow, which he discounts at an 8% nominal discount rate:

   $$PV = 100,000/1.08 = \$92,593$$

   The inflation rate is 4%.

   Calculate the PV of Mr. Deco's payment using the equivalent real cash flow and real discount rate. (You should get exactly the same answer as he did.)

7. **Real and nominal flows (S6.1)** Restate the net cash flows in Table 6.3 in real terms. Discount the restated cash flows at a real discount rate. Assume a 20% nominal rate and 10% expected inflation. NPV should be unchanged at +3,806, or $3,806,000.

8. **Real and nominal flows (S6.1)** Guandong Machinery is evaluating a new project to produce encapsulators. The initial investment in plant and equipment is CNY 500,000.[12] Sales of encapsulators in year 1 are forecasted at CNY 200,000 and costs at CNY 100,000. Both are expected to increase by 10% a year in line with inflation. Profits are taxed at 25%. Working capital in each year consists of inventories of raw materials and is forecasted at 20% of sales in the following year. The project will last five years, and the equipment at the end of this period will have no further value. For tax purposes, the equipment can be depreciated straight-line over these five years. If the nominal discount rate is 15%, show that the net present value of the project is the same whether calculated using real cash flows or nominal flows.

---

[12]CNY is the code used by currency dealers to denote the Chinese yuan.

9. **Working capital (S6.1)** Each of the following statements is true. Use an example to explain why they are consistent.

   a. When a company introduces a new product, or expands production of an existing product, investment in net working capital is usually an important cash outflow.

   b. Forecasting changes in net working capital is not necessary if the timing of all cash inflows and outflows is carefully specified.

10. **Working capital (S6.1)** The following table tracks the main components of working capital over the life of a four-year project.

	2021	2022	2023	2024	2025
Accounts receivable	0	150,000	225,000	190,000	0
Inventory	75,000	130,000	130,000	95,000	0
Accounts payable	25,000	50,000	50,000	35,000	0

   Calculate net working capital and the cash inflows and outflows due to investment in working capital.

11. **Taxes and project NPV (S6.2)** In the International Mulch and Compost example (Section 6-3), we assumed that early losses on the project could be used to offset taxable profits elsewhere in the corporation. Suppose that the losses had to be carried forward and offset against future taxable profits from the project. How would the project NPV change? What is the value of the company's ability to use the tax deductions immediately?

12. **Taxes and project NPV (S6.2)** Suppose that Sudbury Mechanical Drifters is proposing to invest $10 million in a new factory. It can depreciate this investment straight-line over 10 years. The tax rate is 40%, and the discount rate is 10%.

   a. What is the present value of Sudbury's depreciation tax shields?

   b. What would be the present value of the tax shield if the government allowed Sudbury to write-off the factory immediately?

13. **Taxes and project NPV (S6.2)** Ms. T. Potts, the treasurer of Ideal China, has a problem. The company has just ordered a new kiln for $400,000. Of this sum, $50,000 is described by the supplier as an installation cost. Ms. Potts does not know whether the company will need to treat this cost as a tax-deductible current expense or as a capital investment. In the latter case, the company could depreciate the $50,000 straight-line over five years. How will the tax authority's decision affect the after-tax cost of the kiln? The tax rate is 25%, and the opportunity cost of capital is 5%.

14. **Project NPV (S6.3)** Better Mousetrap's research laboratories have developed a new trap. The project requires an initial investment in plant and equipment of $6 million. This investment will be depreciated straight-line over five years to a value of zero, but when the project comes to an end at the end of five years, the equipment will, in fact, be sold for $500,000. The firm believes that working capital at each date must be maintained at 10% of next year's forecasted sales starting immediately. Production costs are estimated at 25% of revenues. (There are no marketing expenses.) Sales forecasts are given in the following table. The firm pays tax at 25% and the required return on the project is 12%. What is the NPV?

Year	0	1	2	3	4	5
Sales (millions of dollars)	0	2.0	2.4	4.0	4.0	2.4

15. **Project NPV (S6.3)** A widget manufacturer currently produces 200,000 units a year. It buys widget lids from an outside supplier at a price of $2 a lid. The plant manager believes that it would be cheaper to make these lids rather than buy them. Direct production costs are estimated to be only $1.50 a lid. The necessary machinery would cost $150,000 and would last 10 years. This investment could be written off immediately for tax purposes. The plant manager estimates that the operation would require additional working capital of $30,000 but argues that this sum can be ignored since it is recoverable at the end of the 10 years. If the company pays tax at a rate of 21% and the opportunity cost of capital is 15%, would you support the plant manager's proposal? State clearly any additional assumptions that you need to make.

16. **Project NPV (S6.3)** Marsha Jones has bought a used Mercedes horse transporter for her Connecticut estate. It cost $35,000. The object is to save on horse transporter rentals. Marsha had been renting a transporter every other week for $200 per day plus $1.00 per mile. Most of the trips are 80 or 100 miles in total. Marsha usually gives the driver, Joe Laminitis, a $40 tip. With the new transporter she will only have to pay for diesel fuel and maintenance, at about $0.45 per mile. Insurance costs for Marsha's transporter are $1,200 per year.

    The transporter will probably be worth $15,000 (in real terms) after eight years, when Marsha's horse Spike, will be ready to retire. Is the transporter a positive-NPV investment? Assume a nominal discount rate of 9% and a 3% forecasted inflation rate. Marsha's transporter is a personal outlay, not a business or financial investment, so taxes can be ignored.

17. **Project NPV (S6.3)** United Pigpen (UP) is considering a proposal to manufacture high-protein hog feed. The project would make use of an existing warehouse, which is currently rented out to a neighboring firm. The next year's rental charge on the warehouse is $100,000, and thereafter the rent is expected to grow in line with inflation at 4% a year. In addition to using the warehouse, the proposal envisages an investment in plant and equipment of $1.2 million. This could be depreciated for tax purposes over 10 years. However, UP expects to terminate the project at the end of eight years and to resell the plant and equipment in year 8 for $400,000. Finally, the project requires an initial investment in working capital of $350,000. Thereafter, working capital is forecasted to be 10% of sales in each of years 1 through 7. Year 1 sales of hog feed are expected to be $4.2 million, and thereafter sales are forecasted to grow by 5% a year, slightly faster than the inflation rate. Manufacturing costs are expected to be 90% of sales, and profits are subject to tax at 25%. The cost of capital is 12%. What is the NPV of UP's project?

18. **Project NPV (S6.3)** Imperial Motors is considering producing its popular Rooster model in China. This will involve an initial investment of CNY 4 billion. The plant will start production after one year. It is expected to last for five years and have a salvage value at the end of this period of CNY 500 million in real terms. The plant will produce 100,000 cars a year. The firm anticipates that in the first year, it will be able to sell each car for CNY 65,000, and thereafter the price is expected to increase by 4% a year. Raw materials for each car are forecasted to cost CNY 18,000 in the first year, and these costs are predicted to increase by 3% annually. Total labor costs for the plant are expected to be CNY 1.1 billion in the first year and thereafter will increase by 7% a year. The land on which the plant is built can be rented for five years at a fixed cost of CNY 300 million a year payable at the beginning of each year. Imperial's discount rate for this type of project is 12% (nominal). The expected rate of inflation is 5%. The plant can be depreciated straight-line over the five-year period, and profits will be taxed at 25%. Assume all cash flows occur at the end of each year except where otherwise stated. What is the NPV of the project plant?

19. **Project NPV and IRR (S6.2, S6.3)** A project requires an initial investment of $100,000 and is expected to produce a cash inflow before tax of $26,000 per year for five years. Company A has substantial accumulated tax losses and is unlikely to pay taxes in the foreseeable future. Company B pays corporate taxes at a rate of 21% and can claim 100% bonus depreciation on the investment. Suppose the opportunity cost of capital is 8%. Ignore inflation.

   a. Calculate project NPV for each company.

   b. What is the IRR of the after-tax cash flows for each company? Why are the IRRs for A and B the same?

20. **Project analysis (S6.3)** Go to the Excel spreadsheet versions of Table 6.3 and answer the following questions.

   a. New engineering estimates raise the possibility that capital investment will be more than $12 million, perhaps as much as $15 million. On the other hand, you believe that the 20% cost of capital is unrealistically high and that the true cost of capital is about 11%. Is the project still attractive under these alternative assumptions?

   b. Continue with the assumed $15 million capital investment and the 11% cost of capital. What if sales, cost of goods sold, and net working capital are all 10% higher in each year? Recalculate NPV. (*Note:* Enter the revised sales, cost, and working-capital forecasts in the spreadsheet for Table 6.3.)

21. **Equivalent annual cash flow (S6.4)** When appraising mutually exclusive investments in plant and equipment, financial managers calculate the investments' equivalent annual cash flows and rank the investments on this basis. Why is this necessary? Why not just compare the investments' NPVs? Explain briefly.

22. **Equivalent annual cash flow (S6.4)** Air conditioning for a college dormitory will cost $1.5 million to install and $200,000 per year to operate at current prices. The system should last 25 years. The real cost of capital is 5%, and the college pays no taxes. What is the equivalent annual cost?

23. **Equivalent annual cash flow (S6.4)** In 2022, the California Air Resources Board (CARB) started planning its "Phase 3" requirements for reformulated gasoline (RFG). RFG is gasoline blended to tight specifications designed to reduce pollution from motor vehicles. CARB consulted with refiners, environmentalists, and other interested parties to design these specifications. As the outline for the Phase 3 requirements emerged, refiners realized that substantial capital investments would be required to upgrade California refineries. Assume a refiner is contemplating an investment of $400 million to upgrade its California plant. The investment lasts for 25 years and does not change raw material and operating costs. The real (inflation-adjusted) cost of capital is 7%. How much extra revenue would be needed each year to recover that cost?

24. **Equivalent annual cash flow (S6.4)** Look at Problem 23 where you calculated the equivalent annual cost of producing reformulated gasoline in California. Capital investment was $400 million. Suppose this amount can be depreciated immediately for tax purposes. The marginal tax rate, including California taxes, is 25%, the cost of capital is 7%, and there is no inflation. The refinery improvements have an economic life of 25 years.

   a. Calculate the after-tax equivalent annual cost.

   b. How much extra would retail gasoline customers have to pay to cover this equivalent annual cost? (*Note:* Extra income from higher retail prices would be taxed.)

25. **Equivalent annual cash flow (S6.4)** Deutsche Transport can lease a truck for four years at a cost of €30,000 annually. It can instead buy a truck at a cost of €80,000, with annual maintenance expenses of €10,000. The truck will be sold at the end of four years for €20,000. Ignore taxes.

   a. What is the equivalent annual cost of buying and maintaining the truck if the discount rate is 10%?

   b. Which is the better option: leasing or buying?

26. **Investment timing (S6.4)** You can purchase a scanner today for $400. The scanner provides benefits worth $60 a year. The expected life of the scanner is 10 years. Scanners are expected to decrease in price by 20% per year. Suppose the discount rate is 10%.

   1. Should you purchase the scanner today or wait to purchase?

   2. When is the best purchase time?

27. **Mutually exclusive investments and project lives (S6.4)** The Borstal Company has to choose between two machines that do the same job but have different lives. The two machines have the following costs:

Year	Machine A	Machine B
0	$40,000	$50,000
1	10,000	8,000
2	10,000	8,000
3	10,000 + replace	8,000
4		8,000 + replace

These costs are expressed in real terms.

a. Suppose you are Borstal's financial manager. If you had to buy one or the other machine and rent it to the production manager for that machine's economic life, what annual rental payment would you have to charge? Assume a 6% real discount rate and ignore taxes.

b. Which machine should Borstal buy?

c. Usually the rental payments you derived in part (a) are just hypothetical—a way of calculating and interpreting equivalent annual cost. Suppose you actually do buy one of the machines and rent it to the production manager. How much would you actually have to charge in each future year if there is steady 8% per year inflation? [*Note:* The rental payments calculated in part (a) are real cash flows. You would have to mark up those payments to cover inflation.]

28. **Mutually exclusive investments and project lives (S6.4)** Look again at your calculations for Problem 27. Suppose that technological change is expected to reduce costs by 10% per year. There will be new machines in year 1 that cost 10% less to buy and operate than A and B. In year 2, there will be a second crop of new machines incorporating a further 10% reduction, and so on. How does this change the equivalent annual costs of machines A and B?

29. **Mutually exclusive investments and project lives. (S6.4)** Econo-Cool air conditioners cost $300 to purchase, result in electricity bills of $150 per year, and last for five years. Luxury Air models cost $500, result in electricity bills of $100 per year, and last for eight years. The discount rate is 21%.

a. What is the equivalent annual cost of the Econo-Cool model?

b. What is the equivalent annual cost of the Luxury Air model?

c. Which model is more cost-effective?

d. Now you remember that the inflation rate is expected to be 10% per year for the foreseeable future. Redo parts (a) and (b).

30. **Mutually exclusive investments and project lives (S6.4)** As a result of improvements in product engineering, United Automation is able to sell one of its two milling machines. Both machines perform the same function but differ in age. The newer machine could be sold today for $50,000. Its operating costs are $20,000 a year, but at the end of five years, the machine will require a $20,000 overhaul (which is tax deductible). Thereafter, operating costs will be $30,000 until the machine is finally sold in year 10 for $5,000. The older machine could be sold today for $25,000. If it is kept, it will need an immediate $20,000 (tax-deductible) over-haul. Thereafter, operating costs will be $30,000 a year until the machine is finally sold in year 5 for $5,000. Both machines are fully depreciated for tax purposes. The company pays tax at 21%. Cash flows have been forecasted in real terms. The real cost of capital is 12%. Which machine should United Automation sell? Explain the assumptions underlying your answer.

31. **Mutually exclusive investments and project lives (S6.4)** Machines A and B are mutually exclusive and are expected to produce the following real cash flows:

Cash Flows ($ thousands)			
Machine	C_0	C_1	C_2	C_3
A	−100	+110	+121	
B	−120	+110	+121	+133

The real opportunity cost of capital is 10%.

a. Calculate the NPV of each machine.

b. Calculate the equivalent annual cash flow from each machine.

c. Which machine should you buy?

32. **Replacement decisions (S6.4)** Machine C was purchased five years ago for $200,000 and produces an annual real cash flow of $80,000. It has no salvage value but is expected to last another five years. The company can replace machine C with machine B (see Problem 31) either now or at the end of five years. Which should it do?

33. **Replacement decisions (S6.4)** Hayden Inc. has a number of copiers that were bought four years ago for $20,000. Currently maintenance costs $2,000 a year, but the maintenance agreement expires at the end of two years, and thereafter, the annual maintenance charge will rise to $8,000. The machines have a current resale value of $8,000, but at the end of year 2, their value will have fallen to $3,500. By the end of year 6, the machines will be valueless and would be scrapped. Hayden is considering replacing the copiers with new machines that would do essentially the same job. These machines cost $25,000, and the company can take out an eight-year maintenance contract for $1,000 a year. The machines would have no value by the end of the eight years and would be scrapped. Both machines are depreciated using seven-year straight-line depreciation, and the tax rate is 39%. Assume for simplicity that the inflation rate is zero. The real cost of capital is 7%. When should Hayden replace its copiers?

34. **Replacement decisions (S6.4)** You are operating an old machine that is expected to produce a cash inflow of $5,000 in each of the next three years before it fails. You can replace it now with a new machine that costs $20,000 but is much more efficient and will provide a cash flow of $10,000 a year for four years. Should you replace your equipment now? The discount rate is 15%.

35. **Replacement decisions. (S6.4)** A forklift will last for only two more years. It costs $5,000 a year to maintain. For $20,000 you can buy a new forklift that can last for 10 years and should require maintenance costs of only $2,000 a year.

a. If the discount rate is 4% per year, should you replace the forklift?

b. What if the discount rate is 12% per year?

36. **The cost of excess capacity (S6.4)** The president's executive jet is not fully utilized. You judge that its use by other officers would increase direct operating costs by only $20,000 a year and would save $100,000 a year in airline bills. On the other hand, you believe that with the increased use the company will need to replace the jet at the end of three years rather than four. A new jet costs $1.1 million and (at its current low rate of use) has a life of six years. Assume that the company does not pay taxes. All cash flows are forecasted in real terms. The real opportunity cost of capital is 8%. Should you try to persuade the president to allow other officers to use the plane?

CHALLENGE

37. **Effective tax rates (S6.2)** One measure of the effective tax rate is the difference between the IRRs of pretax and after-tax cash flows, divided by the pretax IRR. Consider, for example, an investment I generating a perpetual stream of pretax cash flows C. The pretax IRR is C/I, and the after-tax IRR is $C(1 - T_C)/I$, where T_C is the statutory tax rate. The effective rate, call it T_E, is

$$T_E = \frac{C/I - C(1 - T_C)/I}{C/I} = T_C$$

In this case, the effective rate equals the statutory rate.

   a. Calculate T_E the effective tax rate for the guano project in Section 6-3.

   b. How does the effective rate depend on the tax depreciation schedule? On the inflation rate?

   c. Consider a project where all of the up-front investment is treated as an expense for tax purposes. Does this definition of the effective tax rate make sense for such a project?

38. **Equivalent annual costs (S6.4)** We warned that equivalent annual costs should be calculated in real terms. We did not fully explain why. This problem will show you.

   Look back to the cash flows for machines A and B (in "The Choice between Long- and Short-Lived Equipment"). The present values of purchase and operating costs are 28.37 (over three years for A) and 21.00 (over two years for B). The real discount rate is 6% and the inflation rate is 5%.

   a. Calculate the three- and two-year *level nominal* annuities which have present values of 28.37 and 21.00. Explain why these annuities are *not* realistic estimates of equivalent annual costs. (*Hint:* In real life, machinery rentals increase with inflation.)

   b. Suppose the inflation rate increases to 25%. The real interest rate stays at 6%. Recalculate the level nominal annuities. Note that the *ranking* of machines A and B appears to change. Why?

• • • • •

SOLUTIONS TO SELF-TEST QUESTIONS

6.1

			$000s			
Year	0	1	2	3	4	5
Investment	−250					
Sales		250	300	300	240	240
Operating expenses		−200	−200	−200	−200	−200
Cash flow	−250	50	100	100	40	40

Since each machine is forecast to generate $40,000 of cash flow in years 4 and 5, it makes sense to keep operating.

6.2

	Period			
	1	2	3	4
Accounting income	0	+40	+40	+40
− Investment in inventories	−60	0	0	0
− Investment in receivables	0	−100	+0	0
= Cash flow	−60	−60	+40	+40

The company keeps the same *level* of inventories and there is no investment after year 0. Similarly it continues to be owed the same amount by customers and there is no further investment in receivables after year 1.

6.3 The *extra* impact of Fuse2 on sales of Fuse1 is a decline of $1.0 billion. The incremental income from Fuse2 is, therefore, $2.5 - 1.0 = \$1.5$ billion.

6.4 a. The site and buildings could have been sold or put to another use. Their values are opportunity costs, which should be treated as incremental cash outflows.

b. Demolition costs are incremental cash outflows.

c. The cost of the access road is sunk and not incremental.

d. Lost cash flows from other projects are incremental cash outflows (though not easily estimated).

e. Depreciation is not a cash expense and should not be included, except as it affects taxes. (Taxes are discussed later in this chapter.)

f. The reduction in tax due to depreciation is an addition to cash flow.

g. The initial investment in inventories is a cash outflow.

h. The expenditure on design is a sunk cost and not an incremental cash flow.

6.5 Pretax income is $4 - 1.5 - (9 \div 6) = \$1.0$ million. The company will pay tax of $0.3 \times 1.0 = \$0.3$ million.

6.6 From Eq. (6.3B), Operating cash flow = after-tax profit + depreciation = $\$1,539 + \$2,000 = \$3,539$ ($000s).
From Eq. (6.3C), Operating cash flow = (revenues − cash expenses) × (1 − tax rate) + (tax rate × depreciation) = $(\$12,887 - \$8,939) \times (1 - 0.21) + (0.21 \times \$2,000) = \$3,539$ ($000s).

6.7 The only effect that accelerated depreciation has on the cash flow is that it results in a lower tax charge in the early years of the project and a correspondingly higher charge in the later years. With a positive opportunity cost of capital, the discounted value of the cash flows increases.

6.8 C's equivalent annual cost = $5,000 + (\$15,000 \div 8\text{-year annuity factor}) = \$5,000 + \$15,000/6.2098 = \$7,416$, which is less than the annual cost of A or B. Choose C.

MINI-CASE ● ● ●

New Economy Transport (A)

The New Economy Transport Company (NETCO) was formed in 1959 to carry cargo and passengers between ports in the Pacific Northwest and Alaska. By 2021, its fleet had grown to four vessels, including a small dry-cargo vessel, the *Vital Spark*.

The *Vital Spark* is 25 years old and badly in need of an overhaul. P. Handy, the finance director, has just been presented with a proposal that would require the following expenditures:

Overhaul engine and generators	$340,000
Replace radar and other electronic equipment	75,000
Repairs to hull and superstructure	310,000
Painting and other repairs	95,000
	$820,000

Mr. Handy believes that all these outlays could be written off immediately for tax purposes.

NETCO's chief engineer, McPhail, estimates the postoverhaul operating costs as follows:

Fuel	$ 450,000
Labor and benefits	480,000
Maintenance	141,000
Other	110,000
	$1,181,000

These costs generally increase with inflation, which is forecasted at 2.5% a year.

The *Vital Spark* is carried on NETCO's books at a net depreciated value of only $100,000, but it could probably be sold "as is," along with an extensive inventory of spare parts, for $200,000. The book value of the spare parts inventory is $40,000. Sale of the *Vital Spark* would generate an immediate tax liability on the difference between sale price and book value.

The chief engineer also suggests installation of a brand-new engine and control system, which would cost an extra $600,000.[13] This additional equipment would not substantially improve the *Vital Spark*'s performance, but would result in the following reduced annual fuel, labor, and maintenance costs:

Fuel	$ 400,000
Labor and benefits	405,000
Maintenance	105,000
Other	110,000
	$1,020,000

Overhaul of the *Vital Spark* would take it out of service for several months. The overhauled vessel would resume commercial service next year. Based on past experience, Mr. Handy believes that it would generate revenues of about $1.4 million next year, increasing with inflation thereafter.

But the *Vital Spark* cannot continue forever. Even if overhauled, its useful life is probably no more than 10 years, 12 years at the most. Its salvage value when finally taken out of service will be trivial.

NETCO is a conservatively financed firm in a mature business. It normally evaluates capital investments using an 11% cost of capital. This is a nominal, not a real, rate. NETCO's tax rate is 21%.

QUESTION

1. Calculate the NPV of the proposed overhaul of the *Vital Spark,* with and without the new engine and control system. To do the calculation, you will have to prepare a spreadsheet table showing all costs after taxes over the vessel's remaining economic life. Take special care with your assumptions about depreciation tax shields and inflation.

New Economy Transport (B)

There is no question that the *Vital Spark* needs an overhaul soon. However, Mr. Handy feels it unwise to proceed without also considering the purchase of a new vessel. Cohn and Doyle Inc., a Wisconsin shipyard, has approached NETCO with a design incorporating a Kort nozzle,

---

[13]This additional outlay would also qualify for an immediate 100% bonus depreciation.

extensively automated navigation and power control systems, and much more comfortable accommodations for the crew. Estimated annual operating costs of the new vessel are:

Fuel	$380,000
Labor and benefits	330,000
Maintenance	70,000
Other	105,000
	$885,000

The crew would require additional training to handle the new vessel's more complex and sophisticated equipment. Training would probably cost $50,000 next year.

The estimated operating costs for the new vessel assume that it would be operated in the same way as the *Vital Spark*. However, the new vessel should be able to handle a larger load on some routes, which could generate additional revenues, net of additional out-of-pocket costs, of as much as $100,000 per year. Moreover, a new vessel would have a useful service life of 20 years or more.

Cohn and Doyle offered the new vessel for a fixed price of $3,000,000, payable half immediately and half on delivery next year.

Mr. Handy stepped out on the foredeck of the *Vital Spark* as it chugged down the Cook Inlet. "A rusty old tub," he muttered, "but it's never let us down. I'll bet we could keep it going until next year while Cohn and Doyle are building its replacement. We could use up the spare parts to keep it going. We might even be able to sell or scrap it for book value when its replacement arrives.

"But how do I compare the NPV of a new ship with the old *Vital Spark*? Sure, I could run a 20-year NPV spreadsheet, but I don't have a clue how the replacement will be used by the end of that time. Maybe I could compare the overall *cost* of overhauling and operating the *Vital Spark* to the cost of buying and operating the proposed replacement."

QUESTIONS

1. Calculate and compare the equivalent annual costs of (a) overhauling and operating the *Vital Spark* for 12 more years, and (b) buying and operating the proposed replacement vessel for 20 years. What should Mr. Handy do if the replacement's annual costs are the same or lower?

2. Suppose the replacement's equivalent annual costs are higher than the *Vital Spark*'s. What additional information should Mr. Handy seek in this case?

CHAPTER

Introduction to Risk, Diversification, and Portfolio Selection

We have managed to go through six chapters without directly addressing the problem of risk, but now the game is up. We can no longer be satisfied with vague statements like "The opportunity cost of capital depends on the risk of the project." We need to know how risk is defined and managed, what the links are between risk and the opportunity cost of capital, and how the financial manager can cope with risk in practical situations. In this chapter, we concentrate on the first of these issues and leave the other two to Chapters 8 and 9.

Section 7-1 The relationship between risk and return
We start by summarizing 121 years of evidence on rates of return in financial markets, and we measure the risk premium that risky securities have earned over safer securities.

Section 7-2 How to measure risk
We then look at how to measure risk and use our insights to consider past evidence on the risk of different investments.

Section 7-3 How diversification reduces risk
We show how risk can be reduced by portfolio diversification. The risk of an individual security can be separated into *specific* risk, which can be diversified away, and *systematic* risk, which cannot be reduced by diversification.

Section 7-4 Systematic risk is market risk
We show more precisely how the risk of a portfolio depends on the risk of its component securities. Investors can choose from an infinite number of portfolios offering different combinations of risk and expected return. However, it turns out that an investor's willingness to bear risk does not affect which combination of risky securities the investor holds, but only how much of his wealth is put in them.

Section 7-5 Should companies diversify?
For the most part in this chapter, we take the view of the individual investor. We conclude by turning the problem around: Does diversification make sense as a corporate objective? It doesn't, because investors can, and do, easily diversify on their own.

7-1 The Relationship between Risk and Return

How are risk and return linked? Financial analysts are blessed with an enormous quantity of data, which allows us to answer this question, at least retrospectively. There are comprehensive databases of the returns on U.S. stocks, bonds, options, and commodities, as well as data for returns in other countries.

We start by studying the historical performance of three portfolios of U.S. securities:[1]

1. A portfolio of Treasury bills—that is, U.S. government debt securities maturing in less than one year.[2]
2. A portfolio of U.S. long-term Treasury bonds.
3. A portfolio of U.S. stocks.

These investments offer different degrees of risk. Treasury bills are about as safe an investment as you can make. There is no risk of default, and their short maturity means that prices are relatively stable. An investor who wishes to lend money for, say, three months can achieve a perfectly certain payoff by purchasing a Treasury bill maturing in three months.

In contrast, long-term government bonds bear the risk of interest rate changes. Bond prices fall when interest rates rise and rise when interest rates fall. Stocks are riskier still, because their value depends on the evolution of the stock market and on the performance of the issuing companies.

Over a Century of Capital Market History

Figure 7.1 shows how your money would have grown if you had invested $1 at the start of 1900 and reinvested all dividend or interest income in each of the three portfolios.[3]

Figure 7.2 is identical to Figure 7.1, except that it shows the growth in the *real* value of the portfolios—that is, growth in dollars of constant purchasing power. The average rate of inflation over 121 years was only about 3%, but a comparison of Figures 7.1 and 7.2 shows the difference that "only 3%" inflation makes.

We can also calculate the rate of return from these portfolios for each year from 1900 to 2020. Averages of the 121 annual rates of return are shown in Table 7.1.

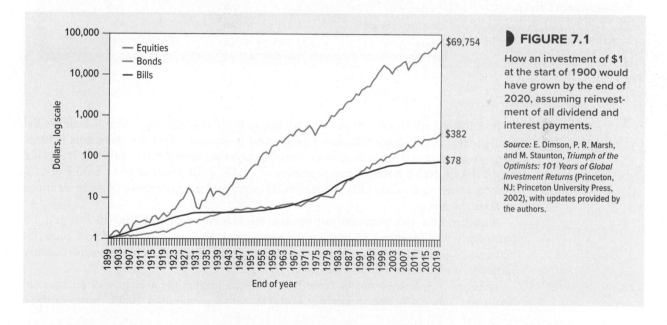

▶ **FIGURE 7.1**

How an investment of $1 at the start of 1900 would have grown by the end of 2020, assuming reinvestment of all dividend and interest payments.

Source: E. Dimson, P. R. Marsh, and M. Staunton, *Triumph of the Optimists: 101 Years of Global Investment Returns* (Princeton, NJ: Princeton University Press, 2002), with updates provided by the authors.

---

[1] There are two widely used sources of historical investment returns. 1. *Stocks, Bonds, Bills and Inflation, SBBI Yearbook,* published annually by Duff & Phelps. 2. E. Dimson, P. R. Marsh, and M. Staunton (DMS), *Triumph of the Optimists: 101 Years of Global Investment Returns* (Princeton, NJ: Princeton University Press, 2002). Updated summaries are published annually as the *Credit Suisse Global Investment Returns Yearbook.* The SBBI Yearbooks summarize U.S. returns from 1926 in great and useful detail. We use the DMS returns, with updates supplied by the authors. DMS provide less detail for the U.S. than the SBBI Yearbooks but cover a longer period—from 1900 vs. 1926—and also provide returns for many other countries.

[2] Treasury bills were not issued before 1919. Before that date, the interest rate used is the commercial paper rate.

[3] Portfolio values are plotted on a log scale. If they were not, the ending values for the common stock portfolio would run off the top of the page.

▶ **FIGURE 7.2**

How an investment of $1 at the start of 1900 would have grown *in real terms* by the end of 2020, assuming reinvestment of all dividend and interest payments. Compare this plot with Figure 7.1, and note how inflation has eroded the purchasing power of returns to investors.

Source: E. Dimson, P. R. Marsh, and M. Staunton, *Triumph of the Optimists: 101 Years of Global Investment Returns* (Princeton, NJ: Princeton University Press, 2002), with updates provided by the authors.

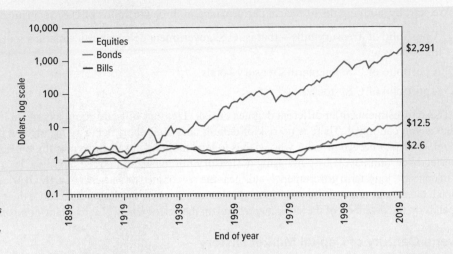

▶**TABLE 7.1**   Average annual rates of return on U.S. Treasury bills, government bonds, and stocks, 1900–2020.

Source: E. Dimson, P. R. Marsh, and M. Staunton, *Triumph of the Optimists: 101 Years of Global Investment Returns* (Princeton, NJ: Princeton University Press, 2002), with updates provided by the authors.

	Average Annual Rate of Return		
	Nominal	Real	Average Risk Premium (Extra Return versus Treasury Bills)
Treasury bills	3.7%	0.9%	0%
Government bonds	5.4	2.6	1.7
Stocks	11.5	8.5	7.8

Investment performance coincides with our intuitive risk ranking. Table 7.1 shows the average return on Treasury bills was 3.7% per year in *nominal* terms. An investment in long-term government bonds would have produced an average nominal return of 5.4%. By taking on the risk of stocks, investors earned a return of 11.5%, a *risk premium* of 11.5 – 3.7 = 7.8% over the return on Treasury bills. Average inflation reduced the *real* returns on these securities by about 3% a year.

Was this 7.8% risk premium just because the U.S. stock market happened to perform particularly well? Figure 7.3 illustrates the average risk premiums for 20 different countries between 1900 and 2020.[4] There is no evidence here that U.S. investors have been particularly fortunate; the U.S. risk premium was about average.

In Figure 7.3, Spanish stocks come bottom of the league; the average risk premium in Spain was only 5.4%. The winner was Portugal, with a premium of 10.0%. Some of these

---

[4]We are concerned here with the difference between the nominal market return and the nominal interest rate. Sometimes you will see *real* risk premiums quoted—that is, the difference between the *real* market return and the *real* interest rate. If the inflation rate is *i*, then the real risk premium is $(r_m - r_f)/(1 + i)$. For countries such as Italy that have experienced a high degree of inflation, this real risk premium may be significantly lower than the nominal premium.

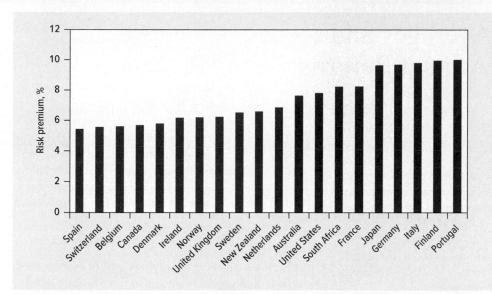

▶ **FIGURE 7.3**

Average market risk premiums (nominal return on stocks minus nominal return on bills), 1900–2020.

Source: E. Dimson, P. R. Marsh, and M. Staunton, *Triumph of the Optimists: 101 Years of Global Investment Returns* (Princeton, NJ: Princeton University Press, 2002), with updates provided by the authors.

differences between countries may reflect differences in risk. They may also reflect pure chance, the long string of positive and negative surprises over the 121 years. Spanish investors probably did not *expect* to be at the bottom of Figure 7.3, nor Portugal at the top.

Why do we look back over such a long period to measure average rates of return? Because the annual rates of return for stocks fluctuate so much that averages over short periods are unreliable. The return in any particular year was affected by one-off events. For example, U.S. stocks fell by 38% in 2008 due to the financial crisis; they rose by 36% in 1995 at the start of the Internet bubble, which burst in 2000. A long period averages out these surprises and gives a more accurate picture of the return that investors can expect to receive in a "normal" year.

Using Historical Evidence to Evaluate Today's Cost of Capital

Suppose there is an investment project that has the same risk as the stock market, represented by the Standard and Poor's Composite Index (S&P 500). What rate should you use to discount this project's forecasted cash flows?

You should use the expected *future* rate of return on the S&P. It's the future return that's relevant because the alternative to investing in the project is to pay out the cash as dividends and allow shareholders to invest in the S&P—in which case, they'd earn the future return on the S&P. Let's call this return r_m, where the subscript m stands for "market."

But how do we predict this future return? One approach is to assume that the future will be like the past, and so today's investors can expect to receive the average historic rate of return shown in Table 7.1. In this case, you'd set r_m at 11.5%.

Unfortunately, that's *not* the way to do it, because r_m won't be stable over time. Remember that it's the sum of the risk-free interest rate, which we label as r_f, and a premium for risk. We know that r_f varies. For example, in 1981 the interest rate on Treasury bills was 15%. Investors wouldn't have been willing to hold stocks if their expected future return in that year was only 11.5%.

Arithmetic Averages and Compound Annual Returns

❭ The average returns shown in Table 7.1 are *arithmetic averages*. In other words, we simply added the 121 annual returns and divided by 121 to get our average return of 11.5%. However, financial analysts may also quote the *geometric average* (also known as the *compound rate of return*). Over the 121-year period stock values multiplied 69,754 times. The geometric average return is calculated by taking the 121st root of 69,754. This gives 9.7%, 1.8 percentage points below the arithmetic average of 11.5%.[5]

Why did we quote the arithmetic average of 11.5%, rather than the geometric average of 9.7%? To understand this, let's use a simple example.

Suppose that Big Pharma's stock price is $100. There is an equal chance that at the end of the year the stock will be worth $90, $110, or $130; there are no dividends. Therefore, the return could be −10%, +10%, or +30%. The *expected* return is ⅓ (−10 + 10 + 30) = +10%. This is the arithmetic average.

If we run the process in reverse and discount the expected cash flow by the expected rate of return, we get back to Big Pharma's current stock price, so this checks out:

$$PV = \frac{110}{1.10} = \$100$$

The expected return of 10% is therefore the correct rate at which to discount the expected cash flow from Big Pharma's stock. It is also the opportunity cost of capital for investments that have the same degree of risk as Big Pharma.

Now suppose that we observe the returns on Big Pharma stock over a large number of years. If the odds are unchanged, the return will be −10% in a third of the years, +10% in a further third, and +30% in the remaining years. The arithmetic average of these yearly returns is

$$\frac{-10 + 10 + 30}{3} = +10\%$$

The arithmetic average of past returns gives you exactly the same answer as the expected return. Thus, it correctly measures the opportunity cost of capital for investments of similar risk to Big Pharma stock.[6]

The geometric average return on Big Pharma stock would be

$$(0.9 \times 1.1 \times 1.3)^{1/3} - 1 = 0.088, \text{ or } 8.8\%$$

which is less than the opportunity cost of capital. Thus, if the cost of capital is estimated from historic returns, only the arithmetic average gives the right answer, not the geometric average.[7]

---

[5]*Technical note:* For log normally distributed returns the annual compound return is equal to the arithmetic average return minus half the variance. For example, the annual standard deviation of returns on the U.S. market was 0.195, or 19.5%. Variance was therefore 0.195², or 0.038. The compound annual return is about 0.038/2 = 0.019, or 1.9 percentage points less than the arithmetic average.

[6]You sometimes hear that the arithmetic average correctly measures the opportunity cost of capital for one-year cash flows, but not for more distant ones. Let us check. Suppose that you expect to receive a cash flow of $121 in year 2. We know that one year hence investors will value that cash flow by discounting at 10% (the arithmetic average of possible returns). In other words, at the end of the year they will be willing to pay PV₁ = 121/1.10 = $110 for the expected cash flow. But we already know how to value an asset that pays off $110 in year 1—just discount at the 10% opportunity cost of capital. Thus PV₀ = PV₁/1.10 = 110/1.1 = $100. Our example demonstrates that the arithmetic average (10% in our example) provides a correct measure of the opportunity cost of capital regardless of the timing of the cash flow.

[7]Our discussion assumed that we *knew* that the returns of −10, +10, and +30% were equally likely. For an analysis of the effect of uncertainty about the expected return see I. A. Cooper, "Arithmetic versus Geometric Mean Estimators: Setting Discount Rates for Capital Budgeting," *European Financial Management* 2 (1996), pp. 157–167; and E. Jacquier, A. Kane, and A. J. Marcus, "Optimal Estimation of the Risk Premium for the Long Run and Asset Allocation: A Case of Compounded Estimation Risk," *Journal of Financial Econometrics* 3 (2005), pp. 37–55. When future returns are forecasted to distant horizons, the historical arithmetic means are upward-biased. This bias is small in most corporate-finance applications, however.

A more sensible method is to take the current interest rate on Treasury bills and add 7.8%, the average *risk premium* shown in Table 7.1. For example, suppose that the current interest rate on Treasury bills is 2%. Adding the average risk premium gives

$$r_S = r_f + \text{normal risk premium}$$
$$= 0.02 + 0.078 = 0.098, \text{ or } 9.8\%$$

This method gives a lower expected future return because interest rates are currently low—2% in this example—compared with the historic average of 3.7% in Table 7.1. This gap of 1.7%

explains why the expected future return on stocks (9.8%) is also 1.7% lower than the historic average of 11.5%.

The crucial assumption here is that there is a stable risk premium on equities, so that the expected *future* risk premium can be measured by the average past risk premium (7.8%). But this assumption may not hold. For example, investors might be less averse to holding stocks today than in the past. Perhaps the growth in mutual funds and ETFs has made it easier for individuals to diversify away risks, or perhaps pension funds can diversify by investing overseas. If these investors can eliminate more of their risk than in the past, they may be content with a lower risk premium.

What all this means is that estimating future returns is part science, but also part art. The "science" is that we can use past returns to guide us. Given a set of past returns, there is a single, scientific "correct" way to calculate the average past return. The "art" comes in two forms. The first is knowing how far back to go when gathering past data. We pointed out an advantage of longer histories—they're less skewed by outlier years. But a disadvantage is that they may be less relevant for today. Perhaps stock returns 100 years ago were from a different era, when it was much harder to diversify, so investors required a higher risk premium to hold stocks.

The second art form is knowing how much to adjust historic data when forecasting the future. Let's say you decided to estimate stock returns over the past 70 years. You believe the risk premiums demanded by investors have come down from the first half of the last century, which included the Great Depression of the 1930s and two World Wars. So you focus on the 70 years since 1950. But even those past 70 years aren't a perfect guide to the future. You may think that risk premiums will come down even more as diversification continues to become easier. Or you may fear the opposite, that stocks will become less safe going forward due to climate change risk.

There's no formula to tell us what will happen next, nor how much we should increase or decrease the historical average by analysis of future risks. Indeed, that's where the skill of investing lies. It is also why professional investors can disagree wildly on the future direction of stocks, even though they all see the same data. In turn, this can explain why there's so much trade in financial markets: One investor is willing to buy and another is willing to sell, yet both sides believe they've got a good deal because they have different predictions for the future.

The difficulty of estimating expected returns is particularly important for growth stocks, which pay no (or few) dividends today. Since the bulk of their dividends will arise far into the future, those dividends will be heavily discounted, and so their present value is particularly sensitive to the discount rate.[8] This is one reason there is particular disagreement over the value of growth stocks, and why there can be bubbles and crashes in such stocks (such as the Internet bubble of the late 1990s and its subsequent bursting).[9] For the same reason, estimates of future returns have outsized effects on the NPV of projects with cash flows that occur far into the future, such as the earnings of an oil producer finally moving to clean energy. Indeed, a common criticism is that managers use too high discount rates, and so underinvest in long-term projects.

To sum up this discussion: Estimating the risk premium is just as much of an art as a science. History contains valuable clues, but the future may be different from the past. Many financial economists rely on the evidence of history and therefore work with a risk premium of about 7%. The remainder generally use a somewhat lower figure. We have no official position on the issue, but we believe that a range of 5% to 8% is reasonable for the risk premium in the United States. We will use 7% in the examples in this and the next chapter.

---

[8] More precisely, a dividend in year t will be discounted by $(1 + r)^t$, so small changes in the estimate of r will be compounded t times. That's why Figure 2.2 showed that the effect of different discount rates is greater the more years you go out.

[9] Of course, a second reason is disagreement over the growth rate g.

BEYOND THE PAGE

Market risk
premium
survey

mhhe.com/brealey14e

7.1 Self-Test

Suppose that in the past Standard and Poor's Index had returned 10.5% per year and the risk-free rate averaged 2%. The risk-free rate is now 3%. You are considering a project with the same risk as the S&P. What should its discount rate be?

7-2   How to Measure Risk

You now have a couple of benchmarks. You know the discount rate for safe projects is the risk-free rate of interest, and you have an estimate of the rate for projects that are just as risky as the stock market —simply the expected future return on the market. But how do we estimate discount rates for assets that don't fit these simple cases? To answer this question, we need to understand (1) how to measure risk and (2) the relationship between risks borne and risk premiums demanded.

The higher returns for stocks in Figure 7.1 and Table 7.1 did not come for free, because stocks were riskier than long-term government bonds or Treasury bills. Figure 7.4 shows the 121 annual rates of return for U.S. stocks. The fluctuations in year-to-year returns are remarkably wide. The highest annual return was 57.6% in 1933—a partial rebound from the stock market crash of 1929–1932. However, there were losses exceeding 25% in six years, the worst being the –43.9% return in 1931.

Another way to present these data is by a histogram or frequency distribution. This is done in Figure 7.5, where the volatility of year-to-year returns shows up in the wide "spread" of outcomes.

Variance and Standard Deviation

So investors require a higher return for taking on more risk. But what's the relevant way to measure risk? Take a look at Figure 7.6, which shows a histogram of the daily returns on IBM stock from 1997 to 2019. On this histogram we have superimposed a bell-shaped normal distribution. The result is typical: When measured over a short interval, the past returns on any stock conform fairly closely to a normal distribution.[10]

> ▌ **FIGURE 7.4**
>
> The stock market has been a profitable but volatile investment.
>
> *Source:* E. Dimson, P. R. Marsh, and M. Staunton, *Triumph of the Optimists: 101 Years of Global Investment Returns* (Princeton, NJ: Princeton University Press, 2002), with updates provided by the authors.

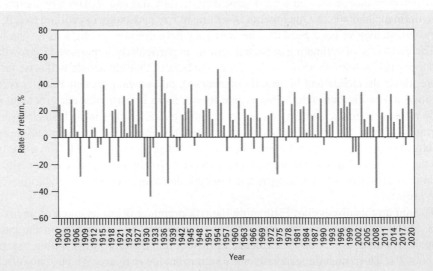

[10]If you were to measure returns over *long* intervals, the distribution would be skewed to the right. For example, you would encounter returns greater than 100% but none less than –100%. The distribution of returns over periods of, say, one year would be better approximated by a *lognormal* distribution. The lognormal distribution, like the normal, is completely specified by its mean and standard deviation. You would also find that the distribution of price changes has a longer tails than the normal and lognormal distributions. Extreme events or "black swans" crop up with alarming frequency. This "tail risk" shows up in Figure 7.6. Note that the frequency of gains and losses is lower than the normal distribution calls for, *except* at the extreme ends of the distribution.

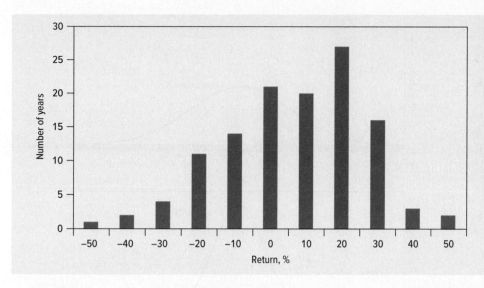

FIGURE 7.5

Histogram of annual rates of return from the U.S. stock market for 1900–2020, showing the wide spread of returns from investment in stocks.

Source: E. Dimson, P. R. Marsh, and M. Staunton, *Triumph of the Optimists: 101 Years of Global Investment Returns* (Princeton, NJ: Princeton University Press, 2002), with updates provided by the authors.

Normal distributions can be completely defined by two numbers. One is the overall level of the distribution, which is captured by the average or expected value. The second is the spread of the distribution, which is measured by the **variance** or **standard deviation**. The variance of the market return is the expected squared deviation from the expected return. In other words,

$$\text{Variance } (\tilde{r}_i) = \text{the expected value of } (\tilde{r}_i - r_i)^2 \qquad (7.1)$$

where $(\tilde{r}_i)$ is the actual return of stock i (IBM in this case) and r_i is the expected return.[11] The standard deviation is the square root of the variance:

$$\text{Standard deviation of } \tilde{r}_i = \sqrt{\text{variance } (\tilde{r}_i)} \qquad (7.2)$$

Standard deviation is usually denoted by σ and variance by σ^2.

Figure 7.7 pictures the distribution of possible returns from three investments. Investments A and B offer the same expected return of 10%, which is why the "peak" of each distribution

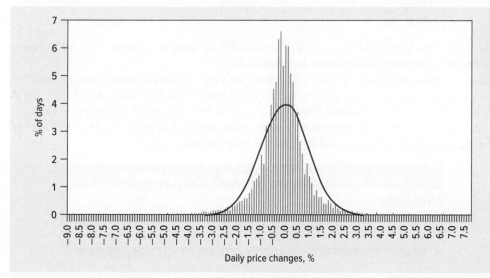

FIGURE 7.6

Daily price changes for IBM are approximately normally distributed. This plot spans 1997 to 2019.

---

[11]One more technical point. When variance is estimated from a sample of *observed* returns, we add the squared deviations and divide by $N-1$, where N is the number of observations. We divide by $N-1$ rather than N to correct for what is called *the loss of a degree of freedom.* The formula is Variance $(\tilde{r}^m) = \frac{1}{N-1}\sum_{t=1}^{N}(\tilde{r}^m_t - r^m)^2$ where $\tilde{r}^m_t$ is the market return in period t and r^m is the mean of the values of $\tilde{r}^m_t$.

▶ **FIGURE 7.7**

Investments A and B both
have an *expected* return of
10%, but because investment
A has the greater spread
of possible returns, it is
more risky than B. We can
measure this spread by
the standard deviation.
Investment A has a standard
deviation of 15%; B, 7.5%.
Most investors would prefer B
to A. Investments B and C
both have the same standard
deviation, but C offers a higher
expected return. Most investors would prefer C to B.

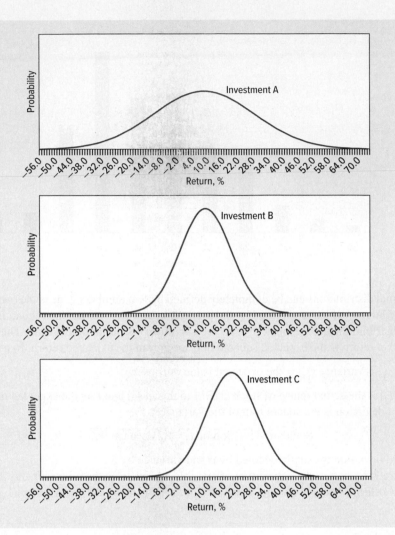

is the same. However, A has a standard deviation of 15% while B's is only 7.5%. Most investors dislike uncertainty and therefore prefer B to A.

Now compare investments B and C. Both have the same standard deviation, but the expected
return is 20% from C and only 10% from B. C's distribution has the same spread as B's, but is
shifted to the right. Most investors like high expected return and therefore prefer C to B.

We'll now move from these hypothetical stocks to our three actual portfolios. Over 1900–2020,
the annual standard deviations and variances of each portfolio were:[12]

Portfolio	Standard Deviation (σ)	Variance (σ^2)
Treasury bills	2.8%	8.1
Government bonds	8.9	79.7
Stocks	19.5	381.8

[12]In discussing the riskiness of *bonds,* be careful to specify the time period and whether you are speaking in real or nominal terms.
The *nominal* return on a long-term Treasury bond is absolutely certain to an investor who holds on until maturity; in other words, it
is risk-free if you forget about inflation. After all, the U.S. government can always print money to pay off its debts. However, the real
return on Treasury securities is uncertain because no one knows how much each future dollar will buy.

The bond returns used to construct this table were measured annually. The returns reflect year-to-year changes in bond prices as
well as interest received. The *one-year* returns on long-term bonds are risky in *both* real and nominal terms.

Unlike the choice among stocks A, B, and C, here there's no unambiguous choice. Stocks, which Table 7.1 showed to have the highest expected return, also have the highest risk. Similarly, Treasury bills' low expected return is offset by the fact that they're risk-free.

Calculating Risk

We'll now show how you can apply Eq. (7.1) and Eq. (7.2) to calculate variance and standard deviation, using a simple example. Consider the following game. You start by investing $100. Then two coins are flipped. For each head, you get back your starting balance *plus* 20%, and for each tail, you get back your starting balance *less* 10%. So there are four equally likely outcomes:

- Head + head: You gain 40%.
- Head + tail: You gain 10%.
- Tail + head: You gain 10%.
- Tail + tail: You lose 20%.

There is a chance of 1 in 4, or 0.25, that you'll make 40%; a chance of 2 in 4, or 0.5, that you will make 10%; and a chance of 1 in 4, or 0.25, that you will lose 20%. The game's expected return is a weighted average of the possible outcomes:

$$\text{Expected return} = (0.25 \times 40) + (0.5 \times 10) + (0.25 \times -20) = +10\%$$

Table 7.2 shows that the variance of the percentage returns is 450. Standard deviation is the square root of 450, or 21. This figure is in the same units as the rate of return, so we can say that the game's risk is 21%.

Now think of a second game, the same as the first except that each head means a 35% gain and each tail means a 25% loss. Again, there are four equally likely outcomes:

- Head + head: You gain 70%.
- Head + tail: You gain 10%.
- Tail + head: You gain 10%.
- Tail + tail: You lose 50%.

For this game, the expected return is 10%, the same as the first. But its standard deviation is double that of the first game, 42% versus 21%. The second game is twice as risky as the first.

(1) Percent Rate of Return ($\tilde{r}$)	(2) Deviation from Expected Return ($\tilde{r}-r$)	(3) Squared Deviation ($\tilde{r}-r$)^2	(4) Probability	(5) Probability × Squared Deviation
+40	+30	900	0.25	225
+10	0	0	0.5	0
−20	−30	900	0.25	225
		Variance = expected value of ($\tilde{r}-r$)^2 = 450		
		Standard deviation = $\sqrt{\text{variance}} = \sqrt{450} = 21$		

❯ **TABLE 7.2**
The coin-tossing game: calculating variance and standard deviation.

BEYOND THE PAGE

How to calculate variance and standard deviation

mhhe.com/brealey14e

Estimating Future Risk

Just as investors are concerned with the *future* expected return, it's the *future* risk of returns that they also care about. But looking at the volatility of returns in the past may be a helpful guide to the volatility of returns that may occur in the future. We have reported the historical standard deviation for U.S. stocks as 19.5%. But what about other countries? Figure 7.8 compares the standard deviation of stock market returns in 20 countries over the same 121-year period. Portugal occupies high field with a standard deviation of 38.2%, but most of the other countries cluster in the low 20s.

Again, data on past volatility are only a starting point for estimating the volatility of returns that might occur in the future. We may need to adjust past volatility if we think the future will be different. For example, Germany, Italy, and Japan now have much more stable economies than before and during the Second World War. Figure 7.9 illustrates that, even in the U.S., a relatively stable economy, volatility has been anything but stable.[13] Instead there have been

▶ **FIGURE 7.8**

The risk (standard deviation of annual returns) of markets around the world, 1900–2020.

Source: E. Dimson, P. R. Marsh, and M. Staunton, *Triumph of the Optimists: 101 Years of Global Investment Returns* (Princeton, NJ: Princeton University Press, 2002), with updates provided by the authors.

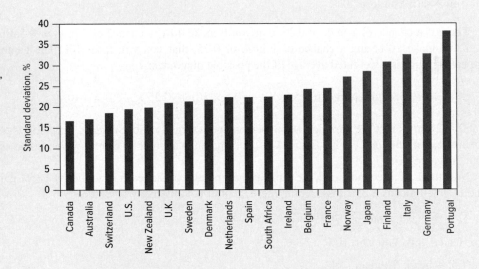

▶ **FIGURE 7.9**

Annualized standard deviation of the preceding 52 weekly market returns, June 1927 to January 2021.

Source: Authors' calculations, using data from Prof. Kenneth French's website, https://mba.tuck.dartmouth.edu/pages/faculty/ken.french/data_library.html.

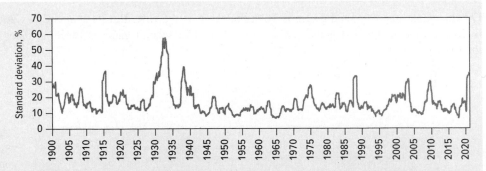

---

[13]These estimates are derived from *weekly* rates of return. The weekly variance is converted to an annual variance by multiplying by the number of weeks in the year. That is, the variance of the annual return is 52 times the weekly variance. The longer you hold a security or portfolio, the more risk you have to bear.

This conversion assumes that successive weekly returns are statistically independent. This is, in fact, a good assumption, as we will show in Chapter 12. Because variance is approximately proportional to the length of time interval over which a security or portfolio return is measured, standard deviation is proportional to the square root of the interval.

periods of both calm and turbulence. In 1995, an unusually tranquil year, the standard deviation of returns was less than 8%. Later, in the financial crisis and the COVID pandemic, the standard deviation spiked at over 30%.

Market turbulence over shorter daily, weekly, or monthly periods can be amazingly high. On Black Monday, October 19, 1987, the U.S. market fell by 23% *on a single day*. That is around twice the dramatic drop on March 16, 2020, in the wake of fear stemming from COVID-19. The market standard deviation for the week surrounding Black Monday was equivalent to 89% per year. Fortunately, volatility reverted to normal levels within a few weeks after the crash.

7.2 Self-Test

Calculate the mean and standard deviation of the score of a regular six-sided die.

7-3   How Diversification Reduces Risk

We can calculate our measures of risk equally well for individual securities. Table 7.3 uses monthly data to estimate standard deviations for 10 well-known common stocks for a recent five-year period.[14] Do these standard deviations look high to you? They should. The market portfolio's standard deviation was just over 12% during this period. All of our individual stocks had higher volatility. Five of them were more than twice as risky as the market.

Take a look also at Table 7.4, which shows the standard deviations of some well-known stocks from different countries and of the markets in which they trade. Once again, every stock is more risky than its domestic market index.

This raises an important question: The market portfolio is made up of individual stocks, so why doesn't its risk reflect the average risk of these stocks? The answer is that *diversification reduces risk.*

BEYOND THE PAGE

Covid and the risk of travel company stocks

mhhe.com/brealey14e

Stock	Standard Deviation (σ)	Stock	Standard Deviation (σ)
United States Steel	76.4%	Wells Fargo	21.6%
Tesla	48.1	ExxonMobil	19.4
Newmont	36.7	Consolidated Edison	16.5
Southwest Airlines	30.5	Johnson & Johnson	14.4
Amazon	28.3	Coca-Cola	12.6

〉TABLE 7.3   Standard deviations for selected U.S. common stocks, March 2015–February 2020 (figures in percent per year).

[14]Stocks that were particularly affected by the COVID-19 pandemic experienced dramatic increases in risk. Therefore, in Table 7.3 we show standard deviations for the pre-pandemic period ending in February 2020. The nearby App link shows how much risk measures changed for the stocks of companies in the travel industry.

》TABLE 7.4
Standard deviations for selected foreign stocks and market indexes, March 2015–February 2020 (figures in percent per year).

	Standard Deviation (σ)				
	Stock	Market		Stock	Market
BHP Billiton (Australia)	26.2%	10.9%	Sanofi (France)	17.5%	14.0%
BP (U.K.)	22.8	11.3	Nestlé (Switzerland)	13.6	10.9
Siemens (Germany)	22.5	15.5	Sony (Japan)	27.6	16.4
Hyundai Heavy Industry (Korea)	40.7	12.5	Toronto-Dominion Bank (Canada)	12.0	9.1
Agricultural Bank (China)	25.5	18.5	Tata Motors (India)	45.3	15.0

EXAMPLE 7.1 • How diversification reduces risk

To see the benefits of diversification more clearly, consider a simple example. There are two companies, Izy's Ice Cream and Ursula's Umbrellas. Assume for now that profits depend on only one variable—whether the weather is sunny or rainy. This is illustrated in the following table.

	Expected Returns, %	
Stock	Sun	Rain
Izy's Ice Cream	14	6
Ursula's Umbrellas	8	16
Portfolio	11	11

Running an ice cream company is risky: You make a lot of money when the sun shines, but you are likely to lose a lot in the rain. Selling umbrellas is similarly mixed: You're profitable in rainy weather but making close to nothing in the sun. So if you owned only one of these companies, your income would be highly dependent on the weather. But instead of owning 100% of one company, an alternative would be to own half of each. This reduces your risk because, while rain hurts Izy's Ice Cream, it's a boon for Ursula's Umbrellas. Your overall income is shown in the Portfolio row of the table. In a heatwave, you earn $1/2 \times 14 + 1/2 \times 8 = 11$, and in a rainstorm, you earn the same amount. So you can sleep soundly at night, knowing that you'll be able to pay the rent come rain or shine.

• • • • •

This is, of course, an extreme example. Izy's Ice Cream and Ursula's Umbrellas are only affected by the weather, and weather affects them in opposite ways, so you can reduce risk all the way to zero. But in reality, you won't be able to totally eradicate risk because stocks don't move in exactly opposite directions. So how much does diversification reduce risk generally? That's what we'll now explore, using real-life companies.

Take Southwest Airlines and Amazon. Between March 2015 and February 2020, the standard deviation of Southwest Airlines was 30.5% and that of Amazon was 28.3%. Suppose you believe these figures are good predictors of future risk. You invest 60% of your portfolio in Southwest Airlines and the remainder in Amazon. The standard deviation of your portfolio will generally *not* be a weighted average of the standard deviations of the individual securities, because diversification reduces risk below this weighted average.

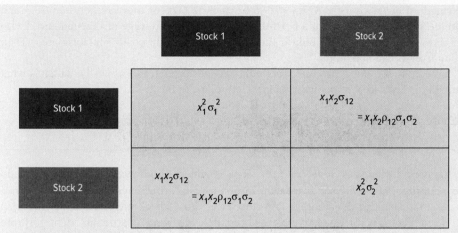

FIGURE 7.10

The variance of a two-stock portfolio is the sum of these four boxes.

x_1, x_2 = proportions invested in stocks 1 and 2;

σ_1^2, σ_2^2 = variance of stock returns;

σ_{12} = covariance of returns ($\rho_{12} \sigma_1 \sigma_2$);

ρ_{12} = correlation between returns on stocks 1 and 2.

Figure 7.10 shows how to calculate the risk of a two-stock portfolio, by summing up four boxes. To complete the top-left box, you weight the variance of the returns on stock 1 (σ_1^2) by the *square* of the proportion invested in it (x_1^2). Similarly, to complete the bottom-right box, you weight the variance of the returns on stock 2 (σ_2^2) by the *square* of the proportion invested in that stock.

The entries in these diagonal boxes depend on the variances of stocks 1 and 2; the entries in the other two boxes depend on their **covariance**. As you might guess, the covariance measures the degree to which the two stocks "covary" or in other words move together. It's the product of the **correlation coefficient** ρ_{12} and the two standard deviations:[15]

$$\text{Covariance between stocks 1 and 2} = \sigma_{12} = \rho_{12}\,\sigma_1\,\sigma_2 \tag{7.3}$$

The two standard deviations σ_1 and σ_2 define the risk of each stock in isolation, not how they covary together. So the key variable that determines covariance is the correlation coefficient ρ_{12}. A positive correlation coefficient indicates that, when stock 1 goes up, stock 2 tends to go up. If ρ_{12} is at its highest value of $+1$, we have perfect positive correlation: When stock 1 goes up, stock 2 always goes up proportionally. A negative correlation coefficient indicates that, when stock 1 goes up, stock 2 tends to go down. If ρ_{12} is at its lowest value of -1, we have perfect negative correlation: When stock 1 goes up, stock 2 always goes down, as in the umbrella and ice cream example. When ρ_{12} is zero, the returns on the two stocks are wholly unrelated.

Just as we weight the variances by the square of the proportion invested, so we weight the covariance by the *product* of the two proportionate holdings x_1 and x_2.

Once you've completed these four boxes, you simply add the entries to obtain the portfolio variance:

$$\text{Portfolio variance} = x_1^2\sigma_1^2 + x_2^2\sigma_2^2 + 2(x_1 x_2 \rho_{12}\sigma_1\sigma_2)$$

Now we can try putting in some figures for Southwest Airlines and Amazon. Let's start with the case of perfect positive correlation, $\rho_{12} = +1$.

The variance of your portfolio is the sum of these entries:

$$\begin{aligned}\text{Portfolio variance} &= (0.6^2 \times 30.5^2) + (0.4^2 \times 28.3^2) + 2(0.6 \times 0.4 \times 1 \times 30.5 \times 28.3)\\ &= 877.3\end{aligned}$$

BEYOND THE PAGE

How to calculate correlation coefficients

mhhe.com/brealey14e

---

[15] Another way to define the covariance is as follows:

Covariance between stocks 1 and 2 = σ_{12} = expected value of $(\tilde{r}_1 - r_1) \times (\tilde{r}_2 - r_2)$

Note that any security's covariance with itself is just its variance:

$$\begin{aligned}\sigma_{11} &= \text{expected value of } (\tilde{r}_1 - r_1) \times (\tilde{r}_1 - r_1)\\ &= \text{expected value of } (\tilde{r}_1 - r_1)^2 = \text{variance of stock 1} = \sigma_1^2\end{aligned}$$

The standard deviation is $\sqrt{877.3} = 29.6\%$ which is 60% of the way between 28.3 and 30.5. So the standard deviation of a portfolio is the weighted average of the standard deviations of individual stocks if and only if the stocks are perfectly positively correlated. Then there's no diversification benefit.[16]

Let's now go to the other extreme of perfect negative correlation ($\rho_{12} = -1$), which is what we assumed for Izy's Ice Cream and Ursula's Umbrellas. In this case,

$$\text{Portfolio variance} = (0.6^2 \times 30.5^2) + (0.4^2 \times 28.3^2) + 2[0.6 \times 0.4 \times (-1) \times 30.5 \times 28.3]$$
$$= 48.7$$

The standard deviation is $\sqrt{48.7} = 7.0\%$. Risk is almost eliminated. But you can still do better by putting 48.9% of your investment in Southwest Airlines and 51.1% in Amazon.[17] In that case, the standard deviation is almost exactly zero. (Check the calculation yourself.) Indeed, when there is perfect negative correlation, there is always a particular set of portfolio weights that will completely eliminate risk. Unfortunately, perfect negative correlation almost never occurs in the real world.

Reality is between the two extremes. Southwest Airlines and Amazon neither move in perfect lockstep nor are diametrically opposed. The recent correlation between the two stocks is 0.38; let's assume that this will continue in the future. If we go through the same exercise again with $\rho_{12} = 0.38$, we find

$$\text{Portfolio variance} = (0.6^2 \times 30.5^2) + (0.4^2 \times 28.3^2) + 2(0.6 \times 0.4 \times 0.38 \times 30.5 \times 28.3)$$
$$= 620.5$$

The standard deviation is $\sqrt{620.5} = 24.9\%$. The risk is now less than 60% of the way between 28.3 and 30.5.

Specific and Systematic Risk

You still might be a little disappointed. Why doesn't diversification reduce risk all the way to zero, as it did with Izy's Ice Cream and Ursula's Umbrellas? Your portfolio still bears some risk, so you might suffer the occasional sleepless night. The answer is that there are two types of risk—specific and systematic—and diversification can only get rid of one of them.

Specific risk is also known as *idiosyncratic risk, residual risk, unique risk,* or *unsystematic risk.* These are risks that affect only one company, or only companies in a single industry or of a particular type. For example, a pilot strike would hurt Southwest but have negligible effect on Amazon. Successful expansion of Alibaba into the United States would erode Amazon's profits but barely impact Southwest. An investor can reduce exposure to these risks by diversifying into unrelated companies. That's why specific risk is also known as *diversifiable risk.*

The second type is **systematic risk.** These are risks that are shared by most other businesses. For example, a downturn in the economy or a collapse of the overall stock market would adversely affect both Amazon and Southwest. As a result, you can't diversify these risks away, no matter how many other companies you move into. That's why systematic risk is also known as *undiversifiable risk.* Total risk (σ) is the sum of specific and systematic risk.

---

[16]We prove this result by substituting $\rho_{12} = 1$ into the portfolio variance formula:

Portfolio variance $= x_1^2\sigma_1^2 + x_2^2\sigma_2^2 + 2(x_1x_2\sigma_1\sigma_2) = (x_2\sigma_1 + x_2\sigma_2)^2$

Portfolio standard deviation $= x_1\sigma_1 + x_2\sigma_2$

[17]The standard deviation of Southwest is 30.5/28.3 = 1.078 times the standard deviation of Amazon. Therefore, you have to invest 1.078 times more in Amazon than in Southwest to eliminate all risk in a two-stock portfolio. The portfolio weights that *exactly* eliminate risk are 0.519 for Amazon and 0.481 for Southwest.

We assumed away systematic risk in the ice cream and umbrella example by saying that profits depend only on the weather. In reality, they'll also be affected by economic conditions. The following table expands the example to recognize that both companies do better in a boom than in a recession. You can see that holding a portfolio of the two businesses does not get rid of all risk; you're still exposed to the possibility of a recession, which is a systematic risk. However, regardless of the state of the economy, you're no longer exposed to weather conditions, which is a specific risk.

Expected Returns, %				
	Boom		Recession	
Stock	Sun	Rain	Sun	Rain
Izy's Ice Cream	18	10	10	2
Ursula's Umbrellas	12	20	4	12
Portfolio	15	15	7	7

7.3 Self-Test

a. Applebaum and Banana have standard deviations of 10% and 20%, respectively, and are less than perfectly correlated. You have a portfolio invested equally in each company. Will its standard deviation be 15%, higher than 15%, or lower than 15%?

b. What correlation coefficient between Applebaum and Banana would lead to the lowest portfolio standard deviation?

7.4 Self-Test

Are these following risks specific or systematic?
a. Purchases of luxury watches rise when executives receive higher bonuses.
b. A pandemic reduces the demand for air travel.
c. A football club loses its star striker to injury.
d. A chemicals company loses an asbestos lawsuit.

Diversification with Many Stocks

The method for calculating portfolio risk can easily be extended to portfolios of three or more securities. We just need to fill in more boxes. Each of those down the diagonal—the red boxes in Figure 7.11—contains the variance weighted by the square of the proportion invested. Each of the other boxes contains the covariance between that pair of securities, weighted by the product of the proportions invested.[18]

---

[18] The formal equivalent to "add up all the boxes" is Portfolio variance $= \sum_{i=1}^{N} \sum_{j=1}^{N} x_i x_j \sigma_{ij}$. Notice that when $i = j$, σ_{ij} is just the variance of stock i.

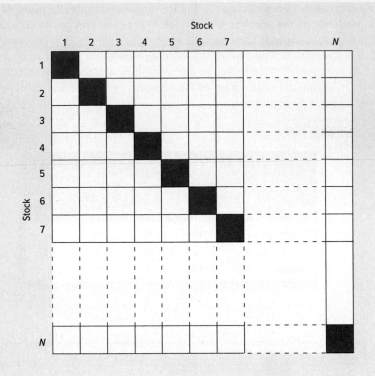

FIGURE 7.11

To find the variance of an *N*-stock portfolio, we must add the entries in a matrix like this. The diagonal cells contain variance terms ($x^2\sigma^2$) and the off-diagonal cells contain covariance terms ($x_i x_j \sigma_{ij}$).

EXAMPLE 7.2 • Limits to diversification

Did you notice in Figure 7.11 how much more important the covariances become as we add more securities to the portfolio? When there are just two securities, there are equal numbers of variance and covariance boxes. When there are many securities, the number of covariances is much larger than the number of variances. Thus the risk of a well-diversified portfolio reflects mainly the covariances.

Suppose we're dealing with portfolios in which equal investments are made in each of *N* stocks. The proportion invested in each stock is, therefore, $1/N$. So in each variance box we have $(1/N)^2$ times the variance, and in each covariance box we have $(1/N)^2$ times the covariance. There are *N* variance boxes and $N^2 - N$ covariance boxes. Therefore,

$$\text{Portfolio variance} = N\left(\frac{1}{N}\right)^2 \times \text{average variance}$$

$$+ (N^2 - N)\left(\frac{1}{N}\right)^2 \times \text{ average covariance}$$

$$= \frac{1}{N} \times \text{average variance} + \left(1 - \frac{1}{N}\right) \times \text{average covariance}$$

BEYOND THE PAGE

Try it!
Risk and increasing diversification

mhhe.com/brealey14e

Notice that as *N* increases, the portfolio variance steadily approaches the average covariance. This illustrates how specific risk is eliminated by combining individual stocks into portfolios, but systematic risk remains. It is the average covariance that constitutes the bedrock of risk remaining after diversification has done its work.

• • • • •

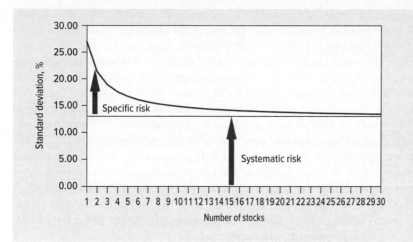

BEYOND THE PAGE

> **FIGURE 7.12**
>
> Average risk (standard deviation) of portfolios containing different numbers of stocks. The stocks were selected randomly from stocks traded on the New York Stock Exchange from 2010 through 2019. Notice that diversification reduces risk rapidly at first, then more slowly. This is because diversification can only eliminate *specific risk*. It cannot eliminate *systematic risk*.

Figure 7.12 compares the standard deviations between 2007 and 2019 of randomly selected one-stock portfolios, two-stock portfolios, five-stock portfolios, and so forth. Adding a second stock significantly reduces your portfolio risk, as we saw when adding Southwest to Amazon. Adding a third stock, let's say Coca-Cola, lowers your risk even further. That's because Coca-Cola doesn't bear the specific risks of either Amazon or Southwest; it's little affected by, Alibaba's expansion, or a pilot strike. Adding more and more stocks further reduces specific risk and thus portfolio risk. But there are diminishing returns. After about 20 or 30 companies, you've pretty much "maxed out" the benefits of diversification. No matter how many companies you add, you can't escape fluctuations in financial markets and the overall economy. The key lesson is this: *You can only diversify away specific risk, not systematic risk.*

International diversification

mhhe.com/brealey14e

7-4 Systematic Risk Is Market Risk

"Adding up the boxes" in Figure 7.11 sounds simple enough, until you remember that there are around 6,000 companies listed on the New York and NASDAQ stock exchanges. A portfolio manager who tried to include every one of those companies' stocks would have to fill up about $6,000 \times 6,000 = 36,000,000$ boxes! Of course, the boxes above the diagonal line of red boxes in Figure 7.11 match the boxes below. Nevertheless, getting accurate estimates of 18,000,000 covariances is impossible. Getting unbiased forecasts of rates of return for nearly 6,000 stocks is likewise impossible.

But it turns out that we don't have to. If investors have the same information, the logic of systematic risk and diversification leads them to invest in the **market portfolio**, which contains all stocks. Investors know what the market portfolio is; they can observe its returns and volatility. They don't have to compute market risk by adding up millions of boxes.

We now work through the logic for this result. The big-picture insight from the last two sections is this. The *total risk* of an individual company is measured by its standard deviation σ. If you held that stock in isolation, that's the amount of risk you'd bear. But investors don't hold individual stocks. They hold portfolios. The risk that a stock adds to a diversified portfolio isn't its total risk but only the systematic risk that's shared with the rest of the portfolio. Specific risk is diversified away.

We therefore only need to worry about a stock's systematic risk. But how do we measure it? Systematic risk is the risk that's shared with the rest of the portfolio, so we first need to know what the rest of the portfolio is before we can estimate it. It's a bit like choosing a wine. Neither red wine nor white wine is better in isolation; what matters is how the wine pairs with the rest of your meal. You need to decide what you're eating first before you pick your pairing.

So let's find out which what portfolio investors will choose. We'll do so using the Nobel Prize–winning insights of Harry Markowitz.[19] Think back to Section 7-3, where you were wondering whether to invest 60% of your savings into Southwest Airlines and 40% into Amazon. Recall that Southwest Airlines has a standard deviation of 30.5% and Amazon's risk is 28.3%. Assume that the future expected returns are 10.0% and 8.0%, respectively. The expected return on the 60–40 portfolio is 9.2%, a simple weighted average of the expected returns on the two holdings. With a correlation of 0.38, we previously calculated a standard deviation of 24.9%.[20]

But what about other splits than 60–40? The curved blue line in Figure 7.13 shows the combinations of expected return and risk that you could achieve by different pairings of the two stocks. It's known as the **investment opportunity set.**

We saw in Section 7-3 that the gain from diversification depends on how highly the stocks are correlated. The blue curve is based on the correlation coefficient $\rho = +0.38$. If both stocks moved in exact lockstep ($\rho = +1$), there would be no gains from diversification. You can see this by the gold dotted line in Figure 7.13. The red dotted line in the figure shows a second extreme case in which the returns on the two stocks are perfectly *negatively* correlated ($\rho = -1$). If this were so, there is a combination of the two stocks that would have no risk.

In practice, you're not limited to investing in just two stocks. For example, you could decide to choose a portfolio from the 10 stocks listed in the first column of Table 7.5. Your forecasts of their returns and standard deviations are shown in the table.[21]

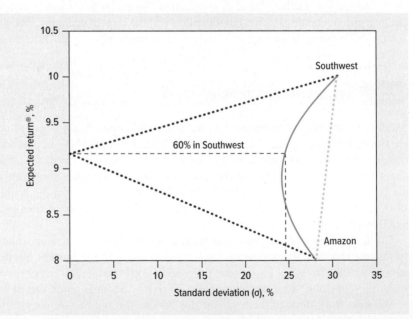

▶ **FIGURE 7.13**

The curved line illustrates how expected return and standard deviation change as you hold different combinations of two stocks. For example, if you invest 60% of your money in Southwest Airlines and the remainder in Amazon, your expected return is 9.2%, which is 60% of the way between the expected returns on the two stocks. The standard deviation is 24.9%, which is less than that of either stock. This is because diversification reduces risk.

---

[19]H. M. Markowitz, "Portfolio Selection," *Journal of Finance* 7 (March 1952), pp. 77–91.

[20] We pointed out in Section 7-3 that the correlation between Southwest Airlines and Amazon has been 0.38. The variance of a portfolio that is invested 60% in Southwest and 40% in Amazon is Variance $= x_1^2\sigma_1^2 + x_2^2\sigma_2^2 + 2x_1x_2\rho_{12}\sigma_1\sigma_2 = [(0.6)^2 \times (30.5)^2] + [(0.4)^2 \times (28.3)^2] + 2(0.6 \times 0.4 \times 0.38 \times 30.5 \times 28.3) = 620.5$. The portfolio standard deviation is $\sqrt{620.5} = 24.9\%$.

[21]There are 45 different correlation coefficients, so we have not listed them in Table 7.5.

Now look at Figure 7.14. Each dot marks the combination of risk and return offered by one of the securities in Table 7.5 (we have omitted United States Steel, whose standard deviation is off the scale).

By holding different proportions of the 10 securities, you can obtain a very wide selection of risk and return. Which combination will you choose out of this menu? You want to go up (to increase expected return) and to the left (to reduce risk). The red curve shows, for every level of risk, the highest expected return that you can obtain by forming a portfolio of the

Three Efficient Portfolios—Percentages Allocated to Each Stock (%)					
	Expected Return (%)	Standard Deviation (%)	A	B	T
United States Steel	6.0	76.4		0	0
Tesla	6.5	48.1		1	5
Newmont	5.0	36.7		7	9
Southwest Airlines	10.0	30.5	100	0	17
Amazon	8.0	28.3		1	10
Wells Fargo	6.8	21.6		21	23
ExxonMobil	5.3	19.4		0	0
Consolidated Edison	5.5	16.5		20	33
Johnson & Johnson	4.4	14.4		7	0
Coca-Cola	4.8	12.6		43	5
Expected portfolio return			10.0	5.4	6.8
Portfolio standard deviation			30.5	10.5	12.5

》TABLE 7.5   Examples of efficient portfolios chosen from 10 stocks.

Note: Standard deviations and the correlations between stock returns were estimated from monthly returns, March 2015–February 2020. Efficient portfolios are calculated assuming that short sales are prohibited.

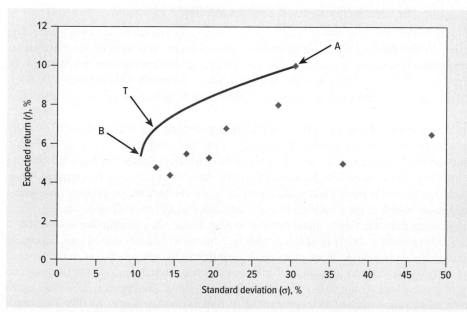

▶ FIGURE 7.14

Each dot shows the expected return and standard deviation of stocks in Table 7.5. There are many possible combinations of expected return and standard deviation from investing in a mixture of these stocks. If you like high expected returns and dislike high standard deviations, you will prefer portfolios along the red line. These are *efficient* portfolios. We have marked the three efficient portfolios described in Table 7.5 (A, T, and B).

Calculating the Efficient Frontier

❭ We won't calculate the efficient frontier here, but you may be interested in how to do it. Think back to the capital rationing problem in Section 5-4. There we wanted to deploy a limited amount of capital investment in a portfolio of projects to give the highest NPV. Here we want to deploy an investor's funds to give the highest expected return for a given standard deviation. To solve the capital rationing problem, we employ linear programming; to solve the portfolio problem, we turn to a variant of linear programming known as *quadratic programming*. Given the expected return and standard deviation for each stock, as well as the correlation between each pair of stocks, we could use a standard quadratic computer program (such as Excel's Goal Seek) to search out the set of efficient portfolios.

10 stocks. Markowitz called the portfolios that lie on this red curve **efficient portfolios** and the red curve itself the **efficient frontier**.

So, out of the millions of possible combinations of the 10 stocks that we could choose from, each with their different weights, we've made substantial progress. We've narrowed the choice set down to the red curve in Figure 7.14 —all investors will choose from this red curve; they won't pick anything below it. We've highlighted three portfolios on this curve and their compositions are summarized in Table 7.5.

- Portfolio A offers the highest expected return. It is invested entirely in one stock, Southwest Airlines.
- Portfolio B offers the minimum risk. You can see from Table 7.5 that it has large holdings in Consolidated Edison, Coca-Cola, and Wells Fargo, which have low standard deviations. However, the portfolio also has a small holding in Newmont and Tesla, even though they are individually risky, because they have very little correlation with other stocks and so provide diversification.
- Portfolio T is a third efficient portfolio with intermediate levels of risk and expected return. (We will explain shortly why portfolio T is important.)

But even though we've narrowed the choice set down to the red curve, it seems we can't go any further. Which point on the curve an investor chooses seems to depend on his preferences. It appears that a risk-averse investor (a "chicken") might hold the minimum risk Portfolio B. A risk-tolerant investor (a "lion") might own Portfolio A. Someone with medium risk tolerance might opt for T. And other investors will choose other points on the curve between A and B.

Thus it may seem that how much of a stock's risk is systematic—is shared with the rest of an investor's portfolio—depends on who's holding the stock. For a risk-averse chicken, systematic risk is the risk that's shared with Portfolio B, a big piece of which is Coca-Cola. For a risk-tolerant lion, it's the risk that's shared with Southwest Airlines. Another drinks company, such as Pepsi-Cola, would be viewed as having high systematic risk by the chicken but not the lion. So it seems that we'll never be able to get a measure of systematic risk that all investors agree on.

This problem dilemma might sound familiar to you. Recall the dilemma we considered in Chapter 1, where investors might disagree on what investments a company should take, depending on their individual preferences. Back then, we showed that introducing well-functioning capital markets turned discord into harmony. If investors can use capital markets (borrowing and lending or buying and selling shares) to satisfy their individual preferences, they'll all agree on how to measure the value of an investment by its impact on shareholder wealth. That result was the *Fisher separation theorem,* which shows that you can separate the investment decision from shareholder preferences.

And it's well-functioning capital markets that also turn discord into harmony here. If investors use borrowing and lending to satisfy their individual preferences, they'll agree on how to measure systematic risk. Let's see why.

Portfolio Choice with Borrowing and Lending

Figure 7.14 showed the efficient portfolios that an investor can choose from by selecting different combinations of 10 stocks. We continue with this example for the moment. What happens if we introduce a risk-free asset?

Suppose that you can lend money by purchasing Treasury bills yielding a risk-free rate of interest r_f. If you invest some of your wealth in stocks and place the remainder in Treasury bills, what does the set of possible risk-return combinations look like? Figure 7.13 showed that, when you combine two risky assets, the investment opportunity set is a curve. But when you combine a risky asset or portfolio with a risk-free asset, you obtain a straight line.[22]

This is illustrated in Figure 7.15, which repeats the efficient portfolios from Figure 7.14. For example, perhaps you wonder about investing in portfolio A, which is an efficient portfolio. The straight line running from the risk-free rate through A shows the combinations of return and risk that you could obtain by holding a mixture of portfolio A and the risk-free rate.

Let's put some numbers on this. Portfolio A has an expected return of 10.0% and a standard deviation of 30.5%. Treasury bills offer an interest rate $r_f = 2\%$ and are risk-free (standard deviation = 0). If you invest half your money in portfolio A and half in Treasury bills, the expected return on your investment is halfway between the expected return on each investment:

$$r = \left(\frac{1}{2} \times \text{expected return on A}\right) + \left(\frac{1}{2} \times \text{interest rate}\right)$$
$$= 6.0\%$$

And the standard deviation is halfway between the standard deviations of each investment:

$$\sigma = 1/2 \times \text{standard deviation of A} + \frac{1}{2} \times \text{standard deviation of bills} = 15.2\%$$

Or suppose that you strive for very large returns: You *borrow* at the Treasury bill rate[23] an amount equal to your initial wealth and invest everything in portfolio A. You have twice your own money invested in A, but you have to *pay* interest on the loan. Therefore your expected return increases to:

$$r = (2 \times \text{expected return on A}) - (1 \times \text{interest rate})$$
$$= 18.0\%$$

The standard deviation of your portfolio increases also:

$$\sigma = (2 \times \text{standard deviation of A}) - (1 \times \text{standard deviation of bills})$$
$$= 30.2\%$$

---

[22]If you want to check this, write down the formula for the standard deviation of a two-stock portfolio:

Standard deviation $= \sqrt{x_1^2\sigma_1^2 + x_2^2\sigma_2^2 + 2x_1x_2\rho_{12}\sigma_1\sigma_2}$. Now see what happens when security 2 is riskless, that is, when $\sigma_2 = 0$.

[23]We are clearly simplifying here. Only the U.S. Treasury can borrow at the Treasury bill rate. But investors can borrow at rates a percentage point or two higher if they post their portfolios as collateral. The higher rates for borrowing mean that in practice the slope of the borrowing segment of the line is a little less than shown in Figure 7.14.

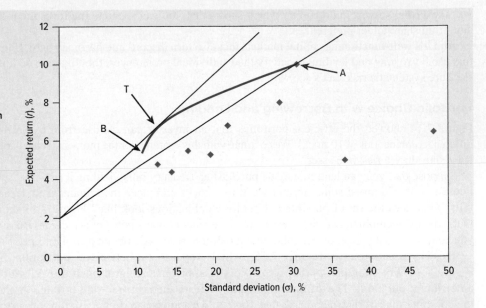

FIGURE 7.15

Lending and borrowing extend the range of investment possibilities. If you invest in portfolio A and lend or borrow at the risk-free interest rate, r_f, you can achieve any point along the straight line from r_f through A. By investing in r_f, and T you can do even better. Since this is the steepest line possible, it is the best combination of risk and return that you can obtain.

By moving money from Treasury bills into the risky portfolio, you increase your risk, but also your expected return. The slope of the straight line shows how much money you earn from each dollar invested—how much your expected return rises when your risk (σ) goes up by 1%. This slope is known as the *Sharpe ratio:*

$$\text{Sharpe ratio} = \frac{\text{Risk premium}}{\text{standard deviation}} = \frac{r - r_f}{\sigma}$$

The lending-borrowing line opens up new portfolio choices that were not apparent in Figure 7.14. You can locate your portfolio anywhere on the line that passes through portfolio A. But the choices on that line are *not* choices you would end up taking. You can draw a straight line between the risk-free rate and *any* portfolio on the efficient frontier of stocks. All stock portfolios to the left of A in Figure 7.15 are better destinations for lending-borrowing lines anchored at the risk-free rate.

As you move left from A to lower-risk efficient stock portfolios, you rotate the lending-borrowing line counterclockwise, increasing its slope and Sharpe ratio. You want the steepest possible slope and highest Sharpe ratio. The slope and Sharpe ratio keep increasing as you keep moving the line left along the red line of efficient stock portfolios. The limit is reached when the lending-borrowing line is just on the edge of the red curve. The line just touches a *tangency portfolio* of stocks, which we label T.

The *best* stock portfolio to combine with the risk-free asset is the tangency portfolio T. This stock portfolio offers the highest Sharpe ratio of risk premium to standard deviation and allows the investor to choose his place on the tangent line. All investors will choose from this tangency line, rather than the straight line through any other portfolio, or from the initial curve that we constructed in Figure 7.14 that included stocks only.

This is a powerful result. What it means is that *all investors will hold the same portfolio of stocks:* the tangency portfolio T. Even though investors have different preferences for risk and return, they'll satisfy their preferences by borrowing and lending different amounts (choosing different points on the lending-borrowing line), not by changing their choice of stocks.

Measuring Investment Manager Performance

❯ How do we measure the investment performance of a fund manager? The simple answer would be to look at her past returns over a long time period. Indeed, most mutual funds advertise themselves by quoting past performance figures. However, as we've shown, an investor may obtain a high return simply by taking on more risk, rather than through skilled stock selection.

The Sharpe ratio is a way to measure the manager's risk-adjusted return, which is a more accurate measure of skill than the raw return.

As long as investors all have the same information and make the same assessments of expected returns, standard deviations, and correlations, then everyone sees the same investment opportunity set and efficient frontier, and everyone sees the same tangency portfolio T. Simply put, if all investors have access to the same information, all should hold the same portfolio of stocks.

Here's why. A lion hunts for high returns and is willing to take on high risk. So you might think she'd prefer A to T because it offers higher returns. But recall that A consists of Southwest Airlines only. Holding one stock is a foolish way to pursue high returns because the lion bears *specific risk*. Any serious setback to Southwest Airlines will torpedo her entire portfolio. (Risk-tolerant investors still dislike risk, just not as much as risk-averse ones). So she should add other companies to diversify away this risk and move from A to T in Figure 7.14. If these additions reduce her risk and return below her desired levels, she can then increase them by borrowing and moving up from T on the tangency line. It's better to take on risk by borrowing more rather than by bearing specific risk. (We'll show formally in Chapter 8 that investors aren't offered higher returns for bearing specific risk because they can get rid of it by diversifying.) As a result, borrowing to invest more than her wealth in portfolio T offers a higher return than A.

Similarly, a chicken might seek safety by running away from tech stocks and investing his entire portfolio in Coca-Cola, which has the lowest standard deviation in Table 7.5. But that's actually unsafe because he bears the specific risks of the utilities sector, such as a change in regulation. It's better for him to diversify away this specific risk by holding some more volatile stocks and moving to T. While this action alone could make his portfolio too volatile, he has a solution: Take some of his money out of stocks and instead invest it in Treasury bills. It's better to decrease risk by buying Treasury bills rather than holding only utilities and bearing specific risk.

To reiterate, *all investors should hold the same stock portfolio.* Investors should differ in *how much* of that portfolio they hold. Chickens will only put some of their money into the portfolio, and the rest into Treasury bills. Lions will borrow to invest more than their initial wealth into the portfolio. But, to the extent that they hold stocks, they will hold the same stocks.

Market Risk

The lessons of our 10-stock portfolio apply to the market as a whole. If investors share the same information, all will hold the portfolio of stocks with the highest Sharpe ratio—that is, the portfolio that is tangent to a lending-borrowing line. This outcome is summarized in Figure 7.16.

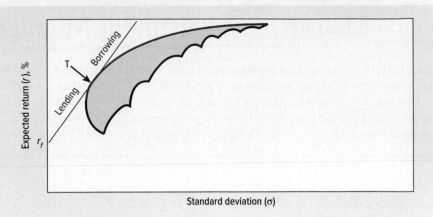

▶ FIGURE 7.16

Lending and borrowing extend the range of investment possibilities. If you invest in the tangent portfolio T and lend or borrow at the risk-free interest rate, r_f, you can achieve any point along the straight line from r_f through T. This gives you the highest expected return for any level of risk.

What does portfolio T look like? If all investors should hold the same stocks, and all stocks are held, this means that *all investors should hold the market portfolio.* The **market portfolio** is the portfolio of all stocks in the economy, where the weights correspond to the fraction of the overall market that each stock represents. For example, if Apple comprises 3% of the value of all traded stocks in the United States, then Apple will be 3% of the market portfolio, and 3% of the stock portfolio held by both chickens and lions.

So we have another separation theorem. We separate the investor's job into two stages. The first is to select the best portfolio of stocks, which is the portfolio T with the highest Sharpe ratio. The second step is to blend this portfolio with borrowing or lending to match the investor's willingness to bear risk. Each investor holds just two investments—the market portfolio T and the amount of lending or borrowing. This result is known as the *two-fund separation theorem.*

Because investors hold the entire stock market, all unsystematic risk is diversified away. *All of the remaining systematic risk is market risk.*

The straight line through T is thus known as the *capital market line.* It shows the trade-off between risk and return that an investor faces when he decides how to allocate his savings between lending or borrowing and the market portfolio. The Sharpe ratio of the capital market line is:[24]

$$\text{Sharpe ratio} = \frac{\text{Risk premium}}{\text{standard deviation}} = \frac{r_M - r_f}{\sigma_M}$$

The equation for the line itself:

$$r_p = r_f + \frac{r_M - r_f}{\sigma_M}\sigma_p \tag{7.4}$$

The subscripts M, which now replaces T, stands for "market" and p for the portfolios along the capital market line.

---

[24]Since 1900, the risk premium on the U.S. market has averaged 7.8% a year (Table 7.1) and the standard deviation of these returns has been 19.5% (Table 7.3). Thus, the Sharpe ratio of the capital market line has been 7.8/19.5 = 0.40. An investor who was prepared to take on an extra percentage point of standard deviation could have earned an extra 0.40% return.

Equation (7.4) means this: Suppose you're more risk-averse than average. Rather than playing it safe and putting your entire savings in Treasury bills, you've chosen to put part of your savings in the market, and as a result, your portfolio bears risk of σ_p. What return can you expect on your portfolio for bearing this risk? Recall the Sharpe ratio is your extra return for each dollar invested, the extra return that you get for bearing risk. So, if you're bearing risk of σ_p, your extra return is σ_p times the Sharpe ratio. This extra return is over and above the risk-free rate that you'd get if you played it totally safe. So, your overall expected return is given by Eq. (7.4).

The same logic applies to a risk-tolerant investor, although that investor may borrow to increase her stake in the market portfolio of stocks.

7.5 Self-Test

There are two stocks in the economy. One makes champagne, another shoelaces. Which of the two stocks will a risk-tolerant lion choose? Which would a risk-averse chicken choose? Both can borrow and lend at the risk-free rate.

7-5   Should Companies Diversify?

We've seen how diversification reduces risk and thus makes sense for investors. You might think that this means that companies should diversify since they're supposed to act in shareholders' interest. Perhaps an energy company should buy a media firm to reduce its exposure to climate change.

But the fact that diversification is good for investors does *not* mean that companies should pursue it. This is because investors can diversify themselves. An investor who wants to reduce his climate change risk can take some of his money out of energy stocks and reallocate it to media. To be sure, he'd have to pay brokerage costs, but this is much cheaper than if the energy company diversifies. As we'll discuss in Chapter 32, if it buys a media firm, it has to hire investment banks, pay a premium over the media company's stock price, and spend time and money integrating the two companies. Starting up a media operation would similarly be slow and expensive.

Because investors can diversify on their own account, they won't pay any extra for a firm that is diversified. The whole is worth no more than the sum of its parts. A conglomerate with both energy and media divisions is worth exactly the same as if those divisions were separate companies. If it cost more, no investor would buy the conglomerate because he'd simply buy energy and media companies separately.

This is a crucial result because it implies *value additivity*. If the market values asset A (say, an energy business) at PV(A) and asset B (say, a media business) at PV(B), value additivity means that the market value of a firm that holds only these two assets is

$$PV(AB) = PV(A) + PV(B)$$

Why is this concept so important? Because it means that a manager can evaluate new investment opportunities in isolation. Let's say the company currently has business A and

---

[25]The fund organizations have other ways of making money on index funds, for example by charging fees for lending out stocks to short-sellers.

is considering whether to invest in a new project, B. She only needs to calculate the PV of project B because that's how much the value of her company increases if she takes the project. The whole is the sum of its parts. She doesn't need to take into account how project B meshes with her existing business A. It doesn't matter whether it is negatively correlated and allows the company to diversify away from its current operations, or positively correlated and would mean doubling down.

The idea of value additivity can be proved formally in several ways.[26] Moreover, it can be extended for any number of assets. For example, a three-asset firm combining assets A, B, and C would be worth PV(ABC) = PV(A) + PV(B) + PV(C), and so on. The bottom line is this: It doesn't matter how many existing businesses a company has, or what these businesses are. The value of a new project depends only on its own discounted cash flows.

7.6 Self-Test

Izy's Ice Cream (from Section 7-3) is worth $40 million and Ursula's Umbrellas is worth $60 million. Their cash flows are perfectly negatively correlated. They decide to merge. What will the value of the merged firm be?

● ● ● ● ●

KEY TAKEAWAYS

- **Historical-average rates of return depended on risk.** Returns to investors have varied according to the risks the investors have borne. Safe securities like U.S. Treasury bills have provided a long-term average return of only 3.7% a year. The stock market provided an average return of 11.5% and a risk premium of 7.8% over the safe rate of interest.

- **Risks can be measured by the standard deviation or variance of returns.** The historical-average standard deviation of the U.S. stock market has been just under 20%. Market standard deviations have been lower in recent decades, but spikes of high volatility have arrived unexpectedly—for example, at the start of the COVID pandemic.

- **Specific vs. systematic risk.** Most of the specific risk of individual stocks is eliminated in a well-diversified portfolio. The systematic risk that remains depends on shared risks of the stocks in the portfolio. Shared risks are measured by the covariance between each pair of stocks. Covariance depends on the standard deviations of the stocks' returns (σ_i and σ_j) and the correlation coefficient between them (ρ_{ij}).

  Covariance of stocks i and j = $\sigma_{ij} = \rho_{ij}\sigma_i\sigma_j$

- **Portfolio risk.** This is computed as a weighted sum of variances and covariances for all stocks in the portfolio. The general formula is:

  Portfolio variance = $\sigma^2 = \sum x_i^2\sigma_i^2 + \sum\sum x_i x_j\, \rho_{ij}\, \sigma_i\, \sigma_j$

  Portfolio standard deviation σ is the square root of variance.

- **Efficient portfolios.** Efficient portfolios offer the highest expected rate of return for each possible level of portfolio risk. Investors can combine investment in efficient stock portfolios with lending or borrowing. By doing so they can identify *one* optimal stock portfolio

---

[26]You may wish to refer to the Appendix to Chapter 32, which discusses diversification and value additivity in the context of mergers.

from the set of efficient portfolios. The optimal stock portfolio is the one with the highest Sharpe ratio:

$$\text{Sharpe ratio} = \frac{\text{Risk premium}}{\text{standard deviation}} = \frac{r - r_f}{\sigma}$$

- **The optimal portfolio is the market portfolio.** Investors who share the same information will all buy the same portfolio of stocks, and adjust its risk by also lending or borrowing depending on their personal risk tolerance. If all investors have the same information, they will all buy the market portfolio of all traded common stocks. They can do so in practice by buying an index fund that tracks a broad market index.

  The relevant risk of a stock is not its total risk, but systematic risk as only this risk cannot be diversified away. Since all investors hold the market portfolio, systematic risk is market risk—it is the risk of a stock that is shared with the overall market.

- **Diversification makes sense for investors, not for corporations.** Almost all serious investors diversify. This does not imply that *firms* should diversify. Corporate diversification is redundant if investors can diversify cheaply and easily on their own. Since diversification does not affect the value of the firm, present values add even when risk is explicitly considered. Thanks to *value additivity,* the net present value rule for capital budgeting works even under uncertainty.

  In this chapter, we have introduced you to a number of formulas. They are reproduced in the endpapers to the book. You should take a look and check that you understand them.

  Near the end of Chapter 9, we list some Excel functions that are useful for measuring the risk of stocks and portfolios.

• • • • •

FURTHER READING

For international evidence on market returns since 1900, see:

E. Dimson, P. R. Marsh, and M. Staunton, *Triumph of the Optimists: 101 Years of Global Investment Returns* (Princeton, NJ: Princeton University Press, 2002). More recent data are available in the *Credit Suisse Global Investment Returns Yearbook Summary,* https://www.credit-suisse.com/about-us/en/reports-research/studies-publications.html.

The Ibbotson Yearbook is a valuable record of the performance of U.S. securities since 1926 and is now published by Duff and Phelps:

R. Ibbotson, R. J. Grabowski, J. P. Harrington, and C. Nunes, *Duff and Phelps 2020 Stocks, Bonds, Bills, and Inflation SBBI Yearbook,* https://www.duffandphelps.com/insights/publications/cost-of-capital/2020-sbbi-yearbook.

Useful books and reviews on the equity risk premium include:

P. Fernandez, E. de Apellaniz, and I. Fernández Acín, "Market Risk Premium and Risk-Free Rate Used for 81 Countries in 2020: A Survey," March 25, 2020. Available at SSRN: https://ssrn.com/abstract=3560869.

W. Goetzmann and R. Ibbotson, *The Equity Risk Premium: Essays and Explorations* (Oxford, U.K.: Oxford University Press, 2006).

R. Mehra (ed.), *Handbook of the Equity Risk Premium* (Amsterdam: North-Holland, 2007).

R. Mehra and E. C. Prescott, "The Equity Risk Premium in Retrospect," in *Handbook of the Economics of Finance,* eds. G. M. Constantinides, M. Harris, and R. M. Stulz (Amsterdam: North-Holland, 2003) Vol. 1, Part 2, pp. 889–938.

PROBLEM SETS

Select problems are available in McGraw-Hill's *Connect*.
Please see the preface for more information.

1. **Rate of return (S7.1)** The level of the Syldavia market index is 21,000 at the start of the year and 25,500 at the end. The dividend yield on the index is 4.2%.

   a. What is the return on the index over the year?

   b. If the interest rate is 6%, what is the risk premium over the year?

   c. If the inflation rate is 8%, what is the *real* return on the index over the year?

2. **Real versus nominal returns (S7.1)** The Costaguana stock market provided a return of 95%. The inflation rate in Costaguana during the year was 80%. In Ruritania the stock market return was 12%, but the inflation rate was only 2%. Which country's stock market provided the higher real rate of return?

3. **Arithmetic average and compound returns (S7.1)** Integrated Potato Chips (IPC) does not pay a dividend. Its current stock price is $150 and there is an equal probability that the return over the coming year will be –10%, +20%, or +50%.

   a. What is the *expected* price at year-end?

   b. If the probabilities of future returns remain unchanged and you could observe the returns of IPC over a large number of years, what would be the (arithmetic) average return?

   c. If you were to discount IPC's expected price at year-end from part (a) by this number, would you underestimate, overestimate, or correctly estimate the stock's present value?

   d. If you could observe the returns of IPC over a large number of years, what would be the compound (geometric average) rate of return?

   e. If you were to discount IPC's expected price at year-end from part (a) by this number, would you underestimate, overestimate, or correctly estimate the stock's present value?

4. **Risk premium (S7.1)** Here are inflation rates and U.S. stock market and Treasury bill returns between 1929 and 1933:

Year	Inflation, %	Stock Market Return, %	T-Bill Return, %
1929	–0.2	–14.5	4.8
1930	–6.0	–28.3	2.4
1931	–9.5	–43.9	1.1
1932	–10.3	–9.9	1.0
1933	0.5	57.3	0.3

   a. What was the real return on the stock market in each year?

   b. What was the average real return?

   c. What was the risk premium in each year?

   d. What was the average risk premium?

5. **Risk Premium (S7.1)** Suppose that in year 2030, investors become much more willing than before to bear risk. As a result, they require a return of 8% to invest in common stocks rather than the 10% that they had required in the past. This shift in risk aversion causes a 15% change in the value of the market portfolio.

   a. Do stock prices rise by 15% or fall?

   b. If you now use past returns to estimate the expected risk premium, will the inclusion of data for 2030 cause you to underestimate or overestimate the return that investors required in the past?

c. Will the inclusion of data for 2030 cause you to underestimate or overestimate the return that investors require in the future?

6. **Stocks vs. bonds (S7.1)** Each of the following statements is dangerous or misleading. Explain why.

   a. A long-term U.S. government bond is always absolutely safe.

   b. All investors should prefer stocks to bonds because stocks offer higher long-run rates of return.

   c. The best practical forecast of future rates of return on the stock market is a 5- or 10-year average of historical returns.

7. **Expected return and standard deviation (S7.2)** A game of chance offers the following odds and payoffs. Each play of the game costs $100, so the net profit per play is the payoff less $100.

Probability	Payoff	Net Profit
0.10	$500	$400
0.50	100	0
0.40	0	−100

What are the expected cash payoff and expected rate of return? Calculate the variance and standard deviation of this rate of return. (Do not make the adjustment for degrees of freedom described in footnote 12.)

8. **Average returns and standard deviation (S7.2)** The following table shows the nominal returns on Brazilian stocks and the rate of inflation.

   a. What was the standard deviation of the market returns? (Do not make the adjustment for degrees of freedom described in footnote 12.)

   b. Calculate the average *real* return.

Year	Nominal Return (%)	Inflation (%)
2015	−41.4	10.7
2016	66.2	6.3
2017	26.9	2.9
2018	15.0	2.7
2019	32.6	3.7
2020	2.1	3.7

9. **Average returns and standard deviation (S7.2)** During the boom years of 2010–2014, ace mutual fund manager Diana Sauros produced the following percentage rates of return. Rates of return on the market are given for comparison.

   a. Calculate the average return and standard deviation of Ms. Sauros's mutual fund.

   b. Why do you need to know the interest rate to judge whether Ms. Sauros performed better or worse than the market?

	2010	2011	2012	2013	2014
Ms. Sauros	+24.9	−0.9	+18.6	+42.1	+15.2
S&P 500	+17.2	+1.0	+16.1	+33.1	+12.7

   c. Would you be more likely to congratulate if the interest rate was high or low?

10. **Risk and diversification (S7.3)** Hippique s.a., which owns a stable of racehorses, has just invested in a mysterious black stallion with great form but disputed bloodlines. Some experts in horseflesh predict the horse will win the coveted Prix de Bidet; others argue that it should be put out to grass. Is this a risky investment for Hippique shareholders?

11. **Diversification (S7.3)** Here are the percentage returns on two stocks.

   a. Calculate the monthly variance and standard deviation of each stock. Which stock is the riskier if held on its own?

   b. Now calculate the variance and standard deviation of the returns on a portfolio that invests an equal amount each month in the two stocks.

   c. Is the variance more or less than half way between the variance of the two individual stocks?

Month	Digital Cheese	Executive Fruit
January	+15%	+7%
February	−3	+1
March	+5	+4
April	+7	+13
May	−4	+2
June	+3	+5
July	−2	−3
August	−8	−2

12. **Risk and diversification (S7.3)** In which of the following situations would you get the largest reduction in risk by spreading your investment across two stocks?

   a. The two shares are perfectly correlated.

   b. There is no correlation.

   c. There is modest negative correlation.

   d. There is perfect negative correlation

13. **Portfolio risk (S7.3–S7.4)** True or false?

   a. Investors prefer diversified companies because they are less risky.

   b. If stocks were perfectly positively correlated, diversification would not reduce risk.

   c. Diversification over a large number of assets completely eliminates risk.

   d. Diversification works only when assets are uncorrelated.

   e. Diversification reduces systematic risk.

f. A stock with a low standard deviation always contributes less to portfolio risk than a stock with a higher standard deviation.

g. The contribution of a stock to the risk of a well-diversified portfolio depends on its market risk.

14. **Portfolio risk (S7.4)** To calculate the variance of a three-stock portfolio, you need to add nine boxes:

Use the same symbols that we used in this chapter; for example, x_1 = proportion invested in stock 1 and σ_{12} = covariance between stocks 1 and 2. Now complete the nine boxes.

15. **Portfolio risk (S7.4)**

a. How many variance terms and how many different covariance terms do you need to calculate the risk of a 100-share portfolio?

b. Suppose all stocks had a standard deviation of 30% and a correlation with each other of 0.4. What is the standard deviation of the returns on a portfolio that has equal holdings in 50 stocks?

c. What is the standard deviation of a fully diversified portfolio of such stocks?

16. **Portfolio risk (S7.4)** Suppose that the standard deviation of returns from a typical share is about 0.4 (or 40%) a year. The correlation between the returns of each pair of shares is about 0.3.

a. Calculate the variance and standard deviation of the returns on a portfolio that has equal investments in two shares, three shares, and so on, up to 10 shares.

b. Use your estimates to draw a graph like Figure 7.12. How large is the underlying market variance that cannot be diversified away?

c. Now repeat the problem, assuming that the correlation between each pair of stocks is zero.

17. **Portfolio risk (S7.4)** Table 7.6 shows standard deviations and correlation coefficients for seven stocks from different countries. Calculate the variance of a portfolio with equal investments in each stock.

	BHP Billiton	BP	Siemens	Nestlé	Sony	Sanofi	Agricultural Bank
BHP Billiton	1.00	0.44	0.21	−0.05	0.21	0.15	0.24
BP		1.00	0.40	0.24	0.27	0.36	0.27
Siemens			1.00	0.26	0.33	0.29	0.21
Nestlé				1.00	0.34	0.27	−0.06
Sony					1.00	0.27	0.35
Sanofi						1.00	0.17
Agricultural Bank							1.00
Standard deviation, %	26.1	22.8	22.5	13.6	27.6	17.5	25.5

❭**TABLE 7.6** Standard deviations of returns and correlation coefficients for a sample of seven stocks

Note: Correlations and standard deviations were calculated using returns in each country's own currency. In other words, they assume that the investor is protected against exchange risk.

18. **Portfolio risk (S7.4)** Your eccentric Aunt Claudia has left you $50,000 in BP shares plus $50,000 cash. Unfortunately, her will requires that the BP stock not be sold for one year and the $50,000 cash must be entirely invested in one of the stocks shown in Table 7.6. What is the safest attainable portfolio under these restrictions?

19. **Portfolio risk (S7.4)** Hyacinth Macaw invests 60% of her funds in stock I and the balance in stock J. The standard deviation of returns on I is 10%, and on J it is 20%. Calculate the variance and standard deviation of portfolio returns, assuming

   a. The correlation between the returns is 1.0.

   b. The correlation is 0.5.

   c. The correlation is 0.

20. **Efficient portfolios (S7.4)** Figure 7.17 purports to show the range of attainable combinations of expected return and standard deviation.

   a. Which diagram is incorrectly drawn and why?

   b. Which is the efficient set of portfolios?

   c. If r_f is the rate of interest, mark with an X the optimal stock portfolio.

▶ **FIGURE 7.17**

See Problem 21

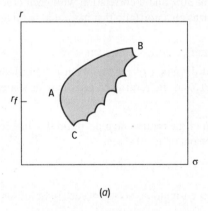

(a)

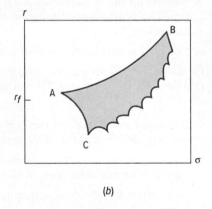

(b)

21. **Efficient portfolios (S7.4)**

   a. Plot the following risky portfolios on a graph:

	A	B	C	D	E	F	G	H
Expected return (r), (%)	10	12.5	15	16	17	18	18	20
Standard deviation (σ), (%)	23	21	25	29	29	32	35	45

   b. Five of these portfolios are efficient, and three are not. Which are inefficient ones?

   c. Suppose you can also borrow and lend at an interest rate of 12%. Which of the portfolios has the highest Sharpe ratio?

d. Suppose you are prepared to tolerate a standard deviation of 25%. What is the maximum expected return that you can achieve if you cannot borrow or lend?

e. What is your optimal strategy if you can borrow or lend at 12% and are prepared to tolerate a standard deviation of 25%? What is the maximum expected return that you can achieve with this risk?

22. **Portfolio risk and return (S7.4)** Look back at the calculation for Southwest Airlines and Amazon in Section 7.4.

   a. Recalculate the expected portfolio return and standard deviation for different values of x_1 and x_2, assuming the correlation coefficient $\rho_{12} = 0$. Plot the range of possible combinations of expected return and standard deviation as in Figure 7.12.

   b. Repeat the problem for $\rho_{12} = +0.5$.

23. **Portfolio risk and return (S7.4)** George Dupree proposes to invest in two shares, X and Y. He expects a return of 12% from X and 8% from Y. The standard deviation of returns is 8% for X and 5% for Y. The correlation coefficient between the returns is 0.2.

   a. Compute the expected return and standard deviation of the following portfolios:

Portfolio	Percentage in X	Percentage in Y
1	50	50
2	25	75
3	75	25

   b. Sketch the set of portfolios composed of X and Y.

   c. Suppose that Mr. Dupree can also borrow or lend at an interest rate of 5%. Show on your sketch how this alters his opportunities. Given that he can borrow or lend, what proportions of the common stock portfolio should be invested in X and Y?

24. **Portfolio risk and return (S7.4)** Ebenezer Scrooge has invested 60% of his money in share A and the remainder in share B. He assesses their prospects as follows:

	A	B
Expected return (%)	15	20
Standard deviation (%)	20	22
Correlation between returns	0.5	

   a. What are the expected return and standard deviation of returns on his portfolio?

   b. How would your answer change if the correlation coefficient were 0 or −0.5?

   c. Is Mr. Scrooge's portfolio better or worse than one invested entirely in share A, or is it not possible to say?

25. **Sharpe ratio (S7.4)** Calculate the Sharpe ratios for portfolios A, B, and T in Table 7.5. Which portfolio offers the highest ratio?

26. **Portfolio risk and return (S7.4)** Here are returns and standard deviations for four investments.

	Return (%)	Standard Deviation (%)
Treasury bills	6	0
Stock P	10	14
Stock Q	14.5	28
Stock R	21	26

Calculate the standard deviations of the following portfolios.

a. 50% in Treasury bills, 50% in stock P.

b. 50% each in Q and R, assuming the shares have

   • Perfect positive correlation.

   • Perfect negative correlation.

   • No correlation.

c. Plot a figure like Figure 7.12 for Q and R, assuming a correlation coefficient of 0.5.

d. Stock Q has a lower return than R but a higher standard deviation. Does that mean that Q's price is too high or that R's price is too low?

27. **Portfolio risk and return (S7.4)** Percival Hygiene has $10 million invested in long-term corporate bonds. This bond portfolio's expected annual rate of return is 9%, and the annual standard deviation is 10%. Amanda Reckonwith, Percival's financial adviser, recommends that Percival consider investing in an index fund that closely tracks the Standard & Poor's 500 Index. The index has an expected return of 14%, and its standard deviation is 16%.

a. Suppose Percival puts all his money in a combination of the index fund and Treasury bills. Can he thereby improve his expected rate of return without changing the risk of his portfolio? The Treasury bill yield is 6%.

b. Could Percival do even better by investing equal amounts in the corporate bond portfolio and the index fund? The correlation between the bond portfolio and the index fund is +0.1.

28. **Portfolio risk and return (S7.4)** Suppose that Treasury bills offer a return of about 6% and the expected market risk premium is 8.5%. The standard deviation of Treasury-bill returns is zero and the standard deviation of market returns is 20%. Use the formula for portfolio risk to calculate the standard deviation of portfolios with different proportions in Treasury bills and the market. (*Note:* The covariance of two rates of return must be zero when the standard deviation of one return is zero.) Graph the expected returns and standard deviations.

CHALLENGE

29. **Portfolio risk (S7.4)** Here are some historical data on the risk characteristics of Ford and Harley Davidson:

	Ford	Harley Davidson
Yearly standard deviation of return (%)	23.5	26.4

The standard deviation of the return on the market was 12.3%.

a. The correlation coefficient of Ford's return versus Harley Davidson was 0.40. What is the standard deviation of a portfolio invested half in each share?

b. What is the standard deviation of a portfolio invested one-third in Ford, one-third in Harley Davidson, and one-third in risk-free Treasury bills?

c. What is the standard deviation if the portfolio is split evenly between Ford and Harley Davidson and is financed at 50% margin, that is, the investor puts up only 50% of the total amount and borrows the balance from the broker?

d. What combination of Ford and Harley Davidson offers the minimum risk.

30. **Efficient portfolios (S7.4)** Look again at the set of the three efficient portfolios that we calculated in Section 7-4.

a. If the interest rate is 5%, which of the three efficient portfolios has the highest Sharpe ratio?

b. How would your answer to part (a) change if the interest rate were 2%?

c. Can the minimum risk portfolio ever offer the highest Sharpe ratio?

31. **Sharpe ratio (S7.4)** Look back at the calculations for Southwest Airlines and Amazon in Section 7.4. What combination of the two stocks offers the highest Sharpe ratio if the interest rate is 2%?

SOLUTIONS TO SELF-TEST QUESTIONS

7.1 The historic risk premium is 10.5% − 2% = 8.5%. With a current risk-free rate of 3%, the hurdle rate should be 3% + 8.5% = 11.5%.

7.2 The mean is $(1 + 2 + 3 + 4 + 5 + 6)/6 = 3.5$.

The variance is $[(1\text{-}3.5)^2 + (2\text{-}3.5)^2 + (3\text{-}3.5)^2 + (4\text{-}3.5)^2 + (5\text{-}3.5)^2 + (6\text{-}3.5)^2]/6 = 2.92$, which corresponds to a standard deviation of $\sqrt{2.92} = 1.71$.

7.3 a. If Applebaum and Banana were perfectly correlated, there would be no diversification benefit, so the portfolio standard deviation would be a (weighted) average of the individual standard deviations—that is, 15%. Since Applebaum and Banana are less than perfectly correlated, there is a diversification benefit, which reduces the portfolio standard deviation to lower than 15%.

b. −1: perfect negative correlation.

7.4 a. Systematic; b. systematic; c. specific; d. specific.

7.5 Both investors will invest in both stocks in the same proportion. They will instead satisfy their preferences for risk through borrowing and lending.

7.6 $100 million. The whole is worth the sum of its parts, no more. While there is a diversification benefit, because the cash flows are less than perfectly positively correlated, shareholders can diversify themselves; there is no need for the companies to do so.

• • • • •

You can download data for Questions 1 and 2 from **finance.yahoo.com.** Refer to the Useful Spreadsheet Functions box near the end of Chapter 9 for information on Excel functions.

1. Download to a spreadsheet the last three years of monthly adjusted stock prices for Coca-Cola (KO), Citigroup (C), and Pfizer (PFE).

   a. Calculate the monthly returns.

   b. Calculate the monthly standard deviation of those returns (see Section 7-2). Use the Excel function STDEV.P to check your answer. Find the annualized standard deviation by multiplying by the square root of 12.

   c. Use the Excel function CORREL to calculate the correlation coefficient between the monthly returns for each pair of stocks. Which pair provides the greatest gain from diversification?

   d. Calculate the standard deviation of returns for a portfolio with equal investments in the three stocks.

2. A large mutual fund group such as Fidelity offers a variety of funds. They include *sector funds* that specialize in particular industries and *index funds* that simply invest in the market index. Log on to **www.fidelity.com** and find first the standard deviation of returns on the Fidelity Spartan 500 Index Fund, which replicates the S&P 500. Now find the standard deviations for different sector funds. Are they larger or smaller than the figure for the index fund? How do you interpret your findings?

CHAPTER

The Capital Asset Pricing Model

In Chapter 7, we began to come to grips with the problem of measuring risk. Here is the story so far.

The stock market is risky because there is a wide spread of possible future rates of return. This spread is measured by the standard deviation or variance of return. The risk of any stock can be broken down into the *specific* or *diversifiable risk* that is peculiar to that stock, and the *systematic* or *market risk* from market-wide fluctuations. Investors can eliminate specific risk by holding a well-diversified portfolio, but they cannot eliminate market risk. All the risk of a fully diversified portfolio is market risk.

We showed how investors can build efficient portfolios, which offer the highest expected return for each level of portfolio risk (and also the lowest risk for each level of expected return). Investors can combine investment in risky stock portfolios with borrowing and lending. Then there is one efficient stock portfolio that is better than all the others. It is the "tangent" portfolio with the highest Sharpe ratio—that is, the efficient portfolio with the highest expected risk premium per unit of standard deviation. If all investors share the same information, they will all hold this tangent portfolio. In this case, all investors will hold the market portfolio of all stocks.

In this chapter, we build on this newfound knowledge.

Section 8.1 Market risk is measured by beta
A stock's market risk is measured by its beta. The average beta of all stocks is 1.0. Returns on stocks with betas greater

than 1.0 tend to amplify market returns. Returns on stocks with betas less than 1.0 tend to move less than the market. The beta of a portfolio equals the weighted-average beta of the stocks in the portfolio.

Section 8.2 The relation between risk and return
The capital asset pricing model (CAPM) states that the expected risk premium offered by a stock equals its beta multiplied by the expected market risk premium. The CAPM was a breakthrough theory that is widely used in corporate finance. (Chapter 9 explores how the CAPM can be used to estimate the cost of capital.)

Section 8.3 Does the CAPM hold in the real world?
The CAPM "works" in several important respects, but average returns on high-beta stocks have been less than the CAPM predicts. Average returns on small-cap and value stocks have been more than the CAPM predicts.

Section 8.4 Some alternative theories
The main competing theory is arbitrage pricing theory (APT), which relates expected risk premiums to two or more macroeconomic factors. The Fama-French three-factor model is a widely used example of APT.

8-1 Market Risk Is Measured by Beta

Chapter 7 built up to the following punchline: *The risk that a stock contributes to a well-diversified portfolio is its market risk.* Tattoo that statement on your forehead if you can't remember it any other way. It is one of the most important ideas in this book.

So how do we measure market risk? Let's go back to the definition: Market risk is the risk that a stock shares with the market. We measure it by estimating how sensitive a stock is to market movements—how much its price changes when the market moves up or down. This sensitivity is called **beta** (β), which is defined as:

$$\beta_i = \sigma_{iM}/\sigma_M^2 \qquad (8.1)$$

Here σ_{iM} is the *covariance* between the stock's return and the market's return and σ_M^2 is the variance of the market's return.

What's the intuition behind this definition? By now you should understand that the market risk of a stock depends on how it covaries with the market. So the covariance σ_{iM} in the numerator makes sense. But why do we scale it by σ_M^2? There are two ways to see this.

The first is a simple decomposition. To find the market risk of security i, we decompose its total risk as measured by its standard deviation into its market risk and specific risk:

$$
\begin{array}{ccccc}
\sigma_i & = & \rho_{iM}\sigma_i & + & (1-\rho_{iM})\sigma_i \\
\textit{Total risk} & = & \textit{market risk} & + & \textit{specific risk}
\end{array}
$$

Market risk is $\rho_{iM}\sigma_i$ because the correlation coefficient ρ_{iM} measures the part of total risk σ_i that comes from the market portfolio. Recall from Eq. (7.3) that the correlation coefficient between two returns is the covariance divided by the product of the individual standard deviations. This gives us:

$$\textit{Market risk} = \rho_{iM}\sigma_i = \frac{\sigma_{iM}}{\sigma_i\sigma_M}\sigma_i = \frac{\sigma_{iM}}{\sigma_M^{\,2}}\sigma_M = \beta_i\sigma_M \qquad (8.2)$$

where $\beta_i = \sigma_{iM}/\sigma_M^2$.

The second way to explain Eq. (8.1) is by what it means. Take any month, and plot the return of Amazon that month on the y-axis and the return of the market on the x-axis. Repeat this many times for many different months. You'll get a scatter plot as shown in Figure 8.1.

You can draw a best-fit line between the individual dots to show the overall relationship between Amazon's return and the market return. You don't need to draw the best-fit line by eye, but can calculate its slope by running a regression of Amazon's return on the market's return:

$$r_i = \alpha + \beta_i r_m + \varepsilon_i$$

As you may know from statistics, the best estimate of β_i—the regression *coefficient* that captures the average effect of the market return on Amazon's return—is the covariance divided by the variance, $\beta_i = \sigma_{im}/\sigma_m^2$. So, just as we wrote at the start of this section, beta measures the sensitivity of a stock's return to the market's return - how much a company's stock return goes up, *on average*, when the market goes up by 1%.

Figure 8.1 shows that, over the five years from March 2015 to February 2020, the best fit line for Amazon has a slope of 1.55—Amazon's beta was 1.55. If the future resembles the past, then when the market rises an extra 1%, Amazon's stock price will rise by an extra 1.55% *on average*. When the market falls an extra 2%, Amazon's stock price will fall on average by an extra $2 \times 1.55 = 3.1\%$.

Of course, Amazon's stock returns are not perfectly correlated with market returns. The company is also subject to specific risk, so the actual returns are scattered about the line in Figure 8.1. Sometimes, Amazon will head south while the market goes north, and vice versa. While beta measures the *slope* of the best fit line, an alternative variable, R-squared, measures the *goodness of fit* of

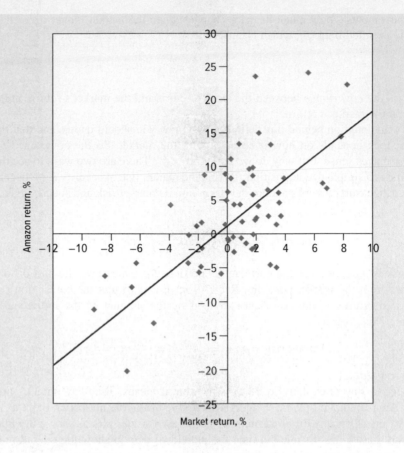

FIGURE 8.1

The return on Amazon stock changes on average by 1.55% for each additional 1% change in the market return. Beta is therefore 1.55.

the best fit line—how close the returns are to the line, or how little specific risk there is. R-squared is calculated as $R^2 = \sigma_{im}^2/\sigma_i\sigma_m$, or alternatively the square of the correlation coefficient ρ_{im}.

Let's get back to betas, and now discuss what they tell us about how stocks behave. Stocks with betas more than 1.0 move more than one-for-one with the overall market. Examples include "luxury" companies such as Porsche. When the economy does well, consumers can buy luxury goods, but they scale back when times are tight. Stocks with betas between 0 and 1.0 still go up with the market, but less than one-for-one. Examples include "necessity" companies, such as Con Edison. In a boom, companies will produce more goods and use more electricity, so the beta is still positive. However, this sensitivity will be low. When bankers get bonuses in economic upswings, they're more likely to celebrate it by buying a Porsche than by turning on the lights for longer.

In theory, betas can be negative. Such a stock does well when the economy does badly, such an insolvency company that helps restructure businesses that go bankrupt. Perhaps you might also say a baseball bat company, because in downturns, borrowers can't pay back lenders, and so loan sharks might hire bailiffs to go round with baseball bats to seize the borrowers' property. In practice, finding such companies is difficult—insolvency practices are typically part of accountancy firms who have consulting businesses that do well in upswings, and are not traded anyway.

Of course, the market is the portfolio of all stocks, so the "average" stock has a beta of 1.0. Table 8.1 reports betas for the 10 well-known stocks discussed in Chapter 7.[1] By considering what business each company is in, we can sanity check whether it makes sense if the beta is above or below 1.

---

[1]We show estimated betas for five years before the start of the pandemic. As the accompanying app below shows, betas for some stocks changed dramatically during the pandemic.

Stock	Beta (β)	Stock	Beta (β)
United States Steel	2.98	Johnson & Johnson	0.75
Southwest Airlines	1.58	Tesla	0.50
Amazon	1.55	Coca-Cola	0.46
Wells Fargo	1.14	Consolidated Edison	0.31
ExxonMobil	1.14	Newmont	0.16

❯**TABLE 8.1**
Estimated betas for selected U.S. stocks, March 2015– February 2020.

Stock	Beta (β)	Stock	Beta (β)
Tata Motors (India)	1.83	Sony (Japan)	0.82
Hyundai Heavy Industry (Korea)	1.44	BHP Billiton (Australia)	0.80
BP (UK)	1.33	Agricultural Bank (China)	0.74
Siemens (Germany)	1.21	Sanofi (France)	0.55
Toronto Dominion Bank (Canada)	0.89	Nestlé (Switzerland)	0.11

❯**TABLE 8.2**
Betas for selected foreign stocks, March 2015–February 2020 (beta is measured relative to the stock's home market).

Of the 10 stocks in Table 8.1, U.S. Steel has the highest beta of 2.98. It also won the prize for the highest standard deviation of 76.4% in Table 7.3 from the previous chapter. Newmont Mining is at the other extreme. Its beta is only 0.16, which may well be a surprise, given its third-place standard deviation of 36.7% in Table 7.3. The combination of high standard deviation and low beta means that most of Newmont's risk was specific and diversifiable, not systematic market risk. Newmont was a dangerous stock held alone, but a relatively safe addition to a diversified portfolio.

Just as we can measure how the returns of U.S. stocks are affected by fluctuations in the U.S. market, so we can measure how stocks in other countries are affected by movements in *their* markets. Table 8.2 shows betas for the sample of stocks from other countries.

BEYOND THE PAGE

COVID and the risk of travel company stocks

mhhe.com/brealey14e

8.1 Self-Test

Sealink has a covariance with the market of 0.03. Its standard deviation is 0.30 (30%), and the standard deviation of the market is 0.20 (20%). What is Sealink's beta?

EXAMPLE 8.1 • Calculating Beta—A Simple Example

When financial analysts estimate beta, they generally obtain past weekly or monthly rates of return for the stock and a market index and then deploy a statistical package to determine the slope of a line relating the stock and market returns. For Amazon, the slope was $\beta = 1.55$.

It may be helpful to see what's going on inside those statistical packages. The following numerical example illustrates beta calculations step by step. Columns 2 and 3 in Table 8.3 show the returns over a six-month period on the market index and the stock of the Anchovy Queen restaurant chain. Although both investments provided an average return of 2%, Anchovy Queen's stock was particularly sensitive to market movements, rising more when the market rose and falling more when it fell.

Columns 4 and 5 show the deviations of each month's return from the average. To calculate the market variance, we need to average the squared deviations of the market returns (column 6). And to calculate the covariance between the stock returns and the market, we need to average the product of the two deviations (column 7). Beta is the ratio of the covariance to the market variance, or 76/50.67 = 1.50. A diversified portfolio of stocks with the same beta as Anchovy Queen would be 1.5 times as volatile as the market.

BEYOND THE PAGE

Try It! Table 8.3: Calculating Anchovy Queen's beta

mhhe.com/brealey14e

)TABLE 8.3
Calculating the variance of the market returns and the covariance between the returns on the market and returns on Anchovy Queen. Beta is the ratio of the covariance to the variance $(\beta = \sigma_{iM}/\sigma_M^2)$.

1	(1)	(2)	(3)	(4)	(5)	(6)	(7)
2							Product of
3				Deviation	Deviation	Squared	Deviations
4				from	from Average	Deviation	from Average
5		Market	Anchovy Q	Average	Anchovy Q	from Average	Returns
6	Month	Market Return	Anchovy Q Return	Deviation from Market Return	Deviation from Average Anchovy Q Return	Squared Deviation from Average Market Return	Product of Deviations from Average Returns (cols 4 × 5)
7	1	−8%	−11%	−10	−13	100	130
8	2	4	8	2	6	4	12
9	3	12	19	10	17	100	170
10	4	−6	−13	−8	−15	64	120
11	5	2	3	0	1	0	0
12	6	8	6	6	4	36	24
13	Average	2	2		Total	304	456
14				Variance $= \sigma_M^2 = 304/6 = 50.67$			
15				Covariance $= \sigma_{iM} = 456/6 = 76$			
16				Beta $(\beta) = \sigma_{iM}/\sigma_M^2 = 76/50.67 = 1.5$			

The Market Portfolio

We should pause to clarify what is meant by "market portfolio." Section 7-5 explained that all investors who share the same information will hold the same portfolio of stocks; since all stocks must be held, all investors must hold the market portfolio.

But that discussion concerned only stocks. In reality, investors can invest in many types of risky assets, including bonds, commodities, and real estate, not just in the investor's home country, but around the world. They can also invest in nontradable assets such as private equity. Institutional investors such as pension funds, sovereign wealth funds, and university endowments hold all these asset classes. The true market portfolio contains all the world's risky assets, not just U.S. stocks.

In practice, there's no index that measures the value of all risky assets. So, in practice, investors often use a *proxy*—an approximation—for the market portfolio. Then, the beta of an asset (stock, bond, etc.) an estimate of how much that asset moves with the proxy for the market portfolio. Most investors' portfolios are concentrated in their home countries' stocks, so most investors use a domestic index as the market proxy. For example, U.S. investors use a U.S. stock index, such as the S&P Composite Index, as their benchmark. Investors in the other large stock markets, including Japan, China, and the U.K., also generally measure betas relative to their own markets. Investors in smaller countries are more likely to use regional indexes. For example, an investor living in Liechtenstein would probably define beta relative the European stock market as a whole. We return to these international topics in Chapter 28.

Why Betas Determine Portfolio Risk

Let's review the two crucial points about security risk and portfolio risk:

- The risk of a well-diversified portfolio is given by its market risk.
- The market risk of a stock is measured by its beta.

We add a third crucial point: *The beta of a portfolio is the weighted average of the betas of the individual stocks within that portfolio.*[2] We could give a mathematical proof of this, but we'd much rather give a common-sense one. Remember the intuition for why the total risk (σ_p) of a portfolio is lower than the average of the total risks of the individual stocks. That's because some of the total risk of an individual stock is diversifiable and so goes away when you add it to a portfolio. But since beta measures undiversifiable risk to begin with, there's no diversification effect when adding a stock to a portfolio. So the beta of a portfolio is simply the weighted-average beta of the stocks in the portfolio—no more, no less. The weight for each stock holding is its market value as a percentage of portfolio value.

The beta of a well-diversified portfolio in turn determines its risk. Suppose we construct a portfolio containing a large number of stocks drawn randomly from the whole market. What will we get? Remember that the average stock has a beta of 1.0, so we'd get a portfolio with a beta of 1.0. Because all of the risk of a well-diversified portfolio is market risk, Eq. (8.3) tells us that its standard deviation is $\beta\sigma_M$, that is, $1.0 \times \sigma_M = \sigma_M$. If the standard deviation of the market is 20% (roughly its average for 1900–2020), then the portfolio standard deviation is also 20%. This is shown by the green line in Figure 8.2.

But suppose we construct the portfolio from stocks with an average beta of 1.5. Then the portfolio beta is 1.5 and its standard deviation is $1.5 \times 20\% = 30\%$.[3] A well-diversified portfolio with a beta of 1.5 will end up with 150% of the market's risk. The upper red line in Figure 8.2 shows this case.

Of course, we could repeat the same experiment with stocks with a beta of 0.5 and end up with a well-diversified portfolio half as risky as the market—a standard deviation of 20%. You can see this also in Figure 8.2.

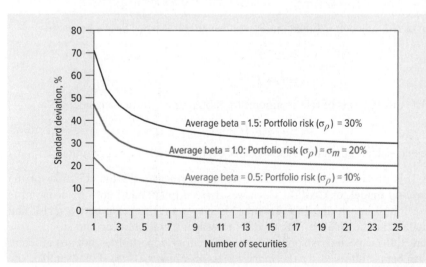

FIGURE 8.2

The green line shows that a well-diversified portfolio of randomly selected stocks ends up with $\beta = 1$ and a standard deviation equal to the market's—in this case 20%. The upper red line shows that a well-diversified portfolio with $\beta = 1.5$ has a standard deviation of about 30%—1.5 times that of the market. The lower blue line shows that a well-diversified portfolio with $\beta = 0.5$ has a standard deviation of about 10%—half that of the market.

Note: In this figure we assume for simplicity that the total risks of individual stocks are proportional to their market risks.

---

[2]As a result, adding a low-beta stock to your portfolio lowers the risk of the overall portfolio. However, this is not "diversification," which refers specifically to the removal of specific risk. Instead, it is "de-risking," which refers to the removal of market risk. Investing more of your wealth into Treasury bills is another way to de-risk.

[3]A 500-stock portfolio with β = 1.5 still has some specific risk, because it is concentrated by industry and in growth rather than income stocks. Its actual standard deviation would be a bit higher than 30%. If that worries you, relax; you can construct a fully diversified portfolio with a beta of 1.5 by borrowing and investing in the market portfolio.

The general point is this: The risk of a well-diversified portfolio is proportional to the portfolio beta, which equals the average beta of the securities included in the portfolio.

8.2 Self-Test

a. Applebaum and Banana have betas of 1.0 and 2.0, respectively. Their returns are less than perfectly correlated. You have a portfolio invested equally in each company. Will its beta be 1.5, higher than 1.5, or lower than 1.5?

b. Given these betas, what correlation coefficient between Applebaum and Banana returns would lead to the lowest portfolio beta?

8-2   The Relationship between Risk and Return

The last section showed that the market risk of a stock is measured by beta. Now we ask one of the most crucial questions in finance: How much extra return should an investor expect for bearing market risk?

Let's go back to the equation of the capital market line from Chapter 7:

$$r_p = r_f + \frac{r_M - r_f}{\sigma_M} \sigma_p \tag{7.4}$$

That equation gave the expected return for an efficient portfolio that combines lending or borrowing and the market portfolio.

Equation (7.4) doesn't apply to individual stocks because they are *not* efficient as standalone assets. Part of their risk can be diversified away, so an investor should not be rewarded for bearing it. Therefore, the capital market line equation doesn't apply to them.

An investor should only be rewarded for bearing a stock's market risk, because only this risk can't be gotten rid of through diversification. Thus, when applying Eq. (7.4) to an individual stock i, we have to replace total risk by market risk only:

$$r_i = r_f + \frac{r_M - r_f}{\sigma_M} \, (market\ risk\ of\ stock\ i)$$

What's the market risk of stock i? Equation (8.2) shows that it is $\beta_i \sigma_M$. So we have:

$$r_i = r_f + \frac{r_M - r_f}{\sigma_M} \, (\beta_i\, \sigma_M)$$
$$r_i = r_f + \beta_i\, (r_M - r_f)$$

We can also write this in terms of risk premiums by subtracting r_i from each side:

$$r_i - r_f = \beta_i\, (r_M - r_f) \tag{8.3}$$

Expected risk premium on stock = beta × expected market risk premium

Equation (8.3) is one of the most famous equations in finance. It's the equation for the **capital asset pricing model**, or **CAPM**, which was derived in the mid-1960s by economists William Sharpe, John Lintner, and Jack Treynor.[4] It shows a relationship between risk and return that's fundamental to finance. The model's message is both startling and simple. In a competitive market, the expected risk premium on *any* security or portfolio—not just efficient portfolios—is its beta multiplied by the *market risk premium $r_M - r_f$*. For example, the expected risk premium on an investment with a beta of 0.5 is half the expected risk premium on the market; the expected risk premium on an investment with a beta of 2 is twice the expected risk premium on the market. This is why beta is such a useful measure of risk.

---

[4]W. F. Sharpe, "Capital Asset Prices: A Theory of Market Equilibrium under Conditions of Risk," *Journal of Finance* 19 (1964), pp. 425–442; and J. Lintner, "The Valuation of Risk Assets and the Selection of Risky Investments in Stock Portfolios and Capital Budgets," *Review of Economics and Statistics* 47 (1965), pp. 13–37. Treynor's article has not been published.

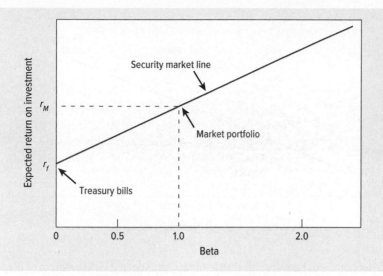

FIGURE 8.3

The capital asset pricing model states that the expected risk premium on each investment is proportional to its beta. This means that each investment should lie on the sloping security market line connecting Treasury bills and the market portfolio.

This relationship is plotted in Figure 8.3, which is known as the **security market line** (**SML**). Treasury bills have a beta of 0 and a risk premium of 0. The market portfolio has a beta of 1.0 and a risk premium of $r_M - r_f$. The risk premium of any security or portfolio is directly proportional to its beta.

The CAPM equation is striking for not only what it contains, but also what it does not. It shows that the risk premium of a stock depends on its market risk and only on its market risk. No other term is on the right-hand side of Eq. (8.3). Diversifiable risk should not affect expected returns, nor should any other firm characteristics. We'll revisit this point in Section 8-3, when testing whether the CAPM's predictions hold up in the real world.

8.3 Self-Test

The risk-free rate is 2%, and the expected return on the market is 8%. What is the expected return of a stock with a beta of (a) 1.5, (b) 0, or (c) –2/3?

What If a Stock Did Not Lie on the Security Market Line?

The CAPM is a theory. There is no legislation forcing a stock's expected return to be given by Eq. (8.3). Why might we expect this theory to hold in practice?

Imagine that you encounter stock A in Figure 8.4. Would you buy it? We hope not—unless we were selling it. Buying A alone would leave you undiversified and with an inferior return. Adding it to a diversified portfolio would cure the lack of diversification but not the inferior return. If you want a portfolio with a beta of 0.5, you could get a higher expected return by investing half your money in Treasury bills and half in the market portfolio. If everyone shares your view of the stock's prospects, the price of A will have to fall, increasing the expected return until it matches what you can get on the security market line.

What about stock B in Figure 8.4? Would you be tempted by its high return? You shouldn't be. You could get a higher expected return for the same beta by borrowing 50 cents for every dollar of your own money and investing 1.5 times your initial wealth in the market portfolio. B has an inferior return, so no investor would want to buy it on its own or add it to a diversified portfolio. Thus, the price of stock B cannot hold. It will have to fall until the expected return on B rises to equal the expected return on the combination of borrowing and the market portfolio that has the same beta as B.

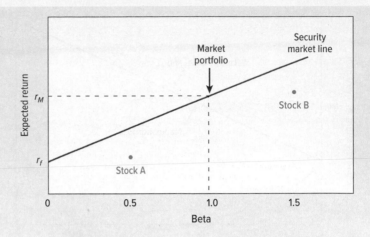

> **FIGURE 8.4**

In equilibrium, no stock can lie below the security market line. For example, instead of buying stock A, investors would prefer to lend part of their money and put the balance in the market portfolio. And instead of buying stock B, they would prefer to borrow and invest in the market portfolio.

We have made our point. An investor can always obtain an expected risk premium of $\beta(r_M - r_f)$ by holding a mixture of the market portfolio and the risk-free asset. So in well-functioning markets nobody will hold a stock that offers an expected risk premium of *less* than $\beta(r_M - r_f)$. But what about the other possibility? Are there stocks that offer a higher expected risk premium and therefore lie *above* the security market line in Figure 8.4? Suppose there were. Then those stocks would offer a higher return than other stocks of the same systematic risk. Investors would pile into those stocks, pushing the price up and the expected return down, until they lay on the security market line and offered the appropriate return for their beta. Overall, every stock must lie on the security market line and command an expected risk premium of:

$$r - r_f = \beta \, (r_M - r_f)$$

The Capital Market Line and the Security Market Line

People often get confused between the security market line and the capital market line. Both lines have expected returns on the vertical axis, but the capital market line has total risk σ_i on the horizontal axis, while the security market line has market risk β_i.

The capital market line applies to *efficient portfolios only*. Inefficient portfolios that bear specific risk, including individual stocks, lie below the line. They carry more risk than efficient portfolios that give the same expected return. But investors are still willing to hold these inefficient stocks because part of their risk is diversifiable. That risk goes away when held as part of a well-diversified portfolio. So, stocks can lie below the capital market line and investors are still willing to hold them.

In contrast, the security market line applies to all stocks and portfolios, efficient or not. That's because the horizontal axis is market risk β_i. Since this risk is undiversifiable, every ounce of it must be rewarded, else an investor would be unwilling to bear it. Thus, the investor needs to be given the risk premium $r_M - r_f$ on the entire amount of market risk β_i. The equation of the security market line, which is the capital asset pricing model, holds for all assets.

In everyday language, being "efficient" is a good thing. We like products or processes that are efficient. In finance also, being efficient is a good thing: We want to get the highest possible return for a given level of risk. However, "efficiency" only matters at a portfolio level. An investor may be perfectly willing to hold inefficient assets, which is why individual assets lie below the capital market line, because these inefficiencies (specific risk) wash away when you hold them as part of a portfolio. An efficient portfolio is comprised of individually inefficient assets.

The Logic behind the Capital Asset Pricing Model

A common job interview question for MBAs is, "Explain the CAPM to your grandparents." Stepping back from the equations, what's the logic behind the CAPM? Let's review the basics.

1. Investors like high expected return and low risk. Portfolios that offer the highest expected return for a given level of risk are known as *efficient portfolios*.

2. If the investor can lend or borrow at the risk-free rate of interest, one efficient portfolio is better than all the others: the portfolio that offers the highest ratio of risk premium to standard deviation (portfolio T in Figure 7.14). A risk-averse investor will put part of his money in this efficient portfolio and part in the risk-free asset. A risk-tolerant investor may put all her money in this portfolio or she may borrow and put in even more.

3. Since everyone holds the same portfolio of stocks, it must be the market portfolio. Everyone holds the market portfolio. Only market risk is relevant.

   Now we'll go back to the risk of individual stocks:

4. Investors don't hold individual stocks, they hold portfolios. So what matters isn't the total risk of a stock because part of this risk is specific to that stock and diversified away when held as part of a portfolio. What's left is the systematic risk that's shared with the rest of the investor's portfolio.

5. Since all investors hold the market portfolio, systematic risk is market risk, the sensitivity of a stock to changes in the market. This sensitivity is known as *beta*.

Intuition: Why Do High Beta and High Returns Go Together?

Why do investors demand a higher return for a stock that has a high beta? Economists would say that high-beta stocks pay off more than low-beta stocks in economic booms, when investors' marginal utility of more money (i.e., the extra happiness from greater returns) is low, and less in recessions, when marginal utility is high. Investors compensate by requiring a higher expected rate of return from high-beta stocks. The opportunity cost of capital from high-beta investments is likewise higher.

A high-beta stock pays off most when the market is booming. Because investors hold the market, their portfolio does well in a boom, when they're probably doing well personally and their marginal utility of more money is relatively low. If they're already able to pay the rent, afford their kids' school fees, and go on a couple of holidays, then the extra return from the high-beta stock isn't as valuable to them as it would be in tougher times. In contrast, when the market crashes, investors' portfolios plummet at the same time when they're probably not doing so well personally and the marginal utility of more money is relatively high. But if a stock is high beta, then it's also likely to suffer more in a market crash. The stock may lose more money precisely at the time when you need it. A high-beta stock is like a fair-weather friend who goes to your garden party when the weather is sunny and everyone else is showing up, but ditches you when it's rainy and you'd really appreciate the company.

In contrast, a low-beta stock is less sensitive to the market. It doesn't do so well when the market is booming and the marginal utility of more money is relatively low. The strength of the low-beta stock is in bad times. That's when your portfolio is underperforming and you really need the money and marginal utility is relatively high. That's when the low-beta stock is likely to deliver more than high-beta stocks. Since it provides valuable insurance against tough times, you're willing to hold it even if its overall return, averaged across booms and recessions, is lower.

When choosing stocks, you don't just care about *how much you get* (the expected return), but *when you get it* (whether returns arise in good or bad times). That's what beta measures.

8.4 Self-Test

Why does a stock's expected return depend only on its market risk β, not its total risk σ?

Can Expected Returns Be Negative?

❭ Let's go back to the CAPM formula:

$$r - r_f = \beta \, (r_M - r_f)$$

If beta is negative—which Section 8.1 argued is possible—then the expected return on a stock can be *less* than the risk-free rate. Indeed, if beta is sufficiently negative, then the expected return might even be less than zero. Does that make sense? Why would anyone be willing to hold a stock that's expected to lose money?

Because of insurance. Ordinary insurance is a useful analogy here. Let's say you have a house worth $1 million,

and it has a 1% chance of burning down. You're offered an insurance policy that pays out the value of your house if it burns down. The expected payoff to the policy is 1% of $1 million = $10,000. If the insurance policy costs $20,000, many households will still be willing to buy it, even though its expected return is *minus* 50%. (You pay $20,000 and get back something with an expected value of $10,000.) Households haven't miscalculated, nor are they being foolish. They buy the insurance contract because it pays off when their house has burned down and they really need the money.

Applying the Capital Asset Pricing Model

Now that we've understood the logic behind the CAPM, let's now *use* it by plugging in actual numbers. The CAPM requires three inputs: β, r_f, and $r_M - r_f$. Let's tackle these in turn:

β: Table 8.1 shows betas for 10 stocks.

r_f: We assume that the interest rate on Treasury bills is 2%.[5]

$r_M - r_f$: We assume that the expected market risk premium is 7%.

Table 8.4 puts these numbers together to give an estimate of the expected return on each stock.[6] The stock with the highest beta in our sample is U.S. Steel. Our estimate of the expected return from U.S. Steel is 22.9%. The stock with the lowest beta is Newmont. Our estimate of its expected return is just 3.1%.

❭ TABLE 8.4
These estimates of the returns expected by investors in February 2020 are based on the capital asset pricing model. We assume 2% for the interest rate r_f and 7% for the expected risk premium $r_M - r_f$.

Stock	Beta (β)	Expected Return $r_f = \beta(r_M - r_f)$
United States Steel	2.98	22.9
Southwest Airlines	1.58	13.0
Amazon	1.55	12.8
Wells Fargo	1.14	10.0
ExxonMobil	1.14	10.0
Johnson & Johnson	0.75	7.3
Tesla	0.50	5.5
Coca-Cola	0.46	5.2
Consolidated Edison	0.31	4.1
Newmont	0.16	3.1

[5] Notice that it is the current interest rate that is relevant. The level of interest rates in the past has nothing to do with the returns that investors expect today.

[6] These expected returns are not the same as the forecasts assumed in Table 7.5 to generate efficient portfolios. Those forecasts were the opinions of a fictitious investor who has not discovered the CAPM.

Pick a stock, and assume a capital investment project with the same risk—same beta—as the stock. The opportunity cost of capital for such a project is calculated in Table 8.4. Given the table's assumptions, the cash flows from a project with the same risk as Southwest Airlines should be discounted at 13%.

We cover the use of the CAPM in capital budgeting in much more detail in Chapter 9.

8-3 Does the CAPM Hold in the Real World?

The CAPM is only a theory. Like any theory, it makes several assumptions. Some of them we've stated explicitly; others we've made implicitly along the way. Let's make them all explicit and in one place:

1. Investors choose their portfolios based on expected return and risk, measured by variance of return.

2. All investors have the same estimates of the mean returns, variances, and covariances of all assets.

3. Investors trade in perfect capital markets. There are no frictions such as taxes, transaction costs, or restrictions on short sales. Investors can both borrow and lend at the same risk-free rate.

4. Investors are price takers and cannot influence prices.

5. The supply of all assets is fixed.

These assumptions don't hold perfectly in the real world, so the CAPM may seem unrealistic. But the straight lines of subway transit systems, such as the New York subway or the London Underground, are also unrealistic because the subway trains don't go in a straight line between stations. Yet the maps remain practically useful even though they are not fully realistic.

So the key question is this: Is the CAPM a sufficiently valid description of the real world that practitioners can use it in practice? To answer this question, let's look at the data. First, it is indeed the case that asset classes with more market risk command a higher expected return. We saw this in Section 7-1: Stocks offer a higher return than government bonds, which in turn offer a higher return than Treasury bills. This relationship is true in all developed economies over long time periods. Moreover, within the broad category of stocks, shares with high betas earn greater returns than those with low betas.

Second, recall from Section 8-2 that the CAPM is important not only for what it does include, but also for what it does not. The CAPM equation $r_i - r_f = \beta_i(r_M - r_f)$ not only means that a security's expected return should depend on its beta, but also that it shouldn't depend on anything else. In particular, it shouldn't depend on diversifiable risk. This prediction is confirmed in practice. Stock prices don't increase when two firms merge just to spread their risks; investment companies, which invest in shares of other firms, aren't more highly valued than the underlying shares that they hold. Investors don't pay a premium for actions that reduce diversifiable risk because they can diversify cheaply and easily on their own.

So we start with two victories for the CAPM: Expected returns are positively related to market risk and unrelated to idiosyncratic risk. The CAPM captures these facts in a simple way. That's why nearly three-quarters of financial managers use it to estimate the cost of capital.[7]

But the CAPM actually makes stronger predictions. Not only does it argue that expected returns increase with beta, but it predicts *how much* they increase. An increase in beta of 1.0 should raise the expected return by $r_M - r_f$. Does this stronger prediction hold in the real world?

---

[7] See J. R. Graham and C. R. Harvey, "The Theory and Practice of Corporate Finance: Evidence from the Field," *Journal of Financial Economics* 60 (2001), pp. 187–243. A number of the managers surveyed reported using more than one method to estimate the cost of capital. Seventy-three percent used the capital asset pricing model, while 39% stated they used the average historical stock return and 34% used the capital asset pricing model with some extra risk factors.

How Large Is the Return for Risk?

Imagine that, in 1931, 10 investors gathered together in a Wall Street bar and agreed to establish investment trust funds for their children. Each investor decided to follow a different strategy. Investor 1 bought the 10% of stocks with the lowest estimated betas; investor 2 chose the 10% with the next-lowest betas; and so on, up to investor 10, who proposed to buy the stocks with the highest betas. At the end of each year, they would re-estimate the betas of all NYSE stocks and reconstitute their portfolios. And so they parted with much cordiality and good wishes.

In time, the 10 investors all passed away, but their children met in early 2020 in the same bar to compare the performance of their portfolios. Figure 8.5 shows how they had fared. Investor 1's portfolio turned out to be much less risky than the market; its beta was only 0.48. However, he also realized the lowest return, 8.1% above the risk-free rate of interest. At the other extreme, the beta of investor 10's portfolio was 1.55, about three times investor 1's beta. But she was rewarded with the highest return, averaging 14.6% a year above the interest rate. So over this 88-year period, returns did indeed increase with beta.

As you can see from Figure 8.5, the market portfolio over the same 89-year period provided an average return of 11.9% above the interest rate[8] and (of course) had a beta of 1.0. The CAPM predicts that the risk premium should increase in proportion to beta, so that the returns of each portfolio should lie on the upward-sloping security market line in Figure 8.5. Since the market provided a risk premium of 11.9%, investor 1's portfolio, with a beta of 0.48, should have provided a risk premium of 5.7% and investor 10's portfolio, with a beta of 1.55, should have given a premium of 18.5%. You can see that, while high-beta stocks performed better than low-beta stocks, the difference was not as great as the CAPM predicts. The additional return for a unit of risk was *less* than the 11.9% predicted by the CAPM.

Although Figures 8.5 provides broad support for the CAPM, critics point out that the slope of the line has been particularly flat in the last 50 years. For example, Figure 8.6 shows how our 10 investors fared between 1966 and 2019. Now it is less clear who is buying the drinks. Returns are more or less in line with CAPM predictions, with the important exception of the two highest beta portfolios. Investor 10, who rode the roller coaster of the highest beta portfolio, earned a return that was barely above the market. Of course before 1966, the line was correspondingly steeper. This is also shown in Figure 8.6.

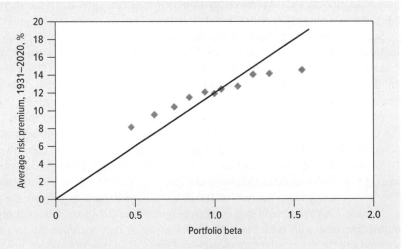

▶ FIGURE 8.5

The capital asset pricing model states that the expected risk premium from any investment should lie on the security market line. The dots show the actual average risk premiums from portfolios with different betas. The high-beta portfolios generated higher average returns, just as predicted by the CAPM. But the high-beta portfolios plotted below the market line, and the low-beta portfolios plotted above. A line fitted to the 10 portfolio returns would be "flatter" than the security market line.

Source: F. Black, "Beta and Return," *Journal of Portfolio Management* 20 (Fall 1993), pp. 8–18. Updates courtesy of Adam Kolasinski.

[8] In Figure 8.5, the stocks in the "market portfolio" are weighted equally. Since the stocks of small firms have provided higher average returns than those of large firms, the risk premium on an equally weighted index is higher than on a value-weighted index. This is one reason for the difference between the 11.9% market risk premium in Figure 8.5 and the 7.7% premium reported in Table 7.1. Also, our 10 investors were lucky to set up their trust funds in 1931, just before stock prices rebounded from the Great Crash of 1929.

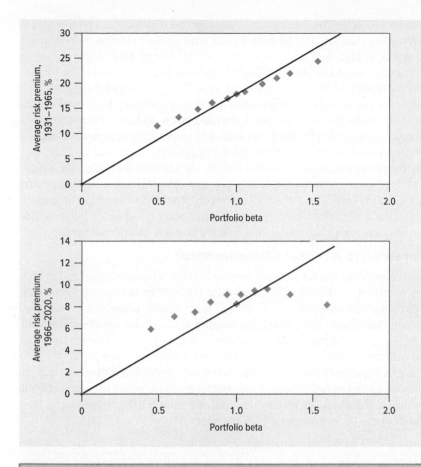

FIGURE 8.6

The relationship between beta and actual average return has been weaker since the mid 1960s. Stocks with the highest betas have provided poor returns.

Source: F. Black, "Beta and Return," *Journal of Portfolio Management* 20 (Fall 1993), pp. 8–18. Updates courtesy of Adam Kolasinski.

8.5 Self-Test

Suppose investors 9 and 10 had an infallible crystal ball in 1931 that predicted the results shown in Figures 8.5 and 8.6. How could they have improved their investment strategies (if allowed by the rules of their game)? Assume that all CAPM assumptions held exactly.

What is going on in the bottom of Figure 8.6? It is hard to say. Defenders of the CAPM emphasize that it predicts *expected* returns, whereas we can observe only *actual* returns. Maybe investors in high-beta stocks got unlucky after 1966, and happened to receive lower returns than they expected. Perhaps the best we can do is to focus on the longest period for which we have reasonable data. This takes us back to Figures 8.5, which suggests that expected returns do increase with beta, though less rapidly than the CAPM predicts.

Another difficulty is that the market definition used in CAPM tests is a proxy for the market portfolio that investors focus on. As we noted in the last section, the market should ideally include all foreign as well as domestic stocks, all bonds as well as stocks, and all other asset classes. It turns out that using an imperfect market proxy can generate results that seem to disprove the CAPM even when the theory is working perfectly.[9]

One key assumption of the CAPM is that investors can both borrow and lend at the risk-free rate. Then, a stock's beta doesn't matter because an investor can borrow or lend to get whatever beta he desires. The chicken only invests some of his money in the stock and puts the remainder in the risk-free rate; the lion borrows to invest more than her initial wealth into the stock. But, if

---

[9] This point is known as the Roll critique: R. Roll, "A Critique of the Asset Pricing Theory's Tests Part 1: On Past and Potential Testability of the Theory," *Journal of Financial Economics* 4 (1977), pp. 129–176.

some investors can't borrow at the risk-free rate, the only way that they can get a high-beta is to buy high-beta stocks—they can't buy low beta stocks and lever up their position by borrowing. This increases the prices of high-beta stocks, and reduces their return. Thus, high-beta stocks have lower returns than they should do under the CAPM, and low-beta stocks have higher returns than they should do under the CAPM—which is exactly what Figures 8.5 and 8.6 suggest.[10]

Indeed, the evidence in Figures 8.5 and 8.6 gives rise to a simple trading strategy: buy low-beta stocks, and sell high-beta stocks. It also means that if you *can* borrow at close to the risk-free rate, the best way to get a high-beta portfolio is not to buy high-beta stocks (they're expensive, because they're sought after by investors who can't borrow) but to buy low-beta stocks and lever up.

This is precisely the strategy pursued by Warren Buffett. He's famous for liking safe companies, and generates a high return by borrowing at very low rates. How? Because he owns several insurance businesses, such as GEICO and National Indemnity. Running an insurance business is effectively borrowing, since you collect the premiums up front and pay out on the policies later. Since his insurance business is very successful, he's able to borrow at exceptional terms.

Are Returns Unrelated to All Other Characteristics?

The CAPM has also come under fire on a second front: Although returns are unrelated to idiosyncratic risk, they're related to other firm characteristics. The red line in Figure 8.7 shows the cumulative difference between the returns on small and large stocks, where size is measured by a stock's market capitalization. You can see that small-cap stocks did not always do well, but over the long haul they have significantly outperformed large-caps. Since the end of 1926, the average annual difference between the returns on the two groups has been 3.1%.

Now look at the green line in Figure 8.7, which shows the cumulative difference between the returns on value stocks and growth stocks. Value stocks are those with high ratios of book value to market value, and growth stocks have low ratios.[11] Since 1926, value stocks have outperformed growth stocks by an average of 4.0% per year.

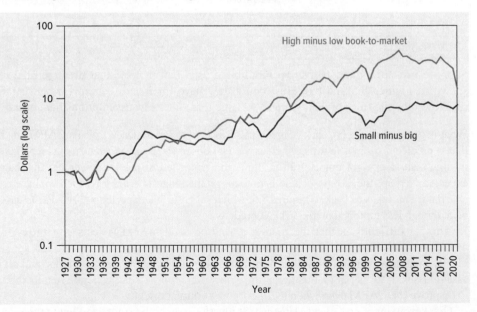

▶ FIGURE 8.7

The red line shows the cumulative difference between the returns on small-firm and large-firm stocks from 1926 to 2020. The green line shows the cumulative difference between the returns on high book-to-market-value stocks (value stocks) and low book-to-market-value stocks (growth stocks).

Source: Kenneth French's website, mba.tuck.dartmouth.edu/pages/faculty/ken.french/data_library.html.

[10] The supply of high-beta stocks in the market portfolio is fixed. If risk-tolerant investors are determined to hold more than the market proportion of high-beta stocks, then conservative investors have to hold less than the market proportion. The risk-tolerant investors have to bid up the prices of high-beta stocks in order the convince the conservative investors to sell them.

[11] Fama and French calculated the returns on portfolios designed to measure the size and value effects. See E. F. Fama and K. R. French, "The Cross-Section of Expected Stock Returns," *Journal of Finance* 47 (1992), pp. 427–465. When calculating the returns on these portfolios, Fama and French control for differences in firm size when comparing stocks with low and high book-to-market ratios. Similarly, they control for differences in the book-to-market ratio when comparing small- and large-firm stocks. For details of the methodology and updated returns on the size and book-to-market factors see Kenneth French's website (mba.tuck.dartmouth.edu/pages/faculty/ken.french/data_library.html).

How seriously is the CAPM damaged by these findings? If you look long and hard at past returns, you're bound to find some strategy that just by chance would have worked in the past. If the returns to the strategy are due to luck—a "spurious correlation"—rather than a risk that investors care about, they should not persist going forward. There's some evidence that this is the case. For example, if you look again at Figure 8.7, you will see that since the mid-1980s, small-firm stocks have underperformed just about as often as they have overperformed.

The CAPM is widely used in corporate finance. It's simple. It makes sense. It seems to generate sensible estimates of costs of capital. On the other hand, the CAPM doesn't hold perfectly in the real world. It's time to consider other theories of risk and return.

BEYOND THE PAGE

The momentum factor

mhhe.com/brealey14e

8-4 Some Alternative Theories

The capital asset pricing model argues that the only risk that investors are concerned about is market risk and that only one measure of risk (beta) is needed. We now turn to an alternative theory that accommodates several sources of risk.

BEYOND THE PAGE

The consumption CAPM

mhhe.com/brealey14e

Arbitrage Pricing Theory

The CAPM begins with an analysis of how investors construct efficient portfolios. Stephen Ross's **arbitrage pricing theory**, or **APT**, comes from a different family entirely. It does not ask which portfolios are efficient. Instead, it starts by *assuming* that each stock's risk premium depends on pervasive macroeconomic "factors," for example the factors that drive returns on small stocks. Stock returns are assumed to obey the following simple relationship:

$$Return = a + b_1 (r_{factor\ 1}) + b_2 (r_{factor\ 2}) + b_3 (r_{factor\ 3}) + \ldots + noise \qquad (8.4)$$

"Noise" stands for specific, diversifiable risk.

APT theory does not say what the factors are: There could be an oil price factor, an interest-rate factor, and a small stock factor. The return on the market portfolio *might* be one factor, but then again it might not.

Some stocks are more sensitive to a particular factor than other stocks. ExxonMobil would be more sensitive to an oil price factor than, say, Coca-Cola. If factor 1 picks up unexpected changes in oil prices, b_1 will be higher for ExxonMobil.

The APT agrees with the CAPM that there are two sources of risk for an individual stock. The first is the risks specific to the company. Since specific risk can be eliminated by diversification, it doesn't affect a stock's risk premium. The second is the risk that stems from the macroeconomic factors. These "macro" risks can't be eliminated by diversification and therefore determine expected risk premiums.

The APT states that the expected risk premium on a stock depends on the expected risk premium associated with each factor and the stock's sensitivity to each factor ($b_1, b_2, b_3, \ldots$). Thus the formula is

$$\begin{aligned} Expected\ risk\ premium &= r - r_f \\ &= b_1 (r_{factor\ 1} - r_f) + b_2 (r_{factor\ 2} - r_f) + \ldots \end{aligned} \qquad (8.5)$$

Notice that this formula makes two statements:

1. If all of the b's in the formula are zero, the expected risk premium is zero. A diversified portfolio that has zero sensitivity to each macroeconomic factor is essentially risk-free (any risk is specific and thus can be diversified away) and therefore must offer the risk-free return. If the portfolio offered a higher return, you could make a risk-free

(or "arbitrage") profit by borrowing to buy the portfolio. If it offered a lower return, you could make an arbitrage profit by running the strategy in reverse: You would *sell* the diversified zero-sensitivity portfolio and *invest* the proceeds at the risk-free rate of interest. This explains why the model is known as arbitrage pricing theory.

2. The risk premium of a diversified portfolio will vary in direct proportion to its sensitivity to each factor. For example, assume that two portfolios, A and B, are sensitive only to factor 1. If portfolio A has a sensitivity of 0.6 and portfolio B a sensitivity of 0.3, portfolio A has double the sensitivity and so must offer double the risk premium.

   Suppose that this wasn't the case, and that A offers a risk premium of 7% but B offers a risk premium of only 3%. Then, an investor who owns B could make an arbitrage profit by selling it and investing the proceeds 50–50 in the risk-free rate and A. The risk of the new portfolio is $50\% \times 0 + 50\% \times 0.6 = 0.3$, the same as before. But the risk premium is $50\% \times 0 + 50\% \times 7\% = 3.5\%$, which is greater than before.

The arbitrage that we have described applies to well-diversified portfolios that have no specific risk. But if the arbitrage pricing relationship holds for all diversified portfolios, it must generally hold for individual stocks, because individual stocks are held in portfolios and their specific risk is diversified away. Each stock must offer an expected return commensurate with its contribution to portfolio risk. In the APT, this contribution depends on the sensitivity of the stock's return to unexpected changes in the macroeconomic factors.

A Comparison of the Capital Asset Pricing Model and Arbitrage Pricing Theory

Both the CAPM and APT claim that a stock's risk premium depends only on its systematic risk. The CAPM argues that there is only one source of systematic risk—that is, a stock's exposure to the risk of the market portfolio. The APT argues that there could be many sources of systematic risk. The sensitivity to the market portfolio could be one of them, but need not be.

How do the two theories stack up? The APT has some attractive features. For example, the market portfolio that plays such a central role in the CAPM does not feature in arbitrage pricing theory. We do not have to worry about the dangers of using a poor market proxy.

Unfortunately, you win some and lose some. The APT does not tell us what the underlying factors are—unlike the CAPM, which collapses *all* macroeconomic risks into a well-defined *single* factor, the return on the market portfolio.[12] One way to use the APT in practice is to try out plausible factors to see which candidates seem to explain past stock returns. The danger with that approach is that some of these factors will end up significant by chance—their correlation with returns is spurious. If so, investors don't actually require a risk premium for exposure to those factors, and the factors will not predict future returns reliably.

Macroeconomic factors can be measured directly or indirectly. Direct measures might include unexpected changes in energy prices, inflation, or long-term interest rates. Indirect measures use returns on specific portfolios of stocks. Suppose, for example, that the higher historical returns on value stocks are traced back to the stocks' exposure to business-cycle risks. The returns on value stocks could then be used as a proxy for business-cycle risks. That may be their role in the following example.

8.6 Self-Test

What does APT theory say about specific risk? Should a firm's specific risk be included as a factor explaining the expected risk premium?

---

[12] The CAPM does not deny the importance of "macro" risks. Macro risks move the market. The CAPM says that fluctuations in the market portfolio incorporate the effects of all relevant macro risks. The investor can worry about a single market risk measure instead of the macro risks separately.

The Three-Factor Model

Look back at the equation for APT. To estimate expected returns, you first need to follow three steps:

Step 1: Identify a reasonably short list of macroeconomic factors that could affect stock returns.

Step 2: Estimate the expected risk premium on each of these factors ($r_{\text{factor 1}} - r_f$, etc.).

Step 3: Measure the sensitivity of each stock to the factors (b_1, b_2, etc.).

One way to shortcut this process is to take advantage of the research by Fama and French, which showed that stocks of small firms and those with a high book-to-market ratio have provided above-average returns. This could simply be a coincidence. But there is also some evidence that these factors are related to company profitability—small and value stocks are less profitable in downturns—and therefore may be picking up risk factors that are left out of the simple CAPM.[13]

If investors do demand an extra return for taking on exposure to these factors, then we can plug these factors into the formula for the APT:

$$r - r_f = b_{\text{market}}\left(r_{\text{market factor}}\right) + b_{\text{size}}\left(r_{\text{size factor}}\right) + b_{\text{book-to-market}}\left(r_{\text{book-to-market factor}}\right)$$

This is commonly known as the Fama–French three-factor model. Using it to estimate expected returns is the same as applying the APT. Here is an example.[14]

Step 1: Identify the Factors   Fama and French have already identified the three factors that appear to determine expected returns. The returns on each of these factors are

Factor	Measured by
Market factor	Return on market index *minus* risk-free interest rate
Size factor	Return on small-firm stocks *less* return on large-firm stocks
Book-to-market factor	Return on high book-to-market-ratio stocks *less* return on low book-to-market-ratio stocks

Step 2: Estimate the Risk Premium for Each Factor   We will keep to our figure of 7% for the market risk premium. History may provide a guide to the risk premium for the other two factors. As we saw earlier, between 1926 and 2019, the difference between the annual returns on small and large stocks averaged 3.1% a year. The difference between the returns on stocks with high and low book-to-market ratios averaged 4.0%.

Step 3: Estimate the Factor Sensitivities   Some stocks are more sensitive than others to fluctuations in the returns on the three factors. You can see this from the first three columns of numbers in Table 8.5, which show some estimates of the factor sensitivities of 10 industry groups for the 60 months ending in February 2020. For example, an increase of 1% in the return on the book-to-market factor *reduces* the return on pharmaceutical stocks by 0.38% but *increases* the return on oil and gas stocks by 0.49%. In other words, when value stocks (high book-to-market) outperform growth stocks (low book-to-market), computer stocks tend to perform relatively badly and oil and gas stocks do relatively well.

---

[13] E. F. Fama and K. R. French, "Size and Book-to-Market Factors in Earnings and Returns," *Journal of Finance* 50 (1995), pp. 131–155.

[14] The three-factor model was first used to estimate the cost of capital for different industry groups by Fama and French. See E. F. Fama and K. R. French, "Industry Costs of Equity," *Journal of Financial Economics* 43 (1997), pp. 153–193. Fama and French emphasize the imprecision in using either the CAPM or an APT-style model to estimate the returns that investors expect.

| | Three-Factor Model | | | | CAPM |
| | Factor Sensitivities | | | | |
	b_{market}	b_{size}	$b_{book\text{-}to\text{-}market}$	Expected Return[a]	Expected Return[b]
Autos	1.12	0.26	0.31	11.9%	10.2%
Banks	1.18	0.09	0.65	13.1	10.5
Chemicals	1.19	0.26	0.41	12.8	10.7
Computers	1.30	−0.18	0.03	10.5	10.9
Construction	0.96	0.49	0.04	10.4	9.3
Food	0.67	−0.38	0.02	5.6	6.3
Oil and gas	1.17	0.49	0.90	15.3	11.0
Pharmaceuticals	0.91	0.20	−0.38	7.5	8.5
Telecoms	0.78	−0.24	0.12	7.2	7.2
Utilities	0.46	−0.36	−0.08	3.7	4.8

❯TABLE 8.5   Estimates of expected equity returns for selected industries using the Fama–French three-factor model and the CAPM.

[a] The expected return equals the risk-free interest rate plus the factor sensitivities multiplied by the factor risk premiums, that is, $2.0 + (b_{market} \times 7.0) + (b_{size} \times 3.1) + (b_{book\text{-}to\text{-}market} \times 4.0)$.

[b] Estimated as $r_f + \beta(r_m - r_f)$, that is, $r_f + \beta \times 7.0$. Note that we used *simple* regression to estimate β in the CAPM formula. This beta may, therefore, be different from b_{market} that we estimated from a multiple regression of stock returns on the three factors.

Source: The industry indexes are value-weighted indexes from Kenneth French's website, mba.tuck.dartmouth.edu/pages/faculty/ken.french/data_library.xhtml.

Once you have estimated the factor sensitivities, multiply each of them by the expected factor return and add up the results. For example, the expected risk premium on oil and gas stocks is:

$$r - r_f = (1.17 \times 7.0) + (0.49 \times 3.1) - (0.90 \times 4.0) = 13.3\%$$

To calculate the expected return we need to add on the risk-free interest rate, which we assume to be 2%. This yields an expected return of $2.0 + 13.3 = 15.3\%$.

Compare this figure with the expected return estimate using the CAPM (the final column of Table 8.5). The three-factor model provides a higher estimate of the expected return for oil and gas stocks. Why? Largely because they are value stocks with a high exposure (0.90) to the book-to-market factor. The three-factor model produces a higher expected return for value stocks, but it produces a lower figure for growth stocks such as pharmaceutical companies that have low book-to-market ratios.[15]

This Fama–French APT model is not widely used in practice to estimate a company's cost of equity. The model requires three betas and three risk premiums instead of one beta and one market risk premium in the CAPM. Also the three Fama–French betas are not as easy to predict and interpret as the CAPM beta, which measures market risk, and there's a logical reason for why investors should be compensated for bearing market risk. The logic for using Fama–French risk factors is sometimes elusive.

---

[15] A stock's factor sensitivities depend on the *covariances* of the stock's return with the factor returns, not on the stock's market capitalization or other attributes. For example, a large-cap stock can *behave* like a portfolio of small stocks; its return can covary positively with the return on the small-stock portfolio. Returns on some growth stocks can covary more positively with value stocks than with growth stocks generally. For further details, see K. Daniel, and S. Titman, "Evidence on the Characteristics of Cross-Sectional Returns," *Journal of Finance* 52 (1997), pp. 1–33.

The Fama–French model finds its widest use as a way of measuring the performance of *investors,* such as mutual funds, pension funds, and other professionally managed portfolios. If a portfolio manager "beats the S&P," it may be because he simply held small stocks at a time that small stocks soared, not because of any skill in picking individual stocks. Since an investor can buy a passive small-stock index fund, she would not wish to pay a portfolio manager to do so. She can evaluate the manager's performance by estimating the portfolio's b_{market}, b_{size}, and $b_{book-to-market}$ and then checking whether the portfolio return is better than the return on a computer-managed portfolio with the same exposures to the Fama–French factors.

● ● ● ● ●

KEY TAKEAWAYS

- **A stock's market risk is measured by its beta**.

$$\beta_i = \sigma_{iM}/\sigma_M^2 \qquad (8.1)$$

where σ_{iM} is the *covariance* between the return on stock i and the market return and σ_M^2 is the variance of the market return. Beta describes how sensitive the stock's return is to unexpected market returns. The average beta of all stocks is 1.0. The beta of a portfolio is the weighted average of the betas of the individual stocks within that portfolio.

- **The capital asset pricing model (CAPM) states that stocks are priced to offer expected risk premiums that are proportional to beta.**

$$\text{Expected risk premium} = \text{beta} \times \text{market risk premium}$$

$$r - r_f = \beta \, (r_m - r_f) \qquad (8.3)$$

The CAPM says that beta is a complete and sufficient measure of risk. Diversifiable risk does not matter. Other attributes—for example, whether the stock is small or large-cap—do not matter.

- **Real-world evidence supports the CAPM, but with important exceptions.** Market risk clearly matters in practice. Diversifiable risk does not. These facts are good news for the CAPM. Average past stock returns increase as beta increases but by less than the CAPM predicts. The relationship between beta and average returns is especially weak for the highest-beta stocks. Stocks of small-cap companies, and stocks with high book values relative to market values, appear to have risks not captured by the CAPM.

- **Arbitrage pricing theory (APT).** The APT theory states that the expected risk premium on a stock should depend on the stock's exposure to several macroeconomic factors that affect stock returns:

$$\text{Expected risk premium} = b_1 \, (r_{factor\,1} - r_f) + b_2 \, (r_{factor\,2} - r_f) + \ldots \qquad (8.5)$$

Here b's represent the stock's sensitivities to the factors, and $r_{factor} - r_f$ is the risk premium demanded by investors who are exposed to this factor.

Arbitrage pricing theory does not say what the factors are. It asks for economists to hunt for unknown game with their statistical toolkits. Fama and French have suggested three factors:

- The market risk premium.

- The difference between the return on small- and large-cap stocks.

- The difference between the return on stocks with high book-to-market ratios and stocks with low book-to-market ratios.

In the Fama–French three-factor model, the expected risks premium depends on the exposures to the three factors.

The CAPM and APT theories both have their fan clubs. However, all financial economists agree on two basic ideas: (1) Investors require extra expected return for taking on risk, and (2) they are concerned predominantly with the risk that they cannot eliminate by diversification.

FURTHER READING

A number of textbooks on portfolio selection explain both Markowitz's original theory and some ingenious simplified versions. See, for example,

E. J. Elton, M. J. Gruber, S. J. Brown, and W. N. Goetzmann: *Modern Portfolio Theory and Investment Analysis,* 9th ed. (New York: John Wiley & Sons, 2014).

The literature on the capital asset pricing model is enormous. There are dozens of published texts of the capital asset pricing model. Fischer Black's paper is a very readable example. Discussions of the theory tend to be more uncompromising. Two excellent but advanced examples are Campbell's survey paper and Cochrane's book.

F. Black, "Beta and Return," *Journal of Portfolio Management* 20 (Fall 1993), pp. 8–18.

J. Y. Campbell, "Asset Pricing at the Millennium," *Journal of Finance* 55 (2000), pp. 1515–1567.

J. H. Cochrane, *Asset Pricing,* revised ed. (Princeton, NJ: Princeton University Press, 2009).

PROBLEM SETS

  Select problems are available in McGraw-Hill's *Connect.* Please see the preface for more information.

1. **Stock betas (S8.1)** What is the beta of each of the stocks shown in Table 8.6?

Stock	Stock Return if Market Return Is:	
	−10%	+10%
A	− 5	+ 5
B	−20	+20
C	−8	+8
D	+5	+5
E	+10	−10

❯**TABLE 8.6**   Stock betas. See Problem 1.

2. **Stock betas (S8.1)** There are few, if any, real companies with negative betas. But suppose you found one with $\beta = -0.25$.

a. How would you expect this stock's rate of return to change if the overall market rose by an extra 5%? What if the market fell by an extra 5%?

b. You have $1 million invested in a well-diversified portfolio of stocks. Now you receive an additional $20,000 bequest. Which of the following actions will yield the safest overall portfolio return?

   i. Invest $20,000 in Treasury bills (which have $\beta = 0$).

  ii. Invest $20,000 in stocks with $\beta = 1$.

 iii. Invest $20,000 in the stock with $\beta = -0.25$.

Explain your answer.

3. **Portfolio betas (S8.1)** A portfolio contains equal investments in 10 stocks. Five have a beta of 1.2; the remainder have a beta of 1.4. What is the portfolio beta?

   a. 1.3.

   b. Greater than 1.3 because the portfolio is not completely diversified.

   c. Less than 1.3 because diversification reduces beta.

4. **Portfolio betas (S8.1)** Suppose the standard deviation of the market return is 20%.

   a. What is the standard deviation of returns on a well-diversified portfolio with a beta of 1.3?

   b. What is the standard deviation of returns on a well-diversified portfolio with a beta of 0?

   c. A well-diversified portfolio has a standard deviation of 15%. What is its beta?

   d. A poorly diversified portfolio has a standard deviation of 20%. What can you say about its beta?

5. **Portfolio betas (S8.1)** Refer to Table 8.1.

   a. What is the beta of a portfolio that has 40% invested in ExxonMobil and 60% in Newmont?

   b. Would you invest in this portfolio if you had no superior information about the prospects for these stocks? Devise an alternative portfolio with the same expected return and less risk.

   c. Now repeat parts (a) and (b) with a portfolio that has 40% invested in Coca-Cola and 60% in Amazon.

6. **CAPM (S8.2)** True or false? Explain or qualify as necessary.

   a. Investors demand higher expected rates of return on stocks with more variable rates of return.

   b. The CAPM predicts that a security with a beta of 0 will offer a zero expected return.

   c. An investor who puts $10,000 in Treasury bills and $20,000 in the market portfolio will have a beta of 2.0.

   d. The CAPM predicts that investors demand higher expected rates of return from stocks with returns that are highly exposed to business-cycle risk.

   e. Investors demand higher expected rates of return from stocks with returns that are very sensitive to fluctuations in the stock market.

7. **CAPM (S8.2)** True or false?

   a. The CAPM implies that if you could find an investment with a negative beta, its expected return would be less than the interest rate.

   b. The expected return on an investment with a beta of 2.0 is twice as high as the expected return on the market.

   c. If a stock lies below the security market line, it is undervalued.

8. **CAPM (S8.2)** Suppose that the Treasury bill rate is 6% rather than the 2% assumed in earlier examples. Assume that the expected return on the market stays at 9%. Use the betas in Table 8.1.

   a. Calculate the expected return from Johnson & Johnson.

   b. Find the highest expected return that is offered by one of these stocks.

   c. Find the lowest expected return that is offered by one of these stocks.

   d. Would U.S. Steel offer a higher or lower expected return if the interest rate were 6% rather than 2%? Assume that the expected market return stays at 9%.

   e. Would Coca-Cola offer a higher or lower expected return if the interest rate were 6%?

9. **CAPM (S8.2)** The Treasury bill rate is 4%, and the expected return on the market portfolio is 12%. Using the CAPM:

   a. Draw a graph similar to Figure 8.3 showing how the expected return varies with beta.

   b. What is the risk premium on the market?

   c. What is the required return on an investment with a beta of 1.5?

   d. If an investment with a beta of 0.8 offers an expected return of 9.8%, does it have a positive NPV?

   e. If the market expects a return of 11.2% from stock X, what is its beta?

10. **Security market line (S8.2)** Briefly explain the difference between the security market line and the capital market line. *Hint:* One applies to efficient portfolios only.

11. **Evidence for or against the CAPM (S8.3)** True or false?

   a. Long-run average rates of return have been higher for high-beta stocks than for low-beta stocks.

   b. Low-beta stocks have earned lower rates of return than the CAPM predicts.

   c. The CAPM predicts that investors do not bid up the values of diversified firms. This prediction is confirmed in practice.

   d. Small-cap stocks have earned higher rates of return than the CAPM predicts.

   e. The historical performance of small-cap stocks does not disprove the CAPM, which allows for factors in addition to the market factor.

12. **APT (S8.4)** Consider a three-factor APT model. The factors and associated risk premiums are

Factor	Risk Premium (%)
Change in gross national product (GNP)	+5
Change in energy prices	−1
Change in long-term interest rates	+2

Calculate expected rates of return on the following stocks. The risk-free interest rate is 7%.

   a. A stock whose return is uncorrelated with all three factors.

   b. A stock with average exposure to each factor ($b = 1$ for each).

   c. A pure-play energy stock with high exposure to the energy factor ($b = 2$) but zero exposure to the other two factors.

   d. An aluminum company stock with average sensitivity to changes in interest rates and GNP, but negative exposure of $b = -1.5$ to the energy factor. (The aluminum company is energy-intensive and suffers when energy prices rise.)

13. **APT (S8.4)** Some true or false questions about the APT:

   a. The APT factors cannot reflect diversifiable risks.

   b. The market rate of return cannot be an APT factor.

   c. There is no theory that specifically identifies the APT factors.

   d. The APT model could be true but not very useful, for example, if the relevant factors change unpredictably.

14. **APT (S8.4)** Consider the following simplified APT model:

Factor	Expected Risk Premium (%)
Market	6.4
Interest rate	−0.6
Yield spread	5.1

Calculate the expected return for the following stocks. Assume $r_f = 5\%$.

	Factor Risk Exposures		
	Market	Interest Rate	Yield Spread
Stock	(b_1)	(b_2)	(b_3)
P	1.0	−2.0	−0.2
P^2	1.2	0	0.3
P^3	0.3	0.5	1.0

15. **APT (S8.4)** Look again at Problem 14. Consider a portfolio with equal investments in stocks P, P^2, and P^3.

   a. What are the factor risk exposures for the portfolio?

   b. What is the portfolio's expected return?

16. **Three-factor model (S8.4)** The following table shows the sensitivity of four stocks to the three Fama–French factors. Estimate the expected return on each stock assuming that the interest rate is 2%, the expected risk premium on the market is 7%, the expected risk premium on the size factor is 3.0%, and the expected risk premium on the book-to-market factor is 4.5%.

	Ford	Walmart	Citigroup	Apple
Market	1.24	0.41	1.52	1.25
Size	−0.07	−0.47	−0.01	−0.67
Book-to-market	0.28	−0.25	0.85	−0.72

CHALLENGE

17. **Evaluating investment performance (S8.4)** Between 2008 and 2017, the returns on Micro-fund averaged 10% a year. In his 2017 discussion of performance, the fund president noted that this was 2.5% a year better than the return on the U.S. market, a result that he attributed to the fund's strategy of buying only stocks with outstanding management.

   The following table shows the returns on the market, the size and book-to-market factors, and the interest rate during this period:

	Market Risk Premium	Return on Size Factor	Return on Book-to-Market Factor	Interest Rate
2008	−38.34	3.26	0.97	1.60
2009	28.26	9.28	−9.14	0.10
2010	17.37	13.77	−5.17	0.12
2011	0.44	−6.04	−8.41	0.04
2012	16.28	−1.22	9.89	0.06
2013	35.2	7.35	1.54	0.02
2014	11.7	−7.75	−1.65	0.02
2015	0.07	−3.73	−9.48	0.02
2016	13.3	6.66	23.33	0.20
2017	21.5	−4.85	−13.85	0.80

   The fund had marketed itself as a way to invest in small and medium-sized stocks, and this was reflected in a beta relative to the size factor of 1.4. It had also traditionally adopted a conservative approach to risk with an estimated market beta of 0.9. The fund's beta relative to the book-to-market factor was –0.4. Evaluate the performance of the fund during this period.

18. **APT (S8.4)** The following question illustrates the APT. Imagine that there are only two pervasive macroeconomic factors. Investments X, Y, and Z have the following sensitivities to these two factors:

Investment	b_1	b_2
X	1.75	0.25
Y	–1.00	2.00
Z	2.00	1.00

We assume that the expected risk premium is 4% on factor 1 and 8% on factor 2. Treasury bills obviously offer zero risk premium.

a. According to the APT, what is the risk premium on each of the three stocks?

b. Suppose you buy $200 of X and $50 of Y and sell $150 of Z. What is the sensitivity of your portfolio to each of the two factors? What is the expected risk premium?

c. Suppose you buy $80 of X and $60 of Y and sell $40 of Z. What is the sensitivity of your portfolio to each of the two factors? What is the expected risk premium?

d. Finally, suppose you buy $160 of X and $20 of Y and sell $80 of Z. What is your portfolio's sensitivity now to each of the two factors? And what is the expected risk premium?

e. Suggest two possible ways that you could construct a fund that has a sensitivity of 0.5 to factor 1 only. (*Hint:* One portfolio contains an investment in Treasury bills.) Now compare the risk premiums on each of these two investments.

f. Suppose that the APT did *not* hold and that X offered a risk premium of 8%, Y offered a premium of 14%, and Z offered a premium of 16%. Devise an investment that has zero sensitivity to each factor and that has a positive risk premium.

• • • • •

SOLUTIONS TO SELF-TEST QUESTIONS

8.1 $\beta_i = \sigma_{im}/\sigma_M^2 = 0.03/0.2^2 = 0.75$

8.2
a. 1.5. The beta of a portfolio is the (weighted) average of the betas of the individual securities.

b. The portfolio beta is a weighted average of the individual betas regardless of correlation.

8.3
a. $2\% + 1.5 \times (8\% - 2\%) = 11\%$

b. 2%

c. $2\% - 2/3 \times (8\% - 2\%) = -2\%$

8.4 Investors should not expect compensation for a stock's total risk σ because part of that risk can be diversified away. They should only expect compensation for undiversifiable risk, which is captured by β.

8.5 Investors 9 and 10 could hold the market portfolio, then borrow to bring their portfolio betas up to the betas of stock portfolios 9 and 10. Their average return would move up to the security market line. Implementing this strategy in real life would have been extremely difficult, however, as we point out later in this section.

8.6 No. APT theory assumes that all specific risk—all risk unrelated to the factors—is eliminated by diversification.

You can download data for the following questions from **finance.yahoo.com** or any financial website that provides stock data.

1. Find a low-risk stock—Walmart or Kellogg would be a good candidate. Use monthly returns for the most recent three years to confirm that the beta is less than 1.0. Now estimate the annual standard deviation for the stock and the S&P index, and the correlation between the returns on the stock and the index. Forecast the expected return for the stock, assuming the CAPM holds, with a market return of 12% and a risk-free rate of 5%.

   a. Plot a graph like Figure 8.5 showing the combinations of risk and return from a portfolio invested in your low-risk stock and the market. Vary the fraction invested in the stock from 0 to 100%.

   b. Suppose that you can borrow or lend at 5%. Would you invest in some combination of your low-risk stock and the market, or would you simply invest in the market? Explain.

   c. Suppose that you forecasted a return on the stock that is 5 percentage points higher than the CAPM return used in part (b). Redo parts (a) and (b) with the higher forecasted return.

   d. Find a high-risk stock and redo parts (a) and (b).

2. Recalculate the betas for the stocks in Table 8.1 using the latest 60 monthly returns. Recalculate expected rates of return from the CAPM formula, using a current risk-free rate and a market risk premium of 7%. How have the expected returns changed from Table 8.1?

CHAPTER

9

Risk and the Cost of Capital

Long before the development of modern theories linking risk and return, smart financial managers adjusted for risk in capital budgeting. They knew that risky projects are, other things equal, less valuable than safe ones—that's just common sense. Therefore, they demanded higher rates of return from risky projects, or they based their decisions about risky projects on conservative forecasts of project cash flows.

In this chapter, we consider how to incorporate risk into investment decisions. There are a number of pitfalls in including risk in capital budgeting analyses that are important to understand and avoid.

Section 9.1 Company and project costs of capital

Today, most companies start with the company cost of capital as a benchmark discount rate for new investments. The company cost of capital is the right discount rate only for investments that have the same risk as the company's overall business. For riskier projects, the cost of capital is greater than the company cost of capital. For safer projects, it is less.

One way to estimate the company cost of capital is to estimate the company's asset beta, which is a weighted average of its debt and equity betas. The asset beta can then be plugged into the capital asset pricing model to derive the company cost of capital. A more convenient alternative is to calculate a weighted average of the returns demanded by investors in the company's debt and equity.

Section 9.2 Estimating beta and the cost of capital

The hardest part of estimating the weighted-average cost of capital is figuring out the cost of equity—that is, the expected rate of return to investors in the firm's common stock. Many firms turn to the capital asset pricing model (CAPM) for an answer. The CAPM states that the expected rate of return equals the risk-free interest rate plus a risk premium that depends on beta and the market risk premium.

You can look up betas on financial websites like Yahoo! Finance and Bloomberg, but it's important to remember that these betas are estimates and liable to statistical errors. We look at how to estimate betas and to check the reliability of these estimates.

Section 9.3 Analyzing project risk

Suppose you're responsible for a specific investment project. How do you know if the project is average risk or above- or below-average risk? We suggest you to check whether the project's cash flows are more or less sensitive to the business cycle than the average project. Also check whether the project has higher or lower fixed operating costs (higher or lower operating leverage) and whether it requires large future investments.

Remember that a project's cost of capital depends only on market risk. Diversifiable events can affect project cash flows but they do not increase the cost of capital. Also don't be tempted to add arbitrary fudge factors to discount rates to try to adjust for risk. A fudge factor is a figure included in a calculation to account for an unquantified influence. They are too often added to discount rates for projects in unstable parts of the world, for example.

Section 9.4 Certainty equivalents

Financial managers usually use a risk-adjusted discount rate for all future cash flows. An alternative is to estimate certainty-equivalent cash flows that can then be discounted at the risk-free interest rate. Although rarely used for standard DCF calculations, certainty equivalents are vital for valuing options and futures. We also use them to illustrate the deductions for risk that are assumed when we use a single risk-adjusted discount rate.

9-1   Company and Project Costs of Capital

The **company cost of capital** is the opportunity cost of capital for an investment in all the firm's assets and is the correct discount rate for its average-risk projects.

If the company has no debt outstanding, the company cost of capital equals its cost of equity, the expected rate of return on the company's common stock. A few large, successful companies pretty well fit this no-debt special case, including Johnson & Johnson (J&J).[1] Its market-value balance sheet at the end of the third quarter of 2020 boiled down to:

J&J Market Value, billions			
Assets: A = $380	$\beta_A = 0.75$	Equity: E = $380	$\beta_E = 0.75$

The equity value of $380 billion was a market capitalization, not a book (accounting) value. The value of assets and equity on J&J's book balance sheet was only about $60 billion. We can't observe the market value of J&J's assets on its book financial statements, but we can infer it from the market cap.

We estimated J&J's equity beta in Table 8.1 as 0.75. Therefore its asset beta must also be $\beta_A = 0.75$. J&J's shareholders bear all the risks of J&J's assets. Beta must be the same on both sides of its balance sheet, in this case $\beta_E = \beta_A = 0.75$.

We can use the CAPM to calculate J&J's company cost of capital r_A. If the risk-free interest rate is 2% and the market risk premium is 7%,

$$r_A = r_f + \beta_A (r_m - r_f) = 2 + 0.75 \times 7 = 7.3\%$$

If J&J considers an average-risk investment, it makes sense to discount the forecasted cash flows at 7.3%.

Company Cost of Capital for CSX

Now let's try the same exercise for the railroad CSX, which has both debt and equity outstanding. Its balance sheet at the end of the third quarter of 2020 included $16.5 billion of debt. The market value of CSX's equity was $60.0 billion, well above the $12.7 billion book equity value. So its debt-to-value ratio was 22%, much lower than a debt ratio calculated from its financial statements.

CSX Market Value, billions			
Assets: A = $76.5	$\beta_A = ?$	Debt: D = $16.5 (22%)	$\beta_D = 0.2$
		Equity: E = $60 (78%)	$\beta_E = 1.18$
Total: V = $76.5		Total: V = $76.5	

What was CSX's asset beta? Not the debt beta because debt has a senior claim on the assets and is therefore safer than the assets. Not the equity beta because debt amplifies shareholders' risk. Shareholders bear both business and *financial risk* because borrowing increases the volatility and beta of equity.

We can't reach the asset beta by looking at debt or equity betas separately. We need a *portfolio* of all of CSX's debt and equity financing. Suppose you purchased a portfolio of 100% of the debt and 100% of the equity. Then you would own 100% of the assets, and the portfolio

---

[1] J&J's market cap at the end of the third quarter of 2020 was about $380 billion, its long-term debt about $30 billion. It also had $12 billion invested in marketable debt securities, so its net debt was only $18 billion.

beta would equal the asset beta. The weights of debt and equity in such a portfolio would be D/V and E/V calculated from *market* values. (Investors can't buy CSX shares for book value.)

CSX's equity beta was $\beta_E = 1.18$, and we will assume a debt beta of $\beta_D = 0.2$. The asset beta is:

$$\beta_A = \beta_D \, D/V + \beta_E \, E/V = 0.2 \times 0.22 + 1.18 \times 0.78 = 0.96$$

The company cost of capital for CSX, using the same risk-free rate and market risk premium as for J&J, is:

$$r_A = r_f + \beta_A \, (r_m - r_f) = 2 + 0.96 \times 7 = 8.8, \text{ about } 9\%$$

9.1 Self-Test

Suppose you mistakenly use a debt ratio from book financial statements instead of market values. Are your estimates of the company cost of capital likely to be too high or too low? Assume you are analyzing a successful public company.

A Weighted Average of Betas, or a Weighted Average of Returns?   We have introduced a fundamental relationship: Risk must be the same on both sides of the balance sheet. If risk means beta, the formula is:

$$\text{Asset beta} = \beta_A = \beta_D \, D/V + \beta_E \, E/V \qquad (9.1)$$

We used the asset beta β_A to calculate the company cost of capital for J&J and CSX.

Yet we have skipped over an important practical problem. We assumed a debt beta. How does a financial manager know what the debt beta is?[2] She won't find debt betas quoted in *The Wall Street Journal,* Yahoo! Finance, or other standard sources of financial data.

Most financial managers avoid this problem. Why go to the trouble of estimating debt betas when the cost of debt appears in plain sight? It is the interest rate paid on corporate borrowing. CSX's CFO knew in 2020 what the interest rate would be on a new bond issue. The CFO did not need a debt beta to estimate that interest rate.

A CFO is usually better off averaging the *costs* of debt and equity, not their betas. We can still use the CAPM to calculate the cost of equity from CSX's equity beta of 1.18:

$$r_E = r_f + \beta_E \, (r_m - r_f) = 2 + 1.18 \times 7 = 10.3\%$$

If the cost of debt is $r_D = 3.4\%$, the company cost of capital is:

$$r_A = r_D \, D/V + r_E \, E/V = 3.4 \times 0.22 + 10.3 \times 0.78 = 8.8, \text{ about } 9\%$$

which in this case is identical to the cost of capital calculated using the asset beta:[3]

---

[2]Sometimes practitioners assume without thinking or checking that $\beta_D = 0$. This can be a decent approximation for the most creditworthy corporations when interest rates are stable. The approximation breaks down as the spread between treasury and corporate interest rates increases. The spread reflects several issues, including default risk and the illiquidity of corporate bonds.

[3]It is identical because the 3.4% cost of debt is consistent with a debt beta of $\beta_D = 0.2$. The two calculations diverge if the observed cost of debt differs from the cost of debt that would be calculated from the CAPM.

We have a second fundamental relationship: The expected rate of return is the same on both sides of the balance sheet:

$$\text{Company cost of capital} = r_A = r_D \, D/V + r_E \, E/V \qquad (9.2)$$

The two relationships in Eqs. (9.1) and (9.2) are both important, and we will use both in various settings later in the book. Equation (9.2), which averages expected returns rather than betas, is more common in practice for estimating the company cost of capital. It has two practical advantages. First, estimating the cost of debt for Eq. (9.2) does not require a debt beta. The equation uses the actual cost of borrowing. Second, although the CAPM is widely used to estimate the cost of equity, it is not required in Eq. (9.2). The financial manager may decide to use a DCF model from Chapter 4, for example.

9.2 Self-Test

Viking Runeship's book balance sheet reports 50% debt and 50% equity. The debt is trading close to book value at a current interest rate of 4%. The market cap of Runeship's equity is double book value. The equity beta is $\beta_E = 1$. The risk-free interest rate is 2%, and the market risk premium is 7%. What is Runeship's company cost of capital?

Three Warnings

Is debt cheap finance? The formula for the company cost of capital blends the costs of debt and equity. Therefore, you might think that the average cost of capital could be reduced by substituting cheap debt for expensive equity. For example, you might expect that CSX could reduce its cost of capital by substituting debt costing only 3.4% for equity which costs more than 10%.

It doesn't work that way! As the debt ratio D/V increases, the cost of the remaining equity also increases, offsetting the apparent advantage of more cheap debt. We show how and why this offset happens in Chapter 16.

What is the risk-free rate? The next issue is what value to use for the risk-free interest rate. Interest rates at the end of 2020 were at a record low—much lower than the 2% rate used in the J&J and CSX examples. The three-month Treasury bill rate was barely positive at 0.1%. Yields on 20-year U.S. Treasury bonds were about 1.4%.

The CAPM is a short-term model. It works period by period and calls for a short-term interest rate. But could a 0.1% three-month risk-free rate give the right discount rate for cash flows 10 or 20 years in the future? Well, now that you mention it, probably not.

Financial managers have to muddle through this problem. Most use a long-term risk-free rate in the CAPM formula.[4] If this short-cut is used, then the market risk premium must be restated as the difference between market returns and returns on *long-term* Treasuries.[5] Table 7.1 shows that over the past century, this risk premium has averaged 6.2%.

Interest is tax deductible. Equation (9.2) is a weighted-average cost of capital (WACC). But it is not the same thing as the *after-tax* weighted-average cost of capital (after-tax WACC),

---

[4]The other muddle would use a forecast of future short rates in the CAPM formula. Making such a forecast in late 2020, with interest rates at record lows at the height of the COVID-19 pandemic, was foolhardy at best. If a long-term forecast of short rates was needed, it was probably better to use some average, "normal" rate, say 2%, as in our examples above.

[5]This approach gives a security market line with a higher intercept and a lower market risk premium. Using a "flatter" security market line is perhaps a better match to the historical evidence, which shows that the slope of average returns against beta is not as steeply upward-sloping as the CAPM predicts. See Figure 8.5.

which uses the *after-tax* cost of debt to capture the value of taxes saved by deducting interest from taxable income. Many companies use the after-tax WACC as a standard discount rate for average-risk investment projects.

We defer discussion of the after-tax WACC to Chapter 18, after we have covered the pros and cons of debt financing in detail. That chapter also covers the adjusted present value (APV) valuation method, in which tax savings from interest deductions are forecasted and valued separately. The company cost of capital is the correct APV discount rate for average-risk investments. In this chapter, we defer consideration of interest tax deductions and keep the focus on the company cost of capital.

What about Investments That Are Not Average Risk?

The company cost of capital is *not* the correct discount rate if a new investment project is more or less risky than the firm's existing business. Each project should, in principle, be evaluated at its *own* opportunity cost of capital. This is a clear implication of the value-additivity principle introduced in Chapter 5. For a firm composed of assets A and B, the firm value is

$$\text{Firm value} = PV(AB) = PV(A) + PV(B)$$
$$= \text{sum of separate asset values}$$

Here, PV(A) and PV(B) are valued just as if they were mini-firms that stockholders could invest in directly. Investors would value A by discounting its forecasted cash flows at a rate reflecting the risk of A. They would value B by discounting at a rate reflecting the risk of B. The two discount rates will, in general, be different. If the present value of an asset depended on the identity of the company that bought it, present values would *not* add up, and we know they do add up. (Think of a portfolio of $1 million invested in J&J and $1 million invested in CSX. Would any reasonable investor say that the portfolio is worth anything more or less than $2 million?)

If the firm considers investing in a third project C, it should also value C as if C were a mini-firm. That is, the firm should discount the cash flows of C at the expected rate of return that investors would demand if they could make a separate investment in C. *The opportunity cost of capital depends on the use to which that capital is put.*

Perhaps we're saying the obvious. Think of J&J: It is a massive health care and consumer products company, with over $80 billion in sales. J&J has well-established consumer products, including Band-Aid® bandages, Tylenol®, and products for skin care and babies. It also invests heavily in much chancier ventures, such as biotech research and development (R&D). Do you think that a new production line for baby lotion has the same cost of capital as an investment in biotech R&D? We don't, though we admit that estimating the cost of capital for biotech R&D could be challenging. We will come back to the problems of valuing R&D investments in Chapter 10, when we discuss decision trees, and again in Chapter 23, when we discuss options.

Suppose we measure the risk of each project by its beta. Then J&J should accept any project lying above the upward-sloping security market line that links expected return to risk in Figure 9.1. If the project is high risk, J&J needs a higher prospective return than if the project is low risk. That is not the same as accepting any project *regardless of its risk* as long as it offers a higher return than the *company's* cost of capital. In that case, J&J would accept any project above the horizontal cost of capital line in Figure 9.1—that is, any project offering a return of more than 7.3%.

It wouldn't make sense to suggest that J&J should demand the same rate of return from a very safe project as from a very risky one. If J&J used the company cost of capital rule, it would reject many good low-risk projects and accept many poor high-risk projects. It also wouldn't make sense to suggest that just because another company has a still lower company cost of capital, it is justified in accepting projects that J&J would reject.

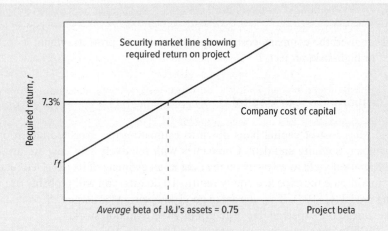

J&J's company cost of capital is about 7.3%. This is the correct discount rate only if the project beta is 0.75. In general, the correct discount rate increases as project beta increases. J&J should accept projects with rates of return above the security market line relating required return to beta.

Perfect Pitch and the Cost of Capital

The true cost of capital depends on project risk, not on the company undertaking the project. So why is so much time spent estimating the company cost of capital?

There are two reasons. First, many projects can be treated as average risk—that is, neither more nor less risky than the average of the company's other assets. For these projects, the company cost of capital is the right discount rate. Second, the company cost of capital is a useful starting point for setting discount rates for unusually risky or safe projects. It is easier to add to, or subtract from, the company cost of capital than to estimate each project's cost of capital from scratch.

There is a good musical analogy here. Most of us, lacking perfect pitch, need a well-defined reference point, like middle C, before we can sing on key. But anyone who can carry a tune gets *relative* pitches right. Businesspeople have good intuition about *relative* risks, at least in industries they are used to, but not about absolute risk or required rates of return. Therefore, they set a companywide cost of capital as a benchmark. This is not the right discount rate for everything the company does, but adjustments can be made for more or less risky ventures.

Measuring differences in risk is difficult to do objectively, and financial managers shy away from intracorporate squabbles. (You can imagine the bickering: "My projects are safer than yours! I want a lower discount rate!" "No they're not! Your projects are riskier than a naked call option!")[6] As a result, many companies use the company cost of capital not just as a benchmark, but as an all-purpose discount rate for every project proposal. In this case, they use too low a discount rate for high-risk projects and too high a rate for safer projects. They invest too much in high-risk projects and too little in low-risk projects. Research shows that diversified companies that rely on a single company cost of capital make exactly that mistake and harm shareholders by doing so.[7]

When firms force the use of a single company cost of capital, risk adjustment shifts from the discount rate to project cash flows. Top management may demand extra-conservative cash-flow forecasts from extra-risky projects. Or they may refuse to sign off on an extra-risky project unless NPV, computed at the company cost of capital, is well above zero. Such rough-and-ready risk adjustments may be better than none at all.

---

[6]A "naked" call option is an option purchased with no offsetting (hedging) position in the underlying stock or in other options. We discuss options in Chapter 21.

[7]P. Krüger, A. Landier, and D. Thesmar, "The WACC Fallacy: The Real Effects of Using a Unique Discount Rate," *Journal of Finance* 70 (June 2015), pp. 1253–1285.

9.3 Self-Test

If Johnson & Johnson used the company cost of capital to value all projects, would it accept too many low-risk, or high-risk, projects?

9-2 Estimating Beta and the Company Cost of Capital

Estimating the company cost of capital boils down to estimating the expected return on a portfolio of the company's equity and debt. Companies with relatively safe debt are usually content to use the promised yield to maturity on the debt as an estimate of its expected return. The harder part is to estimate the expected equity return. To do this, you will probably use the capital asset pricing model (CAPM). If so, you are in good company: Most large U.S. companies use the CAPM to estimate the expected rate of return on their common stock.[8]

We used the CAPM to calculate costs of capital for J&J and CSX in Section 9-1, using estimated equity betas for each company. We did not ask how such betas are estimated in practice. That is our topic now.

Estimating Beta

BEYOND THE PAGE

How to
estimate beta

mhhe.com/brealey14e

BEYOND THE PAGE

Try It!
Comparing
beta estimates

mhhe.com/brealey14e

In principle, we are interested in the future beta of the company's stock, but lacking a crystal ball, we turn first to historical evidence. For example, look at the scatter diagram at the top left of Figure 9.2. Each dot represents the return on U.S. Steel stock and the return on the market in a particular month. The plot starts in March 2010 and runs to February 2015, so there are 60 dots in all.

The second diagram on the left shows a similar plot for the returns on ExxonMobil stock, and the third shows a plot for Consolidated Edison. In each case, we have fitted a line through the points. The slope of this line is an estimate of beta. It tells us how much on average the stock price changed when the market return was 1% higher or lower.

The right-hand diagrams show similar plots for the same three stocks during the subsequent period ending in February 2020. The estimated betas change. For example, the estimate for U.S. Steel is lower in the first period than in the second. You would have been off target if you had blindly used its beta during the earlier period to predict its beta in the later years. However, you could have been pretty confident that ConEd's beta was much less than U.S. Steel's and that ExxonMobil's beta was somewhere between the two.[9]

Only a portion of each stock's total risk comes from movements in the market. The rest is firm-specific, diversifiable risk, which shows up in the scatter of points around the fitted lines in Figure 9.2. *R-squared* (R^2) measures the proportion of the total variance in the stock's returns that can be explained by market movements. For example, for the first five years the R^2 for ExxonMobil was 0.51. In other words, 51% of ExxonMobil's risk was market risk and 49% was diversifiable risk. The variance of the returns on ExxonMobil stock was 248.[10] So we could say that the variance in stock returns that was due to the market was $0.51 \times 248 = 126$, and the variance of diversifiable returns was $0.49 \times 248 = 122$.

The estimates of beta shown in Figure 9.2 are just that. They are based on the stocks' returns in 60 particular months. The noise in the returns can obscure the true beta. Therefore,

---

[8]The CAPM is not the last word on risk and return, of course, but the principles and procedures covered in this chapter work just as well with other models such as the Fama–French three-factor model. See Section 8-4.

[9]Remember that to estimate beta, you must regress the *returns* on the stock (the *y* variable) on the market *returns* (the *x* variable). You would get a very similar estimate if you simply used the percentage *changes* in the stock price and the market index. But sometimes, people make the mistake of regressing the stock price *level* on the *level* of the index and obtain nonsense results.

[10]This is an annual figure; we annualized the monthly variance by multiplying by 12 (see footnote 14 in Chapter 7). The standard deviation was $\sqrt{248} = 15.8\%$.

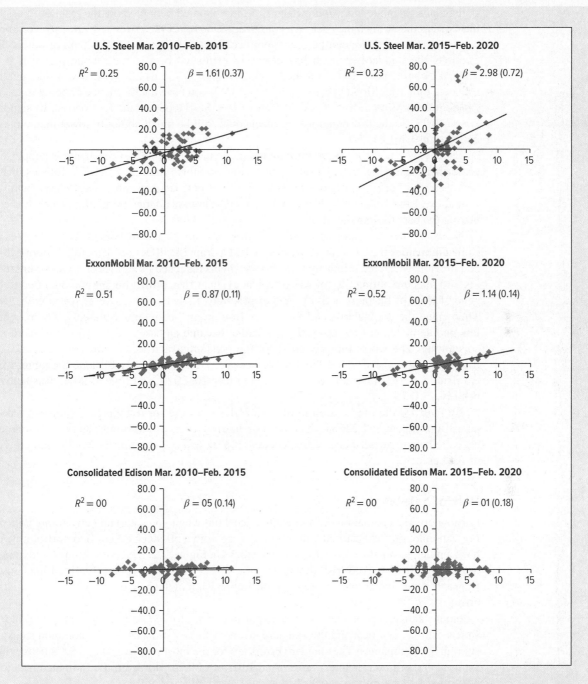

▶ **FIGURE 9.2**   We used past returns to estimate the betas of three stocks for the two pre-pandemic periods March 2010 to February 2015 (left-hand diagrams) and March 2015 to February 2020 (right-hand diagrams). In each case the line is fitted by regressing the returns on the stock on returns on the market. Beta is the slope of the fitted line. Notice that in both periods, U.S. Steel had the highest beta and Consolidated Edison the lowest. Standard errors are in parentheses beside the betas. The standard error measures the range of possible error in the beta estimate. We also report the proportion of total risk that is due to market movements (R^2).

statisticians calculate the *standard error* of the estimated beta to show the extent of possible mismeasurement. Then they set up a *confidence interval* of the estimated value plus or minus two standard errors. We can be much more confident of some estimates than of others. For example, the standard error on ExxonMobil's estimated beta in the second period is 0.14. Thus, the confidence interval for the beta is 1.14 plus or minus 2×0.14. If you state that the *true* beta for ExxonMobil is between 0.86 and 1.42, you have a 95% chance of being right. We can be much less confident of our estimate of U.S. Steel's beta in the first period. Its standard error is 0.37. So the true beta for U.S. Steel could well be much higher or lower than our estimated figure of 1.61.[11]

Usually, you will have more information (and thus more confidence) than this simple, and somewhat depressing, calculation suggests. For example, you know that ConEd's estimated beta was well below 1 in two successive five-year periods. U.S. Steel's estimated beta was well above 1 in both periods. Nevertheless, there is always a large margin for error when estimating the beta for individual stocks.

Note also that a company's risk may change from period to period. For example, for some companies the COVID-19 pandemic had a dramatic effect on risk. Take Zoom, which had previously catered primarily to corporate clients that used its services for videoconferencing and telecommuting. Zoom was a typical cyclical firm with a business model tied to the general level of business activity; not surprisingly, its beta was above 1, specifically 1.82. Then came the coronavirus and the "work from home" economy. Suddenly, Zoom, which few people had heard of before the pandemic, became an essential tool for both work and socializing. The worse the prognosis for the pandemic (and as a result for the economy), the greater was the demand for Zoom's services. Zoom suddenly became a countercyclical firm, and its beta estimated between February 20, 2020, and June 1, 2020, was actually negative, −0.30.[12]

By the way, the imprecision in beta estimates cries out for rounding. If someone reports an estimated beta at 1.22664, that someone hasn't looked at the standard error. No one can estimate beta to an accuracy of five decimal places. Savvy practitioners would round to 1.23 or further to 1.2.

Portfolio Betas

Fortunately, the estimation errors tend to cancel out when you estimate betas of *portfolios*.[13] For example, the beta estimate for a mutual fund with a 50-stock diversified portfolio would have a much lower standard error than the stocks in Figure 9.2. Diversification would remove most of the firm-specific risk that causes the scatter of points around the fitted lines in the figure. It's this scatter that accounts for the imprecision in the beta estimates and the standard errors.

Financial managers sometimes turn to portfolio betas for *industries*. For example, Table 9.1 shows estimates of beta and the standard errors of these estimates for the common stocks of six railroad companies. The standard errors are for the most part over 0.2. CSX's beta, which we used earlier in the chapter, had a standard error of 0.24. However, the estimated beta for a portfolio of all six railroad stocks had a lower standard error of 0.14.

---

[11]For this reason, statisticians would generally adjust this estimate of U.S. Steel's beta down toward 1.0. Similarly, they would adjust upward any estimated beta that was below 1.0. For simplicity, in this book we use unadjusted betas, but if you are interested in how to make the adjustment, take a look at the Beyond the Page feature, "How to estimate beta."

[12]See Karen Langley, "For Some Stocks, Bad News Is Now Good News," *The Wall Street Journal,* July 20, 2020.

[13]If the observations are independent, the standard error of the estimated mean beta declines in proportion to the square root of the number of stocks in the portfolio.

	Beta	Standard Error
Canadian Pacific	1.07	0.18
CSX	1.18	0.24
Kansas City Southern	0.97	0.20
Norfolk Southern	1.33	0.18
Union Pacific	1.09	0.16
Industry portfolio	1.13	0.14

❭ **TABLE 9.1**   Estimates of betas and standard errors for a sample of railroad companies and for an equally weighted portfolio of these companies, based on monthly returns from March 2015 to February 2020. The portfolio beta may be more reliable than the betas of the individual companies. Note the lower standard error for the portfolio.

EXAMPLE 9.1 • A Railroad Industry Cost of Capital for Berkshire Hathaway

Industry betas are particularly helpful for conglomerate companies investing in many different industries. Berkshire Hathaway is today's largest U.S. conglomerate, with investments in insurance, electric utilities, pipelines, jewelry, chemicals, paints, candies, batteries—the list goes on and on. It also owns BNSF, the Burlington Northern Santa Fe railroad. BNSF is one of the largest U.S. railroads and would have been included in Table 9.1 if it were still an independent public company. BNSF and the other railroads in the table face similar business and operating risks. The cost of capital for the comparable portfolio of railroads should be a good discount rate for Berkshire Hathaway's investments in BNSF.

9.4 Self-Test

Why does diversification increase the accuracy of beta estimates? Explain briefly.

9-3   Analyzing Project Risk

In Section 9.1, we estimated the asset beta for CSX and its company cost of capital. This asset beta is an estimate of the average risk of CSX's railroad business and the company cost of capital is a measure of the expected return on the company as a whole. Not all railroad investments are average risk, however. And if you are the first to use railroad-track networks as deep-space transmission antennas, you will have no asset beta to start with and the company cost of capital will not provide a useful guide to the return that you should demand.

How can you make informed judgments about costs of capital for projects or lines of business when you suspect that risk is *not* average? That is our next topic.

A company that wants to set a cost of capital for one particular line of business typically looks for *pure plays* in that line of business. Pure-play companies are public firms that specialize in one activity. For example, suppose that CSX needs to assess the risk of investing in a new company headquarters. The asset beta for railroads is not helpful. You need to know the beta of commercial real estate. Fortunately, portfolios of commercial real estate are traded. For example, you could estimate asset betas from returns on Real Estate Investment Trusts

(REITs) specializing in office buildings.[14] The REITs would serve as traded *comparables* for the proposed office building. You could also turn to indexes of real estate prices and returns derived from sales and appraisals of commercial properties.[15]

We pointed out earlier that Johnson & Johnson produces a range of consumer products as well as investing in pharmaceuticals and biotech R&D. Suppose that J&J wants to set a cost of capital for its pharmaceutical business. Its company cost of capital could be too low. However, it could estimate the average asset beta or cost of capital for pharmaceutical companies that have *not* diversified into consumer products.

Overall company costs of capital are almost useless for *conglomerates*. Conglomerates diversify into several unrelated industries, so they have to consider industry-specific costs of capital. They therefore look for pure plays in the relevant industries. We have noted Berkshire Hathaway as one example. Take Richard Branson's Virgin Group as another. The group combines many different companies, including airlines (Virgin Atlantic) and train services (Virgin Rail Group). Fortunately, there are examples of pure-play airlines and train operators. The trick is picking the comparables with business risks that are most similar to Virgin's companies.

Sometimes good comparables are not available or are not a good match to a particular project. Then the financial manager has to exercise her or his judgment. Here we offer the following advice:

1. *Think about the determinants of asset betas.* Often, the characteristics of high- and low-beta assets can be observed when the beta itself cannot be.

2. *Don't be fooled by diversifiable risk.*

3. *Avoid fudge factors in discount rates.* Don't give in to the temptation to add fudge factors to the discount rate to offset things that could go wrong with the proposed investment. Adjust cash-flow forecasts instead.

1. The Determinants of Asset Betas

Cyclicality   Many people's intuition associates risk with the variability of earnings or cash flow. But much of this variability reflects diversifiable risk. Lone prospectors searching for gold look forward to extremely uncertain future income, but whether they strike it rich is unlikely to depend on the performance of the market portfolio. Even if they do find gold, they do not bear much market risk. Therefore, an investment in gold prospecting has a high standard deviation but a relatively low beta. (Remember from Chapter 7 that Newmont Mining had a high standard deviation, but its beta was close to zero.)

What really counts is the strength of the relationship between the firm's earnings and the aggregate earnings on all real assets. We can measure this either by the *earnings beta* or by the *cash-flow beta*. These are just like a real beta except that changes in earnings or cash flow are used in place of rates of return on securities. Firms with high earnings or cash-flow betas are more likely to have high asset betas.

This means that cyclical firms—firms whose revenues and earnings are strongly dependent on the state of the business cycle—tend to be high-beta firms. Thus, you should demand a higher rate of return from investments whose performance is strongly tied to the performance of the economy.

---

[14]REITs are investment funds that invest in real estate. You would have to be careful to identify REITs investing in commercial properties similar to the proposed office building. There are also REITs that invest in other types of real estate, including apartment buildings, shopping centers, and timberland.

[15]See Chapter 23 in D. Geltner, N. G. Miller, J. Clayton, and P. Eichholtz, *Commercial Real Estate Analysis and Investments,* 3rd ed. (South-Western College Publishing, 2014).

Examples of cyclical businesses include airlines, luxury resorts and restaurants, construction, and steel. (Much of the demand for steel depends on construction and capital investment. Note U.S. Steel's sky-high beta in Figure 9.2.) Examples of less-cyclical businesses include food and tobacco products and established consumer brands such as J&J's baby products. A countercyclical example is MBA programs because spending a year or two at a business school is an easier choice when jobs are scarce. Applications to top MBA programs increase in recessions.

9.5 Self-Test

Would you expect a firm of bankruptcy lawyers to have a high or low beta? Explain.

Operating Leverage   A production facility with high fixed costs, relative to variable costs, is said to have high *operating leverage*. High operating leverage means a high asset beta. Let us see how this works.

The cash flows generated by an asset can be broken down into revenue, fixed costs, and variable costs:

$$\text{Cash flow} = \text{revenue} - \text{fixed cost} - \text{variable cost}$$

Costs are variable if they depend on the rate of output. Examples are raw materials, sales commissions, and some labor and maintenance costs. Fixed costs are cash outflows that occur regardless of whether the asset is active or idle, for example, property taxes or the wages of workers under contract. Costs that are fixed do not decline along with sales, and, therefore, any shortfall in sales has a greater impact on profitability.

EXAMPLE 9.2 • Operating Leverage and Risk

The Stamboard Group is comparing two technologies for producing prefabricated housing. Table 9.2 shows the forecasted cash flows. Both technologies generate the same *expected* level of sales and costs, but the costs of Technology A are a constant proportion of sales. By contrast the costs of Technology B are fixed at $135 million. This higher operating leverage results in a higher asset beta.

	Cash flows ($ millions)		
	Boom	Slump	Expected
Technology A			
Sales	200	100	150
Costs	180	90	135
Net cash flow	20	10	15
Technology B			
Sales	200	100	150
Costs	135	135	135
Net cash flow	65	−35	15

❯ **TABLE 9.2**   Technologies A and B have the same expected cash flows, but, since B's costs are fixed, its cash flows are hit harder by economic downturns and have a higher beta.

Now you have a rule of thumb for judging the relative risks of alternative designs or technologies for producing the same project. Other things being equal, the alternative with the higher level of fixed costs will have the higher project beta. Empirical tests confirm that companies with high operating leverage actually do have high betas.[16] We will look more closely at the measurement of operating leverage in the next chapter.

We have interpreted fixed costs as costs of production, but fixed costs can show up in other forms, for example, as future investment outlays. Suppose that an electric utility commits to build a large electricity-generating plant. The plant will take several years to build. During this period the construction costs are fixed obligations. The commitment to invest therefore increases the plant's asset beta. Of course, the commitment disappears when the plant is up and running. Therefore the plant's asset beta is only temporarily high during construction.

Other Sources of Risk   So far we have focused on cash flows. Cash-flow risk is not the only risk. A project's value is equal to the expected cash flows discounted at the risk-adjusted discount rate r. If either the risk-free rate or the market risk premium changes, then r will change and so will the project value. We saw in Chapter 3 that prices of long-duration bonds are more exposed to a shift in interest rates than short-duration bonds. In just the same way a project with very long-term cash flows is more exposed to shifts in the discount rate than one with short-term cash flows. This project will, therefore, have a high beta even though it may not have high operating leverage or cyclicality.[17]

You cannot hope to estimate the relative risk of assets with any precision, but good managers examine each project from a variety of angles and look for clues as to its riskiness. They know that high market risk is a characteristic of cyclical ventures, of projects with high fixed costs and of projects that are sensitive to market-wide changes in the discount rate. They think about the major uncertainties affecting the economy and consider how their projects are affected by these uncertainties.

2. Don't Be Fooled by Diversifiable Risk

In this chapter, we have defined risk as the asset beta for a firm, industry, or project. But in everyday usage, "risk" simply means "bad outcome." People think of the risks of a project as a list of things that can go wrong. For example,

- A geologist looking for oil worries about the risk of a dry hole.

- A pharmaceutical-company scientist worries about the risk that a new drug will have unacceptable side effects.

- A plant manager worries that new technology for a production line will fail to work, requiring expensive changes and repairs.

- A telecom CFO worries about the risk that a communications satellite will be damaged by space debris. (This was the fate of an Iridium satellite in 2009, when it collided with Russia's defunct Cosmos 2251. Both were blown to smithereens.)

Notice that these risks are all diversifiable. For example, the Iridium-Cosmos collision was definitely a zero-beta event. These hazards do not affect asset betas and should not affect the discount rate for the projects.

Sometimes, financial managers increase discount rates in an attempt to offset these risks. This makes no sense. Diversifiable risks do not increase the cost of capital. They do affect expected cash flows, however.

---

[16]See B. Lev, "On the Association between Operating Leverage and Risk," *Journal of Financial and Quantitative Analysis* 9 (September 1974), pp. 627–642; and G. N. Mandelker and S. G. Rhee, "The Impact of the Degrees of Operating and Financial Leverage on Systematic Risk of Common Stock," *Journal of Financial and Quantitative Analysis* 19 (March 1984), pp. 45–57.

[17]See J. Y. Campbell and J. Mei, "Where Do Betas Come From? Asset Price Dynamics and the Sources of Systematic Risk," *Review of Financial Studies* 6 (Fall 1993), pp. 567–592. Cornell discusses the effect of duration on project risk in B. Cornell, "Risk, Duration and Capital Budgeting: New Evidence on Some Old Questions," *Journal of Business* 72 (April 1999), pp. 183–200.

EXAMPLE 9.3 • Allowing for Possible Bad Outcomes

Project Z will produce just one cash flow, forecasted at $1 million at year 1. It is regarded as average risk, suitable for discounting at a 10% company cost of capital:

$$PV = \frac{C_1}{1+r} = \frac{1,000,000}{1.1} = \$909,100$$

But now you discover that the company's engineers are behind schedule in developing the technology required for the project. They are confident it will work, but they admit to a small chance that it will not. You still see the *most likely* outcome as $1 million, but you also see some chance that project Z will generate *zero* cash flow.

Now the project's prospects are clouded by your new worry about technology. It must be worth less than the $909,100 you calculated before that worry arose. But how much less? There is *some* discount rate (10% plus a fudge factor) that will give the right value, but we do not know what that adjusted discount rate is.

We suggest you reconsider your original $1 million forecast for project Z's cash flow. Project cash flows are supposed to be *unbiased* forecasts that give due weight to all possible outcomes, favorable and unfavorable. Managers making unbiased forecasts are correct on average. Sometimes, their forecasts will turn out high, other times low, but their errors will average out over many projects.

If you forecast a cash flow of $1 million for projects like Z, you will overestimate the average cash flow, because every now and then you will hit a zero. Those zeros should be "averaged in" to your forecasts.

For many projects, the most likely cash flow is also the unbiased forecast. If there are three possible outcomes with the probabilities shown below, the unbiased forecast is $1 million. (The unbiased forecast is the sum of the probability-weighted cash flows.)

Possible Cash Flow	Probability	Probability-Weighted Cash Flow	Unbiased Forecast
1.2	0.25	0.3	
1.0	0.50	0.5	1.0, or $1 million
0.8	0.25	0.2	

This might describe the initial prospects of project Z. But if technological uncertainty introduces a 10% chance of a zero cash flow, the unbiased forecast could drop to $900,000:

Possible Cash Flow	Probability	Probability-Weighted Cash Flow	Unbiased Forecast
1.2	0.225	0.27	
1.0	0.45	0.45	0.90, or $900,000
0.8	0.225	0.18	
0	0.10	0.0	

The present value is

$$PV = 0.9/1.1 = 0.818, \text{ or } \$818,000$$

Managers often work out a range of possible outcomes for major projects, sometimes with explicit probabilities attached. But even when outcomes and probabilities are not explicitly written down, the manager can still consider the good and bad outcomes as well as the most likely one. When the bad outcomes outweigh the good, the cash-flow forecast should be reduced until balance is regained.

Step 1, then, is to do your best to make unbiased forecasts of a project's cash flows. Unbiased forecasts incorporate all possible outcomes, including those that are specific to your project and those that stem from economywide events. Step 2 is to consider whether *diversified* investors would regard the project as more or less risky than the average project. In this step only market risks are relevant.

3. Avoid Fudge Factors in Discount Rates

Think back to our example of project Z, where we reduced forecasted cash flows from $1 million to $900,000 to account for a possible failure of technology. The project's PV was reduced from $909,100 to $818,000. You could have gotten the right answer by adding a fudge factor to the discount rate and discounting the original forecast of $1 million at this higher rate. But you have to think through the possible cash flows to get the fudge factor, and once you forecast the cash flows correctly, you don't need the fudge factor.

Fudge factors in discount rates are dangerous because they displace clear thinking about future cash flows. Here is an example.

EXAMPLE 9.4 • Correcting for Optimistic Forecasts

The chief financial officer (CFO) of EZ^2 Corp. is disturbed to find that cash-flow forecasts for its investment projects are almost always optimistic. On average they are 10% too high. He therefore decides to compensate by adding 10% to EZ^2's company cost of capital, increasing it from 12% to 22%.

Suppose the CFO is right about the 10% upward bias in cash-flow forecasts. Can he just add 10% to the discount rate?

Project ZZ has level forecasted cash flows of $1,000 per year lasting for 15 years. The first two lines of Table 9.3 show these forecasts and their PVs discounted at 12%. Lines 3 and 4 show the corrected forecasts, each reduced by 10%, and the corrected PVs, which are (no surprise) also reduced by 10% (line 5). Line 6 shows the PVs when the uncorrected forecasts are discounted at 22%. The final line 7 shows the percentage reduction in PVs at the 22% discount rate, compared to the unadjusted PVs in line 2.

Line 5 shows the correct adjustment for optimism (10%). Line 7 shows what happens when a 10% fudge factor is added to the discount rate. The effect on the first year's cash flow is a PV

Year	1	2	3	4	5	...	10	...	15
1. Original cash-flow forecast	$1,000.00	$1,000.00	$1,000.00	$1,000.00	$1,000.00	...	$1,000.00	...	$1,000.00
2. PV at 12%	$ 892.90	$ 797.20	$ 711.80	$ 635.50	$ 567.40	...	$ 322.00	...	$ 182.70
3. Corrected cash-flow forecast	$ 900.00	$ 900.00	$ 900.00	$ 900.00	$ 900.00	...	$ 900.00	...	$ 900.00
4. PV at 12%	$ 803.60	$ 717.50	$ 640.60	$ 572.00	$ 510.70	...	$ 289.80	...	$ 164.40
5. PV correction	−10.0%	−10.0%	−10.0%	−10.0%	−10.0%	...	−10.0%	...	−10.0%
6. Original forecast discounted at 22%	$ 819.70	$ 671.90	$ 550.70	$ 451.40	$ 370.00	...	$ 136.90	...	$ 50.70
7. PV "correction" at 22% discount rate	−8.2%	−15.7%	−22.6%	−29.0%	−34.8%	...	−57.5%	...	−72.3%

)TABLE 9.3   The original cash-flow forecasts for the ZZ project (line 1) are too optimistic. The forecasts and PVs should be reduced by 10% (lines 3 and 4). But adding a 10% fudge factor to the discount rate reduces PVs by far more than 10% (line 6). The fudge factor overcorrects for bias and would penalize long-lived projects.

"haircut" of about 8%, 2% less than the CFO expected. But later present values are knocked down by much more than 10%, because the fudge factor is compounded in the 22% discount rate. By years 10 and 15, the PV haircuts are 57% and 72%, far more than the 10% bias that the CFO started with.

Did the CFO really think that bias accumulated as shown in line 7 of Table 9.3? We doubt that he ever asked that question. If he was right in the first place, and the true bias is 10%, then adding a 10% fudge factor to the discount rate understates PV dramatically. The fudge factor also makes long-lived projects look much worse than quick-payback projects.[18]

Discount Rates for International Projects

In this chapter, we have concentrated on investments in the United States. In Chapter 28, we say more about investments made internationally. Here, we simply warn against adding fudge factors to discount rates for projects in developing economies. Such fudge factors are too often seen in practice.

It's true that markets are more volatile in developing economies, but much of that risk is diversifiable for investors in the United States, Europe, and other developed countries. It's also true that more things can go wrong for projects in developing economies, particularly in countries that are unstable politically. Expropriations happen. Sometimes governments default on their obligations to international investors. Thus it's especially important to think through the downside risks and to give them weight in cash-flow forecasts.

9.6 Self-Test

The present value of a project has been estimated at $10 million at a discount rate of 8%, but now the company lawyers point out that there is a 40% chance that the project could result in a costly lawsuit. The CFO therefore increases the discount rate for the project to 9%.
  a. Is the CFO correct in his approach?
  b. If the lawsuit would result in costs of $500,000, all occurring in year 1, what is the PV of the project?

9-4   Certainty Equivalents

In practical capital budgeting, managers use a risk-adjusted rate to discount future cash flows. This is also the procedure that we have described in this chapter. For example, the discount rate may be calculated from the capital asset pricing model:

$$r = r_f + \beta(r_m - r_f)$$

The resulting r is then substituted directly into the standard discounted cash-flow formula:

$$PV = \sum_{t=1}^{T} \frac{C_t}{(1 + r)^t}$$

The risk-adjusted discount rate, r, adjusts for both time and risk in one step. This is illustrated by the clockwise route in Figure 9.3.

There is an alternative way to value risky cash flows, which makes *separate* adjustments for risk and time. Rather than changing the discount rate, you convert the expected cash flows to **certainty equivalents**, which are then discounted using the risk-free interest rate. This is illustrated by the anti-clockwise route in Figure 9.3. The certainty-equivalent cash flow, or CEQ, is the smallest certain payoff that you would be willing to accept in place of the risky payoff. Since CEQ is a certain payoff, it can be discounted at the risk-free rate.

---

[18]The optimistic bias could be worse for distant than near cash flows. If so, the CFO should make the time-pattern of bias explicit and adjust the cash-flow forecasts accordingly.

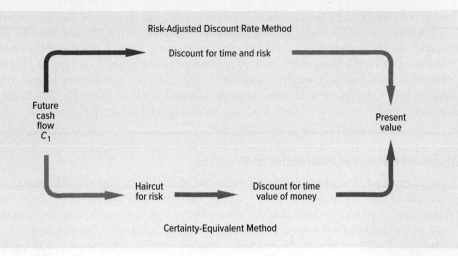

FIGURE 9.3

Two ways to calculate present value. "Haircut for risk" is financial slang referring to the reduction of the cash flow from its forecasted value to its certainty equivalent.

This gives us two identical expressions for the present value of a cash flow t periods away:[19]

$$PV = \frac{C_t}{(1 + r)^t} = \frac{CEQ_t}{(1 + r_f)^t}$$

BEYOND THE PAGE

Certainty equivalents and the CAPM

mhhe.com/brealey14e

Although the certainty-equivalent method is rarely used in everyday project valuation, an understanding of certainty equivalents will allow us to uncover what we are really assuming when we use the same discount rate to value each of a series of future cash flows. It will also become important when we cover options in Chapters 21 through 23 and forward and futures pricing in Chapter 27. Option-pricing formulas discount certainty equivalents. Forward and futures prices *are* certainty equivalents.

EXAMPLE 9.5 • Certainty Equivalent Valuation

Think back to the simple real estate investment that we used in Chapter 2 to introduce the concept of present value. You are considering construction of an office building that you plan to sell after one year for $800,000. That cash flow is uncertain with the same risk as the market, so $\beta = 1$. The risk-free interest rate is $r_f = 7\%$, but you discount the $800,000 payoff at a risk-adjusted rate of $r = 12\%$. This gives a present value of $800,000/1.12 = \$714,286$.

Suppose a real estate company now approaches and offers to fix the price at which it will buy the building from you at the end of the year. This guarantee would remove any uncertainty about the payoff on your investment. So you would accept a lower figure than the uncertain payoff of $800,000. But how much less? If the building has a present value of $714,286 and the interest rate is 7%, then

$$PV = \$714,286 = \frac{\text{certain cash flow}}{1.07}$$

$$\text{Certain cash flow} = \$764,286$$

A project with a guaranteed cash flow of $764,286 has exactly the same present value as an expected but uncertain cash flow of $800,000. The cash flow of $764,286 is therefore known as the *certainty-equivalent cash flow*.

• • • • •

---

[19]CEQ1 can be calculated directly from the capital asset pricing model. The certainty-equivalent value of the cash flow C_1 is $C_1 - \lambda \, cov(\tilde{C}_1, \tilde{r}_m)$. $Cov(\tilde{C}_1, \tilde{r}_m)$ is the covariance between the uncertain cash flow and the return on the market. Lambda, λ, is a measure of the market price of risk. It is defined as $(r_m - r_f)/\sigma_m^2$. For example, if $r_m - r_f = 0.08$ and the standard deviation of the market is $\sigma_m = 0.20$, then lambda $= 0.08/0.20^2 = 2$.

You often hear it said that distant cash flows are more risky than nearby flows and should be discounted at a higher rate. An understanding of certainty equivalents can help to see whether this is correct.

Column 2 in Table 9.4 shows that a project is expected to produce a cash inflow of $100 million for each of three years. The risk-free interest rate is 6%, the market risk premium is 8% and the project's beta is 0.75. You therefore calculate A's cost of capital as:

$$r = r_f + \beta(r_m - r_f) = 6 + 0.75(8) = 12\%$$

Column 3 of Table 9.4 shows the present values of these cash flows at a risk-adjusted discount rate of 12%. Summing these figures gives a total present value for the project of $240.2.

Column 4 of the table shows the certainty-equivalent cash flows. You can see, for example, that a certain cash flow of 94.6 in year 1 has the same present value as an uncertain cash flow of 100:

$$94.6/1.06 = 100/1.12 = 89.3$$

Since the two cash flows have the same present value, investors must be prepared to give up $100 - 94.6 = 5.4$ of expected income to eliminate uncertainty. Similarly, in year 2 they are prepared to give up $100 - 89.6 = 10.4$ to eliminate uncertainty. This is shown in the final column of Table 9.3, headed "Deduction for Risk."

When we valued the project, we used the same risk-adjusted discount rate for each year's cash flow. Now you can see from the final column that this implies a larger deduction for risk from the later cash flows. The reason is that the discount rate compensates for the risk borne *per period.* The more distant the cash flows, the greater the number of periods and the larger the *total* risk adjustment.

1.	2.	3.	4.	5.
Year	Forecasted Project Cash Flow	PV at 12%	Certainty-Equivalent Cash Flow	Deduction for Risk
1	100	89.3	94.6	5.4
2	100	79.7	89.6	10.4
3	100	71.2	84.8	15.2
		240.2		

❭ **TABLE 9.4** This project has a PV of 240.2 when the uncertain cash flows are discounted at a risk-adjusted rate of 12%. It has the same PV when the certainty equivalents are discounted at the risk-free rate of 6%.

9.7 Self-Test

True or false? Assume the project beta is positive.
   a. Discounting certainty-equivalent cash flows at the project's cost of capital would double-count risk and understate PV.
   b. If beta is constant, the ratio of certainty-equivalent to expected cash flows is the same in every year of the project's life.
   c. The ratio of certainty-equivalent to expected cash flow is not affected by diversifiable risks.

In Chapter 8, we set out the basic principles for valuing risky assets. This chapter shows you how to apply those principles when valuing capital investment projects.

- **The company cost of capital (r_A)** is the expected rate of return that investors require on a portfolio of all of the company's outstanding debt and equity. It is the opportunity cost of capital for investment in the firm as a whole. It can be calculated as an average of the expected returns on the firm's equity and debt, weighted by the relative market values of debt and equity:

$$\text{Company cost of capital} = r_A = r_D D/V + r_E E/V$$

- **When should the company cost of capital be used?** Absent taxes, the company cost of capital is the correct discount rate for projects that have the same market risk as the company's existing business. If debt interest is deductible for tax, the company cost of capital must be adjusted for this tax benefit or the value of the tax shield must be added in separately. We explain how to do this in Chapters 17 and 18.

- **How to find the cost of equity (r_E)** Many firms use the CAPM to estimate the cost of equity (r_E). This requires an estimate of the company's beta. Estimates of beta are typically derived from regressions of past stock returns on market returns.

- **Alternative way of finding the company cost of capital (r_A)** Instead of estimating the expected return on both the debt and the equity, managers occasionally estimate the firm's asset beta and substitute this into the CAPM to measure the company cost of capital. The asset beta is a weighted average of the betas of the firm's debt and equity:

$$\beta_A = \beta_D D/V + \beta_E E/V$$

- **When should company cost of capital be used?** Sometimes firms use the same discount rate to value all projects. If this procedure is followed strictly, the firm will accept too many high-risk projects and reject too many low-risk projects. It is *project* risk that counts: The true cost of capital depends on the use to which the capital is put.

- **What determines project risk?** Managers, therefore, need to understand why a particular project may have above- or below-average risk. Cyclical projects and those with high fixed costs generally have high betas.

- **Diversifiable risks and fudge factors** We added two other pieces of advice. Don't be fooled by diversifiable risk. These do not affect the cost of capital, but the possibility of bad outcomes should be incorporated in the cash-flow forecasts. Also be careful not to offset worries about a project's future performance by adding a fudge factor to the discount rate. Such worries should be reflected in the expected cash flows.

- **Certainty equivalents** Rather than adjusting the discount rate for risk, an alternative is to convert the expected cash flows to certainty equivalents which can then discounted at the risk-free interest rate. Although seldom used for making capital investment decisions, certainty-equivalents are essential when valuing options. We also used certainty-equivalents to demonstrate how the use of a single risk-adjusted discount rate implies proportionately larger risk deductions for the later cash flows.

- **Finding stock and market risk** The nearby box provides some useful spreadsheet functions for estimating stock and market risk.

• • • • •

Estimating Stock and Market Risk

❯Spreadsheets such as Excel have some built-in statistical functions that are useful for calculating risk measures. You can find these functions by clicking *fx* on the Excel toolbar. If you then click on the function that you wish to use, Excel will ask you for the inputs that it needs. At the bottom left of the function box, there is a Help facility with an example of how the function is used.

Here is a list of useful functions for estimating stock and market risk. You can enter the inputs for all these functions as numbers or as the addresses of cells that contain the numbers. Note that different versions of Excel may use slightly different names for these functions.

1. **VAR.P** and **STDEV.P:** Calculate variance and standard deviation of a series of numbers, as shown in Section 7-2.

2. **VAR.S** and **STDEV.S:** Footnote 12 of Chapter 7 noted that when variance is estimated from a sample of observations (the usual case), a correction should be made for the loss of a degree of freedom. VAR.S and STDEV.S provide the corrected measures. For any large sample VAR.S and VAR.P will be similar.

3. **SLOPE:** Useful for calculating the beta of a stock or portfolio.

4. **CORREL:** Useful for calculating the correlation between the returns on any two investments.

5. **COVARIANCE.P** and **COVARIANCE.S:** Portfolio risk depends on the covariance between the returns on each pair of stocks. These functions calculate the covariance.

6. **RSQ:** R-squared is the square of the correlation coefficient and is useful for measuring the proportion of the variance of a stock's returns that can be explained by the market.

7. **AVERAGE:** Calculates the average of any series of numbers.

If, say, you need to know the standard error of your estimate of beta, you can obtain more detailed statistics by going to the *Tools* menu and clicking on *Data Analysis* and then on *Regression*.

Spreadsheet Questions

The following questions provide opportunities to practice each of the Excel functions.

1. (VAR.P and STDEV.P) Choose two well-known stocks and download the latest 61 months of adjusted prices from **finance.yahoo.com**. Calculate the monthly returns for each stock. Now find the variance and standard deviation of the returns for each stock by using VAR.P and STDEV.P. Annualize the variance by multiplying by 12 and the standard deviation by multiplying by the square root of 12.

2. (AVERAGE, VAR.P, and STDEV.P) Now calculate the annualized variance and standard deviation for a portfolio that each month has equal holdings in the two stocks. Is the result more or less than the average of the standard deviations of the two stocks? Why?

3. (SLOPE) Download the Standard & Poor's index for the same period (its symbol is ˆGSPC). Find the beta of each stock and of the portfolio. (*Note:* You need to enter the stock returns as the Y-values and market returns as the X-values.) Is the beta of the portfolio more or less than the average of the betas of the two stocks?

4. (CORREL) Calculate the correlation between the returns on the two stocks. Use this measure and your earlier estimates of each stock's variance to calculate the variance of a portfolio that is evenly divided between the two stocks. (You may need to reread Section 7-3 to refresh your memory of how to do this.) Check that you get the same answer as when you calculated the portfolio variance directly.

5. (COVARIANCE.P) Repeat Question 4, but now calculate the covariance directly rather than from the correlations and variances.

SLOPE	▼ X ✓ *fx*	=SLOPE(B1:B9,A1:A9)						
	A	B	C	D	E	F	G	H
1	0.8	20.1						
2	-7.5	-25.4						
3	-16.8	-21.3						
4	-9.2	-10.0						
5	1.2	5.9						
6	-1.0	4.1						
7	-8.6	-10.2						
8	1.1	3.8						
9	4.8	10.3						
10								
11	A1:A9)							
12								

Function Arguments ✕

SLOPE

Known_y's B1:B9 ▦ = {20.0936768149883

Known_x's A1:A9 ▦ = {0.78215656520575

= 1.83972892

Returns the slope of the linear regression line through the given data points.

Known_x's is the set of independent data points and can be numbers or names, arrays, or references that contain numbers.

Formula result =   1.83972892

Help on this function   [OK]   [Cancel]

Microsoft Excel

6. (RSQ) For each of the two stocks calculate the proportion of the variance explained by the market index. Do the results square with your intuition?

7. Use the *Regression* facility under the *Data Analysis* menu to calculate the beta of each stock and of the portfolio (beta here is called the coefficient of the X-variable). Look at the standard error of the estimate in the cell to the right. How confident can you be of your estimates of the betas of each stock? How about your estimate of the portfolio beta?

FURTHER READING

For a useful survey of the issues covered in this chapter, see:

R. Jagannathan, J. Liberti, B. Liu, and I. Meier, "A Firm's Cost of Capital," *Annual Review of Financial Economics* 9 (November 2017), pp. 259–282.

Levi and Welch provide some recommendations for estimating betas in:

Y. Levi and I. Welch, "Best Practice for Cost-of-Capital Estimates," *Journal of Financial and Quantitative Analysis* 52 (April 2017), pp. 427–463.

PROBLEM SETS

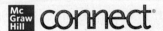

Select problems are available in McGraw-Hill's *Connect*. Please see the preface for more information.

1. **Definitions (S9.1–S9.3)** Define the following terms:

   a. Cost of debt.

   b. Cost of equity.

   c. Company cost of capital.

   d. Equity beta.

   e. Asset beta.

   f. Pure-play comparable.

2. **True/false (S9.1–S9.3)** True or false?

   a. The company cost of capital is the correct discount rate for all projects because the high risks of some projects are offset by the low risk of other projects.

   b. Adding fudge factors to discount rates undervalues long-lived projects compared with quick-payoff projects.

3. **Company cost of capital (S9.1)** Quark Productions ("Give your loved one a quark today.") uses its company cost of capital to evaluate all projects. Will it underestimate or overestimate the value of high-risk projects?

4. **Company cost of capital (S9.2)** The total market value of the common stock of the Okefenokee Real Estate Company is $6 million, and the total value of its debt is $4 million. The treasurer estimates that the beta of the stock is currently 1.5 and that the expected risk premium on the market is 6%. The Treasury bill rate is 4%. Assume for simplicity that Okefenokee debt is risk-free and the company does not pay tax.

   a. What is the required return on Okefenokee stock?

   b. Estimate the company cost of capital.

   c. What is the discount rate for an expansion of the company's present business?

   d. Suppose the company wants to diversify into the manufacture of rose-colored spectacles. The beta of optical manufacturers that have no debt is 1.2. Estimate the required return on Okefenokee's new venture.

5. **Company cost of capital (S9.2)** You are given the following information for Golden Fleece Financial:

Long-term debt outstanding:	$300,000
Current yield to maturity (r_{debt}):	8%
Number of shares of common stock:	10,000
Price per share:	$50
Book value per share:	$25
Expected rate of return on stock (r_{equity}):	15%

Calculate Golden Fleece's company cost of capital.

6. **Company cost of capital (S9.2)** Nero Violins has the following capital structure:

Security	Beta	Total Market Value ($ millions)
Debt	0	$100
Preferred stock	0.20	40
Common stock	1.20	299

a. What is the firm's asset beta? (*Hint:* What is the beta of a portfolio of all the firm's securities?)

b. Assume that the CAPM is correct. What discount rate should Nero set for investments that expand the scale of its operations without changing its asset beta? Assume a risk-free interest rate of 5% and a market risk premium of 6%. Ignore taxes.

7. **Company cost of capital (S9.2)** A company is 40% financed by risk-free debt. The interest rate is 10%, the expected market risk premium is 8%, and the beta of the company's common stock is 0.5. What is the company cost of capital?

8. **Company cost of capital (S9.2)** Binomial Tree Farm's financing includes $5 million of bank loans. Its common equity is shown in Binomial's Annual Report at $6.67 million. It has 500,000 shares of common stock outstanding, which trade on the Wichita Stock Exchange at $18 per share. What debt ratio should Binomial use to calculate its company cost of capital or asset beta? Explain.

9. **Measuring risk (S9.2)** Refer to the top-right panel of Figure 9.2. What proportion of U.S. Steel's returns was explained by market movements? What proportion of risk was diversifiable? How does the diversifiable risk show up in the plot? What is the range of possible errors in the estimated beta?

10. **Measuring risk (S9.2)** Figure 9.4 shows plots of monthly rates of return on three stocks versus those of the market index. The beta and standard deviation of each stock is given beside the plot.

a. Which stock is safest for a diversified investor?

b. Which stock is safest for an undiversified investor who puts all her money in one of these stocks?

c. Consider a portfolio with equal investments in each stock. What would be this portfolio's beta?

d. Consider a well-diversified portfolio composed of stocks with the same beta and standard deviation as Tesla. What are the beta and standard deviation of this portfolio's return? The standard deviation of the market portfolio's return is 20%.

e. Use the capital asset pricing model to estimate the expected return on each stock. The risk-free rate is 4%, and the market risk premium is 8%.

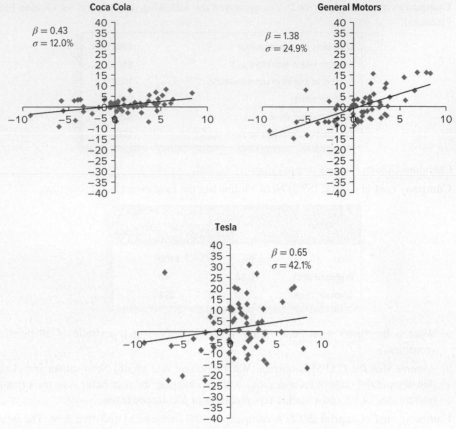

FIGURE 9.4

11. **Measuring risk (S9.2)** The following table shows estimates of the risk of two well-known Canadian stocks:

	Standard Deviation (%)	R^2	Beta	Standard Error of Beta
Sun Life Financial	18.3	0.34	0.89	0.16
Suncor Energy	23.4	0.32	1.11	0.21

a. What proportion of each stock's risk was market risk, and what proportion was specific risk?

b. What is the variance of the returns for Sun Life Financial stock? What is the specific variance?

c. What is the confidence interval on Suncor's beta? (See Section 9-2 on Estimating Beta for a definition of "confidence interval.")

d. If the CAPM is correct, what is the expected return on Sun Life? Assume a risk-free interest rate of 5% and an expected market return of 12%.

e. Suppose that next year, the market provides a 20% return. Knowing this, what return would you expect from Sun Life?

12. **Measuring risk (S9.1)** Look again at Table 9.1. This time we will concentrate on Union Pacific.

    a. Calculate Union Pacific's cost of equity from the CAPM using its own beta estimate and the industry beta estimate. How different are your answers? Assume a risk-free rate of 2% and a market risk premium of 7%.

    b. Can you be confident that Union Pacific's true beta is not the industry average?

    c. Under what circumstances might you advise Union Pacific to calculate its cost of equity based on its own beta estimate?

    d. You now discover that the estimated beta for Union Pacific in the previous five-year period was 1.3. Does this influence your answer to part (c)?

13. **Asset betas (S9.2)** EZCUBE Corp. is 50% financed with long-term bonds and 50% with common equity. The debt securities have a beta of .15. The company's equity beta is 1.25. What is EZCUBE's asset beta?

14. **Asset betas (S9.3)** Which of these projects is likely to have the higher asset beta, other things equal? Why?

    a. The sales force for project A is paid a fixed annual salary. Project B's sales force is paid by commissions only.

    b. Project C is a first-class-only airline. Project D is a well-established line of breakfast cereals.

15. **Asset betas (S9.3)** What types of firms need to estimate industry asset betas? How would such a firm make the estimate? Describe the process step by step.

16. **Betas and operating leverage (S9.3)** You run a perpetual encabulator machine, which generates revenues averaging $20 million per year. Raw material costs are 50% of revenues. These costs are variable—they are always proportional to revenues. There are no other operating costs. The cost of capital is 9%. Your firm's long-term borrowing rate is 6%. Now you are approached by Studebaker Capital Corp., which proposes a fixed-price contract to supply raw materials at $10 million per year for 10 years.

    a. What happens to the operating leverage and business risk of the encabulator machine if you agree to this fixed-price contract?

    b. Calculate the present value of the encabulator machine with and without the fixed-price contract.

17. **Diversifiable risk (S9.3)** Many investment projects are exposed to diversifiable risks. What does "diversifiable" mean in this context? How should diversifiable risks be accounted for in project valuation? Should they be ignored completely?

18. **Fudge factors (S9.3)** Mario Barleycorn estimates his firm's company cost of capital at only 8%. Nevertheless, he sets a 15% companywide discount rate to offset the optimistic biases of project sponsors and to impose "discipline" on the capital budgeting process. Suppose Mr. Barleycorn is correct about the project sponsors, who are, in fact, optimistic by 7% on average. Explain why the increase in the discount rate from 8% to 15% will not offset the bias. (*Note:* The firm is entirely equity financed.)

19. **Fudge factors (S9.3)** Mom and Pop Groceries has just dispatched a year's supply of groceries to the government of the Central Antarctic Republic. Payment of $250,000 will be made one year hence after the shipment arrives by snow train. Unfortunately, there is a good chance of a coup d'état, in which case the new government will not pay. Mom and Pop's controller therefore decides to discount the payment at 40% rather than at the company's 12% cost of capital.

    a. What's wrong with using a 40% rate to offset political risk?

    b. How much is the $250,000 payment really worth if the odds of a coup d'état are 25%?

20. **Fudge factors (S9.3)** An oil company is drilling a series of new wells on the perimeter of a producing oil field. About 20% of the new wells will be dry holes. Even if a new well strikes

oil, there is still uncertainty about the amount of oil produced: 40% of new wells that strike oil produce only 1,000 barrels a day; 60% produce 5,000 barrels per day.

a. Forecast the annual cash revenues from a new perimeter well. Use a future oil price of $100 per barrel.

b. A geologist proposes to discount the cash flows of the new wells at 30% to offset the risk of dry holes. The oil company's normal cost of capital is 10%. Does this proposal make sense? Briefly explain why or why not.

21. **Certainty equivalents (S9.4)** A project has a forecasted cash flow of $110 in year 1 and $121 in year 2. The interest rate is 5%, the estimated risk premium on the market is 10%, and the project has a beta of 0.5. If you use a constant risk-adjusted discount rate, what is

a. The PV of the project?

b. The certainty-equivalent cash flow in years 1 and 2?

c. The ratio of the certainty-equivalent cash flows to the expected cash flow?

22. **Certainty equivalents (S9.4)** A project has the following forecasted cash flows:

Cash Flows ($ thousands)			
C_0	C_1	C_2	C_3
−100	+40	+60	+50

The estimated beta is 1.5. The market return is 16%, and the risk-free rate is 7%.

a. Estimate the cost of capital for the project and the project's PV.

b. What are the certainty-equivalent cash flows in each year?

c. What is the ratio of the certainty-equivalent cash flow to the expected cash flow in each year?

d. Explain why this ratio declines.

CHALLENGE

23. **Beta of costs (S9.2)** Suppose that you are valuing a future stream of high-risk (high-beta) cash *outflows*. High risk means a high discount rate. But the higher the discount rate, the less the present value. This seems to say that the higher the risk of cash outflows, the less you should worry about them! Can that be right? Should the sign of the cash flow affect the appropriate discount rate? Explain.

24. **Fudge factors (S9.3)** An oil company executive is considering investing $10 million in one or both of two wells: Well 1 is expected to produce oil worth $3 million a year for 10 years; well 2 is expected to produce $2 million for 15 years. These are real (inflation-adjusted) cash flows.

The beta for producing wells is 0.9. The market risk premium is 8%, the nominal risk-free interest rate is 6%, and expected inflation is 4%.

The two wells are intended to develop a previously discovered oil field. Unfortunately there is still a 20% chance of a dry hole in each case. A dry hole means zero cash flows and a complete loss of the $10 million investment.

Ignore taxes and make further assumptions as necessary.

a. What is the correct real discount rate for cash flows from developed wells?

b. The oil company executive proposes to add 20 percentage points to the real discount rate to offset the risk of a dry hole. Calculate the NPV of each well with this adjusted discount rate.

c. What do you say the true NPVs of the two wells are?

d. Is there any single fudge factor that could be added to the discount rate for developed wells that would yield the correct NPV for both wells? Explain.

9.1 Too low. The market value of equity is generally well above book value, and the expected return on equity is always higher than that on debt.

9.2 $D/V = 0.33$ and $E/V = 0.67$. $r_D = 4\%$ and $r_E = 2 + 1 \times 7 = 9\%$. The company cost of capital, therefore, equals $r_A = r_D D/V + r_E E/V = 4 \times 0.33 + 9 \times 0.67 = 7.33\%$.

9.3 Too many high-risk projects, too few low-risk projects.

9.4 Diversification reduces portfolio-specific risks, which reduces the scatter of returns around the line relating portfolio and market returns. This makes it easier to locate the line and measure its slope, which is beta.

9.5 Bankruptcy lawyers are likely to have more business in recessions. Their firms may even have negative betas.

9.6 a. No, the chance of a lawsuit is unlikely to be related to the state of the economy and is not a market risk.

   b. PV should be reduced by $(0.4 \times 500{,}000)/1.08 = \$185{,}000$.

9.7 a. True

   b. False

   c. True

You can download data for the following questions from **finance.yahoo.com** or any site that provides financial data.

1. Look at the companies listed in Table 8.4. Calculate monthly rates of return for two successive five-year periods. Calculate betas for each subperiod using the Excel SLOPE function. How stable was each company's beta? Suppose that you had used these betas to estimate expected rates of return from the CAPM. Would your estimates have changed significantly from period to period?

2. Identify a sample of food companies. For example, you could try Campbell Soup (CPB), General Mills (GIS), Kellogg (K), Mondelez International (MDLZ), and Tyson Foods (TSN).

   a. Estimate beta and R^2 for each company, using five years of monthly returns and Excel functions SLOPE and RSQ.

   b. Average the returns for each month to give the return on an equally weighted portfolio of the stocks. Then calculate the industry beta using these portfolio returns. How does the R^2 of this portfolio compare with the average R^2 of the individual stocks?

   c. Use the CAPM to calculate an average cost of equity (r_{equity}) for the food industry. Use current interest rates—take a look at the discussion of what is the risk-free rate? in Section 9-1—and a reasonable estimate of the market risk premium.

MINI-CASE

The Jones Family Incorporated

The Scene: It is early evening in the summer of 2021, in an ordinary family room in Manhattan. Modern furniture, with old copies of *The Wall Street Journal* and the *Financial Times* scattered around. Autographed photos of Jerome Powell and George Soros are prominently displayed.

A picture window reveals a distant view of lights on the Hudson River. John Jones sits at a computer terminal, glumly sipping a glass of chardonnay and putting on a carry trade in Japanese yen over the Internet. His wife Marsha enters.

Marsha: Hi, honey. Glad to be home. Lousy day on the trading floor, though. Dullsville. No volume. But I did manage to hedge next year's production from our copper mine. I couldn't get a good quote on the right package of futures contracts, so I arranged a commodity swap.

John doesn't reply.

Marsha: John, what's wrong? Have you been selling yen again? That's been a losing trade for weeks.

John: Well, yes. I shouldn't have gone to Goldman Sachs's foreign exchange brunch. But I've got to get out of the house somehow. I'm cooped up here all day calculating covariances and efficient risk-return trade-offs while you're out trading commodity futures. You get all the glamour and excitement.

Marsha: Don't worry, dear, it will be over soon. We only recalculate our most efficient common stock portfolio once a quarter. Then you can go back to leveraged leases.

John: You trade, and I do all the worrying. Now there's a rumor that our leasing company is going to get a hostile takeover bid. I knew the debt ratio was too low, and you forgot to put on the poison pill. And now you've made a negative-NPV investment!

Marsha: What investment?

John: That wildcat oil well. Another well in that old Sourdough field. It's going to cost $5 million! Is there any oil down there?

Marsha: That Sourdough field has been good to us, John. Where do you think we got the capital for your yen trades? I bet we'll find oil. Our geologists say there's only a 30% chance of a dry hole.

John: Even if we hit oil, I bet we'll only get 75 barrels of crude oil per day.

Marsha: That's 75 barrels day in, day out. There are 365 days in a year, dear.

John and Marsha's teenage son Johnny bursts into the room.

Johnny: Hi, Dad! Hi, Mom! Guess what? I've made the junior varsity derivatives team! That means I can go on the field trip to the Chicago Board Options Exchange. (*Pauses.*) What's wrong?

John: Your mother has made another negative-NPV investment. A wildcat oil well, way up on the North Slope of Alaska.

Johnny: That's OK, Dad. Mom told me about it. I was going to do an NPV calculation yesterday, but I had to finish calculating the junk-bond default probabilities for my corporate finance home-work. (*Grabs a financial calculator from his backpack.*) Let's see: 75 barrels a day times 365 days per year times $100 per barrel when delivered in Los Angeles . . . that's $2.7 million per year.

John: That's $2.7 million *next* year, assuming that we find any oil at all. The production will start declining by 5% every year. And we still have to pay $20 per barrel in pipeline and tanker charges to ship the oil from the North Slope to Los Angeles. We've got some serious operating leverage here.

Marsha: On the other hand, our energy consultants project increasing oil prices. If they increase with inflation, price per barrel should increase by roughly 2.5% per year. The wells ought to be able to keep pumping for at least 15 years.

Johnny: I'll calculate NPV after I finish with the default probabilities. The interest rate is 6%. Is it OK if I work with the beta of 0.8 and our usual figure of 7% for the market risk premium?

Marsha: I guess so, Johnny. But I am concerned about the fixed shipping costs.

John: (*Takes a deep breath and stands up.*) Anyway, how about a nice family dinner? I've reserved our usual table at the Four Seasons.

Everyone exits.

Announcer: Is the wildcat well really negative NPV? Will John and Marsha have to fight a hostile takeover? Will Johnny's derivatives team use Black–Scholes or the binomial method? Find out in the next episode of The Jones Family Incorporated.

You may not aspire to the Jones family's way of life, but you will learn about all their activities, from futures contracts to binomial option pricing, later in this book. Meanwhile, you may wish to replicate Johnny's NPV analysis.

QUESTIONS

1. Calculate the NPV of the wildcat oil well, taking account of the probability of a dry hole, the shipping costs, the decline in production, and the forecasted increase in oil prices. How long does production have to continue for the well to be a positive-NPV investment? Ignore taxes and other possible complications.

2. Now consider operating leverage. How should the shipping costs be valued, assuming that output is known and the costs are fixed? How would your answer change if the shipping costs were proportional to output? Assume that unexpected fluctuations in output are zero-beta and diversifiable. (*Hint:* The Jones's oil company has an excellent credit rating. Its long-term borrowing rate is only 7%.)

CHAPTER

10

Project Analysis

Having read the earlier chapters on capital budgeting, you may have concluded that the choice of which projects to accept is a simple one. You just draw up a set of cash-flow forecasts, choose the right discount rate, and crank out net present value. But finding projects that create value for the shareholders can never be reduced to a mechanical exercise. We therefore devote the next two chapters to ways in which companies can stack the odds in their favor when making investment decisions.

When managers are presented with investment proposals, they do not accept the cash flow forecasts at face value. Instead, they try to understand what makes a project tick and what could go wrong with it. Remember Murphy's law, "if anything can go wrong, it will," and O'Reilly's corollary, "at the worst possible time."

Once you understand why a venture may go wrong, you can decide whether it is worth trying to rule out the possible causes of failure. Maybe further expenditure on market research would clear up those doubts about acceptance by consumers, or maybe some further work on the test bed would confirm the durability of those welds.

Even if you decide that it is worth going ahead without further analysis, you do not want to be caught by surprise if things go wrong later. You want to know the danger signals and the actions that you might take.

10.1 Sensitivity and scenario analysis

Our first task in this chapter is to show how managers use *sensitivity analysis* to identify the effect on project NPV of a misestimate in one of the forecasts.

In the case of larger projects, managers may also want to think about how project profitability would be affected by possible changes in the environment in which the project operates. We show how managers use *scenario analysis* to construct a limited number of plausible future scenarios and to examine their impact on project profitability.

10.2 Break-even analysis and operating leverage

Sensitivity analysis asks how serious it would be if sales or costs turn out to be worse than expected. Managers sometimes rephrase the question and ask how bad things could get before the project becomes a loser. This is called *break-even analysis*. More often than not "a loser" is defined in terms of accounting profits. We suggest that it makes more sense to define a loser as a project with a negative NPV.

A project's break-even point depends on the extent to which a decline in sales is matched by a decline in costs. If the costs are largely fixed, the business is said to have high *operating leverage*. We show how to measure operating leverage.

10.3 Real options and the value of flexibility

Discounted cash flow analysis commonly assumes that companies hold assets passively, and it ignores the opportunities to expand the project if it is successful or to bail out if it is not. However, wise managers look for ways to capitalize on success and reduce the costs of failure, and they are prepared to pay up for projects that give them this flexibility. Opportunities to modify projects as the future unfolds are known as *real options*. In the final section of the chapter, we describe several important real options, and we show how to use *decision trees* to set out the possible future choices. We will come back to the subject in Chapter 23, where we show how to value real options.

10-1 Sensitivity and Scenario Analysis

Uncertainty means that more things can happen than will happen. Therefore, whenever managers are given a cash-flow forecast, they try to determine what else may happen and the implications of these possible surprise events. This is called **sensitivity analysis.**

Put yourself in the well-heeled shoes of the financial manager of the Otobai Company in Osaka. You are considering the introduction of a high-performance electric scooter for city use. Your staff members have prepared the cash-flow forecasts shown in Table 10.1. Since NPV is positive at the 20% opportunity cost of capital, it appears to be worth going ahead, but before you decide, you want to delve into these forecasts and identify the key variables that determine whether the project succeeds or fails.

The project requires an initial investment of ¥15 billion in plant and machinery, which will have negligible further value when the project comes to an end. As sales build up in the early and middle years of the project, the company will need to make increasing investments in net working capital, which is recovered in later years. After year 6, the company expects sales to tail off as other companies enter the market, and the company will probably need to reduce the price of the scooter. The cost of goods sold is forecast to be 50% of sales; in addition, there will be fixed costs each year that are unrelated to the level of sales. Taxes at a 40% rate are computed after deducting straight-line depreciation.

					Cash Flow in Years						
	0	**1**	**2**	**3**	**4**	**5**	**6**	**7**	**8**	**9**	**10**
1 Cash flow from investment in plant and equipment	−15.00	0.0	0.0	0.0	0.0	0.0	0.0	0.0	0.0	0.0	0.0
2 Cash flow from investment in working capital		−4.10	−1.30	−0.20	−0.30	−0.20	−0.40	1.60	1.90	1.80	1.20
3 Number of units sold		6,800	10,000	16,000	21,500	24,000	25,400	23,400	16,000	10,500	6,000
4 Unit price (¥ millions)		1.50	1.55	1.59	1.64	1.69	1.74	1.80	1.85	1.80	1.75
5 Revenue (3 × 4)		10.20	15.50	25.44	35.26	40.56	44.20	42.12	29.60	18.90	10.50
6 Cost of goods sold (50% of revenue)		5.10	7.75	12.72	17.63	20.28	22.10	21.06	14.80	9.45	5.25
7 Fixed costs	3.00	4.40	4.53	4.67	4.81	4.95	5.10	5.25	5.41	5.57	5.74
8 Depreciation		1.50	1.50	1.50	1.50	1.50	1.50	1.50	1.50	1.50	1.50
9 Pretax profit (5 − 6 − 7 − 8)	−3.00	−0.80	1.72	6.55	11.32	13.83	15.50	14.31	7.89	2.38	−1.99
10 Tax at 40%	−1.20	−0.32	0.69	2.62	4.53	5.53	6.20	5.72	3.16	0.95	−0.80
11 Profit after tax (9 −10)	−1.80	−0.48	1.03	3.93	6.79	8.30	9.30	8.58	4.73	1.43	−1.19
12 Operating cash flow (8 + 11)	−1.80	1.02	2.53	5.43	8.29	9.80	10.80	10.08	6.23	2.93	0.31
13 Net cash flow (1 + 2 + 12)	−16.80	−3.08	1.23	5.23	7.99	9.60	10.40	11.68	8.13	4.73	1.51
14 Present value (at 20%)	−16.80	−2.57	0.85	3.03	3.85	3.86	3.48	3.26	1.89	0.92	0.24
NPV	2.02										

❭**TABLE 10.1**   Preliminary cash-flow forecasts for Otobai's electric scooter project (figures in ¥ billions unless stated otherwise).

These seem to be the important things you need to know, but look out for unidentified variables that could affect these estimates. Perhaps there could be patent problems, or perhaps you will need to invest in service stations that will recharge the scooter batteries. The greatest dangers often lie in these unknown unknowns, or "unk-unks," as scientists call them.

Having found no unk-unks (no doubt you will find them later), you conduct a sensitivity analysis with respect to the required investment in plant and working capital and the forecast sales volume, price, and costs. To do this, the marketing and production staffs are asked to give optimistic and pessimistic estimates for each of the underlying variables. These are set out in the second and third columns of Table 10.2. For example, it is possible that sales of scooters could be 25% below forecast, or you may be obliged to cut the price by 15%. The fourth and fifth columns of the table show what happens to the project's net present value if the variables are set one at a time to their optimistic and pessimistic values. Your project appears to be by no means a sure thing. The most dangerous variables are cost of goods sold and sales volume. If the cost of goods sold is 70% of sales (and all other variables are as expected), then the project has an NPV of − ¥10.7 billion. If unit sales each year turn out to be 25% less than you forecast (and all other variables are as expected), then the project has an NPV of − ¥5.9 billion.

Trendy consultants sometimes use a *tornado diagram* such as Figure 10.1 to illustrate the results of a sensitivity analysis. The bars at the summit of the tornado show the range of NPVs due to uncertainty about the level of sales. At the base of the tornado, you can see the more modest effect of uncertainty about investment in working capital and the level of fixed costs.[1]

10.1 Self-Test

Suppose that capital investment for the Otobai project could be as high as ¥20 billion. Recalculate NPV under this changed assumption. (*Hint:* Don't forget the change in the depreciation tax shield.)

Variable	Possible Deviations from Forecast, %		NPV (¥billions)	
	Optimistic	Pessimistic	Optimistic	Pessimistic
Capital investment	−30%	+50%	5.77	−4.22
Change in working capital	−40	+40	3.37	0.68
Number of units sold	+30	−25	11.57	−5.94
Unit price	+10	−15	5.20	−2.75
Cost of goods sold (% of sales)	30	70	14.75	−10.71
Fixed costs	−30	+30	6.21	−2.17

❭**TABLE 10.2**   To undertake a sensitivity analysis of the electric scooter project, we set each variable in turn at its most pessimistic or optimistic value and recalculate the NPV of the project.

---

[1]Notice that the term "fixed costs" does not imply that they are certain or cannot change from year to year. It indicates that the costs are not related to the level of sales.

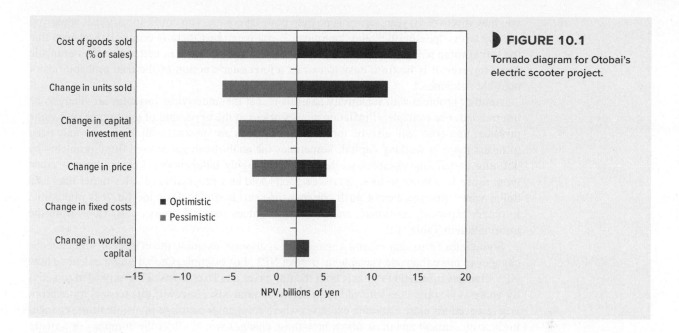

▶ FIGURE 10.1
Tornado diagram for Otobai's electric scooter project.

Value of Information

The world is uncertain, and accurate cash-flow forecasts are unattainable. So, if a project has a positive NPV based on your best forecasts, shouldn't you go ahead with it regardless of the fact that there may be later disappointments? Why spend time and effort focusing on the things that could go wrong?

Sensitivity analysis is not a substitute for the NPV rule, but if you know the danger points, you may be able to modify the project or resolve some of the uncertainty before your company undertakes the investment. For example, suppose that the pessimistic value for the cost of goods sold partly reflects the production department's worry that a particular machine will not work as designed and that the operation will need to be performed by other methods. The chance of this happening is only 1 in 10. But, if it does occur, the extra cost would reduce the NPV of your project by ¥2.5 billion, putting the NPV underwater at $+2.02 - 2.50 = -¥0.48$ billion. Suppose that a ¥100 million pretest of the machine would resolve the uncertainty and allow you to clear up the problem. It clearly pays to invest ¥100 million to avoid a 10% probability of a ¥2.5 billion fall in NPV. You are ahead by $-0.1 + 0.10 \times 2.5 = ¥0.15$ billion. On the other hand, the value of additional information about working capital is small. Because the project is only marginally unprofitable even under pessimistic assumptions about working capital, you are unlikely to be in trouble if you have misestimated that variable.

Limits to Sensitivity Analysis

Sensitivity analysis boils down to expressing cash flows in terms of key project variables and then calculating the consequences of misestimating those variables. It forces the manager to identify the crucial determinants of the project's success and indicates where additional information would be most useful or where design changes may be needed.

One drawback to sensitivity analysis is that it always gives somewhat ambiguous results. For example, what exactly does *optimistic* or *pessimistic* mean? The marketing department may be interpreting the terms in a different way from the production department. Ten years from now, after hundreds of projects, hindsight may show that the marketing department's pessimistic limit was exceeded twice as often as that of the production department, but what you may discover 10 years hence is no help now. Of course, you could specify that when you use the terms "pessimistic" and "optimistic," you mean that there is only a 10% chance that the actual value will prove to be worse than the pessimistic figure or better than the optimistic one. However, it is far from easy to extract a forecaster's notion of the true probabilities of possible outcomes.[2]

Another problem with sensitivity analysis is that the underlying variables are likely to be interrelated. For example, if inflation pushes prices to the upper end of your range, it is quite probable that costs will also be inflated. And if sales are unexpectedly high, you may need to invest more in working capital. Sometimes the analyst can get around these problems by defining underlying variables so that they are roughly independent. For example, it made more sense for Otobai to look at cost of goods sold as a proportion of sales rather than as a dollar value. But you cannot push one-at-a-time sensitivity analysis too far. It is impossible to obtain expected, optimistic, and pessimistic values for total project cash flows from the information in Table 10.2.

Sometimes firms may extend a sensitivity analysis to examine the effects of simultaneous changes in more than one variable on project NPV. For example, Otobai might calculate how NPV changes if inflation impacts both the unit price and fixed costs. This expanded sensitivity analysis is sometimes referred to as **scenario analysis.** However, this term is more properly reserved for more elaborate exercises where companies envisage plausible future changes in the environment and think about how those changes would affect the company or a major investment project.

Stress Tests and Scenario Analysis

Since the banking crisis of 2007–2009, the Federal Reserve has undertaken an annual *stress test* of the ability of major banks to weather another storm. Every year the Fed asks each bank to assess whether it could cope with three possible macroeconomic scenarios (baseline, adverse, and severely adverse). For example, in 2019 the toughest scenario involved a worldwide recession with an 8% decline in GDP, together with sharp falls in interest rates, share prices, and real estate prices. The bank's responses are used by the Fed to assess the likely effect of economic catastrophe on the bank's balance sheet, income, and capital adequacy.

Similarly, companies may construct possible future scenarios to explore how their major projects might be affected by unexpected future developments. These scenarios are not best forecasts; they are, however, plausible representations of an uncertain future. For example, Otobai might investigate a scenario where a growing awareness of climate change results in more car-free city centers, falling prices of electric cars, competition from e-bikes, and new regulations on road usage and speed. Such a scenario might prompt a number of questions. How would the company's scooter fare in such a world? Could the design be modified to make it more attractive for scooter-sharing systems? Would speed restrictions make the scooter uncompetitive with public transport, or would the door-to-door feature of scooter transport offset any speed issues?

Unlike sensitivity analysis, scenario analysis does not restrict Otobai to changing one variable at a time. Each scenario might imply a change in sales volume, unit price, costs, and so on. Also, in contrast to sensitivity analysis, scenario analysis does not generally focus on the best and worst outcomes. Instead it tries to identify how a project would be affected by possible major, mutually consistent changes in a project's environment.

---

[2]If you doubt this, try some simple experiments. Ask the person who repairs your dishwasher to state a numerical probability that it will work for at least one more year. Or construct your own subjective probability distribution of the number of telephone calls you will receive next week. That ought to be easy. Try it. We will also refer in Chapter 11 to evidence that people tend to be overconfident in their forecasts and to understate the possible errors.

Such scenario analysis can prompt the company to think more widely about the future and how it might be affected by credible unexpected developments. Shell, a long-time proponent of scenario analysis, suggests that it offers "an alternative to the 'official' view of the future—the business-as-usual outlook—[which] both reflects an optimism bias and is based on the human tendency to see familiar patterns and be blind to the unexpected."[3] Uncertainty around the future due to COVID-19 has given special importance to this type of analysis. For example, the outlook for airlines due to the spread of mutations and resulting quarantine restrictions, the desire of people to travel, the use of Zoom and other similar programs to hold business meetings, and many other uncertainties make scenario analysis very useful. The same is true for many other industries.

A better understanding of how a project might be affected by a changing world could prompt you to revise your original cash flow forecasts and to devise strategies for the way that you might respond to these changes. Later in the chapter we will look at how companies can build flexibility into a project's design that will allow them to modify the project in the future. Scenario analysis can suggest where such flexibility may be needed.

But there are also limitations to such analysis. The analyst needs to reduce an infinite number of possible future scenarios to no more than two or three scenarios that capture the main uncertainties surrounding the project. But constructing even a limited number of scenarios and identifying their effects can soak up a lot of analyst time. Not surprisingly, formal scenario analysis tends to be reserved for major projects or for possible strategies for the entire business.

BEYOND THE PAGE

Monte Carlo simulation

mhhe.com/brealey14e

10.2 Self-Test

What is the difference between sensitivity and scenario analysis?

10-2   Break-Even Analysis and Operating Leverage

Break-Even Analysis

When we undertake a sensitivity analysis of a project or when we look at alternative scenarios, we are asking how serious it would be if the future turns out to be worse than we forecast. Managers sometimes prefer to rephrase this question and ask how bad things can get before the project becomes a loser. This exercise is known as **break-even analysis.**

We saw earlier that the profitability of Otobai's project could be damaged if sales volume is unexpectedly low. Therefore, management might look at how far volume could fall before the project had a negative NPV. The calculations in our sensitivity analysis provide the data that Otobai needs. Table 10.2 shows that the projected NPV for the project is ¥2.02 billion and that NPV would fall by ¥7.96 billion if there was a 25% reduction in sales volume. Therefore, NPV would be exactly zero if each year sales fell by $25\% \times (2.02)/(7.96) = 6.3\%$ below forecast. That is the sales volume break-even point.

Break-even points are most often calculated in terms of sales, but they can equally well be calculated for other variables. Table 10.3 shows the break-even points for each variable in our Otobai example. You can see, for example, that quite small errors in your forecasts for volume, price, and variable costs could cause your project to become a loser. On the other hand, the project would still break even (NPV = 0) if you have underestimated working capital by 60%.

BEYOND THE PAGE

Try It! Scooter project spreadsheets

mhhe.com/brealey14e

---

[3]A. Wilkinson and R. Kupers, "Living in the Futures," *Harvard Business Review* 91 (May 2013), p. 121.

)TABLE 10.3 The percentage change in the estimated value of each variable that produces an NPV of zero for the electric scooter project.

	Change in Estimated Value
Capital investment	+16.2%
Working capital	+60.1
Sales	−6.3
Cost of goods sold (% of sales)	+3.2
Fixed costs	+14.5

Table 10.3 defines *break even* as the point at which NPV would be exactly zero. But managers frequently calculate the break-even points in terms of accounting profits rather than net present values. For example, look at Table 10.4, which shows the minimum level of sales that Otobai needs each year to avoid a loss on its scooter project. You can see that in year 1, Otobai needs sales of ¥11.80 billion to cover costs and depreciation. In year 2, the break-even sales level rises to ¥12.06 billion.[4]

Should Otobai's manager be relaxed if the project breaks even each year in accounting terms? It is true that its revenues will then be sufficient to cover the operating costs and repay the initial investment. But they will not be sufficient to repay the opportunity cost of capital on that ¥15 billion. A project that breaks even in accounting terms will surely have a negative NPV.

10.3 Self-Test

What would be the accounting break-even level of sales in year 1 if the capital investment in Otobai's project was only ¥10 billion?

Operating Leverage

A project's break-even point depends on the extent to which its costs vary with the level of sales. Suppose that electric scooters fall out of favor. The bad news is that Otobai's sales revenue is less than you had hoped, but you have the consolation that the cost of goods sold is also lower. But, any costs that are fixed do *not* decline along with sales, and, therefore, any shortfall in sales has a greater impact on profitability. Of course, a high proportion of fixed costs is not all bad. The firm whose costs are largely fixed fares poorly when demand is low but makes a killing during a boom.

						Cash Flows in Year (¥ billions)					
	0	1	2	3	4	5	6	7	8	9	10
Revenues	6.00	11.80	12.06	12.34	12.62	12.90	13.20	13.51	13.82	14.15	14.48
Cost of goods sold (50% of sales)	3.00	5.90	6.03	6.17	6.31	6.45	6.60	6.75	6.91	7.07	7.24
Fixed costs	3.00	4.40	4.53	4.67	4.81	4.95	5.10	5.25	5.41	5.57	5.74
Depreciation	0.00	1.50	1.50	1.50	1.50	1.50	1.50	1.50	1.50	1.50	1.50
Pretax profit	0.00	0.00	0.00	0.00	0.00	0.00	0.00	0.00	0.00	0.00	0.00

)TABLE 10.4 A project's accounting break-even point is the minimum level of sales required to avoid an accounting loss.

[4]Notice that because fixed costs change from year to year, so does the break-even level of sales.

A business with high fixed costs is said to have high *operating leverage*. Operating leverage is usually defined in terms of accounting profits rather than cash flows and is measured by the percentage change in profits for each 1% change in sales. Thus the **degree of operating leverage (DOL)** is

$$DOL = \frac{\text{percentage change in profits}}{\text{percentage change in sales}}$$

The following simple formula[5] shows how DOL is related to the business's fixed costs (including depreciation) as a proportion of pretax profits:

$$DOL = 1 + \frac{\text{fixed costs including depreciation}}{\text{pretax profits}} \qquad \text{(10.1)}$$

For example, in year 2 of the scooter project,

$$DOL = 1 + \frac{(4.5 + 1.5)}{1.72} = 4.50$$

A 1% increase in the project's year 2 revenues would result in a 4.5% rise in profits.

EXAMPLE 10.1 • How Fixed Costs Translate Into High Operating Leverage

The following table shows how the profits of two auto producers, X and Y, vary between boom and slump. The only difference between the two companies is that a greater proportion of X's costs are fixed.

	X = High Fixed Cost			Y = Low Fixed Cost		
	Slump	Normal	Boom	Slump	Normal	Boom
Revenue	22.5	30	40	22.5	30	40
− Variable cost	9	12	16	12	16	21.3
− Fixed cost	8	8	8	4	4	4
− Depreciation	6	6	6	6	6	6
= Pretax profit	−0.5	4	10	0.5	4	8.7

In normal times, the two companies earn the same profits, but X's high fixed costs mean that it suffers more in a slump and gains more in a boom. As the economy moves from normal to boom, revenues for both companies increase by 33.3%. For X with its high fixed costs, profits increase by 150%, 4.5 times the increase in revenues. So DOL = 4.5. We get exactly the same figure using the formula—that is, DOL = 1 + fixed costs including depreciation/ profits = 1 + 14/4 = 4.5.

---

[5]This formula for DOL can be derived as follows. If sales increase by 1%, then variable costs will also increase by 1%, and profits will increase by 0.01 × (sales − variable costs) = 0.01 × (pretax profits + fixed costs). Now recall the definition of DOL:

$$DOL = \frac{\text{percentage change in profits}}{\text{percentage change in sales}} = \frac{(\text{change in profits})/(\text{level of profits})}{0.01}$$

$$= 100 \times \frac{\text{change in profits}}{\text{level of profits}} = 100 \times \frac{0.01 \times (\text{profits} + \text{fixed costs})}{\text{level of profits}}$$

$$= 1 + \frac{\text{fixed costs}}{\text{profits}}$$

For Y with its low fixed costs, the 33.3% increase in revenues translates into a 116.7% in profits, 3.5 times the increase in revenues. Our formula gives the same figure for DOL—that is, DOL = 1 + 10/4 = 3.5.

• • • • •

> ### 10.4 Self-Test
>
> What is the degree of operating leverage in year 3 of the scooter project? Why has it changed from year 2?

10-3 Real Options and the Value of Flexibility

When you use discounted cash flow (DCF) to value a project, you implicitly assume that the firm will hold the assets passively. But managers are not paid to do nothing. After they have invested in a new project, they do not simply sit back and watch the future unfold. If things go well, the project may be expanded; if they go badly, the project may be cut back or abandoned altogether. Projects that can be modified in these ways are more valuable than those that do not provide such flexibility. The more uncertain the outlook, the more valuable this flexibility becomes.

That sounds obvious, but notice that sensitivity analysis does not recognize the opportunity to modify projects. For example, think back to the Otobai electric scooter project. In real life, if things go wrong with the project, Otobai would abandon to cut its losses. If so, the worst outcomes would not be as devastating as our sensitivity analysis suggested.

Options to modify projects are known as **real options.** Managers may not always use the term "real option" to describe these opportunities; for example, they may refer to ensuring that projects can be adapted if circumstances change. But when they review major investment proposals, the benefit of flexibility is often the key to their decisions.

The Option to Expand

Long-haul airfreight businesses such as UPS need to move a massive amount of goods each day. To handle the growing demand, UPS announced in 2016 that it had agreed to purchase 14 Boeing freighter aircraft to add to its fleet of more than 500 planes. If business continued to expand, UPS would need more aircraft. But rather than placing an additional firm order, the company secured a place in Boeing's production line by acquiring options to buy an additional 14 aircraft at a predetermined price. These options did not commit UPS to expand but gave it the flexibility to do so.[6]

You can probably think of many other investments that take on added value because of the additional options they provide. For example,

- When launching a new product, companies often start with a pilot program to iron out possible design problems and to test the market. The company can evaluate the pilot project and then decide whether to expand to full-scale production.

- When designing a factory, it can make sense to provide extra land or floor space to reduce the future cost of a second production line.

- When building a four-lane highway, it may pay to build six-lane bridges so that the road can be converted later to six lanes if traffic volumes turn out to be higher than expected.

- When building production platforms for offshore oil and gas fields, companies usually allow ample vacant deck space. The vacant space costs more up front but reduces the cost of installing extra equipment later. For example, vacant deck space could provide an option to install water-flooding equipment if oil or gas prices are high enough to justify this investment.

---

[6]In 2018, UPS decided to exercise the options.

Expansion options do not show up on accounting balance sheets, but managers and investors are well aware of their importance. For example, in Chapter 4 we showed how the present value of growth opportunities (PVGO) contributes to the value of a company's common stock. PVGO equals the forecasted total NPV of future investments. But it is better to think of PVGO as the value of the firm's *options* to invest and expand. The firm is not obliged to grow. It can invest more if the number of positive-NPV projects turns out high, or it can slow down if that number turns out low. The flexibility to adapt investment to future opportunities is one of the factors that makes PVGO so valuable.

The Option to Abandon

If the option to expand has value, what about the decision to bail out? Projects do not just go on until assets expire of old age. The decision to terminate a project is usually taken by management, not by nature. Once the project is no longer profitable, the company will cut its losses and exercise its option to abandon the project.

Some assets are easier to bail out of than others. Tangible assets are usually easier to sell than intangible ones. It helps to have active secondhand markets, which exist mainly for standardized items. Real estate, airplanes, trucks, and certain machine tools are likely to be relatively easy to sell. On the other hand, the knowledge accumulated by a software company's research and development program is a specialized intangible asset and probably would not have significant abandonment value. (Some assets, such as old mattresses, even have *negative* abandonment value; you have to pay to get rid of them. It is costly to decommission nuclear power plants or to reclaim land that has been strip-mined.)

EXAMPLE 10.2 • Bailing out of the outboard-engine project

Managers should recognize the option to abandon when they make the initial investment in a new project or venture. For example, suppose you must choose between two technologies for production of an advanced dual-induction outboard motor for boats.

1. Technology A uses computer-controlled machinery custom-designed to produce the engines in high volumes and at low cost. But if the outboard does not sell, this equipment will be worthless.

2. Technology B uses standard machine tools. Labor costs are much higher, but the machinery can be sold for $17 million if demand turns out to be low.

Just for simplicity, assume that the initial capital outlays are the same for both technologies. If demand in the first year is buoyant, technology A will provide a payoff of $24 million. If demand is sluggish, the payoff from A is $16 million. Think of these payoffs as the project's cash flow in the first year of production plus the value in year 1 of all future cash flows. The corresponding payoffs to technology B are $22.5 million and $15 million:

Payoffs from Producing Outboard ($ millions)		
	Technology A	Technology B
Buoyant demand	$24.0	$22.5[a]
Sluggish demand	16.0	15.0[b]

[a]Composed of a cash flow of $3 million and a PV in year 1 of $19.5 million.
[b]Composed of a cash flow of $1.5 million and a PV in year 1 of $13.5 million.

Technology A looks better in a DCF analysis of the new product because it was designed to have the lowest possible cost at the planned production volume. Yet you can sense the advantage of the flexibility provided by technology B if you are unsure whether the new outboard will sink or swim in the marketplace. If you adopt technology B and the outboard is not a success, you are better off collecting the first year's cash flow of $1.5 million and then selling the plant and equipment for $17 million.

Figure 10.2 summarizes Example 10.2 as a **decision tree**. The abandonment option occurs at the right-hand boxes for technology B. The decisions are obvious: Continue if demand is buoyant, abandon otherwise. Thus the payoffs to technology B are

Buoyant demand → continue production   → payoff of $22.5 million
Sluggish demand → exercise option to sell assets → payoff of 1.5 + 17 = $18.5 million

Technology B provides an insurance policy: If the outboard's sales are disappointing, you can abandon the project and receive $18.5 million. The total value of the project with technology B is its DCF value, assuming that the company does not abandon, *plus* the value of the option to sell the assets for $17 million. When you value this abandonment option, you are placing a value on flexibility.

▶ **FIGURE 10.2**

Decision tree for the dual-induction outboard motor project. Technology B allows the firm to abandon the project and recover $18.5 million if demand is sluggish.

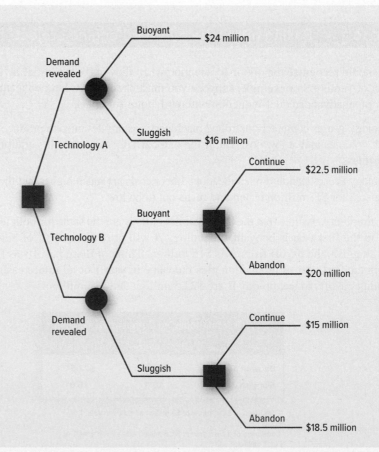

Production Options

When companies undertake new investments, they generally think about the possibility that they may wish to modify the project at a later stage. After all, today everybody may be demanding round pegs, but, who knows, tomorrow square ones may be all the rage. In that case, you need a plant that provides the flexibility to produce a variety of peg shapes.

EXAMPLE 10.3 • Production Options in the Knitwear Industry

In recent years, fashion changes—especially in new sports and active wear collections—have made the pattern of demand in the knitwear industry difficult to predict, and firms have increasingly invested in computer-controlled knitting machines. These provide an option to vary the product mix as demand changes.

In just the same way, it may be worth paying up front for the flexibility to vary the inputs. For example, in Chapter 23, we will describe how electric utilities often build in the option to switch between burning oil and burning natural gas. We refer to these opportunities as *production options*.

Timing Options

The fact that a project has a positive NPV does not mean that it is best undertaken now. It might be even more valuable to delay.

Timing decisions are fairly straightforward under conditions of certainty. You need to examine alternative dates for making the investment and calculate its net future value at each of these dates. Then, to find which of the alternatives would add most to the firm's *current* value, you must discount these net future values back to the present:

$$\text{Net present value of investment if undertaken at time } t = \frac{\text{net future value at date } t}{(1 + r)^t}$$

The optimal date to undertake the investment is the one that maximizes its contribution to the value of your firm today. This procedure should already be familiar to you from Chapter 6, where we worked out when it was best to cut a tract of timber.

In the timber-cutting example, we assumed that there was no uncertainty about the cash flows so that you knew the optimal time to exercise your option. When there is uncertainty, the timing option is much more complicated. An investment opportunity not taken at $t = 0$ might be more or less attractive at $t = 1$; there is rarely any way of knowing for sure. Perhaps it is better to strike while the iron is hot even if there is a chance that it will become hotter. On the other hand, if you wait a bit you might obtain more information and avoid a bad mistake. The greater the uncertainty that may be resolved, the greater the value in waiting. That is why you often find that managers choose not to invest today in projects where the NPV is only marginally positive and there is much to be learned by delay.

10.5 Self-Test

Investments in new products or production capacity often include an option to expand. What other types of options are encountered in capital investment decisions?

More on Decision Trees

We will return to all these real options in Chapter 23, after we have covered the theory of option valuation in Chapters 21 and 22. But we will end this chapter with a closer look at decision trees.

Decision trees are commonly used to describe the real options embedded in capital investment projects. But decision trees were used in the analysis of projects years before real options were first explicitly identified. Decision trees can help to illustrate project risk and the effect of future decisions on project cash flows. Even if you never learn or use option valuation theory, decision trees belong in your financial toolkit.

The best way to appreciate how decision trees can be used in project analysis is to work through a detailed example.

EXAMPLE 10.4 • A Decision Tree for Pharmaceutical R&D

Drug development programs may last several years. Usually, hundreds of thousands of compounds may be tested to find a few with promise. Then these compounds must survive several stages of investment and testing to gain approval from the Food and Drug Administration (FDA). Only then can the drug be sold commercially. The stages are as follows?[7]

1. *Phase I clinical trials.* After laboratory and clinical tests are concluded, the new drug is tested for safety and dosage in a small sample of humans.

2. *Phase II clinical trials.* The new drug is tested for efficacy (Does it work as predicted?) and for potentially harmful side effects.

3. *Phase III clinical trials.* The new drug is tested on a larger sample of humans to confirm efficacy and to rule out harmful side effects.

4. *Prelaunch.* If FDA approval is gained, there is investment in production facilities and initial marketing. Some clinical trials continue.

5. *Commercial launch.* After making a heavy initial investment in marketing and sales, the company begins to sell the new drug to the public.

Once a drug is launched successfully, sales usually continue for about 10 years, until the drug's patent protection expires and competitors enter with generic versions of the same chemical compound. The drug may continue to be sold off-patent, but sales volume and profits are much lower.

The commercial success of FDA-approved drugs varies enormously. The PV of a "blockbuster" drug at launch can be 5 or 10 times the PV of an average drug. A few blockbusters can generate most of a large pharmaceutical company's profits.

No company hesitates to invest in R&D for a drug that it *knows* will be a blockbuster. But the company will not find out for sure until after launch. Occasionally, a company thinks it has a blockbuster only to discover that a competitor has launched a better drug first.

Sometimes the FDA approves a drug but limits its scope of use. Some drugs, though effective, can only be prescribed for limited classes of patients; other drugs can be prescribed much more widely. Thus the manager of a pharmaceutical R&D program has to assess the odds of clinical success and the odds of commercial success. A new drug may be abandoned if it fails clinical trials—for example, because of dangerous side effects—or if the outlook for profits is discouraging.

---

[7]The website of the Tufts Center for the Study of Drug Development (**http://csdd.tufts.edu**) provides a wealth of information about the costs and risks of pharmaceutical R&D.

Figure 10.3 is a decision tree that illustrates these decisions. We have assumed that a new drug has passed phase I clinical trials with flying colors. Now it requires an investment of $18 million for phase II trials. These trials take two years. The probability of success is 44%.

If the trials are successful, the manager learns the commercial potential of the drug, which depends on how widely it can be used. Suppose that the forecasted PV at launch depends on the scope of use allowed by the FDA. These PVs are shown at the far right of the decision tree: an upside outcome of NPV = $700 million if the drug can be widely used, a most likely case with NPV = $300 million, and a downside case of NPV = $100 million if the drug's scope is greatly restricted.[8] The NPVs are the payoffs at launch after investment in marketing. Launch comes three years after the start of phase III if the drug is approved by the FDA. The probabilities of the upside, most likely, and downside outcomes are 25%, 50%, and 25%, respectively.

A further R&D investment of $130 million is required for phase III trials and for the prelaunch period. (We have combined phase III and prelaunch for simplicity.) The probability of FDA approval and launch is 80%.

Now let's value the investments in Figure 10.3. We assume a risk-free rate of 4% and market risk premium of 7%. If FDA-approved pharmaceutical products have asset betas of 0.8, the opportunity cost of capital is $4 + 0.8 \times 7 = 9.6\%$.

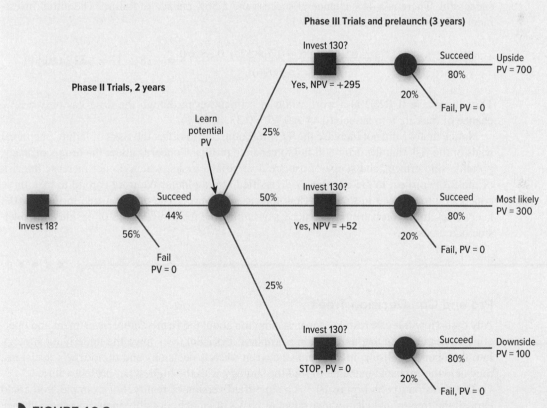

▶ FIGURE 10.3

A simplified decision tree for pharmaceutical R&D. A candidate drug requires an $18 million investment for phase II clinical trials. If the trials are successful (44% probability), the company learns the drug's scope of use and updates its forecast of the drug's PV at commercial launch. The investment required for the phase III trials and prelaunch outlays is $130 million. The probability of success in phase III and prelaunch is 80%.

[8]The most likely case is not the average outcome because PVs in the pharmaceutical business are skewed to the upside. The average PV is $0.25 \times 700 + 0.5 \times 300 + 0.25 \times 100 = \$350$ million.

We work back through the tree from right to left. The NPVs at the start of phase III trials are:

$$\text{NPV (upside)} \quad = -130 + 0.8 \times \frac{700}{(1.096)^3} = +\$295 \text{ million}$$

$$\text{NPV (most likely)} = -130 + 0.8 \times \frac{300}{(1.096)^3} = +\$52 \text{ million}$$

$$\text{NPV (downside)} \quad = -130 + 0.8 \times \frac{100}{(1.096)^3} = -\$69 \text{ million}$$

BEYOND THE PAGE

Try It! Figure 10.3: Decision tree for the pharmaceutical project

mhhe.com/brealey14e

Since the downside NPV is negative at −$69 million, the $130 million investment at the start of phase III should *not* be made in the downside case. There is no point investing $130 million for an 80% chance of a $100 million payoff three years later. Therefore the value of the R&D program at this point in the decision tree is not −$69 million, but zero.

Now calculate the NPV at the initial investment decision for phase II trials. The payoff two years later depends on whether the drug delivers on the upside, most likely, or downside: a 25% chance of NPV = +$295 million, a 50% chance of NPV = +$52 million, and a 25% chance of cancellation and NPV = 0. These NPVs are achieved only if the phase II trials are successful: There is a 44% chance of success and a 56% chance of failure. The initial investment is $18 million. Therefore, NPV is

$$\text{NPV} = -18 + 0.44 \times \frac{0.25 \times 295 + 0.5 \times 52 + 0.25 \times 0}{(1.096)^2} = -18 + 37 = +\$19 \text{ million}$$

Thus the phase II R&D is a worthwhile investment, even though the drug has only a 33% chance of making it to launch ($0.44 \times 0.75 = 0.33$, or 33%).

Notice that we did not increase the 9.6% discount rate to offset the risks of failure in clinical trials or the risk that the drug will fail to generate profits. Concerns about the drug's efficacy, possible side effects, and scope of use are diversifiable risks, which do not increase the risk of the R&D project to the company's diversified stockholders. We were careful to take these concerns into account in the cash-flow forecasts, however. The decision tree in Figure 10.3 keeps track of the probabilities of success or failure and the probabilities of upside and downside outcomes.[9]

• • • • •

Pro and Con Decision Trees

Any cash-flow forecast rests on some assumption about the firm's future investment and operating strategy. Often that assumption is implicit. Decision trees force the underlying strategy into the open. By displaying the links between today's decisions and tomorrow's decisions, they help the financial manager to find the strategy with the highest net present value.

The decision tree in Figure 10.3 is a simplified version of reality. For example, you could expand the tree to include a wider range of NPVs at launch, possibly including some chance of a blockbuster or of intermediate outcomes. You could allow information about the NPVs to arrive gradually, rather than just at the start of phase III. You could introduce the investment decision at phase I trials and separate the phase III and prelaunch stages. You may wish to draw a new decision tree covering these events and decisions. You will see how fast the circles, squares, and branches accumulate.

---

[9]The market risk attached to the PVs at launch is recognized in the 9.6% discount rate.

The trouble with decision trees is that they get so complex so quickly (insert your own expletives). Life is complex, however, and there is very little we can do about it. Our criticism is reserved for analysts who let the complexity become overwhelming. The point of decision trees is to allow explicit analysis of possible future events and decisions. They should be judged not on their comprehensiveness but on whether they show the most important links between today's and tomorrow's decisions. Decision trees used in real life will be more complex than Figure 10.3, but they will nevertheless display only a small fraction of possible future events and decisions. Decision trees are like grapevines: They are productive only if they are vigorously pruned.

● ● ● ● ●

**KEY
TAKEAWAYS**

Good capital budgeting practice tries to identify the major uncertainties in project proposals. An awareness of these uncertainties may suggest ways that the project can be reconfigured to reduce the dangers, or it may point to some additional research that will confirm whether the project is truly worthwhile.

- **Sensitivity analysis** Sensitivity analysis offers a simple way to identify the threats to a project's success. Here the manager considers in turn each cash-flow variable and recalculates NPV at optimistic and pessimistic values of that variable.

- **Scenario analysis** With scenario analysis the manager focuses on a few plausible stories about how the future could unfold and considers the effect of each on the project (or the entire business). Whereas sensitivity analysis looks at only one variable at a time, scenario analysis recognizes that many aspects of a project and the environment may change.

- **Break-even analysis** Suppose the manager is concerned about a possible shortfall in sales. Then it may be helpful to calculate the sales level at which the project just breaks even (NPV = 0) and to consider the odds that sales will fall that far. Break-even analysis is often done in terms of accounting income, although we do not recommend this.

- **Operating leverage** Projects with a high proportion of fixed costs are likely to have higher break-even points. Because a shortfall in sales results in a larger decline in profits when the costs are largely fixed, such projects are said to have high *operating leverage*. The degree of operating leverage (DOL) is commonly defined as the percentage change in profits for a 1% change in sales. It is measured as

$$DOL = 1 + \frac{\text{fixed costs including depreciation}}{\text{profits}}$$

- **Real options** Discussions of capital budgeting sometimes create the impression that once the manager has made an investment decision, there is nothing to do but sit back and watch the cash flows unfold. In practice, companies are constantly modifying their operations. If cash flows are better than anticipated, the project may be expanded; if they are worse, it may be contracted or abandoned altogether. Options to modify projects are known as *real options*. In this chapter, we introduced the main categories of real options: *expansion* options, *abandonment* options, *timing* options, and options providing *flexibility in production*.

- **Decision trees** One convenient way to summarize real options and their cash-flow consequences is to create a *decision tree*. You identify the things that could happen to the project and the main counteractions that you might take. Then, working back from the future to the present, you consider which action you *should* take in each case.

**FURTHER
READING**

Shell Oil has for a long time been a proponent of scenario analysis for prompting managers to think about possible future states. See, for example,

A. Wilkinson and R. Kupers, "Living in the Futures," *Harvard Business Review* 91 (May 2013), pp. 119–127.

Three not-too-technical references on real options are listed below. Additional references follow Chapter 23.

A. Dixit and R. Pindyck, "The Options Approach to Capital Investment," *Harvard Business Review* 73 (May–June 1995), pp. 105–115.

W. C. Kester, "Today's Options for Tomorrow's Growth," *Harvard Business Review* 62 (March–April 1984), pp. 153–160.

A. Triantis and A. Borison, "Real Options: State of the Practice," *Journal of Applied Corporate Finance* 14 (Summer 2001), pp. 8–24.

PROBLEM SETS

Select problems are available in McGraw-Hill's *Connect*.
Please see the preface for more information.

1. **Terminology (S10.1–10.3)** Match each of the following terms to one of the definitions or descriptions listed below: sensitivity analysis, scenario analysis, break-even analysis, operating leverage, decision tree, real option, tornado diagram.

   a. Recalculation of project NPV by changing several inputs to new but consistent values.

   b. Opportunity to modify a project at a future date.

   c. Analysis of how project NPV changes if different assumptions are made about sales, costs, and other key variables.

   d. The degree to which fixed costs magnify the effect on profits of a shortfall in sales.

   e. A graphical technique for displaying possible future events and decisions taken in response to those events.

   f. A graphical technique that is often used to display the results of a sensitivity analysis.

   g. Determination of the level of future sales at which project profitability or NPV equals zero.

2. **Project analysis (S10.1–10.2)** True or false?

   a. Sensitivity analysis is unnecessary for projects with asset betas that are equal to zero.

   b. Sensitivity analysis can be used to identify the variables most crucial to a project's success.

   c. If only one variable is uncertain, sensitivity analysis gives "optimistic" and "pessimistic" values for project cash flow and NPV.

   d. The break-even sales level of a project is higher when break-even is defined in terms of NPV rather than accounting income.

   e. Risk is reduced when most of the costs are fixed.

3. **Sensitivity analysis (S10.1)** Otobai's staff (see Section 10-1) has come up with the following revised estimates for the electric scooter project:

	Optimistic	Pessimistic
% change in capital investment	−20.00	60.00
% change in working capital	−50.00	50.00
% change in units sold	25.00	−20.00
% change in price	20.00	−25.00
Cost of goods sold as % of sales	40.00	75.00
% change in fixed costs	−50.00	70.00

Conduct a sensitivity analysis using the spreadsheets (available in Connect). What are the principal uncertainties in the project?

4. **Sensitivity analysis (S10.1)** The Rustic Welt Company is proposing to replace its old welt-making machinery with more modern equipment. The new equipment costs $9 million (the existing equipment has zero salvage value). The attraction of the new machinery is that it is expected to cut manufacturing costs from their current level of $8 a welt to $4. However, as the following table shows, there is some uncertainty both about future sales and about the performance of the new machinery:

	Pessimistic	Expected	Optimistic
Sales (millions of welts)	0.4	0.5	0.7
Manufacturing cost with new machinery (dollars per welt)	6	4	3
Economic life of new machinery (years)	7	10	13

Conduct a sensitivity analysis of the replacement decision, assuming a discount rate of 12%. Rustic Welt does not pay taxes.

5. **Sensitivity analysis (S10.1)** Use the spreadsheet for the guano project in Chapter 6 to undertake a sensitivity analysis of the project. Make whatever assumptions seem reasonable to you. What are the critical variables? What should the company's response be to your analysis?

6. **Sensitivity analysis (S10.1)** Emperor's Clothes Fashions can invest $5 million in a new plant for producing invisible makeup. The plant has an expected life of five years, and expected sales are 6 million jars of makeup a year. Fixed costs are $2 million a year, and variable costs are $1 per jar. The product will be priced at $2 per jar. The plant will be depreciated straight-line over five years to a salvage value of zero. The opportunity cost of capital is 10%, and the tax rate is 40%.

   a. What is project NPV under these base-case assumptions?

   b. What is NPV if variable costs turn out to be $1.20 per jar?

   c. What is NPV if fixed costs turn out to be $1.5 million per year?

   d. At what price per jar would project NPV equal zero?

7. **Sensitivity analysis (S10.1)** A project currently generates sales of $10 million, variable costs equal 50% of sales, and fixed costs are $2 million. The firm's tax rate is 21%. What are the effects of the following changes on cash flow?

   a. Sales increase from $10 million to $11 million.

   b. Variable costs increase to 65% of sales.

8. **Scenario analysis (S10.1)** Recalculate the NPV of the electric scooter project in a scenario where the outcome is as follows:

   a. Unit sales are 20% below expectations, and

   b. Unit price is 10% below expectations, and

   c. Unit variable cost remains at 50% of revenue, and

   d. Fixed costs increase by 5%, and

   e. Investment in plant and equipment and in working capital are unchanged.

9. **Scenario analysis (S10.1)** You are considering a proposal to produce and market a new sluffing machine. The most likely outcomes for the project are as follows:

   a. Expected sales: 30,000 units per year

   b. Unit price: $50

   c. Variable cost: $30

   d. Fixed cost: $300,000

The project will last for 10 years and requires an initial investment of $1 million, which will be depreciated straight-line over the project life to a final value of zero. The firm's tax rate is 30%, and the required rate of return is 12%.

    However, you recognize that some of these estimates are subject to error. In one scenario a sharp rise in the dollar could cause sales to fall 30% below expectations for the life of the project and, if that happens, the unit price would probably be only $40. The good news is that fixed costs could be as low as $200,000, and variable costs would decline in proportion to sales.

   a. What is project NPV if all variables are as expected?

   b. What is NPV in the bad-case scenario?

10. **Break-even analysis (S10.2)** Break-even calculations are most often concerned with the effect of a shortfall in sales, but they could equally well focus on any other component of cash flow. Dog Days is considering a proposal to produce and market a caviar-flavored dog food. It will involve an initial investment of $90,000 that can be depreciated for tax straight-line over 10 years. In each of years 1 to 10, the project is forecast to produce sales of $100,000 and to incur variable costs of 50% of sales and fixed costs of $30,000. The corporate tax rate is 30%, and the cost of capital is 10%.

   a. Calculate the NPV and accounting break-even levels of fixed costs.

   b. Suppose that you are worried that the corporate tax rate will be increased immediately after you commit to the project. Calculate the break-even rate of taxes.

   c. How would a rise in the tax rate affect the accounting break-even point?

11. **Break-even analysis (S10.2)** Dime-a-Dozen Diamonds makes synthetic diamonds by treating carbon. Each diamond can be sold for $100. The materials cost for a synthetic diamond is $40. The fixed costs incurred each year for factory upkeep and administrative expenses are $200,000. The machinery costs $1 million and is depreciated straight-line over 10 years to a salvage value of zero.

   a. What is the accounting break-even level of sales in terms of number of diamonds sold?

   b. What is the NPV break-even level of sales assuming a tax rate of 35%, a 10-year project life, and a discount rate of 12%?

12. **Break-even analysis (S10.2)** Modern Artifacts can produce keepsakes that will be sold for $80 each. Non-depreciation fixed costs are $1,000 per year, and variable costs are $60 per unit. The initial investment of $3,000 will be depreciated straight-line over its useful life of five years to a final value of zero, and the discount rate is 10%.

   a. What is the accounting break-even level of sales if the firm pays no taxes?

   b. What is the NPV break-even level of sales if the firm pays no taxes?

   c. What is the accounting break-even level of sales if the firm's tax rate is 20%?

   d. What is the NPV break-even level of sales if the firm's tax rate is 20%?

   e.   What is the degree of operating leverage?

13. **Break-even analysis (S10.2)** Define the cash-flow break-even point as the sales volume (in dollars) at which cash flow equals zero.

   a. Is the cash-flow break-even level of sales higher or lower than the zero-profit (accounting) break-even point?

   b. If a project operates at cash-flow break-even [see part (a)] for all future years, is its NPV positive or negative?

14. **Break-even analysis (S10.2)** A financial analyst has computed both accounting and NPV break-even sales levels for a project using straight-line depreciation over a six-year period. The project manager wants to know what will happen to these estimates if the firm can write off the entire investment in the year that it is made. The firm is in a 21% tax bracket.

    a. Would the accounting break-even level of sales in the first years of the project increase or decrease?

    b. Would the NPV break-even level of sales in the first years of the project increase or decrease?

    c. If you were advising the analyst, would the answer to part (a) or (b) be important to you? Specifically, would you say that the switch to immediate expensing makes the project more or less attractive?

15. **Operating leverage (S10.2)** In a slow year, Deutsche Burgers will produce 2 million hamburgers at a total cost of $3.5 million. In a good year, it can produce 4 million hamburgers at a total cost of $4.5 million.

    a. What are the fixed costs of hamburger production?

    b. What are the variable costs?

    c. What is the average cost per burger when the firm produces 1 million hamburgers?

    d. What is the average cost when the firm produces 2 million hamburgers?

    e. Why is the average cost lower when more burgers are produced?

16. **Operating leverage (S10.2)** You estimate that your cattle farm will generate $1 million of profits on sales of $4 million under normal economic conditions and that the degree of operating leverage is 8.

    a. What will profits be if sales turn out to be $3.5 million?

    b. What if they are $4.5 million?

17. **Operating leverage (S10.2)** Look again at Modern Artifacts in Problem 12.

    a. What is the degree of operating leverage of Modern Artifacts when sales are $7,000?

    b. What is the degree of operating leverage when sales are $12,000?

    c. Why is operating leverage different at these two levels of sales?

18. **Operating leverage (S10.2)** What is the lowest possible value for the degree of operating leverage for a profitable firm? Show with a numerical example that if Modern Artifacts (see Problem 12) has zero fixed costs and zero depreciation, then DOL = 1 and, in fact, sales and profits are directly proportional, so a 1% change in sales results in a 1% change in profits.

19. **Operating leverage (S10.2)** A project has fixed costs of $1,000 per year, depreciation charges of $500 a year, annual revenue of $6,000, and variable costs equal to two-thirds of revenues.

    a. If sales increase by 10%, what will be the increase in pretax profits?

    b. What is the degree of operating leverage of this project?

20. **Real options (S10.3)** Explain why options to expand or contract production are most valuable when forecasts about future business conditions are most uncertain.

21. **Real options (S10.3)** Describe the real option in each of the following cases:

    a. Moda di Milano postpones a major investment. The expansion has positive NPV on a discounted cash-flow basis, but top management wants to get a better fix on product demand before proceeding.

    b. Western Telecom commits to production of digital switching equipment specially designed for the European market. The project has a negative NPV, but it is justified on strategic grounds by the need for a strong market position in the rapidly growing, and potentially very profitable, market.

c. Western Telecom vetoes a fully integrated, automated production line for the new digital switches. It relies on standard, less-expensive equipment. The automated production line is more efficient overall, according to a discounted cash-flow calculation.

d. Mount Fuji Airways buys a jumbo jet with special equipment that allows the plane to be switched quickly from freight to passenger use or vice versa.

22. **Real options (S10.3)** True or false?

a. Decision trees can help identify and describe real options.

b. The option to expand increases PV.

c. High abandonment value decreases PV.

d. If a project has positive NPV, the firm should always invest immediately.

23. **Real options (S10.3)** A silver mine can yield 10,000 ounces of silver at a variable cost of $32 per ounce. The fixed costs of owning the mine are $40,000 per year regardless of whether the mine is open or closed. In half the years, silver can be sold for $48 per ounce; in the other years, silver can be sold for only $24 per ounce. Ignore taxes.

a. What is the average cash flow you will receive from the mine if it is always kept in operation and the silver always is sold in the year it is mined?

b. Now suppose you can costlessly shut down the mine in years of low silver prices. What happens to the average cash flow from the mine?

24. **Real options (S10.3)** An auto plant that costs $100 million to build can produce a line of electric cars. The investment will produce cash flows with a present value of $140 million if the line is successful but only $50 million if it is unsuccessful. You believe that the probability of success is only about 50%. You will learn whether the line is successful immediately after building the plant.

a. Would you build the plant?

b. Suppose that the plant can be sold for $95 million to another automaker if the auto line is not successful. Now would you build the plant?

c. Illustrate the option to abandon in part (b) using a decision tree.

25. **Decision trees (S10.3)** Your midrange guess as to the amount of oil in a prospective field is 10 million barrels, but there is a 50% chance that the amount of oil is 15 million barrels and a 50% chance of 5 million barrels. If the actual amount of oil is 15 million barrels, the present value of the cash flows from drilling will be $8 million. If the amount is only 5 million barrels, the present value will be only $2 million. It costs $3 million to drill the well. Suppose that a seismic test costing $100,000 can immediately verify the amount of oil under the ground. Is it worth paying for the test? Use a decision tree to justify your answer.

26. **Decision trees (S10.3)** Look again at the decision tree in Figure 10.3. Expand the possible outcomes as follows:

- Blockbuster: PV = $1.5 billion with 5% probability.
- Above average: PV = $700 million with 20% probability.
- Average: PV = $300 million with 40% probability.
- Below average: PV = $100 million with 25% probability.
- "Dog": PV = $40 million with 10% probability.

Redraw the decision tree. Is the $18 million investment in phase II trials still positive NPV?

27. **Decision trees (S10.3)** Look again at the example in Figure 10.3. The R&D team has put forward a proposal to invest an extra $20 million in expanded phase II trials. The object is to

prove that the drug can be administered by a simple inhaler rather than as a liquid. If successful, the scope of use is broadened and the upside PV increases to $1 billion. The probabilities of success are unchanged. Go to the Beyond the Page Excel spreadsheet version of Figure 10.3. Is the extra $20 million investment worthwhile? Would your answer change if the probability of success in the phase III trials falls to 75%?

CHALLENGE PROBLEMS

28. **Project analysis (S10.1–S10.2)** New Energy is evaluating a new biofuel facility. The plant would cost $4,000 million to build and has the potential to produce up to 40 million barrels of synthetic oil a year. The product is a close substitute for conventional oil and would sell for the same price. The market price of oil currently is fluctuating around $100 per barrel, but there is considerable uncertainty about future prices. Variable costs for the organic inputs to the production process are estimated at $82 per barrel and are expected to be stable. In addition, annual upkeep and maintenance expenses on the facility will be $100 million regardless of the production level. The plant has an expected life of 15 years, and it will be depreciated straight-line over 10 years. Salvage value net of clean-up costs is expected to be negligible. Demand for the product is difficult to forecast. Depending on consumer acceptance, sales might range from 25 million to 35 million barrels annually. The discount rate is 12% and New Energy's tax bracket is 25%.

    a. Find the project NPV for the following combinations of oil price and sales volume. Which source of uncertainty seems most important to the success of the project?

	Oil Price		
Annual Sales (millions of barrels)	**$80/Barrel**	**$100/Barrel**	**$120/Barrel**
25			
30			
35			

    b. At an oil price of $100, what level of annual sales, maintained over the life of the plant, is necessary for NPV break-even? (This will require trial and error unless you are familiar with more advanced features of Excel such as the Goal Seek command.)

    c. At an oil price of $100, what is the accounting break-even level of sales in each year? Why does it change each year? Does this notion of break-even seem reasonable to you?

    d. If each of the sales figures in the table in part (a) is equally likely, what is the NPV of the facility?

    e. Why might the facility be worth building despite your answer to part (d)? (*Hint:* What real option may the firm have to avoid losses in low-oil-price scenarios?)

29. **Decision trees (S10.3)** Magna Charter is a new corporation formed by Agnes Magna to provide an executive flying service for the southeastern United States. The founder thinks there will be a ready demand from businesses that cannot justify a full-time company plane but nevertheless need one from time to time. However, the venture is not a sure thing. There is a 40% chance that demand in the first year will be low. If it is low, there is a 60% chance that it will remain low in subsequent years. On the other hand, if the initial demand is high, there is an 80% chance that it will stay high. The immediate problem is to decide what kind of plane to buy. A turboprop costs $550,000. A piston-engine plane costs only $250,000 but has less capacity. Moreover, the piston-engine plane is an old design and likely to depreciate rapidly. Ms. Magna thinks that next year secondhand piston aircraft will be available for only $150,000.

》TABLE 10.5
The possible payoffs from Ms. Magna's flying service. (All figures are in thousands. Probabilities are in parentheses.)

Payoffs from the Turboprop					
Year 1 demand		High (0.6)			Low (0.4)
Year 1 payoff		$150			$30
Year 2 demand	High (0.8)		Low (0.2)	High (0.4)	Low (0.6)
Year 2 payoff	$960		$220	$930	$140
Payoffs from the Piston Engine					
Year 1 demand		High (0.6)			Low (0.4)
Year 1 payoff		$100			$50
Year 2 demand	High (0.8)		Low (0.2)	High (0.4)	Low (0.6)
Year 2 payoff	$410		$180	$220	$100

Table 10.5 shows how the payoffs in years 1 and 2 from both planes depend on the pattern of demand. You can see, for example, that if demand is high in both years 1 and 2, the turbo will provide a payoff of $960,000 in year 2. If demand is high in year 1 but low in year 2, the turbo's payoff in the second year is only $220,000. Think of the payoffs in the second year as the cash flow that year plus the year-2 value of any subsequent cash flows. Assume that these cash flows can be discounted at 10%.

Ms. Magna now has an idea: Why not start out with one piston-engine plane? If demand is low in the first year, Magna Charter can sit tight with this one relatively inexpensive aircraft. On the other hand, if demand is high in the first year she can buy a second piston-engine plane for only $150,000. In this case, if demand continues to be high, the payoff in year 2 from the two piston planes will be $800,000. However, if demand in year 2 were to decline, the payoff would be only $100,000.

a. Draw a decision tree setting out Magna Charter's choices.

b. If Magna Charter buys a piston plane, should it expand if demand turns out to be high in the first year?

c. Given your answer to part (b), would you recommend that Ms. Magna buy the turboprop or the piston-engine plane today?

d. What would be the NPV of an investment in a piston plane if there were no option to expand? How much extra value is contributed by the option to expand?

● ● ● ● ●

SOLUTIONS TO SELF-TEST QUESTIONS

10.1 Annual depreciation tax shield on the extra investment = 0.4 × 5/10 = ¥0.2 billion
PV additional tax shield = [1/0.2 − 1/(0.2 × 1.2^{10})] × 0.2 = ¥ 0.84 billion
NPV declines by 5 − 0.84 = 4.16 to −¥2.14 billion

10.2 In contrast to sensitivity analysis, scenario analysis does not simply look at the best and worst outcomes but at how the project would fare in particular plausible scenarios. Typically, these scenarios would result in changes in several of the variables (sales volume, price, etc).

10.3 Depreciation falls to 1.0 and the break-even sales falls to 10.8 (i.e., Pretax profit = revenues − variable cost − fixed cost − depreciation = 10.8 − 5.4 − 4.4 − 1.0 = ¥0 billion).

10.4 DOL = 1 + (4.67 + 1.5)/6.55 = 1.94
Operating leverage has declined because fixed costs are a much smaller proportion of profits.

10.5 a. The option to abandon;

b. production options (the option to vary the output or one of the inputs);

c. the timing option (when to undertake a project).

MINI-CASE ● ● ● ● ●

Waldo County

Waldo County, the well-known real estate developer, worked long hours, and he expected his staff to do the same. So George Chavez was not surprised to receive a call from the boss just as George was about to leave for a long summer's weekend.

Mr. County's success had been built on a remarkable instinct for a good site. He would exclaim "Location! Location! Location!" at some point in every planning meeting. Yet finance was not his strong suit. On this occasion, he wanted George to go over the figures for a new $90 million outlet mall designed to intercept tourists heading downeast from Bar Harbor through southern Maine. "First thing Monday will do just fine," he said as he handed George the file. "I'll be in my house in Bar Harbor if you need me."

George's first task was to draw up a summary of the projected revenues and costs. The results are shown in Table 10.6. Note that the mall's revenues would come from two sources: The company would charge retailers an annual rent for the space they occupied and, in addition, it would receive 5% of each store's gross sales.

Construction of the mall was likely to take three years. The construction costs could be depreciated straight-line over 15 years starting in year 3. As in the case of the company's other developments, the mall would be built to the highest specifications and would not need to be rebuilt until year 17. The land was expected to retain its value, but could not be depreciated for tax purposes.

Construction costs, revenues, operating and maintenance costs, and local real estate taxes were all likely to rise in line with inflation, which was forecasted at 2% a year. Local real estate taxes are deductible for corporate tax. The company's corporate tax rate was 25% and the cost of capital was 9% in nominal terms.

George decided first to check that the project made financial sense. He then proposed to look at some of the things that might go wrong. His boss certainly had a nose for a good retail project, but he was not infallible. The Salome project had been a disaster because store sales had turned out to be 40% below forecast. What if that happened here? George wondered just how far sales could fall short of forecast before the project would be underwater.

Inflation was another source of uncertainty. Some people were talking about a zero long-term inflation rate, but George also wondered what would happen if inflation jumped to, say, 10%.

A third concern was possible construction cost overruns and delays due to required zoning changes and environmental approvals. George had seen cases of 25% construction cost overruns and delays up to 12 months between purchase of the land and the start of construction. He decided that he should examine the effect that this would have on the project's profitability. But he realized

		Year				
	0	1	2	3	4	5–17
Investment:						
Land	30					
Construction	20	30	10			
Operations:						
Rentals				12	12	12
Share of retail sales				24	24	24
Operating and maintenance costs	2	4	4	10	10	10
Local real estate taxes	2	2	3	4	4	4

❯TABLE 10.6 Projected revenues and costs in real terms for the Downeast Tourist Mall (figures in $ millions).

that building a spreadsheet and running scenarios was not enough. He had to figure out how to summarize and present his results to Mr. County.

QUESTIONS

1. What is the project's NPV, given the projections in Table 10.6?
2. Conduct a sensitivity and a scenario analysis of the project. What do these analyses reveal about the project's risks and potential value?

How to Ensure That Projects Truly Have Positive NPVs

Many investment decisions, such as the decision to replace one machine with another, are fairly uncomplicated. It is relatively straightforward to write down the cost savings, estimate the opportunity cost of capital, and calculate the net present value. But think of Boeing's decision to develop the 787 Dreamliner, or Apple's decision to produce the iWatch, or Verizon's decision to deploy 5G fiber-optic-based broadband technology. These differ in several important ways from the simple machine replacement problem.

- They have a very large scale.
- The decision is likely to determine the shape of the company for many years ahead.
- It is difficult to project the cash flow consequences of the decision.

In this chapter we discuss some of the problems with making these strategic choices, and we suggest some aids to good decision making.

Section 11.1 Behavioral biases in investment decisions

Senior management needs to be closely involved in strategic investment decisions, but it must rely heavily on information that is provided by project proposers. This information may not be as complete as management would like, and the project's proposers may be subject to behavioral biases that affect their forecasts. In Section 11.1, we discuss some of the problems for management in securing the required information.

Section 11.2 Avoiding forecast errors

Strategic investment decisions, such as those to launch a new product, inevitably involve considerable uncertainty. The forecasts on which they are based will therefore be liable to large errors. The problem is to prevent these forecast errors from swamping genuine information. In Section 11.2, we suggest that managers should look first to market values.

Section 11.3 How competitive advantage translates into positive NPVs

We then ask how managers can distinguish projects that truly have positive NPVs from those that appear worthwhile merely because of forecasting errors. In a fully competitive environment, companies can expect to earn no more than the cost of capital. Positive NPVs arise only when the company has a competitive advantage that allows it to earn more than the cost of capital. So, in Section 11.3, we suggest that when faced with strategic investment decisions, managers need to focus on competitive advantage and how long it will endure.

Section 11.4 Marvin Enterprises decides to exploit a new technology—an example

We conclude in Section 11.4 with a fictional case study describing how Marvin Enterprises, the gargle blaster company, assessed its competitive advantage in a new technology in order to calculate the NPV of a radically new product. Whereas in earlier chapters you were given the cash flow forecasts, in Marvin's case we look at how to derive them. We draw several important lessons from the Marvin case.

11-1 Behavioral Biases in Investment Decisions

Many investment projects carry a high price tag and may determine the shape of the firm's business 10 or 20 years in the future. Because top management needs to be closely involved in these strategic decisions, major investment decisions are seldom delegated. The result is that the head office may receive several hundred investment proposals each year. To assess all these proposals, management must rely on the information that it receives from more junior staff.

As each proposal has traveled up the organization, alliances are likely to have been formed. Thus, once a division has screened its own plants' proposals, the plants in that division may unite in competing against rival schemes. The final proposal that reaches management is, therefore, apt to be a selling document presented by a united front and designed to persuade. The forecasts may have been doctored to ensure that NPV appears positive. The proposal will probably be silent on questions and doubts that were raised at earlier stages. And it won't list the many variants of the project that were considered and rejected.

The ability of senior management to judge the merits of these proposals is further hampered by the fact that project sponsors are liable to behavioral biases. One problem is that most people tend to be overconfident when they forecast. Events they think are almost certain to occur may actually happen only 80% of the time, and events they believe are impossible may happen 20% of the time. Therefore, project proposals are likely to understate the risks.

EXAMPLE 11.1 ● Overconfidence Bias

Overconfidence bias pervades many financial judgments. For example, a group of chief financial officers was asked each year to predict one-year rates of return on the S&P 500 index and to give 80% confidence limits. Perhaps unsurprisingly, the CFOs had essentially no ability to predict returns on the stock market. What is more disturbing is that they also had no self-awareness of their lack of predictive skills. If the CFOs had well-calibrated forecasts, the actual stock market return would fall outside their confidence limits only 20% of the time. Instead, the actual outcome fell outside the limits on 64% of the occasions.[1]

● ● ● ● ●

Anyone who is keen to get a project accepted is also likely to look on the bright side when forecasting the project's cash flows. Such overoptimism seems to be a common feature in financial forecasts. It afflicts governments too, probably more than private businesses. How often have you heard of a new dam, highway, or military aircraft that actually cost less than was originally forecasted?

EXAMPLE 11.2 ● Optimism Bias

There are many examples of optimism bias in financial decisions. For instance, getting a new business off the ground is challenging, and only about half of all startups survive more than three years. But entrepreneurs are congenitally optimistic. About two-thirds of them think that their start-up is more likely to succeed than comparable enterprises, while only 5% believe that their odds of success are worse. A third of entrepreneurs view their success as essentially guaranteed.[2]

● ● ● ● ●

[1] I. Ben-David, J. R. Graham, and C. R. Harvey, "Managerial Miscalibration," *Quarterly Journal of Economics* 128 (2013), pp. 1547–1584.
[2] A. C. Cooper, C. Y. Woo, and W. C. Dunkelberg, "Entrepreneurs' Perceived Chances for Success," *Journal of Business Venturing* 3 (1988), pp. 97–108.

These cognitive biases are likely to be reinforced by the fact that upwardly mobile junior managers have an incentive to promote their pet projects. The result is not altogether bad. Psychologists stress that optimism and confidence are likely to increase effort, commitment, and persistence. The problem is that, while management needs to be closely involved in the final decision, it is forced to rely on biased forecasts.

BEYOND THE PAGE

Overoptimism
and cost
overruns

mhhe.com/brealey14e

11.1 Self-Test

Which of the following observations suggest overconfidence or optimism?
  a. In the energy industry, actual construction costs, on average, turn out to be more than double forecast costs.
  b. Managers are tempted to spend wastefully on perks such as lavish office accommodation.
  c. Many unsuccessful mergers are undertaken because managers wrongly believe they can manage the target company more efficiently.

One response of senior managers to these problems is to impose rigid expenditure limits on individual plants or divisions. These limits force the subunits to choose among projects. Thus the firm ends up using capital rationing not because capital is unobtainable, but as a way of decentralizing decisions.

Sometimes senior managers try to offset overoptimism by increasing the hurdle rate for capital expenditure. Suppose the true cost of capital is 10%, but the CFO is frustrated by the large fraction of projects that don't subsequently earn 10%. She therefore directs project sponsors to use a 15% discount rate. In other words, she adds a 5% fudge factor in an attempt to offset forecast bias. It doesn't work; it simply invites the project sponsor to exaggerate further.

11.2 Self-Test

Suppose that you add a 5% fudge factor to the true 10% cost of capital. By what proportion do you reduce the estimated PV of the cash flow in year 1? What about a cash flow in year 10? Does adding a fudge factor to the cost of capital favor quick-payback projects or longer-lived projects? (*Hint:* See Example 9-4.)

11-2   Avoiding Forecast Errors

Let us suppose that you have persuaded all your project sponsors to give honest forecasts. Although those forecasts are unbiased, they are still likely to contain errors, some positive and others negative. The average error will be zero, but that is little consolation because you want to accept only projects with *truly* superior profitability.

Think, for example, of what would happen if you were to jot down your estimates of the cash flows from operating various lines of business. You would probably find that about half *appeared* to have positive NPVs. This may not be because you personally possess any superior skill in running an airline or a chain of fast-food outlets but because you have inadvertently introduced large errors into your estimates of the cash flows. The more projects you contemplate, the more likely you are to uncover projects that *appear* to be extremely worthwhile.

What can you do to prevent the forecast errors from swamping genuine information? As a senior manager, you can't be expected to check every cash-flow forecast, but you can ask some questions to ensure that each project really does have a positive NPV. We suggest that you begin by looking at market values.

The following parable should help to illustrate what we mean. Your local BMW dealer is announcing a special offer. For $95,000, you get not only a brand-new BMW 8-Series convertible, but also the chance to enjoy a day with your celebrity idol. You wonder how much you are paying for that day.

There are two possible approaches to the problem. You could evaluate each of the BMW's features, starting with the Turbo V8 engine and ending with the exclusive Nappa leather interior, and conclude that the car is worth $90,000. This would seem to suggest that the day with your hero is costing you $5,000. Alternatively, you might nip round to a couple other BMW dealers and discover that the going market price for the car is $95,000 so that the special offer is costing you nothing. As long as there is a competitive market for BMWs, the latter approach makes more sense.

Security analysts face a similar problem whenever they value a company's stock. They must consider the information that is already known to the market about a company, *and* they must evaluate the information that is known only to them. Investors have already evaluated the information that is generally known. Security analysts do not need to evaluate this information again. They can *start* with the market price of the stock and concentrate on valuing their private information.

While most people would instinctively accept the BMW's market value of $95,000, the financial manager is trained to enumerate and value all the costs and benefits from an investment and is therefore tempted to substitute her own opinion for the market's. Unfortunately, this approach increases the chance of error. Many capital assets are traded in a competitive market, so it makes sense to *start* with the market price and then ask *why* you can earn more than your rivals from these assets.

EXAMPLE 11.3 • Investing in a New Clothing Store

We encountered a clothing store chain that estimated the present value of the expected cash flows from each proposed store, including the price at which it could eventually sell the store. Although the firm took considerable care with these estimates, it was disturbed to find that its conclusions were heavily influenced by the forecasted selling price of each store. Management disclaimed any particular real estate expertise, but it discovered that its investment decisions were unintentionally dominated by its assumptions about future real estate prices.

Once the financial managers realized this, they always checked the decision to open a new store by asking the following question: "Let us assume that the property is fairly priced. What is the evidence that it is best suited to one of our stores rather than to some other use?" In other words, *if an asset is worth more to others than it is to you, then beware of bidding for the asset against them.*

Let us take the store problem a little further. Suppose that the new store costs $100 million.[3] You forecast that it will generate after-tax cash flow of $8 million a year for 10 years. Real estate prices are estimated to grow by 3% a year, so the expected value of the real estate at the end of 10 years is $100 \times (1.03)^{10} = \$134$ million. At a discount rate of 10%, your proposed department store has an NPV of $1 million:

$$\text{NPV} = -100 + \frac{8}{1.10} + \frac{8}{(1.10)^2} + \ldots + \frac{8 + 134}{(1.10)^{10}} = \$1 \text{ million}$$

Notice how sensitive the decision is to the ending value of the real estate. For example, an ending value of $120 million implies an NPV of −$5 million.

---

[3]For simplicity, we assume the $100 million goes entirely to real estate. In real life, there would also be substantial investments in fixtures, information systems, training, and start-up costs.

It is helpful to imagine such a business as divided into two parts—a real estate subsidiary that buys the building and a retailing subsidiary that rents and operates it. Then figure out how much rent the real estate subsidiary would have to charge, and ask whether the retailing subsidiary could afford to pay the rent.

In some cases, a fair market rental can be estimated from real estate transactions. For example, we might observe that similar retail space recently rented for $10 million a year. In that case, we would conclude that our department store was an unattractive use for the site. Once the site had been acquired, it would be better to rent it out at $10 million than to use it for a store generating only $8 million.

Suppose, on the other hand, that the property could be rented for only $7 million per year. The department store could pay this amount to the real estate subsidiary and still earn a net operating cash flow of 8 − 7 = $1 million. It is therefore the best *current* use for the real estate.[4]

Will it also be the best *future* use? Maybe not, depending on whether retail profits keep pace with any rent increases. Suppose that real estate prices and rents are expected to increase by 3% per year. The real estate subsidiary must charge 7 × 1.03 = $7.21 million in year 2, 7.21 × 1.03 = $7.43 million in year 3, and so on.[5] Figure 11.1 shows that the store's income fails to cover the rental after year 5.

If these forecasts are right, the store has only a five-year economic life; from that point on, the real estate is more valuable in some other use. If you stubbornly believe that the store is the best long-term use for the site, you must be ignoring potential growth in income from the store.[6]

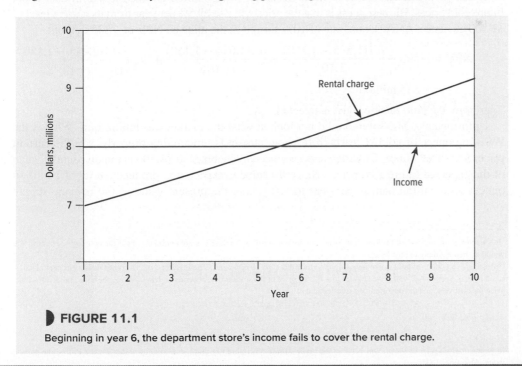

▶ **FIGURE 11.1**

Beginning in year 6, the department store's income fails to cover the rental charge.

---

[4]The fair market rent equals the profit generated by the real estate's *second*-best use.

[5]This rental stream yields a 10% rate of return to the real estate subsidiary. Each year it gets a 7% "dividend" and 3% capital gain. Growth at 3% would bring the value of the property to $134 million by year 10.

The present value (at $r = 0.10$) of the growing stream of rents is

$$\text{PV} = \frac{7}{r - g} = \frac{7}{0.10 - 0.03} = \$100 \text{ million}$$

This PV is the initial market value of the property.

[6]Another possibility is that real estate rents and values are expected to grow at less than 3% a year. But in that case, the real estate subsidiary would have to charge more than $7 million rent in year 1 to justify its $100 million real estate investment. That would make the department store even less attractive.

There is a general point here as illustrated in Example 11.1. Whenever you make a capital investment decision, think what bets you are placing. Our department store example involved at least two bets—one on real estate prices and another on the firm's ability to run a successful store. But that suggests some alternative strategies. For instance, it would be foolish to make a lousy store investment just because you are optimistic about real estate prices. You would do better to buy real estate and rent it out to the highest bidders. The converse is also true. You shouldn't be deterred from going ahead with a profitable store because you are pessimistic about real estate prices. You would do better to sell the real estate and *rent* it back for the store. We suggest that you separate the two bets by first asking, "Should we open a clothing store on this site, assuming that the real estate is fairly priced?" and then deciding whether you also want to go into the real estate business.[7]

Let us look at another example of how market prices can help you make better decisions.

EXAMPLE 11.4 • Opening a Gold Mine

Kingsley Solomon is considering a proposal to open a new gold mine. He estimates that the mine will cost $500 million to develop and that in each of the next 10 years, it will produce 100,000 ounces of gold at a cost, after mining and refining, of $1,150 an ounce. Although the extraction costs can be predicted with reasonable accuracy, Mr. Solomon is much less confident about future gold prices. His best guess is that the price will rise by 5% per year from its current level of $1,500 an ounce. At a discount rate of 10%, this gives the mine an NPV of −$35 million:

$$\text{NPV} = -500 + \frac{0.1(1{,}575 - 1{,}150)}{1.10} + \frac{0.1(1{,}654 - 1{,}150)}{(1.10)^2} + \dots + \frac{0.1(2{,}443 - 1{,}150)}{(1.10)^{10}}$$

$$= -\$35 \text{ million}$$

Therefore, the gold mine project is rejected.

Unfortunately, Mr. Solomon did not look at what the market was telling him. What is the PV of an ounce of gold? Clearly, if the gold market is functioning properly, it is the current price, $1,500 an ounce. Gold does not produce any income, so $1,500 is the discounted value of the expected future gold price.[8] Since the mine is expected to produce a total of 1 million ounces (0.1 million ounces per year for 10 years), the present value of the revenue stream

---

[7]In Chapter 28 we argue that it is foolish to invest in a foreign business because you are optimistic about the country's currency. You would do better simply to buy the currency.

[8]Investing in an ounce of gold is like investing in a stock that pays no dividends: The investor's return comes entirely as capital gains. Look back at Section 4-2, where we showed that P_0, the price of the stock today, depends on DIV_1 and P_1, the expected dividend and price for next year, and the opportunity cost of capital r:

$$P_0 = \frac{\text{DIV}_1 + P_1}{1 + r}$$

But for gold $\text{DIV}_1 = 0$, so

$$P_0 = \frac{P_1}{1 + r}$$

In words, *today's price is the present value of next year's price.* Therefore, we don't have to know either P_1 or r to find the present value. Also since $\text{DIV}_2 = 0$,

$$P_1 = \frac{P_2}{1 + r}$$

and we can express P_0 as

$$P_0 = \frac{P_1}{1 + r} = \frac{1}{1 + r}\left(\frac{P_2}{1 + r}\right) = \frac{P_2}{(1 + r)^2}$$

In general,

$$P_0 = \frac{P_t}{(1 + r)^t}$$

This holds for any asset that pays no dividends, is traded in a competitive market, and costs nothing to store. Storage costs for gold or common stocks are very small compared to asset value.

We also assume that guaranteed future delivery of gold is just as good as having gold in hand today. This is not quite right. As we will see in Chapter 27, gold in hand can generate a small "convenience yield."

is $1 \times 1,500 = \$1,500$ million.[9] Suppose that 10% is an appropriate discount rate for the relatively certain extraction costs. Then

$$\text{NPV} = -\text{initial investment} + \text{PV revenues} - \text{PV costs}$$
$$= -500 + 1,500 - \sum_{t=1}^{10} \frac{0.1 \times 1,150}{(1.10)^t} = \$293 \text{ million}$$

It looks as if Kingsley Solomon's mine is not such a bad bet after all.[10]

● ● ● ● ●

Mr. Solomon's gold, in Example 11.4, was just like anyone else's gold. So there was no point in trying to value it separately. By taking the PV of the gold sales as given, Mr. Solomon was able to focus on the crucial issue: Were the extraction costs sufficiently low to make the venture worthwhile? That brings us to another of those fundamental truths: If others are producing a good or service profitably and (like Mr. Solomon) you can make it more cheaply than them, then you don't need any NPV calculations to know that you are probably onto a good thing.

We confess that our example of Kingsley Solomon's mine is somewhat special. Unlike gold, most commodities are not kept solely for investment purposes, and therefore you cannot automatically assume that today's price is equal to the present value of the future price.

However, here is another way that you may be able to tackle the problem. Suppose that you are considering investment in a new copper mine and that someone offers to buy the mine's future output at a fixed price. If you accept the offer—and the buyer is completely creditworthy—the revenues from the mine are certain and can be discounted at the risk-free interest rate.[11] That takes us back to Chapter 9, where we explained that there are two ways to calculate PV:

- Estimate the expected cash flows and discount at a rate that reflects the risk of those flows.
- Estimate what sure-fire cash flows would have the same values as the risky cash flows. Then discount these *certainty-equivalent* cash flows at the risk-free interest rate.

When you discount the fixed-price revenues at the risk-free rate, you are using the certainty-equivalent method to value the mine's output. By doing so, you gain in two ways: You don't need to estimate future mineral prices, and you don't need to worry about the appropriate discount rate for risky cash flows.

But here's the question: What is the fixed price at which you could agree today to sell your future output? In other words, what is the certainty-equivalent price? Fortunately, for many commodities, there is an active market in which firms fix today the price at which they will buy or sell copper and other commodities in the future. This market is known as the *futures market,* which we will cover in Chapter 27. Futures prices are certainty equivalents, and you can track them in real time every day the markets are open. So you don't need to make elaborate forecasts of copper prices to work out the PV of the mine's output. The market has already done the work for you; you simply calculate future revenues using the current price of copper futures and discount these revenues at the risk-free interest rate.

---

[9]We assume that the extraction rate does not vary. If it can vary, Mr. Solomon has a valuable operating option to increase output when gold prices are high or to cut back when prices fall. Option pricing techniques are needed to value the mine when operating options are important. See Chapter 23.

[10]As in the case of our department store example, Mr. Solomon is placing two bets: one on his ability to mine gold at a low cost and the other on the price of gold. Suppose that he really does believe that gold is overvalued. That should not deter him from running a low-cost gold mine as long as he can place separate bets on gold prices. For example, he might be able to enter into a long-term contract to sell the mine's output or he could sell gold futures.

[11]We assume that the *volume* of output is certain (or does not have any market risk).

Of course, things are never as easy as textbooks suggest. Trades in organized futures exchanges are largely confined to deliveries over the next year or so; therefore, your source for market pricing won't show the price at which you could sell output beyond this period. But financial economists have developed techniques for using the prices in the futures market to estimate the amount that buyers would agree to pay for more-distant deliveries.[12]

Our two examples of gold and copper producers are illustrations of a universal principle of finance: When you have the market value of an asset, *use it,* at least as a starting point, in your analysis.

11.3 Self-Test

A company's headquarters are located in a downtown office building. What is the cost to the company of occupying that building?

11-3   How Competitive Advantage Translates into Positive NPVs

Discounted cash flow techniques are fairly easily applied to straightforward investment problems such as choosing between two machines or the decision to replace an existing machine. Strategic investment decisions such as the decision to enter a new market are much more complex. Not only is the level of uncertainty about the cash flows inherently greater, but managers must be able to cope with incomplete and possibly biased information. How then can managers distinguish which major investment proposals truly have positive NPVs? We suggest that they ask some probing questions about the source of the economic gain.

We start with some definitions. Call PV_t the present value at the end of year t of all subsequent cash flows. Then the economic income that you earn from an investment in year t is equal to the cash flow from that investment plus the change in its value.

$$\text{Economic income in year } t = C_t + (PV_t - PV_{t-1}) \tag{11.1}$$

Most assets *depreciate* in value as the end of their life gets closer, so $(PV_t - PV_{t-1})$ is generally negative.

To satisfy its shareholders, a company needs to earn at least the opportunity cost of capital on each investment. When the realized economic income is more than the income that shareholders require, the company is said to earn an **economic rent:**

$$\text{Economic rent} = \text{actual economic income} - \text{cost of shareholders' capital} \tag{11.2}$$

Companies add value whenever their economic income is greater than the cost of capital. Positive-NPV projects are those that earn economic rents.

11.4 Self-Test

Suppose the investment is not a piece of equipment, but is instead a share of stock. At the start of the year the stock price is $50. At the end of the year, the company pays a $5 dividend and the stock price rises to $60. What is the stock's economic income? If investors required a return of 10%, what is the stock's economic rent that year?

---

[12]After reading Chapter 27, check out E. S. Schwartz, "The Stochastic Behavior of Commodity Prices: Implications for Valuation and Hedging,"*Journal of Finance* 52 (July 1997), pp. 923–973; and A. J. Neuberger, "Hedging Long-Term Exposures with Multiple Short-Term Futures Contracts,"*Review of Financial Studies* 12 (1999), pp. 429–459.

The problem is that competition between companies erodes economic rents and drives them down to zero. Positive rents arise only when the company is able to identify and exploit some competitive advantage. For example, suppose that demand takes off unexpectedly and that your firm can expand production capacity more quickly and cheaply than your competitors. This stroke of luck is pretty sure to generate economic rents until other firms manage to catch up.

Some competitive advantages are longer lived. They include a protected market that competitors can't enter, patents or proprietary technology, the skills and experience of employees, durable relationships with customers or suppliers, reputations that may be reflected in a respected brand name, or strategic assets that competitors can't easily duplicate.

EXAMPLE 11.5 • Strategic assets in the cargo business

Think of the difference between railroads and trucking companies. It's easy to enter the trucking business but nearly impossible to build a brand-new, long-haul railroad.[13] The interstate lines operated by U.S. railroads are strategic assets. With these assets in place, railroads were able to increase revenues and profits rapidly when shipments surged and energy prices increased in the early years of this century. The high cost of diesel fuel was more burdensome for trucks, which are less fuel efficient than railroads. Thus, high energy prices actually handed the railroads a competitive advantage.

• • • • •

A competitive advantage will protect a firm only if it is durable and can be sustained against competition from other businesses. Warren Buffett stresses that successful businesses require the equivalent of a castle moat to deter marauders:

> I want a business with a moat around it with a very valuable castle in the middle. And then I want the duke who's in charge of that castle to be honest and hard-working and able.
>
> Our managers of the businesses we run, I've got one message to them, which is to widen the moat. And we want to throw crocodiles and sharks and everything else, gators, I guess, into the moat to keep away competitors. And that comes about through service, it comes about through quality of product, it comes about through cost, it comes about sometimes through patents, it comes about through real estate location.[14]

You can see how business strategy and finance reinforce each other. Managers who have a clear understanding of their firm's competitive strengths (and the moats that protect their products and services) are better placed to separate those projects that have a positive NPV from those that do not. Therefore, when you are presented with a project that appears to have a positive NPV, do not just accept the calculations at face value. Probe behind the cash-flow estimates, and *try to identify the source of economic rents and how long they will endure.* A positive NPV for a new project is believable only if you believe that your company has some special advantage.

Thinking about competitive advantage can also help ferret out negative-NPV calculations that are negative by mistake. For example, if you are the lowest-cost producer of a profitable product in a growing market, you should invest to expand along with the market. If your calculations show a negative NPV for such an expansion, you have probably made a mistake.

---

[13]The Dakota, Minnesota & Eastern Railroad developed plans to build a new line to transport coal from Wyoming to the Midwest. Although the plans were approved by the regulatory authorities, the project was abandoned in 2012 after the railroad was acquired by the Canadian Pacific Railway.

[14]Berkshire Hathaway 2000 Annual Report and 2007 talk to students at the University of Florida.

We will shortly work through an extended example that shows how a firm's analysis of its competitive position confirmed that a major investment had a positive NPV. But first we look at an example in which the analysis helped a firm to identify a negative-NPV transaction and avoid a costly mistake.

EXAMPLE 11.6 • How One Company Avoided a $100 million Mistake

A U.S. chemical producer was about to modify an existing plant to produce a specialty product, polyzone, which was in short supply on world markets.[15] At prevailing raw material and finished-product prices, the expansion would have been strongly profitable. Table 11.1 shows a simplified version of management's analysis. Note the assumed constant spread between selling price and the cost of raw materials. Given this spread, the resulting NPV was about $64 million at the company's 8% real cost of capital—not bad for a $100 million outlay.

	Year 0	Year 1	Year 2	Years 3–10
Investment	100			
Production (millions of pounds per year)[a]	0	0	40	80
Spread ($ per pound)	1.20	1.20	1.20	1.20
Net revenues	0	0	48	96
Production costs[b]	0	0	30	30
Transport[c]	0	0	4	8
Other costs	0	20	20	20
Cash flow	−100	−20	−6	38
NPV (at $r = 8\%$) = $63.56 million				

⟩TABLE 11.1 NPV calculation for proposed investment in polyzone production by a U.S. chemical company (figures in $ millions except as noted).

Note: For simplicity, we assume no inflation and no taxes. Plant and equipment have no salvage value after 10 years.
[a] Production capacity is 80 million pounds per year.
[b] Production costs are $0.375 per pound after start up ($0.75 per pound in year 2, when production is only 40 million pounds).
[c] Transportation costs are $0.10 per pound to European ports.

BEYOND THE PAGE

Try It!
Polyzone
project

mhhe.com/brealey14e

Then doubt began to creep in. Notice the outlay for transportation costs. Some of the project's raw materials were commodity chemicals, largely imported from Europe, and much of the polyzone production would be exported back to Europe. Moreover, the U.S. company had no long-run technological edge over potential European competitors. It had a head start perhaps, but was that really enough to generate a positive NPV?

Notice the importance of the price spread between raw materials and finished product. The analysis in Table 11.1 forecasted the spread at a constant $1.20 per pound of polyzone for 10 years. That had to be wrong: European producers, who did not face the U.S. company's transportation costs, would see an even larger NPV and expand capacity. Increased competition would almost surely squeeze the spread. The U.S. company decided to calculate the *competitive* spread—the spread at which a European competitor would see polyzone capacity as zero NPV. Table 11.2 shows management's analysis. The resulting spread of about $0.95 per pound was the best *long-run* forecast for the polyzone market, other things constant of course.

---

[15]This is a true story, but names and details have been changed to protect the innocent.

	Year 0	Year 1	Year 2	Years 3–10
Investment	100			
Production (millions of pounds per year)	0	0	40	80
Spread ($ per pound)	0.95	0.95	0.95	0.95
Net revenues	0	0	38	76
Production costs	0	0	30	30
Transport	0	0	0	0
Other costs	0	20	20	20
Cash flow	−100	−20	−12	+26
NPV (at $r = 8\%$) = 0				

〉TABLE 11.2   What is the competitive spread to a European producer? About $0.95 per pound of polyzone. Note that European producers face no transportation costs. Compare Table 11.1 (figures in $ millions except as noted).

How much of a head start did the U.S. producer have? How long before competitors forced the spread down to $0.95? Management's best guess was five years. It prepared Table 11.3, which is identical to Table 11.1 except for the forecasted spread, which would shrink to $0.95 by the start of year 5. Now the NPV was negative.

	Year 0	Year 1	Year 2	Year 3	Year 4	Years 5–10
Investment	100					
Production (millions of pounds per year)	0	0	40	80	80	80
Spread ($ per pound)	1.20	1.20	1.20	1.20	1.10	0.95
Net revenues	0	0	48	96	88	76
Production costs	0	0	30	30	30	30
Transport	0	0	4	8	8	8
Other costs	0	20	20	20	20	20
Cash flow	−100	−20	−6	38	30	18
NPV (at $r = 8\%$) = −9.8						

〉TABLE 11.3   Recalculation of NPV for polyzone investment by U.S. company (figures in $ millions except as noted). If expansion by European producers forces competitive spreads by year 5, the U.S. producer's NPV falls to −$9.8 million. Compare Table 11.1.

The project might have been saved if production could have been started in year 1 rather than 2 or if local markets could have been expanded, thus reducing transportation costs. But these changes were not feasible, so management canceled the project, albeit with a sigh of relief that its analysis had not stopped at Table 11.1.

This is a perfect example of the importance of thinking through sources of economic rents. Positive NPVs are suspect without some long-run competitive advantage. When a company contemplates investing in a new product or expanding production of an existing product, it should specifically identify its advantages or disadvantages over its most dangerous competitors. It should calculate NPV from those competitors' points of view. If competitors' NPVs come out strongly positive, the company had better expect decreasing prices (or spreads) and evaluate the proposed investment accordingly.

11-4   Marvin Enterprises Decides to Exploit a New Technology—An Example

To illustrate some of the problems involved in predicting economic rents, let us leap forward several years from now and look at the decision by Marvin Enterprises to exploit a new technology.[16]

One of the most unexpected developments in the twenty-first century was the remarkable growth of a completely new industry. By 2044, annual sales of gargle blasters totaled $1.68 billion, or 240 million units. Although it controlled only 10% of the market, Marvin Enterprises was among the most exciting growth companies of the decade. Marvin had come late into the business, but it had pioneered the use of implanted microcircuits to control the genetic engineering processes used to manufacture gargle blasters. This development had enabled producers to cut the price of gargle blasters from $9 to $7 and had thereby contributed to the dramatic growth in the size of the market. The estimated demand curve in Figure 11.2 shows just how responsive demand is to such price reductions.

Table 11.4 summarizes the cost structure of the old and new technologies. While companies with the new technology were earning 20% on their initial investment, those with first-generation equipment had been hit by the successive price cuts. Since all Marvin's investment was in the 2040 technology, it had been particularly well placed during this period.

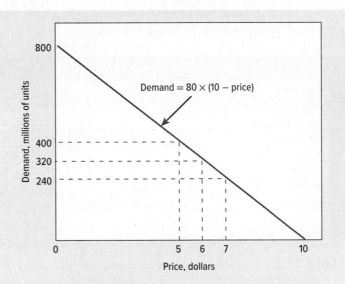

▶ FIGURE 11.2

The demand "curve" for gargle blasters shows that for each $1 cut in price there is an increase in demand of 80 million units.

▶ TABLE 11.4

Size and cost structure of the gargle blaster industry before Marvin announced its expansion plans.

Note: Selling price is $7 per unit. One unit means one gargle blaster.

Technology	Capacity (Millions of Units)		Capital Cost per Unit ($)	Manufacturing Cost per Unit ($)	Salvage Value per Unit ($)
	Industry	Marvin			
First generation (2032)	120	—	17.50	5.50	2.50
Second generation (2040)	120	24	17.50	3.50	2.50

[16]We thank Stewart Hodges for permission to adapt this example from a case prepared by him, and we thank the BBC for permission to use the term *gargle blasters.*

Rumors of new developments at Marvin had been circulating for some time, and the total market value of Marvin's stock had risen to $460 million by January 2045. At that point, Marvin called a press conference to announce another technological breakthrough. Management claimed that its new third-generation process involving mutant neurons enabled the firm to reduce capital costs to $10 and manufacturing costs to $3 per unit. Marvin proposed to capitalize on this invention by embarking on a huge $1 billion expansion program that would add 100 million units to capacity. The company expected to be in full operation within 12 months.

Before deciding to go ahead with this development, Marvin had undertaken extensive calculations on the effect of the new investment. The basic assumptions were as follows:

1. The cost of capital was 20%.

2. The production facilities had an indefinite physical life.

3. The demand curve and the costs of each technology would not change.

4. There was no chance of a fourth-generation technology in the foreseeable future.

5. The corporate income tax, which had been abolished in 2035, was not likely to be reintroduced.

Marvin's competitors greeted the news with varying degrees of concern. There was general agreement that it would be five years before any of them would have access to the new technology. On the other hand, many consoled themselves with the reflection that Marvin's new plant could not compete with an existing plant that had been fully depreciated.

Suppose that you were Marvin's financial manager. Would you have agreed with the decision to expand? Do you think it would have been better to go for a larger or smaller expansion? How do you think Marvin's announcement is likely to affect the price of its stock?

You have a choice. You can go on *immediately* to read *our* solution to these questions. But you will learn much more if you stop and work out your own answer first. Try it.

Forecasting Prices of Gargle Blasters

Up to this point in any capital budgeting problem, we have always given you the set of cash-flow forecasts. In the present case, you have to *derive* those forecasts.

The first problem is to decide what is going to happen to the price of gargle blasters. Marvin's new venture will increase industry capacity to 340 million units. From the demand curve in Figure 11.2, you can see that the industry can sell this number of gargle blasters only if the price declines to $5.75:

$$\text{Demand} = 80 \times (10 - \text{price})$$
$$= 80 \times (10 - 5.75) = 340 \text{ million units}$$

If the price falls to $5.75, what will happen to companies with the 2032 technology? They also have to make an investment decision: Should they stay in business, or should they sell their equipment for its salvage value of $2.50 per unit? With a 20% opportunity cost of capital, the NPV of staying in business is

$$\text{NPV} = -\text{investment} + \text{PV (price} - \text{manufacturing cost)}$$
$$= -2.50 + \frac{5.75 - 5.50}{0.20} = -\$1.25 \text{ per unit}$$

Smart companies with 2032 equipment will, therefore, see that it is better to sell off capacity. No matter what their equipment originally cost or how far it is depreciated, it is more profitable to sell the equipment for $2.50 per unit than to operate it and lose $1.25 per unit.

As capacity is sold off, the supply of gargle blasters will decline and the price will rise. An equilibrium is reached when the price gets to $6. At this point 2032 equipment has a zero NPV:

$$NPV = -2.50 + \frac{6.00 - 5.50}{0.20} = \$0 \text{ per unit}$$

How much capacity will have to be sold off before the price reaches $6? You can check that by going back to the demand curve:

$$Demand = 80 \times (10 - price)$$
$$= 80 \times (10 - 6) = 320 \text{ million units}$$

Therefore Marvin's expansion will cause the price to settle down at $6 a unit and will induce first-generation producers to withdraw 20 million units of capacity.

But after five years, Marvin's competitors will also be in a position to build third-generation plants. As long as these plants have positive NPVs, companies will increase their capacity and force prices down once again. A new equilibrium will be reached when the price reaches $5. At this point, the NPV of new third-generation plants is zero, and there is no incentive for companies to expand further:

$$NPV = -10 + \frac{5.00 - 3.00}{0.20} = \$0 \text{ per unit}$$

Looking back once more at our demand curve, you can see that with a price of $5 the industry can sell a total of 400 million gargle blasters:

$$Demand = 80 \times (10 - price) = 80 \times (10 - 5) = 400 \text{ million units}$$

The effect of the third-generation technology is, therefore, to cause industry sales to expand from 240 million units in 2044 to 400 million five years later. But that rapid growth is no protection against failure. By the end of five years, any company that has only first-generation equipment will no longer be able to cover its manufacturing costs and will be *forced* out of business.

The Value of Marvin's New Expansion

We have shown that the introduction of third-generation technology is likely to cause gargle blaster prices to decline to $6 for the next five years and to $5 thereafter. We can now set down the expected cash flows from Marvin's new plant:

	Year 0 (Investment)	Years 1–5 (Revenue – Manufacturing Cost)	Year 6, 7, 8, . . . (Revenue – Manufacturing Cost)
Cash flow per unit ($)	−10	6 − 3 = 3	5 − 3 = 2
Cash flow (100 million units, $ millions)	−1,000	600 − 300 = 300	500 − 300 = 200

Discounting these cash flows at 20% gives us

$$NPV = -1000 + \sum_{t=1}^{5}\frac{300}{(1.20)^t} + \frac{1}{(1.20)^5}\left(\frac{200}{0.20}\right) = \$299 \text{ million}$$

It looks as if Marvin's decision to go ahead was correct. But there is something we have forgotten. When we evaluate an investment, we must consider *all* incremental cash flows. One effect of Marvin's decision to expand is to reduce the value of its existing 2040 plant.

If Marvin decided not to go ahead with the new technology, the $7 price of gargle blasters would hold until Marvin's competitors started to cut prices in five years' time. Marvin's decision, therefore, leads to an immediate $1 cut in price. This reduces the present value of its 2040 equipment by

$$24 \text{ million} \times \sum_{t=1}^{5} \frac{1.00}{(1.20)^t} = \$72 \text{ million}$$

Considered in isolation, Marvin's decision has an NPV of $299 million. But it also reduces the value of existing plant by $72 million. The net present value of Marvin's venture is, therefore, $299 - 72 = \$227$ million.

Alternative Expansion Plans

Marvin's expansion has a positive NPV, but perhaps Marvin would do better to build a larger or smaller plant. You can check that by going through the same calculations as above. First you need to estimate how the additional capacity will affect gargle blaster prices. Then you can calculate the net present value of the new plant and the change in the present value of the existing plant. The total NPV of Marvin's expansion plan is

Total NPV = NPV of new plant + change in PV of existing plant

We have undertaken these calculations and plotted the results in Figure 11.3. You can see how total NPV would be affected by a smaller or larger expansion.

When the new technology becomes generally available in 2050, firms will construct a total of 280 million units of new capacity.[17] But Figure 11.3 shows that it would be foolish for Marvin to go that far. If Marvin added 280 million units of new capacity in 2045, the discounted value of the cash flows from the new plant would be zero *and* the company would have reduced the value of its old plant by $144 million. To maximize NPV, Marvin should

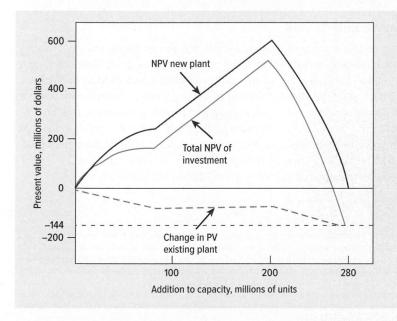

> **FIGURE 11.3**
>
> Effect on net present value of alternative expansion plans. Marvin's 100-million-unit expansion has a total NPV of $227 million (total NPV = NPV new plant + change in PV existing plant = 299 − 72 = 227). Total NPV is maximized if Marvin builds 200 million units of new capacity. If Marvin builds 280 million units of new capacity, total NPV is −$144 million.

[17]Total industry capacity in 2050 will be 400 million units. Of this, 120 million units are second-generation capacity, and the remaining 280 million units are third-generation capacity.

construct 200 million units of new capacity and set the price just below \$6 to drive out the 2032 manufacturers. Output is, therefore, less and price is higher than either would be under free competition.[18]

The Value of Marvin Stock

Let us think about the effect of Marvin's announcement on the value of its common stock. Marvin has 24 million units of second-generation capacity. In the absence of any third-generation technology, gargle blaster prices would hold at \$7 and Marvin's existing plant would be worth

$$PV = 24 \text{ million} \times \frac{7.00 - 3.50}{0.20}$$

$$= \$420 \text{ million}$$

Marvin's new technology reduces the price of gargle blasters initially to \$6 and after five years to \$5. Therefore the value of existing plant declines to

$$PV = 24 \text{ million} \times \left[\sum_{t=1}^{5} \frac{6.00 - 3.50}{(1.20)^t} + \frac{5.00 - 3.50}{0.20 \times (1.20)^5} \right]$$

$$= \$252 \text{ million}$$

But the *new* plant makes a net addition to shareholders' wealth of \$299 million. So after Marvin's announcement its stock will be worth

$$252 + 299 = \$551 \text{ million}[19]$$

Now here is an illustration of something we talked about in Chapter 4: Before the announcement, Marvin's stock was valued in the market at \$460 million. The difference between this figure and the value of the existing plant represented the present value of Marvin's growth opportunities (PVGO). The market valued Marvin's ability to stay ahead of the game at \$40 million even before the announcement. After the announcement PVGO rose to \$299 million.[20]

The Lessons of Marvin Enterprises

Marvin Enterprises may be just a piece of science fiction, but the problems that it confronts are very real. Whenever Intel considers developing a new microprocessor or Pfizer considers developing a new drug, these firms must face up to exactly the same issues as Marvin. We have tried to illustrate the *kind* of questions that you should be asking when presented with a set of cash-flow forecasts. Of course, no economic model is going to predict the future with accuracy. Perhaps Marvin can hold the price above \$6. Perhaps competitors will not appreciate the rich pickings to be had in the year 2050. In that case, Marvin's expansion would be even more profitable. But would you want to bet \$1 billion on such possibilities? We don't think so.

Here are some general lessons that we can draw from Marvin's experience.

---

[18]Notice that we are assuming that all customers have to pay the same price for their gargle blasters. If Marvin could charge each customer the maximum price that that customer would be willing to pay, output would be the same as under free competition. Such direct price discrimination is illegal and, in any case, difficult to enforce. But firms do search for indirect ways to differentiate between customers. For example, stores often offer free delivery, which is equivalent to a price discount for customers who live at an inconvenient distance.

[19]To finance the expansion, Marvin is going to have to sell \$1,000 million of new stock. Therefore the *total* value of Marvin's stock will rise to \$1,551 million. But investors who put up the new money will receive shares worth \$1,000 million. The value of Marvin's old shares after the announcement is therefore \$551 million.

[20]The market value of Marvin stock will be greater than \$551 million if investors expect the company to expand again within the five-year period. In other words, PVGO after the expansion may still be positive. Investors may expect Marvin to stay one step ahead of its competitors or to successfully apply its special technology in other areas.

An investment's NPV depends on the time before competition erodes any advantage.
Investments often turn out to earn far more than the cost of capital because of a favorable surprise. This surprise may in turn create a temporary opportunity for further investments that earn more than the cost of capital. But anticipated and more prolonged rents will naturally lead to the entry of rival producers. That is why you should be suspicious of any investment proposal that predicts a stream of economic rents into the indefinite future. Try to estimate *when* competition will drive the NPV down to zero, and think what that implies for the price of your product.

Investments in high tech industries are particularly exposed to innovation by competitors.
Many companies try to identify the major growth areas in the economy and then concentrate their investment in these areas. But the sad fate of first-generation gargle blaster manufacturers illustrates how rapidly existing plants can be made obsolete by changes in technology. It is fun being in a growth industry when you are at the forefront of the new technology, but a growth industry has no mercy on technological laggards.

   Therefore, do not simply follow the herd of investors stampeding into high-growth sectors of the economy. Think of the fate of the dot-com companies in the "new economy" of the late 1990s. Optimists argued that the information revolution was opening up opportunities for companies to grow at unprecedented rates. The pessimists pointed out that competition in e-commerce was likely to be intense and that competition would ensure that the benefits of the information revolution would go largely to consumers. The Finance in Practice box emphasizes that rapid growth is no guarantee of superior profits.

   We do not wish to imply that good investment opportunities don't exist. For example, they frequently arise because the firm has invested money in the past, which gives it the option to develop new products or to expand cheaply in the future. Perhaps the firm can increase its output just by adding an extra production line, whereas its rivals would need to construct an entirely new factory. Perhaps its research capability gives it the opportunity to be first with a new product.

New investments may impact the value of existing assets.
Marvin also reminds us to include a project's impact on the rest of the firm when estimating incremental cash flows. By introducing the new technology immediately, Marvin reduced the value of its existing plant by $72 million.

   Sometimes the losses on existing plants may completely offset the gains from a new technology. That is why we may see established, technologically advanced companies deliberately slowing down the rate at which they introduce new products. But this can be a dangerous game to play if it opens up opportunities for competitors. For example, for many years Bausch & Lomb was the dominant producer of contact lenses and earned large profits from glass contact lenses that needed to be sterilized every night. Because its existing business generated high returns, the company was slow to introduce disposable lenses. This delay opened up an opportunity for competitors and enabled Johnson & Johnson to introduce disposable lenses.

11.5 Self-Test

If the speed at which new technology can be introduced is increased, how does this affect the present value of existing equipment? What does this imply for companies in growth industries?

Opportunity costs include the salvage value of existing assets.
Marvin's economic rents were equal to the difference between its costs and those of the marginal producer. The costs of the marginal 2032-generation plant consisted of the manufacturing costs plus the opportunity cost of not selling the equipment. Therefore, if the salvage value of

FINANCE IN PRACTICE

● ● ● ● ●

Cautionary Tales

❯ What would be your list of growth industries that have transformed people's lives over the past century? One obvious candidate is the automobile industry. Sales of vehicles in the United States have grown from almost nothing 120 years ago to more than 17 million a year today. Many companies foresaw this rapid growth and concluded that it offered a likely source of juicy profits. Wikipedia lists 1,800 U.S. car manufacturers that were established at some point in the United States, with exotic names such as Ben Hur, O-We-Go, and Motor Bob. Almost all these companies blossomed briefly and then withered. Only a handful of U.S. car companies remain today, two of which filed for bankruptcy in 2009 and had to be rescued by the U.S. government.[21]

An equally profitless growth industry has been the aviation sector. Since 1948, the number of passenger miles flown by U.S. airlines has multiplied nearly 300 times. Yet since that date more than 150 airlines have entered into Chapter 11 bankruptcy, in some cases two or three times.[22] While a number of smaller airlines continue to operate, the sector today is dominated by just four companies: American, Delta, United, and Southwest.

A third and more recent example of a growth industry is the manufacture of computers. With the exception of IBM, the giants of the industry today barely existed in the 1970s. At that time, investors in the industry referred to Snow White and the seven dwarfs.

IBM was Snow White and the seven hefty and well-respected dwarfs were the other major mainframe manufacturers—Burroughs, UNIVAC, NCR, Control Data, Honeywell, General Electric, and RCA. In addition to these major producers, there were a number of glamorous dwarflets, such as Amdahl, Wang Laboratories, Data General, and DEC. As the role of the mainframe changed, only Snow White survived as a major force, while the dwarfs and most of their smaller brethren either no longer exist or have exited computer manufacturing.

Do these cautionary stories mean that companies should seek out stagnant or declining industries? Of course not; other things equal, it is better to operate in a growth industry than a declining one. The problem is that the prospect of rapid industry growth attracts competition. And, if the industry is also characterized by rapidly changing technology or consumer taste, then competitive advantage is likely to be less persistent. Think, for example, of Nokia and BlackBerry, whose phones once dominated the smartphone market until they were quickly overtaken by Apple's iPhone and Android phones. The message, in Warren Buffett's words, is that "the key to investing is not assessing how much an industry is going to affect society, or how much it will grow, but rather determining the competitive advantage of any given company and, above all, the durability of that advantage."[23]

---

the 2032 equipment was higher, Marvin's competitors would incur higher costs and Marvin could earn higher rents. It might seem odd to describe the salvage value as a cost, but remember that when a company considers an investment, it needs to include the opportunity costs of any assets that it already owns and that could otherwise be sold. This is equally true when the company is considering whether to continue with an activity *after* the investment has been made.

We took the salvage value as given, but it in turn depends on the cost savings from substituting outdated gargle blaster equipment for some other asset. In a well-functioning economy, assets will be used so as to minimize the *total* cost of producing the chosen set of outputs. The economic rents earned by any asset are equal to the total extra costs that would be incurred if that asset were withdrawn.

---

[21]Profitless growth in the auto and aviation industries is the subject of a very insightful and entertaining article by Warren Buffett. See C. Loomis, "Mr. Buffett on the Stock Market," *Fortune* (November 22, 1999), pp. 110–115.

[22]Transworld Airlines (TWA) went into Chapter 11 bankruptcy three times, prompting jokes about "Chapter 22" and "Chapter 33." TWA is one of nearly 450 U.S. airlines that are no longer operating. See https://en.wikipedia.org/wiki/List_of_defunct_airlines_of_the_United_States.

[23]C. Loomis, "Mr. Buffett on the Stock Market," op. cit.

11.6 Self-Test

We said that if equipment has a high salvage value, the cost of production is higher. In what sense is this true? If existing producers operate equipment that is readily sold (or used profitably elsewhere in the business), what are the implications for a potential new entrant?

A fully depreciated plant is no better placed to compete than a partially depreciated one. When Marvin announced its expansion plans, many owners of first-generation equipment took comfort in the belief that Marvin could not compete with their fully depreciated plant. Their comfort was misplaced. Regardless of past depreciation policy, it paid to scrap first-generation equipment rather than keep it in production. Do not expect that numbers in your balance sheet can protect you from harsh economic reality.

• • • • •

KEY TAKEAWAYS

- **Behavioral biases in cash flow forecasts** Investment decisions often involve large sums of money and may affect the shape of the company many years into the future. Therefore, senior managers rarely delegate decisions about major investments. However, managers' ability to distinguish between proposals is hampered by the fact that they are often presented with sales documents with little discussion of the potential risks or alternatives. Their task is made harder by the fact that project proposers may be subject to behavioral biases such as overconfidence and overoptimism.

- **Look first to market values** To ensure that project proposals truly add value, we suggest that, where possible, managers should start with the asset's market value and then ask why the company can earn more from those assets than its rivals.

- **Economic rents** A project's *economic income* in any year is equal to the cash flow plus the change in the asset's present value

  Economic income in year $t = C_t + (PV_t - PV_{t-1})$

  The difference between a project's economic income and the cost of capital is the project's *economic rent*. Projects that earn economic rents have positive NPVs.

- **Competitive advantage** Competition tends to eliminate economic rents; so the company can expect to earn rents only when it has some competitive advantage. When assessing strategic investments, it is important to identify that advantage, and think about how long it will be before the economic rents are eroded by the firm's competitors.

• • • • •

FURTHER READING

For a very readable discussion of the problem of overconfidence and other behavioral traits in financial decision making, see:

J. S. Hammond, R. L. Keeney, and H. Raiffa, "The Hidden Traps in Decision Making," *Harvard Business Review* 84 (January 2006), pp. 118–126.

The following papers discuss capital investment and strategy:

P. Barwise, P. Marsh, and R. Wensley, "Must Finance and Strategy Clash?" *Harvard Business Review,* September–October 1989, pp. 85–90.

M. Porter, "What is Strategy?" *Harvard Business Review,* November–December 1996, pp. 61–78.

S. C. Myers, "Finance Theory and Financial Strategy," *Midland Corporate Finance Journal* 5 (Spring 1987), pp. 6–13. Reprinted from *Interfaces* (January–February 1984).

R. Rumelt, *Good Strategy/Bad Strategy: The Difference and Why It Matters* (London, U.K.: Profile Books, 2017)

The following book discusses how to identify economic rents and positive NPVs:

S. Woolley, *Sources of Value* (Cambridge, U.K.: Cambridge University Press, 2009).

PROBLEM SETS

Select problems are available in McGraw-Hill's *Connect*.
Please see the preface for more information.

1. **Behavioral biases (S11.1)** Explain why setting a higher discount rate is not a cure for upward-biased cash-flow forecasts.

2. **Behavioral biases (S11.1)** Look back to the cash flows for projects F and G in Section 5-3. The cost of capital was assumed to be 10%. Assume that the forecasted cash flows for projects of this type are overstated by 8% on average. That is, the forecast for each cash flow from each project should be reduced by 8%. But a lazy financial manager, unwilling to take the time to argue with the projects' sponsors, instructs them to use a discount rate of 18%.

   a. What are the projects' true NPVs?
   b. What are the NPVs at the 18% discount rate?
   c. Are there any circumstances in which the 18% discount rate would give the correct NPVs? (*Hint:* Could upward bias be more severe for more-distant cash flows?)

3. **Market values (S11.2)** Your brother-in-law wants you to join him in purchasing a building on the outskirts of town. You and he would then develop and run a Taco Palace restaurant. Both of you are extremely optimistic about future real estate prices in this area, and your brother-in-law has prepared a cash-flow forecast that implies a large positive NPV. This calculation assumes sale of the property after 10 years. What further calculations should you do before going ahead?

4. **Market values (S11.2)** Suppose that you are considering investing in an asset for which there is a reasonably good secondary market. Specifically, your company is Delta Airlines, and the asset is a Boeing 767—a widely used airplane. How does the presence of a secondary market simplify your problem in principle? Do you think these simplifications could be realized in practice? Explain.

5. **Market values (S11.2)** There is an active, competitive leasing (i.e., rental) market for most standard types of commercial jets. Many of the planes flown by the major domestic and international airlines are not owned by them but leased for periods ranging from a few months to several years. Gamma Airlines, however, owns two long-range DC-11s just withdrawn from Latin American service. Gamma is considering using these planes to develop the potentially lucrative new route from Akron to Yellowknife. A considerable investment in terminal facilities, training, and advertising will be required. Once committed, Gamma will have to operate the route for at least three years. One further complication: The manager of Gamma's international division is opposing commitment of the planes to the Akron–Yellowknife route because of anticipated future growth in traffic through Gamma's new hub in Ulaanbaatar. How would you evaluate the proposed Akron–Yellowknife project? Give a detailed list of the necessary steps in your analysis. Explain how the airplane leasing market would be taken into account. If the project is attractive, how would you respond to the manager of the international division?

6. **Market values (S11.2)** Suppose the current price of gold is $1,200 an ounce. Hotshot Consultants advises you that gold prices will increase at an average rate of 12% for the next two years. After that the growth rate will fall to a long-run trend of 3% per year. What is the present value of 1 million ounces of gold produced in eight years? Assume that gold prices have a beta of 0 and that the risk-free rate is 5.5%.

7. **Market values (S11.2)** On the London Metals Exchange, the price for copper to be delivered in one year is $5,500 a ton. (*Note:* Payment is made when the copper is delivered.) The risk-free interest rate is 2% and the expected market return is 8%.

   a. Suppose that you expect to produce and sell 10,000 tons of copper next year. What is the PV of this output? Assume that the sale occurs at the end of the year.
   b. If copper has a beta of 1.2, what is the expected price of copper at the end of the year? What is the certainty-equivalent end-year price?

8. **Market values (S11.2)** Photographic laboratories recover and recycle the silver used in photographic film. Stikine River Photo is considering purchase of improved equipment for their laboratory at Telegraph Creek. Here is the information they have:

   - The equipment costs $100,000 and will cost $80,000 per year to run.

   - It has an economic life of 10 years but can be depreciated over five years by the straight-line method (see Section 6-2).

   - It will recover an additional 5,000 ounces of silver per year.

   - Silver is selling for $40 per ounce. Over the past 10 years, the price of silver has appreciated by 4.5% per year in real terms. Silver is traded in an active, competitive market.

   - Stikine's marginal tax rate is 25%.

   - Stikine's company cost of capital is 8% in real terms. The nominal interest rate is 6%.

   - What is the NPV of the new equipment?

   Make additional assumptions as necessary.

9. **Market values (S11.2)** The Cambridge Opera Association has come up with a unique door prize for its December 2023 fund-raising ball: Twenty door prizes will be distributed, each one a ticket entitling the bearer to receive a cash award from the association on December 31, 2024. The cash award is to be determined by calculating the ratio of the level of the Standard and Poor's Composite Index of stock prices on December 31, 2024, to its level on June 30, 2024, and multiplying by $100. Thus, if the index turns out to be 5000 on June 30, 2024, and 5,500 on December 31, 2024, the payoff will be $100 \times (5,400/5,000) = \$110$.

   After the ball, a black market springs up in which the tickets are traded. What will the tickets sell for on January 1, 2024? On June 30, 2024? Assume the risk-free interest rate is 10% per year. Also assume the Cambridge Opera Association will be solvent at year-end 2024 and will, in fact, pay off on the tickets. Make other assumptions as necessary.

   Would ticket values be different if the tickets' payoffs depended on the Dow Jones Industrial Index rather than the Standard and Poor's Composite?

10. **Market values (S11.2)** You are asked to value a large building in northern New Jersey. The valuation is needed for a railroad bankruptcy settlement. Here are the facts:

    - The settlement requires that the building's value equal the PV of the net cash proceeds the railroad would receive if it cleared out the building and sold it for its highest and best non-railroad use, which is as a warehouse.

    - The building has been appraised at $1 million. This figure is based on actual recent selling prices of a sample of similar New Jersey buildings used as, or available for use as, warehouses.

    - If rented today as a warehouse, the building could generate $80,000 per year. This cash flow is calculated after out-of-pocket operating expenses and after real estate taxes of $50,000 per year:

Gross rents	$180,000
Operating expenses	50,000
Real estate taxes	50,000
Net	$80,000

    Gross rents, operating expenses, and real estate taxes are uncertain but are expected to grow with inflation.

    - However, it would take one year and $200,000 to clear out the railroad equipment and prepare the building for use as a warehouse. The $200,000 would have to be invested immediately.

    - The property will be put on the market when ready for use as a warehouse. Your real estate adviser says that properties of this type take, on average, one year to sell after they are put on the market. However, the railroad could rent the building as a warehouse while waiting for it to sell.

- The opportunity cost of capital for investment in real estate is 8% in real terms.

- Your real estate adviser notes that selling prices of comparable buildings in northern New Jersey have declined, in real terms, at an average rate of 2% per year over the last 10 years.

- A 5% sales commission would be paid by the railroad at the time of the sale.

- The railroad pays no income taxes. It would have to pay property taxes.

11. **Market values (S11.2)** Sulphur Ridge Mining is considering the development of a new calonium mine at Moose Bend in northern Alberta. The mine would require an upfront investment of $110 million and would produce 100,000 tons of high-grade calonium a year, which is small compared with the current annual worldwide production of 9 million tons. Proved reserves of calonium at the Moose Bend mine are 1.2 million tons. The extraction cost is estimated at $120 a ton and is expected to remain constant in real terms. The market price of calonium is currently $240 a ton, and the consultancy firm, Powder River Associates, is estimating that the real price of calonium will increase by 3% a year in real terms for the foreseeable future. There are several other producers of calonium. Several Canadian mines are believed to be barely breaking even. Others with costs in the $150 to $200 a ton range are making good profits. There are no taxes and the real cost of capital is estimated as 8%. Calonium mining is an environmentally friendly activity, and there are zero costs to shutting down a mine. Should Sulphur Ridge go ahead with the project? Make whatever additional assumptions you think are needed.

12. **Economic rents (S11.3)** True or false?

    a. A firm that earns the opportunity cost of capital is earning economic rents.

    b. A firm that invests in positive-NPV ventures expects to earn economic rents.

    c. Financial managers should try to identify areas where their firms can earn economic rents, because it is there that positive-NPV projects are likely to be found.

    d. Economic rent is the equivalent annual cost of operating capital equipment.

13. **Economic rents (S11.3)** The following table shows the expected cash flows from a project. There are no cash flows beyond year 4. The cost of capital is 7%.

    a. Calculate the project's NPV.

    b. Calculate the economic rent in year 1.

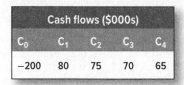

Cash flows ($000s)				
C_0	C_1	C_2	C_3	C_4
−200	80	75	70	65

14. **Economic rents (S11.3)** We characterized the interstate rail lines owned by major U.S. railroads as "strategic assets" that could generate increased profits. In what conditions would you expect these assets to generate economic rents? Keep in mind that railroads compete with trucking companies as well as other railroads. Trucking companies have some advantages, including flexibility.

15. **Economic rents (S11.3)** Thanks to acquisition of a key patent, your company now has exclusive production rights for barkelgassers (BGs) in North America. Production facilities for 200,000 BGs per year will require a $25 million immediate capital expenditure. Production costs are estimated at $65 per BG. The BG marketing manager is confident that all 200,000 units can be sold for $100 per unit (in real terms) until the patent runs out five years hence. After that the marketing manager hasn't a clue about what the selling price will be. What is the NPV of the BG project? Assume the real cost of capital is 9%. To keep things simple, also make the following assumptions:

- The technology for making BGs will not change. Capital and production costs will stay the same in real terms.
- Competitors know the technology and can enter as soon as the patent expires, that is, they can construct new plants in year 5 and start selling BGs in year 6.
- If your company invests immediately, full production begins after 12 months, that is, in year 1.
- There are no taxes.
- BG production facilities last 12 years. They have no salvage value at the end of their useful life.

16. **Economic rents (S11.3)** How would your answer to Problem 15 change if technological improvements reduce the cost of new BG production facilities by 3% per year? Thus a new plant built in year 1 would cost only 25 (1 − 0.03) = $24.25 million, a plant built in year 2 would cost $23.52 million, and so on. Assume that production costs per unit remain at $65.

17. **Economic rents (S11.3)** Reevaluate the NPV of the proposed polyzone project (Example 11.6) under each of the following assumptions. What's the right management decision in each case?

a. Spread in year 4 holds at $1.20 per pound.

b. The U.S. chemical company can start up polyzone production at 40 million pounds in year 1 rather than year 2.

c. The U.S. company makes a technological advance that reduces its annual production costs to $25 million. Competitors' production costs do not change.

18. **Equilibrium prices (S11.3)** Demand for concave utility meters is expanding rapidly, but the industry is highly competitive. A utility meter plant costs $50 million to set up, and it has an annual capacity of 500,000 meters. The production cost is $5 per meter, and this cost is not expected to change. The machines have an indefinite physical life and the cost of capital is 10%. What is the competitive price of a utility meter?

a. $5

b. $10

c. $15

19. **Opportunity costs (S11.3)** New-model commercial airplanes are much more fuel-efficient than older models. How is it possible for airlines flying older models to make money when its competitors are flying newer planes? Explain briefly.

CHALLENGE PROBLEMS

20. **Economic rents (S11.3)** Accidental setbacks can result in negative rents in any year. But can a project have *expected* positive rents in some years and negative expected rents in other years? Explain.

21. **Economic rents (S11.3)** The manufacture of polysyllabic acid is a competitive industry. Most plants have an annual output of 100,000 tons. Operating costs are $0.90 a ton, and the sales price is $1 a ton. A 100,000-ton plant costs $100,000 and has an indefinite life. Its current scrap value of $60,000 is expected to decline to $57,900 over the next two years.

Phlogiston Inc. proposes to invest $100,000 in a plant that employs a new low-cost process to manufacture polysyllabic acid. The plant has the same capacity as existing units, but operating costs are $0.85 a ton. Phlogiston estimates that it has two years' lead over each of its rivals in use of the process but is unable to build any more plants itself before year 2. Also it believes that demand over the next two years is likely to be sluggish and that its new plant will therefore cause temporary overcapacity.

You can assume that there are no taxes and that the cost of capital is 10%.

a. By the end of year 2, the prospective increase in acid demand will require the construction of several new plants using the Phlogiston process. What is the likely NPV of such plants?

b. What does that imply for the price of polysyllabic acid in year 3 and beyond?

c. Would you expect existing plant to be scrapped in year 2? How would your answer differ if scrap value were $40,000 or $80,000?

d. The acid plants of United Alchemists Inc. have been fully depreciated. Can it operate them profitably after year 2?

e. Acidosis Inc. purchased a new plant last year for $100,000 and is writing it down by $10,000 a year. Should it scrap this plant in year 2?

f. What would be the NPV of Phlogiston's venture?

22. **Economic rents (S11.3)** Taxes are a cost, and, therefore, changes in tax rates can affect consumer prices, project lives, and the value of existing firms. The following problem illustrates this. It also illustrates that tax changes that appear to be "good for business" do not always increase the value of existing firms. Indeed, unless new investment incentives increase consumer demand, they can work only by rendering existing equipment obsolete.

The manufacture of bucolic acid is a competitive business. Demand is steadily expanding, and new plants are constantly being opened. Expected cash flows from an investment in a new plant are as follows:

	0	1	2	3
1. Initial investment	100			
2. Revenues		100	100	100
3. Cash operating costs		50	50	50
4. Tax depreciation		33.33	33.33	33.33
5. Income pretax		16.67	16.67	16.67
6. Tax at 40%		6.67	6.67	6.67
7. Net income		10	10	10
8. After-tax salvage				15
9. Cash flow (7 + 8 + 4 − 1)	−100	+43.33	+43.33	+58.33
NPV at 20% = 0				

Assumptions:
1. Tax depreciation is straight-line over three years.
2. Pretax salvage value is 25 in year 3 and 50 if the asset is scrapped in year 2.
3. Tax on salvage value is 40% of the difference between salvage value and depreciated investment.
4. The cost of capital is 20%.

a. What is the value of a one-year-old plant? Of a two-year-old plant?

b. Suppose that the government now changes tax depreciation to allow a 100% write-off in year 1. How does this affect the value of existing one- and two-year-old plants? Existing plants must continue using the original tax depreciation schedule.

c. Would it now make sense to scrap existing plants when they are two rather than three years old?

d. How would your answers change if the corporate income tax were abolished entirely?

23. **Equilibrium prices (S11.3)** The world airline system is composed of the routes X and Y, each of which requires 10 aircraft. These routes can be serviced by three types of aircraft—A, B, and C. There are 5 type A aircraft available, 10 type B, and 10 type C. These aircraft are identical except for their operating costs, which are as follows:

Aircraft Type	Annual Operating Cost ($ millions)	
	Route X	Route Y
A	1.5	1.5
B	2.5	2.0
C	4.5	3.5

The aircraft have a useful life of five years and a salvage value of $1 million.

The aircraft owners do not operate the aircraft themselves but rent them to the operators. Owners act competitively to maximize their rental income, and operators attempt to minimize their operating costs. Airfares are also competitively determined. Assume the cost of capital is 10%.

a. Which aircraft would be used on which route, and how much would each aircraft be worth?

b. What would happen to usage and prices of each aircraft if the number of type A aircraft increased to 10?

c. What would happen if the number of type A aircraft increased to 15?

d. What would happen if the number of type A aircraft increased to 20?

State any additional assumptions you need to make.

• • • • •

SOLUTIONS
TO SELF-TEST
QUESTIONS

11.1 a. An example of overoptimism

b. Probably overconfidence. But it could be a rational (but regrettable) way for managers to try to maximize the benefits of their position

c. An example of overconfidence

11.2 A project with a cash flow of $100 in year 1 is worth $100/1.10 = \$90.91$ at a 10% discount rate and is worth $100/1.15 = \$86.96$ at a 15% discount rate, a reduction of 4.4%. One with a cash flow of $100 in year 10 is worth $100/1.10^{10} = \$38.55$ at a 10% discount rate and is worth $100/1.15^{10} = \$24.72$ at a 15% discount rate, a reduction of 35.9%. Adding a fudge factor to the discount rate penalizes long-lived projects.

11.3 The annual rent charged on similar buildings.

11.4 Economic income $= C_t + (PV_t - PV_{t-1}) = 5 + 60 - 50 = \$15$
Economic rent $= (C_t + PV_t - PV_{t-1}) - r\,PV_{t-1} = (5 + 60 - 50) - (0.1 \times 50) = \$10$

11.5 The value of existing assets declines faster. In a growth industry, companies will prosper only if their technological advantage allows them to find projects with positive NPVs that more than offset the decline in the value of their existing assets.

11.6 The salvage value of an asset is an opportunity cost of staying in business. The higher this opportunity cost, the easier it is for new entrants to replace existing producers, who can sell their existing assets or redeploy them more profitably.

MINI-CASE •••••

Ecsy-Cola[24]

Libby Flannery, the regional manager of Ecsy-Cola, the international soft drinks empire, was reviewing her investment plans for Central Asia. She had contemplated launching Ecsy-Cola in the ex-Soviet republic of Inglistan in 2025. This would involve a capital outlay of $20 million in 2024 to build a bottling plant and set up a distribution system there. Fixed costs (for manufacturing, distribution, and marketing) would then be $3 million per year from 2025 onward. This would be sufficient to make and sell 200 million liters per year—enough for every man, woman, and child in Inglistan to drink four bottles per week! But there would be few savings from building a smaller plant, and import tariffs and transport costs in the region would keep all production within national borders.

The variable costs of production and distribution would be 12 cents per liter. Company policy requires a rate of return of 25% in nominal dollar terms, after local taxes but before deducting any costs of financing. The sales revenue is forecasted to be 35 cents per liter.

Bottling plants last almost forever, and all unit costs and revenues were expected to remain constant in nominal terms. Tax would be payable at a rate of 30%, and under the Inglistan corporate tax code, capital expenditures can be written off on a straight-line basis over four years.

All these inputs were reasonably clear. But Ms. Flannery racked her brain trying to forecast sales. Ecsy-Cola found that the "1–2–4" rule works in most new markets. Sales typically double in the second year, double again in the third year, and after that remain roughly constant. Her best guess was that, if she went ahead immediately, initial sales in Inglistan would be 12.5 million liters in 2026, ramping up to 50 million in 2028 and onward.

Ms. Flannery also worried whether it would be better to wait a year. The soft drink market was developing rapidly in neighboring countries, and in a year's time she should have a much better idea whether Ecsy-Cola would be likely to catch on in Inglistan. If it didn't catch on and sales stalled below 20 million liters, a large investment probably would not be justified.

Ms. Flannery had assumed that Ecsy-Cola's keen rival, Sparky-Cola, would not also enter the market. But last week she received a shock when, in the lobby of the Kapitaliste Hotel, she bumped into her opposite number at Sparky-Cola. Sparky-Cola would face costs similar to Ecsy-Cola. How would Sparky-Cola respond if Ecsy-Cola entered the market? Would it decide to enter also? If so, how would that affect the profitability of Ecsy-Cola's project?

Ms. Flannery thought again about postponing investment for a year. Suppose Sparky-Cola were interested in the Inglistan market. Would that favor delay or immediate action?

Maybe Ecsy-Cola should announce its plans before Sparky-Cola has a chance to develop its own proposals. It seemed that the Inglistan project was becoming more complicated by the day.

QUESTIONS

1. Calculate the NPV of the proposed investment, using the inputs suggested in this case. How sensitive is this NPV to future sales volume?

2. What are the pros and cons of waiting for a year before deciding whether to invest? (*Hint:* What happens if demand turns out high and Sparky-Cola also invests? What if Ecsy-Cola invests right away and gains a one-year head start on Sparky-Cola?)

---

[24]We thank Anthony Neuberger for suggesting this topic.

12

Efficient Markets and Behavioral Finance

Up to this point, we have concentrated almost exclusively on the left-hand side of the balance sheet—the firm's capital investment decision. Now we move to the right-hand side and to the problems involved in financing the capital investments. To put it crudely, you've learned how to spend money; now learn how to raise it.

Of course, we haven't totally ignored financing in earlier chapters. We introduced the weighted-average cost of capital, for example. But in most places, we took the opportunity cost of capital as given. We didn't ask how the cost of capital might be affected by financing.

Now we are turning the problem around. We take the firm's present portfolio of real assets and its future investment strategy as given, and then we determine the best financing strategy. For example,

- Should the firm reinvest most of its earnings in the business, or distribute the cash to shareholders?

- Is it better to distribute cash to stockholders by paying out dividends or by repurchasing stock?

- If the firm needs more money, should it issue more stock or should it borrow?

The purpose of holding the firm's capital investment decision constant is to separate that decision from the financing decision. Strictly speaking, this assumes that investment and financing decisions are *independent*. In many circumstances, this is a reasonable assumption. The firm is generally free to change its capital structure by repurchasing one security and issuing another. In that case, there is no need to associate a particular investment project with a particular source of cash. The firm can think, first,

about which projects to accept and, second, about how they should be financed.

Sometimes decisions about capital structure depend on project choice or vice versa, and in those cases, the investment and financing decisions have to be considered jointly. However, we defer discussion of such interactions of financing and investment decisions until Chapter 18.

12.1 Differences between Investment and Financing Decisions

We start this chapter by contrasting investment and financing decisions. The objective in each case is the same—to maximize NPV. However, if markets are efficient, the financial manager can assume that financial assets are fairly priced, so that it may be hard to find positive-NPV financing opportunities.

12.2 The Efficient Market Hypothesis

We define the efficient market hypothesis more carefully in Section 12.2. The hypothesis comes in three forms, weak, semistrong, and strong, depending on the types of information available to investors.

12.3 Implications of Market Efficiency

Market efficiency has a number of important implications. In particular, it implies that the paths followed by stock prices are random walks and their serial correlation will be near zero. Another implication is that all securities are fairly priced and there are no good or bad investments. This suggests investors should maximize the benefits of diversification by holding the market portfolio. Stock prices can be trusted by investors because they indicate fundamental values of firms. Finally, firm financing decisions neither create nor destroy value.

12.4 Are Markets Efficient? The Evidence
In this section we consider the evidence for market efficiency. While there is much evidence that is consistent with it, there is also some evidence that is difficult to reconcile with it.

12-5 Behavioral Finance
Given this mixed evidence for market efficiency, we look at whether human psychology combined with costs of arbitrage can help to explain how anomalies that are inconsistent with market efficiency can persist. This approach is known as behavioral finance. We consider the challenge it poses to market efficiency.

• • • • •

12-1   **Differences between Investment and Financing Decisions**

A fundamental difference between investment and financing decisions is that it's easier to make money through the former. When a firm considers investment decisions, it does *not* face perfect, competitive product markets. It may have only a few competitors that specialize in the same line of business in the same geographical area. And it may own some unique assets that give it an edge over its competitors. Often, these assets are intangible, such as patents, expertise, or reputation. All of these open up the opportunity to make superior profits and find projects with positive NPVs—for example, launching a new product that uses the firm's specific expertise.

Financial markets are much more competitive than product markets. In financial markets, your competition is all other corporations seeking funds, to say nothing of the state, local, and federal governments that go to New York, London, Singapore, and other financial centers to raise money. The investors who supply financing are comparably numerous, and they are smart. Money attracts brains.

Due to this competition, it's much harder for a company to find positive-NPV financing strategies than positive-NPV investment strategies. For example, attempting to sell your shares for a higher price than their true value is unlikely to be fruitful; smart investors will realize that your shares are overpriced and simply buy those of your competitors. This suggests that companies should focus more on real decisions—making great products, developing a strong brand, and investing in human capital—rather than fine-tuning their financing.

The heart of this argument is the assumption that prices of financial assets are right, or as right as humans can get them. In other words, we assume that prices are set in *efficient financial markets*. To explain what this assumption means for the financial manager a bit more precisely, let's go back to perhaps her most fundamental responsibility: evaluating investment decisions.

NPV Matters for Both Investment and Financing Decisions

Any investment decision also involves a financing decision. If a company builds a new factory, it may need to issue a bond to finance the construction. Even if the company has cash ready and waiting in the bank, spending that cash on the factory is still a financing decision: The cash could otherwise be used to repay a loan or buy back shares.

Both investment and financing decisions involve trading an *asset*—something that gives you a claim to future cash flows. The factory is a real asset and the company is buying it. The bond is a financial asset and the company is selling it. But these real versus financial, buying versus selling distinctions don't matter. Any decision to buy or sell an asset should depend on its NPV. For the factory, the NPV is the future cash flows from the factory minus the cost of building it. For the bond, the NPV is the cash received up-front minus the future interest and principal repayments to the bondholders. We always come back to NPV.

The NPV of Financing Decisions Is Zero in Efficient Markets

As a result, when deciding whether to build the factory, the financial manager needs to calculate two separate NPVs: one for the factory and one for the bond. Part One of this book explained how to do the former, so here we'll focus on the latter. Let's consider a new 10-year bond issue by GENZ Corporation. The issue will raise $100 million for a new factory. The interest rate is 7%. GENZ tried to negotiate a lower rate, but potential investors pointed out that 7% is the prevailing market interest rate on 10-year bonds issued by other companies with the same financial strength and bond rating as GENZ. If GENZ wants to sell the new bonds for $1,000 each, it will have to pay 7% interest on that $1,000.

Would you purchase the bond at this price? Before doing so, you decide to do an NPV calculation. You write out investment and interest payments.

NPV = −$1,000 + PV of interest payments at 7% of $1,000 + PV of principal ($1,000 repaid in year 10)

$$NPV = -\$1,000 + \sum_{t=1}^{10} \frac{\$70}{1.07^t} + \frac{\$1,000}{1.07^{10}} = 0$$

NPV = 0 because buying a GENZ bond gives you the prevailing market rate of return.

GENZ's CFO now decides to calculate the NPV of the bond issue for GENZ. Her calculation is similar to yours, with signs reversed of course. The NPV of each bond that GENZ sells is:

$$NPV = +\$1,000 - \sum_{t=1}^{10} \frac{\$70}{1.07^t} - \frac{\$1,000}{1.07^{10}} = 0$$

Again we have NPV = 0. This makes sense: If the bond is fairly priced for investors, it must likewise be fairly priced for her company.

It's important to highlight the assumptions embedded in our example. We've ignored transaction costs, which we cover in Chapter 15. We've ignored taxes. We'll see in Chapter 18 that interest payments create valuable tax deductions. But our most important assumption was to trust the bond market. We accepted the prevailing interest rate of 7% and assumed that it is the correct discount rate for the cash flows from GENZ bonds—that it reflects the return that we could earn on bonds of similar risk, and so it reflects the opportunity cost of investing in GENZ. In other words, we accepted the *efficient market hypothesis* for bonds.

When the above assumptions hold, there is an important implication: *Financing decisions are zero-NPV.* Recall that every investment decision involves a financing decision and, thus, potentially two complex calculations. But if the NPV of the financing decision is zero, it can be ignored, and the CFO only needs to calculate the NPV of the investment.

The NPV of Financing Decisions in Inefficient Markets

What if the efficient market hypothesis doesn't hold? Then GENZ may be able to get an interest rate *less* than the prevailing market rate. One reason may be a subsidy. Suppose New York State offers to lend at 3% if GENZ locates the new factory in New York instead of New Jersey. That offer is positive-NPV:

$$NPV = +\$1,000 - \sum_{t=1}^{10} \frac{\$30}{1.07^t} + \frac{\$1,000}{1.07^{10}} = \$281$$

The subsidized rate of 3% means that the future interest payments are only $30 rather than $70. Importantly, the discount rate remains at 7%, and so the denominators of the NPV calculation are unchanged. That's because the risk of GENZ is unchanged, so the opportunity cost of lending to GENZ is still 7%. If, instead of lending to GENZ, New York State bought the bonds of another company with similar risk, it would receive a 7% return. Recall that the opportunity cost, and thus the correct discount rate, depends only on what investors could receive elsewhere and is unaffected by what they're actually receiving.

"Intentional" loan subsidies like the one just discussed are rare and mainly given by governments wanting to encourage particular types of investment. But "unintentional" loan subsidies can be common if markets are inefficient. Investors should be charging GENZ 7% because it's a risky company. But what if credit rating agencies incorrectly judge it as being low-risk and give it an AAA credit rating? Then, investors might only charge 3%; as we've shown, you'll have taken out a positive-NPV loan.

Why does this matter? If the only implication is that GENZ's new bondholders lose and GENZ (and thus its shareholders) gain, we might not be too concerned, since this is simply a transfer from one set of investors to another. But there's a much more serious consequence. If investing in the factory was a negative-NPV decision, when we add in the NPV of the loan it now might become positive-NPV overall. Then, GENZ may make the investment even though it destroys value.[1] Indeed, mispricing of loans is believed to be a major contributor to the financial crisis of 2007–2009. Because banks could obtain cheap financing, they made investments that they wouldn't have done otherwise—for example, lending to risky borrowers who ended up being unable to repay.

So whether the efficient markets hypothesis holds isn't just an academic debate. It has profound implications for financial managers and the functioning of the economy as a whole. We'll shortly discuss other practical implications of market efficiency and then review the evidence both for and against it. But, before we do so, it's important that we define market efficiency precisely so that we know what we're debating. It's to this topic that we now turn.

12.1 Self-Test

A company operating in efficient capital markets can choose one of two mutually exclusive projects. Project A has an NPV of $20 million, lasts for 7 years, and can be financed entirely by a bank loan with an 8% interest rate. Project B has an NPV of $50 million, lasts for 10 years, and can be financed entirely by equity with a 15% cost of capital.

   a. Which project should the firm undertake?

   b. Assume now that A lasts for 10 years and B lasts for 7 years; all other details are unchanged. Which project should the firm undertake now?

12-2   The Efficient Market Hypothesis

What does it mean for the market to be efficient? The most common definition is thanks to Eugene Fama, who shared the 2013 Nobel Prize for his contributions to the topic. He defined an efficient market as one in which prices reflect *all available information*.[2] In this chapter, we'll focus on whether the stock market is efficient, but the hypothesis also applies to markets for bonds and other securities. Focusing on stocks, Fama's definition implies the following for a stock price:

$$P_0 = \sum_{t=0}^{\infty} \frac{D_t}{(1+r)^t} I_0 \tag{12.1}$$

---

[1]In Section 12-4, we'll explain that the implications are actually more complicated than this. Even if the loan is positive-NPV, it need not mean that GENZ should undertake a negative-NPV investment if it had the option to simply hold onto the cash (or invest it in another zero-NPV decision).

[2]Fama, Eugene F. (1970): "Efficient Capital Markets: A Review of Theory and Empirical Work." *Journal of Finance* 25, 383-417; Fama, Eugene F. (1976): "Efficient Capital Markets: Reply". *Journal of Finance* 31, 143-145.

We've seen most of this equation before, in Section 4-2. Back then we explained that the stock price equals the expected value of future dividends, discounted at a rate that reflects their risk. Equation 12-1 contains two new elements: the vertical bar means "given," and the I_0 means "all information available at time 0." When the market forecasts future dividends and risk, it uses all information that is available today. So the "price is right"—it contains all relevant information.

What sort of information? Let's consider a trader valuing Apple stock. Relevant information might be the state of the U.S. economy, customer reviews of the iPhone versus its competitors, and the market consensus on the quality of Apple management. But the crucial word in Fama's definition is "all." It means that every bit of information that's relevant to forecasting Apple's dividends—even if it's only tangentially relevant—should be reflected in the stock price. For example, let's say that there's the possibility of a military coup in Peru. That's relevant information, since Apple might sell 0.5% of its iPhones there. So if a coup occurs, this would hit the Peruvian economy and reduce iPhone sales. We can immediately see how market efficiency is far from a foregone conclusion and might not hold in practice. Perhaps the main investors who trade Apple stock are based in the United States and don't know what's happening in Peru.

A second definition of market efficiency is thanks to Michael Jensen.[3] He defined a market as efficient if it's impossible to make excess returns by trading on available information. This definition means the following:

$$E(R_1|I_0) = E(R_1) \tag{12.2}$$

If markets are efficient, the expected return to a trading strategy that uses some information equals the expected return without that information. In other words, information won't help you increase your expected return. Let's say that CEOs with MBA (Master of Business Administration) degrees perform better. Then it might seem a good idea to painstakingly gather the educational background of every CEO in the S&P 500, buy the firms headed by an MBA-minted CEO, and sell all other stocks. But if the market is efficient, then it knows that companies run by MBA-minted CEOs will be more profitable. So their shares will be more expensive—again, "the price is right"—so your trading strategy won't make any money.

What's the difference between the two definitions? Under Fama's, if the present value of future dividends equals $300, the price must be exactly $300. But under Jensen, the price might be $299.95 and the market could still be efficient. The crux is the phrase "*excess returns*," which means returns after adjusting for taxes, transactions costs, and risk.[4] Even though the educational background of CEOs is publicly available, you'll also need to pay transactions costs to put on your trading strategy. If these costs exceed 5 cents per share, then you can't make excess returns.

In most developed markets, and for large investors who are particularly relevant for determining stock prices, these costs are small. So we'll use both definitions interchangeably in this chapter, but will point out the cases in which they differ.

Forms of Market Efficiency

We've already emphasized one important component of the market efficiency definition: An efficient market incorporates *all* available information. But what about the second component, "available"? What do we mean by available information? There are three ways to define it, which in turn implies three forms of market efficiency.

Weak-form efficiency defines "available information" as "information contained in past prices." If the market is weak-form efficient, then any information you could have inferred

---

[3]Jensen, Michael C. (1978): "Some Anomalous Evidence Regarding Market Efficiency." *Journal of Financial Economics* 6, 95-101.
[4]Note that risk is also taken into account in Fama's definition, since risk determines the appropriate discount rate in Equation 12-1.

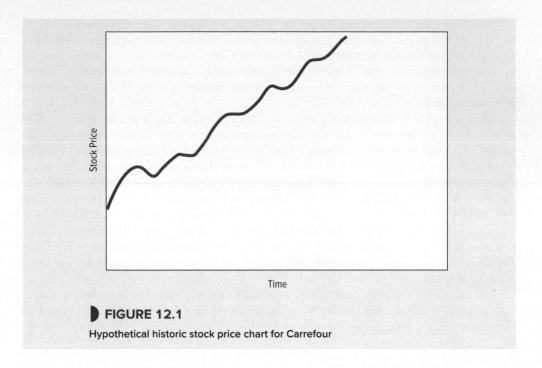

▶ **FIGURE 12.1**

Hypothetical historic stock price chart for Carrefour

from past prices is already in the current stock price. So, knowing past stock prices doesn't help you predict future returns.

Let's give an example. Say the stock price chart of French supermarket Carrefour is as shown in Figure 12.1. The stock price has risen over the past month. You might think that the stock has "momentum" and will continue to rise. In other words, a recent price increase is a buy signal. But if the stock market is efficient, then knowing that recent returns were high tells you nothing about future returns—Carrefour is just as likely to go up in the future as it is to go down.[5] What happened in the past is irrelevant because *markets have no memory.*

And remember that market efficiency refers to "*all* available information." If the market is weak-form efficient, *no* information about past prices is useful—not just Carrefour's past month return, but its return over the past year, its 52-week high, its 20-day moving average, and so on. The stock market is like a coin flip. If you have a fair coin, knowing how many heads there were in the past 10 flips doesn't help you predict whether the next toss will be heads or tails. The same is true for the past 22, 37, or 639 flips.

Some traders, known as technical analysts, or more informally "chartists," use stock price charts to devise trading strategies. Even traders who look at a broader set of information, such as the state of the U.S. economy and customer reviews, typically still look at stock price charts. That's why charts are available on Yahoo! Finance and Bloomberg. But if markets are weak-form efficient, these charts don't help you formulate your trading strategy because *technical analysis* does not produce excess returns. You often see the phrase "past performance is not a guide to future performance" in advertisements for financial products, and you might think that it's just a legal disclaimer. But if markets are weak-form efficient, this statement holds true.

---

[5]This assumes that there is no "drift" to the stock price, i.e. the expected return is zero. If Carrefour has an expected monthly return is 1%, then the statement continues to hold with a small modification: Carrefour's stock return is just as likely to exceed 1% over the next month than it is to fall below 1%.

Semistrong-form efficiency defines "available information" as "public information." This includes past prices, but also any other information available from public sources, such as the Internet, annual reports, and the media. For example, it could include the company's credit rating, recent profits, analyst earnings forecasts, and newspaper speculation on a potential change in CEO.

If markets are semistrong-form efficient, then *fundamental analysis* does not produce excess returns. Fundamental analysis, as the name suggests, scrutinizes a company's fundamentals, such as its management quality, competitive position, and financial strength, using public information. Most professional investors, such as hedge funds and mutual funds, engage in fundamental analysis. But, if markets are semistrong-form efficient, such activity is fruitless. You'd be just as well off holding the market portfolio, as we advocated in Chapter 8. We'll revisit this implication in Section 12-3.

Strong-form efficiency defines "available information" as both public and private information. Private information is information that's not publicly available, such as a pharmaceutical company's executives knowing how its R&D efforts are progressing. If the market is strong-form efficient, then even insiders wouldn't be able to make money.

Whether a piece of information counts as public or private is sometimes a gray area, so the line between strong-form and semistrong-form efficiency is blurred. If a hedge fund uses public information to form its own valuation of a stock, some people say it's using public information; others say the information is private (particularly if the hedge fund uses a proprietary valuation model). However, this distinction won't matter for most of the implications that we will discuss.

The relationship between the different forms of market efficiency can be seen in Figure 12.2. Weak-form efficiency holds if prices incorporate information contained in past prices, which is the small circle. Semistrong-form efficiency holds if prices incorporate public information. Public information is reflected by the large circle, which contains everything in the small circle plus additional information outside the small circle (e.g., credit rating, recent profits, analyst earnings forecasts). Strong-form efficiency holds if prices incorporate both public and private information, which is reflected by the square.

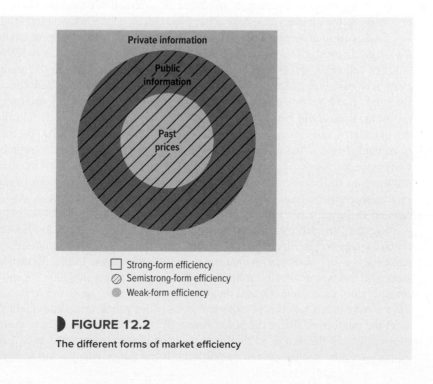

☐ Strong-form efficiency
⊘ Semistrong-form efficiency
● Weak-form efficiency

▶ **FIGURE 12.2**

The different forms of market efficiency

As a result, if markets are strong-form efficient, they must also be semistrong-form efficient. If prices contain everything in the square, they'll automatically contain everything in the large circle. Similarly, if markets are semistrong-form efficient, they must also be weak-form efficient. If prices contain everything in the large circle, they'll automatically contain everything in the small circle.

Conversely, when we talk about *inefficiency,* the implications go in the opposite direction. If markets are not weak-form efficient, they can't be semistrong-form efficient. If prices don't even contain everything in the small circle, they can't hope to contain everything in the large circle. Similarly, if markets aren't semistrong-form efficient, they can't be strong-form efficient. If prices don't even contain everything in the large circle, they can't hope to contain everything in the square.

12.2 Self-Test

Assume the following statements are true. Which forms of market efficiency do they violate? Ensure that you state all applicable forms.

    a. The price of a company rises just before a takeover bid on it (previously known to the negotiating parties) is announced.

    b. Companies included in the list of the Best Companies to Work For beat the market.

    c. Stocks earn higher returns on average than bonds.

    d. Companies with corporate jets underperform the market

    e. Stocks that have performed well recently continue to outperform in the future.

Why Do We Expect Markets to Be Efficient?

In Section 12-4, we'll study the evidence for whether the efficient markets hypothesis holds in the real world. But before testing it with the data, let's test it with common sense: Are there plausible reasons to think that this hypothesis might be valid?

There are indeed—because of *arbitrage.* If prices don't take into account all available information, then traders can make money by trading on the information ignored by the market. Let's consider semistrong-form efficiency, but you can construct analogous examples for weak- or strong-form efficiency. Assume that Apple's stock price is $299, but its present value of future dividends is $300 because news has just broken out that political tensions in Peru have eased. A hedge fund noticing this will see that Apple is underpriced and will buy the stock. If it buys one share, it can only expect to make $1, so it doesn't seem worth it. But the hedge fund could buy 1 million shares, and expect to make a tidy $1 million. The act of buying shares will cause the stock price to go up, let's say to $299.90. Yet there's still money to be made because the stock is still underpriced. So the hedge fund continues to buy shares. Only once the stock price has risen to $300 (i.e., it incorporates all available information) are there no further incentives to buy and sell. So the "selfish" actions of the hedge fund— buying shares to make money for itself—have a social benefit in making markets efficient. (In Section 12-3, we'll explain why efficient markets in turn are good for society).

Note that this arbitrage is different from the one in Chapter 3. In that chapter, we dealt with risk-free bonds. Since the future payoff from such bonds is guaranteed, we had a *riskless arbitrage*—a sure-fire way of making money. With shares, future dividends are uncertain. Based on the best available information, their present value is $300. But the economy could unexpectedly take a tumble, and the present value actually turns out to be $240. So we only have a *risky arbitrage;* the $1 expected profit is not guaranteed. You might think this would limit the number of shares the hedge fund will buy, and if it buys fewer shares, then it won't move prices all the way to $300. But, if the hedge fund is very large, even 1 million shares in Apple would be a small part of its portfolio. It can put on many arbitrage trades on different stocks. As we saw in Chapter 7, the specific risk of each trade will wash away in a large portfolio. What about market risk? That will also wash away if the hedge fund pursues a *market-neutral* strategy. Some arbitrages will involve buying underpriced stock; others will involve selling overpriced stock. So it can construct an arbitrage portfolio that has a zero beta and, thus, bears neither specific nor market risk.

This discussion has two important implications. The first is that market efficiency is a theory of "sharks," not of the average investor. The efficient market hypothesis doesn't assume that every investor uses all available information. All four of your authors are unremarkably average investors. None of us knows the political situation in every country relevant for the stocks we hold. And even if we did have perfect information, we might make mistakes when processing it, as we'll discuss in Section 12-5. But we don't matter for market prices because, being poor academics, we only trade small amounts. The efficient market hypothesis only requires a few large investors—experts, similar to card sharks in a card game—to be able to spot mispricings and trade on them. It assumes markets are Darwinian: These investors became large because they're skilled at noticing relevant information and processing it correctly; as a result, they've made money and grown big. So the large traders who drive market prices are traders who correctly use all available information, so their trades put this information into prices.

The second implication is that market efficiency can never be perfect. You might notice there's a bit of a paradox in the preceding example. It's the trades of the hedge fund that make markets efficient. But the hedge fund only has incentives to trade if markets aren't fully efficient to begin with—if its information isn't currently in the stock price. So markets must be at least a little bit inefficient to provide incentives for investors to gather and trade on information to make efficient.

If you noticed this paradox, good job. Unfortunately, you're more than 40 years too late. This paradox was discovered by one of the most famous finance papers of all time, published by Grossman and Stiglitz in 1980, called "On the Impossibility of Informationally Efficient Markets," which helped Joseph Stiglitz win the Nobel Prize in 2001.[6] Too bad you weren't born a few decades earlier.

Regrets aside, what this discussion means is that market efficiency isn't a black-and-white concept because markets can never be perfectly efficient. Market efficiency is more about the *speed* at which information is incorporated into prices. If the hedge fund is the only large trader, then its information is incorporated quickly, so the market is relatively efficient. But there could be lots of other investors trading randomly for reasons other than information, such as selling shares to buy a house. These so-called *noise traders* will dilute the impact of the hedge fund's trades. Its information will have little effect on prices, so the market is relatively inefficient. Thus, we can talk about a market becoming more or less efficient or compare the efficiency of two markets. But there's no clear cutoff speed that a market has to cross to be classified as "efficient" or "inefficient."

12-3   Implications of Market Efficiency

Having defined market efficiency, we now discuss why it matters. Why do we care about whether the efficient market hypothesis holds in the real world? There are several important implications of market efficiency for both investors and managers.

Stock Prices Follow Random Walks   As is so often the case with important ideas, the concept of efficient capital markets stemmed from a chance discovery. In 1953, Maurice Kendall, a British

---

[6]Grossman, Sanford J., and Joseph E. Stiglitz. "On the Impossibility of Informationally Efficient Markets." *The American Economic Review* 70, no. 3 (1980): 393–408. http://www.jstor.org/stable/1805228.

statistician, presented a controversial paper to the Royal Statistical Society on the behavior of stock and commodity prices.[7] Kendall had expected to find regular price cycles, but to his surprise they did not seem to exist. Each series appeared to be "a 'wandering' one, almost as if once a week the Demon of Chance drew a random number . . . and added it to the current price to determine the next week's price." In other words, prices seemed to follow a *random walk*.

He had stumbled upon an implication of weak-form efficiency. If markets are weak-form efficient, then stock prices are random walks—price changes are random and, in particular, are unrelated to past price changes. A stock moves similar to a beach ball being kicked on a windy day (or for baseball fans, a knuckleball pitch thrown in baseball; or for physicists, the Brownian motion of a particle).

Figure 12.3 illustrates this for four stocks from different markets—Microsoft, BP, Sony, and Deutsche Bank. Each panel shows the change in price of the stock on successive days. The circled dot in the southeast quadrant of the Microsoft panel refers to a pair of days in which a 2.9% increase was followed by a 2.9% decrease. If there were a systematic tendency for increases to be followed by decreases, there would be many dots in the southeast quadrant and few in the northeast quadrant. It is obvious from a glance that there's very little pattern in these price movements, but we can test this more precisely by calculating the correlation coefficient between each day's price change and the next. If price movements persisted, the correlation would be positive; if there were no relationship, it would be 0. In our example, the correlation between successive price changes in Microsoft stock was −0.047; there was a negligible tendency for price rises to be followed by price falls.[8] For the three other stocks, the correlation was also very close to zero.

Figure 12.3 suggests that successive price changes of all four stocks were effectively uncorrelated. Today's price change gave investors almost no clue as to the likely change tomorrow. Does that surprise you? If so, imagine that it were not the case and that changes in Microsoft's stock price were expected to persist for several months. Figure 12.4 provides an example of such a predictable cycle. You can see that an upswing in Microsoft's stock price started last month, when the price was $40, and it is expected to carry the price to $80 next month. What will happen when investors perceive this bonanza? It will self-destruct. Since investors think that Microsoft's stock will rise to $80, it is a bargain at $60 so they'll rush to buy. They'll only stop buying once the stock price is the present value of $80, so that it offers a normal risk-adjusted rate of return. Therefore, as soon as a cycle becomes apparent to investors, they immediately eliminate it by their trading.

You should see now why prices in competitive markets must follow a random walk. If past price changes could be used to predict future price changes, investors could make easy profits. But in competitive markets, there are no such free lunches. As investors try to take advantage of any information in past prices, prices adjust immediately until the superior profits from studying price movements disappear. As a result, all the information in past prices will be reflected in today's stock price, not tomorrow's. Patterns in prices will no longer exist, and price changes in one period will be independent of changes in the next. In other words, the share price will follow a random walk.

The next four implications follow from semistrong-form efficiency.

---

[7]See M. G. Kendall, "The Analysis of Economic Time Series, Part I. Prices," *Journal of the Royal Statistical Society* 96 (1953), pp. 11–25. Kendall's idea was not wholly new. It had been proposed in an almost forgotten thesis written 53 years earlier by a French doctoral student, Louis Bachelier. Bachelier's accompanying development of the mathematical theory of random processes anticipated by five years Einstein's famous work on the random Brownian motion of colliding gas molecules. See L. Bachelier, *Théorie de la Speculation* (Paris: Gauthiers-Villars, 1900). Reprinted in English (A. J. Boness, trans.) in P. H. Cootner (ed.), *The Random Character of Stock Market Prices* (Cambridge, MA: MIT Press, 1964), pp. 17–78.

[8]The correlation coefficient between successive observations is known as the *autocorrelation coefficient*. An autocorrelation of −.037 implies that, if Microsoft's stock price rose by 1% more than the average yesterday, your best forecast of today's change would be a mere .037% *less* than the average.

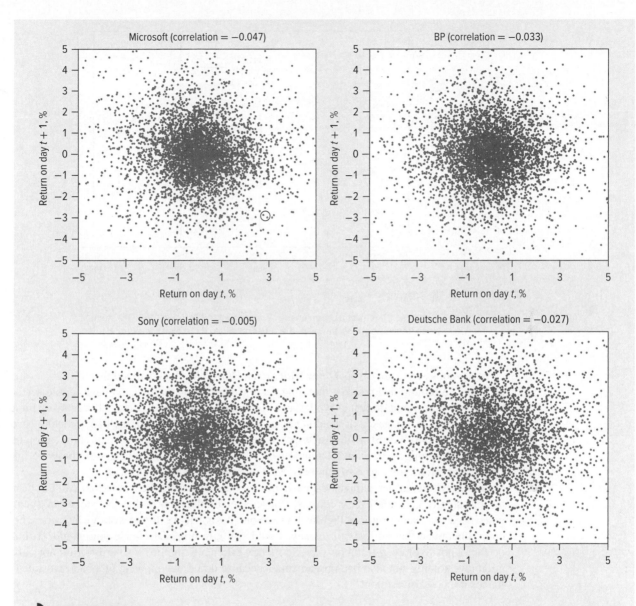

▶ FIGURE 12.3

Each dot shows a pair of returns for a stock on two successive days between January 2000 and December 2019. The circled dot for Microsoft records a daily return of +2.9% and then −2.9% on the next day. The scatter diagram shows no significant relationship between returns on successive days.

Good and Bad Investments Are Hard to Find In the real world, there are such things as good and bad companies. Apple is a good company because the iPhone is a market leader; Philip Morris is a bad company because tobacco usage is on the decline.

But if markets are efficient, there are no such things as good and bad investments. Everyone (or, more precisely, the sharks who drive prices) know that Apple is a good company, so its price is high. As a result, it's not a good investment—you're no better off buying Apple than any other stock. Conversely, everyone knows that Philip Morris's markets are shrinking, so its price is low. Because the "price is right," Philip Morris is no worse (or better) an investment than Apple.

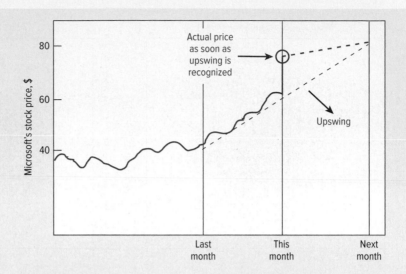

▶ FIGURE 12.4

Cycles self-destruct as soon as they are recognized by investors. The stock price instantaneously jumps to the present value of the expected future price.

In his book *A Random Walk Down Wall Street,* Burton Malkiel claimed that, if markets are efficient, "a blindfolded monkey throwing darts at a newspaper's financial pages could select a portfolio that would do just as well as one carefully selected by experts."[9] If a monkey hit a bad company "by mistake," it wouldn't actually be a mistake because the bad company isn't a bad investment. Indeed, British newspaper *The Observer* ran an investment competition in 2012 where a ginger cat named Orlando beat professional wealth managers by throwing his favorite toy mouse on a grid of numbers, each representing a different stock.

Similarly, we earlier explained that if markets are efficient, then investors can't expect to consistently generate excess returns. But another implication is that investors can't generate *negative* excess returns (before transactions costs). If we found you an investor who could guarantee that he lost you money, would you hire him? Of course you would! You'd do the opposite of everything he says. So market efficiency implies it's hard to find not only good investments, but also bad investments—because doing the opposite of a bad investment makes it a good investment.

Investors Should Hold the Market Portfolio   When citizens invest in mutual funds, they can choose between two main types. An *actively managed fund* has a fund manager who makes discretionary decisions on which stocks to buy and which to avoid based on fundamental analysis. All this takes time and effort and costs money. The fund needs to hire the manager and his team of analysts, and they need to fly around to meet with companies, crunch the numbers, and keep their eyes open for even peripheral information such as the political situation in Peru. So, in return, the fund will charge its investors an *annual management fee* of, say, 1% of total fund value.[10]

But if markets are efficient, then this fee is a waste of money because fundamental analysis doesn't produce excess returns. Any information that the fund manager is using to guide his

[9]B. Malkiel, *A Random Walk Down Wall Street* (New York: W. W. Norton, 1973).
[10]Hedge funds will also charge a *performance fee*. In addition to the annual management fee (which is typically 2% for a hedge fund), it will also charge 20% of any increase in fund value. The common rationale is to provide it with greater incentives to make correct investment decisions.

trading decisions is already incorporated in prices. The manager is no better than Orlando the cat. Rather than paying him fat fees to select particular stocks, investors should instead set a *passively managed fund,* otherwise known as an *index fund.* Such a fund doesn't pick particular companies but, instead, simply replicates an index—for example, the S&P 500 in the United States or the FTSE All-Share Index in the United Kingdom. There's no need to hire a fund manager, so index funds typically charge much lower fees, typically around 0.1%. (In September 2018, Fidelity launched index funds with zero fees.)

Not only does an index fund save fees, but it achieves the benefits of diversification. In Chapter 8, we saw that portfolio theory recommends that investors passively hold the market portfolio. Indeed, we've seen index funds become increasingly popular in recent years. In the European Union, the proportion of total assets owned by index funds doubled from 15% in 2007 to 30% in 2017. For the United States, the rise has been even faster, from 19% to 43%.[11] So market efficiency and portfolio theory aren't just "theories" dreamed up by academics; they're something that many investors believe hold in the real world.

How far could indexing go? Not to 100%, because of the Grossman-Stiglitz paradox we discussed earlier. If all investors hold index funds, then nobody will be collecting information, and prices won't respond to new information when it arrives. An efficient market needs some smart investors who gather information and attempt to profit from it. To provide incentives to gather costly information, prices cannot reflect *all* information. There must be some profits available to allow the costs of information to be recouped. But if the costs are small, relative to the total market value of traded securities, then the financial market can still be close to fully efficient.

Prices Are a Signal of a Firm's Fundamental Value   Imagine you've become a hugely successful financial manager by putting the principles of corporate finance into practice. You end up retiring in five years. (Or perhaps you might get unlucky and it takes you six years before you can start devoting more time to your golf handicap.) You spend some of your time as a non-executive director of a company. One of your main responsibilities is to evaluate the CEO to decide how much she should be paid and, in the extreme, if she should be fired.

This task seems pretty demanding because there are many relevant dimensions to the CEO's performance. You'd have to analyze the company's financial results, read equity analyst opinions, study how its products are doing relative to the competition, talk to her employees to see how they're being treated, and so on. The list is nearly endless. But if the market is efficient, there's less need to do that. The stock price captures almost all relevant information about the company's performance, so you can rely on the stock price. (However, if markets are only semistrong-form efficient, you can't exclusively rely on the stock price because there may be private information relevant for assessing CEO performance that's not in the price.) The same holds true for investors assessing the CEO's performance to decide whether to push for her dismissal.

The stock price is useful not only for evaluating the CEO, but to decide whether to enter into a relationship with a company in the first place. Doing so is an investment, and it's only worth it if there are enough future payoffs to justify the cost.

- Employees, upon receiving a job offer, want to know whether the company is likely to be around in the future. It takes time to settle into a new company, learn its systems, and build trust with your colleagues, and this is only worth it if you'll stay for a long haul.

- Customers, when buying a durable good such as a car, want to know if the company will still be there to provide spare parts and after-sales service.

- Suppliers, when contemplating whether to build a new factory to manufacture bespoke inputs for a customer, will want to know if that company will be around to buy the inputs.

---

[11]V. Sushko and G. Turner, "The Implications of Passive Investing for Securities Markets," *BIS Quarterly Review*, March 2018.

The parties that can learn from an efficient stock price include managers themselves. A CEO has more information about her company than anyone else, but she doesn't have perfect information—hence, the scope for learning. Most important decisions involve a combination of both internal and external factors. For example, when deciding whether to undertake a major expansion, a company should consider its own capacity to expand (internal) and market demand (external). CEOs have excellent internal information, but rarely have perfect external information, which is why they typically seek advice from management consultants and other advisers. While consultants cost millions, the stock price is a free source of information. Even for external information, a CEO may know more than an individual trader. But the stock price accumulates the views of millions of investors who, collectively, might have information that the manager doesn't.[12] Because stock prices are forward-looking, a high price indicates that the firm's prospects are good, so it should expand. Indeed, evidence shows that firms invest more when stock prices are high, especially if the market is efficient.[13]

Event Studies and Abnormal Returns   If prices are a signal of a firm's fundamental value, good events will increase the stock price and bad events will lower it. Let's turn this around. If an event takes place, and we're not sure whether it's good or bad, we can see how the market responds to ascertain its value. If the market is efficient, the stock price will rise upon a good event and fall upon a bad event. This is indeed what an *event study* does.

Let's take an example. Suppose the company Radstock had already fired its CEO and drawn up a shortlist. It then appoints Beatriz Vasquez as the next CEO and the market falls 3% that same day. That would seem to imply that Beatriz was a disastrous choice. How might the board defend its decision to hire Beatriz in the face of apparent market disapproval?

By attributing the negative return to other factors. Radstock's shares may have fallen due to a general market downturn rather than Beatriz's appointment. Indeed, the key to an event study is to isolate the impact of the event by controlling for what happened in the broader market. Chapter 8 showed us how to do this. Recall the CAPM:

$$r - r_f = \beta(r_m - r_f)$$

This means that the return on Radstock (above the risk-free rate) should equal its beta times the return on the market (again, less the risk-free rate). So, any discrepancy or *abnormal return* can be attributed to Beatriz's appointment. This discrepancy is given by alpha in the following equation:

$$\alpha = r - r_f - \beta(r_m - r_f) \tag{12.3}$$

In practice, the risk-free rate for one day is approximately zero. So if the market return on the day of Beatriz's appointment is 4% and Radstock's beta is 1.5, it should have fallen by 6% in the absence of any firm-specific news. Since Radstock fell by 3%, the alpha is 3%. The market believes that Beatriz's appointment adds, rather than subtracts, 3% of firm value.

Assessing whether a corporate event adds value isn't just of intellectual interest; it's of practical use as well. As mentioned earlier, CEOs can learn from the stock price and change course if the market thinks that an action destroys value. For example, when Hewlett-Packard announced that it was in negotiations to buy PwC's consulting business, its stock price fell by 6% that day. This signaled to CEO Carly Fiorina that the market disapproved

[12] The idea that the stock price accumulates the views of millions of investors was pioneered by the Nobel prizewinning economist Friedrich Hayek. F. A. Hayek, "The Use of Knowledge in Society," *American Economic Review* 35 (September 1945), pp. 519–530.

[13] See, for example, Q. Chen, I. Goldstein, and W. Jiang, "Price Informativeness and Investment Sensitivity to Stock Price," *Review of Financial Studies* 20 (May 2007), pp. 619–650; A. Edmans, S. Jayaraman, and J. Schneemeier, "The Source of Information in Prices and Investment-Price Sensitivity," *Journal of Financial Economics* 126 (October 2017), pp. 74–96. This literature on how decision markers learn from prices is surveyed by P. Bond, A. Edmans, and I. Goldstein, "The Real Effects of Financial Markets." *Annual Review of Financial Economics* 4 (October 2012), pp. 339–360.

of the acquisition, so she ended up dropping her bid. As she justified her change of heart, investors "simply voted with their positions in the stock . . . I realize [they] made some valid points." More broadly, evidence shows that acquirers are less likely to complete merger and acquisition (M&A) deals, the more the stock price declines upon announcement.[14]

Event studies can be used to study the value created by not only one action taken by one firm, but that action in general across lots of firms. In Chapter 31, we'll discuss the evidence on whether M&A creates value. This question is of interest to CEOs contemplating an M&A deal, investors speculating on whether a company will engage in a deal, and policymakers deciding whether to regulate M&A deals more closely. Event studies help answer this question by calculating the abnormal return to hundreds of companies that undertake M&A.

Note that Equation 12-3, and the concept of abnormal returns, measured by alpha, can be used to evaluate the performance of fund managers as well as corporate events. Radstock's shares falling doesn't imply that Beatriz was a bad appointment because the market could have fallen. Similarly, a fund manager losing money doesn't mean he's incompetent because that could similarly be attributable to the market. The alpha of a fund manager is his excess returns after taking into account the performance of the market and the fund's beta—the systematic risk of its portfolio. Alpha is a measure of the manager's skill. If markets are efficient, the alpha over a long time period should be zero because he shouldn't be able to systematically beat the market.

Firm Financing Decisions Neither Create Nor Destroy Value   We discussed in Section 12-1 that if markets are efficient, then financing decisions create no value. You can trust market prices—whenever you issue or repurchase debt or equity, you receive or pay a fair price. Then, the value of an investment decision is given purely by the NPV of that investment; the NPV of the accompanying financial decision is zero. Managers should just stick to managing (making correct investment decisions) and not get distracted by worrying about financing.

In practice, managers often act as if they believe that markets are not efficient. If the stock market has gone up recently, they say that the market is "hot" and they should issue equity.[15] The idea is to catch the market while it is high; if they're too slow, it will fall and they'll have missed the sweet spot. Similarly, they're often reluctant to issue stock after a fall in price, and instead, they wait for a rebound. But, if the market is weak-form efficient, recent price movements are irrelevant. After a price fall, the market is no more likely to rebound as it is to fall further, so there's no particular reason to delay selling shares.[16]

Some managers act as if the market is not semistrong-efficient. They may decide on the firm's exchange rate or financing policy, believing that they can predict exchange rates or interest rates better than the market. But, in an efficient market, there's no way to consistently achieve superior rates of return.

Procter & Gamble is a costly example of this point. In 1993, P&G's treasury staff believed that interest rates would be stable and decided to gamble on this belief. They entered into highly complex derivative contracts with Bankers Trust that reduced P&G's borrowing costs by 40 basis points. But the flipside was that P&G had to agree to compensate Bankers Trust if interest rates rose sharply. This is indeed what happened in early 1994, and P&G lost $102 million. It only had itself to blame for trying to swim with sharks. Think of P&G's competition when it traded in the fixed-income markets. Its competition included the trading

---

[14]Y. Luo, "Do Insiders Learn from Outsiders? Evidence from Mergers and Acquisitions," *Journal of Finance* (August 2005), pp. 1951–1982.

[15]See, for example, P. Asquith and D. W. Mullins Jr., "Equity Issues and Offering Dilution," *Journal of Financial Economics* 15 (January–February 1986), pp. 61–89; and (for the U.K.) P. R. Marsh, "The Choice between Equity and Debt: An Empirical Study," *Journal of Finance* 37 (March 1982), pp. 121–144.

[16]If high stock prices signal expanded investment opportunities and the need to finance these new investments, we would expect to see firms raise more money *in total* when stock prices are historically high. But this does not explain why firms prefer to raise the extra cash at these times by an issue of equity rather than debt.

desks of all the major investment banks, hedge funds, and fixed-income portfolio managers. P&G's expertise is in consumer goods, not predicting interest rates. As we argued in Chapter 11, a corporation should not enter a market unless it can identify a competitive advantage and a source of economic rents.

Another action that assumes semistrong-form inefficiency is buying other companies. One firm may purchase another simply because its management thinks that the stock is undervalued. Half of the time, the stock of the target will, in hindsight, turn out to be undervalued. But on the other half, it will be overvalued. On average, the value will be correct, so the acquirer won't systematically make money (in fact, it will lose money given the costs of the acquisition).

What Market Efficiency Does *Not* Imply

Market efficiency seems a pivotal concept since several important implications arise if it holds. However, it's important to understand what market efficiency does *not* imply since many takeaways are commonly misattributed.

Prices Are Stable   When we suggest that stock "prices are right," it only means that prices are right *at the time they are set;* they incorporate all relevant information available at that time. A price that's right today will change tomorrow when new information arrives. For example, Apple's stock price might be $300 based on all available information. But if, unexpectedly, the economy enjoys a boom, Apple's stock price will rise to $360. So Apple's stock price ends up being wrong in hindsight, but was right at the time.

By analogy, let's say you're asked to predict the number of heads over the next 10 coin tosses. Five is the right estimate, based on the information that you have at the time—the relevant information is that the coin is fair, so the probability of a head is ½. After the fact, you end up being wrong, because you get seven heads. But that doesn't change the fact that your guess was right at the time.

Investors Can't Make or Lose Money   Because prices aren't stable, investors might end up making or losing money on individual trades. An investor who buys Apple at $300 ends up lucky if the price unexpectedly rises to $360. What market efficiency implies is that an investor can't *systematically* make or lose money. The next stock he buys might fall by 20% rather than rising by 20% because of unexpectedly bad news. Returning to the analogy, let's say you pay $5, and in return, you receive $1 for every head in the next 10 coin tosses. Sometimes they'll be more than five heads and you'll make money, but it's just as likely that there will be fewer than five and you'll lose money. Going back to the P&G example in the preceding section, P&G lost from its financing decision on that occasion, but it was equally probable that it could have gained.

All Investors Agree   We explained earlier that market efficiency is a theory of "sharks," not the average investor. A mom-and-pop investor might disagree with a shark due to not having or understanding relevant information (e.g., the political situation in Peru). But even if we focus only on "sharks," market efficiency still allows them to disagree. All it means is that dissenting opinions are equally valid, so no shark will be systematically right or wrong. Let's say that sharks are asked to guess the number of heads in the next three tosses. One may guess two; another may wager one. Both guesses are equally reasonable, even though only one will end up right. All market efficiency means is that sharks won't guess zero or three.

All Securities Offer the Same Return   Remember the no-arbitrage argument we used to justify market efficiency in Section 12-2? That would seem to imply that all securities should offer the same return, otherwise there would be an arbitrage—all investors would flock to the higher-yielding securities. But this won't be the case. As we explained in Chapter 8, some securities rationally offer higher returns because of their systematic risk; that's why stocks yield more than Treasury bills. Efficient markets only imply that investors can't earn *excess* returns or alpha, which are returns after taking into account risk and other costs.

12.3 Self-Test

Assume the market is semistrong-form efficient. Which of the following implications are valid?

    a. Investors with a long time horizon should choose growth stocks; investors with a short time horizon should choose value stocks.

    b. The expected return from a stock next year is the same as its realized return last year.

    c. You should buy stocks of toy companies just before December holidays.

    d. We can study whether a merger creates long-term value by studying the short-term market reaction.

12.4 Self-Test

Assume the market is strong-form efficient. Which of the following implications are valid?

    a. Managers should not raise equity to undertake a positive-NPV project if they believe the stock price is too low.

    b. Companies should buy back their shares after they have fallen and issue shares after they have risen.

    c. A CEO should invest in artificial intelligence if her long-term investors have a preference for artificial intelligence stocks.

What if Markets Are Not Efficient? Implications for the Financial Manager

Having discussed what market efficiency does and doesn't imply, we now turn to the implications that follow if markets are *not* efficient. It's clear what investors should do: Buy shares that are underpriced and sell shares that are overpriced. What should a financial manager do?

If the market is not strong-form efficient, then the financial manager will have inside information about the value of her own company's shares. How this affects her actions depend on whether she thinks her stock is overpriced or underpriced.

Let's first consider *overpricing*. Going back to the GENZ CFO of Section 12-1, she might think aloud like this:

> Great! This means we can raise capital cheaply and invest in the factory. Our high stock price gives us a big advantage over our competitors who could not possibly justify building another factory.

In other words, even if Project X is negative-NPV, this may seem to be outweighed by the equity issuance being positive-NPV, so the overall NPV is also positive. This was the conclusion we speculated in Section 12-1. But let's think about this a little more deeply. If GENZ's stock is truly overpriced, it's true that issuing equity creates value for existing shareholders. But it doesn't then need to throw away some of this value by investing the cash in a negative-NPV project. It could instead keep the cash in its bank account or invest it in other securities. Since both of these options yield a fair return for their risk, they're zero-NPV. It's better to combine a positive-NPV financing decision with a zero-NPV investment decision rather than a negative-NPV one. So, the conclusion that we drew in Section 12-1—that inefficient markets spill over into inefficient investment decisions—seems a little premature.

But this spillover *will* occur if the investment and financing decisions are linked—if the only way you could obtain the financing is if you made the investment. One example is the subsidized loan we considered in Section 12-1, where New York State would only lend at 3% if GENZ built a new factory in New York. A second example is a large equity issuance. When a company issues new shares, it has to explain what it will use the money for. If it says it will simply hold onto the cash or invest it in other securities, the market will suspect that the issuance is motivated by overvaluation. Then, it won't be able to issue at a high price, and so the financing decision would no longer be positive-NPV. (Putting this another way, investors won't give a company money to invest in cash or other securities, since they could make these investments directly themselves.) So, when companies are overvalued, they might issue equity to buy another company. Even if that acquisition is negative-NPV, it might disguise the true motives for the issuance, allowing for a positive-NPV financing decision.

One extreme example where this arguably happened is AOL's acquisition of Time Warner at the height of the dot-com bubble in 2000. AOL was a classic dot-com company. Its stock rose from $2.34 at the end of 1995 to $75.88 at the end of 1999. Time Warner's stock price also increased during this period, but only from $18.94 to $72.31. AOL's total market capitalization was a small fraction of Time Warner's in 1995 but overtook Time Warner's in 1998. By the end of 1999, AOL's outstanding shares were worth $173 billion, compared with Time Warner's $95 billion. AOL managed to complete the acquisition before the Internet bubble burst. AOL-Time Warner's stock then plummeted, but not by nearly as much as the stocks of dot-com companies that had not managed to acquire safer partners.[17]

Let's now turn to *underpricing*. Here, investment and financing decisions *are* linked—if the company has no spare cash, it can't invest unless it raises financing—so the implications are stronger. If a company has a positive-NPV project, but selling shares to finance it would be negative-NPV, the CFO should turn down the project. Again, mispricing has negative real effects. But these consequences are mitigated if the CFO could instead finance the investment by raising debt. In this case, the market inefficiency would affect the firm's choice of financing (debt versus equity) but not its real investment decisions. In Chapter 15, we will have more to say about the financing choice when managers believe their stock is mispriced.

Overpricing and underpricing directly affect a company's financing decisions and only spill over into investment decisions if they are linked. However, other types of market inefficiency may directly affect investment decisions, even if the company doesn't need to raise financing to undertake them. One important potential inefficiency, which we briefly discussed in Chapter 1, is that the stock market is myopic; it overweights short-term cash flows relative to long-term cash flows.[18] It may be that the financial manager knows that a project will generate long-term payoffs based on her internal analysis, but the market is unable to forecast these payoffs because they are too far off. Then, even if the project increases shareholder value, the stock price will fall.

Now a falling stock price alone won't lead to the manager avoiding the investment, so myopic stock markets don't, by themselves, lead to myopic investment decisions. If the company's major shareholders are expected to hold onto their shares for the long term, they're not worried about blips in the short-term price. But it may be that investors themselves have short horizons, for rational reasons. For example, a pension fund may need to generate sufficient returns to pay its beneficiaries now. In this case, the manager will place at least some weight on the short-term stock price. As a result, she may turn down some positive-NPV projects that the market undervalues.

Equally, she may take some negative-NPV projects that the market overvalues. An example is Enron venturing into broadband video-on-demand. *The New York Times* explained that "The start of the broadband division helped send the stock leaping still further from $40 in

---

[17]Savor and Lu provide evidence that many other firms were able to benefit from stock acquisitions. See P. Savor and Q. Lu, "Do Stock Mergers Create Value for Acquirers?" *Journal of Finance* 64 (June 2009), pp. 1061–1097.

[18]While stock market myopia is a common concern, the evidence is far from unambiguous. See, for example, M. Roe, "Stock Market Short-Termism's Impact," Harvard University Working Paper (2018); and S. N. Kaplan, "Are U.S. Companies Too Short-Term Oriented? Some Thoughts," *Journal of Applied Corporate Finance* 30 (Fall 2018), pp. 8–18.

January [2001] to $90 several months later, when Enron announced a 20-year partnership with Blockbuster Entertainment to provide video-on-demand services for consumers and subsequently announced a high-speed Internet deal with the Microsoft Network." In the same article, a spokesperson admitted that Enron hoped to capitalize on the dot-com frenzy for online entertainment stocks.[19]

12.5 Self-Test

Assume the market is inefficient. How does the financial manager's decisions change if:

a. Her firm's shares are overpriced?

b. Her firm's shares are underpriced?

c. The market is myopic and undervalues distant cash flows?

12-4   Are Markets Efficient? The Evidence

Having defined market efficiency and explained why it's important, we now examine the evidence. Are markets actually efficient in the real world? Let's consider each form in turn.

Weak-Form Efficiency

Weak-form efficiency implies that future price changes can't be predicted using past price changes. In other words, the *serial correlation* between successive price changes must be zero. In Figure 12.3, we showed that this was the case for four particular stocks, but what matters is whether it holds for stocks in general. So, many tests of market efficiency have estimated this serial correlation across entire markets. One of these early tests was by Fama himself. He studied each of the 30 stocks in the Dow Jones Industrial Average between 1957 and 1962. Averaging across the stocks, he found the following:[20]

Interval	Serial Correlation
1-day change	0.03
4-day change	−0.04
9-day change	−0.05
16-day change	0.01

Market efficiency is a heroic concept to defend because almost any evidence could contradict it. The serial correlation must be zero. It can't be positive because that would imply a trading strategy—you'd buy a stock after it rose in price. But it can't be negative either because that would also imply a trading strategy—you'd buy a stock after it fell in price. Moreover, it has to be zero across every time horizon. The change over the past one day shouldn't predict the change over the next one day; the change over the past four days shouldn't predict the change over the next four days, and so on, just as the number of heads over the past 22, 37, or 639 coin flips is irrelevant for predicting the future. And indeed Fama found this: All of these estimated correlations were statistically indistinguishable from zero. That's why Fama argues markets to be efficient.

---

[19]P. Bolton, J. Scheinkman, and W. Xiong, "Executive Compensation and Short-Termist Behaviour in Speculative Markets," Review of Economic Studies (July 2006), pp. 577–610.

[20]E. F. Fama, "The Behavior of Stock-Market Prices," *Journal of Business* 38, (January 1965), pp. 34–105.

However, there's increasing evidence that even weak-form efficiency doesn't hold. Fama considered several serial correlations, but only over short intervals, from 1 to 16 days. What about longer timeframes? For this, we'll turn to the work of Richard Thaler, who won the 2017 Nobel Prize for his contributions to market efficiency, but in the other direction to Fama, arguing that markets are inefficient. One of Thaler's early papers, with Werner de Bondt, found evidence for *reversal*. They sorted stocks according to their performance over the past 36 months. The stocks that had done the best, they called the "winners," and the ones that had performed the worst were dubbed the "losers." They found that, over the next 36 months, past losers outperform past winners; there's a reversal of fortunes where recent dogs become future stars. Their paper implied a profitable trading strategy: Buy past losers and sell past winners. This implies weak-form inefficiency because you can make money without even knowing the name of a company or what industry it is in. All you need to do is look at its stock price chart to figure out whether to buy or sell it.

In 1993, Jegadeesh and Titman found further evidence of inefficiency, but in the other direction. They also sorted stocks into winners and losers, but now on performance over the past six months, not 36 months. Instead of reversal, they found evidence of *momentum:* Past winners continue to be winners, while recent losers keep dropping. What this means is that stock prices paths tend to be as in Figure 12.5. If a company announces good news that causes its fundamental value to increase by 20%, its stock price will initially underreact. So if you buy a stock that's risen over the past six months, it has further upside. But, after a while, the stock price overshoots. So, a stock that's risen over the past 36 months has gone up too much and you should sell it. Research hasn't reliably found where the crossover point is where a stock turns from underreacting to overreacting; it changes from stock to stock. But one message is clear: The market underreacts in the short term but overreacts in the long term.

The direct implication of these trading strategies is that markets are weak-form inefficient. An indirect implication is that markets are also semistrong-form and strong-form inefficient.

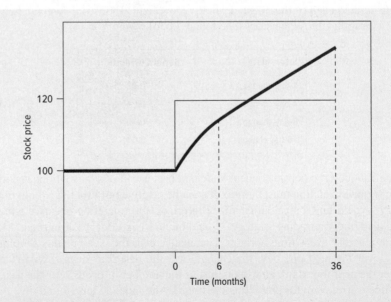

▶ **FIGURE 12.5**

Short-term underreaction and long-term overreaction. The solid black line shows how the market should react to news that increases the stock price from 100 to 120. The red line shows how the market actually reacts. After 6 months, it has underreacted; after 36 months, it has overreacted

The Risk of Momentum Strategies

❭ It's an important caveat that neither reversal nor momentum are risk-free arbitrages. They sometimes lose, and when they do, they lose pretty big. For example, between March and May 2009, the past-six-month losers generated 163% returns, but the winners generated only 8% returns. As a result, some hedge funds that followed the momentum strategy ended up collapsing. So, a momentum strategy is like picking up nickels in front of a steamroller. Most of the time you make a little money, but there's a risk of being flattened.

But a more recent study showed that you might be able to see the steamroller coming.[21] It found that "momentum crashes" occur in periods of market stress, when the market has recently declined or when market volatility is high. The intuition is as follows. If the market has recently declined, the loser portfolio must have fallen faster than the broader market. Thus, it has a high beta. The winner portfolio has a relatively low beta, which is why it didn't decline so much. After times of market stress, the market typically recovers. The loser portfolio, which has high beta stocks, does especially well in the market recovery due to its high beta, and so the momentum strategy fails. Getting out of the momentum strategy in times of market stress doubles the Sharpe ratio of this strategy from 0.6 to 1.2.

As Figure 12.2 showed, the violation of any one form of market efficiency also implies the violation of all stronger forms.

Semistrong-Form Efficiency

There are three sets of tests of semistrong-form efficiency: the performance of actively managed mutual funds, the market's reaction to information, and the performance of trading strategies based on public information. Let's consider each in turn.

The Performance of Active Funds Recall that semistrong-form efficiency implies that fundamental analysis shouldn't earn excess returns. We can test this by studying the performance of active funds since they perform fundamental analysis and trade primarily on public information. Table 12.1 illustrates the percentage of U.S. active funds that don't beat their benchmark.

Most of these numbers are greater than 50%, suggesting that most active funds actually underperform the market, consistent with semistrong-form efficiency. The underperformance is predominantly due to fees. If it were due to poor stock selection, then you could simply do the opposite of a typical mutual fund and hope to make money.

Fund Category	Comparison Index	1 Year	3 Years	5 Years
All domestic funds	S&P Composite 1500	59.07%	67.01%	72.80%
Large cap funds	S&P 500	60.33%	69.71%	75.25%
Mid cap funds	S&P MidCap 400	50.68%	53.49%	59.68%
Small cap funds	S&P SmallCap 600	45.52%	57.04%	65.12%

❭**TABLE 12.1**   Percentage of U.S. Active Equity Funds Outperformed by Benchmarks

Source: S&P Funds Scorecard, Year-End 2020.

---

[21]Daniel, Kent, Moskowitz, Tobias, Momentum Crashes, *Journal of Financial Economics*, Vol. 122, Issue 2, Nov. 2016, 222-247.

OK, maybe mutual funds in general don't earn superior returns, but surely some managers are smarter than others and can be relied on to beat their less competent brethren? Perhaps Table 12.1 combines sharks and minnows—if we just focused on sharks, would we find that they consistently beat the market? Unfortunately, it seems difficult to spot the sharks. For example, a top-quartile fund in one year has no more than an average chance of being in the top quartile the following year.[22] It seems that the top-performing managers in one period have about an average chance of falling on their faces in the next period.

Recall from Section 12-2 that it's not clear whether analyzing the performance of mutual funds tests semistrong-form or strong-form efficiency because, even though mutual funds use public information, they may feed it into a proprietary model. So, one might argue that mutual funds trade on private information; thus, Table 12.1 is evidence in support of strong-form efficiency. But recall also from Figure 12.2 that strong-form efficiency implies semistrong-form efficiency, so even under this interpretation, the implications for semistrong-form efficiency don't change.

Market Reactions to Information   Let's move to the second set of tests of market efficiency. Since semistrong-form efficiency argues that prices contain all available public information, one might think another way to test it is to study how quickly stock prices respond to breaking news. Take Volkswagen's (VW's) diesel emissions scandal as an example. On Friday, September 18, 2015, the U.S. Environmental Protection Agency (EPA) announced that VW had installed "defeat devices" in several models of diesel cars that reduced emissions only when emissions tests were under way. VW's stock price dropped immediately from about $160 to about $130 per share. There was another drop to about $110 per share on Monday, when VW admitted that it had sold 11 million cars worldwide with the defeat device. VW lost nearly one-third of its stock market value in two days' trading.

But actually that's not a complete test of semistrong-efficiency. We can't just show that prices react to events. For prices to "reflect" all available information, they need to *fully* react to the event. There should be no *post-event drift:* After the initial reaction, prices should be equally likely to go up or down. If the emissions scandal erodes $30 of value, the stock price should drop by $30 that same day. There should be no underreaction, where the price initially falls by $20 and drifts down by another $10 over the next few weeks. Nor should there be overreaction, where the price plummets by $40 and then later corrects. Of course the price may still change in the future—remember that market efficiency doesn't imply that prices are stable—but it should be equally likely to go up or down. Future price changes must be caused by new information, not delayed reaction or corrected overreaction to the EPA announcement. Indeed, the subsequent price fall on Monday was due to the additional disclosure that 11 million cars are affected.

To test for the presence of post-event drift, we need to study hundreds of cases, not a single anecdote. Let's take the "event" as a company being the subject of a takeover bid. Acquiring firms usually have to pay a substantial *takeover premium* to get the deal done, so the target firm's stock price increases as soon as the takeover bid is announced. Figure 12.6 shows the average pattern of the target's stock returns before and after the announcement of a takeover (day 0 in the figure). Stock prices drift up before date 0 as investors gradually realize that a takeover may be coming. On the day of the announcement and the following day, prices jump up by 18.0%.[23] The adjustment to the stock price is immediate and complete. There is no significant further drift in the price, either upward or downward. Thus, within the day, the new stock prices reflect (at least on average) the magnitude of the takeover premium.

---

[22]See, for example, the Persistence Scorecard, which is published by Standard & Poor's twice a year.

[23]Investors will respond on day 0 if the announcement is made during that day's hours of trading. Otherwise, they will respond on day 1.

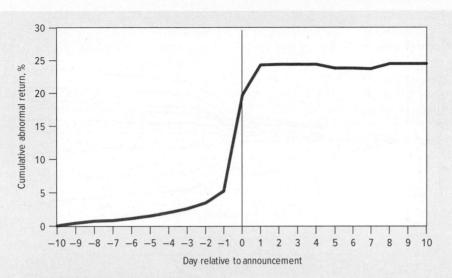

▶ FIGURE 12.6

The abnormal performance of the stocks of takeover targets around the announcement date. The prices of target stocks jump up on the day following the announcement, but from then on, there are no unusual price movements. The figure shows the cumulative abnormal returns for 9,944 U.S. targets between 1975 and 2019.

Source: WRDS.

Recall that market efficiency isn't an absolute concept, but about the speed at which information is incorporated. And it seems that some information is incorporated extremely quickly. CNBC broadcasts a daily Morning and Midday Call that summarizes security-analyst reports and other information about individual stocks. A study of 322 stocks that were discussed in these calls found that positive reports triggered a price increase seconds after the positive news was first broadcast. Investors could make a small profit after expenses only if they were able to buy in the first 15 seconds.[24] After that short window, there's no further post-event drift.

But remember that market efficiency is a heroic position to defend because almost any evidence could contradict it. Not only must the market fully react to announcements of takeover bids and CNBC calls, but other events as well. A famous paper found that the market doesn't even fully react to one of the most important and visible corporate events: quarterly earnings announcements. Every three months, a company announces its earnings—an event that the market pays substantial attention to. (Indeed, we'll argue in Chapter 20 that the market might pay *too much* attention to quarterly earnings.) Now even if earnings rise relative to the last quarter, that might not be "news" if the increase were predictable. The only new information that should move the stock price is the unexpected portion of the new announcement. How do we strip out this component? Before the announcement, equity analysts (such as those at Goldman Sachs and Morgan Stanley) will forecast what they think quarterly earnings will be. The average forecast is known as *analyst consensus*. The new information in the earnings announcement is the actual earnings minus the analyst consensus, known as the *earnings surprise*.

How does the market respond to earnings surprises? Figure 12.7 illustrates.

BEYOND THE PAGE

Long-run IPO returns

mhhe.com/brealey14e

---

[24]The price response to negative reports took longer, 15 minutes on average, probably because of the costs and delays of short-selling. See J. A. Busse and T. C. Green, "Market Efficiency in Real Time," *Journal of Financial Economics* 65 (September 2002), pp. 415–437.

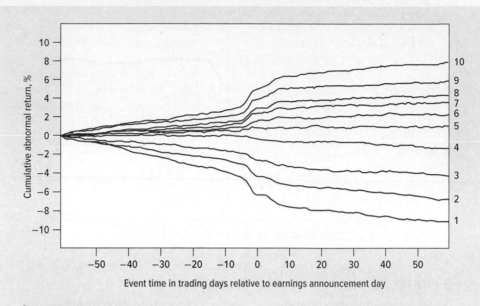

▶ FIGURE 12.7

Cumulative abnormal returns to portfolios of companies sorted by their earnings surprise. Portfolio 10 contains firms with the most positive earnings surprises, and portfolio 1 contains firms with the most negative earnings surprises.

Source: V.L. Bernard and J.K. Thomas, "Post-Earnings-Announcement-Drift: Delayed Price Response or Risk Premium?" *Journal of Accounting Research* 27 (1989), pp. 1–36.

If earnings end up above expectations—a *positive earnings surprise*—the stock price should jump on the announcement but then be flat afterward. But as Figure 12.7 shows, this isn't the case; it continues to drift up afterward. (It also rises before the announcement, similar to Figure 12.6 for takeovers, perhaps because of market anticipation). Similarly, a *negative earnings surprise* causes the stock price to drop, and to continue to fall afterward. This *post-earnings announcement drift* seems extremely puzzling. Because earnings announcements are such important events, it seems bizarre that the market doesn't respond to them. If you told your friend to short a stock because last month it had a bad earnings announcement, she might think that's a dumb idea since it's old news—and very public old news. But Figure 12.7 shows that the idea may be sound since the stock price continues to drop even after 30 days. We'll discuss potential reasons for this slow reaction in Section 12-5.

The Performance of Trading Strategies Based on Public Information   The third set of tests examines the performance of trading strategies based on public information. The reversal and momentum strategies use public information since past prices are a subset of public information. That's why they violate not only weak-form efficiency, but also semistrong-form efficiency (and thus also strong-form efficiency). But there are many other pieces of public information, other than past prices, that investors may use to guide trading decisions.

One such piece of information is valuation multiples, such as P/E. In Chapter 4, we explained how, in an efficient market, there are two reasons for why one stock might have a higher multiple than another: It is less risky, and it is higher-growth (has greater PVGO). But if markets are inefficient, there's a third reason: It's overvalued. A study disentangled these three explanations by studying the long-term performance of stocks with high and low valuation ratios.[25] Regardless of whether they looked at P/E, P/B, or price-to-cash-flow, they found a consistent result. High-valuation (or "glamour") companies underperform low-valuation (or "value") companies over the next five years, implying that they were indeed overvalued.

Now any test of the excess returns to a trading strategy isn't conclusive. That's because excess returns need to be calculated relative to a risk model that tells us what the strategy should be yielding in an efficient market. A study might use the CAPM, as in Equation 12-3, and control for only the market beta when calculating excess returns. But it may be that truth is the three-factor model of Section 8-4. Maybe value companies appear to perform well, but they have high sensitivities to the size and book-to-market factors, and these excess returns disappear after taking these sensitivities into account. And even if we controlled for all three factors, it might be that high returns are due to some additional risk factor that economists haven't yet discovered. As Fama explained, we have a "joint hypothesis" problem.[26] Any test of market efficiency is actually a joint test of *both* whether markets are efficient *and* whether we're using the correct risk model. What appears to be a violation of efficiency may in fact be a result of using the wrong model.

The authors thus tried to find additional evidence of mispricing. They didn't use a risk model since there's no way of knowing whether they had the right model. They instead showed that value stocks outperformed glamour in nearly all of the 22 years that they studied, rejecting the idea that they are riskier. In particular, they did at least as well as glamour in recessions where investors are especially concerned about underperformance. In a follow-up paper, they found that value stocks enjoy positive future earnings surprises, suggesting that equity analysts under-predicted their future earnings, also consistent with market undervaluation.

In Chapters 19 and 20, we'll discuss studies suggesting that using certain environmental, social, and governance (ESG) factors—which are also public information—can also generate excess returns.

12.6 Self-Test

Assume the following statements are true. Do they support semistrong-form efficiency, contradict it, or are inconclusive?

a. A company announces a bad new strategy; the stock price falls.

b. Warren Buffett consistently beats the market every year trading on public information.

c. Companies whose names begin with A perform as well as companies that begin with B, after adjusting for risk.

d. Companies with good governance beat companies with poor governance, after adjusting for risk.

e. The price of a stock trades at greater than the present value of its future dividends, because the market is anticipating that it will be taken over.

Strong-Form Efficiency

Tests of strong-form efficiency investigate whether corporate insiders, such as executives and directors, can beat the market. There's widespread evidence that they do.[27] This is why most

---

[25]J. Lakonishok, A. Shleifer, and R. W. Vishny, "Contrarian Investment, Extrapolation, and Risk," *Journal of Finance* 49 (December 1994), pp. 1541–1578.

[26]E. F. Fama, "Market Efficiency, Long-Term Returns, and Behavioral Finance," *Journal of Financial Economics* 49 (September 1998), pp. 283–306.

[27]Jaffe found that legal insider trades, that occur in intensive trading periods where many insiders trade, enjoy an eight-month abnormal return of 3%. Meulbroek documented that illegal insider trades earned a return of 6.85%. See J. F. Jaffe, "Special Information and Insider Trading," *Journal of Business* 47 (July 1974), pp. 410–428; and L. K. Meulbroek, "An Empirical Analysis of Illegal Insider Trading," *Journal of Finance* 47 (December 1992), pp. 1661–1699.

developed countries have strict insider trading rules, such as the U.S. Securities Exchange Act of 1934. Moreover, insiders also include investment banks that might be advising a company on an M&A deal and thus have private information that one is about to break. The U.S. Global Analyst Research Settlement of 2003 required investment banks to establish "ethical walls" between the M&A department of an investment bank and its trading division. If markets weren't strong-form efficient, then insiders wouldn't be able to make money on their information anyway, so these rules wouldn't be necessary.

With insider trading laws, the market isn't strong-form efficient under Fama's definition in Section 12-1 since prices don't contain insiders' information. But it is strong-form efficient under Jensen's definition since insiders can't trade on their information due to the law.

12-5   Behavioral Finance

Section 12-4 showed that while markets are generally efficient, there's nontrivial evidence of inefficiency. Why might prices depart from fundamental values? Some believe that the answer lies in human psychology. Hedge fund traders might only work 23 hours a day, so they won't be able to gather all relevant information—such as the political situation in Peru—and process it correctly. Even if they use computer models to help them, they can't assess qualitative factors such as a company's management or strategy. So, even in the digital age, prices are still determined in large part by human judgement. Humans may depart from Equation 12-1 in two ways: their preferences and their beliefs.

1. *Preferences.* Equation 12-1 says that investors only care about the discounted future dividends of a stock. The original purchase price doesn't matter—it's a "sunk cost" (see Section 6-1). If you bought a stock at $100 and its price is now $90, but you think it's worth only $85, you should sell it. It doesn't matter that you're making a loss of $10; if you think it's heading further south to $85, not selling will cause your loss to widen to $15. But psychologists have observed that investors don't focus solely on this "fundamental" value, but also whether the stock is showing a profit or a loss compared to the initial purchase price. In particular, they're particularly reluctant to take losses. If I sell my IBM shares for $90, I may feel elated if they only cost me $50, but disappointed if they cost $100.

   That the purchase price matters is the basis for *prospect theory,* discovered by 2002 Nobel Laureate Daniel Kahneman and his coauthor Amos Tversky.[28] Prospect theory states that the value of a share *to an investor* is not only determined by its fundamental value (which is common to all investors, since all receive the same dividends), but by whether he's made gains or losses since his original purchase. It also argues that investors are *loss averse*—they don't like taking even a small loss and will gamble to avoid one even if this risks further losses. Indeed, we see this behavior in casinos; a gambler who's lost money won't call it quits because she doesn't want to end her day in the red. Instead, she throws good money after bad in the hope of recouping her past losses.

   What does this mean for stock prices? If a share has gone up recently, investors want to lock in their profits. They don't want to risk the stock price reversing and falling into the red. So they'll sell their shares. This may explain momentum and post-earnings-announcement-drift; a company that's announced good news may only have enjoyed a small stock price rise because investors sold their shares to take profits.

---

[28]Prospect theory was first set out in D. Kahneman and A. Tversky, "Prospect Theory: An Analysis of Decision under Risk," *Econometrica* 47 (1979), pp. 263–291.

But what if a stock has fallen? Then, investors won't sell as they're reluctant to take a loss. They might even double down and buy more to give themselves a greater chance of recouping that loss. (If they buy more, the stock doesn't need to bounce all the way back for them to break even.) This may explain momentum and post-earnings-announcement-drift on the downside: A company that's announced bad news may only have enjoyed a small stock price fall because investors doubled down to try to recoup their losses.[29]

2. *Beliefs.* Equation 12-1 also says that that when investors form expectations of future dividends, these expectations are rational and based on all available information. But investors may have limited information—they simply don't notice what's happening in Peru. Or they may have limited capacity to process the information—they can't assess how the Peruvian political situation affects the value of Apple.

The difference between these two errors is similar to the difference between poker and chess. Poker is a game of limited information. You might make the wrong call because you don't see the other players' cards. You could go all in because you have a flush, but that turns out to be a mistake if an opponent has a full house. In chess, everyone has perfect information, but people still lose as they're not good at processing this information. This difference is important. Some people think that behavioral finance will become irrelevant now that information is more and more available. While this should indeed reduce inefficiencies, prices will never be perfect because investors may not be able to process the information correctly.

Defenders of efficient markets will acknowledge that people make mistakes. But they'd argue that mistakes shouldn't affect prices because they're idiosyncratic. If Andrea is overoptimistic about a stock and buys too much, and Bimal is pessimistic and sells too much, they'll cancel each other out. But advocates of behavioral finance argue that what causes mistakes is human psychology. Because Andrea and Bimal are both humans, they're affected by the same psychological biases. They'll make mistakes in the same direction and reinforce rather than neutralize each other; in the language of Chapter 7, mistakes are systematic, not idiosyncratic.

Examples of Biases: Overreaction and Underreaction Let's look at some biases that have been extensively documented by psychologists. One is *overreaction.* People overextrapolate from small patterns in the data. If you go to a sports stadium this weekend and see a manager lose for the third straight game, fans will call for his head. More precisely, they're overattributing the stream of losses to the manager's ability rather than luck. Even a high-ability manager, who wins more than 50% of his games, will still have streaks of three losses due to chance—just as a fair coin will still have streaks of three tails. As Nassim Taleb explained in a book of the same name, people are "fooled by randomness."[30] They make inferences from patterns in the data that are actually random.

Now translate this from the sports stadium to the stock market. A tech company announces an increase in sales. This increase is due to luck (good economic conditions), but investors mistakenly attribute it to product quality. They think sales will continue to rise and pour money into the stock, causing its price to soar. The soaring stock price triggers its own overreaction as investors expect the price rise to continue. Such overreaction may explain the success of the *reversal* strategy. A recent "winner" may have enjoyed mildly good news, but

---

[29] Barberis and Huang show that the link between prospect theory and the readiness to sell winners over losers (known as the "disposition effect") is more ambiguous than the above explanation. They propose an alternative driver of the disposition effect, "realization utility." Investors receive a burst of pleasure when they realize a gain and a burst of pain when they realize a loss. N. Barberis and W. Xiong, "What Drives the Disposition Effect? An Analysis of a Long-Standing Preference-Based Explanation," *Journal of Finance* 64 (April 2009), pp. 751–784; and N. Barberis and W. Xiong, "Realization Utility," *Journal of Financial Economics* 104 (May 2012), pp. 251–271.

[30] N. N. Taleb, *Fooled by Randomness: The Hidden Role of Chance in Life and in the Markets* (New York: Random House, 2008).

investors mistakenly thought it was very good news and drove its price up too high. That's why it subsequently underperforms. Overreaction may also explain why stock market bubbles form and then burst, such as the Internet bubble of the late 1990s.

A second common bias is *underreaction*. People are too slow to update their beliefs in the face of new data. This may be due to *confirmation bias*—the tendency to reject any data that contradicts their prior beliefs and accept data that supports them. If you're a climate change denier and you hear of a study that concludes that climate change is a hoax, you instantly accept it. If you see research claiming that climate change is real, you read it trying to poke holes in every argument you encounter. So your beliefs don't change.

Now translate this from science to the stock market. It's 1981 and sales of the film company Kodak have just crossed $10 billion per year. But Sony has just released the Mavica, the first ever electronic camera (a precursor to the digital camera). How did investors respond? Many didn't respond at all. Kodak was one of the world's largest companies; it seemed unfathomable that they'd be threatened by such an untried invention. So the stock price stayed high.

Underreaction may cause post-earnings announcement drift and momentum. When bad news happens, investors underreact to it, and the stock price only partially falls. It only fully reacts when the full extent of the bad news eventually seeps out—digital cameras become a success and eat into Kodak's film sales. The opposite is true for good news.

Are the Effects of Biases Real? Data Mining and Spurious Correlation   The idea that human beings sometimes overreact and sometimes underreact seems plausible given how the human mind works. But you might also find it confusing. How do we know when they over-react and when they underreact? This seems pretty crucial since they have different predictions for stock prices. Indeed, critics of behavioral finance argue that the discipline is actually undisciplined. There are so many psychological biases that you can always find one to explain any apparent violation of market efficiency. This is a particular problem given the possibility of *data mining*. A professor has strong incentives to find a variable that predicts stock returns as it's likely to be published. So there's an incentive to mine the data. Run hundreds of regressions, correlating stock performance with many variables, and try to find something that's significant.

Some of these variables might be sensible, such as the CEO's incentives or education. But even if you ran 100 regressions on nonsense variables, such as the CEO's shoe size, the number of letters in her last name, or her favorite color, five will likely be significant at the 5% level by pure chance. These chance results are known as *spurious correlations*. You might find that CEOs who like red perform better—a spurious correlation because there's no reason for why red-liking should improve performance. But *after* uncovering a relationship, you can mine the psychological literature and find a study showing that red triggers dominance and thus can enhance performance. Indeed, such a study exists.[31] Or if you found CEOs who like red perform worse, you could find a study showing that red is associated with the danger of failure and leads to fear. Indeed, such a study exists.[32]

Turning back to momentum and reversal, since the data finds short-term momentum and long-term reversal, it seems awfully convenient for behavioral economists to claim that investors underreact in the short term and overreact in the long term. If the data found long-term momentum and short-term reversal, they'd have claimed the opposite.

So there are two ways in which behavioral finance tries to show that psychology—rather than an omitted risk factor—explains both overreaction and underreaction. One is to construct

---

[31]R. A. Hill and R. A. Barton, "Psychology: Red Enhances Human Performance in Contests," *Nature* 435 (2005), p. 293.
[32]A. J. Elliot, M. A. Maier, A. C. Moller, and J. Meinhardt, "Color and Psychological Functioning: The Effect of Red on Performance Attainment," *Journal of Experimental Psychology: General* 136 (February 2007), pp. 154–168.

models, based on psychological biases, that explain the precise patterns of short-term under-reaction and long-term overreaction found in the data.[33]

A second way to do so is to conduct "out-of-sample" tests that find the same violation of market efficiency in a different dataset. You may think that Jegadeesh and Titman were ingenious for discovering the momentum strategy, but also foolish. Why did they share this secret with the rest of the world by publishing their 1993 paper? As we showed in Figure 12.4, upon reading their paper, investors should buy recent winners because they're expected to go up in the future. That would drive up their price, so there's no further upside by buying them. Jegadeesh and Titman should have jealously guarded their strategy and traded on it in secret. But they repeated the same analysis in a 2001 paper, using fresh data from a later time period, and found that momentum continued to be just as profitable. This suggests that the initial 1993 finding wasn't due to luck or data mining. It also suggests that momentum may indeed be due to psychology. It's hard to change people's biases because people are hardwired. Even when their 1993 paper came out suggesting that investors should react more to contradictory information, people are unlikely to take heed. Research shows that contradictory information causes the amygdala to light up—the same part of the brain that's triggered by a tiger attacking you.[34] Thus, investors may respond to contradictory information about their favorite stock in the same way they'd respond to a tiger attack—an automatic response that's hard to correct with an academic study.

And you can do "out-of-sample" tests on not only different periods, but also different securities. A 2013 study, entitled "Value and Momentum Everywhere," showed that both the momentum and value strategies work almost everywhere. "Everywhere" meant along two dimensions: different asset classes (bonds, currencies, and commodities—the initial studies focused on stocks) and different regions (the U.K., Europe, and Japan—the initial studies focused on the U.S.). This is also consistent with a behavioral explanation: If confirmation bias is a human phenomenon, it's just as likely to affect a European currency trader as a Japanese stock trader. Similarly, *post-event drift* has been documented not only for earnings surprises, but also dividend changes,[35] share repurchases,[36] and stock splits.[37]

12.7 Self-Test

What might be the behavioral explanations for the following occurrences?

 a. When news broke out in early 2020 about a potential coronavirus pandemic, markets initially only fell slightly.

 b. The price of Bitcoin reached a record $20,000 in December 2017.

Sentiment

So far, we've argued that the market might be inefficient by showing that it doesn't respond to information that it should, such as past prices, valuation ratios, and earnings announcements.

---

[33]Three influential models in this spirit are N. Barberis, A. Shleifer, and R. Vishny, "A Model of Investor Sentiment," *Journal of Financial Economics* 49 (September 1998), pp. 307–343; H. Hong and J. C. Stein, "A Unified Theory of Underreaction, Momentum Trading, and Overreaction in Asset Markets," *Journal of Finance* 54 (December 1999), pp. 2143–2184; and K. Daniel, D. Hirshleifer, and A. Subrahmanyam, "Investor Psychology and Security Market Under- and Overreactions," *Journal of Finance* 53 (December 1998), pp. 1839–1885.

[34]J. T. Kaplan, S. I. Gimbel, and S. Harris, "Neural Correlates of Maintaining One's Political Beliefs in the Face of Counterevidence," *Scientific Reports* 6 (2016), pp. 39589.

[35]R. Michaely, R. H. Thaler, and K. L. Womack, "Price Reactions to Dividend Initiations and Omissions: Overreaction or Drift?" *Journal of Finance* 50 (June 1995), pp. 573–608.

[36]D. Ikenberry, J. Lakonishok, and T. Vermaelen, "Market Underreaction to Open Market Share Repurchases," *Journal of Financial Economics* 39 (October–November 1995), pp. 181–208.

[37]D. L. Ikenberry, G. Rankine and E. K. Stice, "What Do Stock Splits Really Signal?" *Journal of Financial and Quantitative Analysis* 31 (September 1996), pp. 357–375.

A second way to do so is to show that the market does respond to information that it should not. Equation 12-1 shows that the stock price should *only* depend on expected future dividends and not other factors such as the purchase price (as argued by prospect theory) or the sentiment of investors—whether they happen to be happy or sad on the day they trade.

Yet some studies have suggested that sentiment may affect the stock market. One shows that the market falls when the clock changes from spring to fall or fall to spring.[38] Their interpretation is that clock changes mess up traders' sleep patterns and they go to work in a depressed mood. Another finds that the stock market declines on cloudy days and conducts the analysis across several countries to mitigate concerns of data mining.[39]

But you might still have concerns of spurious correlation. Are clock changes and weather strong enough to affect how investors trade? Certainly, sleep is important for your mood, but traders are pretty good at getting by on little sleep. After a late night, they can simply have another shot of espresso. Similarly, weather is not correlated across a country. It could be sunny in New York but cloudy in Chicago, and it might be Chicago fund managers who are driving stock prices even though the stock exchanges are located in New York.

A separate study thus investigates the effect of international soccer results.[40] Studies show that sports defeats lead to serious effects—people suffer heart attacks,[41] commit suicide,[42] and even murder each other[43]—that are unlikely to be neutralized by even the freshest espresso. Moreover, international defeats affect the whole country in the same way; when an English team loses, the whole of England is upset, regardless of what city they live in. (That's why the authors couldn't look at regional competitions such as Major League Baseball or Premier League soccer.) They find that when a country loses an international soccer game, the market falls significantly the next day, even after controlling for what happened in the world market.

Note that these studies do not argue that the financial manager's decisions should be affected by clock changes or soccer results. Instead, they investigate these variables because they are clean measures of sentiment, that are unlikely to affect economic fundamentals.[44] Thus, if the market responds to them, it suggests that it is not fully rational. Other measures of sentiment do affect economic fundamentals, such as a consumer confidence index, and the manager should respond to them. However, showing that those measures affect the market needn't imply irrationality, as the market could be simply responding to their economic content.

So where do we stand? In Section 12-3 we discussed the implications for the financial manager if markets are efficient and how the implications are different if market are inefficient. Section 12-4 documented *some* inefficiencies, and this section has suggested where the inefficiencies might stem from. However, we stress that a financial manager aiming to exploit inefficiencies should do so with caution. She should only attempt to do so if she has very good reasons to believe that she has information that the market doesn't. This is plausible for internal information: If she knows that her firm has strong intangible assets that the market is ignoring, she may wish to buy back shares. However, it is less plausible for external information. Believing that markets are inefficient because they fail to take into account likely changes in the interest rate may lead to a P&G-type disaster.

---

[38]M. J. Kamstra, L. A. Kramer, and M. D. Levi, "Losing Sleep at the Market: The Daylight Saving Anomaly," *American Economic Review* 12 (September 2000), pp. 1005–1011.

[39]D. Hirshleifer and T. Shumway, "Good Day Sunshine: Stock Returns and the Weather," *Journal of Finance* 58 (June 2003), pp. 1009–1032.

[40]A. Edmans, D. Garcia, and O. Norli, "Sports Sentiment and Stock Returns," *Journal of Finance* 62 (August 2007), pp. 1967–1998.

[41]D. Carroll, E. Shah, K. Tilling, J. Macleod, and G. Davey Smith, "Admissions for Myocardial Infarction and World Cup Football: Database Survey," *British Medical Journal* 325 (December 2002), pp. 1439–1442.

[42]F. Trovato, "The Stanley Cup of Hockey and Suicide in Quebec," *Social Forces* 77 (September 1998), pp. 105–127.

[43]G. F. White, "Media and Violence: The Case of Professional Football Championship Games," *Aggressive Behavior* 15 (1989), pp. 423–433.

[44]While soccer results do affect certain industries (e.g. sales of sports equipment might rise if a country wins the World Cup), the authors conduct further tests to rule out a rational economic interpretation of their findings.

Limits to Arbitrage

We earlier explained an important challenge to behavioral finance; even if investors make mistakes, they cancel each other out. We defended this challenge by explaining that mistakes are systematic, rather than idiosyncratic, so investors will make mistakes in the same direction. Efficient market advocates accept this for amateur investors. But there are plenty of hard-headed professional investors managing huge sums of money. They rarely make mistakes—indeed, that's why they became successful and large. Why don't these professionals correct the mistakes of the amateurs? One reason is that there are *limits to arbitrage*—that is, limits on their ability to exploit market inefficiencies.

In Section 12-2, we claimed that, if prices get out of line, arbitrage forces them back. But arbitrage is harder than it looks. Trading costs can be significant, and some trades are difficult to execute. For example, suppose that you identify an overpriced security that is *not* in your existing portfolio. You want to "sell high," but how do you sell a stock that you don't own? It can be done, but you have to *sell short.*

To sell a stock short, you borrow shares from another investor, sell them, and then wait until the price falls and you can buy the stock back for less than you sold it for. You return the borrowed shares and pocket the difference. Sounds easy, but there are costs and fees to be paid, and in some cases, you won't be able to find shares to borrow.[45] And if you're wrong and the stock price increases, then sooner or later you will be forced to repurchase the stock at a higher price (therefore at a loss) to return the borrowed shares to the lender.

The perils of selling short were dramatically illustrated in 2008. Given the gloomy outlook for the automobile industry, several hedge funds decided to sell Volkswagen (VW) shares short. Then in a surprise announcement, Porsche revealed that it had effectively gained control of 74% of VW's shares. Since a further 20% was held by the state of Lower Saxony, there wasn't enough stock available for the short sellers to buy back. As they scrambled to cover their positions, the price of VW stock rose in just two days from €209 to a high of €1,005, making VW the most highly valued company in the world. Although the stock price drifted rapidly down, those short-sellers who were caught in the *short squeeze* suffered large losses.[46]

These risks exist even for "riskless" arbitrage. We earlier explained that for stocks, most arbitrage is risky, but seemingly riskless arbitrages do exist. One example is "Siamese twins," two securities with claims on the same cash flows, which nevertheless trade separately. Before they fully merged in July 2005, Dutch company Royal Dutch Petroleum and British company Shell only pooled their assets. They remained separate companies, and shared all dividends from their assets 60–40. So in theory, the market value of Royal Dutch at all times should be 1.5 times the market value of Shell. But the theoretical valuation might not hold in practice. It may be that the Dutch economy takes a tumble, which causes the price of Royal Dutch to fall in line with the overall Dutch market, and the market might "forget" that the price of Royal Dutch should always be 1.5 times the price of Shell. Indeed, as you can see from Figure 12.8, the prices of the two shares sometimes diverged substantially.[47]

It might seem that there's a riskless arbitrage here. Suppose that you were a professional money manager in 1980 when Royal Dutch was about 12% below the "correct" ratio of 1.5. You sell Shell short, buy 1.5 times the amount of Royal Dutch, and wait confidently for the price ratio to converge back to 1.5, a so-called *convergence trade*. In the long run, this trade

BEYOND THE PAGE

Short sales

mhhe.com/brealey14e

---

[45]Investment and brokerage firms identify shares eligible for lending and arrange to make them available to short-sellers. The supply of shares that can be borrowed is limited. You are charged a fee for borrowing the stock, and you are required to put up collateral to protect the lender in case the share price rises and the short-seller is unable to repurchase and return the shares. Putting up collateral is costless if the short-seller gets a market interest rate, but sometimes only lower interest rates are offered.

[46]See F. Allen, M. Haas, E. Nowak, and A. Tengulov, "Market Efficiency and Limits to Arbitrage: Evidence from the Volkswagen Short Squeeze," *Journal of Financial Economics* 142, 2021, pp. 166–194.

[47]For evidence on the pricing of Siamese twins, see K. A. Froot and E. Dabora, "How Are Stock Prices Affected by the Location of Trade?" *Journal of Financial Economics* 53 (August 1999), pp. 189–216; and, for more recent data, A. De Jong, L. Rosenthal, and M. A. Van Dijk, "The Risk and Return of Arbitrage in Dual-Listed Companies," *Review of Finance* 13 (2009), pp. 495–520.

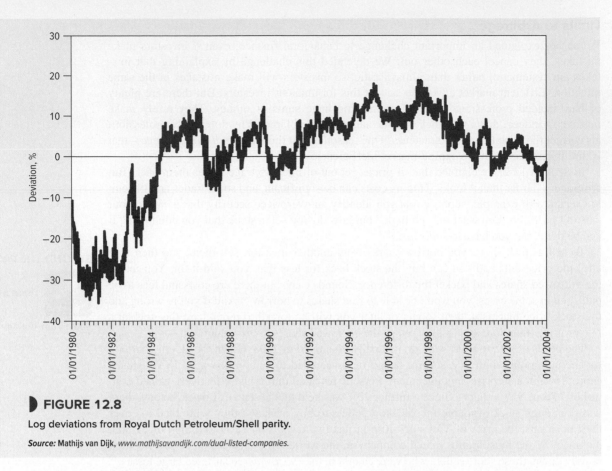

FIGURE 12.8

Log deviations from Royal Dutch Petroleum/Shell parity.

Source: Mathijs van Dijk, *www.mathijsavandijk.com/dual-listed-companies.*

is risk-free, because in the long run, the dividends received by Royal Dutch will be exactly 1.5 times the dividends received by Shell. But the long run can be a long time. The first time you would have seen any profit on your position was in 1983. In the meantime, the mispricing got worse, not better. Royal Dutch fell to more than 30% below 1.5 in mid-1981. Investors have to "mark-to-market"—report the interim value of any long and short positions, even if you haven't closed them out. Therefore, you had to report a substantial loss on your "arbitrage" strategy in that year. You pleaded with investors to be patient; you claimed that you had a great long-term strategy that would eventually pay off but had just been unlucky in the short term. But an incompetent manager with a bad long-term strategy would have given exactly the same excuse. Investors didn't believe you and withdrew their money, causing your fund to collapse. Moreover, other money managers, fearing the same risk, chose not to undertake the convergence trade and so didn't correct prices.

The demise in 1998 of Long Term Capital Management (LTCM) provides another example of the problems with convergence trades. LTCM, one of the largest and most profitable hedge funds of the 1990s, believed that interest rates in the different eurozone countries would converge when the euro replaced the countries' previous currencies. LTCM had taken massive positions to profit from this convergence and other pricing discrepancies. After the Russian government announced a moratorium on some of its debt payments in August 1998, there was great turbulence in the financial markets, and many of the discrepancies that LTCM was betting on suddenly got much larger.[48] LTCM was losing hundreds of millions of dollars daily.

---

[48]The Russian debt moratorium was unexpected and unusual because the debt had only recently been issued and was denominated in *roubles*. The Russian government could have printed roubles to service the debt, but decided to default instead.

The Federal Reserve Bank of New York arranged for a group of LTCM's creditor banks to take over LTCM's remaining assets and shut it down.

12.8 Self-Test

Two years ago, a 5-year Treasury note was issued and so it has three years left until maturity. A newly-issued 3-year Treasury note is trading at a higher price than the two-year-old 5-year note.

    a. What strategy would you implement to exploit the mispricing?

    b. Why might such a strategy be risky?

Agency and Incentive Problems

Another important reason financial markets can be inefficient is agency and incentive problems. In many countries, particularly those with sophisticated financial systems, investors do not directly invest their own wealth in stock, bond, or other financial markets. Instead, they use financial intermediaries that invest the wealth on their behalf. These include banks, insurance companies, pension funds, mutual funds, private equity funds, hedge funds, and various other types of institutions. This intermediation introduces agency and incentive problems that can get in the way of a rational focus on fundamentals and distort markets. In particular, they can lead to mispricing and potentially asset price bubbles.[49]

One major aspect of incentive problems that intermediation introduces is due to the use of debt and other related contracts. If the intermediaries (the agents) actually making the investment decision have debt contracts with the people providing the funds (the principals), they have an incentive to take risks since they receive the upside in the payoff but can default if the investment is unsuccessful with the providers of funds bearing the loss. This is known as "risk shifting." Other contracts where the agents investing the wealth are rewarded for gains but are not fully penalized for losses provide similar risk shifting incentives.

These risk shifting incentives appear particularly important in real estate markets where the purchasers borrow most or all the purchase price from a bank or other intermediary using a mortgage. If the price of the real estate goes up, the borrower makes a profit while if it goes down, they can default and the bank (or the government providing an implicit or explicit guarantee) bears the loss. Many people argue that the origin of the financial crisis of 2008–2009 was due to this and other incentive problems in the real estate market.

Although U.S. house prices had risen nearly threefold in the decade prior to 2006, few homeowners foresaw a collapse in the price of their home. After all, the average house price in the United States had not fallen since the Great Depression of the 1930s. But in 2006 the bubble burst. By March 2009, U.S. house prices had fallen by nearly a third from their peak.[50]

How could such a boom and crash arise? In part it was because banks, credit rating agencies, and other financial institutions all had distorted incentives. Purchases of real estate are generally financed with mortgage loans from banks. In most parts of the United States, borrowers can default on their mortgages with relatively small penalties. If property prices fall, they can simply walk away. But if prices rise, they make money. Thus, borrowers may be willing to take large risks, especially if the fraction of the purchase price financed with their own money is small.

Why, then, are banks willing to lend money to people who are bound to default if property prices fall significantly? Since the borrowers benefited most of the time, they were willing to pay up-front fees to banks to get mortgage loans. But the banks could pass on the default risk

---

[49]See F. Allen, "Do Financial Institutions Matter?" *Journal of Finance* 56 (2001), pp. 1165–1175.

[50]Investors who did foresee that the fall in house prices would lead to the subprime debacle were able to earn high profits. For example, John Paulson, the hedge fund manager, earned $3.7 billion in 2007 as a result (Financial Times, January 15, 2008, and June 18, 2008).

to somebody else by packaging and reselling the mortgages as mortgage-backed securities (MBSs). Many MBS buyers assumed that they were safe investments because the credit rating agencies said so. As it turned out, the credit ratings were a big mistake. (The rating agencies introduced another agency problem because the issuers paid the agencies to rate the MBS issues, and the agencies consulted with issuers over how MBS issues should be structured.)

The "somebody else" was also the government. Many subprime mortgages were sold to FNMA and FHLMC (Fannie Mae and Freddie Mac). These were private corporations with a special advantage: government credit backup. (The backup was implicit but quickly became explicit when Fannie and Freddie got into trouble in 2008. The U.S. Treasury had to take them over.) Thus, these companies were able to borrow at artificially low rates, channeling money into the mortgage market.

The government was also on the hook because large banks that held subprime MBSs were "too big to fail" in a financial crisis. So the original incentive problem—the temptation of home buyers to take out a large mortgage and hope for higher real estate prices—was never corrected. The government could have cut its exposure by reining in Fannie and Freddie before the crisis but did not do so, perhaps because the government was happy to see more people able to buy their homes.

Agency and incentive problems are widespread in the financial services industry. In the United States and many other countries, people engage financial institutions such as pension funds and mutual funds to invest their money. These institutions are the investors' agents, but the agents' incentives do not always match the investors' interests. These agency and incentive problems can lead to significant market inefficiency.

- - - - -

KEY TAKEAWAYS

- **It's much easier to find positive-NPV investments in product markets than in financial markets.**
  Financial markets are much more competitive than product markets. As a result, positive-NPVs are competed away in financial markets but may not be in product markets if non-financial firms have monopoly power of some kind.

- **An efficient market is one where prices reflect all available information**

$$P_0 = \sum_{t=0}^{\infty} \frac{D_t}{(1+r)^t} I_0 \tag{12.1}$$

There are three types of market efficiency, weak-form, semi-strong, and strong. *Weak-form efficiency* defines "available information" as "information contained in past prices." In this case it is impossible to earn superior returns by looking for patterns in stock prices. *Semistrong-form efficiency* defines "available information" as "public information." This includes past prices, but also any other information available from public sources. *Strong-form efficiency* defines "available information" as both public and private information. Private information is information that's not publicly available.

- **We expect markets to be efficient because of arbitrage.**
  Competition between traders will tend to produce an efficient market. In such a market, prices will rapidly impound any new information, and it will be difficult to make consistently superior returns.

- **If markets are weak-form efficient, then stock prices are random walks and price changes are random and are unrelated to past price changes.**
  Prices in competitive markets must follow a random walk. If past price changes could be used to predict future price changes, investors could make easy profits. But in competitive markets, there are no such opportunities. As investors try to take advantage of any information in past prices, prices adjust immediately until the superior profits from studying price movements disappear.

- **In an efficient market, prices adjust so on average stocks earn their risk adjusted expected returns.**
  The process of arbitrage ensures there are no good or bad investments and investors are only rewarded for the risk they bear.

- **Investors should hold the market portfolio to maximize the benefits of diversification.**
  Since, in an efficient market, stocks on average only earn their risk adjusted return, investors should hold a portfolio that is as well-diversified as possible. This is the market portfolio.

- **Stock prices reflect firms' fundamental values.**
  Since stock prices incorporate all available information, they reflect fundamental values.

- **Financing decisions cannot create or destroy value.**
  Another implication of the fact that stock prices reflect all information is that debt and equity are fairly priced, so financing decisions cannot create or destroy value.

- **While there is much evidence that is consistent with weak-form and semistrong-form market efficiency, there is also some evidence that is not.**
  There is a wide range of evidence that stock prices follow a random walk in the short run. However, at longer horizons there is evidence for reversal and momentum, which run counter to stocks being random walks and markets being weak-form efficient. Most active mutual funds underperform the market consistently, which is consistent with semistrong efficiency. However, post-earnings announcement drift is not consistent with this type of efficiency.

- **There is considerable evidence against strong-form efficiency.**
  There is considerable evidence that corporate insiders, such as executives and directors, can beat the market through insider trading.

- **Various behavioral biases and sentiment factors can lead to mispricing.**
  There is considerable psychological evidence that people do not behave rationally and have various biases and are affected by sentiment factors.

- **Limits to arbitrage can ensure that rational investors cannot overcome behavioral factors.**
  Arbitrage is the force that underlies efficient markets. However, there are often limitations to arbitrage such as transaction costs and risks that cannot be hedged, which prevent arbitrage from occurring.

- **Agency and incentive problems can lead to significant inefficiencies.**
  In many countries, financial intermediaries play an important role in investing funds. This leads to agency and incentive problems that can result in asset price bubbles and other kinds of mispricing.

● ● ● ● ●

FURTHER READING

Malkiel's book is an-easy-to-read book on market efficiency. Fama has written two classic review articles on the topic:

B. G. Malkiel, *A Random Walk Down Wall Street,* 11th ed. (New York: W. W. Norton, 2016).

E. F. Fama, "Efficient Capital Markets: A Review of Theory and Empirical Work," *Journal of Finance* 25 (May 1970), pp. 383–417.

E. F. Fama, "Efficient Capital Markets: II," *Journal of Finance* 46 (December 1991), pp. 1575–1617.

There are several useful surveys of behavioral finance:

N. Barberis and R. H. Thaler, "A Survey of Behavioral Finance," in G. M. Constantinides, M. Harris, and R. M. Stulz (eds.), *Handbook of the Economics of Finance* (Amsterdam: Elsevier Science, 2003).

M. Baker, R. S. Ruback, and J. Wurgler, "Behavioral Corporate Finance: A Survey," in B. E. Eckbo (ed.), *The Handbook of Empirical Corporate Finance* (Amsterdam: Elsevier/North-Holland, 2007), Chapter 4.

R. J. Shiller, "Human Behavior and the Efficiency of the Financial System," in J. B. Taylor and M. Woodford (eds.), *Handbook of Macroeconomics* (Amsterdam: North-Holland, 1999).

A. Shleifer, *Inefficient Markets: An Introduction to Behavioral Finance* (Oxford: Oxford University Press, 2000).

R. H. Thaler (ed.), *Advances in Behavioral Finance* (New York: Russell Sage Foundation, 1993).

D. Hirshleifer, "Behavioral Finance," *Annual Review of Financial Economics* 7 (December 2015), pp. 133–159.

Some conflicting views on market efficiency are provided by:

G. W. Schwert, "Anomalies and Market Efficiency," in G. M. Constantinides, M. Harris, and R. M. Stulz (eds.), *Handbook of the Economics of Finance* (Amsterdam: Elsevier Science, 2003).

M. Rubinstein, "Rational Markets: Yes or No? The Affirmative Case?" *Financial Analysts Journal* 57 (May–June 2001), pp. 15–29.

B. G. Malkiel, "The Efficient Market Hypothesis and Its Critics," *Journal of Economic Perspectives* 17 (Winter 2003), pp. 59–82.

R. J. Shiller, "From Efficient Markets Theory to Behavioral Finance," *Journal of Economic Perspectives* 17 (Winter 2003), pp. 83–104.

E. F. Fama and K. R. French, "Dissecting Anomalies," *Journal of Finance* 63 (August 2008), pp. 1653–1678.

Bubbles are discussed in:

M. Brunnermeier, *Asset Pricing under Asymmetric Information: Bubbles, Crashes, Technical Analysis, and Herding* (Oxford: Oxford University Press, 2001).

A. Scherbina, "Asset Price Bubbles: A Selective Survey," IMF Working Paper 13/45, 2013.

R. J. Shiller, *Irrational Exuberance,* 2nd ed. (Princeton, NJ: Princeton University Press, 2005).

For discussions of the rationality of prices in particular bull markets, see

L. Pastor and P. Veronesi, "Was There a Nasdaq Bubble in the Late 1990s?" *Journal of Financial Economics* 81 (2006), pp. 61–100.

M. Richardson and E. Ofek, "DotCom Mania: The Rise and Fall of Internet Stock Prices," *Journal of Finance* 58 (2003), pp. 1113–1138.

K. French and J. M. Poterba, "Were Japanese Stock Prices Too High?" *Journal of Financial Economics* 29 (October 1991), pp. 337–363.

● ● ● ● ●

PROBLEM SETS

 **Select problems are available in McGraw Hill's *Connect*. Please see the preface for more information.**

1. **Market efficiency (S12.1 and S12.2)*** True or false?

   a. Financing decisions are less easily reversed than investment decisions.

   b. Tests have shown that there is almost perfect negative correlation between successive price changes.

   c. The semistrong form of the efficient-market hypothesis states that prices reflect all publicly available information.

   d. In efficient markets, the expected return on each stock is the same.

2. **Market efficiency (S12.2)** True or false? The efficient-market hypothesis assumes that

   a. There are no taxes.

   b. There is perfect foresight.

   c. Successive price changes are independent.

   d. Investors are irrational.

   e. There are no transaction costs.

   f. Forecasts are unbiased.

3. **Market efficiency (S12.2)** Which (if any) of these statements are true? Stock prices appear to behave as though successive values

   a. Are random numbers.

   b. Follow regular cycles.

   c. Differ by a random number.

4. **Market efficiency (S12.2)** Supply the missing words: "There are three forms of the efficient-market hypothesis. Tests of randomness in stock returns provide evidence for the _____ form of the hypothesis. Tests of stock price reaction to well-publicized news provide evidence for the _____ form, and tests of the performance of insiders provide evidence for the _____ form. Market efficiency results from competition between investors. Many investors search for new information about the company's business that would help them to value the stock more accurately. Such research helps to ensure that prices reflect all publicly available information; in other words, it helps to keep the market efficient in the _____ form. Other investors study past stock prices for recurrent patterns that would allow them to make superior profits. Such research helps to ensure that prices reflect all the information contained in past stock prices; in other words, it helps to keep the market efficient in the _____ form."

5. **Market efficiency (S12.2)** How would you respond to the following comments?

   a. "Efficient market, my eye! I know lots of investors who do crazy things."

   b. "Efficient market? Balderdash! I know at least a dozen people who have made a bundle in the stock market."

   c. "The trouble with the efficient-market theory is that it ignores investors' psychology."

   d. "Despite all the limitations, the best guide to a company's value is its written-down book value. It is much more stable than market value, which depends on temporary fashions."

6. **Market efficiency (S12.2)** Respond to the following comments:

   a. "The random-walk theory, with its implication that investing in stocks is like playing roulette, is a powerful indictment of our capital markets."

   b. "If everyone believes you can make money by charting stock prices, then price changes won't be random."

   c. "The random-walk theory implies that events are random, but many events are not random. If it rains today, there's a fair bet that it will rain again tomorrow."

7. **Market efficiency (S12.2)** "If the efficient-market hypothesis is true, the pension fund manager might as well select a portfolio with a pin." Explain why this is not so.

8. **Market efficiency implications (S12.3)** Two financial managers, Alpha and Beta, are contemplating a chart showing the actual performance of the Standard and Poor's Composite Index over a five-year period. Each manager's company needs to issue new shares of common stock sometime in the next year.

   Alpha: My company's going to issue right away. The stock market cycle has obviously topped out, and the next move is almost surely down. Better to issue now and get a decent price for the shares.

   Beta: You're too nervous; we're waiting. It's true that the market's been going nowhere for the past year or so, but the figure clearly shows a basic upward trend. The market's on the way up to a new plateau.

   What would you say to Alpha and Beta?

9. **Market efficiency implications (S12.3)** What does the efficient-market hypothesis have to say about these two statements?

   a. "I notice that short-term interest rates are about 1% below long-term rates. We should borrow short-term."

   b. "I notice that interest rates in Japan are lower than rates in the United States. We would do better to borrow Japanese yen rather than U.S. dollars."

10. **Market efficiency implications (S12.3)*** True or false?

   a. If markets are efficient, shareholders should expect to receive only the risk-free interest rate on their investment.

   b. If markets are efficient, investment in the stock market is a mug's game.

   c. If markets are efficient, investors should just invest in firms with good management and an above-average track record.

   d. In an efficient market, investors should expect stocks to sell at a fair price.

11. **Abnormal returns (S12.3)*** Analysis of 60 monthly rates of return on United Futon common stock indicates a beta of 1.45 and an alpha of −0.2% per month. A month later, the market is up by 5%, and United Futon is up by 6%. What is Futon's abnormal rate of return?

12. **Abnormal returns (S12.3)** The second column in Table 12.2 shows the monthly return on the British FTSE 100 index from January 2015 through July 2017. The remaining columns show returns on the stocks of two firms—Executive Cheese and Paddington Beer. Both firms announced their earnings in July 2017. Calculate the average abnormal return of the two stocks during the month of the earnings announcement. The earnings of one of these stocks slightly disappointed investors and the earnings of the other were slightly better than expected. Which was which?

⟩TABLE 12.2   See Problem 16. Rates of return in percent per month.

Month	Market Return	Executive Cheese Return	Paddington Beer Return
January 2015	2.8	3.6	1.6
February	2.9	7.0	1.5
March	−2.5	−2.2	−0.7
April	2.8	3.1	3.0
May	0.3	0.2	0.1
June	−3.9	−6.5	1.1
July	−0.2	0.1	0.6
August	−6.7	−9.8	−4.6
September	−3.0	−7.2	−5.3
October	4.9	5.8	6.1
November	−0.1	0.2	0.1
December	−1.8	−1.0	−1.2
January 2016	−2.5	−3.1	0.6
February	0.2	0.3	1.7
March	1.3	1.7	2.1
April	1.1	1.1	3.0
May	−0.2	0.1	1.6
June	4.4	7.4	2.8
July	3.4	4.0	0.9
August	0.8	1.2	1.0
September	1.7	5.1	1.3
October	0.8	3.7	−1.6
November	−2.4	−2.7	−1.2
December	5.3	10.7	1.8
January 2017	−0.6	−0.4	−0.7
February	2.3	2.8	2.4
March	0.8	0.7	0.8
April	−1.6	−1.0	−1.2
May	4.4	6.2	−3.7
June	−2.8	−3.2	−1.3
July	2.7	3.0	2.9

13. **Abnormal returns (S12.3)** Here are alphas and betas for Estée Lauder and Caterpillar Tractor for the 60 months ending June 2017. Alpha is expressed as a percent per month.

	Alpha	Beta
Estée Lauder	0.48	0.70
Caterpillar Tractor	−0.41	1.26

Explain how these estimates would be used to calculate an abnormal return.

14. **Market efficiency evidence (S12.4)** Fama and French show that average stock returns on firms with small market capitalizations have been significantly higher than average returns for "large-cap" firms. What are the possible explanations for this result? Does the result disprove market efficiency? Explain briefly.

15. **Market efficiency evidence (S12.4)** Which of the following observations appear to indicate market inefficiency? Explain whether the observation appears to contradict the weak, semi-strong, or strong form of the efficient-market hypothesis.

    a. Tax-exempt municipal bonds offer lower pretax returns than taxable government bonds.

    b. Managers make superior returns on purchases of their company's stock.

    c. There is a positive relationship between the return on the market in one quarter and the change in aggregate profits in the next quarter.

    d. There is some evidence that stocks that have appreciated unusually in the recent past continue to do so in the future.

    e. The stock of an acquired firm tends to appreciate in the period before the merger announcement.

    f. Stocks of companies with unexpectedly high earnings appear to offer high returns for several months after the earnings announcement.

    g. Very risky stocks on average give higher returns than safe stocks.

16. **Market efficiency evidence (S12.4)** Give two or three examples of research results or events that raise doubts about market efficiency. Briefly explain why.

17. **Behavioral finance (S12.5)** Explain how incentive and agency problems might contribute to mispricing of securities or to bubbles. Give examples.

18. **Behavioral finance (S12.5)** True or false?

    a. Psychologists have found that once people have suffered a loss, they are more relaxed about the possibility of incurring further losses.

    b. Psychologists have observed that people tend to put too much weight on recent events when forecasting.

    c. Behavioral biases open up the opportunity for easy arbitrage profits.

19. **Behavioral finance (S12.5)** Many commentators have blamed the subprime crisis on "irrational exuberance." What is your view? Explain briefly.

CHALLENGE

21. **Market efficiency (S12.2)** "The strong form of the efficient-market hypothesis is nonsense. Look at mutual fund X; it has had superior performance for each of the last 10 years." Does the speaker have a point? Suppose that there is a 50% probability that X will obtain superior performance in any year simply by chance.

    a. If X is the only fund, calculate the probability that it will have achieved superior performance for each of the past 10 years.

    b. Now recognize that there are nearly 10,000 mutual funds in the United States. What is the probability that by chance there is at least 1 out of 10,000 funds that obtained 10 successive years of superior performance?

22. **Bubbles (S12.3)** Some extreme bubbles are obvious with hindsight, *after* they burst. But how would you *define* a bubble? There are many examples of good news and rising stock prices, followed by bad news and falling stock prices. Can you set out rules and procedures to distinguish bubbles from the normal ups and downs of stock prices?

• • • • •

SOLUTIONS TO SELF-TEST QUESTIONS

12.1 a. Project B: It has a higher NPV. The NPV is all that matters in efficient capital markets. It already takes into account the cost of capital and when the cash flows arise.

    b. Project B, for the same reasons as above.

12.2 a. Strong form.

    b. Semistrong form, and thus also strong form.

    c. None. The higher returns are due to risk.

    d. Semistrong form, and thus also strong form.

    e. Weak form, and thus also semistrong and strong forms.

12.3 a. No. Both growth and value stocks are fairly priced.

    b. No. The expected return from a stock depends on its current beta and the current risk-free rate and market risk premium. Last year's realized return is irrelevant.

    c. No. The stock price incorporates the fact that toy sales are higher in December.

    d. Yes. As soon as the merger is announced, the stock price should reflect its expected long-term value.

12.4 a. No. If the market is strong-form efficient, the stock price will already reflect any private information causing managers to have a negative assessment.

    b. No. Strong-form efficiency implies weak-form efficiency, and if the market is weak-form efficient, you cannot make money trading on past price movements.

    c. No. A CEO should only invest in artificial intelligence projects if their NPV is positive. Investor preferences do not matter due to the Fisher Separation Theorem.

12.5 a. The manager issues stock when she believes it is overpriced and may invest the proceeds in negative-NPV projects to hide the motive for the stock issue.

    b. The manager repurchases stock when she believes it is underpriced and may turn down positive-NPV investments if they can only be financed by issuing equity.

    c. The manager may turn down positive-NPV projects with positive distant cash flows and take negative-NPV projects with positive near-term cash flows.

12.6 a. Inconclusive. Semistrong-form efficiency requires the stock price to *fully* respond to new information. We don't know whether the stock price fall is too much, too little, or just right.

    b. Contradict.

    c. Support.

    d. Contradict.

    e. Inconclusive. Semistrong-form efficiency requires the stock price to rise by the probability of a takeover multiplied by the premium if a takeover occurs. We don't know whether the price rise is too much, too little, or just right.

12.7 a. Confirmation bias. Investors ignored information suggesting the pandemic might be serious because they did not want it to be true.

b. Overextrapolation. Investors overextrapolated from recent price rises and expected the price to continue to rise.

12.8 a. Buy the (cheap) two-year-old 5-year note and short-sell the (expensive) 3-year note.

b. The mispricing might temporarily widen, that is the 5-year note becomes even cheaper and the 3-year note becomes even more expensive, and you are forced to liquidate your position before the mispricing corrects.

Visit https://www.gresham.ac.uk/series/psychology-of-finance for a Gresham College public lecture series entitled "The Psychology of the Stock Market" by Alex Edmans.

FINANCE ON THE WEB

CHAPTER

An Overview of Corporate Financing

We now begin our analysis of long-term financing decisions—an undertaking we will not complete until Chapter 26. This chapter provides an introduction to corporate financing. It broadly reviews several topics that we will explore more carefully later on.

Section 13.1 Patterns of corporate financing

We start the chapter by looking at aggregate data on the sources of financing. Most of the money for new investments comes from profits that companies retain and reinvest. The remainder can come either from borrowing or from selling new shares. We will see that in aggregate, companies are paying out more money to shareholders through dividends and repurchases than they raise through issuing shares.

Section 13.2 Equity

Our second task in the chapter is to review some of the essential features of equity and debt. Lenders and stockholders have different *cash-flow rights* and also different *control rights*. The lenders have first claim on cash flow because they are promised definite cash payments for interest and principal. After the lenders have been paid, whatever cash is left over belongs to the stockholders. Stockholders, on the other hand, have complete control of the firm, providing that they keep their promises to lenders. Of course, in large public corporations, the stockholders delegate most decisions to the board of directors, who in turn appoint senior management. In these cases, *effective* control often ends up with the company's management. We revisit this topic in Chapter 19 when we discuss corporate governance.

Section 13.3 Debt

Debt has a prior claim on cash flows, but its claim is limited to the amount of the debt. In contrast to equity, it does not have residual cash-flow rights, and it does not participate in the upside of the business. Also, unlike equity, debt offers no control rights unless the firm defaults or violates debt covenants.

Companies can choose from an enormous variety of debt securities. They may borrow for only a few days or for many years; they may borrow dollars, euros, or some other currency; they may pay a fixed or floating rate of interest; and so on. We will sketch out these choices in this chapter, but look at them in more detail in Chapter 25.

Section 13.4 The role of the financial system

An important function of the financial system is to channel funds from investors to companies in the form of new equity or debt. These funds are then used to finance real investment. But the financial system fulfills several other functions that are necessary for our well-being. For example, it allows individuals and firms to make payments to each other quickly, and it offers ways for firms or individuals to share their risks. When markets and intermediaries cease to operate properly, the economy can suffer badly. A box on the financial crisis of 2007–2009 illustrates this.

Section 13.5 Financial markets and intermediaries

The financial manager is the link between the firm and the financial institutions and markets that provide much of the funds that the companies need. We, therefore, introduce you to the major financial institutions and look at the roles that these institutions play in corporate financing and in the economy at large.

Section 13.6 Financial markets and intermediaries around the world

Financial markets and institutions vary significantly from country to country. This section documents how the various functions of the financial system such as risk sharing, funding of investment, and so forth, are achieved in different parts of the world.

Section 13.7 The fintech revolution

The role of financial markets and intermediaries is being challenged by new technologies that seek to automate their functions. These technologies are known collectively as *fintech*. We show how these technologies are changing the way finance is conducted in payment systems, person-to-person lending, crowdfunding, credit scoring, recording transactions, and initial coin offerings.

● ● ● ● ●

13-1   Patterns of Corporate Financing

Corporations invest in long-term assets, such as property, plant, and equipment, and in current assets, such as inventory and accounts receivable. Figure 13.1 shows where U.S. corporations get the cash to pay for these investments. The green bars show the cash that is generated internally. That is, it comes from earnings that are retained and not paid out as dividends.[1]

Internal funds are by far the principal source of cash for most corporations, but cash also moves between companies and investors. It flows from investors to companies whenever companies sell debt or new shares. It flows in the other direction back to investors whenever companies repay maturing debt or repurchase their shares.

You can see from the grey bars in Figure 13.1 that in each year the corporate sector is raising net new cash from debt investors. By contrast, the red bars show that for the most part the amount that companies raise by new share issues has been smaller than the cash spent on repurchasing stock.[2]

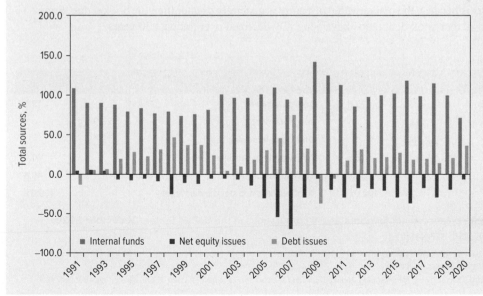

▶ **FIGURE 13.1**

Flow of funds for U.S. nonfinancial corporations.

Source: Board of Governors of the Federal Reserve System, Division of Research and Statistics, "Financial Accounts of the United States," Table F.103, at www.federalreserve.gov/releases/z1/current/data.htm.

---

[1] In Figure 13.1, internally generated cash was calculated by adding depreciation to retained earnings. Depreciation is a noncash expense. Thus, retained earnings understate the cash flow available for investment.

[2] Both dividends and stock repurchases distribute cash to shareholders. Therefore in Figure 13.1, we could have added dividends to internal funds and deducted them from net share issues. Cash flows to corporations would have been even more negative.

The flows shown in Figure 13.1 represent the sum of the financing decisions by thousands of individual companies. Some firms with cash shortages may have sold additional shares (we describe what is involved in such issues in Chapter 14). Others with surplus cash may have distributed it to shareholders by repurchasing stock (we discuss payout policy in Chapter 15). And others may have adjusted their cash holdings by selling new debt or repurchasing existing debt (we discuss debt policy in Chapters 16 and 17).

13.1 Self-Test

Which of the following sources of financing is most important to U.S. corporations as a whole: internal funds, net new borrowing, or stock issues?

How Much Do Firms Borrow?

The mix of debt and equity financing varies widely from industry to industry and from firm to firm. Debt ratios also vary over time for particular firms. These variations are a fact of life: There is no constant, standard debt ratio, and if there were, it would change. But a few aggregate statistics about the debt and equity for nonfinancial corporations will do no harm.

Table 13.1 shows the aggregate balance sheet of U.S. nonfinancial corporations. If all these businesses were merged into a single gigantic firm, Table 13.1 would be its balance sheet. The entries are shown as percentages of the total assets of this hypothetical corporation. All the items in the table are book values, that is, accounting values. These do not generally equal market values. The numbers are nevertheless instructive. Notice that long-term debt constituted 26.9% of the balance-sheet total, while equity accounted for 40.8%. The ratio of long-term debt to long-term debt plus equity was, therefore, $26.9/(26.9 + 40.8) = 0.40.$[3]

Table 13.1 is, of course, only a snapshot. Figure 13.2 provides a longer-term perspective. Notice that the debt ratios are lower when computed from market values rather than book values. This is because the market value of equity is generally greater than the book value. Figure 13.2 shows that book debt ratios have generally declined over the past 30 years.

Assets	%	Liabilities	%
Current assets[a]	25.8	Current liabilities[a]	19.1
Fixed assets	33.9	Long-term debt	26.9
Less depreciation	18.4	Other long-term liabilities[b]	13.1
Net fixed assets	15.5	Total long-term liabilities[b]	40.0
Other long-term assets	58.7	Stockholders' equity	40.8
Total assets	100.0%	Total liabilities and stockholders' equity	100.0%

❱ **TABLE 13.1**   Aggregate balance sheet for nonfinancial corporations in the United States, December 2020 (figures are percentages of total assets).

[a] See Table 31.1 for a breakdown of current assets and liabilities.
[b] Includes deferred taxes and several miscellaneous categories

Source: U.S. Census Bureau, *Quarterly Financial Report, Manufacturing, Mining, Trade, and Selected Service Industries,* 2020, Fourth Quarter, issued March 2021 (www.census.gov/econ/qfr).

---

[3] This debt ratio may be understated, because "Other long-term liabilities" probably include some debt-equivalent claims. We will not pause to sort through these other liabilities, however.

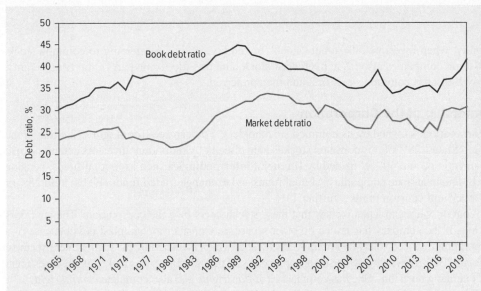

▶ **FIGURE 13.2**

Ratio of debt to debt plus net worth for nonfinancial corporations, 1965–2020.

Source: Board of Governors of the Federal Reserve System, Division of Research and Statistics, Flow of Funds Accounts Table B.103 at www.federalreserve.gov/releases/z1/current/default.htm.

13.2 Self-Test

How is it possible for debt ratios to decline when companies, on average, are issuing new debt and paying out cash to shareholders?

It is interesting to compare debt levels of U.S. companies with those of their foreign counterparts. In those countries that do not have well-developed bond markets, debt means principally short-term bank debt. Therefore, rather than focusing on just long-term debt, it is more instructive to compare the ratio of *total* liabilities to total liabilities plus equity. Figure 13.3 is taken from a study by Claessens, Djankov, and Nenova of 11,000 companies in 46 countries. Korean and Indian companies are among the most highly indebted; those in the United States are relatively conservative in their use of debt.

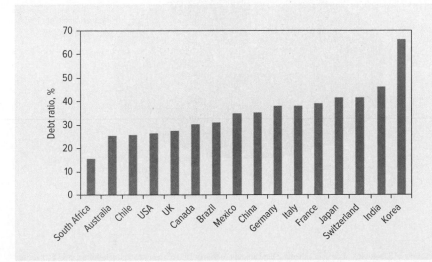

▶ **FIGURE 13.3**

Median ratios of total liabilities to total liabilities plus equity in different countries, 1995–1996.

Source: S. Claessens, S. Djankov, and T. Nenova, "Corporate Risk around the World," World Bank Policy Research Working Paper 2271, 2000, http://documents.worldbank.org/curated/en/907571468739464629/Corporate-risk-around-the-world.

13-2   Equity

Usually, when investors talk about "stock" or "equity," they are referring to common stock. But some companies also issue **preferred stock**, and this too forms part of the firms' equity. We will discuss common stock first and then preferred.

Ownership of the Corporation

A corporation is owned by its common stockholders. You can see from Figure 13.4 that in the United States, 38% of this common stock is held directly by individual investors and non-profit organizations, and 40% is owned by **financial intermediaries** such as mutual funds, pension funds, and insurance companies. Mutual funds and exchange traded funds (ETFs) hold 28% of the stock and pension funds a further 11%.[4]

What do we mean when we say that these stockholders *own* the corporation? The answer is obvious if the company has issued no other securities. Consider the simplest possible case of a corporation financed solely by common stock, all of which is owned by the firm's chief executive officer (CEO). This lucky owner-manager receives all the cash flows and makes all the investment and operating decisions. She has complete *cash-flow rights* and also complete *control rights*.

These rights are split up and reallocated as soon as the company borrows money. If it takes out a bank loan, it enters into a contract with the bank promising to pay interest and eventually repay the principal. The bank gets a privileged, but limited, right to cash flows; the residual cash-flow rights are left with the stockholder. Thus common stock is a *residual claim* on the firm's assets and cash flow.

The bank typically protects its claim by imposing restrictions on what the firm can or cannot do. For example, it may require the firm to limit future borrowing, and it may forbid the firm to sell off assets or to pay excessive dividends. The stockholders' control rights are thereby limited. However, the contract with the bank can never restrict or determine all the operating and investment decisions necessary to run the firm efficiently. (No team of lawyers,

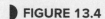
FIGURE 13.4

Holdings of corporate equities, December 2020.

Source: Board of Governors of the Federal Reserve System, Division of Research and Statistics, *Financial Accounts of the United States—Z1,* Table L.223, at https://www.federalreserve.gov/releases/z1/current/default.htm.

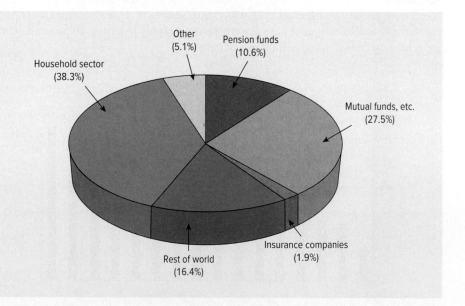

---

[4] Figure 13.4 does not show U.S. holdings of overseas shares. These amount to nearly 20% of the total equity holdings of U.S. investors.

no matter how long they scribbled, could ever write a contract covering all possible contingencies.[5]) The owner of the common stock retains the residual rights of control over these decisions. For example, she may choose to increase the selling price of the firm's products, to hire temporary rather than permanent employees, or to construct a new plant in Miami Beach rather than Hollywood.[6]

Ownership of the firm can of course change. If the firm fails to make the promised payments to the bank, it may be forced into bankruptcy. Once the firm is under the "protection" of a bankruptcy court, shareholders' cash-flow and control rights are tightly restricted and may be extinguished altogether. Unless some rescue or reorganization plan can be implemented, the bank becomes the new owner of the firm and acquires the cash-flow and control rights of ownership. (We discuss bankruptcy in Chapter 33.)

No law of nature says residual cash-flow rights and residual control rights have to go together. For example, one could imagine a situation where the debtholder gets to make all the decisions. But this would be inefficient. Since the benefits of good decisions are felt mainly by the common stockholders, it makes sense to give them control over how the firm's assets are used. Because they have the ultimate right of control and simultaneously have the residual cash flow entitlement, shareholders have an incentive to ensure that management maximizes wealth.

Public corporations may be owned by tens of thousands of stockholders. The common stockholders in these corporations still have the residual rights over the cash flows and have the ultimate right of control over the company's affairs. In practice, however, their control is limited to an entitlement to vote on appointments to the *board of directors,* and on other crucial matters such as the decision to merge. Many stockholders do not bother to vote. They reason that because they own so few shares, their vote will have little impact on the outcome. The problem is that, if all shareholders think in the same way, they cede effective control and management gets a free hand to look after its own interests.

This free-rider problem was highlighted in a book written in 1932 by Berle and Means.[7] They warned of the emergence of a powerful class of managers that were insulated from outside pressure. Economists today are less convinced that managers enjoy the degree of liberty that Berle and Means envisaged. The majority of corporations have large shareholders who are prepared to challenge self-serving or incompetent managers. For example, Clifford Holderness found that 96% of a sample of U.S. public corporations have *blockholders* with at least 5% of the outstanding shares.[8] In many other countries blockholders are even more important. Look, for example, at Figure 13.5, which is taken from a comprehensive study of share ownership in 85 countries. You can see that in the United States, the largest shareholder owns, on average, just over 21% of the outstanding shares.

In many of these cases, investors may take comfort from the fact that there are large shareholders with an incentive to keep a watchful eye on management. But the presence of blockholders is not always good news. In countries where the rule of law is weak, they may be able to profit at the expense of small shareholders, and their existence may be more a concern than a comfort. We will return to this topic of ownership when we review different governance systems in Chapter 19.

BEYOND THE PAGE

Empty voting

mhhe.com/brealey14e

---

[5] Theoretical economists therefore stress the importance of *incomplete contracts.* Their point is that contracts pertaining to the management of the firm are inevitably incomplete and that someone must exercise residual rights of control. See, for example, O. Hart, *Firms, Contracts, and Financial Structure* (Oxford: Oxford University Press, 1995).

[6] Of course, the bank manager may suggest that a particular decision is unwise, or even threaten to cut off future lending, but the bank does not have any *right* to make these decisions.

[7] A. A. Berle and G. C. Means, *The Modern Corporation and Private Property* (New York: The Macmillan Company, 1932).

[8] See C. Holderness, "The Myth of Diffuse Ownership in the United States," *Review of Financial Studies* 22 (April 2009), pp. 1377–1408; and R. La Porta, F. Lopez-de-Silanes, and A. Shleifer, "Corporate Ownership around the World," *Journal of Finance* 54 (1999), pp. 471–517. For a review of the extent and influence of blockholders, see A. Edmans and C. G. Holderness, "Blockholders: A Survey of Theory and Evidence," *The Handbook of the Economics of Corporate Governance,*1 (2017), pp. 541–636.

Equity in Disguise

❭ Common stocks are issued by corporations, but a few equity securities are issued not by corporations but by partnerships or trusts. We will give three examples.

Partnerships Plains All American Pipeline LP is a *master limited partnership* that owns crude oil pipelines in the United States and Canada. You can buy "units" in this partnership on the New York Stock Exchange, thus becoming a *limited partner* in Plains All American. The most the limited partners can lose is their investment in the company.[9] In this and most other respects, the partnership units are just like the shares in an ordinary corporation. They share in the profits of the business and receive cash distributions (such as dividends) from time to time.

Partnerships avoid corporate income tax; any profits or losses are passed straight through to the partners' tax returns. But various limitations offset this tax advantage. For example, the law regards a partnership merely as a voluntary association of individuals; like its partners, it is expected to have a limited life. A corporation, on the other hand, is an independent legal "person" that can, and often does, outlive all its original shareholders.

Trusts and REITs Would you like to own a part of the oil in the Prudhoe Bay field on the north slope of Alaska? Just call your broker and buy a few units of the BP Prudhoe Bay Royalty Trust. BP set up this trust and gave it a royalty interest in production from BP's share of the Prudhoe Bay revenues. As the oil is produced, each trust unit gets its share of the revenues.

This trust is the passive owner of a single asset: the right to a share of the revenues from the first 90,000 barrels of oil from BP's Prudhoe Bay operation that are produced each day. Operating businesses, which cannot be passive, are rarely organized as trusts, though there are exceptions, notably *real estate investment trusts,* or *REITs* (pronounced "reets").

REITs were created to facilitate public investment in commercial real estate; there are shopping center REITs, office building REITs, apartment REITs, and REITs that specialize in lending to real estate developers. REIT "shares" are traded just like common stocks. The REITs themselves are not taxed, so long as they distribute at least 95% of earnings to the REITs' owners, who must pay whatever taxes are due on the dividends. However, REITs are tightly restricted to real estate investment. You cannot set up a widget factory and avoid corporate taxes by calling it a REIT.

---

[9] A partnership can offer limited liability only to its limited partners. The partnership must also have one or more general partners, who have unlimited liability. However, general partners can be corporations. This puts the corporation's shield of limited liability between the partnership and the human beings who ultimately own the general partner.

❭ **FIGURE 13.5**

Average percentage of equity owned by largest shareholders. (Shareholders from one family are grouped together).

Source: G. Aminadav and E. Papaioannou, "Corporate Control around the World," *Journal of Finance* 75 (January 2020), pp. 1191–1246.

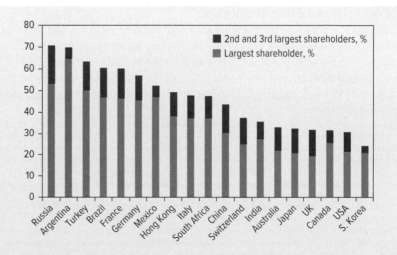

Preferred Stock

Despite its name, preferred stock provides only a small part of most companies' cash needs, and it will occupy less time in later chapters. However, it can be a useful method of financing in mergers and certain other special situations.

Like debt, preferred stock offers a series of fixed payments to the investor. The company can choose *not* to pay a preferred dividend, but in that case it may not pay a dividend to its common stockholders. Most issues of preferred are known as *cumulative preferred stock*. This means that the firm must pay *all* past preferred dividends before common stockholders get a cent. If the company does miss a preferred dividend, the preferred stockholders generally gain some voting rights, so that the common stockholders are obliged to share control of the company with the preferred holders. Directors are also aware that failure to pay the preferred dividend earns the company a black mark with investors, so they do not take such a decision lightly.

Companies cannot deduct preferred dividends when they calculate taxable income. Like common stock dividends, preferred dividends are paid from after-tax income. For most industrial firms, this is a serious deterrent to issuing preferred stock. However, regulated public utilities can take tax payments into account when they negotiate the rates that they are allowed to charge customers. So they can effectively pass the tax disadvantage of preferred on to the consumer. Preferred stock also has a particular attraction for banks because regulators allow banks to lump preferred in with common stock when calculating whether they have sufficient equity capital.

Preferred stock does have one tax advantage. If one corporation buys another's stock, only 50% of the dividends it receives are taxed. This rule applies to both common and preferred stock, but it is most important for preferred, for which returns are dominated by dividends rather than capital gains.

13-3   Debt

When companies borrow money, they promise to make regular interest payments and to repay the principal. However, this liability is limited. Stockholders have the right to default on the debt if they are willing to hand over the corporation's assets to the lenders. Clearly, they will choose to do this only if the value of the assets is less than the amount of the debt.[10]

Debt has a prior claim on cash flows, but its claim is limited to the amount of the debt. Therefore, in contrast to equity, it does not have residual cash-flow rights and it does not participate in the upsides of the business. Also, unlike equity, debt offers no control rights unless the firm defaults or violates debt covenants. Because lenders are not considered to be owners of the firm, they do not normally have any voting power.

The company's payments of interest are regarded as a cost and are deducted from taxable income. Thus interest is paid from *before-tax* income, whereas dividends on common and preferred stock are paid from *after-tax* income. Therefore, the government provides a tax subsidy for debt that it does not provide for equity (and from time to time complains that companies borrow too much). We discuss debt and taxes in detail in Chapter 17.

13.3 Self-Test

A company in a 21% tax bracket can buy a bond yielding 10% or a preferred stock of the same firm yielding 9%. Which will provide the higher after-tax yield?

---

[10] In practice, this handover of assets is far from straightforward. Sometimes thousands of lenders have different claims on the firm. Administration of the handover is usually left to the bankruptcy court (see Chapter 33).

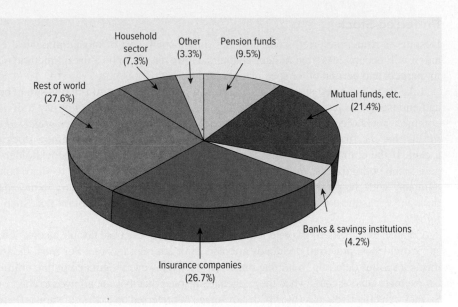

▶ **FIGURE 13.6**

Holdings of bonds issued in the United States by U.S. and foreign corporations, December 2020.

Source: Board of Governors of the Federal Reserve System, Division of Research and Statistics, *Financial Accounts of the United States—Z1,* Table L.213, at https://www.federalreserve.gov/releases/z1/current/default.htm.

We have seen that financial intermediaries own the majority of corporate equity. Figure 13.6 shows that this is also true of the company's bonds. In this case, it is the insurance companies that own the largest stake.[11]

The Different Kinds of Debt

There are two basic kinds of debt, though the distinction is not always clear-cut. The company may issue bonds or notes that may generally be traded by investors in the financial markets. Alternatively it may arrange a loan from a financial institution such as a bank or insurance company.

In either case the precise terms of the debt need to reflect the financial manager's response to a number of questions:

1. *Should the company borrow short-term or long-term?* If your company simply needs to finance a temporary increase in inventories ahead of the holiday season, then it may make sense to take out a short-term bank loan. But suppose that the cash is needed to pay for expansion of an oil refinery. Refinery facilities can operate more or less continuously for 15 or 20 years. In that case, it would be more appropriate to issue a long-term bond.[12]

   Some debts are repaid in a steady, regular way; in other cases, the entire debt is repaid at maturity. Occasionally the borrower has the option to repay the debt early.

2. *Should the debt be fixed or floating rate?* The interest payment, or coupon, on long-term bonds is commonly fixed at the time of issue. If a $1,000 bond is issued when long-term interest rates are 10%, the firm continues to pay $100 per year regardless of how interest rates fluctuate.

   Most bank loans and some bonds offer a variable, or *floating,* rate. For example, the interest rate in each period may be set at 1% above the secured overnight financing rate (SOFR). When SOFR changes, the interest rate on the loan also changes.

---

[11] Figure 13.6 does not include shorter-term debt such as bank loans. Almost all short-term debt issued by corporations is held by financial intermediaries.

[12] A company might choose to finance a long-term project with short-term debt if it wished to signal its confidence in the future. Investors would deduce that, if the company anticipated declining profits, it would not take the risk of being unable to take out a fresh loan when the first one matured. See D. Diamond, "Debt Maturity Structure and Liquidity Risk," *Quarterly Journal of Economics* 106 (1991), pp. 709–737.

13.4 Self-Test

Would you expect the value of a floating-rate loan to be more or less sensitive to interest rate changes than the value of a fixed-rate loan?

3. *Should you borrow dollars or some other currency?* Many firms in the United States borrow abroad. Often they may borrow dollars abroad (foreign investors have large holdings of dollars), but firms with overseas operations may decide to issue debt in a foreign currency. After all, if you need to spend foreign currency, it probably makes sense to borrow foreign currency.

   International bonds have usually been marketed by the London branches of international banks, and have traditionally been known as **eurobonds**. A eurobond may be denominated in dollars, yen, or any other currency. Unfortunately, when the single European currency was established, it was called the *euro*. It is, therefore, easy to confuse a *eurobond* (a bond that is sold internationally) with a bond that is denominated in euros.

4. *What promises should you make to the lender?* Lenders want to make sure that their debt is as safe as possible. Therefore, they may demand that their debt is *senior* to other debt. If default occurs, senior debt is first in line to be repaid. The *junior,* or *subordinated,* debtholders are paid only after all senior debtholders are satisfied (though all debtholders rank ahead of the preferred and common stockholders).

   The firm may also set aside some of its assets specifically for the protection of particular creditors. Such debt is said to be *secured,* and the assets that are set aside are known as *collateral.* Thus, a retailer might offer inventory or accounts receivable as collateral for a bank loan. If the retailer defaults on the loan, the bank can seize the collateral and use it to help pay off the debt.

   Usually, the firm also provides assurances to the lender that it will not take unreasonable risks. For example, a firm that borrows in moderation is less likely to get into difficulties than one that is loaded up with debt. So the borrower may agree to limit the amount of extra debt that it can issue. Lenders are also concerned that, if trouble occurs, others will push ahead of them in the queue. Therefore, the firm may agree not to create new debt that is senior to existing debtholders or to put aside assets for other lenders.

5. *Should you issue straight or convertible bonds?* Companies often issue securities that give the owner an option to convert them into other securities. These options may have a substantial effect on value. The most dramatic example is provided by a **warrant**, which is *nothing but* an option. The owner of a warrant can purchase a set number of the company's shares at a set price before a set date. Warrants and bonds are often sold together as a package.

   A **convertible bond** gives its owner the option to exchange the bond for a predetermined number of shares. The convertible bondholder hopes that the issuing company's share price will zoom up so that the bond can be converted at a big profit. But if the shares zoom down, there is no obligation to convert; the bondholder remains a bondholder.

   In Chapter 25, we will look more closely at these different types of debt.

13.5 Self-Test

Steerforth Corp. has issued a 5% bond with a face value of $1,000 that can be converted into 50 shares of common stock. If the stock price is $72 when the bond matures, would you recommend conversion?

A Debt by Any Other Name

The word *debt* sounds straightforward, but companies make a number of promises that look suspiciously like debt but are treated differently in the accounts. Some of these disguised debts are easily spotted. For example, accounts payable are simply obligations to pay for goods that have already been delivered and are, therefore, like short-term debt.

Other arrangements are less obvious. For example, instead of borrowing to buy new equipment, the company may rent or **lease** it on a long-term basis. In this case, the firm promises to make a series of lease payments to the owner of the equipment. This is just like the obligation to make payments on an outstanding loan. If the firm gets into deep water, it can't choose to miss out on its debt interest, and it can't choose to skip those lease payments.

Pension obligations are another disguised debt because companies are obligated to make the future payments to retired employees. These commitments can be huge. For example, in December 2020 the present value of GE's pension liabilities was $106 billion, significantly larger than the company's long-term debts.

There is nothing underhanded about lease or pension obligations. They either appear on the corporation's balance sheet or are explained in the notes to the financial statements. Careful investors recognize the debt-equivalent obligations and the financial risks that they create.[13]

But now and then, companies work hard to hide their debt to ensure that investors do *not* know how much the company has borrowed. For example, Enron was able to borrow $658 million by setting up *special-purpose entities (SPEs),* which raised cash by a mixture of equity and debt and then used these debts to help fund the parent company. None of this debt showed up on Enron's balance sheet, but the debt showed up with a vengeance in Enron's death spiral toward bankruptcy in 2001. Hiding debt is a way of cheating investors. No reputable company should do this.

13-4   The Role of the Financial System

We have seen that the financial system channels funds from investors to companies in the form of new equity or debt. These funds are then used to finance real investment. But other functions of the financial system may not be quite so obvious. Financial markets and intermediaries contribute in many ways to our individual well-being and the smooth functioning of the economy. Here are some examples.

The Payment Mechanism

Think how inconvenient life would be if all payments had to be made in cash. Fortunately, checking accounts, credit cards, and electronic transfers allow individuals and firms to send and receive payments quickly and safely over long distances. Banks are the obvious providers of payments services, but issuers of credit and debit cards, and services such as Alipay, PayPal, Google Wallet, Apple Pay, Venmo, WeChat pay, and Zelle all make it easier to transfer money.

We will have somewhat more to say about payment mechanisms in Chapter 31.

Borrowing and Lending

Financial institutions do not lend only to companies. They also channel savings toward individuals who can best use them. Thus, if Ms. Chen has more money than she needs now and wishes to save for a rainy day, she can put the money in a bank savings deposit. If Mr. Singh wants to buy a car now and pay for it later, he can borrow money from the bank. In other words, banks provide Chen and Singh with a time machine that allows them to transport their

---

[13] For example, see L. Jin, R. C. Merton, and Z. Bodie, "Do a Firm's Equity Returns Reflect the Risk of its Pension Plan?" *Journal of Financial Economics* 81 (2006), pp. 1–26.

wealth backward and forward over time. Both are happier than if they were forced to spend cash as it arrived.

This facility is important for a company's objectives. As we saw in Chapter 1, when individuals have access to borrowing and lending, companies do not have to worry that shareholders may have different time preferences. Companies can simply focus on maximizing firm value and investors can choose separately when they want to spend their wealth.

In principle, you don't need financial institutions to provide borrowing and lending. Individuals with cash surpluses, for example, could take out newspaper advertisements to find those with cash shortages. But it can be cheaper and more convenient to use a financial intermediary, such as a bank, to link up the borrower and lender. For example, banks are equipped to check out the would-be borrower's creditworthiness and to monitor the use of cash lent out.[14]

Pooling Risk

Financial markets and institutions allow firms and individuals to pool their risks. For instance, insurance companies make it possible to share the risk of an automobile accident or a household fire.

Here is another example. Suppose that you have only a small sum to invest. You could buy the stock of a single company, but then you would be wiped out if that company went belly-up. It is generally better to buy shares in a mutual fund that invests in a diversified portfolio of common stocks or other securities. In this case you are exposed only to the risk that security prices as a whole will fall.

Some financial markets specialize in risk transfer. For example, suppose that a producer of catalytic converters will need to buy 400 ounces of platinum next April but is worried that the price may spiral in the meantime. The company can fix the price of its purchase by buying April platinum futures on an exchange such as the Nymex futures exchange. We discuss futures markets in Chapter 27.

Information Provided by Financial Markets

In well-functioning financial markets, you can *see* what securities and commodities are worth, and you can see—or at least estimate—the rates of return that investors can expect on their savings. The information that financial markets provide is often essential to a financial manager's job. For example, stock prices summarize investors' collective assessment of how well a company is doing, both its current performance and its future prospects. Thus an increase in the stock price sends a positive signal from investors to managers.[15] That is why top management's compensation is linked to stock prices. A manager who owns shares in his or her company will be motivated to increase the company's market value. This reduces agency costs by aligning the interests of managers and stockholders. This is one important advantage of going public. A private company can't use its stock price as a measure of performance. It can still compensate managers with shares, but the shares will not be valued in a financial market. We discuss incentive compensation in Chapter 19.

BEYOND THE PAGE

Prediction markets

mhhe.com/brealey14e

---

[14] However, in the past decade a number of *peer-to-peer* lending firms (P2PLs), such as Prosper and Lending Club, have been established. These firms receive applications for loans from individuals or small businesses and then advertise on the Web for interested lenders. Lenders do not know the identity of the borrower, but the peer-to-peer intermediary does provide a credit score and its own credit assessment of the borrower, which is reflected in the interest rate being offered. The P2PL provides a market place that links borrowers and lenders. In addition, it offers credit information, and collects payments from borrowers and forwards them to the lenders. By contrast a bank *owns* its portfolio of loans and offers its depositors instant access to their money.

[15] We can't claim that investors' assessments of value are always correct. Finance can be a risky and dangerous business—dangerous for your wealth, that is. With hindsight we see horrible mistakes by investors. On average, however, it appears that financial markets collect and assess information quickly and accurately.

When Financial Markets Fail:
The Crisis of 2007–2009

❭ The financial crisis of 2007–2009 raised many questions, but it settled one question conclusively: Financial markets and institutions are important. When financial markets and institutions ceased to operate properly, the world was pushed deeper into a global recession.

BEYOND THE PAGE

Time line of the financial crisis

mhhe.com/brealey14e

The financial crisis had its roots in the easy-money policies that were pursued by the U.S. Federal Reserve and other central banks following the collapse of the Internet and telecom stock bubble in 2000. At the same time, large balance-of-payments surpluses in Asian economies were invested back into U.S. debt securities. This also helped to push down interest rates and contribute to the lax credit.

Banks took advantage of this cheap money to expand the supply of subprime mortgages to low-income borrowers. Many banks tempted would-be homeowners with low initial payments, offset by significantly higher payments later.[16] (Some home buyers were betting on escalating housing prices so that they could resell or refinance before the higher payments kicked in.)

Most subprime mortgages were then packaged together into mortgage-backed securities that could be resold. But, instead of selling these securities to investors who could best bear the risk, many banks kept large quantities of the loans on their own books or sold them to other banks.

BEYOND THE PAGE

U.S. house prices

mhhe.com/brealey14e

The widespread availability of mortgage finance fueled a dramatic increase in house prices, which doubled in many places in the five years ending June 2006. At that point, prices started to slide and homeowners began to default on their mortgages. A year later, Bear Stearns, a large investment bank, announced huge losses on the mortgage investments that were held in two of its hedge funds. By the spring of 2008, Bear Stearns was on the verge of bankruptcy, and the U.S. Federal Reserve arranged for it to be acquired by JPMorgan Chase.

---

[16] With a so-called option ARM loan, the minimum mortgage payment was often not even sufficient to cover that month's interest on the loan. The unpaid interest was then added to the amount of the mortgage, so the homeowner was burdened by an ever-increasing mortgage that one day would need to be paid off.

The crisis peaked in September 2008, when the U.S. government was obliged to take over the giant federal mortgage agencies Fannie Mae and Freddie Mac, both of which had invested several hundred billion dollars in subprime mortgage-backed securities. Over the next few days, the financial system started to melt down. Both Merrill Lynch and Lehman Brothers were in danger of failing. On September 14, the government arranged for Bank of America to take over Merrill in return for financial guarantees. However, it did nothing to rescue Lehman Brothers, which filed for bankruptcy protection the next day. Two days later, the government reluctantly lent $85 billion to the giant insurance company AIG, which had insured huge volumes of mortgage-backed securities and other bonds against default. The following day, the Treasury unveiled its first proposal to spend $700 billion to purchase "toxic" mortgage-backed securities.

BEYOND THE PAGE

The rise and fall of Lehman Brothers

mhhe.com/brealey14e

As the crisis unfolded through 2007 and 2008, uncertainty about which domino would be next to fall made banks reluctant to lend to one another, and the interest rate that they charged for such loans rose to 4.6% above the rate on U.S. Treasury debt. (Normally, this spread above Treasuries is less than 0.5%.) The bond market and the market for short-term company borrowing effectively dried up. This had an immediate knock-on effect on the supply of credit to industry, and the economy suffered one of its worst setbacks since the Great Depression.

Few developed economies escaped the crisis. As well as suffering from a collapse in their own housing markets, many foreign banks had made large investments in U.S. subprime mortgages. A roll call of all the banks that had to be bailed out by their governments would fill several pages, but here are just a few members of that unhappy band: the Royal Bank of Scotland in the United Kingdom, UBS in Switzerland, Allied Irish Bank in Ireland, Fortis in Belgium, ING in the Netherlands, Hypo Group in Austria, and WestLB in Germany.

Who was responsible for the financial crisis? In part, the U.S. Federal Reserve for its policy of easy money. The U.S. government also must take some of the blame for encouraging banks to expand credit for low-income housing.[17] The rating agencies were at fault for providing triple-A ratings for many mortgage bonds that shortly afterward went into default. Last but not least, the bankers themselves were guilty of promoting and reselling the subprime mortgages.

The banking crisis and subsequent recession left many governments with huge mountains of debt. By 2010, investors were becoming increasingly concerned about the position of Greece, where for many years government spending had been running well ahead of revenues. Greece's position was complicated by its membership in the single-currency eurozone. Although much of the country's borrowing was in euros, the government had no control over its currency and could not simply print more euros to service its debt. Investors began to contemplate the likelihood of a Greek government default and the country's possible exit from the eurozone. The failure of eurozone governments to deal decisively with the Greek problem prompted investors to worry about the prospects for other heavily indebted eurozone countries, such as Ireland, Portugal, Italy, and Spain. After several rescue attempts, Greece finally defaulted in 2011. But it was not the end of the story, and four years later, after failing to get further assistance, Greece defaulted on a loan from the IMF.

At least with hindsight, we can see that the run-up to the financial crisis saw plenty of examples of foolishness

---

[17]A rapid expansion of low-income home ownership is generally popular in government circles, and it chimed well with the aspirations set out in President Bush's goals of an "Ownership Society."

and greed. More than a decade after the crisis, bankers remain at the bottom of everyone's popularity list. That position has been reinforced by the revelations that several major banks

BEYOND THE PAGE

The Dodd-Frank Act

mhhe.com/brealey14e

had been rigging the interest rate and foreign exchange markets. But the lesson of the financial crisis and the subsequent scandals is not that we don't need a financial system; it is that we need it to work honestly and well.

Financial markets in the United States and most developed countries work well most of the time, but just like the little girl in the Longfellow poem, "when they are good, they are very good indeed, but when they are bad, they are horrid." During the financial crisis, markets were very horrid indeed. Think of some of the problems that you would have faced as a financial manager:

- Many of the world's largest banks teetered on the edge or had to be rescued so that there were few, or no, safe havens for cash.

- Stock and bond prices bounced around like Tigger on stimulants.

- Periodically, markets for some types of security dried up altogether, making it tough to raise cash.

- From the peak in 2006, manufacturing profits fell away sharply and the number of business bankruptcies tripled.

It must have seemed to financial managers as if they were being assailed from all sides.

13-5 Financial Markets and Intermediaries

The flow of savings from investors to public corporations is illustrated in Figure 13.7. Notice that these savings may travel through financial markets, financial intermediaries, or both. Suppose, for example, that Bank of America raises $300 million by a new issue of shares. An Italian investor buys 6,000 of the new shares for $10 per share. Now Bank of America takes that $60,000, along with money raised by the rest of the issue, and makes a $300 million loan to ExxonMobil. The Italian investor's savings end up flowing through financial markets (the stock market), to a financial intermediary (Bank of America), and finally to Exxon.

Of course, our Italian friend's $60,000 doesn't literally arrive at Exxon in an envelope marked "From L. DaVinci." Investments by the purchasers of the Bank of America's stock issue are pooled, not segregated. Sr. DaVinci would own a share of all of Bank of America's assets, not just one loan to Exxon. Nevertheless, investors' savings are flowing through the financial markets and then the bank to finance Exxon's capital investments.

Suppose that another investor decides to open a checking account with Bank of America. The bank can take the money in this checking account and also lend it on to ExxonMobil.

BEYOND THE PAGE

Stock exchanges: From clubs to commercial companies

mhhe.com/brealey14e

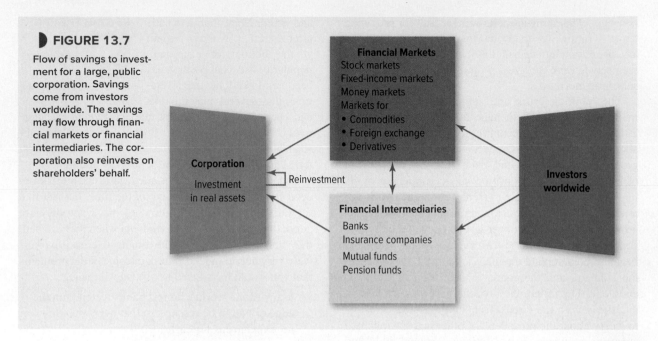

FIGURE 13.7

Flow of savings to investment for a large, public corporation. Savings come from investors worldwide. The savings may flow through financial markets or financial intermediaries. The corporation also reinvests on shareholders' behalf.

In this case, the savings bypass the financial markets and flow directly to a financial intermediary (the bank) and from there to Exxon.

A **financial market** is a market where financial assets are issued and traded. In addition to helping companies to raise cash, financial markets also allow investors to trade stocks or bonds among themselves. For example, Mr. Rosencrantz might decide to raise some cash by selling his Bank of America stock at the same time that Mr. Guildenstern invests his savings in the stock. So they make a trade. The result is simply a transfer of ownership from one person to another, which has no effect on the company's cash, assets, or operations. Such purchases and sales are known as *secondary transactions*.

Some financial assets have less active secondary markets than others. For example, when a bank lends money to a company, it acquires a financial asset (the company's promise to repay the loan with interest). Banks do sometimes sell packages of these loans to other banks, but generally they retain the loan until it is repaid by the borrower. Other financial assets are regularly traded. Some, such as shares of stock, are traded on organized exchanges like the New York, London, or Singapore stock exchanges. In other cases, there is no organized exchange, and the assets are traded by a network of dealers. Such markets are known as *over-the-counter (OTC)* markets. For example, in the United States, most government and corporate bonds are traded OTC. Foreign currency is traded OTC and not on an organized exchange.

Some financial markets are not used to raise cash but, instead, help firms to manage their risks. In these markets firms can buy or sell derivatives, whose payoffs depend on the prices of other securities or commodities. For example, we noted earlier how a manufacturer can use the futures markets to fix the price at which it buys its future platinum requirements.

13.6 Self-Test

Which of the following are financial markets?

    a. NASDAQ

    b. Vanguard Explorer Fund

    c. JPMorgan Chase

    d. London Metal Exchange

Financial Intermediaries

A **financial intermediary** is an organization that raises money from investors and provides financing for individuals, companies, and other organizations. Banks, insurance companies, and investment funds are all intermediaries. These intermediaries are important sources of financing for corporations. They are a stop on the road between savings and real investment.

Why is a financial intermediary different from a manufacturing corporation? First, it may raise money in different ways, for example, by taking deposits or selling insurance policies. Second, it invests that money in *financial* assets, for example, in stocks, bonds, or loans to businesses or individuals. In contrast, a manufacturing company's main investments are in plant, equipment, or other *real* assets.

Look at Table 13.2, which shows the financial assets of the different types of intermediaries in the United States. It gives you an idea of the relative importance of different intermediaries. Of course, these assets are not all invested in nonfinancial businesses. For example, banks make loans to individuals as well as to businesses.[18]

Investment Funds

We look first at investment funds, such as mutual funds, hedge funds, and pension funds. **Mutual funds** raise money by selling shares to investors.[19] This money is then pooled and invested in a portfolio of securities. Investors in a mutual fund can increase their stake in the fund's portfolio by buying additional shares, or they can sell their shares back to the fund if they wish to cash out. The purchase and sale prices depend on the fund's net asset value (NAV) on the day of purchase or redemption. If there is a net flow of cash into the fund, the manager will use it to buy more stocks or bonds; if there is a net outflow, the fund manager will need to raise the money by selling some of the fund's investments.

There are about 8,000 equity and bond mutual funds in the United States. In fact, there are more mutual funds than public companies! The funds pursue a wide variety of investment strategies. Some funds specialize in safe stocks with generous dividend payouts. Some specialize in high-tech growth stocks. Some "balanced" funds offer mixtures of stocks and bonds. Some specialize in particular countries or regions. For example, the Fidelity Investments mutual fund group sponsors funds for Canada, Japan, China, Europe, and Latin America.

Mutual funds offer investors low-cost diversification and professional management. For most investors, it's more efficient to buy a mutual fund than to assemble a diversified

	$ Billions
Mutual funds	$19,563
Money market funds	4,336
Closed-end funds	279
ETFs	5,449
Hedge funds[a]	2,700
Pension funds	25,666
Banks and savings institutions	23,454
Insurance companies	12,279

〉TABLE 13.2 Financial assets of intermediaries in the United States, December 2020.

[a] estimated

Sources: Board of Governors of the Federal Reserve System, Division of Research and Statistics, *Financial Accounts of the United States—Z1*, www.federalreserve.gov.

[18] Intermediaries often invest in each other also. For instance, an investor might buy shares in a mutual fund that then invests in Bank of America's new share issue. If the money then finds its way from Bank of America to Exxon, it would show up as a financial asset of both Bank of America (its loan to Exxon) and the mutual fund (its shareholding in Bank of America).

[19] Mutual funds are not corporations but investment companies. They pay no tax, providing that all income from dividends and price appreciation is passed on to the funds' shareholders. The shareholders pay personal tax on this income.

portfolio of stocks and bonds. Most mutual fund managers also try their best to "beat the market"—that is, to generate superior performance by finding the stocks with better-than-average returns. Whether they can pick winners consistently is another question, which we addressed in Chapter 12. In exchange for their services, the fund's managers take out a management fee. There are also the expenses of running the fund. For mutual funds that invest in stocks, fees and expenses typically add up to nearly 1% per year.

BEYOND THE PAGE

Mutual fund assets

mhhe.com/brealey14e

Most mutual funds invest in shares or in a mixture of shares and bonds. However, one particular type of mutual fund, called a money market fund, invests only in short-term safe securities, such as Treasury bills or bank certificates of deposit. Money market funds offer individuals and small- and medium-sized businesses a convenient home in which to park their spare cash. There are over 1,000 money market funds in the United States. Some of these funds are huge. For example, the Goldman Sachs U.S. Government Money Market Fund had $225 billion in assets in 2020.

Mutual funds are **open-end funds**—they stand ready to issue new shares and to buy back existing shares. In contrast, a **closed-end fund** has a fixed number of shares that are traded on an exchange. If you want to invest in a closed-end fund, you cannot buy new shares from the fund; you must buy existing shares from another stockholder in the fund.

BEYOND THE PAGE

Exchange traded funds

mhhe.com/brealey14e

If you simply want low-cost diversification, one option is to buy a mutual fund that invests in all the stocks in a stock market index. For example, the Vanguard Index Fund holds all the stocks in the Standard & Poor's Composite Index. An alternative is to invest in an **exchange traded fund**, or **ETF**, which is a portfolio of stocks that can be bought or sold in a single trade. For example, you could buy Standard & Poor's Depository Receipts (SPDRs, or "spiders"), which are portfolios matching Standard & Poor's stock market indexes; or you could buy DIAMONDS, which track the Dow Jones Industrial Average.

ETFs are, in some ways, more efficient than mutual funds. To buy or sell an ETF, you simply make a trade, just as if you bought or sold shares of stock. In this respect, ETFs are like closed-end investment funds. But, with rare exceptions, ETFs do not have managers with the discretion to try to "pick winners." ETF portfolios are tied down to indexes or fixed baskets of securities. ETF issuers make sure that the ETF price tracks the price of the underlying index or basket.

Like mutual funds, **hedge funds** also pool the savings of different investors and invest on their behalf. But they differ from mutual funds in at least three ways. First, because hedge funds usually follow complex investment strategies, access is restricted to knowledgeable investors such as pension funds, endowment funds, and wealthy individuals. Don't try to send a check for $3,000 or $5,000 to a hedge fund; most hedge funds are not in the "retail" investment business. Second, hedge funds are generally established as limited partnerships. The investment manager is the general partner and the investors are the limited partners. Third, hedge funds try to attract the most talented managers by compensating them with potentially lucrative, performance-related fees.[20] In contrast, mutual funds usually charge a fixed percentage of assets under management.

Hedge funds follow many different investment strategies. Some try to make a profit by identifying *overvalued* stocks or markets that they then sell short. Some hedge funds take bets on firms involved in merger negotiations, others look for mispricing of convertible bonds, and some take positions in currencies and interest rates. "Vulture funds" specialize in the securities of distressed corporations. Hedge funds manage less money than mutual funds, but they sometimes take very big positions and have a large impact on the market.

There are other ways to pool and invest savings. Consider a pension plan set up by a corporation or other organization on behalf of its employees. The most common type of plan is

---

[20] Sometimes these fees can be very large indeed. For example, hedge fund manager James Simons of Renaissance Technologies earned an estimated $1.8 billion in 2019.

the *defined-contribution* plan. In this case, a percentage of the employee's monthly paycheck is contributed to a **pension fund**. (The employer and employee may each contribute 5%, for example.) Contributions from all participating employees are pooled and invested in securities or mutual funds. (Usually, the employees can choose from a menu of funds with different investment strategies.) Each employee's balance in the plan grows over the years as contributions continue and investment income accumulates. The balance in the plan can be used to finance living expenses after retirement. The amount available for retirement depends on the accumulated contributions and on the rate of return earned on the investments.[21]

Pension funds are designed for long-run investment. They provide professional management and diversification. They also have an important tax advantage: Contributions are tax-deductible, and investment returns inside the plan are not taxed until cash is finally withdrawn.[22]

All these investment funds provide a stop on the road from savings to corporate investment. For example, suppose your mutual fund purchases part of that new issue of shares by Bank of America. The orange arrows show the flow of savings to investment:

Financial Institutions

Banks and insurance companies are *financial institutions*.[23] A financial institution is an intermediary that does more than just pool and invest savings. Institutions raise financing in special ways, for example, by accepting deposits or selling insurance policies, and they provide additional financial services. Unlike most investment funds, they not only invest in securities but also lend money directly to individuals, businesses, or other organizations.

Commercial Banks   There are just under 5,000 commercial banks in the United States. They vary from giant ones such as JPMorgan Chase with $3.4 trillion of assets to small ones like the Oakwood Bank of Texas with $640 million.

Commercial banks are major sources of loans for corporations. (In the United States, they are generally not allowed to make equity investments in corporations, although banks in most other countries can do so.) Suppose that a local forest products company negotiates a nine-month bank loan for $2.5 million. The flow of savings is

BEYOND THE PAGE

World bank rankings

mhhe.com/brealey14e

---

[21] In a *defined-benefit* plan, the employer promises a certain level of retirement benefits (set by a formula), and the *employer* invests in the pension plan. The plan's accumulated investment value has to be large enough to cover the promised benefits. If not, the employer must put in more money. Defined-benefit plans are gradually giving way to defined-contribution plans.

[22] Defined-benefit pension plans share these same advantages, except that the employer invests rather than the employees. In a defined-benefit plan, the advantage of tax deferral on investment income accrues to the employer. This deferral reduces the cost of funding the plan.

[23] We may be drawing too fine a distinction between financial intermediaries and institutions. A mutual fund could be considered a financial institution. But "financial institution" usually suggests a more complicated intermediary, such as a bank.

The bank provides debt financing for the company and, at the same time, provides a place for depositors to park their money safely and withdraw it as needed.

We will have plenty more to say about bank loans in Chapter 25.

Investment Banks   We have discussed commercial banks, which raise money from depositors and other investors and then make loans to businesses and individuals. *Investment banks* are different.[24] Investment banks do not take deposits, and they do not usually make loans to companies. Instead, they advise and assist companies in raising financing. For example, investment banks *underwrite* stock offerings by purchasing the new shares from the issuing company at a negotiated price and reselling the shares to investors. Thus, the issuing company gets a fixed price for the new shares, and the investment bank takes responsibility for distributing the shares to thousands of investors. We discuss share issues in more detail in Chapter 14.

Investment banks also advise on takeovers, mergers, and acquisitions. They offer investment advice and manage investment portfolios for individual and institutional investors. They run trading desks for foreign exchange, commodities, bonds, options, and derivatives.

Investment banks can invest their own money in start-ups and other ventures. For example, the Australian Macquarie Bank has invested in airports, toll highways, electric transmission and generation, and other infrastructure projects around the world.

The largest investment banks are financial powerhouses. They include Goldman Sachs, Morgan Stanley, Lazard, Nomura (Japan), and Macquarie Bank.[25] In addition, the major commercial banks, including Bank of America and Citigroup, all have investment banking operations.[26]

Insurance Companies   Insurance companies are more important than banks for the *long-term* financing of business. They are massive investors in corporate stocks and bonds, and they often make long-term loans directly to corporations.

Suppose a company needs a loan of $2.5 million for nine years, not nine months. It could issue a bond directly to investors, or it could negotiate a nine-year loan with an insurance company:

The money to make the loan comes mainly from the sale of insurance policies. Say you buy a fire insurance policy on your home. You pay cash to the insurance company and get a financial asset (the policy) in exchange. You receive no interest payments on this financial asset, but if a fire does strike, the company is obliged to cover the damages up to the policy limit. This is the return on your investment. (Of course, a fire is a sad and dangerous event that

---

[24] Banks that accept deposits and provide financing to businesses are called *commercial* banks. *Savings banks* accept deposits and savings accounts and loan the money out mostly to individuals, for example, as mortgage loans to home buyers. Investment banks do not take deposits and do not loan money to businesses or individuals, except as *bridge loans* made as temporary financing for takeovers or other transactions.

[25] Strictly speaking, Goldman Sachs and Morgan Stanley are not investment banks. In 2008, they handed in their investment banking charter in exchange for a banking charter that allows them to accept deposits. However, their principal focus is on investment banking activities.

[26] Bank of America owns Merrill Lynch, one of the largest investment banks. Merrill was rescued by Bank of America in 2008 after making huge losses from mortgage-related investments.

you hope to avoid. But if a fire does occur, you are better off getting a return on your investment in insurance than not having insurance at all.)

The company will issue not just one policy but thousands. Normally the incidence of fires "averages out," leaving the company with a predictable obligation to its policyholders as a group. Of course, the insurance company must charge enough for its policies to cover selling and administrative costs, pay policyholders' claims, and generate a profit for its stockholders.

13-6 Financial Markets and Intermediaries around the World

The basic functions of financial markets and institutions are universal and enduring, but the markets and intermediaries that deliver these financial services vary from country to country.

In most of this text, we have assumed that a large part of debt financing comes from public bond markets. Nothing in principle changes when a firm borrows from a bank instead. But in some countries, bond markets are small and bank financing is more important. Figure 13.8 shows the total values of bank loans, private (nongovernment) bonds, and stock markets in different parts of the world in 2019. To measure these financial claims on a comparable basis, the amounts are scaled by gross domestic product (GDP).

Company financing in the United States is different from that in most other countries. The United States not only has a large amount of bank loans outstanding, but there is also a large stock market and a large corporate bond market. Thus, the United States is said to have a market-based financial system. Stock market value is also high in the United Kingdom, but bank loans are much more important than the bond market. However, this is because the UK is an international banking center, so the bank loan figure includes eurocurrency loans and does not represent just domestic loans. In Europe, Japan, and China, bank financing again outpaces bond markets, but the stock markets are relatively small. Thus, most countries in Europe, including Germany, France, Italy, and Spain, have bank-based financial systems. So do many Asian countries, including Japan, China, and India.

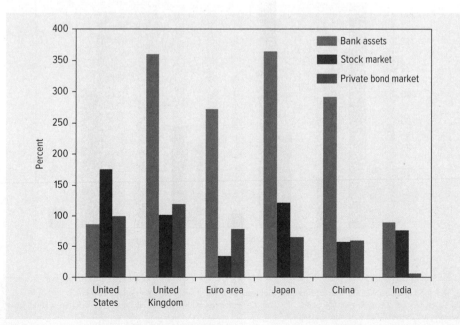

▶ **FIGURE 13.8**

Value of financial claims in 2019, percentage of GDP.

Source: Data from World Bank and national authorities. We are grateful to Michael Chui for this figure.

Let's look at these regions from a different perspective. Figure 13.9 shows the financial investments made by households, again scaled by GDP.[27] ("Households" means individual investors.) Household portfolios are divided into four categories: bank deposits, insurance policies and mutual and pension funds, equity securities, and "other." Notice the differences in the total amounts of financial assets in Figure 13.9. Summing the columns for each country and region, the amount of financial assets is 374% of GDP in the United States, 292% in the United Kingdom, 200% in Europe, and 310% in Japan. This does not mean that European investors are poor, just that they hold less wealth in the form of financial assets. Figure 13.9 excludes other important investment categories, such as real estate or privately owned businesses. It also excludes the value of pensions provided by governments.

In the United States, a large fraction of households' portfolios is held directly in equity securities, mostly common stocks. Therefore, individual investors can potentially play an important role in corporate governance. Direct equity holdings are smallest in Japan. Japanese households could not play a significant direct role in corporate governance even if they wanted to. They can't vote shares that they don't own.

Where direct equity investment is small, household investments in bank deposits, insurance policies, and mutual and pension funds are correspondingly large. In the United Kingdom, the insurance and funds category dominates, with bank deposits in second place. In Europe, bank deposits and insurance and funds run a close race for first. In Japan, bank deposits win by a mile, with insurance and funds in second place and equities a distant third.

Figure 13.9 tells us that in many parts of the world, there are relatively few individual stockholders. Most individuals don't invest directly in equity markets, but indirectly, through insurance companies, mutual funds, banks, and other financial intermediaries. Of course, the thread of ownership traces back through these intermediaries to individual investors. All assets are ultimately owned by individuals. There are no Martian or extraterrestrial investors that we know of.[28]

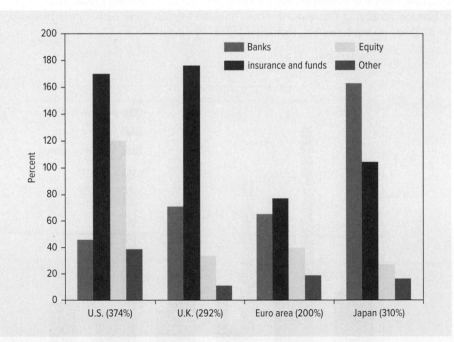

▶ **FIGURE 13.9**

Household portfolio allocations, 2000–2019, percentage of GDP.

Source: Bank of Japan, EUROSTAT, Federal Reserve Board, and the IMF. We are grateful to Michael Chui for this figure.

---

[27] Data for China and India are not available for this and the following figures that summarize portfolio allocations.

[28] There may be owners not yet present on this planet, however. For example, endowments of educational, charitable, and religious organizations are partly held in trust for future generations.

Now let's look at financial institutions. Figure 13.10 shows the financial assets held by financial institutions, including banks, mutual funds, insurance companies, pension funds, and other intermediaries. These investments are smaller in the United States, relative to GDP, than in other countries (as expected in the U.S. market-based system). Financial institutions in the United Kingdom, Europe, and Japan have invested large sums in loans and in deposits. Institutional holdings of equity are high in the United Kingdom. These holdings are mainly owned by insurance companies and pension funds.

We've covered households and financial institutions. Is there any other source for corporate financing? Yes, financing can come from other corporations. Take a look at Figure 13.11, which shows the financial assets held by nonfinancial corporations. Perhaps the most striking feature is the large amount of equity held by firms in Europe. The amount of equity held in Japan and the United Kingdom is also large. In the United States, it is relatively small. As we will see in Chapter 19, these holdings of shares by other nonfinancial corporations have important implications for corporate ownership and governance.

Another interesting aspect of Figure 13.11 is the large amount of intercompany loans and trade credit in Europe and Japan. Many Japanese firms rely heavily on trade-credit financing— that is, on accounts payable to other firms. Of course, the other firms see the reverse side of trade credit: They are providing financing in the form of accounts receivable.

Figures 13.8 to 13.11 show that just drawing a line between market-based, "Anglo-Saxon" financial systems (like the United States, United Kingdom, Australia, Canada, and New Zealand) and bank-based financial systems is simplistic. We need to dig a little deeper when comparing financial systems. For example, more equity is held directly by households in the United States than in the United Kingdom, and the portfolio allocations of households, nonfinancial corporations, and financial institutions are also significantly different. In addition, we noted the large cross-holdings of shares among European corporations. Finally, Japanese households put significantly more of their savings in banks, and corporations in Japan use trade credit much more than in other advanced economies.

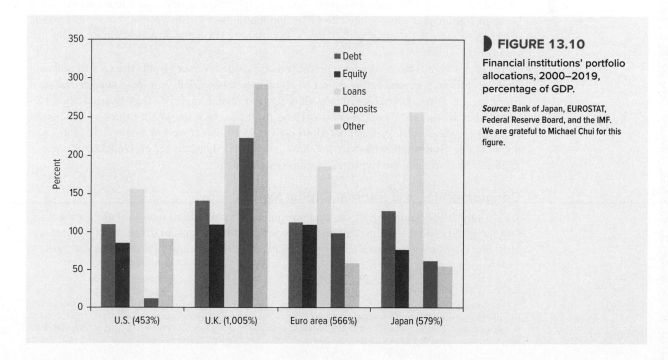

▶ **FIGURE 13.10**

Financial institutions' portfolio allocations, 2000–2019, percentage of GDP.

Source: Bank of Japan, EUROSTAT, Federal Reserve Board, and the IMF. We are grateful to Michael Chui for this figure.

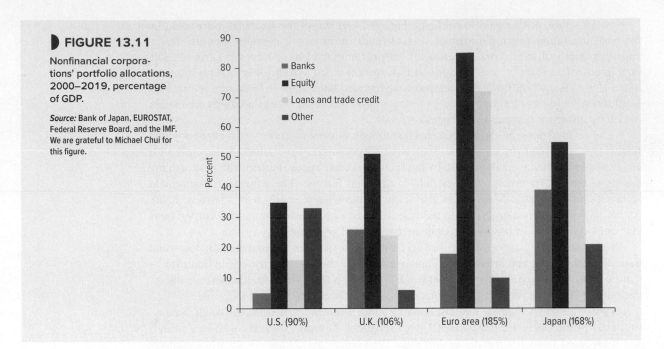

FIGURE 13.11

Nonfinancial corpora-tions' portfolio allocations, 2000–2019, percentage of GDP.

Source: Bank of Japan, EUROSTAT, Federal Reserve Board, and the IMF. We are grateful to Michael Chui for this figure.

What explains the importance of financial markets in some countries, while other countries rely less on markets and more on banks and other financial institutions? One answer is inves-tor protection. Stock and bond markets thrive where investors in these markets are protected reasonably well. Investors' property rights are much better protected in some parts of the world than others. La Porta, Lopez-de-Silanes, Shleifer, Vishny, and others have developed quantitative measures of investor protection based on shareholders' and creditors' rights and the quality of law enforcement.[29] Countries with poor scores generally have smaller stock markets, measured by aggregate market value relative to GDP, and the numbers of listed firms and initial public offerings are smaller relative to population. Poor scores also mean less debt financing for pri-vate firms.

It's easy to understand why poor protection of outside investors stunts the growth of finan-cial markets. A more difficult question is why protection is good in some countries and poor in others. La Porta, Lopez-de-Silanes, Shleifer, and Vishny point to the origin of legal sys-tems. They distinguish legal systems derived from the common-law tradition, which origi-nated in England, from systems based on civil law, which evolved in France, Germany, and Scandinavia. Both shareholders and creditors, it is argued, are better protected by the law in countries that adopted the English common-law tradition.

Conglomerates and Internal Capital Markets

As we saw at the beginning of the chapter, financial markets and intermediaries are not the only way that capital can flow; internal finance is also important. In many countries, particu-larly those without fully developed financial markets, there are groups of firms that operate

[29] R. La Porta, F. Lopez-de-Silanes, A. Shleifer, and R. Vishny, "Legal Determinants of External Finance," *Journal of Finance* 52 (July 1997), pp. 1131–1150, and "Law and Finance," *Journal of Political Economy* 106 (December 1998), pp. 1113–1155; S. Djankov, C. McLiesh, and A. Shleifer, "Private Credit in 129 Countries," *Journal of Financial Economics* 84 (2007), pp. 299–329; and R. Rajan and L. Zingales, *Saving Capitalism from the Capitalists* (New York: Crown Business, 2003).

in several different industries. Funds can easily flow between them because these industrial groups are really conglomerates.

In Korea, for example, the 20 largest conglomerates own about 40% of the country's total corporate assets. These *chaebols* are also strong exporters: Names like Samsung and Hyundai are recognized worldwide. Conglomerates are also common in Latin America. One of the more successful, the Chilean holding company Quinenco, is a dizzying variety of businesses, including hotels and brewing, mobile telephone services, banking, and the manufacture of copper cable. Widely diversified groups are also common in India. The largest, the Tata Group, spans 80 companies in various industries, including steel, electric power, real estate, telecommunications, and financial services. All of these companies are public, but control rests with the group and ultimately with the Tata family.

The United States had a conglomerate merger wave in the 1960s and 1970s, but diversification didn't deliver value in the longer run, and most of the conglomerates of that era have dissolved. But conglomerates survive and grow in developing economies. Why?

Family ownership is part of the answer. A wealthy family can reduce risk while maintaining control and expanding the family business into new industries. Of course, the family could also diversify by buying shares of other companies. But where financial markets are limited and investor protection is poor, internal diversification can beat financial diversification. Internal diversification means running an internal capital market, but if a country's financial markets and institutions are substandard, an internal capital market may not be so bad after all.

"Substandard" does not just mean lack of scale or trading activity. It may mean government regulations limiting access to bank financing or requiring government approval before bonds or shares are issued.[30] It may mean poor information. If accounting standards are loose and companies are secretive, monitoring by outside investors becomes especially costly and difficult, and agency costs proliferate.

Internal diversification may also be the only practical way to grow. You can't be big *and* focused in a small, closed economy because the scale of one-industry companies is limited by the local market. Size can be an advantage if larger companies have easier access to international financial markets, which is important if local financial markets are inefficient. Size also means political power, which is especially important in managed economies or in countries where the government economic policy is unpredictable.

13-7 The Fintech Revolution

Innovation in finance is often driven by new technology, which makes it possible to automate the traditional roles of financial markets and intermediaries.

Today, three developments are serving to drive innovation. One is the availability of large volumes of data about the consumers of financial services. The second is the advances in artificial intelligence and machine learning (AI/ML), which offer new ways to extract information from these data. The third is the availability of cloud computing and cloud storage. Cloud computing enables small firms to share the cost with other firms, and has therefore leveled the playing field.

The application of these new technologies to finance is called *fintech*. We will briefly review seven ways that fintech is changing financial practice.

---

[30] In the United States, the SEC does *not* have the power to deny share issues. Its mandate is only to ensure that investors are given adequate information.

Payment Systems

Until recently cash or checks were the principal way to pay for purchases, but in many countries these are fast disappearing. For example, in Sweden cash transactions make up barely 2% of the value of all payments. You can't use cash to buy a bus ticket or a ticket on the Stockholm metro, and retailers are not legally obliged to accept coins and notes. The majority of Sweden's bank branches no longer keep cash on hand or take cash deposits—and many branches no longer have ATMs. Instead of cash, Swedes use either a card or a mobile phone app to transfer money from one bank account to another in real time.

New payment methods are also helping to improve access for the 2 billion people who have been excluded from modern financial systems. For example, in Kenya, Vodaphone launched M-PESA, a system for payments and storage of value using basic mobile phones. M-PESA customers are assigned an electronic money account linked to their mobile phone number, which allows them to deposit and withdraw money at a network of retail shops. They can also transfer money to other users and make a wide range of payments. Within four years of launch, over two-thirds of Kenya's adult population had M-PESA accounts.[31]

Person-to-Person Lending

Low-income households are not alone in being excluded from the financial system. In every country, small and medium-sized enterprises (SMEs) may also have problems obtaining loans. However, individuals and SMEs that have been denied credit by banks have increasingly been able to obtain it from fintech platforms.[32]

Person-to-person (P2P) lending platforms allow consumers and small businesses to bypass the banking system by connecting lenders and borrowers directly through the web.[33] For example, in the United States, would-be borrowers can apply to Lending Club for a personal loan of up to $40,000 or a business loan of up to $300,000. The company then assigns a credit score to that customer, and on the basis of this score, potential investors can choose whether to participate in the loan. Thus, Lending Club cuts banks out of the lending equation entirely. It does not lend itself; instead, it matches up borrowers and lenders, uses the credit score to set the interest rate for the loan, and services the loan.

Crowdfunding

A new source of financing, known as *crowdfunding,* uses the Internet to raise money directly for start-up businesses from a group of individuals. Initially, companies were not permitted to use crowdfunding to sell shares. Instead, investors received a return in the form of early samples of the company's product. However, this was changed in 2016 by the JOBS Act. For the first time, crowdfunding websites could offer small investors the opportunity to back start-up companies in return for an equity participation in the firm.

The SEC sets the rules for Regulation Crowdfunding (Reg CF) offers. The company is restricted to raising a maximum of $1,070,000 in a 12-month period, which limits the use of crowdfunding to early-stage companies. The most that any individual can invest is set at $107,000. Also, there are requirements on the disclosure of information, and all transactions must take place online through an SEC-registered intermediary.

---

[31] I. Mas and D. Radcliffe, "Mobile Payments Go Viral: M-PESA in Kenya," *Capco Institute's Journal of Financial Transformation* 32 (2011), pp. 169–182.

[32] M. Schweitzer and B. Barkley, "Is Fintech Good for Small Business Borrowers? Impacts on Firm Growth and Customer Satisfaction," 2017, Federal Reserve Bank of Cleveland Working Paper.

[33] There are two mechanisms for pricing the loans. The first is an auction and the second, more common approach, is posted prices. An auction process typically relies on the relative strength of lenders and borrowers to determine the price, whereas posted prices are predetermined by complex algorithms used by the lending platforms.

EXAMPLE 13.1 • How crowdfunding provided finance for a young company

PT Motion Works is typical of the companies that have used crowdfunding to raise cash. It was founded in 2007 to produce and market elliptical and stand-up bikes. Ten years later, it was generating almost $5 million of sales, but it was burning cash rapidly. It then approached StartEngine, an equity crowdfunding site, to arrange a Reg CF issue. The offering memorandum for the issue was published in December 2019, and it set out the company's plans to raise up to $1,070,000, before expenses, by the sale of convertible preferred shares at a price of $7 a share. When the offer closed in March 2020, the company had raised $564,000.

• • • • •

AI/ML Credit Scoring

Credit scores provide essential information for lending decisions. But about 26 million Americans either do not have a bank account or have thin credit files. Thus, many households and small businesses are effectively excluded from borrowing. New techniques to predict default combine the use of artificial intelligence (AI) and machine learning (ML) with soft data about would-be borrowers, such as information on social media, online shopping, payment applications, and cell phone accounts. This widens the possible access to credit.

Distributed Ledgers and Blockchains

A distributed ledger is a database that is distributed across several computers, or nodes. Thus, there is no central party that is responsible for the ledger. Each node has an identical copy of the data and can update the ledger. However, a transaction is only recorded once other nodes have verified the transaction.

   The best-known form of distributed ledger is the blockchain. The blockchain allows nodes to add data, but they cannot alter or delete existing data. Thus, a historical record is maintained of every transaction. Many believe that the technology offers a new way to create, exchange, and track ownership of financial assets. The effect could be lower costs of trading, faster transfers of ownership, and more accurate records.

Cryptocurrencies

A cryptocurrency is a digital currency in which transactions are verified and records maintained in a distributed ledger outside the reach of governments. A familiar example is Bitcoin. Although not very practical as a means of transacting, its price has risen from a few cents a coin after it came into existence in 2009 to more than $63,000 in April 2021.

   Private-sector cryptocurrencies like Bitcoin have caused a potential headache for central banks because of the threat they pose to their control of monetary policy. One of the main issues is the problem posed for financial stability because of the volatility of private cryptocurrency prices. These threats from private cryptocurrencies have prompted debates among policymakers about whether central banks should play a role in issuing central bank digital currencies. Many central banks are progressing from conceptual work into experimentation.[34] For example, the People's Bank of China wants to run city-level trials of a central bank digital currency in 2021 and 2022 so that the e-yuan is ready for use by the 2022 Beijing Winter Olympic Games.

BEYOND THE PAGE

DLT and
blockchains

mhhe.com/brealey14e

---

[34] See C. Barontini and H. Holden, "Proceeding with Caution—A Survey on Central Bank Digital Currency," BIS Paper 101, 2019; and R. Auer, G. Cornelli, and J. Frost, "Rise of the Central Bank Digital Currencies: Drivers, Approaches, and Technologies," BIS Working Paper No. 880, August 2020.

EXAMPLE 13.2 • Wootrade sells blockchain tokens

In October 2020, Wootrade raised an initial amount of $10.7 million by the sales of Woo block-chain tokens. The company offers a platform for trading cryptocurrencies. This platform claims to provide significantly above-average liquidity, tighter spreads than the major exchanges, and zero (or even negative) fees. Holders of the tokens can enjoy fee reductions or sell their tokens on a number of crypto exchanges. The Woo tokens were not registered with the SEC as a security, and therefore, the company did not issue a prospectus. It did, however, publish a white paper describing the business and the initial coin offering.

• • • • •

Initial Coin Offerings

Equity crowdfunding raises cash for start-up ventures by selling stock over the Internet. Companies developing new blockchain-based products and services can instead raise cash by selling tokens in an initial coin offering or ICO. Here is how it works. The start-up company employs a blockchain platform such as Ethereum to create a new digital cryptocurrency (there are about 10,000 of them already in existence). This currency is in the form of digital tokens. To raise funds, the company offers these tokens on the Internet in exchange for cash or an existing cryptocurrency such as Bitcoin or Ether. The company can then use the cryptocurrency to pay its staff, or it can fund the project by selling the cryptocurrency for dollars. Investors who have purchased the tokens can spend them on the software service that is provided by the start-up, or they can resell them on a cryptocurrency exchange. If the business proves profitable, the issuer may subsequently offer to buy back a portion of the tokens at an enhanced price.

The first initial coin offering occurred in 2013, but the market surged in 2017 and 2018. Some of these issues raised just a few hundred thousand dollars. At the other extreme, Swiss-based company Tezos raised $232 million in just a few days to develop a better blockchain for digital currencies. By October 2020, Tezos had a market capitalization of $1.6 billion. However, it was not all that easy for Tezos. Three months after the issue, its value plunged when a management spat led the company to disclose that recruitment had come to a standstill and little work had been done on the product. In November, a lawsuit asserted that Tezos had contravened U.S. securities law by selling unregistered securities, committing securities fraud, and engaging in false advertising. As the experience of Tezos illustrates, most ICO businesses involve high risks, and a few cases are simply scams. Almost half of ICOs sold in 2017 had failed by February 2018.

13.7 Self-Test

We listed seven examples of Fintech. Which of these has depended on the availability of large amounts of data about the users of financial services?

• • • • •

KEY TAKEAWAYS

In this chapter, we have provided a broad overview of the corporation's main sources of funds and some of the markets and intermediaries that provide these funds.

- **Sources of Financing.** Figure 13.1 summarizes how U.S. corporations raise and spend money. Have another look at it and try to get a feel for the numbers. Notice that internally generated cash is the major source of financing for investment. Borrowing is also significant. Net equity issues have been negative, however—that is, share repurchases have been larger than share issues.

- **Common Stock.** A corporation is owned by its common stockholders. They have the rights to control the company's actions, although, in practice, they delegate these rights to the board of directors. They also are entitled to the company's cash flows after its debts have been paid.

- **Debt.** Debt has a prior claim on cash flows, but its claim is limited to the amount of the debt. Therefore, in contrast to equity, it does not have residual cash-flow rights and it does not participate in the upsides of the business. Also, unlike equity, debt offers no control rights unless the firm defaults on its debt. The variety of debt instruments is almost endless. The instruments differ by maturity, interest rate (fixed or floating), currency, seniority, security, and whether the debt can be converted into equity.

- **Who are the investors?** On average nearly 40% of a U.S. company's shares are owned by individuals or nonprofit organizations, and a roughly similar proportion are owned by intermediaries such as mutual funds and pension funds. In contrast to common stock, individuals hold very few corporate bonds. The major bondholders are insurance companies, other intermediaries, and foreign investors.

- **Functions of the financial systems.** In addition to providing companies with funds for investment, a financial system performs a number of basic functions. It operates the payment system, it offers a way for individuals to postpone or accelerate their expenditures, it allows risks to be shared, and it is a valuable source of information about economic activity. In this chapter, we introduced the financial markets and intermediaries that provide these functions.

- **Varieties of financial systems.** The functions of the financial system are universal, but the structure of the system differs from one country to another. Banks play a more important role in Europe and many Asian countries and equity markets are less developed than in the United States.

- **Fintech.** Fintech operates at a small scale in most countries, but it has the potential to upend traditional financial institutions and fundamentally change the way finance is conducted.

● ● ● ● ●

FURTHER READING

A useful article for comparing financial structure in the United States and other major industrial countries is:

R. G. Rajan and L. Zingales, "What Do We Know about Capital Structure? Some Evidence from International Data," *Journal of Finance* 50 (December 1995), pp. 1421–1460.

For a discussion of the allocation of control rights and cash-flow rights between stockholders and debtholders, see:

O. Hart, *Firms, Contracts, and Financial Structure* (Oxford: Oxford University Press, 1995).

Robert Merton gives an excellent overview of the functions of financial institutions in:

R. Merton, "A Functional Perspective of Financial Intermediation," *Financial Management* 24 (Summer 1995), pp. 23–41.

The Winter 2009 issue of the *Journal of Financial Perspectives* contains several articles on the crisis of 2007–2009. See also:

V. V. Acharya and M. W. Richardson, eds., *Restoring Financial Stability* (Hoboken, NJ: John Wiley & Sons, 2009).

F. Allen and E. Carletti, "An Overview of the Crisis: Causes, Consequences and Solutions," *International Review of Finance* 10 (March 2010), pp. 1–26.

The following works cover financial crises more generally:

F. Allen and D. Gale, *Understanding Financial Crises* (Oxford: Oxford University Press, 2007).

C. M. Reinhart and K. Rogoff, "The Aftermath of Financial Crises," *American Economic Review* 99 (May 2009), pp. 466–472.

C. M. Reinhart and K. Rogoff, *This Time Is Different: Eight Centuries of Financial Folly* (Princeton: Princeton University Press, 2009).

For a survey of the literature on fintech see:

F. Allen, X. Gu, and J. Jagtiani, "A Survey of Fintech Research and Policy Discussion," *Review of Corporate Finance,* forthcoming.

● ● ● ● ●

**PROBLEM
SETS**

Mc Graw Hill connect®   **Select problems are available in McGraw-Hill's *Connect*.
Please see the preface for more information.**

1. **Patterns of Corporate Financing (S13.1)** True or false?

   a. Net stock issues by U.S. nonfinancial corporations in most years are small but positive.

   b. Most new capital investment by U.S. companies is funded by retained earnings.

   c. Debt ratios in the United States are lower than in most other developed economies.

2. **Patterns of Corporate Financing** (S13.1) Do you think firms rely too much on internal funds? Would it be better if they had to go back to shareholders when they needed cash?

3. **Patterns of Corporate Financing** (S13.1) In Figure 13.1, would it have been better to have deducted dividends from the net cash raised from shareholders? Should we then have deducted interest payments from net cash raised from debtholders? If so, how would you have defined "internal funds"?

4. **Terminology (S13.2–S13.3)** Fill in the blanks, using the following terms: floating rate, common stock, convertible, subordinated, preferred stock, senior, warrant.

   a. If a lender ranks behind the firm's general creditors in the event of default, his or her loan is said to be _____.

   b. Interest on many bank loans is based on a _____ of interest.

   c. A(n) _____ bond can be exchanged for shares of the issuing corporation.

   d. A(n) _____ gives its owner the right to buy shares in the issuing company at a predetermined price.

   e. Dividends on _____ cannot be paid unless the firm has also paid any dividends on its _____.

5. **Security holdings (S13.2–S13.5)** True or false?

   a. Banks are huge investors in corporate equity.

   b. Insurance companies are huge investors in corporate debt.

   c. Rather than investing directly in corporate equities, most households prefer to pool their risk in a hedge fund.

   d. Many individuals have a current account with an investment bank that then uses the cash to lend to industry.

6. **Common stock (S13.2)** True or false?

   a. In the United States, most common shares are owned by individual investors.

   b. The majority of corporations have large shareholders who are prepared to challenge incompetent managers

   c. Investments in partnerships cannot be publicly traded.

7. **Common stock (S13.2)** What do we mean when we say that stockholders have control rights and residual cash flow rights? How in practice do they exercise their control rights?

8. **Common stock** (S13.2) Large blockholders can either encourage or discourage value maximization. Explain.

9. **Preferred stock (S13.2)** In 2021, Beta Corporation earned gross profits of $760,000.

   a. Suppose that Beta was financed by a combination of common stock and $1 million of debt. The interest rate on the debt was 10%, and the corporate tax rate in 2021 was 21%. How much profit was available for common stockholders after payment of interest and corporate taxes?

b. Now suppose that instead of issuing debt, Beta was financed by a combination of common stock and $1 million of preferred stock. The dividend yield on the preferred was 8%, and the corporate tax rate was still 21%. Recalculate the profit available for common stock-holders after payment of preferred dividends and corporate taxes.

10. **Corporate debt (S13.3)** Which of the following features would increase the value of a corporate bond? Which would reduce its value?

a. The bond is convertible into shares.

b. The bond is secured by a mortgage on real estate.

c. The bond is subordinated.

11. **Financial markets and intermediaries. (S13.5)** True or false?

a. Financing for public corporations must flow through financial markets.

b. Financing for private corporations must flow through financial intermediaries.

c. Almost all foreign exchange trading occurs on the floors of the FOREX exchanges in New York and London.

d. Derivative markets are a major source of finance for many corporations.

12. **Financial markets and intermediaries (S13.5)** True or false?

a. Exchange traded funds are hedge funds that can be bought and sold on the stock exchange.

b. Hedge funds provide small investors with low-cost diversification.

c. The sale of insurance policies is a source of financing for insurance companies.

d. In defined-contribution pension plans, the pension pot depends on the rate of return earned on the contributions by the employer and employee.

13. **Financial markets and intermediaries (S13.5)** Financial markets and intermediaries channel savings from investors to corporate investment. The savings make this journey by many different routes. Give a specific example for each of the following routes:

a. Investor to financial intermediary, to financial markets, and to the corporation.

b. Investor to financial markets, to a financial intermediary, and to the corporation.

c. Investor to financial markets, to a financial intermediary, back to financial markets, and to the corporation.

14. **Financial markets and intermediaries (S13.5)** Explain briefly how each of the following allow individuals or companies to spread their risk:

a. An exchange traded fund.

b. Commodity markets.

c. A life insurance company.

15. **Financial markets and intermediaries (S13.5)** Some individuals are eager to spend income before it arrives; others want to postpone consumption. Give some examples of intermediaries that provide services to these individuals.

16. **Financial markets and intermediaries around the world (S13.6)** Which major countries have

a. The largest stock markets?

b. The largest bond markets?

c. The smallest direct holdings of shares by individual investors?

d. The largest holdings of bank deposits by individual investors?

e. The largest holdings of shares by other corporations?

     f. The largest use of trade credit for financing?

In each case, define "largest" or "smallest" as total value relative to GDP.

17. **Financial markets and intermediaries around the world (S13.6)**

     True/false?

     a. Direct holdings of equity by households are larger in Japan than in the United States.

     b. Bank financing of corporations is relatively important in Japan and continental Europe.

     c. Intercompany loans and trade credit are particularly important in the United States.

18. **Fintech (S13.7)**

     True/false?

     a. A blockchain is a form of cryptocurrency.

     b. Equity crowdfunding can be used to raise cash for start-up ventures by selling stock over the internet.

     c. An initial coin offering is used to sell newly mined bitcoins.

     d. P2P lending platforms are primarily used by banks to make small loans to individuals.

● ● ● ● ●

SOLUTIONS TO SELF-TEST QUESTIONS

13.1 Internal funds are most important, followed by net borrowing.

13.2 Internal funds add to the firm's equity and more than offset the outflow of funds in the form of stock repurchases.

13.3 Because corporations are taxed on only 50% of dividends on their holdings of preferred, the net return is $9 - (0.21 \times .5 \times 9) = 8.06\%$. The net return on the bond is $(1 - 0.21) \times 10 = 7.90\%$.

13.4 The value of a floating-rate loan is less sensitive to interest rate changes because the interest payment and discount rate both vary together. With a fixed-rate loan, only the discount rate varies.

13.5 If you convert, you receive stock worth $50 \times \$72 = \$3,600$. This is much higher than the $1,000 that you receive by letting the bond mature.

13.6 a. and d.

13.7 Soft data about consumer behavior is used by artificial intelligence measures of credit risk. They may also be used for credit scores provided by P2P platforms.

● ● ● ● ●

FINANCE ON THE WEB

1. Use data from finance.yahoo.com to work out the financing proportions given in Figure 13.1 for a particular industrial company for some recent year.

2. The website www.federalreserve.gov/releases/z1/current/default.htm provides data on sources of funds and an aggregate balance sheet for nonfarm nonfinancial corporations. Look at Table F.102 for the latest year. What proportion of the cash that companies needed was generated internally, and how much had to be raised on the financial markets? Is this the usual pattern? Now look at "new equity issues." Were companies, on average, issuing new equity or buying their shares back?

3. An aggregate balance sheet for U.S. manufacturing corporations can be found on www.census.gov/econ/qfr. Find the balance sheet for the latest year. What was the ratio of long-term debt to long-term debt plus equity? What about the ratio of all long-term liabilities to long-term liabilities plus equity?

14

How Corporations Issue Securities

As companies proceed from infancy to adulthood, they need to raise increasing amounts of capital. In this chapter, we explain how they do so.

Section 14.1 Venture capital

Growing firms need to finance that awkward adolescent period before they are large enough to go public. We start by describing how a young firm might go about raising venture capital. We show how entrepreneurs signal their commitment to the project and how venture capitalists structure the deal to ensure that entrepreneurs are well motivated. We then look at the composition of the venture capital market.

Section 14.2 The initial public offering

For a successful firm, there is likely to come a time when it needs to tap a wider source of capital by making its first public issue of common stock. Section 14.2 describes what is involved in an IPO in the United States. We explain the process for registering the offering with the Securities and Exchange Commission, and we introduce the underwriters who buy the issue and resell it to the public. We also see that new issues are generally sold below the price at which they subsequently trade. To understand why that is so, we need to briefly discuss the field of auction procedures.

Section 14.3 Security sales by public companies

A company's first issue of stock is seldom its last. In Chapter 13, we saw that corporations face a persistent financial deficit, which they meet by selling securities. We therefore look at how established public corporations go about raising more capital. In the process, we encounter another puzzle: When companies announce a new issue of stock, the stock price generally falls. We suggest that the explanation lies in the information that investors read into the announcement.

Section 14.4 Private placements

If a stock or bond is sold publicly, it can then be traded on the securities markets. But sometimes investors intend to hold on to their securities and are not concerned about whether they can sell them. In these cases, there is little advantage to a public issue, and the firm may prefer to place the securities directly with one or two financial institutions. At the end of this chapter, we explain how companies arrange a private placement.

14-1   Venture Capital

In 1976, two college dropouts, Steve Jobs and Steve Wozniak, sold their van and a couple of calculators, and used the cash to start manufacturing computers in a garage. Today Apple is valued at $2.3 trillion. In 1996, two Stanford computer science students, Larry Page and Sergey Brin, decided to collaborate to develop a web search engine. To help turn their idea into a commercial product, they were able to raise almost $1 million. Today Google (renamed

Alphabet) is worth $1.6 trillion. In 2004, Mark Zuckerberg launched a website for fellow Harvard students to share ideas and news. Today Facebook is valued at $0.9 trillion. Such stories illustrate that the most important asset of a new firm is often a good idea. But that is not sufficient. To take an idea from the drawing board to a prototype and through to large-scale operations requires increasing amounts of capital.

To demonstrate how emerging companies raise the necessary finance, we will follow the progress of an imaginary company from its start-up to a successful corporation.

In 2034 three college dropouts met to celebrate the incorporation of Marvin Enterprises.[1] By this point, the three entrepreneurs had raised $100,000 from savings and personal bank loans and had purchased 1 million shares in the new company. The company's only other asset was the *idea* for a new product, the household gargle blaster.

Marvin Enterprises' bank account steadily drained away as design and testing proceeded. Local banks did not see Marvin's idea as adequate collateral, so a transfusion of equity capital was clearly needed. The company therefore decided to apply to First Meriam Venture Partners, a venture capital firm that specialized in providing finance for small, start-up firms with high growth potential. Before approaching First Meriam, Marvin needed to prepare a *business plan,* which described the proposed product, its potential market, the underlying technology, and the resources (time, money, employees, and plant and equipment) needed for success.

Most entrepreneurs are able to spin a plausible yarn about their company. But it is as hard to convince a venture capitalist that your business plan is sound as to get a first novel published.[2] Marvin's managers were able to point to the fact that they were prepared to put their money where their mouths were. Not only had they staked all their savings in the company, but they had fully mortgaged everything they could. This *signaled* their faith in the business.

First Meriam Venture Partners was impressed with Marvin's management team and its business plan and agreed to buy 1 million new shares for $1 each. After this *first-stage* financing, the company's market-value balance sheet looked like this:

Marvin Enterprises' First-Stage Balance Sheet (Market Values in $ millions)

Cash from new equity	$1	$1	New equity from venture capital
Other assets, mostly intangible	1	1	Original equity held by entrepreneurs
Value	$2	$2	Value

By agreeing to pay $1 a share for Marvin's stock, First Meriam placed a *pre-money valuation* of $1 million on the entrepreneurs' original shareholdings. This was First Meriam's estimate of the value of the entrepreneurs' original idea and their commitment to the enterprise. If the estimate was right, the entrepreneurs could congratulate themselves on a $900,000 paper gain over their original $100,000 investment. The injection of $1 million by First Meriam produced a *post-money valuation* for Marvin of $2 million.[3]

In exchange for the injection of funds, the entrepreneurs gave up half their company and accepted First Meriam's representatives to the board of directors.[4] Since First Meriam was taking a large stake in an immature business, it demanded a majority on the board. This is not always the case. A common compromise gives an equal number of seats to the founders and

---

[1] We first encountered Marvin Enterprises in Chapter 11.

[2] For evidence on what venture capitalists look for in a potential investment see P. Gompers, W. Gornall, S. N. Kaplan, and I. A. Strebulaev, "How Do Venture Capitalists Make Decisions?" *Journal of Financial Economics,* 135 (January 2020), pp. 169–190.

[3] This calculation may exaggerate the post-money valuation. If First Meriam's equity has superior rights to the original equity, the investment by the entrepreneurs would be worth less than $1 million, and the post-money valuation of the company would be less than $2 million.

[4] Venture capital investors do not necessarily demand a majority on the board of directors. Whether they do depends, for example, on how mature the business is and on what fraction they own. Regardless of whether they have a majority of directors, venture capital companies are seldom silent partners; their judgment and contacts can often prove useful to a relatively inexperienced management team.

to outside investors; the two parties then agree to one or more additional directors to serve as tie-breakers in case a conflict arises.

Venture capital firms tend to specialize in young high-tech businesses like Marvin that are difficult to evaluate, and they monitor these firms closely. Regardless of whether they have a majority of directors, they are not passive investors. They provide ongoing advice and often play a major role in recruiting the senior management team. Thus, in Marvin's early years, First Meriam's judgment and contacts proved valuable to the company and helped it to bring its products more quickly to market.[5]

If Marvin's management had demanded watertight employment contracts and fat salaries, they would not have found it easy to raise venture capital. Instead, the Marvin team agreed to put up with modest salaries. They could cash in only from appreciation of their stock. If Marvin failed, they would get nothing because First Meriam actually bought 1 million shares of *Series A preferred stock* designed to convert into 1 million shares of common stock. This raised even further the stakes for the company's management.[6]

Venture capitalists rarely give a young company up front all the money it will need. At each stage they give enough to reach the next major checkpoint. Thus, in spring 2036, having designed and tested a prototype, Marvin Enterprises was back asking for more money for pilot production and test marketing. First Meriam, the original backers, had insisted on pro-rata rights, which gave it the right to participate in subsequent financings. It, therefore, chose to invest $1.5 million in the *second-stage* financing, and a further $2.5 million came from two other venture capital partnerships and wealthy individual investors. The balance sheet just after the second stage was as follows:

Marvin Enterprises' Second-Stage Balance Sheet (Market Values in $ millions)

Cash from new equity	$ 4	$ 4	Series B convertible preferred stock
Other assets	10	5	Series A convertible preferred stock
		5	Original equity held by entrepreneurs
Value	$14	$14	Value

Now the post-money valuation was $14 million. First, Meriam marked up its original investment to $5 million, and the founders noted an additional $4 million accounting gain.

14.1 Self-Test

Why might the venture capital company prefer to put up only part of the funds up front? Would this affect the amount of effort put in by the entrepreneur? Is the entrepreneur's willingness to accept only part of the needed capital a good signal of the likely success of the venture?

Does this begin to sound like a (paper) money machine? It was so only with hindsight. At stage 1, it wasn't clear whether Marvin would ever get to stage 2. If the prototype hadn't worked, First Meriam could have fired the management and gotten someone else to try to develop the business. It could have refused to put up more funds and effectively closed down the business.[7] Or it could have advanced stage 2 money in a smaller amount on less favorable terms.

---

[5] For evidence on the role of venture capitalists in assisting new businesses, see T. Hellman and M. Puri, "The Interaction between Product Market and Financing Strategy: The Role of Venture Capital," *Review of Financial Studies* 13 (2000), pp. 959–984; and S. N. Kaplan and P. Stromberg, "Characteristics, Contracts and Actions: Evidence from Venture Capitalist Analyses," *Journal of Finance* 59 (October 2004), pp. 2177–2210.

[6] First Meriam also demanded a liquidation preference clause that ensured that they not only had precedence in the event of bankruptcy, but also if the company was sold out at a loss.

[7] If First Meriam had refused to invest at stage 2, it would have been an exceptionally hard sell convincing another investor to step in. The other outside investors knew they had less information about Marvin than First Meriam and would have read its refusal as a bad omen for Marvin's prospects.

EXAMPLE 14.1 • Down rounds and anti-dilution provisions

Suppose that following the initial financing, Marvin found that development of the prototype was proving more costly than anticipated and that the cash *burn rate* was unexpectedly high. In this case, the company might have needed to undertake a *down round* of financing, in which further shares were issued at only $0.80 each. For example, the down round might have involved the sale of $4 million of Series B preferred stock that could be converted into 5 million shares. In this case, the second stage balance sheet would be as follows:

Marvin Enterprises' Second-Stage Balance Sheet following a down round (Market Values in $ millions)

Cash from new equity	$ 4	$ 4	Series B convertible preferred stock
Other assets	1.6	0.8	Series A convertible preferred stock
	__	0.8	Original equity held by entrepreneurs
Value	$5.6	$5.6	Value

The holdings of First Meriam and the original entrepreneurs would now be worth only $0.8 million each, and their share of the company's equity would have fallen from 50% to $0.8/5.6 = 14\%$.

To protect themselves against dilution of their investment in a down round, it is common for the initial providers of venture capital to include an anti-dilution provision that adjusts the conversion price on their preferred stock and limits the reduction in their percentage ownership. For example, First Meriam could have maintained the value of its investment by ensuring that it was entitled to the same conversion terms as the new Series B stock.[8] The effect of such anti-dilution clauses is to load an increasing proportion of the fall in value on the entrepreneurs.

• • • • •

In Chapter 13, we pointed out that stockholders and lenders differ in their cash-flow rights and control rights. The stockholders are entitled to whatever cash flows remain after paying off the other security holders. They also have control over how the company uses its money, and it is only if the company defaults that the lenders can step in and take control of the company. When a new business raises venture capital, these cash-flow rights and control rights are usually negotiated separately. The venture capital firm will want a say in how that business is run and will demand representation on the board and a significant number of votes. The venture capitalist may agree that it will relinquish some of these rights if the business subsequently performs well. However, if performance turns out to be poor, it may automatically get a greater say in how the business is run and whether the existing management should be replaced.

Notice two features of the venture capital funding. First, the venture capital firm would like to ensure that only confident and motivated entrepreneurs apply for funding, and second it would like to create high-powered incentives for the entrepreneurs to work hard. Therefore, the deal with Marvin was designed so that failure would have been costly for management, while success would come largely in appreciation of their equity in the business. Since only part of the money was advanced at each stage, there were no opportunities to sit back and relax. First Meriam's board representation also allowed it to keep in close touch with firm progress and gave it considerable influence on company policy.

For Marvin, fortunately, everything went according to plan. Third-stage **mezzanine financing** was arranged,[9] full-scale production began on schedule, and gargle blasters were acclaimed by music critics worldwide. Marvin Enterprises went public on February 3, 2040.

BEYOND THE PAGE

Facebook's funding rounds

mhhe.com/brealey14e

---

[8] This is known as *full ratchet protection*.

[9] Mezzanine financing does not necessarily come in the third stage; there may be four or five stages. The point is that mezzanine investors come in late, in contrast to venture capitalists who get in on the ground floor.

Once its shares were traded, the paper gains earned by First Meriam and the company's founders turned into fungible wealth. But before we go on to this initial public offering, we will look briefly at the venture capital markets today.

The Venture Capital Market

Like Marvin, most new companies rely initially on family funds and bank loans. Some of them continue to grow with the aid of equity investment provided by wealthy individuals known as *angel investors*. In recent years these individuals have increasingly invested through *angel groups*. The groups not only allow the investors to diversify, but they provide the capacity to make larger investments and to make the follow-on investments that may be needed to take a business to a successful exit from this early stage financing to another form of financing such as venture capital.

Many adolescent companies, like Marvin, raise capital from venture-capital firms, which pool funds from a variety of investors, seek out fledgling companies to invest in, and then work with these companies as they try to grow. In addition, many large firms act as *corporate venturers* by providing equity capital to new innovative companies. For example, GV, the venture capital arm of Alphabet, has funded more than 500 companies.

Figure 14.1 shows that the level of venture capital investment fluctuates sharply. During the giddy days of the dot-com boom, funds invested about $120 billion; two years later the figure had fallen to $16 billion.

Most venture capital funds are organized as limited private partnerships with a fixed life of about 10 years. Pension funds and other investors are the limited partners.[10] The management company, which is the general partner, is responsible for making and overseeing the investments and, in return, receives a fixed fee and a share of the profits, called the *carried interest*.[11] These venture capital partnerships are often grouped together with similar partnerships that provide funds for companies in distress or that buy out whole companies or divisions of public companies and then take them private. The general term for these activities is *private equity investing*.

BEYOND THE PAGE

U.S. venture capital investment

mhhe.com/brealey14e

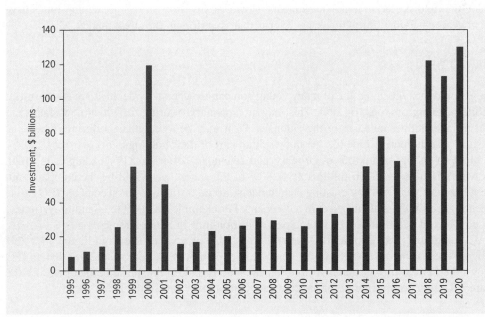

▶ **FIGURE 14.1**

Venture capital investment in the United States.

Source: Thomson Reuters data in MoneyTree Report, Q4, 2020, PricewaterhouseCoopers, National Venture Capital Association.

---

[10] Some pension funds and mutual funds also have their own venture capital arms that largely invest in later stage ventures.

[11] A typical arrangement might be for the management company to receive a fee of 2% *plus* 20% of the profits.

14.2 Self-Test

As a limited partner in a venture capital fund, would you prefer the management company to charge just a fixed fee or to receive carried interest?

Venture capitalists may cash in on their investment in two ways. Once the new business has established a track record, it is most commonly sold out to a larger firm. However, many entrepreneurs do not fit easily into a corporate bureaucracy and would prefer instead to remain the boss. In this case, the company may decide, like Marvin, to go public and so provide the original backers with an opportunity to "cash out" by selling their stock and leaving the original entrepreneurs in control. Approximately 50% of companies going public have been backed by a venture capital company. A thriving venture capital market therefore needs an active stock exchange, such as Nasdaq, that specializes in trading the shares of young, rapidly growing firms.[12]

For every 10 first-stage venture capital investments, only two or three may survive as successful, self-sufficient businesses. From these statistics come two rules for success in venture capital investment. First, don't shy away from uncertainty; accept a low probability of success. But don't buy into a business unless you can see the chance of a big, public company in a profitable market. There's no sense taking a long shot unless it pays off handsomely if you win. Second, cut your losses; identify losers early, and if you can't fix the problem—by replacing management, for example—do not continue to throw good money after bad.

Venture capital firms have had plenty of failures, but they have also provided early financing for many glamorous growth companies such as Intel, Apple, Microsoft, Facebook, and Google (now renamed Alphabet). One study of companies that were supported in their early days with venture capital estimated that in 2014, these companies accounted for 20% of the market capitalization of U.S. public companies and 44% of spending on R&D.[13]

How successful in general is venture capital investment? It is hard to say for at least two reasons. First, until a company has gone public or has been sold, any estimate of its value is subjective. Second, the return on venture capital varies dramatically according to the date at which the fund started to make investments. However, investors in venture capital funds have mostly earned significantly higher net returns than investors in the stock market.

14-2 The Initial Public Offering

There comes a stage in the life of many young companies when they decide to make an **initial public offering** of stock, or **IPO**. This may be a primary offering, in which new shares are sold to raise additional cash for the company. Or it may be a secondary offering, where the existing shareholders decide to cash in by selling part of their holdings.

Many IPOs are a mixture of primary and secondary offerings. For example, in 2020, McAfee's IPO raised $740 million. Over 80% of the shares were sold by the company, but the remainder were sold by existing shareholders. Some of the biggest secondary IPOs arise when a government sells its stake in a company. For example, in 2019 the Saudi government raised a record $29.4 billion by selling part of its holdings in Saudi Aramco.

An important motive for an IPO is to raise cash, but as you can see from Figure 14.2, this is by no means the only objective for going public. Commonly cited reasons are that an IPO allows the firm to use its shares for future acquisitions and establishes a market price for the shares. Raising equity capital for the company comes fairly low in the list of motives.

---

[12] This argument is developed in B. Black and R. Gilson, "Venture Capital and the Structure of Capital Markets: Banks versus Stock Markets," *Journal of Financial Economics* 47 (March 1998), pp. 243–277.

[13] See W. Gornall and I. A. Strebulaev, "The Economic Impact of Venture Capital: Evidence from Public Companies," 2015, Stanford University Working Paper.

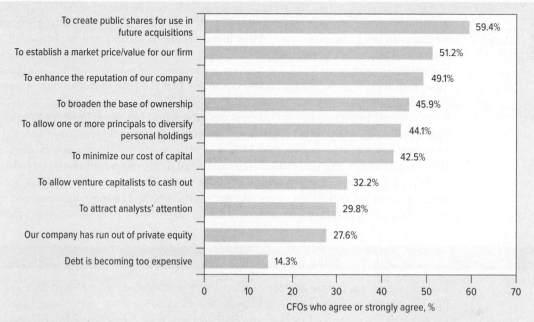

FIGURE 14.2   Survey evidence on the motives for going public.

Source: J. C. Brau and S. E. Fawcett, "Evidence on What CFOs Think about the IPO Process: Practice, Theory and Managerial Implications," *Journal of Applied Corporate Finance* 18 (October 2006), pp. 107–117.

The Public-Private Choice

Although there are advantages to becoming a public corporation, there are also drawbacks. Managers of public companies often chafe at the constant pressure from shareholders to report increases in profits, and they complain at the red tape involved in running a public company. The complaints about red tape have become more vocal since the passage of the Sarbanes–Oxley Act (SOX), which sought to prevent a repeat of the corporate scandals that brought about the collapse of Enron and WorldCom.

Some large U.S. companies—such as Cargill, Koch Industries, and Mars Inc.—have been private all their corporate lives, but you should not think of the issue process in the United States as a one-way street; public firms often go into reverse and return to being privately owned. For example, Dell became a public company in 1988 and then reverted to being private in 2013, when Michael Dell and a private-equity firm bought out the business.

EXAMPLE 14.2 • The public-private choice

For an extreme example of switching between public and private ownership, consider the food service company, Aramark. It began life in 1936 as a private company and went public in 1960. In 1984, a management buyout led to the company going private, and it remained private until 2001 when it had its second public offering. But the experiment did not last long: Five years later, Aramark was once again the object of a buyout that took the company private again. In 2013, Aramark went public for the third time and in 2021 it still is.

• • • • •

For some years before the pandemic, fewer U.S. companies went public, and many new growth companies that are worth a billion dollars or more chose to remain private.[14] As we write this in 2021, there are about 500 of these so-called unicorns around the world, including such well-known U.S. names as SpaceX, Stripe, and Epic Games. While the majority of large businesses in the United States are public corporations, the number of public corporations has more than halved since its high in 1996. It looks as if the case for remaining private may be stronger than it once was.

In response to such concerns Congress passed the Jumpstart Our Business Startups (JOBS) Act, which eased some of the regulations for small companies that had been enacted in SOX. However, not everyone agrees that SOX was responsible for the decline in the number of IPOs. For example, one study observed that the fall in the number of companies going public is concentrated among small venture-backed firms.[15] This may indicate that it is becoming more difficult for such firms to operate in today's rapidly changing markets, and therefore, rather than going public, it makes more sense for these firms to sell out to larger firms.

EXAMPLE 14.3 ● The German Mittelstand

In many countries, private companies are more important than in the United States. For example, Germany's medium-sized manufacturers, collectively known as the Mittelstand, account for about 50% of national income and 80% of the workforce. These Mittelstand companies are typically privately held, family-owned businesses that rely heavily on bank borrowing to make good any financial deficit.[16] Increasingly, private equity firms have been stepping in to provide the equity capital that they need.

● ● ● ● ●

14.3 Self-Test

What are the advantages and disadvantages of going public?

Arranging an Initial Public Offering

We can illustrate the procedure for going public by returning to our example of Marvin Enterprises. By 2040, the company had grown to the point at which it needed still more capital to implement its second-generation production technology. At the same time, the company's founders were looking to sell some of their shares.[17] In the previous few months, there had been a spate of IPOs by high-tech companies, and the shares had generally sold like hotcakes. So Marvin's management hoped that investors would be equally keen to buy the company's stock.

Management's first task was to select the *underwriters*. Underwriters act as financial midwives to a new issue. Usually they play a triple role: First they provide the company with procedural and financial advice, then they buy the issue, and finally they resell it to the public.

---

[14] Interestingly, during the pandemic the pace of IPOs has increased significantly. See https://www.tradersmagazine.com/am/a-record-pace-for-ipos/.

[15] See X. Gao, J. R. Ritter, and Z. Zhu, "Where Have All the IPOs Gone?" *Journal of Financial and Quantitative Analysis* 48 (December 2013), pp. 1663–1692.

[16] Many larger German companies have also chosen to remain private, including the retailers Schwarz Gruppe and Aldi, and the media giant Bertelsmann. For a discussion of the financing of the Mittelstand, see U. Hommel and H. Schneider, "Financing the German Mittelstand," *EIB Papers* 8 (2003), pp. 53–90.

[17] First Meriam also wanted to cash in on its investment, but venture capital companies usually believe that selling out at the time of the IPO would send a bad signal to investors. Therefore, First Meriam planned to wait until well after the IPO and then either sell its holding or distribute its shares in Marvin to the investors in the First Meriam fund.

After some discussion, Marvin settled on Klein Merrick as the managing underwriter and Goldman Stanley as the co-manager. Klein Merrick then formed a syndicate of underwriters who would buy the entire issue and reoffer it to the public.

In choosing Klein Merrick to manage its IPO, Marvin was influenced by Merrick's proposals for making an active market in the stock in the weeks after the issue.[18] Merrick also planned to generate continuing investor interest in the stock by distributing a major research report on Marvin's prospects.[19] Marvin hoped that this report would encourage investors to hold its stock.

Together with Klein Merrick and firms of lawyers and accountants, Marvin prepared a **registration statement** for the approval of the Securities and Exchange Commission (SEC).[20] This statement is a detailed and somewhat cumbersome document that presents information about the proposed financing and the firm's history, existing business, and plans for the future.

The most important sections of the registration statement are distributed to investors in the form of a **prospectus**. In the appendix to this chapter, we have reproduced the prospectus for Marvin's first public issue of stock. Real prospectuses would go into much more detail on each topic, but this example should give you some feel for the mixture of valuable information and redundant qualification that characterizes these documents. The Marvin prospectus also illustrates how the SEC insists that investors' eyes are opened to the dangers of purchase (see "Certain Considerations" in the prospectus). Some investors have joked that if they read each prospectus carefully, they would not dare to buy any new issue.

In addition to registering the issue with the SEC, Marvin needed to check that the issue complied with the so-called blue-sky laws of each state that regulate sales of securities within the state.[21] It also arranged for its newly issued shares to be traded on the Nasdaq exchange.

BEYOND THE PAGE

Twitter's IPO prospectus

mhhe.com/brealey14e

The Sale of Marvin Stock

While Marvin was responding to the SEC's comments on the registration statement, the company and its underwriters began to firm up the issue price. First they looked at the price–earnings ratios of the shares of Marvin's principal competitors. Then they worked through a number of discounted-cash-flow calculations like the ones we described in Chapter 4. Most of the evidence pointed to a market price in the region of $74 to $76 a share, and the company therefore included this provisional figure in an amended version of the prospectus.[22]

Following the issue of the prospectus, Marvin and Klein Merrick arranged a *road show* to talk to potential investors. These were mostly institutional investors, such as managers of mutual funds and pension funds. The investors gave their reactions to the issue and indicated to the underwriters how much stock they wished to buy. Some stated the maximum price that they were prepared to pay, but others said that they just wanted to invest so many dollars in Marvin at whatever issue price was chosen. These discussions with fund managers allowed

---

[18] On average, the managing underwriter accounts for 40% to 60% of trading volume in the stock during the first 60 days after an IPO. See K. Ellis, R. Michaely, and M. O'Hara, "When the Underwriter Is the Market Maker: An Examination of Trading in the IPO Aftermarket," *Journal of Finance* 55 (June 2000), pp. 1039–1074.

[19] The 40 days after the IPO are designated as a *quiet period*. Merrick is obliged to wait until after this period before commenting on the valuation of the company. Survey evidence suggests that in choosing an underwriter, firms place considerable importance on its ability to provide follow-up research reports. See L. Krigman, W. H. Shaw, and K. L. Womack, "Why Do Firms Switch Underwriters?" *Journal of Financial Economics* 60 (May 2001), pp. 245–284.

[20] The rules governing the sale of securities derive principally from the Securities Act of 1933. The SEC is concerned solely with disclosure and it has no power to prevent an issue as long as there has been proper disclosure. Some public issues are exempt from registration. These include issues by small businesses and loans maturing within nine months.

[21] In 1980, when Apple Computer Inc. went public, the Massachusetts state government decided the offering was too risky and barred the sale of the shares to individual investors in the state. The state relented later after the issue was out and the price had risen. Needless to say, this action was not acclaimed by Massachusetts investors. States do not usually reject security issues by honest firms through established underwriters. We cite the example to illustrate the potential power of state securities laws and to show why underwriters keep careful track of them.

[22] The company is allowed to circulate a preliminary version of the prospectus (known as a *red herring*) before the SEC has approved the registration statement.

Klein Merrick to build up a book of potential orders.[23] Although the managers were not bound by their responses, they knew that, if they wanted to keep the underwriters' goodwill, they should be careful not to go back on their expressions of interest. The underwriters also were not obliged to treat all investors equally. Some investors who were keen to buy Marvin stock were disappointed in the allotment that they subsequently received.

Immediately after it received clearance from the SEC, Marvin and the underwriters met to fix the issue price. Investors had been enthusiastic about the story that the company had to tell and it was clear that they were prepared to pay more than $76 for the stock. Marvin's managers were tempted to go for the highest possible price, but the underwriters were more cautious. Not only would they be left with any unsold stock if they overestimated investor demand, but they also argued that some degree of underpricing was needed to tempt investors to buy the stock. Marvin and the underwriters therefore compromised on an issue price of $80. Potential investors were encouraged by the fact that the offer price was higher than the $74 to $76 proposed in the preliminary prospectus and decided that the underwriters must have encountered considerable enthusiasm for the issue.

Although Marvin's underwriters were committed to buy only 900,000 shares from the company, they chose to sell 1,035,000 shares to investors. This left the underwriters short of 135,000 shares or 15% of the issue. If Marvin's stock had proved unpopular with investors and traded below the issue price, the underwriters could have bought back these shares in the marketplace. This would have helped to stabilize the price and would have given the underwriters a profit on the sale of these extra shares. As it turned out, investors fell over themselves to buy Marvin stock, and by the end of the first day, the stock was trading at $105. The underwriters would have incurred a heavy loss if they had been obliged to buy back the extra shares at $105. However, Marvin had provided underwriters with a *greenshoe* option that allowed them to buy an additional 135,000 shares from the company. This ensured that the underwriters were able to sell the extra shares to investors without fear of loss.

After a mandatory "quiet period" of 40 days following the sale, several of Marvin's underwriters published research reports on the company and recommended buying the stock.

The Underwriters

Marvin's underwriters were prepared to enter into a firm commitment to buy the stock and then offer it to the public. Thus they took the risk that the issue might flop and they would be left with unwanted stock. Occasionally, where the sale of common stock is regarded as particularly risky, the underwriters may be prepared to handle the sale only on a *best-efforts* basis. In this case, the underwriters promise to sell as much of the issue as possible, but they do not guarantee to sell the entire amount.[24]

Successful underwriting requires financial muscle and considerable experience. The names of Marvin's underwriters are, of course, fictitious, but Table 14.1 shows that underwriting is dominated by the major investment banks and large commercial banks. Foreign players are also heavily involved in underwriting securities, particularly those that are sold internationally.

Underwriting is not always fun. In April 2008, a British bank, HBOS, offered its shareholders two new shares at a price of £2.75 for each five shares that they currently held.[25] The underwriters to the issue, Morgan Stanley and Dresdner Kleinwort, guaranteed that at the end of eight weeks they would buy any new shares that the stockholders did not want. At the time of the offer, HBOS shares were priced at about £5, so the underwriters felt confident that they would not have to honor their pledge. Unfortunately, they reckoned without the turbulent market in bank shares that year. The bank's shareholders worried that the money they were asked

---

[23] The managing underwriter is therefore often known as the *bookrunner*.

[24] The alternative is to enter into an *all-or-none* arrangement. In this case, either the entire issue is sold at the offering price or the deal is called off and the issuing company receives nothing.

[25] This arrangement is known as a *rights issue*. We describe rights issues later in the chapter.

Top Managing Underwriters of U.S. Equity Issues, 2020
1 Goldman Sachs
2 Morgan Stanley
3 JPMorgan
4 BofA Securities
5 Citigroup
6 Credit Suisse

❭**TABLE 14.1** The top managing underwriters of U.S. equity issues, 2020.

Source: Financial Times.

to provide would go to bailing out the bondholders and depositors. By the end of the eight weeks, the price of HBOS stock had slumped below the issue price, and the underwriters were left with 932 million unwanted shares worth £3.6 billion.

Companies get to make only one IPO, but underwriters are in the business all the time. Wise underwriters, therefore, realize that their reputation is on the line and will not handle an issue unless they believe the facts have been presented fairly to investors. So, when a new issue goes wrong, the underwriters may be blamed for overhyping the issue and failing in their "due diligence." For example, in December 1999, software company Va Linux went public at $30 a share. The next day, trading opened at $299 a share, but then the price began to sag. Within two years, it had fallen below $2. Disgruntled Va Linux investors sued the underwriters, complaining that the prospectus was "materially false." These underwriters had plenty of company because following the collapse of the dot-com stocks in 2000, investors in many other high-tech IPOs sued the underwriters. As the nearby box explains, there was further embarrassment when it emerged that several well-known underwriters had engaged in "spinning"—that is, allocating stock in popular new issues to managers of their important corporate clients. The underwriter's seal of approval for a new issue no longer seemed as valuable as it once had.

Costs of a New Issue

We have described Marvin's underwriters as filling a triple role—providing advice, buying the new issue, and reselling it to the public. In return, they received payment in the form of a *spread;* that is, they were allowed to buy the shares for less than the *offering price* at which the shares were sold to investors.[26] The syndicate manager kept 20% of this spread. A further 25% of the spread was used to pay those underwriters who bought the issue. The remaining 55% went to the firms that provided the sales force.

The underwriting spread on the Marvin issue amounted to 7% of the total sum raised from investors. Since many of the costs incurred by underwriters are fixed, you would expect that the percentage spread would decline with issue size. This, in part, is what we find. For example, a $5 million IPO might carry a spread of 10%, while the spread on a $300 million issue might be only 5%. However, for almost every IPO between $20 and $80 million the spread has been exactly 7%.[27] Since it is difficult to believe that there are no scale economies, this clustering at 7% is a puzzle.[28]

---

[26] In the more risky cases, the underwriter usually receives some extra noncash compensation, such as warrants to buy additional common stock in the future.

[27] H. C. Chen and J. R. Ritter, "The Seven Percent Solution," *Journal of Finance* 55 (June 2000), pp. 1105–1131.

[28] Chen and Ritter argue that the fixed spread suggests the underwriting market is not competitive, and the U.S. Department of Justice was led to investigate whether the spread constituted evidence of price-fixing. Robert Hansen disagrees that the market is not competitive. Among other things, he provides evidence that the 7% spread is not abnormally profitable and argues that it is part of a competitive and efficient market. See R. Hansen, "Do Investment Banks Compete in IPOs? The Advent of the '7% Plus Contract,'" *Journal of Financial Economics* 59 (2001), pp. 313–346.

How Scandal Hit the Investment Banking Industry

❱ 1999 looked to be a wonderful year for investment banks. Not only did they underwrite a near-record number of IPOs, but the stocks that they sold leapt by an average of 72% on their first day of trading, earning the underwriters some very grateful clients. Just three years later, the same investment banks were in disgrace. Probing by New York State Attorney General Eliot Spitzer uncovered a chronicle of unethical and shameful behavior during the boom years.

As the dot-com stock market boom developed, investment banking analysts had begun to take on the additional role of promoters of the shares that they analyzed, in the process becoming celebrities with salaries to match. The early run-up in the stock price of dot-com IPOs therefore owed much to hype by the underwriters' analysts, who strongly promoted stocks that they sometimes privately thought were overpriced. One superstar Internet analyst was revealed in internal e-mails to have believed that stocks he was peddling to investors were "junk" and "piece[s] of crap." In many cases, the stocks were indeed junk, and the underwriters who had puffed the IPOs soon found themselves sued by disgruntled investors who had bought at the inflated prices.

The underwriters' troubles deepened when it was disclosed that in a number of cases they had allocated stock in hot new issues to the personal brokerage accounts of the CEOs of major corporate clients. This stock could then be sold, or "spun," for quick profits. Five senior executives of leading telecom companies were disclosed to have received a total of $28 million in profits from their allocation of stocks in IPOs underwritten by one bank. Over the same period, the bank was awarded more than $100 million of business from these five companies. Eliot Spitzer argued that such lucrative perks were really attempts by the banks to buy future business and that the profits therefore belonged to the companies' shareholders rather than the executives. Soon, top executives of several other companies were facing demands from disgruntled shareholders that they return to their companies the profits that they had pocketed from hot initial public offerings.

These scandals that engulfed the investment banking industry resulted in a $1.4 billion payout by the banks and an agreement to separate investment banking and research departments, hire independent consultants, and select independent research providers. But the revelations also raised troubling questions about ethical standards and the pressures that can lead employees to unscrupulous behavior.

In addition to the underwriting fee, new issues entail substantial administrative costs. Preparation of the registration statement and prospectus involve management, legal counsel, and accountants, as well as the underwriters and their advisers. In addition, the firm has to pay fees for registering the new securities, printing and mailing costs, and so on. You can see from the first page of the Marvin prospectus (see this chapter's appendix) that these administrative costs totaled $820,000 or just over 1% of the proceeds.

Underpricing of IPOs

New issues are costly in yet another way. If the offering price is less than the true value of the issued securities, investors who buy the issue get a bargain at the expense of the firm's original shareholders.

These costs of *underpricing* are hidden but nevertheless real. For IPOs, they generally exceed all other issue costs. Whenever any company goes public, it is very difficult to judge how much investors will be prepared to pay for the stock. Sometimes the underwriters misjudge dramatically. For example, in 2020 Airbnb went public with the sale of 51.3 million shares at $68 each. As soon as trading opened, dealers were flooded with orders to buy the stock; 70 million shares traded, and the stock closed the day at a price of $144.71, a gain of 113%.

BEYOND THE PAGE

Hot IPOs

mhhe.com/brealey14e

We admit that the Airbnb issue was somewhat unusual.[29] But researchers have found that investors who buy at the issue price on average realize very high returns over the following days. For example, one study of nearly 9,000 U.S. IPOs from 1980 to 2020 found average underpricing of 18.4%.[30]

Figure 14.3 shows that the United States is not the only country in which IPOs are underpriced. In Saudi Arabia, the gains from buying IPOs have averaged 240%.

You might think that shareholders would prefer not to sell stock in their company for less than its market price, but many investment bankers and institutional investors argue that underpricing is in the interests of the issuing firm. They say that a low offering price on an IPO raises the price when it is subsequently traded in the market and enhances the firm's ability to raise further capital.

There is another possible reason that it may make sense to underprice new issues. Suppose that you successfully bid for a painting at an art auction. Should you be pleased? It is true that you now own the painting, which was presumably what you wanted, but everybody else at the auction apparently thought that the painting was worth less than you did. In other words, your success suggests that you may have overpaid. This problem is known as the *winner's curse*. Unless bidders recognize this in their bids, the successful buyer will, on average, overpay. If bidders are aware of the danger, they are likely to adjust their bids down correspondingly.

The same problem arises when you apply for a new issue of securities. For example, suppose that you decide to apply for every new issue of common stock. You will find that you have no difficulty in getting stock in the issues that no one else wants. But, when the issue is attractive, the underwriters will not have enough stock to go around, and you will receive less stock than you wanted. The result is that your money-making strategy may turn out to be a loser. If you are smart, you will play the game only if there is substantial underpricing on average. Here then we have a possible rationale for the underpricing of new issues.[31] Uninformed investors who cannot distinguish which issues are attractive are exposed to the winner's curse. Companies and their underwriters are aware of this and need to underprice on average to attract the uninformed investors.

BEYOND THE PAGE

Chinese IPOs

mhhe.com/brealey14e

BEYOND THE PAGE

Facebook's IPO

mhhe.com/brealey14e

14.4 Self-Test

Suppose that you can earn an immediate 15% on underpriced IPOs and lose 10% on overpriced IPOs. But because of high demand, you only get half the shares that you apply for when the issue is underpriced. Suppose you bid for $1000 of shares in each of two issues, one underpriced and the other overpriced. What is the net dollar gain or loss on your investment?

These arguments could well justify some degree of underpricing, but it is not clear that they can account for the occasional underpricing of 100% or more. Skeptics point out that such underpricing is largely in the interests of the underwriters, who want to reduce the risk that they will be left with unwanted stock and also to court popularity by allotting stock to favored clients.[32]

If the skeptics are right, you might expect issuing companies to rebel at being asked to sell stock for much less than it is worth. Think back to our example of Airbnb. If the company had

---

[29] It does not, however, hold the record. That honor goes to VA Linux.

[30] Our figure is an equally weighted average of first-day returns and is taken from data on Jay Ritter's website, https://site.warrington.ufl.edu/ritter/ipo-data/.

[31] This explanation for underpricing was first proposed in K. Rock, "Why New Issues Are Underpriced," *Journal of Financial Economics* 15 (1986), pp. 197–212.

[32] The winner's curse would disappear if only investors knew what the market price was going to be. One response is to allow trading in a security before it has been issued. This is known as the *gray market,* which in the United States is most common for debt issues. Investors can observe the price in the gray market and can be more confident that they are not overbidding when the actual issue takes place.

FIGURE 14.3

Average initial returns from investing in IPOs in different countries.

Source: T. Loughran, J. R. Ritter, and K. Rydqvist, "Initial Public Offerings: International Insights," *Pacific-Basin Finance Journal* 2 (May 1994), pp. 165–199, extended and updated February 2021 on bear.cba.ufl.edu/ ritter.

sold 513 million shares at the market price of $144 rather than $68, it would have raised an additional $7.2 billion. This is called *the money left on the table.* The cost of the underpricing to Airbnb co-founders was about 43% of this figure, or just over $3 billion. So why weren't they and other shareholders hopping mad? Loughran and Ritter suggest that the explanation lies in behavioral psychology and argue that the cost of underpricing may be outweighed in share-holders' minds by the happy surprise of finding that they are wealthier than they thought.[33]

14.5 Self-Test

Look at the appendix to this chapter. What are the administrative costs and underwriting costs of the Marvin issue as a percentage of the issue amount? At the end of the first day, the stock traded at $105. How much money was left on the table?

Hot New-Issue Periods

Figure 14.4 shows that the degree of underpricing fluctuates sharply from year to year. In 1999, around the peak of the dot-com boom, new issues raised $65 billion, and the average first-day return on IPOs was 71%. About $37 billion was left on the table that year. But, as the number of new issues slumped, so did the amount of underpricing.

Some observers believe that these hot new-issue periods arise because investors are prone to periods of excessive optimism and would-be issuers time their IPOs to coincide with these periods. Other observers stress the fact that a fall in the cost of capital or an improvement in the economic outlook may mean that a number of new or dormant projects suddenly become profitable. At such times, many entrepreneurs rush to raise new cash to invest in these projects.[34]

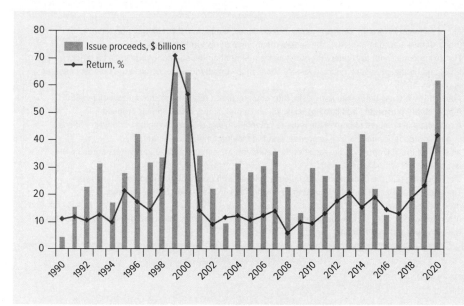

▶ **FIGURE 14.4**

IPO proceeds in the United States and average first-day returns, 1980–2020.

Source: J. R. Ritter, "Monthly Number of IPOs and the average first-day return," December 29, 2020, bear.cba.ufl.edu/ritter.

---

[33] T. Loughran and J. Ritter, "Why Don't Issuers Get Upset about Leaving Money on the Table in IPOs?" *Review of Financial Studies* 15 (2002), pp. 413–444.

[34] For examples of these explanations, see A. P. Ljungqvist, V. Nanda, and R. Singh, "Hot Markets, Investor Sentiment, and IPO Pricing," *Journal of Business* 79 (July 2006), pp. 1667–1702; and L. Pastor and P. Veronesi, "Rational IPO Waves," *Journal of Finance* 60 (2005), pp. 1713–1757.

The Long-Run Performance of IPO Stocks

On average investors who buy IPO stocks at the issue price realize high immediate returns, but how do they fare over the longer run? During the period 1980–2018, investors who bought the stock of an IPO at the close of the first day's trading would have lost 2.1% a year relative to other small growth companies.[35] This suggests that the initial reaction to the new issues was overenthusiastic. Why investors do not seem to have learned is a puzzle.

Alternative Issue Procedures

Table 14.2 summarizes the main steps involved in making an initial public offering of stock in the United States. You can see that Marvin's new issue was a typical IPO in almost every respect. In particular, most IPOs in the United States use the *bookbuilding* method in which the underwriter builds a book of likely orders and uses this information to set the issue price.

The bookbuilding method is, in some ways, like an auction since potential buyers indicate how many shares they are prepared to buy at given prices. However, these indications are not binding and are used only as a guide to fix the price of the issue. The advantage of the book-building method is that it allows underwriters to give preference to those investors whose bids are most helpful in setting the issue price and to offer them a reward in the shape of underpricing.[36] Critics of bookbuilding point to the abuses of the 1990s and emphasize the dangers of allowing the underwriter to decide who is allotted stock.

Although bookbuilding has rapidly gained popularity throughout the world, it is not the only way to sell new stock. For example, when Spotify wanted to give its existing holders the opportunity to sell their shares, it did not engage underwriters to buy and resell the stock. Instead it registered its shares with the SEC and arranged a *direct share listing* on the New York Stock Exchange.[37] Thus all existing shareholders became free to sell their stock

> **TABLE 14.2**
> The main steps involved in making an initial public offering of stock in the United States.

1. About one year before the company expects to go public, it appoints the managing underwriter (bookrunner) and co-manager(s). The underwriting syndicate is formed.
2. The arrangement with the underwriters includes agreement on the spread (typically 7% for medium-sized IPOs) and on the greenshoe option (typically allowing the underwriters to increase the number of shares bought by 15%).
3. About three months before the issue date, the company files a registration statement with the SEC. A preliminary prospectus (red herring) is issued, and a preliminary price range is proposed.
4. A roadshow is arranged to market the issue to potential investors. The managing underwriter builds a book of potential demand and, if appropriate, sets a new preliminary price range.
5. As soon as the SEC approves the registration statement, the company and underwriters agree on the issue price.
6. The following day, the underwriters allot stock (typically with overallotment), and trading starts.
7. The underwriters cover any short position by buying stock in the market or by exercising their greenshoe option.
8. After the 40-day quiet period, the underwriters are permitted to make forward-looking statements about the company and recommendations to buy the stock.

---

[35] See, for example, M. Lowry, R. Michaely, and E. Volkova, "Initial Public Offerings: A Synthesis of the Literature and Directions for Future Research," *Foundations and Trends in Finance,* 11 (February 2017), pp. 154–320.

[36] See L. M. Benveniste and P. A. Spindt, "How Investment Bankers Determine the Offer Price and Allocation of New Issues," *Journal of Financial Economics* 24 (1989), pp. 343–361; and F. Cornelli and D. Goldreich, "Bookbuilding and Strategic Allocation," *Journal of Finance* 56 (December 2001), pp. 2337–2369.

[37] See M. D. Jaffe, G. Rodgers, and H. Gutierrez, "Spotify Case Study: Structuring and Executing a Direct Listing," Harvard Law School Forum on Corporate Governance, July 5, 2018, available on https://corpgov.law.harvard.edu/2018/07/05/spotify-case-study-structuring-and-executing-a-direct-listing/.

immediately. In contrast to a traditional IPO, there was no issue price available for investors, but by providing ample information about the company, Spotify hoped that its share price would quickly settle down to a natural equilibrium.[38]

A direct listing is not feasible when the company wishes to raise cash by the issue of additional shares. In this case, an alternative to bookbuilding is to conduct an open auction in which investors are invited to submit their bids, stating how many shares they wish to buy and the price. The securities are then sold to the highest bidders. Most governments, including the U.S. Treasury, sell their bonds by auction. In the United States, auctions of common stock are rare. However, in 2004, Google simultaneously raised eyebrows and $1.7 billion in the world's largest initial public offering to be sold by auction.[39]

Fans of auctions often point to countries such as France, Israel, and Japan, where auctions were once commonly used to sell new issues of stock. Japan is a particularly interesting case because the bookbuilding method was widely used until it was revealed that investment banks had been allocating shares in hot IPOs to government officials. In 1989, the finance ministry responded to this scandal by ruling that in the future all IPOs were to be auctioned. This resulted in a sharp fall in underpricing. However, in 1997, the restrictions were lifted, bookbuilding returned to favor, and the level of underpricing increased.[40]

Types of Auction: A Digression

Suppose that a government wishes to auction 4 million bonds and three would-be buyers submit bids. Investor A bids $1,020 each for 1 million bonds, B bids $1,000 for 3 million bonds, and C bids $980 for 2 million bonds. The bids of the two highest bidders (A and B) absorb all the bonds on offer and C is left empty-handed. What price do the winning bidders, A and B, pay?

The answer depends on whether the sale is a *discriminatory auction* or a *uniform-price auction*. In a discriminatory auction, every winner is required to pay the price that he or she bid. In this case, A would pay $1,020 and B would pay $1,000. In a uniform-price auction, both would pay $1,000, which is the price of the lowest winning bidder (investor B).

It might seem from our example that the proceeds from a uniform-price auction would be lower than from a discriminatory auction. But this ignores the fact that the uniform-price auction provides better protection against the winner's curse. Wise bidders know that there is little cost to overbidding in a uniform-price auction, but there is potentially a very high cost to doing so in a discriminatory auction.[41] Economists therefore often argue that the uniform-price auction should result in higher proceeds.[42]

Sales of bonds by the U.S. Treasury used to take the form of discriminatory auctions so that successful buyers paid their bid. However, in 1998, the government switched to a uniform-price auction.[43]

---

[38] In the event, Spotify share price drifted down 10% from its first day opening price and then traded within a narrow range for the following month.

[39] Google's issue was followed in 2005 by a $140 million auction of stock by Morningstar.

[40] T. Kaneko and R. Pettway, "Auctions versus Book Building of Japanese IPOs," *Pacific-Basin Journal* 11 (2003), pp. 439–462.

[41] In addition, the price in the uniform-price auction depends not only on the views of B, but also on those of A (e.g., if A had bid $990 rather than $1,020, then both A and B would have paid $990 for each bond). Since the uniform-price auction takes advantage of the views of both A and B, it reduces the winner's curse.

[42] Sometimes auctions reduce the winner's curse by allowing uninformed bidders to enter noncompetitive bids, whereby they submit a quantity but not a price. For example, in U.S. Treasury auctions, investors may submit noncompetitive bids and receive their full allocation.

[43] Experience in the United States with uniform-price auctions suggests that they do indeed reduce the winner's curse problem and realize higher prices for the seller. See D. Goldreich, "Underpricing in Discriminatory and Uniform-Price Treasury Auctions," *Journal of Financial and Quantitative Analysis* 42 (June 2007), pp. 443–466.

〉SPACs

〉When Virgin Galactic went public in 2019, it did not do so by a traditional IPO. Instead, it raised close to $800 million by merging with a SPAC, a special-purpose acquisition vehicle, called Social Capital. The bulk of this sum was provided by the SPAC, but the founder of Social Capital invested an additional $100 million of his personal wealth in Virgin Galactic.

The sponsor of the SPAC raises funds through its own IPO, and goes public with just this cash and no underlying commercial operations. The SPAC then searches for an acquisition target, and in the meantime puts the money in a trust account, which is invested in safe securities.[44] Once the SPAC identifies its target, it usually raises additional funds to help finance the takeover. By merging into the SPAC, the target of the takeover becomes publicly listed.

Investors in the SPAC's initial IPO usually receive options to buy additional shares of the merged firm. In addition, the sponsor of the SPAC usually receives a share of the equity of the merged firm.

The advantage of this model is that once an attractive target is identified, it can be taken public much faster and at lower cost than in a traditional IPO. Of course, investors in the SPAC must trust the sponsor, as the ultimate acquisition is still unknown when the SPAC raises its own funds.[45] The reputation of the SPAC's sponsor is, therefore, crucial.

SPAC activity exploded in 2020, with $80 billion of shares issued, about half the amount raised in IPOs that year. In January 2021 alone, SPACs raised an additional $26 billion. Many of these SPACs were sponsored by celebrities such as NBA all-star Shaquille O'Neal and tennis champion Serena Williams.

SPACs are clearly popular, but are they good deals for their investors? So far, the jury is still out. On average, they have underperformed the post-listing returns of conventional IPOs, but there is some evidence that "high-quality" SPACs, for example, those sponsored by large, and presumably more knowledgeable, private-equity firms, have outperformed.

---

[44] If by the end of two years, the SPAC has not identified a target, the cash must usually be returned to its shareholders.

[45] For this reason, SPACs are often called blank-check firms.

14.6 Self-Test

Helicell Inc. proposes to go public by auctioning 1 million shares of stock. It receives the following bids:

Bidder	Number of Shares (000s)	Price
Eta Investments	350	$45
Kappa Fund	300	50
Nu Group	300	60
Omicron Growth	400	70

Who would receive stock and at what price, if

a. The auction was a discriminatory auction?

b. It was a uniform price auction?

14-3 Security Sales by Public Companies

A company's first public issue of stock is seldom its last. As the firm grows, it is likely to make further issues of debt and equity. Public companies can issue securities either by offering them to investors at large or by making a rights issue that is limited to existing stockholders. We begin by describing public offers, which are now used for almost all debt and equity issues in the United States. We then describe rights issues, which are often used in other countries for issues of common stock.

Public Offers

When a corporation makes a general cash offer of debt or equity in the United States, it goes through much the same procedure as when it first went public. In other words, it registers the issue with the SEC[46] and then sells the securities to an underwriter (or a syndicate of underwriters), which in turn offers the securities to the public. Before the price of the issue is fixed, the underwriter will build up a book of likely demand for the securities, just as in the case of Marvin's IPO.

The SEC's Rule 415 allows large companies to file a single registration statement covering financing plans for up to three years into the future. The actual issues can then be done with scant additional paperwork, whenever the firm needs the cash or thinks it can issue securities at an attractive price. This is called *shelf registration*—the registration statement is "put on the shelf," to be taken down and used as needed.

Think of how you as a financial manager might use shelf registration. Suppose your company is likely to need up to $200 million of new long-term debt over the next year or so. It can file a registration statement for that amount. It then has prior approval to issue up to $200 million of debt, but it isn't obligated to issue a penny. Nor is it required to work through any particular underwriters; the registration statement may name one or more underwriters that the firm thinks it may work with, but others can be substituted later.

Now you can sit back and issue debt as needed, in bits and pieces if you like. Suppose Morgan Stanley comes across an insurance company with $10 million ready to invest in corporate bonds. Your phone rings. It's Morgan Stanley offering to buy $10 million of your bonds, priced to yield, say, 8.5%. Morgan Stanley then resells the bonds to the insurance company, it hopes at a higher price than it paid for them, thus earning an intermediary's profit.

Here is another possible deal: Suppose that you perceive a window of opportunity in which interest rates are temporarily low. You invite bids for $100 million of bonds. Some bids may come from large investment banks acting alone; others may come from ad hoc syndicates. But that's not your problem; if the price is right, you just take the best deal offered.

Not all companies eligible for shelf registration actually use it for all their public issues. Sometimes they believe they can get a better deal by making one large issue through traditional channels, especially when the security has some unusual feature or when the firm believes that it needs the investment banker's counsel or stamp of approval on the issue. Consequently, shelf registration is less often used for issues of common stock or convertible securities than for garden-variety corporate bonds.

The Costs of a Public Offer

Whenever a firm makes a public offer of securities, it incurs substantial administrative costs, and it needs to compensate the underwriters by selling them securities below the price that they expect to receive from investors.

In addition to these direct costs, the offer price for seasoned stock issues is on average set at about 2% below the previous night's close.[47] While this underpricing is far less than in the case of an IPO, it remains a significant proportion of the cost of an issue of stock.

---

[46] In 2005, the SEC created a new category of firm termed "a well-known seasoned issuer" (or WKSI). These firms are exempt from certain filing requirements.

[47] See O. Altinkilic and R. S. Hansen, "Discounting and Underpricing in Seasoned Equity Offers," *Journal of Financial Economics* 69 (2003), pp. 285–323.

Type	Company	Issue Amount ($ millions)	Underwriting Spread (%)
Common Stock			
IPO	Alibaba Group	$21,767	1.2%
IPO	Airbnb	3,490	2.1
IPO	Beam Therapeutics	180	7.0
IPO	Velocity Financial	94	7.0
IPO	OneWater Marine	55	7.0
IPO	Happiness Biotech	11	7.0
Seasoned	General Mills	1,000	3.0
Seasoned	National Retail Properties	396	4.0
Seasoned	UniQure	225	6.0
Seasoned	iRhythm Technologies	100	6.0
Debt			
2.85% First Mortgage Bonds 2029	Southern California Edison	$ 100	0.7%
2.95% Notes 2049	Walmart	985	0.9
4.50% Senior Notes 2049	Unum Group	450	0.9
2% Convertible Notes 2024	Tesla	1,600	1.1

❭**TABLE 14.3**   Gross underwriting spreads of selected issues. Spreads are percentages of gross proceeds.

Table 14.3 lists underwriting spreads for a few recent issues. Notice that the underwriting spreads for debt securities are lower than for common stocks—less than 1% for many issues. Larger issues tend to have lower spreads than smaller issues. This may partly stem from the fact that there are fixed costs to selling securities, but large issues are generally made by large companies, which are better known and easier for the underwriter to monitor. So do not assume that a small company could make a jumbo issue at a negligible percentage spread.[48]

Figure 14.5 summarizes a study of total issue costs (spreads plus administrative costs) for several thousand issues between 2014 and 2019.

Rights Issues

Instead of making an issue of stock to investors at large, companies sometimes give their existing shareholders the right of first refusal. Such issues are known as *privileged subscription,* or *rights, issues.* In the United States, rights issues are largely confined to closed-end investment companies. However, in most countries outside the United States, rights issues are the most common method for seasoned equity issues. For example, rights offerings predominate in China, Germany, France, and Brazil.[49]

We have already come across one example of a rights issue—the offer by the British bank HBOS, which ended up in the hands of its underwriters. Let us look more closely at another issue.

---

[48] This point is emphasized in O. Altinkilic and R. S. Hansen, "Are There Economies of Scale in Underwriting Fees? Evidence of Rising External Financing Costs," *Review of Financial Studies* 13 (Spring 2000), pp. 191–218.

[49] See M. Massa, T. Vermaelen, and M. Xu, "Rights Offerings, Trading, and Regulation: A Global Perspective," INSEAD Working Paper 2013/120/FIN, December 13, 2013, available at SSRN: https://ssrn.com/abstract=2340504.

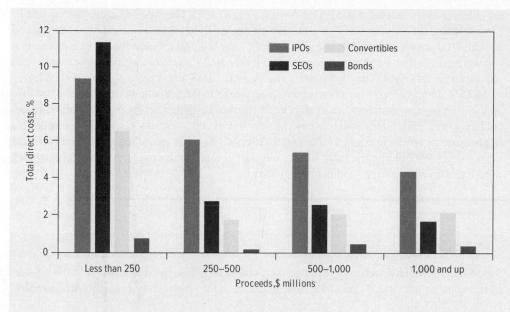

▶ FIGURE 14.5

Total direct costs as a percentage of gross proceeds. The total direct costs for initial public offerings (IPOs), seasoned equity offerings (SEOs), convertible bonds, and straight bonds are composed of underwriter spreads and other direct expenses.

Source: SDC Platinum. We thank Tong Yu for his help with this figure.

EXAMPLE 14.4 ● Rights issues

In 2019, the British retailer, Marks & Spencer (M&S) wished to raise £601 million of equity to finance its development of online retailing. It did so by offering its existing shareholders the right to buy one new share for every five shares that they currently held. The new shares were priced at £1.85, 28% below the pre-announcement market price of £2.57.

Imagine that just before the rights issue you held five shares of M&S valued at $5 \times £2.57 = £12.85$. The offer by M&S would give you rights to buy one new share for an additional outlay of £1.85. If you take up the offer, your holding increases to six shares, and the value increases by the amount of the extra cash to $£12.85 + 1.85 = £14.70$. Therefore, after the issue the value of each share is no longer £2.57 but a little lower at $£14.70/6 = £2.45$. This is termed the ex-rights price.

What is the value of the right to buy a new share for £1.85.? The answer is $£2.45 - £1.85 = £0.60$.[50] An investor who could buy a share worth £2.45 for £1.85 would be willing to pay £0.60 for the privilege.[51]

It should be clear on reflection that M&S could have raised the same amount of money on a variety of terms. For example, it could have offered shareholders the right to buy one new share at £0.37 for every share that they held. In this case, shareholders would buy five times as many shares at a fifth of the price. Our shareholder who initially held five shares would end up with

---

[50] In fact, he should be prepared to pay slightly more because he is not compelled to buy the stock and can choose not to do so. In practice, since the option is usually well in the money and its time to expiration is short, its value is usually negligible.

[51] There is a minor, but potentially confusing, difference between North American and European rights issues. In the M&S issue, shareholders needed one right to buy a new share, but they needed to own five shares to receive this right. A similar issue in North America would generally give shareholders one right for each share held. However, they would need more than one right to buy a new share, and each right would be worth correspondingly less. For example, if M&S had been a U.S. company, shareholders would have received one right for every share owned, but they would have needed five of these rights to buy one new share. Each right would have been only one fifth as valuable. You may encounter formulas for the value of a right. Remember to check whether the formula is referring to a U.S. or a European issue. Better still, work out the value of a right for yourself.

ten shares, worth, in total, $5 \times £2.57 + 5 \times £0.37 = £14.70$. The value of each share would be £14.70/10 = £1.47. Under this new arrangement, the ex-rights share price is lower, but you end up with 10 shares rather than 6. The total value of your holding remains the same. Suppose that you wanted to sell your right to buy one new share for £0.37. Investors would be prepared to pay you £1.10 for this right. They would then pay £0.37 to M&S and receive a share worth £1.47.

M&S's shareholders were given about three weeks to decide whether they wished to take up the offer of new shares. If the stock price in the meantime fell below the issue price, shareholders would have no incentive to buy the new shares. For this reason, companies making a rights issue generally arrange for the underwriters to buy any unwanted stock. Underwriters are not often left holding the baby, but we saw earlier that in the case of the HBOS issue, they were left with a very large (and bouncing) baby.

• • • • •

14.7 Self-Test

Suppose that a naive shareholder held five shares of M&S before the rights issue, but did not take up the rights or sell them. What, if any, would have been the change in this shareholder's wealth?

Our example illustrates that as long as the company successfully sells the new shares, the issue price in a rights offering is irrelevant. That is not the case in a public offer. If the company sells stock to new shareholders for less than the market will bear, the buyer makes a profit at the expense of existing shareholders. As we noted earlier, public offers are typically sold at a small discount of 2% on the previous day's closing price, so underpricing is not a major worry. But since this cost can be avoided completely by using a rights issue, we are puzzled by the apparent preference of U.S. companies for public offers.

Market Reaction to Stock Issues

Why does the stock price fall when a new issue is announced in the United States? One view is that the price of the stock is simply depressed by the prospect of the additional supply. On the other hand, there is little sign that the extent of the price fall increases with the size of the stock issue. There is an alternative explanation that seems to fit the facts better.

Suppose that the CFO of a restaurant chain is strongly optimistic about its prospects. From her point of view, the company's stock price is too low. Yet the company wants to issue shares to finance expansion into the new state of Northern California.[52] What is she to do? All the choices have drawbacks. If the chain sells common stock, it will favor new investors at the expense of old shareholders. When investors come to share the CFO's optimism, the share price will rise, and the bargain price to the new investors will be evident.

If the CFO could convince investors to accept her rosy view of the future, then new shares could be sold at a fair price. But this is not so easy. CEOs and CFOs always take care to sound upbeat, so just announcing "I'm optimistic" has little effect. But supplying detailed information about business plans and profit forecasts is costly and is also of great assistance to competitors.

The CFO could scale back or delay the expansion until the company's stock price recovers. That too is costly, but it may be rational if the stock price is severely undervalued and a stock issue is the only source of financing.

If a CFO knows that the company's stock is *over* valued, the position is reversed. If the firm sells new shares at the high price, it will help existing shareholders at the expense of the new ones. Managers might be prepared to issue stock even if the new cash is just put in the bank.

---

[52] Northern California seceded from California and became the fifty-second state in 2027.

Of course, investors are not stupid. They can predict that managers are more likely to issue stock when they think it is overvalued and that optimistic managers may cancel or defer issues. Therefore, when an equity issue is announced, they mark down the price of the stock accordingly. Thus the decline in the price of the stock at the time of the new issue may have nothing to do with the increased supply but simply with the information that the issue provides.[53]

Cornett and Tehranian devised a natural experiment that pretty much proves this point.[54] They examined a sample of stock issues by commercial banks. Some of these issues were necessary to meet capital standards set by banking regulators. The rest were ordinary, voluntary stock issues designed to raise money for various corporate purposes. The necessary issues caused a much smaller drop in stock prices than the voluntary ones, which makes perfect sense. If the issue is outside the manager's discretion, announcement of the issue conveys no information about the manager's view of the company's prospects.[55]

In the United States companies are not obliged to seek shareholder approval before making an issue of common stock. The same in Canada, Japan, and Israel. But in many other countries, shareholder approval is required and in these countries the announcement of an issue results in a *rise* in the stock price. It seems that, when shareholders are obliged to buy in to the issue decision, companies will ask for their approval only when they have a good and convincing story to tell.[56]

Most financial economists now interpret the change in the stock price on equity issue announcements as an information effect. But what about an issue of preferred stock or debt? Are they equally likely to provide information to investors about company prospects? A pessimistic manager might be tempted to get a debt issue out before investors become aware of the bad news, but how much profit can you make for your shareholders by selling overpriced debt? Perhaps 1% or 2%. Investors know that a pessimistic manager has a much greater incentive to issue equity rather than preferred stock or debt. Therefore, when companies announce an issue of preferred or debt, there is a barely perceptible fall in the stock price.[57]

14-4   Private Placements

Whenever a company makes a public offering, it is obliged to register the issue with the SEC. It could avoid this costly process by selling the securities privately. The rules on what constitutes a *private placement* are complicated. The securities can generally be sold to an unlimited number of financial institutions, but there are restrictions on the number of less wealthy private individuals who can participate.

One of the drawbacks of a private placement is that the investor cannot easily resell the security. However, institutions such as life insurance companies invest huge amounts in corporate debt for the long haul and are less concerned about its marketability. Consequently, an active private placement market has evolved for corporate debt. Often, this debt is negotiated directly between the company and the lender, but if the issue is too large to be absorbed by

---

[53] This explanation was developed in S. C. Myers and N. S. Majluf, "Corporate Financing and Investment Decisions When Firms Have Information That Investors Do Not Have," *Journal of Financial Economics* 13 (1984), pp. 187–221.

[54] M. M. Cornett and H. Tehranian, "An Examination of Voluntary versus Involuntary Security Issuances by Commercial Banks," *Journal of Financial Economics* 35 (1994), pp. 99–122.

[55] The "involuntary issuers" did make a choice: They could have forgone the stock issue and run the risk of failing to meet the regulatory capital standards. The banks that were more concerned with this risk were more likely to issue. Thus it is no surprise that Cornett and Tehranian found some drop in stock price even for the involuntary issues.

[56] C. G. Holderness, "Equity Issuances and Agency Costs: The Telling Story of Shareholder Approval around the World," *Journal of Financial Economics* 129 (2018), pp. 415–439.

[57] See L. Shyam-Sunder, "The Stock Price Effect of Risky vs. Safe Debt," *Journal of Financial and Quantitative Analysis* 26 (December 1991), pp. 549–558.

one institution, the company will generally employ an investment bank to draw up a prospectus and identify possible buyers.

As you would expect, it costs less to arrange a private placement than to make a public issue. This is a particular advantage for companies making smaller issues.

In 1990, the SEC adopted Rule 144A, which relaxed its restrictions on who can buy and trade unregistered securities. The rule allows large financial institutions (known as *qualified institutional buyers*) to trade unregistered securities among themselves. Rule 144A was intended to increase liquidity and reduce interest rates and issue costs for private placements. It was aimed largely at foreign corporations deterred by registration requirements in the United States. The SEC argued that such firms would welcome the opportunity to issue unregistered stocks and bonds that could then be freely traded by large U.S. financial institutions. Rule 144A has been successful in increasing the liquidity of stocks and bonds issued in this way.

KEY TAKEAWAYS

In this chapter, we have summarized the various procedures for financing a company's operations. We first looked at how infant companies raise angel financing and/or venture capital to carry them through to the point at which they can make their first public issue of stock. We then looked at how companies can make further public issues of securities by a general cash offer. Finally, we reviewed the procedures for a private placement.

- Financing for young growing companies may be provided by wealthy individuals, known as angel investors, or by venture capital partnerships. Venture capital deals are structured to provide high-powered incentives to the entrepreneurs and to deter the lazy and no hopers.

- Most venture capital funds are organized as limited private partnerships with a fixed life of about 10 years. Pension funds and other investors are the limited partners. Venture capitalists may cash in on their investment if the company is sold to a larger firm or if it has an initial public offering (IPO).

- Before undertaking an IPO, the company must register the issue with the SEC. It typically engages one or more investment banks to provide advice and to build a book of investor demand. The banks serve as underwriters to the issue by buying the stock from the company before reselling it to investors.

- IPOs are commonly underpriced, which is costly for the issuing company. A suggested rationale for underpricing is that the issue needs to attract investors, who find it difficult to value the issue and who worry that they are likely to receive a larger allocation of the overpriced issues. This problem is called the *winners' curse.*

- In the United States, most security issues by public companies use the bookbuilding method. In the case of common stock issues, an alternative is to make a *rights issue,* in which stock is offered first to existing shareholders in proportion to their holdings. Rights issues are rare in the United States but are widely used in some other countries.

- In the United States, announcement of a common stock issue prompts a fall in the stock price. We suggest that this is due to the information that investors read into the decision. However, the stock price is more likely to rise on the announcement in countries that require the firm to seek shareholder approval for the issue.

- Companies may avoid the process of registration by making a private placement of securities. There are limits on the trading of privately placed securities, but SEC Rule 144A allows the resale of privately placed securities to qualified institutional buyers.

● ● ● ● ●

FURTHER READING

Metrick and Yasuda, Megginson, Gompers, and Gompers and Lerner provide an overview of the venture capital industry, while Sahlman looks at the form of the venture capital contract:

A. Metrick and A. Yasuda, *Venture Capital and the Finance of Innovation,* 3rd ed. (New York: John Wiley & Sons, 2021).

W. L. Megginson, "Toward a Global Model of Venture Capital?" *Journal of Applied Corporate Finance* 16 (Winter 2004), pp. 89–107.

P. Gompers, "Venture Capital," in B. E. Eckbo, ed., *Handbook of Corporate Finance: Empirical Corporate Finance* (Amsterdam: Elsevier/North Holland, 2007).

P. Gompers and J. Lerner, "The Venture Capital Revolution," *Journal of Economic Perspectives* 15 (Spring 2001), pp. 145–168.

W. A. Sahlman, "Aspects of Financial Contracting in Venture Capital," *Journal of Applied Corporate Finance* (Summer 1988), pp. 23–36.

Here are some comprehensive surveys of the literature on new issues:

K. W. Hanley, "The Economics of Primary Markets," available at SSRN: https://ssrn.com/abstract=3046256.

M. Lowry, R. Michaely, and E. Volkova, "Initial Public Offering: A Synthesis of the Literature and Directions for Future Research," *Foundations and Trends in Finance* 11 (February 10, 2017), pp. 154–320.

B. E. Eckbo, R. W. Masulis, and Ø. Norli, "Security Offerings:" in B. E. Eckbo, ed., *Handbook of Corporate Finance: Empirical Corporate Finance* (Amsterdam: Elsevier/North-Holland, 2007).

J. R. Ritter, "Investment Banking and Securities Issuance," in G. M. Constantinides, M. Harris, and R. Stulz, eds., *Handbook of the Economics of Finance* (Amsterdam: Elsevier Science, 2003).

T. Jenkinson and A. P. Ljungqvist, *Going Public: The Theory and Evidence on How Companies Raise Equity Finance,* 2nd ed. (Oxford: Oxford University Press, 1999).

Two useful articles on IPOs are:

R. G. Ibbotson, J. L. Sindelar, and J. R. Ritter, "The Market's Problems with the Pricing of Initial Public Offerings," *Journal of Applied Corporate Finance* 7 (Spring 1994), pp. 66–74.

L. M. Benveniste and W. J. Wilhelm Jr., "Initial Public Offerings: Going by the Book," *Journal of Applied Corporate Finance* 10 (Spring 1997) pp. 98–108.

A useful introduction to the design of auctions is:

P. Milgrom, "Auctions and Bidding: A Primer," *Journal of Economic Perspectives* 3 (1989), pp. 3–22.

● ● ● ● ●

PROBLEM SETS

Mc Graw Hill connect®   Select problems are available in McGraw-Hill's *Connect.* Please see the preface for more information.

1. **Vocabulary (S14.1–S14.4)** Each of the following terms is associated with one of the events beneath. Can you match them up?

    a. Best efforts

    b. Bookbuilding

    c. Shelf registration

    d. Rule 144A

    Events:

    A. Investors indicate to the underwriter how many shares they would like to buy in a new issue and these indications are used to help set the price.

    B. The underwriter accepts responsibility only to try to sell the issue.

C. Some issues are not registered but can be traded freely among qualified institutional buyers.

D. Several tranches of the same security may be sold under the same registration. (A "tranche" is a batch, a fraction of a larger issue.)

2. **Vocabulary (S14.1–S14.4)** Explain what each of the following terms or phrases means:

    a. Venture capital

    b. Bookbuilding

    c. Underwriting spread

    d. Registration statement

    e. Winner's curse

3. **Vocabulary (S14.1–S14.4)** Here is a further vocabulary quiz. Briefly explain each of the following:

    a. Pre-money valuation

    b. Carried interest

    c. Rights issue

    d. Road show

    e. Best-efforts offer

    f. Qualified institutional buyer

    g. Blue-sky laws

    h. Greenshoe option

4. **Stock issues (S14.1–S14.4)** True or false?

    a. Venture capitalists typically provide first-stage financing sufficient to cover all development expenses. Second-stage financing is provided by stock issued in an IPO.

    b. Underpricing in an IPO is only a problem when the original investors are selling part of their holdings.

    c. Stock price generally falls when the company announces a new issue of shares. This is attributable to the information released by the decision to issue.

    d. The rights issue will give the shareholder the opportunity to buy one new share for less than the market price.

5. **Venture capital (S14.1)** Ethelbert.com is a young software company owned by two entrepreneurs. It currently needs to raise $400,000 to support its expansion plans. A venture capitalist is prepared to provide the cash in return for a 40% holding in the company. Under the plans for the investment, the VC will hold 10,000 shares in the company, and the two entrepreneurs will have combined holdings of 15,000 shares.

    a. What is the total after-the-money valuation of the firm?

    b. What value is the venture capitalist placing on each share?

6. **Venture capital (S14.1)** Look at Marvin's first attempt to raise financing. (Refer to Section 14.1 and the Marvin Prospectus in the appendix at the end of this chapter.) Suppose that First Meriam decides that Marvin's shares are worth only $0.80 each.

    a. How many shares will Marvin need to sell to raise the additional $1 million?

    b. What fraction of the firm will Marvin's managers own after the VC investment?

7. **Venture capital (S14.1)** True or false?

    a. Venture capital companies know that managers are more likely to work hard if they can be assured of a good steady salary.

b. Venture capital companies generally advance the money in stages.

c. Venture capital companies are generally passive investors and are happy to let the companies in which they are invested get on with the job.

d. Some young companies grow with the aid of equity investment provided by wealthy individuals known as angel investors.

8. **Venture capital (S14.1)** Complete the passage using the following terms: limited partners, venture capital, private, underwriters, general partners, private equity, corporate venturers, partnerships, private, angel investors. (*Note:* Not all terms will be used.)

Equity capital in young businesses is known as ____(a)____, and it is provided by specialist firms; wealthy individuals, known as ____(b)____; and large technology companies that act as ____(c)____. Venture capital funds are organized as ____(d)____. The management companies are the ____(e)____, and pension funds and other investors are the ____(f)____. Venture capital partnerships are often lumped together with similar partnerships that buy whole companies and take them ____(g)____. The general term for these firms is ____(h)____ companies.

9. **Venture capital (S14.1)**

a. "A signal is credible only if it is costly." Explain why management's willingness to invest in Marvin's equity was a credible signal. Was its willingness to accept only part of the venture capital that would eventually be needed also a credible signal?

b. "When managers take their reward in the form of increased leisure or executive jets, the cost is borne by the shareholders." Explain how First Meriam's financing package tackled this problem.

10. **IPOs (S14.2)** Refer to Section 14.1 and the Marvin Prospectus appendix at the end of this chapter to answer the following questions.

a. If there is unexpectedly heavy demand for the issue, how many extra shares can the underwriters buy?

b. How many shares are to be sold in the primary offering? How many will be sold in the secondary offering?

c. One day post-IPO, Marvin shares traded at $105. What was the degree of underpricing? How does that compare with the average degree of underpricing for IPOs in the United States?

d. There are three kinds of cost to Marvin's new issue—underwriting expense, administrative costs, and underpricing. What was the total dollar cost of the Marvin issue?

11. **IPOs (S14.2)** Find the prospectus for a recent IPO. How do the issue costs compare with

a. Those of the Marvin issue?

b. Those shown in Table 14.3?

Can you suggest reasons for the differences?

12. **Issue costs (S14.2–S14.4)** For each of the following pairs of issues, which is likely to involve the lower proportionate underwriting and administrative costs?

a. A large issue/a small issue.

b. A bond issue/a common stock issue.

c. Initial public offering/subsequent issue of stock.

d. A small private placement of bonds/a small general cash offer of bonds.

13. **Issue costs (S14.2)** In April 2019, Van Dyck Exponents offered 100 shares for sale in an IPO. Half of the shares were sold by the company and the other half by existing shareholders, each of whom sold exactly half of their existing holding. The offering price to the public was $50,

and the underwriters received a spread of 7%. The issue was heavily oversubscribed, and on the first day of trading, the stock price rose to $160.

a. What were the proceeds of the issue to the company? To the shareholders?

b. How much commission did the underwriters receive?

c. How much money was left on the table?

d. What was the cost of the underpricing to the selling shareholders?

14. **Underpricing (S14.2)** In some U.K. IPOs, any investor may be able to apply to buy shares. Mr. Bean has observed that, on average, these stocks are underpriced by about 9% and, for some years, has followed a policy of applying for a constant proportion of each issue. He is therefore disappointed and puzzled to find that this policy has not resulted in a profit. Explain to him why this is so.

15. **Underpricing (S14.2)** Having heard about IPO underpricing, I put in an order to my broker for 1,000 shares of every IPO he can get for me. After three months, my investment record is as follows:

IPO	Shares Allocated to Me	Price per Share	Initial Return
A	500	$10	7%
B	200	20	12
C	1,000	8	−2
D	0	12	23

a. What is the average underpricing in dollars of this sample of IPOs?

b. What is the average initial return on my "portfolio" of shares purchased from the four IPOs that I bid on? When calculating this average initial return, remember to weight by the amount of money invested in each issue.

c. "You have just encountered the problem of the winners' curse." True or false?

16. **Underpricing (S14.2)** Fishwick Enterprises has 200,000 shares outstanding, half of which are owned by Jennifer Fishwick and half by her cousin. The two cousins have decided to sell 100,000 shares in an IPO. Half of these shares would be issued by the company to raise new cash, and half would be shares that are currently held by Jennifer Fishwick. Suppose that the shares are sold at an issue price of $50 but rise to $80 by the end of the first day's trading. Suppose also that investors would have been prepared to buy the issue at $80.

a. What percentage of the company will Jennifer own after the issue?

b. What will her holding be worth at the end of the first day's trading?

c. Suppose the issue had been priced at $80. How many shares would the company have needed to sell to raise the same gross proceeds from the IPO?

d. What in this case would be Jennifer's wealth (cash plus the value of her remaining holding)? Assume Jennifer also needs to sell her shares to raise the same gross proceeds from the IPO.

e. What is the cost of underpricing to Jennifer in dollars?

17. **Underpricing (S14.2)** Construct a simple example to show the following:

a. Existing shareholders are made worse off when a company makes a cash offer of new stock below the market price.

b. Existing shareholders are not made worse off when a company makes a rights issue of new stock below the market price even if the new stockholders do not wish to take up their rights.

18. **Auctions (S14.2)** Spike Equino is the CEO of a private medical equipment company that is proposing to sell 100,000 shares of its stock in an open auction. Suppose the company receives the bids in the following table.

Shares	Price
20,000	$80
10,000	78
15,000	73
25,000	70
10,000	69
8,000	67
14,000	66
15,000	65
30,000	61

    a. What will be the company's total receipts from the sale if the auction is a discriminatory auction?

    b. What if it is a uniform price auction?

    c. In practice, would investors tend to be more cautious in their bidding in a discriminatory or uniform price auction?

19. **Types of seasoned issue (S14.3)** After each of the following issue methods, we have listed two types of issue. Choose the one more likely to employ that method.

    a. Rights issue (*initial public offer/further sale of an already publicly traded stock*).

    b. Rule 144A issue (*international bond issue/U.S. bond issue by a foreign corporation*).

    c. Private placement (*issue of existing stock/bond issue by an industrial company*).

    d. Shelf registration (*initial public offer/bond issue by a large industrial company*).

20. **Costs of a public offer (S14.3)** Why are the costs of debt issues less than those of equity issues? List the possible reasons.

21. **Market reaction to stock issues (S14.3)** There are three reasons that a common stock issue might cause a fall in price:

    a. The price fall is needed to absorb the extra supply.

    b. The issue causes temporary price pressure until it has been digested.

    c. Management has information that stockholders do not have.

    Explain these reasons more fully. Which do you find most plausible? Is there any way that you could seek to test whether you are right?

22. **Rights issues (S14.3)** Associated Breweries is planning to market alcohol-free beer. To finance the venture, it proposes to make a rights issue at $10 of one new share for each two shares held. (The company currently has outstanding 100,000 shares priced at $40 a share.) Assuming that the new money is invested to earn a fair return, give values for the following:

    a. Number of new shares

    b. Amount of new investment

    c. Total value of company after issue

    d. Total number of shares after issue

    e. Stock price after the issue

23. **Rights issues (S14.3)** In 2012, the Pandora Box Company made a rights issue at €5 a share of one new share for every four shares held. Before the issue there were 10 million shares outstanding and the share price was €6.

    a. What was the total amount of new money raised?

    b. The rights issue gave the shareholder the opportunity to buy one new share for less than the market price. What was the value of this opportunity?

c. What was the prospective stock price after the issue?

d. How far could the total value of the company fall before shareholders would be unwilling to take up their rights?

24. **Rights issues (S14.3)** Problem 23 contains details of a rights offering by Pandora Box. Suppose that the company had decided to issue new stock at €4. How many new shares would it have needed to sell to raise the same sum of money? Recalculate the answers to parts (b) to (d) in Problem 23. Show that the shareholders are just as well off if the company issues the shares at €4 rather than €5.

25. **Rights issues vs. cash offers (S14.3)** Suppose that instead of having a rights issue of new stock at €4 (see Problem 24), Pandora decided to make a general cash offer at €4. Would existing shareholders still be just as well off? Explain.

26. **Private placements (S14.4)** You need to choose between making a public offering and arranging a private placement. In each case, the issue involves $10 million face value of 10-year debt. You have the following data for each:

- *A public issue:* The interest rate on the debt would be 8.5%, and the debt would be issued at face value. The underwriting spread would be 1.5%, and other expenses would be $80,000.

- *A private placement:* The interest rate on the private placement would be 9%, but the total issuing expenses would be only $30,000.

a. What is the difference in the proceeds to the company net of expenses?

b. Other things being equal, which is the better deal?

c. What other factors beyond the interest rate and issue costs would you wish to consider before deciding between the two offers?

CHALLENGE PROBLEMS

27. **Venture capital (S14.1)**

a. Why do venture capital companies prefer to advance money in stages? If you were the management of Marvin Enterprises, would you have been happy with such an arrangement? With the benefit of hindsight did First Meriam gain or lose by advancing money in stages?

b. The price at which First Meriam would invest more money in Marvin was not fixed in advance. But Marvin could have given First Meriam an *option* to buy more shares at a preset price. Would this have been better?

c. At the second stage, Marvin could have tried to raise money from another venture capital company in preference to First Meriam. To protect themselves against this, venture capital firms sometimes demand first refusal on new capital issues. Would you recommend this arrangement?

28. **Auctions (S14.3)** Explain the difference between a uniform-price auction and a discriminatory auction. Why might you prefer to sell securities by one method rather than another?

29. **Dilution (S14.3)** Here is recent financial data on Pisa Construction Inc.

Stock price	$40	Market value of firm	$400,000
Number of shares	10,000	Earnings per share	$4
Book net worth	$500,000	Return on investment	8%

Pisa has not performed spectacularly to date. However, it wishes to issue new shares to obtain $80,000 to finance expansion into a promising market. Pisa's financial advisers think a stock issue is a poor choice because, among other reasons, "sale of stock at a price below book value per share can only depress the stock price and decrease shareholders' wealth." To prove the point they construct the following example:

"Suppose 2,000 new shares are issued at $40 and the proceeds are invested. (Neglect issue costs.) Suppose return on investment does not change. Then

$$\text{Book net worth} = \$580{,}000$$
$$\text{Total earnings} = 0.08(580{,}000) = \$46{,}400$$
$$\text{Earnings per share} = \frac{46{,}400}{12{,}000} = \$3.87$$

Thus, EPS declines, book value per share declines, and share price will decline proportionately to $38.70."

Evaluate this argument with particular attention to the assumptions implicit in the numerical example.

• • • • •

**SOLUTIONS
TO SELF-TEST
QUESTIONS**

14.1 Each stage gives the venture capitalist the opportunity to refuse further funding if progress is unsatisfactory, demand a change in management, or require policy changes. The entrepreneur's willingness to go ahead despite this is a signal of her confidence.

14.2 If the management company receives carried interest, it has a greater incentive to maximize the profitability of the venture. Some level of profit-related compensation is in the interests of the limited partners.

14.3 Public ownership allows the founders and venture capitalists to cash out, facilitates further funding, provides a market price for the stock that can be used for incentive compensation schemes, and allows the stock to be used for acquisitions. Disadvantages include the red tape of running a public company and short-term pressure from shareholders to report increasing profits. The firm may also be exposed to a hostile takeover.

14.4 You invest $500 in the underpriced issue and gain $0.15 \times 500 = \$75$. You invest $1,000 in the overpriced issue and lose $0.10 \times 1{,}000 = \$100$. Your net loss is –$25.

14.5 Administrative costs as percent of issue amount were $100 \times \$820/72{,}000 = 1.1\%$. Percentage underwriting costs were $100 \times 5{,}040/72{,}000 = 7.0\%$. The money left on the table was $900{,}000 \times (\$105 - \$80) = \$22.5$ million.

14.6 a. Under a discriminatory auction, Omicron would pay $70 for 400 shares, Nu would pay $60 for 300, and Kappa would pay $50 for 300.
  b. Under a uniform price auction, Omicron, Nu, and Kappa would each pay $50.

14.7 Before the issue the share price was £2.57. The issue reduced the value of each share to £2.45. By not exercising her rights or not selling them, the shareholder would have lost $5 \times £0.12 = £0.60$. This was the value of the rights to buy one share.

• • • • •

**FINANCE ON
THE WEB**

The website of the Angel Capital Association at www.angelcapitalassociation.org provides useful material on trends in angel investing.

Look up a recent IPO on **biz.yahoo.com/ipo** and then use the Edgar database to find the prospectus. (You may find it easiest to look up the company on **finance.yahoo.com** and use the link to SEC filings. In any case, finding the final prospectus can be a matter of trial and error.) Compare the IPO with that of Marvin. For example, who were the existing shareholders? Was the company raising more capital, or were existing shareholders selling? Were existing shareholders prevented by a lock-up agreement from selling more shares? How did the underwriting and other costs compare with those of Marvin? Did the underwriters have a greenshoe option? Did the issue turn out to be underpriced? (The Yahoo! website should help here.) If so, how much money was left on the table?

APPENDIX • • •

Marvin's New-Issue Prospectus[58]

PROSPECTUS
900,000 Shares
Marvin Enterprises Inc.
Common Stock ($.10 par value)

Of the 900,000 shares of Common Stock offered hereby, 500,000 shares are being sold by the Company and 400,000 shares are being sold by the Selling Stockholders. See "Principal and Selling Stockholders." The Company will not receive any of the proceeds from the sale of shares by the Selling Stockholders.

Before this offering there has been no public market for the Common Stock. **These securities involve a high degree of risk. See "Certain Considerations."**

THESE SECURITIES HAVE NOT BEEN APPROVED OR DISAPPROVED BY THE SECURITIES AND EXCHANGE COMMISSION NOR HAS THE COMMISSION PASSED ON THE ACCURACY OR ADEQUACY OF THIS PROSPECTUS. ANY REPRESENTATION TO THE CONTRARY IS A CRIMINAL OFFENSE.

	Price to Public	Underwriting Discount	Proceeds to Company[1]	Proceeds to Selling Stockholders[1]
Per share	$80.00	$5.60	$74.40	$74.40
Total[2]	$72,000,000	$5,040,000	$37,200,000	$29,760,000

[1] Before deducting expenses payable by the Company estimated at $820,000, of which $455,555 will be paid by the Company and $364,445 will be paid by the Selling Stockholders.
[2] The Company and the Selling Stockholders have granted to the Underwriters an option to purchase up to an additional 135,000 shares at the initial public offering price, less the underwriting discount, solely to cover overallotment.

The Common Stock is offered subject to receipt and acceptance by the Underwriters, to prior sale, and to the Underwriters' right to reject any order in whole or in part and to withdraw, cancel, or modify the offer without notice.

Klein Merrick Inc.   February 3, 2040

No person has been authorized to give any information or to make any representations, other than as contained therein, in connection with the offer contained in this Prospectus, and, if given or made, such information or representations must not be relied upon. This Prospectus does not constitute an offer of any securities other than the registered securities to which it relates or an offer to any person in any jurisdiction where such an offer would be unlawful. The delivery of this Prospectus at any time does not imply that information herein is correct as of any time subsequent to its date.

IN CONNECTION WITH THIS OFFERING, THE UNDERWRITERS MAY OVERALLOT OR EFFECT TRANSACTIONS WHICH STABILIZE OR MAINTAIN THE MARKET PRICE OF THE COMMON STOCK OF THE COMPANY AT A LEVEL ABOVE THAT WHICH MIGHT OTHERWISE PREVAIL IN THE OPEN MARKET. SUCH STABILIZING, IF COMMENCED, MAY BE DISCONTINUED AT ANY TIME.

---

[58] Most prospectuses have content similar to that of the Marvin prospectus but go into considerably more detail. Also we have omitted Marvin's financial statements.

Prospectus Summary

The following summary information is qualified in its entirety by the detailed information and financial statements appearing elsewhere in this Prospectus.

The Offering

Common Stock offered by the Company ....500,000 shares
Common Stock offered by the Selling Stockholders ....400,000 shares
Common Stock to be outstanding after this offering ....4,100,000 shares

Use of Proceeds

For the construction of new manufacturing facilities and to provide working capital.

The Company

Marvin Enterprises Inc. designs, manufactures, and markets gargle blasters for domestic use. Its manufacturing facilities employ integrated nanocircuits to control the genetic engineering processes used to manufacture gargle blasters.

The Company was organized in Delaware in 2034.

Proceeds

The net proceeds of this offering are expected to be $36,744,445. Of the net proceeds, approximately $27.0 million will be used to finance expansion of the Company's principal manufacturing facilities. The balance will be used for working capital.

Certain Considerations

Investment in the Common Stock involves a high degree of risk. The following factors should be carefully considered in evaluating the Company:

Substantial Capital Needs The Company will require additional financing to continue its expansion policy. The Company believes that its relations with its lenders are good, but there can be no assurance that additional financing will be available in the future.

Licensing The expanded manufacturing facilities are to be used for the production of a new imploding gargle blaster. An advisory panel to the U.S. Food and Drug Administration (FDA) has recommended approval of this product for the U.S. market but no decision has yet been reached by the full FDA committee.

Dividend Policy

The company has not paid cash dividends on its Common Stock and does not anticipate that dividends will be paid on the Common Stock in the foreseeable future.

Management

The following table sets forth information regarding the Company's directors, executive officers, and key employees.

Name	Age	Position
George Marvin	32	President, Chief Executive Officer, & Director
Mildred Marvin	28	Treasurer & Director
Chip Norton	30	General Manager
Michael Brown	53	Partner First Meriam Venture Partners
David Miller	47	Partner First Meriam Venture Partners
Evan Makinov	43	Senior partner MicroGenetics

George Marvin—George Marvin established the Company in 2034 and has been its Chief Executive Officer since that date. He is a past president of the Institute of Gargle Blasters and has recently been inducted into the Confrérie des Gargarisateurs.

Mildred Marvin—Mildred Marvin has been employed by the Company since 2034.

Chip Norton—Mr. Norton has been General Manager of the Company since 2034. He is a former vice-president of Amalgamated Blasters, Inc.

Executive Compensation

The following table sets forth the cash compensation paid for services rendered for the year 2039 by the executive officers:

Name	Capacity	Cash Compensation
George Marvin	President and Chief Executive Officer	$300,000
Mildred Marvin	Treasurer	220,000
Chip Norton	General Manager	220,000

Certain Transactions

At various times between 2035 and 2038, First Meriam Venture Partners invested a total of $8.5 million in the Company. In connection with this investment, First Meriam Venture Partners was granted certain rights to registration under the Securities Act of 1933, including the right to have their shares of Common Stock registered at the Company's expense with the Securities and Exchange Commission.

Principal and Selling Stockholders

The following table sets forth certain information regarding the beneficial ownership of the Company's voting Common Stock as of the date of this prospectus by (i) each person known by the Company to be the beneficial owner of more than 5 percent of its voting Common Stock, and (ii) each director of the Company who beneficially owns voting Common Stock. Unless otherwise indicated, each owner has sole voting and dispositive power over his or her shares.

	Common Stock					
	Shares Beneficially Owned prior to Offering			Shares Beneficially Owned after Offer[1]		
Name of Beneficial Owner	Number	Percent	Shares to Be Sold	Number	Percent
George Marvin	375,000	10.4	60,000	315,000	7.7
Mildred Marvin	375,000	10.4	60,000	315,000	7.7
Chip Norton	250,000	6.9	80,000	170,000	4.1
First Meriam Venture Partners	1,700,000	47.2	—	1,700,000	41.5
TFS Investors	260,000	7.2	—	260,000	6.3
Centri-Venture Partnership	260,000	7.2	—	260,000	6.3
Henry Pobble	180,000	5.0	—	180,000	4.4
Georgina Sloberg	200,000	5.6	200,000	—	—

[1] Assuming no exercise of the Underwriters' overallotment option.

Lock-up Agreements

The holders of the Common Stock have agreed with the underwriters not to sell, pledge, or otherwise dispose of their shares, other than as specified in this prospectus, for a period of 180 days after the date of the prospectus without the prior consent of Klein Merrick.

Description of Capital Stock

The Company's authorized capital stock consists of 10,000,000 shares of voting Common Stock.

As of the date of this Prospectus, there are 10 holders of record of the Common Stock.

Under the terms of one of the Company's loan agreements, the Company may not pay cash dividends on Common Stock except from net profits without the written consent of the lender.

Underwriting

Subject to the terms and conditions set forth in the Underwriting Agreement, the Company has agreed to sell to each of the Underwriters named below, and each of the Underwriters, for whom Klein Merrick Inc. are acting as Representatives, has severally agreed to purchase from the Company, the number of shares set forth opposite its name below.

Underwriters	Number of Shares to Be Purchased
Klein Merrick Inc.	300,000
Goldman Stanley	300,000
Medici Bank	100,000
Canary Wharf Securities	100,000
Bank of New England	100,000

In the Underwriting Agreement, the several Underwriters have agreed, subject to the terms and conditions set forth therein, to purchase all shares offered hereby if any such shares are purchased. In the event of a default by any Underwriter, the Underwriting Agreement provides that, in certain circumstances, purchase commitments of the nondefaulting Underwriters may be increased or the Underwriting Agreement may be terminated.

There is no public market for the Common Stock. The price to the public for the Common Stock was determined by negotiation between the Company and the Underwriters and was based on, among other things, the Company's financial and operating history and condition, its prospects and the prospects for its industry in general, the management of the Company, and the market prices of securities for companies in businesses similar to that of the Company.

Legal Matters

The validity of the shares of Common Stock offered by the Prospectus is being passed on for the Company by Dodson and Fogg and for the Underwriters by Kenge and Carboy.

Experts

The consolidated financial statements of the Company have been so included in reliance on the reports of Hooper Firebrand, independent accountants, given on the authority of that firm as experts in auditing and accounting.

Financial Statements
[Text and tables omitted.]

CHAPTER

Payout Policy

Payout policy resolves two questions. First, how much cash should the corporation pay out to its shareholders? Second, should the cash be distributed by paying cash dividends or by repurchasing shares? We will cover these questions in reverse order, "how" before "how much."

Companies are not required to pay out cash to their shareholders. Suppose you collect a sample of young, profitable, rapidly growing firms. Most of them will neither pay dividends nor repurchase stock. They will reinvest all their earnings to expand their operations, pay down debt or build up a cushion of cash for a rainy day. But as these firms mature—assuming they stay profitable—they will eventually generate surplus cash. Some will start repurchase programs. Some will initiate cash dividends. Some will use both payout channels.

Section 15-1 Facts about payout

We start by summarizing the basic facts about payout. We set out the steps required to pay dividends and repurchase shares, and we review the rapid growth of repurchases in the twenty-first century. We also explain how dividends are smoothed and stabilized.

Investors expect a firm that has made regular dividend payments to continue doing so and to increase those payments steadily as earnings increase. Dividends are rarely cut back unless the firm suffers significant, continuing losses, and managers don't increase dividends unless they are confident that the dividend can be maintained. Therefore, the announcement of a dividend increase is good news for shareholders, who infer that managers are confident about the future. Repurchases, on the other hand, are more flexible and do not convey as much information to investors.

Section 15-2 Dividends or repurchases? Does the choice affect shareholder value?

Which is most valuable for shareholders, dividends or repurchases? We show that the two payout channels are equally good, at least in an ideal, frictionless financial market.

Section 15-3 Dividend clienteles

We ask why the choice of payout channel may matter in practice. A possible reason is that some clienteles of investors such as retirees depend on quarterly dividend checks and therefore prefer dividends to repurchases. However, it is not clear that such clienteles have to pay extra for dividend-paying stocks or that a company can increase its value by providing these dividends.

Section 15-4 Taxes and payout policy

Repurchases are tax-advantaged. Cash dividends are received by all shareholders, but each shareholder can *choose* whether to sell shares to a repurchase program. Shareholders can postpone sale and thereby defer taxes. When they do sell, they pay tax at capital-gains rates, which have been lower historically than tax rates on dividends.

Section 15-5 Payout policy and the life cycle of the firm

We conclude by considering how much cash should be paid out? Before deciding to pay dividends or repurchase shares, the manager needs to ask a series of questions. First, is the business generating positive free cash flow after making all investments with positive NPVs? Is that positive free cash flow likely to continue? Second, is the firm's debt ratio prudent? If the ratio is too high, paying down debt usually takes priority. Third, are the company's holdings of cash a sufficient cushion for unexpected setbacks and a sufficient war chest for unexpected opportunities? If the answer to all three questions is yes, then the cash is truly surplus. If a corporation has surplus cash, it's best to pay the cash back to shareholders. Paying out surplus cash reassures shareholders that the cash will not be wasted on questionable investments or consumed by perks or excessive compensation.

• • • • •

15-1   Facts about Payout

Corporations pay out cash by distributing dividends or by buying back some of their outstanding shares. Repurchases were rare in the early 1980s, but Figure 15.1 shows that more recently the total value of repurchases in the United States has been similar to the total value of dividends.

Dividends are more stable than repurchases. For example, repurchases were cut back sharply in the banking crisis of 2007–2009 and then again with the arrival of the COVID-19 pandemic. Dividends also fell in 2007–2009 and 2020, but by less than repurchases.

Cash-rich corporations sometimes undertake massive repurchase programs, but they may increase dividends at the same time. Here are four examples from 2019, a busy year for repurchases:

- Apple: $67 billion of repurchases and a 5% increase in dividends.
- Cisco Systems: $22 billion of repurchases and a 6% increase in dividends.
- Citigroup: $20 billion of repurchases and a 41% dividend increase.
- Microsoft: $20 billion of repurchases and a 10% dividend increase.

Here is a table of payout practices, by nonfinancial firms, from 2011 to 2020:

BEYOND THE PAGE

The growth in repurchases

mhhe.com/brealey14e

		Pay Dividend?	
		Yes	No
Repurchase?	Yes	24.1%	23.7%
	No	12.0%	40.1%

Source: Compustat.

BEYOND THE PAGE

How companies pay out

mhhe.com/brealey14e

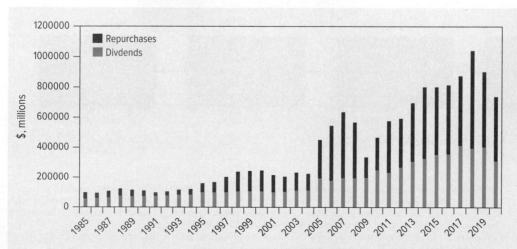

▶ **FIGURE 15.1**

Dividends and stock repurchases by nonfinancial companies in the United States, 1985–2020 (figures in $ millions).

Source: Standard & Poor's Compustat.

On average in any year, 24.1% of the firms paid a dividend and also repurchased shares. The fraction that paid dividends but did not repurchase was 12.0%. The corresponding fraction for repurchases but no dividends was 23.7%. But 40.1% of firms did not pay dividends or repurchase shares. These figures are for nonfinancial companies. The fraction of banks that pay dividends has been much higher than for industrial companies, but the fraction of banks that repurchase has been about the same.[1]

Who are the nondividend payers? Some are companies that used to pay dividends, but then fell on hard times and had to cut back. However, most nondividend payers are growth companies that have never paid a dividend and will not pay one in the foreseeable future. The zero-dividend companies include such household names as Berkshire Hathaway, Alphabet (Google), and Amazon.

How Firms Pay Dividends

On December 11, 2020, Pfizer's board of directors announced a quarterly cash dividend of $0.39 per share. Who received this dividend? That may seem an obvious question, but shares trade constantly, and the firm's records of who owns its shares are never fully up to date. So corporations specify a particular day's roster of shareholders who qualify to receive each dividend. For example, Pfizer announced that it would send a dividend check on March 5, 2021 (the payment date), to all shareholders recorded in its books on January 29 (the record date).

One day before the record date, Pfizer stock began to trade **ex-dividend**. Investors who bought shares on or after that date did not have their purchases registered by the record date and were not entitled to the dividend. Other things equal, a stock is worth less if you miss out on the dividend. So when a stock "goes ex-dividend," its price falls by about the amount of the dividend. Figure 15.2 illustrates the sequence of the key dividend dates. This sequence is the same whenever companies pay a dividend (though of course the actual dates will differ).

Corporations are not free to declare whatever dividend they choose. In some countries, such as Brazil and Chile, companies are obliged by law to pay out a *minimum* proportion of their earnings. Conversely, some restrictions may be imposed by lenders, who are concerned that excessive dividend payments would not leave enough in the kitty to repay their loans. U.S. state law also helps to protect the firm's creditors against excessive dividend payments. For example, companies are not allowed to pay a dividend out of legal capital, which is generally defined as the par value of outstanding shares.[2]

Most U.S. companies pay a *regular* cash dividend each quarter, but occasionally this is supplemented by a one-off *extra* or *special dividend*. Many companies offer shareholders automatic

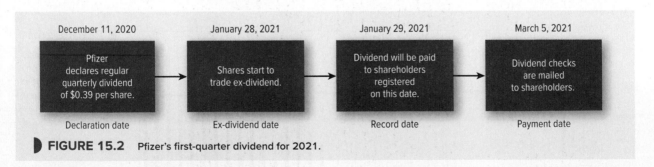

▶ **FIGURE 15.2**   Pfizer's first-quarter dividend for 2021.

[1] E. Floyd, N. Li, and D. J. Skinner, "Payout Policy through the Financial Crisis: The Growth of Repurchases and the Resilience of Dividends," *Journal of Financial Economics* 118 (November 2015), pp. 299–316, Table 1. In Europe, the decline in dividend payers has been especially steep in Germany. See D. J. Denis and I. Osobov, "Why Do Firms Pay Dividends? International Evidence on the Determinants of Dividend Policy," *Journal of Financial Economics* 89 (July 2008), pp. 62–82.

[2] Where there is no par value, legal capital is defined as part or all of the receipts from the issue of shares. Companies with wasting assets, such as mining companies, are sometimes permitted to pay out legal capital.

dividend reinvestment plans (DRIPs). Often, the new shares are issued at a 5% discount from the market price. Sometimes 10% or more of total dividends will be reinvested under such plans.[3]

Dividends are not always in the form of cash. Companies may also declare *stock dividends*. For example, if the firm pays a stock dividend of 5%, it sends each shareholder 5 extra shares for every 100 shares currently owned. A stock dividend is essentially the same as a stock split. Both increase the number of shares but do not affect the company's assets, profits, or total value. So both reduce value *per share*.[4] Stock dividends are now rare in the United States,[5] and in this chapter we focus on *cash* dividends.

15.1 Self-Test

Marina Padrowsky buys 100 shares of United Stores on Tuesday, June 2. The company has declared a dividend of $1 a share payable on June 30 to shareholders of record on Wednesday, June 3. If the ex-dividend date is June 1, is Marina entitled to the dividend? When will the checks go out in the mail?

How Firms Repurchase Stock

Instead of paying a dividend to its stockholders, the firm can use the cash to repurchase stock. The reacquired shares are kept in the company's treasury and may be resold if the company needs money. There are four main ways to repurchase stock. By far the most common method is for the firm to announce that it plans to buy its stock in the open market, just like any other investor.[6] However, companies sometimes use a tender offer where they offer to buy back a stated number of shares at a fixed price, which is typically set at about 20% above the current market level. Shareholders can then choose whether to accept this offer. A third procedure is to employ a *Dutch auction*. In this case, the firm states a series of prices at which it is prepared to repurchase stock. Shareholders submit offers declaring how many shares they wish to sell at each price and the company calculates the lowest price at which it can buy the desired number of shares. Finally, repurchase sometimes takes place by direct negotiation with a major shareholder.

In the past, many countries banned or severely restricted the use of stock repurchases. As a result, firms that had amassed large amounts of cash were tempted to invest it at low rates of return rather than hand it back to shareholders, who could have reinvested it in firms that were short of cash. While most of these limitations have now been removed, you can see from Figure 15.3 that repurchases remain relatively less common outside the United States.

The Information Content of Dividends

A survey in 2004 asked senior executives about their companies' dividend policies. Figure 15.4 paraphrases their responses. Three themes stand out:

1. Managers are reluctant to make dividend changes that may have to be reversed. They are particularly worried about having to rescind a dividend increase and, if necessary, would issue shares or borrow to maintain the dividend.

---

[3] Sometimes companies not only allow shareholders to reinvest dividends, but also allow them to buy additional shares at a discount. For an amusing and true rags-to-riches story, see M. S. Scholes and M. A. Wolfson, "Decentralized Investment Banking: The Case of Discount Dividend-Reinvestment and Stock-Purchase Plans," *Journal of Financial Economics* 23 (September 1989), pp. 7–35.

[4] The distinction between a stock dividend and a stock split is technical. A stock dividend is shown in the accounts as a transfer from retained earnings to equity capital. A split is shown as a reduction in the par value of each share.

[5] In recent years, less than 0.2% of U.S. firms have offered stock dividends. See A. Kalay and F. Zhang, "Vanishing Stock Dividends," 2016, available at SSRN: http://ssrn.com/abstract=2722115.

[6] The U.S. Securities and Exchange Commission's Rule 10b-18 protects repurchasing firms from accusations of share-price manipulation. Open-market repurchases are subject to several restrictions, however. For example, repurchases cannot exceed a small fraction of daily trading volume.

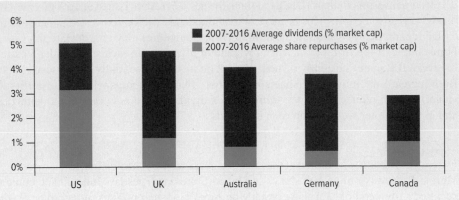

> **FIGURE 15.3**

Repurchases as a percentage of market capitalization.

Source: "Share Repurchases, Executive Pay and Investment," UK Department for Business, Energy and Industrial Strategy, Research Paper Number 2019/011.

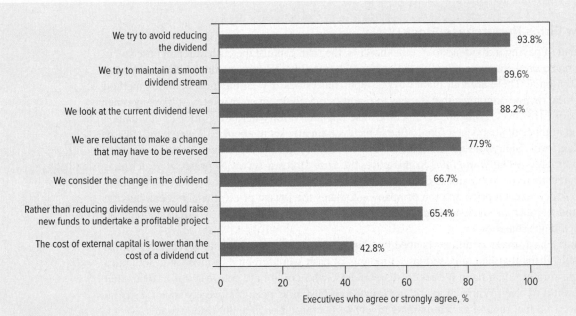

> **FIGURE 15.4**   A survey of financial executives on dividend policy.

Source: A. Brav, J. R. Graham, C. R. Harvey, and R. Michaely, "Payout Policy in the 21st Century," *Journal of Financial Economics* 77 (September 2005), pp. 483–527.

2. Managers "smooth" dividends. Dividend changes follow shifts in long-run, sustainable earnings. Transitory earnings changes are unlikely to affect dividends.

3. Managers focus more on dividend *changes* than on absolute dividend levels. Thus paying a dividend of $2.00 per share is an important financial decision if last year's dividend was $1.50, but no big deal if last year's dividend was also $2.00.

From these responses, you can see why announcement of a dividend increase is good news to investors. Investors know that managers are reluctant to reduce dividends and will not increase them unless they are confident that the payment can be maintained. Therefore, announcement of a higher dividend signals managers' confidence in future profits. That is why investors and financial managers refer to the *information content of dividends.*

The information content of dividends implies that dividend increases predict future profitability. Evidence on this point is somewhat elusive. But Healy and Palepu, who focus on companies that paid a dividend for the first time, find that, on average, earnings jumped 43% in the year that the first dividend was paid. If managers thought that this was a temporary windfall, they might have been cautious about committing themselves to paying out cash. But it looks as if these managers had good reason to be confident about prospects, for earnings continued to rise in the following years.[7] On the other hand, it appears that dividend increases by companies already paying regular dividends do not predict increases in future earnings. Instead the increases predict *safer* earnings. Managers are more likely to increase dividends when they expect future earnings and cash flow to be less volatile and uncertain than usual. They are less likely to increase dividends, and more likely to cut dividends, when they see unusual risks ahead.[8]

Investors certainly appear to take comfort from an increase in dividends. It is no surprise, therefore, to find that a higher dividend prompts a rise in the stock price, whereas a dividend cut results in a fall in price. For example, in the case of the dividend initiations studied by Healy and Palepu, the dividend announcement resulted in a 4% stock-price increase on average.[9]

Notice that investors do not get excited about the *level* of a company's dividend; they worry about the *change,* which they view as an important indicator of the sustainability of earnings. Do not assume, however, that all dividend cuts are bad news. For example, when in April 2020 Harley-Davidson announced a 95% cut in its dividend payment and the postponement of its repurchase program, the stock rose 15%. Investors were relieved that the company was taking prompt action to protect itself against the pandemic.

The Information Content of Share Repurchases

Announcement of a share repurchase is not a commitment to continue repurchases in later years. So the information content of a repurchase announcement is less strongly positive than the announcement of a dividend increase. Nevertheless, a study by Comment and Jarrell, who looked at the announcements of open-market repurchase programs, found that, on average, they resulted in an abnormal price rise of 2%.[10]

Stock repurchases may also be used to signal a manager's confidence in the future. Suppose that you, the manager, believe that your stock is substantially undervalued. You announce that the company is prepared to buy back a fifth of its stock at a price that is 20% above the current market price. But (you say) you are certainly not going to sell any of your own stock at that price. Investors jump to the obvious conclusion—you must believe that the stock is a good value even at 20% above the current price.

When companies offer to repurchase their stock at a premium, senior management and directors usually commit to hold on to their stock.[11] So it is not surprising that researchers have found that announcements of offers to buy back shares above the market price have prompted a larger rise in the stock price, averaging about 11%.[12]

BEYOND THE PAGE

Repurchase motives

mhhe.com/brealey14e

---

[7] P. Healy and K. Palepu, "Earnings Information Conveyed by Dividend Initiations and Omissions," *Journal of Financial Economics* 21 (1988), pp. 149–175. For an example of a study that finds no information in dividend changes, see G. Grullon, R. Michaely, and B. Swaminathan, "Are Dividend Changes a Sign of Firm Maturity?" *Journal of Business* 75 (July 2002), pp. 387–424.

[8] R. Michaely, S. Rossi, and M. Weber, "The Information Content of Dividends: Safer Profits, Not Higher Profits," Chicago Booth Research Paper 17-30, January 2018.

[9] The 4% average return was adjusted for market returns. Healy and Palepu also looked at companies that *stopped* paying a dividend. In this case, the stock price on average declined by 9.5% on the announcement, and earnings fell over the next four quarters.

[10] R. Comment and G. Jarrell, "The Relative Signalling Power of Dutch-Auction and Fixed Price Self-Tender Offers and Open-Market Share Repurchases," *Journal of Finance* 46 (September 1991), pp. 1243–1271. There is also evidence of continuing superior performance during the years following a repurchase announcement. See D. Ikenberry, J. Lakonishok, and T. Vermaelen, "Market Underreaction to Open Market Share Repurchases," *Journal of Financial Economics* 39 (October 1995), pp. 181–208.

[11] Not only do managers hold on to their stock; on average, they also add to their holdings *before* the announcement of a repurchase. See D.S. Lee, W. Mikkelson, and M. Partch, "Managers' Trading around Repurchases," *Journal of Finance* 47 (December 1992), pp. 1947–1961.

[12] See Comment and Jarrell, op. cit.

15-2   Dividends or Repurchases? Does the Choice Affect Shareholder Value?

Announcements of dividends and repurchases can convey information about management's confidence and so affect the stock price. But eventually, the stock price change would happen anyway as information seeps out through other channels. Does the choice between dividends and repurchases affect market value in any fundamental way?

One of the charming features of economics is its ability to accommodate not just two, but three opposing points of view. And so it is with the choice between dividends and repurchases. Some argue that investors pay more for firms with generous, stable dividends. Another group argues that repurchases are better because dividends are taxed at higher effective rates than capital gains. And in the middle are those who believe that the choice between dividends and repurchases has no effect on value.

The middle-of-the-road party was founded in 1961 by Miller and Modigliani (always referred to as "MM"), when they published a proof that payout policy is value-irrelevant in a world without taxes, transaction costs, and other market imperfections.[13]

MM insisted that one must consider dividend policy only after holding the firm's assets, investments, and borrowing policy fixed. Suppose they were not fixed. For example, suppose that the firm decides to reduce capital investment and to pay out the cash saved as a dividend. In this case, the effect of the dividend on shareholder value is tangled up with the profitability of the foregone investment. Or suppose that the firm decides to borrow more aggressively and to pay out the debt proceeds as dividends. In this case, the effect of the dividend can't be separated from the effect of the additional borrowing.

Think what happens if you want to up the dividend *without* changing the investment policy or capital structure. The extra cash for the dividend must come from somewhere. If the firm fixes its borrowing, the only way it can finance the extra dividend is to sell more shares. Alternatively, rather than *increasing* dividends and selling new shares, the firm can pay *lower* dividends. With investment policy and borrowing fixed, the cash that is saved can only be used to buy back some of the firm's existing shares. Thus any change in dividend payout must be offset by the sale or repurchase of shares.

Repurchases were rare when MM wrote in 1961, but we can easily apply their reasoning to the choice between dividends and repurchases. A simple example is enough to show MM's result that the choice is irrelevant in this case. Then we will show that value is also unaffected if the company increases the dividend and finances the increase with an issue of shares.

Dividends or Repurchases? An Example

Rational Demiconductor has, at this moment, 1 million shares outstanding and the following market-value balance sheet:

Rational Demiconductor Balance Sheet ($ millions)

Surplus cash	$ 1.0	$ 0	Debt
Fixed assets and net working capital	10.0	11.0	Equity market capitalization (1 million shares at $11 per share)
	$11.0	$11.0	

The share price is $11 and therefore the total market capitalization is $11 million. If it now pays out the $1 million of surplus cash, the market capitalization must fall to $10 million.

---

[13] M. H. Miller and F. Modigliani, "Dividend Policy, Growth and the Valuation of Shares," *Journal of Business* 34 (October 1961), pp. 411–433. MM's results were anticipated by J. B. Williams, *The Theory of Investment Value* (Cambridge, MA: Harvard University Press, 1938). Also a proof similar to MM's was developed in J. Lintner, "Dividends, Earnings, Leverage, Stock Prices and the Supply of Capital to Corporations," *Review of Economics and Statistics* 44 (August 1962), pp. 243–269. MM recognized that dividends could convey information, but their proofs focused on value, not information about value. The examples in this section put aside the information content of dividends.

Rational Demiconductor Balance Sheet ($ millions)

Surplus cash	$ 0	$ 0	Debt
Fixed assets and net working capital	10.0	10.0	Equity market capitalization
	$10.0	$10.0	

That is true regardless of whether the cash is paid out as a dividend or used to repurchase shares. However, the effect on the price *per share does* depend on how the cash is paid out. If Rational pays a dividend of $1 per share, 1 million shares will still be outstanding, and the share price will fall to $10. Shareholders' wealth, including the cash dividends, is $10 + 1 = $11 per share.

Suppose Rational pays no cash dividend, but repurchases shares instead. It spends $1 million to repurchase 90,909 shares at $11 each, leaving 909,091 shares outstanding. The share price remains at $11 ($1,000,000 divided by 909,091 shares). Therefore, shareholders' wealth is $11 per share. It doesn't matter whether a particular shareholder decides to sell her shares back to the firm. If she sells, she gets $11 per share in cash. If she doesn't sell, she retains shares worth $11 each.

Thus, shareholder wealth is the same with dividends as with repurchases. If Rational pays a cash dividend, wealth is $10 + 1 = $11, including the dividend. If Rational repurchases, there is no dividend, but each share is worth $11.

You may hear a claim that share repurchases should increase the stock price. That's not quite right, as our example illustrates. A repurchase does not increase the stock price, but it avoids the fall in stock price that would occur on the ex-dividend day if the amount spent on repurchases were paid out as cash dividends. Repurchases do not guarantee a higher stock price, but only a stock price higher than if a dividend were paid instead. Repurchases also reduce the number of shares outstanding, so future earnings per share are higher than if the same amount were paid out as dividends.

If MM are correct and payout policy does not affect value, then the choice between dividends and repurchases is merely tactical. A company will decide to repurchase if it wants to retain the flexibility to cut back payout if valuable investment opportunities arise. Another company may commit to pay regular dividends to assure stockholders that it will run a tight ship, paying out free cash flow to limit the temptation for careless spending.

15.2 Self-Test

Suppose that Demiconductor pays out only $0.5 million in cash.

- a. What would happen to the value of the company if it pays it out as a dividend? What if it pays it out by repurchasing stock?
- b. What would happen to the price per share if it pays the money out as a dividend? What if it is paid out by a stock repurchase?

Stock Repurchases and DCF Valuation Models

As we pointed out in Chapter 4, there are two ways to value a share of common stock:

1. Calculate the PV of future dividends paid to holders of that share. If the company is also repurchasing shares, make sure your dividend per share forecasts take account of the reduction in outstanding shares resulting from the repurchases. If total dividend payout is fixed, then fewer shares means more dividends per share.

2. Calculate market capitalization (the market value of *all* shares) by forecasting and discounting all the free cash flow paid out to shareholders. Then calculate price per share by dividing market capitalization by the number of shares currently outstanding. With this approach you don't need to worry about how payout of free cash flow is split between dividends and repurchases.

In Praise of Repurchases

❯ Every now and again you will come across investment commentators who argue that repurchases are a powerful engine lifting stock prices. Here, for example, is a quote from *Money Crashers*.

> Announcements of companies buying back its own shares are usually seen as a good sign by Wall Street and market investors. A share buyback shows that a company's management thinks that its shares are undervalued. The company has to buy the shares on the open market and return them to the company's treasury which essentially takes them out of circulation, thereby reducing the total number

of shares outstanding. So there are two effects going on here: (1) Each share now becomes more valuable because each share now holds a greater percentage of ownership in the company (whose underlying profitability and economics has not changed). (2) The laws of supply and demand go into effect. There is an increase in demand for the company's shares of stock by the company itself and perhaps other investors as well, while the supply is being reduced. Thus, economic theory states that prices will rise as a result.

How would you respond to this argument?

BEYOND THE PAGE

Repurchases and the dividend discount model

mhhe.com/brealey14e

The second valuation method is much easier and more reliable when repurchases are likely to fluctuate. Notice that the method effectively assumes that MM are correct. It assumes that value depends on free cash flow, and not on whether the cash flow is paid out by dividends or by repurchases. The wide use of valuation models based on free cash flow amounts to an endorsement of MM in practice.

Dividends and Share Issues

We have considered dividend policy as the choice between cash dividends and repurchases. If we hold total payout constant, smaller dividends mean larger repurchases. But, as we noted earlier, MM derived their dividend-irrelevance theorem when repurchases were rare. So MM asked whether a corporation could increase value by paying *larger* cash dividends. But they still insisted on holding investment and debt-financing policy fixed.

Suppose a company like Rational Demiconductor has paid out any surplus cash. Now it wants to impress investors by paying out an even larger dividend. The extra money must come from somewhere. If the firm fixes its borrowing, the only way it can finance the extra dividend is to print some more shares and sell them. The new stockholders are going to part with their money only if you can offer them shares that are worth as much as they cost. But how can the firm sell more shares when its assets, earnings, investment opportunities, and, therefore, market value are all unchanged? The answer is that there must be a *transfer of value* from the old to the new stockholders. The new ones get the newly printed shares, each one worth less than before the extra dividend was announced, and the old ones suffer a capital loss on their shares. The capital loss borne by the old shareholders just offsets the extra cash dividend they receive.

Turn back to the first Rational Demiconductor balance sheet, which shows the company starting with $1 million of surplus cash, $1 per share. Suppose it decides to pay an annual dividend of $2 per share. To do so it will have to issue new shares (sooner or later) to replace the extra $1 million of cash that just went out the door. The ex-dividend stock price is $9, so it will have to issue 111,111 shares to raise $1 million. The issue brings Rational's equity market capitalization back to $1,111,111 \times \$9 = \$10$ million. Thus, Rational's shareholders receive a dividend of $2 versus $1 per share, but the extra cash in their pockets is exactly offset by a lower stock price. They own a smaller fraction of the firm, because Rational had to finance the extra dividend by issuing 111,111 new shares.

Figure 15.5 shows how this transfer of value occurs. Assume that Company Z pays out a third of its total value as a dividend and it raises the money to do so by selling new shares. The capital loss suffered by the old stockholders is represented by the reduction in the size of the red boxes. But that capital loss is exactly offset by the fact that the new money raised (the blue boxes) is paid over to them as dividends. The firm that sells shares to pay higher dividends is simply recycling cash by selling shares with a zero NPV. To suggest that this makes shareholders better off is like advising the cook to cool the kitchen by leaving the refrigerator door open.

Does it make any difference to the old stockholders that they receive an extra dividend payment plus an offsetting capital loss? It might if that were the only way they could get their hands on cash. But as long as there are efficient capital markets, they can raise the cash by selling shares. Thus, the old shareholders can cash in either by persuading the management to pay a higher dividend or by selling some of their shares. In either case there will be a transfer of value from old to new shareholders. The only difference is that in the former case, this transfer is caused by a dilution in the value of each of the firm's shares, and in the latter case, it is caused by a reduction in the number of shares held by the old shareholders. The two alternatives are compared in Figure 15.6.

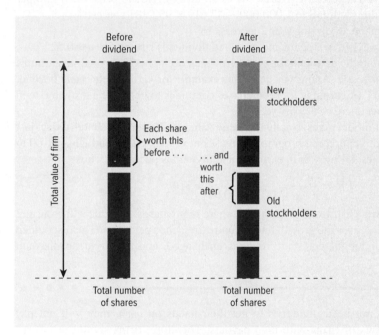

▶ **FIGURE 15.5**

Company Z pays out a third of its worth as a dividend and raises the money by selling new shares. The transfer of value to the new stockholders is equal to the dividend payment. The total value of the firm is unaffected.

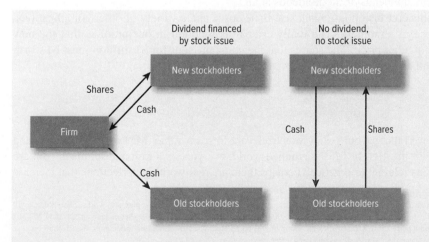

▶ **FIGURE 15.6**

Two ways of raising cash for the firm's original shareholders. In each case the cash received is offset by a decline in the value of the old stockholders' claim on the firm. If the firm pays a dividend, each share is worth less because more shares have to be issued against the firm's assets. If the old stockholders sell some of their shares, each share is worth the same but the old stockholders have fewer shares.

EXAMPLE 15.1 • Do repurchases invalidate the dividend discount model?

If the company pays out surplus cash by repurchasing stock, dividends must be lower than they would otherwise be. So how is it possible that the share price continues to be equal to the present value of future dividends? We illustrate by continuing the Rational Demiconductor example.

Suppose that Rational has just paid a cash dividend of $1 per share, reducing the ex-dividend market capitalization to $10 million. Investors forecast that Rational will earn $1 per share in perpetuity, all of which will be paid out as a dividend. If investors require a return of 10% on their investment in Rational, the present value of the future dividend stream is $10/0.10 = $10 per share.

Rational now announces that henceforth it will pay out exactly 50% of earnings as dividends and 50% as repurchases. (We assume that stockholders who sell their stock back to the company do so immediately after receiving that year's dividend.) This means that next year's dividend will be only $0.50. On the other hand, Rational will use $500,000 (50% of earnings) to buy back shares in year 1. It will repurchase 47,619 shares at the ex-dividend price of $10.50 per share, and shares outstanding will fall to 1,000,000 − 47,619 = 952,381 shares.[14]

Thus expected earnings *per share* for year 2 increase to
$1 million ÷ 952,381 = $1.05 per share and expected dividends rise by 5% to $0.525.

So the $0.50 reduction in the dividend for year 1 has been offset by 5% growth in earnings and dividends per share in year 2. And if you carry this example forward to year 3 and beyond, you will see that using 50% of earnings for repurchases continues to generate a growth rate in earnings and dividends per share of 5% per year.

The dividend discount model gives exactly the same value for Rational's shares today, just as MM would predict. The repurchase program decreases next year's dividend from $1.00 to $.50 per share but generates 5% growth in earnings and dividends per share. Thus

$$PV = \frac{DIV_1}{r - g} = \frac{0.50}{0.10 - 0.05} = \$10$$

Whenever a firm diverts cash from dividends to share repurchases, it reduces the current dividend per share, but increases the growth rate in future dividends per share. The discounted value of the stream of dividends per share remains unchanged, and the dividend discount model survives unscathed.

• • • • •

Because investors do not need dividends to get their hands on cash, they will not pay higher prices for the shares of firms with high payouts. Therefore, firms should not worry about paying low dividends or no dividends at all.

Of course, this conclusion ignores taxes, issue costs, and a variety of other complications. We turn to these in a moment. The really crucial assumption in our proof is that the new shares are sold at a fair price. The shares that the company sells for $1 million must be worth $1 million. In other words, we have assumed efficient markets.

15-3 Dividend Clienteles

When they showed that payout policy was irrelevant for firm value, MM assumed perfect and efficient financial markets. In MM's assumed world, everyone is a rational optimizer. But are these assumptions relevant in practice? Perhaps there are real-world imperfections that increase

---

[14] You can check that next year's ex-dividend price of $10.50 per share is the only price at which repurchase works. Shareholders will not sell their shares for less than $10.50 because then $500,000 would purchase more than 47,619 shares, leaving less than 952,381 shares outstanding and a price above $10.50 when the repurchase is completed. The firm should not offer more than $10.50 because that would repurchase fewer than 47,619 shares and hand a free gift to selling stockholders.

the value of stocks paying generous and steady dividends compared to those that repurchase. For example, some trusts and endowments may prefer high-dividend stocks because dividends are regarded as spendable "income," whereas capital gains are locked up as "additions to principal." In this section we consider some of these real-world imperfections that can make dividends preferred to repurchases or vice-versa. Our conclusion is the same that payout policy doesn't matter.

There is a natural clientele of investors, including retirees, who look to their stock portfolios as a steady source of cash.[15] In principle, as the example comparing dividends and repurchases in the previous section showed, in an ideal world this cash could be easily generated from stocks paying no dividends at all but with repurchases instead; the investors could just sell off a small fraction of their holdings from time to time. But it is simpler and cheaper for the company to send a quarterly check than for its shareholders to sell, say, one share every three months. Regular dividends relieve many of its shareholders of transaction costs and considerable inconvenience.

Some observers have appealed to behavioral psychology to explain why we may prefer to receive those regular dividends rather than sell small amounts of stock.[16] We are all, they point out, liable to succumb to temptation. Some of us may have a weakness for fattening foods, while others may be craving for a drink. We could seek to control these cravings by willpower, but that can be a painful struggle. Instead, it may be easier to set simple rules for ourselves ("cut out chocolate," or "wine with meals only"). In just the same way, we may welcome the self-discipline that comes from spending only dividend income, and thereby sidestep the difficult decision of how much we should dip into capital.

Clearly, some clienteles of investors prefer stocks with regular and stable cash dividends. These investors might be willing to pay more for stocks of companies that paid out cash by dividends rather than repurchases. But do they have to pay more? Corporations are free to adjust the supply of dividends to demand. If they could increase their stock prices simply by shifting payout from repurchases to cash dividends, they would presumably have done so already. The investors who prefer cash dividends already have a wide choice of dividend-paying stocks. If the supply of such stocks is sufficient to satisfy those investors, then additional firms have no incentive to switch from repurchases to cash dividends.

If this is indeed the outcome, then, despite the presence of investor clienteles that prefer dividends, the choice between dividends and repurchases has no impact on value, just as MM argued. Firms that pay dividends will be worth the same as ones that repurchase shares instead.

BEYOND THE PAGE

Designer funds

mhhe.com/brealey14e

15.3 Self-Test

Georgehouse Inc. currently repurchases shares each year and pays no dividends. Suppose the firm switches its payout policy to stop repurchasing and pays generous cash dividends instead. If a shareholder did not need income and so did not sell any shares under the old policy, what could the shareholder do now under the new policy that would be equivalent?

15-4   Taxes and Payout Policy

As the example in Section 15-2 showed, shifting payout from dividends to repurchases results in a higher stock price (but not higher firm value) because the stock price drop on the ex-dividend date is avoided. Investors thus receive a capital gain in place of a cash payment. This has two tax advantages in the United States. First, for those investors who do not sell

---

[15] See, for example, J. R. Graham and A. Kumar, "Do Dividend Clienteles Exist? Evidence on Dividend Preferences of Retail Investors," *Journal of Finance* 61 (June 2006), pp. 1305–1336; and M. Baker, S. Nagel, and J. Wurgler, "The Effect of Dividends on Consumption," *Brookings Papers on Economic Activity* (2007), pp. 231–291.

[16] See H. Shefrin and M. Statman, "Explaining Investor Preference for Cash Dividends," *Journal of Financial Economics* 13 (June 1984), pp. 253–282.

their stock back to the company, tax is deferred until the shares are sold and gains realized. Second, U.S. tax rates on capital gains have been much lower historically than tax rates on dividends. Some commentators have therefore wondered why U.S. companies pay any dividends at all.[17] Why not direct all payout to repurchases?[18]

Tax rates on capital gains used to be much lower than on dividends. For example, in the 1950s, the wealthiest investors paid tax at 90% on dividends and only 25% on realized capital gains. In the 1970s, the top rates were 50% on dividends and 35% on capital gains. But tax rates have come down, and this difference has disappeared for the moment. The maximum rate is now 20% for both.[19] Taxes on capital gains can still be deferred, however. The longer shareholders wait to sell, the lower the present value of their tax liability.[20]

BEYOND THE PAGE

U.S. tax rates

mhhe.com/brealey14e

The distinction between dividends and capital gains is not important for many financial institutions, which operate free of all taxes. For example, pension funds are not taxed. These funds hold over $9 trillion of common stocks, so their clout in the U.S. stock market is enormous. Only corporations have a tax reason to *prefer* cash dividends. They pay corporate income tax on only 50% of dividends received.[21] So, for each $1 of dividends received, the firm gets to keep $1 − (0.50 × 0.21) = 0.895. Thus the effective tax rate is only 10.5%. But corporations have to pay 21% tax on interest income or realized capital gains.

Empirical Evidence on Payout Policies and Taxes

It is hard to deny that taxes have some importance to investors. You can see that in the bond market. Interest on municipal bonds is not taxed, and so municipals usually sell at low pretax yields. Interest on federal government bonds is taxed, so these bonds sell at higher pretax yields. It does not seem likely that investors in bonds just forget about taxes when they enter the stock market.

There is some evidence that in the past taxes have affected U.S. investors' choice of stocks.[22] Lightly taxed institutional investors have tended to hold high-yield stocks and retail investors have preferred low-yield stocks. Moreover, this preference for low-yield stocks has been somewhat more marked for high-income individuals. Nevertheless, taxes have not deterred individuals in high-tax brackets from holding substantial amounts of dividend-paying stocks.

If investors are concerned about taxes, we might also expect that when the tax penalty on dividends is high, companies would think twice about increasing dividend payout. Only about a fifth of U.S. financial managers cite investor taxes as an important influence when the firm makes its dividend decision. On the other hand, firms have sometimes responded to major shifts in the way that investors are taxed. For example, when Australia introduced

---

[17] For example, see Fischer Black, "The Dividend Puzzle," *Journal of Portfolio Management* 2 (Winter 1976), pp. 5–8.

[18] A firm that eliminates dividends and makes regular repurchases may find that the Internal Revenue Service interprets the repurchases as de facto dividends and taxes the payout accordingly. However, in practice this tax risk is a threat only for privately held firms. Nevertheless, public corporations do not usually announce that they are repurchasing shares to save investor taxes on dividends. They may say, "Our stock is a good investment" or "We want to have shares available to finance possible future acquisitions." What do you think of these rationales?

[19] Many investors will also pay a 3.8% Medicare surtax on investment income, bringing the total maximum rate on dividends and capital gains to 23.8%.

[20] When securities are sold, capital gains tax is paid on the difference between the selling price and the purchase price or *basis*. Shares purchased in 2010 for $20 (the basis) and sold in 2020 for $30 would generate a capital gain of $10 per share and a tax of $2.38 at a 23.8% tax rate. Suppose the sale is deferred one year to 2021. If the interest rate is 5%, the PV of the tax viewed from 2020 falls to 2.38/1.05 = $2.27. The effective capital gains tax rate is 22.7%. The longer sale is deferred, the lower the effective tax rate. The effective tax rate falls to zero if the investor dies before selling because under current U.S. estate tax law, any heirs get to "step-up" the basis without realizing any capital gain. Suppose the price is still $30 when the investor dies. The heirs could sell for $30 and pay no tax because they could step-up to a $30 basis. The investor's stock holdings may be subject to estate taxes, however.

[21] The taxable fraction of dividends is reduced to 35% if the corporation owns more than 20% of the dividend payer and is eliminated if it owns more than 80%.

[22] See, for example, Y. Grinstein and R. Michaely, "Institutional Holdings and Payout Policy," *Journal of Finance* 60 (June 2005), pp. 1389–1426; and J. R. Graham and A. Kumar, "Do Dividend Clienteles Exist? Evidence on Dividend Preferences of Retail Investors," *Journal of Finance* 61 (June 2006), pp. 1305–1336.

a tax change in 1987 that effectively eliminated the tax penalty on dividends for Australian investors, firms became more willing to increase dividend payout.[23] Or consider the case of the 2011 tax reform in Japan, which raised the top marginal tax rate on dividend income from 10% to 43.6% for individuals who owned between 3% and 5% of the company's stock. More than 50% of these investors sold their stock before the tax hike, and companies that continued to have such large investors rapidly adjusted their payout policies.[24]

If tax considerations are important, we would expect to find a tendency for high-dividend stocks to sell at lower prices and, therefore, to offer higher pretax returns, at least in past decades when tax rates on dividends were much higher than on capital gains. Unfortunately, the evidence for this effect is ambiguous at best.[25]

Taxes are important, but cannot be the whole story of payout. Many companies paid generous dividends in the 1960s and 1970s, when U.S. tax rates on dividends were much higher than today. The shift from dividends to repurchases accelerated in the 2000s, when tax rates on both dividends and capital gains were much lower than historical levels. Payout has also shifted to repurchases in countries such as Australia which have imputation tax systems that remove the double taxation of dividends.

Nevertheless, it seems safe to say that the tax advantages of repurchases are one reason that they have grown so much in the United States and other developed economies.

Alternatives to the U.S. Tax System

In the United States, shareholders' returns are taxed twice. They are taxed at the corporate level (corporate tax) and in the hands of the shareholder (income tax or capital gains tax). These two tiers of tax are illustrated in Table 15.1, which shows the after-tax return to the shareholder if the company distributes all its income as dividends. We assume the company earns $100 a share before tax and therefore pays corporate tax of $0.21 \times 100 = \$21$. This leaves $79 a share to be paid out as a dividend, which is then subject to a second layer of tax. For example, a shareholder who is taxed at 15% pays tax on this dividend of $0.15 \times 79 = \$11.85$. Only a tax-exempt pension fund or charity would retain the full $79.

15.4 Self-Test

Suppose the company in Table 15.1 did not pay out any cash in dividends. How much higher would the return to the shareholder have been in that year?

Of course, dividends are regularly paid by companies that operate under very different tax systems. In some countries, such as Australia and New Zealand, shareholders' returns are not taxed twice. For example, in Australia, shareholders are taxed on dividends, but they may deduct from this tax bill their share of the corporate tax that the company has paid. This is known as an *imputation tax system*. Table 15.2 shows how the imputation system works.

Suppose that an Australian company earns pretax profits of A$100 a share. After it pays corporate tax at 30%, the profit is A$70 a share. The company now declares a net dividend of A$70

---

[23] K. Pattenden and G. Twite, "Taxes and Dividend Policy under Alternative Tax Regimes," *Journal of Corporate Finance* 14 (2008), pp. 1–16.

[24] See K. Onji and M. Orihara, "Taxes, Stock Ownership, and Payout Policy: Evidence from a 2011 Tax Reform in Japan," April 5, 2016, available at: https://www.mof.go.jp/pri/research/discussion_paper/ron278.pdf.

[25] Two influential early studies found conflicting results. Litzenberger and Ramaswamy estimated that investors priced stocks as if dividend income attracted an extra 14% to 23% of tax. Miller and Scholes used a different methodology and came up with a negligible 4% difference in the tax rate. See R. H. Litzenberger and K. Ramaswamy, "The Effects of Dividends on Common Stock Prices: Tax Effects or Information Effects," *Journal of Finance* 37 (May 1982), pp. 429–443; and M. H. Miller and M. Scholes, "Dividends and Taxes: Some Empirical Evidence," *Journal of Political Economy* 90 (1982), pp. 1118–1141. Subsequent research on dividend taxation and common-stock returns is reviewed in J. Farre-Mensa, R. Michaely, and M. Schmalz, "Payout Policy," in A. Lo and R. C. Merton, eds., *Annual Review of Financial Economics* 6 (December 2014), pp. 75–134.

Operating income	$100	
Corporate tax at 21%	21	◄——— Corporate tax
After-tax income (paid out as dividends)	$ 79	
Income tax paid by investor at 15%	11.85	◄——— Second tax paid by investor
Net income to shareholder	$ 67.15	

❭ **TABLE 15.1**   In the United States, returns to shareholders are taxed twice. This example assumes that all income after corporate taxes is paid out as cash dividends (figures in dollars per share).

	Rate of Income Tax Paid by Investor		
	15%	**30%**	**47%**
Operating income	$100	$100	$100
Corporate tax ($T_c = 0.30$)	30	30	30
After-tax income	$ 70	$ 70	$ 70
Grossed-up dividend	100	100	100
Income tax	15	30	47
Tax credit for corporate payment	−30	−30	−30
Tax due from shareholder	−$15	$ 0	$ 17
Available to shareholder	85	70	53

❭ **TABLE 15.2**   Under imputation tax systems, such as that in Australia, shareholders receive a tax credit for the corporate tax that the firm has paid (figures in Australian dollars per share).

and sends each shareholder a check for this amount. This dividend is accompanied by a tax credit saying that the company has already paid A$30 of tax on the shareholder's behalf. Thus shareholders are treated as if they received a total, or gross, dividend of $70 + 30 = $ A$100 and paid tax of A$30. If the shareholder's tax rate is 30%, there is no more tax to pay and the shareholder retains the net dividend of A$70. If the shareholder pays tax at the top personal rate of 47%, then he or she is required to pay an additional $17 of tax; if the tax rate is 15% (the rate at which Australian pension funds are taxed), then the shareholder receives a *refund* of $30 − 15 = $ A$15.[26]

Under an imputation tax system, millionaires have to pay the extra personal tax on dividends. If this is more than the tax that they would pay on capital gains, then millionaires would prefer that the company does not distribute earnings. If it is the other way around, they would prefer dividends.[27] Investors with low tax rates have no doubts about the matter. If the company pays a dividend, these investors receive a check from the revenue service for the excess tax that the company has paid; therefore, they prefer high payout rates.

Look once again at Table 15.2 and think what would happen if the corporate tax rate were zero. The shareholder with a 15% tax rate would still end up with A$85, and the shareholder

---

[26] In Australia, shareholders receive a credit for the full amount of corporate tax that has been paid on their behalf. In other countries, the tax credit is less than the corporate tax rate. You can think of the tax system in these countries as lying between the Australian and U.S. systems.
[27] In the case of Australia, the tax rate on capital gains is the same as the tax rate on dividends. However, for securities that are held for more than 12 months, only half of the gain is taxed.

with the 47% rate would still receive A$53. Thus, under an imputation tax system, when a company pays out all its earnings, there is effectively only one layer of tax—the tax on the shareholder. The revenue service collects this tax through the company and then sends a demand to the shareholder for any excess tax or makes a refund for any overpayment.[28]

15-5 Payout Policy and the Life Cycle of the Firm

MM said that payout policy does not affect shareholder value. Shareholder value is driven by the firm's investment policy, including its future growth opportunities. Financing policy, including the choice between debt and equity, can also affect value, as we will see in Chapter 17.

In MM's analysis, payout is a residual, a by-product of other financial policies. The firm should make investment and financing decisions, and then pay out whatever cash is left over. Therefore, decisions about how much to pay out should change over the life cycle of the firm.

MM assumed a perfect and rational world, but many of the complications discussed in this chapter actually reinforce the life cycle of payout. Let's review the life-cycle story.[29]

Young growth firms have plenty of profitable investment opportunities. During this time, it is efficient to retain and reinvest all operating cash flow. Why pay out cash to investors if the firm then has to replace the cash by borrowing or issuing more shares? Retaining cash avoids costs of issuing securities and minimizes shareholders' immediate tax bill. Investors are not worried about wasteful overinvestment because investment opportunities are good, and managers' compensation is tied to stock price.

As the firm matures, positive-NPV projects become scarcer relative to cash flow. The firm begins to accumulate cash. Now investors begin to worry about overinvestment or excessive perks. The investors pressure management to start paying out cash. Sooner or later, managers comply—otherwise, stock price stagnates. The payout may come as share repurchases, but initiating a regular cash dividend may send a stronger and more reassuring signal of financial discipline.

As the firm ages, more and more payout is called for. The payout may come as higher dividends or larger repurchases. Sometimes the payout comes as the result of a takeover. Shareholders are bought out, and the firm's new owners generate cash by selling assets and restructuring operations. We discuss takeovers in Chapter 32.

The life cycle of the firm is not always predictable. It's not always obvious when the firm is "mature" and ready to start paying cash back to shareholders. The following three questions can help the financial manager decide:

1. Is the company generating positive free cash flow after making all investments with positive NPVs, and is the positive free cash flow likely to continue?

2. Is the firm's debt ratio prudent?

3. Are the company's holdings of cash a sufficient cushion for unexpected setbacks and a sufficient war chest for unexpected opportunities?

If the answer to all three questions is yes, then the free cash flow is surplus, and payout is called for.

As the nearby box shows, in March 2012, Apple's answer to all three questions was yes. Yes, it was continuing to accumulate cash at a rate of $30 billion per year. Yes, because it had no debt to speak of. Yes, because no conceivable investment or acquisition could soak up its excess cash flow.

---

[28] This is only true for earnings that are paid out as dividends. Retained earnings are subject to corporate tax. Shareholders get the benefit of retained earnings in the form of capital gains.

[29] Here we are following a life-cycle theory set out in H. DeAngelo, L. DeAngelo, and D. Skinner, "Corporate Payout Policy," *Foundations and Trends in Finance* 3 (2008), pp. 95–287.

Apple Commits to Dividends and Repurchases

❯ Figure 15.7 shows how Apple's holdings of cash and marketable securities have grown over the past decade. By the start of 2012, Apple Inc. had accumulated cash and long-term securities of about $100 billion. Steve Jobs, the architect of Apple's explosive growth, had preferred to keep the war chest of cash for investment or possible acquisitions. Jobs's fiscal conservatism may seem quaint when Apple's forecasted income for 2012 was over $40 billion. But Jobs could remember tough times for Apple; the company was near bankruptcy when Jobs took over in 1997. Apple had paid cash dividends in the early 1990s but was forced to stop in 1995 as its cash reserves dwindled.

After Jobs died in October 2011, the pressure from investors for payout steadily increased. "They have a ridiculous amount of cash," said Douglas Skinner, a professor of accounting at the Chicago Booth School of Business. "There is no feasible acquisition that Apple could do that would need that much cash."

On March 19, 2012, Apple announced that it would pay a quarterly dividend of $2.65 per share and spend $10 billion for share buybacks. It forecasted $45 billion in payout over the following three years. Apple's stock price jumped by $15.53 to $601 by the close of trading on the announcement day. Apple's dividend yield went from zero to $(2.65 \times 4)/601 = 1.8\%$.

Was Apple's payout sufficiently generous? Analysts' opinions varied. "A pretty vanilla return-of-cash program" (A. M. Sacconaghi, Bernstein Research). "It's not too piddling, and on the other hand not so large to signal that growth prospects are not what they thought" (David A. Rolfe, Wedgewood Partners).

Apple more than kept its payout promise. In the eight years to 2020, it distributed almost $500 billion through dividends and repurchases. Nevertheless, by the end of the period, its cash mountain was even higher than at the time of the 2012 announcement.

Source: N. Wingfield, "Flush with Cash, Apple Declares a Dividend and Buyback," *The New York Times*, March 20, 2012, pp. B1, B9.

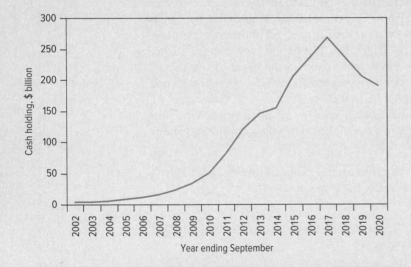

❯ **FIGURE 15.7**

The growth in Apple's holdings of cash and marketable securities, 2002–2020.

Some critics had argued that Apple should pay out the cash because it was earning interest at less than 1% per year. That was a spurious argument because shareholders had no better opportunities. Safe interest rates were extremely low, and neither Apple nor investors could do anything about it.

Note also two further points. First, Apple did not just initiate a cash dividend. It announced a combination of dividends and repurchases. This two-part payout strategy is now standard for large, mature corporations. Second, Apple did not initiate repurchases because its stock was undervalued but because it had surplus cash. You will hear critics who claim that companies should repurchase shares in bad times, when profits disappoint, and forbear in good times when profits are high. It is true that repurchases are sometimes triggered by management's view that their company's stock is underappreciated by investors. But repurchases are primarily a device for distributing surplus cash to investors. It's no surprise that repurchases increase when profits are high and more surplus cash is available.

The Agency Costs of Idle Cash

The managers of a corporation with plenty of cash on hand but few valuable investment opportunities face a potential agency cost. The managers may be tempted to continue investing, building a larger empire but not a more valuable one. In such cases, investors will favor larger cash payouts in order to keep the firm on a cash diet and force more disciplined investment.

Increased payout is often in the managers' interest. Top management compensation is strongly linked to stock price performance. The managers know that stock price is likely to fall if shareholders sense that cash is being spent wastefully. The threat of a falling stock price is an excellent incentive for the managers to pay out surplus cash.

These are arguments for greater cash payouts. The arguments do not say that dividends are necessarily better than repurchases for this purpose. But corporations that increase dividends now are reluctant to cut back dividends later. Share repurchases are more flexible. Therefore, a dividend increase today is the more credible assurance of increased payout in the future.

On the other hand, managers with valuable stock options may prefer repurchases because option payoffs depend on stock price at the option's maturity, and cash spent on repurchases leaves stock prices higher than the same amount of cash paid out as dividends.

15.5 Self-Test

Which of the following suggests that the firm is "mature" and ready to start paying dividends?
    a. Company has borrowed heavily and bonds have been downrated.

    b. The company has had a one-off cash windfall.

    c. If the final trials of a drug work out as promised, the company will need to invest in marketing and production.

Payout and Corporate Governance

This chapter has considered payout policy in developed economies with good corporate governance. Payout can play a still more important role in countries where corporations are more opaque and governance less effective.

In some countries, you cannot always trust the financial information that companies provide. A passion for secrecy and a tendency to construct multilayered corporate organizations can produce earnings figures that are doubtful and sometimes meaningless.

How does an investor separate the winners and losers when governance is weak and corporations are opaque? One clue is payout. Investors can't read managers' minds, but they can learn from their actions. They know that a firm that reports good earnings and pays out a significant fraction of the earnings is putting its money where its mouth is. We can understand, therefore, why investors would be skeptical about reported earnings unless they were backed up by consistent payout policy.

Of course, firms can cheat in the short run by overstating earnings and scraping up cash for payout. But it is hard to cheat in the long run because a firm that is not making money will not have cash to pay out. If a firm pays a high dividend or commits to substantial repurchases without generating sufficient cash flow, it will ultimately have to seek additional debt or equity financing. The requirement for new financing would reveal management's game to investors.

The implications for payout in developing countries could go either way. On the one hand, managers who are committed to shareholder value have a stronger motive to pay out cash when corporate governance is weak and corporate financial statements are opaque. Payout makes the firm's reported earnings more credible. On the other hand, weak corporate governance may also weaken managers' commitment to shareholders. In this case, they will pay out less and, instead, deploy cash more in their own interests. It turns out that dividend payout ratios are on average smaller where governance is weak.[30]

This evidence suggests that good governance encourages dividend payout and retards the agency costs of idle cash.

---

[30] See R. LaPorta, F. Lopez de Silanes, A. Shleifer, and R. W. Vishny, "Agency Problems and Dividend Policy around the World," *Journal of Finance* 55 (February 2000), pp. 1–33.

● ● ● ● ●

KEY TAKEAWAYS

A corporation's payout policy is the answer to two questions. First, how much cash should the company pay out to its stockholders? Second, should the cash be distributed by paying cash dividends or by repurchasing shares?

- **How much should be paid out?** The answer to "How much?" is often zero. Younger companies with profitable growth opportunities do not pay out cash and rarely repurchase stock. They finance investment as much as possible with internally generated cash flow. But as they mature, growth opportunities gradually fade away and surplus cash accumulates. Then the *agency costs* of free cash flow loom larger. Investors worry that surplus cash will be soaked up by negative-NPV investment, and they push harder for payout.

- **Surplus cash.** Cash is surplus when these three criteria are met:

  1. Free cash flow is reliably positive. Recall that free cash flow is the operating cash flow left over after the firm has made all positive-NPV investments.

  2. The firm's debt level is prudent and manageable. Otherwise, free cash flow is better used to pay down debt.

  3. The firm has a sufficient war chest of cash or unused debt capacity to cover unexpected opportunities or setbacks.

- **How dividend and repurchase programs are managed.** Repurchases are more flexible than dividends. Repurchases can be accelerated or slowed down as the corporation's profits and cash position fluctuate. Financial managers do not set regular cash dividends unless they are confident that the dividends can be maintained. Announcements of dividend increases therefore signal managers' confidence and usually cause a stock-price increase.

  The stock-price response to a dividend increase does not imply that dividends are better than repurchases for shareholders. The increase merely accelerates release of good news that would have come out sooner or later through other channels.

- **Dividends vs. repurchases and shareholder value.** The choice between dividends and repurchases has no impact on shareholder value in a perfect, frictionless financial market. For example, when a company shifts payout from repurchases to dividends, the shareholders' cash in hand from dividends is exactly offset by a lower stock price. Or suppose a firm tries to make its shareholders happy by paying a higher dividend but then ends up issuing new shares to pay for the payout. The result is the same: more shares outstanding and a lower price per share, just offsetting the higher dividend.

- **Taxes and payout policy.** U.S. tax rates on dividends have in the past been much higher than rates on capital gains. By 2021, the top tax rate on both dividends and capital gains was equal, although the *effective* tax rate on capital gains was lower because payment could be deferred until the shares were sold. Thus, taxes have favored repurchases.

  Taxes alone cannot explain payout policy, however. For example, corporations paid out massive sums in cash dividends even in the 1960s, 1970s, and early 1980s, when the top income-tax rate on dividends was 70% or more.

- **Dividend clienteles.** Some investors—widows and orphans, for example—may depend on regular cash dividends. But the supply of dividends should expand to satisfy this clientele, and if the supply of dividends already meets demand, then no single firm can increase its market value simply by paying dividends.

- **Concluding comments.** It is difficult to be assertive about payout. But remember, if investment and capital structure decisions are held constant, then arguments about payout policy are largely about shuffling money from one pocket to another. Unless large tax consequences accompany these shuffles, it's unlikely that firm value is much affected by the choice between dividends and repurchases. The short-run choice is tactical. Longer-run payout strategy depends on the life cycle of the firm from youth and growth to profitable maturity.

FURTHER READING

For comprehensive reviews of the literature on payout policy, see:

F. Allen and R. Michaely, "Payout Policy," in G. Constantinides, M. Harris, and R. Stulz, eds., *Handbook of the Economics of Finance: Corporate Finance* (Amsterdam: North-Holland, 2003).

H. DeAngelo, L. DeAngelo, and D. Skinner, "Corporate Payout Policy," *Foundations and Trends in Finance* 3 (2008), pp. 95–287.

J. Farre-Mensa, R. Michaely, and M. Schmalz, "Payout Policy," in A. Lo and R. Merton, eds., *Annual Review of Financial Economics* 6 (December 2014), pp. 75–134.

For a survey of managers' attitudes to the payout decision, see:

A. Kalay and M. Lemmon, "Payout Policy," in B. E. Eckbo, ed., *Handbook of Empirical Corporate Finance* (Amsterdam: Elsevier/North-Holland, 2007), Chapter 10.

A. Brav, J. R. Graham, C. R. Harvey, and R. Michaely, "Payout Policy in the 21st Century," *Journal of Financial Economics* 77 (September 2005), pp. 483–527.

PROBLEM SETS

Mc Graw Hill connect® Select problems are available in McGraw-Hill's *Connect.* Please see the preface for more information.

1. **Dividend payments (S15.1)** In 2021, Entergy paid a regular quarterly dividend of $0.95 per share.

   a. Match each of the following dates.

(A1) Friday, January 29	(B1) Record date
(A2) Thursday, February 11	(B2) Payment date
(A3) Friday, February 12	(B3) Ex-dividend date
(A4) Monday, March 1	(B4) Declaration date

   b. Suppose that you were told that on one of these dates, the stock price fell by about $0.95. Which would be the likely date? Why?

   c. Entergy's stock price in January 2021 was about $98. What was the dividend yield?

   d. Entergy's forecasted earnings per share for 2021 were about $5.90. What was the payout ratio?

2. **Dividend payments (S15.1)** Seashore Salt Co. has surplus cash. Its CFO decides to pay back $4 per share to investors by initiating a regular dividend of $1 per quarter or $4 per year. The stock price jumps to $90 when the payout is announced.

   a. Why does the stock price increase?

   b. What happens to the stock price when the stock goes ex dividend?

3. **Repurchases (S15.1)** Look again at Problem 2. Assume instead that the CFO announces a stock repurchase of $4 per share instead of a cash dividend.

   a. What happens to the stock price when the repurchase is announced? Would you expect the price to increase to $90? Explain briefly.

   b. Suppose the stock is repurchased immediately after the announcement. Would the repurchase result in an additional stock-price increase?

4. **Dividends payments and repurchases (S15.1)** Go to the Apple website or to a financial source such as Yahoo! Finance.

   a. Has Apple's dividend increased from the initial quarterly rate?

   b. What was the announcement date of the most recent dividend?

   c. When did Apple stock last go ex-dividend?

   d. What happened to the stock price on the ex-dividend date? When was the dividend actually paid?

   e. What is Apple's dividend yield?

   f. Look up estimates of Apple's EPS for the next year. What is the dividend payout ratio?

   g. How much does Apple plan to spend on repurchases in the next year? What is the overall payout ratio (dividends plus repurchases)?

5. **Company dividend policy (S15.1)** Here are several "facts" about typical corporate dividend policies. Which are true and which false?

   a. Companies decide each year's dividend by looking at their capital expenditure requirements and then distributing whatever cash is left over.

   b. Managers and investors seem more concerned with dividend changes than with dividend levels.

   c. Managers often increase dividends temporarily when earnings are unexpectedly high for a year or two.

   d. Companies undertaking substantial share repurchases usually finance them with an offsetting reduction in cash dividends.

6. **Company dividend policy (S15.1)** Investors and financial managers focus more on changes in cash dividends than on the level of cash dividends. Why?

7. **Information content of dividends (S15.1)** What is meant by "the information content of dividends"? Explain.

8. **Information content of dividends (S15.1)** Does the good news conveyed by the announcement of a dividend increase mean that a firm can increase its stock price in the long run simply by paying cash dividends? Explain.

9. **Information content of dividends (S15.1)** Generous dividend payouts and high price–earnings multiples are correlated positively. Does this imply that paying out cash as dividends instead of repurchases increases share price? (*Hint:* Could the level of dividends be telling investors something about long-run earnings?)

10. **Payout policy in perfect capital markets (S15.2)** MM insisted that payout policy should be analyzed holding debt and investment policy constant. Why? Explain.

11. **Payout policy in perfect capital markets (S15.2)** Go back to the first Rational Demiconductor balance sheet. Now assume that Rational wins a lawsuit and is paid $1 million in cash. Its market capitalization rises by that amount. It decides to pay out $2 per share instead of $1 per share. Explain what happens to Rational's stock price over the period of the announcement and over the period of the payment if the payout comes (a) as a cash dividend or (b) as a share repurchase.

12. **Payout policy in perfect capital markets (S15.2)** Go back to the first Rational Demiconductor balance sheet one more time. Assume that Rational does not win the lawsuit (see Problem 11) and is left with only $1 million in surplus cash. Nevertheless, Rational decides to pay a cash dividend of $2 per share. What must Rational do to finance the $2 dividend if it holds its debt and investment policies constant? What happens to price per share?

13. **Payout policy in perfect capital markets (S15.2)** Respond to the following comment: "It's all very well saying that I can sell shares to cover cash needs, but that may mean selling at the bottom of the market. If the company pays a regular cash dividend, investors avoid that risk."

14. **Payout policy in perfect capital markets (S15.2)** Here are key financial data for House of Herring Inc.:

Earnings per share for 2027	$5.50
Number of shares outstanding	40 million
Target payout ratio	50%
Planned dividend per share	$2.75
Stock price, year-end 2027	$130

House of Herring plans to pay the entire dividend early in January 2028. All corporate and personal taxes were repealed in 2026.

a. Other things equal, what will be House of Herring's stock price after the planned dividend payout?

b. Suppose the company cancels the dividend and announces that it will use the money saved to repurchase shares. What happens to the stock price on the announcement date? Assume that investors learn nothing about the company's prospects from the announcement. How many shares will the company need to repurchase?

c. Suppose that, instead of canceling the dividend, the company increases dividends to $5.50 per share and then issues new shares to recoup the extra cash paid out as dividends. What happens to the with- and ex-dividend share prices? How many shares will need to be issued? Again, assume investors learn nothing from the announcement about House of Herring's prospects.

15. **Repurchases and the DCF model (S15.2)** Hors d'Age Cheeseworks has been paying a regular cash dividend of $4 per share each year for over a decade. The company is paying out all its earnings as dividends and is not expected to grow. There are 100,000 shares outstanding selling for $80 per share. The company has sufficient cash on hand to pay the next annual dividend.

Suppose that, starting in year 1, Hors d'Age decides to cut its cash dividend to zero and announces that it will repurchase shares instead.

a. What is the immediate stock price reaction? Ignore taxes, and assume that the repurchase program conveys no information about operating profitability or business risk.

b. How many shares will Hors d'Age purchase?

c. Project and compare future stock prices for the old and new policies. Do this for years 1, 2, and 3.

16. **Repurchases and the DCF model (S15.2)** Surf & Turf Hotels is a mature business, although it pays no cash dividends. Next year's earnings are forecasted at $56 million. There are 10 million outstanding shares. The company has traditionally paid out 50% of earnings by repurchases and reinvested the remaining earnings. With reinvestment, the company has generated steady growth averaging 5% per year. Assume the cost of equity is 12%.

    a. Calculate Surf & Turf's current stock price, using the constant-growth DCF model from Chapter 4. (*Hint:* Take the easy route and estimate overall market capitalization.)

    b. Now Surf & Turf's CFO announces a switch from repurchases to a regular cash dividend. Next year's dividend will be $2.80 per share. The CFO reassures investors that the company will continue to pay out 50% of earnings and reinvest 50%. All future payouts will come as dividends, however. What would you expect to happen to Surf & Turf's stock price? Why?

17. **Repurchases and the DCF model (S15.2)** House of Haddock has 5,000 shares outstanding and the stock price is $140. The company is expected to pay a dividend of $20 per share next year, and thereafter, the dividend is expected to grow indefinitely by 5% a year. The president, George Mullet, now makes a surprise announcement: He says that the company will henceforth distribute half the cash in the form of dividends, and the remainder will be used to repurchase stock. The repurchased stock will not be entitled to the dividend.

    a. What is the total value of the company before and after the announcement? What is the value of one share?

    b. What is the expected stream of dividends per share for an investor who plans to retain his shares rather than sell them back to the company? Check your estimate of share value by discounting this stream of dividends per share.

18. **Repurchases and the DCF model (S15.2)** Little Oil has 1 million shares outstanding with a total market value of $20 million. The firm is expected to pay $1 million of dividends next year, and thereafter the amount paid out is expected to grow by 5% a year in perpetuity. Thus, the expected dividend is $1.05 million in year 2, $1.1025 million in year 3, and so on. However, the company has heard that the value of a share depends on the flow of dividends, and therefore, it announces that next year's dividend will be increased to $2 million and that the extra cash will be raised immediately afterward by an issue of shares. After that, the total amount paid out each year will be as previously forecasted—that is, $1.05 million in year 2 and increasing by 5% in each subsequent year.

    a. At what price will the new shares be issued in year 1?

    b. How many shares will the firm need to issue?

    c. What will be the expected dividend payments on these new shares, and what therefore will be paid out to the *old* shareholders after year 1?

    d. Show that the present value of the cash flows to current shareholders remains $20 million.

19. **Repurchases and EPS (S15.2)** Many companies use stock repurchases to increase earnings per share. For example, suppose that a company is in the following position:

Net profit	$10 million
Number of shares before repurchase	1 million
Earnings per share	$10
Price–earnings ratio	20
Share price	$200

The company now repurchases 200,000 shares at $200 a share. The number of shares declines to 800,000 shares and earnings per share increase to $12.50. Assuming the price–earnings ratio stays at 20, the share price must rise to $250. Discuss.

20. **Dividends and value (S15.2)** We stated in Section 15-2 that MM's proof of dividend irrelevance assumes that new shares are sold at a fair price. Look back at Problem 18. Assume that new shares are issued in year 1 at $10 a share. Show who gains and who loses. Is dividend policy still irrelevant? Why or why not?

21. **Payout and valuation (S15.2)** Look back one last time at Problem 18. How would you value Little Oil if it paid out $500,000 in cash dividends year in and year out, with no expected growth or decline? Remaining free cash flow will be used to repurchase shares. Assume that Little Oil's free cash flow continues to grow at 5% as in Problem 18.

22. **Stock repurchases (S15.2)** An article on stock repurchase in the *Los Angeles Times* noted: "An increasing number of companies are finding that the best investment they can make these days is in themselves." Discuss this view. How is the desirability of repurchase affected by company prospects and the price of its stock?

23. **Payout policy and the cost of capital (S15.2)** Comment briefly on each of the following statements:

    a. "Unlike American firms, which are always being pressured by their shareholders to increase dividends, Japanese companies pay out a much smaller proportion of earnings and so enjoy a lower cost of capital."

    b. "Unlike new capital, which needs a stream of new dividends to service it, retained earnings have zero cost."

    c. "If a company repurchases stock instead of paying a dividend, the number of shares falls and earnings per share rise. Thus stock repurchase must always be preferred to paying dividends."

24. **Dividend clienteles (S15.3)** Mr. Milquetoast admires Warren Buffett and believes that Berkshire Hathaway is a good investment. He wants to invest $100,000 in Berkshire Hathaway B shares but hesitates because Berkshire Hathaway has never paid a dividend. He needs to generate $5,000 per year in cash for living expenses. What should Mr. Milquetoast do?

25. **Dividend clienteles (S15.3)** Some types of investors prefer dividend-paying stocks because dividends provide a regular, convenient source of income. Does demand from these investors necessarily lift the prices of dividend-paying stocks relative to stocks of companies that pay no dividends but repurchase shares instead? Explain briefly.

26. **Payout and taxes (S15.4)** Which of the following U.S. investors have tax reasons to prefer companies that pay out cash by repurchases instead of cash dividends? Which should not care?

    a. A pension fund.

    b. An individual investor in the top income-tax bracket.

    c. A corporation.

    d. An endowment for a charity or university.

27. **Payout policy and taxes (S15.4)** Some hold that payout policy doesn't matter because the *supply* of high-, medium-, and low-payout stocks has already adjusted to satisfy investors' demands. Investors who like generous dividends hold stocks that give them all the dividends that they want. Investors who want capital gains see ample low-payout stocks to choose from. Thus, high-payout firms cannot gain by transforming to low-payout firms, or vice versa.

    Suppose the government reduces the tax rate on dividends but not on capital gains. Suppose that before this change the supply of dividends matched investor needs. How would you expect the tax change to affect the total cash dividends paid by U.S. corporations and the proportion of high-versus low-payout companies? Would payout policy still be irrelevant after any dividend supply adjustments are completed? Explain.

28. **Dividends and the firm's life cycle (S15.5)** Halfshell Seafood is still generating good profits, but growth is slowing down. How should its CFO decide when to start up a program of paying out cash to stockholders? What questions should the CFO ask?

CHALLENGE

29. **Dividend policy and the dividend discount model (S15.2)** Consider the following two statements: "Dividend policy is irrelevant," and "Stock price is the present value of expected future dividends." (See Chapter 4.) They *sound* contradictory. This question is designed to show that they are fully consistent.

    The current price of the shares of Charles River Mining Corporation is $50. Next year's earnings and dividends per share are $4 and $2, respectively. Investors expect perpetual growth at 8% per year. The expected rate of return demanded by investors is $r = 12\%$.

    We can use the perpetual-growth model to calculate stock price:

$$P_0 = \frac{\text{DIV}}{r - g} = \frac{2}{0.12 - 0.08} = 50$$

    Suppose that Charles River Mining announces that it will switch to a 100% payout policy, issuing shares as necessary to finance growth. Use the perpetual-growth model to show that current stock price is unchanged.

• • • • •

SOLUTIONS TO SELF-TEST QUESTIONS

15.1   Marina buys after the ex-dividend date and is not entitled to the dividend. Checks will be mailed on June 30.

15.2   a. $10.5 million; also $10.5 million. b. 10.5/1 = $10.5 if paid as a dividend. If paid out as a repurchase, Rational spends $0.5 million to buy back 45,455 shares at $11. The number of remaining shares is (1,000,000 − 45,455) = 954,545, and share price is 10,500,000/954,545 = $11.

15.3   The shareholder can use the cash to reinvest (or, if Georgehouse has a DRIP with its new policy, the shareholder can automatically reinvest).

15.4   If the money had not been paid out, shareholders would have been entitled to the full after-tax income of $79. (Of course, at some future date, they may have become liable for capital gains tax.)

15.5   None of these cases suggests that the firm should start to pay dividends.

    a. The company would do better to use cash to pay down debt.

    b. The company could distribute the windfall by a one-off repurchase, but it should not increase its dividend unsustainably.

    c. If the company will need cash, it should not initiate a dividend program.

• • • • •

FINANCE ON THE WEB

Visit https://www.gresham.ac.uk/lectures-and-events/does-finance-benefit-society for a Gresham College public lecture entitled "Does Finance Benefit Society?" by Alex Edmans, on the subject of share repurchases.

Does Debt Policy Matter?

A corporation's mix of debt and equity financing is called its *capital structure*. When the corporation uses debt, it is said to employ *financial leverage* or *gearing*. What happens if the financial manager uses more or less financial leverage? Is there an ideal mix of debt and equity financing that maximizes the market value of the firm?

There is a traditional view—still lurking in some corners of finance—that debt financing adds value just because the interest rate paid to debt holders is less than the cost of equity. But Modigliani and Miller (MM) proved that market value does *not* depend on capital structure in perfect, frictionless financial markets. MM's famous Proposition 1 states that the total value of outstanding debt and equity depends on the value of the firm's real assets, operations, and growth opportunities, but not on the proportions of debt and equity.

MM's Proposition 1 allows complete separation of investment and financing decisions. It implies that any firm could use the capital budgeting procedures presented in Chapters 5 through 11 without worrying about where the money for capital expenditures comes from. In those chapters, we assumed all-equity financing without really thinking about it. If MM are correct, that is exactly the right approach. If the firm uses a mix of debt and equity financing, its overall cost of capital will be exactly the same as if it were financed entirely with equity.

Financing decisions do matter in practice, for reasons detailed in Chapters 17 and 18. But we devote this chapter to MM because their proposition is the starting point for all applied capital structure theory. If you don't understand the starting point, you won't understand the destination.

Section 16-1 Financial leverage and shareholder value

Section 16-1 introduces capital-structure decisions and explains when maximizing the *total* market value of the firm also maximizes shareholder value.

Section 16-2 Modigliani and Miller's Proposition 1

Section 16-2 sets out MM's Proposition 1 that capital structure is irrelevant to value. We provide a simple numerical example to illustrate MM's argument.

Section 16-3 Leverage and expected returns: MM's Proposition 2

Financial leverage creates *financial risk*. When a corporation finances with more debt and less equity, the risk of the remaining equity goes up and its cost goes up to compensate. MM showed that the increased cost of equity exactly offsets the advantage of borrowing at interest rates lower than the cost of equity.

Section 16-4 No magic in financial leverage

Section 16-4 considers whether some special types of corporate securities could have extra value to investors, thus undercutting MM's logic. We can't rule out this possibility, but, if managers spot an opportunity to issue such securities, there will be an increase in supply that eliminates any gains from further issues of these. This kind of supply response to meet demand should reassure financial managers that MM's proposition is at least approximately correct most of the time.

Section 16-5 A final word on the cost of capital

Throughout this chapter we ignore corporate income taxes, except in Section 16-5, where we recognize the tax deductibility of interest expense on corporate borrowing. We show how this interest tax shield is accounted for in the *after-tax weighted average cost of capital* (WACC).

16-1   Financial Leverage and Shareholder Value

Financial managers try to find the combination of debt and equity financing that maximizes the total value of the firm, debt and equity combined. Before tackling this problem, we should confirm that the financing policy that maximizes total value also maximizes shareholder value.

Example A simplified example will suffice. Let D and E represent the market values of the debt and equity of the Wapshot Wind Farms Company. Wapshot's 1,000 shares sell for $50 apiece. Thus, Wapshot's equity is

$$E = 1,000 \times 50 = \$50,000$$

Wapshot has also borrowed $25,000, and so V, the total market value of all Wapshot's outstanding securities, is

$$V = D + E = \$75,000$$

Wapshot's stock is known as *levered equity*. Its stockholders face the benefits and costs of **financial leverage**, or *gearing*. Suppose that Wapshot "levers up" still further by borrowing an additional $10,000 and paying the proceeds to shareholders as a special dividend of $10 per share. This substitutes debt for equity capital with no impact on Wapshot's assets.

What will Wapshot's equity be worth after the special dividend is paid? We have two unknowns, E and V:

Old debt	$25,000	$35,000 = D
New debt	$10,000	
Equity		? = E
Firm value		? = V

If V is $75,000 as before, then E must be $V - D = 75,000 - 35,000 = \$40,000$. Stockholders have suffered a capital loss that exactly offsets the $10,000 special dividend. But if V *increases* to, say, $80,000 as a result of the change in capital structure, then $E = \$45,000$ and the stockholders are $5,000 ahead. In general, because the new debtholders can demand only a fair rate of return, any increase or decrease in V caused by a shift in capital structure accrues to the firm's stockholders. We conclude that *the policy that maximizes the market value of the firm is also best for the firm's stockholders.*

16.1 Self-Test

Ventone invests in a new project with an NPV of $5 million. It partly finances the venture by borrowing $3 million. The remaining investment of $10 million is financed out of retained earnings. Does the value of the equity increase by $5 million, or by less? Do the new debtholders get a share of the NPV?

This conclusion rests on two important assumptions: First, that Wapshot's shareholders do not gain or lose from payout policy and, second, that after the change in capital structure the old and new debt are together *worth* $35,000.

Payout policy may or may not be relevant, but there is no need to repeat the discussion of Chapter 15. We need only note that shifts in capital structure sometimes force important decisions about payout policy. Perhaps Wapshot's cash dividend has costs or benefits that should be considered in addition to the benefits, if any, achieved by its increased financial leverage.

Our second assumption that old plus new debt ends up worth $35,000 seems unimportant. But it could be wrong. Perhaps the new borrowing has increased the risk of the old bonds. If the holders of old bonds cannot demand a higher rate of interest to compensate for the increased risk, the value of their investment is reduced. In this case, Wapshot's stockholders gain at the expense of the holders of old bonds, even though the overall value of the firm is unchanged.

But this anticipates issues better left to Chapter 17. In this chapter, we assume that any new issue of debt has no effect on the market value of existing debt.

16-2   Modigliani and Miller's Proposition 1

Let us accept that the financial manager would like to find the capital structure that maximizes the value of the firm. How is this done? MM's answer is that the financial manager should stop worrying: In a perfect market, any financing package is as good as another. The value of the firm is unaffected by its choice of capital structure.[1] That is not such an odd statement as it may initially sound. In Chapter 12, we pointed out that when newly issued securities are fairly priced, the issue has zero NPV. In that case, you would not expect a financial manager to be able to add value by substituting one zero-NPV security for another. For example, suppose that a company changes its capital structure by issuing bonds. The investors who buy those bonds must have calculated that they offered fair value and therefore had a zero NPV. Issuing a bond at zero NPV cannot enhance the company's value.

We need to look more closely at why this is the case. Imagine two firms that generate the same stream of operating profits and differ only in their capital structure. Firm U is unlevered. Therefore, the total value of its equity E_U is the same as the total value of the firm V_U: $E_U = V_U$. Firm L, on the other hand, is levered. The value of its equity is, therefore, equal to the value of the firm less the value of the debt: $E_L = V_L - D_L$.

Now think which of these firms you would prefer to invest in. If you don't want to take much risk, you can buy common stock in the unlevered firm U. For example, if you buy 1% of firm U's shares, your investment is $0.01\ V_U$ and you are entitled to 1% of the operating profits:

Dollar Investment	Dollar Return
$0.01\ V_U$	$0.01 \times$ Profits

Now compare this with an alternative strategy. This is to purchase the same fraction of *both* the debt and the equity of firm L. Your investment and return are then:

	Dollar Investment	Dollar Return
Debt	$0.01\ D_L$	$0.01 \times$ Interest
Equity	$0.01\ E_L$	$0.01 \times$ (Profit – Interest)
Total	$0.01(D_L + E_L)$	$0.01 \times$ Profits
	$= 0.01\ V_L$	

Both strategies offer the same payoff: 1% of the firm's profits. The law of one price tells us that in well-functioning markets two investments that offer the same payoff must have the

[1]F. Modigliani and M. H. Miller, "The Cost of Capital, Corporation Finance and the Theory of Investment," *American Economic Review* 48 (June 1958), pp. 261–297. MM's basic argument was anticipated in 1938 by J. B. Williams and to some extent by David Durand. See J. B. Williams, *The Theory of Investment Value* (Cambridge, MA: Harvard University Press, 1938); and D. Durand, "Cost of Debt and Equity Funds for Business: Trends and Problems of Measurement," *Conference on Research in Business Finance* (New York: National Bureau of Economic Research, 1952, pp. 215–262).

same price. Therefore, $0.01\ V_U$ must equal $0.01\ V_L$: The value of the unlevered firm must equal the value of the levered firm.

Suppose that you are willing to run a little more risk. You decide to buy 1% of the outstanding shares in the *levered* firm. Your investment and return are now:

Dollar Investment	Dollar Return
$0.01\ E_L$ $= 0.01(V_L - D_L)$	$0.01 \times (\text{Profit} - \text{Interest})$

Again, there is an alternative strategy. This is to borrow $0.01\ D_L$ on your own account and purchase 1% of the stock of the unlevered firm.[2] In this case, your strategy gives you 1% of the profits from V_U, but you have to pay interest on your loan equal to 1% of the interest that is paid by firm L. Your total investment and net return are:

	Dollar Investment	Dollar Return
Borrowing	$-0.01\ D_L$	$-0.01 \times \text{Interest}$
Equity	$0.01\ V_U$	$0.01 \times \text{Profits}$
Total	$0.01(V_U - D_L)$	$0.01 \times (\text{Profits} - \text{Interest})$

Once more, both strategies offer the same payoff: 1% of profits after interest. Therefore, both investments must have the same cost. The investment $0.01(V_U - D_L)$ must equal $0.01(V_L - D_L)$ and V_U must equal V_L.

This picture of individual investors borrowing money to buy shares in firm U may seem unrealistic. If so, think instead of a large institutional investor—for example, a pension fund. Such a fund rarely borrows money. It is a lender because it invests in bonds as well as stocks. Suppose the fund wants to buy 1% of the stock of firm U, but "lever up" so that its investment outlay equals only the cost of buying 1% of the stock of firm L. Instead of borrowing, it sells bonds equal to 1% of the debt of firm L and uses the proceeds of the sale to pay for part of its investment in U's equity. By doing so, it loses bond interest equal to what it would pay to borrow 1% of D_L. The result is:

	Dollar Investment	Dollar Return
Sale of bonds	$-0.01\ D_L$	$-0.01 \times \text{Interest foregone}$
Equity	$0.01\ V_U$	$0.01 \times \text{Profits}$
Total	$0.01(V_U - D_L)$	$0.01 \times (\text{Profits} - \text{Interest})$

Again we have the MM result. The payoffs from buying firm U's stock, partly financed by selling some bonds, are the same as the payoffs from buying L's stock (and also the same as buying U's stock with borrowed money). U and L must therefore be worth the same overall.

As long as investors can borrow or lend on the same terms as the firm, they can "undo" the effect of any changes in the firm's capital structure. This is how MM arrived at their famous Proposition 1: *The market value of any firm is independent of its capital structure.*

The Law of the Conservation of Value

MM's argument that debt policy is irrelevant is an application of an astonishingly simple idea. If we have two streams of cash flow, A and B, then the present value of $A + B$ is equal to the

---

[2]Rather than borrow on your own account, you might be able to lend $0.01\ D_L$ less than you commonly do. The effect is the same.

present value of *A* plus the present value of *B*. That's common sense: If you have a dollar in your left pocket and a dollar in your right, your total wealth is $2. We met this principle of *value additivity* in our discussion of capital budgeting, where we saw that the present value of two assets combined is equal to the sum of their present values considered separately.

In the present context, we are not combining assets but splitting them up. But value additivity works just as well in reverse. We can slice a cash flow into as many parts as we like; the values of the parts will always sum back to the value of the unsliced stream. (Of course, we have to make sure that none of the stream is lost in the slicing. We cannot say, "The value of a pie is independent of how it is sliced," if the slicer is also a nibbler.)

This is really a *law of the conservation of value*. The value of an asset is preserved regardless of the nature of the claims against it. Thus, Proposition 1: Firm value is determined on the *left-hand* side of the balance sheet by real assets—not by the proportions of debt and equity securities issued to buy the assets.

The simplest ideas often have the widest application. For example, we could apply the law of the conservation of value to the choice between raising $100 million by issuing preferred stock, common stock, or some combination. The law implies that the choice is irrelevant, assuming perfect capital markets and providing that the choice does not affect the firm's investment and operating policies. If the total value of the equity "pie" (preferred and common combined) is fixed, the firm's owners (its common stockholders) do not care how this equity pie is sliced.

The law also applies to the mix of debt securities issued by the firm. The choices of long-term versus short-term, secured versus unsecured, senior versus subordinated, and convertible versus nonconvertible debt all should have no effect on the overall value of the firm.

Combining assets and splitting them up will not affect values as long as they do not affect investors' choices. When we showed that capital structure does not affect choice, we implicitly assumed that both companies and investors can borrow and lend at the same risk-free rate of interest. As long as this is so, investors can undo the effect of any changes in the firm's capital structure.

16.2 Self-Test

Endo Horrocks has operating income of $12.5 million. It is financed solely by equity that has a market value of $100 million. Suppose that the company now issues $50 million of debt at an interest rate of 10% and uses the cash to pay a special dividend to stockholders. The pie chart below show the operating income and the company value before the debt issue. Draw two similar pies to show how MM would predict the income and company value to be divided after the debt issue.

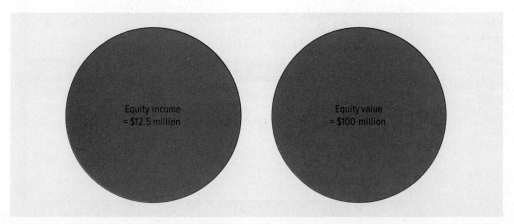

》TABLE 16.1 Macbeth Spot Removers is entirely equity financed. Although it expects to have an income of $1,500 a year in perpetuity, this income is not certain. This table shows the return to the shareholder under different assumptions about operating income. We assume no taxes.

Macbeth Spot Removers				
Number of shares	1,000			
Price per share	$ 10			
Market value of shares	$10,000			
	Outcomes			
Operating income ($)	500	1,000	**1,500**	2,000
Earnings per share ($)	0.50	1.00	**1.50**	2.00
Return on shares (%)	5	10	**15**	20
			Expected outcome	

An Example of Proposition 1

Macbeth Spot Removers is reviewing its capital structure. Table 16.1 shows its current position. The company has no leverage, and all the operating income is paid as dividends to the common stockholders (we assume still that there are no taxes). The expected earnings and dividends per share are $1.50, but this figure is by no means certain—it could turn out to be more or less than $1.50. The price of each share is $10. Because the firm expects to produce a level stream of earnings in perpetuity, the expected return on the share is equal to the earnings-price ratio, $1.50/10.00 = 0.15$, or 15%.

Ms. Macbeth, the firm's president, has concluded that shareholders would be better off if the company had equal proportions of debt and equity. She therefore proposes to issue $5,000 of debt at an interest rate of 10% and to use the proceeds to repurchase 500 shares. To support her proposal, Ms. Macbeth has analyzed the situation under different assumptions about operating income. The results of her calculations are shown in Table 16.2.

》TABLE 16.2 Macbeth Spot Removers is wondering whether to issue $5,000 of debt at an interest rate of 10% and repurchase 500 shares. This table shows the return to the shareholder under different assumptions about operating income.

Possible Payoffs to Equity				
Number of shares	500			
Price per share	$ 10			
Market value of shares	$5,000			
Market value of debt	$5,000			
Interest at 10%	$ 500			
	Outcomes			
Operating income ($)	500	1,000	1,500	2,000
Interest ($)	500	500	500	500
Equity earnings ($)	0	500	1,000	1,500
Earnings per share ($)	0	1.00	2.00	3.00
Return on shares (%)	0	10	20	30
			Expected outcome	

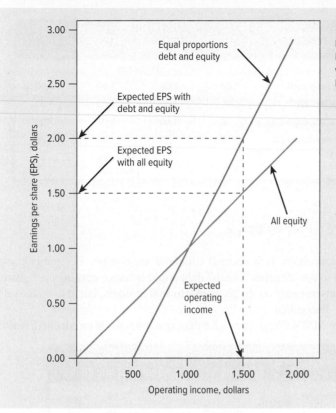

FIGURE 16.1   Borrowing increases Macbeth's EPS (earnings per share) when operating income is greater than $1,000 and reduces EPS when operating income is less than $1,000. Expected EPS rises from $1.50 to $2.

To illustrate how leverage would affect earnings per share, Ms. Macbeth has also produced Figure 16.1. The brown line shows how earnings per share would vary with operating income under the firm's current all-equity financing. It is, therefore, simply a plot of the data for the four outcomes of operating income and earnings per share in Table 16.1. The green line shows how earnings per share would vary with operating income given equal proportions of debt and equity. It is, therefore, a plot of the data in Table 16.2.

Ms. Macbeth reasons as follows: "It is clear that the effect of leverage depends on the company's income. If income is greater than $1,000, the return to the shareholder is *increased* by leverage. If it is less than $1,000, the return is *reduced* by leverage. The return is unaffected when operating income is exactly $1,000. At this point the return on the market value of the assets is 10%, which is exactly equal to the interest rate on the debt. Our capital structure decision, therefore, boils down to what we think about the company's prospects. Since we expect operating income to be above the $1,000 break-even point, I believe we can best help our shareholders by going ahead with the $5,000 debt issue."

As financial manager of Macbeth Spot Removers, you reply: "Your argument ignores the fact that investors could borrow on their own account. For example, suppose that an investor puts up $10 of his own money, borrows a further $10, and then invests the total in two unlevered Macbeth shares. This is exactly the same set of payoffs as the investor would get by buying one share in the levered company. [Compare the last two lines of Tables 16.2 and 16.3.] Therefore, a share in the levered company must also sell for $10. If Macbeth goes ahead and borrows, it will not allow investors to do anything that they could not do already, and so it will not increase value."

The argument that you are using is exactly the same as the one MM used to prove Proposition 1.

)TABLE 16.3   Any investor can
replicate Macbeth's leverage.

Payoffs from borrowing to buy Macbeth shares				
		Outcomes		
Earnings on two shares($)	1.00	2.00	3.00	4.00
Less interest at 10% ($)	1.00	1.00	1.00	1.00
Net earnings on investment ($)	0	1.00	2.00	3.00
Return on $10 investment (%)	0	10	20	30
			Expected outcome	

16-3   Leverage and Expected Returns: MM's Proposition 2

When MM first proposed Proposition 1, it seemed a radical suggestion. Economists and financial managers were used to the idea that "cheap" debt could enhance earnings per share. But the *value* of a share depends not only on the payments to shareholders, but also on the rate at which those cash flows are discounted.

Consider the implications of MM's Proposition 1 for the expected returns on Macbeth stock:

	Current Structure: All Equity	Proposed Structure: Equal Debt and Equity
Expected earnings per share ($)	1.50	2.00
Price per share ($)	10	10
Expected return on share (%)	15	20

Leverage increases the expected stream of earnings per share but *not* the share price. The reason is that the change in the expected earnings stream is exactly offset by a change in the rate at which the earnings are discounted. The expected return on the share (which for a perpetuity is equal to the earnings–price ratio) increases from 15% to 20%. We now show how this comes about.

The expected return on Macbeth's assets r_A is equal to the expected operating income calculated before interest expense, divided by the total market value of the firm's securities:

$$\text{Expected return on assets} = r_A = \frac{\text{expected operating income}}{\text{market value of all securities}}$$

We have seen that in perfect capital markets the company's borrowing decision does not affect *either* the firm's operating income *or* the total market value of its securities. Therefore, the borrowing decision also does not affect the expected return on the firm's assets r_A.

Suppose that an investor holds all of a company's debt and all of its equity. This investor is entitled to all the firm's operating income; therefore, the expected return on the portfolio is just r_A.

The expected return on a portfolio is equal to a weighted average of the expected returns on the individual holdings. Therefore, the expected return on a portfolio consisting of *all* the firm's securities is

$$\text{Expected return on assets} = \frac{\text{(proportion in debt} \times \text{expected return on debt)}}{\text{+ (proportion in equity} \times \text{expected return on equity)}}$$

$$r_A = \left(\frac{D}{D + E} \times r_D\right) + \left(\frac{E}{D + E} \times r_E\right) \tag{16.1}$$

This formula is, of course, an old friend from Chapter 9. The expected returns on debt and equity are called the *cost of debt* and the *cost of equity*. The overall expected return r_A is called the *company cost of capital*. MM's Proposition 1 says that r_A does not depend on capital structure. In this case, the company cost of capital is equal to the opportunity cost of capital—that is, the cost of capital with all-equity financing.

We can turn the formula for r_A around to solve for r_E, which is the expected return to equity:

Expected return on equity = expected return on assets

+ (expected return on assets − expected return on debt)

× debt-equity ratio

$$r_E = r_A + (r_A - r_D)\frac{D}{E} \tag{16.2}$$

Proposition 2

This is MM's Proposition 2: The expected rate of return on the common stock of a levered firm increases in proportion to the debt-equity ratio (*D/E*), expressed in market values; the rate of increase depends on the spread between r_A, the expected rate of return on a portfolio of all the firm's securities, and r_D, the expected return on the debt. Note that $r_E = r_A$ if the firm has no debt.

We can check out this formula for Macbeth Spot Removers. Before the decision to borrow

$$r_E = r_A = \frac{\text{expected operating income}}{\text{market value of all securities}}$$

$$= \frac{1,500}{10,000} = 0.15, \text{ or } 15\%$$

If the firm goes ahead with its plan to borrow at $r_D = 10\%$, the expected return on assets r_A is still 15%, but the expected return on equity is

$$r_E = r_A + (r_A - r_D)\frac{D}{E}$$

$$= 0.15 + (0.15 - 0.10)\frac{5,000}{5,000} = 0.20, \text{ or } 20\%$$

When the firm was unlevered, equity investors demanded a return of r_A. When the firm is levered, they require a premium of $(r_A - r_D)D/E$ to compensate for the extra risk.

MM's Proposition 1 says that financial leverage has no effect on shareholders' wealth. Proposition 2 says that the rate of return they can expect to receive on their shares increases as the firm's debt-equity ratio increases. How can shareholders be indifferent to increased leverage when it increases their expected return? The answer is that any increase in expected return is exactly offset by an increase in financial risk and therefore in shareholders' *required* rate of return.

You can see financial risk at work in our Macbeth example. Compare the risk of earnings per share in Table 16.2 versus Table 16.1. Or look at Table 16.4, which shows how a shortfall in operating income affects the payoff to the shareholders. If the firm is all-equity-financed, a decline of $1,000 in the operating income reduces the return on the shares by 10 percentage points. If the firm issues risk-free debt with a fixed interest payment of $500 a year, then a decline of $1,000 in the operating income reduces the return on the shares by 20 percentage points. In other words, the effect of the proposed leverage is to double the amplitude of the swings in Macbeth's shares. Whatever the risk of the firm's shares before the refinancing, it would be twice as high afterward.

> **TABLE 16.4**   Financial leverage increases the risk of Macbeth shares. A $1,000 drop in operating income reduces earnings per share by $1 with all-equity financing, but by $2 with 50% debt.

If Operating Income Falls From	$1,500	to	$500	Change
No debt: Earnings per share	$1.50		$.50	−$1.00
Return (r_E)	15%		5%	−10%
50% debt: Earnings per share	$2.00		0	−$2.00
Return (r_E)	20%		0	−20%

Now you can see why investors require higher returns on levered equity. The required return simply rises to match the increased financial risk.

Leverage and the Cost of Equity

Consider a company with the following market-value balance sheet:

Asset value	$100	Debt (D)	$33.3	at $r_D = 7.25\%$
		Equity (E)	$66.7	at $r_E = 15.5\%$
Asset value	$100	Firm value (V)	$100	

and an overall company cost of capital of

$$r_A = r_D\, D/V + r_E\, E/V$$
$$= (7.25 \times 33.3/100) + (15.5 \times 66.7/100) = 12.75\%$$

If the firm is considering a project that has the same risk as the firm's existing business, the appropriate discount rate for the cash flows is 12.75%, the firm's cost of capital.

Suppose the firm changes its capital structure by issuing more debt and using the proceeds to repurchase stock. The implications of MM's Proposition 2 are shown in Figure 16.2. The required return on equity increases with the debt-equity ratio (D/E).[3] Yet, no matter how much the firm borrows, the required return on the package of debt and equity, r_A, remains constant at 12.75%. How is it possible for the required return on the package to stay constant when the required return on the individual securities is changing? Answer: Because the proportions of debt and equity in the package are also changing. More debt means that the cost of equity increases but at the same time the *proportion* of equity declines.

In Figure 16.2, we have drawn the rate of interest on the debt as constant no matter how much the firm borrows. This is not wholly realistic. It is true that most large, conservative companies could borrow a little more or less without noticeably affecting the interest rate that they pay. But at higher debt levels, lenders become concerned that they may not get their money back, and they demand higher rates of interest to compensate. Figure 16.3 modifies Figure 16.2 to account for this. You can see that as the firm borrows more, the risk of the debt slowly increases. Proposition 2 continues to predict that the expected return on the package of debt and equity does not change. However, the slope of the r_E line now tapers off as D/E increases. Why? Essentially because holders of risky debt begin to bear part of the firm's operating risk. As the firm borrows more, more of that risk is transferred from stockholders to bondholders.

---

[3]Note that the firm's debt ratio (D/V) of 0.333 corresponds to a debt-equity ratio (D/E) of 0.333/0.667 = 0.5. Figure 16.2 shows that the required return on equity is 15.5% when the debt-equity ratio = 0.5.

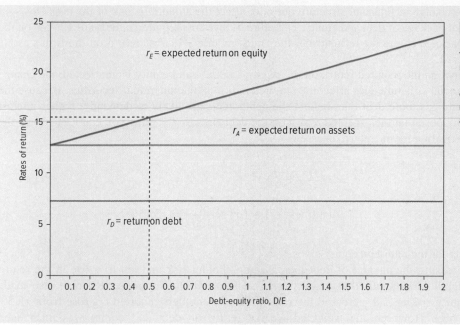

FIGURE 16.2
MM's Proposition 2 predicts that if debt is risk-free, the required return on equity, r_E, increases linearly with the debt-equity ratio, but the return on the package of debt and equity does not change.

Let's assume that the firm issues an additional $16.7 of debt and uses the cash to repurchase $16.7 of its equity. The revised market-value balance sheet has debt of $50 rather than $33.3:

Asset value	$100	Debt (*D*)	$50
		Equity (*E*)	$50
Asset value	$100	Firm value (*V*)	$100

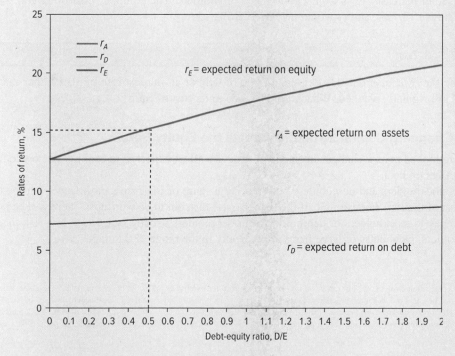

FIGURE 16.3
If leverage increases, the risk of the debt increases and debtholders demand a higher interest rate. As lenders take on the extra risk, the expected return on equity increases more slowly. MM's Proposition 2 continues to predict that the expected return on the package of debt and equity is unchanged.

The change in financial structure does not affect the amount or risk of the cash flows on the total package of debt and equity. Therefore, if investors required a return of 12.75% on the total package before the refinancing, they must require a 12.75% return on the firm's assets afterward.

Although the required return on the *package* of debt and equity is unaffected, the change in financial structure does affect the required return on the individual securities. Because the company has more debt than before, the debtholders are likely to demand a higher interest rate. Suppose that the expected return on the debt rises to 8%. Now you can write down the basic equation for the return on assets:

$$r_A = r_D \frac{D}{V} + r_E \frac{E}{V}$$

$$= \left(8.0 \times \frac{50}{100}\right) + \left(r_E \times \frac{50}{100}\right) = 12.75\%$$

Solving for the return on equity gives $r_E = 17.5\%$.

Increasing the amount of debt increased debtholder risk and led to a rise in the return that debtholders required (r_D rose from 7.25% to 8.0%). The higher leverage also made the equity riskier and increased the return that shareholders required (r_E rose from 15.5% to 17.5%). However, the weighted-average return on debt and equity was unchanged at 12.75%:

$$r_A = r_D \frac{D}{V} + r_E \frac{E}{V}$$

$$= \left(8.0 \times \frac{50}{100}\right) + \left(17.5 \times \frac{50}{100}\right) = 12.75\%$$

Suppose that the company decided instead to repay all its debt and replace it with equity. In that case, all the cash flows would go to the equityholders. The company cost of capital, r_A, would stay at 12.75%, and r_E would also be 12.75%.

16.3 Self-Test

Suppose that Macbeth decides to issue $4,000 of debt at an interest rate of 10% rather than $5,000 as originally planned. What would happen to its cost of equity?

How Changing Capital Structure Affects the Equity Beta

We have looked at how changes in financial structure affect expected return. Let us now look at the effect on beta.

The stockholders and debtholders both receive a share of the firm's cash flows, and both bear part of the risk. For example, if the firm's assets turn out to be worthless, there will be no cash to pay to stockholders or debtholders. But debtholders usually bear much less risk than stockholders. Debt betas of large firms are typically in the range of 0 to 0.2.[4]

---

[4]Debt betas are often close to zero but can move into positive territory for two reasons. First, if the risk of default increases, more of the firm's business risk is shifted to lenders. Thus, "junk" debt issues typically have positive betas. Second, changes in interest rates can affect both stock and bond prices, creating a positive correlation between returns on bonds and returns on the stock market. This second reason is most important when long-term interest rates are unusually volatile, as in the United States in the 1970s and early 1980s.

If you owned a portfolio of all the firm's securities, you wouldn't share the cash flows with anyone. You wouldn't share the risks with anyone either; you would bear them all. The beta of this hypothetical portfolio is just a weighted average of the debt and equity betas:

$$\beta_A = \beta_{\text{portfolio}} = \beta_D \frac{D}{V} + \beta_E \frac{E}{V} \qquad \text{(16.3)}$$

Think back to our example. If the debt before the refinancing has a beta of .1 and the equity has a beta of 1.1, then

$$\beta_A = \left(0.1 \times \frac{33.3}{100}\right) + \left(1.1 \times \frac{66.7}{100}\right) = 0.767$$

What happens after the refinancing? The risk of the total package is unaffected, but both the debt and the equity are now more risky. Suppose that the debt beta changes to 0.15. We can work out the new equity beta:

$$\beta_A = \beta_{\text{portfolio}} = \beta_D \frac{D}{V} + \beta_E \frac{E}{V}$$

$$0.767 = \left(0.15 \times \frac{50}{100}\right) + \left(\beta_E \times \frac{50}{100}\right)$$

Solve for the formula for β_E. You will see that it parallels MM's Proposition 2 exactly:

$$\beta_E = \beta_A + (\beta_A - \beta_D)D/E$$
$$= 0.767 + (0.767 - 0.15)(50/50) = 1.384 \qquad \text{(16.4)}$$

Our example shows how borrowing creates financial leverage or gearing. Financial leverage does not affect the risk or the expected return on the firm's assets, but it does push up the risk of the common stock. Shareholders demand a correspondingly higher return because of this *financial risk*.

You can use our formulas to *unlever* betas—that is, to go from an observed β_E to β_A. You have the equity beta of 1.384. You also need the debt beta, here 0.15, and the relative market values of debt (D/V) and equity (E/V). If debt accounts for 50% of overall value V, then the unlevered beta is

$$\beta_A = \left(0.15 \times \frac{50}{100}\right) + \left(1.384 \times \frac{50}{100}\right) = 0.767$$

This runs the previous example in reverse. Just remember the basic relationship:

$$\beta_A = \beta_{\text{portfolio}} = \beta_D \frac{D}{V} + \beta_E \frac{E}{V}$$

16.4 Self-Test

Suppose that before the financing Macbeth's stock has a beta of 0.9. Macbeth now issues $5,000 of debt with a beta of zero. What happens to
   a. The beta of Macbeth's assets?
   b. The beta of its equity?

Watch Out for Hidden Leverage

MM did not say that borrowing is a bad thing. But they insisted that financial managers stay on the lookout for the financial risk created by borrowing. That risk can be especially dangerous when the borrowing is not in plain sight. For example, most long-term leases are debt-equivalent obligations, so leases can hide debt. Long-term contracts with suppliers can also be debts in disguise when prices and quantities are fixed. For many firms pension liabilities and liabilities for employees' post-retirement health care are massive off-balance-sheet, debt-equivalent obligations.

EXAMPLE 16.1 ● Reeby Sports' bocce project

Here is an example of how hidden leverage can fool a company into poor decisions. Reeby Sports is considering launch of a carbon-fiber bocce shoe. The product will require investment of $500,000 in up-front marketing expenses and $500,000 for new equipment. Jorge Reeby prepares a simple spreadsheet for the new product's expected five-year life and discounts at Reeby Sports' normal 10% cost of capital.[5]

Bocce Shoe Proposal						
	Cash Flow ($1,000s)					
	0	**1**	**2**	**3**	**4**	**5**
Marketing	−500	+260	+260	+260	+260	+260
Equipment	−500					
Total	−1,000					
NPV at 10% = −14, or −$14,000						
IRR = 9.4%						

Jorge notes the negative NPV, then calls the equipment salesperson to cancel Reeby Sports' order. The salesperson, anxious to keep her sale, offers to let Reeby Sports buy the equipment now and pay later. She asks whether Jorge will commit to five fixed payments of $122,000 per year. She argues that this will reduce the up-front investment and improve profitability. Jorge revises his spreadsheet:

Bocce Shoe Proposal (Revised)						
	Cash Flow ($1,000s) **(Fixed payments of $122,000 per year subtracted)**					
	0	**1**	**2**	**3**	**4**	**5**
Marketing	−500	+260	+260	+260	+260	+260
Equipment	0	−122	−122	−122	−122	−122
Total	−500	+138	+138	+138	+138	+138
NPV at 10% = +23, or $23,000						
IRR = 11.8%						

---

[5]Reeby Sports has massive tax losses carried forward from the disastrous recession of 2025. Therefore, Jorge's cash-flow projections assume no taxes and ignore depreciation tax shields.

Now Jorge is inclined to go ahead—the NPV and IRR look much better—but Jenny, his investment-banker daughter, points out that the manufacturer is really just lending $500,000 to Reeby Sports at the same 7% interest rate that Reeby Sports would pay to a bank. She explains that the manufacturer would advance $500,000 now in exchange for later fixed payments totaling $5 \times 122,000 = \$610,000$ undiscounted. The payments are obligatory, just like debt service on a bank loan. The effective interest rate is 7%. (You can check that the IRR to the manufacturer from agreeing to payment by installments is 7%.)

Jenny chides her father for mixing up investment and financing decisions. She upbraids him for forgetting about the financial risk created by a debt-financed equipment purchase. She berates him for discounting the cash flows of $138,000 per year (after installment payments) at the 10% cost of capital, which is designed to value *unlevered* cash flows. "Go back to your first spreadsheet, Dad," she instructs.[6] Jorge, fearing chastisement, reproach, and remonstration, agrees.

The hidden leverage in this example is, of course, only thinly disguised. The leverage would be harder to see if, for example, it were wrapped up in a financial lease transaction. See Chapter 26 and the mini-case at the end of this chapter.

• • • • •

16-4   No Magic in Financial Leverage

MM's propositions boil down to the simple warning: *There is no magic in financial leverage.* Financial managers who ignore this warning can be sucked into practical mistakes. For example, suppose that someone says, "Shareholders demand—and deserve—higher expected rates of return than bondholders. Therefore, debt is the cheaper source of capital. We can reduce the company cost of capital by borrowing more." Unfortunately, that doesn't follow if the extra borrowing leads shareholders to demand a still higher expected rate of return. According to MM's Proposition 2, the cost of equity capital, r_E, increases by just enough to keep the company cost of capital constant. Thus, there are actually two costs of debt. One is the interest rate that lenders require; the other is the higher return that equityholders demand to compensate them for the extra risk resulting from leverage. Mistakes arise when you ignore this second cost.

This is not the only logical short circuit that you are likely to encounter. We have cited two others in Problem 10 at the end of this chapter.

Few financial managers believe that the company cost of capital can be reduced by higher and higher leverage. But is it possible to stake out an intermediate position, in which a moderate degree of leverage increases the expected equity return, r_E, but by less than predicted by MM's Proposition 2? In this case, there would be an optimal amount of leverage that minimizes the weighted average cost of capital.

Two arguments could be advanced in support of this position. First, perhaps shareholders do not notice or appreciate the financial risk created by moderate borrowing, although they wake up when debt is "excessive." If so, shareholders in moderately leveraged firms may accept a lower rate of return than they really should.

---

[6]Jorge might try discounting the cash flows in his second spreadsheet at a cost of *equity.* We discuss the "flow to equity" valuation method in Chapter 18. This method mixes investment and financing decisions, however, and is rarely used to value individual projects. Jorge is well-advised to calculate NPV from his first spreadsheet and *then* ask whether the installment sale adds value, compared with other sources of financing.

Does MM Apply to Banks?

❯ Healthy industrial corporations typically operate with debt ratios of around 35%. Most financial managers would not be too concerned if the ratio was a few percentage points higher or lower and would probably find it difficult to put a precise figure on the optimal debt ratio. As we pointed out in Chapter 1, shareholder value is largely created by the company's choice of real assets, not by its financial structure.

This is not so for bankers. Banks operate with very high debt ratios. For example, just before the 2007–2009 financial crisis, many major banks had book debt-to-asset ratios of about 97% to 98%. So, it needed only a 2% to 3% fall in the value of their assets to wipe out the total value of the equity. With this sort of leverage, it is not surprising that banks often get into difficulties. This does not mean that banks could, or should, operate with the levels of debt that are typical in industrial companies, because a central part of their business is the issue of debt in the form of customer deposits. However, banks could reduce leverage without needing to reduce their deposits or increase their assets.

Bank regulators meeting in Basel, Switzerland, have established limits on the amount of leverage that banks should be allowed to have. Following the crisis, these limits were revised downward in the Basel III Accord.

Several countries have imposed even lower limits on the amount of leverage that their banks can undertake.

These moves to make banks issue more equity capital have been vigorously opposed by bankers, who have argued that higher capital ratios would add considerably to their costs. One complaint is that a reduction in leverage would reduce their return on equity. This may be true, but it is beside the point. Increased capital would lower the expected return on equity, but MM would note that it would also reduce the risk of the equity and the return that shareholders require. In a perfect world, these two effects would cancel out so that lower leverage would not increase the cost of capital for banks and would not make shareholders any worse off.

Does bankers' opposition to higher capital requirements simply reflect a failure to understand MM's arguments, or are there other, more valid reasons for their views? One possibility is tax. Debt interest carries with it a tax shield, which may be important to a financial institution that operates on relatively fine margins. But that raises a further question: Does it make sense for the government to offer a subsidy that encourages banks to borrow if the effect of that borrowing is to cause periodic banking crises?[7] Would it be better for the government to offer the same tax advantage to banks if they issue extra equity?

It seems unlikely that most investors are that unsophisticated.[8] The second argument is better. It accepts MM's reasoning as applied to perfect capital markets but holds that actual markets are imperfect. Because of these imperfections, firms that borrow may provide a valuable opportunity for investors. If so, levered shares might trade at premium prices compared with their theoretical values in perfect markets.

Suppose that corporations can borrow more cheaply than investors. Then investors who want to borrow should do so indirectly by holding the stock of levered firms. They might be willing to live with expected rates of return that do not fully compensate them for the business and financial risk they bear.

Is corporate borrowing really cheaper? It's hard to say. Interest rates on home mortgages are not too different from rates on high-grade corporate bonds.[9] Rates on margin debt

---

[7]For a discussion of these issues by four proponents of higher bank capital requirements, see A. R. Admati, P. M. DeMarzo, M. F. Hellwig, and P. Pfleiderer, "Fallacies and Irrelevant Facts in the Debate on Capital Regulation" in C. Goodhart, D. Gabor, J. Vestergaard and I. Erturk, eds., *Central Banks at a Crossroads: Europe and Beyond* (London: Anthem Press, 2014).

[8]This first argument may reflect a confusion between financial risk and the risk of default. Default is not a serious threat when borrowing is moderate; stockholders worry about it only when the firm goes "too far." But as our Macbeth example in Section 16-2 illustrated, stockholders bear financial risk—in the form of increased volatility of rates of return and a higher beta—even when the chance of default is nil.

[9]One of the authors once obtained a home mortgage at a rate 1/2 percentage point *less* than the contemporaneous yield on long-term AAA bonds.

(borrowing from a stockbroker with the investor's shares tendered as security) are not too different from the rates firms pay banks for short-term loans. And any investor, individual or institutional, who holds bonds can "lever up" by selling bonds and investing the proceeds in stocks. Suppose the bonds are corporate bonds. Then the rate of interest foregone on the bonds that are sold is identical to the interest rate that corporations pay on their outstanding debt.

There could nevertheless be a clientele of individual investors who would prefer corporations to borrow on their behalf. Perhaps the investors want to retain *limited liability,* which means that they are not personally liable for a corporation's debts if it defaults. Such investors might be willing to pay a premium for levered shares *if the supply of levered shares were insufficient to meet their demands.* But all public corporations provide limited liability and most borrow. Therefore it is unlikely that financing more with debt and less with equity would induce these individual investors to pay more for *your* company.

Maybe the market for corporate leverage is like the market for automobiles. Americans need millions of automobiles and are willing to pay thousands of dollars apiece for them. But that doesn't mean that you could strike it rich by going into the automobile business. You're at least 100 years too late.

Today's Unsatisfied Clienteles Are Probably Interested in Financial Innovation

So far, we have made little progress in identifying cases where firm value might plausibly depend on financing. But our examples illustrate what smart financial managers look for. They look for an *unsatisfied* clientele, investors who want a particular kind of financial instrument but because of market imperfections can't get it or can't get it cheaply.

MM's Proposition 1 does not hold when the firm, by imaginative design of its capital structure, can offer some *financial service* that meets the needs of such a clientele. Either the service must be new and unique or the firm must find a way to provide some old service more cheaply than other firms or financial intermediaries can. In these cases, the basic requirement of Proposition 1 that investors can borrow and lend on the same terms as the firm is not satisfied and so the result does not hold.

Now, is there an unsatisfied clientele for garden-variety debt or levered equity? We doubt it. But perhaps you can invent a new security and uncover a latent demand for it.

Imperfections and Opportunities

The most serious capital market imperfections are often those created by government. An imperfection that supports a violation of MM's Proposition 1 *also* creates a money-making opportunity. Firms and intermediaries will find some way to reach the clientele of investors frustrated by the imperfection.

For many years, the U.S. government imposed a limit on the rate of interest that could be paid on savings accounts. It did so to protect banks and savings institutions by limiting competition for their depositors' money. The fear was that depositors would run off in search of higher yields, causing a cash drain that savings institutions would not be able to meet. But interest-rate regulation provided financial institutions with an opportunity to create value by offering money market funds. These are mutual funds that invest in Treasury bills, commercial paper, and other high-grade, short-term debt instruments. Any saver with a few thousand dollars to invest can gain access to these instruments through a money market fund and can withdraw money at any time by writing a check against his or her fund balance. Thus, the fund resembles a checking or savings account that pays close to market

BEYOND THE PAGE

Bank
regulation
and CDOs

mhhe.com/brealey14e

interest rates.[10] These money market funds became enormously popular. At the peak of their popularity in 2008, they managed $3.3 trillion of assets.

Long before all interest-rate ceilings were finally removed in 1986, most of the gains had gone out of issuing money-market funds to individual investors because the supply of them had increased to meet the demand. Once the clientele was finally satisfied, MM's Proposition 1 was restored (until the government creates a new imperfection). The moral of the story is this: If you ever find an unsatisfied clientele, do something right away, or capital markets will evolve and steal it from you.

This is actually an encouraging message for the economy as a whole. If MM are right, investors' demands for different types of securities are satisfied at minimal cost. The cost of capital will reflect only business risk. Capital will flow to companies with positive-NPV investments, regardless of the companies' capital structures. This is the efficient outcome.

16-5 A Final Word on the Cost of Capital

MM left us a simple message. When the firm changes its mix of debt and equity securities, the risk and expected returns of these securities change, but the company's overall cost of capital does not change.

Now if you think that message is too neat and simple, you're right. The complications are spelled out in the next two chapters. But we must note one complication here: In the United States and most other countries, interest paid on a firm's borrowing can be deducted from taxable income. Thus, the *after-tax* cost of debt is $r_D(1 - T_c)$, where T_c is the marginal corporate tax rate. So, when companies discount an average-risk project, they may not use the company cost of capital as we have just computed it. Instead they use the after-tax cost of debt to compute the **after-tax weighted-average cost of capital** or **WACC:**

$$\text{After-tax WACC} = r_D(1 - T_c)\frac{D}{V} + r_E\frac{E}{V}$$

The company cost of capital that we calculated in Section 16-3 is the expected return on the company's assets (r_A). It is equal to the average of the returns to the company's debt and equity investors. Unlike the company cost of capital, the after-tax WACC does *not* equal the expected rate of return to all of the company's debt and equity investors and does not measure the opportunity cost of capital for investment in the company's assets. The after-tax WACC is lower than the opportunity cost of capital because it includes a downward tax adjustment.

EXAMPLE 16.2 • Calculating WACC for CSX

We calculated the company cost of capital for the railroad CSX in Chapter 9. The costs of debt and equity for CSX were $r_D = 3.4\%$ and $r_E = 10.3\%$. The debt-to-value ratio was 0.22. Therefore:

Company cost of capital = $r_A = r_D$ D/V + r_E E/V = 8.8%

Using the corporate tax rate of 21%, the after-tax cost of debt was $3.4 \times (1 - 0.21) = 2.7\%$, so WACC is:

$$\text{After-tax WACC} = r_D(1 - T_c)\frac{D}{V} + r_E\frac{E}{V}$$

$$= 3.4 \times (1 - 0.21) \times 0.22 + 10.3 \times 0.78 = 8.6\%$$

• • • • •

---

[10]Money market funds are not totally safe. In 2008, the Reserve Primary Fund incurred heavy losses on its holdings of Lehman Brothers debt and became only the second money market fund in history to "break the buck" by paying investors only 97 cents on the dollar. Since then, additional regulations have been introduced to prevent a repetition of this failure.

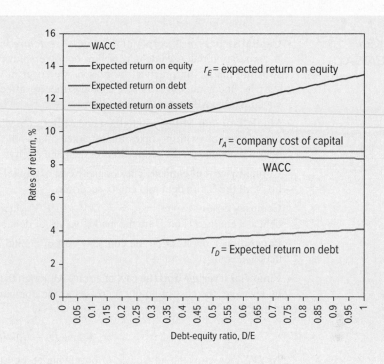

▶ **FIGURE 16.4**

Estimated after-tax WACC for CSX at different debt-equity ratios. The figure assumes r_E = 10.3% at a 22% debt ratio (equivalent to a 28% debt-equity ratio) and a borrowing rate of r_D = 3.4%. We assume that the debt interest rate is effectively constant at lower debt levels but increases at higher debt-equity ratios.

MM's Proposition 2 states that *in the absence of taxes,* the company cost of capital stays the same regardless of the amount of leverage. But if companies receive a tax shield on their interest payments, then the after-tax WACC declines as debt increases. This is illustrated in Figure 16.4, which shows how CSX's WACC changes as the debt–equity ratio changes.

We have now introduced three measures of the cost of capital:

BEYOND THE PAGE

Try It!
Figure 16.4:
Changing
leverage and
the cost of
capital

mhhe.com/brealey14e

- *The opportunity cost of capital* The opportunity cost of capital is the cost of capital for a company or a project if it is all-equity financed.

- *The company cost of capital* (r_A) The company cost of capital is the weighted average of the costs of equity and of debt. MM tell us that in perfect markets the company cost of capital is identical to the opportunity cost for investing in the company.

- *The weighted average cost of capital (WACC)* The weighted average cost of capital is the weighted average of the cost of equity and the *after-tax* cost of debt.

You now know how to *calculate* these measures. In Chapter 18, we will explain how to *use* them.

16.5 Self-Test

CSX's company cost of capital in Figure 16.4 is 8.8%. What is its opportunity cost of capital?

KEY TAKEAWAYS

- **Capital structure** A corporation's *capital structure* is its mix of debt and equity financing. A corporation that uses debt as well as equity employs *financial leverage* or *gearing*. Capital structure matters in practice, for reasons we cover in Chapters 17 and 18. But it's critical to start by understanding whether capital structure affects value in perfect financial markets, which is what MM set out to determine.

- **Modigliani and Miller** Modigliani and Miller's (MM's) Proposition 1 showed that in perfect capital markets with no taxes total market value—the value of debt and equity combined—does not depend on the proportions of debt and equity.

- **Company cost of capital** The company cost of capital, r_A, is the expected return on a portfolio of all the firm's debt and equity securities:

  Company cost of capital $= r_A = r_D\ D/V + r_E\ E/V$ where r_D and r_E are the expected returns on debt and equity, D and E are the market values of debt and equity, and $V = D + E$.

  Proposition 1 implies that the company cost of capital does not depend on the proportions of debt and equity.

- **Financial leverage and the cost of equity** Although the company cost of capital is not affected by leverage, the cost of equity increases as the company borrows more. MM's Proposition 2 states:

$$r_E = r_A + (r_A - r_D)D/E$$

  As D/E increases, the advantage of borrowing at a cost of debt less than the cost of equity is exactly offset by the increase in the cost of equity, leaving the company cost of capital constant.

- **Financial risk** The beta of the company's assets is a weighted average of the betas of the debt and the equity:

$$\beta_A = \beta_D \frac{D}{V} + \beta_E \frac{E}{V}$$

  where β_A is the beta of the firm's assets and β_D and β_E are the betas of its debt and equity. The beta of the company's assets is determined by the company's business and does not depend on the debt-equity ratio. However, the beta of the common stock does increase with the debt-equity ratio: $\beta_E = \beta_A + (\beta_A - \beta_D)D/E$

- **After-tax WACC** Do not confuse the company cost of capital with the after-tax weighted average cost of capital (WACC).

$$\text{After-tax WACC} = r_D\ (1 - T_C)D/V + r_E E/V$$

  where T_C is the corporate tax rate. The after-tax WACC declines with financial leverage because debt interest is tax-deductible. We cover WACC in detail in Chapter 18.

FURTHER READING

The fall 1988 issue of the Journal of Economic Perspectives *contains a collection of articles, including one by Modigliani and Miller, that review and assess the MM propositions. The summer 1989 issue of* Financial Management *contains three more articles under the heading "Reflections on the MM Propositions 30 Years Later."*

Two surveys of financial innovation include:

F. Allen and G. Yago, *Financing the Future: Market-Based Innovations for Growth,* Wharton School Publishing-Milken Institute Series on Financial Innovations (Upper Saddle River, NJ: Pearson Education, 2010).

P. Tufano, "Financial Innovation," in G. M. Constantinides, M. Harris, and R. Stulz, eds., *Handbook of the Economics of Finance,* vol. 1A (Amsterdam: Elsevier/North-Holland, 2003), pp. 307–335.

Miller reviews the MM propositions in:

M. H. Miller, "The Modigliani-Miller Propositions after Thirty Years," *Journal of Economic Perspectives,* 2 (Autumn 1988), pp. 99–120.

For a skeptic's view of MM's arguments see:

S. Titman, "The Modigliani and Miller Theorem and the Integration of Financial Markets," *Financial Management* 31 (Spring 2002), pp. 101–115.

 **Select problems are available in McGraw Hill's *Connect*. Please see the preface for more information.**

PROBLEM SETS

1. **Homemade leverage (S16-2)** Sentry Insurance owns 50,000 shares of the common stock of Copperhead Corporation with a market value of $20 per share, or $1 million overall. Copperhead is currently financed as follows:

Market Value	
Common stock (8 million shares)	$16 million
Short-term loans	$ 2 million

   Copperhead now announces that it is replacing $1 million of short-term debt with an issue of common stock. What action can Sentry take to ensure that it is entitled to exactly the same proportion of profits as before?

2. **Homemade leverage (S16-2)** Companies A and B differ only in their capital structure. A is financed 30% debt and 70% equity; B is financed 10% debt and 90% equity. The debt of both companies is risk-free.

   a. Rosencrantz owns 1% of the common stock of A. What other investment package would produce identical cash flows for Rosencrantz?

   b. Guildenstern owns 2% of the common stock of B. What other investment package would produce identical cash flows for Guildenstern?

   c. Show that neither Rosencrantz nor Guildenstern would invest in the common stock of B if the total value of company A were less than that of B.

3. **Corporate leverage (S16-2)** Suppose that Macbeth Spot Removers issues only $2,500 of debt and uses the proceeds to repurchase 250 shares.

   a. Rework Table 16-2 to show how earnings per share and share return now vary with operating income.

   b. If the beta of Macbeth's assets is 0.8 and its debt is risk-free, what would be the beta of the equity after the debt issue?

4. **Corporate leverage (S16-2)** Reliable Gearing currently is all-equity-financed. It has 10,000 shares of equity outstanding, selling at $100 a share. The firm is considering a capital restructuring. The low-debt plan calls for a debt issue of $200,000 with the proceeds used to buy back stock. The high-debt plan would exchange $400,000 of debt for equity. The debt will pay an interest rate of 10%. The firm pays no taxes.

   a. What will be the debt-to-equity ratio if it borrows $200,000?

   b. If earnings before interest and tax (EBIT) are $110,000, what will be earnings per share (EPS) if Reliable borrows $200,000?

   c. What will EPS be if it borrows $400,000?

5. **MM Proposition 1 (S16-2)** Executive Chalk is financed solely by common stock and has outstanding 25 million shares with a market price of $10 a share. It now announces that it intends to issue $160 million of debt and to use the proceeds to buy back common stock.

    a. How is the market price of the stock affected by the announcement?

    b. How many shares can the company buy back with the $160 million of new debt that it issues?

    c. What is the market value of the firm (equity plus debt) after the change in capital structure?

    d. What is the debt ratio after the change in structure?

    e. Who (if anyone) gains or loses? Now try the next question.

6. **MM Proposition 1 (S16-2)** Executive Cheese has issued debt with a market value of $100 million and has outstanding 15 million shares with a market price of $10 a share. It now announces that it intends to issue a further $60 million of debt and to use the proceeds to buy back common stock. Debtholders, seeing the extra risk, mark the value of the existing debt down to $70 million.

    a. How is the market price of the stock affected by the announcement?

    b. How many shares can the company buy back with the $60 million of new debt that it issues?

    c. What is the market value of the firm (equity plus debt) after the change in capital structure?

    d. What is the debt ratio after the change in structure?

    e. Who (if anyone) gains or loses?

7. **MM Proposition 1 (S16-2)** "MM totally ignore the fact that as you borrow more, you have to pay higher rates of interest." Explain carefully whether this is a valid objection.

8. **MM Proposition 1 (S16-2)** Here is a limerick:

    There once was a man named Carruthers,

    Who kept cows with miraculous udders.

    He said, "Isn't this neat? They give cream from one teat,

    And skim milk from each of the others!"

    What is the analogy between Mr. Carruthers's cows and firms' financing decisions? What would MM's Proposition 1, suitably adapted, say about the value of Mr. Carruthers's cows? Explain.

9. **MM's propositions (S16-2–S16-3)** True or false?

    a. MM's propositions assume perfect financial markets, with no distorting taxes or other imperfections.

    b. MM's Proposition 1 says that corporate borrowing increases earnings per share but reduces the price-earnings ratio.

    c. MM's Proposition 2 says that the cost of equity increases with borrowing and that the increase is proportional to D/V, the ratio of debt to firm value.

    d. MM's Proposition 2 assumes that increased borrowing does not affect the interest rate on the firm's debt.

    e. Borrowing does not increase financial risk and the cost of equity if there is no risk of bankruptcy.

    f. Borrowing always increases firm value if there is a clientele of investors with a reason to prefer debt.

10. **MM's propositions (S16-2–S16-3)** What is wrong with the following arguments?

    a. As the firm borrows more and debt becomes risky, both stock- and bondholders demand higher rates of return. Thus, by reducing the debt ratio, we can reduce both the cost of debt and the cost of equity, making everybody better off.

    b. Moderate borrowing doesn't significantly affect the probability of financial distress or bankruptcy. Consequently, moderate borrowing won't increase the expected rate of return demanded by stockholders.

c. A capital investment opportunity offering a 10% internal rate of return is an attractive project if it can be 100% debt-financed at an 8% interest rate.

d. The more debt the firm issues, the higher the interest rate it must pay. That is one important reason that firms should operate at conservative debt levels.

11. **MM Proposition 2 (S16-3)** Spam Corp. is financed entirely by common stock and has a beta of 1.0. The firm is expected to generate a level, perpetual stream of earnings and dividends. The stock has a price-earnings ratio of 8 and a cost of equity of 12.5%. The company's stock is selling for $50. Now the firm decides to repurchase half of its shares and substitute an equal value of debt. The debt is risk-free, with a 5% interest rate. The company is exempt from corporate income taxes. Assuming MM are correct, calculate the following items after the refinancing:

   a. The cost of equity.

   b. The overall cost of capital.

   c. The price-earnings ratio.

   d. The stock price.

   e. The stock's beta.

12. **MM Proposition 2 (S16-3)** "Increasing financial leverage increases both the cost of debt (r_{debt}) and the cost of equity (r_{equity}). So the overall cost of capital cannot stay constant." This problem is designed to show that the speaker is confused. Buggins Inc. is financed equally by debt and equity, each with a market value of $1 million. The cost of debt is 5%, and the cost of equity is 10%. The company now makes a further $250,000 issue of debt and uses the proceeds to repurchase equity. This causes the cost of debt to rise to 5.5% and the cost of equity to rise to 10.83%. Assume the firm pays no taxes.

   a. How much debt does the company now have?

   b. How much equity does it now have?

   c. What is the overall cost of capital?

   d. What is the percentage increase in earnings per share after the refinancing?

   e. What is the new price-earnings multiple? (*Hint:* Has anything happened to the stock price?)

13. **MM Proposition 2 (S16-3)** The common stock and debt of Northern Sludge are valued at $50 million and $30 million, respectively. Investors currently require a 16% return on the common stock and an 8% return on the debt. If Northern Sludge issues an additional $10 million of common stock and uses this money to retire debt, what happens to the expected return on the stock? Assume that the change in capital structure does not affect the risk of the debt and that there are no taxes.

14. **MM Proposition 2 (S16-3)** Look back to Section 16-2. Suppose that Ms. Macbeth's investment bankers have informed her that since the new issue of debt is risky, debtholders will demand a return of 12.5%, which is 2.5% above the risk-free interest rate.

   a. What are r_A and r_E?

   b. Suppose that the beta of the unlevered stock was 0.6. What will β_A, β_E, and β_D be after the change to the capital structure?

15. **MM Proposition 2 (S16-3)** Rodriguez Pet Foods is financed 80% by common stock and 20% by bonds. The expected return on the common stock is 12% and the rate of interest on the bonds is 6%. Assuming that the bonds are default-risk-free, draw a graph that shows the expected return of Rodriguez's common stock (r_E) and the expected return on the package of common stock and bonds (r_A) for different debt-equity ratios.

16. **MM Proposition 2 (S16-3)** Imagine a firm that is expected to produce a level stream of operating profits. As leverage is increased, what happens to

   a. The ratio of the market value of the equity to income after interest?

   b. The ratio of the market value of the firm to income before interest if (i) MM are right and (ii) the traditionalists are right?

17. **MM Proposition 2 (S16-3)** Archimedes Levers is financed by a mixture of debt and equity. You have the following information about its cost of capital:

$$r_E = \underline{\hspace{1cm}} \qquad r_D = 12\% \qquad r_A = \underline{\hspace{1cm}}$$
$$\beta_E = 1.5 \qquad \beta_D = \underline{\hspace{1cm}} \qquad \beta_A = \underline{\hspace{1cm}}$$
$$r_f = 10\% \qquad r_m = 18\% \qquad D/V = 0.5$$

Can you fill in the blanks?

18. **MM Proposition 2 (S16-3)** Look back to Problem 17. Suppose now that Archimedes repurchases debt and issues equity so that $D/V = 0.3$. The reduced borrowing causes r_D to fall to 11%. How do the other variables change?

19. **Debt clienteles (S16-4)** Can you invent any new kinds of debt that might be attractive to investors? Why do you think they have not been issued?

20. **After-tax WACC (S16-5)** Gaucho Services starts life with all-equity financing and a cost of equity of 14%. Suppose it refinances to the following market-value capital structure:

Debt (D) 45% at $r_D = 9.5\%$

Equity (E) 55%

   a. Use MM's Proposition 2 to calculate the new cost of equity. Gaucho pays taxes at a marginal rate of $T_c = 40\%$.

   b. Calculate Gaucho's after-tax weighted-average cost of capital.

21. **After-tax WACC (S16-5)** Omega Corporation has 10 million shares outstanding, now trading at $55 per share. The firm has estimated the expected rate of return to shareholders at about 12%. It has also issued long-term bonds at an interest rate of 7% and has a debt value of $200 million. It pays tax at a marginal rate of 21%.

   a. What is Omega's after-tax WACC?

   b. How much higher would WACC be if Omega used no debt at all? (*Hint:* For this problem, you can assume that the firm's overall beta[β_A] is not affected by its capital structure or by the taxes saved because debt interest is tax-deductible.)

22. **After-tax WACC (S16-5)** Gamma Airlines has an asset beta of 1.5. The risk-free interest rate is 6%, and the market risk premium is 8%. Assume the capital asset pricing model is correct. Gamma pays taxes at a marginal rate of 25%. Draw a graph plotting Gamma's cost of equity and after-tax WACC as a function of its debt-to-equity ratio D/E, from no debt to $D/E = 1.0$. Assume that Gamma's debt is risk-free up to $D/E = 0.25$. Then the interest rate increases to 6.5% at $D/E = 0.5$, 7% at $D/E = 0.8$, and 8% at $D/E = 1.0$. As in Problem 21, you can assume that the firm's overall beta (β_A) is not affected by its capital structure or the taxes saved because debt interest is tax-deductible.

CHALLENGE

23. **Investor choice (S16-4)** Consider the following three tickets: Ticket A pays $10 if is _____ elected as president, ticket B pays $10 if is _____ elected, and ticket C pays $10 if neither is elected. (Fill in the blanks yourself.) Could the three tickets sell for less than the present value of $10? Could they sell for more? Try auctioning off the tickets. What are the implications for MM's Proposition 1?

24. **Investor choice (S16-4)** People often convey the idea behind MM's Proposition 1 by various supermarket analogies, for example, "The value of a pie should not depend on how it is sliced," or, "The cost of a whole chicken should equal the cost of assembling one by buying two drumsticks, two wings, two breasts, and so on."

   Actually Proposition 1 doesn't work in the supermarket. You'll pay less for an uncut whole pie than for a pie assembled from pieces purchased separately. Supermarkets charge more for chickens after they are cut up. Why? What costs or imperfections cause Proposition 1 to fail in the supermarket? Are these costs or imperfections likely to be important for corporations issuing securities on the U.S. or world capital markets? Explain.

25. **Investor choice (S16-4)** Suppose that new security designs could be patented.[11] The patent holder could restrict use of the new design or charge other firms royalties for using it. What effect would such patents have on MM's capital-structure irrelevance theory?

• • • • •

**SOLUTIONS
TO SELF-TEST
QUESTIONS**

16.1 The value of the equity increases by $5 million as long as debtholders can demand only a fair (zero-NPV) rate of interest (and the value of any existing debt is unaffected).

16.2 Debt interest is $0.10 \times 50 = \$5$ million (40% of earnings). The remaining $7.5 million (or 60% of earnings) goes to the equity holders. The value of the debt is $5/0.1 = \$50$ million or half of the company's value. Debt investors put up half the capital, but because their investment is safer, they are entitled to less than half the firm's income.

16.3 $r_E = r_A + (r_A - r_D)D/E$
$$= 15 + (15 - 10) \times (4/10) = 17\%$$

16.4 a. The beta of the assets does not change.

b. $\beta_E = \beta_A + (\beta_A - \beta_D)D/E$
$$= 0.9 + (0.9 - 0) \times (50/50) = 1.8$$

16.5 Also 8.8%. MM would say that in the absence of taxes, the company cost of capital is the same when there is no debt.

MINI-CASE • • • •

Claxton Drywall Comes to the Rescue

A law firm (not Dewey, Cheatem, and Howe) is expanding rapidly and must move to new office space. Business is good, and the firm is encouraged to purchase an entire building for $10 million. The building offers first-class office space, is conveniently located near their most important corporate clients, and provides space for future expansion. The firm is considering how to pay for it.

Claxton Drywall, a consultant, encourages the firm not to buy the building but to sign a long-term lease for the building instead. "With lease financing, you'll save $10 million. You won't have to put up any equity investment," Drywall explains.

The senior law partner asks about the terms of the lease. "I've taken the liberty to check," Drywall says. "The lease will provide 100% financing. It will commit you to 20 fixed annual payments of $950,000, with the first payment due immediately."

"The initial payment of $950,000 sounds like a down payment to me," the senior partner observes sourly.

"Good point," Drywall says amiably, "but you'll still save $9,050,000 up front. You can earn a handsome rate of return on that money. For example, I understand you are considering branch offices in London and New Delhi. The $9 million would pay the costs of setting up the new

---

[11]So far, security designs cannot be patented, but other financial applications have received patent protection. See J. Lerner, "Where Does *State Street* Lead? A First Look at Finance Patents, 1971–2000," *Journal of Finance* 57 (April 2002), pp. 901–930.

offices, and the cash flows from the new offices should more than cover the lease payments. And there's no financial risk—the cash flows from the expansion will cover the lease payments with a safety cushion. There's no reason for you or your partners to worry or to demand a higher-than-normal rate of return."

QUESTIONS

Suppose the present value of the building equals its purchase price of $10 million. Assume that the law firm can finance the offices in London and New Delhi from operating cash flow, with cash left over for the lease payments. The firm will not default on the lease payments. For simplicity you can ignore taxes.

1. If the law firm takes the lease, it will invest $950,000 and, in effect, borrow $9,050,000, repaid by 19 installments of $950,000. What is the interest rate on this disguised loan?

2. The law firm could finance 80% of the purchase price with a conventional mortgage at a 7% interest rate. Is the conventional mortgage better than the lease?

3. Construct a simple numerical example to convince Drywall that the lease would expose the law firm to financial risk. [*Hint:* What is the rate of return on the firm's equity investment in the office building if a recession arrives and the market value of the (leased) office building falls to $9 million after one year? What is the rate of return with conventional mortgage financing? With all-equity financing?]

4. Do the investments in London and New Delhi have anything to do with the decision to finance the office building? Explain briefly.

CHAPTER

17

How Much Should a Corporation Borrow?

In Chapter 16, we found that debt policy has no effect on firm values in well-functioning capital markets with no frictions or imperfections. Few financial managers would accept that conclusion as a practical guideline. If debt policy doesn't matter, then they shouldn't worry about it—financing decisions could be routine or erratic—it wouldn't matter. Yet financial managers do worry about debt policy. This chapter explains why.

If debt policy is irrelevant, then actual debt ratios should vary randomly from firm to firm and industry to industry. Yet in some industries, companies borrow much more heavily than in others. Look, for example, at Table 17.1. You can see that telecoms companies, retailers, and utilities are large issuers of debt. On the other hand, drug companies and computer software businesses finance largely with equity. Glamorous growth companies rarely use much debt despite rapid expansion and often heavy requirements for capital.

The explanation for these patterns lies partly in the things we left out of the last chapter. We mostly ignored taxes. We assumed bankruptcy was cheap, quick, and painless. We did not discuss conflicts of interest or information and incentive problems. Now we will put all these things back in: taxes first, then the costs of bankruptcy and financial distress. This will lead us to conflicts of interest and to information and incentive problems. In the end, we will have to admit that debt policy does matter.

However, we will not throw away the MM theory we developed so carefully in Chapter 16. We're shooting for a theory *combining* MM's insights plus the effects of taxes, costs of bankruptcy and financial distress, and various other complications. We're not dropping back to a theory based on inefficiencies in the capital market. Instead, we want to see how

Industry	Book Debt Ratio
Pharmaceuticals	0.07
Semiconductors	0.24
Computer software	0.26
Food	0.32
Oil	0.35
Machinery	0.35
Construction	0.39
Transportation	0.40
Paper	0.40
Aerospace	0.40
Chemicals	0.41
Autos	0.46
Clothing	0.46
Utilities	0.49
Retail	0.53
Telecoms	0.55

❱**TABLE 17.1**   Median book-value ratios of debt to debt-plus-equity by industry, 2020.

Source: WRDS Financial Ratios Suite.

well-functioning capital markets respond to taxes and other factors that impact managers' decisions. We proceed as follows:

Section 17-1 Debt and taxes The interest on a company's debt can be deducted when calculating corporate tax. This interest tax shield offers an inducement for companies to use debt financing.

Section 17-2 Costs of financial distress Debt also has its disadvantages. High debt levels bring the risk of financial distress and ultimately bankruptcy. Both are costly.

Section 17-3 The trade-off theory of capital structure The trade-off theory of capital structure suggests that firms should weigh the tax benefits of debt against the possible costs of financial distress.

Section 17-4 The pecking order of financing choices The pecking order theory offers an alternative to the trade-off

theory. If managers are better informed than investors, then an issue of common stock may indicate that managers believe the stock is overpriced. In this case, companies may prefer to issue debt if internally generated cash is insufficient.

Section 17-5 The capital structure decision Studies of capital structure decisions suggest that the motives for these decisions can be complex. We conclude with some considerations that CEOs need to take into account when setting financing strategy.

● ● ● ● ●

17-1 Debt and Taxes

Debt financing has one important advantage under the corporate income tax system in the United States and many other countries. The interest that the company pays is a tax-deductible expense. Thus, the return to bondholders escapes taxation at the corporate level.

There is one restriction on this tax benefit. The net amount of interest that U.S. companies can deduct is limited to 30% of earnings before interest and taxes (EBIT).[1] For most large companies, interest payments will not hit this constraint, but a few may do so, with painful results. For now, we will assume that the constraint on interest deductions is not binding. The constraint will merit more thought later in this chapter, however, and also in Chapters 18 and 33.

Table 17.2 shows simple income statements for firm U, which has no debt, and firm L, which has borrowed $1,000 at 8%. L's tax bill is $17 less than U's. This is the tax shield provided by the debt of L:

$$\text{Annual tax shield} = T_C \times r_D \times D = 0.21 \times 0.08 \times \$1,000 = \$17$$

In effect the government pays 21% of the interest expense of L. The total income that L can pay out to its bondholders and stockholders increases by that amount.

Tax shields can be valuable assets. Suppose that the debt of firm L is fixed and permanent. (That is, the company commits to refinance its present debt obligations when they mature and

	Income Statement of Firm U	Income Statement of Firm L
Earnings before interest and taxes	$1,000	$1,000
Interest paid to bondholders	0	80
Pretax income	$1,000	$920
Tax at 21%	210	193
Net income to stockholders	$790	$727
Total income to both bondholders and stockholders	$0 + 790 = $790	$80 + 727 = $807
Interest tax shield (0.21 × interest)	$0	$17

❭**TABLE 17.2**   The tax deductibility of interest increases the total income that can be paid out to bondholders and stockholders.

---

[1]The limitation was first imposed in 2018 when it was set at 30% of EBITDA. It was temporarily lifted during the COVID pandemic.

to keep rolling over its debt obligations indefinitely.) Then L can look forward to a permanent stream of cash flows of $17 per year. The risk of these flows is likely to be less than the risk of the operating assets of L. The tax shields depend only on the corporate tax rate[2] and on the ability of L to earn enough to cover interest payments. The corporate tax rate has been pretty stable. Moreover, the ability of L to earn its interest payments must be reasonably sure; otherwise, it could not have borrowed at 8%. Therefore, we should discount the interest tax shields at a relatively low rate.

But what rate? One common assumption is that the risk of the tax shields is the same as that of the interest payments generating them. In this case:

$$PV(\text{tax shield}) = \frac{\text{Annual tax shield}}{\text{Interest rate on debt}} = \frac{T_c \times r_D \times D}{r_D}$$
$$= T_c D = 0.21 \times \$1{,}000 = \$210$$

Assumption check. This calculation follows MM's original calculation of the PV of interest tax shields.[3] It rests on strong simplifying assumptions. Firms do not really commit to borrowing a fixed amount permanently, even if they are confident of having enough taxable income to use all the interest tax shields.[4] The natural alternative assumption is a fixed *ratio* of debt to firm value. If the ratio is fixed, then the future level of debt and the amount of interest tax shields will fluctuate as firm value fluctuates. In that case, projected interest tax shields deserve a discount rate higher than the debt interest rate. We cover this point in the next chapter. For now we continue this numerical example using MM's assumptions.

How Do Interest Tax Shields Contribute to the Value of Stockholders' Equity?

MM's proposition 1 amounts to saying that the value of a pie does not depend on how it is sliced. The pie is the firm's assets, and the slices are the debt and equity claims. If we hold the pie constant, then a dollar more of debt means a dollar less of equity value.

But there is really a third slice, the government's. Look at Table 17.3. It shows an expanded balance sheet with *pretax* asset value on the left and the value of the government's tax claim recognized as a liability on the right. MM would still say that the value of the pie—in this case *pretax* asset value—is not changed by slicing. But anything the firm can do to reduce the size of the government's slice obviously makes stockholders better off. One thing it can do is borrow money, which reduces its tax bill and, as we saw in Table 17.2, increases the cash flows to debt and equity investors. The *after-tax* value of the firm (the sum of its debt and equity values as shown in a normal market value balance sheet) goes up by PV(tax shield).

17.1 Self-Test

Suppose that the Fleetwood Group borrows $15 million at an interest rate of 6%. The corporate tax rate is 25%.

   a. What is the present value of the tax shield if the debt is fixed and permanent?

   b. How would your answer change if the interest rate on the debt was 8%?

---

[2] Always use the marginal corporate tax rate, not the average rate. Average rates are often much lower than marginal rates because of accelerated depreciation and other tax adjustments. For large corporations, the marginal rate is usually taken as the statutory rate, which was changed to 21% from 2018. However, effective marginal rates can be less than the statutory rate, especially for smaller, riskier companies that cannot be sure that they will earn taxable income in the future.

[3] F. Modigliani and M. H. Miller, "Corporate Income Taxes and the Cost of Capital: A Correction," *American Economic Review* 53 (June 1963), pp. 433–443.

[4] If the income of L does not cover interest in some future year, the tax shield is not necessarily lost. The losses can be carried forward and used to shield up to 80% of income in later years.

〉TABLE 17.3   Normal and expanded market value balance sheets. In a normal balance sheet, assets are valued after tax. In the expanded balance sheet, assets are valued pretax, and the value of the government's tax claim is recognized on the right-hand side. Interest tax shields are valuable because they reduce the government's claim.

Normal Balance Sheet (Market Values)	
Asset value (present value of after-tax cash flows)	Debt
	Equity
Total assets	Total value

Expanded Balance Sheet (Market Values)	
Pretax asset value (present value of pretax cash flows)	Debt
	Government's claim (present value of future taxes)
	Equity
Total pretax assets	Total pretax value

c. Suppose that instead of the debt being fixed, it was rebalanced in the future to maintain a constant proportion of Fleetwood's market value. Would you use a higher or lower discount rate to value the tax shields? Would this result in a higher or lower value for these tax shields?

Recasting Johnson & Johnson's Capital Structure

Johnson & Johnson is a large, successful firm that uses relatively modest amounts of long-term debt. Table 17.4A shows simplified book and market value balance sheets for Johnson & Johnson in December 2020.

Suppose that you were Johnson & Johnson's financial manager with complete responsibility for its capital structure. You decide to borrow an additional $10 billion on a permanent basis and use the proceeds to repurchase shares.

Table 17.4B shows the new balance sheets. The book version simply has $10,000 million more long-term debt and $10,000 million less equity. But we know that Johnson & Johnson's assets must be worth more because its tax bill will be reduced by 21% of the interest on the new debt. In other words, Johnson & Johnson has an increase in PV(interest tax shield), which is worth $T_cD = 0.21 \times \$10,000$ million $= \$2,100$ million. If the MM theory holds *except* for

〉TABLE 17.4A   Simplified balance sheets for Johnson & Johnson, December 2020 (figures in millions).

Notes:
1. Market value is assumed equal to book value for net working capital, long-term debt, and other long-term liabilities. The difference between the market and book values of long-term assets is equal to the difference between the market and book values of equity.
2. PV interest tax shield assumes fixed, perpetual debt, and a 21% tax rate.

Book Values			
Net working capital	$ 8,744	$ 32,635	Long-term debt
Long-term assets	123,657	36,488	Other long-term liabilities
		63,278	Equity
Total net assets	$132,401	$132,401	Total value
Market Values			
Net working capital	$ 8,744	$ 32,635	Long-term debt
PV interest tax shield	6,853	36,488	Other long-term liabilities
Long-term assets	462,128	408,602	Equity
Total net assets	$477,725	$477,725	Total value

Book Values			
Net working capital	$ 8,744	$ 42,635	Long-term debt
Long-term assets	123,657	36,488	Other long-term liabilities
		53,278	Equity
Total net assets	$132,401	$132,401	Total value
Market Values			
Net working capital	$ 8,744	$ 42,635	Long-term debt
PV interest tax shield	8,953	36,488	Other long-term liabilities
Long-term assets	462,128	400,702	Equity
Total net assets	$479,825	$479,825	Total value

❭TABLE 17.4B   Balance sheets for Johnson & Johnson with additional $10 billion of long-term debt substituted for stockholders' equity (figures in millions).

taxes, firm value must increase by $2,100 million to $479,825 million. Johnson & Johnson's equity ends up worth $400,702 million.

Now you have repurchased $10 billion worth of shares, but Johnson & Johnson's equity value has dropped by only $7.9 billion. Therefore, Johnson & Johnson's stockholders must be $2.1 billion ahead. Not a bad day's work.[5]

MM and Corporate Tax

We have just developed a version of MM's proposition 1 as corrected by them to reflect corporate income taxes.[6] The new proposition is

$$\text{Value of firm} = \text{value if all-equity-financed} + \text{PV (tax shield)}$$

In the special case of fixed, permanent debt,

$$\text{Value of firm} = \text{value if all-equity-financed} + T_C D$$

Our imaginary financial analysis on Johnson & Johnson provides the perfect illustration of the problems inherent in this "corrected" theory. That $2.1 billion came too easily; it seems to violate the law that there is no such thing as a money machine. And if Johnson & Johnson's stockholders would be richer with $42,635 million of corporate debt, why not $52,635 or $62,635 million? At what debt level should Johnson & Johnson stop borrowing? Our formula implies that firm value and stockholders' wealth continue to go up as D increases. The optimal debt policy appears to be embarrassingly extreme: All firms should be 100% debt-financed.

MM were not that fanatical about it. No one would expect the formula to apply at extreme debt ratios. There are several reasons why our calculations overstate the value of interest tax shields.

- It's wrong to think of debt as fixed and perpetual; a firm's ability to carry debt changes over time as profits and firm value fluctuate.
- Some firms face marginal tax rates less than 21%.

---

[5]Notice that as long as the bonds are sold at a fair price, all the benefits from the tax shield must go to the shareholders.
[6]Interest tax shields are recognized in MM's original article, F. Modigliani and M. H. Miller, "The Cost of Capital, Corporation Finance and the Theory of Investment," *American Economic Review* 48 (June 1958), pp. 261–297. The valuation procedure used in Table 17.4B is presented in their 1963 article, "Corporate Income Taxes and the Cost of Capital: A Correction," *American Economic Review* 53 (June 1963), pp. 433–443.

- You can't use interest tax shields unless there are sufficient profits to shield—and no firm can be absolutely sure of that.
- The amount of interest that can be deducted is limited to 30% of EBIT. Once a company breaches this limit, additional debt has no further tax advantages over equity.

But none of these qualifications explains why the most glamorous growth companies, such as Alphabet, Apple, and Microsoft, survive and thrive at low debt ratios. It's hard to believe that its financial managers are simply missing the boat.

We seem to have argued ourselves into a blind alley. But there may be two ways out:

1. Perhaps a fuller examination of the U.S. system of corporate *and personal* taxation will uncover a tax disadvantage of corporate borrowing, offsetting the present value of the interest tax shield.

2. Perhaps firms that borrow incur other costs—bankruptcy costs, for example.

We first examine personal taxation and in the next section we look at bankruptcy costs and other costs of financial distress.

Corporate and Personal Taxes

When personal taxes are introduced, the firm's objective is no longer to minimize the *corporate* tax bill; the firm should try to minimize the present value of *all* taxes paid on corporate income. "All taxes" include *personal* taxes paid by bondholders and stockholders.

Figure 17.1 illustrates how corporate and personal taxes are affected by leverage. Depending on the firm's capital structure, a dollar of operating income will accrue to investors either as debt interest or as equity income (dividends or capital gains). That is, the dollar can go down either branch of Figure 17.1.

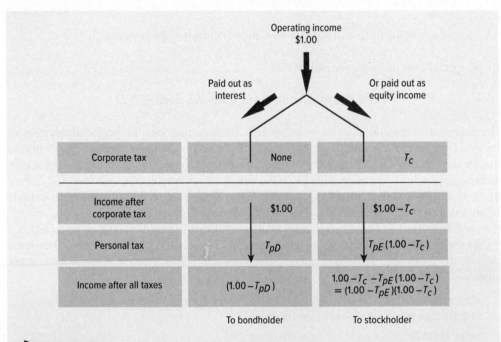

▶ FIGURE 17.1

The firm's capital structure determines whether operating income is paid out as interest or equity income. Interest is taxed only at the personal level. Equity income is taxed at both the corporate and the personal levels. However, T_{pE}, the personal tax rate on equity income, can be less than T_{pD}, the personal tax rate on interest income.

Notice that Figure 17.1 distinguishes between T_{pD}, the personal tax rate on interest, and T_{pE}, the effective personal tax rate on equity income. This rate can be well below T_{pD}, depending on the mix of dividends and capital gains realized by shareholders. The top marginal rate on dividends and capital gains in 2022 is 20% while the top rate on interest income is 37%.[7] Also capital gains taxes can be deferred until shares are sold, so the top *effective* capital gains rate is usually less than 20%.

The firm's objective should be to arrange its capital structure to maximize after-tax income. You can see from Figure 17.1 that corporate borrowing is better if $(1 - T_{pD})$ is more than $(1 - T_{pE}) \times (1 - T_c)$; otherwise, it is worse. The *relative tax* advantage of debt over equity is

$$\text{Relative tax advantage of debt} = \frac{1 - T_{pD}}{(1 - T_{pE})(1 - T_c)}$$

This suggests two special cases. First, suppose that debt and equity income were taxed at the same effective personal rate. With $T_{pE} = T_{pD}$, the relative advantage depends only on the *corporate rate:*

$$\text{Relative advantage} = \frac{1 - T_{pD}}{(1 - T_{pE})(1 - T_c)} = \frac{1}{1 - T_c}$$

In this case, we can forget about personal taxes. The tax advantage of corporate borrowing is exactly as MM calculated it.[8] They do not have to assume away personal taxes. Their theory of debt and taxes requires only that debt and equity income be taxed at the same rate.

The second special case occurs when corporate and personal taxes cancel to make debt policy irrelevant. This requires

$$1 - T_{pD} = (1 - T_{pE})(1 - T_c)$$

This can happen only if T_c, the corporate rate, is less than the personal rate T_{pD} *and* if T_{pE}, the effective rate on equity income, is small. Merton Miller explored this situation at a time when U.S. tax rates on interest and dividends were much higher than now, but we won't go into the details of his analysis here.[9]

In any event, we seem to have a simple, practical decision rule. Arrange the firm's capital structure to move operating income down to where the tax is least (see Figure 17.1). Unfortunately, that is not as simple as it sounds. What's T_{pE}, for example? The shareholder roster of any large corporation is likely to include tax-exempt investors (such as pension funds or university endowments) as well as millionaires and maybe a billionaire or two. All possible tax brackets will be mixed together. And it's the same with T_{pD}, the personal tax rate on interest. The large corporation's "typical" bondholder might be a tax-exempt pension fund, but many taxpaying investors also hold corporate debt.

Some investors may be much happier to buy your debt than others. For example, you should have no problems inducing pension funds to lend; they don't have to worry about personal tax. But taxpaying investors may be more reluctant to hold debt and will be prepared to

---

[7]In practice, the U.S. rate has been higher for investors in the top income brackets. There is an additional net investment income tax of 3.8% plus state income taxes. Proposals for still higher rates were floated by the new Biden administration in 2021. We use 37% for simplicity in these numerical examples.

[8]Personal taxes reduce the dollar amount of corporate interest tax shields, but the appropriate discount rate for cash flows after personal tax is also lower. If investors are willing to lend at a prospective return *before* personal taxes of r_D, then they must also be willing to accept a return *after* personal taxes of $r_D(1 - T_p)$, where T_p is the marginal rate of personal tax. Thus, we can compute the value after personal taxes of the tax shield on permanent debt: PV(tax shield) $= \dfrac{T_c \times r_D D \times (1 - T_p)}{(r_D \times (1 - T_p))} = T_c D$

This brings us back to our previous formula for firm value:

Value of firm = value if all-equity-financed + $T_c D$

[9]M. H. Miller, "Debt and Taxes," *Journal of Finance* 32 (May 1977), pp. 261–275.

do so only if they are compensated by a high rate of interest. Investors paying tax on interest at the top U.S. rate of 37% may be particularly reluctant to hold debt. They will prefer to hold common stock or tax-exempt bonds issued by states and municipalities.

To determine the net tax advantage of debt, companies would need to know the tax rates faced by the *marginal* investor—that is, an investor who is equally happy to hold debt or equity. This makes it hard to put a precise figure on the tax benefit, but we can nevertheless provide a back-of-the-envelope calculation. On average, over the past 10 years, large U.S. companies have paid out about a third of their earnings. Suppose the marginal investor is in the top tax bracket, paying 37% on interest and 20% on dividends and capital gains. Let's assume that deferred realization of capital gains cuts the effective capital gains rate in half, to $20/2 = 10\%$. Therefore, if the investor invests in the stock of a company with a 33% payout, the tax on each $1.00 of equity income is $T_{pE} = (0.33 \times 20) + (0.67 \times 10) = 13\%$.

Now we can calculate the effect of shunting a dollar of income down each of the two branches in Figure 17.1:

BEYOND THE PAGE

Corporate leverage and the Halloween Massacre

mhhe.com/brealey14e

	Interest	Equity Income
Income before tax	$1.00	$1.00
Less corporate tax at $T_c = 0.21$	0	0.21
Income after corporate tax	1.00	0.79
Personal tax at $T_{pD} = 0.37$ and $T_{pE} = 0.13$	0.37	0.103
Income after all taxes	$0.630	$0.687

Advantage to equity = $0.057

In this case, the position is reversed. For highly taxed individuals, the personal tax advantage of equity outweighs the corporate tax advantage of debt. We must emphasize that this back-of-the-envelope calculation is just that. It applies only to an individual investor who is paying the top rate of tax on investment income and can defer capital gains. It does not apply to those financial institutions that do not pay personal tax. They have a clear preference for debt financing.

Most financial managers believe that there is a moderate tax advantage to corporate borrowing, at least for companies that are reasonably sure that they can use the corporate tax shield. For companies that cannot benefit from the corporate tax shield, there is probably a moderate tax disadvantage.

17-2 Costs of Financial Distress

The corporate tax shield on interest payments provides an incentive to borrow, although it diminishes when we recognize personal taxes. We now turn to other factors that may deter companies from taking full advantage of the corporate tax advantage to debt.

Borrowing increases the risk of financial distress, which occurs when promises to creditors are broken or honored with difficulty. Sometimes distress leads to bankruptcy. Sometimes, it only means skating on thin ice.

As we will see, financial distress is costly. Investors know that levered firms may fall into financial distress, and they worry about it. That worry is reflected in the current market value of the levered firm's securities. Thus, the value of the firm can be broken down into three parts:

$$\begin{matrix} \text{Value} \\ \text{of firm} \end{matrix} = \begin{matrix} \text{value if} \\ \text{all-equity-financed} \end{matrix} + \text{PV(tax shield)} - \text{PV}\begin{pmatrix} \text{costs of financial} \\ \text{distress} \end{pmatrix}$$

The costs of financial distress depend on the probability of distress and the magnitude of costs encountered if distress occurs. *Costs of financial distress* cover several specific items. Now we identify these costs and try to understand what causes them.

Bankruptcy Costs

You rarely hear anything nice said about corporate bankruptcy. But there is some good in almost everything. Corporate bankruptcies occur when stockholders exercise their *right to default.* That right is valuable; when a firm gets into trouble, limited liability allows stockholders simply to walk away from it, leaving all its troubles to its creditors. The former creditors become the new stockholders, and the old stockholders are left with nothing.

Stockholders in corporations automatically get *limited liability.* But suppose that this were not so. Suppose that there are two firms with identical assets and operations. Each firm has debt outstanding, and each has promised to repay $1,000 (principal and interest) next year. But only one of the firms, Ace Limited, enjoys limited liability. The other firm, Ace Unlimited, does not; its stockholders are personally liable for its debt.[10]

Figure 17.2 compares next year's possible payoffs to the creditors and stockholders of these two firms. The only differences occur when next year's asset value turns out to be less than $1,000. Suppose that next year, the assets of each company are worth only $500. In this case, Ace Limited defaults. Its stockholders walk away; their payoff is zero. Bondholders get the assets worth $500. But Ace Unlimited's stockholders can't walk away. They have to cough up $500, the difference between asset value and the bondholders' claim. The debt is paid whatever happens.

Suppose that Ace Limited does go bankrupt. Of course, its stockholders are disappointed that their firm is worth so little, but that is an operating problem having nothing to do with financing. Given poor operating performance, the right to go bankrupt—the right to default— is a valuable privilege. As Figure 17.2 shows, Ace Limited's stockholders are in better shape than those of Unlimited.

The example illuminates a mistake people often make in thinking about the costs of bankruptcy. Bankruptcies are thought of as corporate funerals. The mourners (creditors and especially shareholders) look at their firm's present sad state. They think about how valuable their securities used to be and how little is left. But they may also think of the lost value as a cost of bankruptcy. That is the mistake. The decline in the value of assets is what the mourning is really about. That decline has no necessary connection with financing. The bankruptcy is merely a legal mechanism for allowing creditors to take over when the decline in the value of assets triggers a default. Bankruptcy is not the *cause* of the decline in value. It is the result.

We said that bankruptcy is a legal mechanism allowing creditors to take over when a firm defaults. *Bankruptcy costs* are the costs of using this mechanism. There are no bankruptcy costs at all shown in Figure 17.2. Note that only Ace Limited can default and go bankrupt. But, regardless of what happens to asset value, the *combined* payoff to the bondholders and stockholders of Ace Limited is always the same as the *combined* payoff to the bondholders and stockholders of Ace Unlimited. Thus, the overall market values of the two firms now (this year) must be identical. Of course, Ace Limited's stock is worth more than Ace Unlimited's stock because of Ace Limited's right to default. Ace Limited's debt is worth correspondingly less.

Our example was not intended to be strictly realistic. Anything involving courts and lawyers cannot be free. Suppose that court and legal fees are $200 if Ace Limited defaults. The fees are paid out of the remaining value of Ace's assets. Thus, if asset value turns out to be $500, creditors end up with only $300. Figure 17.3 shows next year's *total* payoff to bondholders and stockholders net of this bankruptcy cost. Ace Limited, by issuing risky debt, has

---

[10]Ace Unlimited could be a partnership or sole proprietorship, which does not provide limited liability.

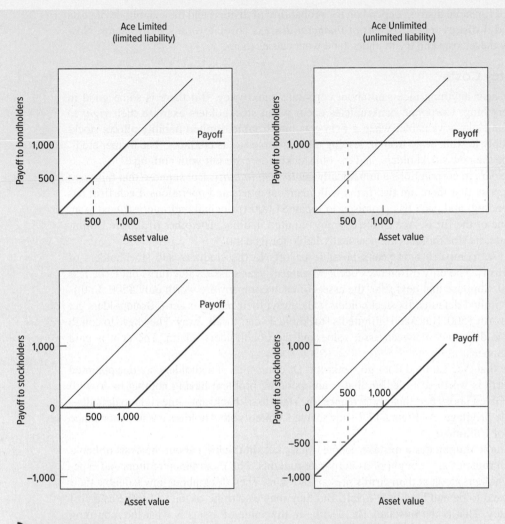

FIGURE 17.2

Comparison of limited and unlimited liability for two otherwise identical firms. If the two firms' asset values are less than $1,000, Ace Limited stockholders default and its bondholders take over the assets. Ace Unlimited stockholders keep the assets, but they must reach into their own pockets to pay off its bondholders. The total payoff to both stockholders and bondholders is the same for the two firms.

given lawyers and the court system a claim on the firm if it defaults. The market value of the firm is reduced by the present value of this claim.

It is easy to see how increased leverage affects the present value of the costs of financial distress. If Ace Limited borrows more, it increases the probability of default and the value of the lawyers' claim. It increases PV (costs of financial distress) and reduces Ace's present market value.

The costs of bankruptcy come out of stockholders' pockets. Creditors foresee the costs and foresee that *they* will pay them if default occurs. For this, they demand compensation in advance in the form of higher payoffs when the firm does *not* default; that is, they demand a higher promised interest rate. This reduces the possible payoffs to stockholders and reduces the present market value of their shares.

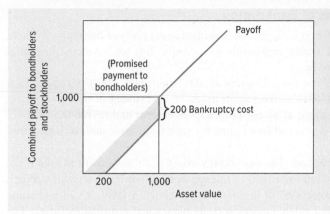

FIGURE 17.3

Total payoff to Ace Limited security holders. There is a $200 bankruptcy cost in the event of default (shaded area).

17.2 Self-Test

Suppose investors foresee $2 million of legal costs if a firm defaults on its bonds. How does this affect the value of the firm's bonds if bankruptcy occurs? How does the possibility of default affect the interest rate demanded by bondholders today? How does this possibility affect today's value of the common stock?

Evidence on Bankruptcy Costs

Bankruptcy costs can add up fast. The failed energy giant Enron paid $757 million in legal, accounting, and other professional fees during the time that it spent in bankruptcy. The estimated direct costs of sorting out the 65,000 claims on the assets of Lehman Brothers was $5.9 billion.[11]

Daunting as such numbers may seem, they are not a large fraction of the companies' asset values. Lawrence Weiss, who studied 31 firms that went bankrupt between 1980 and 1986, found average costs of about 3% of total book assets and 20% of the market value of equity in the year prior to bankruptcy. A study by Andrade and Kaplan of a sample of troubled and highly leveraged firms estimated costs of financial distress amounting to 10% to 20% of pre-distress market value, although they found it hard to decide whether these costs were caused by financial distress or by the business setbacks that led to distress.[12]

Bankruptcy eats up a larger fraction of asset value for small companies than for large ones. There are significant economies of scale in going bankrupt. For example, a study of smaller U.K. bankruptcies by Franks and Sussman found that fees (legal and accounting) and other costs soaked up roughly 20% to 40% of the proceeds from liquidation of the companies.[13]

---

[11]E. Denison, M. J. Fleming, and A. Sarkar, "How Much Value Was Destroyed by the Lehman Bankruptcy," Federal Reserve Bank of New York, Liberty Street Economics blog, https://libertystreeteconomics.newyorkfed.org/2019/01/how-much-value-was-destroyed-by-the-lehman-bankruptcy.html

[12]The pioneering study of bankruptcy costs is J. B. Warner, "Bankruptcy Costs: Some Evidence," *Journal of Finance* 32 (May 1977), pp. 337–347. See also L. A. Weiss, "Bankruptcy Resolution: Direct Costs and Violation of Priority of Claims," *Journal of Financial Economics* 27 (October 1990), pp. 285–314; E. I. Altman, "A Further Empirical Investigation of the Bankruptcy Cost Question," *Journal of Finance* 39 (September 1984), pp. 1067–1089; and G. Andrade and S. N. Kaplan, "How Costly Is Financial (not Economic) Distress? Evidence from Highly Leveraged Transactions That Became Distressed," *Journal of Finance* 53 (October 1998), pp. 1443–1493.

[13]J. Franks and O. Sussman, "Financial Distress and Bank Restructuring of Small to Medium Size UK Companies," *Review of Finance* 9 (2005), pp. 65–96. Karin Thorburn found that the Swedish bankruptcy system is reasonably efficient for smaller firms, however. See "Bankruptcy Auctions: Costs, Debt Recovery and Firm Survival," *Journal of Financial Economics* 58 (December 2000), pp. 337–368.

Direct versus Indirect Costs of Bankruptcy

So far, we have discussed the *direct* (i.e., legal and administrative) costs of bankruptcy. There are indirect costs too, which are nearly impossible to measure. But we have circumstantial evidence indicating their importance.

Managing a bankrupt firm is not easy. Consent of the bankruptcy court is required for many routine business decisions, such as the sale of assets or investment in new equipment. At best, this involves time and effort; at worst, proposals to reform and revive the firm are thwarted by impatient creditors, who stand first in line for cash from asset sales or liquidation of the entire firm.

Sometimes the problem is reversed: The bankruptcy court is so anxious to maintain the firm as a going concern that it allows the firm to engage in negative-NPV activities. When Eastern Airlines entered the "protection" of the bankruptcy court in 1989, it still had some valuable, profit-making routes and salable assets such as planes and terminal facilities. The creditors would have been best served by a prompt liquidation, which probably would have generated enough cash to pay off all debt and preferred stockholders. But the bankruptcy judge was keen to keep Eastern's planes flying at all costs, so he allowed the company to sell many of its assets to fund hefty operating losses. When Eastern finally closed down after two years, it was not just bankrupt, but *administratively* insolvent: There was almost nothing for creditors, and the company was running out of cash to pay legal expenses.[14]

We do not know what the sum of direct and indirect costs of bankruptcy amounts to. We suspect it is a significant number, particularly for large firms for which proceedings would be lengthy and complex. Perhaps the best evidence is the reluctance of creditors to force bankruptcy. In principle, they would be better off to end the agony and seize the assets as soon as possible. Instead, creditors often overlook defaults in the hope of nursing the firm over a difficult period. They do this in part to avoid costs of bankruptcy. There is an old financial saying, "Borrow $1,000 and you've got a banker. Borrow $10,000,000 and you've got a partner."

Creditors may also shy away from bankruptcy because they worry about violations of absolute priority. *Absolute priority* means that creditors are paid in full before stockholders receive a penny. But sometimes reorganizations provide something for everyone, including consolation prizes for stockholders. Sometimes other claimants move up in the queue. For example, after the Chrysler bankruptcy in 2009, the State of Indiana sued (unsuccessfully) on behalf of local pension funds that had invested in Chrysler bonds. The funds complained bitterly about the terms of sale of the bankrupt company's assets to Fiat, arguing that they would get only $.29 on the dollar, while other, more junior claimants fared better. The Chrysler bankruptcy was a special case, however. One of the key players in the proceedings was the U.S. government, which was anxious to protect tens of thousands of jobs in the middle of a severe recession.

We cover bankruptcy procedures in more detail in Chapter 33.

Financial Distress without Bankruptcy

Not every firm that gets into trouble goes bankrupt. As long as the firm can scrape up enough cash to pay the interest on its debt, it may be able to postpone bankruptcy for many years. Eventually the firm may recover, pay off its debt, and escape bankruptcy altogether.

But the mere threat of financial distress can be costly to the threatened firm. Customers and suppliers are extra cautious about doing business with a firm that may not be around for long. Customers worry about resale value and the availability of service and replacement parts. (This was a serious drag on Chrysler's sales before its bankruptcy in 2009.) Suppliers are disinclined to put effort into servicing the distressed firm's account and may demand cash

---

[14]See L. A. Weiss and K. H. Wruck, "Information Problems, Conflicts of Interest, and Asset Stripping: Chapter 11's Failure in the Case of Eastern Airlines," *Journal of Financial Economics* 48 (1998), pp. 55–97.

on the nail for their products. Potential employees are unwilling to sign on and existing staff keep slipping away from their desks for job interviews.

High debt, and thus high financial risk, also appears to reduce firms' appetites for business risk. For example, Luigi Zingales looked at the fortunes of U.S. trucking companies after the trucking industry was deregulated in the late 1970s.[15] The deregulation sparked a wave of competition and restructuring. Survival required new investment and improvements in operating efficiency. Zingales found that conservatively financed trucking companies were more likely to survive in the new competitive environment. High-debt firms were more likely to drop out of the game.

Agency Costs of Financial Distress

When a firm is in trouble, both bondholders and stockholders want it to recover, but in other respects, their interests may be in conflict. In times of financial distress, the security holders are like many political parties—united on generalities but threatened by squabbling on any specific issue.

Financial distress is costly when these agency costs get in the way of proper operating, investment, and financing decisions. Stockholders are tempted to forsake the usual objective of maximizing the overall market value of the firm and to pursue narrower self-interest instead. Just as in fairgrounds there are many games that seem simple to play but where the unwary can be easily caught out and taken advantage of. Stockholders are tempted to play games at the expense of their creditors. We now illustrate how such games can lead to costs of financial distress.

Here is the Circular File Company's book balance sheet:

Circular File Company (Book Values)

Net working capital	$ 20	$ 50	Bonds outstanding
Fixed assets	80	50	Common stock
Total assets	$100	$100	Total value

We will assume there is only one share and one bond outstanding. The stockholder is also the manager. The bondholder is somebody else.

Here is its balance sheet in market values—a clear case of financial distress, since the face value of Circular's debt ($50) exceeds the firm's total market value ($30):

Circular File Company (Market Values)

Net working capital	$20	$27	Bonds outstanding
Fixed assets	10	3	Common stock
Total assets	$30	$30	Total value

If the debt matured today, Circular's owner would default, leaving the firm bankrupt. But suppose that the bond actually matures one year hence, that there is enough cash for Circular to limp along for the year, and that the bondholder cannot "call the question" and force bankruptcy before then.

The one-year grace period explains why the Circular share still has value. Its owner is betting on a stroke of luck that will rescue the firm, allowing it to pay off the debt with something

---

[15] L. Zingales, "Survival of the Fittest or the Fattest? Exit and Financing in the Trucking Industry," *Journal of Finance* 53 (June 1998), pp. 905–938.

left over. The bet is a long shot—the owner wins only if firm value increases from $30 to more than $50.[16] But the owner has a secret weapon: He controls investment and operating strategy.

Risk Shifting: The First Game

Suppose that Circular has $10 cash. The following investment opportunity comes up:

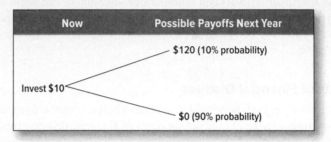

This is a wild gamble and probably a lousy project. But you can see why the owner would be tempted to take it anyway. Why not go for broke? Circular will probably go under anyway, so the owner is essentially betting with the bondholder's money. But the owner gets most of the loot if the project pays off.

Suppose that the project's NPV is −$2 but that it is undertaken anyway, thus depressing firm value by $2. Circular's new balance sheet might look like this:

Circular File Company (Market Values)

Net working capital	$10	$22	Bonds outstanding
Fixed assets	18	6	Common stock
Total assets	$28	$28	Total value

Firm value falls by $2, but the owner is $3 ahead because the bond's value has fallen by $5.[17] The $10 cash that used to stand behind the bond has been replaced by a very risky asset worth only $8.

Thus, a game has been played at the expense of Circular's bondholder. The game illustrates the following general point: Stockholders of levered firms gain when business risk increases. Financial managers who act strictly in their shareholders' interests (and *against* the interests of creditors) will favor risky projects over safe ones. They may even take risky projects with negative NPVs.

This warped strategy for capital budgeting clearly is costly to the firm and to the economy as a whole. Why do we associate the costs with financial distress? Because the temptation to play is strongest when the odds of default are high. A blue-chip company like Microsoft would never invest in our negative-NPV gamble. Its creditors are not vulnerable to one risky project.

EXAMPLE 17.1 • FedEx's gamble

In 1974, Federal Express was a struggling young company with only $5,000 left in its checking account and an upcoming $24,000 bill for its weekly jet fuel payment. Fred Smith took the incentive to gamble literally. He took the firm's remaining $5,000 and boarded a plane for Las Vegas, where he won $27,000.

---

[16]We are not concerned here with how to work out whether $3 is a fair price for stockholders to pay for the bet. We will come to that in Chapter 24 when we discuss risky debt; we will calculate the value of Circular's equity.
[17]We are not calculating this $5 drop. We are simply using it as a plausible assumption. The tools necessary for a calculation come in Chapters 22 and 24.

When asked how he had mustered the nerve to do this, he replied, "What difference did it make? Without the funds for the fuel companies, we couldn't have flown anyway."[18]

The effects of such distorted incentives to take on risk are usually not this blatant, but the results can be the same.

• • • • •

Refusing to Contribute Equity Capital: The Second Game

We have seen how stockholders, acting in their immediate, narrow self-interest, may take projects that reduce the overall market value of their firm. These are errors of commission. Conflicts of interest may also lead to errors of omission.

Assume that Circular cannot scrape up any cash and, therefore, cannot take that wild gamble. Instead, a *good* opportunity comes up: a relatively safe asset costing $10 with a present value of $15 and NPV = +$5.

This project will not, in itself, rescue Circular, but it is a step in the right direction. We might therefore expect Circular to issue $10 of new stock and to go ahead with the investment. Suppose that two new shares are issued to the original owner for $10 cash. The project is taken. The new balance sheet might look like this:

Circular File Company (Market Values)			
Net working capital	$20	$35	Bonds outstanding
Fixed assets	25	10	Common stock
Total assets	$45	$45	Total value

The total value of the firm goes up by $15 ($10 of new capital and $5 NPV). Notice that the Circular bond is no longer worth $27, but $35. The bondholder receives a capital gain of $8 because the firm's assets include a new, safe asset worth $15. The probability of default is less, and the payoff to the bondholder if default occurs is larger.

The stockholder loses what the bondholder gains. Equity value goes up not by $15 but by $15 − $8 = $7. The owner puts in $10 of fresh equity capital but gains only $7 in market value. Going ahead is in the firm's interest but not the owner's.

Again, our example illustrates a general point. If we hold business risk constant, any increase in firm value is shared among bondholders and stockholders. The value of any investment opportunity to the firm's *stockholders* is reduced because project benefits must be shared with bondholders. Thus, it may not be in the stockholders' self-interest to contribute fresh equity capital even if that means forgoing positive-NPV investment opportunities.

A *debt overhang problem* exists whenever value is lost because a levered firm chooses investments to maximize shareholder value rather than the value of the firm. The problem theoretically affects all levered firms, but it is most serious when firms land in financial distress. The greater the probability of default, the more bondholders rather than shareholders gain from investments that increase firm value.

And Three More Games, Briefly

As with other games, the temptation to play the next three games is particularly strong in financial distress.

Cash In and Run   Stockholders may be reluctant to put money into a firm in financial distress, but they are happy to take the money out—in the form of a cash dividend, for example. The market value of the firm's stock goes down by less than the amount of the dividend paid,

---

[18]R. Frock, *Changing How the World Does Business, FedEx's Incredible Journey to Success: The Inside Story* (San Francisco: Berrett-Koehler Publishers, 2006).

because the decline in *firm* value is shared with creditors. This game is just "refusing to contribute equity capital" run in reverse.[19]

Playing for Time   When the firm is in financial distress, creditors would like to salvage what they can by forcing the firm to settle up. Naturally, stockholders want to delay this as long as they can. There are various devious ways to do this—for example, by accounting changes designed to conceal the true extent of trouble; by encouraging false hopes of spontaneous recovery; or by cutting corners on maintenance, research and development, and so on—in order to make this year's operating performance look better.

Bait and Switch   This game is not always played in financial distress, but it is a quick way to get *into* distress. You start with a conservative policy, issuing a limited amount of relatively safe debt. Then you suddenly switch and issue a lot more. That makes all your debt risky, imposing a capital loss on the "old" bondholders. Their capital loss is the stockholders' gain.

A dramatic example of bait and switch occurred in October 1988, when the management of RJR Nabisco announced its intention to acquire the company in a *leveraged buyout* (LBO). This put the company "in play" for a transaction in which existing shareholders would be bought out and the company would be "taken private." The cost of the buyout would be almost entirely debt-financed. The new private company would start life with an extremely high debt ratio.

RJR Nabisco had debt outstanding with a market value of about $2.4 billion. The announcement of the coming LBO drove down this market value by $298 million.[20]

What the Games Cost

Why should anyone object to these games so long as they are played by consenting adults? Because playing them means poor decisions about investments and operations. These poor decisions are *agency costs* of borrowing.

The more the firm borrows, the greater is the temptation to play the games (assuming the financial manager acts in the stockholders' interest). The increased odds of poor decisions in the future prompt investors to mark down the present market value of the firm. The fall in value comes out of the shareholders' pockets. Therefore, it is ultimately in their interest to avoid temptation. The easiest way to do this is to limit borrowing to levels at which the firm's debt is safe or close to it.

Banks and other corporate lenders are also not financial innocents. They are aware of the agency issues and so protect themselves by rationing the amount that they will lend or by imposing restrictions on the company's actions.

EXAMPLE 17.2 • Ms. Crane faces credit rationing

Consider the case of Henrietta Crane, a budding entrepreneur with two possible investment projects that offer the following payoffs:

Now	Investment	Payoff	Probability of Payoff
Project 1	−12	+15	1.0
Project 2	−12	+24	0.5
		0	0.5

---

[19]If stockholders or managers take money out of the firm in anticipation of financial distress or bankruptcy, the bankruptcy court can treat the payout as *fraudulent conveyance* and claw back the money to the firm and its creditors.

[20]We thank Paul Asquith for these figures. RJR Nabisco was finally taken private not by its management but by another LBO partnership. We discuss this LBO in Chapter 33.

Project 1 is surefire and very profitable; project 2 is risky and a rotten project. Ms. Crane now approaches her bank and asks to borrow the present value of $10,000 (she will find the remaining money out of her own purse). The bank calculates that the payoff will be split as follows:

	Expected Payoff to Bank $000	Expected Payoff to Ms. Crane $000
Project 1	+10	+5
Project 2	$(0.5 \times 10) + (0.5 \times 0) = +5$	$0.5 \times (24 - 10) = +7$

If Ms. Crane accepts project 1, the bank's debt is certain to be paid in full; if she accepts project 2, there is only a 50% chance of payment and the expected payoff to the bank is only $5. Unfortunately, Ms. Crane will prefer to take project 2, for if things go well, she gets most of the profit, and if they go badly, the bank bears most of the loss. Unless Ms. Crane can convince the bank that she will not gamble with its money, the bank will limit the amount that it is prepared to lend.[21]

How can Ms. Crane in Example 17.2 reassure the bank of her intentions? The obvious answer is to give it veto power over potentially dangerous decisions. There we have the ultimate economic rationale for all that fine print backing up corporate debt. Debt contracts frequently limit dividends or equivalent transfers of wealth to stockholders. Additional borrowing is almost always limited. For example, many companies are prevented by existing bond indentures from issuing any additional long-term debt unless their ratio of earnings to interest charges exceeds 2.0.

Sometimes firms are restricted from selling assets or making major investment outlays except with the lenders' consent. The risks of playing for time are reduced by specifying accounting procedures and by giving lenders access to the firm's books and its financial forecasts.

Of course, fine print cannot be a complete solution for firms that insist on issuing risky debt. The fine print has its own costs; you have to spend money to save money. Obviously, a complex debt contract costs more to negotiate than a simple one. Afterward it costs the lender more to monitor the firm's performance. Lenders anticipate monitoring costs and demand compensation in the form of higher interest rates; thus, the monitoring costs—another agency cost of debt—are ultimately paid by stockholders.

Perhaps the most severe costs of the fine print stem from the constraints it places on operating and investment decisions. For example, an attempt to prevent the risk-shifting game may also prevent the firm from pursuing *good* investment opportunities. At the minimum, there are delays in clearing major investments with lenders. In some cases, lenders may veto high-risk investments even if net present value is positive. The lenders are tempted to play a game of their own, forcing the firm to stay in cash or low-risk assets even if good projects are forgone.

Debt contracts cannot cover every possible manifestation of the games we have just discussed. Any attempt to do so would be hopelessly expensive and doomed to failure in any event. Human imagination is insufficient to conceive of all the possible things that could go wrong. Therefore, contracts are always *incomplete*. We will always find surprises coming at us on dimensions we never thought to think about.

---

[21]You might think that if the bank suspects Ms. Crane will undertake project 2, it should just raise the interest rate on its loan. In this case, Ms. Crane will not want to take on project 2 (they can't both be happy with a lousy project). But Ms. Crane also would not want to pay a high rate of interest if she is going to take on project 1 (she would do better to borrow less money at the risk-free rate). Therefore, simply raising the interest rate is not the answer.

We hope we have not left the impression that managers and stockholders always succumb to temptation unless restrained. Usually, they refrain voluntarily, not only from a sense of fair play but also on pragmatic grounds: A firm or individual that makes a killing today at the expense of a creditor will be coldly received when the time comes to borrow again. Aggressive game playing is done only by out-and-out crooks and by firms in extreme financial distress. Firms limit borrowing precisely because they don't wish to land in distress and be exposed to the temptation to play.

Costs of Distress Vary with Type of Asset

Suppose your firm's only asset is the Heartbreak Hotel. This a large downtown hotel, which is fully mortgaged. The recession hits, occupancy rates fall, and the mortgage payments cannot be met. The lender takes over and sells the hotel to a new owner and operator. You use your firm's stock certificates for wallpaper.

What is the cost of bankruptcy? In this example, probably very little. The value of the hotel is, of course, much less than you hoped, but that is due to the lack of guests, not to the bankruptcy. Bankruptcy doesn't damage the hotel itself. The direct bankruptcy costs are restricted to items such as legal and court fees, real estate commissions, and the time the lender spends sorting things out.

Suppose we repeat the story of Heartbreak Hotel for Fledgling Electronics. Everything is the same, except for the underlying real assets—not real estate but a high-tech going concern, a growth company whose most valuable assets are technology, investment opportunities, and its employees' human capital.

If Fledgling gets into trouble, the stockholders may be reluctant to put up money to cash in on its growth opportunities. Failure to invest is likely to be much more serious for Fledgling than for the Heartbreak Hotel.

If Fledgling finally defaults on its debt, the lender will find it much more difficult to cash in by selling off the assets. Many of them are intangibles that have value only as a part of a going concern.

Could Fledgling be kept as a going concern through default and reorganization? It may not be as hopeless as putting a wedding cake through a car wash, but there are a number of serious difficulties. First, the odds of defections by key employees are higher than they would be if the firm had never gotten into financial trouble. Special guarantees may have to be given to customers who have doubts about whether the firm will be around to service its products. Aggressive investment in new products and technology will be difficult; each class of creditors will have to be convinced that it is in its interest for the firm to invest new money in risky ventures.

Some assets, like good commercial real estate, can pass through bankruptcy and reorganization largely unscathed[22]; the values of other assets are likely to be considerably diminished. The losses are greatest for the intangible assets that are linked to the health of the firm as a going concern—for example, technology, human capital, and brand image. That may be why debt ratios are low in the pharmaceutical industry, where value depends on continued success in research and development, and in many service industries where value depends on human capital. We can also understand why highly profitable growth companies, such as Microsoft or Alphabet, use mostly equity finance.

---

[22]In 1989, the Rockefeller family sold 80% of Rockefeller Center—several acres of extremely valuable Manhattan real estate—to Mitsubishi Estate Company for $1.4 billion. A REIT, Rockefeller Center Properties, held a $1.3 billion mortgage loan (the REIT's only asset) secured by this real estate. But rents and occupancy rates did not meet forecasts, and by 1995, Mitsubishi had incurred losses of about $600 million. Then Mitsubishi quit, and Rockefeller Center was bankrupt. That triggered a complicated series of maneuvers and negotiations. But did this damage the value of the Rockefeller Center properties? Was Radio City Music Hall, one of the properties, any less valuable because of the bankruptcy? We doubt it.

The moral of these examples is this: *Do not think only about the probability that borrowing will bring trouble. Think also of the value that may be lost if trouble comes.*

17.3 Self-Test

For which of the following companies would the costs of financial distress be most serious? Why?

a. A three-year old biotech company. So far the company has no products approved for sales, but its scientists are busy developing a breakthrough drug.

b. An oil production company with 50 producing wells and 20 million barrels of proven oil reserves.

Heartbreak Hotel for Enron?   Enron was one of the most glamorous, fast-growing, and (apparently) profitable companies of the 1990s. It played a lead role in the deregulation of electric power markets, both in the United States and internationally. It invested in electric power generation and distribution, gas pipelines, telecommunications networks, and various other ventures. It also built up an active energy trading business. At its peak, the aggregate market value of Enron's common stock exceeded $60 billion. By the end of 2001, Enron was in bankruptcy and its shares were worthless.

With hindsight, we see that Enron was playing many of the games that we described earlier in this section. It was borrowing aggressively and hiding the debt in special-purpose entities (SPEs). The SPEs also allowed it to pump up its reported earnings, playing for time while making more and more risky investments. When the bubble burst, there was hardly any value left.

The collapse of Enron didn't really destroy $60 billion in value because that $60 billion wasn't there in the first place. But there were genuine costs of financial distress. Let's focus on Enron's energy trading business. That business was not as profitable as it appeared, but it was nevertheless a valuable asset. It provided an important service for wholesale energy customers and suppliers who wanted to buy or sell contracts that locked in the future prices and quantities of electricity, natural gas, and other commodities.

What happened to this business when it became clear that Enron was in financial distress and probably headed for bankruptcy? It disappeared. Trading volume went to zero immediately. None of its customers was willing to make a new trade with Enron because it was far from clear that Enron would be around to honor its side of the bargain. With no trading volume, there was no trading business. As it turned out, Enron's trading business more resembled Fledgling Electronics than a tangible asset like Heartbreak Hotel.

The value of Enron's trading business depended on Enron's creditworthiness. The value should have been protected by conservative financing. Most of the lost value can be traced back to Enron's aggressive borrowing. This loss of value was, therefore, a cost of financial distress.

17-3   The Trade-Off Theory of Capital Structure

Financial managers often think of the firm's debt–equity decision as a trade-off between interest tax shields and the costs of financial distress. Of course, there is controversy about how valuable interest tax shields are and what kinds of financial trouble are most threatening, but these disagreements are only variations on a theme.

Figure 17.4 shows how the trade-off between the tax benefits and the costs of distress could determine optimal capital structure. PV(tax shield) initially increases as the firm borrows more. At low debt levels, the probability of financial distress should be trivial, and so PV(cost

> ► **FIGURE 17.4**
>
> The value of the firm is equal to its value if all-equity-financed plus PV tax shield minus PV costs of financial distress. According to the trade-off theory of capital structure, the manager should choose the debt ratio that maximizes firm value.

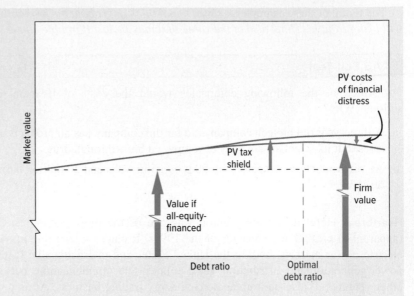

of financial distress) is small and tax advantages dominate. But at some point, the probability of financial distress increases rapidly with additional borrowing; the costs of distress begin to take a substantial bite out of firm value. Also, if the firm can't be sure of profiting from the corporate tax shield, the tax advantage of additional debt is likely to dwindle and eventually disappear. (Once the firm hits the limit on interest deductions at 30% of EBIT, the tax shields from additional borrowing disappear completely.) The theoretical optimum is reached when the present value of tax savings due to further borrowing is just offset by increases in the present value of costs of distress. This is called the *trade-off theory* of capital structure.

This *trade-off theory* of capital structure recognizes that target debt ratios may vary from firm to firm. Companies with safe, tangible assets and plenty of taxable income to shield ought to have high target ratios. Unprofitable companies with risky, intangible assets ought to rely primarily on equity financing.

If there were no costs to adjusting capital structure, then each firm should always be at its target debt ratio. However, there are costs—and, therefore, delays—in adjusting to the optimum. Firms cannot immediately offset the random events that bump them away from their capital structure targets, so we should see random differences in actual debt ratios among firms having the same target debt ratio.

All in all, this trade-off theory of capital structure choice tells a comforting story. Unlike MM's theory, which seemed to say that firms should take on as much debt as possible, it avoids extreme predictions and rationalizes moderate debt ratios. Also, if you ask financial managers whether their firms have target debt ratios, they will usually say yes—although the target may be specified not as a debt ratio but as a debt rating. For example, the firm might manage its capital structure to maintain a single-A bond rating. Ratio or rating, a target is consistent with the trade-off theory.[23]

But what are the facts? Can the trade-off theory of capital structure explain how companies actually behave?

The answer is "yes and no." On the "yes" side, the trade-off theory successfully explains many industry differences in capital structure. High-tech growth companies, whose assets are

---

[23]See J. Graham and C. Harvey, "The Theory and Practice of Corporate Finance: Evidence from the Field," *Journal of Financial Economics* 60 (May 2001), pp. 187–243.

risky and mostly intangible, normally use relatively little debt. Airlines can and do borrow heavily because their assets are tangible and relatively safe.[24]

On the "no" side, there are some things the trade-off theory cannot explain. It cannot explain why some of the most successful companies thrive with little debt. Think of Johnson & Johnson, which, as Table 17.4A shows, has relatively modest amounts of debt. Granted, Johnson & Johnson's most valuable assets are intangible, the fruits of its research and development. We know that intangible assets and conservative capital structures go together. But Johnson & Johnson pays about $2 billion of corporate income tax and has the highest possible credit rating. It could borrow enough to save tens of millions of dollars without raising a whisker of concern about possible financial distress.

Johnson & Johnson illustrates an odd fact about real-life capital structures: The most profitable companies commonly borrow the least.[25] Here the trade-off theory fails because it predicts exactly the reverse. Under the trade-off theory, high profits should mean more debt-servicing capacity and more taxable income to shield and so should give a *higher* target debt ratio.[26]

The tradeoff theory predicts that companies will rebalance their capital structures, issuing or retiring debt and equity to stay close to the optimal debt ratio. The evidence for rebalancing is weak.[27] Perhaps this is not surprising. Figure 17.4 locates the optimum at the top of a gentle curve. How can the financial manager know exactly where that optimum is? Should she be upset if her firm ends above or below it? If the curve is gentle, not much value is lost. In practice, it seems that many financial managers view the value function in Figure 17.4 as not curved but flat over a range of moderate debt ratios.

These shortcomings do not disprove the trade-off theory. As George Stigler emphasized, theories are not rejected by circumstantial evidence; it takes a theory to beat a theory. So we now turn to a completely different theory of financing.

17.4 Self-Test

Rank these industries in order of predicted debt ratios under the trade-off theory of capital structure:

    a. Internet software.

    b. Auto manufacturing.

    c. Regulated utilities.

17-4   The Pecking Order of Financing Choices

The pecking-order theory starts with *asymmetric information*—a fancy term indicating that managers know more about their companies' prospects, risks, and values than do outside investors.

Managers obviously know more than investors. We can prove that by observing the changes in stock prices when managers make announcements. For example, when a company

---

[24]We are not suggesting that all airline companies are safe; many are not. But air*craft* can support debt where air*lines* cannot. If Fly-by-Night Airlines fails, its planes retain their value in another airline's operations. There's a good secondary market in used aircraft, so a loan secured by aircraft can be well protected even if made to an airline flying on thin ice (and in the dark).

[25]For example, in an international comparison, Wald found that profitability was the single largest determinant of firm capital structure. See J. K. Wald, "How Firm Characteristics Affect Capital Structure: An International Comparison," *Journal of Financial Research* 22 (Summer 1999), pp. 161–187.

[26]Here we mean debt as a fraction of the book or replacement value of the company's assets. Profitable companies might not borrow a greater fraction of their market value. Higher profits imply higher market value as well as stronger incentives to borrow.

[27]For a recent example of research on this topic, see B. E. Eckbo and M. Kisser, "Tradeoff Theory and Leverage Dynamics of High-Frequency Debt Issuers," *Review of Finance* 25 (March 2021), pp. 275–324.

announces an increased regular dividend, stock price typically rises because investors interpret the increase as a sign of management's confidence in future earnings. In other words, the dividend increase transfers information from managers to investors. This can happen only if managers know more in the first place.

Asymmetric information affects the choice between internal and external financing and between new issues of debt and equity securities. This leads to a *pecking order,* in which investment is financed first with internal funds (reinvested earnings primarily), then by new issues of debt, and finally with new issues of equity. New equity issues are a last resort when the company runs out of debt capacity, that is, when the threat of costs of financial distress brings regular insomnia to existing creditors and to the financial manager.

We will take a closer look at the pecking order in a moment. First, we look at how asymmetric information can force the financial manager to issue debt rather than common stock.

Debt and Equity Issues with Asymmetric Information

To the outside world, Smith & Company and Jones Inc., our two example companies, are identical. Each runs a successful business with good growth opportunities. The two businesses are risky, however, and investors have learned from experience that current expectations are frequently bettered or disappointed. Current expectations price each company's stock at $100 per share, but the true values could be higher or lower:

	Smith & Co.	Jones, Inc.
True value could be higher, say	$120	$120
Best current estimate	100	100
True value could be lower, say	80	80

Now suppose that both companies need to raise new money from investors to fund capital investment. They can do this either by issuing bonds or by issuing new shares of common stock. How would the choice be made? One financial manager—we will not tell you which one—might reason as follows:

Sell stock for $100 per share? Ridiculous! It's worth at least $120. A stock issue now would hand a free gift to new investors. I just wish those skeptical shareholders would appreciate the true value of this company. Our new factories will make us the world's lowest-cost producer. We've painted a rosy picture for the press and security analysts, but it just doesn't seem to be working. Oh well, the decision is obvious: We'll issue debt, not underpriced equity. A debt issue will save underwriting fees too.

The other financial manager is in a different mood:

Beefalo burgers were a hit for a while, but it looks like the fad is fading. The fast-food division's gotta find some good new products or it's all downhill from here. Export markets are OK for now, but how are we going to compete with those new Siberian ranches? Fortunately, the stock price has held up pretty well—we've had some good short-run news for the press and security analysts. Now's the time to issue stock. We have major investments under way, and why add increased debt service to my other worries?

Of course, outside investors can't read the financial managers' minds. If they could, one stock might trade at $120 and the other at $80.

Why doesn't the optimistic financial manager simply educate investors? Then the company could sell stock on fair terms, and there would be no reason to favor debt over equity or vice versa.

This is not so easy. (Note that both companies are issuing upbeat press releases.) Investors can't be told what to think; they have to be convinced. That takes a detailed layout of the company's plans and prospects, including the inside scoop on new technology, product design, marketing plans, and so on. Getting this across is expensive for the company and also valuable to its competitors. Why go to the trouble? Investors will learn soon enough, as revenues and earnings evolve. In the meantime the optimistic financial manager can finance growth by issuing debt.

Now suppose there are two press releases:

> Jones Inc. will issue $120 million of five-year senior notes.

> Smith & Co. announced plans today to issue 1.2 million new shares of common stock. The company expects to raise $120 million.

As a rational investor, you immediately learn two things. First, Jones's financial manager is optimistic and Smith's is pessimistic. Second, Smith's financial manager is also naive to think that investors would pay $100 per share. The *attempt* to sell stock shows that it must be worth less. Smith might sell stock at $80 per share, but certainly not at $100.[28]

Smart financial managers think this through ahead of time. The end result? Both Smith and Jones end up issuing debt. Jones Inc. issues debt because its financial manager is optimistic and doesn't want to issue undervalued equity. A smart, but pessimistic, financial manager at Smith issues debt because an attempt to issue equity would force the stock price down and eliminate any advantage from doing so. (Issuing equity also reveals the manager's pessimism immediately. Most managers prefer to wait. A debt issue lets bad news come out later through other channels.)

The story of Smith and Jones illustrates how asymmetric information favors debt issues over equity issues. If managers are better informed than investors and both groups are rational, then any company that can borrow will do so rather than issuing fresh equity. In other words, debt issues will be higher in the pecking order.

Taken literally, this reasoning seems to rule out any issue of equity. That's not right because asymmetric information is not always important and there are other forces at work. For example, if Smith had already borrowed heavily, and would risk financial distress by borrowing more, then it would have a good reason to issue common stock. In this case, announcement of a stock issue would not be entirely bad news. The announcement would still depress the stock price—it would highlight managers' concerns about financial distress—but the fall in price would not necessarily make the issue unwise or infeasible.

High-tech, high-growth companies can also be credible issuers of common stock. Such companies' assets are mostly intangible, and bankruptcy or financial distress would be especially costly. This calls for conservative financing. The only way to grow rapidly and keep a conservative debt ratio is to issue equity. If investors see equity issued for these reasons, problems of the sort encountered by Smith's financial manager become much less serious.

With such exceptions noted, asymmetric information can explain the dominance of debt financing over new equity issues, at least for mature public corporations. Debt issues are frequent; equity issues, relatively rare. The bulk of external financing comes from debt, even in the United States, where equity markets are highly information-efficient. Equity issues are even more difficult in countries with less well-developed stock markets.

None of this says that firms ought to strive for high debt ratios—just that it can be better to raise equity by plowing back earnings than issuing stock. In fact, a firm with ample internally generated funds doesn't have to sell any kind of security and thus avoids issue costs and information problems completely.

---

[28]A Smith stock issue might not succeed even at $80. Persistence in trying to sell at $80 could convince investors that the stock is worth even less!

Implications of the Pecking Order

The *pecking-order theory* of corporate financing goes like this.

1. Firms prefer internal finance.

2. They adapt their target dividend payout ratios to their investment opportunities, while trying to avoid sudden changes in dividends.

3. Sticky dividend policies, plus unpredictable fluctuations in profitability and investment opportunities, mean that internally generated cash flow is sometimes more than capital expenditures and other times less. If it is more, the firm pays off debt or invests in marketable securities. If it is less, the firm first draws down its cash balance or sells its holdings of marketable securities.

4. If external finance is required, firms issue the safest security first. That is, they start with debt, then possibly hybrid securities such as convertible bonds, then perhaps equity as a last resort.

In this theory, there is no well-defined target debt–equity mix because there are two kinds of equity, internal and external, one at the top of the pecking order and one at the bottom. Each firm's observed debt ratio reflects its cumulative requirements for external finance.

The pecking order explains why the most profitable firms generally borrow less—not because they have low target debt ratios but because they don't need outside money. Less profitable firms issue debt because they do not have internal funds sufficient for their capital investment programs and because debt financing is first on the pecking order of *external* financing.

In the pecking-order theory, the attraction of interest tax shields is assumed to be second-order. Debt ratios change when there is an imbalance of internal cash flow, net of dividends, and real investment opportunities. Highly profitable firms with limited investment opportunities work down to low debt ratios. Firms whose investment opportunities outrun internally generated funds are driven to borrow more and more.

This theory explains the inverse intra-industry relationship between profitability and financial leverage. Suppose firms generally invest to keep up with the growth of their industries. Then rates of investment will be similar within an industry. Given sticky dividend payouts, the least profitable firms will have less internal funds and will end up borrowing more.

The Bright Side and the Dark Side of Financial Slack

Other things equal, it's better to be at the top of the pecking order than at the bottom. Firms that have worked down the pecking order and need external equity may end up living with excessive debt or passing by good investments because shares can't be sold at what managers consider a fair price.

In other words, *financial slack* is valuable. Having financial slack means having cash, marketable securities, readily salable real assets, and ready access to debt markets or to bank financing. Ready access basically requires conservative financing so that potential lenders see the company's debt as a safe investment.

In the long run, a company's value rests more on its capital investment and operating decisions than on financing. Therefore, you want to make sure your firm has sufficient financial slack so that financing is quickly available for good investments. Financial slack is most valuable to firms with plenty of positive-NPV growth opportunities. That is another reason why growth companies usually aspire to conservative capital structures.

Financial slack is especially available for companies planning a major, multi-year capital investment program. Fu and Smith, in a study of 7,000 U.S. equity issues between 1970 and 2017, found that companies typically issued equity *before* such programs. The fresh equity of course reduced the companies' debt ratios, but the ratios drifted back up as the companies then turned to debt financing to complete the investments.[29]

There is also a dark side to financial slack. Too much of it may encourage managers to take it easy, expand their perks, or empire-build with cash that should be paid back to stockholders. In other words, slack can make agency problems worse.

Michael Jensen has stressed the tendency of managers with ample free cash flow (or unnecessary financial slack) to plow too much cash into mature businesses or ill-advised acquisitions. "The problem," Jensen says, "is how to motivate managers to disgorge the cash rather than investing it below the cost of capital or wasting it in organizational inefficiencies."[30]

If that's the problem, then maybe debt is an answer. Scheduled interest and principal payments are contractual obligations of the firm. Debt forces the firm to pay out cash. Perhaps the best debt level would leave just enough cash in the bank, after debt service, to finance all positive-NPV projects, with not a penny left over.

We do not recommend this degree of fine-tuning, but the idea is valid and important. Debt can discipline managers who are tempted to invest too much. It can also provide the pressure to force improvements in operating efficiency. We pick up this theme again in Chapter 33.

BEYOND THE PAGE

Ford Cashes in on All of Its Financial Slack

mhhe.com/brealey14e

BEYOND THE PAGE

Sealed Air's recapitalization

mhhe.com/brealey14e

17.5 Self-Test

For each of the following observations state whether they better support the trade-off theory or the pecking-order theory.

    a. Utilities with safe and tangible assets borrow relatively heavily.

    b. The most profitable companies borrow least.

    c. Most external financing is in the form of debt rather than equity.

    d. Increases in corporate tax rates appear to have been followed by increases in debt levels.

17-5   **The Capital Structure Decision**

The Evidence

The trade-off theory emphasizes the importance of interest tax shields as an incentive to borrow. However, the evidence on the effect of taxes is mixed. Studies have been unable to identify an effect of tax shields on market values.[31] It seems that taxpaying companies are more likely than nontaxpaying companies to issue debt rather than equity,[32] but the substantial variations over time in an individual company's debt ratio appear to have more to do with the need to finance heavy capital investment than with variations in the tax advantage of debt.[33]

---

[29]Fu and Smith classified about 80% of their sample of issuers as growth companies. Information problems are less severe when growth companies issue stock. They are credible issuers because they need cash for investment. See F. Fu and C. W. Smith, "Strategic Financial Management: Lessons from Seasoned Equity Offerings," *Journal of Applied Corporate Finance* 33 (Winter 2021), pp. 22–35.

[30]M. C. Jensen, "Agency Costs of Free Cash Flow, Corporate Finance and Takeovers," *American Economic Review* 76 (May 1986), pp. 323–329.

[31]A study by E. F. Fama and K. R. French, covering over 2,000 firms from 1965 to 1992, failed to find any evidence that interest tax shields contributed to firm value. See "Taxes, Financing Decisions and Firm Value," *Journal of Finance* 53 (June 1998), pp. 819–843.

[32]MacKie-Mason found that taxpaying companies are more likely to issue debt (vs. equity) than nontaxpaying companies. See J. MacKie-Mason, "Do Taxes Affect Corporate Financing Decisions?" *Journal of Finance* 45 (December 1990), pp. 1471–1493.

[33]Debt ratios for individual companies have fluctuated dramatically when tracked over decades. For example, IBM's book debt ratio peaked at about 40% in the mid-1950s, fell to nearly zero in the mid-1970s, and rose again to about 30% at the turn of the century. International Paper's debt ratio fluctuated between 20% and 40% between 1909 and the end of World War II, then fell to zero until the mid-1960s, when it popped back into the 20–40% range. Such increases in leverage appeared to be a response to heavy capital investment and large requirements for external financing H. DeAngelo and R. Roll, "Capital Structure Instability," *Journal of Applied Corporate Finance* 28 (Fall 2016), pp. 38–52.

There is rather more evidence that the *aggregate* amount of corporate borrowing is affected by changes in tax rates. When the current U.S. system of corporate income taxes was introduced in 1909, the tax rate was set at 1%. By 1968, it had climbed to 52.8% before steadily falling to its current level in 2021 at the time of writing of 21%. So the incentive for companies to borrow has varied considerably over time. A study of company borrowing during these years concluded that companies have responded somewhat to these tax changes. Between 1926 and 2009, a 1% increase in the corporate tax rate was followed by an average increase of 0.2% in corporate leverage so the effect is significant but not huge.[34]

There is also some indirect evidence on alternative theories of capital structure. For example, a study of debt versus equity choices by large firms in seven major economies suggested that differences in debt ratios depended on four factors[35]:

1. *Size.* Large firms tend to have higher debt ratios.

2. *Tangible assets.* Firms with high ratios of fixed assets to total assets have higher debt ratios.

3. *Market-to-book.* Firms with higher ratios of market-to-book value have lower debt ratios.

4. *Profitability.* More profitable firms have lower debt ratios.

These results convey good news for both the trade-off and pecking-order theories. Trade-off enthusiasts note that large companies with tangible assets are less exposed to the costs of financial distress and would be expected to borrow more. They interpret the market-to-book ratio as a measure of growth opportunities and argue that growth companies face high costs of financial distress and, therefore, should borrow less.[36] On the other hand, the observation that the more profitable firms borrow less does not fit so well with the trade-off theory. Instead, pecking-order advocates point to the fact that profitable firms use less debt because they can rely on internal financing, which is higher in the pecking order.

It seems that we have two competing theories, and there is some evidence for both. That's not a comfortable conclusion. So researchers have tried to run horse races between the two theories in order to find the circumstances in which one or the other wins. It seems that the pecking order works best for large, mature firms that have access to public bond markets. These firms rarely issue equity. They prefer internal financing but turn to debt markets if needed to finance investment. Smaller, younger, growth firms are more likely to rely on equity issues when external financing is required.[37]

Neither the trade-off nor the pecking-order theories capture all the considerations that may sway the capital structure choice. For example, there is some evidence that debt ratios incorporate the cumulative effects of *market timing*.[38] Market timing is an example of behavioral

---

[34]See M. Fleckenstein, F. A. Longstaff, and I. A. Strebulaev, "Corporate Taxes and Capital Structure: A Long-Term Historical Perspective," *Critical Finance Review* 9 (2020), pp. 1–28.

[35]R. G. Rajan and L. Zingales, "What Do We Know about Capital Structure? Some Evidence from International Data," *Journal of Finance* 50 (December 1995), pp. 1421–1460. The same four factors seem to work in developing economies. See L. Booth, V. Aivazian, A. Demirguc-Kunt, and V. Maksimovic, "Capital Structures in Developing Countries," *Journal of Finance* 56 (February 2001), pp. 87–130.

[36]As we explain shortly, growth opportunities provide hidden leverage. This hidden leverage is another reason that they may be reluctant to borrow.

[37]L. Shyam-Sunder and S. C. Myers found that the pecking-order hypothesis outperformed the trade-off hypothesis for a sample of large companies in the 1980s. See "Testing Static Trade-off against Pecking-Order Models of Capital Structure," *Journal of Financial Economics* 51 (February 1999), pp. 219–244. M. Frank and V. Goyal found that the performance of the pecking-order hypothesis deteriorated in the 1990s, especially for small growth firms. See "Testing the Pecking Order Theory of Capital Structure," *Journal of Financial Economics* 67 (February 2003), pp. 217–248. See also E. Fama and K. French, "Testing Trade-off and Pecking Order Predictions about Dividends and Debt," *Review of Financial Studies* 15 (Spring 2002), pp. 1–33; and M. L. Lemmon and J. F. Zender, "Debt Capacity and Tests of Capital Structure Theories," *Journal of Financial and Quantitative Analysis* 45 (2010), pp. 1161–1187.

[38]M. Baker and J. Wurgler, "Market Timing and Capital Structure," *Journal of Finance* 57 (February 2002), pp. 1–32.

corporate finance. Suppose that investors are sometimes irrationally exuberant (as in the late 1990s and perhaps in 2021 as pandemic lockdowns end) and sometimes irrationally despondent. If the financial manager's views are more stable than investors', then she can take advantage by issuing shares when the stock price is high and switching to debt when the price is low. Thus, lucky companies with a history of buoyant stock prices will issue less debt and more shares, ending up with low debt ratios. Unfortunate and unpopular companies will avoid share issues and end up with high debt ratios. Market timing could explain why companies tend to issue shares after run-ups in stock prices and also why aggregate stock issues are concentrated in bull markets and fall sharply in bear markets.

There are other behavioral explanations for corporate financing policies. For example, a study of individual CEOs, CFOs, and other top managers found that their individual "styles" persisted as they moved from firm to firm.[39] For example, older CEOs tended to be more conservative and pushed their firms to lower debt. CEOs with MBA degrees tended to be more aggressive. In general, financial decisions depended not just on the nature of the firm and its economic environment, but also on the personalities of the firm's top management.

International comparisons of financing policies have identified a number of institutional differences between countries that may also be important. Debt ratios tend to be higher in countries where the interest tax shield is more valuable, but they are also higher in countries with weaker laws and more government corruption.[40]

Is There a Theory of Optimal Capital Structure?

No. That is, there is no *one* theory that can capture everything that drives thousands of corporations' debt versus equity choices. Instead, there are several theories, each more or less helpful, depending on each particular corporation's assets, operations, and circumstances.

In other words, don't waste time searching for a magic formula for the optimal debt ratio. Remember too that most value comes from the left side of the balance sheet—that is, from the firm's operations, assets, and growth opportunities. Financing is less important. Of course, financing can subtract value rapidly if you screw it up, but you won't do that.

In practice, financing choices depend on the relative importance of the factors discussed in this chapter. In some cases, reducing taxes will be the primary objective. Thus, high debt ratios are found in the lease-financing business (see Chapter 26). Long-term leases are often tax-driven transactions. High debt ratios are also found in developed commercial real estate. For example, modern downtown office buildings can be safe, cash-cow assets if the office space is rented to creditworthy tenants. Bankruptcy costs are small, so it makes sense to lever up and save taxes.

For smaller growth companies, interest tax shields are less important than preserving financial slack. Profitable growth opportunities are valuable only if financing is available when it comes time to invest. Costs of financial distress are high, so it's no surprise that growth companies try to use mostly equity financing.

There's another reason growth companies borrow less. Their growth opportunities are real options—that is, options to invest in real assets. These options contain lots of hidden financial risk. We will see in Chapters 21 through 23 that an option to buy a real asset is equivalent to a claim on a fraction of the asset's value, plus an implicit debt obligation. The implicit debt obligation is usually larger than the net value of the option itself.

A growth company therefore bears financial risk even if it does not borrow a dime explicitly. It makes sense for such a company to offset the financial risk created by growth options

BEYOND THE PAGE

Apple's debt issue

mhhe.com/brealey14e

---

[39]M. Bertrand and A. Schoar, "Managing with Style: The Effect of Managers on Firm Policies," *Quarterly Journal of Economics* 118 (November 2003), pp. 1169–1208.

[40]J. P. H. Fan, S. Titman, and G. Twite, "An International Comparison of Capital Structure and Debt Maturity Choice," *Journal of Financial and Quantitative Analysis* 47 (February 2012), pp. 23–56.

by reducing the amount of debt on its balance sheet. The implicit debt in its growth options ends up displacing explicit debt.

Growth options are less important for mature corporations. Such companies can and usually do borrow more. They often end up following the pecking order. Information problems deter large equity issues, so such firms prefer to finance investment with retained earnings. They issue more debt when investments outrun retained earnings, and pay down debt when earnings outpace investment.

Sooner or later, a corporation's operations age to the point where growth opportunities evaporate. In that case, the firm may issue large amounts of debt and retire equity, to constrain investment and force payout of cash to investors. The higher debt ratio may come voluntarily or be forced by a takeover.

These examples are not exhaustive, but they give some flavor of how a thoughtful CEO can set financing strategy.

- - - - -

KEY TAKEAWAYS

Our task in this chapter was to show why capital structure matters. We did not throw away MM's proposition that capital structure is irrelevant; we added to it. We surveyed the factors that affect the decision to borrow, but we did not arrive at any simple, universal theory of optimal capital structure. However, we did show that there are a number of important factors to be taken into account in choosing capital structure.

- **Interest tax shields** Borrowing reduces taxes because interest is a tax-deductible expense. In the (extreme) case of fixed and permanent debt,

$$\text{PV(tax shield)} = \frac{T_c r_D D}{r_D} = T_c D$$

Tax shields are worth less than $T_C D$ in practice. Debt is not permanent or fixed. Also, the personal tax that lenders pay on interest income can offset the benefits of the corporate tax shield. Interest tax shields nevertheless generally reward borrowing.

- **Financial distress** High debt levels increase the risk of financial distress. The costs of distress are:

  1. The direct costs of bankruptcy and the extra costs of managing a business undergoing bankruptcy and reorganization.

  2. Costs that arise when customers, suppliers, and employees can no longer be confident of a business's viability.

  3. Agency costs that stem from conflicts of interest between shareholders and bondholders.

- **Trade-off theory** The value of the firm can be broken down as:

  Value if all-equity-financed + PV(tax shield) − PV(costs of financial distress)

  The trade-off theory says that the firm should increase debt until the increase in PV(tax shield) is just offset by increases in PV(costs of financial distress). Firms with safe, tangible assets, and plenty of taxable income ought to have high debt ratios. Unprofitable companies with risky, intangible assets ought to rely more on equity.

- **The pecking-order theory** This theory emphasizes the negative information conveyed by an issue of equity. Firms use internal financing when available and choose debt over equity when external financing is required. This explains why the less profitable firms in an industry borrow more—not because they have higher target debt ratios but because they need more external financing and because debt is next in the pecking order when internal funds are exhausted.

- **Financial slack** Financial slack is the ability to get cash on short notice for unexpected opportunities or setbacks. The pecking-order theory stresses the value of financial slack. Without sufficient slack, the firm may be forced to choose between issuing undervalued shares, borrowing and risking financial distress, or passing up positive-NPV investment opportunities. There is, however, a dark side to financial slack. Surplus cash tempts managers to overinvest. In such cases, a high debt ratio can help by forcing the company to disgorge cash and run a tighter ship.

- **The evidence** Debt ratios are higher in mature industries with mostly tangible assets, as the trade-off theory predicts. Interest tax shields encourage borrowing, but the most profitable, tax paying firms that seem best placed to borrow in practice borrow less.

  Debt ratios change as the firm ages. Young firms with plenty of growth opportunities need financial slack and borrow less. Mature firms with few growth opportunities tend to borrow more. Also, mature firms are less likely to issue stock. Instead, they rely more on internal funds and borrowing to finance investment.

● ● ● ● ●

FURTHER READING

The research literature on capital structure is enormous. We cite only a few of the most important and interesting articles. The following review articles give broader surveys:

M. Harris and A. Raviv, "The Theory of Capital Structure," *Journal of Finance* 46 (March 1991), pp. 297–355.

S. C. Myers, "Financing of Corporations," in G. M. Constantinides, M. Harris, and R. Stulz, eds., *Handbook of the Economics of Finance* (Amsterdam: North-Holland, 2003).

M. Frank and V. Goyal, "Trade-off and Pecking Order Theories of Debt," in E. Eckbo, ed., *Handbook of Corporate Finance: Empirical Finance,* vol. 2 (Amsterdam: North-Holland, 2008).

J. R. Graham and M. T. Leary, "A Review of Empirical Capital Structure Research and Directions for the Future," *Annual Review of Financial Economics* 3 (2011), 309–345.

The Fall 2016 issue of the Journal of Applied Corporate Finance *contains several articles on capital structure decisions in practice.*

The following paper surveys chief financial officers' views about capital structure:

J. Graham and C. Harvey, "How Do CFOs Make Capital Budgeting and Capital Structure Decisions?" *Journal of Applied Corporate Finance* 15 (Spring 2002), pp. 8–23.

● ● ● ● ●

PROBLEM SETS

Mc Graw Hill **connect®** Select problems are available in McGraw Hill's *Connect.*
Please see the preface for more information.

1. **Tax shields (S17-1)** The present value of interest tax shields is often written as $T_c D$, where D is the amount of debt and T_c is the marginal corporate tax rate. Under what assumptions is this present value calculation correct?

2. **Tax shields (S17-1)** Compute the present value of interest tax shields generated by these three debt issues. Consider corporate taxes only. Assume that the marginal tax rate is $T_c = 0.30$.

   a. A $1,000, one-year loan at 8%.

   b. A five-year loan of $1,000 at 8%. Assume no principal is repaid until maturity.

   c. A $1,000 perpetuity at 7%.

3. **Tax shields (S17-1)** Here are book and market value balance sheets of the United Frypan Company (UF):

Book				Market			
Net working capital	$ 20	$ 40	Debt	Net working capital	$ 20	$ 40	Debt
Long-term assets	80	60	Equity	Long-term assets	140	120	Equity
	$100	$100			$160	$160	

Assume that MM's theory holds with taxes. There is no growth, and the $40 of debt is expected to be fixed and permanent. Assume a 40% corporate tax rate.

a. How much of the firm's value in dollar terms is accounted for by the debt-generated tax shield?

b. How much better off will UF's shareholders be if the firm borrows $20 more and uses it to repurchase stock?

4. **Tax shields (S17-1)** Look back at the Johnson & Johnson example in Section 17-1. Suppose Johnson & Johnson increases its long-term debt to $50 billion. It uses the additional debt to repurchase shares. Reconstruct Table 17.4B with the new capital structure. How much additional value is added for Johnson & Johnson shareholders if the table's assumptions are correct?

5. **Tax shields (S17-1)** What is the relative tax advantage of corporate debt if the corporate tax rate is $T_c = 0.21$, the personal tax rate on interest is $T_{pD} = 0.37$, but all equity income is received as capital gains and escapes tax entirely ($T_{pE} = 0$)? How does the relative tax advantage change if the company decides to pay out all equity income as cash dividends that are taxed at 20%?

6. **Tax shields (S17-1)** "The firm can't use interest tax shields unless it has (taxable) income to shield." What does this statement imply for debt policy? Explain briefly.

7. **Tax shields (S17-1)** Suppose that Congress sets the top personal tax rate on interest and dividends at 35% and the top rate on realized capital gains at 15%. The corporate tax rate stays at 21%. Compute the difference between the total corporate plus personal taxes paid on debt and the total taxes on equity income if (a) all capital gains are realized immediately and (b) capital gains are deferred forever. Assume capital gains are half of equity income.

8. **Tax shields (S17-1)** "The trouble with MM's argument is that it ignores the fact that individuals cannot deduct interest for personal income tax." Show why this is not an objection if personal tax rates on interest and equity income are the same.

9. **Bankruptcy costs (S17-2)** On February 28, 2025, when PDQ Computers announced bankruptcy, its share price fell from $3.00 to $.50 per share. There were 10 million shares outstanding. Does that imply bankruptcy costs of 10 × (3.00 – 0.50) = $25 million? Explain.

10. **Bankruptcy costs (S17-2)** Look at some real companies with different types of assets. What operating problems would each encounter in the event of financial distress? How well would the assets keep their value?

11. **Financial distress (S17-2)** This question tests your understanding of financial distress.

a. What are the costs of going bankrupt? Define these costs carefully.

b. "A company can incur costs of financial distress without ever going bankrupt." Explain how this can happen.

c. Explain how conflicts of interest between bondholders and stockholders can lead to costs of financial distress.

12. **Financial distress (S17-2)** True or false?

a. If the probability of default is high, managers and stockholders will be tempted to take on excessively risky projects.

b. If the probability of default is high, stockholders may refuse to contribute equity even if the firm has safe positive-NPV opportunities.

c. When a company borrows, the expected costs of bankruptcy come out of the lenders' pockets and do not affect the market value of the shares.

13. **Agency costs (S17-2)** In Section 17-2, we briefly referred to three games: playing for time, cash in and run, and bait and switch.

    For each game, construct a simple numerical example (like the example for the risk-shifting game) showing how shareholders can gain at the expense of creditors. Then explain how the temptation to play these games could lead to costs of financial distress.

14. **Agency costs (S17-2)** Let us go back to Circular File's market value balance sheet:

Net working capital	$20	$27	Bonds outstanding
Fixed assets	10	3	Common stock
Total assets	$30	$30	Total value

Who gains and who loses from the following maneuvers?

a. Circular scrapes up $5 in cash and pays a cash dividend.

b. Circular halts operations, sells its fixed assets, and converts net working capital into $20 cash. Unfortunately, the fixed assets fetch only $6 on the secondhand market. The $26 cash is invested in Treasury bills.

c. Circular encounters an acceptable investment opportunity, NPV = 0, requiring an investment of $10. The firm borrows to finance the project. The new debt has the same security, seniority, and so on, as the old.

d. Suppose that the new project has NPV = +$2 and is financed by an issue of preferred stock.

e. The lenders agree to extend the maturity of their loan from two years to three in order to give Circular a chance to recover.

15. **Agency costs (S17-2)** The Salad Oil Storage (SOS) Company has financed a large part of its facilities with long-term debt. There is a significant risk of default, but the company is not on the ropes yet. Explain:

a. Why SOS stockholders could lose by investing in a positive-NPV project financed by an equity issue.

b. Why SOS stockholders could gain by investing in a negative-NPV project financed by cash.

c. Why SOS stockholders could gain from paying out a large cash dividend.

16. **Agency costs (S17-2)** The possible payoffs from Ms. Crane's projects (see Example 17.2) have not changed but there is now a 40% chance that project 2 will pay off $24 and a 60% chance that it will pay off $0.

a. Recalculate the expected payoffs to the bank and Ms. Crane if the bank lends the present value of $10. Which project would Ms. Crane undertake?

b. What is the maximum amount the bank could lend that would induce Ms. Crane to take project 1?

17. **Covenants (S17-2)**

a. Who benefits from the fine print in bond contracts when the firm gets into financial trouble? Give a one-sentence answer.

b. Who benefits from the fine print when the bonds are issued? Suppose the firm is offered the choice of issuing (1) a bond with standard restrictions on dividend payout, additional borrowing, and so on, and (2) a bond with minimal restrictions but a much higher interest rate? Suppose the interest rates on both (1) and (2) are fair from the viewpoint of lenders. Which bond would you expect the firm to issue? Why?

18. **Trade-off theory (S17-3)** The traditional theory of optimal capital structure states that firms trade off corporate interest tax shields against the possible costs of financial distress due to borrowing. What does this theory predict about the relationship between book profitability and target book debt ratios? Is the theory's prediction consistent with the facts?

19. **Pecking-order theory (S17-4)** "I was amazed to find that the announcement of a stock issue drives down the value of the issuing firm by 20–30%, on average, of the proceeds of the issue. That issue cost dwarfs the underwriter's spread and the administrative costs of the issue. It makes common stock issues prohibitively expensive."

    a. You are contemplating a $100 million stock issue. On past evidence, you anticipate that announcement of this issue will drive down stock price by 3% and that the market value of your firm will fall by 30% of the amount to be raised. On the other hand, additional equity financing is required to fund an investment project that you believe has a positive NPV of $40 million. Should you proceed with the issue?

    b. Is the fall in market value on announcement of a stock issue an *issue cost* in the same sense as an underwriter's spread? Respond to the quote that begins this question.

    Use your answer to part (a) as a numerical example to explain your response to part (b).

20. **Pecking-order theory (S17-4)** Why does asymmetric information push companies to raise external funds by borrowing rather than by issuing common stock?

21. **Pecking-order theory (S17-4)** Fill in the blanks: According to the pecking-order theory,

    a. The firm's debt ratio is determined by _____.

    b. Debt ratios depend on past profitability, because _____.

22. **Financial slack (S17-4)** For what kinds of companies is financial slack most valuable? Are there situations in which financial slack should be reduced by borrowing and paying out the proceeds to the stockholders? Explain.

23. **Financial slack (S17-4)** True or false?

    a. Financial slack means having cash in the bank or ready access to the debt markets.

    b. Financial slack is most valuable to firms with few investment opportunities and poor prospects.

    c. Managers with excessive financial slack may be tempted to spend it on poor investments.

24. **Leverage targets (S17-4)** Some corporations' debt–equity targets are expressed not as a debt ratio but as a target debt rating on the firm's outstanding bonds. What are the pros and cons of setting a target rating rather than a target ratio?

25. **Market timing (S17-5)** Suppose financial managers can use inside information to time equity issues when stock price is unrealistically high. How would capital structure evolve? Explain briefly.

26. **Evidence (S17-5)** A study of capital structure in several developed countries found that debt ratios were positively related to firm size and the proportion of tangible versus intangible assets and negatively related to market-book ratios and profitability. What do these relationships imply for the accuracy of the tradeoff theory? Explain.

CHALLENGE

27. **Trade-off theory (S17-3)** The trade-off theory relies on the threat of financial distress. But why should a public corporation ever have to land in financial distress? According to the theory, the firm should operate at the top of the curve in Figure 17.4. Of course market movements or business setbacks could bump it up to a higher debt ratio and put it on the declining, right-hand side of the curve. But in that case, why doesn't the firm just issue equity, retire debt, and move back up to the optimal debt ratio? What are the reasons companies don't issue stock—or enough stock—quickly enough to avoid financial distress?

28. **Leverage measures (S17-3–S17-4)** Most financial managers measure debt ratios from their companies' book balance sheets. Many financial economists emphasize ratios from market-value balance sheets. Which is the right measure in principle? Does the trade-off theory propose to explain book or market leverage? How about the pecking-order theory?

17.1 a. $T_C D = 0.25 \times 15 = \$3.75$ million.

   b. It would not change, assuming that the bond issue was NPV = 0, apart from taxes, at the new 8% rate.

   c. The future tax shield now varies with the value of the company and is risky. It should be discounted at a higher rate and is therefore less valuable.

17.2 Bond value is reduced in a future bankruptcy. The prospect of legal costs causes bondholders to demand a higher interest rate today. This reduces today's value of the common stock.

17.3 The biotech company. Its assets are intangible. If bankruptcy threatens and the best scientists quit, there may not be much value remaining. On the other hand, bankruptcy would have little effect on the value of the oil wells and reserves.

17.4 From highest to lowest debt ratios: 1. regulated utilities; 2. auto manufacturing; 3. Internet software.

17.5 a. The high debt levels of utilities are consistent with the trade-off theory.

   b. The fact that the most profitable companies borrow least is consistent with the pecking-order theory.

   c. The fact that most external financing is in the form of debt rather than equity is consistent with the pecking-order theory.

   d. The fact that increases in corporate tax rates appear to have been followed by increases in debt levels is consistent with the trade-off theory.

You can download data for the following questions from the Yahoo! Finance website (**www.finance.yahoo.com**).

1. Look up Johnson & Johnson on Yahoo! Finance.

   a. Recalculate book- and market-value balance sheets using the most recent available financial information. Use the same format as for Table 17.3.

   b. Track Johnson & Johnson's long-term debt and debt ratio over the last five years (you will need to go to the company's website to do this). How have they changed? Does it appear that the company has a stable target debt ratio? Do you see any evidence of pecking-order financing?

   c. How much has the company spent to repurchase its own shares? Would the trade-off theory predict share repurchases for a conservatively financed company like Johnson & Johnson?

2. Select three or four companies from the Yahoo! Finance database. Estimate how much more these companies could borrow before they would exhaust taxable profits.

Financing and Valuation

In Chapters 5 and 6, we showed how to value a capital investment project by a four-step procedure:

1. Forecast after-tax cash flows, assuming all-equity financing.

2. Assess the project's risk.

3. Estimate the opportunity cost of capital, that is, the required return with all-equity financing.

4. Calculate NPV, using the opportunity cost of capital as the discount rate.

There's nothing wrong with this procedure, but now we're going to extend it to include value contributed by financing decisions. There are two ways to do this:

1. *Adjust the discount rate.* To take account of the interest tax shields, companies usually adjust the discount rate downward. They do this by calculating an after-tax weighted average cost of capital (WACC).

2. *Adjust the present value.* The *adjusted present value* (APV) method calculates value in two or more steps. You start with a base-case net present value assuming all-equity financing. Then you calculate the present values added or subtracted by financing. APV adds up all the present values to get the complete project value.

Section 18-1 The after-tax weighted-average cost of capital

We explain how to calculate the after-tax weighted-average cost of capital (WACC) and show how to use it to value an investment project.

Section 18-2 Valuing businesses

We work through a realistic example to show how WACC can also be used to value an entire business.

Section 18-3 Using WACC in practice

This section covers some tricks of the trade. It offers helpful suggestions about estimating inputs and adjusting the after-tax WACC when business risk or capital structure changes.

Section 18-4 Using the adjusted present value method

The adjusted present value (APV) method starts by valuing a project or business as if it were all-equity financed and then separately adds in the extra value from financing. We show how to use APV to value an operating business—the same business valued in Section 18-2 using an after-tax WACC. You will be reassured to see that the two valuation approaches lead to the same end result when financing matters only because of taxes and the firm sticks to a constant debt ratio.

Section 18-5 Your questions answered

This is a question-and-answer session designed to clarify points that can often be confusing.

Appendix Discounting Safe Nominal Cash Flows

The appendix covers an important special case, the valuation of safe after-tax cash flows. We explain that the correct discount rate is the *after-tax* interest rate.

This chapter contains several extended numerical examples. To keep things simple, we will follow current (2021) U.S. tax law in all of them, using the 21% corporate tax rate and 100% bonus depreciation implemented in 2018. You can explore the effects of different tax rates and depreciation schedules when you tackle the end-of-chapter problems.

18-1 **The After-Tax Weighted-Average Cost of Capital**

We first addressed problems of valuation and capital budgeting in Chapters 4 and 6. In those early chapters, we said hardly a word about financing decisions. We separated investment from financing decisions. If the investment project was positive-NPV, we assumed that the firm would go ahead, without asking whether the choice of finance for the project would create additional value. We were really assuming a Modigliani–Miller (MM) world in which all financing decisions are irrelevant. In a strict MM world, firms can analyze real investments as if they are all-equity-financed; the actual financing plan is a value-irrelevant detail to be worked out later.

Under MM assumptions, decisions to spend money can be separated from decisions to raise money. Now we reconsider the capital budgeting decision when investment and financing decisions interact and cannot be wholly separated.

One reason financing and investment decisions interact is taxes. Debt interest generates *tax shields* because it is a tax-deductible expense. The tax shields are accounted for in the *after-tax* weighted-average cost of capital:

$$\text{WACC} = r_D(1 - T_c)\frac{D}{V} + r_E\frac{E}{V} \tag{18.1}$$

Here, D and E are the market values of the firm's debt and equity; $V = D + E$ is the total market value of the firm; r_D and r_E are the costs of debt and equity, respectively; and T_c is the marginal corporate tax rate.

Notice that the WACC formula uses the *after-tax* cost of debt $r_D(1 - T_c)$. That is how the after-tax WACC captures the value of interest tax shields. Notice too that all the variables in the WACC formula refer to the firm as a whole. As a result, the formula gives the right discount rate only for projects that are just like the firm undertaking them. The formula works for the "average" project. It is incorrect for projects that are safer or riskier than the average of the firm's existing assets. It is incorrect for projects whose acceptance would lead to an increase or decrease in the firm's target debt ratio.

The WACC is based on the firm's *current* characteristics, but managers use it to discount *future* cash flows. That's fine as long as the firm's business risk and debt ratio (measured in market values) are expected to remain constant, but when the business risk and debt ratio are expected to change, discounting cash flows by the WACC is only approximately correct.

Many firms set a single, companywide WACC but update it if there are major changes in risk and interest rates. The WACC is a common reference point that avoids divisional squabbles about discount rates.[1] But all financial managers need to know how to adjust WACC when business risks and financing assumptions change. We show how to make these adjustments later in this chapter.

EXAMPLE 18.1 • Calculating Sangria's WACC

Sangria is a U.S.-based company whose products aim to promote happy, low-stress lifestyles. Let's calculate Sangria's WACC. Its book and market-value balance sheets are

Sangria Corporation (Book Values, $ millions)			
Asset value	$1,000	$ 500	Debt
		500	Equity
	$1,000	$1,000	

---

[1]See Section 9-1 under "Perfect Pitch and the Cost of Capital."

Sangria Corporation (Market Values, $ millions)			
Asset value	$1,250	$ 500	Debt
		750	Equity
	$1,250	$ 1,250	

We calculated the market value of equity on Sangria's balance sheet by multiplying its current stock price ($7.50) by 100 million, the number of its outstanding shares. The company's future prospects are good, so the stock is trading above book value ($7.50 vs. $5.00 per share). However, interest rates have been stable since the firm's debt was issued, so the book and market values of debt are, in this case, equal.

Sangria's cost of debt (the market interest rate on new borrowing)[2] is 6%. Its cost of equity (the expected rate of return demanded by investors in Sangria's stock) is 12.5%.

The market-value balance sheet shows assets worth $1,250 million. Of course, we can't observe this value directly because the assets themselves are not traded. But we know what they are worth to debt and equity investors ($500 + 750 = $1,250 million). This value is entered on the left of the market-value balance sheet.

Why did we show the book balance sheet? Only so you could draw a big X through it. Do so now.

Think of the WACC as the expected rate of return on a *portfolio* of the firm's outstanding debt and equity. The portfolio weights depend on market values. The expected rate of return on the market-value portfolio reveals the expected rate of return demanded by investors for committing their hard-earned money to the firm's assets and operations.

When estimating the weighted-average cost of capital, you are not interested in past investments but in current values and expectations for the future. Sangria's true debt ratio is not 50%, the book ratio, but 40% because its assets are worth $1,250 million. The cost of equity, $r_E = .125$, is the expected rate of return from purchase of stock at $7.50 per share, the current market price. It is not the return on book value per share. You can't buy shares in Sangria for $5 anymore.

Sangria is consistently profitable and pays taxes at the marginal rate of 21%. This tax rate is the final input for Sangria's WACC. The inputs are summarized here:

Cost of debt (r_D)	0.06
Cost of equity (r_E)	0.125
Marginal tax rate (T_c)	0.21
Debt ratio (D/V)	500/1,250 = 0.4
Equity ratio (E/V)	750/1,250 = 0.6

The company's after-tax WACC is

$$\text{WACC} = 0.06 \times (1 - 0.21) \times 0.4 + 0.125 \times 0.6$$
$$= 0.094, \text{ or } 9.4\%$$

● ● ● ● ●

18.1 Self-Test

Serial Music has a long-standing policy of financing with 50% debt, 50% equity at book values. The average interest rate on existing debt is 4.5%, but new debt can be issued at 3.5%. Its common stock is trading at two times book value per share. The cost of equity is 9.5%. The corporate tax rate is 21%. What is Serial's after-tax WACC?

---

[2] Always use an up-to-date interest rate (yield to maturity), not the interest rate when the firm's debt was first issued and not the coupon rate on the debt's book value.

Now let's see how Sangria would *use* its after-tax WACC.

EXAMPLE 18.2 • Using Sangria's WACC to Value a Project

Sangria's enologists have proposed investing $12.5 million in the construction of a perpetual crushing machine, which (conveniently for us) generates a perpetual stream of earnings and cash flow of $1.487 million per year pretax. The project is average risk, so we can use WACC. The after-tax cash flow is:

Pretax cash flow	$1.487 million
Tax at 21%	0.312
After-tax cash flow	$C = $1.175 million

Note: This after-tax cash flow takes no account of interest tax shields on debt supported by the perpetual crusher project. As we explained in Chapter 6, standard capital budgeting practice separates investment from financing decisions and calculates after-tax cash flows as if the project were all-equity-financed. However, the interest tax shields will not be ignored: We are about to discount the project's cash flows by Sangria's after-tax WACC, in which the cost of debt is entered after tax. The value of interest tax shields is picked up not as higher after-tax cash flows, but in a lower discount rate.

The crusher generates a perpetual after-tax cash flow of $C = $1.175 million, so NPV is

$$NPV = -12.5 + \frac{1.175}{0.094} = 0$$

NPV = 0 means a barely acceptable investment. The annual cash flow of $1.175 million per year amounts to a 9.4% rate of return on investment (1.175/12.5 = 0.094), exactly equal to Sangria's WACC.

If project NPV is exactly zero, the return to equity investors must exactly equal the cost of equity, 12.5%. Let's confirm that Sangria shareholders can actually look forward to a 12.5% return on their investment in the perpetual crusher project.

Suppose Sangria sets up this project as a mini-firm. Its market-value balance sheet looks like this:

Perpetual Crusher (Market Values, $ millions)

Asset value	$12.5	$ 5.0	Debt
		7.5	Equity
	$12.5	$ 12.5	

Calculate the expected dollar return to shareholders:

$$\text{After-tax interest} = r_D(1 - T_c)D$$
$$= 0.06 \times (1 - 0.21) \times 5 = 0.237$$
$$\text{Expected equity income} = C - r_D(1 - T_c)D$$
$$= 1.175 - 0.237 = 0.938$$

The project's earnings are level and perpetual, so the expected rate of return on equity is equal to the expected equity income divided by the equity value:

$$\text{Expected equity return} = r_E = \frac{\text{expected equity income}}{\text{equity value}}$$

$$= \frac{0.938}{7.5} = 0.125, \text{ or } 12.5\%$$

The expected return on equity equals the cost of equity, so it makes sense that the project's NPV is zero.

Review of Assumptions

It is appropriate to discount the perpetual crusher's cash flows at Sangria's WACC only if

- The project's business risks are the same as those of Sangria's other assets and remain so for the life of the project.
- Throughout its life, the project supports the same fraction of debt to value as in Sangria's overall capital structure.

You can see the importance of these two assumptions: If the perpetual crusher had greater business risk than Sangria's other assets, or if the acceptance of the project would lead to a permanent, material change in Sangria's debt ratio, then Sangria's shareholders would not be content with a 12.5% expected return on their equity investment in the project.

But users of WACC need not worry about small or temporary fluctuations in debt ratios. Nor should they be misled by the immediate source of financing. Suppose that Sangria decides to borrow $12.5 million to get a quick start on construction of the crusher. This does not necessarily change Sangria's long-term financing targets. The crusher's debt *capacity* is only $5 million. If Sangria decides for convenience to borrow $12.5 million for the crusher, then sooner or later it will have to borrow $12.5 − $5 = $7.5 million *less* for other projects.

We have illustrated the WACC formula only for a project offering perpetual cash flows. But the formula works for any cash-flow pattern *as long as the firm adjusts its borrowing to maintain a constant debt ratio over time.*[3]

Mistakes People Make in Using the Weighted-Average Formula

The weighted-average formula is very useful, but it is also dangerous. It tempts people to make logical errors. For example, manager Q, who is campaigning for a pet project, might look at the formula

$$\text{WACC} = r_D(1 - T_c)\frac{D}{V} + r_E\frac{E}{V} \qquad (18.1)$$

and think, "Aha! My firm has a good credit rating. It could borrow, say, 90% of the project's cost if it likes. That means $D/V = 0.9$ and $E/V = 0.1$. My firm's borrowing rate r_D is 8%, and the required return on equity, r_E, is 15%. The tax rate is now 21%. Therefore,

$$\text{WACC} = 0.08(1 - 0.21)(0.9) + 0.15(0.1) = 0.072$$

or 7.2%. When I discount at that rate, my project looks great."

---

[3]We can prove this statement as follows. Denote expected after-tax cash flows (assuming all-equity financing) as $C_1, C_2, \ldots, C_T$. With all-equity financing, these flows would be discounted at the opportunity cost of capital r. But we need to value the cash flows for a firm that is financed partly with debt. Start with value in the next to last period: $V_{T-1} = D_{T-1} + E_{T-1}$. The total cash payoff to debt and equity investors is the cash flow plus the interest tax shield. The expected total return to debt and equity investors is

$$\text{Expected cash payoff in } T = C_T + T_c r_D D_{T-1} \qquad (1)$$

$$= V_{T-1}\left(1 + r_D\frac{D_{T-1}}{V_{T-1}} + r_E\frac{E_{T-1}}{V_{T-1}}\right) \qquad (2)$$

Assume the debt ratio is constant at $L = D/V$. Equate (1) and (2) and solve for V_{T-1}

$$V_{T-1} = \frac{C_T}{1 + (1 - T_c)r_D L + r_E(1 - L)} = \frac{C_T}{1 + \text{WACC}}$$

The logic repeats for V_{T-2}. Note that the next period's payoff includes V_{T-1}: Expected cash payoff in $T - 1 = C_{T-1} + T_c r_D D_{T-2} + V_{T-1}$

$$= V_{T-2}\left(1 + r_D\frac{D_{T-2}}{V_{T-2}} + r_E\frac{E_{T-2}}{V_{T-2}}\right)$$

$$V_{T-2} = \frac{C_{T-1} + V_{T-1}}{1 + (1 - T_c)r_D L + r_E(1 - L)} = \frac{C_{T-1} + V_{T-1}}{1 + \text{WACC}} = \frac{C_{T-1}}{1 + \text{WACC}} + \frac{C_T}{(1 + \text{WACC})^2}$$

We can continue all the way back to date 0:

$$V_0 = \sum_{t=1}^{T}\frac{C_t}{(1 + \text{WACC})^t}$$

Manager Q is wrong on several counts. First, the weighted-average formula works only for projects that are carbon copies of the firm. The firm isn't 90% debt-financed.

Second, the immediate source of funds for a project has no necessary connection with the hurdle rate for the project. What matters is the project's overall contribution to the firm's borrowing power. A dollar invested in Q's pet project will not increase the firm's debt capacity by $0.90. If the firm borrows 90% of the project's cost, it is really borrowing in part against its *existing* assets. Any advantage from financing the new project with more debt than normal should be attributed to the old assets, not to the new ones.

Third, even if the firm were willing and able to lever up to 90% debt, its cost of capital would not decline to 7.2%, as Q's naive calculation predicts. You cannot increase the debt ratio without creating financial risk for stockholders and thereby increasing r_E, the expected rate of return they demand from the firm's common stock. Going to 90% debt would certainly increase the borrowing rate, too.

18.2 Self-Test

Look back to your answer to Self-Test 18.1. Serial has accumulated $40 million of surplus cash, which is earning a 1.5% after-tax interest rate. It can use the cash to pay for a new synthesizer line. The line has the same business risk as Serial's other assets. Should the future cash flows from the new line be discounted at the 1.5% interest rate or at Serial's after-tax WACC? Explain briefly.

18-2   Valuing Businesses

On most workdays, the financial manager concentrates on valuing projects, arranging financing, and helping to run the firm more effectively. The valuation of the business as a whole is left to investors and financial markets. But on some days, the financial manager has to take a stand on what an entire business is worth. When this happens, a *big* decision is typically in the offing. For example:

- If firm A is about to make a takeover offer for firm B, then A's financial managers have to decide how much the combined business A + B is worth under A's management. This task is particularly difficult if B is a private company with no observable share price.

- If firm C is considering the sale of one of its divisions, it has to decide what the division is worth in order to negotiate with potential buyers.

- When a firm goes public, the investment bank must evaluate how much the firm is worth in order to set the issue price.

- If a mutual fund owns shares in a company that is not traded, then the fund's directors are obliged to estimate a fair value for those shares. If the directors do a sloppy job of coming up with a value, they are liable to find themselves in court.

In addition, thousands of analysts in stockbrokers' offices and investment firms spend every workday burrowing away in the hope of finding undervalued firms. Many of these analysts use the valuation tools we are about to cover.

In Chapter 4, we took a first pass at valuing free cash flows from an entire business. We assumed then that the business was financed solely by equity. Now we will show how WACC can be used to value a company that is financed by a mixture of debt and equity. You just treat the company as if it were one big project. You forecast the company's free cash flows (the hardest part of the exercise) and discount back to present value. But be sure to remember three important points:

1. If you discount at WACC, cash flows have to be projected just as you would for a capital investment project. Do not deduct interest. Calculate taxes as if the company were all-equity-financed. (The value of interest tax shields is not ignored, because the after-tax cost of debt is used in the WACC formula.)

2. Unlike most projects, companies are potentially immortal. But that does not mean that you need to forecast every year's cash flow from now to eternity. Financial managers usually forecast to a medium-term horizon and add a *terminal* or *horizon value* to the cash flows in the horizon year. The terminal value is the present value at the horizon of all subsequent cash flows. Estimating the terminal value requires careful attention because it often accounts for the majority of the company's value.

3. Discounting at WACC values the assets and operations of the company. If the object is to value the company's equity—that is, its common stock—don't forget to subtract the value of the company's outstanding debt.

Here's an example.

Valuing Rio Corporation

Sangria is tempted to acquire the Rio Corporation, which is also in the business of promoting relaxed, happy lifestyles. Rio has developed a special weight-loss program called the Brazil Diet, based on barbecues, red wine, and sunshine. The firm guarantees that within three months you will have a figure that will allow you to fit right in at Ipanema or Copacabana Beach in Rio de Janeiro. But before you head for the beach, you've got the job of working out how much Sangria should pay for Rio.

Rio is a U.S. company. It is privately held, so Sangria has no stock market price to rely on. Rio is in the same line of business as Sangria, so we will assume that it has the same business risk as Sangria, and, like Sangria, its debt capacity is 40% of firm value. Therefore, we can use Sangria's WACC.

Your first task is to forecast Rio's *free cash flow* (FCF). Free cash flow is the amount of cash that the firm can pay out to investors after making all investments necessary for growth. Free cash flow is calculated assuming the firm is all-equity-financed. Discounting the free cash flows at the after-tax WACC gives the total value of Rio (debt *plus* equity). To find the value of its equity, you will need to subtract the 40% of the firm that can be financed with debt.

We will forecast each year's free cash flow out to a *valuation horizon* (H) and predict the business's value at that horizon (PV_H). The cash flows and horizon value are then discounted back to the present:

$$PV = \underbrace{\frac{FCF_1}{1 + WACC} + \frac{FCF_2}{(1 + WACC)^2} + \cdots + \frac{FCF_H}{(1 + WACC)^H}}_{PV \text{ (free cash flow)}} + \underbrace{\frac{PV_H}{(1 + WACC)^H}}_{PV \text{ (horizon value)}}$$

Of course, the business will continue after the horizon, but it's not practical to forecast free cash flow year by year to infinity. The horizon value PV_H stands in for the value in year H of free cash flow in periods $H + 1, H + 2$, etc.

Free cash flow and net income are not the same. They differ in several important ways:

- Income is the return to shareholders, calculated after interest expense. Free cash flow is calculated assuming all-equity financing.

- Income is calculated after various non-cash expenses, including depreciation. Therefore, we will add back depreciation when we calculate free cash flow.

- Capital expenditures and investments in working capital do not appear as expenses on the income statement, but they do reduce free cash flow.

Free cash flow can be negative for rapidly growing firms, even if the firms are profitable, because investment exceeds cash flow from operations. Negative free cash flow is normally temporary, fortunately for the firm and its stockholders. Free cash flow turns positive as growth slows down and the payoffs from prior investments start to roll in.

Table 18.1 sets out the information that you need to forecast Rio's free cash flows. We will follow common practice and start with a projection of sales. In the year just ended, Rio had sales of $83.6 million. In recent years, sales have grown between 5% and 8% a year. You forecast that sales will grow about 7% a year for the next three years. Growth will then slow to 4% for years 4 to 6 and to 3% starting in year 7.

		Year				Latest			
					Forecast				
		0	1	2	3	4	5	6	7
1	Sales	83.6	89.5	95.8	102.5	106.6	110.8	115.2	118.7
2	Cost of goods sold	63.1	66.2	71.3	76.3	79.9	83.1	87.0	90.8
3	EBITDA (1 − 2)	20.5	23.3	24.4	26.1	26.6	27.7	28.2	27.9
4	Depreciation	3.3	9.9	10.6	11.3	11.8	12.3	12.7	13.1
5	Profit before tax (EBIT) (3 − 4)	17.2	13.4	13.8	14.8	14.9	15.4	15.5	14.8
6	Tax	3.6	2.8	2.9	3.1	3.1	3.2	3.3	3.1
7	Profit after tax (5 − 6)	13.6	10.6	10.9	11.7	11.7	12.2	12.2	11.7
8	Investment in fixed assets (change in gross fixed assets)	11.0	14.6	15.5	16.6	15.0	15.6	16.2	15.9
9	Investment in working capital	1.0	0.5	0.8	0.9	0.5	0.6	0.6	0.4
10	Free cash flow (7 + 4 − 8 − 9)	4.9	5.3	5.2	5.5	8.0	8.3	8.2	8.5
	PV free cash flow, years 1–6	29.0							
	PV horizon value	77.4			(Horizon value in year 6)			132.7	
	PV of company	106.4							
	Assumptions:								
	Sales growth, %	6.7	7.0	7.0	7.0	4.0	4.0	4.0	3.0
	Costs (percent of sales)	75.5	74.0	74.5	74.5	75.0	75.0	75.5	76.5
	Working capital (percent of sales)	13.3	13.0	13.0	13.0	13.0	13.0	13.0	13.0
	Net fixed assets (percent of sales)	79.2	79.0	79.0	79.0	79.0	79.0	79.0	79.0
	Depreciation (percent of net fixed assets)	5.0	14.0	14.0	14.0	14.0	14.0	14.0	14.0
	Tax rate, %	21.0							
	WACC, %	9.4							
	Long-term growth forecast, %	3.0							
	Fixed assets and working capital								
	Gross fixed assets	95.0	109.6	125.1	141.8	156.8	172.4	188.6	204.5
	Less accumulated depreciation	29.0	38.9	49.5	60.8	72.6	84.9	97.6	110.7
	Net fixed assets	66.0	70.7	75.6	80.9	84.2	87.5	91.0	93.8
	Net working capital	11.1	11.6	12.4	13.3	13.9	14.4	15.0	15.4

⟩**TABLE 18.1** Free-cash-flow projections and company value for Rio Corporation ($ millions).

The other components of cash flow in Table 18.1 are driven by these sales forecasts. For example, you can see that costs are forecasted at 74% of sales in the first year with a gradual increase to 76.5% of sales in later years, reflecting increased marketing costs as Rio's competitors gradually catch up.

Increasing sales are likely to require further investment in fixed assets and working capital. Rio's net fixed assets are currently about $0.79 for each dollar of sales. Unless Rio has surplus capacity or can squeeze more output from its existing plant and equipment, its investment in fixed assets will need to grow along with sales. Therefore, we assume that every dollar of sales growth requires an increase of $0.79 in net fixed assets. We also assume that working capital grows in proportion to sales.

Rio's free cash flow is calculated in Table 18.1 as profit after tax, plus depreciation,[4] minus investment. Investment is the change in the stock of (gross) fixed assets and working capital from the previous year. For example, in year 1:

$$\text{Free cash flow} = \text{profit after tax} + \text{depreciation} - \text{investment}$$
$$\text{in fixed assets} - \text{investment in working capital}$$
$$= 10.6 + 9.9 - (109.6 - 95.0) - (11.6 - 11.1)$$
$$= \$5.3 \text{ million}$$

Free cash flow can also be calculated starting with EBITDA, which stands for earnings before interest, taxes, depreciation, and amortization. Here EBITDA = $23.3 million for year 1 in Table 18.1.

$$\text{Free cash flow} = \text{EBITDA} - \text{tax} - \text{investment in fixed}$$
$$\text{assets and working capital}$$
$$= 23.3 - 2.8 - (109.6 - 95.0) - (11.6 - 11.1)$$
$$= \$5.3 \text{ million}$$

Estimating Horizon Value

We will forecast cash flows for each of the first six years. After that, Rio's sales are expected to settle down to stable, long-term growth starting in year 7. To find the present value of the cash flows in years 1 to 6, we discount at the 9.4% WACC:

$$PV = \frac{5.3}{1.094} + \frac{5.2}{1.094^2} + \frac{5.5}{1.094^3} + \frac{8.0}{1.094^4} + \frac{8.3}{1.094^5} + \frac{8.2}{1.094^6} = \$29 \text{ million}$$

Now we need to find the value of the cash flows from year 7 onward. In Chapter 4, we looked at several ways to estimate horizon value. Here we will use the constant-growth DCF formula. This requires a forecast of the free cash flow for year 7, which we have worked out in the final column of Table 18.1, assuming a long-run growth rate of 3% per year.[5] The free cash flow is $8.5 million, so

$$PV_H = \frac{\text{FCF}_{H+1}}{\text{WACC} - g} = \frac{8.5}{0.094 - 0.03} = \$132.7 \text{ million}$$

$$PV \text{ at year 0} = \frac{1}{1.094^6} \times 132.7 = \$77.4 \text{ million}$$

---

[4]For simplicity, we have tied depreciation to growth in sales. We have not tracked bonus depreciation on each year's new investments.
[5]Notice that expected free cash flow increases by about 4% from year 6 to year 7 because the transition from 4% to 3% sales growth reduces required investment. But sales, investment, and free cash flow will all increase at 3% once the company settles into stable growth. Recall that the first cash flow in the constant-growth DCF formula occurs in the next year, year 7 in this case. Growth progresses at a steady-state 3% from year 7 onward. Therefore, it's OK to use the 3% growth rate in the horizon-value formula.

We now have all we need to value the business:

$$PV(\text{company}) = PV(\text{cash flow years 1 to 6}) + PV(\text{horizon value})$$
$$= \$29.0 + 77.4 = \$106.4 \text{ million}$$

This is the total value of Rio. To find the value of the equity, we simply subtract the 40% of firm value that will be financed with debt:

$$\text{Value of debt} = 0.40 \times 106.4 = \$42.6 \text{ million}$$
$$\text{Total value of equity} = \$106.4 - 42.6 = \$63.8 \text{ million}$$

If Rio has 1.5 million shares outstanding, its value per share is:

$$\text{Value per share} = 63.8/1.5 = \$42.53$$

Thus, Sangria could afford to pay up to about $42 per share for Rio.

You now have an estimate of the value of Rio Corporation. But how confident can you be in this figure? Notice that only about a quarter of Rio's value comes from cash flows in the first six years. The rest comes from the horizon value. Moreover, this horizon value can change in response to minor changes in assumptions. For example, if the long-run growth rate is 4% rather than 3%, firm value increases from $106.4 million to $110.5 million.

Thus, faster growth increases Rio's horizon value and PV(company). At this point, we must check the two warnings from the similar Concatenator valuation example that we considered in Chapter 4. Did we account for the extra investment required to support the faster long-run growth? Yes. Growth at 4% instead of 3% increases year 7's investment in fixed assets from $15.9 to $16.9 million and investment in working capital from $0.4 to $0.6 million. (To confirm this, go to the Rio Spreadsheet Beyond the Page and change the long-run growth rate.) Did we assume that Rio can earn more than its cost of capital in perpetuity? Yes, because the increased investment starting in year 7 increased NPV. In other words, the horizon value contains positive PVGO, the present value of growth opportunities.

Will competition eliminate the PVGO? The financial manager will have to think hard about the competitive landscape. Perhaps she will decide that the long-run cost forecast at 76.5% of sales is too optimistic.

Valuation by Comparables

Most of this chapter covers discounted-cash-flow (DCF) valuation models. What about valuation by comparables? In Chapter 4 we described how financial managers use price-earnings (P/E) or price-to-book-value ratios to help value common stocks. These ratios are then averaged for a sample of comparable companies. The average ratios are multiplied by earnings or book value of the stock being valued.

Here we are not valuing common stocks, but an operating business. The financial manager would not use ratios based on net earnings or book value per share, but probably EBIT (earnings before interest and taxes) or, more likely, EBITDA (earnings before interest, taxes, depreciation, and amortization). The numerator of the valuation ratio would not be equity value E, but total company value $D + E$, the sum of the market values of equity and long-term debt. Total company value is often referred to as *enterprise value*.

For example, suppose that lifestyle companies similar to Rio are trading at a ratio of enterprise value to EBITDA of 4.8. Then Sangria's manager could estimate Rio's horizon value at $4.8 \times 27.9 = \$133.9$ million in year 6 and $78.1 million discounted to year 0. This would suggest that Rio is currently worth $29.0 + 78.1 = \$107.1$ million, a trifle higher than our initial DCF estimate.

This valuation is a hybrid, with early free cash flow valued by DCF and horizon value by comparables. It's also possible to bypass DCF entirely. For example, Rio could be valued by multiplying the enterprise value to EBITDA ratio by EBITDA in year 1, which is $23.3 million in line 3 of Table 18.1. This gives a value of $4.8 \times 23.3 = \$111.8$ million, a bit higher still than the DCF and hybrid approaches.

Enterprise-value ratios can be calculated with different denominators. EBIT is often used instead of EBITDA. Operating profit after-tax is also used, but in this case taxes are calculated assuming all-equity financing, as in line 7 of Table 18.1, thus ignoring interest tax shields. The value of interest tax shields is captured elsewhere, for example in the after-tax WACC.

Liquidation Value

Financial managers should also check whether a business is worth more dead than alive. Sometimes a company's *liquidation value* exceeds its value as a going concern. Sometimes financial analysts can ferret out idle or underexploited assets that would be worth much more if sold to someone else. Such assets would be valued at their likely sale price and the rest of the business valued without them.

WACC vs. the Flow-to-Equity Method

When valuing Rio, we forecasted the cash flows assuming all-equity financing and we used the WACC to discount these cash flows. The WACC formula picked up the value of the interest tax shields. Then, to find the equity value, we subtracted the value of debt from the total value of the firm.

If our task is to value a firm's equity, there's an obvious alternative to discounting the total cash flows at the firm's WACC: Discount cash flows to *equity* after interest and after taxes at the cost of equity capital. This is called the **flow-to-equity method**. If the company's debt ratio is constant over time, the flow-to-equity method should give the same answer as discounting total cash flows at the WACC and then subtracting the value of the debt.

BEYOND THE PAGE

Try It!
Cash-flow-
to-equity
method

mhhe.com/brealey14e

It sounds straightforward, but in practice, it can be tricky to do it right. The problem arises because each year's interest payment depends on the amount of debt at the start of the year, and this depends in turn on Rio's *value* at the start of the year (remember Rio's debt is assumed to be a constant proportion of value). So you seem to have a catch-22 situation in which you first need to know Rio's value each year before you can go on to calculate and discount the cash flows to equity. Fortunately, a simple formula allows you to solve simultaneously for the company's value and the cash flow in each year. We won't get into that here, but if you would like to see how the flow-to-equity method can be used to value Rio, click on the nearby Beyond the Page feature to access the worked example.

18-3   Using WACC in Practice

Some Tricks of the Trade

Sangria had just one asset and two sources of financing. A real company's market-value balance sheet has many more entries, for example.[6]

---

[6]This balance sheet is for exposition and should not be confused with a real company's books. It includes the value of growth opportunities, which accountants do not recognize, though investors do. It excludes certain accounting entries, for example, deferred taxes.

Deferred taxes arise when a company uses faster depreciation for tax purposes than it uses in reports to investors. That means the company reports more in taxes than it pays. The difference is accumulated as a liability for deferred taxes. In a sense, there is a liability because the Internal Revenue Service "catches up," collecting extra taxes as assets age. But this is irrelevant in capital investment analysis, which focuses on actual after-tax cash flows and uses accelerated tax depreciation.

Deferred taxes should not be regarded as a source of financing or an element of the weighted-average cost of capital formula. The liability for deferred taxes is not a security held by investors. It is a balance sheet entry created for accounting purposes.

Deferred taxes can be important in regulated industries, however. Regulators take deferred taxes into account in calculating allowed rates of return and the time patterns of revenues and consumer prices.

Current assets, including cash, inventory, and accounts receivable	Current liabilities, including accounts payable and short-term debt
Property, plant, and equipment	Long-term debt (D)
	Preferred stock (P)
Growth opportunities (PVGO)	Equity (E)
Total assets	Total liabilities plus equity

Several questions immediately arise:

How does the formula change when there are more than two sources of financing?   Easy: There is one cost for each element. The weight for each element is proportional to its market value. For example, if the capital structure includes both preferred and common shares,

$$\text{WACC} = r_D(1 - T_c)\frac{D}{V} + r_p\frac{P}{V} + r_E\frac{E}{V}$$

where r_P is investors' expected rate of return on the preferred stock, P is the amount of preferred stock outstanding, and $V = D + P + E$.

What about short-term debt?   Many companies consider only long-term financing when calculating WACC. They leave out the cost of short-term debt. In principle, this is incorrect. The lenders who hold short-term debt are investors who can claim their share of operating earnings. A company that ignores this claim will misstate investors' required return.

But "zeroing out" short-term debt is not a serious error if the debt is only temporary, seasonal, or incidental financing or if it is offset by holdings of cash and marketable securities. Suppose, for example, that one of your foreign subsidiaries takes out a six-month loan to finance its inventory and accounts receivable. The dollar equivalent of this loan will show up as a short-term debt. At the same time, headquarters may be lending money by investing surplus dollars in short-term securities. If this lending and borrowing offset, there is no point in including the cost of short-term debt in the weighted-average cost of capital, because the company is not a *net* short-term borrower.

What about other current liabilities?   Current liabilities are usually "netted out" by subtracting them from current assets. The difference is entered as net working capital on the left-hand side of the balance sheet. The sum of long-term financing on the right is called *total capitalization*.

Net working capital = current assets − current liabilities	Long-term debt (D)
Property, plant, and equipment	Preferred stock (P)
Growth opportunities	Equity (E)
Total assets	Total capitalization (V)

When net working capital is treated as an asset, forecasts of cash flows for capital investment projects must treat increases in net working capital as a cash outflow and decreases as an inflow. This is standard practice, which we followed in Section 6-1. We also did so when we estimated the future investments that Rio would need to make in working capital.

Because current liabilities include short-term debt, netting them out against current assets excludes the cost of short-term debt from the weighted-average cost of capital. We have just explained why this can be an acceptable approximation. But when short-term debt is an important, permanent source of financing—as is common for small firms and firms outside the United States—it should be shown explicitly on the right-hand side of the balance sheet, not netted out against current assets.[7] The interest cost of short-term debt is then one element of the weighted-average cost of capital.

How are the costs of financing calculated?   You can often use stock market data to get an estimate of r_E, the expected rate of return demanded by investors in the company's stock. With that estimate, WACC is not too hard to calculate because the borrowing rate r_D and the debt and equity ratios D/V and E/V can be directly observed or estimated without too much trouble.[8] Estimating the value and required return for preferred shares is likewise usually fairly straightforward.

Estimating the required return on other security types can be troublesome. Convertible debt, where the investors' return comes partly from an option to exchange the debt for the company's stock, is one example. We leave convertibles to Chapter 25.

Junk debt, where the risk of default is high, is likewise difficult. The higher the odds of default, the lower the market price of the debt, and the higher is the *promised* rate of interest. But the weighted-average cost of capital is an *expected*—that is, average—rate of return, not a promised one. For example, early in the COVID crisis, the long-term debt issues of the retail chain Macy's were selling at deep discounts to **par value**. Its 7% coupon bonds maturing in February 2028 were priced at 54% of par value, offering a yield to maturity of 18.5%. (U.S Treasury bonds of the same maturity were yielding less than 1% at that time.) The bonds' low price and high yield to maturity reflected investors' discouraged view of Macy's prospects. But the 18.5% yield was far above the bond's *expected* return. The yield did not average in the losses to investors if Macy's ended up defaulting. Including 18.5% as a "cost of debt" in a calculation of WACC would, therefore, vastly overstate Macy's true cost of capital.

This is bad news: There is no easy way of estimating the true expected rate of return on most junk debt issues. The good news is that for most debt, the odds of default are small. That means the promised and expected rates of return are close, and the promised rate can be used as an approximation in calculating the weighted-average cost of capital.

Should a diversified company use a single, companywide WACC?   It depends on whether the divisions of the diversified company differ significantly in business risk. If they do differ significantly, the higher-risk divisions should be assigned higher WACCs, the lower-risk divisions lower WACCs.

Here is an extreme example. Kansas City Southern used to be a portfolio of (1) the Kansas City Southern Railroad, with operations running from the U.S. Midwest south to Texas and Mexico, and (2) Stillwell Financial, an investment-management company that included the Janus mutual funds. It's hard to think of two more dissimilar businesses. Kansas City Southern's overall WACC was not right for either of them. The company would have been well-advised to set a separate, higher railroad WACC and a lower investment-management WACC. Railroads are riskier than established investment-management operations.

A more recent example: Large electric utilities typically operate in both regulated and unregulated markets. Their unregulated, "merchant" generating plants sell electricity at market prices, which can fluctuate widely. They also operate traditional regulated businesses, which include transmission, local distribution, and also some regulated generation. The regulation stabilizes prices and (in normal times, at least) provides a "floor" on profitability. Applying a single WACC for both businesses would *underestimate* the required return for the

---

[7]Financial practitioners have rules of thumb for deciding whether short-term debt is worth including in WACC. One rule checks whether short-term debt is at least 10% of total liabilities and net working capital is negative. If so, then short-term debt is almost surely being used to finance long-term assets and is explicitly included in WACC.

[8]Most corporate debt is not actively traded, so its market value cannot be observed directly. But you can usually value a nontraded debt security by looking to securities that *are* traded and that have approximately the same default risk and maturity. See Chapter 24.

For healthy firms the market value of debt is usually not too far from book value, so many managers and analysts use book value for D in the weighted-average cost of capital formula. However, be sure to use *market,* not book, values for E.

unregulated merchant business and lead to overinvestment. Conversely, it would result in an *overestimate* of the required return and, therefore, inadequate investment in regulated activities. Thus, such companies typically set two WACCs: a lower one for the safer regulated and a higher one for the riskier merchant business.

Use of an industry WACC for a particular company's investments assumes that the company and industry have approximately the same business risk.[9] Industry WACCs also have to be adjusted (by the three-step procedure given below) if industry-average debt ratios differ from the target debt ratio for the project to be valued.

What tax rate should I use?   Taxes are complicated. Corporations can often reduce average tax rates by taking advantage of special provisions (some say "loopholes") in the tax code. But the WACC formula calls for the *marginal* tax rate—that is, the cash taxes paid as a percentage of each dollar of additional income generated by a capital-investment project.

The examples in this chapter use 21%, the current (2021) U.S. corporate rate. In practice, U.S. corporations add three or four percentage points to cover state taxation. Thus, a corporation operating nationwide—and paying income taxes in most states—might use a 24% or 25% rate to calculate WACC.

What if the company can't use all its interest tax shields?   So far, we have assumed that the company is consistently profitable and will pay taxes at the full statutory rate. Thus, the company can still use a new project's depreciation tax shields even if a project endures a period of start-up losses. The project's depreciation expense shields some of the company's overall taxable income. Interest tax shields on debt supported by the new project can be captured in the same way.

Sometimes interest tax shields from new debt cannot be captured immediately because (1) the company is suffering losses overall or (2) its total interest payments exceed 30% of EBIT.[10] Should the company change its WACC if it finds itself in one or both of these unfortunate states?

Probably not, if the losses or constraint are temporary. Tax losses and nondeductible interest can be carried forward and used to shield future income. (The tax rate in the WACC formula could be reduced to account for delay in using tax shields.) But if the wait to use interest tax shields from additional borrowing is long enough, it may be best to use the APV method, which we explain in the next section.

Adjusting WACC When Debt Ratios and Business Risks Differ

The WACC formula assumes that the project or business to be valued will be financed in the same debt–equity proportions as the company as a whole. What if that is not true? For example, what if Sangria's perpetual crusher project supports only 20% debt versus 40% for Sangria overall?

Moving from 40% to 20% debt may change all the inputs to the WACC formula.[11] Obviously, the financing weights change. But the cost of equity r_E is less because financial risk is reduced. The cost of debt may be lower, too.

Take a look at Figure 18.1, which plots Sangria's WACC and the costs of debt and equity as a function of its debt–equity ratio. The flat line is r_A, the company cost of capital. Remember,

---

[9]Use industry WACCs cautiously. The operations and business risks of the major U.S. and Canadian railroads are similar, so railroad industry WACCs can make sense. But a look into other industry groupings, for example Miscellaneous Consumer Goods, will reveal wide differences in business risks. Levi and Welch argue against using industry-average betas to predict betas for individual companies in Y. Levi and I. Welch, "Best Practice for Cost-of-Capital Estimates," *Journal of Financial and Quantitative Analysis* 52 (April 2017), pp. 427–463.

[10]See the summary of the U.S. Tax Cuts and Jobs Act in Chapter 6.

[11]Even the tax rate could change. For example, Sangria might have enough taxable income to cover interest payments at 20% debt but not at 40% debt. In that case, the effective marginal tax rate would be higher at 20% than 40% debt.

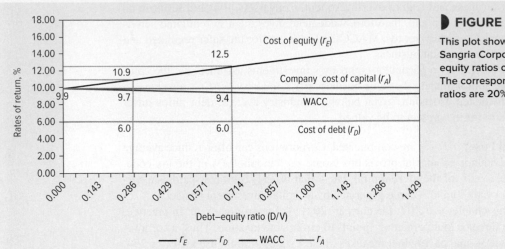

FIGURE 18.1

This plot shows WACC for the Sangria Corporation at debt-to-equity ratios of 25% and 67%. The corresponding debt-to-value ratios are 20% and 40%.

this is the same as the opportunity cost of capital for the company as a whole: the expected rate of return that investors would want from the company if it were all-equity-financed. The company cost of capital depends only on business risk and is the natural reference point.

Suppose Sangria or the perpetual crusher project were all-equity-financed ($D/V = 0$). At that point, WACC and the company cost of capital are identical. Start from that point in Figure 18.1. As the debt ratio increases, the cost of equity increases because of financial risk, but WACC declines. The decline is *not* caused by use of "cheap" debt in place of "expensive" equity. It falls because of the tax shields on debt interest payments. If there were no corporate income taxes, the weighted-average cost of capital would be constant and equal to the company cost of capital at all debt ratios. We showed this in Chapter 16.

Figure 18.1 shows the *shape* of the relationship between financing and WACC, but initially we have numbers only for Sangria's current 40% debt ratio. We want to recalculate WACC at a 20% ratio.

Here is a simple way to do it.

Three-Step Procedure for Finding WACCs at Different Debt Ratios

Step 1   Calculate the company cost of capital. In other words, calculate WACC and the cost of equity at zero debt. This step is called *unlevering* the WACC. The unlevering formula is

$$\text{Company cost of capital} = r_A = r_D \text{D/V} + r_E \text{E/V}$$

This formula comes directly from Modigliani and Miller's proposition 1 (see Section 16-1). If taxes are left out, the weighted-average cost of capital equals the company cost of capital and is independent of leverage.

Step 2   Estimate the cost of debt, r_D, at the new debt ratio, and calculate the new cost of equity.

$$r_E = r_A + (r_A - r_D)D/E$$

This formula is Modigliani and Miller's proposition 2 (see Section 16-3). It calls for *D/E*, the ratio of debt to *equity,* not debt to value.

Step 3   Recalculate WACC at the new financing weights.

Let's do the numbers for Sangria at $D/V = 0.20$.

Step 1. Sangria's current debt ratio is $D/V = 0.4$. So the company cost of capital is:

$$r_A = 0.06(0.4) + 0.125(0.6) = 0.099, \text{ or } 9.9\%$$

Step 2. We will assume that the debt cost stays at 6% when the debt ratio is 20%. Then

$$r_E = r_A + (r - r_D)D/E = 0.099 + (0.099 - 0.06)(0.25) = 0.109, \text{ or } 10.9\%$$

Note that the debt–equity ratio is $0.2/0.8 = 0.25$.
Step 3. Recalculate WACC.

$$WACC = 0.06(1 - 0.21)(0.2) + 0.109(0.8) = 0.097, \text{ or } 9.7\%$$

Figure 18.1 enters these numbers on the plot of WACC versus the debt–equity ratio.

BEYOND THE PAGE

WACC and changing debt ratios

mhhe.com/brealey14e

Unlevering and Relevering Betas

Our three-step procedure for finding WACCS at different debt ratios (1) unlevers and then (2) relevers the cost of equity. Some financial managers find it convenient to (1) unlever and then (2) relever the equity beta. Given the beta of equity at the new debt ratio, the cost of equity can be calculated from the capital asset pricing model (CAPM). We can then compute the WACC at the new debt ratio.

Suppose Sangria's debt and equity betas in our example are $\beta_D = 0.135$ and $\beta_E = 1.07$.[12] If the risk-free rate is 5%, and the market risk premium is 7.0%, then Sangria's cost of equity is

$$r_E = r_f + (r_m - r_f)\beta_E = 0.05 + (0.07)\,1.07 = 0.125, \text{ or } 12.5\%$$

This matches the cost of equity in our example at a 40/60 debt–equity ratio.

To find Sangria's weighted average cost of capital at a 20% debt ratio, we can follow a three-step procedure that pretty much matches the procedure that we used earlier.

Step 1. Unlever beta. The unlevered beta is the *asset beta:* the beta of the equity if the company had zero debt. The formula for unlevering beta was given in Section 16-3.

$$\beta_A = \beta_D(D/V) + \beta_E(E/V)$$

This equation says that the beta of a firm's assets (β_A) is equal to the beta of a portfolio of all of the firm's outstanding debt and equity securities. An investor who bought such a portfolio would own the assets free and clear and absorb only business risks. For Sangria,

$$\beta_A = \beta_D(D/V) + \beta_E(E/V) = 0.135(0.4) + 1.07(0.6) = 0.696$$

Step 2. Estimate the betas of the debt and equity at the new debt ratio. The formula for relevering beta closely resembles MM's proposition 2, except that betas are substituted for rates of return:

$$\beta_E = \beta_A + (\beta_A - \beta_D)D/E$$

Use this formula to recalculate β_E when D/E changes. If the beta of Sangria's debt stays at 0.135 at the new debt–equity ratio of $0.2/0.8 = 0.25$, then

$$\beta_E = \beta_A + (\beta_A - \beta_D)D/E = 0.696 + (0.696 - 0.135)0.25 = 0.836$$

---

[12]Debt betas are generally small, and many managers simplify and assume $\beta_D = 0$. Junk-debt betas can be well above zero, however.

Step 3. Recalculate the cost of equity and the WACC at the new financing weights:

$$r_E = r_f + (r_m - r_f)\beta_E = 0.05 + 0.07(0.836) = 0.109, \text{ or } 10.9\%$$

$$\text{WACC} = 0.06(1 - 0.21)(0.2) + 0.8(0.109) = 0.097, \text{ or } 9.7\%$$

This corresponds to the figure that we calculated above and plotted in Figure 18.1.

Calculating Divisional WACCs

Diversified companies are typically mixes of high- and low-risk divisions. We have noted how discounting at a single, company-average WACC biases investment toward high-risk divisions and away from low-risk divisions. The bias can be canceled out by setting different WACCs for different divisions.

Suppose the financial manager singles out a high-risk division. First she estimates the asset beta β_A for the division and uses the CAPM to set the opportunity cost of capital for that division. Then she sets the target debt ratio for the division, levers up the cost of equity, determines the after-tax cost of debt, and calculates the divisional WACC.

EXAMPLE 18.3 • Calculating a divisional WACC

Suppose that a company is composed of a high-risk division H with $\beta_A = 1.25$ and a low-risk division L with $\beta_A = 0.75$. Suppose the risk-free interest rate is 3% and the market risk premium is 6%. Then the opportunity cost of capital for H is:

$$r_A = r_f + \beta(r_m - r_f) = 0.03 + 1.25 \times 0.06 = 0.105 \text{ or } 10.5\%$$

The financial manager decides on a prudent target debt-to-value ratio of 1/3 (and thus a debt–equity ratio of 0.5) and a cost of debt of $r_D = 4\%$. So the cost of equity is:

$$r_E = r_A + (r_A - r_D) D/E = 0.105 + (0.105 - 0.04)\, 0.5 = 0.1375 \text{ or } 13.75\%$$

Suppose the corporate tax rate is 25%. The divisional after-tax WACC is:

$$\text{WACC} = r_D(1 - T_C)D/V + r_E\, E/V = 0.04(1 - 0.25)(1/3) + 0.1375(2/3) = 0.102, \text{ about } 10\%$$

• • • • •

18.3 Self-Test

Calculate the after-tax WACC for the lower-risk division L with $\beta_A = 0.75$. In this case, the target debt-to-value ratio is 0.5. The cost of debt and tax rate remain at 4% and 25%.

The Assumption of a Constant Debt Ratio in the After-Tax WACC

Does this assumption make sense? A company's after-tax WACC is usually calculated using the company's existing, overall debt ratio. If the company then uses that WACC to discount future cash flows, it must assume that the debt ratio does not change in the future. That assumption, if strictly true, would require the company to rebalance its capital structure to maintain the same market-value debt ratio for the relevant future.

Take Sangria Corporation as an example. It starts with a debt-to-value ratio of 40% and a market value of $1,250 million. Suppose that Sangria's products do unexpectedly well in the marketplace and that market value increases to $1,500 million. Rebalancing means that it will then increase debt to $0.4 \times 1,500 = \$600$ million, thus regaining a 40% ratio.

The proceeds of the additional borrowing could be used to finance other investments or could be paid out to the stockholders. If market value instead falls, Sangria would have to pay down debt proportionally.

Our three-step procedure for recalculating WACC with a different debt ratio makes a similar rebalancing assumption.[13] Whatever the starting debt ratio, the firm is assumed to rebalance to maintain that ratio in the future.[14]

But real companies do not rebalance capital structure in this mechanical and compulsive way. Does their lax rebalancing behavior undermine practical use of the after-tax WACC?

The answer is usually "No." The typical financial manager does not care much if her debt ratio drifts up or down in a range of reasonable financial leverage. She acts as if a plot of WACC against the debt ratio is "flat" (constant) over this range. This makes sense, if we just remember that interest tax shields are the *only* reason why the after-tax WACC declines with leverage in Figure 18.1. The WACC formula doesn't explicitly capture costs of financial distress or any of the other non-tax complications discussed in Chapter 17. The complications may roughly cancel the value added by interest tax shields (within a band of moderate leverage). If so the financial manager is wise to focus on operating and investment decisions, relying on the flat WACC, rather than on fine-tuning the debt ratio.

There is another way to interpret the constant debt ratio in the WACC formula. Assume that a project's **debt capacity** is a constant fraction of project value. ("Capacity" does not mean the maximum amount that could be borrowed, but the amount that the financial manager would optimally choose to borrow.) As the project's value evolves, its debt capacity is assumed to change proportionally, keeping the ratio of debt capacity to value constant at the project level. Discounting at WACC with a fixed debt ratio then gives the project credit for interest tax shields that would be generated by the project's fluctuating future value and debt capacity, even if the firm does not regularly rebalance capital structure to keep its overall debt ratio strictly constant.

---

[13]Similar, but not identical. The basic WACC formula is correct whether rebalancing occurs at the end of each period or continuously. The unlevering and relevering formulas used in steps 1 and 2 of our three-step procedure are exact only if rebalancing is continuous so that the debt ratio stays constant day-to-day and week-to-week. However, the errors introduced from annual rebalancing are very small and can be ignored for practical purposes.

[14]Here's why the formulas work with continuous rebalancing. Think of a market-value balance sheet with assets and interest tax shields on the left and debt and equity on the right, with $D + E = $ PV(assets) + PV(tax shield). The total risk (beta) of the firm's debt and equity equals the blended risk of PV(assets) and PV(tax shield):

$$\beta_D \frac{D}{V} + \beta_E \frac{E}{V} = \alpha\beta_A + (1 - \alpha)\beta_{\text{tax shield}} \qquad (1)$$

where α is the proportion of the total firm value from its assets and $1 - \alpha$ is the proportion from interest tax shields. If the firm readjusts its capital structure to keep D/V constant, then the beta of the tax shield must be the same as the beta of the assets. With rebalancing, an $x\%$ change in firm value V changes debt D by $x\%$. So the interest tax shield $T_c\, r_D\, D$ will change by $x\%$ as well. Thus the risk of the tax shield must be the same as the risk of the firm as a whole:

$$\beta_{\text{tax shield}} = \beta_A = \beta_D \frac{D}{V} + \beta_E \frac{E}{V} \qquad (2)$$

This is our unlevering formula expressed in terms of beta. Since expected returns depend on beta:

$$r_A = r_D \frac{D}{V} + r_E \frac{E}{V} \qquad (3)$$

Rearrange formulas (2) and (3) to get the relevering formulas for β_E and r_E. (Notice that the tax rate T_c has dropped out.)

$$\beta_E = \beta_A + (\beta_A - \beta_E)D/E$$
$$r_E = r_A + (r_A - r_D)D/E$$

All this assumes continuous rebalancing. Suppose instead that the firm rebalances once a year, so that the next year's interest tax shield, which depends on this year's debt, is known. Then you can use a formula developed by Miles and Ezzell:

$$r_{\text{Miles-Ezzell}} = r_A - (D/V) r_D T_t \left(\frac{1 + r_A}{1 + r_D} \right)$$

See J. Miles and J. Ezzell, "The Weighted Average Cost of Capital, Perfect Capital Markets, and Project Life: A Clarification," *Journal of Financial and Quantitative Analysis* 15 (September 1980), pp. 719–730.

The Modigliani–Miller Formula

We have concentrated our attention on the after-tax WACC, which is widely used in practice. But sometimes financial managers turn to other discount-rate formulas, including one derived by Modigliani and Miller (MM). MM considered a company or project generating a level, perpetual stream of cash flows financed with fixed, perpetual debt. There is then a simple relationship between the after-tax discount rate (r_{MM}) and the company cost of capital (r_A):[15]

$$r_{MM} = r_A(1 - T_c D/V)$$

Here it's easy to unlever: just set the debt ratio (D/V) equal to zero.[16]

MM's formula is sometimes still used in practice, but it is exact only in the special case where there is a level, perpetual stream of cash flows and fixed, perpetual debt. However, the formula is not a bad approximation for projects that are not perpetual as long as debt is issued in a fixed amount.[17]

18-4   Adjusted Present Value

We now turn to an alternative way to take account of financing decisions. This is to calculate an **adjusted present value** or **APV**.[18] The idea behind APV is to divide and conquer. Instead of capturing the effects of financing by adjusting the discount rate, APV makes a series of present value calculations. The first calculation establishes a base-case value for the project or firm: its value as a separate, all-equity-financed venture. The discount rate for the base-case value is the opportunity cost of capital for the project being valued, which equals the company cost of capital if the project is average-risk for the company. The discount rate is *not* "levered up" to account for the financial risk created by borrowing. It is an "all-equity" rate. Once the base-case value is set, then each financing side effect is traced out, and the present value of its cost or benefit to the firm is calculated. Finally, all the present values are added together to estimate the project's total contribution to the value of the firm:

$$APV = \text{base-case NPV} + \text{sum of PVs of financing side effects}$$

---

[15]The formula first appeared in F. Modigliani and M. H. Miller, "Corporate Income Taxes and the Cost of Capital: A Correction," *American Economic Review* 53 (June 1963), pp. 433–443. It is explained more fully in M. H. Miller and F. Modigliani: "Some Estimates of the Cost of Capital to the Electric Utility Industry, 1954–1957," *American Economic Review* 56 (June 1966), pp. 333–391. Given perpetual fixed debt,

$$V = \frac{C}{r} + T_c D$$

$$V = \frac{C}{r(1 - T_c D/V)} = \frac{C}{r_{MM}}$$

[16]In this case the relevering formula for the cost of equity is

$$r_E = r_A + (1 - T_c)(r_A - r_D)D/E$$

The unlevering and relevering formulas for betas are

$$\beta_A = \frac{\beta_D(1 - T_c)D/E + \beta_E}{1 + (1 - T_c)D/E}$$

and

$$\beta_E = \beta_A + (1 - T_c)(\beta_A - \beta_D)D/E$$

See R. Hamada, "The Effect of a Firm's Capital Structure on the Systematic Risk of Common Stocks," *Journal of Finance* 27 (May 1972), pp. 435–452.
[17]See S. C. Myers, "Interactions of Corporate Financing and Investment Decisions—Implications for Capital Budgeting," *Journal of Finance* 29 (March 1974), pp. 1–25.
[18]The adjusted-present-value rule was developed in S. C. Myers, "Interactions of Corporate Financing and Investment Decisions—Implications for Capital Budgeting," *Journal of Finance* 29 (March 1974), pp. 1–25.

The most important financing side effect is usually the interest tax shield on the debt supported by the project (a plus). Other possible side effects include the issue costs of securities (a minus) or financing packages subsidized by a supplier or government (a plus).

APV gives the financial manager an explicit view of the factors that are adding or subtracting value. APV can prompt the manager to ask the right follow-up questions. For example, suppose that base-case NPV is positive but less than the costs of issuing shares to finance the project. That should prompt the manager to look around to see if the project can be rescued by an alternative financing plan.

APV for the Perpetual Crusher

APV is easiest to understand in simple numerical examples. Let's apply it to Sangria's perpetual crusher project. We start by showing that APV is equivalent to discounting at WACC if we make the same assumptions about debt policy and taxes.

Earlier we used Sangria's WACC as the discount rate for the crusher's projected cash flows. The WACC calculation assumed that debt will be maintained at a constant 40% of the future value of the project or firm. In this case, the risk of interest tax shields is the same as the risk of the project.[19] Therefore, we can discount the tax shields at the company cost of capital (r_A). We calculated r_A in the last section by unlevering Sangria's WACC to obtain $r_A = 9.9\%$.

The first step is to calculate base-case NPV. This is the project's NPV with all-equity financing. To find it, we discount after-tax project cash flows of $1.175 million at the company cost of capital of 9.9% and subtract the $12.5 million outlay. The cash flows are perpetual, so

$$\text{Base-case NPV} = -12.5 + \frac{1.175}{0.099} = -\$0.63 \text{ million}$$

Thus, the project would not be worthwhile with all-equity financing. But it actually supports debt of $5 million. At a 6% borrowing rate ($r_D = 0.06$) and a 21% tax rate ($T_c = 0.21$), annual tax shields are $0.21 \times 0.06 \times 5 = 0.063$, or $63,000.

What are those tax shields worth? If the firm sticks to a 40% debt ratio, we discount at $r_A = 9.9\%$:[20]

$$\text{PV(interest tax shields, debt rebalanced)} = \frac{63,000}{0.099} = \$0.63 \text{ million}$$

APV is the sum of base-case value and PV(interest tax shields):

$$\text{APV} = -0.63 \text{ million} + 0.63 \text{ million} = 0$$

This is exactly the same as we obtained by one-step discounting with WACC. The perpetual crusher is a break-even project by either valuation method.[21]

But with APV, we don't have to hold debt at a constant proportion of value. Suppose Sangria plans to keep project debt fixed at $5 million. In this case, we assume the risk of the tax shields is the same as the risk of the debt and we discount at the 6% rate on debt:

$$\text{PV(tax shields, debt fixed)} = \frac{63,000}{0.06} = \$1.05 \text{ million}$$

$$\text{APV} = -0.63 + 1.05 = \$0.42 \text{ million}$$

---

[19]That is, $\beta_A = \beta_{\text{tax shields}}$.

[20]Note that we value the tax shields by discounting at the company cost of capital. It would be double counting to discount by WACC.

[21]Calculating the present value of the tax shields is straightforward when the project is a perpetuity. When it is not, the expected value of the project changes as time passes and so does the expected tax shield. With a finite project and debt that is a constant proportion of project value, we would need to calculate the expected project value at each future date before calculating the present value of the tax shields. Therefore, whenever the debt ratio is constant, managers use WACC to account for the interest tax shield, and they save APV for times when debt is repaid on a fixed schedule.

Now the project is more attractive. With fixed debt, the interest tax shields are safe and therefore worth more. (Whether the fixed debt is safer for Sangria is another matter. If the perpetual crusher project fails, the $5 million of fixed debt may end up as a burden on Sangria's other assets.)

18.4 Self-Test

True or false? Explain briefly.

- a. In an APV calculation, you need to use the WACC to discount any tax shields if debt is constantly rebalanced.
- b. The APV is higher when debt is fixed than when it is a constant proportion of value.

Other Financing Side Effects

Suppose Sangria has to finance the perpetual crusher by issuing debt and equity. It issues $7.5 million of equity with issue costs of 7% ($0.53 million) and $5 million of debt with issue costs of 2% ($0.10 million). Assume the debt is fixed once issued, so that interest tax shields are worth $1.05 million. Now we can recalculate APV, taking care to subtract the issue costs:

$$\text{APV} = -0.63 + 1.05 - 0.53 - 0.10 = -0.21 \text{ million, or } -\$210,000$$

The issue costs would result in a negative APV.

Sometimes there are favorable financing side effects that have nothing to do with taxes. For example, suppose that a potential manufacturer of crusher machinery offers to sweeten the deal by leasing it to Sangria on favorable terms. Then, to calculate APV, you would need to add in the NPV of the lease. Or suppose that a local government offers to lend Sangria $5 million at a very low interest rate if the crusher is built and operated locally. The NPV of the subsidized loan could be added in to APV. (We cover leases in Chapter 26 and subsidized loans in the Appendix to this chapter.)

APV for Entire Businesses

APV can also be used to value entire businesses. Let's take another look at the valuation of Rio. In Table 18.1, we assumed a constant 40% debt ratio and discounted free cash flow at Sangria's WACC. Table 18.2 runs the same analysis, but with a fixed debt schedule.

We'll suppose that Sangria has decided to make an offer for Rio. If successful, it plans to finance the purchase with $62 million of debt. It intends to pay down the debt to $53 million in year 6. Recall Rio's horizon value of $132.7 million, which is calculated in Table 18.1 and shown again in Table 18.2. The debt ratio at the horizon is therefore projected at $53/132.7 = 0.40$, or 40%. Thus, Sangria plans to take Rio back to a normal 40% debt ratio at the horizon.[22] But Rio will be carrying a heavier debt load before the horizon. For example, the $62 million of initial debt is about 56% of company value as calculated in Table 18.1.

Let's see how Rio's APV is affected by this more aggressive borrowing schedule. Table 18.2 shows projections of free cash flows from Table 18.1.[23] Now we need Rio's base-case value. This is its value with all-equity financing, so we discount these flows at the company cost of capital (9.9%), not at WACC. The resulting base-case value for Rio is $28.5 + 75.3 = 103.8$ million. Table 18.2 also projects debt levels, interest payments, and interest tax shields.

BEYOND THE PAGE

Try It!
Rio's
spreadsheet

mhhe.com/brealey14e

---

[22]Therefore, we still calculate the horizon value in year 6 by discounting subsequent free cash flows at WACC. The horizon value in year 6 is discounted back to year 0 at the company cost of capital, however.

[23]Many of the assumptions and calculations in Table 18.1 have been hidden in Table 18.2. The hidden rows can be recalled in the Beyond the Page spreadsheets for Tables 18.1 and 18.2.

	Latest Year	Forecast						
	0	1	2	3	4	5	6	7
Free cash flow	4.9	5.3	5.2	5.5	8.0	8.3	8.2	8.5
PV free cash flow, years 1–6	28.5							
PV horizon value	75.3			(Horizon value in year 6)			132.7	
Base-case PV of company	103.8							
Debt	62.0	60.0	60.0	58.0	56.0	54.0	53.0	
Interest		3.72	3.60	3.60	3.48	3.36	3.24	
Interest tax shield		0.78	0.76	0.76	0.73	0.71	0.68	
PV interest tax shields	3.6							
APV	107.5							
Tax rate, %	21.0							
Company cost of capital, %	9.9							
WACC, % (to discount horizon value to year 6)	9.4							
Long-term growth forecast, %	3.0							
Interest rate, % (years 1–6)	6.0							
After-tax debt service		4.94	2.84	4.84	4.75	4.65	3.56	

〉TABLE 18.2   APV valuation of Rio Corporation ($ millions).

If the debt levels are taken as fixed, then the tax shields should be discounted back at the 6% borrowing rate. The resulting PV of interest tax shields is $3.6 million. Thus,

$$APV = \text{base-case NPV} + \text{PV(interest tax shields)}$$
$$= \$103.8 + 3.6 = \$107.5 \text{ million}$$

an increase of $1.0 million from NPV in Table 18.1. The increase can be traced to the higher early debt levels and to the assumption that the debt levels and interest tax shields are fixed and safe.[24]

Now a difference of $1.0 million is not a big deal, considering all the lurking risks and pitfalls in forecasting Rio's free cash flows. But you can see the advantage of the flexibility that APV provides. The APV spreadsheet allows you to explore the implications of different financing strategies without locking into a fixed debt ratio or having to calculate a new WACC for every scenario.

APV is particularly useful when the debt for a project or business is tied to book value or has to be repaid on a fixed schedule. For example, Kaplan and Ruback used APV to analyze

---

[24]But will Rio really *support* debt at the levels shown in Table 18.2? If not, then the debt must be partly supported by Sangria's other assets, and only part of the $3.6 million in PV(interest tax shields) can be attributed to Rio itself.

the prices paid for a sample of leveraged buyouts (LBOs). LBOs are takeovers, typically of mature companies, heavily debt-financed. However, the new debt is not intended to be permanent. LBO business plans call for generating extra cash by selling assets, shaving costs, and improving profit margins. The extra cash is used to pay down the LBO debt. Therefore, you can't use WACC as a discount rate to evaluate an LBO because its debt ratio will not be constant.

APV works fine for LBOs. The company is first evaluated as if it were all-equity-financed. That means that cash flows are projected after tax, but without any interest tax shields generated by the LBO's debt. The tax shields are then valued separately and added to the all-equity value. Any other financing side effects are added also. The result is an APV valuation for the company.[25] Kaplan and Ruback found that APV did a pretty good job explaining prices paid in these hotly contested takeovers, considering that not all the information available to bidders had percolated into the public domain. Kaplan and Ruback were restricted to publicly available data.

APV and Limits on Interest Deductions

The United States now limits the amount of interest that can be deducted for tax to 30% of each year's EBIT. The EU has a similar restriction.

Most companies will not be affected by these limits. But what about the few that are affected? How should a financial manager take limits on interest-expense deductions into account?

Suppose the 30% constraint is and will be binding. Assume the firm is profitable and paying taxes. Then the future interest tax shields generated by a new investment project are proportional to its future EBIT. The financial manager should forecast EBIT and the associated tax shields and discount at a rate depending on the risk of EBIT.[26] The APV formula is the same as before:

$$APV = \text{base-case NPV} + \text{PV(interest tax shields)}$$

but PV(interest tax shields) now depends on the *project's* forecasted EBIT.

Those projects that generate plenty of EBIT are especially valuable to tax-paying firms that are subject to the 30% constraint. The EBIT of the project can relax the constraint for the firm as a whole, thus unlocking interest tax shields on the firm's existing debt.

The APV of an entire business or company subject to the 30% constraint should also include the PV of interest tax shields generated by its expected future EBIT. If the 30% limit on interest deductions is temporary—in one or two low-profit years, for example—then the unused tax shields are not lost but can be carried forward indefinitely and may, therefore, be merely delayed. The financial manager could assign the tax shields to future years, discount to PV and include them in APV.

APV for International Investments

APV is most useful when financing side effects are numerous and important. This is frequently the case for large international investments, which may have custom-tailored *project financing* and special contracts with suppliers, customers, and governments. Here are a few examples of financing side effects resulting from the financing of a project.

---

[25]Kaplan and Ruback actually used "compressed" APV, in which all cash flows, including interest tax shields, are discounted at the opportunity cost of capital. S. N. Kaplan and R. S. Ruback, "The Valuation of Cash Flow Forecasts: An Empirical Analysis," *Journal of Finance* 50 (September 1995), pp. 1059–1093.

[26]In most cases, the risk of EBIT will be similar to the risk of the project's overall cash flows. If so the interest tax shields generated by the project's EBIT can be discounted at the same opportunity cost of capital used to calculate base-case NPV.

We explain project finance in Chapter 25. It typically means very high debt ratios to start, with most or all of a project's early cash flows committed to debt service. Equity investors have to wait. Since the debt ratio will not be constant, you have to turn to APV.

Project financing may include debt available at favorable interest rates. Most governments subsidize exports by making special financing packages available, and manufacturers of industrial equipment may stand ready to lend money to help close a sale. Suppose, for example, that your project requires construction of an on-site electricity generating plant. You solicit bids from suppliers in various countries. Don't be surprised if the competing suppliers sweeten their bids with offers of low interest rate project loans or if they offer to lease the plant on favorable terms. You should then calculate the NPVs of these loans or leases and include them in your project analysis.

Sometimes international projects are supported by contracts with suppliers or customers. Suppose a manufacturer wants to line up a reliable supply of a crucial raw material—powdered magnoosium, say. The manufacturer could subsidize a new magnoosium smelter by agreeing to buy 75% of production and guaranteeing a minimum purchase price. The guarantee is clearly a valuable addition to the smelter's APV: If the world price of powdered magnoosium falls below the minimum, the project doesn't suffer. You would calculate the value of this guarantee (by the methods explained in Chapters 21 to 23) and add it to APV.

Sometimes local governments impose costs or restrictions on investment or disinvestment. For example, Chile, in an attempt to slow down a flood of short-term capital inflows in the 1990s, required investors to "park" part of their incoming money in non-interest-bearing accounts for a period of two years. An investor in Chile during this period could have calculated the cost of this requirement and subtracted it from APV.[27]

18-5 Your Questions Answered

Question: All these cost of capital formulas—which ones do financial managers actually use?

Answer: The after-tax WACC, most of the time. WACC is estimated for the company, or sometimes for an industry. Industry WACCs can be useful when data are available for firms with similar assets, operations, and business risks.

Of course, conglomerate companies, with divisions operating in two or more industries facing different business risks, should not use a single WACC. Such firms should try to estimate a different WACC for each operating division.

Question: But WACC is the correct discount rate only for "average" projects. What if the project's financing differs from the company's or industry's?

Answer: Remember, investment projects are usually not separately financed. Even when they are, you should focus on the project's contribution to the firm's overall debt capacity, not on its immediate financing. (Suppose it's convenient to raise all the money for a particular project with a bank loan. That doesn't mean the project itself supports 100% debt financing. The company is borrowing against its existing assets as well as the project.)

But if the project's debt capacity is materially different from the company's existing assets, or if the company's overall debt policy changes, WACC should be adjusted. The adjustment can be done by the three-step procedure explained in Section 18-3.

Question: Could we do one more numerical example?

Answer: Sure. Suppose that WACC has been estimated as follows at a 30% debt ratio:

$$\text{WACC} = r_D(1 - T_c)\frac{D}{V} + r_E\frac{E}{V}$$

$$= 0.09(1 - 0.21)(0.3) + 0.15(0.7) = 0.126, \text{ or } 12.6\%$$

[27]Such capital controls have been described as financial roach motels: Money can get in, but it can't get out.

What is the correct discount rate at a 50% debt ratio?

Step 1. Calculate the company cost of capital.

$$r_A = r_D D/V + r_E E/V$$
$$= 0.09(0.3) + 0.15(0.7) = 0.132, \text{ or } 13.2\%$$

Step 2. Calculate the new costs of debt and equity. The cost of debt will be higher at 50% debt than 30%. Say it is $r_D = .095$. The new cost of equity is

$$r_E = r_A + (r_A - r_D)D/E$$
$$= 0.132 + (0.132 - 0.095)50/50$$
$$= 0.169, \text{ or } 16.9\%$$

Step 3. Recalculate WACC.

$$\text{WACC} = r_D(1 - T_c)D/V + r_E E/V$$
$$= 0.095(1 - 0.21)(0.5) + 0.169(0.5) = 0.122, \text{ or } 12.2\%$$

Question: How do I use the capital asset pricing model (CAPM) to calculate the after-tax weighted-average cost of capital?

Answer: First plug the equity beta into the CAPM formula to calculate r_E, the expected return to equity. Then use this figure, along with the after-tax cost of debt and the debt-to-value and equity-to-value ratios, in the WACC formula.

Of course, the CAPM is not the only way to estimate the cost of equity. For example, you might be able to use the dividend discount model (see Section 4-4).

Question: But suppose I do use the CAPM? What if I have to recalculate the equity beta for a different debt ratio?

Answer: The formula for the equity beta is

$$\beta_E = \beta_A + (\beta_A - \beta_D)D/E$$

where β_E is the equity beta, β_A is the asset beta, and β_D is the beta of the company's debt. The asset beta is a weighted average of the debt and equity betas:

$$\beta_A = \beta_D(D/V) + \beta_E(E/V)$$

Suppose you needed the opportunity cost of capital r_A. You could calculate β_A and then r_A from the CAPM.

Question: I think I understand how to adjust for differences in debt capacity or debt policy. How about differences in business risk?

Answer: If business risk is different, then r_A, the opportunity cost of capital, is different.

Figuring out the right r_A for an unusually safe or risky project is never easy. Sometimes the financial manager can use estimates of risk and expected return for companies similar to the project. Suppose, for example, that a traditional pharmaceutical company is considering a major commitment to biotech research. The financial manager could pick a sample of biotech companies, estimate their average beta and cost of capital, and use these estimates as benchmarks for the biotech investment.

But in many cases, it's difficult to find a good sample of matching companies for an unusually safe or risky project. Then the financial manager has to adjust the opportunity cost of capital by judgment. Section 9-3 may be helpful in such cases.

Question: When do I need adjusted present value (APV)?

Answer: The WACC formula picks up only one financing side effect: the value of interest tax shields on debt supported by a project. If there are other side effects—subsidized financing tied to a project, for example—you should use APV.

You can also use APV to break out the value of interest tax shields:

$$APV = \text{base-case NPV} + \text{PV(tax shield)}$$

Suppose, for example, that you are analyzing a company just after a leveraged buyout. The company has a very high initial debt level but plans to pay down the debt as rapidly as possible. APV could be used to obtain an accurate valuation.

Question: When should personal taxes be incorporated into the analysis?

Answer: Always use T_c, the marginal corporate tax rate, when calculating WACC as a weighted average of the costs of debt and equity. The discount rate is adjusted *only* for corporate taxes.

In principle, APV can be adjusted for personal taxes by replacing the marginal corporate rate T_c with an effective tax rate that combines corporate and personal taxes and reflects the net tax advantage per dollar of interest paid by the firm. We provided simple calculations of this advantage in Section 17-1. The effective tax rate is almost surely less than T_c, but it is very difficult to pin down the numerical difference. Therefore, in practice T_c is almost always used as an approximation.

Question: Are taxes really that important? Do financial managers really fine-tune the debt ratio to minimize WACC?

Answer: As we saw in Chapter 17, financing decisions reflect many forces beyond taxes, including costs of financial distress, differences in information, and incentives for managers. There may not be a sharply defined optimal capital structure. Therefore, most financial managers don't fine-tune their companies' debt ratios, and they don't rebalance financing to keep debt ratios strictly constant. In effect, they assume that a plot of WACC for different debt ratios is "flat" over a reasonable range of moderate leverage.

• • • • •

KEY TAKEAWAYS

In Chapters 4 and 6, when we first looked at valuing businesses and investment projects, we ignored any effects of financing on value. In effect, we assumed all-equity financing. In this chapter, we show how to take financing, including the interest tax shields from corporate borrowing, into account.

- **After-tax weighted average cost of capital.** When estimating present value, managers can adjust for interest rate tax shields by discounting at the after-tax weighted-average cost of capital (WACC): $WACC = r_D (1 - T_C) D/V + r_E E/V$

  Here $r_D(1 - T_C)$ is the *after-tax* cost of debt and r_E the cost of equity.

  When calculating WACC, remember to use market values for the debt and equity ratios D/V and E/V.

- **WACC vs. the company cost of capital.** Do not confuse WACC with the company cost of capital (that is, the cost of capital in the absence of interest tax shields):

  $$\text{Company cost of capital} = r_A = r_D \, D/V + r_E \, E/V$$

  The company cost of capital is investors' opportunity cost of capital for an all-equity financed investment in the firm.

- **Cost of equity.** The cost of equity r_E depends on the debt–equity ratio:

  $$r_E = r_A + (r_A - r_D)D/E$$

  This formula can be used to lever or unlever the cost of equity. It assumes that the *company* cost of capital does *not* depend on capital structure. But WACC declines as the debt ratio increases, because interest on debt is a tax-deductible expense.

- **Betas.** The formulas for the asset and equity betas are:

$$\beta_A = \beta_D \, D/V + \beta_E E/V$$

$$\beta_E = \beta_A + (\beta_A - \beta_D)D/E$$

- **WACC assumptions.** Discounting at WACC works for projects that are carbon copies of the existing firm—projects with the same business risk that will be financed to maintain the firm's current ratio of debt to market value. But firms can use WACC as a benchmark rate, which is then adjusted for differences in business risk or financing. We gave a three-step procedure for adjusting WACC for different debt ratios.

  All of this chapter's examples reflect assumptions about the amount of debt supported by a project or business. Remember not to confuse "supported by" with the immediate source of funds for investment.

- **Adjusted present value (APV).** APV provides an alternative way to incorporate financing side effects. First calculate a base NPV assuming all-equity financing, and then add the present value of interest tax shields or other financing side effects.

$$APV = \text{base-case NPV} + \text{PV(financing side effects)}$$

  Common financing side effects include interest tax shields, issue costs, and special financing packages offered by suppliers or governments.

- **Valuation based on free cash flow (FCF).** Free cash flow is the amount of cash that can be paid out to all investors, debt as well as equity, after deducting cash needed for new investment or increases in working capital. Free cash flow does not include interest tax shields. The WACC formula accounts for interest tax shields by using the after-tax cost of debt. APV adds PV(interest tax shields) to base-case value.

  Businesses are usually valued in two steps. First, free cash flow is forecasted out to a valuation horizon assuming all-equity financing and is discounted back to present value using WACC. Then a terminal or horizon value is calculated and also discounted back. Be particularly careful to avoid unrealistically high horizon values. By the time the horizon arrives, competitors will have had several years to catch up. Also, when you are done valuing the business, don't forget to subtract its debt to get the value of the firm's equity.

- - - - -

FURTHER READING

The Harvard Business Review *has published a popular account of APV:*

T. A. Luehrman, "Using APV: A Better Tool for Valuing Operations," *Harvard Business Review* 75 (May–June 1997), pp. 145–154.

There have been dozens of articles on the weighted-average cost of capital and other issues discussed in this chapter. Here are three:

J. Miles and R. Ezzell, "The Weighted Average Cost of Capital, Perfect Capital Markets, and Project Life: A Clarification," *Journal of Financial and Quantitative Analysis* 15 (September 1980), pp. 719–730.

R. A. Taggart Jr., "Consistent Valuation and Cost of Capital Expressions with Corporate and Personal Taxes," *Financial Management* 20 (Autumn 1991), pp. 8–20.

R. S. Ruback, "Capital Cash Flows: A Simple Approach to Valuing Risky Cash Flows," *Financial Management* 31 (Summer 2002), pp. 85–103.

The valuation rule for safe, nominal cash flows is developed in:

R. S. Ruback, "Calculating the Market Value of Riskless-Free Cash Flows," *Journal of Financial Economics* 15 (March 1986), pp. 323–339.

Mc Graw Hill **connect**®   Select problems are available in McGraw Hill's *Connect*. Please see the preface for more information.

PROBLEM SETS

1. **WACC (S18-1)** True or false? Use of the WACC formula assumes

   a. A project supports a fixed amount of debt over the project's economic life.

   b. The *ratio* of the debt supported by a project to project value is constant over the project's economic life.

   c. The firm rebalances debt each period, keeping the debt-to-value ratio constant.

2. **WACC (S18-1)** The WACC formula seems to imply that debt is "cheaper" than equity—that is, that a firm with more debt could use a lower discount rate. Does this make sense? Explain briefly.

3. **WACC (S18-1)** Calculate the weighted-average cost of capital (WACC) for Federated Junkyards of America, using the following information:

   • Debt: $75,000,000 book value outstanding. The debt is trading at 90% of book value. The yield to maturity is 9%.

   • Equity: 2,500,000 shares selling at $42 per share. Assume the expected rate of return on Federated's stock is 18%.

   • Taxes: Federated's marginal tax rate is $T_c = 0.21$.

4. **WACC (S18-1)** Suppose Federated Junkyards decides to move to a more conservative debt policy. A year later, its debt ratio is down to 15% ($D/V = 0.15$). The pre-tax cost of debt has dropped to 8.6%. Recalculate Federated's WACC under these new assumptions. The company's business risk, opportunity cost of capital, and tax rate have not changed. Use the three-step procedure explained in Section 18-3.

5. **WACC (S18.1)** Whispering Pines Inc. is all-equity-financed. The expected rate of return on the company's shares is 12%.

   a. What is the opportunity cost of capital for an average-risk Whispering Pines investment?

   b. Suppose the company issues debt, repurchases shares, and moves to a 30% debt-to-value ratio ($D/V = 0.30$). What will be the company's WACC at the new capital structure? The borrowing rate is 7.5% and the tax rate is 21%.

6. **WACC (S18-1)** Table 18.3 shows a *book* balance sheet for the Wishing Well Motel chain. The company's long-term debt is secured by its real estate assets, but it also uses short-term bank loans as a permanent source of financing. It pays 10% interest on the bank debt and

Cash and marketable securities	100	Bank loan	280
Accounts receivable	200	Accounts payable	120
Inventory	50	Current liabilities	400
Current assets	350		
Real estate	2,100	Long-term debt	1,800
Other assets	150	Equity	400
Total	2,600	Total	2,600

⟩TABLE 18.3   Book balance sheet for Wishing Well Inc. (figures in $ millions).

9% interest on the secured debt. Wishing Well has 10 million shares of stock outstanding, trading at $90 per share. The expected return on Wishing Well's common stock is 18%.

Calculate Wishing Well's WACC. Assume that the book and market values of Wishing Well's debt are the same. The marginal tax rate is 21%.

7. **WACC (S18-1)** Table 18.4 shows a simplified balance sheet for the Dutch manufacturer Rensselaer Felt. Calculate this company's weighted-average cost of capital. The debt has just been refinanced at an interest rate of 6% (short term) and 8% (long term). The expected rate of return on the company's shares is 15%. There are 7.46 million shares outstanding, and the shares are trading at €46. The tax rate is 25%.

Cash and marketable securities	1,500	Short-term debt	75,600
Accounts receivable	120,000	Accounts payable	62,000
Inventory	125,000	Current liabilities	137,600
Current assets	246,500		
Property, plant, and equipment	212,000	Long-term debt	208,600
Deferred taxes	45,000		
Other assets	89,000	Shareholders' equity	246,300
Total	592,500	Total	592,500

❭TABLE 18.4   Simplified book balance sheet for Rensselaer Felt (figures in € thousands).

8. **WACC (S18-1)** See Problem 7. How will Rensselaer's WACC and cost of equity change if it issues €50 million in new equity and uses the proceeds to retire long-term debt? Assume the company's borrowing rates are unchanged. Use the three-step procedure from Section 18-3.

9. **WACC (S18-1)** Nevada Hydro is 40% debt-financed and has a weighted-average cost of capital of 10.2%:

$$\text{WACC} = (1 - Tc)\,r_D D/V + r_E E/V = (1-0.21)(0.085)(0.40) + 0.125(0.60) = 0.102$$

Goldensacks Company is advising Nevada Hydro to issue $75 million of preferred stock at a dividend yield of 9%. The proceeds would be used to repurchase and retire common stock. The preferred issue would account for 10% of the pre-issue market value of the firm.

Goldensacks argues that these transactions would reduce Nevada Hydro's WACC to 9.84%:

$$\text{WACC} = (1 - 0.21)(0.085)(0.40) + 0.09(0.10) + 0.125(0.50)$$
$$= 0.0984, \text{ or } 9.84\%$$

Do you agree with this calculation? Explain.

10. **Forecasting cash flow (S18-1)** Suppose Wishing Well (see Problem 6) is evaluating a new motel and resort on a romantic site in Madison County, Wisconsin. Explain how you would forecast the after-tax cash flows for this project. (*Hints:* How would you treat taxes? Interest expense? Changes in working capital?)

11. **Company valuation (S18-2)** Chiara Company's management has made the projections shown in Table 18.5. Use this table as a starting point to value the company as a whole. The WACC for Chiara is 12%, and the forecast long-run growth rate after year 5 is 4%. The company, which is located in South Africa, has ZAR5 million of debt and 865,000 shares outstanding. What is the value per share?

		Historical		Forecast				
Year	−2	−1	0	1	2	3	4	5
1. Sales	35,348	39,357	40,123	36,351	30,155	28,345	29,982	30,450
2. Cost of goods sold	17,834	18,564	22,879	21,678	17,560	16,459	15,631	14,987
3. Other costs	6,968	7,645	8,025	6,797	5,078	4,678	4,987	5,134
4. EBITDA (1 − 2 − 3)	10,546	13,148	9,219	7,876	7,517	7,208	9,364	10,329
5. Depreciation	5,671	5,745	5,678	5,890	5,670	5,908	6,107	5,908
6. EBIT (Pretax profit) (4 − 5)	4,875	7,403	3,541	1,986	1,847	1,300	3,257	4,421
7. Tax at 28%	1,365	2,073	991	556	517	364	912	1,238
8. Profit after tax (6 − 7)	3,510	5,330	2,550	1,430	1,330	936	2,345	3,183
9. Change in working capital	325	566	784	−54	−342	−245	127	235
10. Investment (change in gross fixed assets)	5,235	6,467	6,547	7,345	5,398	5,470	6,420	6,598

〉**TABLE 18.5**   **Cash flow projections for Chiara Corp. (ZAR thousands).**

12. **Flow-to-equity valuation (S18-2)** What is meant by the flow-to-equity valuation method? What discount rate is used in this method? What assumptions are necessary for this method to give an accurate valuation?

13. **APV (S18-4)** True or false? The APV method

    a. Starts with a base-case value for the project.

    b. Calculates the base-case value by discounting project cash flows, forecasted assuming all-equity financing, at the WACC for the project.

    c. Is especially useful when debt is to be paid down on a fixed schedule.

14. **APV (S18-4)** A project costs $1 million and has a base-case NPV of exactly zero (NPV = 0). What is the project's APV in the following cases?

    a. If the firm invests, it has to raise $500,000 by a stock issue. Issue costs are 15% of *net* proceeds.

    b. If the firm invests, there are no issue costs, but its debt capacity increases by $500,000. The present value of interest tax shields on this debt is $76,000.

15. **APV (S18-4)** Consider a project lasting one year only. The initial outlay is $1,000, and the expected inflow is $1,200. The opportunity cost of capital is $r = 0.20$. The borrowing rate is $r_D = 0.10$, and the tax shield per dollar of interest is $T_C = 0.21$.

    a. What is the project's base-case NPV?

    b. What is its APV if the firm borrows 30% of the project's required investment?

16. **APV (S18-4)** To finance the Madison County project (see Problem 10), Wishing Well needs to arrange an additional $80 million of long-term debt and make a $20 million equity issue. Underwriting fees, spreads, and other costs of this financing will total $4 million. How would you take this into account in valuing the proposed investment?

17. **APV (S18-4)** Digital Organics (DO) has the opportunity to invest $1 million now ($t = 0$) and expects after-tax returns of $600,000 in $t = 1$ and $700,000 in $t = 2$. The project will last for two years only. The appropriate cost of capital is 12% with all-equity financing, the borrowing rate is 8%, and DO will borrow $300,000 against the project. This debt must be repaid in two equal installments of $150,000 each. Assume debt tax shields have a net value of $0.30 per dollar of interest paid. Calculate the project's APV using the procedure followed in Table 18.2.

18. **APV (S18-4)** Consider another perpetual project like the crusher described in Section 18-1. Its initial investment is $1,000,000, and the expected cash inflow is $95,000 a year in

perpetuity. The opportunity cost of capital with all-equity financing is 10%, and the project allows the firm to borrow at 7%. The tax rate is 21%.

Use APV to calculate the project's value.

a. Assume first that the project will be partly financed with $400,000 of debt and that the debt amount is to be fixed and perpetual.

b. Then assume that the initial borrowing will be increased or reduced in proportion to changes in the market value of this project.

Explain the difference between your answers to (a) and (b).

19. **Opportunity cost of capital (S18-1)** Suppose the project described in Problem 18 is to be undertaken by a university. Funds for the project will be withdrawn from the university's endowment, which is invested in a widely diversified portfolio of stocks and bonds. However, the university can also borrow at 7%. The university is tax-exempt.

The university treasurer proposes to finance the project by issuing $400,000 of perpetual bonds at 7% and by selling $600,000 worth of common stocks from the endowment. The expected return on the common stocks is 10%. He therefore proposes to evaluate the project by discounting at a weighted-average cost of capital, calculated as

$$r = r_D D/V + r_E E/V$$
$$= 0.07(400,000/1,000,000) + 0.10(600,000/1,000,000)$$
$$= 0.088, \text{ or } 8.8\%$$

What's right or wrong with the treasurer's approach? Should the university invest? Should it borrow? Would the project's value to the university change if the treasurer financed the project entirely by selling common stocks from the endowment?

20. **APV (S18-4)** Consider a project to produce solar water heaters. It requires a $10 million investment and offers a level after-tax cash flow of $1.75 million per year for 10 years. The opportunity cost of capital is 12%, which reflects the project's business risk.

a. Suppose the project is financed with $5 million of debt and $5 million of equity. The interest rate is 8% and the marginal tax rate is 21%. An equal amount of the debt will be repaid in each year of the project's life. Calculate APV.

b. How does APV change if the firm incurs issue costs of $400,000 to raise the $5 million of required equity?

21. **APV and debt capacity (S18-4)** Suppose KCS Corp. buys out Patagonia Trucking, a privately owned business, for $50 million. KCS has only $5 million cash in hand, so it arranges a $45 million bank loan. A normal debt-to-value ratio for a trucking company would be 50% at most, but the bank is satisfied with KCS's credit rating.

Suppose you were valuing Patagonia by APV in the same format as Table 18.2. How much debt would you include? Explain briefly.

22. **APV and issue costs (S18-4)** The Bunsen Chemical Company is currently at its target debt ratio of 40%. It is contemplating a $1 million expansion of its existing business. This expansion is expected to produce a cash inflow of $130,000 a year in perpetuity.

The company is uncertain whether to undertake this expansion and how to finance it. The two options are a $1 million issue of common stock or a $1 million issue of 20-year debt. The flotation costs of a stock issue would be around 5% of the amount raised, and the flotation costs of a debt issue would be around 1½%.

Bunsen's financial manager, Polly Ethylene, estimates that the required return on the company's equity is 14%, but she argues that the flotation costs increase the cost of new equity to 19%. On this basis, the project does not appear viable. On the other hand, she points out that the company can raise new debt on a 7% yield, which would make the cost of new debt 8½%. She therefore recommends that Bunsen should go ahead with the project and finance it with an issue of long-term debt.

Is Ms. Ethylene right? How would you evaluate the project?

23. **APV and limits on interest tax shields (S18-4)** Take another look at the APV calculation for the perpetual crusher project in Section 18-4. This time assume that the corporation investing in the project has hit the 30% constraint on interest deductions as a percentage of EBIT. How does the constraint change the project's APV?

    Notice that the crusher's pretax cash flow of $1.487 million a year is also its EBIT. The project is perpetual, so there is no depreciation or amortization. Assume for simplicity that the constraint is permanently binding, but that the firm will continue to pay tax at the 21% statutory rate.

24. **WACC and APV (S18-1 and S18-4)** Take another look at the valuations of Rio in Tables 18.1 and 18.2. Now use the live spreadsheets in Connect to show how Rio's value depends on:

    a. The forecasted long-term growth rate.

    b. The required amounts of investment in fixed assets and working capital.

    c. The cost of capital. (*Note:* You can vary the cost of capital in Table 18.1.)

    d. Profitability—that is, cost of goods sold as a percentage of sales.

    e. The assumed amount of debt financing.

BEYOND THE PAGE

Try It!
Rio's
spreadsheet

mhhe.com/brealey14e

CHALLENGE

25. **Miles-Ezzell formula (S18-1)** In footnote 14, we referred to the Miles–Ezzell discount rate formula, which assumes that debt is not rebalanced continuously, but at one-year intervals. Derive this formula. Then use it to unlever Sangria's WACC and calculate Sangria's company cost of capital. Your answer will be slightly different from the company cost that we calculated in Section 18-3. Can you explain why?

26. **Horizon value (S18-2)** Modify Table 18.1 on the assumption that competition eliminates any opportunities to earn more than WACC on new investment after year 7 (PVGO = 0). How does the valuation of Rio change?

27. **WACC and Rebalancing (S18-4)** The WACC formula assumes that debt is rebalanced to maintain a constant debt ratio D/V. Rebalancing ties the level of future interest tax shields to the future value of the company. This makes the tax shields risky. Does that mean that fixed debt levels (no rebalancing) are better for stockholders?

● ● ● ● ●

18.1 WACC = 3.5(1 − 0.21)(0.33) + 9.5 × 0.67 = 7.26%

18.2 It should use WACC. The immediate source of funds is irrelevant. What matters is what shareholders could expect to earn by investing in the capital markets in securities with similar risk to the proposed synthesizer.

18.3 $r_A = r_f + \beta (r_m − r_f) = 0.03 + 0.75 \times 0.06 = 0.075$ or 7.5%

So

$r_E = r_A + (r_A − r_D) \, D/E = 0.075 + (0.075 − 0.04)1.0 = 0.11$ or 11.0%

WACC $= r_D(1 − T_C)D/V + r_E \, E/V = 0.04(1 − 0.25)(1/2) + 0.11(1/2) = 0.07$, or 7.0%

18.4 a. False. The tax shields should be discounted at the company cost of capital. To use the WACC would be double-counting.

   b. True. Fixed interest tax shields should be discounted at the rate of interest, usually the interest rate on the company's debt. Take care, however, to check that the debt-financed assets actually support the fixed debt schedule so that the debt does not poach on the debt capacity of other assets.

**SOLUTIONS
TO SELF-TEST
QUESTIONS**

● ● ● ● ●

FINANCE ON THE WEB

Table 18.6 is a simplified book balance sheet for Nike in February 2021. Here is some further information:[28]

Number of outstanding shares (*N*)	1.27 billion
Price per share (*P*)	$138
Beta	0.86
Treasury bill rate	0.1%
20-year Treasury bond rate	2.1%
Cost of debt (r_D)	3.5%
Marginal tax rate	21%

Current assets	$24,700	Current liabilities	$ 8,894
Net property, plant, and equipment	8,107	Long-term debt	12,376
Investments and other assets	3,378	Other liabilities	2,984
		Shareholders' equity	11,931
Total	$36,185	Total	$36,185

⟩**TABLE 18.6** Simplified book balance sheet for Nike, February 2021 (figures in $ millions).

a. Calculate Nike's WACC. Use the capital asset pricing model and the additional information given above. Make additional assumptions and approximations as necessary.

b. What is Nike's opportunity cost of capital?

c. Finally, go to **finance.yahoo.com** and update your answers to parts (a) and (b). (You may also find it necessary to check Nike's most recent financial statements.)

---

[28]Long-term debt includes lease obligations. Property, plant, and equipment includes the value in use of the corresponding leased assets.

APPENDIX • • •

Discounting Safe, Nominal Cash Flows

Suppose you're considering purchase of a $100,000 machine. The manufacturer sweetens the deal by offering to finance the purchase by lending you $100,000 for five years, with annual interest payments of 5%. You would have to pay 13% to borrow from a bank. Your marginal tax rate is 21% ($T_C = 0.21$).

How much is this loan worth? If you take it, the cash flows, in thousands of dollars, are

		Period				
	0	1	2	3	4	5
Cash flow	100	−5	−5	−5	−5	−105
Tax shield		+1.05	+1.05	+1.05	+1.05	+1.05
After-tax cash flow	100	−3.95	−3.95	−3.95	−3.95	−103.95

What is the right discount rate?

Here you are discounting *safe, nominal* cash flows—safe because your company must commit to pay if it takes the loan,[29] and nominal because the payments would be fixed regardless of future inflation. Now, the correct discount rate for safe, nominal cash flows is your company's *after-tax, unsubsidized borrowing rate,*[30] which is $r_D(1 - T_c) = 0.13(1 - 0.21) = 0.1027$. Therefore,

$$NPV = +100 - \frac{3.95}{1.1027} - \frac{3.95}{(1.1027)^2} - \frac{3.95}{(1.1027)^3}$$
$$- \frac{3.95}{(1.1027)^4} - \frac{103.95}{(1.1027)^5}$$
$$= +23.79, \text{ or } \$23,790$$

The manufacturer has effectively cut the machine's purchase price from $100,000 to $100,000 − $23,790 = $76,210. You can now go back and recalculate the machine's NPV using this fire-sale price, or you can use the NPV of the subsidized loan as one element of the machine's adjusted present value.

A General Rule

Clearly, we owe an explanation of why $r_D(1 - T_c)$ is the right discount rate for safe, nominal cash flows. It's no surprise that the rate depends on r_D, the unsubsidized borrowing rate, for that is investors' opportunity cost of capital, the rate they would demand from your company's debt. But why should r_D be converted to an *after-tax* figure?

Let's simplify by taking a *one-year* subsidized loan of $100,000 at 5%. The cash flows, in thousands of dollars, are

	Period 0	Period 1
Cash flow	100	−105
Tax shield on interest of $5		+1.05
After-tax cash flow	100	−103.95

---

[29] In theory, *safe* means literally "risk-free," like the cash returns on a Treasury bond. In practice, it means that the risk of not paying or receiving a cash flow is small.
[30] In Section 12-1, we calculated the NPV of subsidized financing using the *pretax* borrowing rate. Now you can see that was a mistake. Using the pretax rate implicitly defines the loan in terms of its pretax cash flows, violating a rule promulgated way back in Section 6-1: *Always* estimate cash flows on an after-tax basis.

Now ask, What is the maximum amount X that could be borrowed for one year through regular channels if $103,950 is set aside to service the loan?

"Regular channels" means borrowing at 13% pretax and 10.27% after tax. Therefore, you will need 110.27% of the amount borrowed to pay back principal plus after-tax interest charges. If $1.1027X = 103,950$, then $X = 94,269$. Now if you can borrow $100,000 by a subsidized loan, but only $94,269 through normal channels, the difference ($5,731) is money in the bank. Therefore, it must also be the NPV of this one-period subsidized loan.

When you discount a safe, nominal cash flow at an after-tax borrowing rate, you are implicitly calculating the *equivalent loan,* the amount you could borrow through normal channels, using the cash flow as debt service. Note that

$$\text{Equivalent loan} = \text{PV(cash flow available for debt service)}$$
$$= \frac{103,950}{1.1027} = 94,269$$

In some cases, it may be easier to take the lender's side of the equivalent loan rather than the borrower's. For example, you could ask: How much would my company have to invest today to cover next year's debt service on the subsidized loan? The answer is $94,269: If you lend that amount at 13%, you will earn 10.27% after tax, and therefore have $94,269(1.1027) = \$103,950$. By this transaction, you can in effect cancel, or "zero out," the future obligation. If you can borrow $100,000 and then set aside only $94,269 to cover all the required debt service, you clearly have $5,731 to spend as you please. That amount is the NPV of the subsidized loan.

Therefore, regardless of whether it's easier to think of borrowing or lending, the correct discount rate for safe, nominal cash flows is an after-tax interest rate.[31]

In some ways, this is an obvious result once you think about it. Companies are free to borrow or lend money. If they *lend,* they receive the after-tax interest rate on their investment; if they *borrow,* they pay the after-tax interest rate. Thus, the opportunity cost to companies of investing in debt-equivalent cash flows is the after-tax interest rate. This is the adjusted cost of capital for debt-equivalent cash flows.

Some Further Examples

Here are some further examples of debt-equivalent cash flows.

Payout Fixed by Contract

Suppose you sign a maintenance contract with a truck leasing firm, which agrees to keep your leased trucks in good working order for the next two years in exchange for 24 fixed monthly payments. These payments are debt-equivalent flows.

Prejudgment Interest Awards

Court cases involving the award of damages are often complex, and by the time the decision has been reached, many years may have elapsed since the time of the original harm. To compensate for the delay in payment, courts customarily award "prejudgment interest." In other words, they add on an additional award for the return that the claimant could have earned over the period since the offense. This increment is often larger than the amount of the original damage. For example, when GM was held to have infringed a company's patent, it was ordered to pay $8.8 million in royalties and $11 million in prejudgment interest. A company that has to wait for compensation for

---

[31]Borrowing and lending rates should not differ by much if the cash flows are truly safe—that is, if the chance of default is small. Usually your decision will not hinge on the rate used. If it does, ask which offsetting transaction—borrowing or lending—seems most natural and reasonable for the problem at hand. Then use the corresponding interest rate.

damages until long after the damages were incurred has effectively made a debt-equivalent loan to the offender. The award should therefore be increased by the company's *after-tax* interest rate.[32]

Depreciation Tax Shields

Since 2018, U.S. companies have been able to immediately write off most expenditure on capital equipment. In other countries, capital expenditures must generally be written off over their likely life. These deductions generate a depreciation tax shield.

Capital projects are normally valued by discounting the total after-tax cash flows they are expected to generate. Depreciation tax shields contribute to project cash flow, but they are not valued separately; they are just folded into project cash flows along with dozens, or hundreds, of other specific inflows and outflows. The project's opportunity cost of capital reflects the average risk of the resulting aggregate.

However, suppose we ask what depreciation tax shields are worth *by themselves*. For a firm that's sure to pay taxes, depreciation tax shields are a safe, nominal flow. Therefore, they should be discounted at the firm's after-tax borrowing rate.

Perhaps you are CFO of a Polish company that proposes to buy an asset for 500,000 zloty,[33] which can be depreciated straight-line over five years. The corporate tax rate in Poland is 19%. Therefore, the resulting depreciation tax shields are

	Period				
	1	**2**	**3**	**4**	**5**
Percentage deductions	20	20	20	20	20
Deductions (zloty, thousands)	100	100	100	100	100
Tax shields at $T_c = 0.19$ (zloty, thousands)	19	19	19	19	19

If the pretax borrowing rate is 10%, the after-tax discount rate is $r_D(1 - T_c) = 0.10(1 - 0.19) = 0.081$. The present value of these shields is

$$PV = \frac{19}{1.081} + \frac{19}{(1.081)^2} + \frac{19}{(1.081)^3} + \frac{19}{(1.081)^4} + \frac{19}{(1.081)^5}$$
$$= +75.7, \text{ or } 75,700 \text{ zloty}$$

A Consistency Check

You may have wondered whether our procedure for valuing debt-equivalent cash flows is consistent with the WACC and APV approaches presented earlier in this chapter. Yes, it is consistent, as we will now illustrate.

Let's look at another very simple numerical example. You are asked to value a $1 million payment to be received from a blue-chip company one year hence. After taxes at 21%, the cash inflow is $790,000. The payment is fixed by contract.

Because the contract generates a debt-equivalent flow, the opportunity cost of capital is the rate investors would demand on a one-year note issued by the blue-chip company, which happens to

---

[32]Suppose it's determined that company A should have paid B $1 million 10 years ago. B clearly deserves more than $1 million today because it has lost the time value of money. The time value of money should be expressed as an after-tax borrowing or lending rate or, if no risk enters, as the after-tax risk-free rate. The time value of money is *not* equal to B's overall cost of capital. Allowing B to "earn" its overall cost of capital on the payment allows it to earn a risk premium without bearing risk. In practice, courts use a variety of methods for calculating prejudgment interest.

For a broader discussion of these issues, see F. Fisher and R. C. Romaine, "Janis Joplin's Yearbook and the Theory of Damages," *Journal of Accounting, Auditing & Finance* 5 (Winter/Spring 1990), pp. 145–157.

[33]Zloty, the Polish currency, often abbreviated as PLN.

be 8%. For simplicity, we'll assume this is your company's borrowing rate too. Our valuation rule for debt-equivalent flows is therefore to discount at $r_D(1 - T_c) = 0.08(1 - 0.21) = 0.0632$:

$$PV = \frac{650,000}{1.0632} = \$611,362$$

What is the *debt capacity* of this $650,000 payment? Exactly $611,362. Your company could borrow that amount and pay off the loan completely—principal and after-tax interest—with the $650,000 cash inflow. The debt capacity is 100% of the PV of the debt-equivalent cash flow.

If you think of it that way, our discount rate $r_D (1 - T_c)$ is just a special case of WACC with a 100% debt ratio ($D/V = 1$).

$$WACC = r_D(1 - T_c)D/V + r_E E/V$$
$$= r_D(1 - T_c) \text{ if } D/V = 1 \text{ and } E/V = 0$$

Now let's try an APV calculation. This is a two-part valuation. First, the $650,000 inflow is discounted at the opportunity cost of capital, 8%. Second, we add the present value of interest tax shields on debt supported by the project. Because the firm can borrow 100% of the cash flow's value, the tax shield is $r_D T_c$ APV, and APV is:

$$APV = \frac{650,000}{1.08} + \frac{0.08(0.21) \text{ APV}}{1.08}$$

Solving for APV, we get $611,362, the same answer we obtained by discounting at the after-tax borrowing rate. Thus, our valuation rule for debt-equivalent flows is a special case of APV.

PROBLEMS

1. The U.S. government has settled a dispute with your company for $16 million. The government is committed to pay this amount in exactly 12 months. However, your company will have to pay tax on the award at a marginal tax rate of 21%. What is the award worth? The one-year Treasury rate is 5.5%.

2. You are considering a five-year lease of office space for R&D personnel. Once signed, the lease cannot be canceled. It would commit your firm to six annual $100,000 payments, with the first payment due immediately. What is the present value of the lease if your company's borrowing rate is 9% and its tax rate is 21%? The lease payments would be tax-deductible.

CHAPTER

19

Agency Problems and Corporate Governance

So far in this book, we've discussed how the firm's financial managers can add value by good investment and financing decisions. But do they always *want* to add value? They have no special gene that automatically aligns their personal interests with shareholders' investment goals. So how do shareholders ensure that financial managers maximize value and don't fritter the company's money away on plush offices or corporate jets?

A company's system of corporate governance is the set of rules and practices that mitigate the temptations surrounding the company's managers and ensure that they maximize value. In this chapter, we show how companies set incentives for managers, monitor their performance, and sometimes replace them. We also review who controls the corporation and how that control is exercised.

Section 19-1 What agency problems should you look out for?

The separation of ownership and control—ownership by shareholders and control by managers—creates *agency problems*. Managers are human beings, who have their own interests and concerns. Therefore, we start by describing the temptations that can divert managers from maximizing value and the *agency costs* that these temptations create.

Section 19-2 Monitoring by the board of directors

Agency costs can be contained by monitoring managers' actions and intervening when they veer off course. That is one of the board of directors' chief responsibilities.

Section 19-3 Monitoring by shareholders

Shareholders likewise keep a close eye on the company's decisions and performance. If the directors are not up to the job, shareholders can replace them, and another management team can be brought in.

Section 19-4 Monitoring by auditors, lenders, and potential acquirers

The board and shareholders are not the only ones watching the company. The company's auditors scrutinize its financial statements to ensure that its financial condition is fairly reported. Banks and other lenders watch to make sure that the company is able to service its debts. Potential acquirers are always alert for firms that are inefficiently managed in the hope that they can take them over and increase shareholder value.

Section 19-5 Management compensation

No system of monitoring a company's actions can be perfect. It needs to be backed up by incentive compensation that helps to align managers' and shareholders' interests. But incentive systems can also have unpleasant side effects. For example, they can put pressure on managers to worry more about short-term earnings than long-run value.

Section 19-6 Governance regimes around the world

In the United States, shareholders typically diversify by holding small stakes in many companies. They mainly rely on boards and stock-based pay to ensure that managers act in their interests. But in other countries, it is more common for large companies to be owned by a dominant shareholder. If this shareholder is also the manager, the problems that arise from the separation between owner and manager disappear. But the danger is that the dominant shareholder may find ways to profit at the expense of minority shareholders. In this section, we look at how governance regimes around the world cope with these issues.

Section 19-7 Do these differences matter?

We finally discuss whether the governance regime affects a nation's economic performance. It's often believed that market-based systems, such as the United States', lead to short-termism. However, a careful consideration of the evidence shows that reality is much more nuanced. In addition, market-based systems may have distinct advantages, such as reallocating capital more rapidly from declining sectors to growing ones.

● ● ● ● ●

19-1 What Agency Problems Should You Watch Out For?

We explained in Chapter 1 how an *agency problem* arises when an *agent* (such as a CEO) works for *principals* (such as shareholders), and they have conflicting interests. Shareholders would like managers to take all positive-NPV investments and only positive-NPV investments. But managers have their own objectives—they may prefer to take projects that maximize their own pay or prestige, or to avoid decisions that involve hard work.

Agency costs are the reductions in firm value that arise from agency problems. They fall into two categories:

- Value lost because managers don't make value-maximizing decisions.
- Costs of monitoring managers, setting rules and procedures to mitigate agency problems, and intervening when agency problems are sufficiently severe.

We begin by discussing five important agency problems. The manager may:

1. Not put in sufficient effort.
2. Fritter away cash on *perquisites* and private benefits.
3. Overinvest in the search for power or prestige.
4. Be reluctant to take risks or take too many risks.
5. Focus on short-term results at the expense of long-term value.

Reduced Effort

Creating value for shareholders takes effort, and so managers may be tempted to slack off. But how much of a problem is shirking in the real world? CEOs certainly aren't lazy—they frequently work 60-hour weeks and rarely switch off even during weekends or on vacation.

Thus, "reduced effort" doesn't mean the CEO spends her time on the golf course rather than in the office. She might indeed devote most of her waking hours to her company—but those hours may be spent managing existing projects rather than launching new ones. Finding and implementing positive-NPV projects can be a high-effort, high-pressure activity. It's much more comfortable to pursue the "quiet life," coasting along with the status quo, than to head into uncharted territory. While we often think of poor management as involving *errors of commission* (taking bad decisions), even more serious may be *errors of omission* (failing to take good decisions).

EXAMPLE 19.1 ● Kodak's error of omission

In 1981, Sony released a prototype of the electronic camera. Kodak had every ability to respond—after all, it invented the digital camera in 1975 and held patents for it. But it was too tempting to stick with what it knew best, photography film. Why change? A study by Kodak's head of market intelligence predicted that digital would replace film. But this displacement would take 10 years, far too long to bother doing anything about it. Kodak's inertia was an error of omission that led to its bankruptcy in 2012—a huge fall from grace for a company that had been worth $31 billion at its peak and had employed 150,000 people at one point.

Kodak has since emerged from bankruptcy, selling printing products and chemicals and licensing patents and technology. However, its market cap in February 2022 was only $300 million.

● ● ● ● ●

Effort is required not only to take positive-NPV investments, but also to call a halt to negative-NPV ones. It takes effort to identify which projects are underperforming and then close them down. The effort isn't limited to the work required but includes the unpopularity associated with taking tough decisions.

Shutting a business involves job losses and may lead to a public backlash. In November 2018, after GE announced the axing of 14,000 jobs and closure of production facilities in the United States and Canada, it was criticized by the U.S. president, the Canadian prime minister, and the United Automobile Workers trade union.

Reducing the budget of the chief marketing officer may lead to frosty relationships with a colleague that the CEO has to interact with nearly every day. Resisting a trade union's demand for higher wages involves stressful negotiations and the risk of strikes. It may be simplest to cave in, even if this reduces shareholder value.

Evidence confirms that managers tend to prefer the quiet life. For example, when corporations are better protected from takeovers, managers are under less pressure to create shareholder value. In such cases, wages are more likely to increase and productivity and profitability to decline. Fewer new plants are built, and fewer old plants are shut down.[1]

Private Benefits

Managers may be tempted to extract *private benefits,* often in the form of perquisites or "perks." They may spend too much on upscale offices, business meetings at luxury resorts, or redundant corporate jets. For example, RJR Nabisco (featured in the book and movie *Barbarians at the Gate*) had 10 private jets and 36 pilots that flew not only executives, but also the CEO's dog (listed as passenger "G Shepherd") to golf tournaments. The planes were housed in a hangar containing $600,000 of furniture and surrounded by $250,000 of landscaping, complete with a Japanese garden.

Such perks generally destroy value. For example, U.S. companies that disclose the usage of a corporate jet subsequently underperform their peers by 4% per year, which translates into $300 million of value destruction.[2] At first glance, this might seem an overreaction. Under SEC rules, a company needs to disclose even the rental of a jet if it exceeds $50,000. How can something that could cost only $50,000 lead to shareholder value falling by $300 million?

Because the jet is only the tip of the iceberg. A company that allows its CEO to use a corporate jet may also permit other misbehaviors. For example, Westar Energy CEO David Wittig not only had a corporate jet, but also used it for family holidays rather than just business meetings and was paid millions for relocation expenses even though he never moved. He also spent $6.5 million on refurbishing his office, plus $110,000 for window treatments and $1,200 for a bronze alligator in renovating his home.

RJR Nabisco and Westar are, of course, extreme examples. The temptations to enjoy perks are often subtle and mundane. But an agency problem arises whenever managers think a little less hard about spending money that is not their own.

---

[1]M. Bertrand and S., Mullainathan, "Enjoying the Quiet Life? Corporate Governance and Managerial Preferences," *Journal of Political Economy* 111 (2003), pp. 1043–1075.

[2]D. Yermack, "Flights of Fancy: Corporate Jets, CEO Perquisites, and Inferior Shareholder Returns?" *Journal of Financial Economics* 80 (January 2006), pp. 211–242.

Overinvestment

Managers should only take investments if they create value for shareholders. However, they may have personal incentives to pursue projects that do *not* create value. Here are three such temptations.

Compensation   One incentive is pay. There is a strong link between firm size and CEO pay. As a result, a CEO has a strong inducement to grow her firm, either through organic investment or by acquiring another company. She may be reluctant to shrink the company by closing down or selling an unprofitable division.

Prestige   A second inducement is prestige, which can arise from two sources. The first is firm size—bosses of larger firms enjoy greater status. For example, the CEO of the market leader is more likely to be invited to keynote at industry conferences or speak at the World Economic Forum in Davos. The prestige arising from size encourages *empire building*—the CEO to grow her company even if the growth doesn't create value.

The second source of prestige is being viewed as socially responsible. As we'll discuss in Chapter 20, some socially responsible activities (such as investing in employees) ultimately create shareholder value. However, others do not and may, instead, be undertaken to boost the CEO's image. For example, the CEO may donate company money to the local symphony orchestra or art museum to be seen as a pillar of the community.

EXAMPLE 19.2 ● How Countrywide wanted to be the market leader

In 2002, Countrywide Financial was third in U.S. mortgages by market share. CEO Angelo Mozilo was determined to make it number one. Of course, companies should want to be the best in their industry, but for Mozilo, "best" was exclusively about market share—whether the mortgages could be repaid was a secondary consideration. So Countrywide plunged recklessly into subprime mortgages and fell into significant trouble when the financial crisis hit. In January 2008, it was on the verge of bankruptcy and had to be bought out by Bank of America.

● ● ● ● ●

Entrenching Investment   Suppose a CEO, Aditya, considers two expansion plans. One plan requires a manager with special skills that Aditya just happens to have. The other requires general-purpose management skills that Aditya does not possess. Guess which plan Aditya will favor—even if it has a negative NPV? Projects designed to require or reward skills of existing managers are called *entrenching investments*.[3]

Overinvestment is most dangerous when the firm has plenty of cash but limited good investment opportunities. This is known as the *free cash flow* problem.[4]

Risk Taking

We explained in Chapters 7 and 9 why managers should ignore *specific risk* when evaluating investments. Specific risk does not affect NPV because shareholders can diversify it away. But managers may not be able to diversify. Boards typically require them to hold large equity stakes in their firm to ensure they are accountable for performance. Moreover, a manager's

---

[3]A. Shleifer and R. W. Vishny, "Management Entrenchment: The Case of Manager-Specific Investment," *Journal of Financial Economics* 25 (November 1989), pp. 123–140.

[4]M. C. Jensen, "Agency Costs of Free Cash Flow, Corporate Finance and Takeovers," *American Economic Review* 76 (May 1986), pp. 323–329.

job prospects are tied to the firm's prosperity. While a setback at one company has little effect on the wealth of a diversified shareholder, it may cost the CEO their job. So CEOs may be tempted to turn down projects with high specific risk. The "quiet life" beckons.

Conversely, when a business is on the ropes, a manager may have an incentive to take too much risk. For example, suppose that a regional office suffers large, unexpected losses. The regional manager's job is on the line, and in response, she tries a risky strategy that offers a small probability of a big, quick payoff. If the strategy pays off, the losses are covered and her job may be saved. If it fails, she loses her job, but she would have lost it anyway. This behavior is called *gambling for resurrection*.[5]

Companies often hesitate to curtail risky activities that are delivering—at least temporarily—rich profits. The financial crisis of 2007–2009 provides sobering examples. Charles Prince, the pre-crisis CEO of Citigroup, was asked why Citi's leveraged lending business was expanding so rapidly. Prince quipped, "When the music stops . . . things will be complicated. But as long as the music is playing, you've got to get up and dance. We're still dancing." Citi later took a $1.5 billion loss on this line of business.

Short-Termism

A final agency problem is that CEOs may take short-term actions at the expense of long-term value. This problem is believed to be particularly serious today, because intangible assets are increasingly important and they take especially long to nurture. You can observe early on that a tangible asset, such as a factory, is being built. But an intangible asset such as a patent takes years to develop and outside investors can see few signs of interim progress. Indeed, in June 2016, JPMorgan CEO Jamie Dimon and investor Warren Buffett co-wrote a *Wall Street Journal* op-ed entitled "Short-Termism Is Harming the Economy."

Incentive compensation schemes that may alleviate the other four agency problems may exacerbate the agency problem of short-termism. To encourage the CEO to exert effort, eschew private benefits, and avoid overinvestment, the board may pay her according to performance measures such as the stock price or profits. But this may then give her incentives to inflate these performance measures, even at the expense of long-term value, by scrapping an R&D project (an error of commission) or failing to invest in her workforce (an error of omission).

Yet there are other causes of short-termism beyond pay. A CEO's reputation is linked to her company's earnings and stock price. If either slump, the CEO might be fired. If it soars, she might be poached by an even larger firm—and even if the rise is temporary and later reverses, she may not care if she has since moved on.

Executives admit that they might take value-destructive actions in response to these pressures. A survey of 401 CFOs found that 80% would cut discretionary expenditures (such as R&D, advertising, or maintenance) to meet an earnings target.[6] Many managers were also prepared to defer or reject investment projects with positive NPVs. Why are these pressures so strong? The authors of the survey explain it this way:

> The common belief is that a well-run and stable firm should be able to "produce the numbers". . . even in a year that is somewhat down. Because the market expects firms to be able to hit or slightly exceed earnings targets, and on average firms do just this, problems can arise when a firm does not deliver. . . . The market might assume that not delivering [reveals] potentially serious problems (because the firm is apparently so near the edge that it cannot produce the dollars to hit earnings . . .). As one CFO put it, "if you see one cockroach, you immediately assume that there are hundreds behind the walls."

---

[5]Baring Brothers, a British bank with a 200-year history, was wiped out when one of its traders, Nick Leeson, lost $1.4 billion trading in Japanese stock-market indexes from a Barings office in Singapore. Leeson was gambling for redemption. As his losses mounted, he kept doubling and redoubling his trading bets in an attempt to recover his losses.

[6]J. R. Graham, C. R. Harvey, and S. Rajgopal, "The Economic Implications of Corporate Financial Reporting," *Journal of Accounting and Economics* 40 (2005), pp. 3–73.

You might think—or hope—that the market would see through such short-termist behavior rather than taking profits at face value. But it doesn't. A study compared firms that just beat analyst earnings forecasts due to low R&D, low advertising, or high accruals (a way of using accounting policies to boost reported profits) with those who just missed due to high R&D, high advertising, or low accruals. Beaters outperformed missers by 2–4% in the short-term, suggesting that the market took the earnings increase at face value. But over the next three years, beaters underperformed by 15–41%, suggesting that these tricks harm long-run value.[7]

19.1 Self-Test

What are examples of agency problems that exist within corporations?

19-2 Monitoring by the Board of Directors

The company's corporate governance system is the set of rules and practices that seeks to ensure that managers maximize value. Many of the rules are enshrined in law; in some countries, they are buttressed by a corporate governance code that sets out the principles of best practice. These codes are typically "comply or explain"—a company must either comply with the principles or explain why they do not do so. Some guidelines may be issued by influential investors.

A governance system reduces agency costs by either monitoring the manager's actions or providing her with incentives to take value-creating actions. We will first discuss the different types of people who monitor management before turning to the role of incentive compensation.

U.S. and U.K. Boards of Directors

One important governance mechanism is the board of directors. In countries such as the United States and the United Kingdom, there is a single board that is elected by shareholders to monitor managers on their behalf. It consists of both inside *executive directors,* who are also the company's executives (such as the CEO and CFO), and outside *nonexecutive directors,* who serve in a part-time, advisory capacity. Most nonexecutive directors are independent—that is, not linked to the company by a business relationship (e.g., a lucrative consulting contract) that may bias them toward management.

The board's role is to scrutinize managers' actions and intervene when they veer off course. For example, most companies require board approval for any major capital expenditure, strategic initiative, or restructuring. In addition to reacting to proposals from management, the board also proactively monitors the company's profitability, competitive position, and long-term investments to suggest potential changes of direction. The strongest action a board can take is to fire the CEO. In recent years, the CEOs of Boeing, Kraft Heinz, Pacific Gas and Electric, eBay, GE, Expedia, and McDonald's have all left abruptly. Boards outside the United States, which traditionally have been more management friendly, have also become more willing to replace underperforming managers. Recent departures includes the heads of Volkswagen, Deutsche Bank, Nissan, Swedbank, ABB, BMW, and Thyssenkrupp.

Of course, boards themselves may suffer from agency problems. Board members may be long-standing friends of the CEO who won't hold her to account. Research has uncovered a number of factors that impact the effectiveness of a board:

- **Board independence.** Independent directors are more likely to hold management to account. Indeed, the evidence is that when a board contains more outside directors, the

---

[7]S. Bhojraj, P. Hribar, M. Picconi, and J. McInnis, "Making Sense of Cents: An Examination of Firms That Narrowly Miss or Beat Analysts' Forecasts," *Journal of Finance* 64 (2009), pp. 2361–2388.

CEO is more likely to leave following poor performance.[8] As a result, regulations often set a minimum for the fraction of directors that are independent. For example, the New York Stock Exchange and NASDAQ require that a majority of a listed company's directors be independent, and in practice about 85% of directors in large U.S. companies are. China has an independence requirement of one-third.

- **Board size.** A large board may have a free-rider problem, where each director doesn't bother to monitor the CEO because he thinks he can leave it up to other directors. But if all directors reason that way, there's no one to hold the CEO to account. Research shows that companies with smaller boards enjoy higher valuations, and their CEO is more likely to depart after bad performance.[9]

However, we shouldn't conclude that small boards and more independent boards are *always* better. More recent evidence suggests that the optimal board structure isn't one-size-fits-all. A large board is associated with higher firm value if the company is itself large or diversified. If the firm is more complex, you might need more directors to understand its different business lines. In addition, inside directors are good for firm value if the company is R&D-intensive, since such a company is harder for outsiders to understand.[10]

- **Overboarding.** Some directors are highly sought after as board members. However, this may lead to *overboarding,* where the director serves on so many boards that he can't devote sufficient time to each. Research shows that "busy" boards (where a majority of outside directors have at least three directorships) are less profitable and less highly valued, and the CEO is less likely to leave following poor performance.[11]

- **Frequency of Elections.** In about 90% of large U.S. companies, and all U.K. companies, the entire board comes up for reelection each year.[12] Some U.S. companies have *staggered* (or *classified*) *boards,* where only a third of the directors are reelected every year. Proponents of staggered boards argue that they insulate management from short-term pressure and allow the company to innovate and take risks. Shareholder activists, on the other hand, complain that staggered elections entrench management—dissident shareholders can gain only a third of the board seats in any given year and thus must wait two years before they can obtain majority representation. The evidence generally finds that staggered boards reduce firm value.[13] Consequently, in recent years, activists have successfully pressured many companies into destaggering their boards.

19.2 Self-Test

a. Which board characteristics are typically associated with superior company performance?

b. What actions can the board undertake to improve company performance?

---

[8]M. S. Weisbach, "Outside Directors and CEO Turnover," *Journal of Financial Economics* 20 (1988), pp. 431–460.

[9]T. Li, "Outsourcing Corporate Governance: Conflicts of Interest within the Proxy Advisory Industry," *Management Science* 64 (2018), pp. 2951–2971.

[10]J. L. Coles, N. D. Daniel, and L. Naveen, "Boards: Does One Size Fit All?" *Journal of Financial Economics* 87 (2008), pp. 329–356.

[11]E. M. Fich and A. Shivdasani, "Are Busy Boards Effective Monitors?" *Journal of Finance* 61 (2006), pp. 689–724.

[12]There is considerable international variation in the length of director's terms. For example, in Germany and France, directors may be elected for terms of five or six years, respectively.

[13]L. A. Bebchuk and A. Cohen, "The Costs of Entrenched Boards," *Journal of Financial Economics* 78 (2005), pp. 409–433; O. Faleye, "Classified Boards, Firm Value, and Managerial Entrenchment," *Journal of Financial Economics* 83 (2007), pp. 501–529; and A. Cohen and C. C. Y. Wang, "How Do Staggered Boards Affect Shareholder Value? Evidence from a Natural Experiment," *Journal of Financial Economics* 110 (2013), pp. 627–641. However, see Y. Amihud and S. Stoyanov, "Do Staggered Boards Harm Shareholders?" *Journal of Financial Economics* 123 (2017), pp. 432–439, who suggest that the Cohen and Wang results only apply to small stocks or stocks traded over-the-counter rather than on exchanges.

The Effects of Codetermination

❭ In theory at least, codetermination should mean that a firm's decisions take employees into account. Is this the case in practice? A study compared German companies with just over 2,000 workers (and thus 50% worker representation on the supervisory board) with those with just under (and thus 33% worker representation).[14] The latter cut employment by 12% in extreme industry downturns, but the former showed no change. This suggests that employee representation protects workers' jobs in bad times.

But there are a few twists. First, this insurance isn't for free—in firms with greater employee representation, wages are 3–3.5% lower. Second, representation only protects white-collar and skilled blue-collar workers, not unskilled blue-collar workers. This is likely because

not a single employee representative in the sample was an unskilled blue-collar worker. It seems that worker representatives mainly look out for their own.

So there may be better ways to ensure that employees' voices are heard in the boardroom. The 2018 U.K. Corporate Governance Code allows companies to use one of three mechanisms: electing an employee director (as in Germany), assigning this responsibility to a standard shareholder-appointed director, or consulting a formal workforce advisory panel. Indeed, as we'll discuss in Chapter 20, companies with high employee satisfaction also deliver higher long-term stock returns. Thus, shareholders may already have sufficient incentives to ensure a firm invests in its employees; it may not need worker directors to guarantee this.

European Boards of Directors

The U.S. and U.K. practice of a single board that represents shareholders is not universal. German firms have *two* boards of directors: the supervisory board (*Aufsichtsrat*) and management board (*Vorstand*). For companies with fewer than 2,000 employees, one-third of the directors on the supervisory board are elected by employees; the remaining two-thirds are elected by shareholders and often include bank executives. For companies with more than 2,000 employees, half of the board is elected by employees and half by shareholders. In all firms, there's a chairman appointed by shareholders who can cast tie-breaking votes if necessary.

The presence of both shareholder and worker representatives on the supervisory board is known as *codetermination*. The supervisory board is supposed to represent the interests of the company as a whole, not just employees or shareholders. It oversees strategy and elects and monitors the management board, which operates the company. Supervisory boards generally have about 20 members, more than typical U.S. or U.K. boards. Management boards have about 10 members.

In France, firms can elect a single board of directors, as in the United States, or a two-tiered board, as in Germany. The single-tiered board, which is more common, consists mostly of outside directors, who are either shareholders or representatives from financial institutions with which the firm has relationships. The two-board system has a *conseil de surveillance,* which resembles a German supervisory board, and a *directoire,* which is the management board.

19.3 Self-Test

Which companies are more likely to cut employment in extreme industry downturns: those with a high proportion of employees on the supervisory board or those with a small proportion?

---

[14]E. H. Kim, E. Maug, and C. Schneider, "Labor Representation in Governance as an Insurance Mechanism," *Review of Finance* 22 (July 2018), pp. 1251–1289.

Since the board may not always act in shareholders' interests, shareholders may take it upon themselves to monitor the company and press for changes if they believe it is underperforming. Such activity by investors is often referred to as "stewardship." Several countries around the world have Stewardship Codes that investors can choose to sign up to, pledging to undertake a certain level of stewardship in the companies they own.

There are three main stewardship tools at shareholders' disposal: voting, engagement, and exit.

Voting

Shareholders have the ultimate right of control over the company's decisions, but in practice, their formal control is limited to the ability to vote on certain corporate decisions. Some votes, such as on the appointment or reappointment of directors, or the decision to merge, are *binding*. If a majority of the votes cast are against a particular director, he cannot be (re) appointed. Other votes are *advisory* or nonbinding—the company isn't obliged to follow the majority decision, although it will risk a shareholder backlash if it doesn't. As we'll discuss in Section 19-5, some countries give shareholders an advisory vote on executive pay; in some others, they have a binding vote.

Note that shareholders' rights aren't just limited to voting on proposals put forward by management. They can make proposals themselves and try to encourage other investors to support them. For director elections, investors can propose their own slate of candidates to run those nominated by management. This is known as a *proxy fight*. A proxy fight can achieve real change, but launching one is expensive. The incumbents' costs are covered by the company, but the investor must create his own voting instruction form (known as a "ballot") containing his proposed directors and then mail it to the other shareholders.[15] He must also pay for lawyers, consultants, financial advisers, advertising, and proxy solicitation firms (which encourage shareholders to vote a certain way). As a result, the average proxy fight costs over $10 million.[16] Arguably the biggest proxy fight in history, where Trian Partners successfully got Nelson Peltz elected to the Procter & Gamble board, was estimated to have cost both sides a combined $60 million.

Shareholders that meet certain criteria can also put nonbinding proposals to take certain actions onto the company's ballot. Historically, most of these proposals related to governance, such as removing takeover defenses. Nowadays, an increasing number is on environmental and social issues, which comprised 44% of U.S. shareholder proposals in 2021. Examples include taking action on climate change, or introducing a policy to prevent workplace sexual harassment.

Dual-Class Equity   Usually, companies have one class of common stock and each share has one vote. Occasionally, however, a firm may have two classes of stock, which differ in their right to vote—known as *dual-class equity*. For example, when Facebook made its first issue of common stock, the founders were reluctant to give up control of the company. Therefore, the company created two classes of shares. The A shares, which were sold to the public, had 1 vote each, while the B shares, which were owned by the founders, had 10 votes each. Both classes of shares had the same rights to dividends, but different control rights. (An even more extreme case is Snap, where shares sold to the public have no votes at all.)

---

[15]In 2010, the SEC proposed Rule14a-11 that would allow shareholders to add their nominations to the company's proxy material. This was successfully challenged in the courts. However, an SEC rule that allows shareholders to add proposals to change the bylaws was not overturned.

[16]N. Gantchev, "The Costs of Shareholder Activism: Evidence from a Sequential Decision Model," *Journal of Financial Economics* 107 (March 2013), pp. 610–631.

Within the United States, dual-class equity is particularly common in new technology companies where founders wish to protect their entrepreneurial vision and keep control. It's also common in other countries, including Brazil, Canada, Denmark, Finland, Germany, Italy, Mexico, Norway, South Korea, Sweden, and Switzerland. However, research shows that dual-class shares are generally associated with lower firm value, higher CEO pay, worse acquisitions, and poorer investment decisions.[17]

BEYOND THE PAGE

Alibaba and dual-class shares

mhhe.com/brealey14e

When two classes of stock coexist, shareholders with the extra voting power may sometimes use it to toss out bad management or protect good management. But as long as both classes of shares have identical cash-flow rights, all shareholders benefit equally from such changes. So here's the question: If everyone gains equally from better management, why do the shares with more votes typically sell at a premium? The only plausible reason is that there are *private benefits* captured by the owners of these shares. For example, a CEO holding a block of voting shares can resist a challenge to her management position. The shares might have extra bargaining power in an acquisition. Or they might be held by another company, which could use its voting power and influence to secure a business advantage.

BEYOND THE PAGE

The value of voting rights

mhhe.com/brealey14e

These private benefits can be estimated by calculating the difference between the value of ordinary shares and those with extra voting rights. As shown in Table 19.1, this value differs across countries. In the United States, the premium that an investor needed to pay to gain voting control amounted to only 2% of firm value, but in Mexico it was 36%, and in South Korea it was 48%. It appears that in these two countries, majority investors are able to secure large private benefits.

19.4 Self-Test

Suppose that the company receives a juicy takeover offer. Why is it more likely to be opposed if the controlling shareholder is the CEO rather than an outside investor?

Engagement

In addition to voting on corporate decisions, another way to influence a company is to *engage* with managers and directors—discuss company performance, act as a sounding board, and occasionally make suggestions for how the company might be run differently. Small investors, such as households, typically don't bother to do so. They own so few shares that it's not worth

Australia	23%	Italy	29%
Brazil	23%	Korea	48%
Canada	3%	Mexico	36%
Chile	23%	Norway	6%
Denmark	1%	South Africa	7%
Finland	0%	Sweden	1%
France	28%	Switzerland	6%
Germany	9%	United Kingdom	10%
Hong Kong	−3%	United States	2%

❭**TABLE 19.1**   The value of control-block votes as a percentage of firm value.

Source: T. Nenova, "The Value of Corporate Voting Rights and Control: A Cross-Country Analysis," *Journal of Financial Economics* 68 (June 2003), Table 4, p. 336.

---

[17]R. W. Masulis, C. Wang, and F. Xie, "Agency Problems at Dual-Class Companies," *Journal of Finance* 64 (August 2009), pp. 1697–1727.

the time and cost to engage. Moreover, their few shares also means that they have few votes, so managers can ignore their suggestions, or decline to meet with them in the first place, with little consequence.

Although larger investors (such as mutual funds) do, indeed, engage, they recognize that executives are usually better informed and rarely force their ideas on the company. Their expertise is picking stocks, not running corporations. However, there are a growing number of *activist investors* whose expertise is precisely in turning around underperforming firms. Examples include Carl Icahn (Icahn Enterprises), Paul Singer (Elliott Advisors), Daniel Loeb (Third Point), and Nelson Peltz (Trian Partners). Activist investors make suggestions much more frequently and are prepared to make the engagement confrontational and public if management is intransigent. They might write open letters criticizing management and rally support from other investors to threaten a proxy fight. That threat alone may be enough to persuade the company to make changes. For example:

- Nelson Peltz's fund bought a large stake in DuPont and forced DuPont to cut back its operations and research and development and to shed 10% of its worldwide workforce. It agreed to merge with Dow Chemical and to split the merged firm into three new, more focused companies.

- Carl Icahn wrote an open letter to "fellow eBay stockholders" stating that "the complete disregard for accountability at eBay is the most blatant we have ever seen. Indeed, for the first time in our long history, we have encountered a situation where we believe we should not even have to run a proxy fight to change the board composition. Rather, we believe that in any sane business environment these directors would simply resign immediately from the eBay Board, either out of pure decency or sheer embarrassment at the public exposure of the extent of their self-serving activities" (emphasis in original). This led to eBay selling PayPal.

- Third Point engaged in a proxy fight with Campbell Soup, aiming to replace all 12 existing directors. Three days before the AGM, Campbell settled the fight by adding two directors proposed by Third Point, increasing the number of board seats to 14, and giving Third Point a say in the upcoming CEO nomination.

- Other recent targets for activist investors include Bayer (targeted by Elliott), Toshiba (King Street), Olympus (ValueAct), Thyssenkrupp (Cevian), and Papa John's (Starboard Value).

Such activism is controversial. Executives lament that they interfere with their long-term plans and pressure them to deliver short-term returns. Policymakers and the public fear that they force a company to focus entirely on shareholders, ignoring wider society. In 2016, U.S. Senators Tammy Baldwin and Jeff Merkley proposed the Brokaw Act to crack down on activist hedge funds, claiming that they "are leading the short-term charge in our economy" and "only seek to enrich themselves at the expense of workers, communities and taxpayers." Franz Muntefering, chair of the German Social Democratic Party, described activists as "swarms of locusts that fall on companies, stripping them bare before moving on."

Are these concerns actually true? It appears not. When an activist hedge fund takes a large stake in a company, the stock price rises by 7%, with no long-term reversal.[18] These shareholder gains are not from piling on debt to save taxes, but real value creation—plant productivity increases, primarily from a rise in labor productivity.[19] And this isn't achieved by squeezing more out of workers: Wages don't fall, and hours worked don't rise. One potentially worrying finding is that hedge funds cut R&D expenditure, which appears to be the smoking

---

[18]A. Brav, W. Jiang, F. Partnoy, and R. Thomas, "Hedge Fund Activism, Corporate Governance, and Firm Performance," *Journal of Finance* 63 (2008), pp. 1729–1775.

[19]A. Brav, W. Jiang, and H. Kim, "The Real Effects of Hedge Fund Activism: Productivity, Asset Allocation, and Labor Outcomes" *Review of Financial Studies* 28, (2015) 2723–2769.

gun that critics are looking for. But innovation actually rises—more patents are generated, and patent quality increases.[20] The company produces more with less.

Increasingly, activism is on environmental, social, and governance (ESG) issues. For example, in June 2020, activist investor Engine No. 1 won a proxy fight against ExxonMobil, electing three directors to the board that would push the company to decarbonize.

Exit

Voting and engagement are sometimes referred to as "governance through *voice*" as they try to influence how a company is run. However, shareholders can hold managers to account, even without exerting direct influence, by selling out if the firm is underperforming (known as "governance through *exit*" or taking the "Wall Street Walk"). This mechanism can send a powerful message. If enough shareholders bail out, the stock price tumbles. This damages top management's reputation and compensation. Anticipating this, a wise CEO will seek to maximize value to ensure that investors don't exit.

Some critics argue that the threat of investor exit induces managers to inflate short-term profits to deter such selling. They therefore propose mechanisms to encourage investors to hold on to their shares, by granting greater voting rights or "loyalty dividends" after a certain number of years. For example, France's Loi Florange gives investors double voting rights after they have held the stock for two years.

But these suggestions confuse the *holding period* of an investor with his *orientation*. An investor may indeed be selling in the short term (i.e., have a short holding period) but may do so based on an analysis of the company's long-term value (i.e., have a long-term orientation). For example, Ford announced record profits in 2015 followed by its second-highest profits in 2016. Yet investors sold, causing the stock price to fall 21% over those two years, due to concerns that Ford wasn't investing enough in electric or self-driving cars. The stock price decline, despite soaring profits, was a big contributor to CEO Mark Fields being fired in May 2017.

So the crucial question isn't whether investors *hold* for the long-term, but whether they trade on long-term *information*. Investors are more likely to do the latter if they have large stakes. A small investor will base his assessment on freely available information such as earnings—he owns so little that it's not worth it to do more detailed analysis—and take the knee-jerk action of selling a company if it has delivered weak earnings. But large investors, also known as block-holders, have the incentive to do the research first: Figure out whether low profits are due to mismanagement or far-sighted investment. If it's the latter, they won't sell, and may even buy more.

19.5 Self-Test

    a. What are the ways in which shareholders can hold managers to account?

    b. What factors affect shareholders' willingness to do so?

19-4   Monitoring by Auditors, Lenders, and Potential Acquirers

In addition to directors and shareholders, several other parties keep a check on management's performance.

BEYOND THE PAGE

SOX

mhhe.com/brealey14e

Auditors

The audit committee of the board hires external accountants to audit the firm's financial statements and meets with them to discuss their findings. Given the importance of this function,

---

[20]A. Brav, W. Jiang, S. Ma, and X. Tian, "How Does Hedge Fund Activism Reshape Corporate Innovation?" *Journal of Financial Economics* 130 (2018), pp. 237–264.

the 2002 Sarbanes-Oxley Act in the United States stipulates that the audit committee must be comprised entirely of independent directors.

If the audit uncovers no problems, the auditors issue an opinion that the financial statements fairly represent the company's financial condition and are consistent with **generally accepted accounting principles (GAAP)**. If problems are found, the auditors will negotiate changes in assumptions or procedures. Managers almost always agree because if acceptable changes are not made, the auditors may issue a *qualified opinion,* which states that the accounts haven't been fully presented in according with GAAP rules, or worse still an *adverse opinion,* which states that the accounts violate many GAAP rules and contain material misstatements.

Even worse than auditors issuing an adverse opinion is a company admitting to accounting irregularities that escaped detection by the auditors. In December 2019, the British fashion retailer Ted Baker announced that it had discovered accounting irregularities and had overstated its inventory by £25 million. The share price immediately fell by 15%, before recovering to end the day 8% lower—a decline of £14 million. An even more damaging accounting scandal hit the U.K. bakery Patisserie Valerie. In October 2018, it disclosed irregularities, which meant that the accounts overstated its true value by several million pounds. Three months later, it went into administration (the U.K.'s formal bankruptcy process), leading to 70 of its 200 stores being shut down and the loss of 900 jobs.

EXAMPLE 19.3 • The failure of Enron

Enron started as a gas pipeline company but expanded rapidly into trading energy and commodities, and made large investments in electricity generation, broadband communications, and water companies. By the end of 2000, its total stock market value was about $60 billion. A year later, it was bankrupt. But that $60 billion wasn't really lost when Enron failed, because most of that value wasn't there in the first place. By late 2001, Enron was, in many ways, an empty shell. Its stock price was supported more by investors' enthusiasm than by profitable operating businesses. The company had also accumulated large hidden debts. For example, Enron borrowed aggressively through *special-purpose entities* (SPEs). The SPE debts were not reported on its balance sheet, even though many of the SPEs did not meet the requirements for off-balance-sheet accounting. The fall of Enron also brought down its auditor, accounting firm Arthur Andersen.

The bad news started to leak out in the last months of 2001. In October, Enron announced a $1 billion write-down of its water and broadband businesses. In November, it consolidated its SPEs retroactively, which increased the debt on its balance sheet by $658 million and reduced past earnings by $591 million.[21] Its public debt was downgraded to junk ratings on November 28, and on December 2, it filed for bankruptcy.

• • • • •

Lenders

The company's bankers and bondholders also monitor. For example, when a company takes out a syndicated bank loan, the lead bank will keep an eye on the company's activities and profitability. It typically requires the borrower to provide information at least monthly and arrange regular plant visits. If the borrower has provided collateral in the form of inventory or

---

[21]Enron faced other financial problems. For example, it told investors that it had hedged business risks in SPE transactions but failed to say that many of the SPEs were backed up by pledges of Enron shares. When Enron's stock price fell, the hedges unraveled. See P. Healy and K. Palepu, "The Fall of Enron," *Journal of Economic Perspectives* 17 (Spring 2003), pp. 3–26.

receivables, the bank may demand daily information about cash flows.[22] By monitoring the company to protect its loan, the bank generally protects shareholders' interests also.[23]

19.6 Self-Test

In what circumstances might monitoring by the bank not protect shareholders' interests? (You might like to look back at the example of Circular File in Chapter 17 if you are not sure of the answer.)

Takeovers

Other management teams may also check on the performance of a company's management. If they believe that the assets aren't being used efficiently, they can try to take over the business and boot out the existing management. We'll have more to say in Chapters 32 and 33 about the role of takeovers and the market for corporate control.

19-5 Management Compensation

The last three sections have discussed how monitoring by boards, shareholders, and other parties can help ensure that managers create value. This can prevent the more obvious agency costs, such as blatant perks. But monitoring requires time and money. So, while some monitoring is almost always worthwhile, a limit is soon reached at which an extra dollar spent on monitoring would not return an extra dollar of value from reduced agency costs. Like all investments, monitoring encounters diminishing returns.

Some agency costs can't be prevented even with the most thorough monitoring. Suppose a shareholder decides to monitor capital investment decisions. How could he know for sure whether a capital budget approved by top management includes (1) *all* the positive-NPV opportunities open to the firm and (2) *no* projects with negative NPVs due to empire-building? The managers know more about the firm's prospects than outsiders ever can. If the shareholder could identify all projects and their NPVs, then the managers would hardly be needed!

Therefore, compensation plans must be designed to attract competent managers and give them the right incentives. In most companies, compensation is the responsibility of the *compensation committee* or *remuneration committee* of the board of directors. The Securities and Exchange Commission (SEC) and New York Stock Exchange (NYSE) require that all directors on the compensation committee be independent. The committee typically hires outside consultants to advise on both the level of pay (based on general trends and levels in peer firms) and its structure (how pay is linked to performance and what performance measures are used.)

Once the compensation package is approved by the committee, it's described to shareholders. This write-up is called the Compensation Discussion and Analysis (CD&A) in the United States. Most countries then require this report to be put to a shareholder vote, known as "say on pay." In the United States, this vote is nonbinding, but as noted earlier, boards face a shareholder backlash if they don't take heed. For example, in 2018, software company Qualys received 61.2% opposition in its say-on-pay vote. The board reacted by engaging with shareholders and making seven changes to its pay structure, including long-term performance goals; 97% of shareholders approved the adjusted compensation package in the following year.

---

[22]M. Gustafson, I. Ivanov, and R. R. Meisenzahl, "Bank Monitoring: Evidence from Syndicated Loans," *Journal of Financial Economics* 139 (February 2021), pp. 452–477.

[23]The interests of lenders and shareholders are not always aligned—see Chapter 17. But a company's ability to satisfy lenders is normally good news for shareholders, particularly when lenders are well placed to monitor.

In the United Kingdom and European Union, companies must produce two reports. The first is the forward-looking remuneration policy, which explains how the firm will determine pay in the future—for example, how pay will be linked to performance. Here, companies must hold a binding vote at least once every three years. The second is the backward-looking remuneration report, which describes how the board determined actual pay over the past year. Here, companies hold an annual advisory vote.

EXAMPLE 19.4 • Repeated No votes from shareholders are difficult to ignore

In 2014, Bed Bath & Beyond shareholders voted down the pay of CEO Steven Temares, but the company chose to ignore the vote and again increased Temares's compensation in 2015. However, the following year, a second thumbs-down from shareholders led the company to cut CEO compensation by 21% from 2015 to 2017.

• • • • •

For shareholders to be able to vote effectively, they need to be informed. Analyzing whether the level of pay is appropriate and whether performance targets are set correctly is complex. Thus, *proxy advisers* such as Institutional Shareholder Services (ISS) and Glass Lewis advise investors on how they should vote. However, proxy advisers themselves may be imperfect: Because they have to provide advice across thousands of companies, their recommendations may be insufficiently tailored to a company's individual circumstances. In addition, ISS provides consulting services to companies on how to design packages that will be approved by shareholders, and evidence suggests that they may be biased toward their consulting clients.[24]

Compensation Facts and Controversies

In theory, pay can be an effective *solution* to agency problems. By tying a CEO's pay to long-term firm value, it can incentivize her to create value. However, poorly designed pay might exacerbate agency problems by encouraging short-termism as discussed in Section 19-1. Moreover, pay might be a *manifestation* of agency problems—CEOs can influence the board to pay them excessively. Due to these concerns, executive compensation has attracted increasing controversy in recent years, not only from investors who directly bear the cost of excessive pay, but also politicians and the public who fear that it fuels inequality.

Studies of executive pay in the United States suggest three general features:

1. As you can see from Figure 19.1, U.S. CEOs tend to be more highly paid than in other countries. On average, they get double the pay of German CEOs and more than five times the pay of Japanese CEOs.

2. Figure 19.2 shows that average compensation in the United States has risen much more rapidly than inflation. Between 1992 and 2019, total compensation for the CEOs of companies in the Standard & Poor's (S&P) Index has more than tripled in real terms.[25]

---

[24]T. Li, "Outsourcing Corporate Governance: Conflicts of Interest within the Proxy Advisory Industry," *Management Science* 64 (2018), pp. 2951–2971.

[25]This sharp rise in CEO pay started in the 1970s. For the previous 30 years, pay levels were essentially flat. See C. Frydman and R. Saks, "Executive Compensation: A New View from a Long-Term Perspective, 1936–2005," *Review of Financial Studies* 23 (2010), pp. 2099–2138.

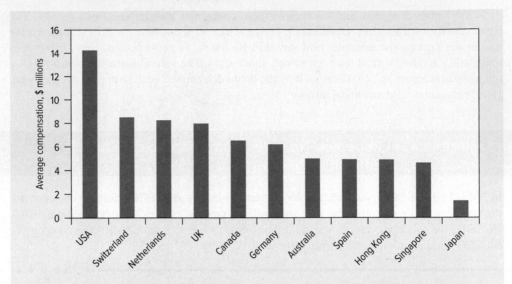

▶ **FIGURE 19.1**   Average annual compensation of CEOs in 2017 by country (in million U.S. dollars).

Source: https://www.statista.com/statistics/424154/average-annual-ceo-compensation-worldwide/.

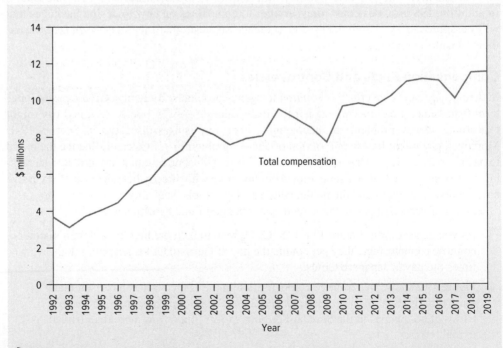

▶ **FIGURE 19.2**   Median total compensation 1992–2019 for CEOs of companies in the S&P Index. Values are shown in inflation-adjusted 2019 dollars.

Source: Execucomp.

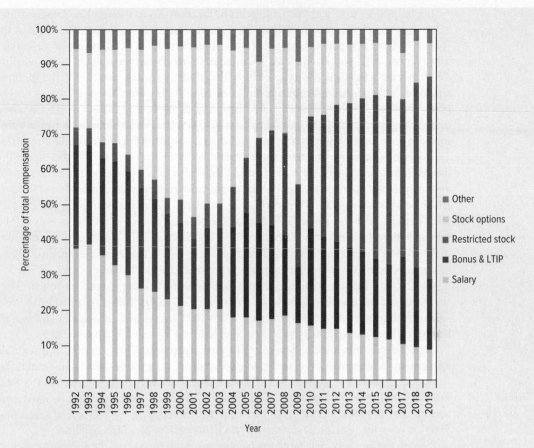

Percentage of total compensation (y-axis)

Legend:
- Other
- Stock options
- Restricted stock
- Bonus & LTIP
- Salary

Year (x-axis): 1992–2019

▶ **FIGURE 19.3**   The average percentage of CEO compensation in the form of salaries, bonuses, long-term incentive plans (LTIPs), stock awards, option awards, and other sources. Stock awards and options are valued at the time of the grant. The sample consists of companies in the S&P Index between 1992 and 2019.

3. Figure 19.3 shows that only 12% of compensation for these CEOs comes from salary. The remainder comes from bonuses, stock grants, stock options, and other performance-linked incentives. This proportion of incentive-based compensation has increased sharply and is much higher than in other countries.

We look first at the size of the pay package and later turn to its contents. The sheer size of executive pay suggests to many that it's out of touch with reality. In the United States, the average S&P 500 CEO earned $14.8 million in 2019, 264 times the average worker, compared with a ratio of only 42 in 1980. In the United Kingdom, the median FTSE 100 CEO earned £3.6 million in 2019, 119 times the median worker.

The rise in the pay ratio since 1980 seems to debunk a common justification for high pay: that it is needed to attract talented CEOs. It's hard to argue that CEOs are much more talented now than in 1980, so why has pay skyrocketed? However, an influential paper by Gabaix and Landier argues that the sharp rise in pay is justified not because CEOs have become more talented, but because talent has become more important.[26]

[26]X. Gabaix and A. Landier, "Why Has CEO Pay Increased So Much?" *Quarterly Journal of Economics* 123 (February 2008), pp. 49–100.

It's helpful to start with an analogy from baseball. Even though LA Angels center fielder Mike Trout is a great player, it's hard to argue that he's substantially more talented than Babe Ruth. Yet Trout gets paid far more than Babe Ruth ever did, even adjusting for inflation. In 2019, Trout signed a 12-year contract for $426 million—the richest contract in U.S. sporting history. That's because baseball is now a multi-billion-dollar industry, due to TV rights, replica merchandise, and a global marketplace, unlike in Babe Ruth's time. Even if Trout is only a tiny bit better than the next-best center fielder, these tiny differences in talent could have a huge effect on LA Angels' profits. If Trout's home runs help win the World Series, that would substantially increase their fan base throughout the world. So it's worth it paying top dollar for top talent.

Now, let's translate this from the ballpark to the boardroom. Just as the baseball industry has gotten much bigger, so have firms. Firms also now compete in a global marketplace, and technology changes so rapidly that the failure to keep pace can be devastating (compare BlackBerry with Apple). Thus, just as in baseball, it's worth paying top dollar for top talent. Average firm size in the S&P 500 is $22 billion. So even if a CEO is only slightly more talented than the next best alternative, and contributes only 1% more to firm value, that's $220 million. In that case, her $14.8 million salary doesn't seem so outrageous. It's expensive to hire a good CEO—but it's even more expensive to hire a bad one.

Gabaix and Landier's argument isn't just an abstract theory; you can test it. The authors show that the increase in pay between 1980 and 2003 can be fully explained by the rise in firm size over that time. An update studying 2004–2011 shows that subsequent changes were also linked to firm size; in 2007–2009, firm size fell by 17% and CEO pay by 28%.

Why doesn't this logic apply to employees? Because a CEO's actions are scalable. If she implements a new production technology or improves corporate culture, this can be rolled out firmwide, and such a decision has a larger effect in a larger firm. One percent is $22 million in a $2.2 billion firm, but $220 million in a $22 billion firm. In contrast, most employees' actions are less scalable. An engineer who has the capacity to service 10 machines creates $50,000 of value regardless of whether the firm has 100 or 1,000 machines.

There is also a less charitable explanation of managerial pay. This view stresses the close links between the CEO and the other members of the board of directors. If directors are too chummy with the CEO, they may find it difficult to get tough when it comes to setting compensation packages. And if shareholders are spread thinly across hundreds of companies, they won't hold directors accountable for not being tough.

So we have two views of the level of managerial pay. One is that it results from competitive forces in a tight market for managerial talent. The other is that poor governance, dispersed shareholders and weak boards allow excessive pay. There is evidence for both views. Supporting the competitive market view, CEOs are not the only group to have seen their compensation increase rapidly in recent years. Pay has risen in many other scalable professions, such as for fund managers, sports stars, and celebrity entertainers, even though their employers don't seem to be poorly governed.[27] Supporting the excessive pay view, the level of CEO pay is increasing in various measures of board ineffectiveness, such as board size and board busyness. In contrast, it's lower if there's an outside blockholder who owns at least 5% of the firm, and thus has strong incentives to monitor pay.

The Structure of CEO Pay

Arguably even more important than the level of CEO pay is its structure—in particular, how it is linked to performance. This is because this linkage affects whether CEO pay attenuates agency problems (if it's closely linked to performance and to the right measures of performance) or exacerbates them (if it's not).

---

[27]S. N. Kaplan and J. D. Rauh, "Wall Street and Main Street: What Contributes to the Rise in the Highest Incomes?" *Review of Financial Studies* 23 (2010), pp. 1004–1050.

The long-term stock price is an attractive measure of performance for many reasons. First, it's what shareholders themselves receive. Second, evidence shows that it is affected by many dimensions of CEO performance—not just current profits, but expected future profits, growth opportunities (PVGO), employee satisfaction, customer satisfaction, environmental steward-ship, patent citations, and so on—and weights them by their relative importance for firm value. So it captures both financial and nonfinancial factors.

As a result, many major companies around the world now link part of their executive pay to the performance of the companies' stock.[28] For example, in 2017, Oracle CEO Larry Ellison received total pay of $21 million. Only $1 of that amount was salary. The lion's share was in the form of stock and option grants. Moreover, as founder of Oracle, Ellison holds more than 1 *billion* shares in the firm. No one can say for certain how hard Ellison would have worked with a different compensation package. But one thing is clear: He has a huge personal stake in the success of the firm—and in increasing its market value.

Critics often point to the fact that there's only a weak link between a CEO's salary and bonus and the performance of the company's stock. But measuring pay-for-performance this way has a fundamental flaw: It ignores the substantial incentives provided by the CEO's hold-ings of stock and options. Ellison's salary may be fixed at $1 per year regardless of Oracle's performance, but he has substantial accountability for performance due to his personal wealth being tied up in Oracle. And Oracle isn't an isolated case. A 10% fall in the stock price costs the average U.S. *Fortune* 500 CEO $6.7 million. Evidence suggests that these incentives work: Companies where the CEO owns a large stake in her firm outperform those who own small stakes by 4–10% per year.[29]

However, there are also disadvantages to paying a manager with shares. One is that the share price depends on many factors outside her control. If the economy takes a tumble, the firm's stock price will fall even if the CEO has performed well. To compensate her for this risk, a firm that wants to pay the CEO with shares will have to offer more than if it paid her in cash. So there's a trade-off—tying CEO wealth more closely to firm value may improve her decision making, but it also costs shareholders more.

And these outside factors don't just matter on the downside, but on the upside as well. Not only might the CEO suffer from poor firm performance outside her control, but she might also be unjustifiably rewarded for good firm performance that's due to luck. A study found that oil company CEOs' pay rises with the oil price, even though it's outside their control. However, this link was weaker when blockholders sat on the board, suggesting that shareholder moni-toring reduces such pay-for-luck.[30]

EXAMPLE 19.5 ● How one CEO reaped a windfall

In December 2017, news broke out that the options of Jeff Fairburn, CEO of U.K. house-builder Persimmon, were now worth £110 million due to Persimmon's strong stock price performance. But this wasn't thanks to Fairburn's genius but because low interest rates and the government's "help-to-buy" scheme had boosted the U.K. housing market. The furor over the announcement forced Chair Nicholas Wrigley to resign.

● ● ● ● ●

---

[28] The major exceptions are in China, Japan, India, and South Korea, where such incentive schemes are less common.

[29] U. von Lilienfeld-Toal and S. Ruenzi, "CEO Ownership, Stock Market Performance, and Managerial Discretion," *The Journal of Finance* 69 (June 2014), pp. 1013–1050.

[30] M. Bertrand and S. Mullainathan, "Are CEOs Rewarded for Luck? The Ones without Principles Are," *Quarterly Journal of Economics* 116 (August 2001), pp. 901–932.

One way to strip out these outside factors is to issue the CEO with *performance shares,* whose value depends upon certain measures of performance, which can be calculated relative to industry peers. For example, one performance metric might be industry-adjusted EPS growth. Performance shares are an example of a more general practice known as a *long-term incentive plan* (LTIP), where the amount paid to the executive depends on hitting certain targets. The plan can pay out either stock (as in the case of performance shares) or, alternatively, cash. In addition to financial targets, LTIPs also allow nonfinancial targets, such as for workplace safety and climate change.

But these performance targets may cause even more problems than they solve. In particular, the CEO may take short-term actions to hit them. Evidence finds that firms that just meet performance targets undertake significantly less R&D and have higher accruals than those that just miss them, suggesting that they engaged in manipulation to reach their goal.[31] Similarly, performance targets can encourage CEOs to focus on the targeted measures and underemphasize other relevant dimensions, particularly those that can't be measured quantitatively. For example, while workplace safety is indeed important, tying pay to this measure may lead to underemphasis on giving employees meaningful work, investing in their skills, and improving corporate culture.

Indeed, while performance shares became increasingly popular in the mid-2000s, there's now increasing concern that they lead to short-termism. In 2019, the U.S. Council of Institutional Investors and the U.K. Investment Association, trade bodies of money managers, independently released policy papers welcoming the use of long-term shares without performance conditions.

But removing performance conditions alone won't be sufficient to deter short-termism. We earlier argued that "the long-term stock price is an attractive measure of performance." The key words are "long-term," because a CEO can artificially inflate the short-term stock price. Studies show that, when CEOs are about to sell their shares, they cut investment, focus on hitting short-term earnings targets, and strategically release good news that temporarily boosts the stock price.[32]

EXAMPLE 19.6 • Cashing out before crashing out

In Section 19-1, we explained how Countrywide's Angelo Mozilo pursued growth at all costs by writing sub-prime loans. This boosted Countrywide's stock price and allowed Mozilo to sell $140 million of shares just before he quit. Even though these loans eventually became delinquent, and led to Countrywide's collapse, Mozilo had already cashed out.

• • • • •

Thus, it is critical for any shares to be locked up for several years before the CEO can sell them, which is known as *restricted stock.* Importantly, this requires the lock-up to extend beyond the CEO's departure so that she plans for succession and undertakes investments even if they won't fully pay off until after she's left.

Indeed, practice is moving in this direction. Unilever CEO Paul Polman had to hold stock worth five times his annual base salary for the first year after he retired in 2018—a shareholding requirement exceeding £5 million—and 2.5 times for the second year. The 2018 revision

---

[31]See B. Bennett, J. C. Bettis, R. Gopalan, and T. Milbourn, "Compensation Goals and Firm Performance," *Journal of Financial Economics* 124 (2017), pp. 307–330.

[32]See, for example, A. Edmans, V. W. Fang, and K. A. Lewellen, "Equity Vesting and Investment," *Review of Financial Studies* 30 (July 2017), pp. 2229–2271; and A. Edmans, L. Goncalves-Pinto, M. Groen-Xu, and Y. Wang, "Strategic News Releases in Equity Vesting Months," *Review of Financial Studies* 31 (November 2018), pp. 4099–4141.

of the U.K. Corporate Governance Code requires companies to develop a formal policy for shareholding requirements post-departure.

19.7 Self-Test

How can executive pay be structured to ensure that managers maximize long-term shareholder value?

19-6   Government Regimes around the World

Thus far in this chapter, we've largely discussed the *market-based* system of corporate governance that is common in the United States and other Anglo-Saxon countries. Since the stock market allows shareholders to diversify, shareholders typically hold small stakes, which reduces their incentive to monitor. So they govern at arm's length, mainly relying on boards and stock-based pay to ensure that managers act in their interests.

But in other countries, shareholders are more concentrated, so direct monitoring by them is particularly important for governance. In others still, a company's main source of financing is from banks rather than shareholders, which gives them a leading role. We now look at different governance regimes around the world, starting with Japan.

Ownership and Control in Japan

Traditionally, the most notable feature of Japanese corporate finance has been the **keiretsu**. A keiretsu is a network of companies, usually organized around a major bank. Japan is said to have a *main bank* system, with long-standing relationships between banks and firms. There are also long-standing business relationships among a keiretsu's companies. For example, a manufacturing company might buy most of its raw materials from group suppliers and, in turn, sell much of its output to other group companies.

The bank and other financial institutions at the keiretsu's center own shares in most of the group companies (though a commercial bank in Japan is limited to 5% ownership of each company). Those companies may, in turn, hold the bank's shares or each other's shares. Because of the cross-holdings, the number of shares available for purchase by outside investors is much lower than the total number outstanding.

The keiretsu is tied together in other ways. Most debt financing comes from the keiretsu's main bank or from affiliated financial institutions. Managers may sit on the boards of directors of other group companies, and a "presidents' council" of the CEOs of the most important group companies meets regularly.

Think of the keiretsu as a system of corporate governance, where power is divided among the main bank, the group's largest companies, and the group as a whole. This confers certain financial advantages. First, firms have access to additional "internal" financing—internal to the group, that is. Thus, a company with a capital budget exceeding operating cash flows can turn to the main bank or other keiretsu companies for financing. This avoids the cost or possible bad-news signal of a public sale of securities. Second, when a keiretsu firm falls into financial distress, with insufficient cash to pay its bills or fund necessary capital investments, a workout can usually be arranged. New management can be brought in from elsewhere in the group, and financing can be obtained, again "internally."

One effect of this structure is that keiretsu companies' investments are more stable and less exposed to the ups and downs of operating cash flows or to episodes of financial distress.[33]

---

[33] T. Hoshi, A. Kashyap, and D. Scharfstein, "Corporate Structure, Liquidity and Investment: Evidence from Japanese Industrial Groups," *Quarterly Journal of Economics* 106 (February 1991), pp. 33–60, and "The Role of Banks in Reducing the Costs of Financial Distress in Japan," *Journal of Financial Economics* 27 (September 1990), pp. 67–88.

It seems that the financial support of the keiretsus enable members to invest for the long run, regardless of temporary setbacks.

Corporation law in Japan resembles that in the United States, but there are some important differences. For example, in Japan, it is easier for shareholders to nominate and elect directors. Also, management remuneration must be approved at general meetings of shareholders.[34] Nevertheless, ordinary shareholders do not, in fact, have much influence. Japanese boards traditionally had 40 or 50 members, with only a handful who are potentially independent of management. However, in recent years, many Japanese companies have changed to U.S.-style boards with fewer members and more independent directors. However, it is still the case that the CEO has tremendous influence. As long as the financial position of a Japanese corporation is sound, the CEO and senior management control the corporation. Outside shareholders have very little influence.

Given this control, plus the cross-holdings within industrial groups, it's no surprise that hostile takeovers are very rare in Japan. Also, Japanese corporations have been stingy with dividends, which probably reflects the relative lack of influence of outside shareholders. On the other hand, Japanese CEOs do not use their power to generate large sums of personal wealth. They are not well paid, compared to CEOs in most other developed countries. (Look back to Figure 19.1 for average top-management compensation levels for Japan and other countries.)

Cross-holdings reached a peak around 1990 when about 50% of corporations' shares were held by other Japanese companies and financial institutions. Starting in the mid-1990s, a banking crisis began to emerge in Japan. This led firms to sell off bank shares because they viewed them as bad investments. Banks and firms in financial distress, such as Nissan, sold off other companies' shares to raise funds. By 2004, the level of cross-holdings had fallen to 20%. They rose again in the next few years as companies in the steel and other industries began to worry about hostile takeovers, which was the original motivation for acquisition of cross-holdings in the 1950s and 1960s.[35]

One of the most important changes in Japan in recent years has been the introduction of economic reforms by former Prime Minister Shinzo Abe, commonly known as Abenomics. Changes in corporate governance have been a major component of these. Their purpose is to make managers more responsible to shareholders and make companies more competitive, profitable and transparent. A new Corporate Governance Code recommended the appointment of two independent outside directors and the disclosure of the company's policy regarding cross-shareholdings in the hope that this would discourage them. While the code is not legally binding, the fact that foreign ownership of Tokyo-listed firms has been above 30% in recent years should increase companies' willingness to adopt it.

Ownership and Control in Germany

Traditionally, banks in Germany played a significant role in corporate governance. This involved providing loans, owning large amounts of equity directly, and the proxy voting of shares held on behalf of customers. Over time, this role has changed significantly. The relationship between the largest German bank, Deutsche Bank, and one of the largest German companies, Daimler AG, provides a good illustration.

Panel *a* of Figure 19.4 shows the 1990 ownership structure of Daimler, or as it was known then, Daimler-Benz. The immediate owners were Deutsche Bank with 28%, Mercedes Automobil Holding with 25%, and the Kuwait Government with 14%. The remaining 32% of the

---

[34] These requirements have led to a unique feature of Japanese corporate life, the *sokaiya,* who are racketeers who demand payment in exchange for not disrupting shareholders' meetings.

[35] See H. Miyajima and F. Kuroki, "The Unwinding of Cross-Shareholding in Japan: Causes, Effects and Implications," in *Corporate Governance in Japan: Institutional Change and Organizational Diversity,* ed. M. Aoki, G. Jackson, and H. Miyajima (Oxford and New York: Oxford University Press, 2007), pp. 79–124. Also see "Criss-Crossed Capitalism," *The Economist* print edition, November 6, 2008.

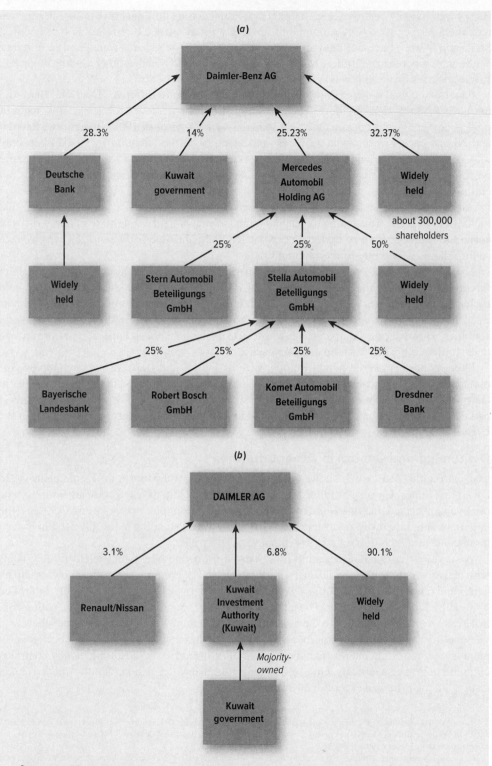

FIGURE 19.4   (*a*) Ownership of Daimler-Benz, 1990. (*b*) Ownership of Daimler, 2014.

Sources: (*a*) J. Franks and C. Mayer, "The Ownership and Control of German Corporations," *Review of Financial Studies* 14 (Winter 2001), Figure 1, p. 949. © 2001 Oxford University Press. (*b*) www.Daimler.com.

shares were widely held by about 300,000 individual and institutional investors. But this was only the top layer. Mercedes Automobil's holding was half owned by two holding companies, Stella and Stern. The rest of its shares were widely held. Stella's shares were, in turn, split four ways: among two banks; Robert Bosch, an industrial company; and another holding company, Komet. Stern's ownership was split five ways but we ran out of space.[36]

Panel *b* shows the ownership structure in 2014. It is quite different. Deutsche Bank did not have a direct stake anymore. The Kuwait government still owned a substantial stake of 6.8%, but that stake is considerably less than the 14% it owned in 1990. In addition, Renault and Nissan each owned about 1.5%. In stark contrast to the situation in 1990, when only 32% of the stock was widely held, in 2014 90% was widely held. The ownership structure has moved a long way toward the U.S. ownership pattern, where many large companies are entirely widely held.

An important reason for this dramatic change in ownership structure was a tax change that took effect in 2002. This exempted capital gains on shares held for more than one year from corporate taxation. Prior to that, the corporate capital gains rate had been 52%, which made selling shares very costly for corporations.

Daimler was not the only company to experience a significant drop in bank ownership. Average bank ownership of equity fell from 4.1% in 1994 to 0.4% in 2005. Board seats held by bank representatives fell from 9.6% to 5.6% of the total. Banks are now primarily interested in using their board representation to promote their lending and investment banking activities. However, the companies on whose boards the bankers sit appear to perform worse than similar companies without such a presence.[37]

Other countries in continental Europe, such as France and Italy, also have complex corporate ownership structures. These countries have not had a dramatic tax change like that in Germany. However, there has been a steady stream of regulatory changes that have mostly had the effect of making the legal framework for corporate governance more like that in the United States.[38]

Ownership and Control in Other Countries

Look at Figure 19.5, which shows the concentration of ownership in different countries. In the United States, Canada, South Korea, and Japan, ownership of listed companies tends to be relatively dispersed, but this is not true everywhere. For example, in France and Germany, the largest shareholder owns, on average, nearly half of the outstanding stock. Ownership is even more concentrated in Russia and Argentina.

A survey of corporate ownership in 27 developed economies found relatively few firms with actively traded shares and dispersed ownership.[39] The pattern of significant ownership by banks and other financial institutions is also uncommon. Instead, firms are typically controlled by wealthy families or the state. The ultimate controlling shareholders have secure voting control even when they do not have the majority stake in earnings, dividends, or asset values.

State involvement is particularly important in China, where the central and local government has a controlling interest in almost a quarter of listed firms. In Europe, family control is common in France, Germany, Greece, and Italy. It is also widespread in South America and in Asia, with the principal exception of Japan.

---

[36]A five-layer ownership tree for Daimler-Benz is given in S. Prowse, "Corporate Governance in an International Perspective: A Survey of Corporate Control Mechanisms among Large Firms in the U.S., U.K., Japan and Germany," *Financial Markets, Institutions, and Instruments* 4 (February 1995), Table 16.

[37]I. Dittmann, E. Maug, and C. Schneider, "Bankers on the Boards of German Firms: What They Do, What They Are Worth, and Why They Are (Still) There," *Review of Finance*, 14 (2010), pp. 35–71.

[38]P.-H. Conac, L. Enriques and M. Gelter, "Constraining Dominant Shareholders? Self-Dealing: The Legal Framework in France, Germany, and Italy," *European Company and Financial Law Review* 4 (2007), pp. 491–528.

[39]R. La Porta, F. Lopez-de-Silanes, and A. Shleifer, "Corporate Ownership around the World," *Journal of Finance* 54 (1999), pp. 471–517.

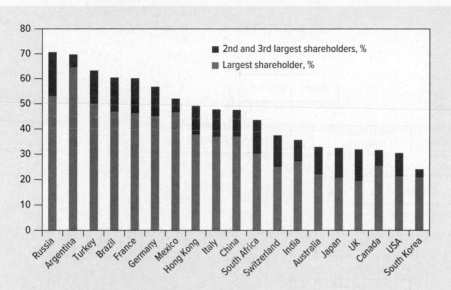

> **FIGURE 19.5**   Average percentage of equity owned by largest shareholders. (Shareholders from one family are grouped together.)

Source: G. Aminadav and E. Papaioannou, "Corporate Control around the World," *Journal of Finance* 75 (June 2020), pp. 1191–1246.

Family control does not usually mean a direct majority stake in the public firm. Control is usually exercised by cross-shareholdings, dual-class shares, and pyramids. We have already discussed cross-holdings and dual-class shares. Pyramids are common in Asian countries as well as several European countries.[40] In a pyramid, control is exercised through a sequence of controlling positions in several layers of companies. The actual operating companies are at the bottom of the pyramid. Above each operating company is a first holding company, then a second one, then perhaps others still higher in the pyramid.[41] Look, for example, at Figure 19.6, which shows the principal shareholders of the French luxury goods company, LVMH. This company is controlled by Financière Jean Goujon, whose only business is to hold a 57.5% stake in LVMH. Jean Goujon is wholly owned by Christian Dior, which in turn is controlled by Semyrhamis, whose main purpose is to hold Christian Dior shares. This company is a wholly owned subsidiary of Financière Agache, which also holds a direct 9.2% stake in Christian Dior. Financière Agache is a 99% controlled subsidiary of the private company Groupe Arnault SAS, which is the holding company of Bernard Arnault and his family. Groupe Arnault SAS also controls 51% of the firm Le Peigne, which holds 1% of the shares of LVMH. In sum, LVMH is controlled by Bernard Arnault and his family, who indirectly hold about a 61.5% stake (57.5% via Financière Jean Goujon, 2% via Financiere Agache, 1% via Groupe Arnault SAS, and 1% via Le Peigne).

The problem with cross-shareholdings, dual-class shares, and pyramids is that minority shareholders may be at a disadvantage; the company's cash flow and potential value may be diverted to management or dominant shareholders with control. In the United States, the law protects minority shareholders from exploitation, but this isn't the case everywhere.[42]

---

[40]L. A. Bebchuk, R. Kraakman, and G. R. Triantis, "Stock Pyramids, Cross-Ownership, and Dual Class Equity," in *Concentrated Corporate Ownership,* ed. R. Morck (Chicago: University of Chicago Press, 2000), pp. 295–318.

[41]A holding company is a firm whose only assets are controlling blocks of shares in other companies.

[42]International differences in the opportunities for dominant shareholders to exploit their position are discussed in S. Johnson et al., "Tunnelling," *American Economic Review* 90 (May 2000), pp. 22–27.

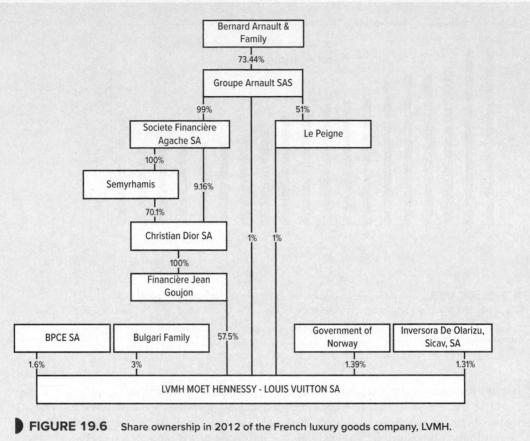

FIGURE 19.6   Share ownership in 2012 of the French luxury goods company, LVMH.

Source: G. Aminadav and E. Papaioannou, "Corporate Control around the World," *Journal of Finance* 75 (June 2020), pp. 1191–1246.

Financial economists sometimes refer to the exploitation of minority shareholders as *tunneling;* the majority shareholder tunnels into the firm and acquires control of the assets for himself. Here is an example of tunneling Russian-style.

EXAMPLE 19.7 • Raiding the minority shareholders

To grasp how the scam works, you first need to understand *reverse stock splits.* These are often used by companies with a large number of low-priced shares. The company making the reverse split simply combines its existing shares into a smaller, more convenient number of new shares. For example, the shareholders might be given two new shares in place of the three shares that they currently own. As long as all shareholdings are reduced by the same proportion, nobody gains or loses by such a move.

However, the majority shareholder of one Russian company realized that the reverse stock split could be used to loot the company's assets. He therefore proposed that existing shareholders receive 1 new share in place of every 136,000 shares they currently held.[43]

Why did the majority shareholder pick the number "136,000"? Answer: Because the two minority shareholders owned less than 136,000 shares and therefore did not have the

---

[43]Since a reverse stock split required only the approval of a simple majority of the shareholders, the proposal was voted through.

right to *any* shares. Instead, they were simply paid off with the par value of their shares, and the majority shareholder was left owning the entire company. The majority shareholders of several other companies were so impressed with this device that they also proposed similar reverse stock splits to squeeze out their minority shareholders.

Such blatant exploitation would not be permitted in the United States or in many other countries.

•••••

19.8 Self-Test

Describe how ownership and control in Germany and Japan are different from in the United States.

19-7 Do These Differences Matter?

It seems clear that a good financial system is crucial for economic growth. Otherwise, entrepreneurs would be unable to find the capital to turn their great idea from a vision into a reality; an established firm could never attract additional funding to grow and move it from good to great. Indeed, industries that are more in need of external financing seem to grow much faster in countries with developed financial systems.[44]

Of course, a good financial system matters. But what counts as a good financial system? A reasonable definition might be one that protects investors' rights (so that they are willing to finance companies) but without restricting managers' freedom to create long-term value. Under this definition, is a market-based or bank-based system better? Does it even matter as long as it is advanced? Indeed, some evidence suggests that it might not. New business formation seems to be accelerated by the quality of a country's legal system, but not by whether the financial regime is market- or bank-based.[45] This suggests that countries should focus on improving their legal system and leave it up to firms to choose to seek financing from the stock market or from banks.

But there *are* differences between market- and bank-based systems. Let's now examine them.

Public Market Myopia

One common criticism of the market-based system is that it leads to short-termism. Small shareholders have little incentive to do their own research and so may rely excessively on quarterly earnings when valuing a company. This may lead to the pressures to inflate earnings that we discussed in Section 19-1. In contrast, if a company is privately held, it doesn't need to report quarterly earnings or worry about sudden drops in the stock price. Shareholders have large stakes and so will look beyond short-term numbers when deciding the CEO's fate. The same is true for banks deciding whether to roll over debt.

The evidence on whether market-based systems lead to short-termism is mixed. One study suggests that they do—public firms invest less than similarly sized private firms and are less responsive to changes in investment opportunities.[46] But other researchers find the opposite

---

[44]R. Levine, "Financial Development and Economic Growth: Views and Agenda," *Journal of Economic Literature* 35 (1997), pp. 688-726; and R. Rajan and L. Zingales, "Financial Dependence and Growth," *American Economic Review* 88 (1998), pp. 559–586.
[45]R. Levine, A. Demirgüç-Kunt, and E. Feyen, "The Evolving Importance of Banks and Markets in Economic Development," *World Bank Economic Review* 27 (2013), pp. 476–490.
[46]J. Asker, J. Farre-Mensa, and A. Ljungqvist, "Corporate Investment and Stock Market Listing: A Puzzle?" *Review of Financial Studies* 28 (2015), pp. 342–390.

result after taking into account differences in firm quality.[47] Rather than comparing public and private firms, a third study investigates what happens to a company after it transitions from private to public. It finds that innovation substantially drops and key employees leave.[48]

At a broader level, if bank-based economies were more long-term, then they should outperform market-based ones. From a Darwinian perspective, we should see most economies moving toward a bank-based system. The fact that we see successful market-based (United States and United Kingdom) and bank-based (Germany and Japan) countries suggests that there are pros and cons of each. Moreover, as far as short-termism is concerned, the United States seems to be the birthplace of more innovative start-ups than any other country. Indeed, the concerns of public market myopia are not new. In the late 1980s and early 1990s, when Japan was performing strongly, commentators advocated that the United States adopt their system of corporate governance.[49] When market-based economies surged ahead in the 1990s, views changed accordingly. In the interim, Japan suffered two decades of stagnation known as the "Lost 20 Years," and former Prime Minister Shinzo Abe's reforms involve adopting the market-based practices.

Moreover, the public versus private distinction is too blunt because a variety of ownership structures are possible for public companies. At one extreme is fully dispersed ownership, where each shareholder holds very few shares. Such a structure may indeed lead to short-termism, as each investor has insufficient incentive to look beyond short-term profit when evaluating companies. However, if public companies have blockholders (large shareholders), they have the incentive to understand the long-term investments that a company is making, and hold them accountable if they're not making them.[50]

Growth Industries and Declining Industries

As mentioned earlier, market-based systems seem to be particularly successful in developing brand-new industries. For example, railways were first developed in the United Kingdom in the nineteenth century, financed largely through the London Stock Exchange. In the twentieth century, the United States led development of mass production in the automobile industry, even though the automobile was invented in Germany. The commercial aircraft industry was also mainly developed in the United States, as was the computer industry after World War II, and more recently the biotechnology and Internet industries.[51] On the other hand, Germany and Japan, two countries with bank-based financial systems, have sustained their competitive advantages in established industries, such as automobiles.

Why are financial markets better at fostering innovative industries?[52] When new products or processes are discovered, there is a wide diversity of opinion about the prospects for a new industry and the best way to develop it. Financial markets accommodate this diversity, allowing young, ambitious companies to search out like-minded investors to fund their growth. This is less likely when financing has to come through a few major banks. If those banks happen not to like your idea, you're stumped.

Market-based systems also seem to be more effective at forcing companies in declining industries to shrink and release capital.[53] When a company cannot earn its cost of capital and

[47]V. Maksimovic, G. Phillips, and L. Yang, "Do Public Firms Respond to Industry Opportunities More than Private Firms? The Impact of Initial Firm Quality," Tuck School of Business Working Paper No. 3093125.

[48]S. Bernstein, "Does Going Public Affect Innovation?" *Journal of Finance* 70 (2015), pp. 1365–1403.

[49]See M. Porter, "Capital Disadvantage: America's Failing Capital Investment System," *Harvard Business Review,* September/October 1992, pp. 65–82.

[50]A. Edmans, "Blockholder Trading, Market Efficiency, and Managerial Myopia," *Journal of Finance* 64 (2009), pp. 2481–2513.

[51]There are counterexamples, such as the development of the chemical industry on a large scale in nineteenth-century Germany.

[52]See F. Allen and D. Gale, "Diversity of Opinion on the Financing of New Technologies," *Journal of Financial Intermediation* 8 (January 1999), pp. 68–69.

[53]See R. Rajan and L. Zingales, "Banks and Markets: The Changing Character of European Finance," in V. Gaspar, P. Hartmann, O. Sleijpen, eds., *The Transformation of the European Financial System,* Second ECB Central Banking Conference, October 2002, Frankfurt, Germany (Frankfurt: European Central Bank, 2003), pp. 123–167.

further growth would destroy value, the stock price drops, and the drop sends a clear negative signal. In his book *Fault Lines,* former Governor of the Central Bank of India Raghu Rajan criticized many elements of the U.S. financial system but acknowledged that: "The ruthlessness of venture capitalists in killing bad ideas . . . is far more important to their success than the ability to identify diamonds in the rough. The arm's length system plants a thousand flowers, uproots hundreds when they do not thrive, and nurtures only a few to bloom. New opportunities abound, while old, tired ways of doing business are ruthlessly eliminated. The system's strength, then, is that it is not heavily biased towards preserving the privileges of incumbent firms and workers."[54]

But in bank-based financial systems, uneconomic firms are often bailed out. When Mazda faltered in the 1970s, Sumitomo Bank guaranteed Mazda's debts and orchestrated a rescue, in part by exhorting employees within its keiretsu to purchase Mazda cars. Sumitomo Bank had an incentive to undertake the rescue because it knew that it would keep Mazda's business when it recovered. In the 1990s, Japanese banks continued to lend to "zombie" firms long after it became clear that prospects for their recovery were hopeless. For example, a coalition of banks kept the Japanese retailer Sogo afloat for years, despite clear evidence of insolvency. When Sogo finally failed in 2000, its debts had accumulated to ¥1.9 trillion.[55]

Market-based financial systems have advantages, but they can only work well when there is transparency. If a firm is transparent to outside investors—if the investors can see its true profitability and prospects—then problems will show up right away in a falling stock price. That, in turn, generates extra scrutiny from security analysts, bond rating agencies, and investors. It may also lead to a takeover.

With transparency, corporate troubles generally lead to corrective action. But the top management of a troubled opaque company may be able to maintain its stock price and postpone the discipline of the market.

Opacity is not so dangerous in a bank-based system. Firms will have long-standing relationships with banks, which can monitor the firm closely and urge it to staunch losses or to cancel excessively risky strategies. But no financial system can avoid occasional corporate meltdowns.

19.9 Self-Test

What are some of the advantages and disadvantages of market- and bank-based financial systems?

● ● ● ● ●

KEY TAKEAWAYS

- **Agency problems and agency costs.** Agency problems exist because managers are tempted to act in their own interests rather than maximizing value. Agency costs include (1) the loss in value because of managers' self-interested decisions and (2) the costs of monitoring managers and acting to reduce agency problems.

- **Common agency problems.** The CEO and other managers may:

   1. Not put in sufficient effort.

   2. Pursue perks and private benefits.

   3. Seek growth to enhance pay and prestige.

[54]R. Rajan, *Fault Lines: How Hidden Fractures Still Threaten the World Economy* (2011), Princeton University Press.
[55]T. Hoshi and A. Kashyap, "Japan's Financial Crisis and Economic Stagnation," *Journal of Economic Perspectives* 18 (Winter 2004), pp. 3–26.

4. Be reluctant to take risks or take too many risks.

5. Focus on short-term results at the expense of long-term value.

- **Corporate governance.** Corporate governance is the system of rules and practices that reduce agency costs and guide managers toward maximizing value. The system provides ways to monitor managers, to limit agency problems and costs, and to provide incentives that align managers' and shareholders' interests.

- **Board of directors.** The board is the first line of monitoring. It approves major decisions. The board's role is usually advisory, but it can replace CEOs when crises hit or performance is systematically poor. Control of the board can mean control of the company. Therefore, activist investors sometimes launch proxy fights, attempting to accumulate enough votes to appoint new directors who will pursue the investors' planned reforms.

- **Shareholders.** Shareholders monitor management and vote for directors. Activist investors buy blocks of shares and attempt to persuade top management to change financial or operating strategies. Shareholders' most powerful action may be the Wall Street Walk: If enough shareholders sell and leave, the stock price falls, which sends a clear and painful message to top managers.

- **Other monitors.** Auditors review and must approve financial statements. Lenders monitor to make sure they are paid in full and on time. Rival firms stay on the lookout for underperforming firms that could be takeover targets.

- **Incentive compensation.** A good incentive system ties management compensation to the value that the manager creates. CEO compensation in the United States has grown steadily in the last 40 years and is now much higher than in other developed economies. This may reflect the effects that differences in talent can have on company values. Others worry that the CEO may have excessive influence on her own compensation.

- **Market- versus bank-based financial systems.** The U.S. and other Anglo-Saxon economies have market-based systems with large, active stock and bond markets. Germany and Japan have bank-based systems in which most debt financing comes from banks. These countries' stock markets are less important.

- **Family control.** In many countries, groups of companies are controlled by families. Control is maintained by cross-shareholdings, pyramids, and issues of shares with extra voting rights to the controlling investors. If the family owner and the management are the same people, then the problem of the separation of owner and manager does not arise. However, there are fewer checks on incompetent managers, and the controlling shareholder may be able to exploit minority shareholders.

- **Other governance systems.** In countries where most debt financing comes from banks, the banks have an important monitoring role. In Russia and China, where the state is often the dominant shareholder, the state may pursue different objectives from the minority shareholders. Particularly unique is the governance systems of the Japanese keiretsu.

- **Which system is better, market-based or bank-based?** This is a complex issue and views have changed on this over the years. Both systems have advantages and disadvantages.

• • • • •

FURTHER READING

The following studies survey or compare financial systems:

F. Allen and D. Gale, *Comparing Financial Systems* (Cambridge, MA: MIT Press, 2000).

M. Aoki, G. Jackson, and H. Miyajima, *Corporate Governance in Japan* (Oxford, UK: Oxford University Press, 2007).

J. P. Krahnen and R. H. Schmidt, eds., *The German Financial System* (Oxford, UK: Oxford University Press, 2004).

R. La Porta, F. Lopez-de-Silanes, and A. Shleifer, "Corporate Ownership around the World," *Journal of Finance* 54 (April 1999), pp. 471–517.

For discussions of corporate governance, see:

A. Edmans, X. Gabaix, and D. Jenter, "Executive Compensation: A Survey of Theory and Evidence" in B. Hermalin and M. Weisbach, eds., *Handbook of the Economics of Corporate Governance* (Amsterdam: North-Holland, 2017), pp. 383–539.

A. Edmans and C. Holderness, "Blockholders: A Survey of Theory and Evidence" in B. Hermalin and M. Weisbach, eds., *Handbook of the Economics of Corporate Governance* (Amsterdam: North-Holland, 2017), pp. 541–636.

A. Shleifer and R. W. Vishny, "A Survey of Corporate Governance," *Journal of Finance* 52 (June 1997), pp. 737–783.

For discussions of the role of law, politics, and finance, see:

R. La Porta, F. Lopez-de-Silanes, and A. Shleifer, "The Economic Consequences of Legal Origins," *Journal of Economic Literature* 46 (2008), pp. 285–332.

R. Rajan and L. Zingales, *Saving Capitalism from the Capitalists* (New York: Crown Business, 2003).

For the evidence on why finance matters for growth, see:

R. Levine, "Financial Development and Economic Growth: Views and Agenda," *Journal of Economic Literature* 35 (1997), pp. 688–726.

R. Rajan and L. Zingales, "Financial Dependence and Growth," *American Economic Review* 88 (June 1998), pp. 559–586.

Finally, if you'd like to read about corporate governance gone wrong. . .

P. Healy and K. Palepu, "The Fall of Enron," *Journal of Economic Perspectives* 17 (Spring 2003), pp. 3–26.

S. Johnson, R. La Porta, F. Lopez-de-Silanes, and A. Shleifer, "Tunneling," *American Economic Review* 90 (May 2000), pp. 22–27.

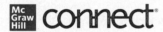 **Select problems are available in McGraw Hill's *Connect*. Please see the preface for more information.**

PROBLEM SETS

1. **Agency problems (S19-1)** Explain the following types of agency problems
   a. Reduced effort
   b. Private benefits
   c. Overinvestment
   d. Risk taking
   e. Short-termism

2. **Monitoring (S19-2–S19-4)** Who monitors the top management of public U.S. corporations?

3. **Monitoring (S19-2–S19-4)** How do European boards of directors differ from U.S. and U.K. boards of directors?

4. **Monitoring (S19-2–S19-4)** Explain how the system of *codetermination* works in Germany.

5. **Monitoring (S19-2–S19-4)** What are the main ways in which shareholders monitor managers?

6. **Monitoring (S19-2–S19-4)** What are the ways in which auditors and lenders ensure managers do what they are supposed to be doing?

7. **Monitoring (S19-2–S19-4)** What is the role of acquisitions in ensuring managers pursue shareholders' interests?

8. **Management compensation (S19-5)** True or false?
   a. U.S. CEOs are paid much more than CEOs in other countries.
   b. A large fraction of compensation for U.S. CEOs comes from grants of restricted shares or performance shares.

c. Stock-option grants give the manager a certain number of shares delivered at annual intervals.

9. **Management compensation (S19-5)** We noted that management compensation must, in practice, rely on results rather than effort. Why? What problems are introduced by not rewarding effort?

10. **Management compensation (S19-5)** Here are a few questions about compensation schemes that tie top management's compensation to the rate of return earned on the company's common stock.

   a. Today's stock price depends on investors' expectations of future performance. What problems does this create?

   b. Stock returns depend on factors outside the managers' control—for example, changes in interest rates or prices of raw materials. Could this be a serious problem? If so, can you suggest a partial solution?

   c. Compensation schemes that depend on stock returns do not depend on accounting data. Is that an advantage? Why or why not?

11. **Management compensation (S19-5)** In recent years, several large banks have paid management bonuses partly in bonds and partly in stock. What do you think is the reason for this? Do you think it is a good idea?

12. **Governance regimes around the world (S19-6)** What is a keiretsu? Give a brief description. What are some of their advantages and disadvantages?

13. **Governance regimes around the world (S19-6)** Do Japanese investors play an important role in corporate financial policy and governance? If not, could they?

14. **Governance regimes around the world (S19-6)** Suppose that a shareholder can gain effective control of a company with 30% of the shares. Explain how a shareholder might gain control of company Z by setting up a holding company X^2 that holds shares in a second holding company X, which in turn holds shares in Z.

15. **Governance regimes around the world (S19-6)** What is tunneling? Why does the threat of tunneling impede the development of financial markets?

16. **Do these differences matter? (S19-7)** Do large blockholders increase company value? Does your answer depend on the structure of the financial system?

17. **Do these differences matter? (S19-7)** Agency problems are inevitable. That is, we can never expect managers to give 100% weight to shareholders' interests and none to their own.

   a. Why not?

   b. List the mechanisms that are used around the world to keep agency problems under control.

● ● ● ● ●

SOLUTIONS TO SELF-TEST QUESTIONS

19.1   The manager may not put in sufficient effort; she may fritter away cash on private benefits; she may overinvest in the search for power or prestige; she may be reluctant to take risks or take excessive risk; she may focus on short-term results.

19.2   a. Small size, independence, less overboarding, annual elections.

   b. Monitor the CEO and fire her if underperformance persists and she has been given fair warning. Advise management and proactively make suggestions.

19.3   Companies with a small proportion of employee-directors are more likely to cut employment.

19.4   The CEO will be unwilling to accept the takeover bid as she will likely lose her job.

19.5   a. Vote against management, engage privately or publicly, sell their shares.

   b. A larger stake size gives investors greater incentives to monitor and greater power to hold management to account (e.g., more votes, ability to sell more shares). Freedom from conflicts of interest also allows investors to hold management to account.

19.6   The bank may be excessively conservative; for example, it may turn down risky projects even if they have a positive NPV.

19.7   The CEO can be paid with a substantial amount of shares that she is required to continue to hold beyond her retirement.

19.8   Banks play a much larger role in Germany and Japan than in the United States.

19.9   Market-based governance systems may lead to myopia if companies focus on short-term earnings, but blockholders (large shareholders) can attenuate this concern. Market-based systems lead to a faster reallocation of capital from declining to growing industries.

Visit **https://www.gresham.ac.uk/series/business-in-society/** for three Gresham College public lectures on corporate governance by Alex Edmans. The most relevant ones for this chapter are entitled "Reforming Corporate Governance," "The Stewardship Role of Investors," and "Executive Pay: What's Right, What's Wrong, and What Could Be Fixed?"

● ● ● ● ●

FINANCE ON THE WEB

CHAPTER

Stakeholder Capitalism and Responsible Business

So far in this book, we've assumed that the manager has a single objective—shareholder value. This objective is consistent with how companies are run in practice, at least in the United States. In Chapter 19, we discussed how institutional features, such as stock-based pay, shareholder-appointed directors, and takeovers, help ensure that executives maximize shareholder value. Indeed, for decades, managers themselves believed this was their only objective. Between 1997 and 2018, the "Statement on the Purpose of a Corporation" issued by the Business Roundtable, an organization of the CEOs of the largest U.S. companies, stated that "The paramount duty of management and of boards of directors is to the corporation's shareholders." A system in which management's objective is to maximize shareholder value is called **shareholder capitalism** or *shareholder primacy*.

Yet policymakers, the public, many executives, and even some shareholders now argue that a corporation should also consider the interests of *stakeholders*—other parties affected by the company, such as employees, customers, suppliers, communities, the government, and the environment—potentially even at the expense of shareholder value. This is known as **stakeholder capitalism.** Indeed, on August 19, 2019, the Business Roundtable radically changed its Statement on the Purpose of a Corporation to embrace stakeholder capitalism. The new statement read: "We commit to: delivering value to our customers . . . investing in our employees . . . dealing fairly and ethically with our suppliers . . . supporting the communities in which we work . . . generating long-term value for shareholders." It put shareholders on a par with stakeholders, rather than ahead of them.

While praised by many, this new statement also attracted strong criticism. The Council of Institutional Investors, an association of U.S. pension funds, foundations, and endowments,

stated that same afternoon that "we respectfully disagree with the statement issued by the BRT earlier today . . . accountability to everyone means accountability to no one."

Who's right? Should a company focus entirely on shareholders, as argued by the Council of Institutional Investors? Or does it have wider responsibilities, as claimed by the Business Roundtable? This chapter reviews the arguments for and against stakeholder capitalism.

Section 20-1 Who are the stakeholders?
We start by summarizing the several classes of stakeholders that a company has responsibility for under stakeholder capitalism.

Section 20-2 The case for shareholder capitalism
This section covers the arguments for shareholder capitalism. We stress that the shareholder value framework we've considered throughout this book places much greater emphasis on stakeholder welfare than often assumed: A company can only create shareholder value if it invests in its stakeholders. Moreover, shareholder value provides a concrete way to evaluate whether a company should undertake such investment.

Section 20-3 The case for stakeholder capitalism
Here we stress that the case for shareholder capitalism relies on three critical assumptions. Since these assumptions aren't always valid, stakeholder capitalism is sometimes justified. But, before advocating stakeholder capitalism, we first need to explain why these assumptions don't hold in a particular setting.

Section 20-4 Responsible business
Both Sections 20-2 and 20-3 show that neither pure shareholder capitalism nor pure stakeholder capitalism is likely to be optimal. Instead, companies should operate somewhere in between. In this section, we describe a mix known

as "responsible business," which seeks to create value for shareholders through creating value for society.

Section 20-5 Responsible business in practice

We discuss how the legal regime affects whether companies are obliged to pursue shareholder or stakeholder value, and how companies can practice responsible business even under shareholder primacy.

Note: Some of this chapter is adapted from Alex Edmans's book on stakeholder capitalism and responsible business, entitled *Grow the Pie: How Great Companies Deliver Both Purpose and Profit.*

● ● ● ● ●

20-1   Who Are the Stakeholders?

Before proceeding further, it's helpful to understand who the key stakeholders are.

Employees

A corporation's survival and profitability depend on the commitment and productivity of its employees. Thus, even a company focused on shareholder value may choose to pay employees more than the legal minimum wage (or what competitors are offering), improve their working conditions, and provide them with meaningful work and skills development. Doing so may lead to its workers becoming more productive and more likely to stay with the firm.

However, under stakeholder capitalism, a company is concerned for employee welfare even if there is no clear link to shareholder value. For example, when Airbnb needed to shed a quarter of its workforce in May 2020 due to the coronavirus pandemic, it spent money on reducing the impact of these layoffs—even though the employees would no longer be working for Airbnb and, thus, wouldn't affect its future profitability. Airbnb gave them a minimum 14 weeks of severance pay and a year's health insurance, allowed them to keep company laptops to help them with the job search, and reassigned part of its recruitment division to outplacement.

Customers

A business that focuses purely on profits will still wish to deliver value to its customers beyond its contractual requirements. It may provide them with free after-sales service, grant refunds even after the official return window, and not increase prices even if demand becomes high in a pandemic. Doing so may increase brand loyalty and reputation, encouraging current customers to stay and attracting new customers.

Under stakeholder capitalism, a company has a responsibility to its customers even if there's no clear benefit. In most countries, households are unable to change their water supplier. Thus, a water company doesn't clearly gain from ensuring that its water quality exceeds the minimum regulatory standards. However, a responsible company may do so because it believes that it has a duty to its customers.

A company's customers might include not only households, but also other companies. For example, clothing manufacturers sell their products to clothing stores rather than only to households directly. In the coronavirus pandemic of 2020, many retailers had to shut their shops and were on the brink of collapse. Chinese sportswear manufacturers Anta and Li Ning supported their retailers by buying back inventory, providing subsidies, cutting or delaying future shipments, and extending credit terms.

Suppliers

Suppliers are instrumental to the success of many companies because they provide high-tech, bespoke inputs. For example, Spirit Aerosystems produces components and subassemblies for

Boeing commercial aircraft, including the entire Boeing 737 aircraft body. Boeing and Spirit are locked together in a customer-supplier stakeholder relationship—neither could operate without the other. The same relationship holds for Spirit and Airbus.

However, suppliers are less material to other companies. Clothing retailers can choose between multiple garment manufacturers, so some don't think twice about squeezing them as much as possible; if one cries foul, the retailer goes elsewhere. As mentioned earlier, clothing retailers shut their stores in the coronavirus pandemic, and many passed on these losses to their suppliers by canceling orders or demanding price reductions. By the end of May 2020, these actions cost Bangladeshi garment factories $3.7 billion of sales, and garment workers worldwide suffered $5.8 billion of unpaid wages. But other retailers followed through on their orders because they felt they had a responsibility to their suppliers.

Local and Regional Communities

The places where a corporation operates contain many stakeholders. A manufacturing plant can be the largest local employer; closure would hurt not just the plant's workers, but also local businesses where they shop, as well as the plant's suppliers. For example, the 2009 shutdown of the General Motors plant in Janesville, Wisconsin, devastated the entire town. Thousands of workers lost their jobs, but the domino effects spread more widely. Lear, which supplied GM with car seats and interiors, also closed. Contributions to local charities plummeted, and children arrived at school hungry and less able to learn. As a result, a firm may decide to keep an aging plant operating, absorbing losses and hoping against hope for recovery, if closing it would severely damage the local economy.[1]

EXAMPLE 20.1 • Cummins and Columbus

The headquarters of Cummins Inc. is in Columbus, Indiana. The Cummins Foundation's Architecture Program has paid fees for prominent architects to design over 50 local schools and other public buildings in Columbus. J. Irwin Miller, Cummins's CEO from 1961 to 1977, ". . . had a lifelong interest in architecture, [and] understood that Cummins' success in retaining the best and brightest employees was closely tied to the company's ability to attract talent to Columbus."[2] The Architecture Program helped make Columbus an attractive community and a good place to live.

In 2017, Cummins announced a $50 million project to renovate its headquarters in Columbus. The state, county, and local governments simultaneously announced plans for a $30 million railroad overpass to improve railroad access to Cummins's manufacturing plants.

• • • • •

The Environment

The environment is different from other stakeholders because it's not a person or group. Corporations can act to improve the environment by cutting back pollution by more than is required by regulations and by investing in energy-efficient production. For example, natural gas leaks out into the atmosphere during production, shipping, and distribution, which

[1] Keeping an unprofitable business alive, at least temporarily, may be a positive-NPV decision that benefits shareholders as well as communities. The ability to close the plant amounts to holding a put option, and it is often optimal to wait before exercising the option. We describe puts in Chapter 21 and put options to close a plant in Chapter 23.
[2] Cummins Foundation Program, https//columbus.in.us/cummins-foundation/.

contributes to global warming. Gas producers that focus just on profits often decide that stopping the leaks is not worth the expense. Stakeholder capitalism urges the producers to pay up to stop leaks, even if shareholder value suffers as a result.

As another example, a paper bag left by the side of a road eventually biodegrades. Most plastic containers don't; they remain as litter for 500 years or more. Thus, a food company that uses plastic packaging imposes an external cost on society. Stakeholder capitalism urges the company to switch to biodegradable containers, even if shareholder value suffers as a result.

The Government

The government is an important stakeholder because a company provides it with tax revenue. Under shareholder capitalism, companies should pay as little tax as they can legally get away with, for example, by locating their intellectual property in low tax jurisdictions. They'll consider the reputational costs of paying low tax, but if the financial damage is less than the tax saved, there's no reason to pay any more.

Under stakeholder capitalism, a company views itself as having a responsibility to contribute to national finances, even if it can get away with contributing less. For example, in 2020, the U.K. government gave companies a tax deduction known as "business rates relief" to help them survive the coronavirus pandemic. Supermarkets Aldi, Morrisons, Sainsbury, and Tesco paid back £1.4 billion of tax relief, even though they were legally entitled to it, because the pandemic boosted their sales and they felt they could survive without it.

Summing up, a company creates value not only for its shareholders, but also for its stakeholders. The value that a company creates to a stakeholder, but doesn't ultimately feed back into profits, is known as *externalities*. The sum of shareholder and stakeholder value (profits plus externalities) can be depicted by a pie, as shown in Figure 20.1. Under shareholder capitalism, a company's objective is to maximize shareholder's slice of the pie. Under stakeholder capitalism, the objective is to maximize the size of the overall pie—the value created to both shareholders and stakeholders.

20.1 Self-Test

Who are a company's stakeholders?

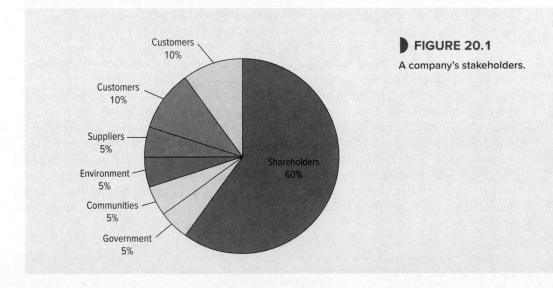

▶ **FIGURE 20.1**

A company's stakeholders.

20-2 The Case for Shareholder Capitalism

In 1970, economist Milton Friedman wrote a provocative article in the *New York Times Magazine* entitled "The Social Responsibility of Business Is to Increase Its Profits."[3] Its closing paragraph said that "there is one and only one social responsibility of business—to use its resources and engage in activities designed to increase its profits so long as it stays within the rules of the game, which is to say, engages in open and free competition without deception or fraud."

This stance, known as the "Friedman doctrine" and viewed as the hallmark of shareholder capitalism, seems at first glance to be extremely narrow-minded. It appears to argue that a company should squeeze every last drop of value from employees, customers, and other stakeholders in its single-minded pursuit of profit. With such a mindset, it's no surprise that that shareholder capitalism is unpopular among many people.

But Friedman never advocated exploiting stakeholders. Indeed, many critics may not have actually read his article, thinking that the title already makes his position clear. Instead, Friedman took stakeholder value seriously but believed that maximizing profits was the best way to create stakeholder value. His argument is based on three points[4]:

1. Government policy ensures companies will engage in socially responsible behavior.
2. Maximizing shareholder value gives shareholders maximum freedom to support the social objectives they care about.
3. Maximizing shareholder value requires companies to invest in stakeholders.

Let's consider each reason in turn.

Government Policy Ensures Companies Will Engage in Socially Responsible Behavior

A nation's prosperity depends on externalities, not just profits. But Friedman argued that externalities should be addressed not by companies, but by governments setting laws and taxes. That's because citizens have different preferences over which externalities are important. Some argue that climate change is society's biggest threat and would advocate closing all coal-fired power stations despite the ensuing job losses; others are more concerned with unemployment and inequality. A democratic government is elected by a nation's citizens, and thus needs to set regulations at the level that best represents their aggregate preferences, else it will be voted out. Since governments still allow coal-fired energy, this must mean that the electorate believes that the social benefits outweigh the costs, according to Friedman.

Under this argument, a company is free to pollute as much as it wants to, as long as it pays any carbon taxes. Investing in reducing emissions (e.g., through carbon capture technology) is costly for society as it uses resources. Thus, it is socially optimal for a company to invest only if the cost of doing so is less than the social cost of the emissions. A profit maximising company will invest only if the cost of doing so is less than the carbon taxes saved by reducing emissions. Thus, if the government sets the carbon tax equal to the social cost of emissions, a profit-maximising company will take the socially optimal investment decision. Similarly, if the electorate believed that the harm from smoking outweighed customers' enjoyment and employees' jobs, it would vote for a government that bans smoking. Supporters of the tobacco industry can argue that since governments tax but don't ban cigarettes, citizens have decided that this industry is legitimate as long as it pays cigarette taxes, which reflect the harm that smoking exerts on society.

---

[3]M. Friedman, "The Social Responsibility of Business is to Increase Its Profits," *New York Times Magazine*, September, 1970.
[4]A. Edmans, "What Stakeholder Capitalism Can Learn From Milton Friedman," *ProMarket* September 10, 2020.

In contrast, Friedman claimed that a CEO who pursues social causes is usurping the role of government: she "is in effect imposing taxes, on the one hand, and deciding how the tax proceeds shall be spent, on the other." She may follow her own preferences, not society's, which is dictatorship rather than democracy. Or she may pursue shareholders' goals, since she is ultimately appointed by shareholders. However, investors disproportionately represent the elite since wealthy people hold more shares, in contrast to the political process where each citizen has one vote. Thus, a CEO who follows shareholders' preferences may ignore the fact that closing a power plant will lead to blue collar job losses, since these employees may not own many shares.

Maximizing Shareholder Value Allows Investors to Pursue Social Objectives

A company's shareholders may have preferences that differ from the electorate as a whole and want it to go beyond simply complying with the law. For example, they may be local and thus are concerned about the company's impact on their community. Regulations are typically decided at a national level and may underweight issues specific to that community, such as job losses from a plant closure. Or shareholders might care about other externalities, such as those on employees or the environment.

However, even if shareholders have social objectives beyond those imposed by the law, this doesn't mean the companies they own should pursue these objectives. Let Carolina and Pierre both be investors in a company called Grindhouse. Carolina cares about cancer prevention, Pierre about the environment. If Grindhouse gave a large donation to the American Cancer Society, this would please Carolina but not Pierre. Instead, Grindhouse should make as high profits as possible, allowing it to pay as high dividends as possible. Then, Carolina can donate some of her dividends to the American Cancer Society, and Pierre his to Greenpeace.[5]

So Friedman did recognize that *individuals* may have social responsibilities beyond profits. He argued that the social responsibility of *business* is to increase profits because doing so gives individuals—Carolina and Pierre—maximum flexibility to choose which social responsibilities they wish to fulfill. This echoes the Fisher Separation Theorem of Chapter 1. There, we argued that managers should maximize shareholder wealth and leave it to investors to decide whether to consume from their wealth now or later. Similarly, managers should maximize shareholder wealth and leave it to investors to decide how much to give to which charity.

Maximizing Shareholder Value Requires a Company to Invest in Stakeholders

What if a company's investors *only* care about shareholder value? That still doesn't mean the company will exploit its stakeholders. Instead, Friedman argued that increasing profits is socially desirable because doing so *requires* a company to take stakeholders seriously. In a competitive environment, the primary condition for the firm's survival is that it looks after its customers. Similarly, if it fails to invest in its employees, they'll be demotivated and unproductive; if it pollutes the environment, its reputation and brand will be hurt. Friedman also argued that companies may find it wise to pay special attention to the local communities where they operate: "[I]t may well be in the long run interest of a corporation that is a major employer in a small community to devote resources to providing amenities to that community or to improving

---

[5]Note that Carolina and Pierre don't need dividends to make charitable contributions. They can sell shares to raise cash. Or they can contribute shares of stock to charity instead of cash. This can have a significant tax advantage. U.S. tax law allows the full market value of contributed shares as a charitable deduction, with no realization of capital gains and no obligation to pay capital gains tax.

its government. That may make it easier to attract desirable employees, it may reduce the wage bill or lessen losses from pilferage and sabotage or have other worthwhile effects."

So Friedman's article doesn't actually advocate the "Friedman doctrine" of ignoring stakeholders. Nor does the shareholder value framework that underpins this book. The NPV rule would give a big green light to investments in employee training programs, customer service centers, and reductions in energy usage, if the benefits outweigh the cost.

20.2 Self-Test

Does the claim that "the social responsibility of business is to increase its profits" imply that:
  a. Businesses should exploit society in the pursuit of profit (to the extent allowed by law)?
  b. Shareholders only care about profit?

Enlightened Shareholder Value

The broader view of value maximization that we've just discussed is often known as *enlightened shareholder value* (ESV). "Enlightened" reminds people that creating shareholder value requires a company to invest in stakeholders. But there's still one and only one objective: shareholder value. Companies should only invest in stakeholders if doing so is positive-NPV. Stakeholders are a means to an end, not an end in themselves. The Business Roundtable's prior statement argues that "[T]he interests of other stakeholders are relevant as a derivative of the duty to stockholders."

Proponents of ESV argue that this single objective has two practical advantages – it offers a clear criterion for making investment decisions and for judging performance.

ESV Offers a Clear Decision Rule   Shareholder capitalism provides a clear decision rule for deciding whether to invest in stakeholders or, indeed, take any decision: Is the NPV positive? For example, suppose Grindhouse considers opening a daycare center for its employees' children. There's a simple decision rule: Grindhouse estimates the cost of the center and compares it with the extra cash flows that it will generate through making employees more productive. If the benefits exceed the costs, the NPV is positive, and Grindhouse should go ahead.

The single NPV objective of shareholder capitalism is particularly attractive since most corporate decisions affect multiple stakeholders. If an energy company shuts down a coal-fired power station, it will help the environment, but it may reduce jobs and also profits due to lower revenues. The NPV criterion combines these effects into one: The company estimates the reputational benefit (in dollar terms) from moving to clean energy, subtracts the reputational cost (also in dollar terms) from firing workers, and also deducts any lost profits. Because all of these effects are in dollar terms, the company is comparing apples with apples. It can add them all up and discount them to get the overall NPV of the closure.

In addition to providing a concrete rule for making a decision, shareholder value provides a concrete rule for deciding how much value to give to each stakeholder. For example, if a company had to balance shareholder value with worker happiness, it's not clear how much it should pay its employees. But a company that seeks to maximize shareholder value needs only to determine what wage will contribute the most to shareholder value. This does not mean that the firm should pay its workers the minimum it can get away with without them quitting. It can be efficient to pay workers more than is necessary because doing so can increase their motivation and, thus, shareholder value. But again there is a clear rule to determine how much to "overpay" workers—only to the extent that it improves the company's value.

EXAMPLE 20.2 • Ford's wage policy

More than a century ago, in the early days of mass-production auto assembly lines, Henry Ford recognized the value of committed and dependable workers. Work on assembly lines was repetitive and difficult. Employee turnover disrupted production, and the costs of finding and training replacements were heavy. Ford decided to pay workers $5 per day, about double the prevailing wage at the time, in order to remove the incentive for workers to quit and move to easier jobs. That $5 wage was motivated by a focus on shareholder value.

• • • • •

ESV Offers a Clear Performance Criterion   Under shareholder capitalism, managers have a single objective: maximize shareholder value. Therefore, there is a clear criterion for judging, after the fact, whether managers have done a good job. When evaluating their performance, we do not need to consider separately whether they have treated other stakeholders well. If they have neglected their customers, employees, and other stakeholders, the effect will show up in the company's profitability and its stock price. Thus, the long-term stock price is the only metric we need to evaluate a manager's performance.

> **20.3 Self-Test**

What are the two advantages of enlightened shareholder value over stakeholder capitalism?

Decision Making under Enlightened Shareholder Value

We've explained how ESV has much more in common with stakeholder capitalism than commonly believed: It takes seriously the importance of investing in stakeholders. Similarly, stakeholder capitalism recognizes that profits are important: Shareholders are part of the pie. The key difference is what comes first. ESV argues that a company's ultimate goal is to create shareholder value; by doing so, it will create value for society as a by-product. Stakeholder capitalism argues that a company's ultimate goal is to create value for society; by doing so, it will increase shareholder value as a by-product. A company's goal under ESV is to maximize shareholders' slice, whereas under stakeholder capitalism it's to maximize the size of the pie—value for society.

Figure 20.2*a* shows the pie for a firm that is tightly managed, with no special regard to stakeholders. Value equals the area of the circle—here, $100 million. For simplicity we consider one class of stakeholders: employees. The employees in Figure 20.2*a* get their market wage, nothing more, and so get no slice of this pie.

Has this Scrooge-like firm really maximized shareholder value? The firm might improve productivity by offering extra wages and job security to employees. Perhaps more generous health insurance or pension contributions would bring forth more effort and loyalty. Then a patient and "enlightened" firm could increase shareholder value by investing more in its employees as stakeholders. Assume this investment costs PV = $10 million. Suppose it increases productivity and expands the pie to $115 million, as in Figure 20.2*b*. Employees now get an extra 9.1% of the pie, worth $10 million, versus nothing extra in Figure 20.2*a*. Shareholders get 90.9%, but the pie is larger, so they gain $5 million. The investment in employees is positive-NPV because both shareholders and employees are better off. Friedman would endorse the outcome in Figure 20.2*b*.

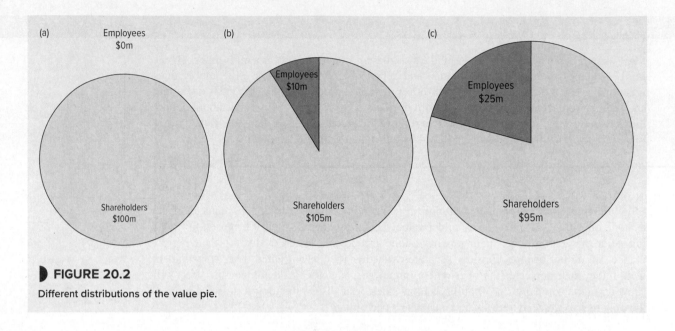

> **FIGURE 20.2**
> Different distributions of the value pie.

Some supporters of stakeholder capitalism regard the pie as fixed, in which case the only way to increase the stakeholders' slice is to reduce shareholders' slice—to them, stakeholder capitalism means "anti-shareholder capitalism." Shareholders must lose from such redistributions. For example, giving employees 10% of the fixed pie in Figure 20.2*a* costs shareholders $10 million.

More sophisticated stakeholder advocates would applaud the win–win gains in Figure 20.2*b* over 20.2*a* but would probably still argue for more. Figure 20.2*c* assumes further investment taking employees' value slice from $10 million to $25 million. The size of the pie increases from $115 million to only $120 million because the additional investment in employees yields diminishing returns. Shareholders' value slice drops back to $95 million, less than in Figure 20.2*a*. Does this negative-sum game create "value for society"? Yes, because the value of the pie is larger. But Figure 20.2*c* is an example of an investment that advocates of enlightened shareholder value would *not* endorse.

20-3   The Case for Stakeholder Capitalism

Given the arguments for shareholder capitalism in the last section, you might think that the case for stakeholder capitalism is dead in the water. But each of the three arguments rests on a crucial assumption, which may not hold in practice.

Yet the Friedman argument is still useful because it highlights that stakeholder capitalism is justified *only if* Friedman's assumptions are violated. Rather than being viewed as a doctrine, Friedman's article should be seen as a theorem, similar to Modigliani-Miller.[6] In Chapters 16–18, we explained how capital structure is relevant in the real world. But the Modigliani-Miller theorem is still useful since it highlights that capital structure is relevant *only if* there

---

[6]See A. Edmans, "What Stakeholder Capitalism Can Learn from Milton Friedman," *ProMarket,* September 10, 2020; and L. Zingales, "Friedman's Legacy: From Doctrine to Theorem," *ProMarket,* October 13, 2020.

are capital market imperfections such as taxes and bankruptcy costs; capital structure cannot be relevant due to reasons unrelated to imperfections such as "debt is cheaper than equity." Similarly, the Friedman theorem argues that companies should pursue social objectives *only if* its assumptions are violated; social objectives cannot be justified by arguments such as "shareholders care about more than just profit," which Friedman already takes into account.

Let's consider each assumption in turn.

Well-Functioning Governments

The Friedman theorem assumes that the political process is perfect, so that the government reflects the nation's aggregate preferences. However, there are several sources of imperfection:

- The government may be influenced by lobbying from companies. If companies are significant donors to political parties, a government may maximize its reelection chances by satisfying companies' goals, not the electorate's. For example, opponents of the tobacco industry argue that most citizens would like smoking to be banned but that the industry's lobbying efforts have prevented such regulation.

- Elections only happen every four or five years. A government may have latitude to deviate significantly from the electorate's preferences midway through a political cycle. Alternatively, it may not have incentives to respond to changes in preferences mid-cycle. For example, the U.K. government published the Dasgupta Report on biodiversity in 2021. However, the next election is not until 2024, so the government could have chosen not to take immediate action.

- Regulation is most effective at addressing measurable issues such as wages and carbon emissions—a government can set a minimum wage and a carbon tax. It's much harder to regulate qualitative issues, such as providing employees with meaningful work and skills development. Thus, even if the electorate views these issues as important, the government may not pass a law to enforce them.

No political process is completely perfect, just like capital markets aren't completely perfect. But the Friedman theorem is still useful because it highlights that stakeholder capitalism is justified *only if* regulation is imperfect. Thus, it's often reasonable for companies to strive to provide meaningful work to their employees. But there are other cases in which regulation is generally effective. If a firm wishes to pay above the minimum wage, even if competitors aren't doing so, it needs to have good arguments for why the government has set it wrongly. Moreover, any government failure to set the wage correctly must outweigh any managerial failure for company action to be justified. Even if shareholders are willing to pay slightly above the minimum wage due to concern for workers, the CEO may pay even more to avoid the effort of tough wage negotiations or reduce the risk that employees protest at her own pay Thus, it can be socially undesirable to allow CEOs to sacrifice profits by giving stakeholders more than what is required by government regulation.

No Comparative Advantage in Serving Society

The only socially responsible action that Friedman considers is donating to charity. He thus implicitly assumes that companies have no *comparative advantage* in serving society: $1 spent on a social initiative creates the same value as $1 spent by anyone else. While that's true for charitable donations, it's not true in two broad cases. First, a company typically has a comparative advantage in any activity it controls directly. If Grindhouse invests a dollar in designing a reduction in its plastic packaging, it helps the environment much more than if it paid out that dollar as dividends and Pierre donated it to Greenpeace to lobby for a tax on plastic bags. Second, a company may have a comparative advantage due to its expertise. During the pandemic, perfume companies pivoted to making sanitizer since they had expertise in manufacturing alcohol-based products. Thus, companies may be justified in sacrificing profits to serve society if they do so in ways that leverage their comparative advantage.

The importance of comparative advantage is often overlooked. Many companies around the world donate millions to charity; India's government requires large companies to spend 2% of their profits on corporate social responsibility (CSR) initiatives.[7] But if you're a drinks company, your expertise is making drinks—not choosing which charitable causes are most worthy.

Instrumental Decision Making Is Effective

We explained in Section 20-2 how enlightened shareholder value advocates investing in stakeholders. However, the motive is *instrumental*. A company exists exclusively to create shareholder value and will only make an investment if it can calculate, at least approximately, the impact it has on future profits. As we've highlighted in this book, calculation works for many investments. When contemplating a new factory, a CEO can forecast how many widgets it will produce and how much it can sell them for. Subtracting the cost gives her the factory's NPV. While the real world is risky, NPV is able to handle risk. As we showed in Chapter 10, the CEO can do a "sensitivity analysis," where she plugs in different assumptions and sees how the conclusion changes.

But this assumes no uncertainty. A risky problem can be analyzed if you have a rough idea of its parameters and can do a sensitivity analysis around them. With uncertainty, you have no idea what the parameters are. Let's go back to Grindhouse's decision to open the daycare center. While the cost is easy to estimate, the benefits are not. How many workers will the daycare center attract, and what's their value to the firm? How much will employee satisfaction rise with onsite childcare, and how much will this greater satisfaction translate into enhanced productivity? How many interactions between colleagues in different departments will the daycare center foster? These questions are almost impossible to answer. There's not even a baseline around which to conduct a sensitivity analysis. So you can't calculate the NPV of the daycare center, and without it, you can't justify the center under shareholder capitalism.

The claim that "increasing shareholder value" will lead a company to invest in stakeholders is only valid if future cash flows can be forecast with some degree of accuracy. For particularly uncertain investments, they can't. Thus, NPV would lead a company to forsake many investments in its employees, and also other stakeholders, ultimately destroying shareholder value. The mindset of maximizing shareholder value may actually lead to companies failing to do so.

That's where stakeholder capitalism comes in. A company with explicit stakeholder objectives makes investments for *intrinsic* reasons—to deliver value to its stakeholders—rather than to *instrumentally* increase shareholder value. Stakeholders are the end itself, not a means to an end. This approach leads it to make many investments that are ultimately profitable but couldn't be justified by a financial calculation. Estimating the contribution of Grindhouse's daycare facility to shareholder value is likely to be challenging, but the company could be fairly certain that it would be good for employees. So the case for the center is much easier to make under stakeholder capitalism. Grindhouse would only need to ask whether the facility creates value for employees, even if it reduces shareholder value. A justification might be: "I know the staff would welcome better daycare. Shareholders have had a good year and we can afford to be generous to our employees." With stakeholder capitalism, what's good for employees (or other stakeholders) is intrinsically good and therefore worth doing.

Importantly, it may ultimately be worth doing for shareholders, not just employees. The daycare center may improve employee recruitment, retention, and motivation, likely increasing shareholder value as a by-product, even if this increase couldn't be quantified at the outset. Thus, *even if* shareholders care only about shareholder value and not externalities, they may surprisingly prefer stakeholder capitalism, because it frees them to make investments that

---

[7]Donating to charity could be in shareholders' interest if doing so supports a key stakeholder (e.g. the local community) or improves the company's brand among its target customer base. However, many charitable donations are unlikely to do so enough to justify the cost.

ultimately improve shareholder value but this improvement was difficult to capture in an NPV analysis. "Maximize shareholder value" is difficult to operationalize for many important decisions, but "create value for stakeholders" can be a valuable decision tool under uncertainty.

The idea that we can have harmonious, win–win outcomes where stakeholders and shareholders simultaneously benefit might seem a "too good to be true" pipe dream. But research shows that investments in stakeholder capital have been rewarded by the stock market.[8]

- Stocks of firms that treat their employees well, as measured by listing on the "100 Best Companies to Work For in America," beat their peers by 2.3% to 3.8% per year from 1984–2011.[9] They also enjoyed positive future earnings surprises, suggesting that the higher stock returns weren't simply due to risk or that employee satisfaction was a result of the company already performing well.

- Companies in the top 20% of the American Customer Satisfaction Index earned just under double the returns of the Dow Jones Industrial Average over 1997–2003.[10]

- A measure of "eco-efficiency" from Innovest Strategic Value Advisors gauges the value of a company's goods and services relative to the waste it generates. Highly ranked stocks beat lowly ranked ones by 5% per year between 1995 and 2003.[11]

- What about the impact of shareholder proposals to improve a company's environmental and social performance? Such proposals increase shareholder value. Stock prices rose by 1.77% on average when a proposal was adopted.[12]

These three reasons are why some *shareholders* advocate stakeholder capitalism. In January 2018, BlackRock CEO Larry Fink wrote an open letter to the CEOs of companies BlackRock invests in, highlighting their need to serve wider society rather than just shareholders. He stressed that "the public expectations of your company have never been greater. Society is demanding that companies, both public and private, serve a social purpose. To prosper over time, every company must not only deliver financial performance, but also show how it makes a positive contribution to society. Companies must benefit all of their stakeholders, including shareholders, employees, customers, and the communities in which they operate."

20.4 Self-Test

What are the three reasons shareholders may prefer stakeholder capitalism to shareholder capitalism?

The Challenge of Stakeholder Capitalism

The potential advantage of stakeholder capitalism is that it frees managers to pursue stakeholder interests even if doing so can't be justified by an NPV calculation. However, this freedom comes at a potentially significant cost—there's no clear rule to replace NPV with,

---

[8]These excess returns require stakeholder capital not only to be valuable to shareholders, but also for this value to be not fully incorporated by the stock market. In an efficient market, the future value of stakeholder capital is fully incorporated in today's stock price, and, therefore, should not affect future returns.

[9]A. Edmans, "Does the Stock Market Fully Value Intangibles? Employee Satisfaction and Equity Prices," *Journal of Financial Economics* 101 (2011), pp. 621–640; and A. Edmans, "The Link between Job Satisfaction and Firm Value, with Implications for Corporate Social Responsibility," *Academy of Management Perspectives* 26 (2012), pp. 1–19.

[10]C. Fornell, S. Mithas, F. V. Morgeson III, and M. S. Krishnan, "Customer Satisfaction and Stock Prices: High Returns, Low Risk," *Journal of Marketing* 70 (2006), pp. 3–14.

[11]J. Derwall, N. Guenster, R. Bauer and K. Koedijk, "The Eco-Efficiency Premium Puzzle," *Financial Analysts Journal* 61 (2005), pp. 51–63.

[12]C. Flammer, "Does Corporate Social Responsibility Lead to Superior Financial Performance? A Regression Discontinuity Approach," *Management Science* 61 (2015), pp. 2549–2568.

leading to arbitrariness. How much shareholder value should managers sacrifice for each shareholder, and how should they assess trade-offs between stakeholders? Should the weight be 50% on shareholders, 15% on employees, and 35% on the environment, or should it be something else? Also, while shareholder value is always expressed in dollars, it's not always clear how to measure stakeholder value. For workers, what matters isn't just their salary, but their overall "utility" or happiness, which includes meaningful work, skills development, and working conditions. For the environment, it's even less clear what the yardstick should be (let's call it "conservation"). So even if we had a clear weighting formula, we'd be hamstrung by the fact that the impacts on different stakeholders are in different terms—profits, utility, and conservation. We're comparing apples and oranges.

As a result, even though a manager under stakeholder capitalism knows she should take externalities into account, it's not clear *how* to do so. If she closes a coal-fired power station, there's no unambiguous way to assess whether the positive externalities to the environment outweigh the negative externalities to workers. Moreover, even if she estimated that an investment yielded positive externalities overall, she doesn't know how much profit she should be willing to sacrifice to create these externalities. Should she choose Figure 20.2c (a bigger pie) over Figure 20.2a (a bigger slice for shareholders)? It's unclear.

Recall the Council of Institutional Investors' worry that "accountability to everyone means accountability to no one." Critics of stakeholder capitalism worry that managers will let their own personal preferences decide which stakeholders the firm should help most. She may end up supporting social causes that she cares about, even if her employees and shareholders don't, or that powerful politicians favor in order to increase the chance of a political appointment after retiring as CEO. (Some cynics have suggested that this is why many CEOs favor stakeholder capitalism.)

Summary

Stakeholder capitalism encourages firms to deal generously with its various stakeholders and to mitigate adverse externalities caused by the firm's operations. It focuses on benefits to society, not just shareholders. However, which externalities they should mitigate, and how much shareholder value to sacrifice to do so, is unclear.

Overall, neither focusing exclusively on the size of the pie nor focusing exclusively on shareholders' slice is likely to be optimal. Corporations in developed economies will probably end up following some blend of shareholder and stakeholder capitalism. Moreover, this blend should recognize the critical importance of growing the pie, not just redistributing it. We stress this point in the next section.

20-4   Responsible Business

Should companies pursue shareholder capitalism or stakeholder capitalism? As with most decisions, the correct answer usually is, "It's a mixture." We now describe a mixture called "responsible business."

Defining Responsible Business

A **responsible business** is one that seeks to *create value for shareholders through creating value for society.* Let's unpack this definition. The need to "create value for society" shouldn't be surprising. However, a responsible business also has a duty to shareholders. Often, shareholders are seen as less worthy than employees or the environment, but they are mostly ordinary citizens (such as parents saving for their children's education) or organizations representing them (such as pension schemes investing for their retirees or insurance companies investing to cover future claims). Shareholders are not "fat cats" who already have more money than they need. Delivering returns to shareholders is a critical social function.

Sometimes responsibility is assumed to mean prioritizing stakeholders and underplaying shareholders, but a responsible business has a duty to both. However, while profits are important, they are a by-product: The primary goal of a responsible business is to create value for society.

Corporate Social Responsibility   Responsible business is sometimes confused with corporate social responsibility (CSR). While there are similarities, there are two fundamental differences. First, CSR typically refers to noncore activities that are delegated to a CSR department in order to improve a company's public image. A tobacco firm could have a CSR department that donates part of its profits to charity. Responsible business is about a company's core activities and ensures that the primary way it generates profits is through offering products and services that create value for society. Thus, a tobacco firm would typically not be viewed as responsible, even if it engages in corporate philanthropy.

Second, CSR focuses on splitting the pie, not growing it. CSR advocates paying workers equitably, not price-gouging customers and not avoiding tax. Indeed, a common dictum of CSR is "do no harm" by not taking from society. Responsible business also stresses that a fair distribution of the pie is important, but it's not enough. It's even more important for a company to *grow the pie*—to "actively do good" by creating value for society. As mentioned in Chapter 1, *errors of omission* (failing to take good actions, such as pursuing excellence in its existing product offerings and inventing new ones) are often even more serious than *errors of commission* (paying the CEO generously).

EXAMPLE 20.3 • Vodafone and M-Pesa

In 2007 Vodafone launched M-Pesa, a mobile-money service in Kenya that allows users to transfer money with their mobile phones. This had a substantial social benefit. Many Kenyans had no access to bank accounts, and so relied on cash, which could be forged or stolen. A study found that M-Pesa lifted 196,000 Kenyan households (2% of the population) out of poverty by 2014.[13] The effect was particularly strong among households headed by women because M-Pesa allowed them to switch from agriculture to retail and other businesses.

• • • • •

The goal of a responsible business to create value for society has important implications for the governance mechanisms discussed in Chapter 19. We discussed how very large executive pay packages are controversial. The controversy has hatched proposals to crack down on the level of pay so that the savings can be redistributed to other stakeholders. But this solution assumes a fixed pie. If reform is needed, it would be better to redesign compensation to incentivize the CEO to create long-term value for society. Indeed, evidence shows that the long-term incentives advocated in Section 19-5 improve not only profitability, but also innovation and the value delivered to suppliers, customers, society, and particularly employees. Thus, they encourage the CEO to create value for both stakeholders and shareholders alike.[14]

---

[13]T. Suri and W. Jack, "The Long-Run Poverty and Gender Impacts of Mobile Money," *Science* 354 (2016), pp. 1288–1292.

[14]C. Flammer and P. Bansal, "Does Long-Term Orientation Create Value? Evidence from a Regression Discontinuity," *Strategic Management Journal* 38 (2017), pp. 1827–1847.

Responsible Business and the Coronavirus Crisis

❯ The coronavirus pandemic of 2020 shrunk the pie for everyone. Many companies responded by reducing compensation to investors and executives and by providing products or services free or at low cost to stakeholders. For example, Unilever donated €100 million of soap, sanitizer, bleach, and food to communities; provided €500 million of liquidity by paying suppliers early and extending credit to customers; and safeguarded the jobs of its 155,000 workers, including contractors such as cleaners and catering staff in addition to direct employees. Executives of companies such as Boeing and United Airlines worked for zero pay for several months.

Such responses were indeed great acts of responsibility. However, not all companies could engage in them. For example, companies in industries unrelated to the crisis didn't have products they could give to communities. Smaller companies didn't have €500 million lying around that they could lend to customers and suppliers. But many companies found ingenious ways to help. Here are some examples:

- The New England Patriots did not have a product that could help in the crisis. Football tickets and replica merchandise were of little value. But it creatively decided to use its plane to fly 1.2 million N95 masks from China to Boston.

- Mercedes's precision engineers typically made pistons and turbochargers for Formula 1 engines, but Formula 1 was canceled at the start of the pandemic. So they teamed up with University College London to reverse-engineer a breathing aid and improve its design so that it could be manufactured at scale. Within 100 hours, they had a prototype, and then repurposed existing machines to mass-produce it.

- Qantas Airways could not afford to keep paying its staff since air travel was almost entirely shut down. It entered into a partnership with Woolworths, a grocery store, to redeploy its furloughed staff. This not only safeguarded their incomes, but also served wider society given the spike in demand for groceries.

- Barry's is a boutique fitness studio. Its fitness instructors offered free live-streamed workouts through Instagram for people who had to self-isolate at home. Some of Barry's desk staff were actors who worked at Barry's to supplement their income given the volatility of an acting career. They used their skills in entertaining to read stories to children using videoconference facilities, taking the load off working parents who had their children at home due to school closures.

Decision Making in Responsible Businesses

We explained earlier that a key argument against ESV is that the NPV rule is very difficult to implement in practice for some investments. That's because it's impossible to forecast, even very roughly, the cash flow implications of these actions. But, under responsible business, there appears to be an even bigger problem: There isn't even a decision rule to begin with. We don't know how to convert the value delivered to different stakeholders into a common unit, nor how to weight the different stakeholders. So you can't measure overall social value and then estimate how a decision will affect it.

Yet nearly every real-life decision involves multiple criteria that can't be weighted. When a worker chooses a job, he doesn't just maximize his income. He also considers his passion for the work, the amount and flexibility of the hours, and the camaraderie with his colleagues. There's no formula telling him how to weight each factor, but this need not matter. Citizens comfortably make decisions with multiple objectives every day using not a *calculation* like NPV but *judgment*—their own internal assessment of the importance of each criterion.

But while a citizen acts for himself, a manager acts for shareholders. The problem with delegating corporate decisions to the manager's judgment is that it gives her freedom to do whatever she pleases. Under responsible business, a manager's judgment is guided by principles, to help ensure that any actions to create value for society also create value for shareholders—or at least don't reduce shareholder value significantly. There are three principles that she should follow:

- The *principle of multiplication* ensures that the social benefits of an investment exceed its private costs, so that the investment delivers value to society.
- The *principle of comparative advantage,* combined with the principle of multiplication, ensures that the social benefits of an investment exceed its social costs, so that the investment creates value for society.
- The *principle of materiality,* combined with the first two principles, makes it more likely that the social value created will ultimately increase shareholder value—the activity creates value for shareholders through creating value for society.

Let's look at these three principles in turn.

Multiplication   The *principle of multiplication* asks the following: If I spend $1 on a stakeholder, does it generate more than $1 of benefit to the stakeholder? In other words, does the activity multiply the money I spend on it? If not, the social benefit is less than the private cost—the social NPV is negative—and the activity doesn't deliver value. The company could instead pay the dollar directly to the stakeholder (e.g., higher wages to employees or lower prices to customers), who can then use it more effectively.

Let's apply this principle to Grindhouse's decision to open a daycare facility. How do we estimate the benefit to the relevant stakeholders (employees in this example)? We could look at membership prices of local daycare facilities and estimate how many workers would use Grindhouse's. Multiplying the two gives a lower bound to the benefit of the facility to the Grindhouse workforce. It's only a lower bound because employees will value an onsite center more highly due to its convenience; as with all decisions, there's a limit to what can be quantified. But the calculation is still useful because it provides a bound on how big the nonquantifiable benefits must be to flip the decision. Say the cost of the Grindhouse center is $2,500 per employee per month, perhaps because few workers are likely to use it, and the highest-quality local facility costs $1,000. It's unlikely that the nonquantifiable benefits will be as much as $1,500, so the principle of multiplication is violated. Rather than building the daycare center, Grindhouse could pay higher wages, which some employees could spend on external daycare.

While the principle of multiplication should help a manager turn down some activities, it alone is too easy to satisfy. Under this principle, Grindhouse should allow the homeless to eat in its staff canteen for free since food likely benefits them more than it costs Grindhouse—in the extreme, $1 of food may save someone's life. Thus, the principle of multiplication is an incomplete decision rule.

Comparative Advantage   The *principle of comparative advantage* asks the following: Can my company deliver more value through an activity than others? If and only if so, undertaking the activity inside the firm creates net value for society. This principle is more stringent than the principle of multiplication because it requires the benefit to stakeholders to exceed not $1 (the private cost of $1 of investment), but the value that others could deliver with $1 (the social opportunity cost). In other words, the company needs to satisfy the principle of multiplication by more than other companies. Only then does it create rather than merely deliver value.

Although feeding the homeless may satisfy the principle of multiplication, it fails the principle of comparative advantage. Food that costs Grindhouse $1 might provide $2 of benefit to the homeless because they're hungry. But a soup kitchen might turn $1 into $3 of benefit because it has a comparative advantage in feeding the homeless: It knows what food best addresses their nutritional needs and is conveniently located. Grindhouse thus doesn't have a comparative advantage in feeding the homeless, so it shouldn't do so. It could instead pay higher wages to employees or deliver higher profits to investors, who can then donate to soup kitchens.

Applying the principle of comparative advantage doesn't require a company to calculate the value it would create with a certain set of resources, and compare it with the value every other company might create. Instead, it needs to *judge* what its comparative advantage is. As discussed earlier, there are two broad cases in which the principle is usually satisfied. First, a company typically has a comparative advantage in any activity it controls directly. While charities can feed the homeless, only Grindhouse affects the plastic packaging it uses for its products. Second, a company may have a comparative advantage due to its expertise, as with perfume companies making sanitizer.

20.5 Self-Test

What is the difference between the principles of multiplication and comparative advantage?

Materiality   Even the principle of comparative advantage could be too weak. A company has a comparative advantage in virtually every activity that it affects directly, so it might invest without limit in everything it controls, leaving few profits for investors.

That's where the *principle of materiality* comes into play. It asks the following: Are the stakeholders the activity benefits material to the company's business? If so they move toward the head of the queue of stakeholders. For example, suppliers such as Corning and Finisar are particularly important to Apple since they provide high-tech, bespoke inputs. Thus, Apple invests in them through a $5 billion Advanced Manufacturing Fund that supports innovation in its suppliers. Suppliers are less important to a plastics or paints manufacturer that uses commodity chemicals as inputs.

While a company has some responsibility to all stakeholders, it's important to prioritize the most material ones because investing in them is more likely to improve profits. Indeed, a study find that firms with high performance across all stakeholders did not actually outperform the stock market—potentially because they are overinvesting in less important stakeholders. Instead, only those that score highly on material stakeholder dimensions and less on immaterial factors beat the market.[15]

Summary

How then is the standard for responsible business different from ESV, which invests in stakeholders only when doing so creates positive NPV for shareholders?

- The primary objective for a responsible business is to create value for society, not just for shareholders. This involves taking investments with significant positive externalities even if they couldn't be fully justified with an NPV calculation, and relieving negative externalities if the cost to shareholders is not too high. In particular, responsible businesses have to act with little thought of profits at times of national crisis, such as war or pandemic (see the earlier box on the coronavirus pandemic.)

- A responsible business also sees intrinsic value in stakeholders but does not assume that more for stakeholders is always better. The stakeholders' slices of the pie have to be designed, and sometimes constrained, to ensure that the firm can stay competitive, expand

---

[15]M. Khan, G. Serafeim, and A. Yoon, "Corporate Sustainability: First Evidence on Materiality," *The Accounting Review* 91 (2016), pp. 1697–1724.

and innovate, and provide shareholders with an adequate return on investment. The principles of multiplication, comparative advantage, and materiality provide such constraints.

- A responsible business believes that acting to create value for society creates value for shareholders in the long run.

Responsible businesses have to manage a balancing act of the interests of shareholders and stakeholders, which will sometimes conflict. The balancing act won't always work, but responsible businesses believe that the balancing act is a better bet than the pure versions of shareholder and stakeholder capitalism.

20-5   Responsible Business in Practice

Even if a company wishes to practice stakeholder capitalism or responsible business, is it legally entitled to do so? We'll first look at what the law allows and then study the steps a company can take to pursue responsible business even if the legal regime is one of shareholder primacy.

Shareholder Primacy in the United States and United Kingdom

Most U.S. public corporations are incorporated in Delaware, where the directors have a *fiduciary duty* to act in the interests of shareholders. In describing directors' responsibilities, the former Chief Justice of the Delaware Supreme Court stated: "[D]irectors must make stockholder welfare their sole end, and . . . other interests may be taken into consideration only as a means of promoting stockholder welfare."[16]

EXAMPLE 20.4 • Craigslist and eBay

In 2004, eBay invested $32 million in the stock of craigslist, the online classified advertising company, and later offered to buy the entire company. Craigslist's founders blocked the purchase. Craigslist explained that it put the interests of its customers ahead of the interests of its shareholders. It feared that eBay would "monetize" classified advertising to generate excessive profits for eBay shareholders. Craigslist lost; an excerpt from the judge's opinion follows.[17]

> I personally appreciate and admire Jim's and Craig's [the founders'] desire to be of service to communities. [But they] opted to form craigslist, Inc. as a *for-profit Delaware corporation* and voluntarily accepted millions of dollars from eBay as part of a transaction whereby eBay became a stockholder. Having chosen a for-profit corporate form, the craigslist directors are bound by the fiduciary duties and standards that accompany that form. These standards include acting to promote the value of the corporation for the benefit of its shareholders.

Craigslist could have avoided this hassle by becoming a *benefit corporation,* which can commit to objectives other than shareholder value. We discuss benefit corporations later in this section.

• • • • •

---

[16]Leo E. Strine, Jr., "The Dangers of Denial: The Need for a Clear-Eyed Understanding of the Power and Accountability Structure Established by Delaware Corporate Law," Institute for Law and Economics, University of Pennsylvania, Research Paper 15-08 (2015), p. 10.

[17]*eBay Domestic Holdings, Inc. v. Newmark,* Delaware Chancery Court 2010.

Importantly, Delaware law (and U.S. law generally) gives directors and managers wide discretion in deciding how to enhance shareholder value. They can take a long-run view of value, not necessarily dancing to the tune of today's stock price. The *business judgment rule* protects them from liability so long as they use judgment to try to benefit shareholders. They can act in the interests of other stakeholders if it promotes shareholder value in the long run. For example, directors may judge it worthwhile to invest significantly in training its employees, because the long-term benefits outweigh shareholders' immediate sacrifice. Moreover, *even if* a company is practicing responsible business, and investing in its employees slightly beyond the point that can be justified with an NPV analysis, it will be very difficult for a court to rule on this, since the benefits to shareholders are almost impossible to quantify.

Shareholder primacy is not guaranteed in all U.S. states. Thirty-five of them states have *constituency statutes,* which allow directors to consider the interests of constituencies (stakeholders) other than shareholders. For example, the constituency statute in Connecticut states that a director may consider "the interests of the corporation's employees, customers, creditors and suppliers, and . . . community and societal considerations." In nearly all cases, constituency statutes are permissive rather than mandatory; directors *may* consider stakeholder interests, but have no obligation to do so.[18]

U.K. law states the following:

> [A] director . . . must act . . . in good faith . . . to promote the success of the company for the benefit of its [shareholders] as a whole, and in doing so have regard to . . . the interest of the company's employees; the need to foster the company's business relationships with suppliers, customers and others; the impact of the company's operations on the community and the environment.[19]

U.K. directors' primary duty is to act for the benefit of shareholders, and "in doing so have regard" to other stakeholders. The corporation is to respect and support the interests of other stakeholders *in order to* benefit shareholders. However, note that the "benefit of shareholders" may include more than shareholder wealth. As discussed previously, shareholder welfare may also include externalities, and so companies should take externalities into account, particularly if shareholders have communicated their important to them. Thus, shareholder primacy does not mean an exclusive focus on shareholder wealth.[20]

In contrast to the U.S. and the U.K., employees have enhanced stakeholder status in several developed countries. For example, German corporate law emphasizes the protection of all stakeholders, especially employees and lenders. A proportion of the members of the supervisory board are elected by employees, not only in Germany, but also in Denmark, Norway, and Sweden. In Japan, managers usually put the interests of employees and customers on a par with, or even ahead of, the interests of shareholders. The Netherlands requires directors to take stakeholders into account, particularly in takeover situations.

---

[18]Even in states without constituency statutes, shareholder primacy has been successfully challenged in some cases. In the 1968 Shlensky vs. Wrigley case, the Illinois Court of Appeal upheld a decision that took stakeholder interests into account, even though Illinois didn't have a constituency statute at the time. The Chicago Cubs baseball team decided not to install lights at Wrigley Field and play night games, despite the potential higher revenues, due to the negative impact on the local community.

[19]From Section 172 of the U.K. Companies Act 2006.

[20]M. Jensen and W. Meckling, "Theory of the Firm: Managerial Behavior, Agency Costs and Ownership Structure," *Journal of Financial Economics* 3 (1976), pp. 305–360.

EXAMPLE 20.5 • Akzo Nobel vs. PPG

In 2017, the Dutch company Akzo Nobel rejected several takeover bids from PPG Industries. CEO Ton Büchner claimed that the bids were not only too low for shareholders, but also made "no substantive commitment to stakeholders" because of the risk of layoffs and PPG's different approach to sustainability. Akzo Nobel's largest shareholder, Elliott Advisors, sued but lost because Dutch law requires directors to consider stakeholder interests. The Dutch Enterprise Chamber ruled that Akzo Nobel's board was fulfilling its duties by considering "the interests of all those involved in the corporation."[21]

• • • • •

Figure 20.3 summarizes the results of a survey of chief financial officers (CFOs) around the world on what they believed was their chief objective. A score of zero means that the CFO focused exclusively on shareholders. A score of 100 means that she focused exclusively on other stakeholders. The modal response is in the 31-50 range, suggesting that CFOs around the world place most weight on shareholders' interests but do not give shareholders absolute primacy.

Shareholder capitalism is often portrayed as a relentless pursuit of profit motivated by the mantra that "greed is good." However, as we've discussed, it requires companies to make substantial investments in their stakeholders. Conversely, under stakeholder capitalism, companies cannot ignore the need to earn the shareholders' cost of capital, otherwise they'd fail to attract financing. The United States and Japan are often portrayed as respective exemplars of shareholder and stakeholder capitalism, but as Figure 20.3 shows, national differences in company objectives are not large. A Martian who compared the business decisions, shareholder returns, and stakeholder performance of Toyota and Ford might find it difficult to believe that the companies had different objectives.

Moreover, differences in national objectives are converging. In Japan, changes in the corporate governance code and the growing involvement of U.S. activist investors have meant an

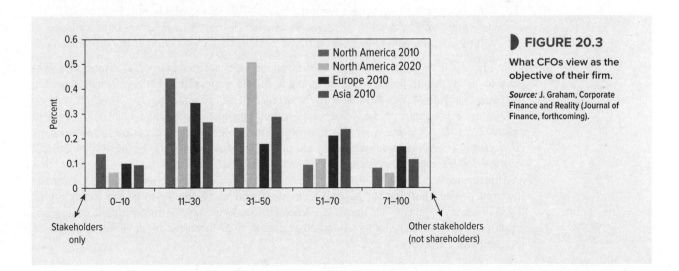

▶ FIGURE 20.3

What CFOs view as the objective of their firm.

Source: J. Graham, *Corporate Finance and Reality* (Journal of Finance, forthcoming).

---

[21]*Elliott International, L.P., et al. v. Akzo Nobel, N.V.,* 200.215.330/01, Amsterdam (2017).

increasing focus by Japanese boards on shareholder value. At the same time, law changes in the United States, combined with shareholder pressure, have made U.S. corporations pay much more attention to employees, communities, and the environment. As Figure 20.3 shows, North American CFOs in 2020 placed much greater weight on stakeholders than they did in 2010.

Overall, while some argue that U.S. and U.K. law needs to be changed away from shareholder primacy for responsible business to become widespread, the law does not appear to impose any significant constraint on company decisions outside of takeover situations. Managers have substantial latitude to serve stakeholders even under shareholder primacy. Many of the examples of responsible behavior discussed in this chapter were undertaken by U.S. and U.K. companies and involve substantial sacrifices of shareholder value, such as Unilever's actions in the coronavirus pandemic.

Benefit Corporations

Suppose a U.S. company does not accept shareholder value as its primary objective. It wants to commit to other goals. It can create a legal obligation to do so by becoming a **benefit corporation**, which is permitted in 36 U.S. states, including Delaware. A benefit corporation states specific public benefits in its articles of incorporation. For example, outdoor apparel company Patagonia states that it will strive "to build the best products and cause no unnecessary harm to the planet or its inhabitants." Crowdfunder Kickstarter pledges to "annually donate 5% of its after-tax profit towards arts and music education, and to organizations fighting to end systemic inequality."

A benefit corporation legally requires directors to deliver its stated benefits, else shareholders (although not other stakeholders) have the right to sue them for failing to do so. It also protects directors from dismissal for poor shareholder returns, as long as the company is fulfilling its stakeholder obligations. Benefit corporations must publish annual *benefit reports* explaining how their commitments were fulfilled, and document their social and environmental performance using a third-party standard.

Other countries have similar arrangements. For example, since 2019, French law provides for the *entreprise à mission* corporation, which requires:

1. Statement of a "mission" in the company's articles of association.

2. A mission committee, distinct from the board of directors, which must include at least one employee. The committee monitors whether the company is acting in accordance with its mission. An independent third party must verify execution of the mission.

In May 2020, the food company Danone became the first listed entreprise à mission, promising to "bring health through food to as many people as possible." Danone North America, its biggest subsidiary, was also the world's largest benefit corporation.

While the concept of benefit corporations seems logical, it is unclear what it means in practice. We are not aware of any cases in which shareholders have successfully sued a benefit corporation for failing to deliver the stated public benefits, potentially because it is difficult to prove failure. How do we know whether Patagonia truly built the "best" products and that any harm that it caused was truly "unnecessary"? Another benefit corporation, Lemonade Inc., has a stated purpose to "harness technology and social impact to be the world's most loved insurance company." It's not clear whether it seeks the love of shareholders, customers, employees, or other stakeholders, or whether it seeks to be loved for its provision of insurance or charitable donations.[22]

---

[22]J. Fisch and S. D. Solomon, "The "Value" of a Public Benefit Company," forthcoming in Research Handbook on Corporate Purpose and Personhood (Elizabeth Pollman & Robert B. Thomson, eds., Elgar).

B Corps

A company that wishes to pursue objectives beyond shareholder value can also become a B Corp. Unlike a benefit corporation or "entreprise à mission," a B Corp has no legal status but is an independent third-party certification by B Lab, a global nonprofit. To be certified, a company must receive a minimum score on the B Impact Assessment, which scrutinizes its societal and environmental performance. (This contrasts with a benefit corporation, where the Benefit Report does not need to be externally certified, and there's no minimum score to be hit.) A B Corp must make a commitment to serve stakeholders other than shareholders, either by becoming a benefit corporation in states that allow it or by including this commitment in the B Corp Agreement for Certification.

Since B Corp certification has no legal status, it doesn't protect directors from being sued for failing to deliver shareholder returns. However, it attracts investors who have broader objectives than financial returns. Thus, a B Corp's shareholders are unlikely to sue its directors for prioritizing stakeholders.

There are over 3,000 B Corps worldwide. It's possible to be a B Corp without being a benefit corporation (Ben & Jerry's ice cream and Burton Snowboards), to be a benefit corporation without being a B Corp (Imperfect Foods, Interface Foundry, and Visionary Organics), and to be both (Patagonia, Kickstarter, and Danone North America).

While there are advantages to becoming a B Corp, it is not necessary to ensure that a company acts responsibly. As we will shortly discuss, companies can commit to reporting on societal and environmental performance even without becoming a B Corp. For a B Corp, breaking such a commitment will lead to the loss of B Corp status. For a standard company, doing so will lead to a significant loss of investor and stakeholder trust. In addition, B Corps are not necessarily more responsible than other companies. Some responsible companies may not view themselves as needing to get certified. In addition, as discussed later, ESG ratings disagree significantly, highlighting the subjectivity in assessing a company's responsibility. The B Lab assessment is only one view.

20.6 Self-Test

What is the difference between a benefit corporation and a B Corp?

Purpose

A simpler way to implement responsible business is for a company to have a public statement of how it seeks to serve society. This is typically referred to as a company's *purpose:* It explains why a company exists, who it serves, its reason for being, and the role it plays in the world.[23] For example, Merck aims "To make a difference in the lives of people globally through our innovative medicines, vaccines, and animal health products." Nestlé's purpose is to "unlock the power of food to enhance quality of life for everyone, today and for generations to come." Importantly, neither company's purpose is to maximize shareholder value. Instead, these companies view shareholder value as the consequence of achieving their mission. Shareholder value is increased if Merck develops innovative medicines or Nestlé produces foods that enhance the quality of life.

Of course, fine words cost little, but a responsible business must put its purpose into practice. For example:

- The pharmacy CVS's purpose is "helping people on their path to better health." In 2014, CVS announced that it would stop selling cigarettes even though they generated $2 billion in sales. As CEO Larry Merlo said, "put simply, the sale of tobacco products is inconsistent with our purpose."

---

[23]Sometimes this is referred to as a company's mission (as in the case of France's "entreprise à mission") or vision.

- In 2013, Barclays Bank closed a division that helped clients avoid tax, sacrificing £1 billion of revenue and contributing to the loss of 2,000 jobs. CEO Antony Jenkins explained: "There are some areas that relied on sophisticated and complex structures, where transactions were carried out with the primary objective of accessing the tax benefits. Although this was legal, going forward such activity is incompatible with our purpose. We will not engage in it again."

Again, even though such actions imposed significant short-term costs on shareholders, it would be difficult for a court to conclusively rule that these costs would not be outweighed by the long-term benefits, and so these actions were entirely feasible under shareholder primacy. Indeed, while CVS's stock fell by 1% on the day after the announcement, it rose steadily over the following weeks.

Often directors' main concern isn't shareholders suing them for pursing a pursuing a purpose beyond shareholder value, but voting them out or selling their shares. One way to mitigate this risk is to put the company's purpose statement to a shareholder vote, which is known as say-on-purpose.[24] For example, the U.K. consumer goods company Unilever put its climate action transition plan to a shareholder vote in May 2021 (to be repeated every three years) to ensure that shareholders concerned about climate believed that it was sufficiently ambitious and also that they were comfortable with any costs that it would entail.

Reporting

Even without becoming a benefit corporation or B Corp, a company is free to report on the value that it delivers to stakeholders. For example, it may disclose quantitative factors, such as the percentage of female employees, greenhouse gas emissions, and the number of new patents generated. However, since many key dimensions of stakeholder value are intangible, qualitative reporting is also critical, such as explaining the mechanisms through which a company involves its workers in decision making.

A significant challenge with nonfinancial reporting is comparability; there's a wide range of potential metrics, and different companies may report different metrics or measure the same one in different ways. To address this issue, several frameworks aim to harmonize reporting by stipulating which items to report and how to measure them. Three examples follow:

- The International Integrated Reporting Council (IIRC) provides principles on how to structure a Sustainability Report or Integrated Report. For example, it states that a company should report the value of six capitals (financial capital, manufacturing capital, human capital, social and relationship capital, intellectual capital, and natural capital or natural resources).

- The Global Reporting Initiative (GRI) provides standards to guide what ESG information to report. For example, for air pollution, it recommends that a company discloses its emissions of nitrogen oxides, sulfur oxides, and persistent organic pollutants.

- The Sustainability Accounting Standards Board (SASB) provides standards that differ by industry. For example, clothing firms should report supply chain water consumption and pollution, labor conditions, and material sourcing; in contrast, banks should disclose data security, financial inclusion, and risk management. The SASB standards are focused on the information that's relevant to investors, while GRI aims to be relevant to both investors and stakeholders. In June 2021, IIRC and SASB merged into a new organization, the Value Reporting Foundation, to further increase comparability.

---

[24]A. Edmans and T. Gosling, "How to Give Shareholders a Say in Corporate Social Responsibility," *The Wall Street Journal*, December 6, 2020.

Even if companies report their ESG performance comprehensively, investors typically like a single number to assess a company with regard to all three, just as a credit rating summarizes all the factors that affect a stock's creditworthiness. This is what ESG ratings aim to do. They are provided by companies such as MSCI, Sustainalytics, Refinitiv, and Vigeo Eiris. Unlike credit ratings, ESG ratings typically disagree quite significantly across providers due to the subjectivity in assessing ESG performance.[25]

● ● ● ● ●

KEY TAKEAWAYS

- **Stakeholders** The stakeholders of a company include employees, customers, suppliers, communities, the government, and the environment.

- **Shareholder capitalism** Advocates of shareholder capitalism argue that the system does not ignore the interests of stakeholders. For example, value is created only when the company has satisfied customers and a motivated workforce. Other stakeholder interests can be addressed by regulation or charitable donations, and maximizing market value maximizes the ability of shareholders to contribute to charities.

  Shareholder capitalism has two further practical advantages. First, it provides a concrete decision rule: Accept all (and only) investments with a positive NPV. Second, since the company has the single objective of increasing shareholder value, management can be judged by the extent that it meets this objective.

- **Stakeholder capitalism** Maximizing shareholder value does not maximize social welfare if there are negative externalities not addressed by regulation and that companies have a comparative advantage in addressing. For example, a company seeking to maximize shareholder value may turn a blind eye to costs of environmental damage not borne by the company. Therefore, supporters of stakeholder capitalism argue that the welfare of *all* stakeholders should be the company's primary objective.

  An additional advantage of stakeholder capitalism is that it may be a practically more useful way to increase shareholder value in a world of uncertainty, because it allows companies to make decisions on intrinsic rather than purely instrumental reasons. However, critics of stakeholder capitalism argue that it leads to arbitrariness: There is no rule stating how the company should weight the interests of different stakeholder groups or how one should judge the performance of a company with multiple objectives.

- **Responsible business** A responsible business seeks to create value for shareholders through creating value for society. It recognizes the need to undertake investments that create stakeholder value, but also to constrain such investments to ensure that managers remain accountable to shareholders. The principles of multiplication, comparative advantage, and materiality provide such constraints.

- **Corporate objectives and the law** In the United States, the United Kingdom, and other Anglo-Saxon economies, the law specifies that shareholders are the owners of the firm and that directors are generally obliged to act in the shareholders' interests by seeking to maximize value, as in shareholder capitalism. By contrast, in Europe and Japan, directors generally have a wider legal responsibility to serve the interests of both shareholders and stakeholders, as in stakeholder capitalism.

- **Implementing responsible business** Some companies may seek to implement responsible business by becoming a benefit corporation or obtaining B Corp certification. Alternatively, they can state a clear purpose, take actions consistent with that purpose, and report on the delivery of its purpose.

---

[25]F. Berg, J. Kölbel and R. Rigobon, "Aggregate Confusion: The Divergence of ESG Ratings," *Review of Finance*, forthcoming.

● ● ● ● ●

FURTHER READING

D. Denis, "Corporate Governance and the Goal of the Firm: In Defense of Shareholder Wealth Maximization," *Financial Review* 51 (November 2016), pp. 467–480.

A. Edmans, *Grow the Pie: How Great Companies Deliver Both Purpose and Profit* (Cambridge, U.K.: Cambridge University Press, 2020).

A. Edmans, "What Stakeholder Capitalism Can Learn from Milton Friedman," *ProMarket,* September 10, 2020.

A. Edmans, "What Stakeholder Capitalism Can Learn from Jensen and Meckling," *ProMarket,* May 9, 2021.

M. Friedman, "The Social Responsibility of Business Is to Increase Its Profits," *New York Times Magazine,* September 13, 1970.

O. Hart and L. Zingales, "Companies Should Maximize Shareholder Welfare Not Market Value," *Journal of Law, Finance, and Accounting* 2 (November 2017), pp. 247–274.

L. Zingales, "Friedman's Legacy: From Doctrine to Theorem," *ProMarket,* October 13, 2020.

● ● ● ● ●

PROBLEM SETS

 **Select problems are available in McGraw Hill's *Connect.* Please see the preface for more information.**

1. **Stakeholder capitalism (S20-1)** Who are the main stakeholders of a company?

2. **Shareholder capitalism (S20-2)** What did Milton Friedman argue in 1970, and how did he support his argument?

3. **Shareholder capitalism (S20-2)** Name two parties that will protect stakeholder welfare under shareholder capitalism.

4. **Shareholder capitalism (S20-2)** Why is enlightened shareholder value referred to as "enlightened"?

5. **Shareholder capitalism (S20-2)** What is the objective of the corporation under

   a. Shareholder capitalism?

   b. Stakeholder capitalism?

6. **Shareholder capitalism (S20-3)** Name two advantages of having shareholder value as the only goal of a corporation.

7. **Stakeholder capitalism (S20-3)** How did the Business Roundtable change its Statement on the Purpose of a Corporation in 2019?

8. **Stakeholder capitalism (S20-3)** Give three reasons stakeholder capitalism might be more effective than shareholder capitalism.

9. **Responsible business (S20-4)** What is the definition of a responsible business?

10. **Responsible business (S20-4)** What principles can a responsible business use to make decisions?

11. **Responsible business in practice (S20-5)** What does shareholder primacy mean? Give examples of countries where shareholder primacy is in operation.

12. **Responsible business in practice (S20-5)** Can companies invest in stakeholders under shareholder primacy?

13. **Responsible business in practice (S20-5)**

    a. What is a benefit corporation?

    b. What is a B Corp?

    c. How do they differ?

14. **Responsible business in practice (S20-5)** What is a company's purpose, and what steps can it take to put purpose into practice?

20.1 A company's stakeholders are its employees, customers, suppliers, communities, the government, and the environment.

20.2 a. No. It is in companies' interest to invest in stakeholders to the extent that the NPV of doing so is positive.

   b. No. Shareholders may care about externalities. However, these externalities are best addressed by regulation, or by the company maximizing shareholder value and shareholders donating to social causes.

20.3 Enlightened shareholder value provides managers with a clear criterion against which to assess any decision: Does it increase NPV? It also provides investors with a clear criterion against which to evaluate a manager's performance: Has she increased shareholder value? Under stakeholder capitalism, there are multiple objectives, and it is unclear how to weight each one.

20.4 a. Shareholders may care about externalities, and the company has a comparative advantage in addressing these externalities.

   b. Shareholders may care about externalities, and the government is unable to regulate them or has failed to regulate them.

   c. Stakeholder capitalism may be a more successful way of increasing shareholder value in a world of uncertainty.

20.5 The principle of multiplication argues that it requires $1 of investment to create more than $1 of social value. The principle of comparative advantage requires $1 of investment to create more value than another company could create with that $1.

20.6 A benefit corporation legally requires a company to pursue the public benefits stated in its articles of association. A B Corp is a certification by B Lab, a global nonprofit, that a company's environmental and social performance is above a certain benchmark.

● ○ ● ● ●
SOLUTIONS TO SELF-TEST QUESTIONS

Visit https://www.gresham.ac.uk/lectures-and-events/purposeful-business for a Gresham College public lecture entitled "Purposeful Business: The Evidence and the Implementation" by Alex Edmans.

● ○ ● ● ●
FINANCE ON THE WEB

Understanding Options

Pop quiz: What do the following events have in common?

- Hershey buys options that put a ceiling on the price that it will pay for its future purchases of cocoa.

- Flatiron offers its president a bonus if the company's year-end stock price exceeds $120.

- Blitzen Computer dips a toe in the water and enters a new market.

- Malted Herring postpones investment in a positive-NPV plant.

- Hewlett-Packard exports partially assembled printers even though it would be cheaper to ship the finished product.

- Dominion installs a dual-fired unit at its Possum Point power station that can use either fuel oil or natural gas.

- Adial Pharmaceuticals issues warrants to purchase 2.1 million shares. The warrants entitle their owner to buy additional shares for $2 each.

- Singapore Airlines issues S$850 million of convertible bonds. Each bond can be exchanged for 174 shares.

Answers: (1) Each of these events involves an option, and (2) each illustrates why the financial manager of a company needs to understand options.

Many capital investments include an embedded option to expand in the future or to abandon the project. For instance, the company may purchase adjoining land that gives it the option in the future to increase capacity. The company is paying money today for the opportunity to make a further investment. To put it another way, the company is acquiring *growth opportunities*.

We took a peek at these *real* options in Chapter 10. We take a more thorough look at them in Chapter 23.

Another important reason that financial managers need to understand options is that they are often tacked on to an issue of corporate securities and so provide the investor or the company with the flexibility to change the terms of the issue. For example, we will see in Chapter 25 how convertibles give their holders an option to exchange their bonds for common stock.

In fact, we explain in Chapter 24 that whenever a company borrows, it gains an option to walk away from its debts and surrender its assets to the bondholders. This is an extremely important insight. It means that anything that we can learn about traded options applies equally to corporate liabilities.

Companies regularly use commodity, currency, and interest-rate options to reduce risk. For example, a meatpacking company that wishes to put a ceiling on the cost of beef might take out an option to buy live cattle at a fixed price. In Chapter 27, we explain how firms employ such options to limit their risk.

In this chapter, we use traded stock options to explain how options work and the variables that affect option values. In the next chapter, we build on these insights to show how these variables can be combined into a precise option valuation model. Then, in Chapter 23, we will look at the real options that may be encountered in capital investment decisions. We divide this chapter into three bite-sized pieces.

Section 21.1 Calls, puts, and shares

In this first section, we introduce you to call and put options, and we show how the payoff on these options depends on the price of the underlying asset.

Section 21.2 Financial alchemy with options

We then show how options can be combined to produce a variety of interesting strategies. It turns out that any set of contingent payoffs—that is, payoffs that depend on the value of some other underlying asset—can be constructed with a simple mixture of options on that asset.

Section 21.3 What determines option values?

We conclude the chapter by identifying the variables that determine option values. You will encounter some surprising and counterintuitive effects. For example, investors are used to thinking that increased risk reduces value. But for options, it is the other way around.

• • • • •

21-1 Calls, Puts, and Shares

Investors regularly trade options on common stocks.[1] These options are not issued by the company. Instead, they are side-bets between two investors, one buying the option and the other selling it. For example, Table 21.1 reproduces quotes for options on the shares of Amazon. com. You can see that there are two types of options—calls and puts. We explain each in turn.

Call Options and Payoff Diagrams

A **call option** gives its owner the *right,* but not the obligation, to buy a share, at a specified *exercise* or *strike price* on or before a specified maturity date. If the option can be exercised only at maturity, it is conventionally known as a *European call;* in other cases (such as the Amazon options shown in Table 21.1), the option can be exercised on, or at any time before, maturity, and it is then known as an *American call.* Notice that these terms imply nothing about where the option is traded. European options may be traded in America and vice versa.

The third column of Table 21.1 sets out the prices in January 2020 of each of the Amazon call options. Look at the quotes for options maturing in April 2020. The first entry says that

Maturity Date	Exercise Price	Price of Call Option	Price of Put Option
April 2020	$1,700	$182.80	$ 33.32
	1,750	149.42	46.37
	1,830	90.28	81.53
	1,900	63.80	113.93
	1,950	49.75	135.79
July 2020	$1,700	$208.45	$53.23
	1,750	200.14	68.50
	1,830	146.20	107.34
	1,900	106.95	135.36
	1,950	83.87	168.70
January 2021[a]	$1,700	$296.78	$110.35
	1,750	263.02	126.13
	1,830	200.28	165.75
	1,900	175.54	195.67
	1,950	147.73	217.05

⟩TABLE 21.1

Selected prices of put and call options on Amazon. com shares in January 2020, when the closing share price was about $1,830.

[a]Long-term options are called "LEAPS."

Source: Yahoo! Finance, finance. yahoo.com.

---

[1]The two principal options exchanges in the United States are the International Securities Exchange (ISE) and the Chicago Board Options Exchange (CBOE).

for $182.80 you could acquire an option to buy one share[2] of Amazon stock for $1,700 on or before April 2020. Moving down to the next row, you can see that an option to buy for $50 more ($1,750 vs. $1,700) costs about $30 less, that is, $149.42. In general, the value of a call option goes down as the exercise price goes up. The more that you need to pay to acquire the share, the less valuable is the option.

Now look at the quotes for options maturing in July 2020 and January 2021. Notice how the option price increases as option maturity is extended. For example, at an exercise price of $1,830, the April 2020 call option costs $90.28, the July 2020 option costs $146.20, and the January 2021 option costs $200.28. The longer before you need to decide whether you want to exercise, the more valuable is the option.

If an option provides a positive payoff if exercised now, it is said to be *in the money*. In Table 21.1, all the Amazon call options with an exercise price below $1,830 were in the money. If the option provides a negative payoff if exercised now, the option is *out of the money*. All the Amazon call options with an exercise price above $1,830 were out of the money. And, if the payoff from exercising would be zero, the option is *at the money*. The Amazon calls with an exercise price of $1,830 were at the money.

Option analysts often draw a *payoff diagram* to illustrate the possible payoffs from an option. For example, the payoff diagram in Figure 21.1*a* shows the possible consequences of investing in Amazon July 2020 call options with an exercise price of $1,830 (boldfaced in Table 21.1). The outcome from investing in Amazon calls depends on what happens to the share price. If the share price at the end of this six-month period turns out to be less than the $1,830 exercise price, it will not make sense to pay the exercise price to obtain the share. Your call will, in that case, be worthless. On the other hand, if the share price turns out to be greater than $1,830, it will pay to exercise your option to buy the share. In this case, when the call expires, it will be worth the market price of the share minus the $1,830 that you must pay to exercise the option. Thus the value of a call option at maturity is the greater of the share price less the exercise price, or zero. If S equals the share price and EX equals the exercise price, then:

$$\text{Call value at maturity} = \max(S - EX, 0) \qquad \textbf{(21.1)}$$

EXAMPLE 21.1 • The payoff from buying a call

Suppose that, by the time that the call option matures, the price of Amazon stock has risen to $2,000. A call with a $1,830 exercise price will then be *in the money* and worth $S - EX = \$2,000 - \$1,830 = \$170$. That is your payoff, but it is not all profit. Table 21.1 shows that you had to pay $146.20 to buy the call.

• • • • •

Notice that the option payoffs depend solely on the price of the underlying asset—in our case, Amazon stock. Therefore, options are often described as derivative instruments, or, more simply, *derivatives*. We will encounter other derivatives in Chapter 27 when we discuss forwards, futures, and swaps.

21.1 Self-Test

Look at the first call option shown in Table 21.1. It gives the owner the right to buy Amazon shares at a price of $1,700. What would be the payoff if exercised today? Is the call *out of the money,* or *at the money*?

---

[2]You can't actually buy an option on a single share. Trades are in multiples of 100. The minimum order would be for 100 options on 100 Amazon shares.

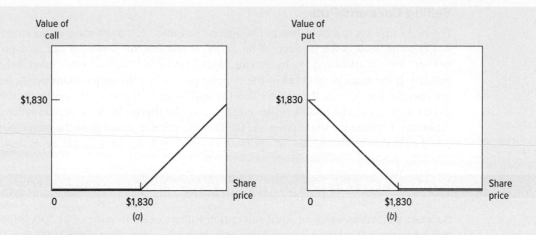

FIGURE 21.1   Payoff diagrams show how payoffs to owners of Amazon calls and puts (shown by the colored lines) depend on the share price. (*a*) Result of buying Amazon call exercisable at $1,830. (*b*) Result of buying Amazon put exercisable at $1,830.

Put Options

Now let us look at the Amazon **put options** in the right-hand column of Table 21.1. Whereas a call option gives you the right to *buy* a share for a specified exercise price, a put gives you the right to *sell* the share. For example, the boldfaced entry in the right-hand column of Table 21.1 shows that for $107.34, you could acquire an option to sell one Amazon share for a price of $1,830 any time before July 2020. The circumstances in which the put turns out to be valuable are just the opposite of those in which the call is profitable. You can see this from the payoff diagram in Figure 21.1*b*. If Amazon's share price immediately before expiration turns out to be *greater* than $1,830, you won't want to sell stock at that price. You would do better to sell the share in the market, and your put option will be worthless. Conversely, if the share price turns out to be *less* than $1,830, it will pay to buy a share at the low price and then take advantage of the option to sell it for $1,830. In this case, the value of the put option on the exercise date is the difference between the $1,830 proceeds from the sale and the market price of the share. Thus, the value of the put option at maturity is the greater of the exercise price minus the stock price, or zero:

$$\text{Put value at maturity} = \max(EX - S, 0) \qquad \textbf{(21.2)}$$

EXAMPLE 21.2 • The payoff from buying a put

Suppose that by the time the put option matures, the price of Amazon stock has fallen to $1,630. A put with a $1,830 exercise price will then be *in the money* and worth $EX - S = \$1,830 - \$1,630 = \$200$. That is your payoff, but you had to pay $107.34 to buy the put. Your profit is $200 − $107.34 = $92.66.

• • • • •

21.2 Self Test

Look again at the put option in the first row of Table 21.1. Suppose that when the option matures in April, Amazon's share price is $1,730. What is the put's value at that point? What is your profit or loss if you bought the put in January 2020?

Selling Calls and Puts

For every investor that buys one of the options in Table 21.1, there must be another that sells it. Let's now look at the position of the seller. If you sell, or "write," a call, you promise to deliver shares if asked to do so by the call buyer. In other words, the buyer's asset is the seller's liability. If the share price is below the exercise price when the option matures, the buyer will not exercise the call and the seller's liability will be zero. If it rises above the exercise price, the buyer will exercise and the seller must give up the shares. In this case, the seller loses the difference between the share price and the exercise price received from the buyer. Notice that it is the buyer who always has the option to exercise; option sellers simply do as they are told.

EXAMPLE 21.3 • The payoff from *selling* a call

Suppose an investor owns an April call option with an exercise price of $1,830. Suppose also that when the call option matures, Amazon's share price turns out to be $2,000. It will pay the call owner to exercise the call. The seller is forced to sell shares worth $2,000 for only $1,830 and so has a payoff of –$170. Of course, that $170 loss is the buyer's gain.

However, the seller has some consolation since they were paid $146.20 in January for selling the call.

• • • • •

Figure 21.2*a* shows how the payoffs to the seller of the Amazon call option vary with the share price. Notice that for every dollar the buyer makes, the seller loses a dollar. Figure 21.2*a* is just Figure 21.1*a* turned on its head.

In just the same way, we can depict the position of an investor who sells, or writes, a put by standing Figure 21.1*b* on its head. The seller of the put has agreed to pay $1,830 for the share if the buyer of the put should request it. Clearly, the seller will be safe as long as the share price remains above $1,830 but will lose money if the share price falls below this number. The worst thing that can happen is that the share becomes worthless. The seller would then be obliged to pay $1,830 for a share worth $0. The payoff to the seller would be –$1,830.

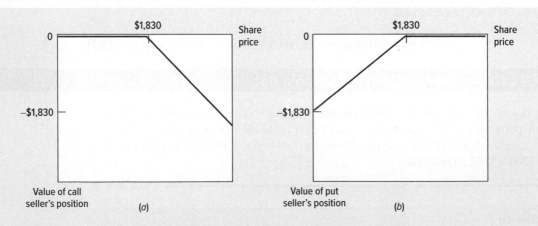

FIGURE 21.2   Payoffs to *sellers* of Amazon calls and puts (shown by the colored lines) depend on the share price. (*a*) Result of selling Amazon call exercisable at $1,830. (*b*) Result of selling Amazon put exercisable at $1,830.

Payoff Diagrams Are Not Profit Diagrams

Payoff diagrams show *only* the payoffs at option exercise; they do not account for the initial cost of buying the option or the initial proceeds from selling it.

This is a common point of confusion. For example, the payoff diagram in Figure 21.1*a* makes purchase of a call *look* like a sure thing—the payoff is at worst zero, with plenty of upside if Amazon's share price goes above $1,830 by July 2020. But compare the *profit diagram* in Figure 21.3*a*, which subtracts the $146.20 *cost* of the call in January 2020 from the payoff at maturity. The call buyer loses money at all share prices less than $1,830 + 146.20 = $1,976.20. Take another example: The payoff diagram in Figure 21.2*b* makes selling a put *look* like a sure loss—the *best* payoff is zero. But the profit diagram in Figure 21.3*b*, which recognizes the $107.34 received by the seller, shows that the seller gains at all prices above $1,830 – 107.34 = $1,722.66.[3]

Profit diagrams like those in Figure 21.3 may be helpful to the options beginner, but options experts rarely draw them.[4] Now that you've graduated from the first options class we won't draw them either. We stick to payoff diagrams, because you have to focus on payoffs at exercise to understand options and to value them properly.

21-2   **Financial Alchemy with Options**

Look now at Figure 21.4*a*, which shows the payoff if you buy an Amazon share at $1,830. You gain dollar-for-dollar if the share price goes up and you lose dollar-for-dollar if it falls. That's obvious; it doesn't take a genius to draw a 45-degree line.

Look now at panel *b,* which shows the payoffs from an investment strategy that retains the upside potential of Amazon stock but gives complete downside protection. In this case, your payoff stays at $1,830 even if the Amazon share price falls to $1,700, $1,000, or zero. Panel *b*'s payoffs are clearly better than panel *a*'s. If a financial alchemist could turn panel *a* into panel *b,* you'd be willing to pay for the service, just as you would be willing to pay a medieval alchemist who turned a base metal into gold.

Now, as you have probably suspected, this financial alchemy is for real. You can make the transformation shown in Figure 21.4. You do it with options, and we will show you how.

BEYOND THE PAGE

Option
payoffs

mhhe.com/brealey14e

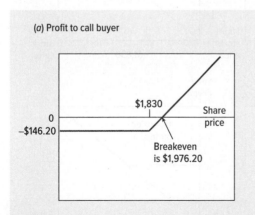

(*a*) Profit to call buyer

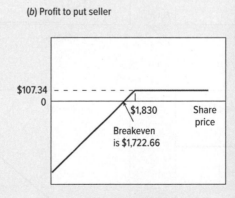

(*b*) Profit to put seller

▶ **FIGURE 21.3**

Profit diagrams incorporate the costs of buying an option or the proceeds from selling one. In panel (*a*), we subtract the $146.20 cost of the Amazon call from the payoffs plotted in Figure 21.1*a*. In panel (*b*), we add the $107.34 proceeds from selling the Amazon put to the payoffs in Figure 21.2*b*.

---

[3]The fact that you have made a profit on your position is not necessarily a cause for congratulation. The profit needs to compensate you for the risk that you took.

[4]Profit diagrams such as Figure 21.3 deduct the initial cost of the option from the final payoff. They therefore ignore the first lesson of finance—"A dollar today is worth more than a dollar in the future."

▶ **FIGURE 21.4**

Payoffs at the end of six months to two investment strategies for Amazon stock. (*a*) You buy one share for $1,830. (*b*) No downside. If the share price falls, your payoff stays at $1,830.

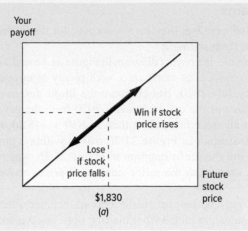

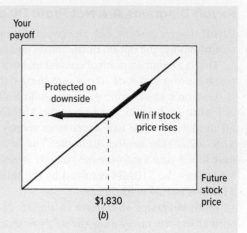

Look at row 1 of Figure 21.5. The first diagram again shows the payoff from buying a share of Amazon stock, while the next diagram in row 1 shows the payoffs from buying an Amazon put option with an exercise price of $1,830. The third diagram shows the effect of combining these two positions. You can see that if Amazon's share price rises above $1,830, your put option is valueless, so you simply receive the gains from your investment in the share. However, if the share price falls below $1,830, you can exercise your put option and sell your share for $1,830. Thus, by adding a put option to your investment in the share, you have protected

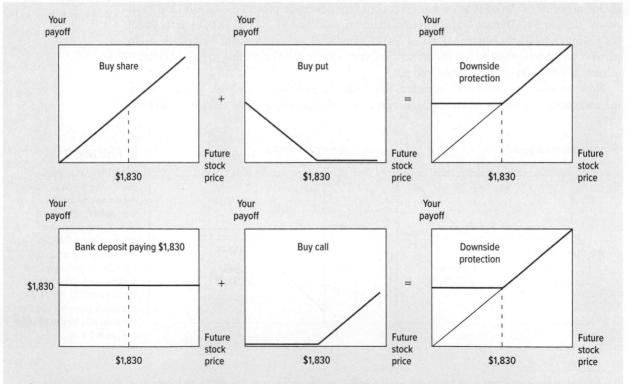

▶ **FIGURE 21.5** Each row in the figure shows a different way to create a strategy where you gain if the share price rises but are protected on the downside (strategy *b* in Figure 21.4).

yourself against loss.[5] This is the strategy that we depicted in Figure 21.4. Of course, there is no gain without pain. The cost of insuring yourself against loss is the amount that you pay for a put option on Amazon stock with an exercise price of $1,830. In January 2020, the price of this put was $107.34. This was the going rate for financial alchemists.

21.3 Self-Test

You own a share of Amazon stock worth $1,830. You would like to protect yourself against a fall in the price of greater than $130 over the coming year. What do you do?

We have just seen how put options can be used to provide downside protection. We now show you how call options can be used to get the same result. This is illustrated in row 2 of Figure 21.5. The first diagram shows the payoff from placing the present value of $1,830 in a bank deposit. Regardless of what happens to the price of Amazon shares, your bank deposit will pay off $1,830. The second diagram in row 2 shows the payoff from a call option on Amazon stock with an exercise price of $1,830, and the third diagram shows the effect of combining these two positions. Notice that if Amazon's share price falls, your call is worthless, but you still have your $1,830 in the bank. For every dollar that Amazon share price rises above $1,830, your investment in the call option pays off an extra dollar. For example, if the share price rises to $2,000, you will have $1,830 in the bank and a call worth $170. Thus you participate fully in any rise in the price of the share, while being fully protected against any fall. So we have just found another way to provide the downside protection depicted in panel *b* of Figure 21.4.

The two rows of Figure 21.5 tell us something about the relationship between a call option and a put option. As long as the two options have the same maturity and exercise price, then regardless of the future share price, both investment strategies provide identical payoffs. In other words, if you buy the share and a put option to sell it for $1,830, you receive the same payoff as from buying a call option and setting aside enough money to pay the $1,830 exercise price. Therefore, if you are committed to holding the two packages until the options expire, the two packages should sell for the same price today. This gives us a fundamental relationship for European options:

$$\text{Value of call} + \text{present value of exercise price} = \text{value of put} + \text{share price}$$
$$C + PV(EX) = P + S$$

(21.3)

To repeat, this relationship holds because the payoff of

buy call for C, invest present value of exercise price PV(EX) in safe asset[6]

is identical to the payoff from

buy put for P, buy share for S.

This basic relationship among share price, call and put values, and the present value of the exercise price is called **put–call parity**.[7]

Put–call parity can be expressed in several ways. Each expression implies two investment strategies that give identical results. For example, suppose that you want to solve for the value of a put. You simply need to twist the put–call parity formula around to give

---

[5]This combination of a stock and a put option is known as a *protective put position*.

[6]The present value is calculated at the *risk-free* rate of interest. It is the amount that you would have to invest today in a bank deposit or Treasury bills to realize the exercise price on the option's expiration date.

[7]Put–call parity holds only if you are committed to holding the options until the final exercise date. It therefore does not hold for American options, which you can exercise *before* the final date. We discuss possible reasons for early exercise in Chapter 22. Also if the stock makes a dividend payment before the final exercise date, you need to recognize that the investor who buys the call misses out on this dividend. In this case the relationship is: Value of call + present value of exercise price = value of put + share price − present value of dividend.

Value of put = value of call + present value of exercise price − share price
$$P = C + PV(EX) - S$$

From this expression you can deduce that

buy put

is identical to

buy call, invest present value of exercise price in safe asset, sell share.

In other words, if puts are not available, you can always create a home-made put by buying calls, putting cash in the bank, and selling shares.

21.4 Self-Test

A one-year European call option on Upsilon stock with an exercise price of $105 costs $20. A one-year put costs $15. The interest rate is 5%? What is the value of the stock? (Upsilon stock does not pay a dividend.)

If you find put–call parity difficult to believe, look at Figure 21.6, which shows the possible payoffs from each position. The diagram on the left shows the payoffs from a call option on Amazon stock with an exercise price of $1,830. The second diagram shows the payoffs from placing the present value of $1,830 in the bank. Regardless of what happens to the share price, this investment will pay off $1,830. The third diagram shows the payoffs from selling Amazon stock. When you sell a share that you don't own, you have a liability—you must sometime buy it back. There is an old saying on Wall Street:

He who sells what isn't his'n
Buys it back or goes to pris'n

Therefore, the best that can happen to you is that the share price falls to zero. In that case, it costs you nothing to buy the share back. But for every extra dollar on the future share price, you will need to spend an extra dollar to buy the share. The final diagram in Figure 21.6 shows that the *total* payoff from these three positions is the same as if you had bought a put option. For example, suppose that when the option matures, the stock price is $1,500. Your

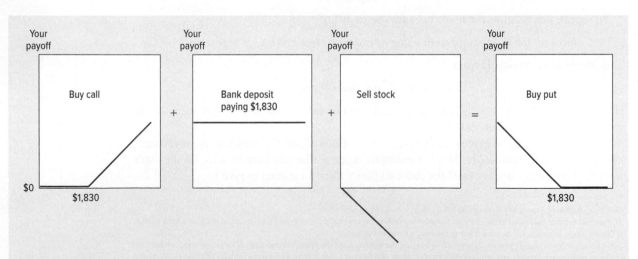

▶ **FIGURE 21.6**   A strategy of buying a call, depositing the present value of the exercise price in the bank, and selling the stock is equivalent to buying a put.

call will be worthless, your bank deposit will be worth $1,830, and it will cost you $1,500 to repurchase the share. Your total payoff is $0 + 1,830 − 1,500 = \$330$, exactly the same as the payoff from the put.

If two investments offer identical payoffs, then they should sell for the same price today. If the law of one price is violated, you have a potential arbitrage opportunity.

EXAMPLE 21.4 • Put-call parity for the six-month at-the-money Amazon options

Let's check whether there are any arbitrage profits to be made from our at-the-money Amazon calls and puts. In January 2020, the price of a six-month call with a $1,830 exercise price was $146.20, the interest rate was about 2% for six months, and Amazon's share price was $1,830. Therefore, the cost of a homemade put was

$$C + PV(EX) - S = P$$
$$146.20 + 1,830/1.02 - 1,830 = \$110.32$$

This is a little bit more than it would have cost you to buy a put directly.

Warning: Trading volume in many listed options is often very low. The latest prices on an options exchange may be very out-of-date, so that it may not be possible in practice to take advantage of apparent arbitrage opportunities.

• • • • •

Spotting the Option

Options rarely come with a large label attached. Often, the trickiest part of the problem is to identify the option. When you are not sure whether you are dealing with a put or a call or a complicated blend of the two, it is a good precaution to draw a payoff diagram. Here is an example.

The Flatiron and Mangle Corporation has offered its president, Ms. Higden, the following incentive scheme: At the end of the year Ms. Higden will be paid a bonus of $50,000 for every dollar that the price of Flatiron stock exceeds its current figure of $120. However, the maximum bonus that she can receive is set at $2 million.[8]

You can think of Ms. Higden as owning 50,000 tickets, each of which pays nothing if the stock price fails to beat $120. The value of each ticket then rises by $1 for each dollar rise in the stock price up to the maximum of $2,000,000/50,000 = \$40$. Figure 21.7 shows the payoffs from just one of these tickets. The payoffs are not the same as those of the simple put and call options that we drew in Figure 21.1, but it is possible to find a combination of options that exactly replicates Figure 21.7. Before going on to read the answer, see if you can spot it yourself. (If you are someone who enjoys puzzles of the make-a-triangle-from-just-two-matchsticks type, this one should be pretty easy.)

The answer is in Figure 21.8. The solid black line represents the purchase of a call option with an exercise price of $120, and the dotted line shows the sale of another call option with an exercise price of $160. The colored line shows the payoffs from a combination of the purchase and the sale—exactly the same as the payoffs from one of Ms. Higden's tickets.

Thus, if we wish to know how much the incentive scheme is costing the company, we need to calculate the difference between the value of 50,000 call options with an exercise price of $120 and the value of 50,000 calls with an exercise price of $160.

---

[8]Bonus schemes in many companies follow a pattern similar to Ms. Higden's scheme. See, for example, A. Edmans, X. Gabaix, and D. Jenter, "Executive Compensation: A Survey of Theory and Evidence," in B. Hermalin and M. Weisbach, eds., *Handbook of the Economics of Corporate Governance* (Amsterdam: North-Holland, 2017).

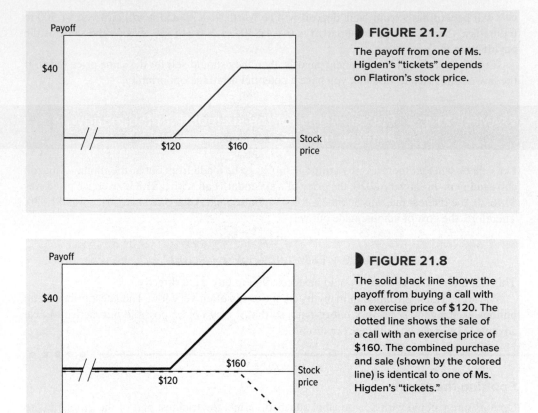

▶ **FIGURE 21.7**

The payoff from one of Ms. Higden's "tickets" depends on Flatiron's stock price.

▶ **FIGURE 21.8**

The solid black line shows the payoff from buying a call with an exercise price of $120. The dotted line shows the sale of a call with an exercise price of $160. The combined purchase and sale (shown by the colored line) is identical to one of Ms. Higden's "tickets."

We could have made the incentive scheme depend in a much more complicated way on the stock price. For example, the bonus could peak at $2 million and then fall steadily back to zero as the stock price climbs above $160.[9] You could still have represented this scheme as a combination of options. In fact, we can state a general theorem:

> Any set of contingent payoffs—that is, payoffs that depend on the value of some other asset—can be constructed with a mixture of simple options on that asset.

In other words, you can create any payoff diagram—with as many ups and downs or peaks and valleys as your imagination allows—by buying or selling the right combinations of puts and calls with different exercise prices.[10]

The practice of packaging different investments to create new tailor-made instruments is called **financial engineering**. Perhaps a German company would like to set a minimum and maximum cost at which it can buy dollars in six-months' time. Or perhaps an oil company would like to pay a lower rate of interest on its debt if the price of oil falls. Options provide the essential building blocks that financial engineers use to create these interesting payoff structures.

---

[9]This is not as nutty a bonus scheme as it may sound. Maybe Ms. Higden's hard work can lift the value of the stock by so much and the only way she can hope to increase it further is by taking on extra risk. You can deter her from doing this by making her bonus start to decline beyond some point. Too bad that before the financial crisis the bonus schemes for some bank CEOs did not contain this feature.

[10]In some cases, you may also have to borrow or lend money to generate a payoff diagram with your desired pattern. Lending raises the payoff line in payoff diagrams, as in the bottom row of Figure 21.5. Borrowing lowers the payoff line.

21-3   What Determines the Value of a Call Option?

So far, we have said nothing about how the value of a call option is determined. We know that when the option matures, its value is the greater of the share price minus the exercise price of zero:

$$\text{Value of call at maturity} = \max{(S - EX, 0)}$$

Consider, for instance, our earlier example of an option to buy Amazon stock at $1,830. If Amazon's share price is below $1,830 on the exercise date, the call will be worthless; if the share price is above $1,830, the call will be worth $1,830 less than the value of the share.

Before maturity a call option must be worth *at least* max$(S - EX, 0)$. This is shown by the heavy, lower line in Figure 21.9. For example, if Amazon shares were priced at $1,960, the lower bound for the call would be max($1,960 - 1,830, 0) = $130. Suppose that you could buy the call for $30, which is less than the lower bound. Then it would pay you to buy the call for $30, pay the exercise price of $1,830, and sell the share for $1,960. You would have made an arbitrage profit of $1,960 - ($30 + $1,830) = $100. The demand for options from investors seeking to exploit this opportunity would quickly force the option price up, at least to the heavy line in the figure. For options that still have some time until expiration, the heavy line is therefore a *lower bound* on the market price of the option. Thus, the lower bound is max$(S - EX, 0)$.

21.5 Self-Test

A call option on Upsilon shares has an exercise price of $80. If the current price of the share is $60, what is the lower bound on the price of the call?

The diagonal line in Figure 21.9 is the *upper bound* to the price of a call option. Why? Because the option cannot give a higher ultimate payoff than the share. If at the option's expiration the share price is *above* the exercise price, the option is worth the share price *less* the exercise price. If the share price ends up *below* the exercise price, the option is worthless, but the share's owner still has a valuable security. For example, if the option's exercise price is $1,830, then the extra dollar returns realized by shareholders are shown in the following table:

	Share Payoff	Call Option Payoff	Extra Payoff from Holding Shares Instead of Options
Option exercised (share price greater than $1,830)	Share price	Share price – $1,830	$1,830
Option expires unexercised (share price less than or equal to $1,830)	Share price	0	Share price

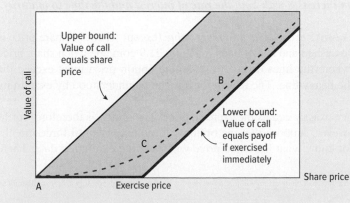

FIGURE 21.9

Value of a call before its expiration date (dashed line). The value depends on the share price. It is always worth more than its value if exercised now (heavy line). It is never worth more than the share price itself.

If the price of the call option is higher than the share price, everyone will rush to sell the option and buy the share. Therefore, the option price must be somewhere in the shaded region of Figure 21.9. In fact, it will lie on a curved, upward-sloping line like the dashed curve shown in the figure. This line begins its travels where the upper and lower bounds meet (at zero). Then it rises, gradually becoming parallel to the upward-sloping part of the lower bound.

But let us look more carefully at the shape and location of the dashed line. Three points, *A, B,* and *C,* are marked on the dashed line in Figure 21.9. As we explain each point you will see why the option price has to behave as the dashed line predicts.

Point *A* *When the share is worthless, the option is worthless.* A share price of zero means that there is no possibility the stock will ever have any future value.[11] If so, the option is sure to expire unexercised and worthless, and it is worthless today.

That brings us to our first important point about option value:

The value of a call option increases as share price increases, if the exercise price is held constant.

That should be no surprise. Owners of call options clearly hope for the share price to rise and are happy when it does.

Point *B* *As the share price increases, the option price approaches the share price less the present value of the exercise price.* Notice that the dashed line representing the option price in Figure 21.9 eventually becomes parallel to the ascending heavy line representing the lower bound on the option price. The reason is as follows: The higher the share price, the higher is the probability that the option will eventually be exercised. If the share price is high enough, exercise becomes a virtual certainty; the probability that the share price will fall below the exercise price before the option expires becomes trivially small.

If you own an option that you *know* will be exchanged for a share of stock, you effectively own the share now. The only difference is that you don't have to pay for the share (by handing over the exercise price) until later, when formal exercise occurs. In these circumstances, buying the call is equivalent to buying the share but financing part of the purchase by borrowing. The amount implicitly borrowed is the present value of the exercise price. The value of the call is therefore equal to the share price less the present value of the exercise price.

This brings us to another important point about options. Investors who acquire stock by way of a call option are buying on credit. They pay the purchase price of the option today, but they do not pay the exercise price until they actually take up the option. The delay in payment is particularly valuable if interest rates are high and the option has a long maturity.

Thus, the value of an option increases with both the rate of interest and the time to maturity.

Point *C* *The option price always exceeds its minimum value* (except when the share price is zero). We have seen that the dashed and heavy lines in Figure 21.9 coincide when share price is zero (point *A*), but elsewhere the lines diverge; that is, the option price must exceed the minimum value given by the heavy line. The reason for this can be understood by examining point *C*.

At point *C,* the share price exactly equals the exercise price. The option is therefore worthless if exercised today. However, suppose that the option will not expire until three months hence. Of course, we do not know what the share price will be at the expiration date. There

---

[11]If a stock *can* be worth something in the future, then investors will pay *something* for it today, although possibly a very small amount.

is roughly a 50% chance that it will be higher than the exercise price and a 50% chance that it will be lower. The possible payoffs to the option are therefore

Outcome	Payoff
Share price rises (50% probability)	Share price less exercise price (option is exercised)
Share price falls (50% probability)	Zero (option expires worthless)

If there is a positive probability of a positive payoff, and if the worst payoff is zero, then the option must be valuable. That means the option price at point *C* exceeds its lower bound, which at point *C* is zero. In general, the option prices will exceed their lower-bound values as long as there is time left before expiration.

One of the most important determinants of the *height* of the dashed curve (i.e., of the difference between actual and lower-bound value) is the likelihood of substantial movements in the stock price. An option on a share whose price is unlikely to change by more than 1% or 2% is not worth much; an option on a share whose price may halve or double is very valuable.

As an option holder, you gain from volatility because the payoffs are not symmetric. If the share price falls *below* the exercise price, your call option will be worthless, regardless of whether the shortfall is a few cents or many dollars. On the other hand, for every dollar that the share price rises *above* the exercise price, your call will be worth an extra dollar. Therefore, the option holder gains from the increased volatility on the upside, but does not lose on the downside.

EXAMPLE 21.5 • Option values increase with share volatility

A simple example may help to illustrate the point. Consider two shares, X and Y, each of which is priced at $100. The only difference is that the outlook for Y is much less easy to predict. There is a 50% chance that the price of X will rise to $130 and a similar chance that it will fall to $90. By contrast, there is a 50–50 chance that the price of Y will either rise to $150 or fall to $70.

Suppose that you are offered a call option on each of these shares with an exercise price of $100. The following table compares the possible payoffs from these options:

	Share Price Falls	Share Price Rises
Payoff from call option on X	$0	$130 – $100 = $30
Payoff from call option on Y	$0	$150 – $100 = $50

In both cases, there is a 50% chance that the share price will decline and make the option worthless but, if the share price rises, the option on Y will give the larger payoff. Because the chance of a zero payoff is the same, the option on Y is worth more than the option on X.

• • • • •

21.6 Self-Test

Rework Example 21.5 assuming that the option is a put rather than a call. Show that option value continues to be higher for the option on the more volatile share.

▶ FIGURE 21.10

Call options on the shares of (*a*) firm X and (*b*) firm Y. In each case, the current share price equals the exercise price, so each option has a 50% chance of ending up worthless (if the share price falls) and a 50% chance of ending up "in the money" (if the share price rises). However, the chance of a large payoff is greater for the option on firm Y's shares because Y's share price is more volatile and therefore has more upside potential.

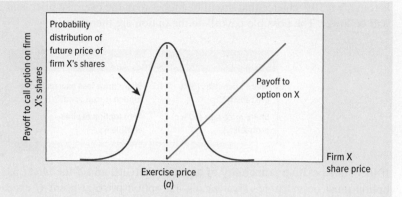

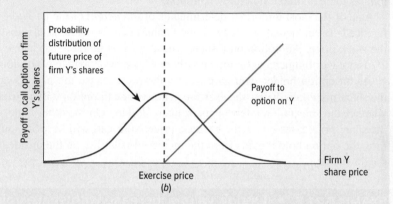

Of course, in practice, future share prices may take on a range of different values. We have recognized this in Figure 21.10, where the uncertain outlook for firm Y's share price shows up in the wider probability distribution of future prices.[12] The greater spread of outcomes for the share price of firm Y again provides more upside potential and, therefore, increases the chance of a large payoff on the option.

Figure 21.11 shows how volatility affects the value of an option. The upper curved line depicts the value of the Amazon call option assuming that Amazon's share price, like that of firm Y's, is highly variable. The lower curved line assumes a lower (and more realistic) degree of volatility.[13]

The probability of large share price changes during the remaining life of an option depends on two things: (1) the variance (i.e., volatility) of the share price *per period* and (2) the number of periods until the option expires. If there are t remaining periods, and the variance per period is σ^2, the value of the option should depend on cumulative variability $\sigma^2 t$.[14] Other things equal, you would like to hold an option on a volatile share (high σ^2). Given volatility, you would like to hold an option with a long life ahead of it (large t).

[12]Figure 21.10 continues to assume that the exercise price on both options is equal to the current stock price. This is not a necessary assumption. Also, in drawing Figure 21.10, we have assumed that the distribution of stock prices is symmetric. This also is not a necessary assumption, and we will look more carefully at the distribution of stock prices in the next chapter.

[13]The option values shown in Figure 21.11 were calculated by using the Black-Scholes option-valuation model. We explain this model in Chapter 22 and use it to value the Amazon option.

[14]Here is an intuitive explanation: If the stock price follows a random walk (Section 12-2), successive price changes are statistically independent. The cumulative price change before expiration is the sum of t random variables. The variance of a sum of independent random variables is the sum of the variances of those variables. Thus, if σ^2 is the variance of the daily price change, and there are t days until expiration, the variance of the cumulative price change is $\sigma^2 t$.

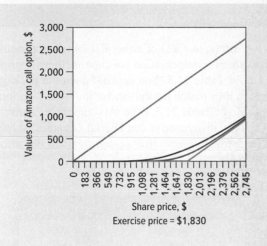

▶ FIGURE 21.11

How the value of the Amazon call option increases with the volatility of the share price. Each of the curved lines shows the value of the option for different initial share prices. The only difference is that the upper line assumes a much higher level of uncertainty about Amazon's future share price.

Thus, the value of an option increases with both the volatility of the share price and the time to maturity.

It's a rare person who can keep all these properties straight at first reading. Therefore, we have summed them up in Table 21.2.

Risk and Option Values

In most financial settings, risk is a bad thing; you have to be paid to bear it. Investors in risky (high-beta) shares demand higher expected rates of return. High-risk capital investment projects have correspondingly high costs of capital and have to beat higher hurdle rates to achieve positive NPV.

For options, it's the other way around. As we have just seen, options written on volatile assets are worth *more* than options written on safe assets.[15] If you can understand and remember that one fact about options, you've come a long way.

1. If There Is an *Increase* in:	The Change in the Call Option Price Is:
Share price (*S*)	Positive
Exercise price (*EX*)	Negative
Interest rate(r_f)	Positive*
Time to expiration (*t*)	Positive
Volatility of share price (σ)	Positive*

2. Other Properties of Call Options:

a. *Upper bound.* The option price is always less than the share price.

b. *Lower bound.* The call price never falls below the payoff to immediate exercise (i.e., max(*S–EX*, 0).

c. If the share is worthless, the call is worthless.

d. As the share price becomes very large, the call price approaches the share price less the present value of the exercise price.

▶ TABLE 21.2

What the price of a call option depends on.

*The direct effect of increases in r_f or σ on option price, given the share price. There may also be indirect effects. For example, an increase in r_f could reduce share price *S*. This in turn could affect option price.

---

[15]This is not as crazy as it may at first sound. *Given the price of the stock,* the option is more valuable when the stock is volatile. However, that same volatility may have reduced the amount that investors are prepared to pay for the stock.

EXAMPLE 21.6 • Volatility and executive stock options

Suppose you have to choose between two job offers, as CFO of either Establishment Industries or Digital Organics. Establishment Industries' compensation package includes a grant of the stock options described on the left side of Table 21.3. You demand a similar package from Digital Organics, and they comply. In fact, they match Establishment Industries' options in every respect, as you can see on the right side of Table 21.3. (The two companies' current share prices just happen to be the same.) The only difference is that Digital Organics' shares are 50% more volatile than Establishment Industries' shares (36% annual standard deviation versus 24% for Establishment Industries).

	Establishment Industries	Digital Organics
Number of options	100,000	100,000
Exercise price	$25	$25
Maturity	5 years	5 years
Current share price	$22	$22
Share price volatility (standard deviation of return)	24%	36%

⟩TABLE 21.3   Which package of executive stock options would you choose?

If your job choice hinges on the value of the executive stock options, you should take the Digital Organics offer. The Digital Organics options are written on the more volatile asset and, therefore, are worth more.

We value these two stock-option packages in the next chapter.

• • • • •

**KEY
TAKEAWAYS**

• • • • •

- **Call and put options** There are two types of options. An American call is an option to buy an asset at a specified exercise price on or before a specified maturity date. Similarly, an American put is an option to sell the asset at a specified price on or before a specified date. European calls and puts are exactly the same except that they cannot be exercised *before* the maturity date.

- **Option value at maturity** When a call option matures, the owner will exercise it only if the stock price is greater than the exercise price. Therefore, at maturity, the value of a call is $\max(S - EX, 0)$. When a put matures, its value is $\max(EX - S, 0)$,

- **Put–call parity** In the case of European options, a strategy of buying a call and borrowing the present value of the exercise price provides an identical payoff to buying both the stock and a put. This basic relationship is called *put–call parity:*

$$C + PV(EX) = P + S$$

Calls and puts are the basic building blocks that can be combined to give any pattern of payoffs.

- **What determines option value?** Common sense tells us that the value of a call should depend on three things:

1. To exercise an option you have to pay the exercise price. Other things equal, the less you are obliged to pay, the better. *Therefore, the value of a call option increases with the asset price and declines with the exercise price.*

2. You do not have to pay the exercise price until you decide to exercise the option. Therefore, a call option gives you a free loan. The higher the rate of interest and the longer the time to maturity, the more this free loan is worth. *So the value of a call option increases with the interest rate and time to maturity.*

3. If the price of the asset falls short of the exercise price, you won't exercise the call option. You will, therefore, lose 100% of your investment in the option no matter how far the asset depreciates below the exercise price. On the other hand, the more the price rises *above* the exercise price, the more profit you will make. Therefore, the option holder does not lose from increased volatility if things go wrong, but gains if they go right. *Therefore, the value of a call increases with $\sigma^2 t$, that is the variance per period of the stock return multiplied by the number of periods to maturity.* Always remember that an option written on a risky (high-variance) asset is worth more than an option on a safe asset. It's easy to forget because, in most other financial contexts, increases in risk reduce present value.

See Further Readings for Chapter 22.

• • • • •

FURTHER READING

• • • • •

 Select problems are available in McGraw Hill's *Connect*. Please see the preface for more information.

PROBLEM SETS

1. **Vocabulary (S21-1)** Complete the following passage:

   A _____ option gives its owner the opportunity to buy a share at a specified price that is generally called the _____ price. A _____ option gives its owner the opportunity to sell a share at a specified price. Options that can be exercised only at maturity are called _____ options.

2. **Option payoffs (S21-1)** Note Figure 21.12 below. Match each diagram, (*a*) and (*b*), with one of the following positions:

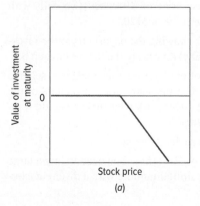

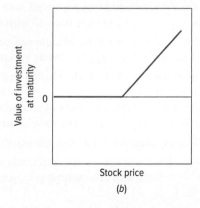

▶ **FIGURE 21.12**

See Problem 2.

- Call buyer.
- Call seller.
- Put buyer.
- Put seller.

3. **Option payoffs (S21-1)** Look again at Figure 21.12. It appears that the investor in panel *b* can't lose and the investor in panel *a* can't win. Is that correct? Explain. (*Hint:* Draw a profit diagram for each panel.)

4. **Option payoffs (S21-1)** What is a call option worth at maturity if (a) the stock price is zero? (b) the stock price is extremely high relative to the exercise price?

5. **Option payoffs (S21-1)** "The buyer of the call and the seller of the put both hope that the stock price will rise. Therefore the two positions are identical." Is the speaker correct? Illustrate with a payoff diagram.

6. **Option combinations (S21-2)** Suppose that you hold a share of stock and a put option on that share. What is the payoff when the option expires if (a) the stock price is below the exercise price? (b) the stock price is above the exercise price?

7. **Option combinations (S21-2)** Dr. Livingstone I. Presume holds £600,000 in East African gold stocks. Bullish as he is on gold mining, he requires absolute assurance that at least £500,000 will be available in six months to fund an expedition. Describe two ways for Dr. Presume to achieve this goal. There is an active market for puts and calls on East African gold stocks, and the rate of interest is 6% per year.

8. **Option combinations (S21-2)** Suppose you buy a one-year European call option on Wombat shares with an exercise price of $100 and sell a one-year European put option with the same exercise price. The current share price is $100, and the interest rate is 10%.

   a. Draw a payoff diagram showing the payoffs from your investments.

   b. How much will the combined position cost you? Explain.

9. **Option combinations (S21-2)** Suppose that Mr. Colleoni borrows the present value of $100, buys a six-month put option on share Y with an exercise price of $150, and sells a six-month put option on Y with an exercise price of $50.

   a. Draw a payoff diagram showing the payoffs when the options expire.

   b. Suggest two other combinations of loans, options, and the underlying stock that would give Mr. Colleoni the same payoffs.

10. **Option combinations (S21-2)** Option traders often refer to "straddles" and "butterflies." Here is an example of each:

    • *Straddle:* Buy one call with exercise price of $100 and simultaneously buy one put with exercise price of $100.

    • *Butterfly:* Simultaneously buy one call with exercise price of $100, sell two calls with exercise price of $110, and buy one call with exercise price of $120.

    Draw payoff diagrams for the straddle and butterfly, showing the payoffs from the investor's net position. Each strategy is a bet on variability. Explain briefly the nature of each bet.

11. **Option combinations (S21-2)** Ms. Higden has been offered yet another incentive scheme (see Section 21-2). She will receive a bonus of $500,000 if the share price at the end of the year is $120 or more; otherwise she will receive nothing. (Don't ask why anyone should want to offer such an arrangement. Maybe there's some tax angle.)

    a. Draw a payoff diagram illustrating the payoffs from such a scheme.

    b. What combination of options would provide these payoffs? (*Hint:* You need to buy a large number of options with one exercise price and sell a similar number with a different exercise price.)

12. **Option combinations (S21-2)** Discuss briefly the risks and payoffs of the following positions:

    a. Buy a share and a put option on the share.

    b. Buy a share.

    c. Buy a call.

   d. Buy a share and sell a call option on the share.

   e. Buy a bond.

   f. Buy a share, buy a put, and sell a call.

   g. Sell a put.

13. **Put–call parity (S21-2)** Which *one* of the following statements is correct?

   a. Value of put + present value of exercise price = value of call + share price.

   b. Value of put + share price = value of call + present value of exercise price.

   c. Value of put – share price = present value of exercise price – value of call.

   d. Value of put + value of call = share price – present value of exercise price.

   The correct statement equates the value of two investment strategies. Plot the payoffs to each strategy as a function of the share price. Show that the two strategies give identical payoffs.

14. **Put-call parity (S21-2)** A European call and put option have the same maturity. Both are at-the-money, so the share price equals the exercise price. The share does not pay a dividend. Which option should sell for the higher price? Explain.

15. **Put–call parity (S21-2)**

   a. If you can't sell a share short, you can achieve exactly the same final payoff by a combination of options and borrowing or lending. What is this combination?

   b. Now work out the mixture of stock and options that gives the same final payoff as investment in a risk-free loan.

16. **Put–call parity (S21-2)** The common stock of Triangular File Company is selling at $90. A 26-week call option written on Triangular File's stock is selling for $8. The call's exercise price is $100. The risk-free interest rate is 10% per year.

   a. Suppose that puts on Triangular stock are not traded, but you want to buy one. How would you do it?

   b. Suppose that puts *are* traded. What should a 26-week put with an exercise price of $100 sell for?

17. **Put–call parity (S21-2)** What is put–call parity and why does it hold? Could you apply the parity formula to a call and put with different exercise prices?

18. **Put–call parity (S21-2)** There is another strategy involving calls and borrowing or lending that gives the same payoffs as the strategy described in Problem 6. What is the alternative strategy?

19. **Put–call parity (S21-1)** It is possible to buy three-month call options and three-month puts on stock Q. Both options have an exercise price of $60 and both are worth $10. If the interest rate is 5% a year, what is the stock price? (*Hint:* Use put–call parity.)

20. **Put–call parity (S21-2)** In September 2020, Facebook's share price was about $250. A nine-month call on the stock, with an exercise price of $250, sold for $38. The risk-free interest rate was 2% a year. How much would you be willing to pay for a put on Facebook stock with the same maturity and exercise price? Assume that the Facebook options are European options. (*Note:* Facebook does not pay a dividend.)

21. **Option bounds (S21-3)** Pintail's share price is currently $200. A one-year *American* call option has an exercise price of $50 and is priced at $75. How would you take advantage of this great opportunity?

22. **Option values (S21-3)** How does the price of a call option respond to the following changes, other things equal? Does the call price go up or down?

   a. Stock price increases.

   b. Exercise price is increased.

c. Risk-free rate increases.

d. Expiration date of the option is extended.

e. Volatility of the stock price falls.

f. Time passes, so the option's expiration date comes closer.

23. **Option values (S21-3)** Respond to the following statements.

a. "I'm a conservative investor. I'd much rather hold a call option on a safe stock like Coca-Cola than a volatile stock like Facebook."

b. "I bought an American call option on Fava Farms stock, with an exercise price of $45 per share and three more months to maturity. Fava Farms' stock has skyrocketed from $35 to $55 per share, but I'm afraid it will fall back below $45. I'm going to lock in my gain and exercise my call right now."

24. **Option values (S21-3)** FX Bank has succeeded in hiring ace foreign exchange trader Lucinda Cable. Her remuneration package reportedly includes an annual bonus of 20% of the profits that she generates in excess of $100 million. Does Ms. Cable have an option? Does it provide her with the appropriate incentives?

25. **Option values (S21-3)** Look at actual trading prices of call options on stocks to check whether they behave as the theory presented in this chapter predicts. For example,

a. Follow several options as they approach maturity. How would you expect their prices to behave? Do they actually behave that way?

b. Compare two call options written on the same stock with the same maturity but different exercise prices.

c. Compare two call options written on the same stock with the same exercise price but different maturities.

26. **Option values (S21-3)** Is it more valuable to own an option to buy a portfolio of shares or to own a portfolio of options to buy each of the individual shares? Say briefly why.

27. **Option values (S21-3)** You've just completed a month-long study of energy markets and conclude that energy prices will be *much* more volatile in the next year than historically. Assuming you're right, what types of option strategies should you undertake? (*Note:* You can buy or sell options on oil-company shares or on the price of future deliveries of crude oil, natural gas, fuel oil, etc.)

28. **Option values (S21-3)** Table 21.4 lists some prices of options on common stocks (prices are quoted to the nearest dollar). The interest rate is 10% a year. Can you spot any mispricing? What would you do to take advantage of it?

)TABLE 21.4
Prices of options on common stocks (in dollars). See Problem 28.

Stock	Time to Exercise (months)	Exercise Price	Share Price	Put Price	Call Price
Drongo Corp.	6	$ 50	$80	$20	$52
Ragwort, Inc.	6	100	80	10	15
Wombat Corp.	3	40	50	7	18
Wombat Corp.	6	40	50	5	17
Wombat Corp.	6	50	50	8	10

CHALLENGE

29. **Option payoffs (S21-1)** Figure 21.13 shows some complicated payoff diagrams. Work out the combination of shares, bonds, and options that produces each of these positions.

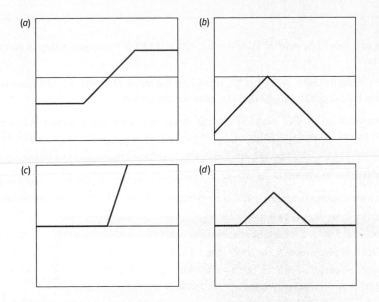

(a) (b) (c) (d)

▶ **FIGURE 21.13**

Some complicated payoff diagrams. See Problem 29.

30. **Option payoffs (S21-1)** Some years ago the Australian firm Bond Corporation sold a share in some land that it owned near Rome for A$110 million and as a result boosted its annual earnings by A$74 million. A television program subsequently revealed that the buyer was given a put option to sell its share in the land back to Bond for A$110 million and that Bond had paid A$20 million for a call option to repurchase the share in the land for the same price.

    a. What happens if the land is worth more than A$110 million when the options expire? What if it is worth less than A$110 million?

    b. Use payoff diagrams to show the net effect of the land sale and the option transactions.

    c. Assume a one-year maturity on the options. Can you deduce the interest rate?

    d. The television program argued that it was misleading to record a profit on the sale of land. What do you think?

31. **Option bounds (S21-3)** Problem 21 considered an arbitrage opportunity involving an American option. Suppose that this option was a European call. Show that there is a similar possible arbitrage profit.

32. **Option values (S21-3)** Three six-month call options are traded on Hogswill stock:

Exercise Price	Call Option Price
$ 90	$ 5
100	11
110	15

How would you make money by trading in Hogswill options? (*Hint:* Draw a graph with the option price on the vertical axis and the ratio of stock price to exercise price on the horizontal axis. Plot the three Hogswill options on your graph. Does this fit with what you know about how option prices should vary with the ratio of stock price to exercise price?) Now look at a financial website at options with the same maturity but different exercise prices. Can you find any money-making opportunities?

• • • • •

SOLUTIONS TO SELF-TEST QUESTIONS

21.1 The call would be worth $1,830 – $1,700 = $130 if exercised today. The call is in the money.

21.2 The option to sell a stock for $1,700 when the stock is worth $1,730 has no value. You would have lost the $33.32 that you paid for the option.

21.3 If you wish to protect yourself against Amazon's stock price falling below $1,700, you need to add to your shareholding a one-year put option with an exercise price of $1,700.

21.4 Put-call parity states that $S = C + \text{PV}(EX) - P$. Thus, the value of Upsilon stock is $20 + $105/1.05 – $15 = $105.

21.5 The lower bound is $\max(S - EX, 0) = \max(60 - 80, 0)$. The lower bound is $0.

21.6

	Stock Price Falls	Stock Price Rises
Payoff from put option on X	$100 – $90 = $10	$0
Payoff from put option on Y	$100 – $70 = $30	$0

• • • • •

FINANCE ON THE WEB

Go to **finance.yahoo.com.** Check out the delayed quotes for Amazon options for different exercise prices and maturities. Take the mean of the bid and ask prices.

a. Confirm that higher exercise prices mean lower call prices and higher put prices.

b. Confirm that longer maturity means higher prices for both puts and calls.

c. Choose an Amazon put and call with the same exercise price and maturity. Confirm that put–call parity holds (it may do so only approximately if some of the prices are out-of-date). (*Note:* You will have to use an up-to-date risk-free interest rate.)

CHAPTER

22

Valuing Options

In Chapter 21, we introduced you to call and put options. Call options give the owner the right to buy an asset at a specified exercise price; put options give the right to sell. We also took the first step toward understanding how options are valued. We saw that the value of a call option depends on five variables:

1. The higher price of the asset, the more valuable an option to buy it.

2. The lower the price that you must pay to exercise the call, the more valuable the option.

3. You do not need to pay the exercise price until the option expires. This delay is most valuable when the interest rate is high.

4. If the stock price is below the exercise price at maturity, the call is valueless regardless of whether the price is $1 below or $100 below. However, for every dollar that the stock price rises above the exercise price, the option holder gains an additional dollar. Thus, the value of the call option increases with the volatility of the stock price.

5. Finally, a long-term option is more valuable than a short-term option. A distant maturity delays the point at which the holder needs to pay the exercise price and increases the chance of a large jump in the stock price before the option matures.

In this chapter, we show how these variables can be combined into an exact option-valuation model—a formula we can plug numbers into and get a definite answer.

The most efficient way to value most options is to use a computer program. But in this chapter, we will work through some simple examples by hand. We do so because unless you understand the basic principles behind option valuation, you are likely to make mistakes in setting up an option problem, and you won't know how to interpret the computer program's answer and explain it to others.

In Chapter 21, we looked at the put and call options on Amazon stock. In this chapter, we stick with these examples and show you how to value the Amazon options. But remember *why* you need to understand option valuation. It is not to make a quick buck trading on an options exchange. It is because many capital budgeting and financing decisions have options embedded in them. We discuss a variety of these options in subsequent chapters.

Section 22-1 A simple option-valuation model

To illustrate the idea behind option valuation, we start by assuming that Amazon shares can take on only two possible future values. We use this example to show that the trick to valuing an option is to devise a combination of the underlying stock and a bank loan that exactly replicates the payoffs on the option. We also show that you get exactly the same result by pretending that investors are risk-neutral and discounting the cash flows that investors would require in this make-believe world. We explain why the two methods are equivalent.

Section 22-2 The binomial method for valuing options

In Section 22-2, we describe the useful binomial method of option valuation, which breaks the option's life into a number of short time periods, in which the stock can take on only one of two possible values.

Section 22-3 The Black–Scholes formula
We next introduce the Black–Scholes formula that assumes stock prices are *continually* changing, and we give four examples of how the formula can help solve practical problems.

Section 22-4 Early exercise and dividend payments
Up until now, we have disregarded the complications that arise when a stock pays a dividend. And we ignored the fact that the value of an American option is not always equal to that of a European one. Section 22-4 addresses these factors.

• • • • •

22-1   A Simple Option-Valuation Model

Why Discounted Cash Flow Won't Work for Options

For many years, economists searched for a practical formula to value options until Fischer Black and Myron Scholes finally hit upon the solution. Later we will show you what they found, but first we should explain why the search was so difficult.

Our standard procedure for valuing an asset is to (1) figure out expected cash flows and (2) discount them at the opportunity cost of capital. Unfortunately, this is not practical for options. The first step is messy but feasible; however, finding *the* opportunity cost of capital is impossible because the risk of an option changes every time the stock price moves.

We will see that when you buy a call, you are effectively borrowing to buy shares. Thus, an option is always riskier than the underlying stock. It has a higher beta and a higher standard deviation of returns. How much riskier the option is depends on the stock price relative to the exercise price. A call option that is deep in the money (stock price greater than exercise price) is almost certain to be exercised, and is therefore safer than a call that is out of the money (stock price less than exercise price). Thus, a stock price increase raises the option's expected payoff *and* reduces its risk. When the stock price falls, the option's payoff falls *and* its risk increases. That is why the expected rate of return investors demand from an option changes day by day, or hour by hour, every time the stock price moves.

We repeat the general rule: The higher the stock price is relative to the exercise price, the safer is the call option, although the option is always riskier than the stock. The option's risk changes every time the stock price changes.

22.1 Self-Test

A one-year call option on Hartness stock has an exercise price of $50. Another one-year call on the stock has an exercise price of $75. Which of the two options is more risky? Is each of them more or less risky than the underlying stock, or can't you say?

Constructing Option Equivalents from Common Stocks and Borrowing

If you've digested what we've said so far, you can appreciate why options are hard to value by standard discounted-cash-flow formulas and why a rigorous option-valuation technique eluded economists for many years. The breakthrough came when Black and Scholes exclaimed, "Eureka! We have found it![1] The trick is to set up an *option equivalent* by a combination of an investment in common stock and borrowing. The net cost of buying the option equivalent must equal the value of the option."

We'll show you how this works with a simple numerical example. We'll travel back to January 2020 and consider a six-month call option on Amazon stock with an exercise price of

---

[1]We do not know whether Black and Scholes, like Archimedes, were sitting in bathtubs at the time.

$1,830. We'll pick a day when Amazon stock was also trading at $1,830, so that this option is *at the money.* The short-term, risk-free interest rate was $r = 2\%$ for six months, or just over 4% a year.

To keep the example as simple as possible, we assume that Amazon stock can do only two things over the option's six-month life. The price could rise by 20% to $1,830 \times 1.20 = \$2,196$. Alternatively, it could fall by the same proportion to $1,830 \div 1.20 = \$1,525$. The upward move is sometimes written as $u = 1.2$, and the downward move as $d = 1/u = 1/1.2 = 0.833$. Note that we are not assuming that the up and down moves are equally likely, a point that we will return to later.

Warning: We will round some of our calculations slightly. So, if you are following along with your calculator, don't worry if your answers differ in the last decimal place.

If Amazon's stock price falls to $1,525, the call option will be worthless, but if the price rises to $2,196, the option will be worth $2,196 - 1,830 = \$366$. The possible payoffs to the option are therefore as follows:

	Stock Price = $1,525	Stock Price = $2,196
1 call option	$0	$366

Now compare these payoffs with what you would get if you bought 0.54545 Amazon share and borrowed the present value of $831.82 from the bank[2]:

	Stock Price = $1,525	Stock Price = $2,196
0.54545 share	$831.82	$1,197.82
Repayment of loan + interest	−831.82	−831.82
Total payoff	$ 0	$ 366.00

Notice that the payoffs from the levered investment in the stock are identical to the payoffs from the call option. Therefore, the law of one price tells us that both investments must have the same value today:

$$\text{Value of call} = \text{ value of 0.54545 shares} - \text{ value of bank loan}$$
$$= 0.54545 \times \$1,830 - 831.82/1.02 = \$998.18 - \$815.51 = \$182.67$$

Presto! You've valued a call option.

To value the Amazon option, we borrowed money and bought stock in such a way that we exactly replicated the payoff from a call option. This is called a **replicating portfolio.** The number of shares needed to replicate one call is called the **hedge ratio or option delta (δ).** In our Amazon example, one call is replicated by a levered position in 0.54545 share. The option delta is, therefore, 0.54545.

We can state the valuation procedure more formally. If the stock price S can rise by a factor of u to S_u or fall by a factor $d = 1/u$ to S_d, then the value of a call is equal to the value of a portfolio composed of an investment of δS in the stock, and debt of B, where the option delta (δ) is given by

$$\delta = \frac{\text{spread of possible option prices}}{\text{spread of possible share prices}} = \frac{C_u - C_d}{S_u - S_d} \qquad \textbf{(22.1)}$$

---

[2]The exact number of shares to buy is $180/330 = 0.54545$, as explained below.

where C_u and C_d are the values of the call option in the "up" and "down" states.[3] The debt is

$$B = \frac{1}{1+r} \times \frac{uC_d - dC_u}{u - d} \qquad (22.2)$$

Plugging in the numbers from our earlier example gives

$$\delta = \frac{366 - 0}{2,196 - 1,525} = 0.54545$$

$$B = \frac{1}{1.02} \times \frac{1.2 \times 0 - 0.833 \times 366}{1.2 - 0.833} = -815.51$$

Value of call $= \delta S + B = 0.54545 \times 1,830 - 815.51 = \$182.67$

Notice that B is negative. Borrowing is equivalent to a negative investment in the risk-free asset.

The replicating portfolio consisted of an investment of just under \$1,000 in the share, which we largely financed by a loan of about \$815. Thus, a call option on a share is equivalent to financing the purchase of the share with borrowed money. That is why the call option is always riskier than the share and why we say that call options create leverage.

This is an extremely important point that does not apply just to options on shares. For example, whenever a company acquires an option to expand in the future, it is creating leverage. That leverage does not appear on the company's balance sheet, but it is nonetheless real for that. We return to this point in Section 23-6.

EXAMPLE 22.1 • Replicating a call option

Over the next year, Foxday shares could either double or halve from their current price of \$200. You own a one-year call option with an exercise price of \$300. The interest rate is 10%. Can you devise a package of borrowing and investment in the share that gives identical payoffs to the option?

If the share price halves the option is worthless; if it doubles, the option is worth $400 - 300 = \$100$. So the option delta is:

$$\delta = \frac{100 - 0}{400 - 100} = 0.3333$$

To replicate the call make an investment in the shares of $\delta \times$ stock price $= 0.33 \times \$200 = \$66.67$ and borrow the present value of $(uC_d - dC_u)/(u - d) = (2 \times 0 - 0.5 \times 100)/(2 - 0.5) = \$33.33$. Therefore, the value of the call is $C = 66.67 - 33.33/1.1 = \$36.36$.

• • • • •

22.2 Self-Test

Look again at Example 22.1. Draw up a table showing that the package of the investment in the share and the loan produces the same payoffs as the call option regardless of whether the share price doubles or halves.

Risk-Neutral Valuation

We stated earlier that the Amazon call option should sell for \$182.67. Notice why this is so. If the option price is higher than \$182.67, you could make a certain profit by buying 0.54545

---

[3]Notice that delta here is the derivative of the option price with respect to the share price.

share of stock, selling a call option, and borrowing the present value of $831.82. Similarly, if the option price is less than $182.67, you could make an equally certain profit by selling 0.54545 share, buying a call, and lending the balance. In either case, there would be an arbitrage opportunity.[4]

If there's a possible arbitrage profit, everyone scurries to take advantage of it. So when we said that the option price had to be $182.67 or there would be an arbitrage opportunity, we did not need to know anything about investor attitudes to risk. Lions and chickens would all jostle each other in the rush to realize a possible arbitrage profit. Thus, the option price *cannot* depend on whether investors embrace risk or are risk-averse. This means that we can make whatever assumption about risk attitudes is most convenient. The most helpful assumption is that investors are risk-neutral because then we can avoid estimating the discount rate for the option and instead just discount at the risk-free rate.

If we can *pretend* that investors are *indifferent* about risk, there is an alternative way to value the option. Simply work out the expected future value of the option in such a world, and discount it back at the risk-free interest rate to give the current value.[5] Let us check that this method gives the same answer.

If investors are indifferent to risk, the expected return on the stock must be equal to the risk-free rate of interest:

$$\text{Expected return on Amazon stock} = 2.0\% \text{ per six months}$$

We know that Amazon stock can either rise by 20% to $2,196 or fall by 16.667% to $1,525. We can, therefore, calculate the probability of a price rise in our hypothetical risk-neutral world. Call this probability p^*. Then

$$\begin{aligned}\text{Expected return} &= [p^* \times 20\%] \\ &\quad + [(1 - p^*) \times (-16.667\%)] \\ &= 2.0\%\end{aligned}$$

Therefore,

$$p^* = 0.50909 \text{ or } 50.909\%$$

Notice that this is *not* the *true* probability that Amazon stock will rise. Investors that dislike risk will require a higher expected return than the risk-free interest rate from Amazon stock. Therefore, the true probability is greater than 0.50909.

The general formula for calculating the risk-neutral probability of a rise in value is

$$p^* = \frac{(1 + \text{interest rate}) - \text{downside change}}{\text{upside change} - \text{downside change}} = \frac{(1 + r) - d}{u - d} \tag{22.3}$$

In the case of Amazon:

$$p^* = \frac{1.02 - 0.8333}{1.20 - 0.8333} = 0.50909$$

We know that if the stock price rises, the call option will be worth $366; if it falls, the call will be worth nothing. Therefore, if investors are risk-neutral, the expected future value of the call option is

$$\begin{aligned}[p^* \times 366] &+ [(1 - p^*) \times 0] \\ &= (0.50909 \times 366) + (0.49091 \times 0) \\ &= \$186.33\end{aligned}$$

---

[4]Of course, you don't get seriously rich by dealing in 0.54545 share. But if you multiply each of our transactions by a million, it begins to look like real money.

[5]Notice that this allows us to sidestep the problem that the risk of the option changes every time the stock price changes. A risk-neutral investor is content to earn the interest rate regardless of the investment's risk.

And the *current* value of the call is

$$\frac{\text{Expected future value}}{1 + \text{interest rate}} = \frac{186.33}{1.02} = \$182.67$$

BEYOND THE PAGE

Try It! The
one- and two-
step binomial
models

mhhe.com/brealey14e

Exactly the same answer that we got earlier!

We now have two ways to calculate the value of an option:

1. Find the combination of stock and loan that replicates an investment in the option. Since the two strategies give identical payoffs in the future, they must sell for the same price today.

2. Pretend that investors do not care about risk so that the expected return on the stock is equal to the interest rate. Calculate the expected future value of the option in this hypothetical *risk-neutral* world, and discount it at the risk-free interest rate. This idea may seem familiar to you. In Chapter 9, we showed how you can value an investment either by discounting the expected cash flows at a risk-adjusted discount rate or by adjusting the expected cash flows for risk and then discounting these **certainty equivalent** flows at the risk-free interest rate. We have just used this second method to value the Amazon option. The certainty equivalent cash flows on the stock and option are the cash flows that would be expected in a risk-neutral world.

EXAMPLE 22.2 ● Calculating the risk-neutral probability of a rise

Over the next year, Foxday shares could either double or halve from their current price of $200. The interest rate is 10%. What is the risk-neutral probability that the share price will rise?

Using the formula for the probability of a rise, gives

$$p^* = \frac{(1 + r) - d}{u - d} = \frac{1.1 - 0.5}{2.0 - 0.5} = 0.40$$

We can check that if the probability of a rise is 40%, then the expected return is equal to the interest rate:

$$0.40 \times 100\% + 0.60 \times -50\% = 10\%$$

● ● ● ● ●

22.3 Self-Test

Look back at Example 22.2. Suppose that a one-year call option on Foxday has an exercise price of $300. Given that the risk-neutral probability of a stock price rise is 40%, what is the expected value of the call at the end of the year? What is its value today?

Valuing the Amazon Put Option

Valuing the Amazon call option may well have seemed like pulling a rabbit out of a hat. To give you a second chance to watch how it is done, we will use the same method to value another option—this time, the six-month Amazon put option with a $1,830 exercise price.[6] We continue to assume that the stock price will either rise to $2,196 or fall to $1,525.

---

[6]When valuing *American* put options, you need to recognize the possibility that it will pay to exercise early. We discuss this complication later in the chapter, but it is unimportant for valuing the Amazon put and we ignore it here.

If Amazon's stock price rises to $2,196, the option to sell for $1,830 will be worthless. If the price falls to $1,525, the put option will be worth $1,830 − 1,525 = $305. Thus, the payoffs to the put are

	Stock Price = $1,525	Stock Price = $2,196
1 put option	$305	$0

We start by calculating the option delta using the formula that we presented previously. If P_u and P_d are the prices of the put option in the "up" and "down" states

$$\delta = \frac{\text{spread of possible option prices}}{\text{spread of possible stock prices}} = \frac{P_u - P_d}{S_u - S_d} = \frac{0 - 305}{2,196 - 1,525}$$
$$= -0.45455$$

Notice that the delta of a put option is equal to the delta of the equivalent call minus 1.0. It is always negative; that is, you need to *sell* delta shares of stock to replicate the put. In the case of the Amazon put, you can replicate the option payoffs by *selling* 0.45455 Amazon share and *lending* the present value of $998.18. Since you have sold the share short, you will need to lay out money at the end of six months to buy it back, but you will have money coming in from the loan. Your net payoffs are exactly the same as the payoffs you would get if you bought the put option:

	Stock Price = $1,525	Stock Price = $2,196
Sale of 0.45455 share	−$693.18	−$998.18
Repayment of loan + interest	+ 998.18	+ 998.18
Total payoff	$305.00	$ 0

Since the two investments have the same payoffs, they must have the same value:

$$\text{Value of put} = -(0.45455) \text{ shares} + \text{value of bank loan}$$
$$= -(0.45455) \times 1,830 + 998.18/1.02 = \$146.79$$

Valuing the Put Option by the Risk-Neutral Method

Valuing the Amazon put option with the risk-neutral method is a cinch. We already know that the probability of a rise in the stock price is 0.50909. Therefore, the expected future value of the put option in a risk-neutral world is

$$[p* \times 0] + [(1 - p*) \times 305]$$
$$= (0.50909 \times 0) + (0.49091 \times \$305)$$
$$= \$149.73$$

And therefore the *current* value of the put is

$$\frac{\text{Expected future value}}{1 + \text{interest rate}} = \frac{149.73}{1.02} = \$146.79$$

The two methods give the same answer.

22.4 Self-Test

Suppose that the possible rise in Amazon's share price is $u = 2.0$ and d changes correspondingly to $1/u = 0.5$. Would you expect the value of the call to be higher or lower? What about the value of the put?

The Relationship between Call and Put Prices

We pointed out earlier that for European options there is a simple relationship between the values of the call and the put.[7]

$$\text{Value of put} = \text{value of call} + \text{present value of exercise price} - \text{share price}$$

Since we had already calculated the value of the Amazon call, we could also have used this relationship to find the value of the put:

$$\text{Value of put} = 182.67 + \frac{1,830}{1.02} - 1,830 = \$146.79$$

Everything checks.

22.5 Self-Test

True or false?
   a. An option is always riskier than the underlying stock.
   b. You can replicate a call option by borrowing to buy delta shares of stock.
   c. The risk-neutral model of option valuation will give the correct option value only if investors are risk-neutral.

22-2   The Binomial Method for Valuing Options

The essential trick in pricing any option is to set up a package of investments in the stock and the loan that will exactly replicate the payoffs from the option. If we can price the stock and the loan, then we can also price the option. Equivalently, we can pretend that investors are risk-neutral, calculate the expected payoff on the option in this fictitious risk-neutral world, and discount by the rate of interest to find the option's present value.

These concepts are completely general, but the example in the last section used a simplified version of what is known as the **binomial method.** The method starts by reducing the possible changes in the next period's stock price to two, an "up" move and a "down" move.

This assumption that there are just two possible prices for Amazon stock at the end of six months is clearly fanciful. We could make the Amazon problem a trifle more realistic by assuming that there are two possible price changes in each three-month period. This would give a wider variety of six-month prices. And there is no reason to stop at three-month periods. We could go on to take shorter and shorter intervals, with each interval showing two possible changes in Amazon's stock price and giving an even wider selection of prices by month 6.

We illustrate this in Figure 22.1. The top diagram shows our starting assumption: just two possible prices at the end of six months. Moving down, you can see what happens when there are two possible price changes every three months. This gives three possible stock prices when the option matures. In Figure 22.1*c*, we have gone on to divide the six-month period into 26 weekly periods, in each of which the price can make one of two small moves. The distribution of prices at the end of six months is now looking much more realistic. As we subdivide the life of the option into shorter and shorter periods, the distribution of possible stock price changes approaches a lognormal distribution.

---

[7]*Reminder:* This formula applies only when the two options have the same exercise price and exercise date.

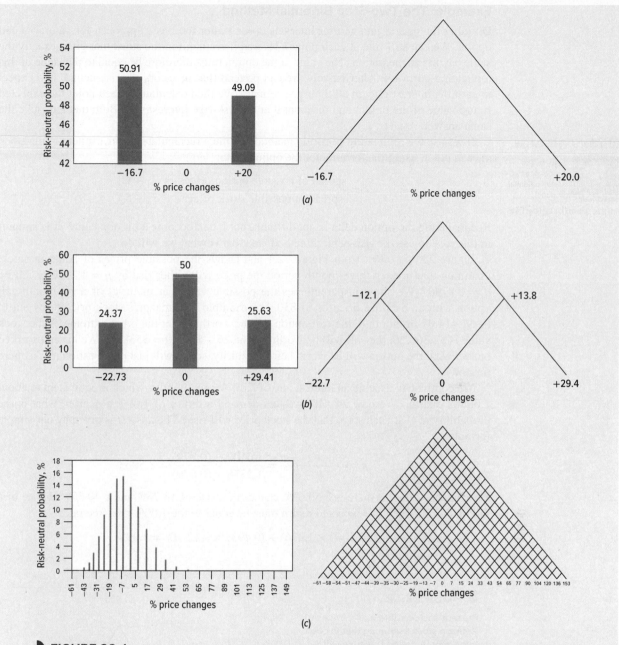

▶ **FIGURE 22.1**   This figure shows the possible six-month price changes for Amazon stock assuming that the stock makes a single up or down move each six months (panel *a*); two moves, one every three months (panel *b*); or 26 moves, one every week (panel *c*). Beside each tree we show a histogram of the possible six-month price changes, assuming investors are risk-neutral.

We could continue in this way to chop the period into shorter and shorter intervals, until eventually we would reach a situation in which the stock price is changing continuously and there is a continuum of possible future stock prices. We demonstrate first with our simple two-step case in Figure 22.1*b*. Then we work up to the situation where the stock price is changing continuously. Don't panic; that won't be as complicated as it sounds.

Example: The Two-Step Binomial Method

Dividing the period into shorter intervals doesn't alter the basic approach for valuing a call option. We can still find at each point a levered investment in the stock that gives exactly the same payoffs as the option. The value of the option must therefore be equal to the value of this replicating portfolio. Alternatively, we can pretend that investors are risk-neutral and expect to earn the interest rate on all their investments. We then calculate at each point the expected future value of the option and discount it at the risk-free interest rate. Both methods give the same answer.

If we use the replicating-portfolio method, we must recalculate the investment in the stock at each point, using the formula for the option delta:

$$\delta = \frac{\text{spread of possible option prices}}{\text{spread of possible stock prices}} = \frac{C_u - C_d}{S_u - S_d}$$

Recalculating the option delta is not difficult, but it can become a bit of a chore. It is simpler in this case to use the risk-neutral method, and that is what we will do.

Figure 22.2 is taken from Figure 22.1 and shows the possible prices of Amazon stock, assuming that in each three-month period the price will either rise by $u = 1.1376$ or fall by $d = 0.8790$.[8] We show in parentheses the possible values at maturity of a six-month call option with an exercise price of $1,830. For example, if Amazon's stock price turns out to be $1,414.07 in month 6, the call option will be worthless; at the other extreme, if the stock value is $2,368.26, the call will be worth $2,368.26 − $1,830 = $538.26. We haven't worked out yet what the option will be worth before maturity, so we will just put question marks there for now.

We continue to assume an interest rate of 2.0% for six months, which is equivalent to about 1.00% a quarter. We now ask: If investors demand a return of 1.00% a quarter, what is the probability ($p*$) at each stage that the stock price will rise? The answer is given by our simple formula:

$$p* = \frac{(1 + r) - d}{u - d} = \frac{1.0100 - (0.879)}{1.1376 - (0.879)} = 0.5063$$

We can check that, if there is a 50.63% chance of a rise of 13.76% and a 49.37% chance of a fall of 12.10%, then the expected return must be equal to the 1.00% risk-free rate:

$$(0.5063 \times 13.76) + (0.4937 \times -12.10) = 1.00\%$$

▶ **FIGURE 22.2**

Present and possible future prices of Amazon stock assuming that in each three-month period the price will either rise by $u = 1.1376$ or fall by $d = 0.8790$. Figures in parentheses show the corresponding values of a six-month call option with an exercise price of $1,830. The interest rate is just under 1% a quarter.

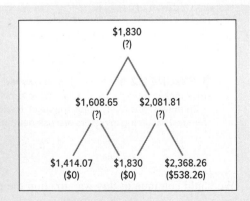

---

[8]We explain shortly why we picked these figures.

Option Value in Month 3   Now we can find the possible option values in month 3. Suppose that by the end of three months, the stock price has risen to $2,081.81. In that case, investors know that when the option finally matures in month 6, the option value will be either $0 or $538.26. We can therefore use our risk-neutral probabilities to calculate the expected option value at month 6:

$$\text{Expected value of call in month 6} = (p^* \times 538.26) + ((1 - p^*) \times 0)$$
$$= (0.5063 \times 538.26) + (0.4937 \times 0)$$
$$= \$272.52$$

And the value in month 3 is 272.52/1.01 = $269.84.

What if the stock price falls to $1,608.65 by month 3? In that case, the option is bound to be worthless at maturity. Its expected value is zero, and its value at month 3 is also zero.

Option Value Today   We can now get rid of two of the question marks in Figure 22.2. Figure 22.3 shows that if the stock price in month 3 is $2,081.81, the option value is $269.84, and if the stock price is $1,608.65, the option value is zero. It only remains to work back to the option value today.

There is a 50.63% chance that the stock price will rise in the first three months in which case the option will be worth $269.84. And there is a 49.37% chance that the stock price will fall, in which case the option will be valueless. So the expected value in month 3 is

$$(0.5063 \times 269.84) + (0.4937 \times 0) = \$136.62$$

And the value today is 136.62/1.01 = $135.27.

The General Binomial Method

Moving to two steps when valuing the Amazon call probably added extra realism. But there is no reason to stop there. We could go on, as in Figure 22.1, to chop the period into smaller and smaller intervals. We could still use the binomial method to work back from the final date to the present. Of course, it would be tedious to do the calculations by hand but simple to do so with a computer program.

Since a stock can usually take on an almost limitless number of future values, the binomial method gives a more realistic and accurate measure of the option's value if we work with a large number of subperiods. But that raises an important question. How do we pick sensible figures for the up and down changes in value? For example, why did we pick figures of +13.76% and −12.1% when we revalued Amazon's option with two subperiods?

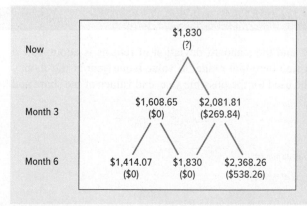

Now			$1,830 (?)		
Month 3		$1,608.65 ($0)		$2,081.81 ($269.84)	
Month 6	$1,414.07 ($0)		$1,830 ($0)		$2,368.26 ($538.26)

▶ FIGURE 22.3

Present and possible future prices of Amazon stock. Figures in parentheses show the corresponding values of a six-month call option with an exercise price of $1,830.

)TABLE 22.1   As the number of steps is increased, you must adjust the range of possible changes in the value of the asset to keep the same standard deviation. But you will get increasingly close to the Black–Scholes value of the Amazon call option.

Note: The standard deviation is $\sigma = 0.25784$.

	Change per Interval (%)		
Number of Steps	Upside	Downside	Estimated Option Value
1	+20.00	−16.67	$182.67
2	+13.76	−12.10	135.27
6	+7.73	−7.17	144.95
26	+3.64	−3.51	149.07
	Black–Scholes value =		150.33

Fortunately, there is a neat little formula that relates the up and down changes to the standard deviation of stock returns:

$$1 + \text{upside change} = u = e^{\sigma\sqrt{h}}$$
$$1 + \text{downside change} = d = 1/u$$

(22.4)

where

e = base for natural logarithms = 2.718
σ = standard deviation of (continuously compounded) future stock returns
h = interval as fraction of a year

When we said that Amazon's stock price could either rise by 20% or fall by 16.667% over six months ($h = 0.5$), our figures were consistent with a figure of 25.784% for the standard deviation of annual returns[9]:

$$1 + \text{upside change (6-month interval)} = u = e^{0.25784\sqrt{0.5}} = 1.2$$
$$1 + \text{downside change} = d = 1/u = 1/1.2 = 0.833$$

To work out the equivalent upside and downside changes when we divide the period into two three-month intervals ($h = 0.25$), we use the same formula:

$$1 + \text{upside change (3-month interval)} = u = e^{0.25784\sqrt{0.25}} = 1.1376$$
$$1 + \text{downside change} = d = 1/u = 1/1.1376 = 0.879$$

BEYOND THE PAGE

Try it! The general binomial model

mhhe.com/brealey14e

The center columns in Table 22.1 show the equivalent up and down moves in the value of Amazon stock if we chop the period into 6 monthly or 26 weekly periods, and the final column shows the effect on the estimated option value. (We explain the Black–Scholes value shortly.)

EXAMPLE 22.3 • Choosing a value for u and d

X shares are currently priced at $100, and the standard deviation of returns is about 40% a year. Suppose we wish to use the two-step binomial model to value a one-year at-the-money call option on X. What values should be used for the possible year-end values of the share and the option?

---

[9]To find the standard deviation given u, we turn the formula around:

$$\sigma = \log(u)/\sqrt{h}$$

where log = natural logarithm. In our example,

$$\sigma = \log(1.20)/\sqrt{(0.5)} = 0.1823/\sqrt{(0.5)} = 0.25784.$$

We need to divide the one-year option maturity into two six-month periods. To calculate the possible upside and downside changes in the share price, we use the formula for u and d, where the interval h is 0.5 years:

$$u = e^{\sigma\sqrt{h}} = e^{0.4\sqrt{0.5}} = 1.327$$
$$d = 1/u = 1/1.327 = 0.754$$

The following figure shows the possible share prices at each six-month period, and in brackets, the possible option values at the end of the year:

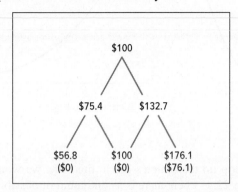

The Binomial Method and Decision Trees

Calculating option values by the binomial method is basically a process of solving decision trees. You start at some future date and work back through the tree to the present. Eventually, the possible cash flows generated by future events and actions are folded back to a present value.

Is the binomial method *merely* another application of decision trees, a tool of analysis that you learned about in Chapter 10? The answer is no, for at least two reasons. First, option pricing theory is absolutely essential for discounting within decision trees. Discounting expected cash flows doesn't work within decision trees for the same reason that it doesn't work for puts and calls. As we pointed out in Section 22-1, there is no single, constant discount rate for options because the risk of the option changes as time and the price of the underlying asset change. There is no single discount rate inside a decision tree because, if the tree contains meaningful future decisions, it also contains options. The market value of the future cash flows described by the decision tree has to be calculated by option pricing methods.

Second, option theory gives a simple, powerful framework for describing complex decision trees. For example, suppose that you have the option to abandon an investment. The complete decision tree would overflow the largest classroom whiteboard. But now that you know about options, the opportunity to abandon can be summarized as "an American put." Of course, not all real problems have such easy option analogies, but we can often approximate complex decision trees by some simple package of assets and options. A custom decision tree may get closer to reality, but the time and expense may not be worth it. Most men buy their suits off the rack even though a custom-made Armani suit would fit better and look nicer.

22-3   The Black–Scholes Formula

Look back at Figure 22.1, which showed what happens to the distribution of possible Amazon stock price changes as we divide the option's life into a larger and larger number of increasingly small subperiods. You can see that the distribution of price changes becomes increasingly smooth.

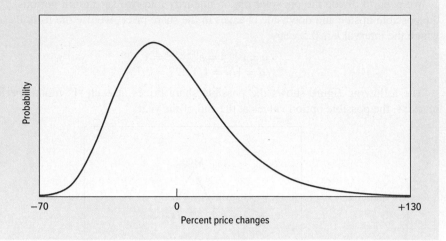

▶ **FIGURE 22.4**

As the option's life is divided into more and more subperiods, the distribution of possible stock price changes approaches a lognormal distribution.

(y-axis) Probability

(x-axis) Percent price changes

−70   0   +130

If we continued to chop up the option's life in this way, we would eventually reach the situation shown in Figure 22.4, where there is a continuum of possible stock price changes at maturity. Figure 22.4 is an example of a lognormal distribution. The lognormal distribution is often used to summarize the probability of different stock price changes.[10] It has a number of good commonsense features. For example, it recognizes the fact that the stock price can never fall by more than 100% but that there is some, perhaps small, chance that it could rise by much more than 100%.

Subdividing the option life into indefinitely small slices does not affect the principle of option valuation. We could still replicate the call option by a levered investment in the stock, but we would need to adjust the degree of leverage continuously as time went by. Calculating option value when there is an infinite number of subperiods may sound a hopeless task. Fortunately, Black and Scholes derived a formula that performs this calculation.[11] It is a complicated-looking formula, but on closer acquaintance you will find it useful and not as daunting as you might think. The formula is

Value of call option (C) = [delta × share price] − [bank loan]

$$[N(d_1) \times S] - [N(d_2) \times PV(EX)]$$
(22.5)

where

$$d_1 = \frac{\log[S/PV(EX)]}{\sigma \sqrt{t}} + \frac{\sigma \sqrt{t}}{2}$$

$$d_2 = d_1 - \sigma \sqrt{t}$$

$N(d)$ = cumulative normal probability density function[12]

---

[10]When we first looked at the distribution of stock price changes in Chapter 7, we depicted these changes as normally distributed. We pointed out at the time that this is an acceptable approximation for very short intervals, but the distribution of changes over longer intervals is better approximated by the lognormal.

[11]The pioneering articles on options are F. Black and M. Scholes, "The Pricing of Options and Corporate Liabilities," *Journal of Political Economy* 81 (May–June 1973), pp. 637–654; and R. C. Merton, "Theory of Rational Option Pricing," *Bell Journal of Economics and Management Science* 4 (Spring 1973), pp. 141–183.

[12]That is, $N(d)$ is the probability that a normally distributed random variable $\tilde{x}$ will be less than or equal to d. $N(d_1)$ in the Black–Scholes formula is the option delta. Thus, the formula tells us that the value of a call is equal to an investment of $N(d_1)$ in the common stock less borrowing of $N(d_2) \times PV(EX)$.

EX = exercise price of option; PV(EX) is calculated by discounting at the risk-free interest
   rate r_f

t = number of periods to exercise date

S = price of stock now

σ = standard deviation per period of (continuously compounded) rate of return on stock

Notice that the value of the call in the Black–Scholes formula has the same properties that
we identified in Chapter 21. It increases with the level of the stock price S and decreases
with the present value of the exercise price PV(EX), which in turn depends on the interest rate and time to maturity. It also increases with the time to maturity and the stock's
variability ($\sigma\sqrt{t}$).

To derive their formula, Black and Scholes assumed that there is a continuum of stock
prices; therefore, to replicate an option, investors must continuously adjust their holding
in the stock.[13] Of course, this is not literally possible, but even so, the formula performs
remarkably well in the real world, where stocks trade only intermittently and prices jump
from one level to another. The Black–Scholes model has also proved very flexible; it can
be adapted to value options on a variety of assets such as foreign currencies, bonds, and
commodities.

It is not surprising, therefore, that it has been extremely influential and has become the
standard model for valuing options. Every day, dealers on the options exchanges use this
formula to make huge trades. These dealers are not for the most part trained in the formula's
mathematical derivation; they just use a computer or a specially programmed calculator to
find the value of the option.

Using the Black–Scholes Formula

The Black–Scholes formula may look difficult, but it is very straightforward to apply. Let us
practice using it to value the Amazon call.

Here are the data that you need:

- Price of stock now = S = 1,830

- Exercise price = EX = 1,830

- Standard deviation of continuously compounded annual returns = σ = 0.25784

- Years to maturity = t = 0.5

- Interest rate per annum = r_f = 2.0% for six months or about 4% per annum[14]

Remember that the Black–Scholes formula for the value of a call is

$$C = [N(d_1) \times S] - [N(d_2) \times PV(EX)]$$

where

$d_1 = \log[S/PV(EX)]/\sigma\sqrt{t} + \sigma\sqrt{t}/2$

$d_2 = d_1 - \sigma\sqrt{t}$

N(d) = cumulative normal probability function

There are three steps to using the formula to value the Amazon call.

---

[13]The important assumptions of the Black–Scholes formula are that (1) the price of the underlying asset follows a lognormal random
walk, (2) investors can adjust their hedge continuously and costlessly, (3) the risk-free rate is known, and (4) the underlying asset does
not pay dividends.

[14]When valuing options, it is more common to use continuously compounded rates to calculate PV(EX) (see Section 2-4). As long
as the two rates are equivalent, both methods give the same answer, so why do we bother to mention the subject here? It is simply
because most computer programs for valuing options call for a continuously compounded rate. If you enter an annually compounded
rate by mistake, the error will usually be small, but you can waste a lot of time trying to trace it.

Step 1   Calculate d_1 and d_2. This is just a matter of plugging numbers into the formula (noting that "log" means *natural* log):

$$d_1 = \log[S/PV(EX)]/\sigma\sqrt{t} + \sigma\sqrt{t}/2$$
$$= \log[1{,}830/(1{,}830/1.02)]/(0.25784 \times \sqrt{0.5}) + 0.25784 \times \sqrt{0.5}/2$$
$$= 0.1998$$
$$d_2 = d_1 - \sigma\sqrt{t} = 0.1998 - 0.25784 \times \sqrt{0.5} = 0.0175$$

Step 2   Find $N(d_1)$ and $N(d_2)$. $N(d_1)$ is the probability that a normally distributed variable will be less than d_1 standard deviations above the mean. If d_1 is large, $N(d_1)$ is close to 1.0 (i.e., you can be almost certain that the variable will be less than d_1 standard deviations above the mean). If d_1 is zero, $N(d_1)$ is 0.5 (i.e., there is a 50% chance that a normally distributed variable will be below the average).

The simplest way to find $N(d_1)$ is to use the Excel function NORMSDIST. For example, if you enter NORMSDIST(0.1998) into an Excel spreadsheet, you will see that there is a 0.5792 probability that a normally distributed variable will be less than 0.1998 standard deviations above the mean.

Again you can use the Excel function to find $N(d_2)$. If you enter NORMSDIST (0.0175) into an Excel spreadsheet, you should get the answer 0.5070. In other words, there is a probability of 0.5070 that a normally distributed variable will be less than 0.0175 standard deviations *below* the mean.

BEYOND THE PAGE

Try It! The Black–Scholes model

mhhe.com/brealey14e

Step 3   Plug these numbers into the Black–Scholes formula. You can now calculate the value of the Amazon call:

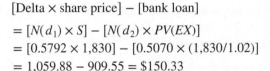

$$[\text{Delta} \times \text{share price}] - [\text{bank loan}]$$
$$= [N(d_1) \times S] - [N(d_2) \times PV(EX)]$$
$$= [0.5792 \times 1{,}830] - [0.5070 \times (1{,}830/1.02)]$$
$$= 1{,}059.88 - 909.55 = \$150.33$$

In other words, you can replicate the Amazon call option by investing \$1,059.88 in the company's shares and borrowing \$909.55. Subsequently, as time passes and the stock price changes, you may need to borrow a little more to invest in the stock or you may need to sell some of your stock to reduce your borrowing.

22.6 Self-Test

What information do you need to apply the Black–Scholes formula?

How Black–Scholes Values Vary with the Stock Price

Suppose you repeat the calculations for the Amazon call for a wide range of stock prices. The result is shown in Figure 22.5. You can see that the option values lie along an upward-sloping curve that starts its travels in the bottom left-hand corner of the diagram. As the stock price increases, the option value rises and gradually becomes parallel to the lower bound for the option value. This is exactly the shape we deduced in Chapter 21 (see Figure 21.9).

The height of this curve depends on share volatility, time to maturity, and the rate of interest. For example, if the risk of Amazon stock had suddenly doubled, the curve shown in Figure 22.5 would rise at every possible stock price. This is shown by the upper curve in Figure 22.5.

The slope of the curve measures the change in the value of the option for a small change in the price of the stock. Since the call option is equivalent to a leveraged position in δ shares, the value of the option changes by δ times the change in the price of the stock. Thus, δ is

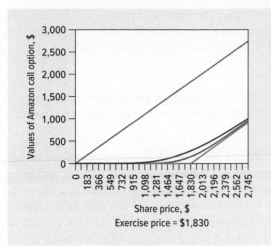

▶ **FIGURE 22.5**

The lower curved line shows the value of the Amazon call option for different levels of Amazon's stock price. The upper curve shows the effect of a doubling in Amazon's risk on values of the call option.

the *slope* of the curve in Figure 22.5. Notice that this slope is always positive. It is close to zero when the stock price is very low. Since the option is unlikely to be exercised, the option holder is unlikely to benefit from stock price rises. The slope approaches 1.0 when the call is deep-in-the-money. Since the option in this case will almost certainly be exercised, the option owner effectively owns the stock (less the present value of the exercise price) and so benefits one-for-one from stock price increases.

The Risk of an Option

How risky is the Amazon call option? We have seen that you can exactly replicate a call by a combination of risk-free borrowing and an investment in the stock. So the risk of the option must be the same as the risk of this replicating portfolio. We know that the beta of any portfolio is simply a weighted average of the betas of the separate holdings. So the beta of the option is just a weighted average of the betas of the investments in the loan and the stock. Thus

$$\beta_c = \frac{\delta S}{\delta S + B} \times \beta_S + \frac{B}{\delta S + B} \times \beta_B \qquad (22.6)$$

where δS is the amount invested in the share and B is the (negative) amount invested in the risk-free loan.

On past evidence, the beta of Amazon stock is $\beta_{stock} = 1.5$; the beta of a risk-free loan is $\beta_{loan} = 0$. You are investing \$1,059.88 in the stock and –909.55 in the loan. (Notice that the investment in the loan is negative—you are *borrowing* money.) Therefore, the beta of the option is $\beta_{option} = (1,059.88 \times 1.5 - 909.55 \times 0)/(1,059.88 - 909.55) = 10.58$. Notice that because a call option is equivalent to a levered position in the stock, it is always riskier than the stock itself. In Amazon's case, the option is about 7 times as risky as the stock and 10 times as risky as the market. As time passes and the price of Amazon stock changes, the risk of the option will also change.

The Black–Scholes Formula and the Binomial Method

Look back at Table 22.1, where we used the binomial method to calculate the value of the Amazon call. Notice that as the number of intervals is increased, the values that you obtain from the binomial method begin to approach the Black–Scholes value of \$150.33.

The Black–Scholes formula recognizes a continuum of possible outcomes. This is usually more realistic than the limited number of outcomes assumed in the binomial method. The formula is also more accurate and quicker to use than the binomial method. So why use

BEYOND THE PAGE

Calculating the risk of corporate debt

mhhe.com/brealey14e

the binomial method at all? The answer is that there are many circumstances in which you cannot use the Black–Scholes formula, but the binomial method will still give you a good measure of the option's value. We will look at several such cases in Section 22-4.

Some Practical Examples

To illustrate the principles of option valuation, we focused on the example of Amazon's options. But financial managers turn to the Black–Scholes model to estimate the value of a variety of different options. Here are four examples.

BEYOND THE PAGE

The perfect payday

mhhe.com/brealey14e

Executive Stock Options   Executive stock options are often an important part of compensation. For many years, companies were able to avoid reporting the cost of these options in their annual statements. However, they must now treat options as an expense just like salaries and wages, so they need to estimate the value of all new options that they have granted. For example, in 2019 Netflix reported that it had awarded its CEO options with a value of $37.4 million. How did it come up with this figure? It just used the Black–Scholes model assuming a standard deviation of about 40%.[15]

Speaking of executive stock options, you can now use the Black–Scholes formula to value the option packages you were offered in Section 21-3 (see Table 21.3). Table 22.2 calculates the value of the options from the safe-and-boring Establishment Industries at $5.26 each. The options from risky-and-glamorous Digital Organics are worth $7.40 each. Congratulations.

Warrants   When Owens Corning emerged from bankruptcy in 2006, the debtholders became the sole owners of the company. But the old stockholders were not left entirely empty-handed. They were given warrants to buy the new common stock at any point in the next seven years for $45.25 a share. Because the stock in the restructured firm was worth about $30 a share, the stock needed to appreciate by 50% before the warrants would be worth exercising. However, this option to buy Owens Corning stock was clearly valuable, and shortly after the warrants started trading, they were selling for $6 each. You can be sure that before shareholders were handed these, all the parties calculated the value of the warrants under different assumptions about the stock's volatility. The Black–Scholes model is tailor-made for this purpose.[16]

⟩TABLE 22.2   Using the Black–Scholes formula to value the executive stock options for Establishment Industries and Digital Organics (see Table 21.3).

	Establishment Industries	Digital Organics
Stock price (S)	$22	$22
Exercise price (EX)	$25	$25
Interest rate (r_f)	0.04	0.04
Maturity in years (t)	5	5
Standard deviation (σ)	0.24	0.36
$d_1 = \log[S/PV(EX)]/\sigma\sqrt{t} + \sigma\sqrt{t}/2$	0.3955	0.4873
$d_2 = d_1 - \sigma\sqrt{t}$	−0.1411	−0.3177
Call value $= [N(d_1) \times S] - [N(d_2) \times PV(EX)]$	$5.26	$7.40

---

[15]The option holders may not have agreed with the Black–Scholes valuation. First, the options were less valuable to the holder if they created substantial undiversifiable risk. Second, if the holder planned to quit the company in the next few years, he may have been liable to forfeit the options. For a discussion of these issues see J. I. Bulow and J. B. Shoven, "Accounting for Stock Options," *Journal of Economic Perspectives* 19 (Fall 2005), pp. 115–134.

[16]Postscript: Unfortunately, Owens Corning's stock price never reached $45 and the warrants expired worthless.

Portfolio Insurance   Your company's pension fund owns an $800 million diversified portfolio of common stocks that moves closely in line with the market index. The pension fund is currently fully funded, but you are concerned that if it falls by more than 20%, it will start to be underfunded. Suppose that your bank offers to insure you for one year against this possibility. What would you be prepared to pay for this insurance? Think back to Section 21-2 (Figure 21.5), where we showed that you can shield against a fall in asset prices by buying a protective put option. In the present case, the bank would be selling you a one-year put option on U.S. stock prices with an exercise price 20% below their current level. You can use the Black–Scholes formula to value that put. (You may have to adjust for dividends, but we'll leave that to the next section.)

BEYOND THE PAGE

The Chinese warrants bubble

mhhe.com/brealey14e

Implied Volatilities   So far, we have used our option pricing model to calculate the value of an option given the standard deviation of the asset's returns. Sometimes it is useful to turn the problem around and ask what the option price is telling us about the asset's volatility. For example, the Chicago Board Options Exchange trades options on several market indexes. As we write this, the Standard and Poor's 500 Index is about 4200, while a six-month at-the-money call on the index is priced at 195. If the Black–Scholes formula is correct, then an option value of 195 makes sense only if investors believe that the standard deviation of index returns is about 19% a year.[17]

The Chicago Board Options Exchange regularly publishes the implied volatility on the Standard and Poor's index, which it terms the VIX (see the nearby box on the "fear index"). There is an active market in the VIX. For example, suppose you feel that the implied volatility is implausibly low. Then you can "buy" the VIX at the current low price and hope to "sell" it at a profit when implied volatility has increased.

You may be interested to compare the current implied volatility that we calculated earlier with Figure 22.6, which shows past measures of implied volatility for the Standard and Poor's index. Notice the sharp increase in investor uncertainty at the height of the credit crunch in 2008 and again at the time of the COVID-19 pandemic. This uncertainty showed up in the price that investors were prepared to pay for options.

BEYOND THE PAGE

The option smile

mhhe.com/brealey14e

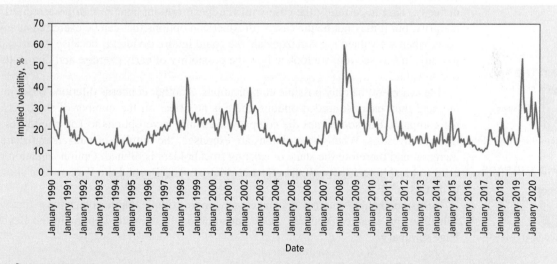

▶ **FIGURE 22.6**   VIX measures the standard deviation of market returns implied by prices of options on the S&P 500 Index.

Source: finance.yahoo.com.

---

[17]In calculating the implied volatility, we need to allow for the dividends paid on the shares. We explain how to take these into account in the next section.

FINANCE IN PRACTICE

The Fear Index*

❭ The Market Volatility Index, or VIX, measures the volatility that is implied by near-term Standard & Poor's 500 Index options and is therefore an estimate of expected *future* market volatility over the next 30 calendar days. Implied market volatilities have been calculated by the Chicago Board Options Exchange (CBOE) since January 1986, though in its current form, the VIX dates back only to 2003.

Investors regularly trade volatility. They do so by buying or selling VIX futures and options contracts. Since these were introduced by the CBOE, combined trading activity in the two contracts has grown to more than 100,000 contracts per day, making them two of the most successful innovations ever introduced by the exchange.

Because VIX measures investor uncertainty, it has been dubbed the "fear index." The market for index options tends to be dominated by equity investors who buy index puts when they are concerned about a potential drop in the stock market. Any subsequent decline in the value of their portfolio is then offset by the increase in the value of the put option. The more that investors demand such insurance, the higher the price of index put options. Thus, VIX is an indicator that reflects the cost of portfolio insurance.

Between January 1990 and April 2021, the VIX has averaged 19.6%, almost identical to the long-term level of market volatility that we cited in Chapter 7. The high point for the index was in March 2020 when the VIX reached 85%,** but there have been several other spikes, for example, in 2008 during the financial crisis.

---

*For a review of the VIX index, see R. E. Whaley, "Understanding the VIX," *Journal of Portfolio Management* 35 (Spring 2009), pp. 98–105.

**On October 19, 1987 (Black Monday), the VIX closed at 150. Fortunately, the market volatility returned fairly rapidly to less exciting levels.

22-4 Early Exercise and Dividend Payments

So far, our discussion of option values has assumed that investors hold the option until maturity. That is certainly the case with European options that *cannot* be exercised before maturity, but it may not be the case with American options that can be exercised at any time. Also, when we valued the Amazon call, we could ignore dividends because Amazon did not pay any. In this section, we look at how the possibility of early exercise and dividends affect option value.

BEYOND THE PAGE

Dilution

mhhe.com/brealey14e

These are not the only possible complications. Another concerns dilution. When investors buy and then exercise traded options, there is no effect on the number of shares issued by the company. But sometimes the company itself may give options to key employees or sell them to investors. When these options are exercised, the number of outstanding shares *does* increase, and therefore the stake of existing stockholders is diluted. Option valuation models need to be able to cope with the effect of dilution. The Beyond the Page feature shows how to do this.

BEYOND THE PAGE

The option menagerie

mhhe.com/brealey14e

Occasionally also you may encounter some more complex options than those that we have valued in this chapter. You can check out some of these exotic options in the Beyond the Page summary.

American Calls—No Dividends Unlike European options, American options can be exercised any time. However, we know that in the absence of dividends, the value of a call option increases with time to maturity. So, if you exercised an American call option early, you would needlessly reduce its value. Because an American call should not be exercised before maturity, its value is the same as that of a European call, and the Black–Scholes model applies to both options.

European Puts—No Dividends   If we wish to value a European put, we can use the put–call parity formula from Chapter 21:

$$\text{Value of put} = \text{value of call} - \text{value of stock} + \text{PV(exercise price)}$$

American Puts—No Dividends   It can sometimes pay to exercise an American put before maturity in order to reinvest the exercise price. For example, suppose that immediately after you buy an American put, the share price falls to zero. In this case, there is no advantage to holding onto the option because it *cannot* become more valuable. It is better to exercise the put and start to earn interest on the exercise money. Thus, an American put is always more valuable than a European put.

Because the Black–Scholes formula does not allow for early exercise, it cannot be used to value an American put exactly, though it will generally provide a good approximation. But you can use the step-by-step binomial method as long as you check at each point whether the option is worth more dead than alive and then use the higher of the two values.

European Calls and Puts on Dividend-Paying Shares   Part of the share value comprises the present value of dividends. The option holder is not entitled to dividends. Therefore, when using the Black–Scholes model to value a European option on a dividend-paying stock, you should reduce the price of the stock by the present value of the dividends to be paid before the option's maturity.

Dividends don't always come with a big label attached, so look out for instances where the asset holder gets a benefit and the option holder does not. For example, when you buy foreign currency, you can invest it to earn interest; but if you own an option to buy foreign currency, you miss out on this income. Therefore, when valuing an option to buy foreign currency, you need to deduct the present value of this foreign interest from the current price of the currency.[18]

American Calls on Dividend-Paying Stocks   We have seen that when the stock does not pay dividends, an American call option is *always* worth more alive than dead. By holding on to the option, you not only keep your option open, but also earn interest on the exercise money. Even when there are dividends, you should never exercise early if the dividend you gain is less than the interest you lose by having to pay the exercise price early. However, if the dividend is sufficiently large, you might want to capture it by exercising the option just before the ex-dividend date.

The only general method for valuing an American call on a dividend-paying stock is to use the step-by-step binomial method. In this case, you must check at each stage to see whether the option is more valuable if exercised just before the ex-dividend date than if held for at least one more period.

---

[18]For example, just suppose that it costs $2 to buy £1 and that this pound can be invested to earn interest of 5%. An investor who holds a one-year option to buy a pound rather than owning the pound itself misses out on interest of $0.05 \times \$2 = \$0.10$. So, before using the Black–Scholes formula to value an option to buy sterling, you must adjust the current price of sterling: Adjusted price of sterling = current price − PV(interest) = $2 − 0.10/1.05 = \$1.905$.

- **Creating a replicating portfolio** We introduced the basic principles of option valuation by considering a call option on a stock that could take on one of two possible values at the option's maturity. The trick is to construct a package of the stock and a loan that would provide exactly the same payoff as the option *regardless* of whether the stock price rises or falls. Therefore, regardless of the investor's attitude to risk, the value of the option must be the same as the value of this replicating portfolio.

- **Risk-neutral valuation** An equivalent way to value an option is to pretend that investors are risk-neutral, in which case the expected return on an asset is equal to the interest rate. You then need to calculate the expected future value of the option in this imaginary risk-neutral world and discount this figure at the interest rate to find the option's present value.

- **The binomial method** The general binomial method adds realism by dividing the option's life into subperiods in each of which the stock price can make one of two possible moves. You can still replicate the call by working back from the option's maturity and calculating its value at each step. Alternatively, you can use the risk-neutral method.

- **The Black–Scholes model** The Black–Scholes formula calculates the option's value when the stock price is constantly changing and takes on a continuum of possible future values.

- **Calculating option risk** An option can be replicated by a package of the underlying asset and a risk-free loan. Therefore, we can measure the risk of any option by calculating the risk of this portfolio. Naked options (i.e., options that are held on their own) are often substantially more risky than the asset itself.

- **Early exercise and dividends** When valuing options in practical situations, there are a number of features to look out for. If they are European options, you cannot exercise before the maturity date. However, if they are American options you can. The ability to exercise early may introduce complications. You may also need to recognize that the option value is reduced by the fact that the holder is not entitled to any dividend or other income on the underlying asset. This chapter has included a number of equations. Here are the more important ones:

- **Replicating portfolio for a call** $C = \delta S + B$, where

$$\delta = \frac{C_u - C_d}{S_u - S_d} \tag{22.1}$$

and

$$B = \frac{1}{1+r} \times \frac{uC_d - dC_u}{u - d} \tag{22.2}$$

- **Risk-neutral probability**

$$p^* = \frac{(1+r) - d}{u - d} \tag{22.3}$$

- **Values for u and d**

$$u = e^{\sigma\sqrt{h}} \tag{22.4}$$
$$d = 1/u$$

- **Black–Scholes formula**

$$C = [N(d_1) \times S] - [N(d_2) \times PV(EX)] \tag{22.5}$$

where

$$d_1 = \frac{\log[S/PV(EX)]}{\sigma\sqrt{t}} + \frac{\sigma\sqrt{t}}{2}$$
$$d_2 = d_1 - \sigma\sqrt{t}$$

Three readable articles about the Black–Scholes model are:

F. Black, "How We Came up with the Option Formula," *Journal of Portfolio Management* 15 (1989), pp. 4–8.

F. Black, "The Holes in Black–Scholes," *RISK Magazine* 1 (1988), pp. 27–29.

F. Black, "How to Use the Holes in Black–Scholes," *Journal of Applied Corporate Finance* 1 (Winter 1989), pp. 67–73.

There are a number of good books on option valuation. They include:

J. Hull, *Options, Futures and Other Derivatives,* 10th ed. (Cambridge, UK: Pearson, 2017).

R. L. McDonald, *Derivatives Markets,* 3rd ed. (Cambridge, UK: Pearson, 2012).

P. Wilmott, *Paul Wilmott on Quantitative Finance,* 2nd ed. (New York: John Wiley & Sons, 2006).

FURTHER READING

Select problems are available in McGraw Hill's *Connect*. Please see the preface for more information.

PROBLEM SETS

1. **One-step binomial model (S22-1)** Over the coming year, Ragwort's stock price will halve to $50 from its current level of $100 or it will rise to $200. The one-year interest rate is 10%.

   a. What is the delta of a one-year call option on Ragwort stock with an exercise price of $100?

   b. What is the amount of the loan in the replicating portfolio?

   c. Use the replicating-portfolio method to value this call.

   d. In a risk-neutral world, what is the probability that Ragwort stock will rise in price?

   e. Use the risk-neutral method to check your valuation of the Ragwort option.

   f. If someone told you that in reality there is a 60% chance that Ragwort's stock price will rise to $200, would you change your view about the value of the option? Explain.

2. **One-step binomial model (S22-1)** Imagine that Amazon's stock price will either rise by 33.3% or fall by 25% over the next six months (see Section 22-1). Recalculate the value of the call option (exercise price = $1,830) using (a) the replicating portfolio method and (b) the risk-neutral method. Explain intuitively why the option value rises from the value computed in Section 22-1.

3. **Binomial model (S22-1)** The share price of Heavy Metal (HM) changes only once a month: Either it goes up by 20% or it falls by 16.7%. Its price now is $40. The interest rate is 1% per month.

   a. What is the value of a one-month call option with an exercise price of $40?

   b. What is the option delta?

   c. Show how the payoffs of this call option can be replicated by buying HM's stock and borrowing.

   d. What is the value of a two-month call option with an exercise price of $40?

   e. What is the option delta of the two-month call over the first one-month period?

4. **One-step binomial model (S22-1)** Suppose a stock price can go up by 15% or down by 13% over the next year. You own a one-year put on the stock. The interest rate is 10%, and the current stock price is $60.

   a. What exercise price leaves you indifferent between holding the put or exercising it now?

   b. How does this break-even exercise price change if the interest rate is increased?

5. **Two-step binomial model (S22-2)** Take another look at our two-step binomial trees for Amazon in Figure 22-2. Use the replicating-portfolio or risk-neutral method to value six-month call and put options with an exercise price of $1,500. Assume the Amazon stock price is $1,830.

6. **Two-step binomial model (S22-2)** Buffelhead's stock price is $220 and could halve or double in each six-month period (equivalent to a standard deviation of 98%). A one-year call option on Buffelhead has an exercise price of $165. The interest rate is 21% a year.

   a. What is the value of the Buffelhead call?

   b. Now calculate the option delta for the second six months if (1) the stock price rises to $440 and (2) the stock price falls to $110.

   c. How does the call option delta vary with the level of the stock price? Explain intuitively why.

   d. Suppose that in month 6, the Buffelhead stock price is $110. How, at that point, could you replicate an investment in the stock by a combination of call options and risk-free lending? Show that your strategy does indeed produce the same returns as those from an investment in the stock.

7. **Two-step binomial model (S22-2)** Suppose that you have an option that allows you to sell Buffelhead stock (see Problem 6) in month 6 for $165 *or* to buy it in month 12 for $165. What is the value of this unusual option?

8. **Two-step binomial model (S22-2)** Johnny Jones's high school derivatives homework asks for a binomial valuation of a 12-month call option on the common stock of the Overland Railroad. The stock is now selling for $45 per share and has an annual standard deviation of 24%. Johnny first constructs a binomial tree like Figure 22-2, in which stock price moves up or down every six months. Then he constructs a more realistic tree, assuming that the stock price moves up or down once every three months, or four times per year.

   a. Construct these two binomial trees.

   b. How would these trees change if Overland's standard deviation were 30%? (*Hint:* Make sure to specify the right up and down percentage changes.)

9. **Option delta (S22-1–S22-2)**

   a. Can the delta of a call option be greater than 1.0? Explain.

   b. Can it be less than zero?

   c. How does the delta of a call change if the stock price rises?

   d. How does it change if the risk of the stock increases?

10. **Option delta (S22-1–S22-2)** Suppose you construct a risk-free investment by buying a share of stock and selling a call option. As the share price changes, the option delta changes, and you will need to adjust your position. You can minimize the cost of adjustments if changes in the stock price have only a small effect on the option delta. Construct an example to show whether the option delta is likely to vary more if you sell in-the-money options, at-the-money options, or out-of-the-money options.

BEYOND THE PAGE

Try it! The Black–Scholes model

mhhe.com/brealey14e

11. **Black–Scholes model (S22-3)**

   a. Use the Black–Scholes formula to find the value of the following call option.

      i. Time to expiration one year.

      ii. Standard deviation 40% per year.

      iii. Exercise price $50.

      iv. Stock price $50.

      v. Interest rate 4% (effective annual yield).

b. Now recalculate the value of this call option, but use the following parameter values. Each change should be considered independently.

   i. Time to expiration two years.

   ii. Standard deviation 50% per year.

   iii. Exercise price $60.

   iv. Stock price $60.

   v. Interest rate 6%.

c. In which case did increasing the value of the input *not* increase your calculation of option value?

12. **Black–Scholes model (S22-3)** Use the Black–Scholes formula to value the following options:

a. A call option written on a stock selling for $60 per share with a $60 exercise price. The stock's standard deviation is 6% per month. The option matures in three months. The risk-free interest rate is 1% per month.

b. A put option written on the same stock at the same time, with the same exercise price and expiration date.

Now for each of these options, find the combination of stock and risk-free asset that would replicate the option.

13. **Binomial and Black–Scholes models (S22-2-S22-3)** The current price of United Carbon (UC) stock is $200. The standard deviation is 22.3% a year, and the interest rate is 21% a year. A one-year call option on UC has an exercise price of $180.

a. Use the Black–Scholes model to value the call option on UC. You may find it helpful to use the spreadsheet version of the model, accessible through the Beyond the Page feature.

b. Use the formula given in Section 22-2 to calculate the up and down moves that you would use if you valued the UC option with the one-period binomial method. Now value the option by using that method.

c. Recalculate the up and down moves and revalue the option by using the two-period binomial method.

d. Use your answer to part (c) to calculate the option delta (1) today, (2) next period if the stock price rises, and (3) next period if the stock price falls. Show at each point how you would replicate a call option with a levered investment in the company's stock.

14. **Option risk (S22-3)** "A call option is always riskier than the stock it is written on." True or false? How does the risk of an option change when the stock price changes?

15. **Option risk (S22-3)**

a. In Section 22-3, we calculated the risk (beta) of a six-month call option on Amazon stock with an exercise price of $1,830. Now repeat the exercise for a similar option with an exercise price of $1,500. Does the risk rise or fall as the exercise price is reduced?

b. Now calculate the risk of a *one-year* call on Amazon stock with an exercise price of $1,500. Does the risk rise or fall as the maturity of the option lengthens?

16. **Warrants (S22-3)** Use the Black–Scholes program from the Beyond the Page feature to value the Owens Corning warrants described in Section 22-3. The standard deviation of Owens Corning stock was 41% a year and the interest rate when the warrants were issued was 5%. Owens Corning did not pay a dividend. Ignore the problem of dilution.

17. **Pension fund insurance (S22-3)** Use the Black–Scholes program to estimate how much you should be prepared to pay to insure the value of your pension fund portfolio for the coming year. Make reasonable assumptions about the volatility of the market and use current interest rates. Remember to subtract the present value of likely dividend payments from the current level of the market index.

18. **American options (S22-4)** For which of the following options *might* it be rational to exercise before maturity? Explain briefly why or why not.

    a. American put on a non-dividend-paying stock.

    b. American call—the dividend payment is $5 per annum, the exercise price is $100, and the interest rate is 10%.

    c. American call—the interest rate is 10%, and the dividend payment is 5% of future stock price. (*Hint:* The dividend depends on the stock price, which could either rise or fall.)

19. **American options (S22-4)** The price of Moria Mining stock is $100. During each of the next two six-month periods the price may either rise by 25% or fall by 20% (equivalent to a standard deviation of 31.5% a year). At month 6, the company will pay a dividend of $20. The interest rate is 10% per six-month period. What is the value of a one-year American call option with an exercise price of $80? Now recalculate the option value, assuming that the dividend is equal to 20% of the with-dividend stock price.

20. **American options (S22-4)** Suppose that you own an American put option on Buffelhead stock (see Problem 6) with an exercise price of $220.

    a. Would you ever want to exercise the put early?

    b. Calculate the value of the put.

    c. Now compare the value with that of an equivalent European put option.

21. **American options (S22-4)** Recalculate the value of the Buffelhead call option (see Problem 6), assuming that the option is American and that at the end of the first six months the company pays a dividend of $25. (Thus, the price at the end of the year is either double or half the ex-dividend price in month 6.) How would your answer change if the option was European?

22. **American options (S22-4)** The current price of the stock of Mont Tremblant Air is C$100. During each six-month period, it will either rise by 11.1% or fall by 10% (equivalent to an annual standard deviation of 14.9%). The interest rate is 5% per six-month period.

    a. Calculate the value of a one-year European put option on Mont Tremblant's stock with an exercise price of C$102.

    b. Recalculate the value of the Mont Tremblant put option, assuming that it is an American option.

23. **American options (S22-4)** Other things equal, which of these American options are you most likely to want to exercise early?

    a. A put option on a stock with a large dividend or a call on the same stock.

    b. A put option on a stock that is selling below exercise price or a call on the same stock.

    c. A put option when the interest rate is high or the same put option when the interest rate is low.

    Illustrate your answer with examples.

24. **Option exercise (S22-4)** Is it better to exercise a call option on the with-dividend date or on the ex-dividend date? How about a put option? Explain.

CHALLENGE

25. **Option delta (S22-1)** Use the put-call parity formula (see Section 21-2) and the one-period binomial model to show that the option delta for a put option is equal to the option delta for a call option minus 1.

26. **Option delta (S22-2)** Show how the option delta changes as the stock price rises relative to the exercise price. Explain intuitively why this is the case. (What happens to the option delta if the exercise price of an option is zero? What happens if the exercise price becomes indefinitely large?)

27. **Option risk (S22-3)** Calculate and compare the risk (betas) of the following investments: (a) a share of Amazon stock; (b) a one-year call option on Amazon; (c) a one-year put option; (d) a portfolio consisting of a share of Amazon stock and a one-year put option; (e) a portfolio consisting of a share of Amazon stock, a one-year put option, and the sale of a one-year call. In each case, assume that the exercise price of the option is $1,830, which is also the current price of Amazon stock.

28. **Option risk (S22-3)** In Section 22-1, we used a simple one-step model to value two Amazon options each with an exercise price of $1,830. We showed that the call option could be replicated by borrowing $815.51 and investing $998.18 in 0.54545 shares of Amazon stock. The put option could be replicated by selling short $693.18 of Amazon stock and lending $988.18.

    a. If the beta of Amazon stock is 1.5, what is the beta of the call according to the one-step model?

    b. What is the beta of the put?

    c. Suppose that you were to buy one call and invest the present value of the exercise price in a bank loan. What would be the beta of your portfolio?

    d. Suppose instead that you were to buy one share and one put option of Amazon. What would be the beta of your portfolio now?

    e. Your answers to parts (c) and (d) should be the same. Explain.

29. **Option maturity (S22-3)** Some corporations have issued *perpetual* warrants. Warrants are call options issued by a firm, allowing the warrant holder to buy the firm's stock.

    a. What does the Black–Scholes formula predict for the value of an infinite-lived call option on a non-dividend-paying stock? Explain the value you obtain. (*Hint:* What happens to the present value of the exercise price of a long-maturity option?)

    b. Do you think this prediction is realistic? If not, explain carefully why. (*Hints:* What about dividends? What about bankruptcy?)

30. **Dividends (S22-4)** Your company has just awarded you a generous stock option scheme. You suspect that the board will either decide to increase the dividend or announce a stock repurchase program. Which do you secretly hope they will decide? Explain. (You may find it helpful to refer back to Chapter 15.)

● ● ● ● ●

SOLUTIONS TO SELF-TEST QUESTIONS

22.1 Both options are more risky than the share. The stock price relative to the exercise price is higher for the option with the $50 exercise price. This is the less risky option. (An option with a zero exercise price is essentially the same as a share and therefore has the same risk as the share.)

22.2

	Stock Price = $100	Stock Price = $400
0.3333 share	$33.33	$133.33
Repayment of loan + interest	−$33.33	−$33.33
Total payoff	$ 0	$100.00

22.3 If the stock price falls, the option is worthless; if it rises, the option value is $400 − $300 = $100. With a 40% probability of a rise, the expected value of the option at the end of the year is 0.40 × $100 = $40. Its value today is $40/1.10 = $36.36.

22.4 A higher value for u implies greater variability, which increases the upside payoff for both the call and the put, without changing the downside. The value of both options increases.

22.5   a. True;
     b. true;
     c. false.

22.6   a. Share price;
     b. exercise price;
     c. standard deviation of continuously compounded returns;
     d. time to maturity;
     e. interest rate.

● ● ● ● ●

FINANCE ON THE WEB

Look at the stocks listed in Table 7.3. Pick at least three stocks, and find call option prices for each of them on **finance.yahoo.com.** Now find monthly adjusted prices and calculate the standard deviation from the monthly returns using the Excel function STDEV.P. Convert the standard deviation from monthly to annual units by multiplying by the square root of 12.

   a. For each stock, pick a traded option with a maturity of about six months and an exercise price equal to the current stock price. Use the Black–Scholes formula and your estimate of standard deviation to value each option. If the stock pays dividends, remember to subtract from the stock price the present value of any dividends that the option holder will miss out on. How close is your calculated value to the traded price of the option?

   b. Your answer to part (a) will not exactly match the traded price. Experiment with different values for the standard deviation until your calculated values match the prices of the traded options as closely as possible. What are these implied volatilities? What do the implied volatilities say about investors' forecasts of future volatility?

MINI-CASE ● ● ● ●

Bruce Honiball's Invention

It was another disappointing year for Bruce Honiball, the manager of retail services at the Gibb River Bank. Sure, the retail side of Gibb River was making money, but it didn't grow at all in 2019. Gibb River had plenty of loyal depositors but few new ones. Bruce had to figure out some new product or financial service—something that would generate some excitement and attention.

Bruce had been musing on one idea for some time. How about making it easy *and safe* for Gibb River's customers to put money in the stock market? How about giving them the upside of investing in equities—at least *some* of the upside—but none of the downside?

Bruce could see the advertisements now:

> How would you like to invest in Australian stocks completely risk-free? You can with the new Gibb River Bank *Equity-Linked Deposit.* You share in the good years; we take care of the bad ones.
>
> Here's how it works. Deposit A$100 with us for one year. At the end of that period, you get back your A$100 *plus* A$5 for every 10% rise in the value of the Australian All Ordinaries stock index. But, if the market index falls during this period, the Bank will still refund your A$100 deposit in full.
>
> There's no risk of loss. Gibb River Bank is your safety net.

Bruce had floated the idea before and encountered immediate skepticism, even derision: "Heads they win, tails we lose—is that what you're proposing, Mr. Honiball?" Bruce had no ready answer.

Could the bank really afford to make such an attractive offer? How should it invest the money that would come in from customers? The bank had no appetite for major new risks.

Bruce has puzzled over these questions for the past two weeks but has been unable to come up with a satisfactory answer. He believes that the Australian equity market is currently fully valued, but he realizes that some of his colleagues are more bullish than he is about equity prices.

Fortunately, the bank had just recruited a smart new MBA graduate, Sheila Liu. Sheila was sure that she could find the answers to Bruce Honiball's questions. First she collected data on the Australian market to get a preliminary idea of whether equity-linked deposits could work. These data are shown in Table 22.3. She was just about to undertake some quick calculations when she received the following further memo from Bruce:

> Sheila, I've got another idea. A lot of our customers probably share my view that the market is overvalued. Why don't we also give them a chance to make some money by offering a "bear market deposit"? If the market goes up, they would just get back their A$100 deposit. If it goes down, they get their A$100 back plus $5 for each 10% that the market falls. Can you figure out whether we could do something like this? Bruce.

QUESTION

1. What kinds of options is Bruce proposing? How much would the options be worth? Would the equity-linked and bear-market deposits generate positive NPV for Gibb River Bank?

Year	Interest Rate	Market Return	Dividend Yield	Year	Interest Rate	Market Return	Dividend Yield
1995	8.0%	20.2%	4.0	2005	5.6%	21.1%	3.8
1996	7.4	14.6	4.1	2006	5.9	25.0	3.8
1997	5.5	12.2	3.7	2007	6.6	18.0	4.3
1998	5.0	11.6	3.6	2008	7.3	−40.4	6.8
1999	4.9	19.3	3.3	2009	3.2	39.6	5.3
2000	5.9	5.0	3.3	2010	4.3	3.3	4.2
2001	5.2	10.1	3.3	2011	4.8	−11.4	4.4
2002	4.6	−8.1	3.5	2012	3.7	18.8	5.1
2003	4.8	15.9	4.2	2013	2.8	19.7	4.5
2004	5.4	27.6	3.7	2014	2.5	5.0	4.5
2005	15.6	21.1	3.8	2015	2.1	3.8	4.7
2006	5.9	25.0	3.8	2016	1.8	11.6	4.8
2007	6.6	18.0	4.3	2017	1.5	12.5	4.4

❭**TABLE 22.3**
Australian interest rates and equity returns, 1995–2017.

CHAPTER

23

Real Options

When you use discounted cash flow (DCF) to value a project, you implicitly assume that your firm will hold the project passively. In other words, you are ignoring the *real options* attached to the project. You could say that DCF does not reflect the value of management. Managers who hold real options do not have to be passive; they can make decisions to capitalize on good fortune or to mitigate loss. The opportunity to make such decisions clearly adds value whenever project outcomes are uncertain.

Chapter 10 gave several simple examples of real options and showed how to use decision trees to set out possible future outcomes and decisions. But we did not show you how to value real options. That is our task in this chapter. We apply the concepts and valuation principles you learned in Chapter 22.

Section 23-1 The option to expand If the immediate investment project succeeds, firms may have an option to expand it or to exploit follow-on investment opportunities. We start with an analysis of a strategic investment in the computer business.

Section 23-2 Options in R&D Research and development seldom generates revenue, but it does give the company an option to make potentially very valuable follow-on investments. As an example, we look at how to value the options created by pharmaceutical R&D.

Section 23-3 The timing option A project may be worth undertaking now, but if you delay, you may acquire additional information that could let you avoid a bad mistake. We look first at a simple invest/don't invest option and then at an option to postpone the choice between two mutually exclusive projects.

Section 23-4 The abandonment option NPV calculations generally assume a fixed project life, but real option techniques make it possible to relax this assumption and to link project life to its profitability. We also look at an example of temporary abandonment, where the company can mothball a project until conditions improve.

Section 23-5 Flexible production and procurement Here we look at the option to vary production inputs or outputs in response to fluctuating demand or prices.

Section 23-6 Valuing real options We start with two conceptual problems. Unlike the options that we valued in Chapter 22, real options are not traded. We check, therefore, that it is still appropriate to use these models. Second, we discuss how taxes should be accounted for. We conclude the chapter with a discussion of the practical challenges in valuing real options.

23-1 The Option to Expand

It is 1982 and the first personal computer has recently been launched. You are assistant to the chief financial officer (CFO) of Blitzen Computers, an established computer manufacturer casting a profit-hungry eye on the PC market. You are helping the CFO evaluate the proposed introduction of the Blitzen Mark I Micro.

⟩TABLE 23.1

Summary of cash flows and financial analysis of the Mark I microcomputer ($ millions).

	Year					
	1982	1983	1984	1985	1986	1987
After-tax operating cash flow (1)		+110	+159	+295	+185	0
Capital investment (2)	450	0	0	0	0	0
Increase in working capital (3)	0	50	100	100	−125	−125
Net cash flow (1) − (2) − (3)	−450	+60	+59	+195	+310	+125
NPV at 20% = −$46.45, or about −$46 million						

The Mark I's forecasted cash flows and NPV are shown in Table 23.1. Unfortunately, the Mark I can't meet Blitzen's customary 20% hurdle rate and has a $46 million negative NPV, contrary to top management's strong gut feeling that Blitzen ought to be in the personal computer market.

The CFO has called you in to discuss the project:

"The Mark I just can't make it on financial grounds," the CFO says. "But we've got to do it for strategic reasons. I'm recommending we go ahead."

"But you're missing the all-important financial advantage, Chief," you reply.

"Don't call me 'Chief.' What financial advantage?"

"If we don't launch the Mark I, it will probably be too expensive to enter the micro market later, when Apple, IBM, and others are firmly established. If we go ahead, we have the opportunity to make follow-on investments that could be extremely profitable. The Mark I gives not only its own cash flows, but also a call option to go on with a Mark II micro. That call option is the real source of strategic value."

"So it's strategic value by another name. That doesn't tell me what the Mark II investment's worth. The Mark II could be a great investment or a lousy one—we haven't got a clue."

"That's exactly when a call option is worth the most," you point out perceptively. "The call lets us invest in the Mark II if it's great and walk away from it if it's lousy."

"So what's it worth?"

"Hard to say precisely, but I've done a rough calculation, which suggests that the value of the option to invest in the Mark II could more than offset the Mark I's $46 million negative NPV. [The calculations are shown in Table 23.2.] If the option to invest is worth $55 million, the total value of the Mark I is its own NPV, −$46 million, plus the $55 million option attached to it, or +$9 million."

"You're just overestimating the Mark II," the CFO says gruffly. "It's easy to be optimistic when an investment is three years away."

"No, no," you reply patiently. "The Mark II is expected to be no more profitable than the Mark I—just twice as big and therefore twice as bad in terms of discounted cash flow. I'm forecasting it to have a negative NPV of about $100 million. But there's a chance the Mark II could be extremely valuable. The call option allows Blitzen to cash in on those upside outcomes. The chance to cash in could be worth $55 million.

"Of course, the $55 million is only a trial calculation, but it illustrates how valuable follow-on investment opportunities can be, especially when uncertainty is high and the product market is growing rapidly. Moreover, the Mark II will give us a call on the Mark III, the Mark III on the Mark IV, and so on. My calculations don't take subsequent calls into account."

"I think I'm beginning to understand a little bit of corporate strategy," mumbles the CFO.

Questions and Answers about Blitzen's Mark II

Question: I know how to use the Black–Scholes formula to value traded call options, but this case seems harder. What number do I use for the stock price? I don't see any traded shares.

> **TABLE 23.2**
Valuing the option to invest in the Mark II microcomputer.

Assumptions
1. The decision to invest in the Mark II investment must be made after three years, in 1985.
2. The Mark II investment is double the scale of the Mark I (note the expected rapid growth of the industry). Investment required is $900 million (the exercise price), which is taken as fixed.
3. Forecasted cash inflows of the Mark II are also double those of the Mark I, with present value of $807 million in 1985 and $807/(1.2)^3 = $467 million in 1982.
4. The future value of the Mark II cash flows is highly uncertain. This value evolves as a stock price does with a standard deviation of 35% per year. (Many high-technology stocks have standard deviations higher than 35%.)
5. The annual interest rate is 10%.

Interpretation
The opportunity to invest in the Mark II is a three-year call option on an asset worth $467 million with a $900 million exercise price.

Valuation

$$\text{PV (exercise price)} = \frac{900}{(1.1)^3} = 676$$

$$\text{Call value} = [N(d_1) \times S] - [N(d_2) \times PV(EX)]$$

$$d_1 = \log [S/PV(EX)]/\sigma \sqrt{t} + \sigma \sqrt{t}/2$$
$$= \log [0.691]/0.606 + 0.606/2 = -0.3072$$
$$d_2 = d_1 - \sigma \sqrt{t} = -0.3072 - 0.606 = -0.9134$$

$$N(d_1) = 0.3793, N(d_2) = 0.1805$$

$$\text{Call value} = [0.3793 \times 467] - [0.1805 \times 676] = \$55.1 \text{ million}$$

BEYOND THE PAGE

Blitzen

mhhe.com/brealey14e

Answer: With traded call options, you can see the value of the *underlying asset* that the call is written on. Here the option is to buy a nontraded real asset, the Mark II. We can't observe the Mark II's value; we have to compute it.

The Mark II's forecasted cash flows are set out in Table 23.3. The project involves an initial outlay of $900 million in 1985. The cash inflows start in the following year and have a present value of $807 million in 1985, equivalent to $467 million in 1982 as shown in Table 23.3. So the real option to invest in the Mark II amounts to a three-year call on an underlying asset worth $467 million, with a $900 million exercise price.

Notice that real options analysis does *not* replace DCF. You typically need DCF to value the underlying asset.

Question: Table 23.2 uses a standard deviation of 35% per year. Where does that number come from?

> **TABLE 23.3**
Cash flows of the Mark II microcomputer, as forecasted from 1982 ($ millions).

		Year					
	1982	**1985**	**1986**	**1987**	**1988**	**1989**	**1990**
After-tax operating cash flow			+220	+318	+590	+370	0
Increase in working capital			100	200	200	−250	−250
Net cash flow			+120	+118	+390	+620	+250
Present value at 20%	+467	← +807					
Investment, PV at 10%	676	← 900					
	(PV in 1982)						
Forecasted NPV in 1985		−93					

Answer: We recommend you look for *comparables*—that is, traded stocks with business risks similar to the investment opportunity.[1] For the Mark II, the ideal comparables would be growth stocks in the personal computer business or perhaps a broader sample of high-tech growth stocks. Use the average standard deviation of the comparable companies' returns as the benchmark for judging the risk of the investment opportunity.[2]

Question: Table 23.3 discounts the Mark II's cash flows at 20%. I understand the high discount rate because the Mark II is risky. But why is the $900 million investment discounted at the risk-free interest rate of 10%? Table 23.3 shows the present value of the investment in 1982 of $676 million.

Answer: Black and Scholes assumed that the exercise price is a fixed, certain amount. We wanted to stick with their basic formula. If the exercise price is uncertain, you can switch to a slightly more complicated valuation formula.[3]

Question: Nevertheless, if I had to decide in 1982, once and for all, whether to invest in the Mark II, I wouldn't do it. Right?

Answer: Right. The NPV of a commitment to invest in the Mark II is negative:

$$\text{NPV}(1982) = \text{PV(cash inflows)} - \text{PV(investment)} = \$467 - 676 = -\$209 \text{ million}$$

The option to invest in the Mark II is "out of the money" because the Mark II's value is far less than the required investment. Nevertheless, the option is worth +$55 million. It is especially valuable because the Mark II is a risky project with lots of upside potential. Figure 23.1 shows the probability distribution of the possible present values of the Mark II in 1985. The expected (mean or average) outcome is our forecast of $807,[4] but the actual value could exceed $2 billion.

Question: Could it also be far below $807 million—$500 million or less?

Answer: The downside is irrelevant because Blitzen won't invest unless the Mark II's actual value turns out higher than $900 million. The net option payoffs for all values less than $900 million are zero.

In a DCF analysis, you discount the expected outcome ($807 million), which averages the downside against the upside, the bad outcomes against the good. The value of a call option depends only on the upside. You can see the danger of trying to value a future investment option with DCF.

Question: What's the decision rule?

Answer: Adjusted present value. The best-case NPV of the Mark I project is −$46 million, but accepting it creates the expansion option for the Mark II. The expansion option is worth $55 million, so

$$\text{APV} = -46 + 55 = +\$9 \text{ million}$$

Of course, we haven't counted other follow-on opportunities. If the Mark I and Mark II are successes, there will be an option to invest in the Mark III, possibly the Mark IV, and so on.

---

[1]You could also use scenario analysis, which we described in Chapter 10. Work out "best" and "worst" scenarios to establish a range of possible future values. Then find the annual standard deviation that would generate this range over the life of the option. For the Mark II, a range from $300 million to $2 billion would cover about 90% of the possible outcomes. This range, shown in Figure 23.1, is consistent with an annual standard deviation of 35%.

[2]Be sure to "unlever" the standard deviations, thereby eliminating volatility created by debt financing. Chapters 16 and 18 covered unlevering procedures for beta. The same principles apply for standard deviation: You want the standard deviation of a portfolio of all the debt and equity securities issued by the comparable firm.

[3]If the required investment is uncertain, you have, in effect, an option to exchange one risky asset (the future value of the exercise price) for another (the future value of the Mark II's cash inflows). See W. Margrabe, "The Value of an Option to Exchange One Asset for Another," *Journal of Finance* 33 (March 1978), pp. 177–186.

[4]We have drawn the future values of the Mark II as a lognormal distribution, consistent with the assumptions of the Black–Scholes formula. Lognormal distributions are skewed to the right, so the average outcome is greater than the most likely outcome. The most likely outcome is the highest point on the probability distribution.

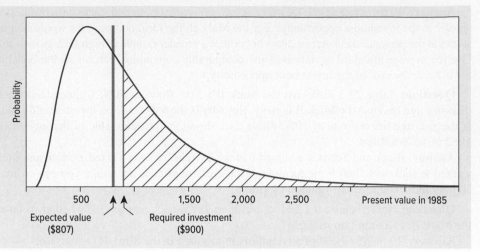

FIGURE 23.1

This distribution shows the range of possible present values for the Mark II project in 1985. The expected value is about $800 million, less than the required investment of $900 million. The option to invest pays off in the shaded area above $900 million.

Expected value
($807)

Required investment
($900)

Present value in 1985

23.1 Self-Test

Suppose that the present value of the Mark II is still more uncertain. Is the option to make the follow-on investment more or less valuable? Confirm your answer by revaluing the option with a standard deviation of 50%.

Other Expansion Options

You can probably think of many other cases where companies spend money today to create opportunities to expand in the future. A mining company may acquire rights to an ore body that is not worth developing today but could be very profitable if ore prices increase. A real estate developer may invest in worn-out farmland that could be turned into a shopping mall if a new highway is built. A pharmaceutical company may acquire a patent that gives the right but not the obligation to market a new drug. In each case, the company is acquiring a real option to expand.

23-2   Options in R&D

For many companies the largest investment they make is in R&D. Take, for example, the pharmaceutical industry, which spends massive amounts on R&D to develop new drugs. We described pharmaceutical R&D in Example 10.4 and in Figure 10.3, which is a simplified decision tree. After you have reviewed that example and figure, take a look at Figure 23.2, which recasts the decision tree as a real option.

The drug candidate in Figure 23.2 requires an immediate investment of $18 million. That investment buys a real option to invest $130 million at year 2 to pay for phase III trials and costs incurred during the prelaunch period. Of course, the real option exists only if phase II trials are successful. There is a 56% probability of failure. So after we value the real option, we will have to multiply its value by the 44% probability of success.

The exercise price of the real option is $130 million. The underlying asset is the PV of the drug, assuming that it passes phase III successfully. Figure 10.3 forecasts the expected PV of the drug at launch (a forecast, not a certain amount) at $350 million in year 5. We multiply this value by 0.8 because the decision whether to exercise the option must be taken in year 2, *before* the company knows whether the drug will succeed or fail in phase III and prelaunch.

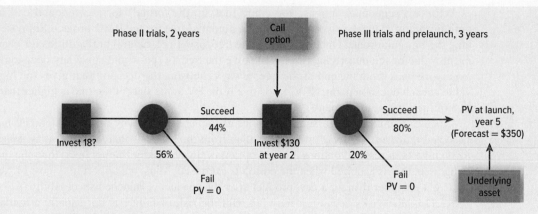

FIGURE 23.2

The decision tree from Figure 10.3 recast as a real option. If phase II trials are successful, the company has a real call option to invest $130 million. If the option is exercised, the company gets an 80% chance of launching an approved drug. The PV of the drug, which is forecasted at $350 million in year 5, is the underlying asset for the call option.

Then we must discount this value back to year 0, because the Black–Scholes formula calls for the value of the underlying asset on the date when the option is valued. The cost of capital is 9.6%, so the PV today is

$$\text{PV at year 0, assuming success in phase II} = 0.8 \times 350/(1.096)^5$$
$$= 177, \text{ or } \$177 \text{ million}$$

To value the real option, we need a risk-free rate (assume 4%) and a volatility of the value of the drug assuming it can be launched (assume 20%). With these inputs, the Black–Scholes value of a two-year call on an asset worth $177 million with an exercise price of $130 million is $58.4 million. (Refer to Section 22.3 if you need a refresher on how to use the Black–Scholes formula.)

But there's only a 44% chance that the drug will pass phase II trials. So the company must compare an initial investment of $18 million with a 44% chance of receiving an option worth $58.4 million. The NPV of the drug at year 0 is

$$\text{NPV} = -18 + (0.44 \times 58.4) = \$7.7 \text{ million}$$

This NPV is less than the $19 million NPV computed from Figure 10.3.[5] Nevertheless, the R&D project is still a "go."

Of course, Figure 23.2 assumes only one decision point, and only one real option, between the start of phase II and the product launch. In practice, there would be other decision points, including a go/no go decision after phase III trials but before prelaunch investment. In this case, the payoff to the first option at the end of phase II is the value at that date of the second option. This is an example of a *compound call*.

[5]Note that the Black–Scholes formula treats the exercise price of $130 million as a fixed amount and calculates its PV at a risk-free rate. In Chapter 10, we assumed this investment was just as risky as the drug's postlaunch cash flows. We discounted the investment at the 9.6% overall cost of capital, reducing its PV and thus increasing NPV overall. This is one reason the Black–Scholes formula gives a lower NPV than we calculated in Chapter 10. Of course, the $130 million is only an estimate, so discounting at the risk-free rate may not be correct. You could move from Black–Scholes to the valuation formula for an exchange option, which allows for uncertain exercise prices (see footnote 3). On the other hand, the R&D investment is probably close to a fixed cost because it is not exposed to the risks of the drug's operating cash flows postlaunch. There is a good case for discounting R&D investment at a low rate, even in a decision tree analysis.

With two sequential options, you could look up the formula for a compound call in an option pricing manual, or you could build a binomial tree for the R&D project. Suppose you take the binomial route. Once you set up the tree, using risk-neutral probabilities for changes in the value of the underlying asset, you solve the tree as you would solve any decision tree. You work back from the end of the tree, always choosing the decision that gives the highest value at each decision point. NPV is positive if the PV at the start of the tree is higher than the $18 million initial investment.

Despite its simplifying assumptions, our example explains why investors demand higher expected returns from R&D investments than from the products that the R&D may generate. R&D invests in real call options.[6] A call option is always riskier (higher beta) than the underlying asset that is acquired when the option is exercised. Thus, the opportunity cost of capital for R&D is higher than for a new product after the product is launched successfully.[7]

R&D is also risky because it may fail. But the risk of failure is not usually a market or macroeconomic risk. The drug's beta or cost of capital does not depend on the probabilities that a drug will fail in phase II or III. If the drug fails, it will be because of medical or clinical problems, not because the stock market is down. We take account of medical or clinical risks by multiplying future outcomes by the probability of success, not by adding a fudge factor to the discount rate.

23.2 Self-Test

Suppose the drug can be launched in year 4, not year 5 as assumed in Figure 23.2. The forecasted value at that time remains at $350 million. The option-exercise decision is still at year 2. How does this change affect the value of the call and of the R&D program?

23-3   The Timing Option

The fact that a project has a positive NPV does not mean that you should go ahead today. It may be better to wait and see how the market develops.

Suppose that you are contemplating a now-or-never opportunity to build a malted herring factory. In this case, you have an about-to-expire call option on the present value of the factory's future cash flows. If the present value exceeds the cost of the factory, the call option's payoff is the project's NPV. But if NPV is negative, the call option's payoff is zero because, in that case, the firm will not make the investment.

Now suppose that you can delay construction of the plant. You still have the call option, but you face a trade-off. If the outlook is highly uncertain, it is tempting to wait and see whether the malted herring market takes off or decays. On the other hand, if the project is truly profitable, the sooner you can capture the project's cash flows, the better. If the cash flows are high enough, you will want to exercise your option right away.

The cash flows from an investment project play the same role as dividend payments on a stock. When a stock pays no dividends, an American call is always worth more alive than dead and should never be exercised early. But payment of a dividend before the option matures reduces the ex-dividend price and the possible payoffs to the call option at maturity. Think of the extreme case: If a company pays out all its assets in one bumper dividend, the stock price

---

[6]You could also value the R&D example as (1) the PV of making all future investments, given success in clinical trials, plus (2) the value of an abandonment put, which will be exercised if clinical trials are successful but the PV of postlaunch cash flows is sufficiently low. NPV is identical because of put–call parity.

[7]The higher cost of capital for R&D is not revealed by the Black–Scholes formula, which discounts certainty-equivalent payoffs at the risk-free interest rate.

must be zero and the call worthless. Therefore, any in-the-money call would be exercised just before this liquidating dividend.

Dividends do not always prompt early exercise, but if they are sufficiently large, call option holders capture them by exercising just before the ex-dividend date. We see managers acting in the same way: When a project's forecasted cash flows are sufficiently large, managers capture the cash flows by investing right away. But when forecasted cash flows are small, managers are inclined to hold on to their call rather than to invest, even when project NPV is positive.[8] This explains why managers are sometimes reluctant to commit to positive-NPV projects. This caution is rational as long as the option to wait is open and sufficiently valuable.

Valuing the Malted Herring Option

We will set up the malted herring example as a simple binomial tree. Figure 23.3 shows the possible cash flows and end-of-year values. If you commit and invest $180 million, you have a project worth $200 million. If demand turns out to be low in year 1, the cash flow is only $16 million and the value of the project falls to $160 million. But if demand is high in year 1, the cash flow is $25 million and value rises to $250 million. Although the project lasts indefinitely, we assume that investment cannot be postponed beyond the end of the first year, and therefore we show only the cash flows for the first year and the possible values at the end of the year. Notice that if you undertake the investment right away, you capture the first year's cash flow ($16 million or $25 million); if you delay, you miss out on this cash flow, but you will gain more information on how the project is likely to work out.

We can use the binomial method to value this option. The first step is to pretend that investors are risk-neutral and to calculate the probabilities of high and low demand in this risk-neutral world. If demand is high in the first year, the malted herring plant has a cash flow of $25 million and a year-end value of $250 million. The total return is $(25 + 250)/200 - 1 = 0.375$, or 37.5%. If demand is low, the plant has a cash flow of $16 million and a year-end value of $160 million. Total return is $(16 + 160)/200 - 1 = -0.12$, or −12%. In a *risk-neutral* world, the expected return would be equal to the interest rate, which we assume is 5%:

$$\text{Expected return} = (\text{probability of high demand}) \times 37.5$$
$$+ (1 - \text{probability of high demand}) \times (-12)$$
$$= 5\%$$

Therefore, the risk-neutral probability of high demand is 34.3%. This is the probability that would generate the risk-free return of 5%.

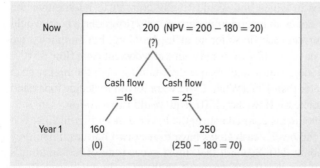

Now

200 (NPV = 200 − 180 = 20)
(?)

Cash flow   Cash flow
=16   = 25

Year 1   160   250
(0)   (250 − 180 = 70)

▶ **FIGURE 23.3**   Possible cash flows and end-of-period values for the malted herring project are shown in black. The project costs **$180 million, either now or later.** The red figures in parentheses show payoffs from the option to wait and to invest later if the project is positive NPV at year 1. Waiting means loss of the first year's cash flows. The problem is to figure out the current value of the option.

[8]We have been a bit vague about forecasted project cash flows. If competitors can enter and take away cash that you could have earned, the meaning is clear. But what about the decision to, say, develop an oil well? Here, delay doesn't waste barrels of oil in the ground; it simply postpones production and the associated cash flow. The cost of waiting is the decline in today's *present value* of revenues from production. Present value declines if the cash flow from production increases more slowly than the cost of capital.

We want to value a call option on the malted herring project with an exercise price of $180 million. We begin, as usual, at the end and work backward. The bottom row of Figure 23.3 shows the possible values of this option at the end of the year. If project value is $160 million, the option to invest is worthless. At the other extreme, if project value is $250 million, option value is $250 − 180 = $70 million.

To calculate the value of the option today, we work out the expected payoffs in a risk-neutral world and discount at the interest rate of 5%. Thus, the value of your option to invest in the malted herring plant is

$$\frac{(0.343 \times 70) + (0.657 \times 0)}{1.05} = \$22.9 \text{ million}$$

But here is where we need to recognize the opportunity to exercise the option immediately. The option is worth $22.9 million if you keep it open, and it is worth the project's immediate NPV (200 − 180 = $20 million) if exercised now. Therefore, we decide to wait and then to invest next year only if demand turns out high.

We have, of course, simplified the malted herring calculations. You won't find many actual investment-timing problems that fit into a one-step binomial tree. But the example delivers an important practical point: A positive NPV is not a sufficient reason for investing. It may be better to wait and see.

23.3 Self-Test

Suppose that the malted herring project required an investment of $170 million. All other inputs are unchanged. Would this change your decision to wait? Explain.

Optimal Timing for Real Estate Development

Sometimes it pays to wait for a long time, even for projects with large positive NPVs. Suppose you own a plot of vacant land in the suburbs.[9] The land can be used for a hotel or an office building, but not for both. A hotel could be later converted to an office building, or an office building to a hotel, but only at significant cost. You are therefore reluctant to invest, even if both investments have positive NPVs.

In this case, you have two options to invest, but only one can be exercised. You therefore learn two things by waiting. First, you learn about the general *level* of cash flows from development—for example, by observing changes in the value of developed properties near your land. Second, you can update your estimates of the *relative* size of the hotel's future cash flows versus the office building's.

Figure 23.4 shows the conditions in which you would finally commit to build either the hotel or the office building. The horizontal axis shows the current cash flows that a hotel would generate. The vertical axis shows current cash flows for an office building. For simplicity, we assume that each investment would have an NPV of exactly zero at a current cash flow of 100. Thus, if you were forced to invest today, you would choose the building with the higher cash flow, assuming the cash flow is greater than 100. (What if you were forced to decide today and each building could generate the same cash flow, say, 150? You would flip a coin.)

If the two buildings' cash flows plot in the colored area at the lower right of Figure 23.4, you build the hotel. To fall in this area, the hotel's cash flows have to beat two hurdles. First, they must exceed a minimum level of about 240. Second, they must exceed the office building's cash flows by a sufficient amount. If the situation is reversed, with office building cash flows

---

[9]The following example is based on P. D. Childs, T. J. Riddiough, and A. J. Triantis, "Mixed Uses and the Redevelopment Option," *Real Estate Economics* 24 (Fall 1996), pp. 317–339.

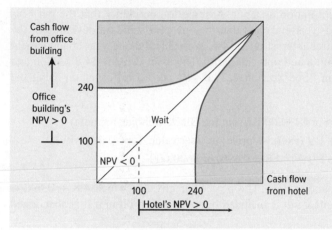

FIGURE 23.4   Development option for vacant land, assuming two mutually exclusive uses, either hotel or office building. The developer should "wait and see" unless the hotel's or office building's cash flows end up in one of the shaded areas.

Source: Adapted from Figure 1 in P. D. Childs, T. J. Riddiough, and A. J. Triantis, "Mixed Uses and the Redevelopment Option," *Real Estate Economics* 24 (Fall 1996), pp. 317–339.

above the minimum level of 240, and also sufficiently above the hotel's, then you build the office building. In this case, the cash flows plot in the colored area at the top left of the figure.

Notice how the "wait and see" region extends upward along the 45-degree line in Figure 23.4. When the cash flows from the hotel and office building are nearly the same, you become *very* cautious before choosing one over the other.

You may be surprised at how high cash flows have to be in Figure 23.4 to justify investment. There are three reasons. First, building the office building means not building the hotel, and vice versa. Second, the calculations underlying Figure 23.4 assumed cash flows that were small, but growing; therefore, the costs of waiting to invest were small. Third, the calculations did not consider the threat that someone might build a competing hotel or office building right next door. In that case, the "relax and wait" area of Figure 23.4 would shrink dramatically.

23-4   The Abandonment Option

Expansion value is important. When investments turn out well, the quicker and easier the business can be expanded, the better. But suppose bad news arrives, and cash flows are far below expectations. In that case, it is useful to have the option to bail out and recover the value of the project's plant, equipment, or other assets. The option to abandon is equivalent to a put option. You exercise that abandonment option if the value recovered from the project's assets is greater than the present value of continuing the project for at least one more period.

Bad News for the Perpetual Crusher

We introduced the perpetual crusher project in Chapter 18 to illustrate the use of the weighted-average cost of capital (WACC). The project cost $12.5 million and generated expected perpetual cash flows of $1.175 million per year. With WACC = 0.094, the project was worth PV = 1.175/0.094 = $12.5 million. Subtracting the investment of $12.5 million gave NPV = 0.

Several years later, the crusher has not panned out. Cash flows are still expected to be perpetual but are now running at only $450,000 a year. The crusher is therefore worth only $450,000/0.094 = $4.8 million. Is this bad news terminal?

Suppose the crusher project can be abandoned, with recovery of $5.2 million from the sale of machinery and real estate. Does abandonment make sense? The immediate gain from abandonment is of course $5.2 − 4.8 = $0.4 million. But what if you can wait and reconsider abandonment later? In this case, you have an abandonment option that does not have to be exercised immediately.

We can value the abandonment option as a put. Assume for simplicity that the put lasts one year only (abandon now or at year-end) and that the one-year standard deviation of the crusher project is 30%. The risk-free interest rate is 4%. We value the one-year abandonment put using the Black–Scholes formula and put–call parity. The asset value is $4.8 million and the exercise price is $5.2 million. (See Section 22.3 if you need a refresher on using the Black–Scholes formula.)

$$\text{Call value} = 0.49 \text{ million or } \$490,000 \quad (\text{from the Black–Scholes formula})$$
$$\text{Put value} = \text{call value} + \text{PV (exercise price)} - \text{asset value} \quad (\text{put–call parity})$$
$$= 0.49 + (5.2/1.04) - 4.8 = 0.690, \text{ or } \$690,000$$

Therefore, you decide not to abandon now. The project, if alive, is worth $4.8 + 0.690 = $5.49 million when the abandonment put is included but only $5.2 million if it is abandoned immediately.

You are keeping the project alive not out of stubbornness or loyalty to the crusher, but because there is a chance that cash flows will recover. The abandonment put still protects on the downside if the crusher project deals up further disappointments.

Of course, we have made simplifying assumptions. For example, the recovery value of the crusher is likely to decline as you wait to abandon. So perhaps we are using too high an exercise price. On the other hand, we have considered only a one-year European put. In fact, you have an American put with a potentially long maturity. A long-lived American put is worth more than a one-year European put because you can abandon in year 2, 3, or later if you wish.

23.4 Self-Test

A sudden rise in raw-materials prices reduces operating cash flow for one of Widgeon Wheel's product lines. Future prospects are highly uncertain, and there is no guarantee that the line will return to normal profitability. A tough-minded CEO proposes to shut it down. How would you analyze her proposal? Explain briefly what you would consider. (You can assume that once shut down, the line cannot be restarted.)

Abandonment Value and Project Life

A project's economic life can be just as hard to predict as its cash flows. Yet NPVs for capital-investment projects usually assume fixed economic lives. For example, in Chapter 6 we assumed that the guano project would operate for exactly seven years. Real-option techniques allow us to relax such fixed-life assumptions. Here is the procedure[10]:

1. Forecast cash flows well beyond the project's expected economic life. For example, you might forecast guano production and sales out to year 15.

2. Value the project, including the value of your abandonment put, which allows, but does not require, abandonment before year 15. The actual timing of abandonment will depend on project performance. In the best upside scenarios, project life will be 15 years—it will make sense to continue in the guano business as long as possible. In the worst downside scenarios, project life will be much shorter than seven years. In intermediate scenarios where actual cash flows match original expectations, abandonment will occur around year 7.

This procedure links project life to the performance of the project. It does not impose an arbitrary ending date, except in the far distant future.

---

[10]See S. C. Myers and S. Majd, "Abandonment Value and Project Life," in *Advances in Futures and Options Research*, F. J. Fabozzi, ed. (Greenwich, CT: JAI Press, 1990).

Temporary Abandonment

Companies are often faced with complex options that allow them to abandon a project *temporarily*—that is, to mothball it (or in other words put it on hold) until conditions improve. Suppose you own an oil tanker operating in the short-term spot market. (In other words, you charter the tanker voyage by voyage, at whatever short-term charter rates prevail at the start of the voyage.) The tanker costs $50 million a year to operate, and at current tanker rates, it produces charter revenues of $52.5 million per year. The tanker is therefore profitable but scarcely cause for celebration. Now tanker rates dip by 10%, forcing revenues down to $47.5 million. Do you immediately lay off the crew and mothball the tanker until prices recover? The answer is clearly yes if the tanker operation can be turned on and off like a faucet. But that is unrealistic. There is a fixed cost to mothballing the tanker. You don't want to incur this cost only to regret your decision next month if rates rebound to their earlier level. The higher the costs of mothballing and the more variable the level of charter rates, the greater the loss that you will be prepared to bear before you call it quits and lay up the boat.

Suppose that eventually you do decide to take the boat off the market. You lay up the tanker temporarily.[11] Two years later, your faith is rewarded; charter rates rise, and the revenues from operating the tanker creep above the operating cost of $50 million. Do you reactivate immediately? Not if there are costs to doing so. It makes more sense to wait until the project is well in the black and you can be fairly confident that you will not regret the cost of bringing the tanker back into operation.

These choices are illustrated in Figure 23.5. The teal line shows how the value of an operating tanker varies with the level of charter rates. The black line shows the value of the tanker when mothballed.[12] The level of rates at which it pays to mothball is given by M and the level at which it pays to reactivate is given by R. The higher the costs of mothballing and reactivating and the greater the variability in tanker rates, the further apart these points will be. You can see that it will pay for you to mothball as soon as the value of a mothballed tanker reaches the value of an operating tanker plus the costs of mothballing. It will pay to reactivate as soon as the value of a tanker that is operating in the spot market reaches the value of a mothballed tanker plus the costs of reactivating. If the level of rates falls below M, the value of the tanker is given by the black line; if the level is greater than R, value is given by the teal line. If rates lie between M and R, the tanker's value depends on whether it happens to be mothballed or operating.

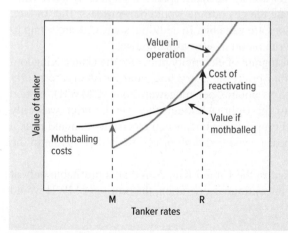

▶ **FIGURE 23.5**   An oil tanker should be mothballed when tanker rates fall to M, where the tanker's value if mothballed is enough above its value in operation to cover mothballing costs. The tanker is reactivated when rates recover to R.

---

[11]We assume it makes sense to keep the tanker in mothballs. If rates fall sufficiently, it will pay to scrap the tanker.
[12]Dixit and Pindyck estimate these thresholds for a medium-sized tanker and show how they depend on costs and the volatility of freight rates. See A. K. Dixit and R. S. Pindyck, *Investment under Uncertainty* (Princeton, NJ: Princeton University Press, 1994), Chapter 7. Brennan and Schwartz provide an analysis of a mining investment that also includes an option to shut down temporarily. See M. Brennan and E. Schwartz, "Evaluating Natural Resource Investments," *Journal of Business* 58 (April 1985), pp. 135–157.

> ### 23.5 Self-Test
>
> Look at Figure 23.5. Suppose that tanker rates are currently just below the level R. Under what circumstances would it make sense to operate the tanker?

23-5   Flexible Production and Procurement

Flexible production means the ability to vary production inputs or outputs in response to fluctuating demand or prices. Firms often build flexibility into their production facilities so that they can use the cheapest raw materials or produce the most valuable set of outputs depending on the circumstances. Having the option to do one or the other can be valuable. There are a number of situations where you can produce at a large scale but with high fixed costs and low marginal costs or at a small scale with low fixed costs and high marginal costs. Which is optimal will depend on the level of demand and prices. Again, having flexibility or, in other words, an option to do either, can be valuable.

As a first example, take the case of CT (combustion-turbine) generating plants, which are designed to deliver short bursts of peak-load electrical power. CTs can't match the thermal efficiency of coal or nuclear power plants, but CTs can be turned on or off on short notice. By contrast, "nukes" are efficient only if operated on "base load" for long periods.

The profits from operating a CT depend on the *spark spread*—that is, on the difference between the price of electricity and the cost of the natural gas used as fuel. CTs are usually money-losers at average spark spreads, but the spreads are volatile and can spike to very high levels when demand is high and generating capacity tight. Thus, a CT delivers a series of call options that can be exercised day by day (even hour by hour) when spark spreads are sufficiently high. The call options are normally out-of-the-money (CTs typically operate only about 5% of the time), but the money made at peak prices makes investment in the CTs worthwhile.[13]

The volatility of spark spreads depends on the correlation between the price of electricity and the price of natural gas used as fuel. If the correlation were 1.0, so that electricity and natural gas prices moved together dollar for dollar, the spark spread would barely move from its average value, and the options to operate the gas turbine would be worthless. But, in fact, the correlation is less than 1.0, so the options are valuable. In addition, some CTs are set up to give a further option because they can be run on oil as well as natural gas.[14]

The top panel of Figure 23.6 shows a histogram of electricity prices for the United Kingdom over a 16-year period. There is a separate price for every half hour, so there are nearly 300,000 prices plotted. Prices are quoted as pounds per megawatt-hour (£/MWH). Notice how strongly the histogram is skewed to the right. Although the average price was only £45 per MWH, prices above £100/MWH crop up regularly when electricity demand peaks. The highest price was £5,003/MWH. These occasional high prices are hardly visible in the top panel of Figure 23.6.

Suppose you have a CT generating plant in the United Kingdom that is profitable only at prices above £60/MWH. If the plant was in continuous operation, the profit per MWH would

---

[13]Here we refer to simple CTs, which are just large gas turbines connected to generators. Combined-cycle CTs add a steam generator to capture exhaust heat from the turbine. The steam is used to generate additional electricity. Combined-cycle units are much more efficient than simple CTs.

[14]Industrial steam and heating systems can also be designed to switch between fuels, depending on relative fuel costs. See N. Kulatilaka, "The Value of Flexibility: The Case of a Dual-Fuel Industrial Steam Boiler," *Financial Management* 22 (Autumn 1993), pp. 271–280.

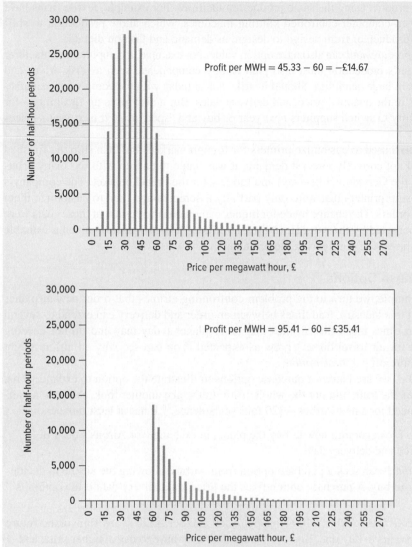

Profit per MWH = 45.33 − 60 = −£14.67

Profit per MWH = 95.41 − 60 = £35.41

▶ **FIGURE 23.6**

In the United Kingdom, electricity prices are set every half hour. The top panel is a histogram of prices (£/MWH) for a 16-year period. Note how the histogram is skewed to the right. If a plant with costs of £60/MWH operated continuously during this period, it would have incurred a loss of £14.67/MWH. The bottom panel shows the prices realized by a plant that operated only when prices exceeded generating costs of £60/MWH. This plant would have made a profit of £35.41/MWH.

be negative at £45.33 − 60 = −£14.67. But it would be better to leave the plant idle when prices are low and to exercise your option to operate only if the price for that half hour is above £60. The bottom panel of Figure 23.6 shows how the revenues per MWH are increased if the plant avoids operating when prices are low. Although the plant would have been idle for nearly three-quarters of the time, it would have reaped an average profit of 95.41 − 60 = £35.41 per MWH when it was producing.

Figure 23.6 assumes that the plant's operating cost is constant at £60. This is accurate only if the cost of natural gas is constant. Otherwise, the payoff to the option to operate depends on the spark spread. Often, the cost of gas is locked in by contract between the generator and the gas supplier. But if the cost of gas is sufficiently volatile, you would replot Figure 23.6 in spark spreads rather than electricity prices. You would operate when the spark spread is positive.

In this example, the output is the same (electricity). Option value comes from the ability to vary the level of output. In other cases, option value comes from the flexibility to switch from product to product using the same production facilities. For example, textile firms have invested heavily in computer-controlled knitting machines, which allow production to shift from product to product, or from design to design, as demand and fashion dictate.

Flexibility in *procurement* can also have option value. For example, a computer manufacturer planning next year's production must also plan to buy components, such as disk drives and microprocessors, in large quantities. Should it strike a deal today with the component manufacturer? This locks in the quantity, price, and delivery dates. But it also gives up flexibility—for example, the ability to switch suppliers next year or buy at a "spot" price if next year's prices are lower.

Hewlett-Packard used to customize printers for foreign markets and then ship the finished printers. If it did not correctly forecast demand, it was liable to end up with too many printers designed for the German market (say) and too few for the French market. The company's solution was to ship printers that were only partially assembled and then to customize them once it had firm orders. The change made for higher manufacturing costs, but these costs were more than compensated by the extra flexibility. In effect, Hewlett-Packard gained a valuable option to delay the cost of configuring the printers.[15]

Aircraft Purchase Options

For our final example, we turn to the problem confronting airlines that order new airplanes for future use. In this industry, lead times between an order and delivery can extend to several years. Long lead times mean that airlines that order planes today may end up not needing them if demand for air travel doesn't grow as expected. You can see why an airline might negotiate for an aircraft purchase *option.*

In Section 10-3, we used aircraft purchase options to illustrate the option to expand. What we said there was the truth, but not the whole truth. Let's take another look. Suppose an airline forecasts a need for a new Airbus A320 four years hence.[16] It has at least three choices.

- *Commit now.* It can commit now to buy the plane, in exchange for Airbus's offer of locked-in price and delivery date.

- *Acquire option.* It can seek a purchase option from Airbus, allowing the airline to decide later whether to buy. A purchase option fixes the price and delivery date if the option is exercised.

- *Wait and decide later.* Airbus will be happy to sell another A320 at any time in the future if the airline wants to buy one. However, the airline may have to pay a higher price and wait longer for delivery, especially if the demand for air travel is high and many planes from other airlines are on order.

The top half of Figure 23.7 shows the terms of a typical purchase option for an Airbus A320. The option must be exercised at year 3, when final assembly of the plane will begin. The option fixes the purchase price and the delivery date in year 4. The bottom half of the figure shows the consequences of "wait and decide later." We assume that the decision will come at year 3. If the decision is "buy," the airline pays the year-3 price and joins the queue for delivery in year 5 or later.

The payoffs from "wait and decide later" can never be better than the payoffs from an aircraft purchase option since the airline can discard the option and negotiate afresh with Airbus if it wishes. In most cases, however, the airline will be better off in the future with the option

---

[15]Hewlett-Packard's decision is described in P. Coy, "Exploiting Uncertainty," *BusinessWeek,* June 7, 1999, pp. 118–122.

[16]The following example is based on J. E. Stonier, "What Is an Aircraft Purchase Option Worth? Quantifying Asset Flexibility Created through Manufacturer Lead-Time Reductions and Product Commonality," in *Handbook of Airline Finance,* G. F. Butler and M. R. Keller, eds. © 1999 Aviation Week Books.

	Year 0	Year 3	Year 4	Year 5 or later
Buy option	Airline and manufacturer set price and delivery date	Exercise? (Yes or no)	Aircraft delivered if option exercised	
Wait	Wait and decide later	Buy now? If yes, negotiate price and wait for delivery.		Aircraft delivered if purchased at year 3

▶ **FIGURE 23.7**   This aircraft purchase option, if exercised at year 3, guarantees delivery at year 4 at a fixed price. Without the option, the airline can still order the plane at year 3, but the price is uncertain and the wait for delivery is longer.

Source: Adapted from Figure 17–17 in J. Stonier, "What Is an Aircraft Purchase Option Worth? Quantifying Asset Flexibility Created through Manufacturer Lead-Time Reductions and Product Commonality," in *Handbook of Airline Finance*, G. F. Butler and M. R. Keller, eds.

than without it; the airline is at least guaranteed a place in the production line, and it may have locked in a favorable purchase price. But how much are these advantages worth today, compared to the wait-and-see strategy?

Figure 23.8 illustrates Airbus's answers to this problem. It assumes a three-year purchase option with an exercise price equal to an A320 price of $45 million. The present value of the purchase option depends on both the NPV of purchasing an A320 at that price and on the forecasted wait for delivery if the airline does *not* have a purchase option but nevertheless decides to place an order in year 3. The longer the wait in year 3, the more valuable it is to have the purchase option today. (Remember that the purchase option holds a place in the A320 production line and guarantees delivery in year 4.)

If the NPV of buying an A320 today is very high (the right-hand side of Figure 23.8), future NPV will probably be high as well, and the airline will want to buy regardless of whether it has a purchase option. In this case, the value of the purchase option comes mostly

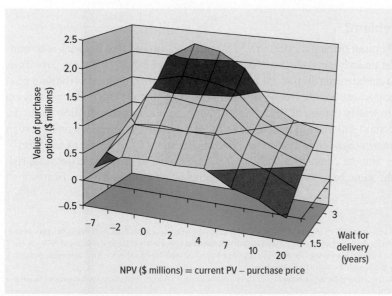

▶ **FIGURE 23.8**

Value of aircraft purchase option—the extra value of the option versus waiting and possibly negotiating a purchase later. (See Figure 23.7.) The purchase option is worth most when NPV of purchase now is about zero and the forecasted wait for delivery is long.

Source: Adapted from Figure 17–20 in J. Stonier, "What Is an Aircraft Purchase Option Worth? Quantifying Asset Flexibility Created Through Manufacturer Lead-Time Reductions and Product Commonality," in *Handbook of Aviation Finance*, G. F. Butler and M. R. Keller, eds.

from the value of guaranteed delivery in year 4.[17] If the NPV is very low, then the option has low value because the airline is unlikely to exercise it. (Low NPV today probably means low NPV in year 3.) The purchase option is worth the most, compared to the wait-and-decide-later strategy, when NPV is around zero. In this case, the airline can exercise the option, getting a good price and early delivery, if future NPV is higher than expected; or it can walk away from the option if NPV disappoints. Of course, if it walks away, it may still wish to negotiate with Airbus for delivery at a price lower than the option's exercise price.

We have cruised by many of the technical details of Airbus's valuation model for purchase options. But the example does illustrate how real-options models are being built and used. By the way, Airbus offers more than just plain-vanilla purchase options. Airlines can negotiate "rolling options," which lock in price but do not guarantee a place on the production line. (Exercise of the rolling option means that the airline joins the end of the queue.) Airbus also offers a purchase option that includes the right to switch from delivery of an A320 to an A319, a somewhat smaller plane.

> ### 23.6 Self-Test
>
> Why does the value of the Airbus option increase as the wait for delivery increases?

23-6 Valuing Real Options

In this chapter, we have presented several examples of important real options. The real-option valuation methods that we described do not replace discounted cash flow (DCF). First, many (perhaps most) investment decisions involve assets whose value depends primarily on forecasted cash flows, not on real options. Second, the starting point in most real-option analyses is the present value of an underlying asset. To value the underlying asset, you typically have to use DCF.

When valuing real options, we used the option-pricing methods developed in Chapter 22, as if the real options were traded calls or puts. Was it right to value the real options as if they were traded? Also we said next to nothing about taxes. Shouldn't the risk-free rate be after-tax? What about the practical problems that managers face when they try to value real options in real life? We now address these questions.

A Conceptual Problem?

When we introduced option pricing models in Chapter 22, we showed that the trick is to construct a package of the underlying asset and a loan that would give exactly the same payoffs as the option. If the two investments do not sell for the same price, then there are arbitrage possibilities. But most real assets are not freely traded. This means that we can no longer rely on arbitrage arguments to justify the use of Black–Scholes or binomial option valuation methods.

The risk-neutral method still makes practical sense for real options, however. It's really just an application of the *certainty-equivalent* method introduced in Chapter 9.[18] The key assumption—implicit until now—is that the company's *shareholders* have access to assets with the same risk characteristics (e.g., the same beta) as the capital investments being evaluated by the firm.

---

[17]The Airbus real-options model assumes that future A320 prices will be increased when demand is high, but only to an upper bound. Thus, the airline that waits and decides later may still have a positive-NPV investment opportunity if future demand and NPV are high. Figure 23.8 plots the *difference* between the value of the purchase option and this wait-and-see opportunity. This difference can shrink when NPV is high, especially if forecasted waiting times are short.

[18]Use of risk-neutral probabilities converts future cash flows to certainty equivalents, which are then discounted to present value at a risk-free rate.

Think of each real investment opportunity as having a "double," a security or portfolio with identical risk. Then the expected rate of return offered by the double is also the cost of capital for the real investment and the discount rate for a DCF valuation of the investment project. Now what would investors pay for a real *option* based on the project? The same as for an identical traded option written on the double. This traded option does not have to exist; it is enough to know how it would be valued by investors, who could employ either the arbitrage or the risk-neutral method. The two methods give the same answer, of course.

When we value a real option by the risk-neutral method, we are calculating the option's value if it could be traded. This exactly parallels standard capital budgeting. Shareholders would vote unanimously to accept any capital investment whose market value *if traded* exceeds its cost, as long as they can buy traded securities with the same risk characteristics as the project. This key assumption supports the use of both DCF and real-option valuation methods.

What about Taxes?

So far, this chapter has mostly ignored taxes, but just for simplicity. Taxes have to be accounted for when valuing real options. Take the Mark II microcomputer in Table 23.2 as an example. The Mark II's forecasted PV of $807 million should be calculated from *after-tax* cash flows generated by the product. The required investment of $900 million should likewise be calculated after-tax.[19]

What about the risk-free discount rate used in the risk-neutral method? It should also be after-tax. Look back to the Chapter 18 Appendix, which demonstrates that the proper discount rate for safe cash flows is the after-tax interest rate. The same logic applies here because projected cash flows in the risk-neutral method are valued as if they were safe.

Recall that the value of a real call option can be expressed as a position in the underlying asset minus a loan. Thus, the call behaves like a claim on the underlying asset partly financed with borrowed money. The borrowing does not show up on the corporation's balance sheet, but it is nevertheless really there. The implicit borrowing is a debt-equivalent obligation that must be valued using an after-tax interest rate.[20]

The implicit borrowing creates off-balance-sheet financial leverage. The resulting financial risk is the reason the real call option's value is more volatile than the value of the underlying asset. (The real option would have a higher beta than the underlying asset if both were traded in financial markets.)

In Chapter 17, we pointed out that highly profitable growth companies like Alphabet and Amazon use mostly equity finance. These companies' real growth options are one explanation. The options contain implicit debt. If the CFOs of these growth firms recognize the implicit debt, or at least the extra financial risk attached to the options, they should reduce ordinary borrowing to compensate. Option leverage therefore displaces ordinary financial leverage. The displacement means that if you forget to count both the debt that is on and off the balance sheet, a growth firm will appear to be less leveraged than it actually is.

Practical Challenges

The challenges in applying real-options analysis are not conceptual but practical. It isn't always easy. We can tick off some of the reasons.

---

[19]If the capital investment cannot be deducted immediately for tax, you should subtract the PV of any depreciation tax shields from the pretax capital investment, thus converting the investment to a net after-tax outlay.

[20]The interest on the option debt is also implicit and therefore not tax-deductible. The proof that the discount rate for real options should be after-tax is in S. C. Myers and J. A. Read Jr., "Real Options, Taxes and Leverage," *Critical Finance Review* 9 (June 2020), pp. 29–76.

First, real options can be complex, and valuing them can absorb a lot of analytical and computational horsepower. Whether you want to invest in that horsepower is a matter for business judgment. Sometimes an approximate answer now is more useful than a "perfect" answer later, particularly if the perfect answer comes from a complicated model that other managers will regard as a black box they don't understand. One advantage of real-options analysis, if you keep it simple, is that it's relatively easy to explain. Complex decision trees can often be described as the payoffs to one or two simple call or put options.

The second problem is lack of *structure*. To quantify the value of a real option, you have to specify its possible payoffs, which depend on the range of possible values of the underlying asset, exercise prices, timing of exercise, etc. In this chapter, we have taken well-structured examples where it is easy to see the road map of possible outcomes. For example, investments in pharmaceutical R&D are well-structured because all new drugs have to go through the same series of clinical trials to get approved by the U.S. Food and Drug Administration. Outcomes are uncertain, but the road map is clear. In other cases, you may not have a road map. For example, reading this book can enhance your personal call option to work in financial management, yet we suspect that you would find it hard to write down how that option would change the binomial tree of your entire future career.

A third problem can arise when your *competitors* have real options. This is not a problem in industries where products are standardized and no single competitor can shift demand and prices. But when you face just a few key competitors, all with real options, then the options can interact. If so, you can't value your options without thinking of your competitors' moves. Your competitors will be thinking in the same fashion.

An analysis of competitive interactions would take us into other branches of economics, including game theory. But you can see the danger of assuming passive competitors. Think of the timing option. A simple real-options analysis will often tell you to wait and learn before investing in a new market. Be careful that you don't wait and learn that a competitor has moved first.[21]

Given these hurdles, you can understand why systematic, quantitative valuation of real options is restricted mostly to well-structured problems like the examples in this chapter. The qualitative implications of real options are widely appreciated, however. Real options give the financial manager a conceptual framework for strategic planning and thinking about capital investments. If you can identify and understand real options, you will be a more sophisticated consumer of DCF analysis and better equipped to invest your company's money wisely.

Understanding real options also pays off when you can *create* real options, adding value by adding flexibility to the company's investments and operations. For example, it may be better to design and build a series of modular production plants, each with capacity of 50,000 tons per year of magnoosium alloy, than to commit to one large plant with capacity of 150,000 tons per year. The larger plant will probably be more efficient because of economies of scale. But with the smaller plants, you retain the flexibility to expand in step with demand and to defer investment when demand growth is disappointing.

Sometimes valuable options can be created simply by "overbuilding" in the initial round of investment. For example, oil-production platforms are typically built with vacant deck space to reduce the cost of adding equipment later. Undersea oil pipelines from the platforms to shore are often built with larger diameters and capacity than production from the platform will require. The additional capacity is then available at low cost if additional oil is found nearby. The extra cost of a larger diameter pipeline is much less than the cost of building a second pipeline later.

---

[21]Being the first mover into a new market is not always the best strategy, of course. Sometimes, later movers win. For a survey of real options and product-market competition, see H. Smit and L. Trigeorgis, *Strategic Investment, Real Options and Games* (Princeton, NJ: Princeton University Press, 2004).

In this chapter we described four real options:

- **The option to make follow-on investments.** Call options to make follow-on investments are often embedded in capital projects. Some expenditures such as research and development have value *only* because they may lead to profitable future investments.

- **The option to wait (and learn) before investing.** This is equivalent to owning a call option on the investment project. Rather than exercising the call immediately, it's often better to defer a positive-NPV project in order to keep the call alive. Deferral is most attractive when uncertainty is great and immediate project cash flows—which are lost or postponed by waiting—are small.

- **The option to abandon.** The option to abandon a project provides partial insurance against failure. This is a put option; the put's exercise price is the value of the project's assets if sold or shifted to a more valuable use. You exercise the put if the value recovered from the project's assets is greater than the present value of continuing the project for at least one more period.

- **The option to vary the firm's output or its production methods.** Firms often build flexibility into their production facilities so that they can use the cheapest raw materials or produce the most valuable set of outputs. In this case, they effectively acquire the option to exchange one asset for another.

- **Valuing real options.** When we value a real option, we are estimating its value if it could be traded. This is the standard approach in corporate finance, the same approach taken in DCF valuations. The key assumption is that shareholders can buy traded securities or portfolios with the same risk characteristics as the real investments being evaluated by the firm. This key assumption supports the use of both DCF and real-option valuation methods.

- The real options that are encountered in practice are often complex. Each real option brings its own issues and trade-offs. Nevertheless, the Black–Scholes formula often suffices to value one-time expansion and abandonment options. For more complex options, it may be easier to switch to binomial trees.

- Call options are equivalent to a claim on the underlying asset partly financed with borrowed money. Thus, growth companies with plenty of call options to expand in the future have additional leverage, even though this leverage does not show up on their balance sheets.

The Further Reading for Chapter 10 lists several introductory articles on real options. The Spring 2005 and 2007 issues of the Journal of Applied Corporate Finance *contain additional articles.*

The Spring 2006 issue contains two further articles:

R. L. McDonald, "The Role of Real Options in Capital Budgeting: Theory and Practice," *Journal of Applied Corporate Finance* 18 (Spring 2006), pp. 28–39.

M. Amram, F. Li, and C. A. Perkins, "How Kimberly-Clark Uses Real Options," *Journal of Applied Corporate Finance* 18 (Spring 2006), pp. 40–47.

The standard texts on real options include:

M. Amran and N. Kulatilaka, *Real Options: Managing Strategic Investments in an Uncertain World* (Boston: Harvard Business School Press, 1999).

T. Copeland and V. Antikarov, *Real Options: A Practitioner's Guide* (New York: Texere, 2003).

A. K. Dixit and R. S. Pindyck, *Investment under Uncertainty* (Princeton, NJ: Princeton University Press, 1994).

H. Smit and L. Trigeorgis, *Strategic Investment, Real Options and Games* (Princeton, NJ: Princeton University Press, 2004).

L. Trigeorgis, *Real Options* (Cambridge, MA: MIT Press, 1996).

Mason and Merton review a range of option applications to corporate finance:

S. P. Mason and R. C. Merton, "The Role of Contingent Claims Analysis in Corporate Finance," in E. I. Altman and M. G. Subrahmanyam, eds., *Recent Advances in Corporate Finance* (Homewood, IL: Richard D. Irwin, 1985).

Brennan and Schwartz have worked out an interesting application to natural resource investments:

M. J. Brennan and E. S. Schwartz, "Evaluating Natural Resource Investments," *Journal of Business* 58 (April 1985), pp. 135–157.

Myers and Read cover the tax and financing implications of real options.

S. C. Myers and J. A. Read, "Real Options, Taxes and Leverage," *Critical Finance Review* 9 (June 2020), pp. 29–76.

• • • • •

PROBLEM SETS

 **Select problems are available in McGraw Hill's *Connect*. Please see the preface for more information.**

1. **Expansion options (S23.1)** Look again at the valuation in Table 23.2 of the option to invest in the Mark II project. Consider a change in each of the following inputs. Would the change increase or decrease the value of the expansion option?

   a. Increased uncertainty (higher standard deviation).

   b. More optimistic forecast (higher expected value) of the Mark II in 1985.

   c. Increase in the required investment in 1985.

2. **Expansion options (S23.1)** Look again at Table 23.2. How does the value in 1982 of the option to invest in the Mark II change if

   a. The investment required for the Mark II is $800 million (vs. $900 million)?

   b. The present value of the Mark II in 1982 is $500 million (vs. $467 million)?

   c. The standard deviation of the Mark II's present value is only 20% (vs. 35%)?

BEYOND THE PAGE

 Try it!
The Black–
Scholes
model

mhhe.com/brealey14e

3. **Expansion options (S23.1)** You own a one-year call option to buy one acre of Los Angeles real estate. The exercise price is $2 million, and the current, appraised market value of the land is $1.7 million. The land is currently used as a parking lot, generating just enough money to cover real estate taxes. The annual standard deviation is 15% and the interest rate 12%. How much is your call worth? Use the Black–Scholes formula. You may find it helpful to go to the spreadsheet for Chapter 22, which calculates Black–Scholes values (see the Beyond the Page feature).

4. **Expansion options (S23.1)** A variation on Problem 3: Suppose the land is occupied by a warehouse generating rents of $150,000 after real estate taxes and all other out-of-pocket costs. The present value of the land plus warehouse is again $1.7 million. Other facts are as in Problem 3. You have a European call option. What is it worth?

5. **R&D (S23.1)** Construct a sensitivity analysis of the value of the pharmaceutical R&D project described in Figure 23.2. What input assumptions are most critical for the NPV of the project? Be sure to check the inputs to valuing the real option to invest at year 2.

6. **Real options and put–call parity (S23.2)** Redo the example in Figure 23.2, assuming that the real option is a put option allowing the company to abandon the R&D program if commercial prospects are sufficiently poor at year 2. Use put–call parity. The NPV of the drug at date 0 should again be +$7.7 million.

7. **Timing options (S23.2)** You own a parcel of vacant land. You can develop it now, or wait.

   a. What is the advantage of waiting?

   b. Why might you decide to develop the property immediately?

8. **Timing options (S23.2)** Look back at the malted herring option in Section 23-3. How did the company's analysts estimate the present value of the project? It turns out that they assumed that the probability of low demand was about 45%. They then estimated the expected payoff as $(0.45 \times 176) + (0.55 \times 275) = 230$. Discounting at the company's 15% cost of capital gave a present value for the project of $230/1.15 = 200$.

   a. How would this present value change if the probability of low demand was 55%? How would it change if the *project's* cost of capital was higher than the company cost of capital at, say, 20%?

   b. Now estimate how these changes in assumptions would affect the value of the option to delay.

9. **Timing options (S23.2)** You have an option to purchase all of the assets of the Overland Railroad for $2.5 billion. The option expires in nine months. You estimate Overland's current (month 0) present value (PV) as $2.7 billion. Overland generates after-tax free cash flow (FCF) of $50 million at the end of each quarter (i.e., at the end of each three-month period). If you exercise your option at the start of the quarter, that quarter's cash flow is paid out to you. If you do not exercise, the cash flow goes to Overland's current owners.

   In each quarter, Overland's PV either increases by 10% or decreases by 9.09%. This PV includes the quarterly free cash flow (FCF) of $50 million. After the $50 million is paid out, PV drops by $50 million. Thus, the binomial tree for the first quarter is (figures in millions):

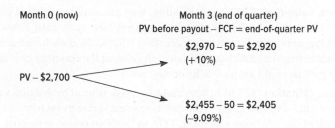

   The risk-free interest rate is 2% per quarter.

   a. Build a binomial tree for Overland, with one up or down change for each three-month period (three steps to cover your nine-month option).

   b. Suppose you can only exercise your option now, or after nine months (not at month 3 or 6). Would you exercise now?

   c. Suppose you can exercise now, or at month 3, 6, or 9. What is your option worth today? Should you exercise today, or wait?

10. **Abandonment options (S23.3)** A start-up company is moving into its first offices and needs desks, chairs, filing cabinets, and other furniture. It can buy the furniture for $25,000 or rent it for $1,500 per month. The founders are of course confident in their new venture, but nevertheless they rent. Why? What's the option?

11. **Abandonment options (S23.3)** Flip back to Tables 6.3 and 6.4, where we assumed an economic life of seven years for IM&C's guano plant. What's wrong with that assumption? How would you undertake a more complete analysis?

12. **Abandonment options (S23.3)** In Section 10-3, we considered two production technologies for a new outboard motor. Technology A was the most efficient but had no salvage value if the new outboards failed to sell. Technology B was less efficient but offered a salvage value of $17 million.

   Figure 10.2 shows the present value of the project as either $24 or $16 million in year 1 if Technology A is used. Assume that the present value of these payoffs is $18 million at year 0.

a. With Technology B, the payoffs at year 1 are $22.5 or $15 million. What is the present value of these payoffs in year 0 if Technology B is used? (*Hint:* The payoffs with Technology B are 93.75% of the payoffs from Technology A.)

b. Technology B allows abandonment in year 1 for $17 million salvage value. You also get cash flow of $1.5 million, for a total of $18.5 million. Calculate abandonment value, assuming a risk-free rate of 7%.

13. **Abandonment options (S23.3)** Take another look at the perpetual crusher example in Section 23-4. Construct a sensitivity analysis showing how the value of the abandonment put changes depending on the standard deviation of the project and the exercise price.

14. **Flexible production and procurement (S23.4)** Gas turbines are among the least efficient ways to produce electricity, much less thermally efficient than coal or nuclear plants. Why do gas-turbine generating stations exist? What's the option?

15. **Valuing real options (S23.6)** Respond to the following comments.

a. "You don't need option pricing theories to value flexibility. Just use a decision tree. Discount the cash flows in the tree at the company cost of capital."

b. "These option pricing methods are just plain nutty. They say that real options on risky assets are worth more than options on safe assets."

c. "Real-options methods eliminate the need for DCF valuation of investment projects."

16. **Valuing real options (S23.6)** Why is quantitative valuation of real options often difficult in practice? List the reasons briefly.

17. **Real option valuation (S23.6)** Josh Kidding, who has only read part of Chapter 10, decides to value a real option by (1) setting out a decision tree, with cash flows and probabilities forecasted for each future outcome; (2) deciding what to do at each decision point in the tree; and (3) discounting the resulting expected cash flows at the company cost of capital. Will this procedure give the right answer? Why or why not?

18. **Real option valuation (S23.6)** In binomial trees, risk-neutral probabilities are set to generate an expected rate of return equal to the risk-free interest rate in each branch of the tree. What do you think of the following statement: "The value of an option to acquire an asset increases with the difference between the risk-free rate of interest and the weighted-average cost of capital for the asset"?

19. **Valuing real options (S23.6)** Alert financial managers can *create* real options. Give three or four possible examples.

20. **Valuing real options (S23.6)** Describe each of the following situations in the language of options:

a. Drilling rights to undeveloped heavy crude oil in Northern Alberta. Development and production of the oil is a negative-NPV endeavor. (Assume a break-even oil price is C$90 per barrel, versus a spot price of C$80.) However, the decision to develop can be put off for up to five years. Development costs are expected to increase by 5% per year.

b. A restaurant is producing net cash flows, after all out-of-pocket expenses, of $700,000 per year. There is no upward or downward trend in the cash flows, but they fluctuate as a random walk, with an annual standard deviation of 15%. The real estate occupied by the restaurant is owned, not leased, and could be sold for $5 million. Ignore taxes.

c. A variation on part (b): Assume the restaurant faces known fixed costs of $300,000 per year, incurred as long as the restaurant is operating. Thus,

$$\text{Net cash flow} = \text{revenue less variable costs} - \text{fixed costs}$$
$$\$700,000 = 1,000,000 - 300,000$$

The annual standard deviation of the forecast error of revenue less variable costs is 10.5%. The interest rate is 10%. Ignore taxes.

d. A paper mill can be shut down in periods of low demand and restarted if demand improves sufficiently. The costs of closing and reopening the mill are fixed.

e. A real estate developer uses a parcel of urban land as a parking lot, although construction of either a hotel or an apartment building on the land would be a positive-NPV investment.

f. Air France negotiates a purchase option for 10 Boeing 787s. Air France must confirm the order by 2024. Otherwise, Boeing will be free to sell the aircraft to other airlines.

21. **Valuing real options (S23.6)** True or false?

   a. Real-options analysis sometimes tells firms to make negative-NPV investments to secure future growth opportunities.

   b. Using the Black–Scholes formula to value options to invest is dangerous when the underlying investment project would generate significant immediate cash flows.

   c. Binomial trees can be used to evaluate options to acquire or abandon an asset. It's OK to use risk-neutral probabilities in the trees even when the asset beta is 1.0 or higher.

   d. It's OK to use the Black–Scholes formula or binomial trees to value real options, even though the options are not traded.

   e. A real-options valuation will sometimes reveal that it's better to invest in a series of smaller plants rather than a single large plant.

22. **Valuing real options (S23.6)** Why is quantitative valuation of real options often difficult in practice? List the reasons briefly.

CHALLENGE

23. **Complex real options (S23.6)** Suppose you expect to need a new plant that will be ready to produce turbo-encabulators in 36 months. If design A is chosen, construction must begin immediately. Design B is more expensive, but you can wait 12 months before breaking ground. Figure 23.9 shows the cumulative present value of construction costs for the two designs up to the 36-month deadline. Assume that the designs, once built, will be equally efficient and have equal production capacity.

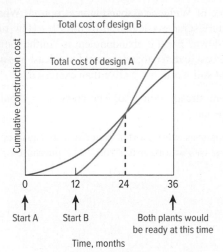

> **FIGURE 23.9**
>
> Cumulative construction cost of the two plant designs. Plant A takes 36 months to build; plant B, only 24. But plant B costs more.

A standard DCF analysis ranks design A ahead of design B. But suppose the demand for turbo-encabulators falls and the new factory is not needed; then, as Figure 23.9 shows, the firm is better off with design B, provided the project is abandoned before month 24.

Describe this situation as the choice between two (complex) call options. Then describe the same situation in terms of (complex) abandonment options. The two descriptions should imply identical payoffs, given optimal exercise strategies.

24. **Options and growth (S23.6)** In Chapter 4, we expressed the value of a share of stock as

$$P_0 = \frac{\text{EPS}_1}{r} + \text{PVGO}$$

where EPS_1 is earnings per share from existing assets, r is the expected rate of return required by investors, and PVGO is the present value of growth opportunities. PVGO really consists of a portfolio of expansion options.[22]

a. What is the effect of an increase in PVGO on the standard deviation or beta of the stock's rate of return?

b. Suppose the CAPM is used to calculate the cost of capital for a growth (high-PVGO) firm. Assume all-equity financing. Will this cost of capital be the correct hurdle rate for investments to expand the firm's plant and equipment, or to introduce new products?

• • • • •

SOLUTIONS TO SELF-TEST QUESTIONS

23.1   Option value increases with uncertainty. (Nothing more is lost if Blitzen does not go ahead with the Mark II. On the other hand, there is more upside.) With a standard deviation of 50%, call value increases from $55.1 million to $102.9 million.

23.2   The call value increases to $74.6 million. The R&D program's PV is $14.8 million.

23.3   If you invest now, the project has an NPV of 200 − 170 = $30 million. The value of the option to delay is now worth

$$\frac{(0.343 \times 80) + (0.657 \times 0)}{1.05} = \$26.1 \text{ million}$$

The lower investment outlay increases NPV and eliminates the advantage of delaying.

23.4   You would have to think through the value of Widgeon's abandonment option. What is the line's PV now? What is the likely future standard deviation of the PV? How much value could Widgeon recover by shutting down? Even if abandonment is "in the money" (recovery value greater than PV), it may be best to defer abandonment for at least one more period. Put options can be in the money but still worth more alive than exercised.

23.5   You would continue to operate if you were already doing so. The costs of mothballing would exceed the costs of continuing to operate.

23.6   Long-dated options are worth more than options with shorter maturities, because uncertainty (standard deviation or variance) increases at longer horizons. The purchase option guarantees a delivery date.

---

[22]If this challenge problem intrigues you, check out two articles by Eduardo Schwartz and Mark Moon, who attempt to use real-options theory to value Internet companies: "Rational Valuation of Internet Companies," *Financial Analysts Journal* 56 (May/June 2000), pp. 62–65; and "Rational Pricing of Internet Companies Revisited," *The Financial Review* 36 (November 2001), pp. 7–25.

Credit Risk and the Value of Corporate Debt

We first looked at how to value bonds way back in Chapter 3. We explained in that chapter what bond dealers mean when they refer to spot rates of interest and yields to maturity. We discussed why long-term and short-term bonds may offer different rates of interest and why prices of long-term bonds are affected more by a change in rates. We looked at the difference between nominal and real (inflation-adjusted) interest rates, and we saw how interest rates respond to changes in the prospects for inflation.

All the lessons of Chapter 3 hold good for both government and corporate bonds, but there is also a fundamental distinction between government and corporate issues. When a government borrows money, you can usually be confident that the debt will be repaid in full and on time. This is not true of corporate borrowing. Look, for example, at Figure 24.1. You can see that in 2009, following the financial crisis, companies defaulted on a record $330 billion of debt. Bondholders are aware of the danger that they will not get their money back and so demand a higher yield. We turn now to consider how much higher these yields are and what determines their level.

Section 24-1 Yields on corporate debt
In Section 24-1, we begin our review of corporate bonds by looking at how yields vary with the likelihood of default. We show that you can think of the yield spread over government bonds as the amount that would be needed to insure against default. Lenders sometimes use credit default swaps to provide this insurance.

Section 24-2 Valuing the option to default
In Section 24-2, we look more carefully at the company's decision to default. We show that default is an *option;* if the

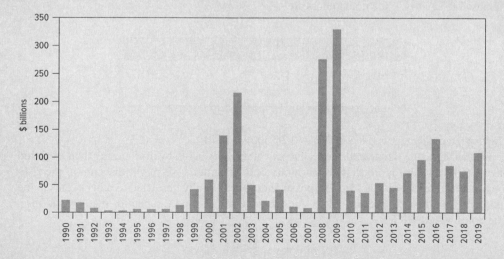

► FIGURE 24.1
Global face value of defaulting debt, 1990–2020, ($ billions).

Source: Moody's Investor Service, "Annual Default Study," February 2021.

going becomes too tough, the company has the option to stop payments on its bonds and hand over the business to the debtholders. We know what determines the value of options; therefore, we know the basic variables that must enter into the valuation of corporate bonds.

Section 24-3 Predicting the probability of default
In Section 24-3, we look at bond ratings and we describe some statistical and structural models that are used to estimate the probability that a corporate bond will default.

• • • • •

24-1 Yields on Corporate Debt

Following its introduction as a public company in 2014, California Resources Corporation incurred large losses and built up a heavy debt load. By 2019, its 8.0% bonds maturing in 2022 were trading at 24% of face value, where they offered a yield to maturity of 54%. A naïve investor who compared this figure with the 2% yield on Treasury bonds might have concluded that the bonds were a wonderful investment. But the owner would earn a 54% return only if the company repaid the debt in full. By 2019, that was looking increasingly doubtful. Because there was a significant risk that the company would default on its bonds, the *expected* yield was much less than 54%.

Distinguishing Promised and Expected Yields

Corporate bonds, such as the California Resources bond, offer a higher **promised yield** than government bonds, but do they necessarily offer a higher **expected yield**? We can answer this question with a simple numerical example. Suppose that the interest rate on one-year *risk-free* bonds is 5%. Backwoods Chemical Company has issued 5% notes with a face value of $1,000, maturing in one year. What will the Backwoods notes sell for?

If the notes are risk-free, the answer is easy—just discount principal ($1,000) and interest ($50) at 5%:

$$PV \text{ of notes} = \frac{\$1,000 + 50}{1.05} = \$1,000$$

Suppose, however, that there is a 20% chance that Backwoods will default and that, if default does occur, holders of its notes receive half the face value of the notes, or $500. In this case, the possible payoffs to the noteholders are

	Payoff	Probability
No default	$1,050	0.8
Default	500	0.2

The expected payment is 0.8($1,050) + 0.2($500) = $940.

We can value the Backwoods notes like any other risky asset, by discounting their expected payoff ($940) at the appropriate opportunity cost of capital. We might discount at the risk-free interest rate (5%) if Backwoods' possible default is totally unrelated to other events in the economy. In this case, default risk is wholly diversifiable, and the beta of the notes is zero. The notes would sell for

$$PV \text{ of notes} = \frac{\$940}{1.05} = \$895$$

An investor who purchased the notes for \$895 would receive a *promised* yield of 17.3%:

$$\text{Promised yield} = \frac{\$1,050}{\$895} - 1 = 0.173$$

That is, an investor who purchased the notes for \$895 would earn a return of 17.3% if Backwoods does not default. Bond traders therefore might say that the Backwoods notes "yield 17.3%." But the smart investor would realize that the notes' *expected* yield is only 5%, the same as on risk-free bonds.

This, of course, assumes that the risk of default with these notes is wholly diversifiable so that they have no market risk. In general, risky bonds do have market risk (i.e., positive betas) because default is more likely to occur in recessions when all businesses are doing poorly. Suppose that investors demand a 3% risk premium giving an 8% expected rate of return. Then the Backwoods notes will sell for 940/1.08 = \$870 and offer a promised yield of (1,050/870) − 1 = 0.207, or 20.7%.

24.1 Self-Test

Suppose that investors receive nothing if Backwoods defaults. If bondholders still demand an 8% expected return, what is the price of the bond, and what is its promised yield?

What Determines the Yield Spread?

Figure 24.2 shows how the yield spread on U.S. corporate bonds varies with the bond's risk. Bonds rated Aaa by Moody's are the highest grade bonds and are issued only by a few blue-chip companies. The promised yield on these bonds has on average been about 1% higher than the yield on Treasuries. Baa bonds are rated three notches lower; the yield spread on these bonds has averaged a little more than 2%. At the bottom of the heap are high-yield or "junk" bonds. There is considerable variation in the yield spreads on junk bonds; a typical spread might be about 6% over Treasuries, but spreads can rocket skyward as companies fall into distress.

Remember these are promised yields; companies don't always keep their promises and many high-yielding bonds have defaulted.

Figure 24.2 also shows that yield spreads can vary quite sharply from one year to the next, particularly for low-rated bonds. For example, they were unusually high in 2000–2002 and

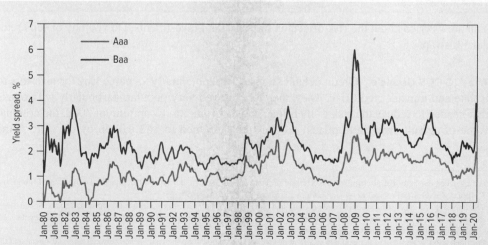

▶ **FIGURE 24.2**

Monthly yield spreads between corporate and 10-year Treasury bonds, 1980–2020.

Source: The Federal Reserve Bank of St. Louis, https://fred.stlouisfed.org/.

2008–2009. Why is this? The main reason is that, as Figure 24.1 shows, these were periods when defaults were more likely. However, the fluctuations in spreads appear to be too large to be due simply to changing probabilities of default. It seems that there are occasions when investors are particularly reluctant to bear the risk of low-grade bonds and so scurry to the safe haven of government debt.[1]

To understand more precisely what the yield spread measures, compare these two strategies:

Strategy 1: Invest $1,000 in a floating-rate default-free bond yielding 9%.[2]

Strategy 2: Invest $1,000 in a floating-rate corporate bond yielding 10%. At the same time, take out an insurance policy to protect yourself against the possibility of default. You pay an insurance premium of 1% a year, but in the event of default, you are compensated for any loss in the bond's value.

The two strategies offer similar payoffs. In the case of strategy 2, you gain a 1% higher yield, but this is exactly offset by the 1% annual premium on the insurance policy. Why does the insurance premium have to be equal to the spread? Because, if it was not equal, one strategy would dominate the other and there would be an arbitrage opportunity. The law of one price tells us that two equivalent risk-free investments must cost the same.

Our example tells us how to interpret the yield spread on corporate bonds. It is equal to the annual premium that would be needed to insure the bond against default.[3]

Insuring Bonds with a CDS   It is possible to insure corporate bonds; you do so with an arrangement called a **credit default swap (CDS).** If you buy a default swap, you commit to pay a regular insurance premium (or *spread*). For example, in January 2020 the spread on a Boeing CDS was quoted at 45 **basis points.** This meant that you needed to pay $45,000 a year to buy protection on $10 million worth of the company's debt ($45,000 = 0.0045 × $10 million). In return, if Boeing subsequently defaulted on its debt, the seller of the swap would pay you the difference between the face value of the debt and its market value. You gain a higher yield by investing in Boeing bonds rather than Treasuries, but that gain is eaten up by the cost of insuring against default. In practice, for a variety of reasons, the CDS spread generally differs somewhat from the yield spread on the bond. This difference is termed the *basis*. For example, if the CDS price is less than the bond spread, the basis is said to be negative.

BEYOND THE PAGE

What Exactly
Is a Default?

mhhe.com/brealey14e

BEYOND THE PAGE

A Most
Controversial
Trade

mhhe.com/brealey14e

24.2 Self-Test

You are worried about the risk of default on your bond investments. Do you buy or sell credit default swaps?

The AIG CDS Debacle   Credit default swaps offer a potentially valuable way for investors to isolate and transfer credit risk. They, therefore, proved very popular, particularly with banks that needed to reduce the risk of their loan books. From almost nothing in 2000, the notional value of default swaps and related products mushroomed to $62 trillion by the start of the

---

[1]For evidence on the effect of changing risk aversion on bond spreads, see A. Berndt, R. Douglas, D. Duffie, and M. Ferguson, "Corporate Credit Risk Premia," *Review of Finance* 22 (March 2018), pp. 419–454.

[2]The interest payment on floating-rate bonds goes up and down as the general level of interest rates changes. Thus, a floating-rate, default-free bond will sell at close to face value on each coupon date. Many governments issue "floaters." The U.S. Treasury does not do so, though some U.S. government agencies do.

[3]For illustration, we have used the example of a floating-rate bond to demonstrate the equivalence between the yield spread and the cost of default insurance. The yield spread on a fixed-rate bond should be very close to the cost of insurance (i.e. the CDS spread).

Dynegy's Credit Default Swaps

❯ In the event of default, the seller of a credit default swap pays the buyer the difference between the face value of the debt and its market value. But finding the market value of defaulting bonds can be tricky. The following example illustrates how this is done.

In 2011, the electric utility, Dynegy, filed for bankruptcy with more than $2 billion of debt and over $700 million net of credit default swaps outstanding. The market value of Dynegy's debt and therefore the loss suffered by the CDS sellers was determined by a two-stage auction. In the first stage, all the participants submitted prices at which they would be prepared to sell or buy a minimum amount of a pre-approved pool of Dynegy bonds. As it turned out, most participants in this auction wished to buy rather than sell the bonds. So a second-stage auction was held to find a price that would tempt sufficient additional sellers.

The resulting equilibrium price from this second stage was 71.25% of face value, so the implied loss on each bond was $100 - 71.25 = 28.75\%$ of face value. Therefore, an investor who had bought a **notional value** of $10 million of Dynegy credit default swaps was entitled to receive compensation from the seller of $2.875 million.[4]

---

financial crisis.[5] Many of these default swaps were sold by **monoline insurers,** which specialize in providing services to the capital markets. The monolines had traditionally concentrated on insuring relatively safe municipal debt but had been increasingly prepared to underwrite corporate debt, as well as many securities that were backed by subprime mortgages. By 2008, insurance companies had sold protection on $2.4 trillion of bonds. As the outlook for many of these bonds deteriorated, investors began to question whether the insurance companies had sufficient capital to make good on their guarantees.

One of the largest providers of credit protection was AIG Financial Products, part of the giant insurance group, AIG, with a portfolio of more than $440 billion of credit guarantees. AIG's clients never dreamt that the company would be unable to pay up: Not only was AIG triple-A rated, but it had promised to post generous collateral if the value of the insured securities dropped or if its own credit rating fell. So confident was AIG of its strategy that the head of its financial products group claimed that it was hard "to even see a scenario within any kind of realm of reason that would see us losing one dollar in any of these transactions." But in September 2008, the unthinkable scenario occurred when the credit rating agencies downgraded AIG's debt, and the company found itself obliged to provide $32 billion of additional collateral within 15 days. Had AIG defaulted, everyone who had bought a CDS contract from the company would have suffered large losses on these contracts. To save AIG from imminent collapse, the Federal Reserve stepped in with an $85 billion rescue package.

24-2 Valuing the Option to Default

The difference between a corporate bond and a Treasury bond is that the company has the option to default, whereas the government supposedly doesn't.[6] That default option is valuable. If you don't believe us, think about whether (other things equal) you would prefer to be

---

[4]For a detailed description of the Dynegy CDS auction, see L. Pollack, "Mechanics," *Financial Times,* January 11, 2012.

[5]*Notional value* refers to the total face value of bonds covered by CDS contacts. The *present value* of a CDS contract at its creation is usually zero. That is, the buyer of credit protection usually pays no money up front. Then the present value fluctuates, increasing as and if credit risk increases, but is always smaller than the notional value unless the bond turns out to be totally worthless. Data on credit derivatives is published by the International Swap Dealers Association (ISDA) at www.isda.org.

[6]Governments cannot print the currencies of other countries, and may be forced into default on their foreign currency debt. For example, in 2001 Argentina defaulted on $95 billion of foreign currency debt, and in 2012 investors in Greek government debt had to accept a write-down of about $100 billion. Governments have occasionally defaulted on their own currency's debt. For example, in 1998, the Russian government defaulted on $36 billion of ruble debt.

a shareholder in a company with limited liability or in a company with unlimited liability. Of course, you would prefer to have the option to walk away from your company's debts. Unfortunately, every silver lining has its cloud, and the drawback to having a default option is that corporate bondholders expect to be compensated for giving it to you. That is why corporate bonds sell at lower prices and offer higher yields than government bonds.

We can illustrate the nature of the default option by returning to the plight of Circular File Company, which we discussed in Chapter 17. Circular File borrowed $50 per share, but then fell on hard times, and the market value of its assets fell to $30. Circular's bond and stock prices fell to $27 and $3, respectively. Thus, Circular's *market-value* balance sheet is:

Circular File Company

Asset value	$30	$27	Bond
	—	3	Stock
	$30	$30	Firm value

If Circular's debt were due and payable now, the firm could not repay the $50 it originally borrowed. It would default, leaving bondholders with assets worth $30 and shareholders with nothing. The reason that Circular stock has a market value of $3 is that the debt is *not* due immediately, but one year from now. A stroke of good fortune could increase firm value enough to pay off the bondholders in full, with something left over for the stockholders.

Circular File is not compelled to repay the debt at maturity. If the value of its assets is less than the $50 that it owes, it will choose to default on the debt and the bondholders will take over the company's assets. Thus, the company has, in effect, issued a safe bond but, at the same time, acquired an option to sell the firm's assets to the bondholders for the amount of the debt. The exercise price of this put option is $50, the face value of the bond. If the value of the company's assets when the bond matures is greater than $50, Circular will not exercise its option to default. If the assets' value is less than $50, it will pay Circular to exercise its option and to hand over the assets in settlement of the debt.

Bond traders, investors, and financial managers refer to *default puts*. When a firm defaults, its stockholders are, in effect, exercising their default put. The put's value is the value of limited liability—the value of the stockholders' right to walk away from their firm's debts in exchange for handing over the firm's assets to its creditors. In the case of Circular File, this option to default is extremely valuable because default is likely to occur. At the other extreme, the value of IBM's option to default is trivial compared with the value of IBM's assets. Default on IBM bonds is possible but extremely unlikely. Option traders would say that for Circular File, the put option is "deep in the money" because today's asset value ($30) is well below the exercise price ($50). For IBM, the put option is far "out of the money" because the value of IBM's assets greatly exceeds the amount of IBM's debt.

24.3 Self-Test

Who owns the default put option—the shareholders or the bondholders?

Finding Bond Values

Valuing corporate bonds should be a two-step process:

$$\text{Bond value} = \text{bond value assuming no chance of default} \tag{24.1}$$
$$- \text{value of put option on assets}$$

The first step is easy: Calculate the bond's value assuming no default risk. (Discount promised interest and principal payments at the rate offered by Treasuries of the same maturity.) The second step requires you to calculate the value of a put written on the firm's assets, where the maturity of the put equals the maturity of the bond and the exercise price of the put equals the promised payment.

In Chapter 17, we *assumed* that the value of Circular's bond was $27. Now we can see where that figure could have come from. Suppose that the standard deviation of the returns on Circular's assets is 60% a year and that the risk-free interest rate is 10%. The current value of Circular's assets is $30, and the exercise price of the default option is $50. If you enter these data into the Black–Scholes model, you find that the value of Circular's default put is $18.6. You can now value its bond:

BEYOND THE PAGE

Try It!
Valuing the
default put

mhhe.com/brealey14e

$$\text{Value of Circular's bond} = \text{value of default-free bond} - \text{value of default put}$$
$$= 50/1.1 \qquad\qquad - 18.6$$
$$= \$26.9 \text{ (about } \$27)$$

Before you get too excited about valuing the default option, we should warn you that, in practice, you would encounter complications that make the valuation of corporate bonds considerably more difficult than it sounds. For example, we assumed that Circular File is committed to making a single payment of $50 at the end of the year. But suppose, instead, that it has issued a 10-year bond that pays interest annually. In this case, there are 10 payments rather than just 1. When each payment comes due, Circular has the option to make the coupon payment or to default. If it makes the first payment, Circular obtains a second option to default when the second interest payment becomes due. The reward to making this payment is that the stockholders get a third put option, and so on. (This is an example of a *compound* put option.)

Of course, if the firm does not make any of these payments when due, bondholders take over, and stockholders are left with nothing. In other words, if Circular decides to exercise its default option, it gives up all subsequent default options.

Valuing the 10-year bond when it is issued is equivalent to valuing the first of the 10 options. But you cannot value the first option without valuing the nine that follow. Even this example understates the practical difficulties because large firms may have dozens of outstanding debt issues with different interest rates and maturities, and before the current debt matures, they may make further issues. Consequently, when bond traders evaluate a corporate bond, they do not reach for their option calculator. They are more likely to start by identifying bonds with similar maturity and risk of default and look at the yield spreads offered by these bonds.

Valuing the default put may be challenging, but, now we know that limited liability is an option, we also know what the value of that option depends on. The following table shows how the value of the option to default depends on the underlying variables:[7]

If there is an increase in:	Value of default put:
Value of company's assets	Declines
Standard deviation of asset value	Rises
Amount of outstanding debt	Rises
Debt maturity	Rises
Default-free interest rate	Declines
Dividend payments	Rises

We have seen that corporate bonds sell at higher promised yields than Treasury bonds with the same maturities. Can we explain the size of these yield spreads in terms of the default put that attaches to corporate bonds? The answer appears to be "yes" in the case of investment-grade bonds. For these bonds, the default risk can do a fairly good job of explaining the typical yield spread.[8] However, yields on junk bonds appear to be higher than their default experience would justify. It seems that investors in junk bonds demand additional yield to compensate for their relative lack of liquidity.

---

[7]Notice that the effect of an interest rate rise on the value of a put option is the opposite of its effect on the value of a call. Circular's option to extinguish the debt is more valuable when interest rates are high. However, the effect on put values of changes in the interest rate is generally modest.

[8]S. M. Schaefer and P. Feldhutter, "The Credit Spread Puzzle—Myth or Reality?" *Review of Financial Studies* 31 (2018), pp. 2897–2942.

Valuing Government Financial Guarantees

❱ When American Airlines declared bankruptcy in 2011, its pension plan had liabilities of $18.5 billion and assets of just $8.3 billion. But the 130,000 workers and retirees did not face a destitute old age. Their pensions were largely guaranteed by the Pension Benefit Guaranty Corporation (PBGC). This is a U.S. federally chartered corporation created in 1974 to ensure the continuity of pension payments in the event of the bankruptcy of an employer.

Pension promises are a long-term liability just like the promises to bondholders. The guarantee by the PBGC changes the pension promises from a risky liability to a safe one. If the company goes belly-up and there are insufficient assets to cover the pensions, the PBGC makes up most of the difference.[9]

The government recognizes that the guarantee provided by the PBGC is costly. Thus, shortly after assuming the liability for the American Airlines plan, the PBGC calculated that the discounted value of payments on all defaulted plans and those close to default amounted to $98 billion.

Unfortunately, these calculations ignore the risk that other firms in the future may fail and hand over their pension liability to the PBGC. To calculate the cost of the guarantee, we need to think about what the value of company pension promises would be without any guarantee:

Value of guarantee = value of guaranteed pensions
− value of pension promises
without a guarantee

With the guarantee, the pensions are as safe as a promise by the U.S. government[10]; without the guarantee, the pensions are like an ordinary debt obligation of the firm. We already know what the difference is between the value of safe government debt and risky corporate debt. It is the value of the firm's right to hand over the assets of the firm and to walk away from its obligations. Thus, the value of the pension guarantee is the value of this put option.

A paper prepared for the Congressional Budget Office showed how option pricing models can help to give a better measure of the cost to the PBGC of pension guarantees.[11] Their estimates suggest that the value of the PBGC's guarantees was much higher than its published estimate.

The PBGC is not the only government body to provide financial guarantees. Fortunately, option pricing is leading to a better way to calculate their cost.

The Value of Corporate Equity

We saw in Chapter 21 that the value of a put option is identical to the value of a call option with the same exercise price, plus the present value of the exercise price, and less the value of the underlying asset. Think what this means for the value of Circular File's default put:

Value of put option to default = value of call option on Circular's assets
+ present value of Circular's debt at the risk-free interest rate
− value of Circular's assets

---

[9]There are limits to pension payments made by the PBGC to retired employees. Employees with large pensions are not made whole.

[10]The pension guarantee is not ironclad. If the PBGC cannot meet its obligations, the government is not committed to providing the extra cash. But few doubt that it would do so.

[11]W. Kiska, D. Lucas, and M. Phaup, "The Risk Exposure of the Pension Benefit Guaranty Corporation" (Washington, D.C.: Congressional Budget Office, September 2005).

If you twist this formula around, you get:

$$
\begin{array}{l}
\begin{matrix} \text{Value of call option} \\ \text{on Circular's assets} \end{matrix} = \begin{matrix} \text{value of} \\ \text{Circular's assets} \end{matrix} - \left(\begin{matrix} \text{present value of} \\ \text{Circular's debt at the} \\ \text{risk-free interest rate} \end{matrix} - \begin{matrix} \text{value of put} \\ \text{option to default} \end{matrix} \right) \\[2em]
\phantom{\begin{matrix} \text{Value of call option} \\ \text{on Circular's assets} \end{matrix}} = \begin{matrix} \text{value of} \\ \text{Circular's assets} \end{matrix} - \begin{matrix} \text{value of} \\ \text{Circular's debt} \end{matrix} = \begin{matrix} \text{value of Circular's} \\ \text{equity} \end{matrix}
\end{array}
$$

The expression on the right-hand side is simply the value of Circular's equity. This tells us that you can think of Circular's bondholders as effectively owning the company now, but the shareholders have the option to buy it back from them at the end of the year by paying off the debt. Thus, the balance sheet of Circular File can be expressed as follows:

Circular File Company (Market Values)

Asset value	$30	$26.9	Bond value = asset value − value of call
		3.1	Stock value = value of call
	$30	$30	Firm value = asset value

24.4 Self-Test

Describe the value of corporate debt and equity in terms of the value of the company's assets and a call option on these assets. What is the exercise price of the call? Assume that the company has just one issue of debt that is due to make just one future payment.

24-3   Predicting the Probability of Default

Banks and other financial institutions not only want to know the value of the loans that they have made, but they also need to know the risk that they are incurring. Some rely on the judgments of specialized bond-rating services. Others have developed their own models for measuring the probability that the borrower will default. We describe bond ratings first and then discuss two classes of models for predicting default.

As discussed in Chapter 3, the relative quality of most traded bonds can be judged by bond ratings. There are three principal rating services—Moody's, Standard & Poor's, and Fitch.[12] Table 24.1 summarizes these ratings. For example, the highest quality bonds are rated triple-A (Aaa) by Moody's, then come double-A (Aa) bonds, and so on. Bonds rated Baa or above are known as *investment-grade* bonds.[13] Many pension funds, and other financial institutions are not allowed to invest in bonds unless they are investment-grade.[14]

Bonds rated below Baa are termed **high-yield** or **junk bonds**. Most junk bonds used to be *fallen angels*—that is, bonds of companies that had fallen on hard times. But during the 1980s, new issues of junk bonds multiplied 10-fold, as more and more companies issued large quantities of low-grade debt to finance takeovers. The result was that for the first time, corporate midgets were able to raise the money to take control of corporate giants.

---

[12]The SEC has been concerned about the power wielded by the three bond-rating agencies. Therefore, it has approved seven new, nationally recognized statistical rating organizations (NRSROs): DBRS, A.M. Best, Egan-Jones Ratings, Morningstar Credit Ratings (previously known as Realpoint), Kroll Bond Rating, HR Ratings de Mexico, and Japan Credit Rating.

[13]Rating services also provide a finer breakdown. Thus, a bond might be rated A-1, A-2, or A-3 (the lowest A rating). In addition, the rating service may announce that it has put an issue on its watch list for a possible upgrade or downgrade.

[14]Investment-grade bonds can usually be entered at face value on the books of banks and life insurance companies.

Moody's	Standard & Poor's and Fitch
Investment-Grade Bonds	
Aaa	AAA
Aa	AA
A	A
Baa	BBB
Junk Bonds	
Ba	BB
B	B
Caa	CCC
Ca	CC
C	C

❭**TABLE 24.1**   Key to bond ratings. The highest quality bonds are rated triple-A. Investment-grade bonds have to be the equivalent of Baa or higher. Bonds that don't make this cut are called "high-yield" or "junk" bonds.

Issuers of these junk bonds often had debt ratios of 90–95%. Many worried that this threatened the health of corporate America, and as default rates on corporate debt rose to 10% in the early 1990s, the market for new issues of junk bonds dried up. Since then, the market for junk debt has had its ups and downs. For example, as interest rates on Treasuries dwindled in the years following the financial crisis, investors sought higher yields, and new issues of junk bonds boomed.

Bond ratings are judgments about firms' financial and business prospects. There is no fixed formula that is used to calculate ratings. Nevertheless, investment bankers, bond portfolio managers, and others who follow the bond market closely can get a fairly good idea of how a bond will be rated by looking at a few key numbers, such as the firm's operating margin, the return on assets, the debt ratio, and the ratio of earnings to interest. Table 24.2 shows how these ratios vary with the firm's bond rating.

24.5 Self-Test

Which of these statements describe(s) investment-grade bonds?
  a. They generally have lower interest coverage.
  b. They generally have lower debt ratios.
  c. They generally have higher operating margins.
  d. They generally have lower return on assets.

Ratio	Aaa	Aa	A	Baa	Ba	B	Caa-C
Operating margin (%)	24.8	24.2	16.9	15.0	11.2	7.6	3.8
Pretax return on assets (%)	12.3	14.7	13.5	10.4	8.8	6.6	4.9
Long- plus short-term debt ratio (%)	42.8	41.5	46.7	48.4	55.9	68.1	94.4
Interest coverage	14.4	24.4	13.7	9.8	6.5	3.3	1.7

❭**TABLE 24.2**   How financial ratios differ according to a firm's bond rating. Median ratios for U.S. non-financial firms by bond rating.

Source: Moody's Financial Metrics, "Key Ratios by Rating and Industry for North American Non-Financial Corporations," December 2017.

Country Credit Ratings

❯ In addition to rating corporate debt, the major credit agencies also assign a rating for sovereign, state and municipal debt. Table 24.3 shows some examples of how Moody's rated the debt of different governments in September 2021.

Countries with highly rated debt share some common characteristics. They have high per capita income, low inflation and low external debt, a high level of economic development, and no history of past defaults.[15]

Rating	Countries	
Aaa	Germany	USA
Aa	France	UK
A	China	Japan
Baa	India	Italy
Ba	Brazil	South Africa
B	Turkey	Pakistan
Caa	Cuba	El Salvador

❯**TABLE 24.3** Examples of Moody's ratings for foreign currency government debt, September 2021.

Source: www.moodys.com.

Figure 24.3 shows that bond ratings do reflect the probability of default. Since 1970, no U.S. bonds that were initially rated triple-A by Moody's have defaulted in the year after issue, and only 1 in 700 have defaulted within 10 years of issue. (The Aaa default rate is not plotted in Figure 24.3. It would be invisible.) At the other extreme, about half of Caa to C bonds have defaulted by year 10. Of course, bonds do not usually fall suddenly from grace. As time passes and the company becomes progressively more shaky, the agencies revise downward the bond's rating to reflect the increasing probability of default.

Rating agencies don't always get it right. When Enron went belly-up in 2001, investors protested that only two months earlier the company's debt had an investment-grade rating. Rating agencies also did not win many friends during the financial crisis of 2007–2009, when many of the mortgage-backed securities that had been given triple-A ratings defaulted. Conversely,

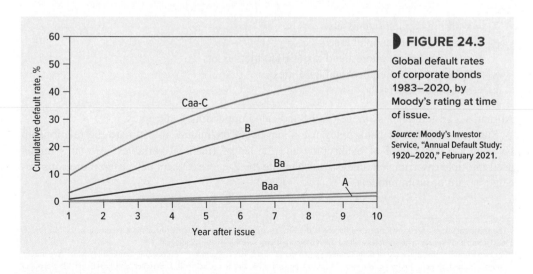

❯ **FIGURE 24.3**

Global default rates of corporate bonds 1983–2020, by Moody's rating at time of issue.

Source: Moody's Investor Service, "Annual Default Study: 1920–2020," February 2021.

---

[15]R. Cantor and F. Packer, "Determinants and Impact of Sovereign Credit Ratings," Federal Reserve Bank of New York, *Economic Policy Review* 2 (October 1996), pp. 37–53.

when agencies *do* downgrade a company's debt, they are often accused of overhasty action that increases the cost of borrowing.

Statistical Models of Default

Financial managers pay attention to bond ratings, but they may also make their own judgments about the chances of default. There are two methods that they use to do this. We first describe statistical models to predict default, and we then describe structural models.

If you apply for a credit card or a bank loan, you will probably be asked to complete a questionnaire that provides details about your job, home, and financial health. This information is then used to calculate an overall credit score.[16] If you do not make the grade on the score, you are likely to be refused credit or subjected to a more detailed analysis. In a similar way, mechanical credit scoring systems are used by banks to assess the risk of their corporate loans and by firms when they extend credit to customers.

Suppose that you are given the task of developing a system that will help to decide which businesses are poor credits. You start by examining the financial statements of companies that went bankrupt over the past 20 years. Figure 24.4 shows what you find. You can see that, on average, bankruptcy was preceded by declining profit margins and return on capital, increasing financial leverage, and deteriorating liquidity.

Rather than focusing on individual ratios, it makes sense to combine the ratios into a single score that can separate the creditworthy sheep from the impecunious goats. In other words, you need to estimate an equation that relates the risk of bankruptcy to a set of different financial variables. Most statistical bankruptcy models focus on a relatively small set of accounting ratios, such as measures of leverage, profitability, and liquidity. For small businesses, there may be little alternative to the use of accounting data, but for large, publicly traded firms, it is also possible to take advantage of the information in security prices. A declining share price, volatile returns, a low market-to-book ratio, and a low share price all seem to indicate a higher probability of impending bankruptcy.[17]

One of the earliest statistical models that is still widely used is the Z-score model proposed by Edward Altman.[18] A company's Z-score is given by the following formula:

$$Z = 1.2\,x_1 + 1.4\,x_2 + 3.3\,x_3 + 0.6\,x_4 + 1.0\,x_5$$

where:

x_1 = working capital/total assets
x_2 = retained earnings/total assets
x_3 = earnings before interest and tax (EBIT)/total assets
x_4 = market value of equity/total liabilities
x_5 = sales/total assets

Altman suggested that a score below 1.8 indicated impending bankruptcy.

Statistical models of bankruptcy use a variety of techniques to estimate the relationship between the occurrence of bankruptcy and the set of financial variables. Altman's model used multiple discriminant analysis to calculate the Z-score. Others have used more sophisticated hazard or probit models.

---

[16]The most commonly used consumer credit score is the FICO score, which is used by the three main credit agencies—Experian, TransUnion, and Equifax. The agencies also use their own proprietry scoring system, VantageScore.

[17]For two examples that make use of both accounting and market data, see T. Shumway, "Forecasting Bankruptcy More Accurately: A Simple Hazard Model," *Journal of Business* 74 (2001), pp. 101–124; and J. Y. Campbell, J. Hilscher, and J. Szilagyi, "In Search of Distress Risk," *Journal of Finance* 63 (December 2008), pp. 2899–2939.

[18]E. Altman, "Financial Ratios, Discriminant Analysis and the Prediction of Corporate Bankruptcy," *Journal of Finance* 23 (September 1968), pp. 589–609.

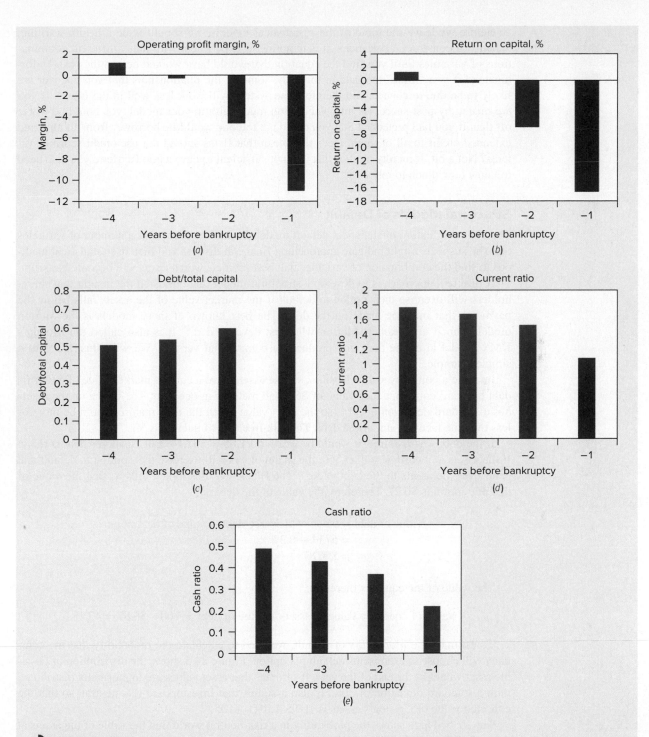

◗ **FIGURE 24.4**   Median financial ratios of 409 firms filing for bankruptcy between 1999 and 2019.

Source: Compustat and WRDS Financial Ratios.

Before we leave the topic of these statistical models, we should issue a health warning. When you construct a risk index, it is tempting to experiment with many different combinations of variables until you find the equation that would have worked best in the past. Unfortunately, if you "mine" the data in this way, some of the relationships that you uncover are likely to be due to chance, and therefore the system will work less well in the future. If you are misled by past successes into placing too much faith in your model, you could be worse off than if you had pretended that you could not tell one would-be borrower from another and extended credit to all of them. Does this mean that firms should not use credit scoring systems? Not a bit. It merely implies that it is not sufficient to have a good system; you also need to know how much to rely on it.

Structural Models of Default

The common feature of statistical default models is that the user picks a number of variables that she suspects might indicate approaching financial distress and then uses statistical methods to find the combination of variables that best predicts which firms will become bankrupt.

A different approach is to develop a structural model that builds on the insight that shareholders will exercise their option to default if the market value of the assets falls below the payments that must be made on the debt. The best known of these models is the Merton model, named after Robert Merton who first developed it.[19] It is also called the Moody's KMV model after the firm that produced a commercial version. We will illustrate with a simple example.

Imagine a company, call it Upsilon, whose assets have a current market value of $100. Its debt has zero coupon, a face value of $60, and matures in one year. The return on the assets has a standard deviation of 30%, so the asset value when the debt matures could be more or less than the face amount of the debt. The risk-free rate of interest is 5%.

If the debt was risk-free, it would be worth 60/1.05 = $57.14. But Upsilon's debt is risky: If the assets are worth less than $60, the shareholders will exercise their option to default and hand over the assets to the debtholders. The Black–Scholes model tells us that the value of this put option is $0.27. Therefore, the value of the debt is:

$$\text{Value of debt} = \text{value of risk-free debt} - \text{value of default put}$$
$$= 57.14 - 0.27$$
$$= \$56.87$$

The value of the equity is therefore:

$$\text{Value of equity} = \text{Value of assets} - \text{value of debt} = 100 - 56.87 = 43.13$$

To estimate the *probability* of default, we need to calculate the probability that the company will choose to exercise its default put option. Figure 24.5 shows the distribution of possible asset values at the end of the year. It assumes that asset values are lognormally distributed with a standard deviation of 30%. It also assumes that investors are risk-neutral, so that the expected value of Upsilon's assets is $100 \times 1.05 = \$105$.[20]

The shaded area shows the probability in a risk-neutral world that the value of the assets at the end of the year will be less than the face value of the debt and that Upsilon will therefore

---

[19]See R. C. Merton, "On the Pricing of Corporate Debt: The Risk Structure of Interest Rates," *Journal of Finance* 29 (1972), pp. 449–470.
[20]If you wish to estimate the actual, rather than risk-neutral, probability that Upsilon will default, you need to use the expected return on the assets rather than the risk-free interest rate.

default. If you look back at the Black–Scholes formula in Section 22.3, you will see the expression $N(d_2)$. The risk-neutral probability that the option will be exercised is equal to $1 - N(d_2)$. In the case of Upsilon,

$$\text{Risk} - \text{neutral probability of default} = 1 - N(d_2) = 0.043, \text{ or } 4.3\% \qquad \textbf{(24.2)}$$

There is a 4.3% risk-neutral chance that Upsilon will default.

24.6 Self-Test

Suppose that Upsilon's debt has a face value of $70. Use the Black–Scholes app from Chapter 22 to recalculate the risk-neutral probability that it will default.

Structural models of default have obvious attractions. They have a theoretical base. So the relevant variables are pretty well known, and you do not need to go prospecting among past data to find variables that may be indications of impending default. But when you apply the model in practice, you inevitably encounter complications. For example, unless you can observe the market value of the company's debts, you can't observe the value of its assets or measure their volatility.[21] Also, companies may have several debt issues, each with a different maturity. Nevertheless, it is possible to adapt the structural model to estimate the probability of default by real companies.[22]

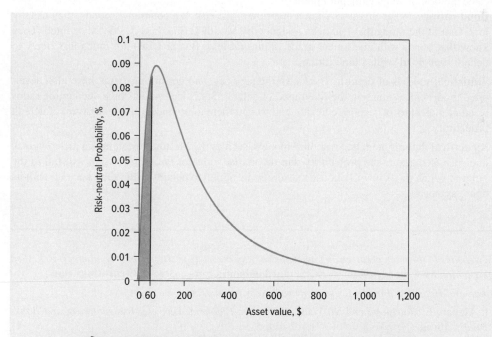

▶ **FIGURE 24.5** Upsilon has issued one-year debt with a face value of $60. The shaded area shows that there is a 4.3% risk-neutral probability that the value of the company's assets at the end of the year will be less than $60. In that case, the company will choose to default.

---

[21]Merton proposed an ingenious way to back out asset value and volatility from the value and volatility of the equity.
[22]In Moody's model, the probability of default is called the *expected default frequency* (*EDF*).

- **Expected yield on a corporate bond.** Corporations have limited liability. Therefore, if companies are unable to pay their debts, they can file for bankruptcy. As a result lenders may receive less than they are owed and the *expected* yield on a corporate bond is less than the *promised yield*.

- **The yield spread on a corporate bond.** Because of the possibility of default, the promised yield on a corporate bond is higher than on a government bond. You can think of this yield spread as the amount that you would need to pay to insure the bond against default. There is a market for insurance policies that protect the debtholder against default. These policies are called credit default swaps. There are few free lunches in financial markets. So the extra yield you get for buying a corporate bond is likely to be eaten up by the cost of insuring against default.

- **The default put.** The company's option to default is equivalent to a put option. If the value of the firm's assets is less than the amount of the debt, it will pay the company to default and to allow the lenders to take over the assets in settlement of the debt. Thus

$$\text{Bond value} = \text{value of risk-free bond} - \text{value of put option on issuer's assets}$$

  This insight tells us what we need to think about when valuing corporate debt—the current value of the firm relative to the point at which it would default, the volatility of the assets, the maturity of the debt payments, and the risk-free interest rate. Unfortunately, most companies have several loans outstanding with payments due at different times. This considerably complicates the task of valuing the put option.

- **Bond ratings.** When investors want a measure of the risk of a company's bonds, they usually look first at the rating that has been assigned by Moody's, Standard & Poor's, or Fitch. They know that bonds with investment-grade ratings (at least Baa or BBB) are much less likely to default than bonds with a junk rating.

- **Statistical models of default.** Banks, rating services, and consulting firms have also developed models for estimating the likelihood of default. Statistical models take accounting ratios or other indicators of corporate health, and weight them to produce a single measure of default probability.

- **Structural default models.** Structural models, such as the Merton model, take a different tack and seek to measure the probability that the market value of the firm's assets will fall to the point at which the firm will choose to exercise its option to default rather than keep up with its debt payments.

The websites of the main credit rating agencies contain a variety of useful reports on credit risk. (*See in particular* **www.moodys.com, www.standardandpoors.com,** and **www.fitchratings.com.**)

Altman and Hotchkiss provide a review of credit scoring models in:

E. I. Altman, E. Hotchkiss, and W. Wang, *Corporate Financial Distress, Restructuring and Bankruptcy,* 4th ed. (New York: John Wiley, 2019).

Books that discuss corporate bonds and credit risk include:

A. Saunders and L. Allen, *Credit Risk Measurement,* 3rd ed. (New York: John Wiley, 2010).

J. B. Caouette, E. I. Altman, P. Narayanan, and R. Nimmo, *Managing Credit Risk,* 2nd ed. (New York: John Wiley, 2008).

D. Duffie, *Measuring Corporate Default Risk* (Oxford, UK: Oxford University Press, 2011).

D. Duffie and K. J. Singleton, *Credit Risk: Pricing, Measurement and Management* (Princeton, NJ: Princeton University Press, 2003).

![McGraw Hill Connect] **Select problems are available in McGraw Hill's *Connect*. Please see the preface for more information.**

1. **Expected yield (S24.1)** You own a 5% bond maturing in two years and priced at 87%. Suppose that there is a 10% chance that at maturity the bond will default and you will receive only 40% of the promised payment. What is the bond's promised yield to maturity? What is its expected yield (i.e., the possible yields weighted by their probabilities)?

2. **Bond ratings (S24.1)** In February 2018, Aaa bonds yielded 2.36%, Baa bonds yielded 3.43%, and Treasuries with the same maturities yielded 0.676%.

   a. What was the credit spread on Aaa bonds?

   b. What was the spread on Baa bonds?

   c. What do you think would be the difference in price (as a percent of face value) between a typical 5% 10-year Baa bond and a similar Treasury bond?

3. **Bond ratings (S24.1)** It is 2030 and the yields on corporate bonds are as follows:

Aaa	A	Ba
8%	10%	12%

   Tau Corp wishes to raise $10 million by an issue of 9% 10-year bonds. What will be the likely issue price (as a percent of face value) if Tau is rated (a) Aaa, (b) A, or (c) Ba?

4. **Default option (S24.2)** The difference between the value of a government bond and a similar corporate bond is equal to the value of an option. What is this option, and what is its exercise price?

5. **Default option (S24.2)** Other things equal, would you expect the difference between the price of a Treasury bond and a corporate bond to increase or decrease with

   a. The company's business risk?

   b. The degree of financial leverage?

   c. The time to maturity?

6. **Default option (S24.2)** Company A has issued a single zero-coupon bond maturing in 10 years. Company B has issued a coupon bond maturing in 10 years. Explain why it is more complicated to value B's debt than A's.

7. **Default option (S24.2)** How much would it cost you to insure the bonds of Backwoods Chemical against default? (See Section 24-1.)

8. **Default option (S24.2)** Digital Organics has 10 million outstanding shares trading at $25 per share. It also has a large amount of debt outstanding, all coming due in one year. The debt pays interest at 8%. It has a face value of $350 million but is trading at a market value of only $280 million. The one-year risk-free interest rate is 6%.

   a. Write out the put–call parity formula for Digital Organics' stock, debt, and assets.

   b. What is the value of the company's option to default on its debt?

9. **Default option (S24.2)** Square File's assets are worth $100. It has $80 of zero-coupon debt outstanding that is due to be repaid at the end of two years. The risk-free interest rate is 5%, and the standard deviation of the returns on Square File's assets is 40% per year. Calculate the present value of the company's debt and equity.

10. **Predicting default probability (S24.3)** A friend has mentioned that she has read somewhere that the following variables can be used to predict bankruptcy: (a) the company debt ratio;

BEYOND THE PAGE

Try It!
The Black–Scholes model

mhhe.com/brealey14e

(b) the interest coverage; (c) the amount of cash relative to sales or assets; (d) the return on assets; (e) the market-to-book ratio; (f) the recent return on the stock; (g) the volatility of the stock returns. The problem is that she can't remember whether a high value of each variable implies a high or a low probability of bankruptcy. Can you help her out?

11. **Predicting default probability (S24.3)** What variables are required to use the Merton model to calculate the risk-neutral probability that a company will default on its debt?

12. **Predicting default probability (S24.3)** Company X has borrowed $150 maturing this year and $50 maturing in 10 years. Company Y has borrowed $200 maturing in five years. In both cases, asset value is $140. Sketch a scenario in which X does not default but Y does.

BEYOND THE PAGE

Try It!
The Black–Scholes model

mhhe.com/brealey14e

13. **Predicting default probability (S24.3)** Discuss the problems with developing a numerical credit scoring system for evaluating personal loans. You can only test your system using data for applicants who have in the past been granted credit. Is this a potential problem?

14. **Predicting default probability (S24.3)** Look back at Section 24.3. Suppose that the standard deviation of the return on Upsilon's assets is 50%. Recalculate the probability that the company will default.

CHALLENGE

15. **Default option (S24.2)** Look back at the first Backwoods Chemical example at the start of Section 24-1. Suppose that the firm's book balance sheet is

Backwoods Chemical Company (Book Values)			
Net working capital	$ 400	$1,000	Debt
Net fixed assets	1,600	1,000	Equity (net worth)
Total assets	$2,000	$2,000	Total value

BEYOND THE PAGE

Try It!
The Black–Scholes model

mhhe.com/brealey14e

The debt has a one-year maturity and a promised interest payment of 9%. Thus, the promised payment to Backwoods's creditors is $1,090. The market value of the assets is $1,200, and the standard deviation of asset value is 45% per year. The risk-free interest rate is 9%. Calculate the value of Backwoods's debt and equity.

SOLUTIONS TO SELF-TEST QUESTIONS

24.1   The expected payoff is $0.8 \times \$1,050 = \$840$. The bond price is $\$840/1.08 = \$778$, and the promised yield is $1,050/778 - 1 = 0.35$, or 35%.

24.4   You *buy* a credit default swap.

24.3   The shareholders have the option to hand over the assets to the bondholders rather than to repay the bonds.

24.4   The value of the equity is a call option on the assets (i.e., shareholders get to own the assets by repaying the debt). The value of the debt is equal to the value of the assets less the value of the shareholders' call option. The exercise price of the call option is the face value of the company's debt.

24.5   b and c.

24.6   If the exercise price of the put is $70, $N(d_2) = 0.8852$. So the risk-neutral probability of default is $1 - 0.8852 = 0.1148$, or 11.48%.

1. Go to **finance.yahoo.com** and select three industrial companies that have been experiencing difficult times.

   a. Are the companies' troubles reflected in their financial ratios? (You may find it helpful to refer to Figure 24.4.)

   b. Now look at the company's bond rating. Do the ratings and ratios provide consistent messages?

25

The Many Different Kinds of Debt

In Chapters 16 and 17, we discussed how much a company should borrow. But companies also need to think about what *type* of debt to issue. They can choose to issue short or long-term debt, straight or convertible bonds; they can issue in the United States or in the international debt market; and they can either sell the debt publicly or place it privately with a few large investors.

As a financial manager, you need to choose the type of debt that makes sense for your company. For example, if a firm has only a temporary need for funds, it will generally issue short-term debt. Firms with a substantial overseas business may prefer to issue foreign currency debt. Sometimes, competition between lenders opens a window of opportunity in a particular sector of the debt market. The effect may be only a few basis points reduction in yield, but on a large issue, that can translate into savings of several million dollars.

This chapter looks principally at bonds and bank loans. But companies have a number of important debt-like liabilities that we do *not* discuss here. For instance, long-term leases are very similar to debt. The user of the equipment agrees to make a series of lease payments, and if it defaults, it may be forced into bankruptcy. We discuss leases in Chapter 26.

Postretirement health benefits and pension promises can also be huge liabilities. For example, in 2003 General Motors had a pension deficit of $19 billion. To reduce this deficit, GM made a large issue of bonds and invested the majority of the proceeds in its pension fund. You could say that the effect was to increase the company's debt, but the economic reality was that it substituted one long-term obligation (the new debt) for another (its pension obligation). Management of pension plans is outside the scope of this book, but financial managers spend a good deal of time worrying about the pension "debt."

Figure 25.1 provides a road map through this chapter. We start with the long-term bond market.

Section 25-1 Long-term corporate bonds

We begin with a look at standard, or *straight,* bonds. We examine the differences between senior and junior bonds and between secured and unsecured bonds, including a special kind of secured bond called an *asset-backed bond*. We describe how bonds may be repaid by means of a sinking fund and how the borrower or the lender may have an option for early repayment. As we review these different features of corporate debt, we explain why sinking funds, repayment options, and the like exist. They are not simply matters of custom or neutral mutations; there are generally good reasons for their use.

Section 25-2 Convertible securities and some unusual bonds

In Section 25-2, we turn to some less common bonds, starting with convertible bonds and their close relative, the package of bonds and warrants. We also illustrate the enormous variety of bond designs by looking at a few unusual bonds and at some of the motives for innovation in the bond market.

Section 25-3 Bank loans

The rest of the chapter is concerned with shorter term debt. We start in Section 25-3 with bank loans, which make up much of the short-term debt market. Companies may arrange a *revolving line of credit* with a bank that allows them to borrow up to an agreed amount whenever they need financing. Lines of credit can tide the firm over when it has a temporary

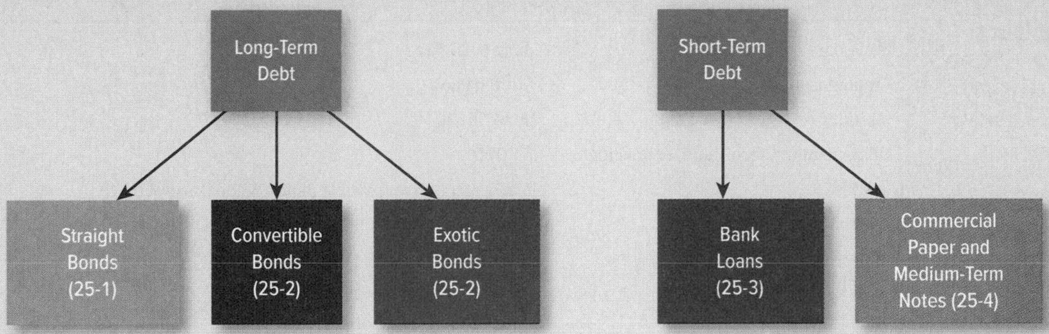

FIGURE 25.1   The principal species of corporate debt and the sections of this chapter in which they are discussed.

shortage of cash. Loans from lines of credit may be repaid in only a few months. Banks also make *term loans* that sometimes extend for five years or more. Some loans are too large to be made by a single bank and are therefore syndicated among a group of banks. We also look at how banks protect their loans by imposing restrictions on the borrower and by requiring security.

Section 25-4 Commercial Paper and Medium-Term Notes

Rather than borrowing from a bank, large blue-chip companies sometimes bypass the banking system and issue their own short-term debt to investors. This is called *commercial paper*. Somewhat longer term loans that are marketed on a regular basis are known as *medium-term notes*. In Section 25-4, we discuss both in turn.

Appendix: Project Finance

In the Appendix to the chapter, we look at another form of private placement known as project finance. The words *project finance* conjure up images of multibillion-dollar loans to finance huge ventures in exotic parts of the world. You'll find there's something to the popular image, but it's not the whole story.

• • • • •

25-1   Long-Term Corporate Bonds

Bond Terms

Applied Materials (AMAT) supplies equipment and software for the manufacture of semiconductors. In 2011, AMAT issued 30-year bonds to help finance an acquisition. The bond was a plain-vanilla issue; in other words, it was pretty well standard in every way. To give you some feel for the bond contract (and for some of the language in which it is couched), we have summarized in Table 25.1 the terms of the issue. We will look in turn at its principal features.

The AMAT bond was issued in 2011 and is due to mature 30 years later in 2041. It was issued in denominations of $1,000. So, at maturity, the company will repay the principal amount of $1,000 to the holder of each bond.

The annual interest or *coupon* payment on the bond is 5.85% of $1,000, or $58.50. This interest is payable semiannually, so every six months the bondholder receives interest of 58.50/2 = $29.25. Most U.S. bonds pay interest semiannually, but in many other countries it is common to pay interest annually.[1]

---

[1]If a bond pays interest semiannually, investors usually calculate a *semiannually* compounded yield to maturity on the bond. In other words, the yield is quoted as twice the six-month yield. When bonds pay interest annually, it is conventional to quote their yields to maturity on an *annually* compounded basis. For more on this, see Section 3-1.

⟩TABLE 25.1
Summary of terms of bond issue by Applied Materials (AMAT).

Issue date	June 8, 2011
Amount issued	$600 million
Maturity	June 15, 2041
Denomination, face value, or principal	$1,000
Interest	5.85% per annum payable June 15 and December 15.
Offered	Issued at a price of 99.592% plus accrued interest (proceeds to company 98.717%)
Joint book-running managers	Citi, JPMorgan
Registered	Issued in fully registered form only
Trustee	U.S. Bank National Association
Security	Not secured. Company will not permit to have any lien on its property or assets without equally and ratably securing the debt securities.
Seniority	Senior notes ranking pari passu with other unsecured unsubordinated debt.
Change of control event	If a change of control occurs and the notes are simultaneously downrated to below investment grade the company will offer to repurchase the notes.
Sinking fund	None.
Callable	At whole or in part at the option of the Company with at least 30 days, but not more than 60 days, notice at the greater of (*i*) 100% of the principal amount or (*ii*) the sum of the scheduled remaining payments discounted at 30 basis points above the Treasury rate.
Moody's rating at issue date	A3

Sometimes bonds are sold with a lower coupon payment but at a significant discount on their face value, so investors receive much of their return in the form of capital appreciation.[2] The ultimate is the zero-coupon bond, which pays no interest at all; in this case, the entire return consists of capital appreciation.[3]

The AMAT interest payment is fixed for the life of the bond, but in some issues the payment varies with the general level of interest rates. For example, the payment may be set at 1% over the U.S. Treasury bill rate or over the secured overnight financing rate (SOFR). SOFR is the interest rate on transactions in the Treasury repurchase market, where investors offer banks overnight loans backed by the bank's bond holdings. Sometimes these *floating-rate notes* specify a minimum (or floor) interest rate, or they may specify a maximum (or cap) on the rate.[4]

The AMAT bonds have a face value of $1,000 and were sold to investors at 99.592% of face value. In addition, buyers had to pay any *accrued interest*. This is the amount of any future interest that has accumulated by the time of the purchase. For example, investors who bought bonds for delivery on December 15 would have to wait only two months before receiving their first interest payment. Therefore, the four months of accrued interest would be

BEYOND THE PAGE

Accrued interest calculations

mhhe.com/brealey14e

---

[2]Any bond that is issued at a discount is known as an *original issue discount bond.* A zero-coupon bond is often called a "pure discount bond." The capital appreciation on a discount bond is not taxed as income as long as it amounts to less than 0.25% a year (IRS Code Section 1272).

[3]The ultimate of ultimates was an issue of a perpetual zero-coupon bond on behalf of a charity.

[4]Instead of issuing a capped floating-rate loan, a company sometimes issues an uncapped loan and at the same time buys a cap from a bank. The bank pays the interest in excess of the specified level.

$(120/360) \times 8.25 = 2.75\%$, and the investor would need to pay the purchase price of the bond plus $2.75\% \times \$1,000$.[5]

Although the AMAT bonds were offered to the public at a price of 99.592%, the company received only 98.717%. The difference represents the underwriters' spread. Of the $597.6 million raised, $592.3 million went to the company and $5.3 million (or about 0.9%) went to the underwriters.

Moving down Table 25.1, you see that the AMAT's bonds are *registered*. This means that the company's registrar records the ownership of each bond and the company pays the interest and final principal amount directly to each owner. Almost all bonds in the United States are issued in registered form, but in many countries, companies may issue *bearer* bonds. In this case, the bond certificate constitutes the primary evidence of ownership, so the bondholder must return the certificate to the company to claim the final repayment of principal.

The AMAT bonds were sold publicly to investors. Before it could sell the bonds, it needed to file a registration statement for approval of the SEC and to prepare a prospectus. The bond was issued under an **indenture**, or **trust deed**, between the company and a trustee that represents the bondholders. The trustee must see that the terms of the indenture are observed and look after the bondholders in the event of default. The bond indenture is a turgid legal document that is bedtime reading only for insomniacs.[6] However, the main provisions are described in the prospectus to the issue.

Security and Seniority

Like most bond issues by industrial and financial companies, the AMAT bonds are unsecured. Unsecured bonds maturing in 10 years or fewer are usually called **notes**, while longer term issues may be called bonds (as in the case of the AMAT bond) or **debentures**.[7] When bonds are unsecured, it is common for the issue to include a *negative-pledge* clause, which promises that the company will not issue any secured bonds without offering the same security to its unsecured bonds. The AMAT bond has a negative-pledge clause.

Sometimes a company sets aside particular assets for the protection of the bondholder. For example, utility company bonds are often secured. In this case, if the company defaults on its debt, the trustee or lender may take possession of the relevant assets. If these are insufficient to satisfy the claim, the remaining debt will have a general claim, alongside any unsecured debt, on the other assets of the firm.

The majority of secured bonds are **mortgage bonds**. These sometimes provide a claim against a specific building, but they are more often secured on all of the firm's property.[8] Of course, the value of any mortgage depends on the extent to which the property has alternative uses. A custom-built machine for producing buggy whips will not be worth much when the market for buggy whips dries up.

---

[5]In the U.S. corporate bond market, accrued interest is calculated on the assumption that a year is composed of twelve 30-day months; in some other markets (such as the U.S. Treasury bond market) calculations recognize the actual number of days in each calendar month.

[6]For example, the indenture for the AMAT bond states, "Unless and until it is exchanged in whole or in part for securities in definitive form, this security may not be transferred except as a whole by the depositary to a nominee of the depositary or by a nominee of the depositary to the depositary or to another nominee of the depositary or by the depositary or any such nominee to a successor depositary or a nominee of such successor depositary. Unless this global security is presented by an authorized representative of the depositary to the company or its agent for registration of transfer, exchange, or payment, and any security issued is registered in the name of any entity as may be requested by an authorized representative of the depositary (and any payment is made to such entity as may be requested by an authorized representative of the depositary), any transfer, pledge, or other use hereof for value or otherwise by or to any person is wrongful inasmuch as the registered owner hereof has an interest herein." Try saying that three times very fast.

[7]In some countries, such as the United Kingdom and Australia, "debenture" means a secured bond.

[8]Many mortgages are secured not only by existing property but also by "after-acquired" property. However, if the company buys only property that is already mortgaged, the bondholder would have only a junior claim on the new property. Therefore, mortgage bonds with after-acquired property clauses also limit the extent to which the company can purchase additional mortgaged property.

Companies that own securities may use them as collateral for a loan. For example, holding companies are firms whose main assets consist of common stock in a number of subsidiaries. So, when holding companies wish to borrow, they generally use these investments as collateral. In such cases, the problem for the lender is that the stock is junior to any debt that the subsidiaries may have issued. Therefore, these *collateral trust bonds* usually include detailed restrictions on the freedom of the subsidiaries to issue debt or preferred stock.

A third form of secured debt is the **equipment trust certificate (ETC).** This was originally used to finance new railroad rolling stock but is now commonly used for the purchase of aircraft and shipping containers. Under this arrangement, a trustee obtains formal ownership of the equipment. The company makes a down payment on the cost of the equipment, and the balance is provided by a package of ETCs with different maturities that might typically run from 1 to 15 years. Only when all these debts have finally been paid off does the company become the formal owner of the equipment. Bond rating agencies such as Moody's or Standard & Poor's usually rate equipment trust certificates one grade higher (better) than the company's regular debt.

Bonds may be senior claims or they may be subordinated to the senior bonds or subordinated to *all* other creditors.[9] If the firm defaults, the senior bonds come first in the pecking order. The subordinated lender gets in line behind the general creditors but ahead of the preferred stockholders and the common stockholders.

As you can see from Figure 25.2, if default does occur, it pays to hold senior secured bonds. On average, investors in these bonds can expect to recover 54% of the amount of the loan. At the other extreme, recovery rates for subordinated bondholders are only 31% of the face value of the debt.

Asset-Backed Securities

Instead of borrowing money directly, companies sometimes bundle up a group of assets and then sell the cash flows from these assets. This issue is known as an *asset-backed security,* or *ABS.* The debt is secured, or backed, by the underlying assets.

The most common type of asset-backed security is the *mortgage-backed security,* or *MBS.* Suppose your company has made a large number of mortgage loans to buyers of homes or commercial real estate. However, you don't want to wait until the loans are paid off; you

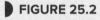 **FIGURE 25.2**

Percentage recovery rates on defaulting debt by seniority and security, 1983–2019.

Source: Moody's, "Annual Default Study: Corporate Default and Recovery Rates, 1920–2019," February 28, 2020.

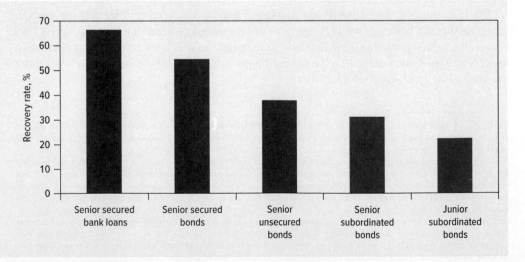

[9]If a bond does not specifically state that it is junior, you can assume that it is senior.

would like to get your hands on the money now. Here is what you do. You establish a separate, special-purpose company that buys a package of the mortgage loans. To finance this purchase, the company sells *mortgage-backed securities*. These securities are pass-through securities; their holders simply receive a share of the mortgage payments. For example, if interest rates fall and the mortgages are repaid early, holders of the bonds are also repaid early. That is not generally popular with these holders because they get their money back just when they don't want it—when interest rates are low.[10]

Instead of issuing one class of bonds, a pool of mortgages can be bundled and then split into different slices (or *tranches*), known as *collateralized mortgage obligations* (CMOs) or, more generally, *collateralized debt obligations* (CDOs). For example, mortgage payments might be used first to pay off one class of security holders and only then will other classes start to be repaid. The senior tranches have first claim on the cash flows and therefore may be attractive to conservative investors such as insurance companies or pension funds. The riskiest (or *equity*) tranche, sometimes humorously called "toxic waste," can then be sold to hedge funds or mutual funds that specialize in low-quality debt.

Real estate lenders are not unique in wanting to turn future cash receipts into upfront cash. Automobile loans, student loans, and credit card receivables are also often bundled and remarketed as CDOs. This process of bundling a number of future cash flows into a single security is called *securitization*. You can see the arguments for securitization. As long as the risks of the individual loans are not perfectly correlated, the risk of the package is less than that of any of the parts. In addition, securitization distributes the risk of the loans widely, and because the package can be traded, investors are not obliged to hold it to maturity.

In the years leading up to the financial crisis of 2007–2008, the proportion of new securitized mortgages expanded sharply, while the quality of the mortgages declined. By 2007, more than half of the new issues of mortgage CDOs involved exposure to subprime mortgages. Because the mortgages were packaged together, investors in these CDOs were protected against the risk of default on an individual mortgage. However, even the senior tranches were exposed to the risk of an economywide slump in the housing market.

Catastrophe struck in the summer of 2007, when the investment bank Bear Stearns revealed that two of its hedge funds had invested heavily in nearly worthless CDOs. Bear Stearns was rescued with help from the Federal Reserve, but it signaled the start of the credit crunch and the collapse of the CDO market. By 2009, issues of CDOs had effectively disappeared, and issuance remains well below pre-crisis levels.[11]

Did this collapse reflect a fundamental flaw in the practice of securitization? A bank that packages and resells its mortgage loans spreads the risk of those loans. However, the danger is that when a bank can earn juicy fees from securitization, it might not worry so much if the loans in the package are junk.[12]

BEYOND THE PAGE

Mortgage-backed securities

mhhe.com/brealey14e

Call Provisions

Back to our AMAT bond. The bond includes a call option that allows the company to repay the debt early. This can be a valuable option if AMAT wishes to reduce its leverage or tidy up its outstanding debt. The price at which companies could call their bonds used to be set at a fixed number. In this case, issuers had an incentive to call the bonds whenever they were worth more than the call price. This was not popular with investors. These days, it is more

---

[10]In Europe, it is common for banks or mortgage institutions to finance them by issuing *covered bonds* or *Pfandbriefe*. These are similar to U.S. mortgage-backed securities except that the mortgages continue to be held by the issuer.

[11]Data on issuance are available on www.sifma.org.

[12]CDO fees for the originating bank were in the region of 1.5–1.75%, more than three times the amount that the bank could earn from underwriting an investment-grade bond. However, many banks during the crisis seem to have persuaded themselves that the underlying mortgages were *not* junk and kept a large portion of the loans on their own books. See, for example, V. Acharya and M. Richardson (eds.), *Restoring Financial Stability* (Hoboken, NJ: Wiley, 2009).

common to link the call price to an estimate of the bond's value. Thus, if interest rates fall and the bond increases in value, AMAT must pay more than face value to buy back its bonds. The formula for determining this price seeks to ensure that AMAT can never buy back the bond for less than it is worth.

Very occasionally you come across bonds that give *investors* the repayment option. Extendible bonds give them the option to extend the bond's life. Retractable (or *puttable*) bonds give investors the right to demand early repayment. Puttable bonds exist largely because bond indentures cannot anticipate every action the company may take that could harm the bondholder. The put option allows the bondholders to demand repayment if the value of their bonds is reduced.

Puttable loans can sometimes get their *issuers* into BIG trouble. During the 1990s, many loans to Asian companies gave their lenders a repayment option. Consequently, when the Asian crisis struck in 1997, these companies were faced by a flood of lenders demanding their money back.

> ### 25.1 Self-Test
>
> The call provision on the AMAT bonds is designed so that the company needs to pay a higher price to call its bonds when interest rates fall. As a bondholder, would you prefer it if the call price on the bonds was fixed? Why or why not?

Sinking Funds

The AMAT bond must be repaid all at once in 2041. But in many cases, a bond issue is repaid in regular steps before maturity. To do this, the company makes a series of payments into a *sinking fund.* If the payment is in the form of cash, the trustee selects bonds by lottery and uses the cash to redeem them at their face value.[13] Alternatively, the company can choose to buy bonds in the marketplace and pay these into the fund. This is a valuable option for the company. If the bond price is low, the firm will buy the bonds in the market and hand them to the sinking fund; if the price is high, it will call the bonds by lottery.

Generally, there is both a mandatory sinking fund that *must* be satisfied and an optional fund that can be satisfied if the borrower chooses. A sinking fund provides a hurdle that the firm must keep jumping. If it cannot pay the cash into the sinking fund, the lenders can demand their money back. That is why long-dated, lower quality issues involve larger sinking funds. Higher quality bonds generally have a lighter sinking fund requirement if they have one at all.[14]

Bond Covenants

Investors in corporate bonds know that there is a risk of default. But they still want to make sure that the company plays fair. They don't want it to gamble with their money. Therefore, the loan agreement usually includes a number of *debt covenants* that prevent the company from purposely increasing the value of its default option.[15] These covenants may be relatively light for blue-chip companies but more restrictive for smaller, riskier borrowers.

Debt covenants set limits on what financial managers can do. But accepting covenants is usually in the company's and shareholders' interest. Covenants reassure lenders, reducing the interest rate they demand and making the debt issue easier to sell. Covenants can also block

---

[13]Every investor dreams of buying up the entire supply of a sinking-fund bond that is selling way below face value and then forcing the company to buy the bonds back at face value. Cornering the market in this way is fun to dream about but difficult to do.

[14]Unfortunately, a sinking fund is a weak test of solvency if the firm is allowed to repurchase bonds in the market. Since the market value of the debt declines as the firm approaches financial distress, the sinking fund becomes a hurdle that gets progressively lower as the hurdler gets weaker.

[15]We described in Section 17-2 some of the games that managers can play at the expense of bondholders.

out the conflicts of interest that arise if the company falls on hard times and financial distress. Such conflicts can tempt the firm to take imprudent risks or other value-destroying actions that benefit stockholders at the expense of lenders.[16] For example, lenders worry that after they have made the loan, the company may pile up more debt and so increase the chance of default. They protect themselves against this risk by prohibiting the company from making further debt issues unless the ratio of debt to equity is below a specified limit.

Not all debts are created equal. If the firm defaults, the senior debt comes first in the pecking order and must be paid off in full before the junior debtholders get a cent. Therefore, when a company issues senior debt, the lenders will place limits on further issues of senior debt. But they won't restrict the amount of *junior* debt that the company can issue. Because the senior lenders are at the front of the queue, they view the junior debt in the same way that they view equity: They would be happy to see an issue of either. Of course, the converse is not true. Holders of the junior debt *do* care both about the total amount of debt and the proportion that is senior to their claim. As a result, an issue of junior debt generally includes a restriction on both total debt and senior debt.

All bondholders worry that the company may issue more secured debt. An issue of mortgage bonds often imposes a limit on the amount of secured debt. This is not necessary when you are issuing unsecured debentures. As long as the debenture holders are given an equal claim, they don't care how much you mortgage your assets. Therefore, unsecured bonds usually include a negative-pledge clause, in which the unsecured holders simply say, "Me too."[17] We saw earlier that the AMAT bonds include a negative pledge clause.

Instead of borrowing money to buy an asset, companies may enter into a long-term agreement to rent or lease it. For the debtholder, this is very similar to secured borrowing. Therefore, debt agreements also include limitations on leasing.

We have talked about how an unscrupulous borrower can try to increase the value of the default option by issuing more debt. But this is not the only way that such a company can exploit its existing bondholders. For example, the value of the default option is increased when the company pays out some of its assets to stockholders. In the extreme case, a company could sell all its assets and distribute the proceeds to shareholders as a bumper dividend. That would leave nothing for the lenders. To guard against such dangers, debt issues may restrict the amount that the company may pay out in the form of dividends or repurchases of stock.[18]

Merger covenants seek to ensure that in the event of a merger the debt obligation remains with the merged company rather than with just a part of the new company. In addition, if there is a change of control, bondholders may have the right to sell their bond back to the company at a premium price.

Take a look at Table 25.2, which summarizes the principal covenants in a large sample of senior bond issues. These covenants prevent the company from taking certain actions that would reduce the value of their bonds. Notice that investment-grade bonds tend to have fewer restrictions than high-yield bonds. For example, restrictions on the amount of any dividends or repurchases are less common in the case of investment-grade bonds.

These debt covenants *do* matter. One study of the effect of leveraged buyouts on the value of the company's debt found that when there were no restrictions on further debt issues, dividend payments, or mergers, the buyout led to a 5.2% fall in the value of existing bonds.[19] Those bonds that were protected by strong covenants against excessive borrowing increased in price by 2.6%.

---

[16]See Section 17-2.

[17]"Me too" is not acceptable legal jargon. Instead, the bond agreement may state that the company "will not consent to any lien on its assets without securing the existing bonds equally and ratably."

[18]A dividend restriction might typically prohibit the company from paying dividends if their cumulative amount would exceed the sum of (1) cumulative net income, (2) the proceeds from the sale of stock or conversion of debt, and (3) a dollar amount equal to one year's dividend.

[19]P. Asquith and T. Wizman, "Event Risk, Covenants, and Bondholder Returns in Leveraged Buyouts," *Journal of Financial Economics* 27 (September 1990), pp. 195–213. Leveraged buyouts (LBOs) are company acquisitions that are financed by large issues of (usually unsecured) debt. We describe LBOs in Chapter 33.

Covenant Loopholes

❯ Bond covenants aim to prevent the issuer from deliberately damaging its bondholders. Unfortunately, it is not easy to cover all loopholes, as the bondholders of Marriott Corporation discovered in 1992. They hit the roof when the company announced plans to divide its operations into two separate businesses. One business, Marriott International, would manage Marriott's hotel chain and receive most of the revenues, while the other, Host Marriott, would own all the company's real estate and be responsible for servicing essentially all of the old company's $3 billion of debt. As a result, the price of Marriott's bonds plunged nearly 30%, and investors began to think about how they could protect themselves against such *event risks*.

Type of Covenant	Percentage of Bonds with Covenants	
	Investment-Grade Bonds	Other Bonds
Merger restrictions	92%	93%
Dividends or other payment restrictions	6	44
Borrowing covenants	74	67
Default-related events[a]	52	71
Change of control	24	74

❯**TABLE 25.2** Percentage of a sample of bonds with covenant restrictions. Sample consists of 4,478 senior bonds issued between 1993 and 2007.

[a]For example, default on other loans, rating changes, or declining net worth.

Source: S. Chava, P. Kumar, and A. Warga, "Managerial Agency and Bond Covenants," *Review of Financial Studies* 23 (2010), pp. 1120–1148.

25.2 Self-Test

Why are borrowers happy to enter into covenants that reassure the lender but constrain the borrower?

Privately Placed Bonds

The AMAT notes were registered with the SEC and sold publicly. However, bonds may also be placed privately with a few financial institutions, though the market for privately placed bonds is much smaller than the public market.[20]

As we saw in Section 14-4, it costs less to arrange a private placement than to make a public debt issue. But there are other differences between a privately placed bond and its public counterpart.

First, if you place an issue privately with one or two financial institutions, it may be necessary to sign only a simple promissory note. This is just an IOU that lays down certain

---

[20]D. J. Denis and V. T. Mihov estimated that the value of privately placed bond issues is less than 20% that of total bond issues. See D. J. Denis and V. T. Mihov, "The Choice among Bank Debt, Non-Bank Private Debt and Public Debt: Evidence from New Corporate Borrowings," *Journal of Financial Economics* 70 (2003), pp. 3–28.

conditions that the borrower must observe. However, when you make a public issue of debt, you must worry about who is supposed to represent the bondholders in any subsequent negotiations and what procedures are needed for paying interest and principal. Therefore, the contract has to be more complicated.

The second characteristic of publicly issued bonds is that they are somewhat standardized products. They *have* to be—investors are constantly buying and selling without checking the fine print in the agreement. This is not so necessary in private placements, so the debt can be custom-tailored for firms with special problems or opportunities. The relationship between borrower and lender is much more intimate. Imagine a $200 million debt issue placed privately with an insurance company, and compare it with an equivalent public issue held by 200 anonymous investors. The insurance company can justify a more thorough investigation of the company's prospects and, therefore, may be more willing to accept unusual terms or conditions.[21]

These features of private placements give them a particular niche in the corporate debt market—namely, relatively low-grade loans to small- and medium-sized firms.[22] These are the firms that face the highest costs in public issues, that require the most detailed investigation, and that may require specialized, flexible loan arrangements.

Of course, the advantages of private placements are not free, for the lenders demand a higher rate of interest to compensate them for holding an illiquid asset. It is difficult to generalize about the difference in interest rates between private placements and public issues, but a typical differential is 50 basis points, or 0.50 of a percentage point.

Foreign Bonds and Eurobonds

AMAT's bonds were registered with the SEC, denominated in dollars, and marketed to investors in the United States and overseas. If the company had needed the cash for a project in another country, it might have preferred to issue debt in that country's currency. For example, it could have sold sterling bonds in the United Kingdom or Swiss franc bonds in Switzerland. Similarly, many foreign companies issue dollar bonds in the United States. Foreign currency bonds that are sold to local investors in the country of that currency (sterling bonds sold in the United Kingdom or dollar bonds sold in the United States) are known as *foreign bonds*. Foreign bonds have a variety of nicknames. For example, a bond sold by a foreign company in the United States is known as a *yankee bond,* a bond sold by a foreign firm in Japan is a *samurai,* and one sold in the United Kingdom is a *bulldog.*

Of course, any firm that raises money from local investors in a foreign country is subject to the rules of that country and oversight by its financial regulator. For example, when a foreign company issues publicly traded bonds in the United States, it must first register the issue with the SEC. However, as long as the bonds are *not* publicly traded, foreign firms borrowing in the United States can avoid registration by complying with the SEC's Rule 144A. Rule 144A bonds can be bought and sold only by large financial institutions.[23]

Instead of issuing a bond in a particular country's market, a company may market a bond issue internationally. Issues that are denominated in one country's currency but marketed internationally outside that country are known as *eurobonds* and are usually made in one of the major currencies, such as the U.S. dollar, the euro, or the yen. For example, AMAT could have issued a dollar bond just to overseas investors. As long as the issue is not sold to U.S. investors, it does not need to be registered with the SEC.[24] Eurobond issues are marketed by

---

[21]Of course, debt with the same terms could be offered publicly, but then 200 separate investigations would be required—a much more expensive proposition.

[22]See D. J. Denis and V. T. Mihov, "The Choice among Bank Debt, Non-Bank Private Debt, and Public Debt: Evidence from New Corporate Borrowings," *Journal of Financial Economics* 70 (2003), pp. 3–28.

[23]We described Rule 144A in Section 14-4.

[24]You should not, however, get the impression that the eurobond market is some lawless wilderness. Eurobond contracts typically state that the issue is subject to either British or New York law.

international syndicates of underwriters, such as the London branches of large U.S., European, and Japanese banks and security dealers. Be careful not to confuse a eurobond (which is outside the oversight of any domestic regulator and may be in any currency) with a bond that is marketed in a European country and denominated in euros.[25] Frequently, companies make a global bond issue, consisting of parallel issues of eurobonds and domestic bonds.

25.3 Self-Test

Other things equal, would you pay more for
- a. A senior bond or a junior bond?
- b. A secured bond or an unsecured bond?
- c. A bond with a mandatory sinking fund or one without?
- d. A publicly issued bond or a privately issued bond?

25-2 Convertible Securities and Some Unusual Bonds

Unlike a straight bond, a convertible security can change its spots. It starts life as a bond (or preferred stock) but subsequently may turn into common stock. For example, in May 2019, Tesla issued $1.8 billion of 2.0% convertible senior notes due in 2024. Each bond can be converted at any time into 3.2276 shares of common stock. Thus, the owner has a five-year option to return the bond to the company and receive 3.2276 shares of common stock in exchange. The number of shares into which each bond can be converted is called the bond's **conversion ratio**. The conversion ratio of the Tesla bond is 3.2276.

To receive these shares, the owner of the convertible must surrender bonds with a face value of $1,000. This means that to receive *one* share, the owner needs to surrender bonds with a face value of $1,000/3.2276 = $309.83. This is the bond's **conversion price**. Anybody who bought the bond at $1,000 to convert it into stock paid the equivalent of $309.83 a share, a *conversion premium* of 27.5% above the stock price at the time of the convertible issue.

You can think of a convertible bond as equivalent to a straight bond plus an option to acquire common stock. When convertible bondholders exercise this option, they do not pay cash; instead they give up their bonds in exchange for shares. If Tesla's bonds had not been convertible, they would probably have been worth about $800 at the time of issue. The difference between the price of a convertible bond and the price of an equivalent straight bond represents the value that investors place on the conversion option. For example, an investor who paid $1,000 in 2019 for the Tesla convertible would have paid about $1,000 − $800 = $200 for the five-year option to acquire 3.2276 shares.

The Value of a Convertible at Maturity

By the time the Tesla convertible matures, investors need to choose whether to stay with the bond or convert to common stock. Figure 25.3*a* shows the possible bond values at maturity.[26] Notice that the bond value is simply the face value as long as Tesla does not default. However, if the value of the company's assets is sufficiently low, the bondholders will receive *less* than the face value and, in the extreme case that the assets are worthless, they will receive nothing. You can think of the bond value as a lower bound, or "floor," to the price of the

---

[25]To make matters more confusing, the term "eurobond" has also been used to refer to bonds that in the future might be issued jointly by eurozone governments.

[26]You may recognize this as the position diagram for a default-free bond *minus* a put option on the assets with an exercise price equal to the face value of the bonds. See Section 24-2.

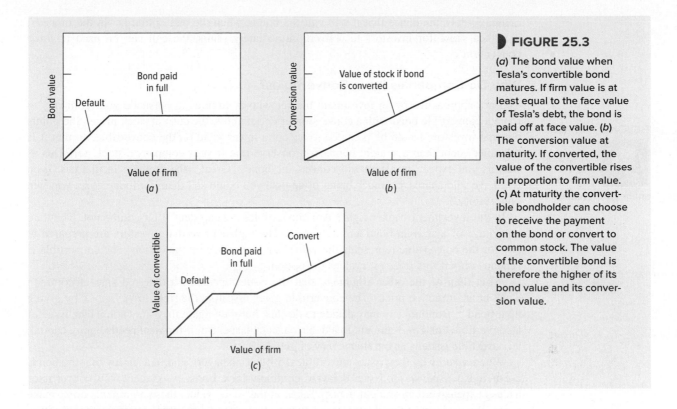

▶ FIGURE 25.3

(*a*) The bond value when Tesla's convertible bond matures. If firm value is at least equal to the face value of Tesla's debt, the bond is paid off at face value. (*b*) The conversion value at maturity. If converted, the value of the convertible rises in proportion to firm value. (*c*) At maturity the convertible bondholder can choose to receive the payment on the bond or convert to common stock. The value of the convertible bond is therefore the higher of its bond value and its conversion value.

convertible. But that floor has a nasty slope and, when the company falls on hard times, the bond may not be worth much.

Figure 25.3*b* shows the value of the shares that investors receive if they choose to convert. If Tesla's assets at that point are worthless, the shares into which the convertible can be exchanged are also worthless. But, as the value of the assets rises, so does the conversion value.

Tesla's convertible cannot sell for less than its conversion value. If it did, investors would buy the convertible, exchange it rapidly for stock, and sell the stock. Their profit would be equal to the difference between the conversion value and the price of the convertible. Therefore, there are two lower bounds to the price of the convertible: its bond value and its conversion value. Investors will not convert if the convertible is worth more as a bond; they *will* do so if the conversion value at maturity exceeds the bond value. In other words, the price of the convertible at maturity is represented by the higher of the two lines in Figure 25.3*a* and *b*. This is shown in Figure 25.3*c*.

25.4 Self-Test

Dulwich's 5% convertible bonds have a face value of $1,000 and a conversion ratio of 25. If the common stock sells at $30 when the bond matures, would you choose to convert? Why or why not?

Forcing Conversion

Many issuers of convertible bonds have an option to buy (or *call*) the bonds back at their face value whenever its stock price is 30% or so above the bond's conversion price.[27] If the

---

[27]The Tesla convertible is not callable.

company does announce that it will call the bonds when the call option is "in the money", it makes sense for investors to convert immediately. Thus, the call can be used to *force* conversion.

Why Do Companies Issue Convertibles?

BEYOND THE PAGE

Why companies issue convertibles

mhhe.com/brealey14e

You are approached by an investment banker who is anxious to persuade your company to issue a convertible bond with a conversion price set above the current stock price. She points out that investors would be prepared to accept a lower yield on the convertible, so that it is "cheaper" debt than a straight bond. You observe that if your company's stock performs as well as you expect, investors will convert the bond. "Great," she replies, "in that case, you will have sold shares at a much better price than you could sell them for today. It's a win-win opportunity."

Is the investment banker right? Are convertibles "cheap debt"? Of course not. They are a package of a straight bond and an option. The higher price that investors are prepared to pay for the convertible represents the value that they place on the option. The convertible is "cheap" only if this price overvalues the option.

What then of the other argument, that the issue represents a deferred sale of common stock at an attractive price? The convertible gives investors the right to buy stock by giving up a bond.[28] Bondholders may decide to do this, but then again they may not. Thus, issue of a convertible bond *may* amount to a deferred stock issue. But if the firm needs equity capital, a convertible issue is an unreliable way of getting it.

When asked why they issue convertibles, 58% of managers said in a survey that the bonds are an inexpensive way to issue "delayed" common stock. Forty-two percent view convertibles as less expensive than straight debt.[29] Taken at their face value, these arguments don't make sense. But we suspect that these phrases encapsulate some more complex and rational motives.

Notice that convertibles tend to be issued by smaller and more speculative firms. These issues are almost invariably unsecured and generally subordinated. Now put yourself in the position of a potential investor. You are approached by a firm with an untried product line that wants to issue some junior unsecured debt. You know that if things go well, you will get your money back, but if they do not, you could easily be left with nothing. Since the firm is in a new line of business, it is difficult to assess the chances of trouble. Therefore, you don't know what the fair rate of interest is. Also, you may be worried that once you have made the loan, management will be tempted to run extra risks. It may take on additional senior debt, or it may decide to expand its operations and go for broke on your money. In fact, if you charge a very high rate of interest, you could be encouraging this to happen.

What can management do to protect you against a wrong estimate of the risk and to assure you that its intentions are honorable? In crude terms, it can give you a piece of the action. You don't mind the company running unanticipated risks as long as you share in the gains as well as the losses.[30] Convertible securities make sense whenever it is unusually costly to assess the risk of debt or whenever investors are worried that management may not act in the bondholders' interest.[31]

---

[28]That is much the same as already having the stock together with the right to sell it for the convertible's bond value. In other words, instead of thinking of a convertible as a bond plus a call option, you could think of it as the stock plus a put option. Now you can see why it is wrong to think of a convertible as equivalent to the sale of stock; it is equivalent to the sale of both stock and a put option. If there is any possibility that investors will want to hold on to their bond, this put option has value.

[29]See J. R. Graham and C. R. Harvey, "The Theory and Practice of Finance: Evidence from the Field," *Journal of Financial Economics* 61 (2001), pp. 187–243.

[30]In the survey referred to above, a further 44% of the respondents reported that an important factor in their decision was the fact that convertibles were attractive to investors who were unsure about the riskiness of the company.

[31]Changes in risk are more likely when the firm is small and its debt is low-grade. Therefore, we should find that convertible bonds of such firms offer their holders a larger potential ownership share. This is indeed the case. See C. M. Lewis, R. J. Rogalski, and J. K. Seward, "Understanding the Design of Convertible Debt," *Journal of Applied Corporate Finance* 11 (Spring 1998), pp. 45–53.

Zero-Coupon Convertibles

❭ A convertible-bond buyer receives a relatively low interest (coupon) rate but gets a valuable option to convert the bond to shares of common stock. For example, if a straight bond pays 5%, an otherwise similar convertible might pay 3%. But in the first half of 2021, a flood of convertible issues was made at unusually low interest rates, often *zero*.

- Airbnb's $2 billion issue in February 2021 had a zero coupon and a 60% conversion premium. (The stock price will have to increase by at least 60% within five years to make conversion worthwhile.)

- Expedia Group's $1 billion issue, also in February, had a zero coupon and a 72.5% conversion premium. Expedia's stock price was up by about 20% by June 2021—only 52.5% to go!

There is nothing odd or illogical about zero-coupon bonds. (Think of U.S. Treasury strips.) But if the coupon is cut to zero, investors have to see an offsetting increase in conversion-option value. Otherwise, the bond cannot be issued at or near par value.

The higher the conversion premium, the less valuable the conversion option, other things equal. The combination of zero coupons and high premiums for the Airbnb and Expedia issues therefore seemed surprising. The average coupon and premium for all convertible issues were 1.41% and 39% in the first part of 2021. On the other hand, Airbnb and Expedia were high-volatility stocks, and volatility adds value to options.

Source: M. Farrell, "Convertible Bond Sales Are Soaring in 2021—Often at 0% Interest," *The Wall Street Journal*, May 28, 2021.

The relatively low coupon rate on convertible bonds may also be a convenience for rapidly growing firms facing heavy capital expenditures.[32] They may be willing to provide the conversion option to reduce immediate cash requirements for debt service. Without that option, lenders might demand extremely high (promised) interest rates to compensate for the probability of default. This would not only force the firm to raise still more capital for debt service but also increase the risk of financial distress. Paradoxically, lenders' attempts to protect themselves against default may actually increase the probability of financial distress by increasing the burden of debt service on the firm.

Valuing Convertible Bonds

We have seen that a convertible bond is equivalent to a package of a bond and an option to buy stock. This means that the option-valuation models that we described in Chapter 22 can also be used to value the option to convert. We don't want to repeat that material here, but we should note three wrinkles that you need to look out for when valuing a convertible:

1. *Dividends.* If you hold the common stock, you may receive dividends. The investor who holds an option to convert into common stock misses out on these dividends. In fact, the convertible holder loses out every time a cash dividend is paid, because the dividend reduces the stock price and thus reduces the value of the conversion option. If the dividends are high enough, it may even pay to convert before maturity to capture the extra income. We showed how dividend payments affect option value in Section 22-4.

2. *Dilution.* The second complication arises because conversion increases the number of outstanding shares. Therefore, exercise means that each shareholder is entitled to

---

[32]Of course, the firm could also make an equity issue rather than an issue of straight debt or convertibles. However, a convertible issue sends a better signal to investors than an issue of common stock. As we explained in Chapter 14, announcement of a stock issue prompts worries of overvaluation and usually depresses the stock price. Convertibles are hybrids of debt and equity and send a less negative signal. If the company is likely to need equity, its willingness to issue a convertible and take the chance that the stock price will rise enough to lead to conversion also signals management's confidence in the future. See J. Stein, "Convertible Bonds as Backdoor Equity Financing," *Journal of Financial Economics* 32 (1992), pp. 3–21.

a smaller proportion of the firm's assets and profits.[33] This problem of *dilution* never arises with traded options. If you buy an option through an options exchange and subsequently exercise it, you have no effect on the number of shares outstanding.

3. *Changing bond value.* When investors convert to shares, they give up their bond. The exercise price of the option is therefore the value of the bond that they are relinquishing. But this bond value is not constant. If the bond value at issue is less than the face value (and it usually is less), it is likely to change as maturity approaches. Also, the bond value varies as interest rates change and as the company's credit standing changes. If there is some possibility of default, investors cannot even be certain of what the bond will be worth *at maturity*. In Chapter 22, we did not get into the complication of uncertain exercise prices.

A Variation on Convertible Bonds: The Bond–Warrant Package

Instead of issuing a convertible bond, companies sometimes sell a package of straight bonds and warrants. Warrants are simply long-term call options that give the investor the right to buy the firm's common stock.

EXAMPLE 25.1 • GM's Warrant Issue

In 2009, General Motors filed for bankruptcy. As part of the bankruptcy settlement, GM's bondholders received shares in the reorganized company plus two issues of warrants. Warrants, like call options. have an exercise price that allows the owner to exchange one warrant for one share of stock. For example, GM "B" warrants expired in July 2019 and had an exercise price of $18.33. Since the price of GM stock on the expiry date was about $38, it paid warrant holders to put up the $18.33 exercise price and receive a share of GM stock.

• • • • •

Convertible bonds consist of a package of a straight bond and an option. An issue of bonds and warrants also contains a straight bond and an option. But there are some differences:

1. *Warrants are usually issued privately.* Packages of bonds with warrants tend to be more common in private placements. By contrast, most convertible bonds are issued publicly.

2. *Warrants can be detached.* When you buy a convertible, the bond and the option are bundled together. You cannot sell them separately. This may be inconvenient. If your tax position or attitude to risk inclines you to bonds, you may not want to hold options as well. Warrants are sometimes also "nondetachable," but usually you can keep the bond and sell the warrant.

3. *Warrants are exercised for cash.* When you convert a bond, you simply exchange your bond for common stock. When you exercise warrants, you generally put up extra cash, though occasionally you have to surrender the bond or can choose to do so. This means that the bond–warrant package and the convertible bond have different effects on the company's cash flow and on its capital structure.

4. *A package of bonds and warrants may be taxed differently.* There are some tax differences between warrants and convertibles. Suppose that you are wondering whether to issue a convertible bond at 100. You can think of this convertible as a package of a

---

[33]In their financial statements, companies recognize the possibility of dilution by reporting fully diluted earnings, which show how earnings would be affected by the issue of the extra shares.

straight bond worth, say, 90 and an option worth 10. If you issue the bond and option separately, the IRS will note that the bond is issued at a discount and that its price will rise by 10 points over its life. The IRS will allow you, the issuer, to spread this prospective price appreciation over the life of the bond and deduct it from your taxable profits. The IRS will also allocate the prospective price appreciation to the taxable income of the bondholder. Thus, by issuing a package of bonds and warrants rather than a convertible, you may reduce the tax paid by the issuing company and increase the tax paid by the investor.

5. *Warrants may be issued on their own.* Warrants do not have to be issued in conjunction with other securities. For example, the GM warrants were not combined with a bond issue. Warrants are often used to compensate investment bankers for underwriting services, and many companies also give their executives long-term options to buy stock. These executive stock options are not usually called warrants, but that is exactly what they are.

Innovation in the Bond Market

Domestic bonds and eurobonds, fixed- and floating-rate bonds, coupon bonds and zeros, callable and puttable bonds, straight bonds and convertible bonds—you might think that this would give you as much choice as you need. Yet almost every day some new type of bond seems to be issued. Table 25.3 lists some of the more interesting bonds that have been invented in recent years.[34] Earlier in the chapter, we described asset-backed securities, and in Chapter 27, we discuss catastrophe bonds whose payoffs are linked to the occurrence of natural disasters.

Some financial innovations appear to serve little or no economic purpose; they may flower briefly but then wither. Many other innovations seem to have a more obvious rationale. Here are some important motives for creating new securities:

1. *Investor choice.* Sometimes new financial instruments are created to widen investor choice. Economists refer to such securities as helping to "complete the market." This was the idea behind the 2016 issue of $100 million of *mortality,* or *death bonds,* by the insurance

Asset-backed securities	Many small loans are packaged together and resold as a bond.
Catastrophe (CAT) bonds	Payments are reduced in the event of a specified natural disaster.
Contingent convertibles (CoCos)	Bonds that convert automatically into equity as the value of the company falls.
Equity-linked bonds	Payments are linked to the performance of a stock market index.
Longevity bonds	Bonds whose payments are reduced or eliminated if there is a fall in mortality rates.
Mortality bonds	Bonds whose payments are reduced or eliminated if there is a jump in mortality rates.
Pay-in-kind bonds (PIKs)	Issuer can choose to make interest payments either in cash or in more bonds with an equivalent face value.
Credit-linked bonds	Coupon rate changes as company's credit rating changes.
Reverse floaters (yield-curve notes)	Floating-rate bonds that pay a higher rate of interest when other interest rates fall and a lower rate when other rates rise.
Step-up bonds	Bonds whose coupon payments increase over time.

❭**TABLE 25.3**   Some examples of innovation in bond design.

---

[34]For a more comprehensive list of innovations, see K. A. Carrow and J. J. McConnell, "A Survey of U.S. Corporate Financing Innovations: 1970–1997," *Journal of Applied Corporate Finance* 12 (Spring 1999), pp. 55–69.

BBVA Issues a CoCo

❯ Here is another example of how bond design can help to solve agency problems. The credit crisis of 2008–2009 drove many of the world's largest banks to the brink of bankruptcy. Yet shareholders were reluctant to put up the cash that was needed to save them. If they did so, they would largely be getting the bondholders and the government off the hook. One suggested remedy is for the banks to issue *contingent convertible bonds* (*CoCos*). These are bonds that convert automatically into equity if the bank hits trouble. For example, in 2016 the Spanish bank, BBVA, issued €500 million of perpetual CoCos. If

BBVA's capital falls below a specified level, the CoCos reduce the bank's leverage by changing into equity.

Regulators and central bankers are fervent champions of CoCos. For example, the Governor of the Bank of England declared, "We, at the Bank, put a lot of weight on the potential contribution that contingent capital can make . . . I see real benefits in working to ensure that in future contingent capital is a major part of the liability structure of the banking system." Bankers and shareholders are not so sure how popular CoCos are likely to be with bondholders.

company Swiss Re. One of the big risks for a life insurance company is a pandemic or other disaster that results in a sharp increase in the death rate. Swiss Re's bond offered investors a higher-than-normal interest rate for taking on some of that risk. Payments on the bonds would be reduced if, during the following five years, death rates in the United Kingdom, Canada, or Australia were unusually high. As coronavirus deaths started to mount in 2020, investors in Swiss Re's bonds began to worry about the likely payout.

Mortality bonds widen investor choice. They allow insurance companies to protect themselves against adverse changes in mortality and they spread the risk widely around the market.

2. *Government regulation and tax.* Merton Miller has described new government regulations and taxes as the sand in the oyster that stimulates the design of new types of security. For example, the eurobond market was a response to the U.S. government's imposition of a tax on purchases of foreign securities.

   Asset-backed securities provide another instance of a market that was encouraged by regulation. To reduce the likelihood of failure, banks are obliged to finance part of their loan portfolios with equity capital. Many banks were able to reduce the amount of capital that they needed to hold by packaging up their mortgage loans or credit-card receivables and selling them off as CDOs. Bank regulators have worried about this. They think that banks may be tempted to sell off their riskiest loans and to keep their safest ones. They have, therefore, introduced new regulations that will link the capital requirement to the riskiness of the loans.

3. *Reducing agency costs.* We have already seen how convertible bonds may reduce agency costs. Here is another example. At the turn of the century, investors were worried by the huge spending plans of telecom companies. So when Deutsche Telecom, the German telecom giant, decided to sell $15 billion of bonds in 2000, it offered a provision to reassure investors. Under this arrangement, Deutsche Telecom was required to increase the coupon rate on the bonds by 50 basis points if ever its bonds were downgraded to below investment grade by Moody's or Standard & Poor's. Deutsche Telecom's bonds protected investors against possible future attempts by the company to exploit existing bondholders by loading on more debt.

Dreaming up these new financial instruments is only half the battle. The other problem is to produce them efficiently. Think, for example, of the problems of packaging together several hundred million dollars' worth of credit card receivables and allocating the cash flows to a diverse group of investors. That requires good computer systems. The deal also needs to be structured so that, if the issuer goes bankrupt, the receivables will not be part of the bankruptcy estate. That depends on the development of legal structures that will stand up in the event of a dispute.

25-3   Bank Loans

Bonds are generally long-term loans and, more often than not, are issued publicly by the borrowing company. It is now time to look at shorter term debt. This is not usually issued publicly and is largely supplied by banks. Whereas the typical bond issue has a maturity of 10 years, the bank loan is more likely to be repaid in about three years.[35] Of course, there is plenty of variation around these figures.

In the United States, bank loans are a less important source of finance than the bond market, but for many smaller firms, they are the *only* source of borrowing. Bank loans come in a variety of flavors. Here are a few of the ways that they differ.

Commitment

Companies sometimes wait until they need the money before they apply for a bank loan, but about 90% of commercial loans by U.S. banks are made under commitment. In this case, the company establishes a line of credit that allows it to borrow up to an established limit from the bank. This line of credit may be an **evergreen credit** with no fixed maturity, but more commonly, it is a **revolving credit** (*revolver*) with a fixed maturity. One common arrangement is a 364-day facility that allows the company, over the following year, to borrow, repay, and reborrow as its need for cash varies.[36]

Credit lines can be expensive; in addition to paying interest on any borrowings, the company must pay a commitment fee on the unused amount. The growth in the use of credit lines has changed the role of banks. They are no longer simply lenders; they are also in the business of providing companies with liquidity insurance.

Maturity

Many bank loans are for only a few months. For example, a short-term loan may be needed to finance a temporary increase in inventory. Such a loan is described as **self-liquidating**; in other words, the sale of goods provides the cash to repay the loan.

Sometimes also a company may need a short-term **bridge loan** to finance the purchase of new equipment or the acquisition of another firm. For example, in 2019 the pharmaceutical company AbbVie took out a huge $38 billion bridge loan to finance its bid for Botox-maker Allergan. AbbVie refinanced this bridge loan through a bond issue split across 10 different maturities.

Banks also provide longer maturity **term loans**. A term loan typically has a maturity of four to five years. Usually it is repaid in level amounts over this period, though there is sometimes a large final *balloon* payment or just a single *bullet* payment at maturity. Term loans are often renegotiated before maturity. Banks are willing to do this if the borrower is an established customer, remains creditworthy, and has a sound business reason for making the change.[37] The ability to renegotiate is an advantage of bank financing over publicly issued

---

[35]See D. J. Denis and V. T. Mihov, "The Choice among Bank Debt, Non-Bank Private Debt, and Public Debt: Evidence from New Corporate Borrowings," *Journal of Financial Economics* 70 (2003), pp. 3–28.

[36]Banks originally promoted 364-day facilities because they did not need to set aside capital for commitments of less than a year.

[37]One study of private debt agreements found that over 90% are renegotiated before maturity. In most cases, this is not because of financial distress, but because of changing circumstances of the borrower. See M. R. Roberts and A. Sufi, "Renegotiation of Financial Contracts: Evidence from Private Credit Agreements," *Journal of Financial Economics* 93 (2009), pp. 159–184.

FINANCE IN PRACTICE

• • • • •

SOFR

❯ For many years it was common to link interest rates on bank loans to the *London interbank offered rate (LIBOR)*, which was used as the reference rate for more than $8 trillion of loans. To calculate LIBOR, a group of international banks in London stated each day the interest rate they would need to pay to borrow funds from another bank. Confidence in these estimates was dealt a blow at the height of the financial crisis, when reports surfaced that banks were substantially understating the interest rate. The scandal led to a new procedure for producing LIBOR, but it became increasingly clear that following the crisis, the level of activity in the interbank market had declined to the point where the LIBOR figures were little more than guesses.

Matters came to a head in 2017 when the regulator of LIBOR in the United Kingdom said that it would not persuade or compel LIBOR panel banks to make submissions beyond the end of 2021. A committee, appointed to come up with an alternative for LIBOR, proposed the *secured overnight financing rate (SOFR)*,

an average of interest rates on overnight Treasury repo transactions. In April 2018, the New York Federal Reserve began publishing the daily SOFR rate, and SOFR futures trading opened on the CME. Three months later, Fannie Mae issued the first bond with an interest rate tied to SOFR.

SOFR differs from LIBOR in three important ways. First, it is based each day on over $700 billion of transactions, whereas LIBOR was based on bankers' estimates. Second, since the repo loans[39] used to calculate SOFR are secured by Treasury securities, they are effectively risk-free, whereas LIBOR was based on unsecured loans. Third, unlike LIBOR, which was calculated for different maturities, SOFR is currently just an overnight rate.

SOFR is not the only game in town. Several challengers have appeared, including a Short-Term Bank Yield Index sponsored by Bloomberg. For example, in April 2021 Bank of America, issued a $1 billion six-month floating rate loan linked to the one-month Yield Index.

---

debt. Renegotiating the terms of a publicly issued note or bond held by hundreds of scattered investors is costly, time-consuming, and usually impractical.

Rate of Interest

Most short-term bank loans are made at a fixed rate of interest, which is often quoted as a discount. For example, if the interest rate on a one-year loan is stated as a discount of 5%, the borrower receives $100 − $5 = $95 and undertakes to pay $100 at the end of the year. The annually compounded rate of interest on such a loan is not 5%, but 5/95 = 0.0526, or 5.26%.

| 25.5 Self-Test |

A bank offers you a one-year loan at a discount of 10%. What is the annually compounded rate of interest?

For longer term bank loans, the interest rate is usually linked to the general level of interest rates. The most common benchmarks are SOFR, the federal funds rate,[38] or the bank's prime rate. Thus, if the rate is set at "1% over SOFR," the borrower may pay 5% in the first three months when SOFR is 4%, 6% in the next three months when SOFR is 5%, and so on. The nearby box describes how SOFR is set and its relationship to the Treasury bill rate.

---

[38]The federal funds rate is the rate at which banks lend excess reserves to each other.

[39]A repo or repurchase agreement is a secured loan. The borrower sells the collateral to the lender and agrees to buy it back at a set date in price. The excess of the buyback price over the selling price is the interest received by the lender. SOFR is based on overnight repos for U.S. Treasuries.

Syndicated Loans

Some bank loans and credit lines are too large for a single lender. In these cases, the borrower may pay an arrangement fee to one or more lead banks, which then parcel out the loan or credit line among a syndicate of banks.[40]

The syndicate arrangers serve as underwriters to the loan. They price the loan, market it to other banks, and may also guarantee to take on any unsold portion. The arrangers' first step is to prepare an *information memo* that provides potential lenders with some facts about the loan. The syndicate desk will then try to sound out the level of interest in the deal before the loan is finally priced and marketed to interested buyers. If the borrower has good credit, or if the arranging bank has a particularly good reputation, the majority of the loan is likely to be syndicated. In other cases, the arranging bank may need to demonstrate its faith in the deal by keeping a high proportion of the loan on its own books.[41]

EXAMPLE 25.2 • Sprint's syndicated loan

In 2017, JPMorgan, Citigroup, Mizuho Bank, and Goldman Sachs arranged a syndicated loan facility for Sprint Communications. The package consisted of a \$4.0 billion, seven-year term loan and a \$2.0 billion revolving credit facility. The term loan was priced at 2.5% over LIBOR. The interest rate on the revolving credit facility was 1.75–2.75% over LIBOR.[42] In addition, Sprint was required to pay a commitment fee of 0.25–0.45% on any unused portion of the revolving credit.

• • • • •

Bank loans used to be illiquid; once the bank had made a loan, it was stuck with it. This is no longer the case so that banks with an excess demand for loans may solve the problem by selling a portion of their existing loans to other institutions. For example, about 20% of syndicated loans are subsequently resold, and these sales are reported weekly in *The Wall Street Journal.*[43]

Security

If a bank is concerned about a firm's credit risk, it will ask the firm to provide security for the loan. This is most common for longer term bank loans, more than half of which are secured.[44] Sometimes the bank will take a *floating lien.* This gives it a general claim if the firm defaults. However, it does not specify the assets in detail, and it sets few restrictions on what the company can do with the assets.

More commonly, banks require specific collateral. For example, suppose that there is a significant delay between the time that you ship your goods and when your customers pay. If you need the money up front, you can borrow by using these receivables as collateral.

---

[40]For a standard loan to a blue-chip company, the fee for arranging a syndicated loan may be as low as 10 basis points, while a complex deal with a highly leveraged firm may carry a fee of up to 250 basis points. For good reviews of the syndicated loan market, see S. C. Miller, "A Guide to the Syndicated Loan Market," Standard & Poor's, September 2005 (www.standardandpoors.com); and B. Gadanecz, "The Syndicated Loan Market: Structure, Development and Implications," *BIS Quarterly Review,* December 2004, pp. 75–89 (www.bis.org).

[41]See A. Sufi, "Information Asymmetry and Financing Arrangements: Evidence from Syndicated Loans," *Journal of Finance* 62 (April 2007), pp. 629–668.

[42]In the case of both facilities, Sprint had the option to link the interest rate to an alternative measure of the short-term interest rate.

[43]Loan sales generally take one of two forms: *assignments* or *participations.* In the former case, a portion of the loan is transferred with the agreement of the borrower. In the second case, the lead bank maintains its relationship with the borrower but agrees to pay over to the buyer a portion of the cash flows that it receives.

[44]The results of a survey of the terms of business lending by banks in the United States are published quarterly in the *Federal Reserve Bulletin* (see www.federalreserve.gov/releases/E2).

First, you must send the bank a copy of each invoice and provide it with a claim against the money that you receive from your customers. The bank may then lend up to 80% of the value of the receivables. Each day, as you make more sales, your collateral increases and you can borrow more money. Each day, some customers also pay their bills. This money is placed in a special collateral account under the bank's control and is periodically used to reduce the amount of the loan. Therefore, as the firm's business fluctuates, so does the amount of the collateral and the size of the loan.

You can also use inventories as security for a loan. For example, if your goods are stored in a warehouse, you need to arrange for an independent warehouse company to provide the bank with a receipt showing that the goods are held on the bank's behalf. The bank will generally be prepared to lend up to 50% of the value of the inventories. When the loan is repaid, the bank returns the warehouse receipt, and you are free to remove the goods.[45]

Banks are naturally choosy about the security that they will accept. They want to make sure that they can identify and sell the collateral if you default. They may be happy to lend against a warehouse full of a standard nonperishable commodity, but they would turn up their nose at a warehouse of ripe Camembert.

Banks also need to ensure that the collateral is safe and that the borrower doesn't sell the assets and run off with the money. Here is an example of how a group of banks failed to make these checks.

BEYOND THE PAGE

Hazards of secured bank lending

mhhe.com/brealey14e

EXAMPLE 25.3 • The great salad oil swindle

When banks fail to check the security for a loan, the result can be very costly. This was the experience of the banks and companies that made nearly $200 million of loans to the Allied Crude Vegetable Oil Refining Corporation. In return, the company agreed to provide security in the form of storage tanks full of valuable salad oil. Unfortunately, cursory inspections failed to notice that the tanks contained largely seawater with only a few feet of salad oil floating on top. The company even transferred oil between different tanks while entertaining the inspectors at lunch. When the fraud was discovered, Allied turned out to have only 110 million pounds of salad oil rather than the 1.8 billion pounds that it claimed to own. The president of Allied went to jail, leaving the 51 lenders out in the cold, looking for their $200 million.

• • • • •

Loan Covenants

We saw earlier that bond issues may contain covenants, which restrict companies from taking actions that would increase the risk of their debt. For publicly issued bonds, these restrictions are often mild and are generally *incurrence covenants*. For example, they might say that the company may not issue more debt unless the interest cover is greater than five times. In the case of privately placed debt, such as the Sprint syndicated loan, the covenants are generally more severe, and include *maintenance covenants*. For example, these may specify that the company is in violation of its covenants if interest cover falls below five times regardless of whether that is a result of taking on more debt or is simply caused by declining earnings.

Since privately placed debt keeps the borrower on a fairly short leash, it is quite common for a covenant to be breached. This is not as calamitous as it may sound. As long as

---

[45]It is not always practicable to keep inventory in a warehouse. For example, automobile dealers need to display their cars in a showroom. One solution is to enter into a floor-planning arrangement in which the finance company or bank holds title to the cars until they are sold. When the cars are sold, the proceeds are used to repay the loan. The interest or "flooring charge" depends on how long the cars have been in the showroom.

the borrower is in good financial health, the lender may simply adjust the terms of the covenant. Only if covenants continue to be violated will the lender choose to take more drastic action.

Covenants on bank loans and privately placed bonds are principally of three kinds.[46] The first and most common covenant sets a maximum fraction of net income that can be paid out as dividends. A second set of covenants, called *sweeps,* state that all or part of the loan must be repaid if the borrower makes a large sale of assets or a substantial issue of debt. The third group places conditions on key financial ratios, such as the borrower's debt ratio, and interest coverage ratio, or current ratio. For example, the Sprint loan required the company to maintain a specified debt ratio and interest cover.

25-4   Commercial Paper and Medium-Term Notes

Commercial Paper

Banks borrow money from one group of firms or individuals (including holders of checking-account and savings-account deposits) and relend the money to another group, for example as mortgage loans or term loans to businesses. They make their profit by charging a higher rate of interest when they lend than they pay when they borrow.[47]

Sometimes it is convenient to have a bank in the middle. It saves depositors and other lenders to the bank the trouble of looking for potential borrowers and assessing their creditworthiness, and it saves the potential borrowers the trouble of looking for lenders. Depositors do not care about the identity of the borrowers: They need only satisfy themselves that the bank as a whole is safe.

There are also occasions on which it is *not* worth paying an intermediary to perform these functions. Large, well-known companies can bypass the banking system by issuing their own short-term unsecured notes. These notes are known as **commercial paper (CP)**. Both foreign and domestic financial institutions, such as bank holding companies and finance companies,[48] also issue commercial paper, sometimes in very large quantities. The major issuers of commercial paper have set up their own marketing departments and sell their paper directly to investors, often using the web to do so. Smaller companies sell through dealers who receive a fee for marketing the issue.

Commercial paper in the United States has a maximum maturity of nine months, though most paper is for less than 60 days. Buyers generally hold it to maturity, but the company or dealer that sells the paper is usually prepared to repurchase it earlier.

Commercial paper is not risk-free. When California was mired in the energy crisis of 2001, Southern California Edison and Pacific Gas and Electric defaulted on $1.4 billion of commercial paper. And in 2008, Lehman Brothers filed for bankruptcy with $3 billion of paper outstanding. But such defaults are rare. The majority of commercial paper is issued by high-grade, nationally known companies,[49] and the issuers generally support their borrowing by arranging a backup line of credit with a bank, which guarantees that they can find the money to repay the paper.

---

[46]For an analysis of loan covenants in privately placed debt see M. Bradley and M. R. Roberts, "The Structure and Pricing of Corporate Debt Covenants," *Quarterly Journal of Finance* 5 (June 2015), pp. 1–37.

[47]Banks now pay little or no interest on checking accounts, but they provide valuable services, including check clearing, cash ATM machines, etc. The cost of providing these services replaces explicit interest paid on the accounts.

[48]A *bank holding company* is a firm that owns both a bank and nonbanking subsidiaries.

[49]Moody's, Standard & Poor's, and Fitch publish quality ratings for commercial paper. For example, Moody's provides three ratings, from P-1 (i.e., Prime 1, the highest grade paper) to P-3. Most investors are reluctant to buy low-rated paper. For example, money-market funds are largely limited to holding P-1 paper.

BEYOND THE PAGE

Commercial paper and the financial crisis

mhhe.com/brealey14e

Because investors are reluctant to buy commercial paper that does not have the highest credit rating, companies cannot rely on the commercial paper market to provide them always with the short-term capital that they need. For example, when the rating services downgraded the commercial paper of Ford and General Motors, both companies were forced to sharply reduce their sales of commercial paper.

When Lehman Brothers filed for bankruptcy in September 2008, the commercial paper market nosedived. The spread between the interest rates on commercial paper and Treasury bills doubled, while the market closed entirely for low-grade issuers. Many firms that found themselves shut out of the commercial paper market rushed to borrow on their bank lines of credit. Firms that had no such alternative source of borrowing were forced to cut back on their investment plans.[50] Only after the Fed announced plans to buy large quantities of high-grade paper did the market begin to return to normal.

In addition to unsecured commercial paper, there is also a market for *asset-backed commercial paper*. In this case, the company sells its assets to a special-purpose vehicle that then issues the paper. For example, as the auto companies reduced their sales of unsecured commercial paper, they increasingly relied on asset-backed paper secured by the firm's receivables. As the customers paid their bills, the cash was passed through to the holders of this paper.

By 2007, asset-backed paper accounted for almost half the commercial paper market, but weaknesses surfaced after a number of banks set up structured investment vehicles (SIVs) that invested in mortgage-backed securities financed by asset-backed paper. Because the buyers of the commercial paper bore the credit risk, the banks had less incentive to worry about the quality of the underlying mortgages. Once it became clear to investors that this quality was very low, many of the SIVs found it impossible to refinance the maturing paper and went into default.

Medium-Term Notes

New issues of securities do not need to be registered with the SEC as long as they mature within 270 days. So by limiting the maturity of commercial paper issues, companies can avoid the delays and expense of registration. However, large blue-chip companies also make regular issues of unsecured **medium-term notes (MTNs)**.

You can think of MTNs as a hybrid between corporate bonds and commercial paper. Like bonds, they are relatively long-term instruments; their maturity is never less than 270 days, though it is typically less than 10 years.[51] On the other hand, like commercial paper, MTNs are not underwritten but are sold on a regular basis either through dealers or, occasionally, directly to investors. Dealers support a secondary market in these MTNs and are prepared to buy the notes back before maturity.[52]

Borrowers such as finance companies, which always need cash, welcome the flexibility of MTNs. For example, a company may tell its dealers the amount of money that it needs to raise that week, the range of maturities that it can offer, and the maximum interest that it is prepared to pay. It is then up to the dealers to find the buyers. Investors may also suggest their own terms to one of the dealers, and, if these terms are acceptable, the deal is done.

---

[50]For an analysis of firm reaction to the collapse of the commercial paper market, see P. Gao and H. Yun, "Commercial Paper, Lines of Credit, and the Real Effects of the Financial Crisis of 2008: Firm-Level Evidence from the Manufacturing Industry," working paper, University of Notre Dame, 2010.

[51]Occasionally, an MTN registration may be used to issue much longer term bonds. For example, Disney has even used its MTN program to issue a 100-year bond.

[52]In Chapter 14, we encountered SEC Rule 415, which allows companies to file a single registration statement covering financing plans for up to three years in the future (*shelf registration*). Since the interest rates on new MTN issues are adjusted frequently, an active MTN market was feasible only after the passage of Rule 415 in 2005.

- **Types of corporate bonds** The detailed bond agreement is set out in the indenture between the issuer and a trustee, but the main provisions are summarized in the prospectus to the issue. Most bonds are unsecured debentures or notes. This means that they are general claims on the corporation. The principal exceptions are utility mortgage bonds, collateral trust bonds, and equipment trust certificates. In the event of default, the trustee to these issues can repossess the company's assets to pay off the debt. Sometimes firms raise money using asset-backed securities, which requires bundling together assets, such as mortgages, and selling the cash flows from them.

- **Repayment provisions** Some long-term bond issues have a sinking fund. This means that the company must set aside enough money each year to retire a specified number of bonds. A sinking fund reduces the average life of the bond, and it provides a yearly test of the company's ability to service its debt. It therefore helps to protect the bondholders against the risk of default.

  Long-dated bonds may be callable before maturity. This option to call the bond may be valuable to a company that wishes to reduce its leverage or tidy up its outstanding debt.

- **Bond covenants protect the lender** Lenders usually seek to prevent the borrower from taking actions that would damage the value of their loans. Here are some examples of debt covenants:

  - A limit on the amount of additional borrowing by the company.

  - A negative pledge clause, which prohibits the company from securing additional debt without giving equal treatment to the existing unsecured bonds.

  - A limit on the company's dividend payments or repurchases of stock.

  - Protection for the bondholder against a potentially damaging merger or change of control.

- **Privately placed bonds and international bond issues** Bonds can be issued in the public markets in the United States, in which case they must be registered with the SEC. Alternatively, if they are issued to a limited number of buyers, they can be privately placed. They can also be issued in a foreign bond market or in the Eurobond market. Eurobonds are marketed simultaneously in a number of foreign countries by the London branches of international banks and security dealers.

- **Convertible bonds** Most bonds start and finish their lives as bonds, but convertible bonds give their owner the option to exchange the bond for common stock. The *conversion ratio* measures the number of shares into which each bond can be exchanged. You can think of a convertible bond as equivalent to a straight bond plus a call option on the stock. Instead of issuing a convertible, companies may decide to issue a package of bonds and options (*warrants*) to buy the stock. If the stock price rises above the exercise price, the investor may then keep the bond and exercise the warrants with cash.

- **Bond innovation** There is an enormous variety of bond issues. By a process of natural selection, some of the new instruments become popular and may even replace existing species. Others are exotic curiosities. Some innovations succeed because they widen investor choice or reduce agency costs. Others owe their origin to tax rules and government regulation.

- **Bank loans** Many corporations, particularly smaller ones, obtain finance from banks. Bank loans usually have shorter maturities than bonds. Frequently, firms pay a commitment fee to keep a credit line open that they can draw upon when they need the cash.

  Many bank loans are short-term and charge a fixed rate of interest. The interest rate on longer-term bank loans is usually linked to SOFR or some other index of interest rates. Bank loans may be provided by a syndicate of banks if the amount needed is too large for a single bank. Loans are frequently secured by collateral such as receivables, inventories, or securities. Covenants on bank loans are usually more restrictive than on bonds.

- **Commercial paper and MTNs** Commercial paper (CP) and medium-term notes (MTNs) are a cheaper alternative to bank loans for many large firms. They can be sold directly to lenders or through dealers. Commercial paper can be unsecured or asset-backed. Medium-term notes are a hybrid between bonds and commercial paper. They are longer term than commercial paper but are sold in a similar way.

FURTHER READING

A useful general work on debt securities is:

F. J. Fabozzi (ed.), *The Handbook of Fixed Income Securities,* 9th ed. (New York: McGraw-Hill, 2021).

For an excellent guide to syndicated lending see:

Standard & Poor's, *A Guide to the Loan Market,* September 2011.

S. J. Lee, D. Li, R R. Meisenzahl, and M. J. Sicilian, "The U.S. Syndicated Term Loan Market: Who Holds What and When?" *FEDS Notes,* November 25, 2019.

For nontechnical discussions of the pricing of convertible bonds and the reasons for their use, see:

M. J. Brennan and E. S. Schwartz, "The Case for Convertibles," *Journal of Applied Corporate Finance* 1 (Summer 1988), pp. 55–64.

C. M. Lewis, R. J. Rogalski, and J. K. Seward, "Understanding the Design of Convertible Debt," *Journal of Applied Corporate Finance* 11 (Spring 1998), pp. 45–53.

For a useful description of the commercial paper market and its difficulties in the crash of 2007–2009, see:

M. Kacperczyk and P. Schnabl, "When Safe Proved Risky: Commercial Paper during the Financial Crisis of 2007–2009," *Journal of Economic Perspectives* 24 (Winter 2010), pp. 29–50.

The readings listed at the end of Chapter 16 include several articles on financial innovation.

PROBLEM SETS

Select problems are available in McGraw Hill's *Connect*. Please see the preface for more information.

1. **Bond terms (S25.1)** Use Table 25.1 (but not the text) to answer the following questions:
   a. Who are the principal underwriters for the AMAT bond issue?
   b. What is the percentage underwriting spread?
   c. How many dollars does the company receive for each bond after deduction of the underwriters' spread?
   d. Is the bond "bearer" or "registered"?
   e. Who is the trustee for the issue?

2. **Bond terms (S25.1)** Look at Table 25.1:
   a. The AMAT bond was issued on June 8, 2011, at 99.592%. How much would you have to pay to buy one bond delivered on June 15? Don't forget to include accrued interest.
   b. When is the first interest payment on the bond, and what is the total dollar amount of the payment?
   c. On what date do the bonds finally mature, and what is the amount to be paid on each bond at maturity?

3. **Bond terms (S25.1)** Find the terms and conditions of a recent bond issue and compare them with those of the AMAT issue.

4. **Bond terms (S25.1)** Select the most appropriate term from within the parentheses:

   a. (High-grade bonds/Low-grade bonds) generally have only light sinking-fund requirements.

   b. Equipment trust certificates are often issued by (railroads/bank holding companies).

   c. Mortgage pass-through certificates are an example of (an asset-backed security/a convertible bond).

5. **Bond terms (S25.1)** Suppose that the AMAT bond was issued at face value and that investors continue to demand a yield of 5.85%. Sketch what you think would happen to the bond price as the first interest payment date approaches and then passes. What about the price of the bond plus accrued interest (sometimes known as the *dirty price*)?

6. **Bond terms (S25.1)** Bond prices can fall either because of a change in the general level of interest rates or because of an increased risk of default. To what extent do floating-rate bonds protect the investor against each of these risks?

7. **Security and Seniority (S25.1)**

   a. As a senior bondholder, would you like the company to issue more junior debt to finance its investment program, would you prefer it not to do so, or would you not care?

   b. You hold debt secured on the company's existing property. Would you like the company to issue more unsecured debt to finance its investments, would you prefer it not to do so, or would you not care?

8. **Security and Seniority (S25.1)** Proctor Power has fixed assets worth $200 million and net working capital worth $100 million. It is financed partly by equity and partly by three issues of debt. These consist of $250 million of First Mortgage Bonds secured only on the company's fixed assets, $100 million of senior debentures, and $120 million of subordinated debentures. (The amounts of the three issues are par or face values.) If the debt were due today, how much would each debtholder be entitled to receive?

9. **Security and Seniority (S25.1)** Elixir Corporation has just filed for bankruptcy. Elixir is a holding company whose assets consist of real estate worth $80 million and 100% of the equity of its two operating subsidiaries. It is financed partly by equity and partly by an issue of $400 million of senior collateral trust bonds that are just about to mature. Subsidiary A has issued directly $320 million of debentures and $15 million of preferred stock. Subsidiary B has issued $180 million of senior debentures and $60 million of subordinated debentures. A's assets have a market value of $500 million, and B's have a value of $220 million. How much will each security holder receive if the assets are sold and distributed strictly according to precedence?

10. **Security and Seniority (S25.1)**

    a. Residential mortgages may stipulate either a fixed rate or a variable rate. As a *borrower*, what considerations might cause you to prefer one rather than the other?

    b. Why might holders of mortgage pass-through certificates prefer mortgages with floating rates?

11. **Sinking funds (S25.1)** For each of the following sinking funds, state whether the fund increases or decreases the value of the bond at the time of issue (or whether it is impossible to say):

    a. An optional sinking fund operating by drawings at par.

    b. A mandatory sinking fund operating by drawings at par *or* by purchases in the market.

    c. A mandatory sinking fund operating by drawings at par.

12. **Call provisions (S25.1)**

    a. Look at Table 25.1. Suppose that AMAT decides to call the bond one year before it is due to expire. The interest rate on one-year Treasury bonds is 2%. What price must AMAT pay to call the bonds?

b. Now suppose that the interest rate on Treasury bonds is 10%. What price must AMAT pay to call its bonds?

13. **Covenants (S25.1)** Alpha Corp. is prohibited from issuing more senior debt unless net tangible assets exceed 200% of senior debt. Currently, the company has outstanding $100 million of senior debt and has net tangible assets of $250 million. How much more senior debt can Alpha Corp. issue?

14. **Covenants (S25.1)** Explain carefully why bond indentures may place limitations on the following actions:

    a. Sale of the company's assets.

    b. Payment of dividends to shareholders.

    c. Issue of additional senior debt.

15. **Private placements (S25.1)** Explain the three principal ways in which the terms of private placement bonds commonly differ from those of public issues.

16. **Convertible bonds (S25.2)** True or false?

    a. Convertible bonds are usually senior claims on the firm.

    b. The higher the conversion ratio, the more valuable the convertible.

    c. The higher the conversion price, the less valuable the convertible.

    d. Convertible bonds do not share fully in the price of the common stock, but they provide some protection against a decline.

17. **Convertible bonds (S25.2)** Maple Aircraft has issued a 4¾% convertible subordinated debenture due 2023. The conversion price is $47.00 and the debenture is callable at 102.75% of face value. The market price of the convertible is 91% of face value, and the price of the common is $41.50. The value of the bond in the absence of a conversion feature is about 65% of face value.

    a. What is the conversion ratio of the debenture?

    b. If the conversion ratio were 50, what would be the conversion price?

    c. What is the conversion value?

    d. At what stock price is the conversion value equal to the bond value?

    e. Can the market price be less than the conversion value?

    f. How much is the convertible holder paying for the option to buy one share of common stock?

    g. By how much does the common have to rise by 2023 to justify conversion?

18. **Convertible bonds (S25.2)** The Surplus Value Company had $10 million (face value) of convertible bonds outstanding in 2020. Each bond has the following features.

Face value	$1,000
Conversion price	$25
Current call price	105 (percent of face value)
Current trading price	130 (percent of face value)
Maturity	2027
Current stock price	$30 (per share)
Interest rate	10% (coupon as percent of face value)

    a. What is the bond's conversion value?

    b. Can you explain why the bond is selling above conversion value?

    c. Should Surplus call? What will happen if it does so?

19. **Convertible bonds (S25.2)** Sweeney Pies has issued a zero-coupon 10-year bond that can be converted into 10 Sweeney shares. Comparable straight bonds are yielding 8%. Sweeney stock is priced at $50 a share.

    a. Suppose that you had to make a now-or-never decision on whether to convert or to stay with the bond. Which would you do?

    b. If the convertible bond is priced at $550, how much are investors paying for the option to buy Sweeney shares?

    c. If, after one year, the value of the conversion option is unchanged, what is the value of the convertible bond?

20. **Convertible bonds (S25.2)** Iota Microsystems' 10% convertible is about to mature. The conversion ratio is 27.

    a. What is the conversion price?

    b. The stock price is $47. What is the conversion value?

    c. Should you convert?

21. **Convertible bonds (S25.2)** Zenco Inc. is financed by 3 million shares of common stock and by $5 million face value of 8% convertible debt maturing in 2029. Each bond has a face value of $1,000 and a conversion ratio of 200. What is the value of each convertible bond at maturity if Zenco's net assets are worth:

    a. $30 million?

    b. $4 million?

    c. $20 million?

    d. $5 million?

    Draw a figure similar to Figure 25.3c showing how the value of each convertible bond at maturity varies with the value of Zenco's net assets.

22. **Convertible bonds (S25.2)** Look back at Tesla's convertible bond that was described in Section 25-2. Use the Black—Scholes app from Chapter 22 to provide an estimate of the value of the conversion option. (Note: Tesla was not expected to pay a dividend in this period.) Do you think the conversion option was fairly priced?

23. **Bank loans (S25.3)** Match each of the following terms with one of the definitions below.

    A. Revolving credit

    B. Bridge loan

    C. Term loan

    D. Syndicated loan

    E. Commitment fee

    F. Maintenance covenant

       a. Requirement that borrower keeps in the future to a certain condition—for example, a minimum debt ratio.

       b. Rather like a corporate credit card, it allows the company to choose to borrow up to a certain limit and to repay.

       c. Loan that is parceled out among a group of banks.

       d. Longer term bank loan with a fixed maturity.

       e. Fee paid on unused portion of a revolving credit.

       f. Short-term bank loan taken out until more permanent funding can be arranged.

24. **Bank loans (S25.3)** Suppose that you are a banker responsible for approving corporate loans. Nine firms are seeking secured loans. They offer the following assets as collateral. Which of these assets are most likely to be good collateral? Which are likely to be poor collateral? Explain.

a. Firm A, a heating oil distributor, offers a tanker load of fuel oil in transit from the Middle East.

b. Firm B, a wine wholesaler, offers 1,000 cases of Beaujolais Nouveau located in a field warehouse.

c. Firm C, a stationer, offers an account receivable for office supplies sold to the City of New York.

d. Firm D, a bookstore, offers its entire inventory of 15,000 used books.

e. Firm E, a wholesale grocer, offers a boxcar full of bananas.

f. Firm F offers 100 ounces of gold.

g. Firm G, a government securities dealer, offers its portfolio of Treasury bills.

h. Firm H, a boat builder, offers a half-completed luxury yacht. The yacht will take four more months to complete.

25. **Bank loans, commercial paper, and medium-term notes (S25.3–S25.4)** Complete the passage below by selecting the most appropriate terms from the following list:

floating lien, revolving credit, medium-term note, warehouse receipt, unsecured, commitment fee, commercial paper.

Companies with fluctuating needs for cash often arrange a _____ with their bank that allows them to borrow up to a specified amount. In addition to paying interest on any borrowings, the company must pay a _____ on any unused amount.

Secured short-term loans are sometimes covered by a _____, which gives it a general claim on the firm's assets. Generally, however, the borrower pledges specific assets. For example, a loan may be secured by inventory. In this case, an independent warehouse company provides the bank with a _____, showing that the goods are held on the bank's behalf and releases those goods only on instructions.

Banks are not the only source of short-term debt. Many large companies issue their own _____ debt directly to investors, often on a regular basis. If the maturity is less than 270 days, the debt does not need to be registered with the SEC and is known as _____. A company may also have a program to sell longer maturity debt to investors on a continuing basis. This is called a _____ program.

26. **Bank loans, commercial paper, and medium-term notes (S25.3–S25.4)** Term loans usually require firms to pay a fluctuating interest rate. For example, the interest rate may be set at 1% over SOFR. SOFR can sometimes vary by several percentage points within a single year. Suppose that your firm has decided to borrow $40 million for five years and that it has three alternatives:

a. Borrow from a bank at 1.5% over SOFR, currently 6.5%. The proposed loan agreement requires no principal payments until the loan matures in year 5.

b. Issue 26-week commercial paper, currently yielding 7%. Since funds are required for five years, the commercial paper will need to be rolled over semiannually; that is, financing the $40 million will require 10 successive commercial paper sales.

c. Issue a five-year medium-term note at a fixed rate of 7.5%. As in the case of the bank loan, no principal has to be repaid until the end of year 5.
   What factors would you consider in analyzing these alternatives? In what circumstances would you prefer each of these possible loans?

CHALLENGE

27. **Bond repurchase (S25.1)** Dorlcote Milling has outstanding a $1 million 3% mortgage bond maturing in 10 years. The coupon on any new debt issued by the company is 10%. The finance director, Mr. Tulliver, cannot decide whether there is a tax benefit to repurchasing

the existing bonds in the marketplace and replacing them with new 10% bonds. What do you think? Does it matter whether bond investors are taxed?

28. **Convertible bonds (S25.2)** This question illustrates that when there is scope for the firm to vary its risk, lenders may be more prepared to lend if they are offered a piece of the action through the issue of a convertible bond. Liu Zhang is proposing to form a new start-up firm with initial assets of $10 million. She can invest this money in one of two projects. Each has the same expected payoff, but one has more risk than the other. The relatively safe project offers a 40% chance of a $12.5 million payoff and a 60% chance of an $8 million payoff. The risky project offers a 40% chance of a $20 million payoff and a 60% chance of a $5 million payoff.

    Ms. Zhang initially proposes to finance the firm by an issue of straight debt with a promised payoff of $7 million. Ms. Zhang will receive any remaining payoff. Show the possible payoffs to the lender and to Ms. Zhang if (a) she chooses the safe project and (b) she chooses the risky project. Which project is Ms. Zhang likely to choose? Which will the lender want her to choose?

    Suppose now that Ms. Zhang offers to make the debt convertible into 50% of the value of the firm. Show that in this case the lender receives the same expected payoff from the two projects.

29. **Convertible bonds (S25.2)** Occasionally, it is said that issuing convertible bonds is better than issuing stock when the firm's shares are undervalued. Suppose that the financial manager of the Butternut Furniture Company does have inside information indicating that the Butternut stock price is too low. Butternut's future earnings will in fact be higher than investors expect. Suppose further that the inside information cannot be released without giving away a valuable competitive secret. Clearly, selling shares at the present low price would harm Butternut's existing shareholders. Will they also lose if convertible bonds are issued? If they do lose in this case, is the loss more or less than it would be if common stock were issued?

    Now suppose that investors forecast earnings accurately but still undervalue the stock because they overestimate Butternut's actual business risk. Does this change your answers to the questions posed in the preceding paragraph? Explain.

• • • • •

SOLUTIONS TO SELF-TEST QUESTIONS

25.1 If the call price is fixed, the company can call the bonds when they are worth more than the call price but will not call them when they are worth less than the call price. This is not in the interests of the bondholder.

25.2 Loans that are "covenant-lite" will carry a higher rate of interest since the lenders will assume that the borrowers will be tempted to borrow heavily or take other actions that reduce loan value. Reputable borrowers will be happy to reassure lenders.

25.3 You would pay more for

a. A senior bond;

b. A secured bond;

c. A bond with a mandatory sinking fund;

d. A publicly issued bond.

25.4 You can convert into $1,000/25 = 40$ shares which are worth $40 \times \$30 = \$1,200$. It would pay to convert rather than receive $1,000 from the maturing bond.

25.5 $r = 100/90 - 1 = 0.111$, or 11.1%.

MINI-CASE · · · · ·

The Shocking Demise of Mr. Thorndike

It was one of Morse's most puzzling cases. That morning, Rupert Thorndike, the autocratic CEO of Thorndike Oil, was found dead in a pool of blood on his bedroom floor. He had been shot through the head, but the door and windows were bolted on the inside, and there was no sign of the murder weapon.

Morse looked in vain for clues in Thorndike's bedroom and office. He had to take another tack. He decided to investigate the financial circumstances surrounding Thorndike's demise. The company's capital structure was as follows:

- 5% debentures: $250 million face value. The bonds mature in 10 years and offer a yield of 12%.
- Stock: 30 million shares, which closed at $9 a share the day before the murder.
- 10% subordinated convertible notes: The notes mature in one year and are convertible at any time at a conversion ratio of 110 (110 shares for each note with $1,000 face value). The day before the murder these notes were priced at 5% more than their conversion value.

Yesterday, Thorndike had flatly rejected an offer by T. Spoone Dickens to buy all of the common stock for $10 a share. With Thorndike out of the way, it appeared that Dickens's offer would be accepted, much to the profit of Thorndike Oil's other shareholders.[53]

Thorndike's two nieces, Doris and Patsy, and his nephew, John, all had substantial investments in Thorndike Oil and had bitterly disagreed with Thorndike's dismissal of Dickens's offer. Their stakes are shown in the following table:

	5% Debentures (Face Value)	Shares of Stock	10% Convertible Notes (Face Value)
Doris	$4 million	1.2 million	$0 million
John	0	0.5	5
Patsy	0	1.5	3

All debt issued by Thorndike Oil would be paid off at face value if Dickens's offer went through. Holders of the convertible notes could choose to convert and tender their shares to Dickens.

Morse kept coming back to the problem of motive. Which niece or nephew, he wondered, stood to gain most by eliminating Thorndike and allowing Dickens's offer to succeed?

QUESTION

1. Help Morse solve the case. Which of Thorndike's relatives stood to gain most from his death?

---

[53]Rupert Thorndike's shares would go to a charitable foundation formed to advance the study of financial engineering and its crucial role in world peace and progress. The managers of the foundation's endowment were not expected to oppose the takeover.

APPENDIX ● ● ●

Project Finance

Project finance loans are loans that are tied as closely as possible to the fortunes of a particular project and that minimize the exposure of the parent. These loans are usually referred to simply as **project finance** and are a specialty of large international banks.

Some Common Features

No two project financings are alike, but they have some common features. Typically, the parent will set up a special-purpose company to own and manage the project. This company will then enter into a package of contracts that ensures the project will generate the cash flows needed to service the debt. Three components of this package are particularly important.

First, the lenders need to be confident that the project will be built on time and to specifications. This is the role of the engineering, procurement, and construction (EPC) contract between the project company and the plant's constructors.

Second, the lenders need to know that the project will be able to generate sufficient revenues to enable it to service the loans. Therefore, the project company will generally enter into a long-term off-take contract with the business that is buying the product (the offtaker).

A third set of contracts involves the government of the host country. The lenders require assurance that the government will not impose new taxes or limit its ability to access the currency markets. If possible, it can be helpful to have the involvement of the World Bank or an international development bank to ensure that the government plays fair.

The effect of this web of contracts is to shift much of the project's risk away from the special-purpose company. As a result, the special-purpose company commonly has very little equity, and about 70% of the capital for the project is typically provided in the form of bank debt or other privately placed borrowing. This debt is supported by the project cash flows; if these flows are insufficient, the lenders do not usually have any recourse against the parent companies.

BEYOND THE PAGE

Revenue guarantees for project finance

mhhe.com/brealey14e

The Role of Project Finance

Project finance is widely used in developing countries to fund power, telecommunications, mining, and transportation projects, but it is also used in major industrialized countries. In the United States, project finance has been most commonly used to fund power plants. For example, an electric utility company may get together with an industrial company to construct a cogeneration plant that provides electricity to the utility and waste heat to a nearby industrial plant. The utility stands behind the cogeneration project and guarantees its revenue stream. Banks are happy to lend a high proportion of the cost of the project because they know that once the project is up and running, the cash flow is insulated from most of the risks facing normal businesses.[54]

Project financing is costly to arrange,[55] and the project debt usually carries a relatively high interest rate. So why don't companies simply finance the projects by borrowing against their existing assets? Notice that most of the projects have limited lives and employ established technologies. They generate substantial free cash flow, and there are few options to make profitable follow-on investments. If such investments are funded with project finance, management has little discretion

---

[54]There are some interesting regulatory implications to this arrangement. When a utility builds a power plant, it is entitled to a fair return on its investment: Regulators are supposed to set customer charges that will allow the utility to earn its cost of capital. Unfortunately, the cost of capital is not easily measured and is a natural focus for argument in regulatory hearings. But when a utility buys electric power, the cost of capital is rolled into the contract price and treated as an operating cost. In this case, the pass-through to the customer may be less controversial.

[55]Total transaction costs for infrastructure projects average 3–5% of the amount invested. See M. Klein, J. So, and B. Shin, "Transaction Costs in Private Infrastructure Projects—Are They Too High?" The World Bank Group, October 1996.

over how the cash flows are used. Instead, the debt-service requirements ensure that the cash must be returned to investors rather than frittered away on unprofitable future ventures.[56]

EXAMPLE 25A.1 • Project finance for an Indonesian power station

In 2004, the Indonesian government passed a law to promote private participation in geothermal power generation. Shortly thereafter, PLN, the government-owned power company, started a bidding process to appoint an independent power company (IPP) to build, own, and operate the huge Sarulla geothermal power station.

The tender was won by Sarulla Operations Ltd. (SOL), a special-purpose consortium owned by Kyushu Electric (a Japanese electric power company), Itochu (a Japanese trading company with major energy interests), INPEX (a Japanese oil company), PT Medco Energi (an Indonesian oil and gas company), and Ormat Technologies (a U.S. geothermal producer).

About three-quarters of the $1.6 billion estimated project cost was provided by a syndicate of banks led by the Japanese Bank for International Cooperation (JBIC) and the Asian Development Bank. The commercial lenders were Sumitomo Mitsui Banking Corporation, Société Générale, National Australian Bank, Bank of Tokyo Mitsubishi UFJ, Mizuho, and ING. Two climate funds also provided concessional loans. The bank loans were to be drawn down over 4 years and then repaid over the following 16 years, and the consortium took out an interest rate swap that protected it against subsequent changes in interest rates.

The high level of bank lending was possible only because the profitability of the project was protected by a series of contracts that reallocated the risks. First, SOL signed a joint operating contract with the project's concession holder, which granted it the right to use the geothermal field for 30 years. The lead contractor for the project, Hyundai Engineering and Construction, then entered into an engineering, procurement, and construction contract that protected SOL against delays or defects in construction. Project revenues were protected by a power purchase agreement with PLN, which agreed to purchase the energy produced by the geothermal power plant for 30 years and to pay higher prices during the early years of operation. To ensure that PLN would meet its obligations, the Indonesian government issued a 20-year business viability guarantee letter (BVGL), and JBIC provided a political risk guaranty for the portion of the loan provided by commercial lenders. SOL's owners also provided a contingent equity facility in which they undertook to provide additional equity in case of cost overruns.

So far the Sarulla project has hit no major snags. By 2018, it had achieved full commercial operation and was generating sufficient electricity to power over 2 million Indonesian households.

• • • • •

QUESTIONS

1. Explain when it makes sense to use project finance rather than a direct debt issue by the parent company.

2. Look back at the Sarulla project. There were many other ways that the project could have been financed. For example, PLN could have invested in the power plant and hired a consortium to run it. Alternatively, the consortium could have owned the power plant directly and funded its cost by a mixture of new borrowing and the sale of shares. What do you think were the advantages of setting up a separately financed company to undertake the project?

---

[56]Because the project is an independent company, it cannot drag down the parent company if something does go badly wrong with the project.

Discussions of project finance include:

B. C. Esty, *Modern Project Finance: A Casebook* (New York: John Wiley, 2003).

B. C. Esty, "Returns on Project-Financed Investments: Evolution and Managerial Implications," *Journal of Applied Corporate Finance* 15 (Spring 2002), pp. 71–86.

R. A. Brealey, I. A. Cooper, and M. Habib, "Using Project Finance to Fund Infrastructure Investments," *Journal of Applied Corporate Finance* 9 (Fall 1996), pp. 25–38.

● ● ● ●

**APPENDIX
FURTHER
READING**

CHAPTER

26

Leasing

Most of us occasionally rent a car, bicycle, or boat. Usually, such personal rentals are short-lived; we may rent a car for a day or week. But in corporate finance, longer term rentals are common. A rental agreement that extends for a year or more and involves a series of fixed payments is called a lease.

Firms lease as an alternative to buying capital equipment. In a typical year, approximately a quarter of U.S. purchases of equipment and software is financed by a lease. Trucks and farm machinery are often leased; so are railroad cars, aircraft, and ships. Just about every kind of asset can be leased. For example, the two pandas in Copenhagen Zoo are leased from the Chinese government at an annual cost of $1 million.

Section 26-1 What is a lease?

In Section 26-1, we introduce the principal lessors, and we catalog the different kinds of leases. One of the key distinctions is between short-term, or *operating,* leases, and long-term, or *financial,* leases that last for most of the economic life of the asset.

Section 26-2 Why lease?

When equipment is needed for only a short time, it is often more convenient to lease than to buy. For long-term leases, the choice is generally to lease rather than borrow.

Section 26-3 Rentals on an operating lease

We show that the key to understanding operating leases is equivalent annual cost. The annual payment on an operating lease should cover the lessor's equivalent annual cost.

Section 26-4 Valuing financial leases

A financial lease is similar to long-term secured borrowing. We show that the net present value of a financial lease is equal to the difference between the financing provided by the lease and that provided by an equivalent loan.

Section 26-5 When do financial leases pay?

When a firm borrows money to buy equipment, it can offset the depreciation against its taxable profits. When it leases the equipment, it is the lessor who makes uses of the depreciation deduction. Financial leases make the most sense when the depreciation tax shield is more valuable to the lessor than to the lessee.

Section 26-6 Setting up a leveraged lease

Big-ticket leases for items such as aircraft, satellites, or rolling stock are usually in the form of a leveraged lease. This is a financial lease in which the lessor borrows part of the purchase price of the leased asset. In this final section of the chapter, we describe the structure of a typical leveraged lease.

26-1   What Is a Lease?

Every lease involves two parties. The *user* of the asset is called the *lessee*. The lessee makes periodic payments to the *owner* of the asset, who is called the *lessor*. For example, if you sign an agreement to rent an apartment for a year, you are the lessee and the owner is the lessor.

You often see references to the *leasing industry*. This refers to lessors. (Almost all firms are lessees to at least a minor extent.) Some of the largest lessors are equipment manufacturers. For example, IBM is a large lessor of computers, and Deere is a large lessor of agricultural and construction equipment.

The other two major groups of lessors are banks and independent leasing companies. Leasing companies play an enormous role in the airline business. For example, in 2021 AerCap owned and leased out more than 2,000 commercial aircraft. The world's airlines rely largely on leasing to finance their fleets.

Leasing companies offer a variety of services. Some act as lease brokers (arranging lease deals) as well as being lessors. Others specialize in leasing automobiles, trucks, and standardized industrial equipment; they succeed because they can buy equipment in quantity, service it efficiently, and if necessary, resell it at a good price.

Leases come in many forms, but in all cases the **lessee** (user) promises to make a series of payments to the **lessor** (owner). The lease contract specifies the monthly or semiannual payments, with the first payment usually due as soon as the contract is signed. When a lease is terminated, the leased equipment reverts to the lessor. However, the lease agreement often gives the user the option to purchase the equipment or take out a new lease.

Some leases are short-term or can be canceled by the lessee before the end of the contract period. These are generally known as **operating leases**. Others extend over most of the estimated economic life of the asset and cannot be canceled or can be canceled only if the lessor is reimbursed for any losses. These are called **financial**, **capital**, or **full-payout leases**.

Financial leases are a *source of financing*. Signing a financial lease contract is like borrowing money. There is an immediate cash inflow because the lessee is relieved of having to pay for the asset. But the lessee is also obliged to make the payments specified in the lease contract. The user could have borrowed the full purchase price of the asset by agreeing to make interest and principal payments to the lender. Thus, the cash-flow consequences of leasing and borrowing are similar. In either case, the firm raises cash now and pays it back later. Later in this chapter, we compare leasing and borrowing as financing alternatives.

Leases also differ in the services provided by the lessor. Under a **full-service lease**, or **rental lease**, the lessor promises to maintain and insure the equipment and to pay any property taxes due on it. In a **net lease**, the lessee agrees to maintain the asset, insure it, and pay any property taxes. Financial leases are usually net leases.

Most financial leases are arranged for brand new assets. A company may lease the asset directly from the manufacturer (e.g., IBM or Deere), or it may arrange for an independent leasing company to buy it from the manufacturer and provide the lease. These are called **direct leases**. In other cases, the firm sells an asset it already owns and leases it back from the buyer. These **sale and lease-back** arrangements are common in real estate.

EXAMPLE 26.1 • Goldman Sachs arranges a sale and lease-back

In 2019, Goldman Sachs sold its new London headquarters for $1.49 billion and arranged to lease the building back for an initial period of 25 years. Legal ownership passed to the new owner, but the right to use it remained with Goldman.

• • • • •

You may also encounter **leveraged leases**. These are financial leases in which the lessor borrows part of the purchase price of the leased asset. This does not change the lessee's obligations, but it can complicate the lessor's analysis considerably.

26.1 Self-Test

Define the following terms: a. financial lease; b. sale-and-leaseback; c. net lease; d. operating lease; e. leveraged lease.

26-2 | **Why Lease?**

You hear many suggestions about why companies should lease equipment rather than buy it. Let us look at some sensible reasons and then at a more dubious one.

Sensible Reasons for Leasing

Short-Term Leases Are Convenient Suppose you want the use of a car for a week. You could buy one and sell it seven days later, but that would be silly. You would spend time selecting a car, negotiating purchase, arranging insurance, and registering ownership. Then at the end of the week you would negotiate resale and cancel the registration and insurance. You might also have a hard time explaining to suspicious would-be buyers why you are selling the car so soon. When you need a car for a short time, it clearly makes sense to rent it. You save the trouble of registering ownership, and you know the effective cost. In the same way, it pays a company to lease equipment that it needs for only a year or two. Of course, this kind of lease is always an operating lease.[1]

Maintenance Is Provided Under a full-service lease, the user receives maintenance and other services. Many lessors are well equipped to provide efficient maintenance. Of course, these benefits will be reflected in higher lease payments.

Standardization Leads to Low Administrative and Transaction Costs Suppose that you operate a leasing company that specializes in financial leases for trucks. You are effectively lending money to a large number of firms (the lessees) that may differ considerably in size and risk. But, because the underlying asset is in each case the same salable item (a truck), you can safely "lend" the money (lease the truck) without conducting a detailed analysis of each firm's business. You can also use a simple, standard lease contract. This standardization makes it possible to "lend" small sums of money without incurring large investigative, administrative, or legal costs.

For these reasons leasing is often a relatively cheap source of cash for the small company with few tangible assets to support a debt issue.[2] It offers secure financing on a flexible, piecemeal basis, with lower transaction costs than in a debt issue.

Tax Shields Can Be Used The lessor owns the leased asset and deducts its depreciation from taxable income. If the depreciation tax shields are more valuable to the lessor than to the asset's user, it may make sense for the lessor to own the equipment and pass on some of the tax benefits to the lessee in the form of low lease payments.

Lessors May Fare Better than Lenders in Bankruptcy Lessors in financial leases are in many ways similar to secured lenders, but lessors may fare better in bankruptcy. If the bankruptcy court decides that the leased asset is "essential" to the lessee's business, it *affirms* the lease. Then the bankrupt firm can continue to use the asset. It must still make the lease

---

[1]The market for used cars suffers from a "lemons" problem since the seller typically knows more about the quality of the car than the would-be buyer. Because off-lease used cars are generally of above-average quality, leasing can help to alleviate this problem. Igal Hendel and Alessandro Lizzeri argue that this may help to explain the prevalence of car leasing. See I. Hendel and A. Lizzeri, "The Role of Leasing under Adverse Selection," *Journal of Political Economy* 110 (February 2002), pp. 113–143. Thomas Gilligan uses a similar argument to analyze the market for aircraft leasing. See T. W. Gilligan, "Lemons and Leases in the Used Business Aircraft Market," *Journal of Political Economy* 112 (2004), pp. 1157–1180.

[2]For evidence that leasing is relatively more common in such firms, see J. R. Graham and M. T. Leary, "A Review of Empirical Capital Structure Research and Directions for the Future," *Annual Review of Financial Economics* 3 (2011), pp. 309–345.

payments, however. This can be good news for the lessor, who is paid while other creditors cool their heels. Even secured creditors are not paid until the bankruptcy process works itself out.

If the lease is not affirmed but *rejected,* the lessor can recover the leased asset. If it is worth less than the present value of the remaining lease payments, the lessor can try to recoup this loss. But in this case the lessor must get in line with unsecured creditors.

Unfortunately for lessors, there is a third possibility. As the following example shows, a lessee in financial distress may be able to renegotiate the lease, forcing the lessor to accept lower lease payments.

EXAMPLE 26.2 • Leases and financial distress

In 2001, American Airlines (AA) acquired most of the assets of Trans World Airlines (TWA). TWA was bankrupt, and AA's purchase contract was structured so that AA could decide whether to affirm or reject TWA's aircraft leases. AA contacted the lessors and threatened to reject. The lessors realized that rejection would put about 100 leased aircraft back in their laps to sell or re-lease, probably at fire-sale prices. (The market for used aircraft was not strong at the time.) The lessors, therefore, ended up accepting renegotiated lease rates that were about half what TWA had been paying.[3]

• • • • •

Lessees May Sidestep the Limitation on Debt Interest The 2017 Tax Cuts and Jobs Act limited the tax deductibility of interest payments to 30% of earnings before interest and depreciation. Companies that are up against this limit may find it convenient to lease new equipment rather than to borrow in order to buy it. The rental payments on the lease are fixed obligations like debt interest, but there is no restriction on the company's ability to deduct them when calculating its tax liability.

A Dubious Reason for Leasing

Leasing Preserves Capital Leasing companies provide "100% financing"; they advance the full cost of the leased asset. Consequently, lessors often claim that leasing preserves capital, allowing the firm to save its cash for other things.

But the firm can also "preserve capital" by borrowing money. If Greymare Bus Lines leases a $100,000 bus rather than buying it, it conserves $100,000 cash. However, it could also (1) buy the bus for cash and (2) borrow $100,000, using the bus as security. Its bank balance ends up the same whether it leases or buys and borrows. It has the bus in either case, and it incurs a $100,000 liability in either case. What's so special about leasing?

26-3 Rentals on an Operating Lease

In Chapter 6, we defined the equivalent annual cost of an asset as the annual rental payment sufficient to cover the present value of all the costs of owning and operating the asset.

In the examples in Chapter 6, the rental payments were hypothetical—just a way of converting a present value to an annual cost. But in the leasing business the payments are real. Suppose you decide to lease a machine tool for one year. What will the rental payment be in a competitive leasing industry? The lessor's equivalent annual cost, of course.

---

[3]If the leases had been rejected, the lessors would have had a claim only on TWA's assets and cash flows, not AA's. The renegotiation of the TWA leases is described in E. Benmelech and N. K. Bergman, "Liquidation Values and the Credibility of Financial Contract Renegotiation: Evidence from U.S. Airlines," *Quarterly Journal of Economics* 123 (2008), pp. 1635–1677.

Example of an Operating Lease

The boyfriend of the daughter of the CEO of Establishment Industries takes her to the senior prom in a pearly white stretch limo. The CEO is impressed. He decides Establishment Industries ought to have one for VIP transportation. Establishment's CFO prudently suggests a one-year operating lease and approaches Acme Limolease for a quote.

Table 26.1 shows Acme's analysis. Suppose it buys a new limo for $75,000 that it plans to lease out for seven years (years 0 through 6). The table gives Acme's forecasts of operating, maintenance, and administrative costs, the latter including the costs of negotiating the lease, keeping track of payments and paperwork, and finding a replacement lessee when Establishment's year is up. For simplicity, we assume zero inflation and use a 7% cost of capital. We also assume that the limo will have zero salvage value at the end of year 6. The present value of all costs, partially offset by the value of depreciation tax shields, is $113,920.[4] How much does Acme need to charge to break even?

Acme can afford to buy and lease out the limo only if the rental payments forecasted over six years have a present value of at least $113,920. We follow common leasing practice and assume rental payments in advance.[5] The problem, then, is to calculate a six-year annuity due with a present value of $113,920.

As Table 26.1 shows, the required annuity is $19,750.[6] This annuity's present value (after taxes) exactly equals the present value of the after-tax costs of owning and operating the limo.

	Year						
	0	**1**	**2**	**3**	**4**	**5**	**6**
Initial cost	−75	0	0	0	0	0	0
Maintenance costs, etc.	−12	−12	−12	−12	−12	−12	−12
Tax shield on costs	+2.52	+2.52	+2.52	+2.52	+2.52	+2.52	+2.52
Depreciation tax shield[a]	+15.75	0	0	0	0	0	0
Total	−68.73	−9.48	−9.48	−9.48	−9.48	−9.48	−9.48
PV at 7% = −113.92[b]							
Break-even rent (level)	−25.01	−25.01	−25.01	−25.01	−25.01	−25.01	−25.01
Tax	+5.25	+5.25	+5.25	+5.25	+5.25	+5.25	+5.25
Break-even rent after tax	−19.75	−19.75	−19.75	−19.75	−19.75	−19.75	−19.75
PV at 7% = −113.92[b]							

❭**TABLE 26.1**   Calculating the zero-NPV rental rate (or equivalent annual cost) for Establishment Industries' pearly white stretch limo (figures in $ thousands). The break-even rent is set so that the PV of after-tax lease payments equals **$113,920**, the PV of the after-tax cost of buying and operating the limo.

Note: We assume no inflation and a 7% cost of capital. The tax rate is 21%.
[a]The depreciation tax shield is calculated assuming that EI can write-off the full amount of the investment immediately. We ignore the special depreciation rules for luxury automobiles.
[b]Note that the first payment of these annuities comes immediately. The standard annuity factor must be multiplied by $1 + r = 1.07$.

---

[4]The depreciation tax shields are safe cash flows if the tax rate does not change and Acme is sure to pay taxes. If 7% is the right discount rate for the other flows in Table 26.1, the depreciation tax shields deserve a lower rate. A more refined analysis would discount safe depreciation tax shields at an after-tax borrowing or lending rate. See the Appendix to Chapter 18 or the next section of this chapter.
[5]In Section 6-4, the hypothetical rentals were paid *in arrears.*
[6]This is a level annuity because we are assuming that (1) there is no inflation and (2) the services of a six-year-old limo are no different from a brand-new limo's. If users of aging limos see them as obsolete or unfashionable, or if purchase costs of new limos are declining, then lease rates have to decline as limos age. This means that rents follow a *declining* annuity. Early users have to pay more to make up for declining rents later.

The annuity provides Acme with a competitive expected rate of return (7%) on its investment. Acme could try to charge Establishment Industries more than $19,750, but if the CFO is smart enough to ask for bids from Acme's competitors, the winning lessor will end up receiving this amount.

Remember that Establishment Industries is not compelled to use the limo for more than one year. Acme may have to find several new lessees over the limo's economic life. Even if Establishment continues, it can renegotiate a new lease at whatever rates prevail in the future. Thus, Acme does not know what it can charge in year 1 or afterward. If pearly white falls out of favor with teenagers and CEOs, Acme is probably out of luck.

In real life, Acme would have several further things to worry about. For example, how long will the limo stand idle when it is returned at year 1? If idle time is likely before a new lessee is found, then lease rates have to be higher to compensate.[7]

In an operating lease, the *lessor* absorbs these risks, not the lessee. The discount rate used by the lessor must include a premium sufficient to compensate its shareholders for the risks of buying and holding the leased asset. In other words, Acme's 7% real discount rate must cover the risks of investing in stretch limos. (As we see in the next section, risk bearing in *financial* leases is fundamentally different.)

BEYOND THE PAGE

Try It!
Leasing
spreadsheets

mhhe.com/brealey14e

26.2 Self-Test

Suppose that the corporate tax rate is 10%. Recalculate the break-even rental rate on Acme's limo.

Lease or Buy?

If you need a car or limo for only a day or a week you will surely rent it; if you need one for five years you will probably buy it. In between, there is a gray region in which the choice of lease or buy is not obvious. The decision rule should be clear in concept, however: If you need an asset for your business, *buy it if the equivalent annual cost of ownership and operation is less than the best lease rate you can get from an outsider.* In other words, buy if you can "rent to yourself" cheaper than you can rent from others. (Again we stress that this rule applies to *operating* leases.)

If you plan to use the asset for an extended period, your equivalent annual cost of owning the asset will usually be less than the operating lease rate. The lessor has to mark up the lease rate to cover the costs of negotiating and administering the lease, the foregone revenues when the asset is off-lease and idle, and so on. These costs are avoided when the company buys and rents to itself.

There are two cases in which operating leases may make sense even when the company plans to use an asset for an extended period. First, the lessor may be able to buy and manage the asset at less expense than the lessee. For example, Amerco, a major truck leasing company, owns nearly 170,000 trucks. That puts it in an excellent bargaining position with truck manufacturers. Such companies also run very efficient service operations, and they know how to extract the most salvage value when trucks wear out and it is time to sell them. A small business, or a small division of a larger one, cannot achieve these economies and often finds it cheaper to lease trucks than to buy them.

Second, operating leases often contain useful options.[8] Suppose Acme offers Establishment Industries the following two leases:

---

[7] If, say, limos were off-lease and idle 20% of the time, lease rates would have to be 25% above those shown in Table 26.1.

[8] McConnell and Schallheim calculate the value of options in operating leases under various assumptions about asset risk, depreciation rates, etc. See J. J. McConnell and J. S. Schallheim, "Valuation of Asset Leasing Contracts," *Journal of Financial Economics* 12 (August 1983), pp. 237–261.

1. A one-year lease for $19,750.

2. A six-year lease for $21,000, *with the option to cancel the lease* at any time from year 1 on.[9]

The second lease has obvious attractions. Suppose Establishment's CEO becomes fond of the limo and wants to use it for a second year. If rates increase, lease 2 allows Establishment to continue at the old rate. If rates decrease, Establishment can cancel lease 2 and negotiate a lower rate with Acme or one of its competitors.

Of course, lease 2 is a more costly proposition for Acme: In effect it gives Establishment an insurance policy protecting it from increases in future lease rates. The difference between the costs of leases 1 and 2 is the annual insurance premium. But lessees may happily pay for insurance if they have no special knowledge of future asset values or lease rates. A leasing company acquires such knowledge in the course of its business and can generally sell such insurance at a profit.

Airlines face fluctuating demand for their services and the mix of planes that they need is constantly changing. Most airlines, therefore, lease a proportion of their fleet on a short-term, cancelable basis and are willing to pay a premium to lessors for bearing the cancellation risk. Specialist aircraft lessors are prepared to bear this risk because they are well-placed to find new customers for any aircraft that are returned to them. Aircraft owned by specialist lessors spend less time parked and more time flying than aircraft owned by airlines.[10]

26-4 Valuing Financial Leases

For operating leases, the decision centers on "lease versus buy." For *financial* leases, the decision amounts to "lease versus borrow." Financial leases extend over most of the economic life of the leased equipment. They are *not* cancelable. Therefore, financial leases make sense only when the company is prepared to take on the business risks of owning and operating the leased asset.

A financial lease is just another way of borrowing money to pay for an asset. If a company takes out a secured loan, it is obliged to make a series of fixed payments. If it fails to make those payments, the lender can repossess the asset. If the company signs a finance lease, it too is obliged to make a series of fixed payments; if it fails to do so, the lessor can repossess the asset. Therefore, in important respects, a financial lease is equivalent to a secured loan.

Having said this, we must immediately qualify. Legal ownership can make a difference when a financial lease expires because the lessor gets the asset. Once a secured loan is paid off, the user owns the asset free and clear.

Example of a Financial Lease

Imagine yourself in the position of Thomas Pierce III, president of Greymare Bus Lines. Your firm was established by your grandfather, who was quick to capitalize on the growing demand for transportation between Widdicombe and nearby townships. The company has owned all its vehicles from the time the company was formed; you are now reconsidering that policy. Your operating manager wants to buy a new bus costing $100,000. The bus will last only eight years before going to the scrap yard. You are convinced that investment in the additional equipment

---

[9]Acme might also offer a one-year lease for $28,000 but give the lessee an option to *extend* the lease on the same terms for up to five additional years. This is, of course, identical to lease 2. It doesn't matter whether the lessee has the (put) option to cancel or the (call) option to continue.

[10]A. Gavazza, "Asset Liquidity and Financial Contracts: Evidence from Aircraft Leases," *Journal of Financial Economics* 95 (January 2010), pp. 62–84.

	Year							
	0	**1**	**2**	**3**	**4**	**5**	**6**	**7**
Cost of new bus	+100							
Lost depreciation tax shield	−21	0	0	0	0	0	0	0
Lease payment	−16.2	−16.2	−16.2	−16.2	−16.2	−16.2	−16.2	−16.2
Tax shield of lease payment	+3.4	+3.4	+3.4	+3.4	+3.4	+3.4	+3.4	+3.4
Cash flow of lease	+66.2	−12.8	−12.8	−12.8	−12.8	−12.8	−12.8	−12.8

❭TABLE 26.2   Cash-flow consequences of the lease contract offered to Greymare Bus Lines (figures in $ thousands).

is worthwhile. However, the representative of the bus manufacturer has pointed out that her firm would also be willing to lease the bus to you for eight annual payments of $16,200 each. Greymare would remain responsible for all maintenance, insurance, and operating expenses.

Table 26.2 shows the cash-flow consequences of signing the lease contract. The consequences are as follows:

1. Greymare does not have to pay for the bus. This is equivalent to a cash inflow of $100,000.

2. Greymare no longer owns the bus and so cannot depreciate it. Therefore it gives up a valuable depreciation tax shield. In Table 26.2, we have assumed that the bus could be written-off immediately for tax.

3. Greymare must pay $16,200 per year for eight years to the lessor. The first payment is due immediately and the last at the end of year 7.

4. However, these lease payments are fully tax-deductible. At a 21% marginal tax rate, the lease payments generate tax shields of $3,400 per year. You could say that the after-tax cost of the lease payment is $16,200 − $3,400 = $12,800.

We must emphasize that Table 26.2 assumes that Greymare will pay taxes at the full 21% marginal rate. If the firm were sure to lose money, and therefore pay no taxes, lines 2 and 4 would be left blank. Table 26.2 also assumes the bus will be worthless when it goes to the scrapyard at the end of year 7. Otherwise, there would be an entry for salvage value lost.

Warning: Notice also that we assume for simplicity that all the cash flows occur on just one day each year. So today, Greymare saves the cost of buying the bus, makes the up-front lease payment, and settles up any tax consequences. Exactly 365 days later, it makes a further lease payment and pays $3,400 less in taxes. Elsewhere in the book, we have made similar simplifying assumptions, but leasing is a business with narrow margins; when you need to calculate the value of a lease, it pays to be precise about the exact timing of each cash flow.

BEYOND THE PAGE

Try It!
Leasing
spreadsheets

mhhe.com/brealey14e

Valuing the Lease Contract

When we left the president of Greymare, he had just set down in Table 26.2 the cash flows of the financial lease proposed by the bus manufacturer.

A lessee might, in principle, end up using a separate discount rate for each line of Table 26.2, each rate chosen to fit the risk of that line's cash flow. But established, profitable firms usually find it reasonable to simplify by discounting the types of flows shown in Table 26.2 at a single rate based on the rate of interest the firm would pay if it borrowed rather than leased.[11] We assume Greymare's borrowing rate is 10%.

---

[11]This assumption is reasonable for the lease payments because the lessor is effectively lending money to the lessee. But the various tax shields might carry enough risk to deserve a higher discount rate. For example, Greymare might be confident that it could make the lease payments but not confident that it could earn enough taxable income to use these tax shields. In that case, the cash flows generated by the tax shields would probably deserve a higher discount rate than the borrowing rate used for the lease payments.

At this point, we must go back to our discussion in the Appendix to Chapter 18 of debt-equivalent flows. When a company lends money, it pays tax on the interest it receives. Its net return is the after-tax interest rate. When a company borrows money, it can deduct interest payments from its taxable income. The net cost of borrowing is the after-tax interest rate. Thus, the after-tax interest rate is the effective rate at which a company can transfer debt-equivalent flows from one time period to another. Therefore, to value the incremental cash flows stemming from the lease, we need to discount them at the after-tax interest rate.

Since Greymare can borrow at 10%, we should discount the lease cash flows at $r_D(1 - T_c) = 0.10(1 - 0.21) = 0.079$, or 7.9%. This gives

$$\text{NPV lease} = +66.2 - \frac{12.80}{1.079} - \frac{12.80}{(1.079)^2} - \frac{12.80}{(1.079)^3} - \frac{12.80}{(1.079)^4}$$

$$- \frac{12.80}{(1.079)^5} - \frac{12.80}{(1.079)^6} - \frac{12.80}{(1.079)^7}$$

$$= -0.66, \text{ or } -\$660$$

Since the lease has a negative NPV, Greymare is better off buying the bus.

The general formula for valuing a financial lease is:

$$\text{NPV of lease} = \text{initial financing provided} - \sum_{t=1}^{N} \frac{\text{lease cash flow}}{[1 + r_D(1 - T_c)]^t} \tag{26.1}$$

where N is the length of the lease. Initial financing provided equals the cost of the leased asset minus any immediate lease payment or other cash outflow attributable to the lease.[12]

26.3 Self-Test

Recalculate the cash flows and NPV of Greymare's lease assuming Greymare pays tax at 30%. Why does NPV decline?

Comparing the Lease with an Equivalent Loan

A positive or negative NPV for a financial lease is not an abstract concept; Greymare's shareholders really are $660 poorer if the company leases. Let us now check how this situation comes about.

Look once more at Table 26.2. The lease cash flows are:

	Year							
	0	1	2	3	4	5	6	7
Lease cash flows, thousands	+66.20	−12.80	−12.80	−12.80	−12.80	−12.80	−12.80	−12.80

The lease payments are contractual obligations like the principal and interest payments on secured debt. Thus, you can think of the incremental lease cash flows in years 1 through 7 as the "debt service" of the lease. Suppose that, instead of paying $12,800 annually to the lessor, Greymare decided to set aside $12,800 to service a loan. Table 26.3 shows how much Greymare could then borrow. The initial amount of the loan is $66.860 thousand. If Greymare borrowed this sum, it would need to pay interest in the first year of $0.10 \times 66.86 = 6.69$ and

---

[12]The principles behind lease valuation were originally set out in S. C. Myers, D. A. Dill, and A. J. Bautista, "Valuation of Financial Lease Contracts," *Journal of Finance* 31 (June 1976), pp. 799–819; and J. R. Franks and S. D. Hodges, "Valuation of Financial Lease Contracts: A Note," *Journal of Finance* 33 (May 1978), pp. 647–669.

					Year			
	0	**1**	**2**	**3**	**4**	**5**	**6**	**7**
Amount borrowed	66.86	59.34	51.23	42.48	33.04	22.85	11.86	0
Interest paid at 10%		−6.69	−5.93	−5.12	−4.25	−3.30	−2.29	−1.19
Interest tax shield at 21%		+1.40	+1.25	+1.08	+0.89	+0.69	+0.48	+0.25
Interest paid after tax		−5.28	−4.69	−4.05	−3.36	−2.61	−1.81	−0.94
Principal repaid		−7.52	−8.11	−8.75	−9.44	−10.19	−10.99	−11.86
Net cash flow of equivalent loan	66.86	−12.80	−12.80	−12.80	−12.80	−12.80	−12.80	−12.80

❭TABLE 26.3   Details of the equivalent loan to the lease offered to Greymare Bus Lines (figures in $ thousands; cash outflows shown with negative sign).

would *receive* a tax shield on this interest of $0.21 \times 6.69 = 1.40$. Greymare could then repay 7.52 of the loan, leaving a net cash outflow of 12.80 (exactly the same as for the lease) in year 1 and an outstanding debt at the start of year 2 of 59.34.

As you walk through the calculations in Table 26.3, you see that it costs exactly the same to service a loan that brings an immediate inflow of 66.86 as it does to service the lease, which brings in only 66.20. That is why we say that the lease has a net present value of $66.20 - 66.86 = -0.66$, or −$660. If Greymare leases the bus rather than raising an *equivalent loan,* there will be $660 less in Greymare's bank account.

Our example illustrates two general points about leases and equivalent loans. First, if you can devise a borrowing plan that gives the same cash flow as the lease in every future period but a higher immediate cash flow, then you should not lease. If, however, the equivalent loan provides the same future cash outflows as the lease but a lower immediate inflow, then leasing is the better choice.

Second, our example suggests two ways to value a lease:

1. *Hard way.* Construct a table like Table 26.3 showing the equivalent loan.
2. *Easy way.* Discount the lease cash flows at the *after-tax* interest rate that the firm would pay on an equivalent loan. Both methods give the same answer—in our case an NPV of −$660.[13]

Notice that the value of the lease is its *incremental* value relative to borrowing via an equivalent loan. A positive lease value means that *if* you acquire the asset, lease financing is advantageous. It does not prove you should acquire the asset.

Notice that our formula applies to net financial leases. Any insurance, maintenance, and other operating costs picked up by the lessor have to be evaluated separately and added to the value of the lease. If the asset has salvage value at the end of the lease, that value should be taken into account also.

Financial Leases When There Are Limits on the Interest Tax Shield

In Table 26.3, we devised a loan that Greymare could take out that had exactly the same cash flows as the lease. In that table, we assumed that Greymare could deduct the interest on this loan when it calculated its taxable income. But the 2017 Tax Cuts and Jobs Act limited the amount of interest that companies can deduct to 30% of earnings before interest and

---

[13]Sometimes the easy way is not possible. For example, the company's tax rate may vary over the period of the lease. In that case, you will need to fall back on the hard way. Later in the section, we will encounter another case where you will need to construct the equivalent loan.

depreciation. Suppose that Greymare has borrowed heavily and cannot deduct interest payments for tax. This restriction applies to interest expense on borrowing by Greymare but not to lease payments, even though they are equivalent to debt service. Therefore, leasing the bus allows Greymare to sidestep the restriction on interest deductibility.

If Greymare borrows to finance the bus, it will not enjoy any interest tax shields until its earnings recover. So the cost of debt during this period is no longer equal to the after-tax interest rate, and it no longer makes sense to value the lease cash flows by discounting them at this rate. Since the easy way to value the lease doesn't work, you need turn to the hard way and calculate out how much Greymare could borrow if it set aside the future lease cash flows to service the loan. If the amount that Greymare could borrow is less than the immediate cash inflow on the lease, then leasing is the better option.[14]

Leasing and the Internal Revenue Service

If Greymare leases the bus, it loses the depreciation shield on the bus but can deduct the lease payment in full. The *lessor,* as legal owner, uses the depreciation tax shield but must report the lease payments as taxable rental income.

However, the Internal Revenue Service is suspicious by nature and will only allow the lessee to deduct the entire lease payment if it is satisfied that the arrangement is a genuine lease and not a disguised installment purchase or secured loan agreement.[15]

Some leases are designed *not* to qualify as a true lease for tax purposes. Suppose a manufacturer finds it convenient to lease a new computer but wants to keep the depreciation tax shields. This is easily accomplished by giving the manufacturer the option to purchase the computer for $1 at the end of the lease.[16] Then the Internal Revenue Service treats the lease as an installment sale, and the manufacturer can deduct depreciation and the interest component of the lease payment for tax purposes. But the lease is still a lease for all other purposes.

26-5   When Do Financial Leases Pay?

We have examined the value of a lease from the viewpoint of the lessee. The lessor's criterion is simply the reverse. As long as lessor and lessee are in the same tax bracket, every cash outflow to the lessee is an inflow to the lessor, and vice versa. In our numerical example, the bus manufacturer would project cash flows in a table like Table 26.2, but with the signs reversed. The value of the lease to the bus manufacturer would be

$$\text{Value of lease to lessor} = -66.20 + \frac{12.80}{1.079} + \frac{12.80}{(1.079)^2} + \frac{12.80}{(1.079)^3}$$

$$+ \frac{12.80}{(1.079)^4} + \frac{12.80}{(1.079)^5} + \frac{12.80}{(1.079)^6} + \frac{12.80}{(1.079)^7}$$

$$= +0.66 \text{ or } \$660$$

In this case, the values to lessee and lessor exactly offset ($-\$660 + \$660 = 0$). The lessor can win only at the lessee's expense.

---

[14]The trick in doing this is to work back from the final year, when the loan will be fully paid off. The amount of the loan at the *start* of that year plus the final interest payment, less any tax shield, can then be set equal to the final lease payment. If you are still not sure how to calculate the equivalent loan, take a look at the Beyond the Page Spreadsheet.

[15]For example, the IRS will disallow the lease if the lessee has an option to acquire the asset for a nominal sum. The lessee will almost certainly exercise such a bargain-purchase option, leaving the lessor with no chance of future ownership. Special-purpose assets that can only be used by the lessee will also be disqualified because the lessee will end up owning them.

[16]Such leases are known as *$1 out leases.*

But both lessee and lessor can win if their tax rates differ. Suppose that Greymare paid no tax ($T_c = 0$). Then the only cash flows of the bus lease would be:

	Year							
	0	1	2	3	4	5	6	7
Cost of new bus	+100							
Lease payment	−16.2	−16.2	−16.2	−16.2	−16.2	−16.2	−16.2	−16.2

These flows would be discounted at 10% because $r_D(1 - T_c) = r_D$ when $T_c = 0$. The value of the lease is

$$\text{Value of lease} = +100 - \sum_{t=0}^{7} \frac{16.2}{(1.10)^t}$$

$$= +100 - 95.07 = +4.93, \text{ or } \$4,930$$

In this case, there is a net gain of $660 to the lessor (who has the 21% tax rate) *and* a net gain of $4,930 to the lessee (who pays zero tax). This mutual gain is at the expense of the government. On the one hand, the government gains from the lease contract because it can tax the lease payments. On the other hand, the contract allows the lessor to take advantage of depreciation and interest tax shields that are of no use to the lessee. Because the depreciation is accelerated and the interest rate is positive, the government suffers a net loss in the present value of its tax receipts as a result of the lease.

26.4 Self-Test

True or false? "Leasing allows companies with a high marginal tax rate to 'sell' their depreciation tax shields."

Now you should begin to understand the circumstances in which the government incurs a loss on the lease and the other two parties gain. Other things being equal, the combined gains to lessor and lessee are highest when

- The lessor's tax rate is substantially higher than the lessee's.
- The depreciation tax shield is received early in the lease period.
- The lease period is long and the lease payments are concentrated toward the end of the period.
- The interest rate r_D is high—if it were zero, there would be no advantage in present value terms to postponing tax.

Leasing around the World

In most developed economies, leasing is widely used to finance investment in plant and equipment.[15] But there are important differences in the treatment of long-term financial leases for tax and accounting purposes. For example, some countries allow the lessor to use depreciation tax shields, just as in the United States. In other countries, the lessee claims depreciation deductions. Accounting usually follows suit.

A number of *big-ticket* leases are cross-border deals. Cross-border leasing can be attractive when the lessor is located in a country that offers generous depreciation allowances. The ultimate cross-border transaction occurs when *both* the lessor *and* the lessee can claim depreciation deductions. Ingenious leasing companies look for such opportunities to *double-dip*. Tax authorities look for ways to stop them.[16]

---

[15]For example, in 2019 leasing in Europe accounted for 28.6% of new investment in vehicles and equipment (**www.leaseurope.org**).
[16]Currently in the United States, the tax authorities seem to be winning. The American Jobs Creation Act (JOBS) of 2004 eliminated much of the profit from cross-border leases.

26-6 Setting Up a Leveraged Lease

Big-ticket leases are usually *leveraged leases*. The structure of a leveraged lease is summarized in Figure 26.1. In this example, the leasing company (or a syndicate of several leasing companies) sets up a special-purpose entity (SPE) to buy and lease a commercial aircraft. The SPE raises up to 80% of the cost of the aircraft by borrowing, usually from insurance companies or other financial institutions. The leasing company puts up the remaining 20% as the equity investment in the lease.

Once the lease is up and running, lease payments begin, and depreciation and interest tax shields are generated. All (or almost all) of the lease payments go to debt service. The leasing company gets no cash inflows until the debt is paid off, but does get all depreciation and interest deductions, which generate tax losses that can be used to shield other income.

By the end of the lease, the debt is paid off and the tax shields exhausted. At this point, the lessee has the option to purchase the aircraft. The leasing company gets the purchase price if the lessee's purchase option is exercised and takes back the aircraft otherwise.

The debt in a leveraged lease is *nonrecourse*. The lenders have first claim on the lease payments and on the aircraft if the lessee can't make scheduled payments but no claim on the leasing company. Thus, the lenders must depend solely on the airline lessee's credit and on the airplane as collateral.

The leasing company puts up only 20% of the money, gets 100% of the tax shields, but is not on the hook if the lease transaction falls apart. Does this sound like a great deal? Don't jump to that conclusion because the lenders will demand a higher interest rate in exchange for giving up recourse. In efficient debt markets, paying extra interest to avoid recourse should be a zero-NPV transaction—otherwise, one side of the deal would get a free ride at the expense of the other. Nevertheless, nonrecourse debt, as part of the overall structure shown in Figure 26.1, is a customary and convenient financing method.[17]

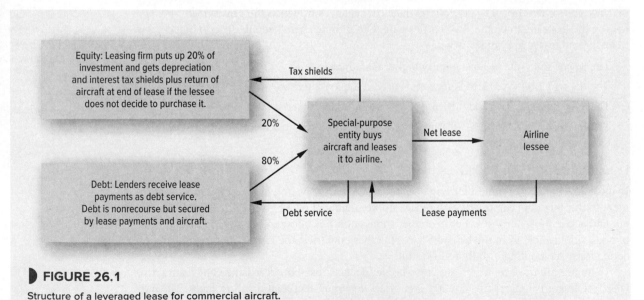

▶ **FIGURE 26.1**

Structure of a leveraged lease for commercial aircraft.

---

[17]Leveraged leases have special tax and accounting requirements, which we won't go into here. Also, the equity investment in leveraged leases can be tricky to value because the stream of after-tax cash flows changes sign more than once. That is no problem if you use the NPV rule, but it causes difficulties if you wish to calculate the internal rate of return (IRR). This requires use of modified internal rates of return, if you insist on using IRRs. We discussed multiple IRRs and modified IRRs in Section 5-3. Also take a look at Problem 24 at the end of this chapter.

- **What is a lease?** A lease is just an extended rental agreement. The owner of the equipment (the *lessor*) allows the user (the *lessee*) to operate the equipment in exchange for regular lease payments.

    Short-term, cancelable leases are known as *operating leases*. In these leases, the lessor bears the risks of ownership. Long-term, noncancelable leases are called *financial, capital,* or *full-payout* leases. Financial leases are *sources of financing* for assets that the firm wishes to acquire and use for an extended period. Many companies have sound reasons for financing via leases. For example, companies that are not paying taxes can usually strike a favorable deal with a tax-paying lessor. Also, it may be less costly and time-consuming to sign a standardized lease contract than to negotiate a long-term secured loan.

- **Operating leases** Operating leases are attractive to equipment users if the after-tax lease payment is less than the equivalent annual cost of buying the equipment. Operating leases make sense when the user needs the equipment only for a short time, when the lessor is better able to bear the risks of obsolescence, or when the lessor can offer a good deal on maintenance.

- **Valuing financial leases** A financial lease extends over most of the economic life of the leased asset and cannot be canceled. Signing a financial lease is like signing a secured loan to finance purchase of the leased asset. With financial leases, the choice is not "lease versus buy" but "lease versus borrow." When a firm borrows money, it pays the after-tax rate of interest on its debt. Therefore, the opportunity cost of entering into a financial lease is the after-tax rate of interest on the firm's bonds. To value a financial lease, we need to discount the incremental cash flows from leasing by the after-tax interest rate.

- **When do financial leases pay?** An equivalent loan is one that commits the firm to exactly the same future cash flows as a financial lease. When we calculate the net present value of the lease, we are measuring the difference between the amount of financing provided by the lease and the financing provided by the equivalent loan:

    Value of lease = financing provided by lease − value of equivalent loan

    If the lessor is in the same tax bracket as the lessee, it will receive exactly the same cash flows but with signs reversed. Thus, the lessee can gain only at the lessor's expense, and vice versa. However, if the lessee's tax rate is lower than the lessor's, then both can gain at the federal government's expense. This is a tax-timing advantage because the lessor gets interest and depreciation tax shields early in the lease.

- **Leveraged leases** Leveraged leases are three-way transactions that include lenders as well as the lessor and lessee. Lenders advance up to 80% of the cost of the leased equipment and lessors put in the rest as an equity investment. The lenders get first claim on the lease payments and on the asset but have no recourse to the equity lessors if the lessee can't pay. The lessor's return comes mostly from interest and depreciation tax shields early in the lease and the value of the leased asset at the end of the lease. Leveraged leases are common in big-ticket, cross-border lease-financing transactions.

A useful general reference on leasing is:

P. K. Nevitt and F. J. Fabozzi, *Equipment Leasing,* 4th ed. (Hoboken, NJ: John Wiley & Sons, 2008).

Smith and Wakeman discuss the economic motives for leasing:

C. W. Smith Jr. and L. M. Wakeman, "Determinants of Corporate Leasing Policy," *Journal of Finance* 40 (July 1985), pp. 895–908.

The options embedded in many operating leases are discussed in:

J. J. McConnell and J. S. Schallheim, "Valuation of Asset Leasing Contracts," *Journal of Financial Economics* 12 (August 1983), pp. 237–261.

S. R. Grenadier, "Valuing Lease Contracts: A Real Options Approach," *Journal of Financial Economics* 38 (July 1995), pp. 297–331.

S. R. Grenadier, "An Equilibrium Analysis of Real Estate Leases," *Journal of Business* 78 (2005), pp. 1173–1214.

PROBLEM SETS

Mc Graw Hill **connect**

Select problems are available in McGraw Hill's *Connect.* Please see the preface for more information.

1. **Types of lease (S26.1)** The following terms are often used to describe leases:

   a. Direct

   b. Full-service

   c. Operating

   d. Financial

   e. Net

   f. Leveraged

   g. Sale and lease-back

   Match one or more of these terms with each of the following statements:

   A. The initial lease period is shorter than the economic life of the asset.

   B. The initial lease period is long enough for the lessor to recover the cost of the asset.

   C. The lessor provides maintenance and insurance.

   D. The lessee provides maintenance and insurance.

   E. The lessor buys the equipment from the manufacturer.

   F. The lessor buys the equipment from the prospective lessee.

   G. The lessor finances the lease contract by issuing debt and equity claims against it.

2. **Reasons for leasing (S26.2)** Some of the following reasons for leasing are rational. Others are irrational or assume imperfect or inefficient capital markets. Which of the following reasons are the rational ones?

   a. The lessee's need for the leased asset is only temporary.

   b. Specialized lessors are better able to bear the risk of obsolescence.

   c. Leasing provides 100% financing and thus preserves capital.

   d. Leasing allows firms with low marginal tax rates to "sell" depreciation tax shields.

   e. Leasing increases earnings per share.

   f. Leasing reduces the transaction cost of obtaining external financing.

3. **Lease treatment in bankruptcy (S26.2)** What happens if a bankrupt lessee affirms the lease? What happens if the lease is rejected?

4. **Lease treatment in bankruptcy (S26.2)** How does the position of an equipment lessor differ from the position of a secured lender when a firm falls into bankruptcy? Assume that the secured loan would have the leased equipment as collateral. Which is better protected, the lease or the loan? Does your answer depend on the value of the leased equipment if it were sold or re-leased?

5. **Operating leases (S26.3)** Explain why the following statements are true:

   a. In a competitive leasing market, the annual operating lease payment equals the lessor's equivalent annual cost.

   b. Operating leases are attractive to equipment users if the lease payment is less than the user's equivalent annual cost.

6. **Operating leases (S26.3)** Acme has branched out to rentals of office furniture to start-up companies. Consider a $3,000 desk. Desks last for six years and can be depreciated immediately. What is the break-even operating lease rate for a new desk? Assume that lease rates for old and new desks are the same and that Acme's pretax administrative costs are $400 per desk in each of years 1 to 6. The cost of capital is 9% and the tax rate is 21%. Lease payments are made in advance, that is, at the start of each year. The inflation rate is zero.

7. **Inflation and operating leases (S26.3)** In Problem 6, we assumed identical lease rates for old and new desks.

   a. How does the initial break-even lease rate change if the expected inflation rate is 5% per year? Assume that the real cost of capital does not change. (*Hint:* Look at the discussion of equivalent annual costs in Chapter 6.)

   b. How does your answer to part (a) change if wear and tear force Acme to cut lease rates by 10% in real terms for every year of a desk's age?

8. **Technological change and operating leases (S26.3)** Look at Table 26.1. How would the initial break-even operating lease rate change if rapid technological change in limo manufacturing reduces the costs of new limos by 5% per year? (*Hint:* We discussed technological change and equivalent annual costs in Chapter 6.)

9. **Valuing financial leases (S26.4)** Look again at Problem 6. Suppose a blue-chip company requests a six-year financial lease for a $3,000 desk. The company has just issued five-year notes at an interest rate of 6% per year. What is the break-even rate in this case? Assume administrative costs drop to $200 per year. Explain why your answers to Problem 6 and this question differ.

10. **Valuing financial leases (S26.4)** Suppose that National Waferonics has before it a proposal for a four-year financial lease. The firm constructs a table like Table 26.2. The bottom line of its table shows the lease cash flows:

	Year 0	Year 1	Year 2	Year 3
Lease cash flow	+62,000	−26,800	−22,200	−17,600

These flows reflect the cost of the machine, depreciation tax shields, and the after-tax lease payments. Ignore salvage value. Assume the firm could borrow at 10% and faces a 21% marginal tax rate.

   a. What is the value of the equivalent loan?

   b. What is the value of the lease?

   c. Suppose the machine's NPV under normal financing is −$5,000. Should National Waferonics invest? Should it sign the lease?

11. **Valuing Financial Leases (S26.4)** Look again at the National Waferonics lease in Problem 10. Suppose that National Waferonics is highly levered and is unable to deduct further interest payments for tax.

   a. Does this make a lease more or less attractive?

   b. Recalculate the NPV of the lease by constructing an equivalent loan. (*Hint:* Start with the final year. The final repayment of the loan with interest should be set equal to the cash flow on the lease.)

Questions 12 to 17 all refer to Greymare's bus lease. To answer them you may find it helpful to use the Beyond the Page live Excel spreadsheets in Connect.

12. **Valuing financial leases (S26.4)** Look again at the bus lease described in Table 26.2.

    a. What is the value of the lease if Greymare's marginal tax rate is $T_c = 0.30$?

    b. What would the lease value be if the tax rate is 21%, but for tax purposes, the initial investment had to be written off in equal amounts over years 1 through 5?

13. **Valuing financial leases (S26.4)** In Section 26-4, we showed that the lease offered to Greymare Bus Lines had a positive NPV of $4,930 if Greymare paid no tax and an NPV of + $660 to a lessor paying 21% tax. What is the minimum lease payment the lessor could accept under these assumptions? What is the maximum amount that Greymare could pay?

14. **Valuing financial leases (S26.4)** In Section 26-5, we stated that if the interest rate were zero, there would be no advantage in postponing tax and therefore no advantage in leasing. Value the Greymare Bus Lines lease with an interest rate of zero. Assume that Greymare does not pay tax. Can you devise any lease terms that would make both a lessee and a lessor happy? (If you can, we would like to hear from you.)

15. **Valuing financial leases (S26.4)** A lease with a varying rental schedule is known as a structured lease. Try structuring the Greymare Bus Lines lease to increase value to the lessee while preserving the value to the lessor. Assume that Greymare does not pay tax. (*Note:* In practice, the tax authorities will allow some structuring of rental payments but might be unhappy with some of the schemes you devise.)

16. **When financial leases pay (S26.5)** In Section 26-5, we listed four circumstances in which there are potential gains from leasing. Check them out by conducting a sensitivity analysis on the Greymare Bus Lines lease, assuming that Greymare does not pay tax. Try, in turn, (a) a lessor tax rate of 50% (rather than 21%), (b) straight-line depreciation in years 1 to 6 (rather than immediate expensing), (c) a four-year lease with four annual rentals (rather than an eight-year lease), and (d) an interest rate of 20% (rather than 10%). In each case, find the minimum rental that would satisfy the lessor and calculate the NPV to the lessee.

17. **Valuing financial leases (S26.4)** Nodhead College needs a new computer. It can either buy it for $250,000 or lease it from Compulease. The lease terms require Nodhead to make six annual payments (prepaid) of $62,000. Nodhead pays no tax. Compulease pays tax at 30%. Compulease can depreciate the computer for tax purposes straight-line over five years. The computer will have no residual value at the end of year 5. The interest rate is 8%.

    a. What is the NPV of the lease for Nodhead College?

    b. What is the NPV for Compulease?

    c. What is the overall gain from leasing?

18. **Valuing financial leases (S26.4)** The Safety Razor Company has a large tax-loss carryforward and does not expect to pay taxes for another 10 years. The company is therefore proposing to lease $100,000 of new machinery. The lease terms consist of eight equal lease payments prepaid annually. The lessor can write the machinery off straight line over seven years. There is no salvage value at the end of the machinery's economic life. The tax rate is 30%, and the rate of interest is 10%. Wilbur Occam, the president of Safety Razor, wants to know the maximum lease payment that his company should be willing to make and the minimum payment that the lessor is likely to accept. Can you help him?

19. **Valuing financial leases (S26.4–S26.5)** True or false?

    a. The cost of capital for a financial lease is the pretax interest rate the company would pay on a bank loan.

    b. An equivalent loan's principal plus after-tax interest payments exactly match the after-tax cash flows of the lease.

c. A financial lease should not be undertaken unless it provides more financing than the equivalent loan.

d. It makes sense for firms that pay no taxes to lease from firms that do.

e. Other things equal, the net tax advantage of leasing increases as nominal interest rates increase.

20. **Nonrecourse debt (S26.6)** Lenders to leveraged leases hold nonrecourse debt. What does "nonrecourse" mean? What are the benefits and costs of nonrecourse debt to the equity investors in the lease?

21. **Leveraged leases (S26.6)** How does a leveraged lease differ from an ordinary, long-term financial lease? List the key differences.

22. **Leveraged leases (S26.6)** How would the lessee in Figure 26.1 evaluate the NPV of the lease? Sketch the correct valuation procedure. Then suppose that the equity lessor wants to evaluate the lease. Again sketch the correct procedure. (*Hint:* APV. How would you calculate the combined value of the lease to lessee and lessor?)

CHALLENGE

23. **Valuing leases (S26.3–S26.5)** Magna Charter has been asked to operate a Beaver bush plane for a mining company exploring north and west of Fort Liard. Magna will have a firm one-year contract with the mining company and expects that the contract will be renewed for the five-year duration of the exploration program. If the mining company renews at year 1, it will commit to use the plane for four more years.

Magna Charter has the following choices:

- Buy the plane for $500,000.
- Take a one-year operating lease for the plane. The lease rate is $118,000, paid in advance.
- Arrange a five-year, noncancelable financial lease at a rate of $75,000 per year, paid in advance.

These are net leases; all operating costs are absorbed by Magna Charter.

How would you advise Agnes Magna, the charter company's CEO? For simplicity assume five-year, straight-line depreciation for tax purposes. The company's tax rate is 30%. The weighted-average cost of capital for the bush-plane business is 14%, but Magna can borrow at 9%. The expected inflation rate is 4%.

Ms. Magna thinks the plane will be worth $300,000 after five years. But if the contract with the mining company is not renewed (there is a 20% probability of this outcome at year 1), the plane will have to be sold on short notice for $400,000.

If Magna Charter takes the five-year financial lease and the mining company cancels at year 1, Magna can sublet the plane, that is, rent it out to another user.

Make additional assumptions as necessary.

24. **Leasing and the Internal Rate of Return (S26.6)** Reconstruct Table 26.2 as a leveraged lease, assuming that the lessor borrows $80,000, 80% of the cost of the bus, nonrecourse at an interest rate of 11%. All lease payments are devoted to debt service (interest and principal) until the loan is paid off. Assume that the bus is worth $10,000 at the end of the lease. Calculate after-tax cash flows on the lessor's equity investment of $20,000. What is the IRR of the equity cash flows? Is there more than one IRR? How would you value the lessor's equity investment?

● ● ● ● ●

SOLUTIONS TO SELF-TEST QUESTIONS

26.1 a. Lease term extends over economic life of asset;

b. user sells asset and leases it back;

c. lessee agrees to maintain the asset, insure it, and pay any property taxes;

d. short-term (or cancelable) lease;

e. lessor borrows part of the asset cost, using the lease as security for the loan.

26.2

		Year					
	0	1	2	3	4	5	6
Initial cost	−75.00						
Maintenance costs, etc.	−12.00	−12.00	−12.00	−12.00	−12.00	−12.00	−12.00
Tax shield on costs	1.2	1.2	1.2	1.2	1.2	1.2	1.2
Depreciation tax shield	7.5						
Total	−78.30	10.8	10.8	10.8	10.8	10.8	10.8
PV	−78.30	−10.09	−9.43	−8.82	−8.24	−7.70	−7.20
Total PV	−129.78						
Break-even rental	−25.01	−25.01	−25.01	−25.01	−25.01	−25.01	−25.01
Tax	2.5	2.5	2.5	2.5	2.5	2.5	2.5
Break-even rental after tax	−22.51	−22.51	−22.51	−22.51	−22.51	−22.51	−22.51
PV	−22.51	−21.03	−19.66	−18.37	−17.17	−16.05	−15.00
Total PV	−129.78						

Since all cash flows (including the initial investment) are taxed at the same 10% rate, the break-even rental is unchanged.

26.3

Cash flow consequence of the lease contract for Greymare (figures in $ thousands)

				Year				
	0	1	2	3	4	5	6	7
Cost of new bus	100							
Lost depreciation tax shield	−30	0.00	0.00	0.00	0.00	0.00	0.00	0.00
Lease payment	−16.20	−16.20	−16.20	−16.20	−16.20	−16.20	−16.20	−16.20
Tax shield of lease payment	4.86	4.86	4.86	4.86	4.86	4.86	4.86	4.86
Cash flow of lease	58.66	−11.34	−11.34	−11.34	−11.34	−11.34	−11.34	−11.34
PV lease cash flows	58.66	−10.60	−9.90	−9.26	−8.65	−8.09	−7.56	−7.06
NPV of lease	−2.45							

Greymare obtains a bigger tax shield on the lease payments, but this is more than offset by the higher upfront loss of the depreciation tax shield.

26.4 False. Leasing allows companies with a low marginal tax rate to "sell" their depreciation tax shields.

Managing Risk

Life is punctuated by unforeseen and unforeseeable shocks. Wars, banking and currency crises, political upheavals, earthquakes, floods, and pandemics can all cause severe economic disruption.

In 2020, COVID-19 struck with almost no warning. In the second quarter of the year, U.S. GDP fell by nearly 10%. Few industries escaped the impact, and some were hit particularly badly. World air travel fell by about 90%. In the United States, occupancy rates in hotels fell to about 25%. Auto producers in all countries were forced to shut down production.

Major catastrophes of this magnitude are, fortunately, rare. However, most businesses are hit from time to time by potentially ruinous shocks. Good managers try to ensure that their companies are not overwhelmed by them. They check that their company is not over-leveraged and has reserve borrowing power to tide them over difficult periods. They also maintain a reserve of liquid assets as an emergency source of cash.

Firms may also be able to reduce risk by building flexibility into their operations. They may ensure that they are not overly dependent on a single source of materials or a single outlet for their products. They may construct production facilities in different locations so that they can maintain output if one plant is out of action. In such cases, the company is acquiring a real option. We discussed real options in Chapter 23.

Our focus in this chapter is on financial contracts designed to *transfer* risk. They include insurance contracts, futures, and swaps. These contracts do not eliminate risk; instead, they pass the risk to other corporations or investors who are better prepared to bear it.

Section 27-1 Why manage risk?

But why bother? Why should shareholders care whether the company's future profits are exposed to future changes in interest rates, exchange rates, or commodity prices? We start the chapter with that question.

Section 27-2 Insurance

Most companies buy insurance against a variety of hazards. Insurance companies can *pool* risks by holding a large, diversified portfolio of policies. However, they cannot diversify away market or macroeconomic risks. Therefore, companies generally use insurance policies to reduce their diversifiable risk. They find other ways to avoid market or macroeconomic risks.

Section 27-3 Reducing risk with financial options

Firms may use options to set a limit on the losses that they can suffer from an adverse change in material prices.

Section 27-4 Forward and futures contracts

Forward or futures contracts are widely used by firms to offset the effect of fluctuations in the price of a commodity or a financial asset. We explain the mechanics of futures trading and show how to value a futures contract.

Section 27-5 Interest rate risk

For many firms, the interest rate that they will need to pay on future borrowing is a major uncertainty. We therefore explain how they can use specialist instruments such as interest rate futures and forward rate agreements to control this risk.

Section 27-6 Swaps

Sometimes a company that pays a fixed interest rate on its debt may prefer to pay a floating rate, or a company that has issued euro debt may prefer an issue of dollar debt. Swaps allow them to make such adjustments.

Section 27-7 How to set up a hedge

Forward, futures, and swap contracts allow firms to offset (or *hedge*) their risks. To do so, companies need to know how large a position to take in each contract. We show how to calculate the hedge ratio.

Section 27-8 Is "derivative" a four-letter word?

Companies use derivatives mainly to reduce risk, but they can also be used for speculation and this can get companies into trouble. Some observers worry that such speculation may threaten the whole financial system. These worries are accentuated by careless measures of the amount of money that is at risk.

● ● ● ● ●

27-1   Why Manage Risk?

Financial transactions undertaken *solely* to reduce risk do not add value in perfect and efficient markets. Why not? There are two basic reasons.

- *Reason 1: Hedging is a zero-sum game.* A corporation that insures or hedges a risk does not eliminate it. It simply passes the risk to someone else. For example, suppose that a heating-oil distributor contracts with a refiner to buy all of next winter's heating-oil deliveries at a fixed price. This contract is a *zero-sum game* because the refiner loses what the distributor gains, and vice versa.[1] If next winter's price of heating oil turns out to be unusually high, the distributor wins from having locked in a below-market price, but the refiner is forced to sell below the market. Conversely, if the price of heating oil is unusually *low,* the refiner wins because the distributor is forced to buy at the high fixed price. Of course, neither party knows next winter's price at the time that the deal is struck, but they consider the range of possible prices, and in an efficient market they negotiate terms that are fair (zero-NPV) on both sides of the bargain.

- *Reason 2: Investors' do-it-yourself alternative.* Corporations cannot increase the value of their shares by undertaking transactions that investors can easily do on their own. When the shareholders in the heating-oil distributor made their investment, they were presumably aware of the risks of the business. If they did not want to be exposed to the ups and downs of energy prices, they could have protected themselves in several ways. Perhaps they bought shares in both the distributor and refiner and do not care whether one wins next winter at the other's expense.

Of course, shareholders can adjust their exposure only when companies keep investors fully informed of the transactions that they have made. For example, when a group of European central banks announced in 1999 that they would limit their sales of gold, the gold price immediately shot up. Investors in gold-mining shares rubbed their hands at the prospect of rising profits. But when they discovered that some mining companies had protected themselves against price fluctuations and would *not* benefit from the price rise, the hand-rubbing by investors turned to hand-wringing.[2]

Some stockholders of these gold-mining companies wanted to make a bet on rising gold prices; others didn't. But all of them gave the same message to management. The first group said, "Don't hedge! I'm happy to bear the risk of fluctuating gold prices because I think gold prices will increase." The second group said, "Don't hedge! I'd rather do it myself." We have seen this do-it-yourself principle before. Think of other ways that the firm could reduce risk. It could do so by diversifying, for example, by acquiring another firm in an unrelated industry.

---

[1]In game theory, "zero-sum" means that the payoffs to all players add up to zero, so that one player can win only at the others' expense.
[2]The news was worst for the shareholders of Ashanti Goldfields, the huge Ghanaian mining company. Ashanti had gone to the opposite extreme and placed a bet that gold prices would fall. The 1999 price rise nearly drove Ashanti into bankruptcy.

But we know that investors can diversify on their own, and so diversification by corporations is redundant.[3]

Corporations can also lessen risk by borrowing less. But we showed in Chapter 16 that just reducing financial leverage does not make shareholders any better or worse off because they can instead reduce financial risk by borrowing less (or lending more) in their personal accounts. Modigliani and Miller (MM) proved that a corporation's debt policy is irrelevant in perfect financial markets. We could extend their proof to say that risk management is also irrelevant in perfect financial markets.

Of course, in Chapter 17, we decided that debt policy *is* relevant, not because MM were wrong, but because of other things, such as taxes, agency problems, and costs of financial distress. The same line of argument applies here. If risk management affects the value of the firm, it must be because of "other things," not because risk shifting is inherently valuable.

27.1 Self-Test

We gave two arguments why *financial* transactions undertaken solely to reduce risk do not add value in perfect and efficient markets. Do the same arguments apply to a company that acquires a real option that allows it to abandon a project. Why or why not?

Let's review the reasons that risk-reducing transactions can make sense in practice.[4]

Reducing the Risk of Cash Shortfalls or Financial Distress

Transactions that reduce risk make financial planning simpler and reduce the odds of an embarrassing cash shortfall. This shortfall might mean only an unexpected trip to the bank, but a financial manager's worst nightmare is landing in a financial pickle and having to pass up a valuable investment opportunity for lack of funds. In extreme cases, an unhedged setback could trigger financial distress or even bankruptcy.

Banks and bondholders recognize these dangers. They try to keep track of the firm's risks, and before lending, they may require the firm to carry insurance or to implement hedging programs. Risk management and conservative financing are therefore substitutes, not complements. Thus, a firm might hedge part of its risk in order to operate safely at a higher debt ratio.

Smart financial managers make sure that cash (or ready financing) will be available if investment opportunities expand. That happy match of cash and investment opportunities does not necessarily require hedging, however. Let's contrast two examples.

Cirrus Oil produces from several oil fields and also invests to find and develop new fields. Should it lock in future revenues from its existing fields by hedging oil prices? Probably not, because its investment opportunities expand when oil prices rise and contract when they fall. Locking in oil prices could leave it with too much cash when oil prices fall and too little, relative to its investment opportunities, when prices rise.

Cumulus Pharmaceuticals sells worldwide and half of its revenues are received in foreign currencies. Most of its R&D is done in the United States. Should it hedge at least some of its foreign exchange exposure? Probably yes, because pharmaceutical R&D programs are very expensive, long-term investments. Cumulus can't turn its R&D program on or off depending on a particular year's earnings, so it may wish to stabilize cash flows by hedging against fluctuations in exchange rates.

---

[3]See Section 7-5 and also our discussion of diversifying mergers in Chapter 32. Note that diversification reduces overall risk, but not market risk.

[4]There may be other, special reasons not covered here. For example, governments are quick to tax profits but may be slow to rebate taxes when there are losses. In the United States, losses cannot be set against earlier tax payments but can only be carried forward and used to shield future profits. Thus, a firm with volatile income and more frequent losses has a higher effective tax rate. A firm can reduce the fluctuations in its income by hedging. For most firms, this motive for risk reduction is not a big deal. See J. R. Graham and C. W. Smith Jr., "Tax Incentives to Hedge," *Journal of Finance* 54 (December 1999), pp. 2241–2262.

Agency Costs May Be Mitigated by Risk Management

In some cases, hedging can make it easier to monitor and motivate managers. Suppose your confectionery division delivers a 60% profit increase in a year when cocoa prices fall by 12%. Does the division manager deserve a stern lecture or a pat on the back? How much of the profit increase is due to good management and how much to lower cocoa prices? If the cocoa prices were hedged, it's probably good management. If they were not hedged, you will have to sort things out with hindsight, probably by asking, "What would profits have been if cocoa prices had been hedged?"

The fluctuations in cocoa prices are outside the manager's control. But she will surely worry about cocoa prices if her bottom line and bonus depend on them. Hedging ties her bonus more closely to risks that she can control and allows her to spend worrying time on these risks.

Hedging external risks that would affect individual managers does not necessarily mean that the *firm* ends up hedging. Some large firms allow their operating divisions to hedge away risks in an internal market. The internal market operates with real (external) market prices, transferring risks from the division to the central treasurer's office. The treasurer then decides whether to hedge the firm's aggregate exposure.

This sort of internal market makes sense for two reasons. First, divisional risks may cancel out. For example, your refining division may benefit from an increase in heating-oil prices at the same time that your distribution division suffers. Second, because operating managers do not trade actual financial contracts, there is no danger that the managers will cause the firm to take speculative positions. For example, suppose that profits are down late in the year, and your hope for end-year bonuses is fading. Could you be tempted to make up the shortfall with a quick score in the cocoa futures market? Well . . . not you, of course, but you can probably think of some acquaintances who would try just one speculative fling.

The dangers of permitting operating managers to make real speculative trades should be obvious. The manager of your confectionery division is an amateur in the cocoa futures market. If she were a skilled professional trader, she would probably not be running chocolate factories.[5]

Risk management requires some degree of centralization. These days many companies appoint a chief risk officer to develop a risk strategy for the company as a whole. The risk manager needs to come up with answers to the following questions:

1. *What are the major risks that the company is facing and what are the possible consequences?* Some risks are scarcely worth a thought, but there are others that might cause a serious setback or even bankrupt the company.

2. *Is the company being paid for taking these risks?* Managers are not paid to avoid all risks, but if they can reduce their exposure to risks for which there are no corresponding rewards, they can afford to place larger bets when the odds are stacked in their favor.

3. *How should risks be controlled?* Should the company reduce risk by building extra flexibility into its operations? Should it change its operating or financial leverage? Or should it insure or hedge against particular hazards?

The Evidence on Risk Management

Which firms use financial contracts to manage risk? Almost all do to some extent. For example, they may have contracts that fix prices of raw materials or output, at least for the near future. Most take out insurance policies against fire, accidents, and theft. In addition, as we

---

[5]Amateur speculation is doubly dangerous when the manager's initial trades are losers. At that point, the manager is already in deep trouble and has nothing more to lose by going for broke. "Going for broke" is often called "gambling for redemption."

shall see, managers employ a variety of specialized tools for hedging risk. These are known collectively as *derivatives.* A survey of the world's 500 largest companies found that most of them use derivatives to manage their risk.[6] Eighty-three percent of the companies employ derivatives to control interest rate risk. Eighty-eight percent use them to manage currency risk, and 49% to manage commodity price risk.

Risk policies differ. For example, some natural resource companies work hard to hedge their exposure to price fluctuations; others shrug their shoulders and let prices wander as they may. Explaining why some hedge and others don't is not easy. A study of the gold-mining industry suggests that managers' personal risk aversion may have something to do with it. Hedging of gold prices appears to be more common when top management has large personal shareholdings in the company. It is less common when top management holds lots of stock options.[7] (Remember that the value of an option falls when the risk of the underlying security is reduced.) A study of oil and gas producers found the firms that hedged the most had high debt ratios, no debt ratings, and low dividend payouts. It seems that for these firms hedging programs were designed to improve the firms' access to debt finance and to reduce the likelihood of financial distress.[8]

BEYOND THE PAGE

Derivatives usage

mhhe.com/brealey14e

27-2 Insurance

Most businesses buy insurance against a variety of hazards—the risk that their plants will be damaged by fire; that their ships, planes, or vehicles will be involved in accidents; that the firm will be held liable for environmental damage, and so on.

When a firm takes out insurance, it is simply transferring the risk to the insurance company. Insurance companies have several advantages in bearing risk. First, they may have considerable experience in insuring similar risks, so they are well placed to estimate the probability of loss and price the risk accurately. Second, they may be skilled at providing advice on measures that the firm can take to reduce the risk, and they may offer lower premiums to firms that take this advice. Third, an insurance company can *pool* risks by holding a diversified portfolio of policies. The claims on any individual policy can be highly uncertain, yet the claims on a portfolio of policies may be stable. Of course, insurance companies cannot diversify away market or macroeconomic risks; firms generally use insurance policies to reduce their diversifiable risk and they find other ways to avoid macro risks.

Insurance companies also suffer some *disadvantages* in bearing risk, and these are reflected in the prices they charge. Suppose your firm owns a $1 billion offshore oil platform. A meteorologist has advised you that there is a 1-in-10,000 chance that in any year the platform will be destroyed in a storm. Thus, the *expected* loss from storm damage is $1 billion/10,000 = $100,000.

The risk of storm damage is almost certainly not a macroeconomic risk and can potentially be diversified away. So you might expect that an insurance company would be prepared to insure the platform against such destruction as long as the premium was sufficient to cover the expected loss. In other words, a fair premium for insuring the platform should not be much above $100,000 a year.[9] Such a premium would make insurance a zero-NPV deal for your company. Unfortunately, no insurance company would offer a policy for only $100,000. Why not?

---

[6]International Swap Dealers Association (ISDA), "2009 Derivatives Usage Survey," www.isda.org.

[7]See P. Tufano, "The Determinants of Stock Price Exposure: Financial Engineering and the Gold Mining Industry," *Journal of Finance* 53 (June 1998), pp. 1014–1052.

[8]See G. D. Haushalter, "Financing Policy, Basis Risk and Corporate Hedging," *Journal of Finance* 55 (February 2000), pp. 107–152.

[9]If the premium is paid at the beginning of the year and the claim is not settled until the end, then the zero-NPV premium equals the discounted value of the expected claim or $100,000/(1 + r)$.

- *Reason 1: Administrative costs.* An insurance company, like any other business, incurs a variety of costs in arranging the insurance and handling any claims. For example, disputes about the liability for environmental damage can eat up millions of dollars in legal fees. Insurance companies need to recognize these costs when they set their premiums.

- *Reason 2: Adverse selection.* Suppose that an insurer offers life insurance policies with "no medical exam needed, no questions asked." There are no prizes for guessing who will be most tempted to buy this insurance. Our example is an extreme case of the problem of *adverse selection.* Unless the insurance company can distinguish between good and bad risks, the latter will always be most eager to take out insurance. Insurers increase premiums to compensate or require the owners to share any losses.

- *Reason 3: Moral hazard.* Once a risk has been insured, the owner may be tempted to take fewer precautions against damage. This temptation is called *moral hazard.* Insurance companies are aware of this danger and factor it into their pricing.

The extreme forms of adverse selection and moral hazard are rarely encountered in professional corporate finance. But the problems arise in more subtle ways. That oil platform may not be a "bad risk," but the oil company knows more about the platform's weaknesses than the insurance company does. The oil company will not purposely scuttle the platform, but once insured it could be tempted to save on maintenance or structural reinforcements. Thus, the insurance company may end up paying for engineering studies or for a program to monitor maintenance. All these costs are rolled into the insurance premium.

When the costs of administration, adverse selection, and moral hazard are small, insurance may be close to a zero-NPV transaction. When they are large, insurance is a costly way to protect against risk.

Many insurance risks are *jump risks;* one day there is not a cloud on the horizon and the next day the hurricane hits. The risks also be huge. For example, the attack on the World Trade Center on September 11, 2001, cost insurance companies about $36 billion; the Japanese tsunami involved payments of $35–$40 billion; Hurricanes Katrina, Harvey, and Irma were each estimated to cost companies in excess of $40 billion. Early estimates of the cost of COVID-19 for insurance companies suggest that it could be similar in magnitude.

If the losses from such disasters can be spread more widely, the cost of insuring them should decline. Therefore, insurance companies have been looking for ways to share catastrophic risks with investors. One solution is for the companies to issue *catastrophe bonds* (or *Cat bonds*). If a catastrophe occurs, the payment on a Cat bond is reduced or eliminated.[10] The insurance company can use the cash otherwise spent on debt service to help cover its losses. For example, in 2019, the insurance company Allstate issued $300 million of Cat bonds. The bonds covered the company for four years against losses from U.S. named storms, earthquakes, severe weather events, fires, and other perils for all states except for Florida.

27.2 Self-Test

Does it generally make sense to take out insurance against specific risks or systematic risks? Why?

---

[10]For a discussion of Cat bonds and other techniques to spread insurance risk, see N. A. Doherty, "Financial Innovation in the Management of Catastrophe Risk," *Journal of Applied Corporate Finance* 10 (Fall 1997), pp. 84–95; K. Froot, "The Market for Catastrophe Risk: A Clinical Examination," *Journal of Financial Economics* 60 (2001), pp. 529–571; and J. D. Cummins, "CAT Bonds and Other Risk-Linked Securities: State of the Market and Recent Developments," *Risk Management and Insurance Review* 11 (Spring 2008), pp. 23–47.

27-3 Reducing Risk with Financial Options

Managers regularly buy options on currencies, interest rates, and commodities to limit downside risk. Consider, for example, the problem faced by the Mexican government. A hefty portion of its revenue comes from Pemex, the state-owned oil company. So, when oil prices fall, the government may be compelled to reduce its planned spending.

The government's solution has been to arrange an annual hedge against a possible fall in the oil price. Although the details of its hedging program are a closely guarded secret, it is reported that in 2019 the Mexican government bought put options that gave it the right to sell around 250 million barrels of oil over the coming year at an exercise price of $55 per barrel. If oil prices rose above this figure, Mexico would reap the benefit. But if oil prices fell below $55, the payoff to the put options would exactly offset the revenue shortfall. In effect, the options put a floor of $55 a barrel on the value of the oil. Of course, the hedge did not come free. The Mexican government was said to have spent $1.2 billion to buy the contracts from a group of international banks.

Figure 27.1 illustrates the nature of Mexico's insurance strategy. Panel *a* shows the revenue derived from selling 250 million barrels of oil. As the price of oil rises or falls, so do the government's revenues. Panel *b* shows the payoffs to the government's options to sell 250 million barrels at $55 a barrel. The payoff on these options rises as oil prices fall below $55 a barrel. This payoff exactly offsets any decline in oil revenues. Panel *c* shows the government's total revenues after buying the put options. For prices below $55 per barrel, revenues are fixed at $250 \times \$55 = \$13,750$ million. But for every dollar that oil prices rise above $55, revenues increase by $250 million. The profile in panel *c* should be familiar to you. It represents the payoffs to the protective put strategy that we first encountered in Section 21-2.[11]

Options open up many other strategies for risk management. Consider a crude-oil refiner. Unlike Pemex, that company worries about unexpectedly *high* crude-oil prices. If crude-oil prices can be passed on to customers by higher prices of refined

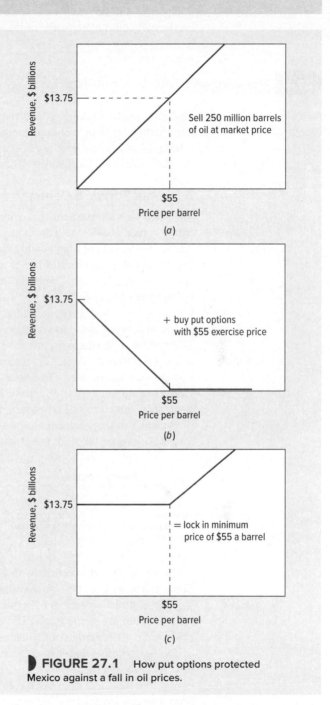

FIGURE 27.1 How put options protected Mexico against a fall in oil prices.

---

[11]The Mexican government option position was slightly more complicated than our description. On some of the production, it agreed to take a hit if prices fell below some minimum price.

products, that worry should not be serious. If higher prices cannot be fully passed on, the company could buy calls on crude oil. If oil prices climb above the call exercise price, profits on the call could offset some of the increased cost of the refiner's main raw material.

27-4 Forward and Futures Contracts

Hedging involves taking on one risk to offset another. It potentially removes all uncertainty, eliminating the chance of both happy and unhappy surprises. We explain shortly how to set up a hedge, but first we give some examples and describe some derivative instruments that are specially designed for hedging. These are forwards, futures, and swaps.

A Simple Forward Contract

We start with an example of a simple **forward contract**. Arctic Fuels, the heating-oil distributor, plans to deliver 1 million gallons of heating oil to its retail customers next January. Arctic worries about high heating-oil prices next winter and wants to lock in the cost of buying its supply. Northern Refineries is in the opposite position. It will produce heating oil next winter but doesn't know what the oil can be sold for. So the two firms strike a deal: Arctic Fuels agrees in September to buy 1 million gallons from Northern Refineries at $2.40 per gallon, to be paid on delivery in January. Northern agrees to sell and deliver 1 million gallons to Arctic in January at $2.40 per gallon.

Arctic and Northern are now the two *counterparties* in a forward contract. The **forward price** is $2.40 per gallon. This price is fixed today, in September in our example, but payment and delivery occur later. (The price for immediate delivery is called the **spot price**.) Arctic, which has agreed to *buy* in January, has the *long* position in the contract. Northern Refineries, which has agreed to *sell* in January, has the *short* position.

We can think of each counterparty's long and short positions in balance-sheet format, with long positions on the right (asset) side and short positions on the left (liability) side.

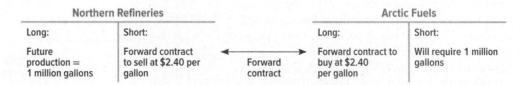

Northern Refineries			**Arctic Fuels**	
Long:	Short:		Long:	Short:
Future production = 1 million gallons	Forward contract to sell at $2.40 per gallon	Forward contract	Forward contract to buy at $2.40 per gallon	Will require 1 million gallons

Northern Refineries starts with a long position because it will produce heating oil. Arctic Fuels starts with a short position because it will have to buy to supply its customers. The forward contract creates an offsetting short position for Northern Refineries and an offsetting long position for Arctic Fuels. The offsets mean that each counterparty ends up locking in a price of $2.40, regardless of what happens to future spot prices.

Do not confuse this forward contract with an option. Arctic does not have the option to buy. It has committed to buy, even if spot prices in January turn out much lower than $2.40 per gallon. Northern does not have the option to sell. It cannot back away from the deal, even if spot prices for delivery in January turn out much higher than $2.40 per gallon. Note, however, that both the distributor and refiner do need to worry about *counterparty risk*—that is, the risk that the other party will not perform as promised.

We confess that our heating oil example glossed over several complications. For example, we assumed that the risk of both companies is reduced by locking in the price of heating oil. But suppose that the retail price of heating oil moves up and down with the wholesale price. In that case the heating-oil distributor is naturally hedged, because costs and revenues move together. Locking in costs with a futures contract could actually make the distributor's profits *more* volatile.

Futures Exchanges

Our heating-oil distributor and refiner do not have to negotiate a one-off, bilateral contract. Each can go to an exchange where standardized forward contracts on heating oil are traded. The distributor would buy contracts and the refiner would sell.

Here we encounter some tricky vocabulary. When a standardized forward contract is traded on an exchange, it is called a **futures contract**—same contract, but a different label. The exchange is called a **futures exchange**. The distinction between "futures" and "forward" does not apply to the contract, but to how the contract is traded. We describe futures trading in a moment.

Table 27.1 lists a few of the most important commodity futures contracts and the exchanges on which they are traded.[12] Our refiner and distributor can trade heating oil futures on the New York Mercantile Exchange (NYMEX). A forest products company and a homebuilder can trade lumber futures on the Chicago Mercantile Exchange (CME). A wheat farmer and a miller can trade wheat futures on the Chicago Board of Trade (CBOT) or on a smaller regional exchange.

27.3 Self-Test

Each of the following businesses may use the commodity futures markets: a. forestry company; b. cable manufacturer; c. furniture manufacturer; d. oil producer; e. milling company; f. airline; g. farmer. Match each business up with one of the following futures contracts and state whether the business is more likely to buy or sell the contract: A. crude oil; B. lumber; C. copper; D. wheat.

For many firms, the wide fluctuations in interest rates and exchange rates have become at least as important a source of risk as changes in commodity prices. Financial futures are similar to commodity futures, but instead of placing an order to buy or sell a commodity at a future date, you place an order to buy or sell a financial asset at a future date. Table 27.2 lists some important financial futures. Like Table 27.1, it is far from complete. For example, you can also trade futures on the Thai stock market index, the Chilean peso, Spanish government bonds, and many other financial assets.

Almost every day, some new futures contract seems to be invented. At first, there may be just a few private deals between a bank and its customers, but if the idea proves popular, one of the futures exchanges will try to muscle in on the business. For example, in 2019 ICE launched the first marine fuel contract.

The Mechanics of Futures Trading

When you buy or sell a futures contract, the price is fixed today but payment is not made until later. You will, however, be asked to put up **margin** in the form of either cash or Treasury bills to demonstrate that you have the money to honor your side of the bargain. As long as you earn the market interest rate on the margined securities, there is no cost to you.

Futures contracts are **marked to market**. This means that each day, any profits or losses on the contract are calculated; you pay the exchange's clearing house any losses and receive any profits. For example, suppose that in September Arctic Fuels buys 1 million gallons of January heating-oil futures contracts at a futures price of $2.40 per gallon. The next day the

---

[12]By the time you read this, the list of futures contracts will almost certainly be out of date because thinly traded contracts are terminated and new contracts are introduced. The list of futures exchanges may also be out of date. There have been plenty of mergers in recent years. In July 2007, the CME and CBOT merged to form the CME Group, and the following year, the group acquired NYMEX Holdings, which operated the NYMEX and COMEX exchanges. Also in 2007, the Intercontinental Exchange (ICE) acquired the New York Board of Trade and NYSE merged with Euronext, which owned the futures exchange, LIFFE. Six years later, NYSE Euronext was itself acquired by the ICE, which kept Euronext's futures business but split off its stock exchange operation.

Future	Exchange	Future	Exchange
Corn	CBOT, Euronext, DCE	Aluminum	LME, SHFE
Wheat	CBOT, Euronext	Copper	COMEX, LME, MCX, SHFE
		Gold	COMEX, MCX
Soybeans	CBOT, TGE	Lead	LME, MCX
Soybean meal	CBOT, DCE	Nickel	LME, MCX
Soybean oil	CBOT, DCE	Silver	COMEX, LME, MCX, TOCOM
		Tin	LME
Lean hogs	CME	Zinc	COMEX, LME, MCX, SHFE
Live cattle	CME		
		Crude oil	ICE, MCX, NYMEX, TOCOM
Cocoa	ICE, NYMEX	Gas oil	ICE
Coffee	ICE	Heating oil	ICE, NYMEX
Cotton	ICE	Natural gas	ICE, NYMEX
Lumber	CME	Unleaded gasoline	ICE, NYMEX, TOCOM
Orange juice	ICE		
Rubber	SHFE, TOCOM	Electricity	NYMEX
Sugar	ICE, NYMEX, ZCE		

❯ TABLE 27.1   Some important commodity futures and some of the exchanges on which they are traded.

Key to abbreviations:

CBOT	Chicago Board of Trade (part of CME Group)	MCX	Multi Commodity Exchange (India)
CME	Chicago Mercantile Exchange	NYMEX	New York Mercantile Exchange (part of CME Group)
COMEX	Commodity Exchange Division (part of CME Group)	SHFE	Shanghai Futures Exchange
DCE	Dalian Commodity Exchange (China)	TGE	Tokyo Grain Exchange
ICE	Intercontinental Exchange	TOCOM	Tokyo Commodity Exchange
LME	London Metal Exchange	ZCE	Zhengzhou Commodity Exchange

price of the January contract increases to $2.44 per gallon. Arctic now has a profit of $0.04 × 1,000,000 = $40,000. The exchange's clearinghouse therefore pays $40,000 into Arctic's margin account. If the price then drops back to $2.42, Arctic's margin account pays $20,000 back to the clearing house.

Of course, Northern Refineries is in the opposite position. Suppose it sells 1 million gallons of January heating-oil futures contracts at a futures price of $2.40 per gallon. If the price increases to $2.44 cents per gallon, it loses $0.04 × 1,000,000 = $40,000 and must pay this amount into the clearinghouse. Notice that neither the distributor nor the refiner has to worry about whether the other party will honor the other side of the bargain. The futures exchange guarantees the contracts and protects itself by settling up profits or losses each day. Futures trading eliminates counterparty risk.

Now consider what happens over the life of the futures contract. We're assuming that Arctic and Northern take offsetting long and short positions in the January contract (not directly with each other, but with the exchange). Suppose that a severe cold snap pushes the spot price of heating oil in January up to $2.60 per gallon. Then the futures price at the end of the contract will also be $2.60 per gallon.[13] So Arctic gets a cumulative profit of (2.60 − 2.40) ×

---

[13]Recall that the spot price is the price for immediate delivery. The futures contract also calls for immediate delivery when the contract ends in January. Therefore, the ending price of a futures or forward contract must converge to the spot price at the end of the contract.

Future	Exchange	Future	Exchange
U.S. Treasury bonds	CBOT	U.S. house prices	CME
U.S. Treasury notes	CBOT		
German government bonds (bunds)	Eurex, ICE	S&P 500 Index	CME
Japanese government bonds (JGBs)	CME, JPX, SGX	French equity index (CAC)	Euronext
British government bonds (gilts)	ICE	German equity index (DAX)	Eurex
U.S. Treasury bills	CME	Japanese equity index (Nikkei)	CME, JPX, SGX
		U.K. equity index (FTSE)	ICE
Eurodollar deposits	CME, ICE		
SOFR	CME, ICE	Euro	CME, Eurex
30-day Federal funds	CME	Japanese yen	CME
		Bitcoins	CME, ICE

)TABLE 27.2   Some important financial futures and some of the exchanges on which they are traded.

Key to abbreviations:

CBOT	Chicago Board of Trade	JPX	Japan Exchange Group
CME	Chicago Mercantile Exchange	SGX	Singapore Exchange
Eurex	Eurex Exchange	TFX	Tokyo Financial Futures Exchange
ICE	Intercontinental Exchange		

1,000,000 = \$200,000. It can take delivery of 1 million gallons, paying \$2.60 per gallon, or \$2,600,000. Its *net* cost, counting the profits on the futures contract, is \$2,600,000 − 200,000 = \$2,400,000, or \$2.40 per gallon. Thus, it has locked in the \$2.40 per gallon price quoted in September when it first bought the futures contract. You can easily check that Arctic's net cost always ends up at \$2.40 per gallon, regardless of the spot price and ending futures price in January.

Northern Refineries suffers a cumulative loss of \$200,000 if the January price is \$2.60. That's the bad news; the good news is that it can sell and deliver heating oil for \$2.60 per gallon. Its net revenues are \$2,600,000 − 200,000 = \$2,400,000, or \$2.40 per gallon, the futures price in September. Again, you can easily check that Northern's net selling price always ends up at \$2.40 per gallon.

Taking delivery directly from an exchange can be costly and inconvenient. For example, the NYMEX heating-oil contract calls for delivery in New York Harbor. Arctic Fuels will be better off taking delivery from a local source such as Northern Refineries. Northern Refineries will likewise be better off delivering heating oil locally rather than shipping it to New York. Therefore, both parties will probably close out their futures positions just before the end of the contract, and take their profits or losses.[14] Nevertheless, the NYMEX futures contract has allowed them to hedge their risks.

The effectiveness of this hedge depends on the correlation between changes in heating-oil prices locally and in New York Harbor. Prices in both locations will be positively correlated because of a common dependence on world energy prices. But the correlation is not perfect. What if a local cold snap hits Arctic Fuels's customers but not New York? A long position in NYMEX futures won't hedge Arctic Fuels against the resulting increase in the local spot price. This is an example of **basis risk**. We return to the problems created by basis risk later in this chapter.

---

[14]Some financial futures contracts *prohibit* delivery. All positions are closed out at the spot price at contract maturity.

Trading and Pricing Financial Futures Contracts

Financial futures trade in the same way as commodity futures. Suppose your firm's pension fund manager thinks that the French stock market will outperform other European markets over the next six months. She forecasts a 10% six-month return. How can she place a bet? She can buy French stocks, of course. But she could also buy futures contracts on the CAC index of French stocks, which are traded on the Euronext exchange. Suppose she buys 15 six-month futures contracts at 4,500. Each contract pays off 10 times the level of the index, so she has a long position of $15 \times 10 \times 4,500 = €675,000$. This position is marked to market daily. If the CAC goes up, the exchange puts the profits into your fund's margin account; if the CAC falls, the margin account falls too. If your pension manager is right about the French market, and the CAC ends up at 5,000 after six months, then your fund's cumulative profit on the futures position is $15 \times (5,000 - 4,500) \times 10 = €75,000$.

If you want to buy a security, you have a choice. You can buy for immediate delivery at the spot price, or you can "buy forward" by placing an order for future delivery at the futures price. You end up with the same security either way, but there are two differences. First, if you buy forward, you don't pay up front, and so you can earn interest on the purchase price.[15] Second, you miss out on any interest or dividend that is paid in the meantime. This tells us the relationship between spot and futures prices:

$$F_t = S_0 \left(1 + r_f - y\right)^t \tag{27-1}$$

where F_t is the futures price for a contract lasting t periods, S_0 is today's spot price, r_f is the risk-free interest rate, and y is the dividend yield or interest rate.[16] The following example shows how and why this formula works.

EXAMPLE 27.1 • Valuing index futures

Suppose that the six-month CAC futures contract trades at 4,459.50 when the current (spot) CAC index is 4,500. The interest rate is 1% per year (about 0.5% over six months) and the dividend yield on the index is 2.8% (about 1.4% over six months). These numbers fit the formula perfectly because

$$F_t = 4,500 \times (1 + 0.005 - 0.014) = 4,459.50$$

But why are the numbers consistent?

Suppose you just buy the CAC index for 4,500 today. Then in six months, you will own the index and also have dividends of $0.014 \times 4,500 = 63.00$. But you decide to buy a futures contract for 4,459.50 instead, and you put €4,500 in the bank. After six months, the bank account has earned interest at 0.5%, so you have $4,500 \times 1.005 = 4,522.50$, enough to buy the index for 4,459.50 with €63.00 left over—just enough to cover the dividend you missed by buying futures rather than spot. You get what you pay for.[17]

• • • • •

---

[15]In the Appendix to Chapter 18, we pointed out that companies effectively earn the after-tax interest rate when they lend and they pay the after-tax interest rate when they borrow. Therefore, when we value a forward contract, we should also use the after-tax rather than the pretax rate. You will generally see the formula for the value of a forward contract written without a tax term. For convenience we have followed that convention here, but when valuing a forward contract, remember to use the after-tax rate. See S. C. Myers and J. A. Read Jr., "Real Options, Taxes and Leverage," *Critical Finance Review* 9 (2020), pp. 29–76.

[16]This formula is strictly true only for forward contracts that are not marked to market. Otherwise, the value of the future depends on the path of interest rates over the life of the contract. In practice, this qualification is usually not important, and the formula works for futures as well as forward contracts.

[17]We can derive our formula as follows. Let S_6 be the value of the index after six months. Today S_6 is unknown. You can invest S_0 in the index today and get $S_6 + yS_0$ after six months. You can also buy the futures contract, put S_0 in the bank, and use your bank balance to pay the futures price F_6 in six months. In the latter strategy you get $S_6 - F_6 + S_0(1 + r_f)$ after six months. Since the investment is the same, and you get S_6 with either strategy, the payoffs must be the same: $S_6 + yS_0 = S_6 - F_6 + S_0(1 + rf)$. Therefore, $F_6 = S_0(1 + r_f - y)$. Here we assume that r_f and y are six-month rates. If they are monthly rates, the general formula is $F_t = S_0(1 + r_f - y)^t$, where t is the number of months. If they are annual rates, the formula is $F_t = S_0(1 + r_f - y)^{t/12}$.

Spot and Futures Prices—Commodities

The difference between buying *commodities* today and buying commodity futures is more complicated. First, because payment is again delayed, the buyer of the future earns interest on her money. Second, she does not need to store the commodities and, therefore, saves warehouse costs, wastage, and so on. On the other hand, the futures contract gives no *convenience yield,* which is the value of being able to get your hands on the real thing. The manager of a supermarket can't stock the shelves with orange juice futures if she runs out of inventory at 1 p.m. on a Saturday.

Let's express storage costs and convenience yield as fractions of the spot price. For commodities, the futures price for t periods ahead is[18]

$$F_t = S_0 \left(1 \times r_f + \text{storage costs} - \text{convenience yield}\right)^t$$

It's interesting to compare this formula with the formula for a financial future. Convenience yield plays the same role as dividends or interest foregone (y) on securities. But financial assets cost nothing to store, and storage costs do not appear in the formula for financial futures.

Usually, you can't observe storage cost or convenience yield, but you can infer the difference between them by comparing spot and futures prices. This difference—that is, convenience yield less storage cost—is called *net convenience yield.*

Net convenience yield for most commodities is generally positive, and futures prices are generally below spot prices. This condition is called *backwardation.* Occasionally, if storage costs are high and there is plenty of the physical commodity available, the futures price is above the spot price and the market is said to be in *contango.*

EXAMPLE 27.2 • Calculating net convenience yield

In May 2020, the spot price of West Texas Intermediate (WTI) crude oil was $24.11 a barrel and the six-month futures price was $30.05 per barrel. The interest rate was about 0.5% for six months. Thus,

$$F_t \quad = \quad S_0\left(1 + r_f + \text{storage costs} - \text{convenience yield}\right)$$
$$\$30.05 \quad = \quad 24.11(1.005 - \text{net convenience yield})$$

So net convenience yield was negative, that is, net convenience yield = convenience yield − storage costs = −0.241 or −24.1% over six months. Therefore, the market was in contango.

In 2020, the major oil producers continued to pump oil even while the coronavirus pandemic caused demand to slump. Storage tanks were close to capacity, and the convenience of having oil in the tanks was much less than the storage cost.

• • • • •

More about Forwards and Futures

Critics and proponents of futures markets sometimes argue about whether the markets provide "price discovery." That is, they argue about whether futures prices reveal traders' forecasts of spot prices when the futures contract matures. If one of these fractious personalities comes your way, we suggest that you respond with a different question: Do futures prices reveal information about future prices that is not already in *today's* spot price? Our formulas reveal the answer to this question. There is useful information in the *difference* between spot and futures prices, but it is information about convenience yields and storage costs, or about dividend or interest payments in the case of financial futures. Futures prices reveal information about

---

[18]This formula could overstate the futures price if no one is willing to hold the commodity, that is, if inventories fall to zero or some absolute minimum.

future spot prices only when a commodity is not stored or cannot be stored. Then the link between spot and futures prices is broken, and futures prices can assist with price discovery.

You cannot easily store electricity, for example. As a result, electricity supplied in, say, six months' time, is a different commodity from electricity available now, and there is no simple link between today's price and that of a futures contract to buy or sell at the end of six months. Of course, generators and electricity users will have their own views of what the spot price is likely to be, and the futures price will reveal these views to some extent.

27-5 Interest Rate Risk

Forward Rates of Interest and the Term Structure

We now consider the risks created by fluctuating interest rates. We start with some definitions.

The t-period spot rate r_t is the rate of interest today on a loan that makes a single payment at time t. Therefore, a dollar invested today for t periods will accumulate to $(1 + r_t)^t$. For example, suppose that the one-year spot rate of interest is $r_1 = 3\%$ and the two-year spot rate is $r_2 = 4\%$. A dollar invested today for one year will accumulate to \$1.03.

Define the *extra* rate of return that you earn by extending a loan from one period to two as the **forward interest rate** $_1f_2$. Then,

$$(1 + r_2)^2 = (1 + 0.04)^2 = (1 + r_1)(1 + {_1f_2}) = 1.082$$

Since $r_1 = 0.03$, you can solve for $_1f_2 = 0.0501$, or 5.01%. You earn 3% for a one-year loan and an additional 5.01% if you lend for an additional year.

The example is easy to generalize.[19] If the three-year spot rate is 4.4%,

$$(1 + r_3)^3 = (1 + 0.044)^3 = 1.138 = (1 + r_2)^2(1 + {_2f_3})$$

$$1 + {_2f_3} = (1 + r_3)^3/(1 + r_2)^2 = 1.138/1.082 = 1.0521, \text{ so } {_2f_3} = 5.21\%$$

27.4 Self-Test

Continue the example. Suppose the four-year spot rate is 4.6%. What is the forward interest rate $_3f_4$?

In our example, we derived forward interest rates from the term structure of spot rates ($r_1 = 0.03$, $r_2 = 0.04$, $r_3 = 0.044$, $r_4 = 0.046 \ldots$). We could turn this around and say that the forward rates *determine* the term structure. In addition, forward rates contain information about future spot rates. Suppose the expectations theory of the term structure holds exactly. Then we can interpret the forward rates as investors' forecasts (expectations) of future one-period spot rates. These forecasts then determine today's spot interest rates for different maturities.

The expectations theory is not the whole story of the term structure, as we explained in Section 3-4. Although expectations about future interest rates are not the only factor that drives the term structure, they're still important, and forward rates can provide a rough and ready guide to investors' interest-rate expectations.

Borrowing and Lending at Forward Interest Rates

Fluctuating interest rates can pose unpleasant challenges for the financial manager. We now show how to "lock in" future interest rates at today's forward rates.

---

[19]Our examples use one-period forward rates for simplicity, but forward rates that span two or more periods can also be calculated. For example, the rate $_1f_3$ is the extra return from investing between dates 1 and 3. In our example, $(1 + {_1f_3})^2 = (1 + r_3)^3/(1 + r_1) = 1.138/1.03 = 1.1049$, which implies $_1f_3 = 0.0511$ or 5.11%. (Note: $1.0511^2 = 1.1049$.)

Suppose you wish to take out a one-year loan for $1,000,000 in one years' time, but you worry that borrowing rates may increase next year. You would like to fix today the interest rate on that loan. The one-year spot rate is $r_1 = 3\%$, and the two-year rate is $r_2 = 4\%$. The forward rate $_1f_2$ is 5.01%. A simple solution is to borrow for two years at 4% and lend the money at 3% until you need it in year 1. The amount you need to borrow today is $\$1,000,000/(1 + r_1) = \$970,870$. If you then lend this amount at 3% for one year, it will accumulate to $1,000,000.

The following table sets out the cash flows:

Figures in $1,000s	Year 0	Year 1	Year 2
Borrow 970.87 for 2 years at 4%	+970.87		−1,050.1
Lend 970.87 for 1 year at 3%	−970.87	+1,000	
Net cash flow	0	+1,000	−1,050.1

By borrowing now for two years and lending the money for one, you have effectively committed today to take out a one-year loan at the end of the year at the forward interest rate of 5.01%. No need now to worry about higher interest rates next year: You have locked in the forward rate.

27.5 Self-Test

The manager of a pension fund portfolio will receive a $1 million contribution from the pension-plan sponsor one year from now. He worries that interest rates will fall before he receives the money. Show how he can lock in the interest rate for year 2 on the $1 million investment. Use the spot interest rates in the table above.

Forward Rate Agreements

There may be simpler ways to fix today the interest rate that you will pay on a future loan. One is to enter into a *forward rate agreement* (FRA) with a bank.

Suppose that at the end of three months you are going to need a six-month loan of $50,000,000. You can lock in the interest rate on that loan by buying a three-against-nine-month (or 3 × 9) FRA.[20] The bank that is selling the FRA might offer you a contract or reference rate of 7% on a notional principal of $50,000,000. Then, if at the end of three months the interest rate is higher than 7%, the bank will pay you the six-month cost of that interest rate rise.[21] For example, if the interest rate rises to 8%, the bank will pay you $50,000,000 × (0.08 − 0.07)/2 = $250,000. This payment protects you against the cost of a general rise in interest rates. If, on the other hand, the interest rate falls to 6%, you pay $250,000 to the bank.

Interest Rate Futures

You can also hedge against changes in interest rates by trading interest-rate futures. For example, a company that plans to issue bonds at the end of the year could protect itself against a general rise in long-term interest rates by selling Treasury bond futures. If Treasury bond prices subsequently fall, then the profit from the sale of futures should offset the lower price that the company is likely to realize on its bond issue.

---

[20]Note that the party that profits from a rise in rates is described as the "buyer." In our example, you would be said to "buy three against nine months" money, meaning that the forward rate agreement is for a six-month loan in three months' time.

[21]Historically, the contract interest rate has generally been measured by LIBOR. LIBOR will be replaced by the Secured Overnight Funding Rate SOFR as the reference rate for FRAs.

There is a wide choice of interest rate futures. They include futures on long-term Treasury notes and bonds, as well as short-term interest rate (STIR) futures on Treasury bills, the federal funds rate, and the *Secured Overnight Financing Rate* (SOFR).[22]

Daily turnover in U.S. interest rate futures is about $4 trillion. As a result, futures offer a low-cost and very liquid means for hedging interest rate exposure. However, the company is almost always left with some basis risk: Hedging the future interest rate on a Treasury note is not the same thing as hedging the interest rate your company will have to pay on a bank loan or debt issue.

The forward pricing formula is:

$$F_t = S_0 \left(1 + r_f - y\right)^t \tag{27-2}$$

We used this formula in Section 27-4 to price stock index futures. The formula is the same for interest rate futures, except that the yield y is the current yield (coupon divided by price). Suppose you buy a one-period future on a Treasury note and hold it until maturity. You earn interest because payment is deferred. But you lose the coupon on the bond because you do not own it yet.

We do not go into the quirks and complications of trading Treasury futures here. Consider instead how a financial manager could use one to cover a future obligation.

EXAMPLE 27.3 • Investing future pension fund contributions

The manager of a pension fund receives and invests contributions from the pension-plan sponsor. The manager must also make periodic distributions from the fund to pay out benefits to retired employees. Suppose a $100 million contribution will arrive at date 1. A $105 million distribution is scheduled for date 2. We have described how the manager could lock in the forward rate $_1f_2$ to eliminate uncertainty about the interest rate earned on the $100 million contribution. This time, the manager wants to use a Treasury note future to hedge.

To keep the arithmetic as simple as possible, assume a flat term structure with $r_1 = r_2 = 5\%$. The forward rate $_1f_2$ also is 5%. The futures contract matures at date 1 and the underlying Treasury note at date 2. The note pays a coupon of 5% per period. The current futures price (percentage of par value) equals the spot price of 100.

$$F_t = S_0 \left(1 + r_f - y\right)^2 = 100(1 + 0.05 - 0.05)^2 = 100$$

The financial manager plans to invest the $100 million contribution at date 1 to cover the $105 million obligation at date 2. What happens if the interest rate falls to 3% at date 1? Then the contribution will grow only to $103 million by date 2, $2 million short.

So the manager takes a $100 million long position in the futures contract. If the interest stays at 5%, there is no gain or loss on the contract and the $100 million contribution can be invested at 5%. If the interest rate falls to 3%, the futures contract closes at a higher note price, which is 105/1.03 = 101.94. The manager can invest the $100 million contribution plus the futures profit of $1.94 million to cover the $105 million obligation (101.94 × 1.03 = 105).

If the interest rate rises to 7%, there is a loss of $1.87 million on the contract, leaving only 100 − 1.87 = $98.13 million to invest. But that is enough: 98.13 × 1.07 = $105 million. You can check to confirm that no matter how the interest rate changes, the manager always has enough (including profits or losses on the futures contract) to get to $105 million at date 2. This outcome is inevitable because the closing price of the futures contract at date 1 equals

---

[22]The most popular futures contract has historically been the eurodollar future, which is linked to the London Interbank Rate (LIBOR). However, LIBOR is due to be phased out by June 2023, so users of eurodollar futures will need to switch to alternative contracts.

the PV of the Treasury note, which is the PV of 105 (principal plus interest on the note) at date 2.

The arithmetic of transactions in real life will be more complicated than our example, but the point of the example holds. Treasury futures can be used to hedge interest rate risk.

* * * * *

Treasury futures contracts can also be used to hedge *investment* risk. For example, suppose the pension fund portfolio includes $500 million of long-term Treasury bonds. The manager worries that bond prices will fall sharply because of higher inflation and tighter monetary policy. She could simply sell the bonds. Or she could hedge by selling Treasury bond futures. As a futures seller, she profits when bond prices decline. The futures profits can offset a bond-price decline.

27-6 Swaps

Some future cash flows are fixed. Others vary with the level of interest rates, rates of exchange, prices of commodities, and so on. These characteristics may not always result in the desired risk profile. For example, a company that pays a fixed rate of interest on its debt might prefer to pay a floating rate, while another company that receives cash flows in euros might prefer to receive them in yen. Swaps allow them to get where they want to go.

The market for swaps is huge. In 2020, the total notional amount of swaps outstanding was more than $350 trillion. By far, the major part of this figure consisted of interest rate swaps.[23]

Interest Rate Swaps

Friendly Bancorp has made a five-year, $50 million loan to fund part of the construction cost of a large cogeneration project. The loan carries a fixed interest rate of 8%. Annual interest payments are therefore $4 million. Interest payments are made annually, and all the principal will be repaid at year 5.

Suppose that instead of receiving fixed interest payments of $4 million a year, the bank would prefer to receive floating-rate payments. It can do so by swapping the $4 million, five-year annuity (the fixed interest payments) into a five-year floating-rate annuity. We show first how Friendly Bancorp can make its own homemade swap. Then we describe a simpler procedure.

The bank (we assume) can borrow at a 6% fixed rate for five years.[24] Therefore, the $4 million interest it receives can support a fixed-rate loan of 4/0.06 = $66.67 million. The bank can now construct the homemade swap as follows: It borrows $66.67 million at a fixed interest rate of 6% for five years and simultaneously lends the same amount at SOFR.[25] We assume that SOFR is initially 5%. SOFR is a short-term interest rate, so future interest receipts will fluctuate as the bank's investment is rolled over.

The net cash flows to this strategy are shown in the top portion of Table 27.3. Notice that there is no net cash flow in year 0 and that in year 5 the principal amount of the short-term investment is used to pay off the $66.67 million loan. What's left? A cash flow equal to the *difference* between the interest earned (SOFR × 66.67) and the $4 million outlay on the fixed

---

[23]Data on swaps are provided by the International Swaps and Derivatives Association (www.isda.org) and the Bank for International Settlements (www.bis.org).

[24]The spread between the bank's 6% borrowing rate and the 8% lending rate is the bank's profit on the project financing.

[25]SOFR (Secured Overnight Funding Rate) has replaced LIBOR as a reference interest rate for financial contracts. SOFR is probably below the five-year interest rate because investors expect interest rates to rise.

			Year			
	0	1	2	3	4	5
Homemade swap:						
1. Borrow $66.67 at 6% fixed rate	+66.67	−4	−4	−4	−4	−(4 + 66.67)
2. Lend $66.67 at SOFR floating rate	−66.67	+0.05 × 66.67	+ $SOFR_1$ × 66.67	+ $SOFR_2$ × 66.67	+ $SOFR_3$ × 66.67	+ $SOFR_4$ × 66.67 + 66.67
Net cash flow	0	−4 +0.05 × 66.67	−4 + $SOFR_1$ × 66.67	−4 + $SOFR_2$ × 66.67	−4 + $SOFR_3$ × 66.67	−4 + $SOFR_4$ × 66.67
Standard fixed-to-floating swap:						
Net cash flow	0	−4 +0.05 × 66.67	−4 + $SOFR_1$ × 66.67	−4 + $SOFR_2$ × 66.67	−4 + $SOFR_3$ × 66.67	−4 + $SOFR_4$ × 66.67

❭TABLE 27.3   The top panel shows the cash flows in millions of dollars to a homemade fixed-to-floating interest rate swap. The bottom panel shows the cash flows to a standard swap transaction.

loan. The bank also has $4 million per year coming in from the project financing, so it has transformed that fixed payment into a floating payment keyed to SOFR.

Of course, there's an easier way to do this, shown in the bottom portion of Table 27.3. The bank can just enter into a five-year swap.[26] Naturally, Friendly Bancorp takes this easier route. Let's see what happens.

Friendly Bancorp calls a swap dealer, which is typically a large commercial or investment bank, and agrees to *swap* the payments on a $66.67 million fixed-rate loan for the payments on an equivalent floating-rate loan. The swap is known as a fixed-to-floating interest rate swap and the $66.67 million is termed the *notional principal* amount of the swap. Friendly Bancorp and the dealer are the counterparties to the swap.

The dealer is quoting a rate for five-year swaps of 6% against SOFR.[27] The fixed rate is sometimes quoted as a spread over the yield on U.S. Treasuries. For example, if the yield on five-year Treasury notes is 5.25%, the swap spread is 0.75%.

The first payment on the swap occurs at the end of year 1 and is based on the starting SOFR rate of 5%. The dealer (who pays floating) owes the bank 5% of $66.67 million, while the bank (which pays fixed) owes the dealer $4 million (6% of $66.67 million). The bank, therefore, makes a net payment to the dealer of 4 − (0.05 × 66.67) = $0.67 million:

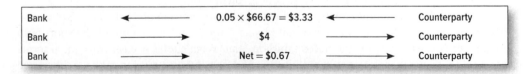

---

[26]Both strategies are equivalent to a series of forward contracts on SOFR. The forward prices are $4 million each for $SOFR_1$ × $66.67, $SOFR_2$ × $66.67, and so on. Separately negotiated forward prices would not be $4 million for any one year, but the PVs of the "annuities" of forward prices would be identical.

[27]Notice that the swap rate always refers to the interest rate on the fixed leg of the swap. Rates may be quoted against SOFR, but dealers will also be prepared to quote rates against other short-term debt.

The second payment is based on SOFR at year 1. Suppose it increases to 6%. Then the net payment is zero:

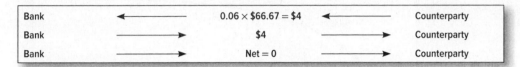

Bank	←	0.06 × \$66.67 = \$4	←	Counterparty
Bank	→	\$4	→	Counterparty
Bank	→	Net = 0	→	Counterparty

The third payment depends on SOFR at year 2, and so on.

The *notional value* of this swap is \$66.67 million. The fixed and floating interest rates are multiplied by the notional amount to calculate dollar amounts of fixed and floating interest. But the notional value vastly overstates the economic value of the swap. At creation, the economic value of the swap is zero because the NPV of the cash flows to each counterparty is zero. The NPV drifts away from zero as time passes and interest rates change. But the economic value will always be far less than notional value. Careless references to notional values give the impression that swap markets are impossibly gigantic; in fact, they are merely very large.

The economic value of a swap depends on the path of long-term interest rates. For example, suppose that after two years, interest rates are unchanged, so a 6% note issued by the bank would continue to trade at its face value. In this case, the swap still has zero value. (You can confirm this by checking that the NPV of a new three-year homemade swap is zero.) But if long rates increase over the two years to 7% (say), the value of a three-year note falls to

$$PV = \frac{4}{1.07} + \frac{4}{(1.07)^2} + \frac{4 + 66.67}{(1.07)^3} = \$64.92 \text{ million}$$

Now the fixed payments that the bank has agreed to make are less valuable and the swap is worth 66.67 − 64.92 = \$1.75 million.

How do we know the swap is worth \$1.75 million? Consider the following strategy:

1. The bank can enter a new three-year swap deal in which it agrees to *pay* SOFR on the same notional principal of \$66.67 million.

2. In return it receives fixed payments at the new 7% interest rate; that is, 0.07 × 66.67 = \$4.67 per year.

The new swap cancels the cash flows of the old one, but it generates an extra \$0.67 million for three years. This extra cash flow is worth

$$PV = \sum_{t=1}^{3} \frac{0.67}{(1.07)^t} = \$1.75 \text{ million}$$

Remember, ordinary interest rate swaps have no initial cost or value (NPV = 0), but their value drifts away from zero as time passes and long-term interest rates change. One counterparty wins as the other loses.

27.6 Self-Test

Suppose that after three years, long-term interest rates fall to 4%. What is the value then of Friendly Bancorp's swap?

In our example, the swap dealer loses from the rise in interest rates. Dealers will try to hedge the risk of interest rate movements by engaging in a series of futures or forward contracts or by entering into an offsetting swap with a third party. As long as Friendly Bancorp and the other counterparty honor their promises, the dealer is fully protected against risk. The recurring nightmare for swap managers is that one party will default, leaving the dealer with a large unmatched position. This is an example of counterparty risk.

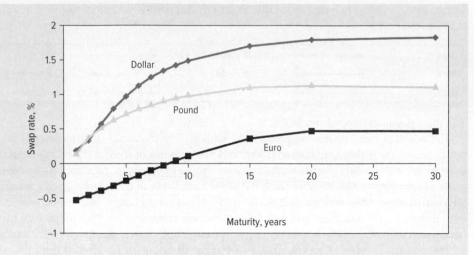

FIGURE 27.2

Swap curves for three currencies, June 2021.

The market for interest rate swaps is large and liquid. Consequently, financial analysts often look at swap rates when they want to know how interest rates vary with maturity. For example, Figure 27.2 shows swap rates in June 2021 for the U.S. dollar, the euro, and the British pound. You can see that in each country, long-term interest rates are much higher than short-term rates.

Currency Swaps

We now look briefly at an example of a currency swap.

Suppose that the Possum Company needs €11 million to help finance its European operations. We assume that the euro interest rate is about 5%, and the dollar rate is about 6%. Since Possum is better known in the United States, the financial manager decides not to borrow euros directly. Instead, the company issues $10 million of five-year 6% notes in the United States. Then it arranges with a counterparty to swap this dollar loan into euros. Under this arrangement. the counterparty agrees to pay Possum sufficient dollars to service its dollar loan, and in exchange Possum agrees to make a series of annual payments in euros to the counterparty.

Here are Possum's cash flows (in millions):

Stock	Year 0		Year 1–4		Year 5	
	Dollars	**Euros**	**Dollars**	**Euros**	**Dollars**	**Euros**
1. Issue dollar loan	+10		−0.6		−10.6	
2. Swap dollars for euros	−10	+8	+0.6	−0.4	+10.6	−8.4
3. Net cash flow	0	+8	0	−0.4	0	−8.4

Look first at the cash flows in year 0. Possum receives $10 million from its issue of dollar notes, which it then pays over to the swap counterparty. In return the counterparty sends Possum a check for €8 million. (We assume that at current rates of exchange, $10 million is worth €8 million.)

Now move to years 1 through 4. Possum needs to pay interest of 6% on its debt issue, which works out at $0.06 \times 10 = \$0.6$ million. The swap counterparty agrees to provide Possum each year with sufficient cash to pay this interest, and in return, Possum makes an annual payment to the counterparty of 5% of €8 million, or €0.4 million. Finally, in year 5 the swap counterparty pays Possum enough to make the final payment of interest and principal on its dollar notes ($10.6 million), while Possum pays the counterparty €8.4 million.

The combined effect of Possum's two steps (line 3) is to convert a 6% dollar loan into a 5% euro loan. You can think of the cash flows for the swap (line 2) as a series of forward contracts to buy euros in years 1 through 5. In each of years 1 through 4, Possum agrees to purchase $0.6 million at a cost of €0.4 million; in year 5 it agrees to buy $10.6 million at a cost of €8.4 million.[28]

Some Other Swaps

While interest rate and currency swaps are the most popular type of contract, there is a wide variety of other possible swaps or related contracts. For example, in Chapter 24 we encountered credit default swaps that allow investors to insure themselves against the default on a corporate bond.

Inflation swaps allow a company to protect against inflation risk. One party in the swap receives a fixed payment while the other receives a payment that is linked to the rate of inflation. In effect, the swap creates a made-to-measure inflation-linked bond, which can be of any maturity.[29]

You can also enter into a *total return swap* where one party (party A) makes a series of agreed payments and the other (party B) pays the total return on a particular asset. This asset might be a common stock, a loan, a commodity, or a market index. For example, suppose that B owns $10 million of IBM stock. It now enters into a two-year swap agreement to pay A each quarter the total return on this stock. In exchange A agrees to pay B interest of SOFR + 1%. B is known as the *total return payer* and A is the *total return receiver*. Suppose SOFR is 5%. Then A must pay B 6% of $10 million, or about 1.5% a quarter. If IBM stock returns more than this, there will be a net payment from B to A; if the return is less than 1.5%, A must make a net payment to B. Although ownership of the IBM stock does not change hands, the effect of this total return swap is the same as if B had sold the asset to A and bought it back at an agreed future date.

27-7   How to Set Up a Hedge

There can be many ways to hedge a risk exposure. Some hedges involve zero maintenance: Once established, the financial manager can walk away and worry about other matters. Other hedges are dynamic: They work only if adjusted at frequent intervals.

The forward contract between Northern Refineries and Arctic Fuels, which we described in Section 27-4, required zero maintenance because each counterparty locked in the price of heating oil at $2.40 per gallon, regardless of the future path of heating-oil prices. Now we look at a case where the financial manager will probably implement a *dynamic hedge*.

Hedging Interest Rate Risk

Potterton Leasing has acquired a warehouse and leased it to a manufacturer for fixed payments of $2 million per year for 20 years. The lease cannot be canceled by the manufacturer, so Potterton has a safe, debt-equivalent asset. The interest rate is 10%, and we ignore taxes for simplicity. The PV of Potterton's rental income is $17 million:

$$PV = \frac{2}{1.1} + \frac{2}{(1.1)^2} + \cdots + \frac{2}{(1.1)^{20}} = 17.0 \text{ million}$$

---

[28]Usually in a currency swap the two parties make an initial payment to each other (i.e., Possum pays the bank $10 million and receives €8 million). However, this is not necessary, and Possum might prefer to buy the €8 million from another bank.

[29]If the inflation swap involves only a single future payment, it is known as a *zero-coupon swap*. If it provides a sequence of payments, each linked to the rate of inflation, it is called a *year-on-year swap*.

The lease exposes Potterton to interest rate risk. If interest rates increase, the PV of the lease payments falls. If interest rates decrease, the PV rises. Potterton's CFO therefore decides to issue an offsetting debt liability:

PV (lease) = $17 million	PV (debt) = $17 million

Thus, Potterton is long $17 million and also short $17 million. But it may not be hedged. Simply borrowing $17 million at some arbitrary maturity does *not* eliminate interest rate risk. Suppose the CFO took out a *one-year,* $17 million bank loan, with a plan to refinance the loan annually. Then she would be borrowing short and lending long (via the 20-year lease), which amounts to a $17 million bet that interest rates will fall. If instead they rise, her company will end up paying more interest in years 2 to 20, with no compensating increase in the lease cash flows.

To hedge interest rate risk, the CFO needs to design the debt issue so that any change in interest rates has the same (and thus offsetting) impact on both the PV of the lease payments and the PV of the debt. There are two ways to accomplish this:

1. *Zero-maintenance hedge.* Issue debt requiring interest and principal payments of exactly $2 million per year for 20 years. This debt would be similar to a real estate mortgage with level payments. In this case, lease payments would exactly cover debt service in each year. The PVs of the lease payments and the offsetting debt would always be identical, regardless of the level of future interest rates.

2. *Duration hedge.* Issue debt with the same *duration* as the lease payments. Here, debt service does not have to match the lease payments in each (or any) year. If durations are matched, then small changes in interest rates—say, from 10% down to 9.5% or up to 10.5%—will have the same impact on the PVs of the lease payments and the debt.

The duration-matching strategy is usually more convenient, but it is not zero maintenance because durations will drift out of line as interest rates change and time passes. Thus, the CFO will have to revisit and reset the hedge. She will have to execute a dynamic strategy to make duration-matching work.

Potterton's CFO first calculates the duration of the lease payments[30]:

$$\text{Duration} = \frac{1}{PV}\{[PV(C_1) \times 1] + [PV(C_2) \times 2] + [PV(C_3) \times 3] + \cdots \}$$

$$= \frac{1}{17.0}\left\{\left[\frac{2}{1.10} \times 1\right] + \left[\frac{2}{1.10^2} \times 2\right] + \cdots + \left[\frac{2}{1.10^{20}} \times 20\right]\right\}$$

$$= 7.5 \text{ years}$$

Therefore, to hedge its interest rate risk, Potterton needs to issue a package of bonds with a duration of 7.5 years. The simplest solution is to issue a 12-year bond with a 10% coupon, which has a 7.5-year duration. But this is not the only possible strategy. For example, the company could issue $7.9 million of 10% 20-year bonds and $9.1 million of 10% 8-year bonds. The duration of this package would also be 7.5 years.[31]

Figure 27.3 plots the PVs of the lease payments and the 12-year bond as a function of the interest rate. Both the PV curves are downward-sloping but convex; note how each curve comes down steeply at low interest rates but flattens out at higher interest rates.

Now compare the slope of the PV curve for the lease payments with the slope of the 12-year bond. The slopes are identical at the current 10% interest rate because the duration

---

[30]Look back at Section 3-2 if you need a review session on calculating duration.
[31]The duration of the 20-year bonds is 9.37 years and that of the 8-year bonds is 5.87 years. The duration of the package is $(7.9 \times 9.37 + 9.1 \times 5.87)/17 = 7.5$ years.

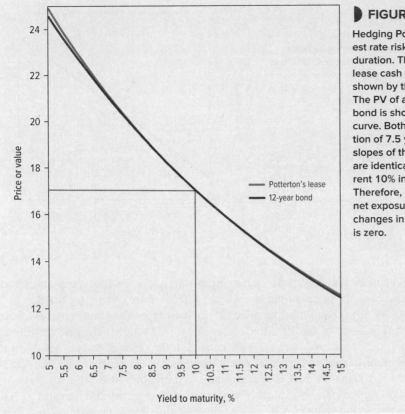

Hedging Potterton's interest rate risk by matching duration. The PV of the lease cash inflows is shown by the blue curve. The PV of a 10% 12-year bond is shown by the red curve. Both have a duration of 7.5 years, so the slopes of the PV curves are identical at the current 10% interest rate. Therefore, Potterton's net exposure to small changes in interest rates is zero.

is identical at this rate. Therefore, so long as the interest rate does not stray too far from the current level of 10%, the PV of the lease cash flows changes by almost the same amount as the PV of the bond. In this case, Potterton is hedged. But you can see from Figure 27.3 that if interest rates change by, say 5%, the value of the lease payments changes by a little bit more than the value of the bond. In this case, Potterton's CFO will have to reset the hedge.

She will also need to reset the hedge at some point even if interest rates do not change because the duration of the 12-year bond will decrease faster than that of the 20-year lease. For example, think forward 12 years: At that point the bond will mature, while the lease will still have 8 years to run.

Duration is not a complete measure of interest rate risk. It measures only exposure to the level of interest rates, not to changes in the shape of the term structure. Duration in effect assumes that the term structure is "flat." It is widely used, however, because it is a good first approximation to interest rate risk exposure. The mini-case at the end of this chapter offers another opportunity to use this concept.

Hedge Ratios and Basis Risk

In our example of Potterton Leasing, the CFO matched lease cash flows worth $17 million against debt worth $17 million. In other words, the *hedge ratio* for Potterton was exactly 1.

Hedge ratios can be much higher or lower than 1. For example, suppose a farmer owns 100,000 bushels of wheat and wishes to hedge by selling wheat futures. In practice, the wheat that the farmer owns and the wheat that he sells in the futures markets are not identical. If he sells wheat futures on the Kansas City exchange, he agrees to deliver hard, red winter wheat in

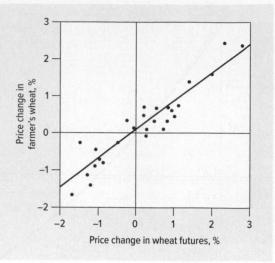

> **FIGURE 27.4**

Hypothetical plot of past changes in the price of the farmer's wheat against changes in the price of Kansas City wheat futures. A 1% change in the futures price implies, on average, a 0.8% change in the price of the farmer's wheat.

Kansas City in September. But perhaps he is growing northern spring wheat many miles from Kansas City; in this case, the prices of the two wheats will not move exactly together.

Figure 27.4 shows how changes in the prices of the two types of wheat may have been related in the past. The slope of the fitted line shows that a 1% change in the price of Kansas wheat was, on average, associated with an 0.8% change in the price of the farmer's wheat. Because the price of the farmer's wheat is relatively less sensitive to changes in Kansas prices, he needs to sell 0.8 × 100,000 bushels of wheat futures to minimize risk.

Let us generalize. Suppose that you already own an asset, A (e.g., wheat), and you wish to hedge against changes in the value of A by making an offsetting sale of another asset, B (e.g., wheat futures). Suppose also that percentage changes in the value of A are related in the following way to percentage changes in the value of B:

$$\text{Expected change in value of A} = \alpha + \delta \,(\text{change in value of B})$$

Delta (δ) measures the sensitivity of A to changes in the value of B. It is also equal to the *hedge ratio*—that is, the number of units of B that should be sold to hedge the purchase of A. You minimize risk if you offset your position in A by the sale of delta units of B. In our wheat example, $\delta = 0.8$.

The trick in setting up a hedge is to estimate the delta or hedge ratio. Our farmer could use past experience to do so, but often a strong dose of judgment is called for. For example, suppose that Antarctic Air would like to protect itself against a hike in oil prices. As the financial manager, you need to decide how much a rise in oil price would affect firm value.

Suppose the company spent $200 million on fuel last year. Other things equal, a 10% increase in the price of oil will cost the company an extra 0.1 × 200 = $20 million. But perhaps you can partially offset the higher costs by charging higher ticket prices, in which case earnings will fall by less than $20 million. Or perhaps an oil price rise will lead to a slowdown in business activity and therefore lower passenger numbers. In that case earnings will decline by more than $20 million. Working out the likely effect on firm value is even trickier because it depends on whether the rise is likely to be permanent. Perhaps the price rise will induce an increase in production or encourage consumers to economize on energy usage.

Whenever the two sides of the hedge do not move exactly together, there will be some basis risk. That is not a problem for the CFO of Potterton. As long as interest rates do not change sharply, any changes in the value of Potterton's lease should be almost exactly offset by changes in the value of the debt. In this case there is no basis risk, and Potterton is perfectly hedged.

BEYOND THE PAGE

🌐 | WTI and Brent
oil futures

mhhe.com/brealey14e

Our wheat farmer is less fortunate. The scatter of points in Figure 27.4 shows that it is not possible for the farmer to construct a perfect hedge using wheat futures. Since the underlying commodity (the farmer's wheat) and the hedging instrument (Kansas City wheat futures) are imperfectly correlated, some basis risk remains.

27.7 Self-Test

Suppose you hold a $1 million portfolio of common stocks with a beta of 1.2. You wish to use index futures to hedge the risk. Should you buy or sell futures? How large a futures position should you take to minimize risk?

27-8   Is "Derivative" a Four-Letter Word?

Our wheat farmer sold wheat futures to reduce business risk. But if you were to copy the farmer and sell futures without an offsetting holding of wheat, you would increase risk, not reduce it. You would be *speculating*.

Speculators in search of large profits (and prepared to tolerate large losses) are attracted by the leverage that derivatives provide. By this we mean that it is not necessary to lay out much money up front and the profits or losses may be many times the initial outlay. "Speculation" has an ugly ring, but a successful derivatives market needs speculators who are prepared to take on risk and provide more cautious people such as farmers or millers with the protection they need. For example, if there is an excess of farmers wishing to sell wheat futures, the price of futures will be forced down until enough speculators are tempted to buy in the hope of a profit. If there is a surplus of millers wishing to buy wheat futures, the reverse will happen. The price of wheat futures will be forced *up* until speculators are drawn in to sell.

Speculation may be necessary to a thriving derivatives market, but it can get companies into serious trouble. The nearby Finance in Practice box describes how the French bank Société Générale took a €4.9 billion bath from unauthorized trading by one of its staff. The bank has plenty of company. In 2011, Swiss bank UBS reported that a rogue trader had notched up losses of $2.3 billion. And in 1995, Baring Brothers, a blue-chip British merchant bank with a 200-year history, became insolvent. The reason: Nick Leeson, a trader in Baring's Singapore office, had placed very large bets on the Japanese stock market index that resulted in losses of $1.4 billion.

These tales of woe have some cautionary messages for all corporations. During the 1970s and 1980s, many firms turned their treasury operations into profit centers and proudly announced their profits from trading in financial instruments. But it is not possible to make large profits in financial markets without also taking large risks, so these profits should have served as a warning rather than a matter for congratulation.

An Airbus 350 weighs 280 tons, flies at nearly 600 miles per hour, and is inherently very dangerous. But we don't ground A350s; we just take precautions to ensure that they are flown with care. Similarly, it is foolish to suggest that firms should ban the use of derivatives, but it makes obvious sense to take precautions against their misuse. Here are two bits of horse sense:

- *Precaution 1: Don't be taken by surprise.* By this we mean that senior management needs to monitor regularly the value of the firm's derivatives positions and to know what bets the firm has placed. At its simplest, this might involve asking what would happen if interest rates or exchange rates were to change by 1%. But large banks and consultants have also developed sophisticated models for measuring the risk of derivatives positions.

- *Precaution 2: Place bets only when you have some comparative advantage that ensures the odds are in your favor.* If a bank were to announce that it was drilling for oil or

BEYOND THE PAGE

Major derivatives losses

mhhe.com/brealey14e

BEYOND THE PAGE

LTCM

mhhe.com/brealey14e

BEYOND THE PAGE

Metallgesell-schaft

mhhe.com/brealey14e

BEYOND THE PAGE

The world's poorest man

mhhe.com/brealey14e

launching a new soap powder, you would rightly be suspicious about whether it had what it takes to succeed. You should be equally suspicious if an oil producer or consumer products company announced that it was placing a bet on interest rates or currencies.

Imprudent speculation in derivatives is undoubtedly an issue of concern for the company's shareholders, but is it a matter for more general concern? Some people believe, like Warren Buffett, that derivatives are "financial weapons of mass destruction." They point to the huge volume of trading in derivatives and argue that speculative losses could lead to major defaults that might threaten the whole financial system. These worries have led to increased regulation of derivatives markets.

Now, this is not the place for a discussion of regulation, but we should warn you about careless measures of the size of the derivatives markets and the possible losses. In June 2020, the *notional value* of outstanding derivative contracts was \$582 trillion.[32] This is a very large sum, but it tells you nothing about the money that was being put at risk. For example, suppose that a bank enters into a \$10 million interest rate swap (\$10 million notional value) and the other party goes bankrupt the next day. How much has the bank lost? Nothing. It hasn't paid anything up front; the two parties simply promised to pay sums to each other in the future. Now the deal is off.

Suppose that the other party does not go bankrupt until a year after the bank entered into the swap. In the meantime interest rates have moved in the bank's favor, so it should be receiving more money from the swap than it is paying out. When the other side defaults on the deal, the bank loses the difference between the interest that it is due to receive and the interest that it should pay. But it doesn't lose \$10 million.[33]

The only meaningful measure of the potential loss from default is the amount that it would cost firms showing a profit to replace their positions.

• • • • •

**KEY
TAKEAWAYS**

As a manager, you are paid to take risks, but you are not paid to take just any risk. Hedging, when practical, can make sense if it reduces the chance of cash shortfalls or financial distress. In some cases, hedging can also make it easier to monitor and motivate operating managers. Relieving managers of risks outside their control helps them concentrate on what they can control.

- **Insurance** Insurance companies specialize in assessing risks and can pool risks by holding a diversified portfolio of policies. Insurance works less well when policies are taken up by companies that are most at risk (*adverse selection*) or when the insured company is tempted to skimp on maintenance or safety procedures (*moral hazard*).

- **Options** Companies can use options to offset adverse shifts in prices of production inputs or outputs. For example, a forest-products company could buy puts to offset a possible fall in construction-lumber prices. A homebuilder could buy calls: if lumber prices take off, profits on the calls could help pay for lumber purchases.

- **Forwards and futures** A forward contract is an advance order to buy or sell an asset. The forward price is fixed today, but payment is not made until the delivery date at the end of the contract. Forward contracts that are traded on organized futures exchanges are called futures contracts. Futures contracts are standardized and traded in huge volumes. Futures markets allow firms to lock in future prices for dozens of different commodities, securities, and currencies.

---

[32]Bank of International Settlements, *Derivatives Statistics* (www.bis.org/statistics/derstats.htm). This sum was for over-the-counter derivatives. Exchange-traded options and other derivatives accounted for about \$30 trillion more.

[33]This does not mean that firms don't worry about the possibility of default, and there are a variety of ways that they try to protect themselves. In the case of swaps, firms are reluctant to deal with banks that do not have the highest credit rating.

- **Interest-rate risk** Forward rate agreements (FRAs) provide protection against changes in interest rates. You can also construct homemade contracts to lock in forward interest rates. For example, if you borrow for two years and at the same time lend for one year, you have effectively taken out a forward loan. You can also hedge interest-rate risk using futures markets for government bills, notes or bonds.

- **Swaps** Firms also hedge with swap contracts. For example, a firm can make a deal to pay interest to a bank at a fixed long-term rate and receive interest from the bank at a floating short-term rate. The firm swaps a fixed for a floating rate. Such a swap could make sense if the firm has relatively easy access to short-term borrowing but dislikes the exposure to fluctuating short-term interest rates. The swap could pay for the fluctuating short-term rates, leaving a fixed-rate obligation.

- **Principles of hedging** Start with a risky long or short position in an asset. Find a closely related asset. Then buy or sell the amount of that asset that minimizes the risk of your net position. If the assets are *perfectly* correlated, you can make the net position risk-free. If they are less than perfectly correlated, you must absorb *basis risk*.

  The trick is to find the *hedge ratio* or *delta*—that is, the number of units of one asset that is needed to offset changes in the value of the other asset.

- **Duration** The effect of a change in interest rates on an asset's value depends on its duration. If two assets have the same duration, they will be equally affected by fluctuations in interest rates, and offsetting positions in the two assets will cancel out interest rate risk. But hedges that match durations are dynamic. As time passes and prices change, you must rebalance your position to maintain the hedge.

- **Does hedging help shareholders?** Hedging and risk reduction sound as wholesome as mom's apple pie. But remember that hedging solely to reduce risk cannot add value. It is a zero-sum game: Risks aren't eliminated; they are just shifted to some counterparty. And remember that your shareholders can also hedge by adjusting the composition of their portfolios or by trading in futures or other derivatives. Investors won't reward the firm for doing something that they can do perfectly well for themselves.

● ● ● ● ●

FURTHER READING

Three general articles on corporate risk management:

K. A. Froot, D. Scharfstein, and J. C. Stein, "A Framework for Risk Management," *Harvard Business Review* 72 (November–December 1994), pp. 59–71.

B. W. Nocco and R. M. Stulz, "Enterprise Risk Management: Theory and Practice," *Journal of Applied Corporate Finance* 18 (Fall 2006), pp. 8–20.

C. H. Smithson and B. Simkins, "Does Risk Management Add Value? A Survey of the Evidence," *Journal of Applied Corporate Finance* 17 (Summer 2005), pp. 8–17.

The Summer 2005 and Fall 2006 issues of the Journal of Applied Corporate Finance *are devoted to risk management, and current news and developments are discussed in* Risk *magazine. You may also wish to refer to the following texts:*

J. C. Hull, *Options, Futures, and other Derivatives,* 10th ed. (Cambridge, UK: Pearson, 2017).

C. H. Smithson, *Managing Financial Risk,* 3rd ed. (New York: McGraw-Hill, 1998).

R. M. Stulz, *Risk Management and Derivatives* (Cincinnati, OH: Thomson-Southwestern Publishing, 2003).

Schaefer's paper is a useful review of how duration measures are used to immunize fixed liabilities:

S. M. Schaefer, "Immunisation and Duration: A Review of Theory, Performance and Applications," *Midland Corporate Finance Journal* 3 (Autumn 1984), pp. 41–58.

PROBLEM SETS

Mc Graw Hill **connect**

Select problems are available in McGraw Hill's *Connect*.
Please see the preface for more information.

1. **Vocabulary check (S27-4)** Define the following terms:

   a. Spot price.

   b. Forward vs. futures contract.

   c. Long vs. short position.

   d. Basis risk.

   e. Mark to market.

   f. Net convenience yield.

2. **Insurance (S27-2)** Large businesses spend millions of dollars annually on insurance. Why? Should they insure against all risks or does insurance make more sense for some risks than others?

3. **Catastrophe bonds (S27-2)** On some catastrophe bonds, payments are reduced if the claims against the issuer exceed a specified sum. In other cases, payments are reduced only if claims against the entire industry exceed some sum. What are the advantages and disadvantages of the two structures? Which involves more basis risk? Which may create a problem of moral hazard?

4. **Futures and options (S27-3–S27-4)** A gold-mining firm is concerned about short-term volatility in its revenues. Gold currently sells for $1,300 an ounce, but the price is extremely volatile and could fall as low as $1,220 or rise as high as $1,380 in the next month. The company will bring 1,000 ounces to the market next month.

   a. What will be total revenues if the firm remains unhedged for gold prices of $1,220, $1,300, and $1,380 an ounce?

   b. The futures price of gold for delivery one month ahead is $1,310. What will be the firm's total revenues at each gold price if the firm enters into a one-month futures contract to deliver 1,000 ounces of gold?

   c. What will be total net revenues if the firm buys a one-month put option to sell gold for $1,300 an ounce? The put option costs $110 per ounce.

5. **Futures and options (S27-3–S27-4)** Parfum Pétrochimique (PP) is concerned about a possible increase in the price of heavy fuel oil, which is one of its major inputs. Show how PP can use either options or futures contracts to protect itself against a rise in the price of crude oil. Show how the payoffs in each case would vary if the oil price were $70, $80, or $90 a barrel. What are the advantages and disadvantages for PP of using futures rather than options to reduce risk? Assume the current price of oil is $70 per barrel, the futures price is $80, and the option exercise price is $80.

6. **Futures contracts (S27-4)** True or false?

   a. Hedging transactions in an active futures market have zero or slightly negative NPVs.

   b. When you buy a futures contract, you pay now for delivery at a future date.

   c. The holder of a financial futures contract misses out on any dividend or interest payments made on the underlying security.

   d. The holder of a commodities futures contract does not have to pay for storage costs, but foregoes convenience yield.

7. **Futures contracts (S27-4)** List some of the commodity futures contracts that are traded on exchanges. Who do you think could usefully reduce risk by buying each of these contracts? Who do you think might wish to sell each contract?

8. **Marking to market (S27-4)** Yesterday, you sold six-month futures on the German DAX stock market index at a price of 15,600. Today, the DAX closed at 15,550 and DAX futures

closed at 15,650. You get a call from your broker, who reminds you that your futures position is marked to market each day. Is she asking you to pay money, or is she about to offer to
pay you?

9. **Futures prices (S27-4)** Calculate the value of a six-month futures contract on a Treasury
bond. You have the following information:

- Six-month interest rate: 10% per year, or 4.9% for six months.

- Spot price of bond: 95.

- The bond pays an 8% coupon, 4% every six months.

10. **Futures prices (S27-4)** In July 2021, six-month futures on the Australian S&P/ASX 200
Index traded at 7,224. Spot was 7,309. The interest rate was about 1% a year, and the dividend
yield was about 3.0% a year. Were the futures fairly priced?

11. **Futures prices (S27-4)** If you buy a nine-month T-bill future, you undertake to buy a
$1 million three-month bill in nine months' time. Suppose that Treasury bills and notes cur-
rently offer the following yields:

Months to Maturity	Annual Yield
3	6%
6	6.5
9	7
12	8

What is the dollar value of a nine-month bill future?

12. **Futures prices (S27-4)** Table 27.4 contains spot and six-month futures prices for several
commodities and financial instruments. There may be some money-making opportunities.
See if you can find them, and explain how you would trade to take advantage of them. The
interest rate is 14.5%, or 7% over the six-month life of the contracts.

Commodity	Spot Price	Futures Price	Comments
Magnoosium	$2,550 per ton	$2,728.50 per ton	Monthly storage cost = monthly convenience yield.
Frozen quiche	$0.50 per pound	$0.514 per pound	Six months' storage costs = $0.10 per pound; six months' convenience yield = $0.05 per pound.
Nevada Hydro 8s of 2024	77	78.39	4% semiannual coupon payment is due just before futures contract expires.
Costaguanan pulgas (currency)	9,300 pulgas = $1	6,900 pulgas = $1	Costaguanan interest rate is 95% per year.
Establishment Industries common stock	$95	$97.54	Establishment pays dividends of $2 per quarter. Next dividend is paid two months from now.
Cheap white wine	$12,500 per 10,000-gal tank	$14,200 per 10,000-gal tank	Six months' convenience yield = $250 per tank. Your company has surplus storage and can store 50,000 gallons at no cost.

〉TABLE 27.4   Spot and six-month futures prices for selected commodities and securities. See
Problem 12.

13. **Futures prices (S27-4)** The following table shows 2021 gold futures prices for varying
contract lengths. Gold is predominantly an investment good, not an industrial commodity.

Investors hold gold because it diversifies their portfolios and because they hope its price will rise. They do not hold it for its convenience yield.

	Contract Length (months)		
	3	6	9
Futures price	$1,796.2	$1,809.6	$1,827.4

Calculate the interest rates faced by traders in gold futures, assuming a zero net convenience yield, for each of the contract lengths shown above. The spot price is $1,787.3 per ounce.

14. **Futures prices (S27-4)** Consider the commodities and financial assets listed in Table 27.5. The risk-free interest rate is 6% a year, and the term structure is flat.

Asset	Spot Price	Comments
Magnoosium	$2,800 per ton	Net convenience yield = 4% per year
Oat bran	$0.44 per bushel	Net convenience yield = 0.5% per month
Biotech stock index	$140.2	Dividend = 0
Allen Wrench Co. common stock	$58.00	Cash dividend = $2.40 per year
5-year Treasury note	$108.93	8% coupon
Westonian ruple	3.1 ruples = $1	12% interest rate in ruples

)TABLE 27.5   Spot prices for selected commodities and financial assets. See Problem 14.

a. Calculate the six-month futures price for each case.

b. Explain how a magnoosium producer would use a futures market to lock in the selling price of a planned shipment of 1,000 tons of magnoosium six months from now.

c. Suppose the producer takes the actions recommended in your answer to part (b), but after one month magnoosium prices have fallen to $2,200. What happens? Will the producer have to undertake additional futures market trades to restore its hedged position?

d. Does the biotech index futures price provide useful information about the expected future performance of biotech stocks?

e. Suppose Allen Wrench stock falls suddenly by $10 per share. Investors are confident that the cash dividend will not be reduced. What happens to the futures price?

f. Suppose interest rates suddenly fall to 4%. The term structure remains flat. What happens to the six-month futures price on the five-year Treasury note? What happens to a trader who shorted 100 notes at the futures price calculated in part (a)?

g. An importer must make a payment of 1 million ruples three months from now. Explain *two* strategies the importer could use to hedge against unfavorable shifts in the ruple–dollar exchange rate.

15. **Convenience yield (S27-4)** Calculate the convenience yield for magnoosium scrap from the following information:

- Spot price: $2,550 per ton.
- Futures price: $2,408 for a one-year contract.
- Interest rate: 12%.
- Storage costs: $100 per year.

16. **Convenience yield (S27-4)** Residents of the northeastern United States suffered record-setting low temperatures throughout November and December 2027. Spot prices of heating oil rose 25%, to over $7 a gallon.

a. What effect did this have on the net convenience yield and on the relationship between futures and spot prices?

b. In late 2028, refiners and distributors were surprised by record-setting *high* temperatures. What was the effect on net convenience yield and spot and futures prices for heating oil?

17. **Convenience yield (S27-4)** After a record harvest, grain silos are full to the brim. Are storage costs likely to be high or low? What does this imply for the net convenience yield?

18. **Convenience yield (S27-4)** In July 2021, four-month bitcoin futures were priced at $33,930. The spot price was $33,645. The six-month interest rate was about 2%.

a. What was the convenience yield?

b. Is your answer to part (a) consistent with what you would expect? Explain.

19. **Interest-rate swaps (S27-6)** A year ago, a bank entered into a $50 million five-year interest rate swap. It agreed to pay company A each year a fixed rate of 6% and to receive in return SOFR. When the bank entered into this swap, SOFR was 5%, but now interest rates have risen, so on a four-year interest rate swap the bank could expect to pay 6.5% and receive SOFR.

a. Is the swap showing a profit or loss to the bank?

b. Suppose that at this point company A approaches the bank and asks to terminate the swap. If there are four annual payments still remaining, how much should the bank charge A to terminate?

20. **Interest rate swaps (S27-6)** In June 2021, swap dealers were quoting a rate for five-year sterling interest-rate swaps of 0.73% against SONIA (the short-term interest rate for sterling loans). SONIA at the time was 0.05%. Suppose that A arranges with a dealer to swap a £10 million five-year fixed-rate loan for an equivalent floating-rate loan.

a. Assume the swap is fairly priced. What is the value of this swap at the time that it is entered into?

b. Suppose that immediately after A has entered into the swap, the long-term interest rate rises by 1%. Who gains and who loses?

c. What is now the value of the swap for each £1,000 of par value?

21. **Total return swaps (S27-6)** Is a total return swap on a bond the same as a credit default swap (see Section 24-1)? Why or why not?

22. **Hedging (S27-7)** "Speculators want futures contracts to be incorrectly priced; hedgers want them to be correctly priced." Why?

23. **Hedging (S27-7)** "Northern Refineries does not avoid risk by selling oil futures. If prices stay above $2.40 a gallon, then it will actually have lost by selling oil futures at that price." Is this a fair comment?

24. **Hedging (S27-7)** What is meant by "delta" (δ) in the context of hedging? Give examples of how delta can be estimated or calculated.

25. **Hedging (S27-7)** You own a $1 million portfolio of aerospace stocks with a beta of 1.2. You are very enthusiastic about aerospace but uncertain about the prospects for the overall stock market. Explain how you could hedge out your market exposure by selling the market short. How much would you sell? How in practice would you go about "selling the market"?

26. **Hedging interest rates (S27-7)**

a. Marshall Arts has just invested $1 million in long-term Treasury bonds. Marshall is concerned about increasing volatility in interest rates. He decides to hedge using bond futures contracts. Should he buy or sell such contracts?

b. The treasurer of Zeta Corporation plans to issue bonds in three months. She is also concerned about interest rate volatility and wants to lock in the price at which her company could sell 5% coupon bonds. How would she use bond futures contracts to hedge?

27. **Hedging with futures (S27-7)** Phoenix Motors wants to lock in the cost of 10,000 ounces of platinum to be used in next quarter's production of catalytic converters. It buys three-month futures contracts for 10,000 ounces at a price of $1,300 per ounce.

    a. Suppose the spot price of platinum falls to $1,200 in three months' time. Does Phoenix have a profit or loss on the futures contract? Has it locked in the cost of purchasing the platinum it needs?

    b. How do your answers change if the spot price of platinum increases to $1,400 after three months?

28. **Hedging with futures (S27-7)** Legs Diamond owns shares in a Vanguard Index 500 mutual fund worth $1 million on July 15. (This is an index fund that tracks the Standard and Poor's 500 Index.) He wants to cash in now, but his accountant advises him to wait six months so as to defer a large capital gains tax. Explain to Legs how he can use stock index futures to hedge out his exposure to market movements over the next six months. Could Legs "cash in" without actually selling his shares?

29. **Hedging (S27-7)** Price changes of two gold-mining stocks have shown strong positive correlation. Their historical relationship is

    Average percentage change in A = 0.001 + 0.75 (percentage change in B)

    Changes in B explain 60% of the variation of the changes in A ($R^2 = 0.6$).

    a. Suppose you own $100,000 of A. How much of B should you sell to minimize the risk of your net position?

    b. What is the hedge ratio?

    c. Here is the historical relationship between stock A and gold prices:

    Average percentage change in A = −0.002 + 1.2 (percentage change in gold price)

    If $R^2 = 0.5$, can you lower the risk of your net position by hedging with gold (or gold futures) rather than with stock B? Explain.

30. **Hedging (S27-7)** Your investment bank has an investment of $100 million in the stock of the Swiss Roll Corporation and a short position in the stock of the Frankfurter Sausage Company. Here is the recent price history of the two stocks:

	Percentage Price Change	
Month	Frankfurter Sausage	Swiss Roll
January	−10	−10
February	−10	−5
March	−10	0
April	+10	0
May	+10	+5
June	+10	+10

On the evidence of these six months, how large would your short position in Frankfurter Sausage need to be to hedge you as far as possible against movements in the price of Swiss Roll?

31. **Duration hedging (S27-7)** Securities A, B, and C have the following cash flows:

	Year 1	Year 2	Year 3
A	$ 40	$40	$ 40
B	120	—	—
C	10	10	110

a. Calculate their durations if the interest rate is 8%.

b. Suppose that you have an investment of $10 million in A. What combination of B and C would hedge this investment against interest rate changes?

c. Now suppose that you have a $10 million investment in B. How would you hedge?

32. **Basis risk (S27-7)** What is basis risk? In which of the following cases would you expect basis risk to be serious?

a. A broker owning a large block of Disney common stock hedges by selling index futures.

b. An Iowa corn farmer hedges the selling price of her crop by selling Chicago corn futures.

c. An importer must pay €900 million in six months. He hedges by buying euros forward.

CHALLENGE

33. **Interest-rate swaps (S27-6)** Phillip's Screwdriver Company has borrowed $20 million from a bank at a floating interest rate of 2 percentage points above three-month Treasury bills, which now yield 5%. Assume that interest payments are made quarterly and that the entire principal of the loan is repaid after five years.

   Phillip's wants to convert the bank loan to fixed-rate debt. It could have issued a fixed-rate five-year note at a yield to maturity of 9%. Such a note would now trade at par. The five-year Treasury note's yield to maturity is 7%.

a. Is Phillip's stupid to want long-term debt at an interest rate of 9%? It is borrowing from the bank at 7%.

b. Explain how the conversion could be carried out by an interest rate swap. What will be the initial terms of the swap? (Ignore transaction costs and the swap dealer's profit.)

   One year from now short and medium-term Treasury yields *decrease* to 6%, so the term structure then is flat. (The changes actually occur in month 5.) Phillip's credit standing is unchanged; it can still borrow at 2 percentage points over Treasury rates.

c. What net swap payment will Phillip's make or receive?

d. Suppose that Phillip's now wants to cancel the swap. How much would it need to pay the swap dealer? Or would the dealer pay Phillip's? Explain.

• • • • •

**SOLUTIONS
TO SELF-TEST
QUESTIONS**

27.1 No, the arguments apply only to financial transactions. By contrast, the option to abandon a project may have a positive NPV. Investors cannot replicate an abandonment option for themselves.

27.2 Insurance is generally used to protect against specific risks, which the insurance company can diversify by holding portfolios of policies.

27.3 a. Sells timber futures;

   b. buys copper futures;

   c. buys timber futures;

   d. sells oil futures;

   e. buys wheat futures;

   f. buys oil futures;

   g. sells wheat futures.

27.4 $(1 + {}_3f_4) = (1 + r_4)^4/(1 + r_3)^3 = 1.197/1.138 = 1.052$, so ${}_3f_4 = 5.2\%$.

27.5 Borrow $970,870 for one year at 3%. Invest this amount for two years at 4%. Cash flows are −$1 million at year 1 (to prepay the one-year loan) and +$1,050,100 at year 2.

27.6   The value of a two-year note is $4/1.04 + (4 + 66.7)/1.04^2 = 69.2$. Therefore, the value of Friendly Bancorp's swap is $66.7 - 69.2 = -\$2.5$ million.

27.7   You should sell $1.2 million of index futures.

● ● ● ● ●

FINANCE ON THE WEB

1. The websites of the major commodities exchanges provide futures prices. Calculate the *annualized* net convenience yield for a commodity of your choice. (*Note:* You may need to use the futures price of a contract that is about to mature as your estimate of the current spot price.)

2. You can find swap rates for the U.S. dollar and the euro on https://fred.stlouisfed.org/. Plot the current swap curves as in Figure 27.3.

3. You can find spot and futures prices for several equity indexes on **www.wsj.com.** Pick one and check whether it is fairly priced. You will need to do some detective work to find the dividend yield on the index and the interest rate.

4. For an interesting commentary by John Parsons and Antonio Mello on news about futures and hedging look at https://bettingthebusiness.com.

MINI-CASE ● ● ● ●

Rensselaer Advisers

You are a vice president of Rensselaer Advisers (RA), which manages portfolios for institutional investors (primarily corporate pension plans) and wealthy individuals. In mid-2025, RA had about $1.1 billion under management, invested in a wide range of common-stock and fixed-income portfolios. Its management fees average 55 basis points (0.55%), so RA's total revenue for 2025 is about $0.0055 \times \$1.1$ billion $= \$6.05$ million.

You are attempting to land a new client, Madison Mills, a conservative, long-established manufacturer of papermaking felt. Madison has established a defined-benefit pension plan for its employees. RA would manage the pension assets that Madison has set aside to cover defined-benefit obligations for retired employees.

Defined benefit means that an employer is committed to pay retirement income according to a formula. For example, annual retirement income could equal 40% of the employee's average salary in the five years prior to retirement. In a defined-benefit plan, retirement income does not depend on the performance of the pension assets. If the assets in the fund are not sufficient to cover pension benefits, the company is required to contribute enough additional cash to cover the shortfall. Thus, the PV of promised retirement benefits is a debt-equivalent obligation of the company.[35]

Table 27.6 shows Madison's obligations to its already retired employees from 2026 to 2047. Each of these employees receives a fixed dollar amount each month. Total dollar payments decline as the employees die off. The PV of the obligations in Table 27.6 is about $89 million at the current long-term interest rate (we assume it is 5%). Table 27.6 also calculates the duration of the obligations at 7.87 years.

Madison has set aside $90 million in pension assets to cover the obligations in Table 27.6, so this part of its pension plan is fully funded.[36] The pension assets are now invested in a diversified portfolio of common stocks, corporate bonds, and notes.

---

[35]In *defined contribution* plans, the corporation contributes to the pension fund on behalf of its employees. Each employee has a claim on part of the fund, just as if the employee held shares in a mutual fund. Employees' retirement benefits depend on their balances in the fund at retirement. If the benefits fall short of an employee's plans or expectations, he or she has no recourse to the company.

[36]Madison must also set pension assets aside for current employees. For this mini-case, we concentrate only on retired employees' benefits.

Year	Date (*t*)	Payment	PV at 5%	PV × *t*
2026	1	10,020,000	9,542,857	9,542,857
2027	2	9,009,500	8,171,882	16,343,764
2028	3	8,522,000	7,361,624	22,084,872
2029	4	8,434,500	6,939,084	27,756,336
2030	5	7,858,500	6,157,340	30,786,702
2031	6	7,794,000	5,816,003	34,896,017
2032	7	7,729,500	5,493,211	38,452,479
2033	8	7,639,500	5,170,714	41,365,714
2034	9	6,440,500	4,151,604	37,364,434
2035	10	6,330,000	3,886,071	38,860,709
2036	11	6,242,500	3,649,860	40,148,465
2037	12	6,205,000	3,455,176	41,462,114
2038	13	5,775,500	3,062,871	39,817,322
2039	14	5,600,700	2,828,734	39,602,277
2040	15	5,432,000	2,354,693	37,675,092
2041	16	5,140,000	23,54,693	37,675,092
2042	17	4,234,900	1,847,673	31,410,438
2043	18	4,123,000	1,713,192	30,837,450
2044	19	3,890,000	1,539,405	29,248,697
2045	20	3,500,600	1,319,339	26,386,786
2046	21	3,400,500	1,220,584	25,632,254
2047	22	3,340,600	1,141,984	25,123,641
			SUM =	703,991,694
			PV =	89,436,787
			DURATION =	7.87

〉TABLE 27.6
Madison Mills Pension Fund, projected benefits for retired employees.

After reviewing Madison's existing portfolio, you schedule a meeting with Hendrik van Wie, Madison's CFO. Mr. van Wie stresses Madison's conservative management philosophy and warns against "speculation." He complains about the performance of the previous manager of the pension assets. He suggests that you propose a plan of investing in safe assets in a way that minimizes exposure to equity markets and changing interest rates. You promise to prepare an illustration of how this goal could be achieved.

Later, you discover that RA has competition for Madison's investment management business. SPX Associates is proposing a strategy of investing 70% of the portfolio ($63 million) in index funds tracking the U.S. stock market and 30% of the portfolio ($27 million) in U.S. Treasury securities. SPX argues that their strategy is "safe in the long run" because the U.S. stock market has delivered an average risk premium of about 7% per year. In addition, SPX argues that the growth in its stock market portfolio will far outstrip Madison's pension obligations. SPX also claims that the $27 million invested in Treasuries will provide ample protection against short-term stock market volatility. Finally, SPX proposes to charge an investment management fee of only 20 basis points (0.20%). RA had planned to charge 30 basis points (0.30%).

QUESTIONS

1. Prepare a memo for Mr. van Wie explaining how RA would invest to minimize both risk and exposure to changing interest rates. Give an example of a portfolio that would accomplish

this objective. Explain how the portfolio would be managed as time passes and interest rates change. Also explain why SPX's proposal is not advisable for a conservative company like Madison.

RA manages several fixed-income portfolios. For simplicity, you decide to propose a mix of the following three portfolios:

- A portfolio of long-term Treasury bonds with an average duration of 14 years.
- A portfolio of Treasury notes with an average duration of seven years.
- A portfolio of short-term Treasury bills and notes with an average duration of one year.

The term structure is flat, and the yield on all three portfolios is 5%.

2. Sorry, you lost. SPX won and implemented its proposed strategy. Now the recession of 2026 has knocked down U.S. stock prices by 20%. The value of the Madison portfolio, after paying benefits for 2026, has fallen from $90 million to $78 million. At the same time interest rates have dropped from 5% to 4% as the Federal Reserve relaxes monetary policy to combat the recession.

Mr. van Wie calls again, chastened by the SPX experience, and he invites a new proposal to invest the pension assets in a way that minimizes exposure to the stock market and changing interest rates. Update your memo with a new example of how to accomplish Mr. van Wie's objectives. You can use the same portfolios and portfolio durations as in Question 1. You will have to recalculate the PV and duration of the pension benefits from 2026 onward. Assume a flat term structure with all interest rates at 4%. (*Hint:* Madison's pension obligations are now *underfunded*. Nevertheless, you can hedge interest rate risk if you increase the duration of the pension assets.)

CHAPTER

28

International Financial Management

Companies that operate internationally face various extra complications. In particular, they must deal with different currencies and interest rates and with the political risks that can arise from operating in less stable parts of the world.

Section 28-1 The foreign exchange market
We start by explaining how spot and forward exchange rates are quoted and traded.

Section 28-2 Some basic relationships
To develop a coherent international policy, the financial manager needs an understanding of the linkages between exchange rates and cross-country differences in interest rates and inflation. We look at some simple theories and at how well they stand up against the data. Most turn out to be not much better than rules of thumb but, nevertheless, are useful guides.

Section 28-3 Hedging currency risk
Exchange rate fluctuations can have a major impact on a company's profitability. We describe how corporations assess and hedge their currency exposures.

Section 28-4 International investment decisions
Currency differences can complicate international capital investment decisions. Cash flows for an investment project in Germany, say, must be forecasted in euros, but what are those cash flows worth in dollars? We describe how companies can value foreign currency cash flows.

Section 28-5 Political risk
We conclude the chapter with a discussion of political risk. Political risk means possible adverse acts by a hostile foreign government—for example, discriminatory taxes or limits on the profits that can be taken out of the country. We explain how companies structure their operations and financing to reduce their exposure to these risks.

28-1   The Foreign Exchange Market

An American company that imports goods from France may need to buy euros to pay for the purchase. An American company exporting to France may receive euros, which it then sells in exchange for dollars. Both firms make use of the foreign exchange market.

The foreign exchange market has no central marketplace. A corporation that wants to buy or sell currency usually does so electronically through a commercial bank. Turnover in the foreign exchange market is huge. In London in April 2019, $3,576 billion of currency changed hands each day. That is equivalent to an annual turnover of about $1,300 trillion

						Forward Rates	
Country	Currency	Symbol	Code	Spot Rate	3 Months	6 Months	1 Year
Europe							
Eurozone	Euro	€	EUR	1.1595	1.1618	1.1645	1.1690
Czech Republic	Koruna	Kč	CZK	22.8420	22.8410	22.8360	22.8310
Russia	Ruble	₽	RUB	70.7987	70.1318	69.4397	68.1211
Sweden	Krona	kr	SEK	8.8655	8.8416	8.3886	8.8230
Switzerland	Franc	fr	CHF	0.9298	0.9274	0.9246	0.9198
United Kingdom	Pound	£	GBP	1.2714	1.2756	1.2765	1.2774
Americas							
Brazil	Real	R$	BRL	5.1101	5.1273	5.1432	5.1937
Canada	Dollar	$	CAD	1.3416	1.3413	1.3410	1.3415
Mexico	Peso	$	MXN	22.2949	22.5591	22.7913	23.2403
Pacific/Middle East/Africa							
Australia	Dollar	$	AUD	0.7151	0.7154	0.7154	0.7152
China	Yuan	¥	CNY	6.9955	542	6.6947	6.7668
India	Rupee	₹	INR	74.6035	74.6107	74.6177	74.6328
Japan	Yen	¥	JPY	107.19	107.06	106.85	106.55
New Zealand	Dollar	$	NZD	0.6670	0.6670	0.6669	0.6665
South Africa	Rand	R	ZAR	16.3958	16.5488	116.6893	16.9753
South Korea	Won	₩	KRW	1,196.03	1196.17	1,195.17	1,193.03
Turkey	Lira	₹	TRY	6.8523	7.0600	7.3799	8.0233

[a]*Rates show the number of units of foreign currency per U.S. dollar, except for the euro, the U.K. pound, and the Australian and New Zealand dollars, which show the number of U.S. dollars per unit of foreign currency.*

❭**TABLE 28.1**   Spot and forward exchange rates, July 2020.

Source: CME GROUP

($1,300,000,000,000,000). New York, Singapore, Hong Kong, and Tokyo together accounted for a further $3,018 billion of turnover per day.[1]

Table 28.1 shows a sample of exchange rates in July 2020. The second column shows the name of each country's currency. For example, the Swedish currency is called the krona, and the Swiss currency is the franc. The next column shows the symbol for that currency. For example, a shop window in Sweden might show that the price of an article was kr5, while in Switzerland it would be shown as fr5. The fourth column in the table shows the abbreviations that are used by foreign exchange dealers. The code for the Swedish krona is SEK and the code for the Swiss franc is CHF.

The next column in the table shows the exchange rate for each currency in July 2020. Generally, foreign exchange quotes state the amount of the foreign currency that you can buy for a dollar. In this case, the dollar is said to be the *base currency* and the foreign currency is said to be the quote *currency*. Thus, Table 28.1 shows that for one dollar (the base currency) you could buy 5.1101 Brazilian reals (the quote currency). This is sometimes written as USD/BRL = 5.1101. The U.S. dollar (shown on the left) is the base currency and the real (shown on the right) is the quote currency.

Generally, in foreign exchange quotes, the U.S. dollar is the base currency so that the stated exchange rate tells you how many units of the other country's currency you can buy for one

---

[1]The results of the triennial survey of foreign exchange business are published on www.bis.org/forum/research.htm.

U.S. dollar. There are four cases where the quote is reversed. When quoting an exchange rate between the U.S. dollar and the euro, the British pound, the Australian dollar, or the New Zealand dollar, dealers commonly state the number of U.S. dollars that you can buy for one unit of the foreign currency. For example, Table 28.1 shows that one euro (the base currency) is equivalent to 1.1595 U.S. dollars (the quote currency).[2] This is generally written as EUR/USD = 1.1595. If €1 buys $1.1595, then $1 must buy 1/1.1595 = €0.8624.[3]

All the currency quotations in Table 28.1 involve the U.S. dollar as one of the two currencies, but sometimes you may need a quote for a pair of currencies that does *not* include the dollar. For example, you might want to know the exchange rate between the euro and Japanese yen. Dealers commonly refer to this as a cross-rate.[4] The cross-rate also consists of a base currency and a quote currency. If the euro is one of the two currencies, then it will be used as the base currency. So we can use the data in Table 28.1 to calculate that the cross-rate between the euro and the yen is EUR/JPY = (EUR/USD) × (USD/JPY) = 1.1595 × 107.19 = 124.287. One euro is equivalent to 124.287 yen.[5]

The exchange rates that we have been looking at in the fifth column of Table 28.1 are the prices of currency for immediate delivery. These are known as **spot rates of exchange**. The spot rate for the real is USD/BRL = 5.1101 and the spot rate for the euro is EUR/USD = 1.1595.

In addition to the spot exchange market, there is a *forward market*. In the forward market you buy and sell currency for future delivery. If you know that you are going to pay out or receive foreign currency at some future date, you can insure yourself against loss by buying or selling forward. Thus, if you need 1 million reals in three months, you can enter into a three-month *forward contract*. The **forward exchange rate** on this contract is the price you agree to pay in three months when the 1 million reals are delivered. If you look again at Table 28.1, you will see that the three-month forward rate for the real is quoted at USD/BRL = 5.1273.[6] If you buy reals for three months' delivery, you get more reals for your dollar than if you buy them spot. In this case, the real is said to trade at a forward *discount* relative to the dollar because forward reals are cheaper than spot ones. Expressed as an annual rate, the forward discount is[7]

$$4 \times \left(\frac{5.1101}{5.1273} - 1 \right) = -0.0134, \text{ or } -1.34\%$$

You could also say that the *dollar* was selling at a *forward premium* on the real.

A forward purchase or sale is a made-to-measure transaction between you and the bank. It can be for any currency, any amount, and any delivery day. You could buy, say, 99,999 Vietnamese dong or Haitian gourdes for a year and a day forward as long as you can find a bank ready to deal. Most forward transactions are for six months or less, but the long-term currency swaps that we described in Chapter 27 are equivalent to a bundle of forward transactions. When firms want to enter into long-term forward contracts, they commonly do so through a currency swap.

---

[2] The euro is the common currency of the European Monetary Union. The 19 members of the Union are Austria, Belgium, Cyprus, Estonia, Finland, France, Germany, Greece, Ireland, Italy, Latvia, Lithuania, Luxembourg, Malta, Netherlands, Portugal, Slovenia, Slovakia, and Spain.

[3] When the dollar is the base currency, the quote is said to be *indirect*. Where the foreign currency is the base, the quote is *direct*.

[4] Strictly, a cross-rate refers to an exchange rate between the currencies of two countries that differ from the place of quotation, but it more commonly refers to any pair of currencies that does not include the dollar.

[5] Foreign exchange dealers use a hierarchy of base currencies for quoting cross-rates. The euro is top of this hierarchy, followed by the pound, Australian dollar, New Zealand dollar, U.S. dollar, and Canadian dollar. For example, the cross-rate between the pound and the Canadian dollar will generally be in terms of the number of dollars you can buy for a pound, while the cross-rate between the Canadian dollar and the yen will be in terms of the number of yen you can buy for a Canadian dollar.

[6] Forward rates are often quoted in terms of "points." To calculate the forward rate, divide the number of points by 10,000 and add the result to the spot rate. For example, if the three-month forward rate on the euro is quoted as +23 points, the rate is 1.1595 + 23/10,000 = 1.1595 + 0.0023 = 1.1618.

[7] Here is an occasional point of confusion. When the U.S. dollar is the base currency, we calculate the premium by taking the ratio of the spot rate to the forward rate. If the U.S. dollar were the *quote* currency, then we would need to calculate the ratio of the forward rate to the spot rate.

There is also an organized market for currency for future delivery known as the currency *futures* market. Futures contracts are highly standardized; they are for specified amounts and for a limited choice of delivery dates.[8]

When you buy a forward or futures contract, you are committed to taking delivery of the currency. As an alternative, you can take out an *option* to buy or sell currency in the future at a price that is fixed today. Made-to-measure currency options can be bought from the major banks, and standardized options are traded on the options exchanges.

28.1 Self-Test

Look at Table 28.1.
  a. How many rupees can you buy for one dollar?
  b. What is the cross exchange rate between the pound and the rupee?
  c. Is the rupee at a forward premium or discount on the dollar?

28-2   **Some Basic Relationships**

You can't develop a consistent international financial policy until you understand the reasons for the differences in exchange rates and interest rates. We consider four problems:

Problem 1. Why is the dollar rate of interest different from the foreign rate?

Problem 2. Why is the forward rate of exchange different from the spot rate?

Problem 3. What determines next year's expected spot rate of exchange?

Problem 4. What is the relationship between the inflation rate in the United States and the foreign inflation rate?

We illustrate by looking at the kingdom of Ruritania and its currency, the rur.[9]

Suppose that individuals were not worried about risk and that there were no barriers or costs to international trade or capital flows. In that case, the spot exchange rates, forward exchange rates, interest rates, and inflation rates would stand in the following simple relationship to one another:

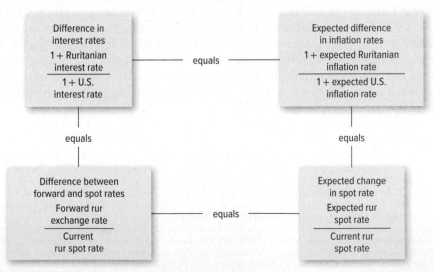

---

[8]See Chapter 27 for a further discussion of the difference between forward and futures contracts.

[9]Ruritania was conceived by Anthony Hope as the setting for his 1894 novel *The Prisoner of Zenda*. The Ruritanian rur was first proposed by Ludwig von Mises in his 1912 book *The Theory of Money and Credit*.

Why should this be so?

Interest Rates and Exchange Rates

Suppose that you have $1,000 to invest for one year. U.S. dollar deposits are offering an interest rate of 5%; Ruritanian rur deposits are offering (an attractive?) 15.5%. Where should you put your money? Does the answer sound obvious? Let's check:

- *Dollar loan.* The rate of interest on one-year dollar deposits is 5%. Therefore, at the end of the year you get $1,000 \times 1.05 = \text{USD1,050}$.

- *Rur loan.* The current exchange rate is USD/RUR = 50. Therefore, for $1,000, you can buy $1,000 \times 50 = \text{RUR50,000}$. The rate of interest on a one-year rur deposit is 15.5%. Therefore, at the end of the year you get $50,000 \times 1.155 = \text{RUR57,750}$. Of course, you don't know what the exchange rate is going to be in one year's time. But that doesn't matter. You can fix today the price at which you sell your rurs. The one-year forward rate is USD/RUR = 55. Therefore, by selling forward, you can make sure that you will receive $57,750/55 = \$1,050$ at the end of the year.

Thus, the two investments offer the same rate of return. They have to—they are both risk-free. If the domestic interest rate were different from the *covered* foreign interest rate, you would have a money machine.

When you make the rur loan, you receive a higher interest rate. But you get an offsetting loss because you sell rurs forward at a lower price than you pay for them today. The interest rate differential in our example is

$$\frac{1 + \text{Ruritanian interest rate}}{1 + \text{U.S. interest rate}}$$

And the differential between the forward and spot exchange rates is

$$\frac{\text{Forward rur exchange rate}}{\text{Current rur spot rate}}$$

Interest rate parity theory says that the difference in interest rates must equal the difference between the forward and spot exchange rates:

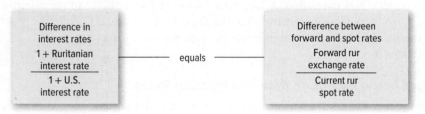

In our example,

$$\frac{1.155}{1.05} = \frac{55}{50}$$

28.2 Self-Test

Suppose that the interest rate on the Ruritanian rur was 10.25%. What would you expect the forward exchange rate to be?

The Forward Premium and Changes in Spot Rates

Now let's consider how the forward premium is related to changes in spot rates of exchange. If people didn't care about risk, the forward rate of exchange would depend solely on what people expected the spot rate to be. For example, if the one-year forward rate on rurs is USD/RUR = 55, that could only be because traders expect the spot rate in one year's time to be USD/RUR = 55. If they expected it to be, say, USD/RUR = 60, nobody would be willing to buy rurs forward. They could get more rurs for their dollar by waiting and buying spot.

Therefore the *expectations theory* of exchange rates tells us that the percentage difference between the forward exchange rate and today's spot rate is equal to the expected change in the spot rate:

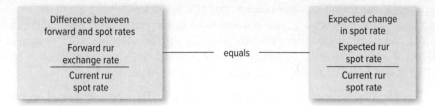

Of course, this assumes that traders don't care about risk. If they do care, the forward rate could be either higher or lower than the expected spot rate. For example, suppose that you have contracted to receive 1 million rurs in three months. You can wait until you receive the money before you change it into dollars, but this leaves you open to the risk that the price of the rur may fall over the next three months. Your alternative is to sell the rur forward. In this case, you are fixing today the price at which you will sell your rurs. Since you avoid risk by selling forward, you may be willing to do so even if the forward price of rurs is a little *lower* than the expected spot price.

Other companies may be in the opposite position. They may have contracted to pay out rurs in three months. They can wait until the end of the three months and then buy rurs, but this leaves them open to the risk that the price of the rur may rise. It is safer for these companies to fix the price today by *buying* rurs forward. These companies may, therefore, be willing to buy forward even if the forward price of the rur is a little *higher* than the expected spot price.

Thus, some companies find it safer to *sell* the rur forward, while others find it safer to *buy* the rur forward. When the first group predominates, the forward price of rurs is likely to be less than the expected spot price. When the second group predominates, the forward price is likely to be greater than the expected spot price. On average you would expect the forward price to underestimate the expected spot price just about as often as it overestimates it.

Changes in the Exchange Rate and Inflation Rates

Now we come to the third side of our quadrilateral—the relationship between changes in the spot exchange rate and inflation rates. Suppose that you notice that silver can be bought in Ruritania for 1,000 rurs a troy ounce and sold in the United States for $30.00. You think you may be on to a good thing. You take $20,000 and exchange it for $20,000 × USD/RUR50 = $20,000 × 50 = 1,000,000 rurs. That's enough to buy 1,000 ounces of silver. You put this silver on the first plane to the United States, where you sell it for $30,000. You have made a gross profit of $10,000. Of course, you have to pay transportation and insurance costs out of this, but there should still be something left over for you.

Money machines don't exist—not for long, anyway. As others notice the disparity between the price of silver in Ruritania and the price in the United States, the price will be forced up in Ruritania and down in the United States until the profit opportunity disappears. Arbitrage ensures that the dollar price of silver is about the same in the two countries. Of course, silver is a standard and easily transportable commodity, but the same forces should act to equalize the domestic and foreign prices of other goods. Those goods that can be bought more cheaply abroad will be imported, and that will force down the price of domestic products. Similarly, those goods that can be bought more cheaply in the United States will be exported, and that will force down the price of the foreign products.

This is called *purchasing power parity*.[10] Just as the price of goods in Walmart stores must be roughly the same as the price of goods in Target, so the price of goods in Ruritania when converted into dollars must be roughly the same as the price in the United States:

$$\text{Dollar price of goods in the United States} = \frac{\text{rur price of goods in Ruritania}}{\text{number of rurs per dollar}}$$

Purchasing power parity implies that any differences in the rates of inflation will be offset by a change in the exchange rate. This is often termed *relative purchasing power parity*. For example, if prices rise by 1.0% in the United States and by 11.1% in Ruritania, the number of rurs that you can buy for \$1 must rise by $1.111/1.01 - 1$, or 10%. Therefore purchasing power parity says that to estimate changes in the spot rate of exchange, you need to estimate differences in inflation rates[11]:

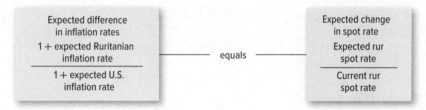

In our example,

$$\text{Current spot rate} \times \text{expected difference in inflation rates} = \text{expected spot rate}$$

$$50 \times \frac{1.111}{1.010} = 55$$

28.3 Self-Test

Suppose that gold currently costs \$1,000 an ounce in New York and £600 in London.
   a. What must be the pound dollar (GBP/USD) exchange rate?

   b. Suppose that gold prices rise by 2% in the United States and by 5% in the United Kingdom. What must be the exchange rate at the end of the year?

Interest Rates and Inflation Rates

Now for the fourth leg! Just as water always flows downhill, so capital tends to flow where returns are greatest. But investors are not interested in *nominal* returns; they care about what their money will buy. So, if investors notice that real interest rates are higher in Ruritania than in the United States, they will shift their savings into Ruritania until the expected real returns are the same in the two countries. If the expected real interest rates are equal, then

---

[10]Economists use the term *purchasing power parity* to refer to the notion that the level of prices of goods in general must be the same in the two countries. They tend to use the phrase *law of one price* when they are talking about the price of a single good.

[11]In other words, the *expected* difference in inflation rates equals the *expected* change in the exchange rate. Strictly interpreted, purchasing power parity also implies that the *actual* difference in the inflation rates always equals the *actual* change in the exchange rate.

the difference in nominal interest rates must be equal to the difference in the expected inflation rates[12]:

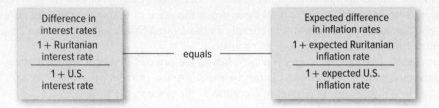

In Ruritania the real one-year interest rate is 4%:

$$\text{Ruritanian expected real interest rate} = \frac{1 + \text{Ruritanian nominal interest rate}}{1 + \text{Ruritanian expected inflation rate}} - 1$$

$$= \frac{1.155}{1.111} - 1 = 0.040$$

In the United States it is also 4%:

$$\text{U.S. expected real interest rate} = \frac{1 + \text{U.S. nominal interest rate}}{1 + \text{U.S. expected inflation rate}} - 1$$

$$= \frac{1.050}{1.010} - 1 = 0.040$$

Is Life Really That Simple?

We have described four theories that link interest rates, forward rates, spot exchange rates, and inflation rates. Of course, such simple economic theories are not going to provide an exact description of reality. We need to know how well they predict actual behavior. Let's check.

Interest Rate Parity Theory   Interest rate parity theory says that the rur rate of interest covered for exchange risk should be the same as the dollar rate. Before the financial crisis of 2007–2009, interest rate parity almost always held, provided money could be moved easily between deposits in the different currencies. In fact, dealers would *set* the forward price of a currency by looking at the difference between the interest rates on deposits. However, since 2007 there appear to have been periods when a shortage of bank regulatory capital has increased the cost of arbitrage and caused the relationship to break down.[13]

The Expectations Theory of Forward Rates   How well does the expectations theory explain the level of forward rates? Scholars who have studied exchange rates have found that forward rates typically exaggerate the likely change in the spot rate. When the forward rate appears to predict a sharp rise in the spot rate (a forward premium), the forward rate tends to overestimate

---

[12]In Section 3-5, we discussed Irving Fisher's theory that money interest rates change to reflect changes in anticipated inflation. Here, we argue that international differences in money interest rates also reflect differences in anticipated inflation. This theory is sometimes known as the *international Fisher effect*.

[13]See W. Du, A. Tepper, and A. Verdelhan, "Deviations from Covered Interest Rate Parity," *Journal of Finance* 73 (June 2018), pp. 915–957. However, for evidence that deviations from interest rate parity theory subsequently faded away, see H. Mance, "Cross-Currency Basis, RIP?" FT Alphaville, October 11, 2017, https://ftalphaville.ft.com/2017/10/11/2194672/cross-currency-basis-rip/.

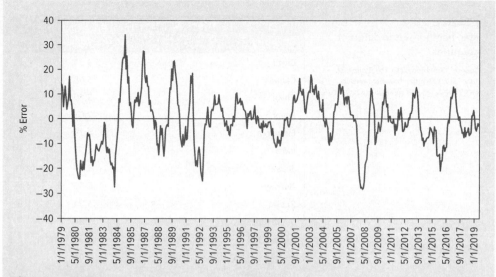

▶ FIGURE 28.1 Percentage error from using the one-year forward rate for U.K. pounds to forecast next year's spot rate. Note that the forward rate overestimates and underestimates the spot rate with about equal frequency.

Source: Bank of England.

the rise in the spot rate. Conversely, when the forward rate appears to predict a fall in the currency (a forward discount), it tends to overestimate this fall.[14]

This finding is *not* consistent with the expectations theory. Instead it looks as if sometimes companies are prepared to give up return to *buy* forward currency and other times they are prepared to give up return to *sell* forward currency. In other words, forward rates seem to contain a risk premium, but the sign of this premium swings backward and forward.[15] You can see this from Figure 28.1. Almost half the time the forward rate for the U.K. pound *overstates* the likely future spot rate and half the time it *understates* the likely spot rate, often by substantial amounts. *On average,* the forward rate and future spot rate are almost identical. In this case a company that *always* uses the forward market to protect against exchange rate movements does not pay any extra for this insurance.

That's the good news. The bad news is that the forward rate is a fairly awful forecaster of the spot rate. For example, in Figure 28.1 the large error in 1985 reflects the total failure of the forward rate to anticipate the 34% rise in the value of sterling.

Relative Purchasing Power Parity What about the third side of our quadrilateral—relative purchasing power parity? No one who has compared prices in foreign stores with prices at home really believes that prices are the same throughout the world. Look, for example, at Table 28.2, which shows the price of a Big Mac in different countries in 2020.

---

[14]Many researchers have even found that, when the forward rate predicts a rise, the spot rate is more likely to fall, and vice versa. For a readable discussion of this puzzling finding, see K. A. Froot and R. H. Thaler, "Anomalies: Foreign Exchange," *Journal of Economic Perspectives* 4 (1990), pp. 179–192.

[15]For evidence that forward exchange rates contain risk premiums that are sometimes positive and sometimes negative, see, for example, E. F. Fama, "Forward and Spot Exchange Rates," *Journal of Monetary Economics* 14 (1984), pp. 319–338.

❯TABLE 28.2 Price of Big Mac hamburgers in different countries.

Source: "Burgernomics," *The Economist,* July 15, 2020, https://www.economist.com/news/2020/07/15/the-big-mac-index.

Country	Local Price Converted to U.S. Dollars ($)
Brazil	3.91
Canada	5.08
China	3.10
Egypt	2.63
Euro area	4.79
India	2.53
Japan	3.64
Norway	5.55
Russia	1.91
South Africa	1.86
Switzerland	6.91
Turkey	2.04
United Kingdom	4.28
United States	5.71

Notice that at current rates of exchange a Big Mac cost $6.91 in Switzerland but only $5.71 in the United States. To equalize prices in the two countries, the number of Swiss francs that you could buy for your dollar needed to increase by 6.91/5.71 − 1 = 0.21, or 21%.

This suggests a possible way to make a quick buck. Why don't you buy a hamburger to-go in (say) South Africa for the equivalent of $1.86 and take it for resale in Switzerland, where the price in dollars is $6.91? The answer, of course, is that the gain would not cover the costs. The same good can be sold for different prices in different countries because transportation is costly and inconvenient.[16]

While exchange-adjusted prices may not be equal, there is rather more support for *relative purchasing power parity.* In other words, there is some relationship between inflation and changes in exchange rates. For example, between 2015 and 2020, the purchasing power of the Turkish lira declined by about 40% relative to that of the dollar. If exchange rates had not adjusted, exporters in Turkey would have found it impossible to sell their goods. But, of course, exchange rates did adjust. In fact, the value of the Turkish lira fell by 60% relative to the U.S. dollar.

In Figure 28.2, we have plotted the relative change in purchasing power for a sample of countries against the change in the exchange rate. Turkey is tucked in the bottom left-hand corner. You can see that although the relationship is far from exact, large differences in inflation rates are generally accompanied by an offsetting change in the exchange rate.[17]

Strictly speaking, purchasing power parity theory implies that the differential inflation rate is always identical to the change in the spot rate. But we don't need to go as far as that. We should be content if the *expected* difference in the inflation rates equals the *expected* change

---

[16]Of course, even within a currency area there may be considerable price variations. The price of a Big Mac, for example, differs substantially from one part of the United States to another.

[17]Note that some of the countries represented in Figure 28.2 have highly controlled economies, so that their exchange rates are not those that would exist in an unrestricted market. The interest rates shown in Figure 28.4 are subject to a similar caveat.

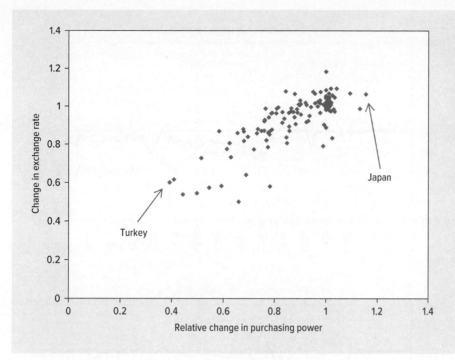

FIGURE 28.2

A decline in the exchange rate and a decline in a currency's purchasing power tend to go hand in hand. In this diagram, each of the 125 points represents the experience of a different country in the period 2015–2020. The vertical axis shows the change in the value of the foreign currency relative to the dollar. The horizontal axis shows the change in the purchasing power relative to that of the United States. The point in the lower left is Turkey.

Source: IMF, International Financial Statistics.

in the spot rate. That's all we wrote on the third side of our quadrilateral. Look, for example, at Figure 28.3. The blue line in the first plot shows that by the end of 2020, £1 sterling bought only 28% of the dollars that it did at the start of 1900. But this decline in the value of sterling was largely matched by the higher inflation rate in the United Kingdom. The red line shows that the inflation-adjusted, or *real,* exchange rate ended the century at roughly the same level as it began.[18] The second and third plots show the experiences of France and Italy, respectively. The fall in nominal exchange rates for both countries is much greater than the fall in the real rates. Adjusting for changes in currency units, the equivalent of one French franc in 2020 bought about 1% of the number of dollars that it did at the start of 1900. The equivalent of one Italian lira bought about 0.4% of the number of dollars. In both cases, the real exchange rates in 2020 are not much different from those at the beginning of the twentieth century. Of course, real exchange rates do change, sometimes quite sharply. For example, the real value of sterling fell by 13% in two weeks following the Brexit vote in 2016. However, if you were a financial manager called on to make a long-term forecast of the exchange rate, you could not have done much better than to assume that changes in the value of the currency would offset the difference in inflation rates.

28.4 Self-Test

Look at Table 28.2. Would the Egyptian pound need to fall or rise against the dollar for the price of hamburgers to be the same in the two countries?

---

[18]The real exchange rate is equal to the nominal exchange rate multiplied by the inflation differential. For example, suppose that the value of sterling falls from $1.65 = £1 to $1.50 = £1 at the same time that the price of goods rises 10% faster in the United Kingdom than in the United States. The inflation-adjusted, or real, exchange rate is unchanged at Nominal exchange rate $\times (1 + i_£)/(1 + i_\$) = 1.5 \times 1.1 = \$1.65/£$.

Source: E. Dimson, P. R. Marsh, and M. Staunton, *Triumph of the Optimist: 101 Years of Global Investment Returns* (Princeton, NJ: Princeton University Press, 2002), with updates provided by the authors.

▶ **FIGURE 28.3**

Nominal versus real exchange rates in the United Kingdom, France, and Italy. December 1899 = 100. (Values are shown on log scale.)

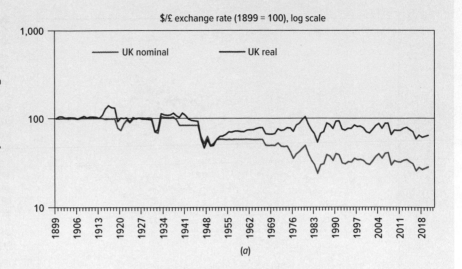

$/£ exchange rate (1899 = 100), log scale

(a)

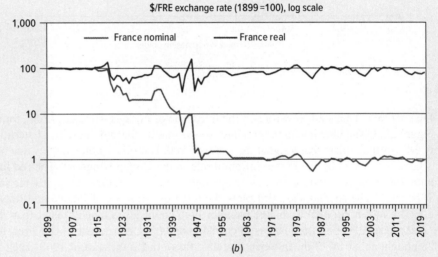

$/FRE exchange rate (1899 =100), log scale

(b)

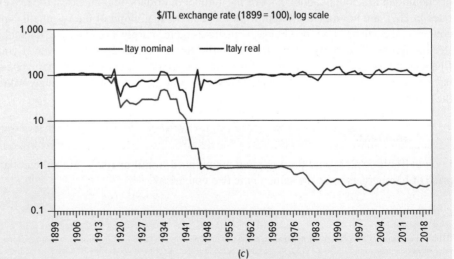

$/ITL exchange rate (1899 = 100), log scale

(c)

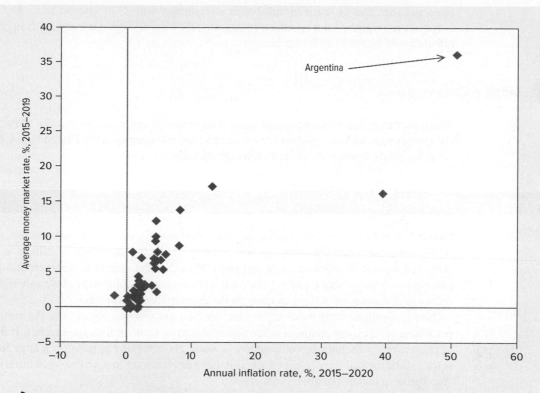

▶ **FIGURE 28.4** Countries with the highest interest rates generally have the highest inflation. In this diagram each of the 45 points represents the experience of a different country.

Source: IMF, International Financial Statistics.

Equal Real Interest Rates Finally we come to the relationship between interest rates in different countries. Do we have a single world capital market with the same *real* rate of interest in all countries? Does the difference in money interest rates equal the difference in the expected inflation rates?

This is not an easy question to answer since we cannot observe *expected* inflation. However, in Figure 28.4, we have plotted the average interest rate in each of 45 countries against the average inflation rate. Switzerland is tucked into the bottom-left corner of the chart, while Argentina is represented by the dot in the top-right corner. You can see that, in general, the countries with the highest interest rates also had the highest inflation rates. There were much smaller differences between the real rates of interest than between the nominal (or money) rates.

This may be a good point at which to offer a warning: Do not naively borrow in currencies with the lowest interest rates. Those low interest rates may reflect the fact that investors expect inflation to be low and the currency to appreciate. In this case, the gain that you realize from "cheap" borrowing is liable to be offset by the high cost of the currency that is needed to service the loan. Many have learned this lesson the hard way. For example, some years ago over 500,000 Poles were lured by low Swiss interest rates into taking out mortgages in Swiss francs. When the Swiss franc jumped by 23% against the Polish zloty, many of those borrowers found themselves in big trouble.

Professional foreign exchange traders may, from time to time, enter into *carry trades* in which they deliberately take on currency risk by borrowing in countries with low interest rates and then use the cash to buy bonds in countries with high interest rates. But careful corporate managers do not speculate in this way; they use foreign currency loans to offset the effect that exchange rate fluctuations have on the company's business.

28-3 Hedging Currency Risk

Sharp exchange rate movements can make a large dent in corporate profits. To illustrate how companies cope with this problem, we look at a typical company in the United States, Outland Steel, and walk through its foreign exchange operations.

EXAMPLE 28.1 ● Outland Steel

Outland Steel has a small but profitable export business. Contracts involve substantial delays in payment, but since the company has a policy of always invoicing in dollars, it is fully protected against changes in exchange rates. Recently, the export department has become unhappy with this practice and believes that it is causing the company to lose valuable export orders to firms that are willing to quote in the customer's own currency.

You sympathize with these arguments, but you are worried about how the firm should price long-term export contracts when payment is to be made in foreign currency. If the value of that currency declines before payment is made, the company may suffer a large loss. You want to take the currency risk into account, but you also want to give the sales force as much freedom of action as possible.

Notice that Outland can insure against its currency risk by selling the foreign currency forward. This means that it can separate the problem of negotiating sales contracts from that of managing the company's foreign exchange exposure. The sales force can allow for currency risk by pricing on the basis of the forward exchange rate. And you, as financial manager, can decide whether the company *ought* to hedge.

What is the cost of hedging? You sometimes hear managers say that it is equal to the difference between the forward rate and *today's* spot rate. That is wrong. If Outland does not hedge, it will receive the spot rate at the time that the customer pays for the steel. Therefore, the cost of insurance is the difference between the forward rate and the expected spot rate when payment is received.

Insure or speculate? We generally vote for insurance. First, it makes life simpler for the firm and allows it to concentrate on its main business. Second, it does not cost much. (In fact, the cost is zero on average if the forward rate equals the expected spot rate, as the expectations theory of forward rates implies.) Third, the foreign currency market seems reasonably efficient, at least for the major currencies. Speculation should be a zero-NPV game, unless financial managers have information that is not available to the pros who make the market.

Is there any other way that Outland can protect itself against exchange loss? Of course. It can borrow foreign currency against its foreign receivables, sell the currency spot, and invest the proceeds in the United States. Interest rate parity theory tells us that in free markets the difference between selling forward and selling spot should be equal to the difference between the interest that you have to pay overseas and the interest that you can earn at home.

● ● ● ● ●

Our discussion of Outland's export business illustrates four practical implications of our simple theories about forward exchange rates. First, you can use forward rates to adjust for exchange risk in contract pricing. Second, the expectations theory suggests that protection against exchange risk is usually worth having. Third, interest rate parity theory reminds us that you can hedge either by selling forward or by borrowing foreign currency and selling spot. Fourth, the cost of forward cover is not the difference between the forward rate and *today's* spot rate; it is the difference between the forward rate and the expected spot rate when the forward contract matures.

Perhaps we should add a fifth implication. You don't make money simply by buying currencies that go up in value and selling those that go down. For example, suppose that you buy Narnian leos and sell them after a year for 2% more than you paid for them. Should you give yourself a pat on the back? That depends on the interest that you have earned on your leos. If the interest rate on leos is 2 percentage points less than the interest rate on dollars, the profit on the currency is exactly canceled out by the reduction in interest income. Thus, you make money from currency speculation only if you can predict whether the exchange rate will change by more or less than the interest rate differential. In other words, you must be able to predict whether the exchange rate will change by more or less than the forward premium or discount.

Transaction Exposure and Economic Exposure

The exchange risk from Outland Steel's export business is due to delays in foreign currency payments and is therefore referred to as *transaction exposure*. Transaction exposure can be easily identified and hedged. Since a 1% fall in the value of the foreign currency results in a 1% fall in Outland's dollar receipts, for every euro or yen that Outland is owed by its customers, it needs to sell forward one euro or one yen.[19]

BEYOND THE PAGE

Operational hedging by auto producers

mhhe.com/brealey14e

However, Outland may still be affected by currency fluctuations even if its customers do not owe it a cent. For example, Outland may be in competition with Swedish steel producers. If the value of the Swedish krona falls, Outland will need to cut its prices in order to compete.[20] Outland may be able to protect itself against such an eventuality by selling the krona forward. In this case the loss on Outland's steel business will be offset by the profit on its forward sale.

Notice that Outland's exposure to the krona is not limited to specific transactions that have already been entered into. Financial managers often refer to this broader type of exposure as *economic exposure*.[21] Economic exposure is less easy to measure than transaction exposure. For example, it is clear that the value of Outland Steel is positively related to the value of the krona, so to hedge its position it needs to borrow kronor or sell kronor forward. But, in practice, it may be hard to say exactly how many kronor Outland needs to borrow.

Large Swiss companies, such as Nestlé or the Swatch Group, sell their products around the world. Therefore, like Outland Steel, they need to manage their economic exposure. One solution is to undertake operational hedging by balancing production closely with sales. Look, for example, at Table 28.3, which summarizes the overseas sales and costs for a sample of well-known Swiss companies. Notice that in the case of Nestlé and Swiss Re, sales and costs were almost perfectly matched. These companies were, therefore, relatively immune to fluctuations in the exchange rate. By contrast, in the case of Swatch and Richemont, a substantial proportion of production costs arose in Switzerland, and therefore both companies were exposed to an appreciation of the Swiss franc.

BEYOND THE PAGE

Operational hedging and the Swiss franc

mhhe.com/brealey14e

These Swiss companies also used financial hedges to reduce currency risk. For example, Richemont stated in 2019 that its policy was to hedge up to 70% of the next year's forecast

---

[19] To put it another way, the hedge ratio is 1.0.

[20] Of course, if purchasing power parity always held, the fall in the value of the krona would be matched by higher inflation in Sweden. The risk for Outland is that the *real* value of the krona may decline so that when measured in dollars, Swedish costs are lower than previously. Unfortunately, it is much easier to hedge against a change in the *nominal* exchange rate than against a change in the *real* rate.

[21] Financial managers also refer to *translation exposure*, which measures the effect of an exchange rate change on the company's financial statements.

		Swiss Franc		Euro		U.S. Dollar		Other	
Company	**Activity**	**Sales**	**Costs**	**Sales**	**Costs**	**Sales**	**Costs**	**Sales**	**Costs**
Adecco	Employment agency	2	2	48	45	20	19	30	34
Holcim	Cement	4	6	10	10	21	25	65	59
Lindt & Sprüngli	Chocolate	5	12	43	35	40	25	12	28
Nestlé	Food producer	2	5	30	30	30	30	38	35
Novartis	Pharmaceuticals	2	15	26	25	36	40	36	20
Richemont	Luxury goods	5	20	30	20	50	40	15	20
Swatch Group	Luxury goods	10	30	30	20	50	25	10	25
Swiss Re	Insurance	3	5	20	20	40	40	37	35

❭**TABLE 28.3**   Estimated proportion of sales and costs in 2017 for major Swiss companies that derive from particular currency areas.

Source: UBS.

currency exposure in U.S. dollars, Hong Kong dollars, Chinese yuan, Japanese yen, UAE dirham, and Singapore dollars.

> **28.5 Self-Test**
>
> A Ford dealer in the United States never needs to buy or sell foreign currency. Does that mean it has no currency risk?

28-4 International Investment Decisions

Suppose that the Swiss pharmaceutical company, Roche, is evaluating a proposal to build a new plant in the United States. To calculate the project's net present value, Roche forecasts the following dollar cash flows from the project:

Cash Flows ($ millions)					
C_0	C_1	C_2	C_3	C_4	C_5
-1,300	400	450	510	575	650

These cash flows are stated in dollars. So to calculate their net present value Roche discounts them at the dollar cost of capital. (Remember dollars need to be discounted at a *dollar* rate, not the Swiss franc rate.) Suppose this cost of capital is 12%. Then

$$\text{NPV} = -1,300 + \frac{400}{1.12} + \frac{450}{1.12^2} + \frac{510}{1.12^3} + \frac{575}{1.12^4} + \frac{650}{1.12^5} = \$513 \text{ million}$$

To convert this net present value to Swiss francs, the manager can simply multiply the dollar NPV by the spot rate of exchange. For example, if the spot rate is USD/CHF = 1.2 then the NPV in Swiss francs is

NPV in francs = NPV in dollars × USD/CHF = 513 × 1.2 = 616 million francs

Notice one very important feature of this calculation. Roche does not need to forecast whether the dollar is likely to strengthen or weaken against the Swiss franc. No currency forecast is needed because the company can hedge its foreign exchange exposure. In that case, the decision to accept or reject the pharmaceutical project in the United States is totally separate from the decision to bet on the outlook for the dollar. For example, it would be foolish for Roche to accept a poor project in the United States just because management is optimistic about the outlook for the dollar; if Roche wishes to speculate in this way it can simply buy dollars forward. Equally, it would be foolish for Roche to reject a good project just because management is pessimistic about the dollar. The company would do much better to go ahead with the project and sell dollars forward. In that way, it would get the best of both worlds.[22]

When Roche ignores currency risk and discounts the dollar cash flows at a dollar cost of capital, it is implicitly assuming that the currency risk is hedged. Let us check this by calculating the number of Swiss francs that Roche would receive if it hedged the currency risk by selling forward each future dollar cash flow.

We need first to calculate the forward rate of exchange between dollars and francs. This depends on the interest rates in the United States and Switzerland. For example, suppose that the dollar interest rate is 6% and the Swiss franc interest rate is 4%. Then interest rate parity theory tells us that the one-year forward exchange rate is

$$\text{USD/CHF} \times (1 + r_{\text{SFr}})/(1 + r_\$) = \frac{1.2 \times 1.04}{1.06} = 1.177$$

Similarly, the two-year forward rate is

$$\text{USD/CHF} \times (1 + r_{\text{SFr}})^2/(1 + r_\$)^2 = \frac{1.2 \times 1.04^2}{1.06^2} = 1.155$$

So, if Roche hedges its cash flows against exchange rate risk, the number of Swiss francs it will receive in each year is equal to the dollar cash flow times the forward rate of exchange:

Cash Flows (millions of Swiss francs)					
C_0	C_1	C_2	C_3	C_4	C_5
$-1{,}300 \times 1.2$	400×1.177	450×1.155	510×1.133	575×1.112	650×1.091
$= -1{,}560$	$= 471$	$= 520$	$= 578$	$= 639$	$= 709$

These cash flows are in Swiss francs and therefore they need to be discounted at the risk-adjusted Swiss franc discount rate. Since the Swiss rate of interest is lower than the dollar rate, the risk-adjusted discount rate must also be correspondingly lower. The formula for converting from the required dollar return to the required Swiss franc return is[23]

$$(1 + \text{Swiss franc return}) = (1 + \text{dollar return}) \times \frac{(1 + \text{Swiss franc interest rate})}{(1 + \text{dollar interest rate})}$$

In our example,

$$(1 + \text{Swiss franc return}) = 1.12 \times \frac{1.04}{1.06} = 1.099$$

---

[22]There is a general point here that is not confined to currency hedging. Whenever you face an investment that appears to have a positive NPV, decide what it is that you are betting on and then think whether there is a more direct way to place the bet. For example, if a copper mine looks profitable only because you are unusually optimistic about the price of copper, then maybe you would do better to buy copper futures or the shares of other copper producers rather than opening a copper mine.

[23]The following example should give you a feel for the idea behind this formula. Suppose the spot rate for Swiss francs is SFr 1.2 = $1. Interest rate parity tells us that the forward rate must be 1.2 × 1.04/1.06 = SFr 1.177/$. Now suppose that a share costs $100 and will pay an expected $112 at the end of the year. The cost to Swiss investors of buying the share is 100 × 1.2 = SFr 120. If the Swiss investors sell forward the expected payoff, they will receive an expected 112 × 1.177 = SFr 131.9. The expected return in Swiss francs is 131.9/120 − 1 = 0.099, or 9.9%. More simply, the Swiss franc return is 1.12 × 1.04/1.06 − 1 = 0.099.

Thus, the risk-adjusted discount rate in dollars is 12%, but the discount rate in Swiss francs is only 9.9%.

All that remains is to discount the Swiss franc cash flows at the 9.9% risk-adjusted discount rate:

$$NPV = -1,560 + \frac{471}{1.099} + \frac{520}{1.099^2} + \frac{578}{1.099^3} + \frac{639}{1.099^4} + \frac{709}{1.099^5}$$

$$= 616 \text{ million francs}$$

Everything checks. We obtain exactly the same net present value by (1) ignoring currency risk and discounting Roche's dollar cash flows at the dollar cost of capital and (2) calculating the cash flows in francs on the assumption that Roche hedges the currency risk and then discounting these Swiss franc cash flows at the franc cost of capital.

To repeat: When deciding whether to invest overseas, separate out the investment decision from the decision to take on currency risk. This means that your views about future exchange rates should *not* enter into the investment decision. The simplest way to calculate the NPV of an overseas investment is to forecast the cash flows in the foreign currency and discount them at the foreign currency cost of capital. The alternative is to calculate the cash flows that you would receive if you hedged the foreign currency risk. In this case, you need to translate the foreign currency cash flows into your own currency *using the forward exchange rate* and then discount these domestic currency cash flows at the domestic cost of capital. If the two methods don't give the same answer, you have probably made a mistake.

When Roche analyzes the proposal to build a plant in the United States, it is able to ignore the outlook for the dollar *only because it is free to hedge the currency risk.* Because investment in a pharmaceutical plant does not come packaged with an investment in the dollar, the opportunity for firms to hedge allows for better investment decisions.

28.6 Self-Test

Aberdeen Corp is evaluating a simple possible project in Ruritania. It costs 90,000 rurs and produces a single certain cash flow of 121,000 rurs in two years. The Ruritanian interest rate is 10% and the U.S. rate is 5%. The current spot exchange rate is USD/RUR = 2. Calculate the project's dollar NPV by first discounting the rur cash flows. Show that you get the same answer if you discount the equivalent dollar cash flows.

The Cost of Capital for International Investments

Roche should discount dollar cash flows at a dollar cost of capital. But how should a Swiss company like Roche calculate a cost of capital in dollars for an investment in the United States? There is no simple, consensus for answering this question, but we suggest the following procedure as a start.

First you need to decide on the risk of a U.S. pharmaceutical investment to a Swiss investor. You could look at the betas of a sample of U.S. pharmaceutical companies *relative to the Swiss market index.*

Why measure betas relative to the Swiss index, while a U.S. counterpart such as Merck would measure betas relative to the U.S. index? The answer lies in Section 7-4, where we explained that risk cannot be considered in isolation; it depends on the other securities in the investor's portfolio. Beta measures risk *relative to the investor's portfolio.* If U.S. investors already hold the U.S. market, an additional dollar invested at home is just more of the same. But if Swiss investors hold the Swiss market, an investment in the United States can reduce their risk because the Swiss and U.S. markets are not perfectly correlated. That explains why an investment in the United States can be lower risk for Roche's shareholders than for Merck's shareholders. It also explains why Roche's shareholders may be willing to accept a relatively low expected return from a U.S. investment.[24]

Suppose that you decide that the investment's beta relative to the Swiss market is 0.8 and that the market risk premium in Switzerland is 7.4%. Then the required return on the project can be estimated as

$$\text{Required return} = \text{Swiss interest rate} + (\text{beta} \times \text{Swiss market risk premium})$$
$$= 4 + (0.8 \times 7.4) = 9.9$$

This is the project's cost of capital measured in Swiss francs. We used it to discount the expected *Swiss franc* cash flows if Roche hedged the project against currency risk. We cannot use it to discount the *dollar* cash flows from the project.

To discount the expected *dollar* cash flows, we need to convert the Swiss franc cost of capital to a dollar cost of capital. This means running our earlier calculation in reverse:

$$(1 + \text{dollar return}) = (1 + \text{Swiss franc return}) \times \frac{(1 + \text{dollar interest rate})}{(1 + \text{Swiss franc interest rate})}$$

In our example,

$$(1 + \text{dollar return}) = 1.099 \times \frac{1.06}{1.04} = 1.12$$

We used this 12% dollar cost of capital to discount the forecasted dollar cash flows from the project.

When a company measures risk relative to its domestic market as in our example, its managers are implicitly assuming that shareholders hold simply domestic stocks. That is not a bad approximation, particularly in the United States. Although U.S. investors can reduce their risk by holding an internationally diversified portfolio of shares, they generally invest only a small proportion of their money overseas. Why they are so shy is a puzzle. It looks as if they are worried about the costs of investing overseas, such as the extra costs involved in identifying which stocks to buy, or the possibility of unfair treatment by foreign companies or governments.

The world is getting smaller and "flatter," however, and investors everywhere are increasing their holdings of foreign securities. Pension funds and other institutional investors have diversified internationally, and dozens of mutual funds have been set up for people who want to invest abroad. If investors throughout the world held the world portfolio, then costs of capital would converge. The cost of capital would still depend on the risk of the investment, but not on the domicile of the investing company. There is some evidence that for large U.S. firms it does not make much difference whether a U.S. or global beta is used. For firms in smaller countries, the evidence is not so clear-cut and sometimes a global beta may be different from the local beta and more appropriate.[25]

28-5   Political Risk

So far, we have focused on the management of exchange rate risk, but managers also worry about political risk. By this they mean the threat that a government will change the rules of the game—that is, break a promise or understanding—*after* the investment is made. Of course, political risks are not confined to overseas investments. Businesses in every country

---

[24]When an investor holds an efficient portfolio, the expected reward for risk on each stock in the portfolio is proportional to its beta *relative to the portfolio*. So if the Swiss market index is an efficient portfolio for Swiss investors, then these investors will want Roche to invest in the United States if the expected rate of return more than compensates for the investment's beta relative to the Swiss index.

[25]See R. M. Stulz, "The Cost of Capital in Internationally Integrated Markets: The Case of Nestlé," *European Financial Management* 1, no. 1 (1995), pp. 11–22; R. S. Harris, R. C. Marston, D. R. Mishra, and T. J. O'Brien, "Ex Ante Cost of Capital Estimates of S&P 500 Firms: The Choice between Global and Domestic CAPM," *Financial Management* (Autumn 2003), pp. 51–66; and Standard & Poor's, "Domestic vs. Global CAPM," *Global Cost of Capital Report,* 4th Quarter 2003.

are exposed to the risk of unanticipated actions by governments or the courts. But in some parts of the world foreign companies are particularly vulnerable.

Several consultancy services offer analyses of political and economic risks and draw up country rankings.[26] For example, Table 28.4 is an extract from the 2019 political risk rankings provided by the PRS Group. Each country is scored on 15 separate dimensions. You can see that Norway comes top of the class overall, while Venezuela languishes near the bottom.

Some managers dismiss political risk as an act of God, like a hurricane or earthquake. But the most successful multinational companies structure their business to reduce political risk. Foreign governments are not likely to expropriate a local business if it cannot operate without the support of its parent. For example, the foreign subsidiaries of American computer manufacturers or pharmaceutical companies would have relatively little value if they were cut off from the know-how of their parents. Such operations are much less likely to be expropriated than, say, a mining operation that can be operated as a stand-alone venture.

We are not recommending that you turn your silver mine into a pharmaceutical company, but you may be able to plan your overseas manufacturing operations to improve your bargaining position with foreign governments. For example, Ford has integrated its overseas operations so that the manufacture of components, subassemblies, and complete automobiles is spread across plants in a number of countries. None of these plants would have much value on its own, and Ford can switch production between plants if the political climate in one country deteriorates.

❯ **TABLE 28.4** Political risk scores for a sample of countries.

Source: International Country Risk Guide, a publication of The PRS Group, Inc. (www.prsgroup.com), June 2019.

Maximum Score 100		
Country	Total Score	Rank
Venezuela	42.5	139
Turkey	58.8	123
Argentina	62.5	112
Brazil	70.8	65
India	71.3	61
China	72.8	54
Russia	73.0	53
France	74.5	45
Italy	75.8	39
United States	77.8	27
United Kingdom	78.0	26
Australia	79.5	23
Japan	81.3	17
Canada	82.0	15
Korea, Republic	82.3	14
Germany	83.3	9
Sweden	84.3	6
Singapore	86.5	4
Switzerland	88.5	2
Norway	89.3	1

---

[26]For a discussion of these services see C. Erb, C. R. Harvey, and T. Viskanta, "Political Risk, Financial Risk, and Economic Risk," *Financial Analysts Journal* 52 (1996), pp. 28–46. Also, Campbell Harvey's webpage (https://people.duke.edu/~charvey/) is a useful source of information on political risk.

Multinational corporations have also devised financing arrangements to help keep foreign governments honest. For example, suppose your firm is contemplating an investment of $500 million to reopen the San Tomé silver mine in Costaguana with modern machinery, smelting equipment, and shipping facilities.[27] The Costaguanan government agrees to invest in roads and other infrastructure and to take 20% of the silver produced by the mine in lieu of taxes. The agreement is to run for 25 years.

The project's NPV on these assumptions is quite attractive. But what happens if a new government comes into power five years from now and imposes a 50% tax on "any precious metals exported from the Republic of Costaguana"? Or changes the government's share of output from 20% to 50%? Or simply takes over the mine "with fair compensation to be determined in due course by the Minister of Natural Resources of the Republic of Costaguana"?

No contract can absolutely restrain sovereign power. But you can arrange project financing to make these acts as painful as possible for the foreign government. For example, you might set up the mine as a subsidiary corporation, which then borrows a large fraction of the required investment from a consortium of major international banks. If your firm guarantees the loan, make sure the guarantee stands only if the Costaguanan government honors its contract. The government will be reluctant to break the contract if that causes a default on the loans and undercuts the country's credit standing with the international banking system.

If possible, you should arrange for the World Bank (or one of its affiliates) to finance part of the project or to guarantee your loans against political risk. Few governments have the courage to take on the World Bank. Here is another variation on the same theme. Arrange to borrow, say, $450 million through the Costaguanan Development Agency. In other words, the development agency borrows in international capital markets and relends to the San Tomé mine. Your firm agrees to stand behind the loan as long as the government keeps its promises. If it does keep them, the loan is your liability. If not, the loan is *its* liability.

Political risk is not confined to the risk of expropriation. Multinational companies are always exposed to the criticism that they siphon funds out of countries in which they do business, and, therefore, governments are tempted to limit their freedom to repatriate profits. This is most likely to happen when there is considerable uncertainty about the rate of exchange, which is usually when you would most like to get your money out. Here, again, a little forethought can help. For example, there are often more onerous restrictions on the payment of dividends to the parent than on the payment of interest or principal on debt. Royalty payments and management fees are less sensitive than dividends, particularly if they are levied equally on all foreign operations. A company can also, within limits, alter the price of goods that are bought or sold within the group, and it can require more or less prompt payment for such goods.

Calculating NPVs for investment projects becomes exceptionally difficult when political risks are significant. You have to estimate expected cash flows and project life with extra caution. You may want to take a look at the payback period (see Chapter 5), on the theory that quick-payback projects are less exposed to political risks. But do not try to compensate for political risks by adding casual fudge factors to discount rates. Fudge factors spawn bias and confusion, as we explained in Chapter 9.

28.7 Self-Test

Moria Mining is considering a proposal to develop a new open-cast mine in Khazaddum. It forecasts that the mine could produce cash flows of 20 million Khazad dollars a year in perpetuity. Normally, Moria would use a discount rate of 10% for such a project. However, in recent instances, the government has expropriated half the cash flows, and therefore, the company discounts the cash flows at 20%. Is this a sensible way to allow for political risk. What do you think is the present value of the mine?

---

[27]The early history of the San Tomé mine is described in Joseph Conrad's *Nostromo.*

● ● ● ● ●

KEY TAKEAWAYS

- **Exchange rates** Spot exchange rates are the prices of foreign currency for immediate delivery. Forward exchange rates are the prices agreed to today for delivery of a currency at a future date. The U.S. dollar is generally the basis for an exchange rate quote. In other words, a dealer will quote the number of units of the foreign currency that can be bought for one dollar. The euro, British pound, and the Australian and New Zealand dollars are exceptions. For example, dealers will quote the number of U.S. dollars that you can buy for one euro.

- **Currencies, interest rates, and inflation** The international financial manager has to cope with different currencies, interest rates, and inflation rates. To produce order out of chaos, the manager needs some model of how they are related. We described four simple theories:

    1. *Interest rate parity* states that the interest differential between two countries must be equal to the difference between the forward and spot exchange rates:

    $$\frac{1 + \text{foreign interest rate}}{1 + \text{domestic interest rate}} = \frac{\text{forward exchange rate}}{\text{spot exchange rate}}$$

    In the international markets, arbitrage ensures that parity generally holds. There are two ways to hedge against exchange risk: One is to take out forward cover; the other is to borrow or lend abroad. Interest rate parity tells us that the costs of the two methods should be the same.

    2. The *expectations theory* of exchange rates states that the forward rate equals the expected spot rate:

    $$\frac{\text{forward exchange rate}}{\text{current spot exchange rate}} = \frac{\text{expected future spot exchange rate}}{\text{current spot exchange rate}}$$

    In practice, forward rates seem to incorporate risk premiums, but for any currency this premium is about equally likely to be negative as positive.

    3. Relative *purchasing power parity* states that the real exchange rate is constant, so that the expected change in the spot exchange rate is matched by the expected change in the inflation rate:

    $$\frac{1 + \text{expected foreign inflation rate}}{1 + \text{expected domestic inflation rate}} = \frac{\text{expected spot exchange rate}}{\text{current spot exchange rate}}$$

    In the short run, real exchange rates can fluctuate sharply. On the other hand, a financial manager who needs to make a long-term forecast of the exchange rate cannot do much better than to assume that the real exchange rate will not change.

    4. In an integrated world, *real rates of interest* would have to be the same. Thus,

    $$\frac{1 + \text{foreign nominal interest rate}}{1 + \text{expected foreign inflation rate}} = \frac{1 + \text{domestic interest rate}}{1 + \text{expected domestic inflation rate}}$$

    In practice, government regulation and taxes can cause differences in real interest rates. But do not simply borrow where interest rates are lowest. Those countries are also likely to have the lowest inflation rates and the strongest currencies.

- **Foreign exchange risk** Fluctuating exchange rates are a potential source of risk. Some companies can mitigate this risk by *operational hedging* so that their foreign currency revenues are matched by their foreign currency costs. *Transaction risk* arises when operational hedging cannot eliminate the risk in future foreign currency cash flows. Forward markets or the loan markets can be used to hedge the transaction exposure that arises from future commitments in a foreign currency. But the company's financing choices also need to reflect the impact of a change in the exchange rate on the value of the entire business. This is known as *economic exposure*.

- **International investment** Because companies can hedge their currency risk, the decision to invest in another country does not involve currency forecasts. There are two ways to calculate the NPV of an overseas project. The first is to forecast the foreign currency cash flows and to discount them at the foreign currency cost of capital. The second is to translate the foreign currency cash flows into domestic currency, assuming that they are hedged against exchange rate risk. These domestic currency flows can then be discounted at the domestic cost of capital. The answers should be identical.

- **Political risk** International investments may also be exposed to political risk. However, firms may be able to structure operations or financing to reduce the chances that foreign governments will change the rules of the game.

● ● ● ● ●

FURTHER READING

There are several useful textbooks in international finance. Here is a small selection:

P. Sercu, *International Finance: Theory into Practice* (Princeton, NJ: Princeton University Press, 2009).

D. K. Eiteman, A. I. Stonehill, and M. H. Moffett, *Multinational Business Finance,* 15th ed. (Cambridge, UK: Pearson, 2020).

A. C. Shapiro and P. Hanouna, *Multinational Financial Management,* 11th ed. (New York: John Wiley & Sons, 2019).

Here are some general discussions of international investment decisions and associated exchange risks:

G. Allayannis, J. Ihrig, and J. P. Weston, "Exchange-Rate Hedging: Financial versus Operational Strategies," *American Economic Review* 91 (May 2001), pp. 391–395.

D. R. Lessard, "Global Competition and Corporate Finance in the 1990s," *Journal of Applied Corporate Finance* 3 (Winter 1991), pp. 59–72.

M. D. Levi and P. Sercu, "Erroneous and Valid Reasons for Hedging Foreign Exchange Exposure," *Journal of Multinational Financial Management* 1 (1991), pp. 25–37.

Listed below are a few of the articles on the relationship between interest rates, exchange rates, and inflation:

Forward and spot exchange rates

M. D. Evans and K. K. Lewis, "Do Long-Term Swings in the Dollar Affect Estimates of the Risk Premia?" *Review of Financial Studies* 8 (1995), pp. 709–742.

Interest rate parity

K. Clinton, "Transaction Costs and Covered Interest Arbitrage: Theory and Evidence," *Journal of Political Economy* 96 (April 1988), pp. 358–370.

W. Du, A. Tepper, and A. Verdelhan, "Deviations from Covered Interest Rate Parity," *Journal of Finance* 73 (June 2018), pp. 915–957.

Purchasing power parity

K. Froot and K. Rogoff, "Perspectives on PPP and Long-Run Real Exchange Rates," in G. Grossman and K. Rogoff (eds.), *Handbook of International Economics* (Amsterdam: North-Holland Publishing Company, 1995).

K. Rogoff, "The Purchasing Power Parity Puzzle," *Review of Economic Literature* 34 (June 1996), pp. 667–668.

A. M. Taylor and M. P. Taylor, "The Purchasing Power Parity Debate," *Journal of Economic Perspectives* 18 (Autumn 2004), pp. 135–158.

PROBLEM SETS

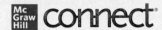

Select problems are available in McGraw Hill's *Connect*.
Please see the preface for more information.

1. **Exchange rates (S28.1)** Look at Table 28.1.

   a. How many Turkish lira do you get for your dollar?

   b. What is the three-month forward rate for the lira?

   c. Is the lira at a forward discount or premium on the dollar?

   d. Use the one-year forward rate to calculate the annual percentage discount or premium on the lira.

   e. If the one-year interest rate on dollars is 2% annually compounded, what do you think is the one-year interest rate on the lira?

   f. According to the expectations theory, what is the expected spot rate for the lira in three months' time?

   g. According to purchasing power parity theory, what then is the expected difference in the three-month rate of price inflation in the United States and Turkey?

2. **Exchange rates (S28.1)** Table 28.1 shows the three-month forward rate on the South African rand.

   a. Is the rand at a forward discount or premium on the dollar?

   b. What is the annual *percentage* discount or premium?

   c. If you have no other information about the two currencies, what is your best guess about the spot rate on the rand three months hence?

   d. Suppose that you expect to receive 100,000 rand in three months. How many dollars is this likely to be worth?

3. **Some basic relationships (S28.2)** Define each of the following theories in a sentence or simple equation:

   a. Interest rate parity.

   b. Expectations theory of forward rates.

   c. Purchasing power parity.

   d. International capital market equilibrium (relationship of real and nominal interest rates in different countries).

4. **Interest rate parity (S28.2)** Look again at Table 28.1. Which countries would you expect to have a lower one-year interest rate than the United States?

5. **Interest rate parity (S28.2)** The following table shows interest rates and exchange rates for the U.S. dollar and the Lilliputian nano. The spot exchange rate is USD/NAN = 15. Complete the missing entries:

	1 Month	3 Months	1 Year
Dollar interest rate (annually compounded)	4.0	4.5	?
Nano interest rate (annually compounded)	8.2	?	9.8
Forward nanos per dollar	?	?	15.6
Forward discount on nano (% per year)	?	4.8	?

6. **Interest rate parity (S28.2)** Look at Table 28.1. If the three-month interest rate on dollars is 0.2%, what do you think is the three-month interest rate on the Brazilian real? Explain what would happen if the rate were substantially above your figure.

〉TABLE 28.5
Interest rates and
exchange rates.

*ªNumber of units of for-
eign currency that can be
exchanged for $1.*

	Interest Rate (%)	Spot Exchange Rate*ª*	1-Year Forward Exchange Rate*ª*
United States (dollar)	3	—	—
Costaguana (pulga)	23	10,000	11,942
Westonia (ruple)	5	2.6	2.65
Gloccamorra (pint)	8	17.1	18.2
Anglosaxophonia (wasp)	4.1	2.3	2.28

7. **Interest rate parity (S28.2)** Table 28.5 shows the annual interest rate (annually compounded) and exchange rates against the dollar for different currencies. Are there any arbitrage opportunities? If so, how would you secure a positive cash flow today, while zeroing out all future cash flows?

8. **Purchasing power parity (S28.2)** In September 2021, the exchange rate for the Narnian leo was USD/LEO = 2,419. Inflation in the year to September 2022 was about 30% in Narnia and 2% in the United States.

   a. If purchasing power parity held, what should have been the nominal exchange rate in September 2022?

   b. The actual exchange rate in September 2022 in the midst of a currency crisis was USD/LEO = 8,325. What was the change in the *real* exchange rate?

9. **Interest rates and exchange rates (S28.2)** Penny Farthing, the treasurer of International Bicycles Inc., has noticed that the interest rate in Japan is below the rates in most other countries. Therefore, she is suggesting that the company should make an issue of Japanese yen bonds. Does this make sense?

10. **Currency risk (S28.3)** Suppose that in 2025, one- and two-year interest rates are 5.2% in the United States and 1.0% in Japan. The spot exchange rate is USD/JPY = 120.22. Suppose that one year later, interest rates are 3% in both countries, while the value of the yen has appreciated to USD/JPY = 115.0.

    a. Benjamin Pinkerton from New York invested in a U.S. two-year zero-coupon bond at the start of the period and sold it after one year. What was his return?

    b. Madame Butterfly from Nagasaki bought some dollars. She also invested in the two-year U.S. zero-coupon bond and sold it after one year. What was her return in yen?

    c. Suppose that Ms. Butterfly had correctly forecasted the price at which she sold her bond and that she hedged her investment against currency risk. How could she have hedged? What would have been her return in yen?

11. **Currency risk (S28.3)** Companies may be affected by changes in the nominal exchange rate or in the real exchange rate. Explain how this can occur. Which changes are easiest to hedge against?

12. **Currency risk (S28.3)** You have bid for a possible export order that would provide a cash inflow of €1 million in six months. The spot exchange rate is EUR/USD = 1.3549 and the six-month forward rate is EUR/USD = 1.3620. There are two sources of uncertainty: (1) the euro could appreciate or depreciate, and (2) you may or may not receive the export order. Illustrate in each case the final payoffs if (a) you sell 1 million euros forward, and (b) you buy a six-month option to sell euros with an exercise price of EUR/USD = 1.3620.

13. **Currency risk (S28.3)** In July 2020, an American investor buys 1,000 shares in a Mexican company at a price of 500 pesos each. The share does not pay any dividend. A year later, she sells the shares for 550 pesos each. The exchange rates when she buys the stock are shown in Table 28.1. Suppose that the exchange rate at the time of sale is USD/MXN = 25.

    a. How many dollars does she invest?

    b. What is her total return in pesos? In dollars?

    c. Do you think that she has made an exchange rate profit or loss? Explain.

14. **Currency hedging (S28.3)** An importer in the United States is due to take delivery of clothing from Mexico in six months. The price is fixed in Mexican pesos. Which of the following transactions could eliminate the importer's exchange risk?

    a. Sell six-month call options on pesos.

    b. Buy pesos forward.

    c. Sell pesos forward.

    d. Sell pesos in the currency futures market.

    e. Borrow pesos; buy dollars at the spot exchange rate.

    f. Sell pesos at the spot exchange rate; lend dollars.

15. **Currency hedging (S28.3)** A U.S. company has committed to pay 10 million kronor to a Swedish company in one year. What is the cost (in present value) of covering this liability by buying kronor forward? The Swedish interest rate is 0.02%, and exchange rates are shown in Table 28.1. Briefly explain.

16. **Currency hedging (S28.3)** A firm in the United States is due to receive payment of €1 million in eight years' time. It would like to protect itself against a decline in the value of the euro, but finds it difficult to get forward cover for such a long period. Is there any other way in which it can protect itself?

17. **Currency hedging (S28.3)** Suppose you are the treasurer of Lufthansa, the German international airline. How is company value likely to be affected by exchange rate changes? What policies would you adopt to reduce exchange rate risk?

18. **Currency hedging (S28.3)** A Ford dealer in the United States may be exposed to a devaluation of the yen if this leads to a cut in the price of Japanese cars. Suppose that the dealer estimates that a 1% decline in the value of the yen would result in a permanent decline of 5% in the dealer's profits. How should she hedge against this risk, and how should she calculate the size of the hedge position? (*Hint:* You may find it helpful to refer to Section 27-7.)

19. **Currency hedging (S28.3)** "Last year we had a substantial income in sterling, which we hedged by selling sterling forward. In the event sterling appreciated. So our decision to sell forward cost us a lot of money. I think that in the future we should either stop hedging our currency exposure or just hedge when we think sterling is overvalued." As financial manager, how would you respond to your chief executive's comment?

20. **Investment decisions (S28.4)** Carpet Baggers Inc. is proposing to construct a new bagging plant in a country in Europe. The two prime candidates are Germany and Switzerland. The forecasted cash flows from the proposed plants are as follows:

	C_0	C_1	C_2	C_3	C_4	C_5	C_6	IRR (%)
Germany (millions of euros)	−60	+10	+15	+15	+20	+20	+20	15.0
Switzerland (millions of Swiss francs)	−120	+20	+30	+30	+35	+35	+35	12.8

The spot exchange rate for euros is EUR/USD = 1.3, while the rate for Swiss francs is USD/CHF = 1.5. The interest rate is 5% in the United States, 4% in Switzerland, and 6% in the euro countries. The financial manager has suggested that, if the cash flows were stated in dollars, a return in excess of 10% would be acceptable.

Should the company go ahead with either project? If it must choose between them, which should it take?

21. **Investment decisions (S28.4)** It is the year 2023 and Pork Barrels Inc. is considering construction of a new barrel plant in Spain. The forecasted cash flows in millions of euros are as follows:

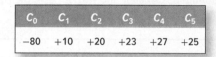

C_0	C_1	C_2	C_3	C_4	C_5
−80	+10	+20	+23	+27	+25

The spot exchange rate is EUR/USD = 1.2. The interest rate in the United States is 8%, and the euro interest rate is 6%. You can assume that pork barrel production is effectively risk-free.

a. Calculate the NPV of the euro cash flows from the project. What is the NPV in dollars?

b. What are the dollar cash flows from the project if the company hedges against exchange rate changes? What is the NPV of these flows?

c. Suppose that the company expects the euro to depreciate by 5% a year. How does this affect the value of the project?

CHALLENGE

22. **Currency hedging (S28.3)** Alpha and Omega are U.S. corporations. Alpha has a plant in Hamburg that imports components from the United States, assembles them, and then sells the finished product in Germany. Omega is at the opposite extreme. It also has a plant in Hamburg, but it buys its raw material in Germany and exports its output back to the United States. How is each firm likely to be affected by a fall in the value of the euro? How could each firm hedge itself against exchange risk?

● ● ● ● ●

28.1 a. USD/INR = 74.6035.

b. GBP/INR = (USD/INR) × (GBP/USD) = (74.6035) × (1.2714) = 94.851.

c. A small discount (you get more rupees for your dollar if you buy forward).

28.2 Forward exchange rate = $\dfrac{1 + \text{Ruritanian interest rate}}{1 + \text{U.S. interest rate}}$ × spot exchange rate

= (1.1025/1.05) × 50 = 52.5.

28.3 a. Because the gold price must be the same in the two countries, GBP600 = USD1,000. Therefore, GBP/USD = 1,000/600 = 1.667.

b. In the United States, price = $1,000 × 1.02 = $1,020. In the United Kingdom, price = $600 × 1.05 = £630. The new exchange rate is therefore GBP/USD = 1,020/630 = 1.619.

28.4 It would need to rise.

28.5 If the euro or the yen depreciates against the dollar, then foreign cars are likely to become cheaper. The Ford dealer, therefore, has economic risk even though it never needs to buy or sell foreign currency.

28.6 1. Discount rur cash flows at rur interest rate: NPV = −90,000 + 121,000/1.10² = RUR10,000, which is equivalent to USD5,000.

2. Interest-rate-parity gives a one-year forward exchange rate of 2 × (1.10/1.05)² = 2.195. Therefore, the dollar cash flows from the project are C_0 = −90,000/2 = −45,000 and C_2 = 121,000/2.195 = +55,125. Discount at the U.S. interest rate: NPV = −45,000 + 55,125/1.05² = USD5,000.

SOLUTIONS TO
SELF-TEST

28.6 If the government is expected to expropriate half the cash flows, the expected cash flow is only 10 million Khazad dollars. Unless the expropriation risk is correlated with the market, this flow can be discounted at the customary 10% to give a PV of 10 /0.10= 100 million Khazad dollars. Doubling the discount rate will not give the right answer.

● ● ● ● ●

FINANCE ON THE WEB

With a little ingenuity you can find recent data for the following question on the Bank of England website (www.bankofengland,co.uk).

1. a. How many U.S. dollars are worth one British pound?

   b. How many British pounds are worth one U.S. dollar?

   c. Suppose that you arrange today to buy British dollars in 90 days. How many pounds could you buy for each U.S. dollar?

   d. If forward rates simply reflect market expectations, what is the likely spot exchange rate for the pound in 90 days' time?

Data for the following question can be found in the foreign exchange rate tables in the online version of *The Wall Street Journal* (**www.wsj.com**).

2. a. How many Swiss francs can you buy for $1?

   b. How many Japanese yen can you buy?

   c. What rate do you think a Swiss bank would quote (CHF/JPY) for buying or selling Japanese yen? Explain what would happen if it quoted a cross-rate that was substantially above your figure.

MINI-CASE ● ● ● ●

Exacta, s.a.

Exacta, s.a., is a major French producer of precision machine tools, based in Lyons. About two-thirds of its output is exported. The majority of these sales are within the European Union. However, the company also has a thriving business in the United States, despite strong competition from several U.S. firms. Exacta usually receives payment for exported goods within two months of the invoice date so that at any point in time, only about one-sixth of annual exports to the United States is exposed to currency risk.

The company believes that its North American business is now large enough to justify a local manufacturing operation, and it has recently decided to establish a plant in South Carolina. Most of the output from this plant will be sold in the United States, but the company believes that there should also be opportunities for future sales in Canada and Mexico.

The South Carolina plant will involve a total investment of $380 million and is expected to be in operation by the year 2024. Annual revenues from the plant are expected to be about $420 million, and the company forecasts net profits of $52 million a year. Once the plant is up and running, it should be able to operate for several years without substantial additional investment.

Although there is widespread enthusiasm for the project, several members of the management team have expressed anxiety about possible currency risk. M. Pangloss, the finance director, reassured them that the company was not a stranger to currency risk; after all, the company was already exporting about $320 million of machine tools each year to the United States and has managed to exchange its dollar revenue for euros without any major losses. But not everybody was convinced by this argument. For example, the CEO, Mme. Bovary, pointed out that the $380 million to be invested would substantially increase the amount of money at risk if the dollar fell relative to the euro. Mme. Bovary was notoriously risk-averse on financial matters and would push for complete hedging if practical.

M. Pangloss attempted to reassure the CEO. At the same time, he secretly shared some of the anxieties about exchange rate risk. Nearly all the revenues from the South Carolina plant would be in U.S. dollars, and the bulk of the $380 million investment would likewise be incurred in the United States. About two-thirds of the operating costs would be in dollars, but the remaining one-third would represent payment for components brought in from Lyons plus the charge by the head office for management services and use of patents. The company has yet to decide whether to invoice its U.S. operation in dollars or euros for these purchases from the parent company.

M. Pangloss is optimistic that the company can hedge itself against currency risk. His favored solution is for Exacta to finance the plant by a $380 million issue of dollar bonds. That way the dollar investment would be offset by a matching dollar liability. An alternative is for the company to sell forward at the beginning of each year the expected revenues from the U.S. plant. But he realizes from experience that these simple solutions might carry hidden dangers. He decides to slow down and think more systematically about the additional exchange risk from the U.S. operation.

QUESTIONS

1. What would Exacta's true exposure be from its new U.S. operations, and how would it change from the company's current exposure?

2. Given that exposure, what would be the most effective and inexpensive approach to hedging?

CHAPTER

Financial Analysis

In Chapter 19, we saw how investors and rival companies monitor a corporation's progress and seek to keep management on its toes. To do so, they rely on the information in the company's financial statements and on the auditor's assurance that the statements are free of material misstatement. If investors can see a firm's profitability and financial health, then problems will show up right away in a falling stock price. This, in turn, alerts the board of directors and generates extra scrutiny. It may also lead to a takeover. With transparency, corporate troubles generally lead to corrective action.

But how can shareholders use the financial statements to judge whether managers are doing a good job or where there may be scope for improvement? They need measures of value added. They also need measures that help to explain where that value added came from. For example, value added depends on profitability, so they need measures of profitability. Profitability in turn depends on how efficiently the firm generates sales from its assets and controls its costs.

Value also depends on sound financing. Value is destroyed if the firm is financed imprudently and can't pay its debts. It is also destroyed if the firm does not maintain adequate liquidity and therefore has difficulty in finding the cash to pay its bills.

There is a danger of being overwhelmed by the quantity of data in a company's financial statements.[1] So, when shareholders and other stakeholders scrutinize the financial statements, they generally start by calculating a few key financial ratios. You have probably heard stories of whizzes who can take a company's accounts apart in minutes, calculate some financial ratios, and divine the company's future. Such people

are like abominable snowmen: often spoken of but never truly seen. The financial ratios that we describe in this chapter are no substitute for a crystal ball. They are just a convenient way to summarize large quantities of financial data and to compare firms' performance. The ratios help you to ask the right questions; they seldom answer them.

Figure 29.1 serves as a road map for this chapter. In each box, we have posed a question and given examples of helpful financial ratios or other measures. We will first discuss the boxes on the left that are concerned with investment and then those on the right that are concerned with financing.

Section 29-1 Understanding financial statements
We start the chapter with a brief review of the company's financial statements that are the data source for most of the financial ratios.

Section 29-2 Measuring company performance
We then look at some measures of how far the firm has created value for its shareholders.

Section 29-3 Measuring efficiency
We show how the return that the firm earns for its shareholders depends on the sales that it can generate from its assets and the profit margin that it earns on these sales. We also look at measures of of how efficiently the firm uses specific types of asset.

Section 29-4 Measuring leverage
Debt has its advantages, but shareholders need to check that the firm's leverage is prudent. We describe the principal measures of leverage.

---

[1]HSBC's 2007 *Annual Report* totaled 454 pages. The *Financial Times* reported that Britain's postal service was obliged to limit the number that its postmen carried in order to prevent back injuries.

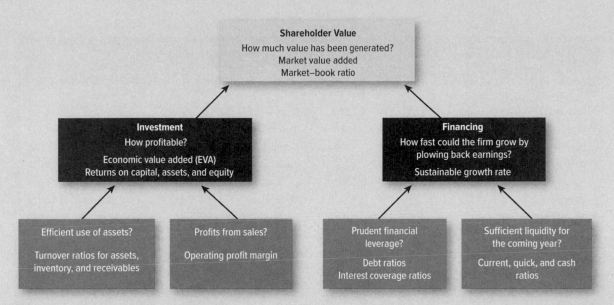

FIGURE 29.1   An organization chart for financial ratios, showing how common financial ratios and other measures relate to shareholder value.

Section 29-5 Measuring liquidity

Some assets are more liquid than others. We therefore look at how easily the firm's assets can be converted into cash.

Section 29-6 Interpreting financial ratios

How do you judge whether a measure is a cause for congratulation or concern? In many cases, there is no natural benchmark, but we suggest some tests that you can apply.

• • • • •

29-1 Understanding Financial Statements

Your task is to assess the financial standing of Kroger, the supermarket company. Perhaps you are the financial manager of Kroger or of one of its competitors. You could be a mutual fund manager trying to decide whether to allocate $25 million of new money to Kroger stock. You could be an investment banker seeking business from the company or a bondholder concerned with its credit standing.

You turn first to Kroger's financial statements. In the United States, public companies such as Kroger provide financial statements to their shareholders quarterly and annually. The annual statements are filed with the SEC on form 10-K, and the quarterly statements are filed on form 10-Q. Therefore, you often hear financial analysts refer loosely to the company's "10-K" or its "10-Q."

The financial statements include the balance sheet, the income statement, the statement of cash flows, and the statement of the shareholders' equity. We will focus on the balance sheet and income statement.

The Balance Sheet

Table 29.1 sets out a simplified balance sheet for Kroger for fiscal years 2019 and 2018. It provides a snapshot of the company's assets at the end of the year and the sources of the money that was used to buy those assets.

BEYOND THE PAGE

The rise and stall in the convergence of accounting standards

mhhe.com/brealey14e

	Fiscal Year			Fiscal Year	
Assets	**2019***	**2018****	**Liabilities and Shareholders' Equity**	**2019***	**2018****
Current assets			Current liabilities		
Cash and marketable securities	$ 1,578	$ 1,610	Debt due for repayment	$ 1,965	$ 3,157
Receivables	1,706	1,589	Accounts payable	6,349	6,059
Inventories	7,084	6,846	Other current liabilities	5,929	5,058
Other current assets	522	758	Total current liabilities	$14,243	$ 14,274
Total current assets	$10,890	$10,803	Long-term debt	$12,111	$ 12,072
Fixed assets			Other long-term liabilities	10,329	3,937
Tangible fixed assets			Total liabilities	$36,683	$ 30,283
Property, plant, and equipment	$45,847	$43,864	Shareholders' equity:		
Less accumulated depreciation	23,976	22,229	Common stock and other paid-in capital	$ 1,918	$ 1,918
Net tangible fixed assets	$21,871	$21,635	Additional paid-in capital	3,337	3,245
Intangible asset (goodwill)	4,142	4,345	Retained earnings	20,309	19,284
Operating lease assets	6,814	—	Treasury stock	(16,991)	(16,612)
Other assets	1,539	1,335	Total shareholders' equity	$ 8,573	$ 7,835
			Total liabilities and shareholders' equity	$45,256	$ 38,118
Total assets	$45,256	$38,118			

❭TABLE 29.1   Balance sheet of The Kroger Co., fiscal 2019 and 2018 (figures in $ millions).

*Year ending February 1, 2020
**Year ending February 2, 2019

The assets are listed in declining order of liquidity. The accountant lists first those assets that are most likely to be turned into cash in the near future. They include cash itself; marketable securities and receivables (i.e., bills to be paid by the firm's customers); and inventories of raw materials, work-in-process, and finished goods. These assets are all known as *current assets*.

The remaining assets on the balance sheet consist of long-term, usually illiquid, assets such as warehouses, stores, fixtures, and vehicles. The balance sheet does not show up-to-date market values of these long-term assets. Instead, the accountant records the amount that each asset originally cost and deducts a fixed annual amount for depreciation of buildings, plant, and equipment. Notice that the assets for 2019 include those financed by short-term operating leases; in previous years, these did not need to be shown.

The balance sheet does not include all the company's assets. Some of the most valuable ones are intangible, such as reputation, skilled management, and a well-trained labor force. Accountants are generally reluctant to record these assets in the balance sheet unless they can be readily identified and reasonably valued.[2]

Now look at the right-hand portion of Kroger's balance sheet, which shows where the money to buy the assets came from. The accountant starts by looking at the liabilities—that

---

[2]Kroger's balance sheet does include an entry for "goodwill." This reflects the difference between the price paid to acquire a company and that company's book value.

is, the money owed by the company. First come those liabilities that need to be paid off in the near future. These *current liabilities* include debts that are due to be repaid within the next year and payables (i.e., amounts owed by the company to its suppliers).

The difference between the current assets and current liabilities is called the *net current assets* or *net working capital*. For Kroger, this figure is negative,

$$\text{Net working capital} = \text{current assets} - \text{current liabilities}$$
$$= 10,890 - 14,243 = -\$3,353$$

The bottom portion of the balance sheet shows the sources of the cash that was used to acquire the net working capital and fixed assets. Some of the cash has come from the issue of bonds and leases that will not be repaid for many years. After all these long-term liabilities have been paid off, the remaining assets belong to the common stockholders. The company's equity is simply the total value of the net working capital and fixed assets less the long-term liabilities. Part of this equity has come from the sale of shares to investors, and the remainder has come from earnings that the company has retained and invested on behalf of the shareholders.

29.1 Self Test

Which of the following are current assets? a. receivables; b. treasury stock; c. goodwill; d. payables; e. inventory.

The Income Statement

If Kroger's balance sheet resembles a snapshot of the firm at a particular point in time, its income statement is like a video. It shows how profitable the firm has been over the past year.

Look at the summary income statement in Table 29.2. You can see that during 2019, Kroger sold goods worth $122,286 million.[3] The total cost of purchasing and selling these goods was $95,294 + $22,092 = $117,386 million. In addition to these out-of-pocket expenses, Kroger also deducted depreciation of $2,649 million for the value of the fixed assets used up in producing the goods. After including a small amount of other income, Kroger's earnings before interest and taxes (EBIT) were

$$\text{EBIT} = \text{total revenues} - \text{costs} - \text{depreciation} + \text{other income}$$
$$= 122,286 - 117,386 - 2,649 + 333$$
$$= \$2,584 \text{ million}$$

Of this sum, $603 million went to pay the interest on the short- and long-term debt (remember debt interest is paid out of pretax income), and a further $469 million went to the government in the form of taxes. The $1,512 million that was left over belonged to the shareholders. Kroger paid out $486 million as dividends and reinvested the remainder in the business.

29.2 Self-Test

If Kroger had paid no dividend in fiscal 2019, what would have been the addition to retained earnings?

---

[3]For simplicity, we have added $74 million of investment income to net sales.

Accounting Practice and Malpractice

❭ U.S. accounting rules are spelled out by the Financial Accounting Standards Board (FASB) in its generally accepted accounting principles. Yet, inevitably, rules and principles leave room for discretion, and managers under pressure to perform are tempted to take advantage of this leeway to satisfy investors. Investors worry about the fact that some companies seem particularly prone to inflate their earnings by playing fast and loose with accounting practice. They refer to such companies as having "low-quality" earnings, and they place a correspondingly lower value on the firms' stock.

Here is just one example of ambiguities in accounting rules that have been used by companies to conceal unflattering information. Firms record a sale when it is made, not when the customer actually pays. But the date of sale is not always obvious. Suppose it is November and you are concerned that if your firm does not meet its sales target, you can forget about your annual bonus. You contact your main customers, and they agree to increase their December orders as long as they have the right to return any unsold goods. Your firm then books these shipments as "sales," even though

there is a high likelihood that many of the goods will be returned. That is almost certainly illegal and will get you into serious trouble. But suppose instead that you tell your customers that the price of your product may rise in the new year and suggest that they place an extra order in December. This practice, known as "channel stuffing," increases this year's sales at the expense of next year's sales.

Many companies have been thought to use channel stuffing to overstate their earnings, but blatant instances are liable to attract the SEC's attention. For example, in 2019, the sportswear company, Under Armour, was accused of pressuring retailers to accept early shipments of its products and of redirecting goods that ordinarily would have been shipped to its own factory stores to discount chains instead so they could be booked as current sales. But those purported sales were effectively "borrowed" against future ones, thus painting an inflated portrait of actual demand for its product, and misleading investors about its future prospects. When the federal investigation of these practices came to light in late 2019, Under Armour's share price suffered a one-day decline of nearly 19%.

❭ **TABLE 29.2** Income statement of The Kroger Co., fiscal 2019 (figures in $ millions).

Net sales$	$122,286
Cost of goods sold	95,294
Selling, general, and administrative expenses	22,092
Earnings before interest, taxes, depreciation, and amortization (EBITDA)	4,900
Depreciation	2,649
Other income	333
Earnings before interest and income taxes (EBIT)	$ 2,584
Interest expense	603
Taxable income	$ 1,981
Taxes	469
Net income	$ 1,512
Allocation of net income	
Dividends	486
Addition to retained earnings	1,026

income.[8] In 2019, Kroger's after-tax interest and net income totaled $(1 - 0.21) \times 603 + 1,512 = \$1,988$ million (the tax rate in 2019 was 21%).[9]

Kroger entered fiscal 2019 with total capital of $19,907 million, which was made up of $12,072 million of long-term debt and $7,835 million of shareholders' equity. This was the cumulative amount that had been invested in the past by the debt- and equityholders. Kroger's weighted-average cost of capital was about 5.5%. Therefore, investors who provided the $19,907 million required the company to earn at least $0.055 \times 19,907 = \$1,095$ million for its debt- and equityholders.

If you deduct the total cost of the company's capital from the income that it earned, you can see that it made $1,988 - 1,095 = \$893$ million, nearly $1 billion more than investors required. This was Kroger's residual income, or EVA:

$$\text{EVA} = (\text{after-tax interest} + \text{net income}) - (\text{cost of capital} \times \text{capital})$$
$$= 1,988 - 1,095 = \$893 \text{ million}$$

Sometimes it is helpful to re-express EVA as follows:

$$\text{EVA} = \left(\frac{\text{after-tax interest} + \text{net income}}{\text{total capital}} - \text{cost of capital} \right) \times \text{total capital}$$

In the case of Kroger, with a 21% tax rate

$$\frac{\text{After-tax interest} + \text{net income}}{\text{total capital}} = \frac{(1 - 0.21) \times 603 + 1,512}{19,907} = 0.100, \text{ or } 10.0\%$$

Kroger's cost of capital was about 5.5%. So,

$$\text{EVA} = \left(\frac{\text{after-tax interest} + \text{net income}}{\text{total capital}} - \text{cost of capital} \right) \times \text{total capital}$$
$$= (0.100 - 0.055) \times 19,907 = \$893$$

The first four columns of Table 29.4 show measures of EVA for our sample of large companies. Apple heads the list. It earned $35.9 billion more than was needed to satisfy investors. By contrast, ExxonMobil was among the laggards. Although it earned an accounting profit of $16.1 billion, this figure was calculated before deducting the cost of the capital that was employed. After deducting the cost of the capital, Exxon made an EVA *loss* of $4.9 billion.

29.3 Self-Test

Evergrid Corporation had operating income (after-tax interest + net income) of $50 million. Its total capital at the start of the year was $220 million. Its cost of capital was 11%. What was its EVA?

Accounting Rates of Return

EVA measures how many dollars a business is earning after deducting the cost of capital. Other things equal, the more assets the manager has to work with, the greater the opportunity to generate a large EVA. The manager of a small division may be highly competent, but if that division has few assets, she is unlikely to rank high in the EVA stakes. Therefore, when comparing managers, it can also be helpful to measure the firm's return *per dollar of investment.*

---

[8]This figure is called the company's net operating profit after tax, or NOPAT:

NOPAT = after-tax interest + net income

[9]The tax advantages of Kroger's debt financing are not lost. They are picked up when we use the weighted-average cost of capital (WACC) to calculate the income that Kroger's investors require. WACC already includes an adjustment for the interest tax shield.

	1. After-Tax Interest + Net Income	2. Cost of Capital (WACC, %)	3. Total Long-Term Capital	4. EVA = 1 − (2 × 3)	5. Return on Capital (ROC, %) (1 ÷ 3)
Apple	$58,081	11.0	$200,882	$35,924	28.9
Microsoft	41,362	9.6	164,653	25,606	25.1
Walmart	17,254	5.0	122,699	11,107	14.1
Johnson & Johnson	15,426	7.3	87,436	9,086	17.6
Coca-Cola	9,732	5.0	42,345	7,611	23.0
Caterpillar	7,022	11.9	39,039	2,361	18.0
Consolidated Edison	2,233	4.2	34,221	806	6.5
ExxonMobil	16,007	9.8	212,332	−4,886	7.5
GM	7,285	11.1	111,920	−5,138	6.5
DuPont	−86	6.1	132,233	−13,005	-0.1

❭TABLE 29.4 Accounting measures of company performance, March 2020 (dollar values in billions). Companies are ranked by economic value added (EVA).

Note: EVAs do not compute exactly because of rounding in column 2.

Source: EVA Dimensions

Three common return measures are the return on capital (ROC), the return on assets (ROA), and the return on equity (ROE). All are based on accounting information and are therefore known as *book rates of return.*

Return on Capital[10]   We have already calculated Kroger's **return on capital (ROC)** in 2019:

$$\text{ROC} = \frac{\text{after-tax interest + net income}}{\text{total capital}} = \frac{(1 - 0.21) \times 603 + 1{,}512}{19{,}907} = 0.100, \text{ or } 10.0\%$$

The company's cost of capital (WACC) was about 5.5%. So we can say that the company earned 4.5% more than shareholders demanded.

Notice that, when we calculated Kroger's return on capital, we summed the company's *after-tax* interest and net income. The reason that we subtracted the tax shield on debt interest was that we wished to calculate the income that the company would have earned with all-equity financing. The tax advantages of debt financing are picked up when we compare the company's return on capital with its weighted-average cost of capital (WACC).[11] WACC already includes an adjustment for the interest tax shield.[12] Financial analysts often ignore this refinement and use the gross interest payment to calculate ROC.

The last column in Table 29.4 shows the return on capital for our sample of well-known companies. Notice that Johnson and Johnson's return on capital was 17.6%, more than 10 percentage points higher than its cost of capital. Although it had a higher return than Walmart, it had a slightly lower EVA. This was because it had far fewer dollars invested than Walmart.

Return on Assets   **Return on assets (ROA)** measures the income available to debt and equity investors per dollar of the firm's *total* assets. Total assets (which equal total liabilities

BEYOND THE PAGE

Biases in accounting measures of performance

mhhe.com/brealey14e

---

[10]The expression, *return on capital,* is commonly used when calculating the profitability of an entire firm. When measuring the profitability of an individual plant, the equivalent measure is generally called *return on investment* (or *ROI*).

[11]For the same reason, we used the after-tax interest payment when we calculated Kroger's EVA.

[12]Remember that WACC is a weighted average of the *after-tax* interest rate and the cost of equity.

plus shareholders' equity) are greater than total capital because total capital does not include current liabilities.[13] With a 21% tax rate the return on Kroger's assets was

$$\text{ROA} = \frac{(\text{after-tax interest} + \text{net income})}{\text{total assets}} = \frac{(1 - 0.21) \times 603 + 1,512}{38,118} = 0.052, \text{ or } 5.2\%$$

When we subtract the tax shield on Kroger's interest payments, we are again asking how much the company would have earned if it were all-equity-financed. This adjustment is helpful when comparing the profitability of firms with very different capital structures. Again, this refinement is ignored more often than not, and ROA is calculated using the gross interest payment. Sometimes analysts take no account of interest payments and measure ROA as the income for equityholders divided by total assets. This measure ignores entirely the income that the assets have generated for debtholders.

Return on Equity   We measure the **return on equity (ROE)** as the income to shareholders per dollar invested. Kroger had net income of $1,512 million in 2019 and stockholders' equity of $7,835 million at the start of the year. So its return on equity was

$$\text{ROE} = \frac{\text{net income}}{\text{equity}} = \frac{1,512}{7,835} = 0.193, \text{ or } 19.3\%$$

Has the company provided an adequate return for shareholders? To answer that question, we need to compare it with the company's cost of equity. Kroger's cost of equity capital in 2019 was about 6.8%, so its return on equity was well above its cost of equity.

When we calculated these book rates of return, we compared a flow measure (income earned over the year) with a snapshot measure (the funds at the start of the year). If the company does not raise any capital during the year, this is exactly the correct procedure. But, if it does raise new capital and this capital contributes to the year's operating income, you may be better to divide by the average of the funds at the start and end of the year.[14]

Problems with EVA and Accounting Rates of Return

Rate of return and economic value added have some obvious attractions as measures of performance. Unlike market-value-based measures, they show current performance and are not affected by the expectations about future events that are reflected in today's stock market prices. Rate of return and economic value added can be calculated for a private company where there is no observable market value, and they can be calculated for a particular plant or division. However, remember that these measures are based on book (balance sheet) values for assets. Debt and equity are also book values. Accountants do not show every asset on the balance sheet, yet our calculations take accounting data at face value. For example, we ignored the fact that Kroger has invested large sums in marketing to establish its brand name. This brand name is an important asset, but its value is not shown on the balance sheet. If it were shown, the book values of assets, capital, and equity would increase, and Kroger would not appear to earn such high returns.

Anyone using accounting measures of performance had better hope that the accounting numbers measure the economic reality. Unfortunately, they do not always do so. Applying EVA or any other accounting measure of performance therefore requires adjustments to the income statements and balance sheets.   For example, think of the difficulties in measuring the profitability of a pharmaceutical research program, where it typically takes 10 to 12 years

BEYOND THE PAGE

Is it better to use average or start-of-year assets?

mhhe.com/brealey14e

---

[13]Although it is sometimes done, it is not correct to compare return on assets with WACC. Current liabilities are ignored when calculating WACC.

[14]In the case of Kroger, the company actually bought back part of its equity during the year. To recognize this, you would need to use a *lower* figure for capital than the value at the start of the year.

to bring a new drug from discovery to final regulatory approval and the drug's first revenues. That means 10 to 12 years of guaranteed losses, even if the managers in charge do everything right. Similar problems occur in start-up ventures, where there may be heavy capital outlays but low or negative earnings in the first years of operation. This does not imply negative NPV, so long as operating earnings and cash flows are sufficiently high later on. But EVA and ROI would be negative in the start-up years, even if the project were on track to a strong positive NPV. The problem in these cases is not with EVA or ROI, but with the accounting data. The pharmaceutical R&D program may be showing accounting losses because generally accepted accounting principles require that outlays for R&D be written off as current expenses. But from an economic point of view, those outlays are an investment, not an expense. If a proposal for a new business predicts accounting losses during a start-up period, but the proposal never-theless shows a positive NPV, then the start-up losses are really an investment—cash outlays made to generate larger cash inflows when the business hits its stride.

Remember also that the balance sheet does not show the current market values of the firm's assets. The assets in a company's books are valued at their original cost less any depre-ciation. Older assets may be grossly undervalued in today's market conditions and prices. So a positive EVA and a high return on assets indicates that the business has performed well by making profitable investments in the past, but it does not necessarily mean that you could buy the same assets today at their reported book values. Conversely, a low return suggests some poor decisions in the past, but it does not always mean that today the assets could be employed better elsewhere.

Finally, remember that a company's book equity is reduced when it repurchases its stock. Companies that have been active repurchasers, such as McDonald's or Home Depot, can have negative book equity. This can make nonsense of measures of EVA or the book rate of return.

29-3 Measuring Efficiency

The DuPont Formula

We began our analysis of Kroger by calculating how much value the company has added for its shareholders and how much profit it is earning after deducting the cost of the capital that it employs. We examined the company's rates of return on capital, equity, and total assets and found that its return has been higher than the cost of capital. Our next task is to probe a little deeper to understand the reasons that a company has earned a high or low return.

The return on the firm's assets depends on the sales that it generates and on the profit that it earns from each dollar of sales. Let's see how this comes about.

Asset Turnover Ratio   The asset turnover, or sales-to-assets, ratio shows how much sales vol-ume is generated by each dollar of total assets, and therefore it measures how hard the firm's assets are working. For Kroger, each dollar of assets produced $3.21 of sales:

$$\text{Asset turnover} = \frac{\text{sales}}{\text{total assets at start of year}} = \frac{122{,}286}{38{,}118} = 3.21$$

Profit Margin   The profit margin measures the proportion of sales that finds its way into profits. It is sometimes defined as

$$\text{Profit margin} = \frac{\text{net income}}{\text{sales}} = \frac{1{,}512}{122{,}286} = 0.0124, \text{ or } 1.24\%$$

This definition can be misleading. When companies are partly financed by debt, a portion of the profits from the sales must be paid as interest to the firm's lenders. We would not want to say that a firm is less profitable than its rivals simply because it employs debt finance and pays out part of its profits as interest. Therefore, when we are calculating the profit margin, it is useful to add back the after-tax debt interest to net income. This gives an alternative measure of profit margin, which is called the **operating profit margin**:

$$\text{Operating profit margin} = \frac{\text{after-tax interest} + \text{net income}}{\text{sales}}$$

$$= \frac{(1 - 0.21) \times 603 + 1{,}512}{122{,}286}$$

$$= 0.0163, \text{ or } 1.63\%$$

Explaining the Return on Assets   We calculated earlier that Kroger has earned a return of 5.2% on its assets. The following equation shows that this return depends on two factors—the sales that the company generates from its assets (asset turnover) and the profit that it earns on each dollar of sales (operating profit margin):

$$\text{Return on assets} = \frac{\text{after-tax interest} + \text{net income}}{\text{assets}} = \underset{\uparrow}{\frac{\text{sales}}{\text{assets}}} \times \underset{\uparrow}{\frac{\text{after-tax interest} + \text{net income}}{\text{sales}}}$$

$$\qquad\qquad\qquad\qquad\text{asset turnover} \quad \text{operating profit margin}$$

This breakdown of ROA into the product of turnover and margin is often called the **DuPont formula**, after the chemical company that popularized it. In Kroger's case, the formula gives the following breakdown of ROA:

$$\text{ROA} = \text{asset turnover} \times \text{operating profit margin} = 3.21 \times 0.0163 = 0.052$$

Any improvement in a firm's return on assets must involve either an improvement in the asset turnover or in the operating profit margin.

All firms would like to earn a higher return on their assets, but their ability to do so is limited by competition. The DuPont formula helps to identify the constraints that firms face. Fast-food chains, which have high asset turnover, tend to operate on low margins. Luxury hotels have relatively low turnover ratios but tend to compensate with higher margins.

Firms sometimes seek to improve their profit margins by acquiring a supplier. The idea is to capture the supplier's profit as well as their own. Unfortunately, unless they have some special skill in running the new business, any gain in profit margin is offset by a decline in asset turnover. Other things equal, vertical integration brings higher profit margins and lower asset turnover.

A few numbers may help to illustrate this point. Table 29.5 shows the sales, profits, and assets of Admiral Motors and its components supplier, Diana Corporation. Both earn a 10% return on assets, though Admiral has a lower operating profit margin (20% versus

	Sales	Profits	Assets	Asset Turnover	Profit Margin	ROA
Admiral Motors	$20	$4	$40	0.50	20%	10%
Diana Corporation	8	2	20	0.40	25	10
Diana Motors (the merged firm)	20	6	60	0.33	30	10

❭**TABLE 29.5**   Merging with suppliers or customers generally increases the profit margin, but this increase is offset by a reduction in asset turnover.

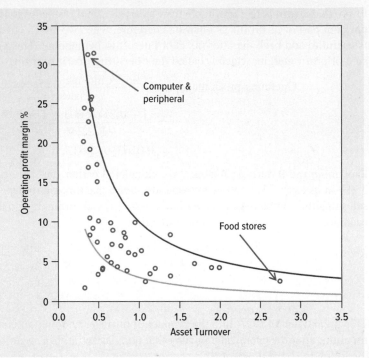

▶ **FIGURE 29.2**

Asset turnover and operating profit margin for 48 U.S. industries in the year ending December 2019. High asset turnover tends to be associated with low profit margins.

Source: Compustat

Diana's 25%). Since all of Diana's output goes to Admiral, Admiral's management reasons that it would be better to merge the two companies. That way, the merged company would capture the profit margin on both the auto components and the assembled car.

The bottom row of Table 29.5 shows the effect of the merger. The merged firm does indeed earn the combined profits. Total sales remain at $20 million, however, because all the components produced by Diana are used within the company. With higher profits and unchanged sales, the profit margin increases. Unfortunately, the asset turnover is *reduced* by the merger since the merged firm has more assets. This exactly offsets the benefit of the higher profit margin. The return on assets is unchanged.

Figure 29.2 shows evidence of the trade-off between asset turnover and operating profit margin. You can see that industries with high average turnover ratios tend to have lower average profit margins. Conversely, high margins are typically associated with low turnover. The two curved lines in the figure trace out the combinations of profit margin and turnover that result in an ROA of either 3% or 10%. Despite the enormous dispersion across industries in both margin and turnover, that variation tends to be offsetting, so for most industries, the return on assets lies between 3% and 10%.

29.4 Self-Test

A supermarket company reduces its prices across the board. What would you expect to happen to its asset turnover, operating profit margin, and return on assets: rise, fall, or can't say?

Other Efficiency Measures

The asset turnover ratio measures how efficiently the business is using its entire asset base. But you also might be interested in how hard *particular types* of assets are being put to use. Here are a couple of examples.

Inventory Turnover Efficient firms don't tie up more capital than they need in raw materials and finished goods. They hold only a relatively small level of inventories, and they turn over those inventories rapidly. When you calculate the inventory turnover, remember that the balance sheet shows the *cost* of inventories rather than the amount that the finished goods will eventually sell for. So it is usual to compare the level of inventories with the cost of goods sold rather than with sales. In Kroger's case,

$$\text{Inventory turnover} = \frac{\text{cost of goods sold}}{\text{inventory at start of year}} = \frac{95,294}{6,846} = 13.9$$

Another way to express this measure is to look at how many days of output are represented by inventories. This is equal to the level of inventories divided by the daily cost of goods sold:

$$\text{Inventory period} = \frac{\text{inventory at start of year}}{\text{daily cost of goods sold}} = \frac{6,846}{95,294/365} = 26.2 \text{ days}$$

Receivables Turnover Receivables are sales for which the company has not yet been paid. The receivables turnover ratio measures the firm's sales as a proportion of its receivables. For Kroger,

$$\text{Receivables turnover} = \frac{\text{sales}}{\text{receivables at start of year}} = \frac{122,286}{1,589} = 77.0$$

If customers are quick to pay, unpaid bills will be a relatively small proportion of sales, and the receivables turnover will be high. Therefore, a comparatively high ratio often indicates an efficient credit department that is quick to follow up on late payers. Sometimes, however, a high ratio indicates that the firm has an unduly restrictive credit policy and offers credit only to customers who can be relied on to pay promptly.[15]

Another way to measure the efficiency of the credit operation is by calculating the average length of time for customers to pay their bills. The faster the firm turns over its receivables, the shorter the collection period. Kroger's customers pay their bills in about 4.7 days:

$$\text{Accounts receivable period} = \frac{\text{receivables at start of year}}{\text{average daily sales}} = \frac{1,589}{122,286/365} = 4.7 \text{ days}$$

The receivables turnover ratio and the inventory turnover ratio may help to highlight particular areas of inefficiency, but they are not the only possible indicators. For example, Kroger might compare its sales per square foot with those of its competitors, an airline might look at revenues per passenger-mile, and a law firm might look at revenues per partner. A little thought and common sense should suggest which measures are likely to produce the most helpful insights into your company's efficiency.

29-4 Measuring Leverage

When a firm borrows money, it promises to make a series of interest payments and then to repay the amount that it has borrowed. If profits rise, the debtholders continue to receive only the fixed interest payment, so all the gains go to the shareholders. Of course, the reverse

---

[15]Where possible, it makes sense to look only at *credit* sales. Otherwise, a high ratio might simply indicate that a small proportion of sales is made on credit.

happens if profits fall. In this case, shareholders bear the greater part of the pain. If times are sufficiently hard, a firm that has borrowed heavily may not be able to pay its debts. The firm is then bankrupt, and shareholders lose most or all of their investment.

Because debt increases the returns to shareholders in good times and reduces them in bad times, it is said to create *financial leverage.* Leverage ratios measure how much financial leverage the firm has taken on. CFOs keep an eye on leverage ratios to ensure that lenders are happy to continue to take on the firm's debt.

Debt Ratio   Financial leverage is usually measured by the ratio of long-term debt to total long-term capital. (Here, "long-term debt" should include not just bonds or other borrowing but also financing from long-term leases.[16]) For Kroger,

$$\text{Long-term debt ratio} = \frac{\text{long-term debt}}{\text{long-term debt} + \text{equity}} = \frac{12,111}{12,111 + 8,573} = 0.59, \text{ or } 59\%$$

This means that 59 cents of every dollar of long-term capital is in the form of debt.

Leverage is also measured by the debt–equity ratio. For Kroger,

$$\text{Long-term debt–equity ratio} = \frac{\text{long-term debt}}{\text{equity}} = \frac{12,111}{8,573} = 1.4, \text{ or } 140\%$$

Kroger's long-term debt ratio is somewhat high for U.S. nonfinancial companies, but the CFO could fairly point out that the book value of the equity has been reduced by its repurchases and substantially understates its market value. If we use market values to calculate Kroger's leverage, its long-term debt ratio is only about 36%.

Some companies deliberately operate at very high debt levels. For example, in Chapter 33, we look at leveraged buyouts (LBOs). Firms that are acquired in a leveraged buyout usually issue large amounts of debt. When LBOs first became popular in the 1990s, these companies had average debt ratios of about 90%. Many of them flourished and paid back their debtholders in full; others were not so fortunate.

Notice also that our measure of leverage ignores short-term debt. That probably makes sense if the short-term debt is temporary or is matched by similar holdings of cash, but if the company is a regular short-term borrower, it may be preferable to widen the definition of debt to include all liabilities. In this case,

$$\text{Total debt ratio} = \frac{\text{total liabilities}}{\text{total assets}} = \frac{36,683}{45,256} = 0.81 \text{ or } 81\%$$

Therefore, Kroger is financed 81% with long- and short-term liabilities and 19% with equity.[17]

Managers sometimes refer loosely to a company's leverage, but we have just seen that leverage may be measured in several different ways. This is not the first time we have come across several ways to define a financial ratio. There is no law stating how a ratio should be defined. So be warned: Do not use a ratio without understanding how it has been calculated. Remember also that a company may have many obligations that provide leverage even though they are not shown as debts on the balance sheet. For example, unfunded pension and health care benefits may be huge fixed obligations though they are not shown as debt on the balance sheet.

Times-Interest-Earned Ratio   Another measure of financial leverage is the extent to which interest obligations are covered by earnings. Banks prefer to lend to firms whose earnings

---

[16]A finance lease is a long-term rental agreement that commits the firm to make regular payments. This commitment is just like the obligation to make payments on an outstanding loan. See Chapter 26.

[17]In this case, the debt consists of all liabilities, including current liabilities.

cover interest payments with room to spare. *Interest coverage* is measured by the ratio of earnings before interest and taxes (EBIT) to interest payments. For Kroger,[18]

$$\text{Times-interest-earned} = \frac{\text{EBIT}}{\text{interest payments}} = \frac{2{,}584}{603} = 4.3$$

The company enjoys a comfortable interest coverage or *times-interest-earned* ratio. Sometimes lenders are content with coverage ratios as low as 2 or 3.

   The regular interest payment is a hurdle that companies must keep jumping if they are to avoid default. Times-interest-earned measures how much clear air there is between hurdle and hurdler. The ratio is only part of the story, however. For example, it doesn't tell us whether Kroger is generating enough cash to repay its debt as it comes due.

Cash Coverage Ratio   In Chapter 6, we pointed out that depreciation is deducted when calculating the firm's earnings, even though no cash goes out the door. Suppose we add back depreciation to EBIT to calculate operating cash flow.[19] We can then calculate a *cash* coverage ratio. For Kroger,

$$\text{Cash coverage} = \frac{\text{EBIT} + \text{depreciation}}{\text{interest payments}} = \frac{2{,}584 + 2{,}649}{603} = 8.7$$

29.5 Self-Test

A firm repays $10 million face value of debt and issues $10 million of debt with a lower rate of interest. What happens to its long-term book debt ratio? What happens to times interest earned and cash coverage ratios?

Leverage and the Return on Equity

When the firm raises cash by borrowing, it must make interest payments to its lenders. This reduces net profits. On the other hand, if a firm borrows instead of issuing equity, it has fewer equityholders to share the remaining profits. Which effect dominates? An extended version of the DuPont formula helps us answer this question. It breaks down the return on equity (ROE) into four parts:

$$\text{ROE} = \frac{\text{net income}}{\text{equity}}$$

$$= \underset{\substack{\uparrow \\ \text{leverage} \\ \text{ratio}}}{\frac{\text{assets}}{\text{equity}}} \times \underset{\substack{\uparrow \\ \text{asset} \\ \text{turnover}}}{\frac{\text{sales}}{\text{assets}}} \times \underset{\substack{\uparrow \\ \text{operating} \\ \text{profit margin}}}{\frac{\text{after-tax interest} + \text{net income}}{\text{sales}}} \times \underset{\substack{\uparrow \\ \text{"debt burden"}}}{\frac{\text{net income}}{\text{after-tax interest} + \text{net income}}}$$

Notice that the product of the two middle terms is the return on assets. It depends on the firm's production and marketing skills and is unaffected by the firm's financing mix. However, the first and fourth terms do depend on the debt–equity mix. The first term, assets/equity, which we call the *leverage ratio,* can be expressed as (equity + liabilities)/equity,

---

[18]The numerator of times-interest-earned can be defined in several ways. Sometimes depreciation is excluded. Sometimes it is just earnings plus interest—that is, earnings before interest but *after* tax. This last definition seems nutty to us because the point of times-interest-earned is to assess the risk that the firm won't have enough money to pay interest. If EBIT falls below interest obligations, the firm won't have to worry about taxes. Interest is paid before the firm pays taxes.

[19]Earnings before interest, taxes, depreciation, and amortization are often termed EBITDA.

which equals 1 + total-debt-to-equity ratio. The last term, which we call the "debt burden," measures the proportion by which interest expense reduces net income.

Suppose that the firm is financed entirely by equity. In this case, both the leverage ratio and the debt burden are equal to 1, and the return on equity is identical to the return on assets. If the firm borrows, however, the leverage ratio is greater than 1 (assets are greater than equity) and the debt burden is less than 1 (part of the profits is absorbed by interest). Thus, leverage can either increase or reduce return on equity. You will usually find, however, that leverage increases ROE when the firm is performing well and ROA exceeds the interest rate.

29-5 Measuring Liquidity

If you are extending credit to a customer or making a short-term bank loan, you need to know whether the company can lay its hands on the cash to repay you. That is why credit analysts and bankers look at several measures of **liquidity**. Liquid assets can be converted into cash quickly and cheaply.

Think, for example, what you would do to meet a large unexpected bill. You might have some money in the bank or some investments that are easily sold, but you would not find it so easy to turn your old sweaters into cash. Companies, likewise, own assets with different degrees of liquidity. For example, accounts receivable and inventories of finished goods are generally quite liquid. As inventories are sold off and customers pay their bills, money flows into the firm. At the other extreme, real estate may be very *illiquid*. It can be hard to find a buyer, negotiate a fair price, and close a deal on short notice.

Managers have another reason to focus on liquid assets: Their book (balance sheet) values are usually reliable. The book value of a catalytic cracker may be a poor guide to its true value, but at least you know what cash in the bank is worth. Liquidity ratios also have some *less* desirable characteristics. Because short-term assets and liabilities are easily changed, measures of liquidity can rapidly become outdated. You might not know what the catalytic cracker is worth, but you can be fairly sure that it won't disappear overnight. Cash in the bank can disappear in seconds.

Also, assets that seem liquid sometimes have a nasty habit of becoming illiquid. This happened during the subprime mortgage crisis in 2007. Some financial institutions had set up funds known as *structured investment vehicles (SIVs)* that issued short-term debt backed by residential mortgages. As mortgage default rates began to climb, the market in this debt dried up and dealers became very reluctant to quote a price. Investors who were forced to sell found that the prices that they received were less than half the debt's estimated value.

Bankers and other short-term lenders applaud firms that have plenty of liquid assets. They know that when they are due to be repaid, the firm will be able to get its hands on the cash. But more liquidity is not always a good thing. For example, efficient firms do not leave excess cash in their bank accounts. They don't allow customers to postpone paying their bills, and they don't leave stocks of raw materials and finished goods littering the warehouse floor. In other words, high levels of liquidity may indicate sloppy use of capital. Here, EVA can help because it penalizes managers who keep more liquid assets than they really need.

Net-Working-Capital-to-Total-Assets Ratio   Current assets include cash, marketable securities, inventories, and accounts receivable. Current assets are mostly liquid. The difference between current assets and current liabilities is known as *net working capital*. It roughly measures the company's potential reservoir of cash. For Kroger, net working capital in 2019 was negative:

$$\text{Net working capital} = 10{,}890 - 14{,}243 = -\$3{,}353 \text{ million}$$

Net working capital was -7.4% of total assets:

$$\frac{\text{Net working capital}}{\text{total assets}} = \frac{-3{,}353}{45{,}256} = -0.074, \text{ or } -7.4\%$$

Current Ratio   The current ratio is just the ratio of current assets to current liabilities:

$$\text{Current ratio} = \frac{\text{current assets}}{\text{current liabilities}} = \frac{10{,}890}{14{,}243} = 0.76$$

Kroger has $0.76 in current assets for every dollar in current liabilities.

   Changes in the current ratio can be misleading. For example, suppose that a company borrows a large sum from the bank and invests it in marketable securities. Current liabilities rise and so do current assets. If nothing else changes, net working capital is unaffected but the current ratio changes. For this reason, it is sometimes preferable to net short-term investments against short-term debt when calculating the current ratio.

Quick (Acid-Test) Ratio   Some current assets are closer to cash than others. If trouble comes, inventory may not sell at anything above fire-sale prices. (Trouble typically comes *because* the firm can't sell its inventory of finished products for more than production cost.) Thus, managers often exclude inventories and other less liquid components of current assets when comparing current assets to current liabilities. They focus instead on cash, marketable securities, and bills that customers have not yet paid. This results in the quick ratio:

$$\text{Quick ratio} = \frac{\text{cash} + \text{marketable securities} + \text{receivables}}{\text{current liabilities}} = \frac{1{,}578 + 1{,}706}{14{,}243} = 0.23$$

Cash Ratio   A company's most liquid assets are its holdings of cash and marketable securities. That is why analysts also look at the cash ratio:

$$\text{Cash ratio} = \frac{\text{cash} + \text{marketable securities}}{\text{current liabilities}} = \frac{1{,}578}{14{,}243} = 0.11$$

A low cash ratio may not matter if the firm can borrow on short notice. Who cares whether the firm has actually borrowed from the bank or whether it has a guaranteed line of credit so it can borrow whenever it chooses? None of the standard measures of liquidity takes the firm's "reserve borrowing power" into account.

29.6 Self-Test

a. A firm has $1.2 million in current assets and $1 million in current liabilities. If it uses $0.5 million of cash to reduce its accounts payable, what will happen to the current ratio? What happens to net working capital?

b. A firm uses cash on hand to pay for additional inventories. What will happen to the current ratio? To the quick ratio?

29-6   Interpreting Financial Ratios

We have shown how to calculate some common summary measures of Kroger's performance and financial condition. Now you need some way to judge whether they are high or low. In some cases, there may be a natural benchmark. For example, if a firm has negative economic value added or a return on capital less than the cost of that capital, it has not created wealth for its shareholders.

But what about some of our other measures? There is no right level for, say, the asset turnover or profit margin, and if there were, it would almost certainly vary from year to year and industry to industry. Therefore, when assessing company performance, managers usually look first at how the financial ratios have changed over time, and then they look at how their measures stack up in comparison with companies in the same line of business.

We will first compare Kroger's position in 2019 with its performance in earlier years. For example, Figure 29.3 shows that Kroger's returns on assets have enjoyed a fairly rocky ride since 2001. We know that ROA = asset turnover × operating profit margin. You can see from Figure 29.3 that while asset turnover has been fairly steady from one year to the next, the fluctuations in the return on assets has been largely due to the sharp variation in profit margins. A better understanding of the variation in costs could be useful here.

Managers also need to ask themselves how the company's performance compares with that of its principal competitors. Table 29.6 sets out some key performance measures for Kroger and a peer group of companies. Some differences stand out. Kroger has a lower return on assets than its competitors. This stems from a lower operating margin rather than from the amount of sales that its assets generate. Kroger also has higher leverage than its typical competitors and has less liquidity.

The companies in Table 29.6 are similar in business, and it makes sense to compare their financial ratios. However, all financial ratios must be interpreted in the context of industry norms. For example, you would not expect a soft-drink manufacturer to have the same profit margin as a jeweler or the same leverage as a finance company. You can see

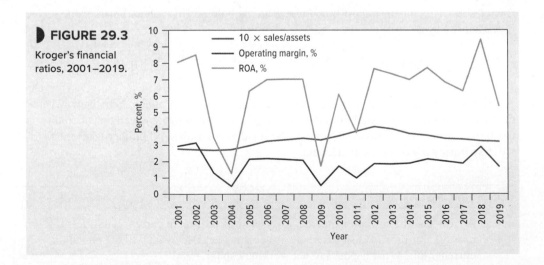

FIGURE 29.3

Kroger's financial ratios, 2001–2019.

		Fiscal 2019	
		Kroger	Peer Group
Performance Measures			
Market-to-book ratio	Market value of equity/book value of equity	2.5	1.0
Return on capital (ROC, %)	(After-tax interest + net income)/total capital	10.0	18.5
Return on assets (ROA, %)	(After-tax interest + net income)/total assets	5.2	11.2
Return on equity (ROE, %)	Net income/equity	19.3	12.6
Efficiency Measures			
Asset turnover	Sales/total assets at start of year	3.21	2.90
Inventory turnover	Cost of goods sold/inventory at start of year	13.9	13.9
Days in inventory	Inventory at start of year/daily cost of goods sold	26.2	26.3
Receivables turnover[a]	Sales/receivables at start of year	77.0	49.9
Average collection period (days)	Receivables at start of year/daily sales	4.7	7.3
Profit margin (%)	Net income/sales	1.24	2.22
Operating profit margin (%)	(After-tax interest + net income)/sales	1.63	2.37
Leverage Measures			
Long-term debt ratio	Long-term debt/(long-term debt + equity)	0.59	0.07
Total debt ratio	Total liabilities/total assets	0.81	0.33
Times-interest-earned	EBIT/interest payments	4.3	10.3
Cash coverage ratio	(EBIT + depreciation)/interest payments	8.7	16.0
Liquidity Measures			
Net-working-capital-to-total-assets ratio	Net working capital/total assets	−0.07	0.08
Current ratio	Current assets/current liabilities	0.76	1.38
Quick ratio	(Cash + marketable securities + receivables)/current liabilities	0.23	0.61
Cash ratio	(Cash + marketable securities)/current liabilities	0.11	0.39

❯TABLE 29.6   Selected financial ratios for Kroger and a peer group of companies, 2019. (Peer group firms have a NAICS classification of 445110, Supermarkets and Other Grocery).

some of these variations in Table 29.7, which presents some financial ratios for a sample of industry groups.

Notice the large variation across industries. Some of these differences, particularly in profitability measures, may arise from chance. But other differences may reflect more fundamental factors. For example, telecoms and utility companies tend to have high debt ratios, which persist in good years and bad. In comparison, business equipment companies tend to borrow far less. We pointed out earlier that some businesses are able to generate a high level of sales from relatively few assets. You can see that this is the case for retail companies. On the other hand, these companies earn a relatively low profit margin on these sales. By contrast, utilities turn over their assets more slowly but earn a much higher margin of profit on their sales.

	Market-to-Book Ratio	Return on Equity (%)	Asset Turnover	Inventory Turnover	Receivables Turnover	Operating Profit Margin (%)	Long-Term Debt Ratio	Total Debt Ratio	Times-Interest-Earned	Current Ratio	Quick Ratio	Cash Ratio
Autos	2.30	18.7	1.30	8.36	6.13	7.9	.44	.40	7.19	1.55	1.10	.20
Beer and liquor	3.30	31.4	0.34	1.79	8.62	16.2	.49	.47	7.14	1.51	.74	.13
Business equipment	3.11	4.9	0.76	3.79	5.94	9.4	.22	.36	6.19	2.41	1.85	1.07
Chemicals	3.85	17.4	0.87	4.53	6.45	14.1	.47	.55	7.27	2.05	1.39	.33
Clothing	3.98	12.4	1.20	2.79	8.07	12.2	.22	.25	15.24	2.38	1.75	.92
Construction	2.00	14.4	1.00	3.01	8.09	11.7	.37	.50	6.71	2.24	1.44	.47
Electrical equipment	2.55	11.2	0.91	3.48	6.35	10.7	.32	.49	8.19	2.37	1.47	.53
Food	2.35	13.9	1.10	5.58	10.25	12.9	.32	.49	6.66	1.76	.88	.19
Oil	1.82	10.8	0.55	14.55	6.29	8.0	.31	.47	4.96	1.62	1.36	.46
Paper	2.58	18.4	1.04	5.71	7.57	9.3	.48	.46	7.18	1.60	1.11	.23
Retail	2.12	12.3	1.92	5.68	26.33	4.0	.34	.35	4.19	1.51	.49	.16
Steel	1.78	14.0	1.38	5.14	8.43	7.5	.40	.49	4.59	2.78	1.21	.42
Telecom	1.77	22.2	0.50	25.04	7.20	15.4	.50	.59	3.35	1.01	.98	.40
Utilities	1.62	8.3	0.25	12.44	9.60	19.1	.46	.49	3.07	.67	.50	.05

❯TABLE 29.7 Median financial ratios for publicly traded North American companies, March 2020.

Source: WRDS Financial Ratios Suite.

- **The role of financial ratios** Managers use financial statements to monitor their own company's performance, to help understand the policies of a competitor, and to check on the financial health of customers. To avoid being overwhelmed by the sheer volume of data in a company's Annual Report, managers start with a few salient ratios to summarize the firm's market valuation, profitability, efficiency, capital structure, and liquidity. Remember, however, that financial ratios seldom provide answers, but they help you to ask the right questions.

- **Market measures of performance** To measure the increase in shareholder value provided by the company, analysts look at the market-value-added and the market-to-book ratio.

- **Accounting measures of performance** Measures of company performance derived from accounting data include economic value added (EVA) and measures of accounting return (return on capital, return on equity, and return on assets).

- **The DuPont formula** To understand the source of the company's performance, analysts often use the DuPont formula to decompose the company's return on assets.

$$\text{Return on assets} = \text{asset turnover} \times \text{operating profit margin}$$
$$= (\text{sales/assets}) \times ((\text{after-tax interest} + \text{net income}) / \text{sales})$$

Other common measures of efficiency include the inventory turnover and the receivables turnover ratios.

- **Leverage measures** Leverage may be measured by the ratio of debt to total capital and by the ratio of earnings to interest payments.

- **Liquidity measures** Analysts check on the company's liquidity by looking at the current ratio, which is the ratio of current assets to current liabilities. They may also calculate the ratio of cash and other liquid assets to current liabilities.

- **Benchmarking the company's performance** You need a standard for assessing a company's financial position. It is generally useful to compare the company's current financial ratios with the equivalent ratios in the past and with the ratios of other firms in the same business.

There are some good general texts on financial statement analysis. See, for example:

K. G. Palepu and P. M. Healy, *Business Analysis and Valuation,* 5th ed. (Cincinnati, OH: South-Western Publishing, 2013).

L. Revsine, D. Collins, B. Johnson, F. Mittelstaedt, and L. Soffer, *Financial Reporting and Analysis,* 7th ed. (New York: McGraw-Hill/Irwin, 2017).

S. Penman, *Financial Statement Analysis and Security Valuation,* 5th ed. (New York: McGraw-Hill/Irwin, 2012).

 Select problems are available in McGraw Hill's *Connect*.
Please see the preface for more information.

1. **Financial Statements (S29.1)** Construct a balance sheet for Galactic Enterprises given the following data:

Cash balances	$25,000
Inventories	$30,000
Net plant and equipment	$140,000
Accounts receivable	$35,000
Accounts payable	$24,000
Long-term debt	$130,000

What is shareholders' equity?

2. **Performance measures (S29.2)** Keller Cosmetics maintains an operating profit margin of 8% and a sales-to-assets ratio of 3. It has assets of $500,000 and equity of $300,000. Assume that interest payments are $30,000 and the tax rate is 25%.

a. What is the return on assets?

b. What is the return on equity?

3. **Performance measures (S29.2)** Table 29.8 gives abbreviated balance sheets and income statements for Walmart. At the end of fiscal 2019, Walmart had 2,832 million shares outstanding with a share price of $94. The company's weighted-average cost of capital was about 5%. Assume the corporate tax rate was 21%. Calculate:

a. Market value added.

b. Market-to-book ratio.

c. Economic value added.

d. Return on start-of-the-year capital.

4. **Performance measures (S29.2)** Describe some alternative measures of a firm's overall performance. What are their advantages and disadvantages? In each case, discuss what benchmarks you might use to judge whether performance is satisfactory.

5. **Measuring efficiency (S29.3)**

a. If a firm's assets of $10,000 represent 200 days' sales, what is its annual sales?

b. What is its asset turnover ratio?

6. **Measuring efficiency (S29.3)** Microcharge's customers take on average 60 days to pay their bills. What is its receivables turnover?

7. **Measuring efficiency (S29.3)** Magic Flutes has total receivables of $3,000, which represent 20 days' sales. Total assets are $75,000. The firm's operating profit margin is 5%. Find the firm's sales-to-assets ratio and return on assets

8. **Measuring leverage (S29.4)** A firm has a long-term debt–equity ratio of 0.4. Shareholders' equity is $1 million. Current assets are $200,000, and total assets are $1.5 million. If the current ratio is 2.0, what is the ratio of debt to total long-term capital?

	Fiscal 2019	Fiscal 2018
Balance Sheet		
Assets		
Current assets		
Cash and marketable securities	$ 9,465	$ 7,722
Accounts receivable	6,284	6,283
Inventories	44,435	44,269
Other current assets	1,622	3,623
Total current assets	$ 61,806	$ 61,897
Fixed assets		
Net fixed assets	$127,049	$ 111,395
Other long-term assets	47,640	46,003
Total assets	$236,495	$ 219,295
Liabilities and Shareholders' Equity		
Current liabilities		
Accounts payable	$ 46,973	$ 47,060
Other current liabilities	30,817	30,417
Total current liabilities	$ 77,790	$ 77,477
Long-term debt	43,714	43,520
Other long-term liabilities	33,439	18,664
Total liabilities	$154,943	$ 139,661
Total shareholders' equity	81,552	79,634
Total liabilities and shareholders' equity	$236,495	$ 219,295
Income Statement		
Net sales	$523,964	
Cost of goods sold	394,605	
Selling, general, and administrative expenses	97,804	
Depreciation	10,987	
Other income/expenses	2,147	
Earnings before interest and tax (EBIT)	$ 22,715	
Interest expense	2,599	
Taxable income	$ 20,116	
Tax	4,915	
Net income	$ 15,201	

❯ **TABLE 29.8**   Balance sheets and income statement for Walmart, fiscal 2019 (figures in $ millions).

9. **Measuring leverage (S29.4)** Consider this simplified balance sheet for Geomorph Trading:

Current assets	$100	$60	Current liabilities
Long-term assets	500	280	Long-term debt
		70	Other liabilities
		190	Equity
	$600	$600	

a. Calculate the ratio of debt to equity.

b. What are Geomorph's net working capital and total long-term capital? Calculate the ratio of debt to total long-term capital.

10. **Measuring leverage (S29.4)** Discuss alternative measures of financial leverage. Should the market value of equity be used or the book value? Is it better to use the market value of debt or the book value? How should you treat off-balance-sheet obligations such as pension liabilities? How would you treat preferred stock?

11. **Measuring leverage (S29.4)** Suppose that a firm has both fixed-rate and floating-rate debt outstanding. What effect will a decline in interest rates have on the firm's times-interest-earned ratio? What about the ratio of the market value of debt to that of equity? Would you judge that leverage has increased or decreased?

12. **Measuring leverage and liquidity (S29.4–S29.5)** Look again at the balance sheet for Geomorph in Problem 9. Suppose that at year-end, Geomorph had $30 in cash and marketable securities. Immediately after the year-end, it used a line of credit to borrow $20 for one year, which it invested in additional marketable securities. Would the company appear to be (a) more or less liquid or (b) more or less highly leveraged? Make any additional assumptions that you need.

13. **Measuring liquidity (S29.5)** Airlux Antarctica has current assets of $300 million, current liabilities of $200 million, and a cash ratio of 0.05. How much cash and marketable securities does it hold?

14. **Measuring liquidity (S29.5)** How would the following actions affect a firm's current ratio?

    a. Inventory is sold.

    b. The firm takes out a bank loan to pay its suppliers.

    c. The firm arranges a line of credit with a bank that allows it to borrow at any time to pay its suppliers.

    d. A customer pays its overdue bills.

    e. The firm uses cash to purchase additional inventories.

15. **Financial ratios (S29.2–S29.5)** Look again at Table 29.8, which gives abbreviated balance sheets and income statements for Walmart. Assume Walmart had a 21% corporate tax rate in 2019. Calculate the following using balance-sheet figures from the start of the year:

    a. Return on assets.

    b. Operating profit margin.

    c. Sales-to-assets ratio.

    d. Inventory turnover.

    e. Debt–equity ratio.

    f. Current ratio.

    g. Quick ratio.

16. **Financial ratios (S29.2–S29.5)** There are no universally accepted definitions of financial ratios, but five of the following ratios are clearly incorrect. Substitute the correct definitions.

    a. Debt–equity ratio = (long-term debt + value of leases)/(long-term debt + value of leases + equity)

    b. Return on equity = (EBIT − tax)/average equity

    c. Profit margin = net income/sales

    d. Days in inventory = sales/(inventory/365)

    e. Current ratio = current liabilities/current assets

    f. Sales-to-net-working-capital = average sales/average net working capital

    g. Quick ratio = (current assets − inventories)/current liabilities

    h. Times-interest-earned = interest earned × long-term debt

17. **Financial ratios (S29.2–S29.5)** True or false?

    a. A company's debt–equity ratio is always less than 1.

    b. The quick ratio is always less than the current ratio.

    c. The return on equity is always less than the return on assets.

18. **Financial ratios (S29.2–S29.5)** Sara Togas sells all its output to Federal Stores. The following table shows selected 2020 financial data, in millions, for the two firms:

	Sales	Interest Payment	Net Income	Assets at Start of Year
Federal Stores	$100	$4	$10	$50
Sara Togas	20	1	4	20

The company's tax rate is 21%. Calculate the sales-to-assets ratio, the operating profit margin, and the return on assets for the two firms. Now assume that the two companies merge. If Federal continues to sell goods worth $100 million, how will the three ratios change?

19. **Financial ratios (S29.2–S29.5)** As you can see, someone has spilled ink over some of the entries in the balance sheet and income statement of Transylvania Railroad (Table 29.9). Can you use the following information to work out the missing entries? (*Note:* For this problem,

	December 2020	December 2019
Balance Sheet		
Cash	▚▙▚	20
Accounts receivable	▚▙▚	34
Inventory	▚▙▚	26
Total current assets	▙▚▚	80
Fixed assets (net)	▚▚▙	25
Total	▚▚▙	105
Notes payable	25	20
Accounts payable	30	35
Total current liabilities	▚▙▚	55
Long-term debt	▚▚▙	20
Equity	▚▙▚	30
Total	115	105
Income Statement		
Sales	▚▚▙	
Cost of goods sold	▚▙▚	
Selling, general, and administrative expenses	10	
Depreciation	20	
EBIT	▚▙▚	
Interest	▚▚▙	
Earnings before tax	▚▙▚	
Tax	▚▚▙	
Earnings available for common stock	▙▚▙	

❭TABLE 29.9 Balance sheet and income statement of Transylvania Railroad (figures in $ millions).

use the following definitions: inventory turnover = COGS/average inventory; receivables collection period = average receivables/[sales/365].)

- Long-term debt ratio: 0.4.
- Times-interest-earned: 8.0.
- Current ratio: 1.4.
- Quick ratio: 1.0.
- Cash ratio: 0.2.
- Inventory turnover: 5.0.
- Receivables collection period: 73 days.
- Tax rate = 0.4.

20. **Interpreting financial ratios (S29.6)** This question reviews some of the difficulties encountered in interpreting accounting numbers.

   a. Give four examples of important assets, liabilities, or transactions that may not be shown on the company's books.

   b. How does investment in intangible assets, such as research and development, distort accounting ratios? Give at least two examples.

21. **Interpreting financial ratios (S29.6)** Here are some data for five companies in the same industry:

	Company Code				
	A	**B**	**C**	**D**	**E**
EBIT	10	30	100	−3	80
Interest expense	5	15	50	2	1

   You have been asked to calculate a measure of times-interest-earned for the industry. Discuss the possible ways that you might calculate such a measure. Does changing the method of calculation make a significant difference to the end result?

22. **Interpreting financial ratios (S29.6)** How would rapid inflation affect the accuracy and relevance of a manufacturing company's balance sheet and income statement? Does your answer depend on how much debt the firm has issued?

23. **Interpreting financial ratios (S29.6)** Suppose that you wish to use financial ratios to estimate the risk of a company's stock. Which of those that we have described in this chapter are likely to be helpful? Can you think of other accounting measures of risk?

24. **Interpreting financial ratios (S29.6)** Look up some firms that have been in trouble. Plot the changes over the preceding years in the principal financial ratios. Are there any patterns?

CHALLENGE

25. **Calculating EVA (S29.2)** We noted that when calculating EVA, you should calculate income as the sum of the after-tax interest payment and net income. Why do you need to deduct the tax shield? Would an alternative be to use a different measure of the cost of capital? Or would you get the same result if you simply deducted the cost of equity from net income (as is often done)?

26. **Return on capital (S29.2)** Sometimes analysts use the average of capital at the start and end of the year to calculate return on capital. Provide some examples to illustrate when this does and does not make sense. (*Hint:* Start by assuming that capital increases solely as a result of retained earnings.)

27. **Measuring leverage (S29.4)** Take another look at Geomorph Trading's balance sheet in Problem 9 and consider the following additional information:

Current Assets		Current Liabilities		Other Liabilities	
Cash	$15	Payables	$35	Deferred tax	$32
Inventories	35	Taxes due	10	Unfunded pensions	22
Receivables	50	Bank loan	15	R&R reserve	16
	$100		$60		$70

The "R&R reserve" covers the future costs of removal of an oil pipeline and environmental restoration of the pipeline route.

There are many ways to calculate a debt ratio for Geomorph. Suppose you are evaluating the safety of Geomorph's debt and want a debt ratio for comparison with the ratios of other companies in the same industry. Would you calculate the ratio in terms of total liabilities or total capitalization? What would you include in debt—the bank loan, the deferred tax account, the R&R reserve, the unfunded pension liability? Explain the pros and cons of these choices.

• • • • •

SOLUTIONS TO SELF-TEST QUESTIONS

29.1 a. receivables and e. inventory.

29.2 The entire net income of $1,512 million.

29.3 $50 - (0.11 \times 220) = \$25.8$ million

29.4 Asset turnover increases, and operating profit margin falls. Return on assets could either rise or fall.

29.5 Long-term debt ratio is unchanged. However, times interest earned and the cash coverage ratio increase.

29.6 a. The current ratio starts at $1.2/1.0 = 1.2$. The transaction will reduce current assets to $0.7 million and current liabilities to $0.5 million. The current ratio increases to $0.7/0.5 = 1.4$. Net working capital is unchanged at $0.2 million.

  b. The current ratio is unaffected. However, the quick ratio will fall because inventories are not included among the most liquid assets.

• • • • •

FINANCE ON THE WEB

Use data from Yahoo! Finance (**finance.yahoo.com**) to answer the following questions.

1. Select two companies that are in a similar line of business and find their simplified balance sheets and income statements. Then draw up financial statements for each company and compute the principal financial ratios. Compare and contrast the companies based on these data.

2. Look up the latest financial statements for a company of your choice and calculate the following ratios for the latest year:

   a. Return on capital.

   b. Return on equity.

   c. Operating profit margin.

    d. Days in inventory.

    e. Debt ratio.

    f. Times-interest-earned.

    g. Current ratio.

    h. Quick ratio.

3. Select five companies and, using their financial statements, compare the days in inventory and average collection period for receivables. Can you explain the differences between the companies?

CHAPTER

30

Financial Planning

This chapter is concerned with financial planning. We look first at short-term planning where the focus is on ensuring that the firm does not run out of cash. Short-term planning is, therefore, often termed *cash budgeting*. In the second half of the chapter, we look at how firms also use financial planning models to help them in developing a coherent *long-term* strategy.

Section 30-1 What are the links between short-term and long-term financing decisions?
Financial managers of firms with a surplus of long-term financing and with cash in the bank enjoy greater liquidity and need to raise less short-term finance. We look at the advantages and disadvantages of this policy.

Section 30-2 Tracing and forecasting changes in cash
Short-term financial planning is about making sure that the company can pay its bills. The starting point for this is an understanding of the sources and uses of cash. We work through an example in which a company forecasts its cash needs over the coming year.

Section 30-3 Developing a short-term financing plan
We continue our example to show how planning models are used to explore the most economical way to raise the needed cash.

Section 30-4 How companies use long-term financial planning models
In this section, we look at a long-term planning model and show how it can be used to understand the financial actions that will be needed to support the company's long-term growth.

Section 30-5 Long-term planning models and company valuation
We show how the financial statements provided by long-term planning models also provide much of the basic data that you need to value the company.

Section 30-6 The relationship between growth and external financing
Faster growth implies a greater financing requirement. We look at how the plowback ratio, the return on equity, and leverage affect the growth rate that the company can maintain.

30-1 | What Are the Links between Short-Term and Long-Term Financing Decisions?

Short-term financial decisions differ in two ways from long-term decisions such as the purchase of plant and equipment or the decision to issue long-dated bonds. First, they generally involve short-lived assets and liabilities, and, second, they are usually easily reversed. Compare, for example, a 60-day bank loan with an issue of 20-year bonds. The bank loan is clearly a short-term decision. The firm can repay it two months later and be right back where

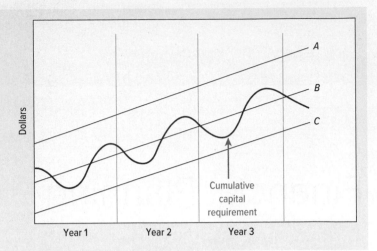

> **FIGURE 30.1**
>
> The firm's cumulative capital requirement (red line) is the cumulative investment in all the assets needed for the business. This figure shows that the requirement grows year by year, but there is some seasonal fluctuation within each year. The requirement for short-term financing is the difference between long-term financing (lines A, B, and C) and the cumulative capital requirement. If long-term financing follows line C, the firm always needs short-term financing. At line B, the need is seasonal. At line A, the firm never needs short-term financing. There is always extra cash to invest.

it started. A firm might conceivably issue a 20-year bond in January and retire it in March, but it would be extremely inconvenient and expensive to do so. In practice, the bond issue is a long-term decision, not only because of the bond's 20-year maturity but also because the decision to issue it cannot be reversed on short notice.

All businesses require capital—that is, money invested in plant, machinery, inventories, accounts receivable, and all the other assets it takes to run a business. These assets can be financed by either long-term or short-term sources of capital. Let us call the total investment the firm's *cumulative capital requirement*. For most firms the cumulative capital requirement grows irregularly, like the wavy line in Figure 30.1. This line shows a clear upward trend as the firm's business grows. But the figure also shows seasonal variation around the trend, with the capital requirement peaking late in each year. In addition, there would be unpredictable week-to-week and month-to-month fluctuations, but we have not attempted to show these in Figure 30.1.

When long-term financing does not cover the cumulative capital requirement, the firm must raise short-term capital to make up the difference. When long-term financing *more* than covers the cumulative capital requirement, the firm has surplus cash available. Thus the amount of long-term financing raised, given the capital requirement, determines whether the firm is a short-term borrower or lender.

Lines *A, B,* and *C* in Figure 30.1 illustrate this. Each depicts a different long-term financing strategy. Strategy *A* implies a permanent cash surplus, which can be invested in short-term securities. Strategy *C* implies a permanent need for short-term borrowing. Under *B,* which is probably the most common strategy, the firm is a short-term lender during part of the year and a borrower during the rest.

What is the *best* level of long-term financing relative to the cumulative capital requirement? It is hard to say. There is no convincing theoretical analysis of this question. We can make practical observations, however. First, most financial managers attempt to "match maturities" of assets and liabilities.[1] That is, they largely finance long-lived assets like plant and machinery with long-term borrowing and equity. Second, most firms make a permanent

[1] A survey by Graham and Harvey found that managers considered that the desire to match the maturity of the debt with that of the assets was the single most important factor in their choice between short- and long-term debt. See J. R. Graham and C. R. Harvey, "The Theory and Practice of Finance: Evidence from the Field," *Journal of Financial Economics* 61 (May 2001), pp. 187–243. Stohs and Mauer confirm that firms with a preponderance of short-term assets do indeed tend to issue short-term debt. See M. H. Stohs and D. C. Mauer, "The Determinants of Corporate Debt Maturity Structure," *Journal of Business* 69 (July 1996), pp. 279–312.

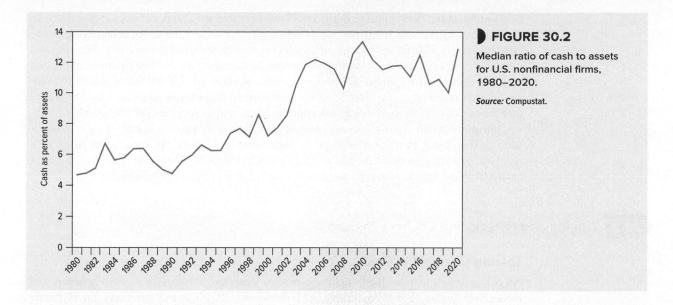

▶ FIGURE 30.2

Median ratio of cash to assets for U.S. nonfinancial firms, 1980–2020.

Source: Compustat.

investment in net working capital (current assets less current liabilities). This investment is financed from long-term sources.

Current assets can be converted into cash more easily than long-term assets. So firms with large holdings of current assets enjoy greater liquidity. Of course, some current assets are more rapidly converted into cash than others. Inventories are converted into cash only when the goods are produced, sold, and paid for. Receivables are more liquid; they become cash as customers pay their outstanding bills. Short-term securities can generally be sold if the firm needs cash on short notice, and are therefore more liquid still.

Whatever the motives for maintaining liquidity, they seem more powerful today than they used to be. You can see from Figure 30.2 that, particularly in the easy-money years before the financial crisis, firms in the United States increased their holdings of cash and marketable securities.

Some firms choose to hold more liquidity than others. For example, many high-tech companies, such as AbbVie and Gilead Sciences, hold huge amounts of short-term securities. On the other hand, firms in old-line manufacturing industries—such as chemicals, paper, or steel—manage with a far smaller reserve of liquidity. Why is this? One reason is that companies with rapidly growing profits may generate cash faster than they can redeploy it in new positive-NPV investments. This produces a surplus of cash that can be invested in short-term securities. Of course, companies faced with a growing mountain of cash may eventually respond by adjusting their payout policies. In Chapter 15, we saw how Apple sought to reduce its cash mountain by paying a special dividend and repurchasing its stock.

There are some advantages to holding a large reservoir of cash, particularly for smaller firms that face relatively high costs of raising funds on short notice. For example, biotech firms require large amounts of cash to develop new drugs. Therefore, these firms generally have substantial cash holdings to fund their R&D programs. These precautionary reasons for holding liquid assets are particularly important for small companies in relatively high-risk industries, and it is these companies that are most likely to hold large cash surpluses.[2]

Financial managers of firms with a surplus of long-term financing and with cash in the bank don't have to worry about finding the money to pay next month's bills. The cash can also

[2]T. Opler, L. Pinkowitz, R. Stulz, and R. Williamson, "The Determinants and Implications of Corporate Cash Holdings," *Journal of Financial Economics* 52 (April 1999), pp. 3–46.

help to protect the firm against a rainy day. However, there are also drawbacks to surplus cash. Holdings of marketable securities are at best a zero-NPV investment for a taxpaying firm.[3] Also, managers of firms with large cash surpluses may be tempted to run a less tight ship and may allow the cash to seep away in a succession of operating losses. For example, at the end of 2007, General Motors held $27 billion in cash and short-term investments. But shareholders valued GM stock at less than $14 billion. It seemed that shareholders realized (correctly) that the cash would be used to support ongoing losses and to service GM's huge debts.

One study found that on average shareholders appear to value a dollar of cash at about $1.20.[4] They seem to place a particularly high value on liquidity in the case of firms with plenty of growth opportunities, but when a firm is likely to face financial distress, a dollar of cash within the firm is generally worth less than a dollar to the shareholders.[5]

30-2 Tracing and Forecasting Changes in Cash

Tracing Changes in Cash

An example will help to illustrate how a company can trace change in its cash holdings and forecast its future cash needs. Table 30.1 shows the 2021 income statement for Dynamic Mattress Company, and Table 30.2 compares the firm's 2020 and 2021 year-end balance sheets. You can see that Dynamic's cash balance increased from $20 million to $30.4 million in 2021.

What caused this increase? Did the extra cash come from Dynamic's issue of long-term debt, from reinvested earnings, from cash released by reducing inventory, or from extra credit extended by Dynamic's suppliers? (Note the increase in accounts payable.) The answer is provided in the company's cash flow statement shown in Table 30.3. A positive sign in the table shows that the activity increased the company's cash balance; a negative sign shows that it reduced the cash balance.

)TABLE 30.1

Income statement for Dynamic Mattress Company, 2021 (figures in $ millions).

		2021
1	Sales	2,200.0
2	Costs	2,024.0
3	Depreciation	23.5
4	EBIT (1 – 2 – 3)	152.5
5	Interest	6.0
6	Pretax income (4 – 5)	146.5
7	Tax at 50%	73.3
8	Net income (6 – 7)	73.3
	Dividend	46.8
	Reinvested earnings	26.5

---

[3] If, as most people believe, there is a tax advantage to borrowing there must be a corresponding tax disadvantage to lending, since the firm must pay tax at the corporate rate on the interest that it receives from Treasury bills. In this case, investment in Treasury bills has a negative NPV. See Section 17-1.

[4] L. Pinkowitz and R. Williamson, "The Market Value of Cash," *Journal of Applied Corporate Finance* 19 (2007), pp. 74–81.

[5] The apparent implication is that the firm should distribute the cash to shareholders. However, debtholders may place restrictions on dividend payments to the shareholders.

	2021	2020	
Assets			
Current assets			
Cash	30.4	20.0	+10.4
Marketable securities	25.0	0.0	+25.0
Accounts receivable	150.0	124.0	+26.0
Inventory	171.6	183.0	−11.4
Total current assets	377.0	327.0	+50.0
Fixed assets			
Property, plant, and equipment	375.0	345.0	+30.0
Less accumulated depreciation	100.0	76.5	+23.5
Net fixed assets	275.0	268.5	+ 6.5
Total assets	652.0	595.5	+56.5
Liabilities and Shareholders' Equity			
Current liabilities			
Bank loans	0.0	25.0	−25.0
Accounts payable	135.0	110.0	+25.0
Total current liabilities	135.0	135.0	0.0
Long-term debt	90.0	60.0	+30.0
Shareholders' equity	427.0	400.5	+26.5
Total liabilities and shareholders' equity	652.0	595.5	+56.5

〉TABLE 30.2
Year-end balance sheets for 2021 and 2020 for Dynamic Mattress Company (figures in $ millions).

Cash flow statements classify cash flows into those from operating activities, investing activities, and financing activities. Dynamic's cash flow statement shows that Dynamic *generated* cash from the following sources:

1. It earned $73.3 million of net income (*operating activity*).
2. It set aside $23.5 million as depreciation. Remember that depreciation is *not* a cash outlay. Thus, it must be added back to obtain Dynamic's cash flow (*operating activity*).
3. It reduced inventory, releasing $11.4 million (*operating activity*).
4. It increased its accounts payable, in effect borrowing an additional $25 million from its suppliers (*operating activity*).
5. It issued $30 million of long-term debt (*financing activity*).

Dynamic's cash flow statement shows that it *used* cash for the following purposes:

1. It allowed accounts receivable to expand by $26 million (*operating activity*). In effect, it lent this additional amount to its customers.
2. It invested $30 million (*investing activity*). This shows up as the increase in gross fixed assets in Table 30.2.
3. It paid a $46.8 million dividend (*financing activity*). (*Note:* The $26.5 million increase in Dynamic's equity in Table 30.2 is due to reinvested earnings: $73.3 million of equity income, less the $46.8 million dividend.)

BEYOND THE PAGE

Try It!
Dynamic
Mattress's
short-term plan

mhhe.com/brealey14e

)TABLE 30.3 Statement of cash flows for Dynamic Mattress Company, 2021 (figures in $ millions).

Cash flows from operating activities	
Net income	+73.3
Depreciation	+23.5
Decrease (increase) in accounts receivable	−26.0
Decrease (increase) in inventories	+11.4
Increase (decrease) in accounts payable	+25.0
Net cash flow from operating activities	+107.2
Cash flows from investing activities	
Investment in fixed assets	−30.0
Cash flows from financing activities	
Dividends	−46.8
Sale (purchase) of marketable securities	−25.0
Increase (decrease) in long-term debt	+30.0
Increase (decrease) in short-term debt	−25.0
Repurchase of common stock	0.0
Net cash flow from financing activities	−66.8
Increase (decrease) in cash balance	+10.4

4. It purchased $25 million of marketable securities (*financing activity*).

5. It repaid $25 million of short-term bank debt (*financing activity*).[6]

Look again at Table 30.3. Notice that to calculate cash flows from operating activities, we start with net income and then make two adjustments. First, since depreciation is *not* a cash outlay, we must add it back to net income.[7] Second, we need to recognize the fact that the income statement shows sales and expenditures when they are made, rather than when cash changes hands. For example, think of what happens when Dynamic sells goods on credit. The company records a profit at the time of sale, but there is no cash inflow until the bills are paid. Because there is no cash inflow, there is no change in the company's cash balance, although there is an increase in working capital in the form of an increase in accounts receivable. No net addition to cash would be shown in a cash flow statement like Table 30.3. The increase in cash from operations would be offset by an increase in accounts receivable. Later, when the bills are paid, there is an increase in the cash balance. However, there is no further profit

---

[6]This is principal repayment, not interest. Sometimes interest payments are explicitly recognized as a use of funds. If so, cash flow from operations would be defined *before* interest—that is, as net income plus interest plus depreciation.

[7]There is a potential complication here because the depreciation figure shown in the company's report to shareholders is rarely the same as the depreciation figure used to calculate tax. The reason is that firms can minimize their current tax payments by using *accelerated* depreciation when computing their taxable income. As a result, the shareholder books (which generally use straight-line depreciation) overstate the firm's current tax liability. Accelerated depreciation does not eliminate taxes; it only delays them. Since the ultimate liability has to be recognized, the additional taxes that will need to be paid are shown on the balance sheet as a deferred tax liability. In the statement of cash flows, any increase in deferred taxes is treated as a source of funds. In the Dynamic Mattress example, we ignore deferred taxes.

at this point and no increase in working capital. The increase in the cash balance is exactly matched by a decrease in accounts receivable.

Table 30.3 adjusts the cash flow from operating activities *downward* by $26 million to reflect the additional credit that Dynamic has extended to its customers. On the other hand, in 2021 Dynamic reduced its inventories and increased the amount that is owed to its suppliers. The cash flow from operating activities is adjusted *upward* to reflect these changes.[8]

30.1 Self-Test

How will the following affect cash and net working capital *(current assets – current liabilities)*?

    a. The firm takes out a short-term bank loan and uses the funds to pay off some of its accounts payable.

    b. The firm uses cash on hand to buy raw materials.

    c. The firm repurchases outstanding shares of stock.

    d. The firm sells long-term bonds and puts the proceeds in its bank account.

Forecasting Dynamic's Cash Needs

Table 30.3 shows why Dynamic's cash balance rose in 2021. But its financial manager also needs to forecast the company's cash needs in 2022 and ensure that the company will be able to pay its upcoming bills. These forecasts are set out in the firm's cash budget and are then used to draw up a plan for investing any cash surpluses or financing any deficit.

There are three steps to preparing a cash budget:

Step 1	Forecast the sources of cash. The largest source of cash usually comes from payments by the firm's customers.
Step 2	Forecast the uses of cash.
Step 3	Calculate whether the firm is facing a cash shortage or surplus. The company then uses these forecasts to draw up a plan for raising or investing cash.

We will illustrate these steps by continuing with the example of Dynamic Mattress.

Step 1. Forecast the Sources of Cash   Most of Dynamic's cash inflow comes from the sales of mattresses. Therefore, we start with a sales forecast by quarter for 2022:[9]

	First Quarter	Second Quarter	Third Quarter	Fourth Quarter
Sales ($ millions)	560	502	742	836

But unless customers pay cash on delivery, these sales will become accounts receivable before they become cash. Cash flow comes from collections on accounts receivable.

Most firms keep track of the average time it takes customers to pay their bills. From this, they can forecast what proportion of a quarter's sales is likely to be converted into cash in that quarter and what proportion is likely to be carried over to the next quarter as accounts receivable.

---

[8]In practice, you will not generally find that you can derive the cash flow statement from the income statement and balance sheets. A common reason for this is the occurrence of mergers.

[9]Most firms would forecast by month instead of by quarter. Sometimes weekly or even daily forecasts are made. But presenting a monthly forecast would triple the number of entries in Table 30.4 and subsequent tables. We wanted to keep the examples as simple as possible.

Suppose that 70% of Dynamic's sales are typically paid for in the immediate quarter and the remaining 30% in the next. Table 30.4 shows forecast collections under this assumption. For example, you can see that in the first quarter, collections from current sales are 70% of $560, or $392 million. But the firm also collects 30% of the previous quarter's sales, or 0.3 × $396.7 = $119.0 million. Therefore, total collections are $392 + $119.0 = $511.0 million.

Dynamic started the first quarter with $150.0 million of accounts receivable. The quarter's sales of $560 million were added to accounts receivable, but $511.0 million of collections were subtracted. Therefore, as Table 30.4 shows, Dynamic ended the quarter with accounts receivable of 150 + 560 − 511 = $199 million. The general formula is

BEYOND THE PAGE

Try It!
Dynamic
Mattress's
short-term plan

mhhe.com/brealey14e

$$\text{Ending accounts receivable} = \text{beginning accounts receivable} + \text{sales} - \text{collections} \quad (30.1)$$

Step 2: Forecast the Uses of Cash   So much for the incoming cash. Now for the outgoing. There always seem to be many more uses for cash than there are sources. The second section of Table 30.5 shows how Dynamic expects to use cash. For simplicity, we have condensed the uses into five categories:

1. *Payments of accounts payable.* Dynamic has to pay its bills for raw materials, parts, electricity, and so on. The cash-flow forecast assumes all these bills are paid on time, although Dynamic could probably delay, or *stretch,* payment to some extent. Stretching payables is one source of short-term financing, but for most firms, it is an expensive source because, by stretching, they lose discounts given to firms that pay promptly. (This is discussed in more detail in Chapter 31.)

2. *Increase in inventories.* The expected increase in sales in 2022 requires additional investment in inventories.

3. *Labor, administrative, and other expenses.* This category includes all other regular business expenses.

4. *Capital expenditures.* Note that Dynamic Mattress plans a major outlay of cash in the first quarter to pay for a long-lived asset.

5. *Taxes, interest, and dividend payments.* This includes dividend payments to stockholders and interest on currently outstanding long-term debt. It does not include interest on any additional borrowing to meet cash requirements in 2022. At this stage in the analysis, Dynamic does not know how much it will have to borrow, or whether it will have to borrow at all.

		First Quarter	Second Quarter	Third Quarter	Fourth Quarter
1	Receivables at start of period	150	199	181.6	253.6
2	Sales	560	502	742	836
	Collections				
	Sales in current period (70%)	392	351.4	519.4	585.2
	Sales in last period (30%)	119[a]	168	150.6	222.6
3	Total collections	511	519.4	670	807.8
4	Receivables at end of period 1 + 2 − 3	199	181.6	253.6	281.8

⟩TABLE 30.4   To forecast Dynamic Mattress's collections on accounts receivable, you have to forecast sales and collection rates in 2022 (figures in $ millions).

[a]We assume that sales in the last quarter of the previous year were $396.7 million.

	First Quarter	Second Quarter	Third Quarter	Fourth Quarter
Sources of cash				
Collections on accounts receivable	511.0	519.4	670.0	807.8
Other	0	0	77.0	0
Total sources	511.0	519.4	747.0	807.8
Uses of cash				
Payments on accounts payable	250.0	250.0	267.0	261.0
Increase in inventory	150.0	150.0	170.0	180.0
Labor and other expenses	136.0	136.0	136.0	136.0
Capital expenditures	70.0	10.0	8.0	14.5
Taxes, interest, and dividends	46.0	46.0	46.0	46.0
Total uses	652.0	592.0	627.0	637.5
Sources minus uses	−141.0	−72.6	120.0	170.3
Calculation of short-term borrowing requirement				
Cash at start of period	30.4	−110.6	−183.2	−63.2
Change in cash balance	−141.0	−72.6	120.0	170.3
Cash at end of period	−110.6	−183.2	−63.2	107.1
Minimum operating balance	25.0	25.0	25.0	25.0
Cumulative financing required	135.6	208.2	88.2	−82.1

❯TABLE 30.5   Dynamic Mattress's cash budget for 2022 (figures in $ millions).

Step 3: Calculate the Cash Balance   The forecasted net inflow of cash (sources minus uses) is shown by the bold face entries in Table 30.5. Note the large negative figure for the first quarter: a $141.0 million forecast outflow. There is a smaller forecast outflow in the second quarter and then substantial cash inflows in the second half of the year.

The bottom part of Table 30.5 calculates how much financing Dynamic will have to raise if its cash-flow forecasts are right. It starts the year with $30.4 million in cash. There is a $141.0 million cash outflow in the first quarter, so Dynamic will have to obtain at least $141.0 − 30.4 = $110.6 million of additional financing. This would leave the firm with a forecasted cash balance of exactly zero at the start of the second quarter.

Most financial managers regard a planned cash balance of zero as driving too close to the edge of the cliff. They establish a minimum operating cash balance to absorb unexpected cash inflows and outflows. We assume that Dynamic's minimum operating cash balance is $25 million. This means it will have to raise $110.6 + $25 = $135.6 million in the first quarter and $72.6 million more in the second quarter. Thus, its *cumulative* financing requirement is $208.2 million by the second quarter. Fortunately, this is the peak: The cumulative requirement declines in the third quarter by $120 million to $88.2 million. In the final quarter, Dynamic is out of the woods: Its cash balance is $107.1 million, well above its minimum operating balance.

30.2 Self-Test

Calculate Dynamic's quarterly cash receipts (as in Table 30.4) if customers pay for only 60% of purchases in the current quarter and pay the remaining 40% in the following quarter.

Our next task is to show how firms develop a short-term financial plan that covers the forecasted requirements in the most economical way. We continue with the example of Dynamic Mattress after two general observations:

1. The large forecast cash outflows in the first two quarters do not necessarily spell trouble for Dynamic Mattress. In part, they reflect the capital investment made in the first quarter: Dynamic is spending $70 million, but it should be acquiring an asset worth that much or more. The cash outflows also reflect low sales in the first half of the year; sales recover in the second half.[10] If this is a predictable seasonal pattern, the firm should have no trouble borrowing to help it get through the slow months.

2. Table 30.5 is only a best guess about future cash flows. It is a good idea to think about the uncertainty in your estimates. For example, you could undertake a sensitivity analysis, in which you inspect how Dynamic's cash requirement would be affected by a shortfall in sales or by a delay in collections.

Dynamic's cash budget defines its problem. Its financial manager must find short-term financing to cover the firm's forecast cash requirements. There are dozens of sources of short-term financing, but, for simplicity, we will assume that Dynamic has just two options:

1. *Bank loan.* Dynamic has an existing arrangement with its bank, allowing it to borrow up to $100 million at an interest rate of 10% per year, or 2.5% per quarter. It can borrow and repay the loan whenever it chooses, but the company may not exceed its credit limit.

2. *Stretching payables.* Dynamic can also raise capital by putting off payment of its bills. The financial manager believes that Dynamic can defer up to $100 million in each quarter. Thus, $100 million can be saved in the first quarter by not paying bills in that quarter. (Note that the cash-flow forecasts in Table 30.5 assumed that these bills will be paid in the first quarter.) If deferred, these payments must be made in the second quarter, but up to $100 million of the second quarter bills can be deferred to the third quarter, and so on.

Stretching payables is often costly, even if no ill will is incurred.[11] The reason is that suppliers may offer discounts for prompt payment. Dynamic loses this discount if it pays late. In this example, we assume the lost discount is 5% of the amount deferred. In other words, if a $100 payment is delayed, the firm must pay $105 in the next quarter. This is similar to borrowing at a quarterly interest rate of 5%, or equivalently at an annualized rate over 20% (more precisely, $1.05^4 - 1 = 0.216$, or 21.6%).

Dynamic Mattress's Financing Plan

With these two options, the short-term financing strategy is obvious. Use the bank loan first, if necessary up to the $100 million limit. If there is still a shortage of cash, stretch payables.

Table 30.6 shows the resulting plan. In the first quarter of 2022, the plan calls for borrowing the full amount from the bank ($100 million) and stretching $10.6 million of payables (see lines 1 and 2 of Panel B). In addition, the company sells the $25 million of marketable securities it held at the end of 2021. Thus, it raises $100 + $10.6 + $25 = $135.6 million of cash in the first quarter (see the last line of Panel B).

[10]Maybe people buy more mattresses late in the year when the nights are longer.
[11]In fact, ill will is likely to be incurred. Firms that stretch payments risk being labeled as credit risks. Since stretching is so expensive, suppliers reason that customers will resort to it only when they cannot obtain credit at reasonable rates elsewhere. Suppliers naturally are reluctant to act as the lender of last resort.

In the second quarter, Dynamic needs to raise an additional $72.6 million to support its operations. It also owes interest of $2.5 million on its bank loan and must retire the payables that it stretched last quarter. With the 5% penalty for late payment to suppliers, this adds $10.6 + $0.5 million to the funds it must raise in the second quarter. Finally, to compensate for the interest it had been earning on the securities it sold in the first quarter, it will require another $0.50 million. In total, therefore, it must come up with $86.7 million in the second quarter.

In the third quarter, the firm generates a $120 million cash-flow surplus from operations. Part of that surplus, $86.7 million, is used to pay off the stretched payables from the second quarter, as it is required to do. A small portion is used to pay interest on its outstanding loans. It uses the remaining cash-flow surplus, $25.9 million (last line of Panel A), to pay down its bank loan. In the fourth quarter, the firm has a surplus from operations of $170.3 million. It pays off the interest and remaining principal on the bank loan and is able to invest $93.9 million in cash and marketable securities.

	First Quarter	Second Quarter	Third Quarter	Fourth Quarter
A. Cash requirements				
Cash required for operations[a]	135.6	72.6	−120.0	−170.3
Interest on bank loan[b]	0	2.5	2.5	1.9
Cost of stretched payables[c]	0	0.5	4.3	0
Repayment of last quarter's stretched payables	0	10.6	86.7	0
Lost interest on securities sold[d]	0	0.5	0.5	0.5
Total cash required	135.6	86.7	−25.9	−167.9
B. Cash raised in quarter from				
Bank loan	100.0	0	0	0
Stretched payables	10.6	86.7	0	0
Securities sold	25.0	0	0	0
Total cash raised	135.6	86.7	0	0
C. Repayments				
Repayment of bank loan	0	0	25.9	74.1
D. Addition to cash balances and security holdings				
Additions	0	0	0	93.9
E. Bank loan outstanding				
Beginning of quarter	0	100.0	100.0	74.1
End of quarter	100.0	100.0	74.1	0

❯TABLE 30.6   Dynamic Mattress's financial plan for 2022 (figures in $ millions).

[a]Cash required for operations in each quarter equals the change in cumulative financing required from the last line of Table 30.5. A negative cash requirement implies a positive cash flow from operations.
[b]The interest rate on the bank loan is 2.5% per quarter, applied to the bank loan outstanding at the start of the quarter. Thus, the interest due in the second quarter is $0.025 \times \$100$ million $= \$2.5$ million.
[c]The cost of the stretched payables is 5% of the payment deferred. For example, in the second quarter, 5% of the $10.6 million of deferred payments is about $0.53 million.
[d]The interest loss on securities sold is 2% per quarter. Thus, in the second quarter, Dynamic needs to find an additional $0.02 \times \$25$ million $= \$0.5$ million.

30.3 Self-Test

    a. Revise Dynamic Mattress's short-term financial plan, assuming that it can borrow only $80 million from the bank.

    b. In the end the bank loan is repaid, whether it is $80 million or $100 million as in Table 30.6. Why, then, does the company end up with a smaller addition to cash balances when it borrows $80 million?

Evaluating the Plan

Does the plan shown in Table 30.6 solve Dynamic's short-term financing problem? No—the plan is feasible, but Dynamic can probably do better. The most glaring weakness is its reliance on stretching payables, an extremely expensive financing device. Remember that it costs Dynamic 5% per quarter to delay paying bills—an effective interest rate of greater than 20% per year.

    The first plan would merely stimulate the financial manager to search for cheaper sources of short-term borrowing. The financial manager would ask several other questions as well. For example:

1. Does Dynamic need a larger reserve of cash or marketable securities to guard against, say, its customers paying more slowly?

2. Does the plan yield satisfactory current and quick ratios?[12] Its bankers may be worried if these ratios deteriorate.

3. Are there intangible costs to stretching payables? Will suppliers begin to doubt Dynamic's creditworthiness?

4. Does the plan for 2022 leave Dynamic in good financial shape for 2023? (Here the answer is yes because Dynamic will have paid off all short-term borrowing by the end of the year.)

5. Should Dynamic try to arrange long-term financing for the major capital expenditure in the first quarter? This seems sensible, following the rule of thumb that long-term assets deserve long-term financing. It would also dramatically reduce the need for short-term borrowing. A counterargument is that Dynamic is financing the capital investment only temporarily by short-term borrowing. By year-end, the investment is paid for by cash from operations. Thus, Dynamic's initial decision not to seek immediate long-term financing may reflect a preference for ultimately financing the investment with retained earnings.

6. Perhaps the firm's operating and investment plans can be adjusted to simplify the short-term financing problem. Is there any easy way of deferring the first quarter's large cash outflow? For example, suppose that the large capital investment in the first quarter is for new mattress-stuffing machines to be delivered and installed in the first half of the year. The new machines are not scheduled to be ready for full-scale use until August. Perhaps the machine manufacturer could be persuaded to accept 60% of the purchase price on delivery and 40% when the machines are installed and operating satisfactorily.

7. Should Dynamic release cash by reducing the level of other current assets? For example, it could reduce receivables by getting tough with customers who are late paying their bills. (The cost is that, in the future, these customers may take their business elsewhere.) Or it may be able to get by with lower inventories of mattresses. (The cost here is that it may lose business if there is a rush of orders that it cannot supply.)

---

[12]These ratios are discussed in Chapter 29.

Short-term financing plans must be developed by trial and error. You lay out one plan, think about it, and then try again with different assumptions on financing and investment alternatives. Trial and error is important because it helps you understand the real nature of the problem the firm faces. Here we can draw a useful analogy between the process of planning and Chapter 10's discussion of project analysis. In Chapter 10, we described sensitivity analysis and other tools used by firms to find out what makes capital investment projects tick and what can go wrong with them. Dynamic's financial manager faces the same kind of task here: not just to choose a plan but to understand what can go wrong and what will be done if conditions change unexpectedly.[13]

Short-Term Financial Planning Models

Working out a consistent short-term plan requires burdensome calculations. Fortunately, much of the arithmetic can be delegated to a computer. Many large firms have built short-term financial planning models to do this. Smaller companies do not face so much detail and complexity and often find it easier to work with a spreadsheet program on a personal computer. In either case, the financial manager specifies forecasted cash requirements or surpluses, interest rates, credit limits, and so on, and the model grinds out a plan like the one shown in Table 30.6.

The computer also produces balance sheets, income statements, and any special reports the financial manager may require. Smaller firms that do not want custom-built models can rent general-purpose models offered by banks, accounting firms, management consultants, or specialized computer software firms.

Most of these models simply work out the consequences of the assumptions specified by the financial manager. *Optimization models* for short-term financial planning are also available. These models are usually linear-programming models that search for the best plan from a range of alternative policies. These models help when the firm faces complex problems where trial and error might never identify the best combination of alternatives.

Of course, the best plan for one set of assumptions may prove disastrous if the assumptions are wrong. Thus, the financial manager always needs to explore the implications of alternative assumptions about future cash flows, interest rates, and so on.

30-4   Using Long-Term Financial Planning Models

It's been said that a camel looks like a horse designed by a committee. If a firm made every decision piecemeal, it would end up with a financial camel. That is why smart financial managers also need to plan for the long term and to consider the financial actions that will be needed to support the company's long-term growth. Here is where finance and strategy come together. A coherent long-term plan demands an understanding of how the firm can generate superior returns by its choice of industry and by the way that it positions itself within that industry.

Long-term planning involves capital budgeting on a grand scale. It focuses on the investment by each line of business and avoids getting bogged down in details.

Why Build Financial Plans?

Firms spend considerable time and resources in long-term planning. What do they get for this investment?

Contingency Planning   Planning is not just forecasting. Forecasting concentrates on the most likely outcomes, but planners also worry about unlikely events. If you think ahead about what

---

[13]This point is even more important in *long-term* financial planning.

could go wrong, then you are less likely to ignore the danger signals, and you can respond faster to trouble. We described in Chapter 10 how firms often consider the effect of different scenarios when considering major projects. Wise managers also think about how the firm as a whole would be affected by changes in the environment in which they operate.

Considering Options   Planners need to consider whether there are opportunities for the company to exploit its existing strengths by moving into a wholly new area. They may often recommend entering a market for "strategic reasons"—that is, not because the immediate investment has a positive NPV, but because it establishes the firm in a new market and creates options for possibly valuable follow-on investments.

Forcing Consistency   Financial plans draw out the connections between the firm's plans for growth and the financing requirements. For example, a forecast of 25% growth might require the firm to issue securities to pay for necessary capital expenditures, while a 5% growth rate might enable the firm to finance these expenditures by using only reinvested profits.

Financial plans should help to ensure that the firm's goals are mutually consistent. For example, the chief executive might say that she is shooting for a profit margin of 10% and sales growth of 20%, but financial planners need to think about whether a high sales growth may require price cuts that will reduce the profit margin.

Moreover, a goal that is stated in terms of accounting ratios is not operational unless it is translated back into what that means for business decisions. For example, a higher profit margin can result from higher prices, lower costs, or a move into new, high-margin products. Why then do managers often define objectives in this way? In part, such goals may be a code to communicate real concerns. For example, a target profit margin may be a way of saying that in pursuing sales growth, the firm has allowed costs to get out of control. The danger is that everyone may forget the code and the accounting targets may be seen as goals in themselves. No one should be surprised when lower-level managers focus on the goals for which they are rewarded. For example, when Volkswagen set a goal of a 6.5% profit margin, some VW groups responded by developing and promoting expensive, high-margin cars. Less attention was paid to marketing cheaper models, which had lower profit margins but higher sales volume. As soon as this became apparent, Volkswagen announced that it would de-emphasize its profit margin goal and would instead focus on return on investment. It hoped that this would encourage managers to get the most profit out of every dollar of invested capital.

Valuing the Firm   In Chapters 4 and 18, we valued a firm by forecasting free cash flows out to a horizon date and estimating the remaining value of the firm at that horizon. The cash flows and horizon value were then discounted back to the present. Financial planning models provide forecasts of income statements and balance sheets, which are the basis for estimating the firm's free cash flows up to the horizon date.

A Long-Term Financial Planning Model for Dynamic Mattress

We will drop in again on the financial manager of Dynamic Mattress to see how she uses a simple spreadsheet program to draw up the firm's long-term plan.

Long-term planning is concerned with the big picture. Therefore, when constructing long-term planning models it is generally acceptable to collapse all current assets and liabilities into a single figure for net working capital. Table 30.7 replaces Dynamic's latest balance sheets with condensed versions that report only net working capital rather than individual current assets or liabilities.

Suppose that Dynamic's analysis of the industry leads it to forecast a 20% annual growth in the company's sales and profits over the next five years. Can the company realistically expect to finance this out of retained earnings and borrowing, or should it plan for an issue of equity? Spreadsheet programs are tailor-made for such questions. Let's investigate.

	2021	2020
Net working capital	242.0	192.0
Fixed assets		
Gross investment	375.0	345.0
Less depreciation	100.0	76.5
Net fixed assets	275.0	268.5
Total net assets	517.0	460.5
Long-term debt	90.0	60.0
Shareholders' equity	427.0	400.5
Long-term liabilities and net worth[a]	517.0	460.5

❭TABLE 30.7 Condensed year-end balance sheets for 2021 and 2020 for Dynamic Mattress Company (figures in $ millions).

[a]When only net working capital appears on a firm's balance sheet, this figure (the sum of long-term liabilities and net worth) is often referred to as total capitalization.

The basic sources and uses relationship tells us that the sources of funds must be sufficient to cover the uses. If the company's operations do not provide sufficient cash to pay for the uses, then it will need to raise additional capital from external sources. Dynamic's external capital requirement equals the difference between the cash that the firm will need for its investments and dividend payments and the funds that it will generate from its business operations.

$$\text{External capital required} = (\text{investment in net working capital} + \text{investment in fixed assets} + \text{dividends}) - \text{cash flow from operations} \tag{30.2}$$

Thus, there are three steps to finding how much extra capital Dynamic will need and the implications for its debt ratio.

Step 1. Project next year's net income plus depreciation, assuming the planned 20% increase in revenues. These projections are shown in Panel A of Table 30.8. The first column shows net income for Dynamic in the latest year (2021) and is taken from Table 30.1. The remaining columns show the forecasted values for the following five years.

Step 2. Project what additional investment in net working capital and fixed assets will be needed to support this increased activity and how much of the net income will be paid out as dividends. The sum of these expenditures gives you the total *uses* of capital. If the total uses of capital exceed the cash flow generated by operations, Dynamic will need to raise additional long-term capital. Panel B of Table 30.8 shows these capital requirements. The first column shows that in 2021 Dynamic needed to raise $30 million of new capital. The remaining columns forecast its capital needs for the following five years. For example, you can see that Dynamic will need to issue $67.9 million of debt in 2022 if it is to expand at the planned rate and not sell more shares.

Step 3. Finally, construct a forecast, or pro forma, balance sheet that incorporates the additional assets and the new levels of debt and equity. For example, the first column of Panel C of Table 30.8 shows the latest condensed balance sheet for Dynamic Mattress. The remaining columns show that the company's equity grows by the additional retained earnings (net income less dividends), while long-term debt increases steadily to $607.8 million.

Over the five-year period, Dynamic Mattress is forecasted to borrow an additional $517.8 million, and by year 2026, its debt ratio will have risen from 17% to 47%. The interest payments would still be comfortably covered by earnings, and most financial managers could live with this amount of debt. However, the company could not continue to borrow at that rate

BEYOND THE PAGE

 Try It!
Dynamic
Mattress's
long-term plan

mhhe.com/brealey14e

	2021	2022	2023	2024	2025	2026
PANEL A						
Income Statement						
1 Revenues	2,200.0	2,640.0	3,168.0	3,801.6	4,561.9	5,474.3
2 Costs (92% of revenues)	2,024.0	2,428.8	2,914.6	3,497.5	4,197.0	5,036.4
3 Depreciation (9% of net fixed assets at start of year)	23.5	24.8	29.7	35.6	42.8	51.3
4 EBIT (1 − 2 − 3)	152.5	186.5	223.7	268.5	322.2	386.6
5 Interest (10% of long-term debt at start of year)	6.0	9.0	15.8	24.0	34.0	46.1
6 Income before tax (4 − 5)	146.5	177.5	207.9	244.4	288.1	340.5
7 Tax at 50%	73.3	88.7	104.0	122.2	144.1	170.2
8 Net income (6 − 7)	73.3	88.7	104.0	122.2	144.1	170.2
9 Dividends (60% of net income)	46.8	53.2	62.4	73.3	86.4	102.1
10 Reinvested earnings (8 − 9)	26.5	35.5	41.6	48.9	57.6	68.1
PANEL B						
Sources of Capital						
11 Net income plus depreciation (8 + 3)	96.8	113.5	133.7	157.9	186.8	221.6
Uses of Capital						
12 Investment in net working capital	50	48.4	58.1	69.7	83.6	100.4
13 Investment in fixed assets	30	79.8	95.7	114.8	137.8	165.4
14 Dividends (9)	46.8	53.2	62.4	73.3	86.4	102.1
15 Total uses of capital	126.8	181.4	216.2	257.9	307.9	367.9
16 External capital required (15 − 11)	30.0	67.9	82.5	100.0	121.0	146.3
PANEL C						
Balance Sheet (year-end)						
Assets						
17 Net working capital	242.0	290.4	348.5	418.2	501.8	602.2
18 Net fixed assets	275.0	330.0	396.0	475.2	570.2	684.3
19 Total assets (17 + 18)	517.0	620.4	744.5	893.4	1,072.1	1,286.5
Liabilities and Equity						
20 Long-term debt[a]	90.0	157.9	240.4	340.4	461.5	607.8
21 Shareholders' equity[b]	427.0	462.5	504.1	553.0	610.6	678.7
22 Total liabilities and shareholders' equity (20 + 21)	517.0	620.4	744.5	893.4	1,072.1	1,286.5
Financial Ratios						
23 Debt ratio	0.17	0.25	0.32	0.38	0.43	0.47
24 Interest cover	25.4	20.7	14.2	11.2	9.5	8.4
Columns may not add because of rounding.						

❯**TABLE 30.8**   Actual (2021) and forecasted operating cash flows for Dynamic Mattress Company (figures in $ millions).

[a]Long-term debt, the balancing item increases by external financing.
[b]Shareholders' equity equals previous year's value plus reinvested earnings.

beyond five years, and the debt ratio might be close to the limit set by the company's banks and bondholders.

An obvious alternative is for Dynamic to issue a mix of debt and equity, but there are other possibilities that the financial manager may want to explore. One option may be to hold back dividends during this period of rapid growth. That is something that you need to decide on now, not later after you have increased the dividend. An alternative may be to investigate whether the company could cut back on net working capital. For example, it may be able to economize on inventories or speed up the collection of receivables. The model makes it easy to examine these alternatives.

We stated earlier that financial planning is not just about exploring how to cope with the most likely outcomes. It also needs to ensure that the firm is prepared for unlikely or unexpected ones. For example, management would certainly wish to check that Dynamic Mattress could cope with a cyclical decline in sales and profit margins. Sensitivity analysis or scenario analysis can help to do this.

> **30.4 Self-Test**
>
> Suppose that Dynamic is committed to a 20% growth rate and to paying out 60% of its income. If it wishes to maintain the same proportions of debt and equity as in 2021, how much equity must be issued in 2022?

Pitfalls in Model Design

The Dynamic Mattress model that we have developed is too simple for practical application. You probably have already thought of several ways to improve it—by keeping track of the outstanding shares, for example, and printing out earnings and dividends per share. Or you might want to distinguish between short-term lending and borrowing opportunities, now buried in working capital.

The model that we developed for Dynamic Mattress is known as a *percentage of sales model.* Almost all the forecasts for the company are proportional to the forecasted level of sales. However, in reality many variables will *not* be proportional to sales. For example, important components of working capital such as inventory and cash balances will generally rise less rapidly than sales. In addition, fixed assets such as plant and equipment are not usually added in small increments as sales increase. The Dynamic Mattress plant may well be operating at less than full capacity, so that the company can initially increase output without *any* additions to capacity. Eventually, however, if sales continue to increase, the firm may need to make a large new investment in plant and equipment.

But beware of adding too much complexity: There is always the temptation to make a model bigger and more detailed. You may end up with an exhaustive model that is too cumbersome for routine use. The fascination of detail, if you give in to it, distracts attention from crucial decisions like stock issues and payout policy.

Choosing a Plan

Financial planning models help the manager to develop consistent forecasts of crucial financial variables. However, a planning model does not tell you whether the plan is optimal. For example, we saw that Dynamic Mattress is planning for a rapid growth in sales and earnings per share. But is that good news for the shareholders? Well, not necessarily; it depends on the opportunity cost of the capital that Dynamic Mattress needs to invest. If the new investment earns more than the cost of capital, it will have a positive NPV and add to shareholder wealth. If the investment earns less than the cost of capital, shareholders will be worse off, even though the company expects steady growth in earnings.

The capital that Dynamic Mattress needs to raise depends on its decision to pay out 60% of its earnings as a dividend. But the financial planning model does not tell us whether this dividend payment makes sense or what mixture of equity or debt the company should issue. In the end the management has to decide.[14]

30-5   Long-Term Planning Models and Company Valuation

Suppose that you need to value Dynamic Mattress. Perhaps the company is privately held and so there is no stock price to rely on. You decide to forecast free cash flows for each of the next five years and then to estimate the value of the company at the end of that time.

Table 30.9 shows that your financial planning model provides much of the basic information that you need to produce those cash flow forecasts.[15]

Notice that free cash flow is negative in each of the first five years. This reflects the rapid level of investment and explains the heavy issues of debt that Dynamic needs to make during these years. The negative flow is not necessarily a cause for concern. Dynamic is acquiring assets during this period that it expects to produce operating cash flows for many years. If investors agree, the rosy prospects should be reflected in the horizon value in year 5.

Estimating horizon value is usually the most difficult part of the exercise. We discussed several ways to do so in Chapters 4 and 18, and we won't repeat those discussions here. Instead, we will simply assume that horizon value is estimated at 10 times the 2026 earnings under all-equity financing:

$$\text{Horizon value} = 10 \times (170.2 + 23.1) = \$1,993.1 \text{ million}$$

This gives us all we need to estimate the total current value of the Dynamic Mattress Company assuming a 15% weighted average cost of capital:

$$\text{PV} = \frac{(-10.2)}{1.15} + \frac{(-12.2)}{1.15^2} + \frac{(-14.7)}{1.15^3} + \frac{(-17.6)}{1.15^4} + \frac{(-21.1+1,933.1)}{1.15^5} = \$912.8 \text{ million}$$

	$ millions				
	2022	2023	2024	2025	2026
1. Depreciation	24.8	29.7	35.6	42.8	51.3
2. Interest after tax[a]	4.5	7.9	12.0	17.0	23.1
3. Net income	88.7	104.0	122.2	144.1	170.2
4. Operating cash flow (1 + 2 + 3)	118.0	141.6	169.9	203.9	244.6
5. Investment in working capital	48.4	58.1	69.7	83.6	100.4
6. Investment in fixed assets	79.8	95.7	114.8	137.8	165.4
7. Free cash flow (4 − 5 − 6)	−10.2	−12.2	−14.7	−17.6	−21.1

⟩TABLE 30.9   Five-year forecasts of Dynamic's free cash flow ($ in millions).

[a]Note that we wish to estimate cash flow assuming all-equity financing. We therefore add back after-tax interest.

---

[14]It is possible to build linear programming models that help search for the best strategy subject to specified assumptions and conditions. These models can be more effective in screening alternative financial strategies.

[15]Look back at Table 18.1, where we set out the free cash flows for Rio Corporation. A financial planning model would be a natural tool for deriving these figures.

To estimate the value of Dynamic's equity, you would need to subtract the value of the debt.

30.5 Self-Test

Use the Beyond the Page spreadsheet to forecast Dynamic's five-year cash flows, assuming that cost of goods sold is 93% of sales. Otherwise, assume that the horizon value is maintained at 10 times the 2026 earnings and keep all other assumptions the same. Reestimate the value of Dynamic Mattress.

30-6 The Relationship between Growth and External Financing

We started this chapter by noting that financial plans force managers to be consistent in their goals for growth, investment, and financing. Before leaving the topic of financial planning, we should look at some general relationships between a firm's growth objectives and its financing needs.

We saw in Table 30.8 that with a 20% growth rate, the firm needs to raise $67.9 million of new capital in 2022. The faster the planned growth rate the greater the need for external financing. Table 30.10 shows how required external financing responds to a changing growth rate. Notice that at a 5.9% growth rate, required external financing is zero. At higher growth rates, the firm requires additional capital. At lower growth rates, reinvested earnings exceed the addition to assets and there is a surplus of funds from internal sources; this shows up as negative required external financing.

We can generalize the relationship between a firm's growth objectives and its financing needs. If net assets are proportional to sales, then the additional assets required to support any growth in sales is

$$\text{Additional net assets required} = \text{growth rate} \times \text{initial net assets}$$

and

$$\text{Required external financing} = (\text{growth rate} \times \text{initial net assets}) - \text{reinvested earnings} \quad (30.1)$$

The maximum growth rate that a firm can achieve without raising external funds is called the internal growth rate. If we set external financing to zero in Equation 30.1, then we can solve for the internal growth rate

$$\text{Internal growth rate} = \frac{\text{reinvested earnings}}{\text{net assets}} \quad (30.2)$$

Growth Rate (%)	Required External Financing ($ millions)
0	−28.5
5.9	0
10	19.7
20	67.9
30	116.1

❯**TABLE 30.10** Required external financing for Dynamic Mattress in 2022. Higher growth rates require more external capital.

We can gain more insight into what determines this growth rate by multiplying the top and bottom of the expression for internal growth rate by *net income* and *equity* as follows:

$$\text{Internal growth rate} = \frac{\text{reinvested earnings}}{\text{net income}} \times \frac{\text{net income}}{\text{equity}} \times \frac{\text{equity}}{\text{net assets}} \quad \textbf{(30.3)}$$

$$= \text{plowback ratio} \times \text{return on equity} \times \text{equity/net assets}$$

A firm can achieve a higher growth rate without raising external capital if (1) it plows back a high proportion of its earnings, (2) it has a high return on equity (ROE), and (3) it has a low debt-to-asset ratio.[16]

EXAMPLE 30.1 • Calculating Dynamic's internal growth rate

Dynamic has chosen a plowback ratio of 40%. The company starts 2022 with equity of $427 million and with net assets of $517 million. Dynamic's return on equity is ROE = 17.9%[17] and its ratio of equity to net assets is 427/517 = 0.826. If it is unwilling to raise new capital, its maximum growth rate is

$$\text{Internal growth rate} = \text{plowback ratio} \times \text{ROE} \times \text{equity/net assets}$$
$$= 0.4 \times 0.179 \times 0.826 = 0.059, \text{ or } 5.9\%$$

Look back at Table 30.10 and you will see that at this growth rate external financing is zero. This growth rate is much lower that the 20% growth rate that Dynamic is planning, which explains the company's heavy requirement for external finance.

• • • • •

Instead of focusing on how rapidly the company can grow without any external financing, Dynamic Mattress's financial manager may be interested in the growth rate that can be sustained without additional equity issues. Of course, if the firm is able to raise enough debt, virtually any growth rate can be financed. It makes more sense to assume that the firm has settled on an optimal capital structure that it will maintain. Thus, the firm issues only enough debt to keep the debt–equity ratio constant. The sustainable growth rate is the highest growth rate the firm can maintain without increasing its financial leverage. It turns out that the sustainable growth rate depends only on the plowback rate and the return on equity:

$$\text{Sustainable growth rate} = \text{plowback ratio} \times \text{return on equity} \quad \textbf{(30.4)}$$

For Dynamic Mattress,

$$\text{Sustainable growth rate} = 0.40 \times 0.1815 = 0.0726, \text{ or } 7.26\%$$

We first encountered this formula in Chapter 4, where we used it to value common stocks.[18]

These simple formulas remind us that firms may grow rapidly in the short term by relying on debt finance, but such growth can rarely be maintained without incurring excessive debt levels.

---

[16]In practice, calculating the internal growth rate and the sustainable growth rate can be a bit tricky since the return on equity *depends* on the growth rate.

[17]Dynamic is forecasting a growth rate of 20% and an ROE of 88.7/427 = 20.8%, but if it grows more slowly, sales, net income, and ROE will all be lower. This means that you need to solve for the growth rate and ROE simultaneously. The solution is easily found using the Excel solver tool.

[18]Since Dynamic's ROE depends on its growth rate, you need to solve for ROE and growth rate simultaneously. See the previous footnote.

30.6 Self-Test

State the formulas for the internal growth rate and the sustainable growth rate. Would you expect the internal growth rate to be higher or lower than the sustainable growth rate? Does this make sense?

- **Short-term planning** Short-term financial planning is concerned with the management of the firm's short-term, or current, assets and liabilities. The most important current assets are cash, marketable securities, accounts receivable, and inventory. The most important current liabilities are short-term loans and accounts payable. The difference between current assets and current liabilities is called net working capital.

- **The choice between short-term and long-term financing** A firm that issues large amounts of long-term capital, or that retains a large part of its earnings, may have permanent excess cash. Such firms are able to buy themselves time to react to a short-term crisis. This may be important for growth firms that find it difficult to raise cash on short notice. However, large cash holdings can lead to complacency.

- **Planning cash needs** The starting point for short-term financial planning is a forecast of sources and uses of cash. Firms forecast their net cash requirements by estimating collections on accounts receivable, adding other cash inflows, and subtracting all cash outlays. If the forecasted cash balance is insufficient to cover day-to-day operations, the company will need to find additional finance. Firms use computerized financial models to help plan future financing needs.

- **Long-term planning models** The financial manager also needs to consider the financial actions that will be needed to support the firm's plans for *long-term* growth. Most firms, therefore, prepare a long-term financial plan. Long-term planning forces the financial manager to consider the combined effects of all the firm's investment and financing decisions and the consequences of unexpected setbacks. We showed how you can use a simple spreadsheet model to analyze Dynamic Mattress's long-term strategy.

- **Planning models and company valuation** Long-term financial plans also provide much of the basic information that you need to estimate a company's value. We showed how forecasts in a long-term planning model can be useful when estimating free cash flow and company value.

- **Feasible growth rates** A company's internal growth rate is the maximum rate at which it can grow without the need for external finance. It is equal to

$$\text{Internal growth rate} = \frac{\text{reinvested earnings}}{\text{net assets}} \tag{30.3}$$
$$= \text{plowback ratio} \times \text{return on equity} \times \text{equity/net assets}$$

The sustainable growth rate is the rate at which it can grow without changing its leverage ratio or issuing new equity. It is equal to

$$\text{Sustainable growth rate} = \text{plowback ratio} \times \text{return one equity} \tag{30.4}$$

Long-term financial models are discussed in:

J. R. Morris and J. P Daley, *Introduction to Financial Models for Management and Planning,* 2nd ed. (Boca Raton, FL: Chapman & Hall/CRC Finance Series, 2017).

PROBLEM SETS

Select problems are available in McGraw Hill's *Connect*.
Please see the preface for more information.

1. **Sources and uses of cash (S30.2)** State whether each of the following events is a source or a use of cash, or neither.

   a. An automobile manufacturer increases production in response to a forecasted increase in demand. Unfortunately, the demand does not increase.

   b. Competition forces the firm to give customers more time to pay for their purchases.

   c. Rising commodity prices increase the value of raw material inventories by 20%.

   d. The firm sells a parcel of land for $100,000. The land was purchased five years earlier for $200,000.

   e. The firm repurchases its own common stock.

   f. The firm doubles its quarterly dividend.

   g. The firm issues $1 million of long-term debt and uses the proceeds to repay a short-term bank loan.

2. **Sources and uses of cash (S30.2)** Table 30.11 shows Dynamic Mattress's year-end 2019 balance sheet, and Table 30.12 shows its income statement for 2020. Work out the statement of cash flows for 2020. Group these items into sources of cash and uses of cash.

Balance Sheet (year-end)	2019	2020
Assets		
Cash	29.0	20.0
Marketable Securities	10.0	0.0
Accounts Receivable	110.0	124.0
Inventory	100.0	183.0
Total Current Assets	249.0	327.0
Fixed Assets		
Property, Plant, and Equipment	330.0	345.0
Less: Accumulated Depreciation	70.0	76.5
Net Fixed Assets	260.0	268.5
Total Assets	509.0	595.5
Liabilities and Equity		
Bank Loans	20.0	25.0
Accounts Payable	75.0	110.0
Total Current Liabilities	95.0	135.0
Long-Term Debt	25.0	60.0
Shareholder's Equity	389.0	400.5
Total Liability and Shareholder's Equity	509.0	595.5

❯**TABLE 30.11** Year-end balance sheet for Dynamic Mattress for 2019 and 2020 (figures in $ millions). See Problem 2.

Sales	$1,500
Operating costs	1,405
	$95
Depreciation	6.5
	$88.5
Interest	5
Pretax income	$83.5
Tax at 50%	41.8
Net income	$41.8

❭TABLE 30.12 Income statement for Dynamic Mattress for 2020 (figures in $ millions). See Problem 2.

Notes: Dividend = $30.
Retained earnings = $11.8.

3. **Sources and uses of cash (S30.2)** What will be the effect of each of the following transactions on cash, net working capital, and the current ratio? Assume that the current ratio is above 1.0.

   a. The firm borrows $1,000 in a short-term loan from its bank and pays $500 in accounts payable.

   b. The firm issues $1,000 in long-term bonds and uses the proceeds to pay $800 in payables and purchase $200 in marketable securities.

4. **Sources and uses of cash and working capital (S30.2)** Listed below are six transactions that Dynamic Mattress might make. Indicate how each transaction would affect (1) cash and (2) working capital.

   a. Pay out an extra $10 million cash dividend.

   b. Receive $2,500 from a customer who pays a bill resulting from a previous sale.

   c. Pay $50,000 previously owed to one of its suppliers.

   d. Borrow $10 million long term and invest the proceeds in inventory.

   e. Borrow $10 million short term and invest the proceeds in inventory.

   f. Sell $5 million of marketable securities for cash.

5. **Collections on receivables (S30.2)** Here is a forecast of sales by National Bromide for the first four months of 2022 (figures in $ thousands):

	Month 1	Month 2	Month 3	Month 4
Cash sales	15	24	18	14
Sales on credit	100	120	90	70

   On average, 50% of credit sales are paid for in the current month, 30% are paid in the next month, and the remainder are paid in the month after that. What is the expected cash inflow from operations in months 3 and 4?

6. **Collections on receivables (S30.2)** If a firm pays its bills with a 30-day delay, what fraction of its purchases will be paid in the current quarter? In the following quarter? What if the delay is 60 days?

7. **Forecasts of payables (S30.2)** Dynamic Futon forecasts the following purchases from suppliers:

	Jan.	Feb.	Mar.	Apr.	May	Jun.
Value of goods ($ millions)	32	28	25	22	20	20

a. Forty percent of goods are supplied cash-on-delivery. The remainder are paid with an average delay of one month. If Dynamic Futon starts the year with payables of $22 million, what is the forecasted level of payables for each month?

b. Suppose that from the start of the year the company stretches payables by paying 40% after one month and 20% after two months. (The remainder continue to be paid cash on delivery.) Recalculate payables for each month assuming that there are no cash penalties for late payment.

8. **Cash budget (S30.2)** Table 30.13 lists data from the budget of Ritewell Publishers. Half the company's sales are for cash immediately; the other half are paid for with a one-month delay. The company pays all its credit purchases with a one-month delay. Credit purchases in January were $30, and total sales in January were $180. Complete the cash budget in Table 30.14.

	February	March	April
Total sales	$200	$220	$180
Purchases of materials			
For cash	70	80	60
For credit	40	30	40
Other expenses	30	30	30
Taxes, interest, and dividends	10	10	10
Capital investment	100	0	0

> TABLE 30.13   Selected budget data for Ritewell Publishers. See Problem 8.

	February	March	April
Sources of cash			
Collections on cash sales			
Collections on accounts receivables			
Total sources of cash			
Uses of cash			
Payments of accounts payable			
Cash purchases of materials			
Other expenses			
Capital expenditures			
Taxes, interest, and dividends			
Total uses of cash			
Net cash inflow			
Cash at start of period	100		
+ Net cash inflow			
= Cash at end of period			
+ Net cash inflow			
+ Minimum operating cash balance	100	100	100
= Cumulative short-term financing required			

> TABLE 30.14   Cash budget for Ritewell Publishers. See Problem 8.

9. **Cash budget (S30.2)**

a. Paymore places orders for goods equal to 75% of its sales forecast for the next quarter. What will orders be in each quarter of the coming year if the sales in the current quarter are expected to be $320 and the sales forecasts for the next five quarters are as follows?

	Quarter in Coming Year				Following Year
	First	Second	Third	Fourth	First Quarter
Sales forecast, $	372	360	336	334	384

b. Paymore pays for two-thirds of the purchases immediately and pays for the remaining purchases in the next quarter. Calculate Paymore's cash payments in the coming year.

c. Paymore's customers pay their bills with a two-month delay. What are the expected cash receipts from sales in the coming year?

d. Now suppose that Paymore's other expenses are $105 a quarter. Calculate the expected net cash flow for each quarter in the coming year.

e. Suppose that Paymore's starting cash balance is $40 and its minimum acceptable balance is $30. Work out the short-term financing requirements for the coming year.

10. **Cash budget (S30.2)** Which items in Table 30.5 would be affected by the following events?

a. Interest rates rise.

b. Suppliers demand interest for late payment.

c. Dynamic receives an unexpected bill in the third quarter from the Internal Revenue Service for underpayment of taxes in previous years.

11. **Short-term financial plans (S30.2–S30.3)** Each of the following events affects one or more tables in Sections 30-2 and 30-3. Show the effects of each event by adjusting the tables listed in parentheses:

a. Dynamic repays only $10 million of short-term debt in 2021 (Tables 30.2 and 30.3).

b. Dynamic issues an additional $40 million of long-term debt in 2021 and invests $25 million in a new warehouse (Tables 30.1, 30.2, and 30.3).

c. At the start of 2021, Dynamic reduces the quantity of stuffing in each mattress. Customers don't notice, but operating costs fall by 10% (Tables 30.1, 30.2, and 30.3).

d. Starting in the third quarter of 2022, Dynamic employs new staff members who prove very effective in persuading customers to pay more promptly. As a result, 90% of sales are paid for immediately and 10% are paid in the following quarter (Tables 30.4, 30.5, and 30.6).

e. Starting in the first quarter of 2022, Dynamic cuts wages by $20 million a quarter (Table 30.5).

f. In the second quarter of 2022, a disused warehouse catches fire mysteriously. Dynamic receives a $50 million check from the insurance company (Table 30.5).

g. Dynamic's treasurer decides he can scrape by on a $10 million operating cash balance (Table 30.5).

12. **Short-term financial plans (S30.3)** Work out a short-term financing plan for Dynamic Mattress Company, assuming the limit on the line of credit is raised from $100 to $120 million. Otherwise, keep to the assumptions used in developing Table 30.6.

13. **Short-term financial plans (S30.3)** Dynamic Mattress decides to lease its new mattress-stuffing machines rather than buy them. As a result, capital expenditure in the first quarter is reduced by $50 million, but the company must make lease payments of $2.5 million for each of the four quarters. Assume that the lease has no effect on tax payments until after the fourth quarter. Construct two tables like Tables 30.5 and 30.6 showing Dynamic's cumulative financing requirement and a new financing plan. Check your answer using Dynamic's spreadsheet.

BEYOND THE PAGE

Try It!
Dynamic
Mattress's
spreadsheet

mhhe.com/brealey14e

BEYOND THE PAGE

Try It!
Dynamic
Mattress's
spreadsheet

mhhe.com/brealey14e

BEYOND THE PAGE

Try It!
Dynamic
Mattress's
spreadsheet

mhhe.com/brealey14e

14. **Long-term financial plans (S30.4)** True or false?

    a. Financial planning should attempt to minimize risk.

    b. The primary aim of financial planning is to obtain better forecasts of future cash flows and earnings.

    c. Financial planning is necessary because financing and investment decisions interact and should not be made independently.

    d. Firms' planning horizons rarely exceed three years.

    e. Financial planning requires accurate forecasting.

    f. Financial planning models should include as much detail as possible.

15. **Long-term financial plans (S30.4)** Corporate financial plans are often used as a basis for judging subsequent performance. What do you think can be learned from such comparisons? What problems are likely to arise, and how might you cope with these problems?

16. **Long-term planning models (S30.4)** The balancing item in the Dynamic long-term planning model is borrowing. What is meant by balancing item? How would the model change if dividends were made the balancing item instead? In that case how would you suggest that planned borrowing be determined?

BEYOND THE PAGE

Try It!
Dynamic
Mattress's
spreadsheet

mhhe.com/brealey14e

17. **Long-term planning models (S30.4)** Construct a new model for Dynamic Mattress based on your answer to Problem 16. Does your model generate a feasible financial plan for 2022? (*Hint:* If it doesn't, you may have to allow the firm to issue stock.)

18. **Long-term planning models (S30.4)**

    a. Use the Dynamic Mattress model in Table 30.8 and the spreadsheets to produce pro forma income statements, balance sheets, and statements of cash flows for 2022–2026. Assume business as usual, except that sales and costs are now planned to expand by 30% per year, as are fixed assets and net working capital. The interest rate is forecasted to remain at 10% and stock issues are ruled out. Dynamic also sticks to its 60% dividend payout ratio.

    b. What are the firm's debt ratio and interest coverage under this plan?

    c. Can the company continue to finance expansion by borrowing?

BEYOND THE PAGE

Try It!
Dynamic
Mattress's
spreadsheet

mhhe.com/brealey14e

19. **Long-term planning models (S30.4)** Table 30.15 summarizes the 2022 income statement and end-year balance sheet of Drake's Bowling Alleys. Drake's financial manager forecasts a 10% increase in sales and costs in 2023. The ratio of sales to average assets is expected to remain at 0.40. Interest is forecasted at 5% of debt at the start of the year.

Income Statement		
Sales	$1,000	(40% of average assets)[a]
Costs	750	(75% of sales)
Interest	25	(5% of debt at start of year)[b]
Pretax profit	225	
Tax	90	(40% of pretax profit)
Net income	$135	
Balance Sheet		
Net assets	$2,600	Debt	$500
		Equity	2,100
Total	$2,600	Total	$2,600

》TABLE 30.15 Financial statements for Drake's Bowling Alleys, 2022 (figures in thousands). See Problem 19.

[a]Assets at the end of 2021 were $2,400,000.
[b]Debt at the end of 2021 was $500,000.

a. What is the implied level of assets at the end of 2023?

b. If the company pays out 50% of net income as dividends, how much cash will Drake need to raise in the capital markets in 2023?

c. If Drake is unwilling to make an equity issue, what will be the debt ratio at the end of 2023?

20. **Long-term planning models (S30.4)** Abbreviated financial statements for Archimedes Levers are shown in Table 30.16. If sales increase by 10% in 2022 and all other items, including debt, increase correspondingly, what must be the balancing item? What will be its value?

Income Statement	
Sales	$4,000
Costs, including interest	3,500
Net income	$500

Balance Sheet, Year-End					
	2021	2020		2021	2020
Net assets	$3,200	$2,700	Debt	$1,200	$1,033
			Equity	2,000	1,667
Total	$3,200	$2,700	Total	$3,200	$2,700

》TABLE 30.16   Financial statements for Archimedes Levers, 2021. See Problem 20.

21. **Long-term planning models (S30.4)** The financial statements of Eagle Sport Supply are shown in Table 30.17. For simplicity, "Costs" include interest. Assume that Eagle's assets are proportional to its sales.

a. Find Eagle's required external funds if it maintains a dividend payout ratio of 50% and plans a growth rate of 15% in 2023.

b. If Eagle chooses not to issue new shares of stock, what variable must be the balancing item? What will its value be?

c. Now suppose that the firm plans instead to increase long-term debt only to $1,100 and does not wish to issue any new shares of stock. Why must the dividend payment now be the balancing item? What will its value be?

Income Statement	
Sales	$950
Costs	250
Pretax income	700
Taxes (at 28.6%)	200
Net income	$500

Balance Sheet, Year-End					
	2022	2021		2022	2021
Net assets	$3,000	$2,700	Debt	$1,000	$ 900
			Equity	2,000	1,800
Total	$3,000	$2,700	Total	$3,000	$2,700

》TABLE 30.17   Financial statements for Eagle Sport Supply, 2022. See Problem 21.

22. **Company valuation (S30.5)** Assume a 10% growth rate in sales and costs for Dynamic. Use the planning model to help value the company. Use the same assumption about the 2026 price/earnings ratio that we used in Section 30.5. How does firm value change? Do you think it was realistic to keep to the same price earnings ratio? Why or why not?

23. **Forecast growth rates (S30.6)** What is the maximum possible growth rate for Archimedes (see Problem 20) if it maintains its return on equity, the payout ratio is set at 50% and

    a. No external debt or equity is to be issued?

    b. The firm maintains a fixed debt ratio but issues no equity?

24. **Forecast growth rates (S30.6)**

    a. What is the internal growth rate of Eagle Sport (see Problem 21) if the dividend payout ratio is fixed at 50% and the equity-to-asset ratio is fixed at two-thirds?

    b. What is the sustainable growth rate?

25. **Forecast growth rates (S30.6)** Bio-Plasma Corp. is growing at 30% per year. It is all-equity-financed and has total assets of $1 million. Its return on equity is 20%. Its plowback ratio is 40%.

    a. What is the internal growth rate?

    b. What is the firm's need for external financing this year?

    c. By how much would the firm increase its internal growth rate if it reduced its payout rate to zero?

    d. By how much would such a move reduce the need for external financing? What do you conclude about the relationship between dividend policy and requirements for external financing?

CHALLENGE

29. **Long-term planning models (S30.5)** Table 30.18 shows the 2022 financial statements for the Executive Cheese Company. Annual depreciation is 10% of fixed assets at the

Income Statement	
Revenue	$1,785
Fixed costs	53
Variable costs (80% of revenue)	1,428
Depreciation	80
Interest (at 11.8%)	24
Taxes (at 40%)	80
Net income	$ 120

Balance Sheet, Year-End		
	2022	2021
Assets		
Net working capital	$ 400	$ 340
Fixed assets	800	680
Total assets	$1,200	$1,020
Liabilities		
Debt	$ 240	$ 204
Book equity	960	816
Total liabilities	$1,200	$1,020

Sources and Uses	
Sources	
Net income	$ 120
Depreciation	80
Borrowing	36
Stock issues	104
Total sources	$ 340
Uses	
Increase in net working capital	$60
Investment	200
Dividends	80
Total uses	$ 340

❯TABLE 30.18   Financial statements for Executive Cheese Company, 2022 (figures in thousands).

beginning of the year, plus 10% of new investment. The company plans to invest a further $200,000 per year in fixed assets for the next five years and net working capital is expected to remain a constant proportion of fixed assets. The company forecasts that the ratio of revenues to total assets at the start of each year will remain at 1.75. Fixed costs are expected to remain at $53, and variable costs at 80% of revenue. The company's policy is to pay out two-thirds of net income as dividends and to maintain a book debt ratio of 20%.

a. Construct a model for Executive Cheese like the one in Table 30.8.

b. Use your model to produce a set of financial statements for 2023.

● ● ● ● ●

SOLUTIONS
TO SELF-TEST
QUESTIONS

30.1 a. This transaction merely substitutes one current liability (short-term debt) for another (accounts payable). Neither cash nor net working capital is affected.

b. This transaction will increase inventory at the expense of cash. Cash falls, but net working capital is unaffected.

c. The firm will use cash to buy back the stock. Both cash and net working capital will fall.

d. The proceeds from the sale will increase both cash and net working capital.

30.2

Quarter	First	Second	Third	Fourth
A. Accounts Receivable				
Receivables (start of period)	150.0	215.3	192.1	288.1
Sales	560.0	502.0	742.0	836.0
Collections				
60% of sales in current period	336.0	301.2	445.2	501.6
40% of sales in previous period	158.7	224.0	200.8	296.8
Total collections	494.7	525.2	646.0	798.4
Receivables (end of period)	215.3	192.1	288.1	325.7

30.3 a.

Quarter:	First	Second	Third	Fourth
A. Cash Requirements				
Cash required for operations	135.6	72.6	−120.0	−170.3
Interest on bank loan	0.0	2.0	2.0	1.9
Interest on stretched payables	0.0	1.5	5.4	0.0
Repayment of last quarter's stretched payables	0.0	30.6	107.2	0.0
Lost interest on sold securities	0.0	0.5	0.5	0.5
Total cash required	135.6	107.2	−4.9	−167.9
B. Cash Raised in Quarter				
Bank loan	80.0	0.0	0.0	0.0
Stretched payables	30.6	107.2	0.0	0.0
Securities sold	25.0	0.0	0.0	0.0
Total cash raised	135.6	107.2	0.0	0.0
C. Repayments				
Of bank loan	0.0	0.0	4.9	75.1
D. Addition to Cash Balances or Security Holdings	0.0	0.0	0.0	92.8
E. Bank Loan				
Beginning of quarter	0.0	80.0	80.0	75.1
End of quarter	80.0	80.0	75.1	0.0

b. The implicit interest rate on stretching payables is higher than the rate on the bank loan. In the first quarter, if the company can borrow only $80 million, it must stretch payables by $30.6 million rather than $10.6 million (as in Table 30.6). Borrowing at the higher interest rate means that Dynamic incurs higher total interest payments and faces a greater need to raise cash in the second quarter. This, in turn, slows the rate at which it can pay off the bank loan. Therefore, the interest due on the bank loan in the fourth quarter is higher, and that higher interest payment absorbs some of the funds that would have been available to invest in cash or securities. The model allows us to trace the chain of implications over the course of the year.

30.4 The total amount of external financing is unchanged because the dividend payout is unchanged. The $103.4 million increase in total assets in 2022 will now be financed by a mixture of debt and equity. In 2021 equity accounted for 427/517 = 0.826 of capital. Therefore, the firm will need to increase equity by 0.826 × $103.4 = $85.4 million and debt by 0.174 × $103.4 = $18.0 million. Because reinvested earnings already increase shareholders' equity by $35.5 million, the firm would issue an additional $49.9 million of new equity and $18.0 million of debt.

30.5

	2022	2023	2024	2025	2026
Free cash flow	−23.4	−28.1	−33.7	−40.4	−48.5
Horizon value					1,659.4
Total cash flow	−23.4	−28.1	−33.7	−40.4	1,610.9
PV at 15%	714.2				

See Self-Test 30.5.

30.6

$$\text{Internal growth rate} = \frac{\text{reinvested earnings}}{\text{net assets}}$$

$$= \text{plowback ratio} \times \text{return on equity} \times \text{equity/net assets} \qquad (30.6)$$

$$\text{Sustainable growth rate} = \text{plowback ratio} \times \text{return on equity}$$

As long as the company has some debt, equity/net assets must be less than 1.0, and the internal growth rate must be less than the sustainable growth rate.

Look up the financial statements for any company on **finance.yahoo.com.** Make some plausible forecasts for future growth and the asset base needed to support that growth. Then use a spreadsheet program to develop a five-year financial plan. What financing is needed to support the planned growth? How vulnerable is the company to an error in your forecasts?

FINANCE ON THE WEB

CHAPTER

Working Capital Management

Most of this book is devoted to long-term financial decisions, including capital budgeting and debt policy. We now turn to the management of current assets and liabilities. "Current" or "short term" means that the asset or liability will mature or be replaced in 12 months or less.

The principal short-term assets are cash and short-term investments, inventories, and accounts receivable (payments due from customers). The main items on the liability side are accounts payable (payments the firm must make to suppliers), short-term borrowing, and the current portion of long-term debt—that is, principal payments that come due in the next 12 months.

Section 31-1 The working capital requirement
All these components of working capital need to be managed. Section 31-1 provides an overview of working capital and shows how the firm's working capital requirements depend on the nature of its operations.

Section 31-2 Managing inventories
We then turn to look at some of the more important elements, beginning in Section 31-2 with inventories. We show that the

management of inventories boils down to a trade-off of the costs of holding inventories against the benefit of having buffer stocks to meet unexpected needs.

Section 31-3 Accounts receivable management
This section looks at the management of accounts receivable. The firm needs to set sensible credit terms, determine which customers are poor credits, and establish a collection system.

Section 31-4 Cash management
We consider how cash is managed. Although cash is needed for day-to-day transactions, it is important to sweep up excess cash that would otherwise sit idle.

Section 31-5 Investing surplus cash
Excess cash is usually invested in short-term financial instruments, including Treasury bills, commercial paper, and repos (repurchase agreements). Section 31-5 concludes the chapter, with a description of these money market securities and shows how to calculate their yields.

31-1   The Working Capital Requirement

Current assets and liabilities are collectively labeled **working capital.** Table 31.1 shows the composition of working capital of all U.S. manufacturing companies in 2020. The asset side of this working capital balance sheet includes cash and short-term investments, inventories, and accounts receivable (payments due from customers). The liability side includes accounts payable (payments the firm must make to suppliers), short-term borrowing, income taxes due, and the portion of long-term debt that comes due in the next 12 months. There is also a large

Current Assets					Current Liabilities
Cash	$ 584	4.9%	$ 216	1.8	Short-term loans
Other short-term financial investments	294	2.5	679	5.7	Accounts payable
Accounts receivable	774	6.5	36	0.3	Accrued income taxes
Inventories	877	7.4	208	1.8	Current payments due on long-term debt
Other current assets	536	4.5	1,131	9.5	Other current liabilities
Total	$3,064	25.8%	$2,270	19.1%	Total
Net working capital	$ 794				

〉TABLE 31.1 Current assets and liabilities for U.S. manufacturing corporations, 4th quarter 2020 ($ billions). Percentages show the size of each short-term asset or liability relative to total book assets.

Source: U.S. Census Bureau, Quarterly Financial Report for U.S. Manufacturing, Mining, and Trade Corporations, Table 1, www.census.gov/econ/qfr/index.html.

entry for various other current liabilities. Current assets are larger than current liabilities, so **net working capital** (current assets minus current liabilities) is on average positive.

The percentages in Table 31.1 show that working capital is not small change. For example, accounts receivable and inventories each accounted for about 7% of total book assets. The sum of all current assets was nearly 26% of total book assets.

The financial manager cannot freely choose the amount of investment in inventories or accounts receivable or the size of accounts payable; the amounts will depend in large part on the nature of the firm's operations and the industry in which it operates. It may also depend on your firm's cumulative free cash flow. A company that generates more cash than it invests will often build up large holdings of cash and short-term investments. We will note shortly the "cash mountains" accumulated by Apple, Facebook, and a few other highly profitable companies.

Figure 31.1 shows the relative importance of working capital in different industries. For example, current assets account for nearly 50% of total book assets for machinery producers but only 6% of book assets for railroads. For some industries, current assets means principally inventory; for others, it means accounts receivable or cash and securities. Retail firms hold large inventories. Receivables are relatively more important for auto producers. Cash and securities make up the bulk of current assets for software companies.

The Cash Cycle

Think about the operations of a typical firm and the resulting need for finance. The firm buys raw materials, processes them into finished goods, and then generally sells these goods on credit. The whole cycle of operations looks like this:

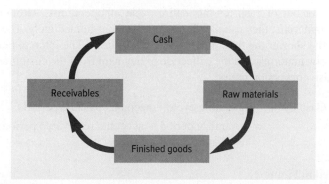

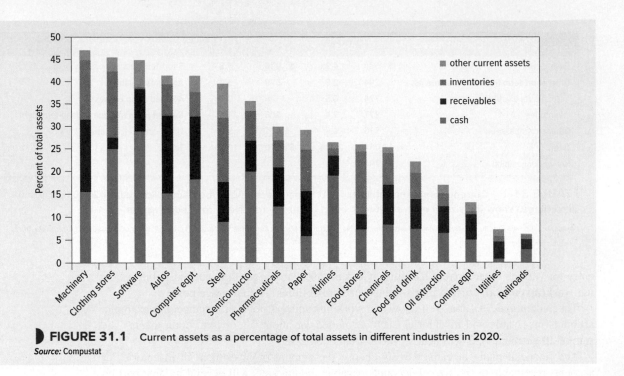

FIGURE 31.1   Current assets as a percentage of total assets in different industries in 2020.
Source: Compustat

If you draw up a balance sheet at the beginning of the process, you see cash. If you delay a little, you find the cash replaced by inventories of raw materials and, still later, by inventories of finished goods. When the goods are sold, the inventories give way to accounts receivable, and, finally, when the customers pay their bills, the firm draws out its profit and replenishes the cash balance.

The delay between the initial investment in inventories and the final sale date is called the *inventory period* (a measure that should be familiar to you from Chapter 29). The delay between the time that the goods are sold and when the customers finally pay their bills is the *accounts receivable period* (another measure that should be familiar). The total length of time from the purchase of raw materials until the final payment by the customer is termed the *operating cycle*:

$$\text{Operating cycle} = \text{inventory period} + \text{accounts receivable period}$$

Companies are not out of cash for this entire cycle of operations. Although they start by purchasing raw materials, they usually do not pay for them immediately. The longer that they defer payment, the shorter the time that they are out of cash. The interval between the firm's payment for its raw materials and the collection of payment from the customer is known as the cash cycle or cash conversion period:

$$
\begin{aligned}
\text{Cash cycle} = {}& \text{operating cycle} - \text{accounts payable period} \\
= {}& (\text{inventory period} + \text{accounts receivable period}) \\
& - \text{accounts payable period}
\end{aligned}
$$

This is illustrated in Figure 31.2.

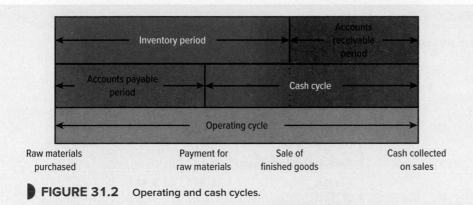

▶ **FIGURE 31.2**   Operating and cash cycles.

EXAMPLE 31.1 • Calculating the cash cycle for U.S. manufacturing companies

Table 31.2 provides the information necessary to calculate the cash cycle for U.S. manufacturers. Call the day on which firms purchase materials day 0. Firms do not pay for these materials until day 39 (payable period = 39 days). By day 59, companies have converted the raw materials into finished products, which are then sold (inventory period = 59 days). Forty-five days later, on day 104, customers pay for their purchases (receivables period = 45 days). Thus, cash goes out of the door on day 39 and does not come back in again until day 104. The cash cycle for U.S. manufacturing firms is

Inventory period + receivables period − payables period = 59 + 45 − 39 = 65 days

In other words, it is taking U.S. manufacturing companies over nine weeks from the time they lay out money on inventories to collect payment from their customers. This shows up in the working capital that companies need to maintain.

Of course, the cash cycle is much shorter in some businesses than in others. For example, aircraft are not manufactured overnight. So aerospace companies typically hold large inventories and offer long payment periods. Their cash cycle is nearly six months, and they need to make a substantial investment in net working capital. By contrast, retail companies with their low investment in receivables often have negative cash cycles.

• • • • •

Income statement	
Sales	$6,133
Cost of goods sold	5,464
Balance sheet, start of year	
Inventory	$ 879
Accounts receivable	764
Accounts payable	682
Average inventory period = inventory at start of year/daily cost of goods sold = 879/(5,464/365) = 59 days	
Average receivables period = receivables at start of year/daily sales = 764/(6,133/365) = 45 days	
Average payables period = payables at start of year/daily cost of goods sold = 682/(5,464/365) = 39 days	

▶**TABLE 31.2**   Data used to calculate the cash cycles for U.S. manufacturing firms in 2020 (figures in billions).

Note: Cost of goods sold includes selling, general, and administrative expenses.
Source: U.S. Department of Commerce, Quarterly Financial Report for Manufacturing, Mining, Trade and Selected Service industries, December 2020, Tables 1.0 and 1.1.

31.1 Self-Test

Here are some recent data for Walmart and Boeing. What are their cash cycles?

(figures in billions)	Walmart	Boeing
Income statement		
Sales	$514.4	$101.1
Cost of goods sold	385.3	81.5
Balance sheet, start of year		
Inventory	$ 43.8	$ 44.3
Accounts receivable	5.6	9.8
Accounts payable	46.1	12.2

31-2   Managing Inventories

Most firms keep inventories of raw materials, work in process, or finished goods awaiting sale and shipment. But they are not obliged to do so. For example, they could buy materials day by day, as needed. But then they would pay higher prices for ordering in small lots, and they would risk production delays if the materials were not delivered on time. They can avoid that risk by ordering more than the firm's immediate needs. Similarly, firms could do away with inventories of finished goods by producing only what they expect to sell tomorrow. But this too could be a dangerous strategy. A small inventory of finished goods may mean shorter and more costly production runs, and it may not be sufficient to meet an unexpected increase in demand.

There are also costs to holding inventories that must be set against these benefits. Money tied up in inventories does not earn interest, storage and insurance must be paid for, and there may be risk of spoilage or obsolescence. Firms need to strike a sensible balance between the benefits of holding inventory and the costs.

EXAMPLE 31.2 • The inventory trade-off

Akron Wire Products uses 255,000 tons a year of wire rod. Suppose that it orders Q tons at a time from the manufacturer. Just before delivery, Akron has effectively no inventories. Just *after* delivery it has an inventory of Q tons. Thus, Akron's inventory of wire rod roughly follows the sawtooth pattern in Figure 31.3.

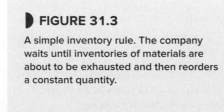

▶ **FIGURE 31.3**

A simple inventory rule. The company waits until inventories of materials are about to be exhausted and then reorders a constant quantity.

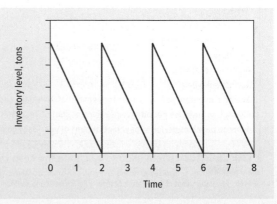

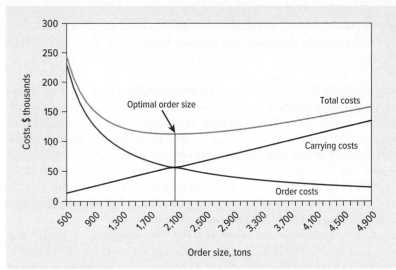

FIGURE 31.4

As the inventory order size is increased, order costs fall and inventory carrying costs rise. Total costs are minimized when the saving in order costs is equal to the increase in carrying costs.

There are two costs to this inventory. First, each order that Akron places involves a handling and delivery cost. Second, there are carrying costs, such as the cost of storage and the opportunity cost of the capital that is invested in inventory. Akron can reduce the order costs by placing fewer and larger orders. On the other hand, a larger order size increases the average quantity held in inventory, so that the carrying costs rise. Good inventory management requires a trade-off between these two types of cost.

This is illustrated in Figure 31.4. We assume here that each order that Akron places involves a fixed order cost of $450, while the annual carrying cost of the inventory works out at about $55 a ton. You can see how a larger order size results in lower order costs but higher carrying costs. The sum of the two costs is minimized when the size of each order is $Q = 2,043$ tons. The optimal order size (2,043 tons in our example) is termed the *economic order quantity,* or *EOQ*.[1]

BEYOND THE PAGE

Try It! Figure 31.4: Akron's inventory costs

mhhe.com/brealey14e

• • • • •

Our Akron example was not wholly realistic. For instance, most firms do not use up their inventory of raw material at a constant rate, and they would not wait until stocks had completely run out before they were replenished. But this simple model does capture some essential features of inventory management:

- Optimal inventory levels involve a trade-off between carrying costs and order costs.

- Carrying costs include the cost of storing goods as well as the cost of capital tied up in inventory.

- A firm can manage its inventories by waiting until they reach some minimum level and then replenish them by ordering a predetermined quantity.[2]

- When carrying costs are high and order costs are low, it makes sense to place more frequent orders and maintain higher levels of inventory.

- Inventory levels do not rise in direct proportion to sales (see footnote 1). As sales increase, the optimal inventory level rises, but less than proportionately.

---

[1]Where the firm uses up materials at a constant rate, as in our example, there is a simple formula for calculating the economic order quantity (or EOQ). Its optimal size $= Q = \sqrt{(2 \times \text{sales} \times \text{cost per order/carrying cost})}$. In our example $Q = \sqrt{(2 \times 255,000 \times 450/55)} = 2,043$ tons.

[2]This is known as a *reorder point* (or *two-bin*) *system.* Some firms use instead a *periodic review system,* where the firm reviews inventory levels periodically and tops the inventory up to the desired amount.

> ### 31.2 Self-Test
>
> If interest rates rise, do order costs or carrying costs change? What would you expect would happen to inventory levels?

Manufacturers today typically get by with slimmer inventories than they used to. Some have adopted a *just-in-time* strategy in which inventories of parts and subassemblies are nearly zero. Just-in-time was pioneered by Toyota. Suppliers deliver parts and subassemblies to Toyota's assembly plants only as needed on the production line. Deliveries are made throughout the day at intervals as short as one hour. Toyota can operate successfully with minimal inventories only because it and its suppliers make sure that traffic snarl-ups, strikes, and other hazards do not interrupt the flow of components and bring production to a standstill. Thus, a just-in-time inventory system has its costs. The company and its suppliers have to maintain systems and procedures to ensure that parts really do arrive just in time.

Just-in-time inventory management works when the flow of production is steady and predictable so that no significant buffer is needed for unexpected changes or requirements. But in most circumstances, inventory buffers are needed. For example, a gas-fired power plant may hold a supply of fuel oil for use in case gas supplies are cut short. (Some power plants in New England switch from natural gas to fuel oil in severe cold snaps, when the demand for gas for residential heating soars.) Department stores hold extra merchandise in case consumer demand is higher than expected. It's better to bear the cost of holding inventory than to bear the risk of disgruntled customers staring at empty shelves. As a rough and general rule, the greater the uncertainty, the larger the inventory buffer should be.

Sometimes it may be possible to reduce inventories of finished goods by producing the goods to order. For example, Dell Computer discovered that it did not need to keep a large stock of finished machines. Its customers are able to use the Internet to specify what features they want on their PCs. The computer is then assembled to order and shipped to the customer.[3]

31-3   Accounts Receivable Management

We continue our tour of current assets with the firm's *accounts receivable.* When one company sells goods to another, it does not usually expect to be paid immediately. These unpaid bills, or **trade credit,** compose the bulk of accounts receivable. The remainder is made up of **consumer credit**—that is, bills awaiting payment by the final customer.

Management of trade credit requires answers to four sets of questions:

1. How long do you give customers to pay their bills? Are you prepared to offer a cash discount for prompt payment?

2. How do you determine which customers are likely to pay their bills?

3. How much credit are you prepared to extend to each customer? Do you play it safe by turning down any doubtful prospects? Or do you accept the risk of a few bad debts as part of the cost of building a large regular clientele?

4. How do you collect the money when it becomes due? What do you do about reluctant payers or deadbeats?

We discuss each of these topics in turn.

---

[3]These examples of just-in-time and build-to-order production are taken from T. Murphy, "JIT When ASAP Isn't Good Enough," *Ward's Auto World,* May 1999, pp. 67–73; R. Schreffler, "Alive and Well," *Ward's Auto World,* May 1999, pp. 73–77; and "A Long March: Mass Customization," *The Economist,* July 14, 2001, pp. 63–65.

Terms of Sale

Not all sales involve credit. For example, if you are supplying goods to a wide variety of irregular customers, you may demand cash on delivery (COD). And, if your product is custom-designed, it may be sensible to ask for cash before delivery (CBD) or to ask for *progress payments* as the work is carried out.

When we look at transactions that do involve credit, we find that each industry seems to have its own particular practices.[4] These norms have a rough logic. For example, firms selling consumer durables may allow the buyer a month to pay, while those selling perishable goods, such as cheese or fresh fruit, typically demand payment in a week. Similarly, a seller may allow more extended payment if its customers are in a low-risk business, if their accounts are large, if they need time to check the quality of the goods, or if the goods are not quickly resold.

To encourage customers to pay before the final date, it is common to offer a cash discount for prompt settlement. For example, pharmaceutical companies commonly require payment within 30 days but may offer a 2% discount to customers who pay within 10 days. These terms are referred to as "2/10, net 30."[5]

31.3 Self-Test

Suppose that a firm sells goods on terms of 2/10, net 20. On May 1, you buy goods from the company with an invoice value of $20,000. How much would you need to pay if you took the cash discount? By what date should you pay for your purchase if you do not take the cash discount?

Cash discounts are often very large. For example, a customer who buys on terms of 2/10, net 30 may decide to forgo the cash discount and pay on the 30th day. This means that the customer obtains an extra 20 days' credit but pays about 2% more for the goods. This is equivalent to borrowing money at an annually compounded rate of 44.6%.[6] Of course, any firm that delays payment beyond the due date gains a cheaper loan but damages its reputation.

EXAMPLE 31.3 • Calculating interest rates on trade credit

What is the implied interest rate on trade credit if the discount for early payment is 5/10, net 60? The cash discount in this case is 5% and customers who choose not to take the discount receive an extra $60 - 10 = 50$ days credit. So the effective annual interest is

$$\text{Annually compounded rate} = \left(1 + \frac{\text{discount}}{\text{discounted price}} \right)^{365/\text{extra days credit}} - 1$$

$$= \left(1 + \frac{5}{95} \right)^{365/50} - 1 = 0.454, \text{ or } 45.4\%$$

In this case, the customer who does not take the discount is effectively borrowing money at an annual interest rate of 45.4%.

• • • • •

---

[4]Standard credit terms in different industries are reported in C. K. Ng, J. K. Smith, and R. L. Smith, "Evidence on the Determinants of Credit Terms Used in Interfirm Trade," *Journal of Finance* 54 (June 1999), pp. 1109–1129.

[5]If goods are bought on a recurrent basis, it may be inconvenient to require separate payment for each delivery. A common solution is to pretend that all sales during the month in fact occur at the end of the month (EOM). Thus, goods may be sold on terms of 8/10 EOM, net 60. This arrangement allows the customer a cash discount of 8% if the bill is paid within 10 days of the end of the month; otherwise the full payment is due within 60 days of the invoice date.

[6]The cash discount allows you to pay $98 rather than $100. If you do not take the discount, you get a 20-day loan, but you pay 2/98 = 2.04% more for your goods. The number of 20-day periods in a year is 365/20 = 18.25. A dollar invested for 18.25 periods at 2.04% per period grows to $(1.0204)^{18.25} = \$1.446$, a 44.6% return on the original investment. If a customer is happy to borrow at this rate, it's a good bet that he or she is desperate for cash (or can't work out compound interest). For a discussion of this issue, see J. K. Smith, "Trade Credit and Information Asymmetry," *Journal of Finance* 42 (1987), pp. 863–872.

> ### 31.4 Self-Test

What would be the annually compounded interest rate in Example 31.3 if the terms of sale were 5/10, net 50? Why is the rate higher?

Credit Analysis

Unfortunately, not all customers pay their bills even by the due date. There are a number of ways to find out whether customers are likely to pay. For existing customers, an obvious indication is whether they have paid promptly in the past. For new customers, you can use the firm's financial statements to make your own assessment, or you may be able to look at how highly investors value the firm.[7] However, the simplest way to assess a customer's credit standing is to seek the views of a specialist in credit assessment. For example, in Chapter 24, we described how bond rating agencies, such as Moody's and Standard and Poor's, provide a useful guide to the riskiness of the firm's bonds.

Bond ratings are usually available only for relatively large firms. However, you can obtain information on many smaller companies from a credit agency. Dun and Bradstreet is by far the largest of these agencies, and its database contains credit information on millions of businesses worldwide. Credit bureaus are another source of data on a customer's credit standing. In addition to providing data on small businesses, they can also provide an overall credit score for individuals.[8]

Finally, firms can also ask their bank to undertake a credit check. It will contact the customer's bank and ask for information on the customer's average balance, access to bank credit, and general reputation.

Of course you don't want to subject each order to the same credit analysis. It makes sense to concentrate your attention on the large and doubtful orders.

The Credit Decision

Let us suppose that you have taken the first three steps toward an effective credit operation. In other words, you have fixed your terms of sale, you have decided on the contract that customers must sign, and you have established a procedure for estimating the probability that they will pay up. Your next step is to work out which of your customers should be offered credit.

If there is no possibility of repeat orders, the decision is relatively simple. Figure 31.5 summarizes your choice. On one hand, you can refuse credit. In this case, you make neither profit

> **FIGURE 31.5**
>
> If you refuse credit, you make neither profit nor loss. If you offer credit, there is a probability p that the customer will pay and you will make REV − COST; there is a probability $(1 - p)$ that the customer will default and you will lose COST.

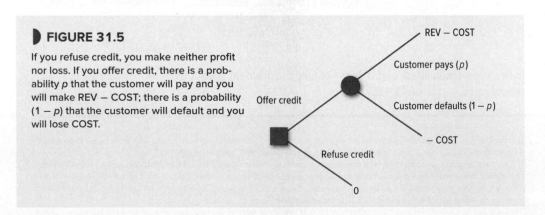

---

[7]We discussed how you can use these sources of information in Chapter 29.
[8]We discussed credit scoring models in Section 24-3.

nor loss. The alternative is to offer credit. Suppose that the probability that the customer will pay up is p. If the customer does pay, you receive additional revenues (REV) and you incur additional costs; your net gain in this case is the present value of REV − COST. Unfortunately, you can't be certain that the customer will pay; there is a probability $(1 − p)$ of default. Default means that you receive nothing and incur the additional costs. The *expected* profit from each course of action is therefore as follows:

	Expected Gain
Refuse credit	0
Grant credit	pPV(REV − COST) − (1 − p)PV(COST)

You should grant credit if the expected gain from doing so is positive.

EXAMPLE 31.4 • The credit decision

Consider the case of the Cast Iron Company. On each nondelinquent sale, Cast Iron receives revenues with a present value of $1,200 and incurs costs with a value of $1,000. Therefore, the company's expected profit, if it offers credit, is

$$p\text{PV(REV − COST)} − (1 − p)\text{PV(COST)} = p \times 200 − (1 − p) \times 1,000$$

If the probability of collection is 5/6, Cast Iron can expect to break even:

$$\text{Expected profit} = \frac{5}{6} \times 200 − \left(1 − \frac{5}{6}\right) \times 1,000 = 0$$

Therefore, Cast Iron's policy should be to grant credit whenever the chances of collection are better than 5 out of 6.

So far, we have ignored the possibility of repeat orders. But one of the reasons for offering credit today is that it may help to get yourself a good, regular customer. Figure 31.6 illustrates the problem. Cast Iron has been asked to extend credit to a new customer. You can find little information on the firm, and you believe that the probability of payment is no better than 0.8. If you grant credit, the expected profit on this customer's order is

$$\text{Expected profit on initial order} = p_1 \text{PV(REV − COST)} − (1 − p_1)\text{PV(COST)}$$
$$= (0.8 \times 200) − (0.2 \times 1,000) = −\$40$$

You decide to refuse credit.

This is the correct decision if there is no chance of a repeat order. But look again at the decision tree in Figure 31.6. If the customer does pay up, there will be a repeat order next year. Because the customer has paid once, we assume that you can be 95% sure that he or she will pay again. For this reason any repeat order is very profitable:

$$\text{Next year's expected profit on repeat order} = p_2 \text{PV(REV − COST)} − (1 − p_2)\text{PV(COST)}$$
$$= (0.95 \times 200) − (0.05 \times 1,000) = \$140$$

Now you can reexamine today's credit decision. If you grant credit today, you receive the expected profit on the initial order *plus* the possible opportunity to extend credit next year:

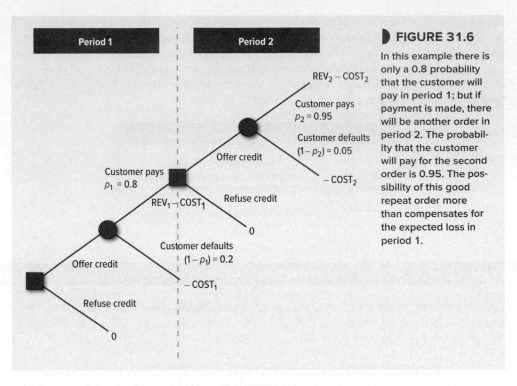

In this example there is only a 0.8 probability that the customer will pay in period 1; but if payment is made, there will be another order in period 2. The probability that the customer will pay for the second order is 0.95. The possibility of this good repeat order more than compensates for the expected loss in period 1.

$$
\begin{aligned}
\text{Total expected profit} &= \text{expected profit on initial order} \\
&\quad + \text{probability of payment and repeat order} \\
&\quad \times \text{PV(next year's expected profit on repeat order)} \\
&= -40 + 0.80 \times \text{PV}(140)
\end{aligned}
$$

At any reasonable discount rate, you ought to extend credit. Notice that you should do so even though you expect to take a loss on the initial order. The expected loss is more than outweighed by the possibility that you will secure a reliable and regular customer. Cast Iron is not committed to making further sales to the customer, but by extending credit today, it gains a valuable *option* to do so. It will exercise this option only if the customer demonstrates its creditworthiness by paying promptly.

• • • • •

Of course real-life situations are generally far more complex than our simple Cast Iron examples. Customers are not all good or all bad. Many of them pay consistently late; you get your money, but it costs more to collect and you lose a few months' interest. Then there is the uncertainty about repeat sales. There may be a good chance that the customer will give you further business, but you can't be sure of that and you don't know for how long she will continue to buy.

Like almost all financial decisions, credit allocation involves a strong dose of judgment. Our examples are intended as reminders of the issues involved rather than as cookbook formulas. Here are the basic things to remember.

1. *Maximize profit.* As credit manager, you should not focus on minimizing the number of bad accounts; your job is to maximize present value. You must face up to the following facts: The best that can happen is that the customer pays promptly; the worst is default. In the best case, the firm receives the full additional revenues from the

sale less the additional costs; in the worst, it receives nothing and loses the costs. You must weigh the chances of these alternative outcomes. If the margin of profit is high, you are justified in a more liberal credit policy; if it is low, you cannot afford many bad debts.[9]

2. *Concentrate on the dangerous accounts.* You should not expend the same effort on analyzing all credit applications. If an application is small or clear-cut, your decision should be largely routine; if it is large or doubtful, you may do better to move straight to a detailed credit appraisal. Most credit managers don't make decisions on an order-by-order basis. Instead, they set a credit limit for each customer. The sales representative is required to refer the order for approval only if the customer exceeds this limit.

3. *Look beyond the immediate order.* The credit decision is a dynamic problem. You cannot look only at the present. Sometimes it may be worth accepting a relatively poor risk as long as there is a good chance that the customer will become a regular and reliable buyer. New businesses must, therefore, be prepared to incur more bad debts than established businesses. This is part of the cost of building a good customer list.

31.5 Self-Test

In the Cast Iron example, the company would break even if the probability of collection was 5/6. Suppose that the cost of each sale is $1,080. Does this change the break-even probability of collection? What can you deduce about the relationship between the profit margin and a company's willingness to grant credit?

Collection Policy

The final step in credit management is to collect payment. To keep track of how promptly bills are paid, firms generally keep an aging schedule, which shows the proportion of accounts that are mildly or badly overdue.

There is always a potential conflict of interest between the collection operation and the sales department. Sales representatives commonly complain that they no sooner win new customers than the collection department frightens them off with threatening letters. The collection manager, on the other hand, bemoans the fact that the sales force is concerned only with winning orders and does not care whether the goods are subsequently paid for.

There are also many instances of cooperation between the sales force and the collection department. For example, the specialty chemical division of a major pharmaceutical company actually made a business loan to an important customer that had been suddenly cut off by its bank. The pharmaceutical company bet that it knew its customer better than the customer's bank did. The bet paid off. The customer arranged alternative bank financing, paid back the pharmaceutical company, and became an even more loyal customer. It was a nice example of financial management supporting sales.

It is not common for suppliers to make business loans in this way, but they lend money indirectly whenever they allow a delay in payment. Trade credit can be an important source of funds for indigent customers that cannot obtain a bank loan. But that raises an important question: If the bank is unwilling to lend, does it make sense for you, the supplier, to continue to extend trade credit? Here are two possible reasons why it may make sense: First, as in the case of our pharmaceutical company, you may have more information than the bank about

---

[9]Look back at our first Cast Iron example, where we concluded that the company is justified in granting credit if the probability of collection is greater than 5/6. If the customer pays, Cast Iron will earn a profit margin of 200/1200 = 1/6. In other words, the company is justified in granting credit if the probability of payment exceeds 1 − profit margin.

the customer's business. Second, you need to look beyond the immediate transaction and recognize that your firm may stand to lose some profitable future sales if the customer goes out of business.[10]

Large firms can reap economies of scale in record keeping, billing, and collection, but the small firm may not be able to support a fully fledged credit operation. However, the small firm may be able to obtain some scale economies by farming out part of the job to a **factor.**

Factoring typically works as follows. The factor and the client agree on a credit limit for each customer. The client then notifies the customer that the factor has purchased the debt. Thereafter, whenever the client makes a sale to an approved customer, it sends a copy of the invoice to the factor, and the customer makes payment directly to the factor. Most commonly the factor does not have any recourse to the client if the customer fails to pay, but sometimes the client assumes the risk of bad debts. There are, of course, costs to factoring, and the factor typically charges a fee of 1% or 2% for administration and a roughly similar sum for assuming the risk of nonpayment. In addition to taking over the task of debt collection, most factoring agreements also provide financing for receivables. In these cases, the factor pays the client 70% to 80% of the value of the invoice in advance at an agreed interest rate. Of course, factoring is not the only way to finance receivables; firms can also raise money by borrowing against their receivables.

Factoring is common in Europe, but in the United States it accounts for only a small proportion of debt collection. It is most common in industries such as clothing and toys. These industries are characterized by many small producers and retailers that do not have long-term relationships. Because a factor may be employed by a number of manufacturers, it sees a larger proportion of the transactions than any single firm, and therefore is better placed to judge the creditworthiness of each customer.[11]

31-4 Cash Management

In December 2021, Amazon held $10.1 billion in cash and $73.6 billion in short-term securities. Short-term securities pay interest; cash doesn't. So why do firms such as Amazon hold such large amounts of cash? Why don't they arrange for the bank to "sweep" the cash at the end of the day into an interest-bearing investment, such as a money-market mutual fund?

There are at least two reasons. First, cash may be left in non-interest-bearing accounts to compensate banks for the services they provide. Second, large corporations may have literally hundreds of accounts with dozens of different banks. It is often better to leave idle cash in these accounts than to monitor every account every day in order to make daily transfers between them.

One major reason for this proliferation of bank accounts is decentralized management. You cannot give a subsidiary operating autonomy without giving its managers the right to spend and receive cash. Good cash management nevertheless implies some degree of centralization. It is impossible to maintain your desired cash inventory if all the subsidiaries in the group are responsible for their own private pools of cash. And you certainly want to avoid situations in which one subsidiary is investing its spare cash at 5% while another is borrowing at 8%. It is not surprising, therefore, that even in highly decentralized companies there is generally central control over cash balances and bank relations.

---

[10]For some evidence on the determinants of the supply and demand for trade credit, see M. A. Petersen and R. G. Rajan, "Trade Credit: Theories and Evidence," *Review of Financial Studies* 10 (1997), pp. 661–692.

[11]If you don't want help with collection but do want protection against bad debts, you can obtain credit insurance. For example, most governments have established agencies to insure export business. In the United States, this insurance is provided by the Export-Import Bank in association with a group of insurance companies known as the Foreign Credit Insurance Association (FCIA). Banks are much more willing to lend when exports have been insured.

Check When you write a check, you are instructing your bank to pay a specified sum on demand to the particular firm or person named on the check.
Credit card A credit card, such as a Visa card or MasterCard, gives you a line of credit that allows you to make purchases up to a specified limit. At the end of each month, either you pay the credit card company in full for these purchases or you make a specified minimum payment and are charged interest on the outstanding balance.
Debit card A debit card allows you to have your purchases from a store charged directly to your bank account. The deduction is usually made electronically and is immediate. Debit cards may be used to make withdrawals from a cash machine (ATM).
Credit transfer With a credit transfer you ask your bank to set up a standing order to make a regular set payment to a supplier. For example, standing orders are often used to make regular fixed mortgage payments.
Direct debit A direct debit (or direct payment) is an instruction to your bank to allow a company to collect varying amounts from your account, as long as you have been given advance notice of the amount and date. For example, an electric utility company may ask you to arrange an automatic payment of your electricity bills from your bank account.

❱**TABLE 31.3**   Small, face-to-face purchases are commonly paid for with paper currency, but here are some of the other ways customers may pay their bills.

How Purchases Are Paid For

Many small, face-to-face purchases are made with paper currency. But you probably would not want to use dollar bills to buy a new car, and you can't use them to make a purchase over the Internet. There are a variety of ways that you can pay for larger purchases or send payments to another location. Some of the more important ways are set out in Table 31.3.

Changes in Check Usage

Look now at Figure 31.6. You can see that there are large differences in the ways that people around the world pay for their purchases. For example, checks are almost unknown in Germany, the Netherlands, and Sweden.[12] Most payments in these countries are by credit transfer or direct debit. By contrast, Americans (and Canadians) love to write checks. Each year, individuals and firms in the United States write about 11 billion checks.

But throughout the world, the use of checks is on the decline. For one-off purchases, they are being replaced by credit or debit cards. In addition, mobile phone technology and the Internet are encouraging the development of new infant payment systems. For example,

- Electronic bill presentment and payment (or EBPP) allows companies to bill customers and receive payments via the Internet. EBPP is forecasted to grow rapidly.

- Stored-value cards (or e-money) let you transfer cash value to a card that can be used to buy a variety of goods and services. For example, Hong Kong's Octopus card system, which was developed to pay for mass transit travel, is now used by 99% of Hong Kongers for payments at retail stores, car parks, and petrol stations.

Speeding Up Check Collections

Although checks are rarely employed for large-value payments, they are still widely used in the United States for smaller, nonrecurring transactions. Handling and transporting checks around the country are cumbersome and labor-intensive tasks. However, the United States

---

[12]For a discussion of the changing pattern of payment methods, see "Innovations in Retail Payments," Committee on Payment and Settlement Systems, Bank for International Settlements, Basel, Switzerland, May 2012.

and many other countries now permit images to be made of physical checks and then cleared electronically.[13]

Firms that receive a large volume of checks have devised a number of ways to ensure that the cash becomes available as quickly as possible. For example, a retail chain may arrange for each branch to deposit receipts in a collection account at a local bank. Surplus funds are then periodically transferred electronically to a **concentration account** at one of the company's principal banks. There are two reasons that concentration banking allows the company to gain quicker use of its funds. First, because the store is nearer to the bank, transfer times are reduced. Second, because the customer's check is likely to be drawn on a local bank, the time taken to clear the check is also reduced.

Concentration banking is often combined with a **lockbox system.** In this case, the firm's customers are instructed to send their payments to a regional post-office box. The local bank then takes on the administrative chore of emptying the box and depositing the checks in the company's local deposit account.

31.6 Self-Test

How will the following conditions affect the price that a firm should be willing to pay for a lockbox service?

    a. The average size of its payments increases, but the number stays the same.

    b. The number of payments per day increases (with no change in average size of payments).

    c. The interest rate increases.

    d. The average mail time saved by the lock-box system increases.

Electronic Payment Systems

Large-value payments are generally made electronically. There are three main ways that this is done: direct debits, direct deposits, and wire transfers.

Recurring expenditures, such as utility bills, mortgage payments, and insurance premiums, are increasingly settled by *direct debit* (also called *automatic debit* or *direct payment*). In this case, the firm's customers simply authorize it to debit their bank account for the amount due. The company provides its bank with a file showing details of each customer, the amount to be debited, and the date. The payment then travels electronically through the **Automated Clearing House (ACH)** system.[14] The firm knows exactly when the cash is coming in and avoids the labor-intensive process of handling thousands of checks.

The ACH system also allows money to flow in the reverse direction. Thus, while a *direct debit* transaction provides an automatic debit, a *direct deposit* constitutes an automatic credit. Direct deposits are used to make bulk payments such as wages or dividends. Again the company provides its bank with a file of instructions. The bank then debits the company's account and transfers the cash via the ACH to the bank accounts of the firm's employees or shareholders.

The volume of direct debits and deposits has increased rapidly. You can see from Table 31.4 that the total value of these transactions is more than double that of checks.[15]

---

[13]In the United States, digital imaging and clearing of checks were permitted in 2004 by the Check Clearing for the 21st Century Act, usually known as Check 21.

[14]The ACH system is operated by the Federal Reserve and by a private-sector operator, the Electronics Payments Network (EPN).

[15]The Automated Clearing House also handles check conversion transactions and nonrecurring transactions made by telephone or over the Internet.

	Volume (millions)	Value ($ trillions)
Checks	11,000	$ 19
ACH direct debits and deposits	22,970	51
Fedwire Funds Service	158	716
CHIPS	115	418

〉TABLE 31.4   Use of payment systems in the United States, 2018.

Source: Bank for International Settlements, "Statistics on Payment, Clearing and Settlement Systems in the CPSS Countries—Figures for 2018," November 2019.

Large-value payments *between* companies are usually made electronically through Fedwire or CHIPS. Fedwire is operated by the Federal Reserve system and connects 6,000 financial institutions to the Fed and, thereby, to each other.[16] CHIPS is a bank-owned system. It mainly handles eurodollar payments and foreign exchange transactions and is used for more than 95% of cross-border payments in dollars. Table 31.4 shows that the *number* of payments by Fedwire and CHIPS is relatively small, but the sums involved are huge.

International Cash Management

Cash management in domestic firms is child's play compared with cash management in large multinational corporations operating in dozens of countries, each with its own currency, banking system, and legal structure.

A single centralized cash management system is an unattainable ideal for these companies, although they are edging toward it. For example, suppose that you are treasurer of a large multinational company with operations throughout Europe. You could allow the separate businesses to manage their own cash, but that would be costly and would almost certainly result in each one accumulating little hoards of cash. The solution is to set up a regional system. In this case, the company establishes a local concentration account with a bank in each country. Any surplus cash is swept daily into a central multicurrency account in London or another European banking center. This cash is then invested in marketable securities or used to finance any divisions that have a cash shortage.

Payments can also be made out of the regional center. For example, to pay wages in each European country, the company needs to send its principal bank a computer file of the payments to be made. The bank then finds the least costly way to transfer the cash from the company's central accounts and arranges for the cash to be credited on the correct day to the employees in each country.

Rather than actually moving cash between local bank accounts and a regional concentration account, the company may employ a multinational bank with branches in each country and then arrange for the bank to *pool* all the cash surpluses and shortages. In this case, no money is transferred between accounts. Instead, the bank just adds together the credit and debit balances and pays the firm interest on any surplus.

When a company's international branches trade with each other, the number of cross-border transactions can multiply rapidly. Rather than having payments flowing in all directions, the company can set up a netting system. Each branch can then calculate its net position and

---

[16]Fedwire is a *real-time, gross settlement system,* which means that each transaction over Fedwire is settled individually and immediately. With a net settlement system, transactions are put into a pot and periodically netted off before being settled. CHIPS is an example of a net system that settles at frequent intervals.

undertake a single transaction with the netting center. Several industries have set up netting systems for their members. For example, more than 200 airlines have come together to establish a netting system for the foreign currency payments that they must make to each other.

Paying for Bank Services

Much of the work of cash management—processing checks, transferring funds, running lockboxes, helping keep track of the company's accounts—is done by banks. And banks provide many other services not so directly linked to cash management, such as handling payments and receipts in foreign currency, or acting as custodian for securities.

All these services need to be paid for. Usually, payment is in the form of a monthly fee, but banks may agree to waive the fee as long as the firm maintains a minimum average balance in an interest-free deposit. Banks are prepared to do this because, after setting aside a portion of the money in a reserve account with the Fed, they can relend the money to earn interest. Demand deposits earmarked to pay for bank services are termed *compensating balances.* They used to be a very common way to pay for bank services, but since banks have been permitted to pay interest on demand deposits, there has been a steady trend away from using compensating balances and toward direct fees.

31-5 Investing Surplus Cash

In June 2021, Apple was sitting on a $192 billion mountain of cash and fixed-income investments, amounting to nearly 60% of the company's total assets. Of this sum, $14.9 billion was kept as cash, and the remainder was invested as follows:

Fixed-Income Investments	Value at Cost ($ billions)
Money market and mutual funds	$ 9.7
U.S. Treasury and agency securities	30.1
Non–U.S. government securities	20.0
Certificates of deposit and time deposits	7.1
Commercial paper	2.1
Corporate debt securities	85.2
Municipal securities	1.0
Mortgage- and asset-backed securities	22.2
Total	$177.4

Apple's massive investments in securities came from the torrent of free cash flow produced each year by its operations.

Investment Choices

BEYOND THE PAGE

Taxing overseas income

mhhe.com/brealey14e

Most companies do not have the luxury of such huge cash surpluses, but they also park any cash that is not immediately needed in short-term investments. The market for these investments is known as the **money market.** The money market has no physical marketplace. It consists of a loose collection of banks and dealers linked together by telephones or through the web. But a huge volume of securities is regularly traded on the money market, and competition is vigorous.

Large corporations generally manage their own money market investments, but small companies sometimes find it more convenient to hire a professional investment management firm or to put their cash into a money market fund. This is a mutual fund that invests only in low-risk, short-term securities.

The relative safety of money market funds has made them particularly popular at times of financial stress. During the credit crunch of 2008, fund assets mushroomed as investors fled from plunging stock markets. Then it was revealed that one fund, the Reserve Primary Fund, had incurred heavy losses on its holdings of Lehman Brothers' commercial paper. The fund became only the second money market fund in history to "break the buck" by offering just 97 cents on the dollar to investors who cashed in their holdings. That week, investors pulled nearly $200 billion out of money market funds, prompting the government to offer emergency insurance to investors.

Calculating the Yield on Money Market Investments

Many money market investments are pure discount securities. This means that they don't pay interest. The return consists of the difference between the amount you pay and the amount you receive at maturity.

Interest rates on money market investments are often quoted on a discount basis. For example, suppose that three-month bills are issued at a discount of 5%. This is a rather complicated way of saying that the price of a three-month bill is $100 - (3/12) \times 5 = 98.75$. Therefore, for every $98.75 that you invest today, you receive $100 at the end of three months. The return over three months is $1.25/98.75 = 0.0127$, or 1.27%. This is equivalent to an annual yield of 5.16%. Note that the return is always higher than the discount. When you read that an investment is selling at a discount of 5%, it is very easy to slip into the mistake of thinking that this is its return.[17]

31.7 Self-Test

A Treasury bill with face value of $100,000 and maturity of six months is selling at a 4% discount. What is the equivalent annual yield on the bill?

Returns on Money Market Investments

When we value long-term debt, it is important to take account of default risk. Almost anything may happen in 30 years, and even today's most respectable company may get into trouble eventually. Therefore, corporate bonds offer higher yields than Treasury bonds.

Short-term debt is not risk-free, but generally, the danger of default is less for money market securities issued by corporations than for corporate bonds. There are two reasons for this. First, the range of possible outcomes is smaller for short-term investments. Even though the distant future may be clouded, you can usually be confident that a particular company will survive for at least the next month. Second, for the most part, only well-established companies can borrow in the money market. If you are going to lend money for just a few days, you can't afford to spend too much time in evaluating the loan. Thus, you will consider only blue-chip borrowers.

Despite the high quality of money market investments, there are often significant differences in yield between corporate and U.S. government securities. Why is this? One answer is that the investments have different degrees of liquidity or "moneyness." Investors like Treasury bills because they are easily turned into cash on short notice. Securities that cannot be converted so quickly and cheaply into cash need to offer relatively high yields. During times of market turmoil investors may place a particularly high value on having ready access to cash. On these occasions the yield on illiquid securities can increase dramatically.

---

[17]To confuse things even more, dealers in the money market often quote rates as if there were only 360 days in a year. So a discount of 5% on a bill maturing in 91 days translates into a price of $100 - 5 \times (91/360) = 98.74\%$.

The International Money Market

In Chapter 25, we pointed out that there are two main markets for dollar bonds. There is the domestic market in the United States, and there is the eurobond market centered in London. There is also an international market for short-term dollar investments, which is known as the *eurodollar* market. Eurodollars have nothing to do with the euro, the currency of the European Monetary Union (EMU). They are simply dollars deposited in a bank in Europe.

Just as there is both a domestic U.S. money market and a eurodollar market, so there is both a domestic Japanese money market and a market in London for euroyen. So, if a U.S. corporation wishes to make a short-term investment in yen, it can deposit the yen with a bank in Tokyo or it can make a euroyen deposit in London. Similarly, there is both a domestic money market in the euro area as well as a money market for euros in London.[18] And so on.

If we lived in a world without regulation and taxes, the interest rate on a eurodollar loan would have to be the same as the rate on an equivalent domestic dollar loan. However, the international debt markets thrive because governments attempt to regulate domestic bank lending. When the U.S. government limited the rate of interest that banks in the United States could pay on domestic deposits, companies could earn a higher rate of interest by keeping their dollars on deposit in Europe. As these restrictions have been removed, differences in interest rates have largely disappeared.

In the late 1970s, the U.S. government was concerned that its regulations were driving business overseas to foreign banks and the overseas branches of American banks. To attract some of this business back to the States, the government in 1981 allowed U.S. and foreign banks to establish *international banking facilities (IBFs)*. An IBF is the financial equivalent of a free-trade zone; it is physically located in the United States, but it is not required to maintain reserves with the Federal Reserve and depositors are not subject to any U.S. tax.[19] However, there are tight restrictions on what business an IBF can conduct. In particular, it cannot accept deposits from domestic U.S. corporations or make loans to them.

Money Market Instruments

The principal money market instruments are summarized in Table 31.5. We describe each in turn.

U.S. Treasury Bills The first item in Table 31.5 is U.S. Treasury bills. These are usually issued weekly and mature in four weeks, three months, six months, or one year.[20] Sales are by a uniform-price auction. This means that all successful bidders are allotted bills at the same price.[21] You don't have to participate in the auction to invest in Treasury bills. There is also an excellent secondary market in which billions of dollars of bills are bought and sold every day.

Federal Agency Securities "Agency securities" is a general term used to describe issues by government agencies and government-sponsored enterprises (GSEs). Although most of this debt is not guaranteed by the U.S. government,[22] investors have generally assumed that the government would step in to prevent a default. That view was reinforced in 2008, when the

---

[18]Occasionally (but only occasionally) referred to as "euroeuros."

[19]For these reasons, dollars held on deposit in an IBF are classed as eurodollars.

[20]Three-month bills actually mature 91 days after issue, six-month bills mature in 182 days, and one-year bills mature in 364 days. For information on bill auctions, see https://www.treasurydirect.gov/tdhome.htm.

[21]A small proportion of bills is sold to *noncompetitive* bidders. Noncompetitive bids are filled at the same price as the successful competitive bids.

[22]Exceptions are the Government National Mortgage Association (Ginnie Mae), the Small Business Administration, the General Services Administration (GSA), the Farm Credit Financial Assistance Corporation, the Agency for International Development, the Department of Veterans' Affairs (VINNIE MAE), and the Private Export Funding Corporation (PEFCO). Their debts are backed by the "full faith and credit" of the U.S. government.

Investment	Borrower	Maturities When Issued	Marketability	Basis for Calculating Interest	Comments
Treasury bills	U.S. government	4 weeks, 3 months, 6 months, or 1 year	Excellent secondary market	Discount	Auctioned weekly
Government agency and Government Sponsored Enterprise (GSE) benchmark bills and discount notes	Ginnie Mae, Fannie Mae, Freddie Mac, etc.	Overnight to 360 days	Very good secondary market	Discount	Benchmark bills by regular auction; discount notes sold through dealers
Tax-exempt municipal notes	Municipalities, states, school districts, etc.	3 months to 1 year	Good secondary market	Usually interest-bearing with interest at maturity	Tax-anticipation notes (TANs), revenue anticipation notes (RANs), bond anticipation notes (BANs), etc.
Tax-exempt variable-rate demand notes (VRDNs)	Municipalities, states, state universities, etc.	10 to 40 years	Good secondary market	Variable interest rate	Long-term bonds with put options to demand repayment
Nonnegotiable time deposits and negotiable certificates of deposit (CDs)	Commercial banks, savings and loans	Usually 1 to 3 months; also longer-maturity, variable-rate CDs	Fair secondary market for negotiable CDs	Interest-bearing with interest at maturity	Receipt for time deposit
Commercial paper (CP) Asset-backed paper (ABP)	Industrial firms, finance companies, and bank holding companies; also municipalities	Maximum 270 days; usually 60 days or less	Dealers or issuer will repurchase paper	Usually discount	Unsecured promissory note; may be placed through dealer or directly with investor
Medium-term notes (MTNs)	Largely finance companies and banks; also industrial firms	Minimum 270 days; usually less than 10 years	Dealers will repurchase notes	Interest-bearing; usually fixed rate	Unsecured promissory note placed through dealer
Bankers' acceptances (BAs)	Major commercial banks	1 to 6 months	Fair secondary market	Discount	Demand to pay that has been accepted by a bank
Repurchase agreements (repos)	Dealers in U.S. government securities	Overnight to about 3 months; also open repos (continuing contracts)	No secondary market	Repurchase price set higher than selling price; difference quoted as repo interest rate	Sales of government securities by dealer with simultaneous agreement to repurchase

❭TABLE 31.5   Money market investments in the United States.

two giant mortgage companies, the Federal National Mortgage Association (Fannie Mae) and the Federal Home Loan Mortgage Corporation (Freddie Mac) ran into trouble and were taken into government ownership.

Agencies and GSEs borrow both short and long term. The short-term debt consists of discount notes, which are similar to Treasury bills. They are actively traded and often held by corporations. These notes have traditionally offered somewhat higher yields than U.S. Treasuries. One reason is that agency debt is not quite as marketable as Treasury issues. In addition, unless the debt has an explicit government guarantee, investors have demanded an extra return to compensate for the (small?) possibility that the government would allow the agency to default.

Short-Term Tax-Exempts   Short-term notes are also issued by states, municipalities, and agencies such as state universities and school districts.[23] These have one particular attraction—the interest is not subject to federal tax.[24] Of course, this tax advantage of municipal debt is usually recognized in its price. For many years, triple-A municipal debt yielded 10% to 30% less than equivalent Treasury debt.

Most tax-exempt debt is relatively low risk, and is often backed by an insurance policy, which promises to pay out if the municipality is about to default.[25] However, in the turbulent markets of 2008, even the backing of an insurance company did little to reassure investors, who worried that the insurers themselves could be in trouble.

Variable-Rate Demand Notes   There is no law preventing firms from making short-term investments in long-term securities. If a firm has $1 million set aside for an income tax payment, it could buy a long-term bond on January 1 and sell it on April 15, when the taxes must be paid. However, the danger with this strategy is obvious. What happens if bond prices fall by 10% between January and April? There you are with a $1 million liability to the Internal Revenue Service, bonds worth only $900,000, and a very red face. Of course, bond prices could also go up, but why take the chance? Corporate treasurers entrusted with excess funds for short-term investments are naturally averse to the price volatility of long-term bonds.

BEYOND THE PAGE

Auction-rate preferred stock

mhhe.com/brealey14e

One solution is to buy municipal variable-rate demand notes (VRDNs). These are long-term securities, whose interest payments are linked to the level of short-term interest rates. Whenever the interest rate is reset, investors have the right to sell the notes back to the issuer for their face value.[26] This ensures that on these reset dates the price of the notes cannot be less than their face value. Therefore, although VRDNs are long-term loans, their prices are very stable. In addition, the interest on municipal debt has the advantage of being tax-exempt. So a municipal variable-rate demand note offers a relatively safe, tax-free, short-term haven for your $1 million of cash.

Bank Time Deposits and Certificates of Deposit   If you make a time deposit with a bank, you are lending money to the bank for a fixed period. If you need the money before maturity, the bank usually allows you to withdraw it but exacts a penalty in the form of a reduced rate of interest.

In the 1960s, banks introduced the **negotiable certificate of deposit (CD)** for time deposits of $1 million or more. In this case, when a bank borrows, it issues a certificate of deposit, which is simply evidence of a time deposit with that bank. If a lender needs the money before maturity, it can sell the CD to another investor. When the loan matures, the new owner of the CD presents it to the bank and receives payment.[27]

Commercial Paper and Medium-Term Notes   As discussed in detail in Chapter 25, these consist of short- and medium-term debt issued by companies on a regular basis.

---

[23]Some of these notes are *general obligations* of the issuer; others are *revenue securities,* and in these cases, payments are made from rent receipts or other user charges.

[24]This advantage is partly offset by the fact that Treasury securities are free of state and local taxes.

[25]Defaults on tax-exempts have been rare and, for the most part, have involved not-for-profit hospitals. However, there have been a number of major defaults of tax-exempt debt. In 1983, the Washington Public Power Supply System (unfortunately known as WPPSS or "WOOPS") defaulted on $2.25 billion of bonds. In 1994, Orange County in California also defaulted after losing $1.7 billion on its investment portfolio. In 2011, Jefferson Country, Alabama, declared bankruptcy with $4.2 billion in municipal debt. The record for municipal bankruptcies is held by Detroit, which filed for bankruptcy in 2013 with $18 to $20 billion of debt.

[26]Issuers generally support their borrowing by arranging a backup line of credit with a bank, which ensures that they can find the money to repay the notes.

[27]Some CDs are not negotiable and are simply identical to time deposits. For example, banks may sell low-value nonnegotiable CDs to individuals.

Bankers' Acceptances Bankers' acceptances (BAs) are commonly used to finance exports or imports. An acceptance begins life as a written request for the bank to guarantee a customer's obligation to pay. Once the bank accepts this demand, it becomes a negotiable security that can be bought or sold through money-market dealers. Acceptances by the large U.S. banks generally mature in one to six months and involve very low credit risk.

Repurchase Agreements Repurchase agreements, or *repos,* are effectively secured loans that are typically made to a government security dealer. They work as follows: The investor buys part of the dealer's holding of Treasury securities and simultaneously arranges to sell them back again at a later date at a specified higher price.[28] The borrower (the dealer) is said to have entered into a *repo*; the lender (who buys the securities) is said to have a *reverse repo*.

Repos sometimes run for several months, but more frequently, they are just overnight (24-hour) agreements. No other domestic money-market investment offers such liquidity. Corporations can treat overnight repos almost as if they were interest-bearing demand deposits.

Suppose that you decide to invest cash in repos for several days or weeks. You don't want to keep renegotiating agreements every day. One solution is to enter into an *open repo* with a security dealer. In this case, there is no fixed maturity to the agreement; either side is free to withdraw at one day's notice. Alternatively, you may arrange with your bank to transfer any excess cash automatically into repos.

---

[28]To reduce the risk of repos, it is common to lend less than the market value of the security. This difference is known as a *haircut.*

- **Working capital** Current assets and liabilities constitute the firm's working capital. The difference between current assets and liabilities is its net working capital. The most important current assets are inventories, accounts receivable, cash and short-term investments. The most important current liabilities are accounts payable and short-term debt, which includes both short-term loans and principal payments on long-term debt coming due in the next 12 months.

- **The cash cycle** The amount of working capital that companies need to maintain depends on the gap between the time that they pay for their raw materials and the time that they receive payment from their customers. This gap is called the *cash cycle*.

- **Inventory management** Inventories consist of raw materials, work in process, and finished goods. There are benefits to holding inventories. For example, a stock of raw materials reduces the risk that the firm will be forced to shut down production because of an unexpected shortage. But inventories also tie up capital and are expensive to store. The task of the production manager is to strike a sensible balance between these benefits and costs. In recent years, many companies have decided that they can get by on lower inventories than before. For example, some have adopted *just-in-time* systems that allow the firm to keep inventories to a minimum by receiving a regular flow of components and raw materials throughout the day.

- **Receivables management** The management of receivables involves four steps:

  1. Establish the length of the payment period and the size of any cash discounts for those customers that pay promptly.

  2. Assess your customer's creditworthiness. You can either do your own homework or rely on the company's bond rating or on the judgement of a credit agency or credit bureau.

  3. Establish sensible credit limits. Remember not to be too shortsighted in reckoning the expected profit. It may be worth accepting marginal applicants if there is a chance that they may become regular and reliable customers.

4. **Collect.** You need to be resolute with the truly delinquent customers, but you do not want to offend the good ones by writing demanding letters just because their check has been delayed in the mail.

- **Cash management** Firms need cash on hand to pay suppliers, meet payrolls, buy equipment, pay debt service and so on. But idle cash earns no interest. Firms therefore establish systems and procedures to transfer excess cash into central accounts at concentration banks. The transfers are almost always made electronically. The central accounts can then provide cash to plants or subsidiaries that will need it.

- **Investment of surplus cash** Surplus cash is invested in the money market, perhaps overnight in repurchase transactions or perhaps in securities such as Treasury bills or CDs with maturities of weeks or months.

● ● ● ● ●

FURTHER READING

Here are some general textbooks on working capital management:

J. S. Sagner, *Working Capital Management: Applications and Case Studies* (New York: John Wiley & Sons, 2014).

J. Zietlow, M. Hill, and T. Maness, *Short-Term Financial Management,* rev. 5th ed., (San Diego, CA: Cognella Publishing, 2016).

For a discussion of credit policy, see:

S. Mian and C. W. Smith, "Extending Trade Credit and Financing," *Journal of Applied Corporate Finance* 7 (Spring 1994), pp. 75–84.

M. A. Petersen and R. G. Rajan, "Trade Credit: Theories and Evidence," *Review of Financial Studies* 10 (1997), pp. 661–692.

The *Red Book, produced periodically by the Bank of International Settlements, provides a useful description of payment systems for different countries.*

Two readable discussions of why some companies maintain more liquidity than others are:

A. Dittmar, "Corporate Cash Policy and How to Manage It with Stock Repurchases," *Journal of Applied Corporate Finance* 20 (Summer 2008), pp. 22–34.

L. Pinkowitz and R. Williamson, "What Is the Market Value of a Dollar of Corporate Cash?" *Journal of Applied Corporate Finance* 19 (Summer 2007), pp. 74–81.

For descriptions of the money-market and short-term lending opportunities, see:

F. J. Fabozzi, *The Handbook of Fixed Income Securities,* 8th ed. (New York: McGraw-Hill, 2012).

F. J. Fabozzi, S. V. Mann, and M. Choudhry, *The Global Money Markets* (New York: John Wiley, 2002).

Chapter 4 of *U.S. Monetary Policy and Financial Markets,* available on the New York Federal Reserve website, **www.ny.frb.org.**

● ● ● ● ●

PROBLEM SETS

Select problems are available in McGraw Hill's *Connect*. Please see the preface for more information.

1. **Components of working capital (S31.1)** Take a look at Figure 31.1. Why do food stores hold large inventories? Why do railroads hold small inventories? Why do you think that pharmaceutical companies hold so much cash and securities? Answer briefly.

2. **Components of working capital (S31.1)** True or false?

   a. Companies with negative net working capital are usually in financial trouble.

   b. Principal payments on long-term debt are shown as current liabilities if due within the next 12 months.

c. Accounts payable are usually a small fraction of the firm's total liabilities.

d. Accounts receivable are usually the largest category of current assets.

e. Less profitable companies typically hold larger cash balances as a precautionary measure.

f. Well-managed companies invest the majority of their excess cash in short-term securities. They avoid the risks of investing in long-term bonds.

3. **Cash cycle (S31.1)** In 2020 and 2021, Colgate Palmolive's financial statements included the following items. What was its cash cycle?

$ millions		
	2021	**2020**
Inventory	$ 1,250	$ 1,221
Receivables	1,400	1,480
Payables	1,222	1,212
Sales	15,693	15,544
Cost of goods sold	6,368	6,313

4. **Cash cycle (S31.1)** What effect will each of the following have on the cash cycle?

a. The inventory turnover falls from 80 to 60 days.

b. Customers are given a larger discount for cash transactions.

c. The firm adopts a policy of reducing accounts payable.

d. The firm starts producing more goods in response to customers' advance orders instead of producing ahead of demand.

e. A temporary glut in the commodity market induces the firm to stock up on raw materials while prices are low.

5. **Cash cycle (S31.1)** A firm is considering several policy changes to increase sales. It plans to increase the variety of goods it keeps in inventory, but this will increase inventory by $100,000. It will offer more liberal sales terms, but this will result in receivables increasing by $650,000. These actions are forecasted to increase sales by $8 million a year. Cost of goods sold will remain at 80% of sales. Because of the firm's increased purchases for its own production needs, payables will increase by $350,000. What effect will these changes have on the firm's cash cycle?

6. **Inventory (S31.2)** True or false?

a. Just-in-time inventory systems reduce the cost of managing inventory to zero.

b. Companies hold larger inventories of finished goods when customer demand fluctuates unpredictably.

c. Other things equal, higher real interest rates should lead to lower inventories.

d. Other things equal, lower costs of storage should lead to lower inventories.

7. **Inventory (S31.2)** What are the trade-offs involved in the decision of how much inventory the firm should carry?

8. **Inventory (S31.2)** Central banks pushed short-term interest rates down to extremely low levels in the financial crisis that started in 2008. Some Treasury bill rates in Europe were negative. Other things equal, how would you expect corporations' inventory levels to respond to such a large reduction in interest rates?

9. **Inventory (S31.2)** Take another look at Example 31.2. Suppose a rise in interest rates increases carrying cost per ton from $55 to $75. What is the effect on economic order quantity?

10. **Inventory (S31.2)** Polar Express Railroad keeps a $5 million inventory of spare parts on hand for repairing unexpected breakdowns and equipment failures. The inventory is held in one centralized warehouse at a storage cost of $330,000 per year. The inventory has been financed by a short-term bank loan at 6.5% interest.

    The operations manager has proposed moving the parts from the centralized warehouse to 10 storage locations at the hubs of the Polar Express network. The required total inventory would increase to $7 million because some parts would have to be held in inventory at all 10 locations. Storage costs would increase to $600,000 per year. But having the parts at the hubs would save $400,000 per year in the labor cost of repairs. Also repairs would be completed quicker, improving customer service.

    Evaluate the operations manager's proposal. Assume the opportunity cost of capital is the interest rate on the bank loan.

11. **Credit terms (S31.3)** Listed below are some common terms of sale. Can you explain what each means?

    a. 2/30, net 60.

    b. 2/5, EOM, net 30.

    c. COD.

12. **Credit terms (S31.3)** Some of the terms in Problem 11 involve a cash discount. For each of these, calculate the rate of interest paid by customers who pay on the due date instead of taking the cash discount.

13. **Credit terms (S31.3)** Phoenix Lambert currently sells its goods cash on delivery. However, the financial manager believes that by offering credit terms of 2/10 net 30 the company can increase sales by 4%, without significant additional costs. If the interest rate is 6% and the profit margin is 5%, would you recommend offering credit? Assume first that all customers take the cash discount. Then assume that they all pay on day 30.

14. **Credit terms (S31.3)** Until recently, Augean Cleaning Products sold its products on terms of net 60, with an average collection period of 75 days. In an attempt to induce customers to pay more promptly, it has changed its terms to 2/10, EOM, net 60. The initial effect of the changed terms is as follows:

	Average Collection Periods (Days)	
Percent of Sales with Cash Discount	**Cash Discount**	**Net**
60	30[a]	80

[a]Some customers deduct the cash discount even though they pay after the specified date.

Calculate the effect of the changed terms. Assume

- Sales volume is unchanged.
- The interest rate is 12%.
- There are no defaults.
- Cost of goods sold is 80% of sales.

15. **Credit terms (S31.3)** Company X sells on a 1/30, net 60 basis. Customer Y buys goods invoiced at $1,000.

    a. How much can Y deduct from the bill if Y pays on day 30?

    b. What is the effective annual rate of interest if Y pays on the due date rather than on day 30?

    c. How would you expect payment terms to change under the following conditions?

    i. The goods are perishable.

    ii. The goods are not rapidly resold.

    iii. The goods are sold to high-risk firms.

16. **Credit policy (S31.3)** The Branding Iron Company sells its irons for $50 apiece wholesale. Production cost is $40 per iron. There is a 25% chance that wholesaler Q will go bankrupt within the next six months. Q now orders 1,000 irons and asks for six months' credit. Should you accept the order? Assume that the discount rate is 10% per year, there is no chance of a repeat order, and Q will pay either in full or not at all.

17. **Credit policy (S31.3)** Look back at Section 31-3. Cast Iron's costs have increased from $1,000 to $1,050. Assuming there is no possibility of repeat orders, answer the following:

    a. When should Cast Iron grant or refuse credit?

    b. If it costs $12 to determine whether a customer is creditworthy, when should Cast Iron undertake such a check?

18. **Credit policy (S31.3)** Look back at the discussion in Section 31-3 of credit decisions with repeat orders. If $p_1 = 0.8$, what is the minimum level of p_2 at which Cast Iron is justified in extending credit?

19. **Credit policy (S31.3)** How should your willingness to grant credit be affected by differences in (a) the profit margin, (b) the interest rate, (c) the probability of repeat orders? In each case, illustrate your answer with a simple example.

20. **Credit policy (S31.3)** As treasurer of the Universal Bed Corporation, Aristotle Procrustes is worried about his bad debt ratio, which is currently running at 6%. He believes that imposing a more stringent credit policy might reduce sales by 5% and reduce the bad debt ratio to 4%. If the cost of goods sold is 80% of the selling price, should Mr. Procrustes adopt the more stringent policy?

21. **Credit policy (S31.3)** Jim Khana, the credit manager of Velcro Saddles, is reappraising the company's credit policy. Velcro sells on terms of net 30. Cost of goods sold is 85% of sales, and fixed costs are a further 5% of sales. Velcro classifies customers on a scale of 1 to 4. During the past five years, the collection experience was as follows:

Classification	Defaults as Percent of Sales	Average Collection Period in Days for Nondefaulting Accounts
1	0	45
2	2.0	42
3	10.0	40
4	20.0	80

The average interest rate was 15%.

    What conclusions (if any) can you draw about Velcro's credit policy? What other factors should be taken into account before changing this policy?

22. **Credit policy (S31.3)** Look again at the last problem. Suppose (a) that it costs $95 to classify each new credit applicant and (b) that an almost equal proportion of new applicants falls into each of the four categories. In what circumstances should Mr. Khana not bother to undertake a credit check?

23. **Credit policy (S31.3)** True or false?

    a. It makes sense to monitor the credit manager's performance by looking at the proportion of bad debts.

    b. If a customer refuses to pay despite repeated reminders, the company usually turns the debt over to a factor or an attorney.

24. **Cash management (S31.4)** Complete the passage that follows by choosing the appropriate terms from the following list: *lockbox banking, Fedwire, CHIPS, concentration banking.*

Firms can increase their cash resources by speeding up collections. One way to do this is to arrange for payments to be made to regional offices that pay the checks into local banks. This is known as_____. Surplus funds are then transferred from the local bank to one of the company's main banks. Transfers can be made electronically by the _____or _____systems. Another technique is to arrange for a local bank to collect the checks directly from a post office box. This is known as_____.

25. **Cash management (S31.4)** True or false?

a. "Money market" refers to the system of electronic cash transfers between corporations and within the banking industry.

b. Most large corporations maintain many bank accounts.

c. Yields quoted on a discount basis are always lower than the true interest rate.

d. The cost of holding excess cash is lower when interest rates are lower.

26. **Cash management (S31.4)** Knob Inc. is a nationwide distributor of furniture hardware. The company now uses a central billing system for credit sales of $180 million annually. First National, Knob's principal bank, offers to establish a new concentration banking system for a flat fee of $100,000 per year. The bank estimates that mailing and collection time can be reduced by three days. By how much will Knob's cash balances be increased under the new system? How much extra interest income will the new system generate if the extra funds are used to reduce borrowing under Knob's line of credit with First National? Assume that the borrowing rate is 12%. Finally, should Knob accept First National's offer if collection costs under the old system are $40,000 per year?

27. **Lockboxes (S31.4)** Anne Teak, the financial manager of a furniture manufacturer, is considering operating a lockbox system. She forecasts that 300 payments a day will be made to lockboxes with an average payment size of $1,500. The bank's charge for operating the lockboxes is $0.40 a check. What reduction in the time to collect and process each check is needed to justify the lockbox system?

28. **Lockboxes (S31.4)** The financial manager of JAC Cosmetics is considering opening a lockbox in Pittsburgh. Checks cleared through the lockbox will amount to $10,000 per day. The lockbox will make cash available to the company three days earlier than is currently the case.

a. Suppose that the bank offers to run the lockbox for a $20,000 compensating balance. Is the lockbox worthwhile?

b. Suppose that the bank offers to run the lockbox for a fee of $0.10 per check cleared instead of a compensating balance. What must the average check size be for the fee alternative to be less costly? Assume an interest rate of 6% per year.

c. Why did you need to know the interest rate to answer part (b) but not to answer part (a)?

29. **Payment systems (S31.4)** A parent company settles the collection account balances of its subsidiaries once a week. (That is, each week it transfers any balances in the accounts to a central account.) The cost of a wire transfer is $10. A check costs $0.80. Cash transferred by wire is available the same day, but the parent must wait three days for checks to clear. Cash can be invested at 12% per year. How much money must be in a collection account before it pays to use a wire transfer?

30. **Money-market yields (S31.5)** In January 2020, three-month (91-day) Treasury bills were selling at a discount of 1.5%. What was the annual yield?

31. **Money-market yields (S31.5)** A three-month Treasury bill and a six-month bill both sell at a discount of 10%. Which offers the higher annual yield?

32. **Money-market yields (S31.5)** In Section 31-5, we described a three-month bill that was issued on an annually compounded yield of 5%. Suppose that one month has passed and the

investment still offers the same annually compounded return. What is the percentage discount? What was your return over the month?

33. **Money-market yields (S31.5)** Look again at Problem 32. Suppose another month has passed, so the bill has only one month left to run. It is now selling at a discount of 3%. What is the yield? What was your realized return over the two months?

34. **Money-market securities (S31.5)** For each item below, choose the investment that best fits the accompanying description:

    a. Maturity often overnight (repurchase agreements/bankers' acceptances).

    b. Maturity never more than 270 days (tax-exempts/commercial paper).

    c. Issued by the U.S. Treasury (tax-exempts/three-month bills).

    d. Quoted on a discount basis (certificates of deposit/Treasury bills).

    e. Sold by auction (tax-exempts/Treasury bills).

35. **Money-market securities (S31.5)** Consider three securities:

    a. A floating-rate bond.

    b. A preferred share paying a fixed dividend.

    c. A floating-rate preferred.

    If you were responsible for short-term investment of your firm's excess cash, which security would you probably prefer to hold? Could your answer depend on your firm's tax rate? Explain briefly.

36. **Money-market securities (S31.5)** Look up current interest rates offered by short-term investment alternatives. Suppose that your firm has $1 million excess cash to invest for the next two months. How would you invest this cash? How would your answer change if the excess cash were $5,000, $20,000, $100,000, or $100 million

37. **Tax-exempts (S31.5)** In 2006, agency bonds sold at a yield of 5.32%, while high-grade tax-exempts of comparable maturity offered 3.7% annually. If an investor receives the same *after-tax* return from corporates and tax-exempts, what is that investor's marginal rate of tax? What other factors might affect an investor's choice between the two types of securities?

38. **After-tax yields (S31.5)** Suppose you are a wealthy individual paying 35% tax on income. What is the expected after-tax yield on each of the following investments?

    a. A municipal note yielding 7.0% pretax.

    b. A Treasury bill yielding 10% pretax.

    c. A floating-rate preferred stock yielding 7.5% pretax.

    How would your answer change if the investor is a corporation paying tax at 35%? What other factors would you need to take into account when deciding where to invest the corporation's spare cash?

CHALLENGE

39. **The cost of capital for current assets (S31.2)** Look again at Problem 10, which asked you to assume that the 6.5% interest rate was the opportunity cost of capital. Was that a reasonable assumption? What should the opportunity cost of capital for inventory depend on? Would it ever make sense to use the firm's overall weighted average cost of capital? What if the inventory was not spare parts for a railroad, but a risky commodity—for example, crude oil stocks held as raw material for a petrochemical plant? Discuss and explain.

40. **Credit policy (S31.3)** Galenic Inc. is a wholesaler for a range of pharmaceutical products. Before deducting any losses from bad debts, Galenic operates on a profit margin of 5%. For a long time, the firm has employed a numerical credit scoring system based on a small number of key ratios. This has resulted in a bad debt ratio of 1%.

Galenic recently commissioned a detailed statistical study of the payment record of its customers over the past eight years and, after considerable experimentation, identified five variables that could form the basis of a new credit scoring system. On the evidence of the past eight years, Galenic calculates that for every 10,000 accounts, it would have experienced the following default rates:

	Number of Accounts		
Credit Score under Proposed System	Defaulting	Paying	Total
Greater than 80	60	9,100	9,160
Less than 80	40	800	840
Total	100	9,900	10,000

By refusing credit to firms with a low credit score (less than 80), Galenic calculates that it would reduce its bad debt ratio to 60/9,160, or just under 0.7%. While this may not seem like a big deal, Galenic's credit manager reasons that this is equivalent to a decrease of one-third in the bad debt ratio and would result in a significant improvement in the profit margin.

a. What is Galenic's current profit margin, allowing for bad debts?

b. Assuming that the firm's estimates of default rates are right, how would the new credit scoring system affect profits?

c. Why might you suspect that Galenic's estimates of default rates will not be realized in practice? What are the likely consequences of overestimating the accuracy of such a credit scoring scheme?

d. Suppose that one of the variables in the proposed scoring system is whether the customer has an existing account with Galenic (new customers are more likely to default). How would this affect your assessment of the proposal?

● ● ● ● ●

SOLUTIONS TO SELF-TEST QUESTIONS

31.1

	Walmart	Boeing
Average inventory period	41.5 days	198.4 days
Average receivables period	4.0	35.4
Average payables period	43.7	54.6
Cash cycle	1.8 days	179.2 days

31.2 Carrying costs rise and inventory levels should fall.

31.3 You pay $19,600. Due date = May 21.

31.4 $= \left(1 + \dfrac{5}{95}\right)^{365/40} - 1 = 0.597$, or 59.7%

In this case, the customer pays the same amount but gains only 40 days extra credit.

31.5 Break-even probability = 0.9 (i.e., $0.9 \times 120 - (1 - 0.9) \times 1,080 = 0$). The lower the profit margin, the higher the break-even probability of collection. Break-even probability = 1 − profit margin = 1 − 120/1,200 = 0.9.

31.6 The benefits of a lockbox system, and therefore the price that you should be prepared to pay, are higher when

a. Payment size is higher (because interest is earned on more funds).

b. Payments per day are higher (because interest is earned on more funds).

c. The interest rate is higher (because the cost of idle money is higher).

d. Mail time saved is higher (because you earn interest on the funds for longer).

31.7 The discount is 4%. So for every $100 that you undertake to repay in month 6, you receive up-front $98. The six-month interest rate is $100/98 - 1 = 0.02041$. The effective annual rate is $1.02041^2 - 1 = 0.0412$ or 4.12%.

FINANCE ON THE WEB

1. The three main credit bureaus maintain useful websites with examples of their business and consumer reports. Log on to **www.equifax.com** and look at the sample report on a small business. What information do you think would be most useful if you were considering granting credit to the firm?

2. Log on to the Federal Reserve site at **www.federalreserve.gov** and look up current money market interest rates. Suppose your business has $7 million set aside for an expenditure in three months. How would you choose to invest it in the meantime? Would your decision be different if there were some chance that you might need the money earlier?

32

CHAPTER

Mergers

Mergers and acquisitions are typically the largest investment decisions that a financial manager undertakes. Successful mergers can transform a company. Unsuccessful ones can destroy the company or hobble it for a decade.

The scale and pace of merger activity in the United States has been remarkable. In 2020, North American companies were involved in over 17,000 deals totaling more than $2 trillion. Some of the more important recent mergers are shown in Table 32.1 . During periods of intense merger activity, management spends significant amounts of time either searching for firms to acquire or worrying about whether some other firm will acquire them.

> **TABLE 32.1**   Some important recent mergers.

Note: Several of these mergers were pending and subject to regulatory approval. In other cases, there may be rival acquirers.

Industry	Acquiring Company	Selling Company	Payment ($ billions)
Media	AT&T	Time Warner	109
Pharmaceuticals	Bristol-Myers Squibb	Celgene	90
Defense	United Technologies	Raytheon	89
Pharmaceuticals	AbbVie	Allergan	86
Media	Disney	21st Century Fox	71
Energy/petrochemicals	Saudi Aramco (Saudi)	Saudi Basic Industries (Saudi)	70
Banking	BB&T Corp	SunTrust	66
Pharmaceuticals	Takeda Pharmaceuticals (Japan)	Shire (UK)	59
Energy	Occidental	Anadarko	54
Autos	Fiat Chrysler	PSA - Peugeot (France)	50
Financial technology	FIS	Worldpay	35
Computing	IBM	Red Hat	34

Section 32-1 Types of merger We start our discussion in Section 32.1 with a brief introduction to the three main types of merger—horizontal, vertical, and conglomerate.

Section 32-2 Some sensible motives for mergers A merger adds value only if the two companies are worth more together than apart. We look at some of the more common reasons why this may be so.

Section 32-3 Some dubious motives for mergers You may also hear some questionable arguments for merger. We discuss several of them.

Section 32-4 Estimating merger gains and costs A merger has a positive NPV if the gains are greater than the costs. Sometimes costs can be tricky to estimate.

Section 32-5 The mechanics of a merger Mergers involve various legal, tax, and accounting issues, which we highlight in this section.

Section 32-6 Takeovers and the market for corporate control Mergers are partly about economies from combining two firms, but they are also about who gets to run the company. Many marriages between companies are amicable, but sometimes one party is dragged unwillingly to the altar. So we also look at what is involved in hostile takeovers.

Section 32-7 Merger waves and merger profitability We look at the possible reasons for merger waves and at who gains and loses from merger activity.

• • • • •

32-1   Types of Merger

Mergers can be *horizontal, vertical,* or *conglomerate.* A **horizontal merger** is one that takes place between two firms in the same line of business. Almost all the mergers listed in Table 32.1 are horizontal.

A **vertical merger** involves companies at different stages of production. The buyer expands back toward the source of raw materials or forward in the direction of the ultimate consumer. An example is the $69 billion 2018 acquisition of Aetna by CVS Health. Aetna specializes in health insurance, while CVS operates pharmacies and is a pharmacy benefits manager. The acquisition gave CVS greater control over two areas of the health care supply chain and allowed it to better manage supply and demand.

A **conglomerate merger** involves companies in unrelated lines of businesses. For example, the Indian Tata Group is a huge, widely diversified company. Its acquisitions have been as diverse as Eight O'Clock Coffee, Corus Steel, Jaguar Land Rover, the Ritz Carlton (Boston), and British Salt. No U.S. company is as diversified as Tata, but in the 1960s and 1970s, it was common in the United States for unrelated businesses to merge. Much of the action in the 1980s and 1990s came from breaking up the conglomerates that had been formed 10 to 20 years earlier.

32.1 Self-Test

Are the following hypothetical mergers horizontal, vertical, or conglomerate?
  a. IBM acquires Dell Computer.
  b. Dell Computer acquires Walmart.
  c. Walmart acquires Tyson Foods.
  d. Tyson Foods acquires IBM.

32-2   Some Sensible Motives for Mergers

Our comments in Chapter 11 about the characteristics of a good investment decision also hold true when you are buying an entire company. You add value only if the merger gives you some competitive edge that other firms can't match and the target firm's managers can't achieve on their own. *Synergies* arise whenever the merged firm is worth more than the sum of its parts. As we review the possible sources of these synergies, bear in mind that two firms do not necessarily need to merge to create synergies. For example, a possible alternative might be to achieve the same end by a strategic alliance supported by long-term contracts.

We will look at five of the most important motives:

- Economies of scale and scope.
- Economies of vertical integration.
- Complementary resources.
- Changes in corporate control.
- Industry consolidation.

Economies of Scale and Scope

Many mergers are intended to achieve economies of scale. These arise whenever the average unit cost of production goes down as production increases. One way to achieve economies of scale is to spread fixed costs over a larger volume of production. For example, when BB&T and SunTrust merged, they claimed that the combined bank would produce annual cost savings of around $1.6 billion by 2022. Some of these savings came about because the bank could serve the same number of customers from a smaller number of branches. In addition, the greater scale would make it economical to increase its investment in new technology. The merged bank also expected to achieve economies from sharing central services such as office management and accounting, financial control, executive development, and top-level management.

Cost savings from economies of scale have been a major motive for mergers between banks.[1] The United States entered the 1980s with far too many banks, largely as a result of outdated restrictions on interstate banking. As these restrictions eroded and communications and technology improved, small banks were swept up into large regional or "super-regional" banks, and the number of banks declined from over 14,000 to little more than 5,000.

Other mergers seek to achieve economies of scope, that arise whenever there is an economic advantage to broadening the firm's range of products. This was the motivation behind the 2018 acquisition by Procter & Gamble of the consumer health business of German company Merck KGaA. P&G reckoned that there would be marketing economies from adding Merck's vitamin and food supplements to P&G's existing over-the-counter medicines.

To achieve these economies of scale and scope, the merged firm may close down overlapping or inefficient operations. Almost half of acquired plants are either closed or sold off in the three years following a merger.[2]

Economies of Vertical Integration

Vertical mergers seek to gain control over the production process by expanding back toward the output of the raw material or forward to the ultimate consumer. One way to achieve this is to merge with a supplier or a customer.

Companies need to work with a variety of suppliers and customers. They can manage these relationships by entering into contracts that specify the volume and quality of goods to be delivered and their price. However, problems may arise when two business activities are inextricably linked. For example, production of components may require the supplying firm to make a large investment in highly specialized equipment. Or a smelter may need to be located next to the mine to reduce the costs of transporting the ore. It may be possible in such cases to organize the activities as separate firms operating under long-term contracts. But such contracts can never allow for every conceivable change in the way that the businesses may need

---

[1]A study of 41 large bank mergers calculated present values of cost savings averaging 12% of the combined market values of the merging banks. See. J. F. Houston, C. M. James, and M. D. Ryngeart, "Where do Merger Gains Come From? Bank Mergers from the Perspective of Insiders and Outsiders," *Journal of Financial Economics* 60 (2001), pp. 285–331.

[2]V. Maksimovic, G. Phillips, and N.R. Prabhala, "Post-Merger Restructuring and the Boundaries of the Firm," *Journal of Financial Economics* 102 (2011), pp. 317–343.

to interact. Therefore, when two parts of an operation are highly dependent on each other, it may make sense to combine them within the same vertically integrated firm, which then has control over how the assets should be used. For example, in 2006 the European Commission challenged Philips's proposed acquisition of Intermagnetics, a producer of superconducting magnets. However, Philips successfully argued that for some years, it had taken over 99% of Intermagnetics output and that the combination of the two companies would facilitate the joint development of new MRI systems.

Not all arguments for vertical integration make sense. For example, sometimes you come across companies that justify the purchase of a supplier with arguments such as the following: "We're paying the supplier $10 per widget. It probably only costs them $6 to make the widget, so they're making $4 profit. If we buy them, then we can pocket this profit ourselves!" Simply merging and continuing to produce the same widgets is unlikely to create value. The supplier is not foolish. If it's making $4 profit per widget, it won't allow the customer to buy it out unless it's paid (at least) the present value of all future profits. So, even though the customer does save on the $4 markup in the future, it has to pay the present value of all future markups to buy the supplier today.

Nowadays the tide of vertical integration seems to be flowing out. Companies are finding it more efficient to *outsource* the provision of many services and various types of production. For example, back in the 1950s and 1960s, General Motors was deemed to have a cost advantage over its main competitors, Ford and Chrysler, because a greater fraction of the parts used in GM's automobiles were produced in-house. By the 1990s, Ford and Chrysler had the advantage: They could buy the parts cheaper from outside suppliers. This was partly because the outside suppliers tended to use nonunion labor at lower wages. But it also appears that manufacturers have more bargaining power versus independent suppliers than versus a production facility that's part of the corporate family. In 1998, GM decided to spin off Delphi, its automotive parts division, as a separate company. After the spin-off, GM continued to buy parts from Delphi in large volumes, but it negotiated the purchases at arm's length.

32.2 Self-Test

Why do you think that R&D departments are typically vertically integrated with their users?

Complementary Resources

Many small firms are acquired by large ones that can provide the missing ingredients necessary for the small firms' success. The small firm may have a unique product but lack the engineering and sales organization required to produce and market it on a large scale. The firm could develop engineering and sales talent from scratch, but it may be quicker and cheaper to merge with a firm that already has ample talent. The two firms have *complementary resources*—each has what the other needs—and so it may make sense for them to merge. Also, the merger may open up opportunities that neither firm could pursue otherwise.

In recent years, many of the major pharmaceutical firms have faced the loss of patent protection on their more profitable products and have not had an offsetting pipeline of promising new compounds. This has prompted an increasing number of acquisitions of biotech firms. For example, in 2017 Bristol Myers acquired IFM Therapeutics, a start-up company with two pre-clinical immunotherapy programs. Bristol Myers calculated that IFM's drugs would fit well with its own range of immunotherapy treatments. At the same time, IFM obtained the resources that it needed to bring its products to market.

Changes in Corporate Control

Some firms have excess cash and do not pay it out to stockholders. Such firms often find themselves targeted for takeover by other firms that propose to redeploy the cash. During the oil price slump of the early 1980s, many cash-rich oil companies found themselves threatened by takeover. This was not because their cash was a unique asset. The acquirers wanted to capture the companies' cash flow to make sure it was not frittered away on negative-NPV oil exploration projects.

Cash is not the only asset that can be wasted by poor management. There are always firms with unexploited opportunities to cut costs and increase sales and earnings. Such firms are natural candidates for acquisition by other firms with better management. In some instances, "better management" may simply mean the determination to force painful cuts or realign the company's operations. Notice that the motive for such acquisitions has nothing to do with benefits from combining two firms. Acquisition is simply the mechanism by which a new management team replaces the old one.

If this motive for merger is important, one would expect to observe that acquisitions often precede a change in the management of the target firm. This seems to be the case. In the year after a takeover, the chief executive is four times more likely to be replaced than in earlier years. Acquired firms have generally been poor performers; in the four years before acquisition, their stock prices lagged behind those of other firms in the same industry by 15%. Apparently, many of these firms fell on bad times and were rescued, or reformed, by merger.[3]

There are other and less costly ways to improve management without having to merge with another company. Incompetent or work-shy managers may be replaced by the board of directors. And, if the board is reluctant to take the responsibility, an activist shareholder may garner enough support to win a proxy fight and impose a management change. (We discuss proxy fights in Section 19.3.) Replacing management by means of an acquisition should be a last resort.

Industry Consolidation

Some of the biggest opportunities to improve efficiency may come in industries with too many firms and too much capacity. These conditions can trigger a wave of mergers and acquisitions, which then force companies to cut capacity and employment and release capital for reinvestment elsewhere in the economy. For example, when U.S. defense budgets fell after the end of the Cold War, a round of consolidating takeovers followed in the defense industry. The merged companies found it easier than the two competing ones to make the necessary cuts.

Logic Does Not Guarantee Success

We have listed several reasons that a merger may make economic sense. But how well a merger works out also depends on whether management can handle the complex task of integrating two firms with different production processes, accounting methods, and corporate cultures. For example, the nearby box shows how these difficulties bedeviled the merger of three Japanese banks.

The value of most businesses depends on *human* assets—managers, skilled workers, scientists, and engineers. If these people are not happy in their new roles in the merged firm, the best of them will leave. Beware of paying too much for assets that go down in the elevator and out to the parking lot at the close of each business day. They may drive into the sunset and never return.

---

[3]K. J. Martin and J. J. McConnell, "Corporate Performance, Corporate Takeovers, and Management Turnover," *Journal of Finance* 46 (1991), pp. 671–687.

EXAMPLE 32.1 • Daimler-Benz/Chrysler—A clash of cultures

Consider the $38 billion merger in 1998 between Daimler-Benz and Chrysler. Although it was hailed as a model for consolidation in the auto industry, the early years were rife with conflicts between two very different cultures:

> German management-board members had executive assistants who prepared detailed position papers on any number of issues. The Americans didn't have assigned aides and formulated their decisions by talking directly to engineers or other specialists. A German decision worked its way through the bureaucracy for final approval at the top. Then it was set in stone. The Americans allowed midlevel employees to proceed on their own initiative, sometimes without waiting for executive-level approval. . . .
>
> Cultural integration also was proving to be a slippery commodity. The yawning gap in pay scales fueled an undercurrent of tension. The Americans earned two, three, and, in some cases, four times as much as their German counterparts. But the expenses of U.S. workers were tightly controlled compared with the German system. Daimler-side employees thought nothing of flying to Paris or New York for a half-day meeting, then capping the visit with a fancy dinner and a night in an expensive hotel. The Americans blanched at the extravagance.[4]

Nine years after acquiring Chrysler, Daimler threw in the towel and announced that it was offloading an 80% stake in Chrysler to a leveraged-buyout firm, Cerberus Capital Management. Daimler actually paid Cerberus $677 million to take Chrysler off its hands. Cerberus in return assumed about $18 billion in pension and employee health care liabilities and agreed to invest $6 billion in Chrysler and its finance subsidiary.

• • • • •

There are also occasions when the merger does achieve gains, but the buyer nevertheless loses because it pays too much. For example, the buyer may overestimate the value of stale inventory or underestimate the costs of renovating old plant and equipment, or it may overlook the warranties on a defective product. Buyers need to be particularly careful about environmental liabilities. If there is pollution from the seller's operations or toxic waste on its property, the costs of cleaning up will probably fall on the buyer.

32-3   Some Dubious Motives for Mergers

The benefits that we have described so far all make economic sense. Other arguments sometimes given for mergers are dubious. For example, sometimes you may come across managers who believe that there are simple rules for identifying good acquisitions. They may say, for example, that they always try to buy into growth industries or that they have a policy of acquiring companies that are selling below book value. But investors can buy into growth industries if they wish to do so. Or they can buy into companies selling below book values. They don't need a merger to help them to do so.

Other dubious reasons for merger include:

- Diversification.
- Increasing earnings per share.
- Lower borrowing costs.
- Management motives.

We will look at each in turn.

---

[4]B. Vlasic and B. A. Stertz, "Taken for a Ride," *BusinessWeek,* June 5, 2000. Used with permission of Bloomberg L.P. ©2017. All rights reserved.

Those Elusive Synergies

❯ When three of Japan's largest banks combined to form Mizuho Bank, the result was a bank with assets of $1.5 trillion, more than twice those of the world leader, Deutsche Bank. The name "Mizuho" means "rich rice harvest," and the bank's management forecasted that the merger would yield a rich harvest of synergies. In a message to shareholders, the bank president claimed that the merger would create "a comprehensive financial services group that will surge forward in the 21st century." He predicted that the bank would "lead the new era through cutting-edge comprehensive financial services . . . by exploiting to the fullest extent the Group's enormous strengths, which are backed by a powerful customer base and state-of-the-art financial and information technologies." The cost of putting the banks together was forecasted at ¥130 billion, but management predicted future benefits of ¥466 billion a year.

Within a few months of the announcement, reports began to emerge of squabbles among the three partners. One problem area was IT. Each of the three merging banks had a different supplier for its computer system. At first, it was proposed to use just one of these three systems, but then the banks decided to connect the three different systems together using "relay" computers.

Three years after the initial announcement, the new company opened for business on April 1, 2002. Five days later, computer glitches resulted in a spectacular foul-up. Some 7,000 of the bank's cash machines did not work, 60,000 accounts were debited twice for the same transaction, and millions of bills went unpaid. *The Economist* reported that two weeks later, Tokyo Gas, the biggest gas company, was still missing ¥2.2 billion in payments, and the top telephone company, NTT, which was looking for ¥12.7 billion, was forced to send its customers receipts marked with asterisks in place of figures because it did not know which of about 760,000 bills had been paid.

One of the objectives behind the formation of Mizuho was to exploit economies in its IT systems. The launch fiasco illustrated dramatically that it is easier to predict such merger synergies than to realize them.

Sources: The creation of Mizuho Bank and its launch problems are described in "Undispensable: A Fine Merger Yields One Fine Mess," *The Economist,* April 27, 2002, p. 72; "Big, Bold, but . . . ", *Euromoney,* December 2000, pp. 30–35; and "Godzilla Bank," *Forbes,* March 20, 2000, pp. 132–133.

Diversification

Unless the two businesses are perfectly related, you would expect a merger between them to spread the risk. Isn't that a gain from merging?

The trouble with this argument is that diversification is easier and cheaper for the stockholder than for the corporation. There is little evidence that investors pay a premium for diversified firms; in fact, discounts are more common. The Appendix to this chapter provides a simple proof that corporate diversification does not increase value in perfect markets as long as investors' diversification opportunities are unrestricted.

Increasing Earnings per Share: The Bootstrap Game

When one company acquires another with a lower P/E ratio, its earnings per share are increased. For this reason, acquisitions that offer no evident economic gains may nevertheless produce several years of rising earnings per share. To see how this can happen, let us look at the acquisition of Muck and Slurry by the well-known conglomerate World Enterprises.

The position before the merger is set out in the first two columns of Table 32.2. Because Muck and Slurry has relatively poor growth prospects, the price–earnings ratio on its shares is lower than that of World Enterprises' (line 3). The merger, we assume, produces no economic benefits, so the firms should be worth exactly the same together as they are apart. The market value of World Enterprises after the merger should be equal to the sum of the separate values of the two firms (line 6).

	World Enterprises before Merger	Muck and Slurry	World Enterprises after Merger
1. Earnings per share	$2.00	$2.00	$2.67
2. Price per share	$40	$20	$40
3. Price–earnings ratio	20	10	15
4. Number of shares	100,000	100,000	150,000
5. Total earnings	$200,000	$200,000	$400,000
6. Total market value	$4,000,000	$2,000,000	$6,000,000
7. Current earnings per dollar invested in stock (line 1 ÷ line 2)	$0.05	$0.10	$0.067

〉TABLE 32.2 Impact of merger on market value and earnings per share of World Enterprises.

Note: When World Enterprises purchases Muck and Slurry, there are no gains. Therefore, total earnings and total market value should be unaffected by the merger. But earnings per share increase. World Enterprises issues only 50,000 of its shares (priced at $40) to acquire the 100,000 Muck and Slurry shares (priced at $20).

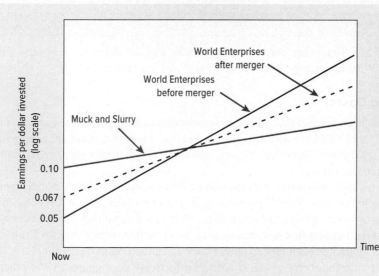

▶ FIGURE 32.1

Effects of merger on earnings growth. By merging with Muck and Slurry, World Enterprises increases current earnings but accepts a slower rate of future growth. Its stockholders should be no better or worse off unless investors are fooled by the bootstrap effect.

Since World Enterprises' stock is selling for double the price of Muck and Slurry stock (line 2), World Enterprises can acquire the 100,000 Muck and Slurry shares for 50,000 of its own shares. Thus, World will have 150,000 shares outstanding after the merger.

Total earnings double as a result of the merger (line 5), but the number of shares increases by only 50%. Earnings *per share* rise from $2.00 to $2.67. We call this the *bootstrap effect* because there is no real gain created by the merger and no increase in the two firms' combined value. Since the stock price is unchanged, the price–earnings ratio falls (line 3).

Figure 32.1 illustrates what is going on here. Before the merger, $1 invested in World Enterprises bought 5 cents of current earnings and rapid growth prospects. On the other hand, $1 invested in Muck and Slurry bought 10 cents of current earnings but slower growth prospects. If the *total* market value is not altered by the merger, then $1 invested in the merged firm gives 6.7 cents of immediate earnings but slower growth than World Enterprises offered alone.

Muck and Slurry shareholders get lower immediate earnings but faster growth. Neither side gains or loses provided everybody understands the deal.

Financial manipulators sometimes try to ensure that the market does *not* understand the deal. Suppose that investors are fooled by the exuberance of the president of World Enterprises and by plans to introduce modern management techniques into its new Earth Sciences Division (formerly known as Muck and Slurry). They could easily mistake the 33% post-merger increase in earnings per share for real growth. If they do, the price of World Enterprises stock rises and the shareholders of both companies receive something for nothing.

This is a "bootstrap" or "chain letter" game. It generates earnings growth not from capital investment or improved profitability, but from purchase of slowly growing firms with low price–earnings ratios. If this fools investors, the financial manager may be able to puff up stock price artificially. But to keep fooling investors, the firm has to continue to expand by merger *at the same compound rate*. Clearly, this cannot go on forever; one day, expansion must slow down or stop. At this point, earnings growth falls dramatically and the house of cards collapses.

This game is not often played these days, but you may still encounter managers who would rather acquire firms with low price–earnings ratios. Buying a firm with a lower price-earnings ratio than your own will always increase immediate earnings per share, but that alone will not add value.

32.3 Self-Test

Suppose that Muck and Slurry has even worse prospects and its share price is only $10. Rework Table 32.2. What happens to World Enterprises' earnings per share?

Lower Borrowing Costs

You often hear it said that a merged firm is able to borrow more cheaply than its separate units could. In part, this is true. We have already seen (in Section 14-3) that there are economies of scale in making new issues. Therefore, if firms can make fewer, larger security issues by merging, there are genuine savings.

But when people say that borrowing costs are lower for the merged firm, they usually mean something more than lower issue costs. They mean that when two firms merge, the combined company can borrow at lower interest rates than either firm could separately. This, of course, is exactly what we should expect in a well-functioning bond market. While the two firms are separate, they do not guarantee each other's debt; if one fails, the bondholder cannot ask the other for money. But after the merger, each enterprise effectively does guarantee the other's debt; if one part of the business fails, the bondholders can still take their money out of the other part. Because these mutual guarantees make the debt less risky, lenders demand a lower interest rate.

Does the lower interest rate mean a net gain to the merger? Not necessarily. Compare the following two situations:

- *Separate issues.* Firm A and firm T each make a $50 million bond issue.
- *Single issue.* Firms A and T merge, and the new firm AT makes a single $100 million issue.

Of course, AT would pay a lower interest rate, other things being equal. But it does not make sense for A and T to merge just to get that lower rate. Although AT's shareholders do gain from the lower rate, they lose by having to guarantee each other's debt. In other words, they get the lower interest rate only by giving bondholders better protection. There is no *net* gain.

In Section 24-2, we showed that

$$\text{Bond value} = \begin{matrix} \text{Bond value} \\ \text{assuming no} \\ \text{chance of default} \end{matrix} - \begin{matrix} \text{Value of} \\ \text{shareholders' (put)} \\ \text{option to default} \end{matrix}$$

A merger of A and T increases bond value (or reduces the interest payments necessary to support a *given* bond value) only by reducing the value of stockholders' option to default. In other words, the value of the default option for AT's $100 million issue is less than the combined value of the two default options on A's and T's separate $50 million issues.

Now suppose that A and T each borrow $50 million and *then* merge. If the merger is a surprise, it is likely to be a happy one for the bondholders. The bonds they thought were guaranteed by one of the two firms end up guaranteed by both. The shareholders lose in this case because they have given bondholders better protection but have received nothing in exchange.

There is one situation in which mergers can create value by making debt safer. Consider a firm that covets interest tax shields but is reluctant to borrow more because of worries about financial distress. (This is the trade-off theory described in Chapter 17.) Merging decreases the probability of financial distress, other things equal. If it allows increased borrowing, and increased value from the interest tax shields, there can be a net gain to the merger.[5]

Management Motives

There is another class of dubious motives for merger. These motives are not ones that you will hear cited by management because the urge to merge may be more a result of the manager's hubris or personal objectives than it is of economic reasoning.

An overconfident manager, or one with excessive self-regard, may come to believe that she can run a target company better than the incumbent management. There is evidence that CEOs who have demonstrated unusual self-esteem or who have been particularly lauded in the media have tended to make more frequent and larger acquisitions, pay higher premiums, and engage in value-destroying mergers.[6]

Warren Buffett summarizes the situation as follows:

Many managements apparently were overexposed in impressionable childhood years to the story in which the imprisoned handsome prince is released from a toad's body by a kiss from a beautiful princess. Consequently, they are certain their managerial kiss will do wonders for the profitability of [the target company]. We've observed many kisses but very few miracles. Nevertheless, many managerial princesses remain serenely confident about the future potency of their kisses—even after their corporate backyards are knee-deep in unresponsive toads.[7]

The effect of such management hubris is reinforced by strong inducements for managers to make acquisitions. As we explained in Chapter 19, there's a strong link between firm size and CEO pay. Bosses of larger firms also enjoy greater prestige and public recognition. What better way to increase your compensation and celebrity status than by a large acquisition?

Sometimes, CEOs are rewarded simply for undertaking an acquisition, regardless of whether it creates value for shareholders. For example, in 2000 Vodafone's Christopher Gent

---

[5]This merger rationale was first suggested by W. G. Lewellen, "A Pure Financial Rationale for the Conglomerate Merger," *Journal of Finance* 26 (1971), pp. 521–537. If you want to see some of the controversy and discussion that this idea led to, look at R. C. Higgins and L. D. Schall, "Corporate Bankruptcy and Conglomerate Merger," *Journal of Finance* 30 (1975), pp. 93–114; and D. Galai and R. W. Masulis, "The Option Pricing Model and the Risk Factor of Stock," *Journal of Financial Economics* 3 (1976), especially pp. 66–69.

[6]The hubris motive for mergers was suggested by Richard Roll in "The Hubris Hypothesis of Corporate Takeovers," *Journal of Business* 59 (1986), pp. 197–216. Empirical evidence is provided by A. Chatterjee and D. C. Hambrick, "It's All about Me: Narcissistic Chief Executive Officers and Their Effects on Company Strategy and Performance," *Administrative Science Quarterly* 52 (2007), pp. 351–386; M. Hayward and D. C. Hambrick, "Explaining the Premiums Paid for Large Acquisitions: Evidence of CEO Hubris," *Administrative Science Quarterly* 42 (1997), pp. 103–127; and U. Malmendier and G. Tate, "Who Makes Acquisitions? CEO Overconfidence and the Market's Reaction," *Journal of Financial Economics* 89 (2008), pp. 20–43.

[7]Warren Buffet, Berkshire Hathaway Annual Report, 1981.

was paid £10 million for buying German rival Mannesmann. In the same year, Chase Manhattan CEO William Harrison was paid a $20 million bonus for negotiating the acquisition of J.P. Morgan, even though the negotiations took only three weeks and Chase's stock price subsequently dropped by one-third. One study found that nearly 40% of acquiring firms compensate their CEOs with a cash bonus for completing the deal.[8] These bonuses are unrelated to the market's reaction to the deal but positively related to deal size—giving CEOs a particular incentive to make large acquisitions.

32-4   Estimating Merger Gains and Costs

Suppose that you are the financial manager of acquirer firm A and you want to analyze the possible purchase of target firm T. The first thing to think about is whether there is an *economic gain* from the merger. There is an economic gain *only if the two firms are worth more together than apart.* If the combined firm would be worth PV_{AT} and the separate firms are worth PV_A and PV_T, then

$$\text{Gain} = PV_{AT} - (PV_A + PV_T) = \Delta PV_{AT}$$

If this gain is positive, there is an economic justification for merger.[9]

In order to buy T, A will almost certainly need to pay T's shareholders more than their firm is currently worth. This *acquisition premium* is the cost to A of the merger. The *net* present value to A of the merger is measured by the difference between the gain and the cost. Therefore, A should go ahead with the merger if

$$NPV = (\Delta PV_{AT} - \text{Cost}) > 0$$

We like to write the merger criterion in this way because it focuses attention on two distinct questions. When you estimate the benefit, you concentrate on whether there are any gains to be made from the merger. When you estimate cost, you are estimating how much of the gain A gets to keep.

Estimating NPV When the Merger Is Financed by Cash

Estimating a merger's NPV is simplest when the target is purchased with cash. We illustrate this with an example.

EXAMPLE 32.2 • Estimating merger NPV when the payment is in cash

Suppose that Firm A has a value of $200 million, and T has a value of $50 million. Merging the two firms would allow cost savings with a present value of $25 million. This is the gain from the merger. Thus,

$$PV_A = \$200$$
$$PV_T = \$50$$
$$PV_{AT} = \$275\text{million}$$
$$\text{Gain} = \Delta PV_{AT} = +\$25 \text{ million}$$

---

[8]Y. Grinstein and P. Hribar, "CEO Compensation and Incentives: Evidence from M&A Bonuses," *Journal of Financial Economics* 73 (2004), pp. 119–143.

[9]When A estimates the merger gains, it makes sense to keep an eye on what investors think the gains from merging are. If A's stock price falls when the deal is announced, then investors are sending the message that the merger benefits are doubtful or that A is paying too much for them.

If A offers to buy T for cash, the cost of the acquisition is equal to the cash payment minus T's value as a separate entity. Thus,

$$\text{Cost} = \text{cash} - PV_T$$

For example, suppose that T is bought for $65 million of cash. Then the cost of the merger is

$$\text{Cost} = \text{cash} - PV_T$$
$$= 65 - 50 = \$15 \text{ million}$$

Note that the shareholders of firm T—the people on the other side of the transaction—are ahead by $15 million. They have captured $15 million of the $25 million merger gain. The NPV to A's shareholders equals the overall gain from the merger less that part of the gain captured by T's shareholders:

$$NPV = 25 - 15 = +\$10 \text{ million}$$

Just as a check, let's confirm that A's shareholders really come out $10 million ahead. They start with a firm worth $PV_A = \$200$ million, and they end up with a firm worth $275 million. However, they have to pay out $65 million to T's shareholders.[10] Thus, NPV is

$$NPV = \text{wealth with merger} - \text{wealth without merger}$$
$$= (PV_{AT} - \text{cash}) - PV_A$$
$$= (\$275 - \$65) - \$200 = +\$10 \text{ million}$$

Suppose investors do not anticipate the merger between A and T. The announcement will cause the value of T's stock to rise from $50 million to $65 million, a 30% increase. If investors share management's assessment of the merger gains, the market value of A's stock will increase by $10 million, only a 5% increase.

32.4 Self-Test

Cislunar Foods makes a surprise cash offer of $22 a share for Targetco. Before the offer, Targetco shares were selling for $18 a share. Targetco has 1 million shares outstanding. What must Cislunar believe about the present value of the improvements it can bring to Targetco's operations?

Estimating NPV When the Merger Is Financed by Stock

Many mergers involve payment wholly or partly in the form of the acquirer's stock. When a merger is financed by stock, the cost depends on the value of the shares in the new company that are received by the shareholders of the selling company. If x is the proportion of the equity in the joint firm that is given to the target, then the cost is

$$\text{Cost} = xPV_{AT} - PV_T$$

EXAMPLE 32.3 • Estimating merger NPV when payment is in the form of stock

Suppose that shareholders in the target firm are offered x = 25% of the equity in the combined company. The remaining 75% will be held by A's shareholders.

---

[10]We are assuming that PV_A includes enough cash to finance the deal, or that the cash can be borrowed at a fair market interest rate. Notice that the value to A's stockholders after the deal is done and paid for is $275 − $65 = $210 million—a gain of $10 million.

The cost of the merger is now

$$\text{Cost} = x\text{PV}_{AT} - \text{PV}_T = 0.25 \times 275 - 50 = \$18.75 \text{ million}$$

And the net gain to A is

$$\text{NPV} = \text{Gain} - \text{Cost} = 25 - 18.75 = \$6.25 \text{ million}$$

• • • • •

BEYOND THE PAGE

Try It!
Merger
calculator

mhhe.com/brealey14e

Notice a key distinction between cash and stock as financing instruments. If cash is offered, the cost of the merger is unaffected by the merger gains. If stock is offered, the cost depends on the gains because the gains show up in the postmerger share price.

Stock financing also mitigates the effect of overvaluation or undervaluation of either firm. Suppose, for example, that A overestimates T's value as a separate entity, perhaps because it has overlooked some hidden liability. Thus, A makes too generous an offer. Other things being equal, A's stockholders are better off if it is a stock offer rather than a cash offer. With a stock offer, the inevitable bad news about T's value will fall partly on the shoulders of T's stockholders.

> **32.5 Self-Test**
>
> See Example 32.3. Suppose A has 600 shares and T has 300. A now offers T shareholders one A share for every T share. What is the cost of the merger to A?

Asymmetric Information

There is a second important difference between cash and stock financing for mergers. A's managers will usually have access to information about A's prospects that is not available to outsiders. Economists call this *asymmetric information.*

Suppose A's managers are more optimistic than outside investors. They may think that A's shares will really be worth $285 million after the merger, $10 million higher than the $275 million market value that we just calculated. If they are right, the true cost of a stock-financed merger with T is

$$\text{Cost} = 0.25 \times 285 - 50 = \$21.25 \text{ million}$$

T's shareholders would get a "free gift" of $21.25 million.

Of course, if A's managers were really this optimistic, they would strongly prefer to finance the merger with cash. Financing with stock would be favored by *pessimistic* managers who think their company's shares are *over* valued.

Does this sound like "win-win" for A—just issue shares when overvalued, cash otherwise? No, it's not that easy, because T's shareholders, and outside investors generally, understand what's going on. Suppose you are negotiating on behalf of T. You find that A's managers keep suggesting stock rather than cash financing. You quickly infer that A's managers are pessimistic, mark down your own opinion of what the shares are worth, and drive a harder bargain.

This asymmetric-information story explains why the share prices of buying firms generally fall when stock-financed mergers are announced.[11] Andrade, Mitchell, and Stafford found an average market-adjusted fall of 1.5% on the announcement of stock-financed mergers between 1973 and 1998. There was a small *gain* (0.4%) for a sample of cash-financed deals.[12]

---

[11]The same reasoning applies to stock issues. See Sections 14-3 and 17-4.

[12]See G. Andrade, M. Mitchell, and E. Stafford, "New Evidence and Perspectives on Mergers," *Journal of Economic Perspectives* 15 (2001), pp. 103–120. This result confirms earlier work, including N. Travlos, "Corporate Takeover Bids, Methods of Payment, and Bidding Firms' Stock Returns," *Journal of Finance* 42 (1987), pp. 943–963; and J. R. Franks, R. S. Harris, and S. Titman, "The Postmerger Share-Price Performance of Acquiring Firms," *Journal of Financial Economics* 29 (1991), pp. 81–96.

More on Estimating Costs—What If the Target's Stock Price Anticipates the Merger?

The cost of a merger is the premium that the buyer pays over the seller's stand-alone value. How can that value be determined? If the target is a public company, you can start with its market value; just observe price per share and multiply by the number of shares outstanding. But bear in mind that if investors *expect* A to acquire T, or if they expect *somebody* to acquire T, the market value of T may overstate its stand-alone value.

This is one of the few places in this book where we draw an important distinction between market value (MV) and the true, or "intrinsic," value (PV) of the firm as a separate entity. The problem here is not that the market value of T is wrong but that it may not be the value of firm T as a separate entity. Potential investors in T's stock will see two possible outcomes and two possible values:

Outcome	Market Value of T's Stock
1. No merger	PV_T: Value of T as a separate firm
2. Merger occurs	PV_T *plus* some part of the benefits of the merger

If the second outcome is possible, MV_T, the stock market value we observe for T, will overstate PV_T. This is exactly what should happen in a competitive capital market. Unfortunately, it complicates the task of a financial manager who is evaluating a merger.

Here is an example: Suppose that just before A and T's merger announcement we observe the following:

	Firm A	Firm T
Market price per share	$200	$100
Number of shares	1,000,000	500,000
Market value of firm	$200 million	$50 million

Firm A intends to pay $65 million cash for T. If T's market price reflects only its value as a separate entity, then we have already seen that

$$\text{Cost} = \text{cash} - PV_T$$
$$= 65 - 50 = \$15 \text{ million}$$

However, suppose that the market value of T's shares has *already* risen by $6 million because of rumors that T might get a favorable merger offer. That means that its intrinsic value is overstated, and its true value, PV_T, is only $44 million. Then

$$\text{Cost} = (65 - 44) = \$21 \text{ million}$$

Since the merger gain is $25 million, this deal still makes A's stockholders better off, but T's stockholders are now capturing the lion's share of the gain.

Notice that if the market made a mistake, and the market value of T was *less* than T's true value as a separate entity, the cost could be negative. In other words, T would be a *bargain* and the merger would be worthwhile from A's point of view, even if the two firms were worth no more together than apart. Of course, A's stockholders' gain would be T's stockholders' loss because T would be sold for less than its true value.

Firms have made acquisitions just because their managers believed they had spotted a company whose intrinsic value was not fully appreciated by the stock market. However, we know from the evidence on market efficiency that "cheap" stocks often turn out to be expensive. It is not easy for outsiders, whether investors or managers, to find firms that are truly undervalued by the market. Moreover, if the shares are really bargain-priced, A doesn't need a merger to profit by its special knowledge. It can just buy up T's shares on the open market and hold them passively, waiting for other investors to wake up to T's true value.

If firm A is wise, it will not go ahead with a merger if the cost exceeds the gain. Firm T will not consent if A's gain is so big that T loses. This gives us a range of possible cash payments that would allow the merger to take place. Whether the payment is at the top or the bottom of this range depends on the relative bargaining power of the two participants.

Right and Wrong Ways to Estimate the Benefits of Mergers

Some companies begin their merger analyses with a forecast of the target firm's future cash flows. Any revenue increases or cost reductions attributable to the merger are included in the forecasts, which are then discounted back to the present and compared with the purchase price:

$$\text{NPV} = \begin{array}{c} \text{DCF valuation} \\ \text{of target, including} \\ \text{merger benefits} \end{array} - \begin{array}{c} \text{cash required} \\ \text{for acquisition} \end{array}$$

This is a dangerous procedure. Even the brightest and best-trained analyst can make large errors in valuing a business. The estimated NPV may come up positive not because the merger makes sense but simply because the analyst's cash-flow forecasts are too optimistic. On the other hand, a good merger may not be pursued if the analyst fails to recognize the target's potential as a stand-alone business.

Our procedure *starts* with the target's stand-alone market value (PV_B) and concentrates on the *changes* in cash flow that would result from the merger. *Ask yourself why the two firms should be worth more together than apart.*

One final piece of horse sense: Often, two companies bid against each other to acquire the same target firm. In effect, the target firm puts itself up for auction. In such cases, ask yourself whether the target is worth more to you than to the other bidder. If the answer is no, you should think carefully about getting into a bidding contest. Winning such a contest may be more expensive than losing it. If you lose, you have simply wasted your time; if you win, you have probably paid too much.

32-5 The Mechanics of a Merger

Buying a company is a more complicated affair than buying a piece of machinery. Thus we should look at some of the problems encountered in arranging mergers. In practice, these arrangements are often *extremely* complex, and specialists need to be consulted. We are not trying to replace those specialists; we simply want to alert you to the kinds of legal, tax, and accounting issues that they deal with.

Mergers, Antitrust Law, and Popular Opposition

Mergers can get bogged down in the federal antitrust laws. The most important statute is the Clayton Act of 1914, which forbids an acquisition whenever "in any line of commerce or in any section of the country" the effect "*may be* substantially to lessen competition, or to *tend* to create a monopoly."

Antitrust law can be enforced by the federal government in either of two ways: by a civil suit brought by the Justice Department or by a proceeding initiated by the Federal Trade

Commission (FTC).[13] The Hart–Scott–Rodino Antitrust Act of 1976 requires that these agencies be informed of all acquisitions of stock greater than about $75 million. Thus, almost all large mergers are reviewed at an early stage.[14] Both the Justice Department and the FTC then have the right to seek injunctions delaying a merger. An injunction is often enough to scupper the companies' plans. For example, when Halliburton proposed a $28 billion acquisition of Baker Hughes in 2014, the Justice Department filed a lawsuit to block the merger. The companies tried to deal with the department's objections by selling off various business lines to other players. But by 2016, it had become obvious that they could not assuage concerns that the merger would create too much market power, and the companies scrapped their merger plan.

Companies that do business outside the United States also have to worry about foreign antitrust laws. For example, GE's $46 billion takeover bid for Honeywell was blocked by the European Commission, which argued that the combined company would have too much power in the aircraft industry.

Sometimes trustbusters will object to a merger but then relent if the companies agree to divest certain assets and operations. For example, in 2020 the Justice Department consented to the merger between United Technologies and Raytheon only on condition that the companies sell their military airborne radios and GPS businesses.

Mergers may also be stymied by political pressures and popular resentment even when no formal antitrust issues arise. In recent years national governments in Europe have become involved in almost all high-profile cross-border mergers and are likely to intervene actively in any hostile bid. For example, the news in 2005 that PepsiCo might bid for Danone aroused considerable hostility in France. The prime minister added his support to opponents of the merger and announced that the French government was drawing up a list of strategic industries that should be protected from foreign ownership. It was unclear whether yogurt production would be one of these strategic industries.

Economic nationalism is not confined to Europe. The Committee on Foreign Investment in the United States (CFIUS) is responsible for reviewing any acquisition by a foreign company which might have major implications for U.S. national interests. For example, in 2018, the United States blocked Singapore-based Broadcom's takeover bid for the U.S. chipmaker Qualcomm. President Trump cited "national security concerns" about giving a foreign entity access to U.S. technology.

The Form of Acquisition

Suppose that company A is confident that the purchase of T will not be challenged on antitrust grounds. The next step is to consider the form of the acquisition.

One possibility is literally to *merge* the two companies, in which case company A automatically assumes *all* T's assets and *all* its liabilities. This so-called *one-step* (or *statutory*) *merger* must have the approval of at least 50% of T's shareholders.[15] Company A also may need shareholder approval if it issues more than 20% of its stock in the deal.

An alternative is simply to make a *takeover* (or *two-step*) offer to buy T's stock in exchange for cash, shares, or other securities. In this case A can deal individually with the shareholders of the selling company. T's managers may not be involved at all. Their approval and cooperation are generally sought, but if they resist, A will attempt to acquire an effective majority of the outstanding shares. If the bid is successful, A gains control of T. It can then vote to complete the merger (*step 2*) and, if necessary, toss out the incumbent management. We discuss the mechanics of takeovers in more detail next.

---

[13]Competitors or third parties who think they will be injured by the merger can also bring antitrust suits.

[14]The target has to be notified also, and it in turn informs investors. Thus the Hart–Scott–Rodino Act effectively forces an acquiring company to "go public" with its bid.

[15]Corporate charters and state laws sometimes specify a higher percentage.

A third approach is to buy some or all of T's assets. In this case, ownership of the assets needs to be transferred, and payment is made to the selling firm T rather than directly to its shareholders.

Merger Accounting

When one company buys another, its management worries about how the purchase will show up in its financial statements. Before 2001, the company had a choice of accounting method, but in that year, the Financial Accounting Standards Board (FASB) introduced new rules that required the buyer to use the *purchase method* of merger accounting. This is illustrated in Table 32.3, which shows what happens when A Corporation buys T Corporation, leading to the new AT Corporation. The two firms' initial balance sheets are shown at the top of the table. Below this we show what happens to the balance sheet when the two firms merge. We assume that T Corporation has been purchased for $18 million, 180% of book value.

Why did A Corporation pay an $8 million premium over T's book value? There are two possible reasons. First, the true values of T's *tangible assets*—its working capital, plant, and equipment—may be greater than $10 million. We will assume that this is *not* the reason; that is, we assume that the assets listed on its balance sheet are valued there correctly.[16] Second, A Corporation may be paying for an *intangible asset* that is not listed on T Corporation's balance sheet. For example, the intangible asset may be a promising product or technology. Or it may be no more than T Corporation's share of the expected economic gains from the merger.

A Corporation is buying an asset worth $18 million. The problem is to show that asset on the left-hand side of AT Corporation's balance sheet. T Corporation's tangible assets are worth only $10 million. This leaves $8 million. Under the purchase method, the accountant takes care of this by creating a new asset category called *goodwill* and assigning $8 million to it.[17] As long as the goodwill continues to be worth at least $8 million, it stays on the balance sheet and the company's earnings are unaffected.[18] However, the company is obliged each year to estimate the fair value of the goodwill. If the estimated value ever falls below $8 million, the goodwill is "impaired" and the amount shown on the balance sheet must be adjusted downward and the write-off deducted from that year's earnings. Some companies have found that this can make a nasty dent in profits. For example, when the new accounting rules were introduced, AOL was obliged to write down the value of its assets by $54 billion.

❯ TABLE 32.3
Accounting for the merger of A Corporation and T Corporation, assuming that A Corporation pays $18 million for T Corporation (figures in $ millions).

Key: NWC = net working capital; FA = net book value of fixed assets; D = debt; E = book value of equity.

Balance Sheet of A Corporation			
NWC	20	30	D
FA	80	70	E
	100	100	

Balance Sheet of T Corporation			
NWC	1	0	D
FA	9	10	E
	10	10	

Balance Sheet of AT Corporation			
NWC	21	30	D
FA	89	88	E
Goodwill	8		
	118	118	

---

[16]If B's tangible assets are worth more than their previous book values, they would be reappraised and their current values entered on AB Corporation's balance sheet.

[17]If part of the $8 million consisted of payment for identifiable intangible assets such as patents, the accountant would place these under a separate category of assets. Identifiable intangible assets that have a finite life need to be written off over their life.

[18]Goodwill is depreciated for tax purposes, however.

Some Tax Considerations

An acquisition may be either taxable or tax-free. If payment is in the form of cash, the acquisition is regarded as taxable. In this case the selling stockholders are treated as having *sold* their shares, and they must pay tax on any capital gains. If payment is largely in the form of shares, the acquisition is tax-free and the shareholders are viewed as *exchanging* their old shares for similar new ones; no capital gains or losses are recognized.

The tax status of the acquisition also affects the taxes paid by the merged firm afterward. After a tax-free acquisition, the merged firm is taxed as if the two firms had always been together. In a taxable acquisition, the assets of the selling firm are revalued, the resulting write-up or write-down is treated as a taxable gain or loss, and tax depreciation is recalculated on the basis of the restated asset values.

A very simple example will illustrate these distinctions.

EXAMPLE 32.4 • A merger's tax status

In 2012, Captain B forms Seacorp, which purchases a fishing boat for $300,000. Assume, for simplicity, that the boat is depreciated for tax purposes over 20 years on a straight-line basis (no salvage value). Thus, annual depreciation is $300,000/20 = $15,000, and in 2022, the boat has a net book value of $150,000. But Captain B finds that owing to careful maintenance, inflation, and good times in the local fishing industry, the boat is really worth $280,000. In addition, Seacorp holds $50,000 of marketable securities.

Now suppose that Captain B sells the firm to Baycorp for $330,000. The possible tax consequences of the acquisition are shown in Table 32.4. In this case, Captain B may ask for a tax-free deal to defer capital gains tax. But Baycorp can afford to pay more in a taxable deal because depreciation tax shields are larger.

	Taxable Merger	Tax-Free Merger
Impact on Captain B	Captain B must recognize a $30,000 capital gain.	Capital gain can be deferred until Captain B sells the Baycorp shares.
Impact on Baycorp	Boat is revalued at $280,000. Tax depreciation increases to $280,000/10 = $28,000 per year (assuming 10 years of remaining life).	Boat's value remains at $150,000, and tax depreciation continues at $15,000 per year.

〉TABLE 32.4   Possible tax consequences when Baycorp buys Seacorp for $330,000. Captain B's original investment in Seacorp was $300,000. Just before the merger Seacorp's assets were $50,000 of marketable securities and one boat with a book value of $150,000 but a market value of $280,000.

• • • • •

32.6 Self-Test

Suppose that the market value of Seacorp's boat is $320,000 and that Captain B sells the firm for $370,000. Rework Table 32.4. to show the tax consequences.

32-6   Takeovers and the Market for Corporate Control

The shareholders are the owners of the firm. But most shareholders do not feel like the boss, and with good reason. Try buying one share of IBM stock and marching into the boardroom for a chat with your employee, the CEO. (However, if you own 50 million IBM shares, the CEO will travel to see you.)

The *ownership* and *management* of large corporations are separated. Shareholders elect the board of directors but have little direct say in most management decisions. Agency costs arise when managers or directors are tempted to make decisions that are not in the shareholders' interests.

As we pointed out in Chapter 19, there are many forces and constraints working to keep managers' and shareholders' interests in line. But what can be done to ensure that the board has engaged the most talented managers? What happens if managers are inadequate? What if the board is derelict in monitoring the performance of managers? Or what if the firm's managers are fine but the resources of the firm could be used more efficiently by merging with another firm? Can we count on managers to pursue policies that might put them out of a job?

These are all questions about the *market for corporate control,* the mechanisms by which firms are matched up with owners and management teams who can make the most of the firm's resources. You should not take a firm's current ownership and management for granted. If it is possible for the value of the firm to be enhanced by changing management or by reorganizing under new owners, there will be incentives for someone to make the change.

There are three ways to change the management of a firm: (1) a successful proxy contest in which a group of shareholders votes in a new board of directors who then pick a new management team, (2) a takeover of one company by another, and (3) a leveraged buyout of the firm by a private group of investors. We discussed proxy contests in Section 19-3, and we will consider buyouts in the next chapter. Here we focus on takeovers

To change a firm's management, the would-be acquirer can make an offer directly to the target's shareholders. If the takeover offer is in cash, it is called a *tender offer;* if it is partly in stock, it is an *exchange offer.* The management of the target firm may advise its shareholders to accept the offer, or it may fight the bid in the hope that the acquirer will either raise its offer or throw in the towel.

The acquirer will usually state that its offer is conditional on receiving at least 50% acceptances from the target's shareholders. If the bidder is successful, it can then proceed with a *two-step* merger that obligates the minority shareholders to accept.[19]

Hostile takeovers are rarely the preferred acquisition strategy. They are expensive not only in the form of legal and other support costs, but in the high premium that the buyer may be forced to pay for the target's stock. Also, in a negotiated merger, the bidder has access to the target's books and is able to conduct a thorough due diligence analysis. In a hostile takeover, the bidder must make do with publicly available information.

In the United States, the rules for tender offers are set largely by the Williams Act of 1968 and by state laws. The Williams Act obliges firms that own 5% or more of another company's shares to tip their hand by reporting their holding to the SEC and to outline their intentions in a Schedule 13(d) filing. This filing is often an invitation for other bidders to enter the fray and to force up the takeover premium. The consolation for the initial bidder is that if its bid is ultimately unsuccessful, it may be able to sell to sell off its toehold in the target at a substantial profit.

---

[19]Under Delaware law, this is most simply achieved if the acquirer owns more than 90% of the target's shares. In this case, a "short form" merger can be completed in a day or two that forces the minority holders to accept the offer. The alternative is for the target to be acquired by a special-purpose subsidiary of the bidder whose shareholders then vote to merge with the main company.

Tender offers present shareholders with a difficult decision. Should they accept, should they wait to see if someone else produces a better offer, or should they sell their stock in the market? This dilemma presents an opportunity for arbitrageurs, such as hedge funds, that specialize in answering such questions. In other words, they buy from the target's shareholders and take on the risk that the deal will not go through.[20] Often, the arbitrageur will become actively involved in the target company's response to the bid and will seek to force the bidder to raise its offer.[21]

Firms that are worried about being taken over usually prepare their defenses in advance. Often, they persuade shareholders to agree to *shark-repellent* changes to the corporate charter. For example, the charter may be amended to require that any merger must be approved by a *supermajority* of 80% of the shares rather than the normal 50%. Firms may also deter potential bidders by devising *poison pills* that make the company unappetizing, typically by giving shareholders the right to buy the company's shares at a discount as soon as a bidder acquires a significant number of shares. The bidder is not entitled to the discount. Thus, the bidder resembles Tantalus—as soon as it has acquired the shares, control is lifted away from its reach.

These days, large companies are reluctant to keep a poison pill permanently in place, but since they can be rapidly approved by the board in the event of a hostile bid, the so-called morning-after pill remains one of the most important takeover defenses. Bidders can circumvent such a defense only by first conducting a proxy fight. Once the new board is in control, the poison pill can then be removed, and the company can recommend acceptance of the tender offer. Thus, proxy fights have increasingly become a step in a hostile takeover.

Table 32.5 summarizes these and other lines of defense. Although shareholders are generally prepared to go along with management's shark-repellant measures, it is doubtful whether they are truly in their interest. Managers who are protected from takeover appear to enjoy higher remuneration and to generate less wealth for their shareholders.[22]

Managers of target companies may act in shareholders' interests by opposing the bid in order to hold out for a better price. Sometimes, however, their opposition to the bid may be prompted by their wish to keep a lucrative job. If that is the case, the solution may be to offer them generous compensation for stepping aside. For example, when Verizon acquired Yahoo! in 2017, Marissa Mayer, Yahoo!'s CEO, received a $23 million golden parachute.

Any management team that tries to develop improved weapons of defense must expect challenge in the courts. Courts do not usually question a board's business judgment unless there is evidence that the decision breached the duties of loyalty, good faith, and due care. However, two landmark cases have imposed particular rules for the board of a takeover target. In the Unocal case, the court stated that the target's board must inform itself fully, and any decision to take defensive action must be the result of a careful evaluation of the hostile bid. Defensive measures by the target should not be coercive or fall outside a range of reasonable responses. The Revlon case imposed a duty for the company to obtain the best value reasonably available. For example, in 1993 a court blocked Viacom's agreed takeover of Paramount on the grounds that Paramount directors did not do their homework before turning down a higher offer from QVC. Paramount was forced to give up its poison-pill defense and the stock options that it had offered to Viacom. Such decisions have led managers to become more careful in opposing bids, and they do not throw themselves blindly into the arms of any white knight.

BEYOND THE PAGE

Valeant's battle for Allergan

mhhe.com/brealey14e

[20]Strictly speaking, an arbitrageur is an investor who takes a fully hedged—that is, riskless—position. But arbitrageurs in merger battles often take very large risks indeed. Their activities are known as "risk arbitrage."

[21]W. Jiang, T. Li, and D. Mei, "Influencing Control: Jawboning in Risk Arbitrage," *Journal of Finance* 73 (2018), pp. 2635–2675.

[22]A. Agrawal and C. R. Knoeber, "Managerial Compensation and the Threat of Takeover," *Journal of Financial Economics* 47 (1998), pp. 219–239; and P. A. Gompers, J. L. Ishii, and A. Metrick, "Corporate Governance and Equity Prices," *Quarterly Journal of Economics* 118 (2003), pp. 107–155.

Pre-Offer Defenses	Description
Shark-repellent charter amendments:	
Supermajority	A high percentage of shares, typically 80%, is needed to approve a merger.
Fair price	Mergers are restricted unless a fair price (determined by formula or appraisal) is paid.
Restricted voting rights	Shareholders who acquire more than a specified proportion of the target have no voting rights unless approved by the target's board.
Waiting period	Unwelcome acquirers must wait for a specified number of years before they can complete the merger.
Other:	
Poison pill	Existing shareholders are issued rights that, if there is a significant purchase of shares by a bidder, can be used to purchase additional stock in the company at a bargain price.
Poison put	Existing bondholders can demand repayment if there is a change of control as a result of a hostile takeover.
Post-Offer Defenses	
Litigation	Target files suit against bidder for violating antitrust or securities laws.
Asset restructuring	Target buys assets that bidder does not want or that will create an antitrust problem.
Liability restructuring	Target issues shares to a friendly third party, increases the number of shareholders, or repurchases shares from existing shareholders at a premium.

❭**TABLE 32.5**   A summary of takeover defenses.

Anglo-Saxon countries used to have a near-monopoly on hostile takeovers. That is no longer the case. Takeover activity in Europe often exceeds that in the United States, and in recent years, some of the most bitterly contested takeovers have involved European companies. For example, Mittal's $27 billion takeover of Arcelor resulted from a fierce and highly politicized five-month battle. Arcelor used every defense in the book—including inviting a Russian company to become a leading shareholder.

Mittal is now based in Europe, but it began operations in Indonesia. This illustrates another change in the merger market. Acquirers are no longer confined to the major industrialized countries. They now include Brazilian, Indian, and Chinese companies. For example, Tetley Tea, Anglo-Dutch steelmaker Corus, and Jaguar and Land Rover have all been acquired by Indian conglomerate Tata Group. In China, Lenovo acquired IBM's personal computer business; Geely bought Volvo from Ford; and China National Chemical bought Syngenta, the Swiss agrichemical business. In Brazil, Vale purchased Inco, the Canadian nickel producer, and Cutrale-Safra bought the U.S. banana company Chiquita Brands.

32-7   Merger Waves and Merger Profitability

Merger Waves

Look at Figure 32.2, which shows the number of mergers in the United States for each year since 1985. Notice that mergers come in waves. There was an upsurge in merger activity in the 1960s and late 1980s (not shown in the figure) and in the 1990s. Another merger boom got under way in 2003, petered out with the onset of the credit crisis, and resumed in 2014. These were generally periods of rising stock prices.

We don't really understand why merger activity is so volatile and why it seems to be associated with booming stock markets. If mergers are prompted by economic motives, at least one

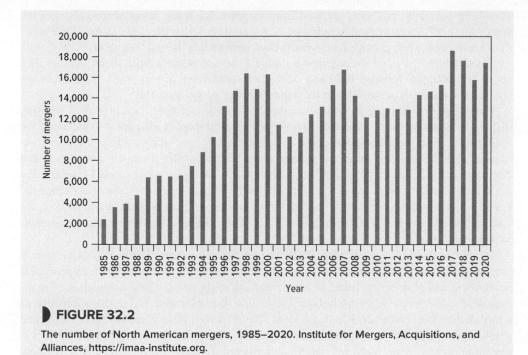

> **FIGURE 32.2**

The number of North American mergers, 1985–2020. Institute for Mergers, Acquisitions, and Alliances, https://imaa-institute.org.

of these motives must be "here today and gone tomorrow," and it must somehow be associated with high stock prices. But none of the economic motives that we review in this chapter has anything to do with the general level of the stock market. None burst on the scene in the 1960s, reappeared for most of the 1980s and again in the mid-1990s and early 2000s. Some mergers may result from mistakes in valuation on the part of the stock market. In other words, the buyer may believe that investors have underestimated the value of the seller or may hope that they will overestimate the value of the combined firm. But we see (with hindsight) that mistakes are made in bear markets as well as bull markets. Why don't we see just as many firms hunting for bargain acquisitions when the stock market is low? It is possible that "suckers are born every minute," but it is difficult to believe that they can be harvested only in bull markets.

Merger activity in each wave tends to be concentrated in a relatively small number of industries and is often prompted by deregulation. For example, deregulation of telecoms and banking in the 1990s led to a spate of mergers in both industries.[23] Changes in technology or the pattern of demand can also prompt a spate of mergers. The reduction in defense expenditures following the end of the cold war led to a wave of consolidations among defense companies.

Who Gains and Loses from Mergers?

Look back at Figure 12.6, which showed the performance of the stocks of U.S. target firms around the time of the merger announcement. On average, the announcement was associated with an abnormal return of 16.1% for the target shareholders. This is the premium that investors expected the acquirer would need to pay to consummate the merger. Of course, this is an average figure; selling shareholders sometimes obtained much higher returns. When Allergan acquired the biotech company Tobira, it paid a premium of 500% for Tobira's stock.

---

[23]See G. Andrade, M. Mitchell, and E. Stafford, "New Evidence and Perspectives on Mergers," *Journal of Economic Perspectives* 15 (Spring 2001), pp. 103–120; and J. Harford, "What Drives Merger Waves?" *Journal of Financial Economics* 77 (2005), pp. 529–560.

Selling shareholders clearly do well from mergers. But what about shareholders of the acquiring firm? A similar picture to Figure 12.6 would show that they have done a little better than break even. Their average return in the days surrounding the bid was about 0.5%.[24]

Thus, it looks as if, on average, the merging firms are worth a little more together than apart. For example, between 1980 and 2005, the overall value of merging U.S. firms, buyer and seller combined, increased over the announcement period by 1.1%.[25]

The returns of merging firms around the deal's announcement date provide a measure of the gains that investors expected from the merger. But there is also some evidence of the anticipated longer term changes in cash flows. For example, one study compared analyst forecasts of cash flows made before the merger announcement with subsequent forecasts.[26] The comparison suggested that analysts expected small tax savings from increased leverage, but the principal merger gains were expected to be in the form of operating synergies. These did not stem from forecast improvements in revenues or operating costs, but the combined firms were expected to realize significant economies in their capital expenditures and investments in working capital.

Of course, there is huge variation in the profitability of mergers. The history of mergers is strewn with some high-profile disasters for the buyers, which makes it difficult to generalize about the effect of mergers. Take, for example, Bank of America's 2008 acquisition of mortgage lender Countrywide for $4 billion. The bank's chief executive hailed the acquisition as a rare chance to become No. 1 in home loans. But after the housing bubble burst, the soured loans made by Countryside ended up costing Bank of America an estimated $40 billion in operating losses, fines, and compensation payments. Equally embarrassing was Hewlett-Packard's (HP) purchase of the British software company Autonomy. HP paid $11.1 billion for Autonomy. Just 13 months later, it wrote down the value of this investment by $8.8 billion. HP claimed that it was misled by improper accounting at Autonomy. Nevertheless, the acquisition was a disastrous investment, and HP's CEO was fired in short order.

Buyers vs. Sellers

Why do buyers earn lower returns than sellers? There are several reasons. First, buying firms are typically larger than selling firms. In many mergers, the buyer is so much larger that even substantial net benefits would not show up clearly in the buyer's share price. Suppose, for example, that company A buys company T, which is only one-tenth A's size. Suppose the dollar value of the net gain from the merger is split equally between A and T.[27] Each company's shareholders receive the same *dollar* profit, but T's receive 10 times A's *percentage* return.

The second reason is the competition among potential bidders. Once the first bidder puts the target company "in play," one or more additional suitors often jump in, sometimes as white knights at the invitation of the target firm's management. Every time one suitor tops another's bid, more of the merger gain slides toward the target. At the same time, the target firm's management may mount various legal and financial counterattacks, ensuring that capitulation, if and when it comes, is at the highest attainable price.

The low returns to buyers may also stem from the nature of the buyer's management. We noted earlier that hubris and excessive self-esteem may lead managers to believe that the target firm is worth far more under their leadership. We also saw that managers have an incentive

---

[24]This poor performance may partly reflect that in the case of mergers financed by stock, investors may deduce that the acquirer's management believe that the stock is overpriced.

[25]S. Betton, B. E. Eckbo, and K. S. Thorburn, "Corporate Takeovers," in B. Espen Eckbo (ed.), *Handbook of Empirical Corporate Finance*, Vol. 2 (Amsterdam: Elsevier/North-Holland, 2008). See also G. Andrade, M. Mitchell, and E. Stafford, "New Evidence and Perspectives on Mergers," *Journal of Economic Perspectives* 15 (Spring 2001), pp. 103–120.

[26]E. Devos, P.-R. Kadapakkam, and S. Krishnamurthy, "How do Mergers Create Value? A Comparison of Taxes, Market Power, and Efficiency Improvements as Explanations for Synergies," *Review of Financial Studies* 22 (2009), pp. 1179–1211.

[27]In other words, the *cost* of the merger to A is one-half the gain ΔPV_{AT}.

to undertake acquisitions that enhance their compensation and their prestige. In such cases, the managers of the acquiring company may not be too concerned about the price that is paid for the target. There is some indirect evidence to support this view. For example, one study documents large losses to the most aggressive acquirers in the merger wave of 1998–2001.[28]

Mergers and Society

Concerns about the volume of merger activity generally focus on its wider effects on society rather than the extent of any gains to shareholders. One survey of popular opinion found that 58% of the population believes that hostile takeovers do more harm than good. Moreover, when asked which one group they thought ought to be protected most from being hurt in a hostile takeover, 63% said "employees."[29] The critical question, therefore, is whether any gains to shareholders come at the expense of other stakeholders. This could happen in several ways:

- *Customers* could lose if competition is reduced so that the merged company is able to use its greater market power to raise prices and reduce product choice. This is why regulatory authorities block even synergistic mergers if they think that the efficiency gains might be outweighed by the loss of competition.

- *Suppliers* may lose if the merged company gains greater purchasing power and can demand lower prices from suppliers.

- *Employees* may be affected in two ways. First, less competition may allow the merged company to get away with paying lower wages. Second, mergers may lead to plant closures and job losses.

- Existing *bondholders* may lose if the acquirer finances the merger by raising more debt.

Are these concerns generally valid? It is hard to say. There is little concrete evidence to back them up, and there is some indication that these different stakeholders may actually benefit from mergers. For example, wages and employment in general appear to rise following a merger, which suggests that some of the efficiency gains are passed onto workers.[30]

The problem is that, even after the event, it is seldom easy to judge whether a merger has benefited society. The following example illustrates this point.

EXAMPLE 32.5 ● Kraft offers to buy British chocolate-maker, Cadbury

In 2009, Kraft offered to buy Cadbury. Although the offer was initially resisted by Cadbury's board, Kraft upped its offer and finally succeeded in acquiring Cadbury's shares at a 50% premium to their market price.

The acquisition was strongly criticized in the British press. Cadbury was an established brand, and the company had a long record of prioritizing employee welfare. To make matters worse, Kraft had pledged not to shut down Cadbury's factory in Somerdale but reversed its decision a week later, leading to 400 job losses.

But, as is so often the case, there are two sides to the story. Cadbury had actually announced the closure of the Somerdale plant in 2007, so it may have occurred without the takeover.

---

[28]See S. B. Moeller, F. P. Schlingemann, and R. M. Stulz, "Wealth Destruction on a Massive Scale: A Study of Acquiring Firm Returns in the Recent Merger Wave," *Journal of Finance* 60 (2005), pp. 757–782.

[29]"Impact of Mergers and Acquisitions," evidence by Louis Harris, Hearing Before the Subcommittee on Telecommunications and Finance of the Committee on Energy and Commerce, House of Representatives, April 1, 1987 (Washington, D.C.: U.S. Government Printing Office, 1987).

[30]For example, Brown and Medoff argue that wages and employment appear to rise following a merger. See C. Brown and J .L. Medoff, "The Impact of Firm Acquisitions on Labor," in Alan J. Auerbach (ed.), *Corporate Takeovers: Causes and Consequences* (Chicago: University of Chicago Press, 1988).

Also, the merged company made substantial improvements to Cadbury's Bournville site, which had, for some years, seen declining productivity and workforce. Following the merger, the company undertook a £75 million modernization and set up an £18 million global research operation inside Bournville. Not only did this modernization safeguard the long-term viability of Bournville, but its gains were also shared with workers. A pay deal, struck shortly after it was completed, was praised by the union as having "set the benchmark for other employers to follow."

KEY TAKEAWAYS

- **Types of merger** There are three main categories of merger: horizontal, vertical, and conglomerate.

- **Reasons to merge** There are many sensible reasons to merge. Important ones include economies of scale and scope, economies of vertical integration, combining complementary resources, effecting a change in corporate control, and industry consolidation.

- **Dubious reasons for merging** There are also many dubious arguments for merger. We listed four: diversification, higher earnings per share, reduced borrowing costs, and increased management prestige or compensation.

- **Gains and costs of a merger** An acquisition adds value if the gain exceeds the cost. If firm A merges with T to form a new entity, AT, then the gain from the merger is:

$$\text{Gain} = PV_{AT} - (PV_A + PV_T) = \Delta_{PVAT}$$

If the merger is financed by cash:

$$\text{Cost} = \text{cash paid} - PV_T$$

When payment is in the form of shares, the cost depends on the fraction of the merged company now owned by the target's shareholders and what their shares are worth after the merger is complete.

- **Mechanics of merging** The mechanics of buying a firm are more complex than those of buying a machine. You need to ensure that the purchase does not fall afoul of antitrust laws and to take account of the tax status of the merger.

- **Forms of merger** You also need to decide on the form of the merger. In a one-step merger, the assets and liabilities of the two companies are merged into a single company. An alternative is to undertake a two-step merger, first buying the stock of the seller rather than the company itself and then merging the businesses. Sometimes the merger is effected by purchase of the assets of the seller.

- **Hostile takeovers** If the target firm opposes a merger, the buyer can decide to make a tender or exchange offer directly to the target's shareholders. The target's defenses may include a poison pill or a supermajority approval for a merger. Faced with a poison-pill defense, the would-be acquirer may engage in a proxy battle to gain control of the board and win the target's acquiescence.

- **Merger profitability** Selling shareholders earn large abnormal returns, while the bidding firm's shareholders appear to make proportionately smaller gains. This suggests that, on average, investors expect mergers to generate some positive net benefits for investors. It is difficult to measure the effect on wider society, but there is little evidence that merger gains are at the expense of employees or customers.

- **Merger waves** Merger activity thrives in periods of economic expansion and buoyant stock prices. Mergers are most frequent in industries that are coping with change—for example, changes in technology or regulation.

Here are three general works on mergers:

R. Bruner, *Applied Mergers and Acquisitions* (Hoboken, NJ: John Wiley & Sons, 2004).

J. F. Weston, M. L. Mitchell, and J. H. Mulherin, *Takeovers, Restructuring and Corporate Governance,* 4th ed. (Upper Saddle River, NJ: Prentice-Hall, 2013).

S. Betton, B. E. Eckbo, and K. S. Thorburn, "Corporate Takeovers," in B. E. Eckbo (ed.), *Handbook of Empirical Corporate Finance* (Amsterdam: Elsevier/North-Holland, 2007), Chapter 15.

Historical information about mergers is reviewed in:

G. Andrade, M. Mitchell, and E. Stafford, "New Evidence and Perspectives on Mergers," *Journal of Economic Perspectives* 15 (Spring 2001), pp. 103–120.

S. J. Everett, "The Cross-Border Mergers and Acquisitions Wave of the Late 1990s," in R. E. Baldwin and L. A. Winters (eds.), *Challenges to Globalization* (Chicago: University of Chicago Press, 2004).

J. Harford, "What Drives Merger Waves?" *Journal of Financial Economics* 77 (2005), pp. 529–560.

B. Holmstrom and S. N. Kaplan, "Corporate Governance and Merger Activity in the U.S.: Making Sense of the 1980s and 1990s," *Journal of Economic Perspectives* 15 (Spring 2001), pp. 121–144.

Finally, here are some informative case studies:

S. N. Kaplan (ed.), *Mergers and Productivity* (Chicago: University of Chicago Press, 2000). This is a collection of case studies.

R. Bruner, "An Analysis of Value Destruction and Recovery in the Alliance and Proposed Merger of Volvo and Renault," *Journal of Financial Economics* 51 (1999), pp. 125–166.

FURTHER READING

PROBLEM SETS

   **Select problems are available in McGraw Hill's *Connect.*
Please see the preface for more information.**

1. **Mergers (S32.2–S32.7)** True or false?

   a. Sellers almost always gain in mergers.

   b. Buyers usually gain more than sellers.

   c. Firms that do unusually well tend to be acquisition targets.

   d. Merger activity in the United States varies dramatically from year to year.

   e. On the average, mergers produce large economic gains.

   f. Tender offers require the approval of the selling firm's management.

   g. The cost of a merger to the buyer equals the gain realized by the seller.

2. **Mergers (S32.2–S32.7)** True or false?

   a. Under purchase accounting any difference between the amount paid for the target's assets and their book value is shown as goodwill in the merged company's balance sheet.

   b. In a tax-free merger, the acquirer can write up the value of the target's assets and deduct a higher depreciation charge.

   c. Both the Justice Department and the FTC can seek injunctions to delay a merger where there may be anti-trust issues.

   d. Stock financing for mergers mitigates the effect of over- or under-valuation of the target.

3. **Merger motives (S32.2–S32.3)** Which of the following motives for mergers make economic sense?

   a. Merging to achieve economies of scale.

   b. Merging to reduce risk by diversification.

    c. Merging to redeploy cash generated by a firm with ample profits but limited growth opportunities.

    d. Merging to combine complementary resources.

    e. Merging to increase earnings per share.

4. **Merger motives (S32.2–S32.3)** Examine several recent mergers and suggest the principal motives for merging in each case.

5. **Merger motives (S32.2–S32.3)** Suppose you obtain special information—information unavailable to investors—indicating that Backwoods Chemical's stock price is 40% undervalued. Is that a reason to launch a takeover bid for Backwoods? Explain carefully.

6. **Merger motives (S32.2–S32.3)** Respond to the following comments.

    a. "Our cost of debt is too darn high, but our banks won't reduce interest rates as long as we're stuck in this volatile widget-trading business. We've got to acquire other companies with safer income streams."

    b. "Merge with Fledgling Electronics? No way! Their P/E's too high. That deal would knock 20% off our earnings per share."

    c. "Our stock's at an all-time high. It's time to make our offer for Digital Organics. Sure, we'll have to offer a hefty premium to Digital stockholders, but we don't have to pay in cash. We'll give them new shares of our stock."

7. **Merger motives (S32.3)** The Muck and Slurry merger has fallen through (see Section 32-3). But World Enterprises is determined to report earnings per share of $2.67. It therefore acquires the Wheelrim and Axle Company. You are given the following facts:

	World Enterprises	Wheelrim and Axle	Merged Firm
Earnings per share	$2.00	$2.50	$2.67
Price per share	$40	$25	?
Price–earnings ratio	20	10	?
Number of shares	100,000	200,000	?
Total earnings	$200,000	$500,000	?
Total market value	$4,000,000	$5,000,000	?

    Once again, there are no gains from merging. In exchange for Wheelrim and Axle shares, World Enterprises issues just enough of its own shares to ensure its $2.67 earnings per share objective.

    a. Complete the table for the merged firm.

    b. How many shares of World Enterprises are exchanged for each share of Wheelrim and Axle?

    c. What is the cost of the merger to World Enterprises?

    d. What is the change in the total market value of the World Enterprises shares that were outstanding before the merger?

8. **Merger gains and costs (S32.4)** Velcro Saddles is contemplating the acquisition of Skiers' Airbags Inc. The values of the two companies as separate entities are $20 million and $10 million, respectively. Velcro Saddles estimates that by combining the two companies, it will reduce marketing and administrative costs by $500,000 per year in perpetuity. Velcro Saddles can either pay $14 million cash for Skiers' or offer Skiers' a 50% holding in Velcro Saddles. The opportunity cost of capital is 10%.

    a. What is the gain from merger?

    b. What is the cost of the cash offer?

   c. What is the cost of the stock alternative?

   d. What is the NPV of the acquisition under the cash offer?

   e. What is its NPV under the stock offer?

9. **Merger gains and costs (S32.4)** As financial manager of Corton Inc., you are investigating a possible acquisition of Denham Lathes. You have the basic data given in the following table. You estimate that investors expect a steady growth of about 6% in Denham's earnings and dividends. Under new management, this growth rate would be increased to 8% per year without the need for additional capital.

	Corton	Denham
Forecast earnings per share	$5.00	$1.50
Forecast dividend per share	$3.00	$0.80
Number of shares	1,000,000	600,000
Stock price	$90	$20

   a. What is the gain from the acquisition?

   b. What is the cost of the acquisition if Corton pays $25 in cash for each share of Denham?

   c. What is the cost of the acquisition if Corton offers one share of Corton for every three shares of Denham?

   d. How would the cost of the cash offer change if the expected growth rate of Corton was not changed by the merger?

   e. How would the cost of the share offer change if the expected growth rate was not changed by the merger?

10. **Merger gains and costs (S32.4)** Gobi Desserts is bidding to take over Universal Puddings. Gobi has 3,000 shares outstanding, selling at $50 per share. Universal has 2,000 shares outstanding, selling at $17.50 a share. Gobi estimates the economic gain from the merger to be $15,000.

   a. If Universal can be acquired for $20 a share, what is the NPV of the merger to Gobi?

   b. What will Gobi sell for when the market learns that it plans to acquire Universal for $20 a share?

   c. What will Universal sell for?

   d. What are the percentage gains to the shareholders of each firm?

   e. Now suppose that the merger takes place through an exchange of stock. On the basis of the premerger prices of the firms, Gobi sells for $50, so instead of paying $20 cash, Gobi issues 0.40 of its shares for every Universal share acquired. What will be the price of the merged firm?

   f. What is the NPV of the merger to Gobi when it uses an exchange of stock? Why does your answer differ from part (a)?

11. **Merger gains and costs (S32.4)** Winterbourne is considering a takeover of Monkton Inc. Winterbourne has 10 million shares outstanding, which sell for $40 each. Monkton has 5 million shares outstanding, which sell for $20 each. If the merger gains are estimated at $25 million, what is the highest price per share that Winterbourne should be willing to pay to Monkton shareholders?

12. **Merger gains and costs (S32.4)** If Winterbourne from Problem 11 has a price-earnings ratio of 12 and Monkton has a P/E ratio of 8, what should be the P/E ratio of the merged firm? Assume in this case that the merger is financed by an issue of new Winterbourne shares. Monkton will get one Winterbourne share for every two Monkton shares held. In the short run, the merger has no effect on the earnings outlook for the two businesses.

13. **Merger gains and costs (S32.4)** Sometimes the stock price of a possible target company rises in anticipation of a merger bid. Explain how this complicates the bidder's evaluation of the target company.

14. **Merger gains and costs (S32.4)** Examine a recent merger in which at least part of the payment made to the seller was in the form of stock. Use stock market prices to obtain an estimate of the gain from the merger and the cost of the merger.

15. **Merger accounting (S32.5)** Look again at Table 32.3. Suppose that T Corporation's fixed assets are reexamined and found to be worth $12 million instead of $9 million. How would this affect the AT Corporation's balance sheet under purchase accounting? How would the value of AT Corporation change? Would your answer depend on whether the merger is taxable?

16. **Taxation (S32.5)** Explain the distinction between a tax-free and a taxable merger. Are there circumstances in which you would expect buyer and seller to agree to a taxable merger?

17. **Taxation (S32.5)** Which of the following transactions are not likely to be classed as tax-free?

    a. An acquisition of assets.

    b. A merger in which payment is entirely in the form of voting stock.

18. **Merger tactics (S32.6)** Connect each term to its correct definition or description.

    a. Poison pill

    b. Tender offer

    c. Shark repellent

    d. Merger

    e. Proxy contest

        A. Changes in the corporate charter that are designed to deter an unwelcome takeover.

        B. Measure in which shareholders are issued rights to buy shares if the bidder acquires a large stake in the firm.

        C. Offer to buy shares directly from stockholders.

        D. One company assumes all the assets and all the liabilities of another.

        E. Attempt to gain control of a firm by winning the votes of its stockholders.

CHALLENGE

19. **Takeover tactics (S32.6)** Examine a hostile acquisition and discuss the tactics employed by both the predator and the target companies. Do you think that the management of the target firm was trying to defeat the bid or to secure the highest price for its stockholders? How did each announcement by the protagonists affect their stock prices?

20. **Merger regulation (S32.6)** How do you think mergers should be regulated? For example, what defenses should target companies be allowed to employ? Should managers of target firms be compelled to seek out the highest bids? Should they simply be passive and watch from the sidelines?

● ● ● ● ●

SOLUTIONS TO SELF-TEST QUESTIONS

32.1   a. horizontal;

    b. conglomerate;

    c. vertical;

    d. conglomerate.

32.2   It is difficult to draw up a contract with another company that specifies the correct investment and management of future research and the sharing of profits if the research is successful (or even to define "successful").

32.3   Earnings per share now rise by 60% to $3.20.

	World Enterprises before Merger	Muck and Slurry	World Enterprises after Merger
1. Earnings per share	$2.00	$2.00	$3.20
2. Price per share	$40	$10	$40
3. Price–earnings ratio	20	5	12.5
4. Number of shares	100,000	100,000	125,000
5. Total earnings	$200,000	$200,000	$400,000
6. Total market value	$4,000,000	$1,000,000	$5,000,000
7. Current earnings per dollar invested in stock (line 1 ÷ line 2)	$0.05	$0.20	$0.08

32.4   The cost of the merger is $4 million—the $4 per share premium offered to Targetco shares times 1 million shares. If the merger has a positive NPV to Cislunar, the gain must be greater than $4 million.

32.5   T's shareholders will now own a third of the combined company. Therefore, cost is $0.33 \times 275 - 50 = \$41.67$ million.

32.6

	Taxable Merger	Tax-Free Merger
Impact on Captain B	Captain B must recognize a $70,000 capital gain.	Capital gain can be deferred until Captain B sells the Baycorp shares.
Impact on Baycorp	Boat is revalued at $320,000. Tax depreciation increases to $320,000/10 = $32,000 per year (assuming 10 years of remaining life).	Boat's value remains at $150,000, and tax depreciation continues at $15,000 per year.

Possible tax consequences when Baycorp buys Seacorp for $370,000. Captain B's original investment in Seacorp was $300,000. Just before the merger, Seacorp's assets were $50,000 of marketable securities and one boat with a book value of $150,000 but a market value of $320,000.

Visit https://www.gresham.ac.uk/lectures-and-events/mergers-acquisitions-value for a Gresham College public lecture entitled "Mergers and Acquisitions: Do They Create or Destroy Value?" by Alex Edmans.

FINANCE ON THE WEB

APPENDIX • • •

Conglomerate Mergers and Value Additivity

A pure conglomerate merger is one that has no effect on the operations or profitability of either firm. If corporate diversification is in stockholders' interests, a conglomerate merger would give a clear demonstration of its benefits. But if present values add up, the conglomerate merger would not make stockholders better or worse off.

In this appendix, we examine more carefully our assertion that present values add. It turns out that values *do* add as long as capital markets are perfect and investors' diversification opportunities are unrestricted.

Call the merging firms A and B. Value additivity implies

$$PV_{AB} = PV_A + PV_B$$

where

PV_{AB} = market value of combined firms just after merger

PV_A, PV_B = separate market values of A and B just before merger

For example, we might have

PV_A = $100 million ($200 per share × 500,000 shares outstanding)

and

PV_B = $200 million ($200 per share × 1,000,000 shares outstanding)

Suppose A and B are merged into a new firm, AB, with one share in AB exchanged for each share of A or B. Thus, there are 1,500,000 AB shares issued. *If* value additivity holds, then PV_{AB} must equal the sum of the separate values of A and B just before the merger—that is, $300 million. That would imply a price of $200 per share of AB stock.

But note that the AB shares represent a portfolio of the assets of A and B. Before the merger, investors could have bought one share of A and two of B for $600. Afterward, they can obtain a claim on *exactly* the same real assets by buying three shares of AB.

Suppose that the opening price of AB shares just after the merger is $200, so that $PV_{AB} = PV_A + PV_B$. Our problem is to determine if this is an equilibrium price—that is, whether we can rule out excess demand or supply at this price.

For there to be excess demand, there must be some investors who are willing to increase their holdings of A and B as a consequence of the merger. Who could they be? The only thing new created by the merger is diversification, but those investors who want to hold assets of A *and* B will have purchased A's and B's stock before the merger. The diversification is redundant and consequently won't attract new investment demand.

Is there a possibility of excess supply? The answer is yes. For example, there will be some shareholders in A who did not invest in B. After the merger they cannot invest solely in A, but only in a fixed combination of A and B. Their AB shares will be less attractive to them than the pure A shares, so they will sell part of or all their AB stock. In fact, the only AB shareholders who will *not* wish to sell are those who happened to hold A and B in exactly a 1:2 ratio in their premerger portfolios!

Since there is no possibility of excess demand but a definite possibility of excess supply, we seem to have

$$PV_{AB} \leq PV_A + PV_B$$

That is, corporate diversification can't help, but it may hurt investors by restricting the types of portfolios they can hold. This is not the whole story, however, since investment demand for AB shares might be attracted from other sources if PV_{AB} drops below $PV_A + PV_B$. To illustrate, suppose there are two other firms, A* and B*, which are judged by investors to have the same risk characteristics as A and B, respectively. Then before the merger,

$$r_A = r_{A*} \quad \text{and} \quad r_B = r_{B*}$$

where r is the rate of return expected by investors. We'll assume $r_A = r_{A*} = 0.08$ and $r_B = r_{B*} = 0.20$.

Consider a portfolio invested one-third in A* and two-thirds in B*. This portfolio offers an expected return of 16%:

$$r = x_{A*} r_{A*} + x_{B*} r_{B*}$$
$$= \frac{1}{3}(.08) + \frac{2}{3}(.20) = .16$$

A similar portfolio of A and B before their merger also offered a 16% return.

As we have noted, a new firm AB is really a portfolio of firms A and B, with portfolio weights of ⅓ and ⅔. It is therefore equivalent in risk to the portfolio of A* and B*. Thus, the price of AB shares must adjust so that it likewise offers a 16% return.

What if AB shares drop below $200, so that PV_{AB} is less than $PV_A + PV_B$? Since the assets and earnings of firms A and B are the same, the price drop means that the expected rate of return on AB shares has risen above the return offered by the A*B* portfolio. That is, if r_{AB} exceeds $\frac{1}{3}r_A + \frac{2}{3}r_B$, then r_{AB} must also exceed $\frac{1}{3}r_{A*} + \frac{2}{3}r_{B*}$. But this is untenable: Investors A* and B* could sell part of their holdings (in a 1:2 ratio), buy AB, and obtain a higher expected rate of return with no increase in risk.

On the other hand, if PV_{AB} rises above $PV_A + PV_B$, the AB shares will offer an expected return less than that offered by the A*B* portfolio. Investors will unload the AB shares, forcing their price down.

A stable result occurs only if AB shares stick at $200. Thus, value additivity will hold exactly in a perfect-market equilibrium if there are ample substitutes for the A and B assets. If A and B have unique risk characteristics, however, then PV_{AB} can fall below $PV_A + PV_B$. The reason is that the merger curtails investors' opportunity to tailor their portfolios to their own needs and preferences. This makes investors worse off, reducing the attractiveness of holding the shares of firm AB.

In general, the condition for value additivity is that investors' opportunity set—that is, the range of risk characteristics attainable by investors through their portfolio choices—is independent of the particular portfolio of real assets held by the firm. Corporate diversification per se can never expand the opportunity set given perfect security markets. Diversification may reduce the investors' opportunity set, but only if the real assets the corporations hold lack substitutes among traded securities or portfolios.

In rare cases, the firm may be able to expand the opportunity set. It can do so if it finds an investment opportunity that is unique—a real asset with risk characteristics shared by few or no other financial assets. In this lucky event, the firm should not diversify, however. It should set up the unique asset as a separate firm so as to expand investors' opportunity set to the maximum extent. If Gallo by chance discovered that a small portion of its vineyards produced wine comparable to Chateau Margaux, it would not throw that wine into the Hearty Burgundy vat.

CHAPTER

Corporate Restructuring

In the last chapter, we described how mergers and acquisitions change a company's ownership and management team and therefore often force major shifts in corporate strategy. But this is not the only way that company structure can be altered. In this chapter, we look at other mechanisms for changing ownership and control.

Section 33-1   Leveraged buyouts We start with leveraged buyouts (LBOs) and leveraged restructurings. The main point of these transactions is not just to change control, although existing management is often booted out, but also to change incentives for managers and improve financial performance.

Section 33-2 The private-equity market Leveraged buyouts are the specialty of private-equity funds. We look at how these funds are structured and how the private-equity business has developed. Private-equity funds usually end up holding a portfolio of companies in different industries. In this respect, they resemble the conglomerates that dominated takeover activity in the 1960s. These conglomerates are mostly gone—it seems that private equity is a superior financial technology for doing the tasks that conglomerates used to do.

Section 33-3 Fusion and fission in corporate finance We look at other ways that companies can change their structure. These include spin-offs, carve-outs, asset sales, and privatizations.

Section 33-4 Bankruptcy Some companies choose to restructure, but others have it thrust upon them. None more so than those that fall on hard times and can no longer service their debts. The chapter therefore concludes by looking at how distressed companies either work out a solution with their debtors or go through a formal bankruptcy process.

33-1   Leveraged Buyouts

Leveraged buyouts (LBOs) differ from ordinary acquisitions in three important ways. First, the target company goes private, and its shares no longer trade on the open market. Second, the acquirer finances a large fraction of the purchase price by bank loans and bonds, which are secured by the assets and cash flows of the target company. Some, if not all, of the bonds are junk—that is, below investment grade. In early LBOs, debt ratios of 90% were not uncommon, though in recent years, LBOs have been financed with nearly equal amounts of debt and equity. Third, equity financing for LBOs comes from private-equity investment partnerships, which we describe shortly. Many of the larger LBOs are *club deals,* in which the target is acquired by a consortium of private-equity firms. For example, in 2007 a consortium

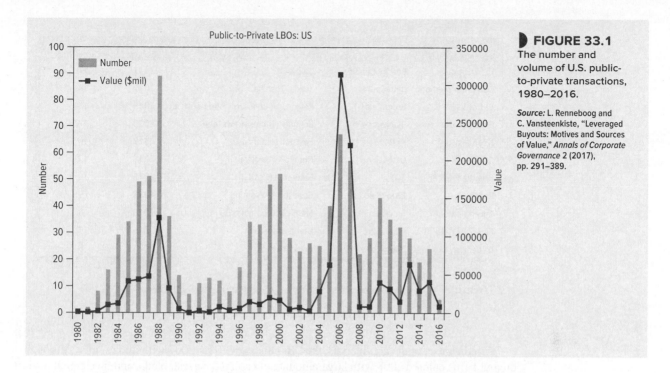

▶ **FIGURE 33.1**
The number and volume of U.S. public-to-private transactions, 1980–2016.

Source: L. Renneboog and C. Vansteenkiste, "Leveraged Buyouts: Motives and Sources of Value," *Annals of Corporate Governance* 2 (2017), pp. 291–389.

of KKR, TPG Capital, and Goldman Sachs jointly put up $32 billion in a record buyout of the utility, TXU.[1]

When a buyout is led by existing management, the transaction is called a **management buyout** or **MBO**. In the 1970s and 1980s, many MBOs were arranged for unwanted divisions of large diversified companies. Smaller divisions outside the companies' main lines of business sometimes failed to attract top management's interest and commitment, and divisional management chafed under corporate bureaucracy. Many such divisions flowered when spun off as MBOs. Their managers, pushed by the need to generate cash for debt service and encouraged by a substantial personal stake in the business, found ways to cut costs and compete more effectively.

LBO activity then shifted to buyouts of entire businesses, including large, mature, public corporations. You can see from Figure 33.1 that the years 2006 and 2007 witnessed an exceptional volume of such deals.

EXAMPLE 33.1 ● The buyout of Chrysler

One of the most interesting deals of 2007 was DaimlerChrysler's decision to sell an 80% stake in Chrysler to Cerberus Capital Management. Chrysler, one of Detroit's original Big Three automakers, merged into DaimlerChrysler in 1998, but the expected synergies between the Chrysler and Mercedes-Benz product lines were hard to grasp. The Chrysler division had some profitable years, but lost $1.5 billion in 2006. Prospects looked grim. So DaimlerChrysler (now Daimler A. G.) *paid* Cerberus $677 million to take Chrysler off its hands. Cerberus assumed about $18 billion in pension and employee health care liabilities, however, and agreed to invest $6 billion in Chrysler and its finance subsidiary.[2] Two years later, Chrysler filed for bankruptcy, wiping out Cerberus's investment. Subsequently, Chrysler was acquired by Fiat.

● ● ● ● ●

---

[1]The buyers hoped that increasing natural gas prices would provide TXU's coal-fired generating plants with an edge. It did not happen. Gas prices declined as fracking took off, and in 2014, TXU became one of the country's largest bankruptcies.
[2]Cerberus had previously purchased a controlling stake in GMAC, General Motors' finance subsidiary.

Industry	Lead Partnership	Target (previous owner)	Year	Value ($ billions)
Electric power	Energy Capital	Calpine	2017	17
Computer memories	Bain Capital	Kioxia (Toshiba)	2017	18
Batteries	Brookfield	Power Solutions (Johnson Controls)	2018	13
Financial data	Blackstone	Refinitiv (Thomson Reuters)	2018	17
Health care	KKR	Envision Healthcare	2018	10
Chemicals	Carlyle	Nouryon (AkzoNobel)	2018	12
Pharmaceutical	EQT	Galderma (Nestlé)	2019	10
Railroads	Brookfield	Genesee & Wyoming	2019	9
Entertainment	Blackstone	Merlin Entertainments	2019	8
Financial data	CC Capital	Dun & Bradstreet	2019	7
Genealogy provider	Blackstone	Ancestry.com	2021	5

❭TABLE 33.1   **Some recent leveraged buyouts (values in $ billions).**

With the onset of the credit crisis, the LBO boom of 2006–2007 withered rapidly. Although buyout firms entered 2008 with large amounts of capital to invest, banks and investment institutions became much more wary of lending to LBOs. By 2009, the value of buyout deals had fallen by 90% from its 2007 high. Since then, the market has slowly recovered, but the targets have generally been tiddlers compared with those of the boom years.

Table 33.1 lists some recent transactions. Notice that some of the targets were stand-alone companies; others were divisions of larger corporations. For example, Galderma was previously Nestlé's skin health care business, and Kioxia was Toshiba's computer-memory business.

The RJR Nabisco LBO

The largest, most dramatic, and best documented LBO of the 1980s was the $25 billion take-over of RJR Nabisco by the private-equity partnership, Kohlberg, Kravis, Roberts (KKR). This LBO is worth reviewing because the players, tactics, and controversies of LBOs are writ large in this case.[3]

The battle for RJR began in October 1988 when the board of directors of RJR Nabisco revealed that Ross Johnson, the company's chief executive officer, had formed a group of investors that proposed to buy all of RJR's stock for $75 per share in cash and take the firm private. RJR's share price immediately moved to about $75, handing shareholders a 36% gain over the previous day's price of $56. At the same time, RJR's bonds fell because it was clear that existing bondholders would soon have a lot more company.[4]

Johnson's offer lifted RJR onto the auction block. Once the company was in play, its board of directors was obliged to consider other offers, which were not long in coming. Four days later, KKR bid $90 per share, $79 in cash plus PIK preferred stock valued at $11. (PIK means "pay in kind." The company could choose to pay preferred dividends with more preferred shares rather than cash.)

---

[3]The whole story is reconstructed by B. Burrough and J. Helyar in *Barbarians at the Gate: The Fall of RJR Nabisco* (New York: Harper & Row, 1990)—see especially Chapter 18—and in a movie with the same title.

[4]N. Mohan and C. R. Chen track the abnormal returns of RJR securities in "A Review of the RJR Nabisco Buyout," *Journal of Applied Corporate Finance* 3 (Summer 1990), pp. 102–108.

Improved Monitoring One problem for a public corporation with several hundred thousand shareholders is that no one shareholder has the incentive or the ability to monitor the company's actions and demand change where necessary. Not only does an LBO change the manager's incentives, but the concentrated shareholding facilitates more effective monitoring.

We have reviewed several motives for LBOs. We do not say that all LBOs are good. On the contrary, there have been many cases of poor judgment, as the bankruptcy of Chrysler illustrated. Yet, we do quarrel with those who portray LBOs solely as undertaken by Wall Street barbarians breaking up the traditional strengths of corporate America.

33.1 Self Test

LBOs tend to focus on mature companies with plenty of free cash flow. Why do you think that this is the case?

Leveraged Restructurings

In 1986, the supermarket company Safeway was the target of a hostile takeover bid. But instead of accepting the bid, it agreed to a leveraged buyout by KKR and a group of Safeway managers. Two years later fellow supermarket company Kroger was also faced with a bid from KKR. However, it decided to take the do-it-yourself route and to avoid the buyout by voluntarily taking on the extra leverage that KKR would have imposed. This is called a *leveraged restructuring* or *recap*.

Both the Safeway and Kroger transactions resulted in a debt-to-value ratio exceeding 90%, but there were important differences in the subsequent company structure. Kroger remained a public company. Its ownership stayed widely dispersed and its board membership did not change. By contrast, Safeway became a private company and only went public again in 1990. About 90% of Safeway's equity after the LBO was owned by KKR, and KKR had a majority of the seats on Safeway's board. Safeway's CEO commented on how these changes led to much more active monitoring:

> I think I had a good board when Safeway was a public company before the LBO. But the level of scrutiny and questioning is just not comparable. In our board meetings with KKR, anything can be brought up, and management has to really work to defend itself. It is just utterly different from what goes on in public companies.[11]

Following the buyout, Safeway linked managerial compensation more closely to firm performance. It also repaid debt by selling assets while only modestly reducing its capital expenditure program. In contrast, Kroger cut back on capital expenditures while selling fewer assets.

The examples of Safeway and Kroger illustrate the similarities and differences between a leveraged buyout and a recap. Both involve taking on large amounts of debt. The requirement to generate cash to service this debt is intended to curb wasteful investment and force improvements in operating efficiency. However, a buyout takes the company private, and the resulting concentration in ownership increases the degree of monitoring by the firm's owners. Also, buyouts are usually accompanied by high-powered incentive compensation packages.

BEYOND THE PAGE

Sealed Air's restructuring

mhhe.com/brealey14e

---

[11]The two restructurings are compared in D. J. Denis, "Organizational Form and the Consequences of Highly Leveraged Transactions: Kroger's Recapitalization and Safeway's LBO," *Journal of Financial Economics,* 36 (1994), pp. 193–224. Denis argues that Safeway's subsequent performance was better than that of Kroger and attributes the difference to the incentive compensation scheme and the enhanced monitoring.

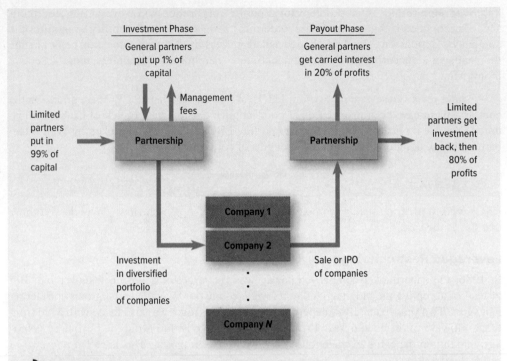

FIGURE 33.2 Organization of a typical private-equity partnership. The limited partners, having put up almost all of the money, get first crack at the proceeds from sale or IPO of the portfolio companies. Once their investment is returned, they get 80% of any profits. The general partners, who organize and manage the partnership, get a 20% carried interest in profits.

33-2 The Private-Equity Market

Private-Equity Partnerships

Figure 33.2 shows how a private-equity investment fund is organized. The fund is a partnership, not a corporation. The *general partner* sets up and manages the partnership, while the *limited partners* put up almost all of the money. Limited partners are generally institutional investors, such as pension funds, endowments, and insurance companies. Wealthy individuals may also participate. The limited partners have limited liability, like shareholders in a corporation, but do not participate in management.

Once the partnership is formed, the general partners seek out companies to invest in. For example, we saw in Chapter 14 how venture capital partnerships look for high-tech start-ups or adolescent companies that need capital to grow. LBO funds, on the other hand, look for mature businesses with ample free cash flow that need restructuring. Some funds specialize in particular industries—for example, real estate, or energy. Other buyout funds like KKR's and Cerberus's look for opportunities almost anywhere.

The partnership agreement has a limited term, typically 10 years. The portfolio companies must then be sold and the proceeds distributed. So the general partners cannot reinvest the limited partners' money. Of course, once a fund is proved successful, the general partners can usually go back to the limited partners, or to other institutional investors, and form another fund.

The general partners of a private-equity fund get a management fee, usually 1% or 2% of capital committed,[12] plus a *carried interest* in 20% of any profits earned by the partnership. In other words, the limited partners get paid off first, but then get only 80% of any further returns. The general partners therefore have a call option on 20% of the partnership's total future payoff, with an exercise price set by the limited partners' investment.[13]

You can see some of the advantages of private-equity partnerships:

- Carried interest gives the general partners plenty of upside. They are strongly motivated to earn back the limited partners' investment and deliver a profit.

- Carried interest, because it is a call option, gives the general partners incentives to take risks. Venture capital funds take the risks inherent in start-up companies. Buyout funds amplify business risks with financial leverage.

- There is no separation of ownership and control. The general partners can intervene in the fund's portfolio companies if performance lags or strategy needs changing.

- There is no free-cash-flow problem: Limited partners don't have to worry that cash from a first round of investments will be dribbled away in later rounds. Cash from the first round *must* be distributed to investors.

33.2 Self-Test

What is carried interest? Why do we say that it is like an option?

The foregoing are good reasons for the growth of private equity. But some contrarians say that rapid growth also came from irrational exuberance and speculative excess. These contrarian investors stayed on the sidelines and waited glumly (but hopefully) for the crash.

The popularity of private equity has also been linked to the costs and distractions of public ownership, including the costs of dealing with Sarbanes-Oxley and other legal and regulatory requirements. Many CEOs and CFOs feel pressured to meet short-term earnings targets. Perhaps they spend too much time worrying about these targets and about day-to-day changes in stock price. Perhaps going private avoids public investors' "short-termism" and makes it easier to invest for the long run. But recall that for private equity, the long run is the life of the partnership, about 10 years. General partners *must* find a way to cash out of the companies in the partnership's portfolio. There are only two ways to cash out: an IPO or a *trade sale* to another company. Many of today's private-equity deals will be future IPOs. Thus, private-equity investors need public markets. The firms that seek divorce from public shareholders may well have to remarry them later.

Are Private-Equity Funds Today's Conglomerates?

A conglomerate is a firm that diversifies across a number of unrelated businesses. Is KKR a conglomerate? Table 33.2, which lists some of KKR's 200 holdings, suggests that it is. KKR funds have invested in dozens of industries.

Does this mean that private-equity firms today perform the tasks that public conglomerates used to do? Before answering that question, let's take a brief look at the history of U.S. conglomerates.

Conglomerates were fashionable in the 1960s, when a merger boom created more than a dozen conglomerates. Table 33.3 shows that by the 1970s, some of these conglomerates had achieved amazing spans of activity. Most were broken up in the 1980s and 1990s.

---

[12]LBO and buyout funds also extract fees for arranging financing for their takeover transactions.

[13]The structure and compensation of private-equity partnerships are described in A. Metrick and A. Yasuda, "The Economics of Private Equity Funds," *Review of Financial Studies* 23 (2010), pp. 2303–2341.

Company	Business	Company	Business
Arnotts (Australia)	Food	EuroKids (India)	Education
BrightSpring Health Services (USA)	Health	feedzai (USA)	Fraud detection
Cardenas (USA)	Food retail	Sector Alarm (Norway)	Security systems
China Outfitters (China)	Menswear	Axel Springer (Germany)	Publishing
Corel (Canada)	Software	Travelopia (USA)	Travel

❭**TABLE 33.2**   KKR invests in many different industries. Here are a few of its portfolio holdings in 2021.

Source: KKR.

❭**TABLE 33.3**   The largest conglomerates of 1979, ranked by sales compared with U.S. industrial corporations. Most of these companies have been broken up.

Source: A. Chandler and R. S. Tetlow (eds.), *The Coming of Managerial Capitalism* (New York: McGraw-Hill, 1985), p. 772. See also J. Baskin and P. J. Miranti Jr., *A History of Corporate Finance* (Cambridge, UK: Cambridge University Press, 1997), ch. 7.

Sales Rank	Company	Number of Industries
8	International Telephone & Telegraph (ITT)	38
15	Tenneco	28
42	Gulf & Western Industries	4
51	Litton Industries	19
66	LTV	18

EXAMPLE 33.2 • The growth and breakup of ITT

One of the largest conglomerates, ITT acquired more than 300 companies during the 1960s. By the end of the 1970s, it was operating in 38 different industries and ranked eighth in sales among U.S. corporations. But by that stage, investors were becoming disillusioned with sprawling conglomerates. In 1995 ITT, which had already sold or spun off several businesses, split what was left into three separate firms. One acquired ITT's interests in hotels and gambling; the second took over ITT's automotive parts, defense, and electronics businesses; and the third specialized in insurance and financial services.

• • • • •

What advantages were claimed for the conglomerates of the 1960s and 1970s? First, diversification across industries was supposed to stabilize earnings and reduce risk. That's hardly compelling because shareholders can diversify much more efficiently on their own.

Second, a widely diversified firm can operate an *internal capital market*. Free cash flow generated by divisions in mature industries (cash cows) can be funneled within the company to those divisions (stars) with plenty of profitable growth opportunities. Consequently, there is no need for fast-growing divisions to raise finance from outside investors.

There are some good arguments for internal capital markets. The company's managers probably know more about its investment opportunities than outside investors do, and transaction costs of issuing securities are avoided. Nevertheless, it appears that attempts by conglomerates to allocate capital investment across many unrelated industries were more likely to subtract value than add it. Trouble is, internal capital markets are not really markets, but combinations of central planning (by the conglomerate's top management and financial staff) and intracompany bargaining. Divisional capital budgets depend on politics as well as pure economics. Large, profitable divisions with plenty of free cash flow may have the most bargaining power; they may get generous capital budgets while smaller divisions with good growth opportunities are reined in.

EXAMPLE 33.3 • Internal capital markets in the oil industry

Misallocation in internal capital markets is not restricted to pure conglomerates. For example, Owen Lamont found that when oil prices fell by half in 1986, diversified oil companies cut back capital investment in their non-oil divisions. The non-oil divisions were forced to "share the pain," even though the drop in oil prices did not diminish their investment opportunities. *The Wall Street Journal* reported one example:[14]

> Chevron Corp. cut its planned 1986 capital and exploratory budget by about 30% because of the plunge in oil prices. . . . A Chevron spokesman said that the spending cuts would be across the board and that no particular operations will bear the brunt.
>
> About 65% of the $3.5 billion budget will be spent on oil and gas exploration and production—about the same proportion as before the budget revision.
>
> Chevron also will cut spending for refining and marketing, oil and natural gas pipelines, minerals, chemicals, and shipping operations.

Why cut back on capital outlays for minerals, say, or chemicals? Low oil prices are generally good news, not bad, for chemical manufacturing, because oil distillates are an important raw material.

Most of the oil companies in Lamont's sample were large, blue-chip companies. They could have raised additional capital from investors to maintain spending in their non-oil divisions. They chose not to.

• • • • •

All large companies must allocate capital among divisions or lines of business. Therefore, they all have internal capital markets and must worry about mistakes and misallocations. But the danger probably increases as the company moves from a focus on one, or a few related industries, to unrelated conglomerate diversification. Look again at Table 33.3: How could top management of ITT keep accurate track of investment opportunities in 38 different industries?

Conglomerates face further problems. Their divisions' market values can't be observed independently, and it is difficult to set incentives for divisional managers. This is particularly serious when managers are asked to commit to risky ventures. For example, how would a biotech start-up fare as a division of a traditional conglomerate? Would the conglomerate be as patient and risk-tolerant as investors in the stock market? How are the scientists and clinicians doing the biotech R&D rewarded if they succeed? We don't mean to say that high-tech innovation and risk-taking are impossible in public conglomerates, but the difficulties are evident.

---

[14]O. Lamont, "Cash Flow and Investment: Evidence from Internal Capital Markets," *Journal of Finance* 52 (March 1997), pp. 83–109. *The Wall Street Journal* quotation appears on pp. 89–90. © 1997 Dow Jones & Company, Inc. A more recent example was the decision in January 2015 by Royal Dutch Shell and Qatar Petroleum to abandon plans to build a $6.5 billion petrochemical plant because it was "commercially infeasible" in the current energy market. There may have been good reasons for the decision, but it was not because oil had become much cheaper in 2015. Lower oil prices would presumably lead to lower production costs for petrochemicals.

33.3 Self-Test

What are the chief problems encountered in managing internal capital markets? Why are these problems most acute in widely diversified, conglomerate firms?

The third argument for traditional conglomerates came from the idea that good managers are fungible; in other words, it was argued that modern management would work as well in the manufacture of auto parts as in running a hotel chain. Thus, conglomerates were supposed to add value by removing old-fashioned managers and replacing them with ones trained in the new management science.

There was some truth in this claim. The best of the conglomerates did add value by targeting companies that needed fixing—companies with slack management, surplus assets, or excess cash that was not being invested in positive-NPV projects. These conglomerates targeted the same types of companies that LBO and private-equity funds would target later. The difference is that conglomerates would buy companies, try to improve them, and then manage them for the long run. The long-run management was the most difficult part of the game. Conglomerates would buy, fix, and hold. Private equity buys, fixes, and sells. By selling (cashing out), private equity avoids the problems of managing the conglomerate firm and running internal capital markets.[15] You could say that private-equity partnerships are temporary conglomerates.

Table 33.4 compares the financial structure of a private-equity fund and of a typical public conglomerate. Both are diversified, but the fund's limited partners do not have to worry that free cash flow will be plowed back into unprofitable investments. The fund has no internal capital market. Monitoring and compensation of management also differ. In the fund, each company is run as a separate business. The managers report directly to the owners, the fund's partners. Each company's managers own shares or stock options in that company, not in the fund. Their compensation depends on their firm's market value in a trade sale or IPO.

Private-Equity Fund	Public Conglomerate
Widely diversified, investment in unrelated industries	Widely diversified, investment in unrelated industries
Limited-life partnership forces sale of portfolio companies	Public corporations designed to operate divisions for the long run
No financial links or transfers between portfolio companies	Internal capital market
General partners "do the deal," then monitor; lenders also monitor	Hierarchy of corporate staff evaluates divisions' plans and performance
Managers' compensation depends on exit value of company	Divisional managers' compensation depends mostly on earnings—"smaller upside, softer downside"

❭TABLE 33.4   Private-equity fund vs. public conglomerate. Both diversify, investing in a portfolio of unrelated businesses, but their financial structures are otherwise fundamentally different.

Source: Adapted from G. Baker and C. Montgomery, "Conglomerates and LBO Associations: A Comparison of Organizational Forms," working paper, Harvard Business School, Cambridge, MA, July 1996.

---

[15]Economists have tried to measure whether corporate diversification adds or subtracts value. Berger and Ofek estimate an average conglomerate discount of 12% to 15%. That is, the estimated market value of the whole is 12% to 15% less than the sum of the values of the parts. The chief cause of the discount seems to be overinvestment and misallocation of investment. See P. Berger and E. Ofek, "Diversification's Effect on Firm Value," *Journal of Financial Economics* 37 (January 1995), pp. 39–65. But not everyone is convinced that the conglomerate discount is real. Other researchers have found smaller discounts or pointed out statistical problems that make the discount hard to measure. See, for example, J. M. Campa and S. Kedia, "Explaining the Diversification Discount," *Journal of Finance* 57 (August 2002), pp. 1731–1762; and B. Villalonga, "Diversification Discount or Premium? Evidence from the Business Information Tracking Service," *Journal of Finance* 59 (April 2004), pp. 479–506.

In a public conglomerate, the businesses would be divisions, not freestanding companies. Ownership of the conglomerate would be dispersed, not concentrated. The divisions would not be valued separately by investors in the stock market, but by the conglomerate's corporate staff, the very people who run the internal capital market. Managers' compensation wouldn't depend on divisions' market values because no shares in the divisions would be traded and the conglomerate would not be committed to selling the divisions or spinning them off.

You can see the arguments for focus and against corporate diversification. But we must be careful not to push the arguments too far. For example, conglomerates, though rare in the United States, are common, and apparently successful, in many parts of the world. They include such giants as Sumitomo in Japan, and Samsung in Korea.

33-3   Fusion and Fission in Corporate Finance

Figure 33.3 shows some of AT&T's acquisitions and divestitures. Before 1984, AT&T controlled most of the local and almost all of the long-distance telephone service in the United States. (Customers used to speak of the ubiquitous "Ma Bell.") Then in 1984, the company accepted an antitrust settlement requiring local telephone services to be spun off to seven new, independent companies. AT&T was left with its long-distance business plus Bell Laboratories, Western Electric (telecommunications manufacturing), and various other assets. As the communications industry became increasingly competitive, AT&T acquired several other businesses, notably in computers, cellular telephone service, and cable television. Some of these acquisitions are shown as the green incoming arrows in Figure 33.3.

AT&T was an unusually active acquirer. It was a giant company trying to respond to rapidly changing technologies and markets. But AT&T was simultaneously *divesting* dozens of other businesses. For example, its credit card operations (the AT&T Universal Card) were sold to Citicorp. AT&T also created several new companies by spinning off parts of its business. For example, in 1996 it spun off Lucent (incorporating Bell Laboratories and Western Electric) and its computer business (NCR). Only six years earlier, AT&T had paid $7.5 billion

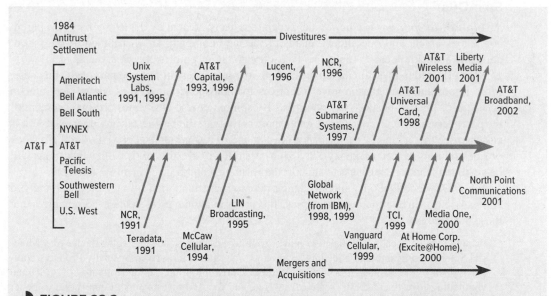

▶ **FIGURE 33.3** The effects of AT&T's antitrust settlement in 1984, and a few of AT&T's acquisitions and divestitures from 1991 to 2003. Divestitures are shown by the outgoing green arrows. When two years are given, the transaction was completed in two steps.

Parent Company	Spun-Off Companies	Value of Spin-Off ($ in billions)	Year
Abbott Labs	AbbVie	56	2013
eBay	PayPal	49	2015
Hutchison Whampoa (Hong Kong)	Cheung Kong Property	37	2015
MetLife	Brighthouse Financial	8	2016
DowDuPont	Dow Inc.	34	2019
DowDuPont	Corteva	22	2019
United Technologies	Carrier Global	11	2020
United Technologies	Otis Worldwide	20	2020

❯**TABLE 33.5**   Some notable recent spinoffs.

to acquire NCR. These and several other important divestitures are shown as the green outgoing arrows in Figure 33.3.

Figure 33.3 is not the end of AT&T's story. In 2004, AT&T was acquired by Cingular Wireless, which retained the AT&T name. In 2005, this company in turn merged with SBC Communications Inc., a descendant of Southwestern Bell. By that point, there was not much left of the original AT&T, but the name survived. AT&T's largest recent acquisitions include Direct TV for $48.5 billion in 2015 and Time Warner for $85 billion in 2018. (But both of these acquisitions were reversed in 2021, as we will see in an example below.)

In the market for corporate control, *fusion*—that is, mergers and acquisitions—gets most of the attention and publicity. But *fission*—the sale or distribution of assets or operating businesses—can be just as important, as the top half of Figure 33.3 illustrates. In many cases, businesses are sold in LBOs or MBOs. But other transactions are common, including spin-offs, carve-outs, divestitures, asset sales, and privatizations. We start with spin-offs.

Spin-Offs

A **spin-off** (or *split-up*) is a new, independent company created by detaching part of a parent company's assets and operations. Shares in the new company are distributed to the parent company's stockholders.[16] Table 33.5 lists a few notable spinoffs of recent years.

Spin-offs widen investor choice by allowing them to invest in just one part of the business. More important, they can improve incentives for managers. Companies sometimes refer to divisions or lines of business as "poor fits." By spinning these businesses off, management of the parent company can concentrate on its main activity. If the businesses are independent, it is easier to see the value and performance of each and to reward managers by giving them stock or stock options in their company. Also, spin-offs relieve investors of the worry that funds will be siphoned from one business to support unprofitable capital investments in another.

When Dow and DuPont announced their plan to merge and then split the proposed merged company into three separate businesses, the accompanying press release commented that these businesses:

> . . . will include a leading global pure-play Agriculture company; a leading global pure-play Material Science company; and a leading technology and innovation-driven Specialty Products company. Each of the businesses will have clear focus, an appropriate capital structure, a distinct and compelling investment thesis, scale advantages, and focused investments in innovation to better deliver superior solutions and choices for customers. (DuPont press release, December 11, 2015)

---

[16]The value of the shares that shareholders receive is taxed as a dividend unless they are given at least 80% of the shares in the new company.

Notice the emphasis on "pure play" and "focus."

Investors generally greet the announcement of a spin-off as good news.[17] Their enthusiasm appears to be justified, because spin-offs seem to bring about more efficient capital investment decisions by each company and improved operating performance.[18]

Carve-Outs

Carve-outs are similar to spin-offs, except that shares in the new company are not given to existing shareholders but are sold in a public offering.

EXAMPLE 33.4 ● Siemens carves out its medical business

Conscious of the growing concerns about widely diversified firms, the German company, Siemens, has been both spinning off and carving out several of its business. As part of this process, in 2018 it carved out 15% of the equity of Healthineers, its medical technology operation. The IPO raised $4.5 billion of cash, which would not have happened if the company had been spun off. Commenting on the move, the CEO said "The listing will make us a pure player, a purebred medical technology company. We will have greater flexibility—and the means to reach our goals faster."

● ● ● ● ●

As in the case of Healthineers, most carve-outs leave the parent with majority control of the subsidiary, usually about 80% ownership.[19] This may not reassure investors who are worried about a lack of focus or a poor fit, but it does allow the parent to set the manager's compensation based on the performance of the subsidiary's stock price. Sometimes companies carve out a small proportion of the shares to establish a market for the subsidiary's stock and subsequently spin off the remainder of the shares. For example, in 2014 Fiat Chrysler announced plans to sell a 10% stake in Ferrari on the stock market and then to spin off the remaining shares to its stockholders. Example 33.5 describes how the computer company, Palm, was first carved and then spun.

EXAMPLE 33.5 ● How Palm was carved and spun

When 3Com acquired U.S. Robotics in 1997, it also became the owner of Palm, a small start-up business developing handheld computers. It was a lucky purchase because over the next three years, the Palm Pilot came to dominate its market. But as Palm began to take up an increasing amount of management time, 3Com concluded that it needed to return to what

---

[17]For example, between 1990 and 2020, the announcement of a spin-off was associated with an average abnormal return of 2.5%. See also P. J. Cusatis, J. A. Miles, and J. R. Woolridge, "Restructuring through Spin-Offs: The Stock-Market Evidence," *Journal of Financial Economics* 33 (Summer 1994), pp. 293–311.

[18]See R. Gertner, E. Powers, and D. Scharfstein, "Learning about Internal Capital Markets from Corporate Spin-Offs," *Journal of Finance* 57 (2003), pp. 2479–2506; L. V. Daley, V. Mehrotra, and R. Sivakumar, "Corporate Focus and Value Creation: Evidence from Spin-Offs," *Journal of Financial Economics* 45 (1997), pp. 257–281; T. R. Burch and V. Nanda, "Divisional Diversity and the Conglomerate Discount: Evidence from Spin-Offs," *Journal of Financial Economics* 70 (2003), pp. 69–78; and A. K. Dittmar and A. Shivdasani, "Divestitures and Divisional Investment Policies," *Journal of Finance* 58 (2003), pp. 2711–2744. But G. Colak and T. M. Whited argue that apparent increases in value are due to econometric problems rather than actual increases in investment efficiency. See "Spin-Offs, Divestitures and Conglomerate Investment," *Review of Economic Studies* 20 (2007), pp. 557–595.

[19]In the United States, the parent must retain an 80% interest to consolidate the subsidiary with the parent's tax accounts. Otherwise, the subsidiary is taxed as a freestanding corporation.

it knew best and focus on its basic business of selling computer network systems. In 2000, it announced that it would carve out 5% of its holding of Palm through an initial public offering and then spin off the remaining 95% of Palm shares by giving 3Com shareholders about 1.5 Palm shares for each 3Com share that they owned.

The Palm carve-out occurred at close to the peak of the high-tech boom and got off to a dazzling start. The shares were issued in the IPO at $38 each. On the first day of trading, the stock price touched $165 before closing at $95. Therefore, anyone owning a share of 3Com stock could look forward later in the year to receiving about 1.5 shares of Palm worth $1.5 \times 95 = \$142.50$. But apparently 3Com's shareholders were not fully convinced that their newfound wealth was for real, for on the same day 3Com's stock price closed at $82, or more than $60 a share *less* than the market value of the shares in Palm that they were due to receive.[20]

Three years after 3Com spun off its holding in Palm, Palm itself entered the spin-off business by giving shareholders stock in PalmSource, a subsidiary that was responsible for developing and licensing the Palm™ operating system. The remaining business, renamed palmOne, would focus on making mobile gadgets. The company gave three reasons for its decision to split into two. First, like 3Com's management, Palm's management believed that the company would benefit from clarity of focus and mission. Second, it argued that shareholder value could "be enhanced if investors could evaluate and choose between both businesses separately, thereby attracting new and different investors." Finally, it seemed that Palm's rivals were reluctant to buy software from a company that competed with them in making handheld hardware.

● ● ● ● ●

Perhaps the most enthusiastic carver-outer of the 1980s and 1990s was Thermo Electron, with operations in health care, power generation equipment, instrumentation, environmental protection, and various other areas. By 1997, it had carved out stakes in seven publicly traded subsidiaries, which in turn had carved out 15 further public companies. The 15 were grandchildren of the ultimate parent, Thermo Electron. The company's management reasoned that the carve-outs would give each company's managers responsibility for their own decisions and expose their actions to the scrutiny of the capital markets. For a while, the strategy seemed to work, and Thermo Electron's stock was a star performer. But the complex structure began to lead to inefficiencies, and in 2000 Thermo Electron went into reverse. It reacquired many of the subsidiaries that the company had carved out only a few years earlier, and it spun off several of its progeny, including Viasys Health Care and Kadant Inc., a manufacturer of paper-making and paper-recycling equipment. Then in November 2006, Thermo Electron merged with Fisher Scientific.

EXAMPLE 33.6 ● AT&T divests DirecTV and Time Warner

In 2015, AT&T acquired DirecTV for $48.5 billion. In 2018, it acquired Time Warner for $85 billion, after successfully fighting off an antitrust challenge from the U.S. Department of Justice. The future at those times looked bright. AT&T planned to offer packages of DirecTV access combined with its wireless services. AT&T said Time Warner was a "perfect match" and praised its "complementary strengths." "We're going to bring a fresh approach to how the media and entertainment industry works for consumers, content creators, distributors and advertisers."

---

[20]This difference would seem to present an arbitrage opportunity. An investor who bought 1 share of 3Com and sold short 1.5 shares of Palm would earn a profit of $60 and own 3Com's other assets for free. The difficulty in executing this arbitrage is explored in O. A. Lamont and R. H. Thaler, "Can the Market Add and Subtract? Mispricing in Tech Stock Carve-Outs," *Journal of Political Economy* 111 (2003), pp. 227–268.

By 2021, delivery of news and entertainment by streaming over the Internet was steadily displacing delivery by satellite. DirecTV was spun off into a new company, jointly owned by AT&T and the private-equity fund TPG. The company was valued at about $16 billion. TPG invested $1.8 billion, and DirecTV took on $6.2 billion of debt. AT&T retained 70% ownership of the new company and received $5.8 billion in cash.

In May 2021, AT&T decided to retreat from the entertainment business and concentrate more on its traditional strengths in telecom. It announced a plan to divest Time Warner, now Warner Media, and merge it with Discovery, Inc., operator of the Discovery, Animal Planet, and other channels. AT&T would receive about $43 billion from the transaction and retain 70% of the new company's shares.[21]

Neither divestment was a simple spin-off or carve-out. In each case, a co-investor was found. For example, Warner Media was, in effect, carved out and then merged with Discovery. But perhaps the most interesting aspect of these deals was how quickly AT&T's strategies had changed.

• • • • •

33.4 Self Test

What is the difference between a spin-off and a carve out? What are the cash consequences of each?

Asset Sales

The simplest way to divest an asset is to sell it. An *asset sale* or *divestiture* means sale of a part of one firm to another. This may consist of an odd factory or warehouse, but sometimes whole divisions are sold.

Maksimovic and Phillips examined a sample of about 50,000 U.S. manufacturing plants between 1974 and 1992. About 35,000 plants in the sample changed hands during that period. One-half of the ownership changes were the result of mergers or acquisitions of entire firms, but the other half resulted from asset sales—that is, sale of part or all of a division.[22]

Asset sales are another way of getting rid of "poor fits." Sometimes asset sales are demanded by the Justice Department as part of the condition for approving a merger. For example, before agreeing to a merger between SunTrust Banks and BB&T, the Justice Department demanded that SunTrust sell 28 branches across North Carolina, Virginia, and Georgia with approximately $2.3 billion in deposits.

Announcements of asset sales are generally good news for investors in the selling firm, and on average, the assets are employed more productively after the sale.[23] It appears that asset sales transfer business units to the companies that can manage them most effectively.

Privatization and Nationalization

A **privatization** is a sale of a government-owned company to private investors. In recent years, almost every government in the world seems to have a privatization program. Here are some examples of privatizations:

- Japan sells the West Japan Railway Company (March 2004).
- Germany privatizes Postbank, the country's largest retail bank (June 2004).

BEYOND THE PAGE

Sprint issues a tracking stock

mhhe.com/brealey14e

---

[21]The Warner Media divestment was not complete when we wrote this example, but no antitrust or other challenges were expected.
[22]V. Maksimovic and G. Phillips, "The Market for Corporate Assets: Who Engages in Mergers and Asset Sales and Are There Efficiency Gains?" *Journal of Finance* 56 (2001), Table 1, p. 2000.
[23]See S. Bhagat, A. Shleifer, and R. Vishny, "Hostile Takeovers in the 1980s: The Return to Corporate Specialization," *Brookings Papers on Economic Activity: Microeconomics,* 1990, pp. 1–12.

- France sells 30% of EDF (Electricité de France; December 2005).
- China sells Industrial and Commercial Bank of China (October 2006).
- Poland sells Tauron Polska Energia (March 2011).
- U.K. sells Royal Mail (October 2013).
- Greece sells 67% stake in port of Piraeus (April 2016).
- Brazil passes bill to privatize its biggest power utility (June 2021).

Most privatizations are more like carve-outs than spin-offs because shares are sold for cash rather than distributed to the ultimate "shareholders"—that is, the citizens of the selling country. But several former communist countries, including Russia, Poland, and the Czech Republic, privatized by means of vouchers distributed to citizens. The vouchers could be used to bid for shares in the companies that were being privatized. Thus, the companies were not sold for cash, but for vouchers.[24]

Privatizations have raised enormous sums for governments. China raised $22 billion from the privatization of the Industrial and Commercial Bank of China. The Japanese government's successive sales of its holding of NTT (Nippon Telegraph and Telephone) brought in $100 billion.

The motives for privatization seem to boil down to the following three points:

1. *Increased efficiency.* Through privatization, the enterprise is exposed to the discipline of competition and insulated from political influence on investment and operating decisions. Managers and employees can be given stronger incentives to cut costs and add value.

2. *Share ownership.* Privatizations encourage share ownership. Many privatizations give special terms or allotments to employees or small investors.

3. *Revenue for the government.* Last but not least.

There were fears that privatizations would lead to massive layoffs and unemployment, but that does not appear to be the case. While it is true that privatized companies operate more efficiently and thus reduce employment, they generally grow faster as privatized companies, which increases employment. In many cases the net effect on employment has been positive.

On other dimensions, the impact of privatization is usually positive. A review of research on the issue concludes that the firms "almost always become more efficient, more profitable, . . . financially healthier and increase their capital investment spending."[25]

The process of privatization is not a one-way street. It can sometimes go into reverse, and publicly owned firms may be taken over by the government. For example, as part of his aim to construct a socialist republic in Venezuela, Hugo Chavez nationalized firms in the banking, oil, power, telecom, steel, and cement sectors. The idea behind public ownership is that the government can represent the wider interests of society and help to safeguard jobs. But you can see the dangers that may arise when the company is subject to political interference.

Sometimes temporary nationalization has been a pragmatic last resort for governments rather than part of a long-term strategy. For example, in 2008, the U.S. government took control of the giant mortgage companies Fannie Mae and Freddie Mac when they were threatened with bankruptcy.[26] In 2012, the Japanese government agreed to provide 1 trillion yen in return for a majority holding in Tepco, operator of the stricken Fukushima nuclear plant.

---

[24]There is extensive research on voucher privatizations. See, for example, M. Boycko, A. Shleifer, and R. Vishny, "Voucher Privatizations," *Journal of Financial Economics* 35 (1994), pp. 249–266; and R. Aggarwal and J. T. Harper, "Equity Valuation in the Czech Voucher Privatization Auctions," *Financial Management* 29 (Winter 2000), pp. 77–100.

[25]W. L. Megginson and J. M. Netter, "From State to Market: A Survey of Empirical Studies on Privatization," *Journal of Economic Literature* 39 (2001), pp. 381–389.

[26]The credit crisis prompted a number of company nationalizations throughout the world, such as that of Northern Rock in the U.K., Hypo Real Estate in Germany, Landsbanki in Iceland, and Anglo-Irish Bank in Ireland.

33-4   Bankruptcy

Some firms are forced to reorganize by the onset of financial distress. At this point they need to agree to a reorganization plan with their creditors or file for bankruptcy. We list the largest nonfinancial U.S. bankruptcies in Table 33.6. The credit crunch also ensured a good dollop of large financial bankruptcies. Lehman Brothers tops the list. It failed in September 2008 with assets of $691.1 billion. Two weeks later, Washington Mutual went the same way with assets of $327.9 billion.

During 2020 the COVID pandemic led to further major bankruptcies. Among the casualties are Neiman Marcus, Brooks Brothers, Hertz, Occitane, and Chesapeake Energy.

Bankruptcy proceedings in the United States may be initiated by the creditors, but in the case of public corporations, it is usually the firm itself that decides to file. It can choose one of two procedures, which are set out in Chapters 7 and 11 of the 1978 Bankruptcy Reform Act. The purpose of Chapter 7 is to oversee the firm's death and dismemberment, while Chapter 11 seeks to nurse the firm back to health.

Most small firms make use of Chapter 7. In this case, the bankruptcy judge appoints a trustee, who then closes the firm down and auctions off the assets. The proceeds from the auction are used to pay off the creditors. Secured creditors can recover the value of their collateral. Whatever is left over goes to the unsecured creditors, who take assigned places in a queue. (Secured creditors join as unsecured to the extent that their collateral is not worth enough to repay the secured debt.) The court and the trustee are first in line. Wages come next, followed by federal and state taxes and debts to some government agencies such as the Pension Benefit Guarantee Corporation. The remaining unsecured creditors mop up any remaining crumbs from the table.[27] Frequently, the trustee needs to prevent some creditors from trying to jump the gun and collect on their debts, and sometimes the trustee retrieves property that a creditor has recently seized.

BEYOND THE PAGE

U.S. bankruptcy filings

mhhe.com/brealey14e

Company	Bankruptcy Date	Total Assets Pre-bankruptcy ($ billions)
WorldCom	July 2002	$103.9
General Motors	June 2009	91.0
Pacific Gas and Electric	January 2019	71.4
Enron	December 2001	65.5
Conseco	December 2002	61.4
Energy Future Holdings	April 2014	41.0
Chrysler	April 2009	39.3
Pacific Gas and Electric	April 2001	36.2
Texaco	April 1987	34.9
Global Crossing	January 2002	30.2
General Growth Properties	April 2009	29.6
Lyondell Chemical Company	January 2009	27.4
Calpine	December 2005	27.2
UAL	December 2002	25.2

❭**TABLE 33.6**
The largest nonfinancial bankruptcies.

Source: New Generation Research, Inc., www.bankruptcydata.com.

---

[27]On average there isn't much left. See M. J. White, "Survey Evidence on Business Bankruptcy," in J. S. Bhandari and L. A. Weiss (eds.), *Corporate Bankruptcy* (Cambridge, UK: Cambridge University Press, 1996).

Managers of small firms that are in trouble know that Chapter 7 bankruptcy means the end of the road and, therefore, try to put off filing as long as possible. For this reason, Chapter 7 proceedings are often launched not by the firm, but by its creditors.

When large public companies can't pay their debts, they generally attempt to rehabilitate the business. This is in the shareholders' interests; they have nothing to lose if things deteriorate further and everything to gain if the firm recovers. The procedures for rehabilitation are set out in Chapter 11. Most companies find themselves in Chapter 11 because they can't pay their debts. But sometimes companies have filed for Chapter 11 not because they run out of cash, but to deal with burdensome labor contracts or lawsuits.

EXAMPLE 33.7 • Delphi files for Chapter 11

Delphi, the automotive parts manufacturer, filed for bankruptcy in 2005. Delphi's North American operations were running at a loss, partly because of high-cost labor contracts with the United Auto Workers (UAW) and partly because of the terms of its supply contract with GM, its largest customer. Delphi sought the protection of Chapter 11 to restructure its operations and to negotiate better terms with the UAW and GM.

• • • • •

BEYOND THE PAGE

Cramdowns

mhhe.com/brealey14e

The aim of Chapter 11 is to keep the firm alive and operating while a plan of reorganization is worked out.[28] During this period, other proceedings against the firm are halted, and the company usually continues to be run by its existing management.[29] The responsibility for developing the plan falls on the debtor firm but, if it cannot devise an acceptable plan, the court may invite anyone to do so—for example, a committee of creditors.

The plan goes into effect if it is accepted by the creditors and confirmed by the court. Each *class* of creditors votes separately on the plan. Acceptance requires approval by at least one-half of votes cast in each class, and those voting "aye" must represent two-thirds of the value of the creditors' aggregate claim against the firm. The plan also needs to be approved by two-thirds of the shareholders. Once the creditors and the shareholders have accepted the plan, the court normally approves it, provided that each class of creditors is in favor and that the creditors will be no worse off under the plan than they would be if the firm's assets were liquidated and the proceeds distributed. Under certain conditions the court may confirm a plan even if one or more classes of creditors votes against it,[30] but the rules for a "cramdown" are complicated, and we will not attempt to cover them here.

The reorganization plan is basically a statement of who gets what; each class of creditors gives up its claim in exchange for new securities or a mixture of new securities and cash. The problem is to design a new capital structure for the firm that will (1) satisfy the creditors and (2) allow the firm to solve the *business* problems that got the firm into trouble in the first place.[31] Sometimes satisfying these two conditions requires a plan of baroque complexity, involving the creation of a dozen or more new securities.

---

[28]To keep the firm alive, it may be necessary to continue to use assets that were offered as collateral, but this denies secured creditors access to their collateral. To resolve this problem, the Bankruptcy Reform Act makes it possible for a firm operating under Chapter 11 to keep such assets as long as the creditors who have a claim on them are compensated for any decline in their value. Thus, the firm might make cash payments to the secured creditors to cover economic depreciation of the assets.

[29]Occasionally, the court appoints a trustee to manage the firm.

[30]But at least one class of creditors must vote for the plan; otherwise, the court cannot approve it.

[31]Although Chapter 11 is designed to keep the firm in business, the reorganization plan often involves the sale or closure of large parts of the business.

The Securities and Exchange Commission (SEC) plays a role in many reorganizations, particularly for large, public companies. Its interest is to ensure that all relevant and material information is disclosed to the creditors before they vote on the proposed plan of reorganization.

Chapter 11 proceedings are often successful, and the patient emerges fit and healthy. But in other cases, rehabilitation proves impossible, and the assets are liquidated under Chapter 7. Sometimes the firm may emerge from Chapter 11 for a brief period before it is once again submerged by disaster and back in the bankruptcy court. For example, the venerable airline TWA came out of Chapter 11 bankruptcy at the end of 1993, was back again less than two years later, and then for a third time in 2001, prompting jokes about "Chapter 22" and "Chapter 33."[32]

BEYOND THE PAGE

Chapter 55

mhhe.com/brealey14e

Is Chapter 11 Efficient?

Here is a simple view of the bankruptcy decision: If the firm is unable to pay its creditors, it files for bankruptcy. If the assets of the bankrupt firm can be put to better use elsewhere, the firm is liquidated and the proceeds are used to pay off the creditors; otherwise, the creditors become the new owners and the firm continues to operate.[33]

In practice, matters are rarely so simple. For example, we observe that firms often petition for bankruptcy even when the equity has a positive value. And firms often continue to operate even when the assets could be used more efficiently elsewhere. The problems in Chapter 11 usually arise because the goal of paying off the creditors conflicts with the goal of maintaining the business as a going concern. We described in Chapter 17 how the assets of Eastern Airlines seeped away in bankruptcy. When the company filed for Chapter 11, its assets were more than sufficient to repay in full its liabilities of $3.7 billion. But the bankruptcy judge was determined to keep Eastern flying. When it finally became clear that Eastern was a terminal case, the assets were sold off and the creditors received less than $900 million. The creditors would clearly have been better off if Eastern had been liquidated immediately; the unsuccessful attempt at resuscitation cost the creditors $2.8 billion.[34]

Here are some further reasons that Chapter 11 proceedings do not always achieve an efficient solution:

1. Although the reorganized firm is legally a new entity, it is entitled to the tax-loss carry-forwards belonging to the old firm. If the firm is liquidated rather than reorganized, the tax-loss carry-forwards disappear. Thus, there is a tax incentive to continue operating the firm even when its assets could be sold and put to better use elsewhere.

2. If the firm's assets are sold, it is easy to determine what is available to pay creditors. However, when the company is reorganized, it needs to conserve cash. Therefore, claimants are often paid off with a mixture of cash and securities. This makes it less easy to judge whether they receive a fair shake.

3. Senior creditors, who know they are likely to get a raw deal in a reorganization, may press for a liquidation. Shareholders and junior creditors prefer a reorganization. They hope that the court will not interpret the creditors' pecking order too strictly and that they will receive consolation prizes when the firm's remaining value is sliced up.

4. Although shareholders and junior creditors are at the bottom of the pecking order, they have a secret weapon—they can play for time. When they use delaying tactics, the junior creditors are betting on a stroke of luck that will rescue their investment. On the

---

[32]One study found that after emerging from Chapter 11, about one in three firms reentered bankruptcy or privately restructured their debt. See E. S. Hotchkiss, "Postbankruptcy Reform and Management Turnover," *Journal of Finance* 50 (1995), pp. 3–21.

[33]If there are several classes of creditors in this simplistic model, the junior creditors initially become the owners of the company and are responsible for paying off the senior debt. They now face exactly the same decision as the original owners. If their newly acquired equity is valueless, they will also default and turn over ownership to the next class of creditors.

[34]These estimates of creditor losses are taken from L. A. Weiss and K. H. Wruck, "Information Problems, Conflicts of Interest, and Asset Stripping: Chapter 11's Failure in the Case of Eastern Airlines," *Journal of Financial Economics* 48 (1998), pp. 55–97.

other hand, the senior claimants know that time is working against them, so they may be prepared to settle for a lower payoff as part of the price for getting the plan accepted. Also, prolonged bankruptcy cases are costly, as we pointed out in Chapter 17. Senior claimants may see their money seeping into lawyers' pockets and decide to settle quickly.

But bankruptcy practices do change, and in recent years, Chapter 11 proceedings have become more creditor-friendly.[35] For example, equity investors and junior debtholders used to find that managers were willing allies in dragging out a settlement, but these days, the managers of bankrupt firms often receive a key-employee retention plan, which provides them with a large bonus if the reorganization proceeds quickly and a smaller one if the company lingers on in Chapter 11. For large public bankruptcies, this has contributed to a reduction in the time spent in bankruptcy from about 840 days in 2007 to 430 in 2017.[36]

While a reorganization plan is being drawn up, the company is likely to need additional working capital. It has, therefore, become increasingly common to allow the firm to buy goods on credit and to borrow money (known as *debtor in possession,* or *DIP,* debt). The lenders, who frequently comprise the firm's existing creditors, receive senior claims and can insist on stringent conditions. DIP lenders therefore have considerable influence on the outcome of the bankruptcy proceedings.

As creditors have gained more influence, shareholders of the bankrupt firms have received fewer crumbs. In recent years, the court has faithfully observed the pecking order of creditors in about 90% of Chapter 11 settlements.

In 2009, GM and Chrysler both filed for bankruptcy. They were not only two of the largest bankruptcies ever, but they were also extraordinary legal events. With the help of billions of fresh money from the U.S. Treasury, the companies were in and out of bankruptcy court with blinding speed, compared with the normal placid pace of Chapter 11. The U.S. government was deeply involved in the rescue and in the financing of New GM and New Chrysler. Both bankruptcies raised a number of financial issues. We illustrate with the example of Chrysler.

EXAMPLE 33.8 • Chrysler files for Chapter 11

Chrysler was the weakest of the Big Three U.S. auto manufacturers. We have noted its purchase in 2007 by the private-equity fund Cerberus. By 2009, in the midst of the financial crisis and recession, Chrysler was headed for the dustbin unless it could arrange a rescue from the U.S. government. The rescue came *after* Chrysler's bankruptcy, however. Cerberus's stake was wiped out.

Chrysler filed for bankruptcy on April 30, 2009. It owed $6.9 billion to secured lenders, $5.3 billion to trade creditors (e.g., parts suppliers), and $10 billion to a Voluntary Employees' Beneficiary Association (VEBA) trust set up to fund health and other benefits promised to retired employees. It also had unfunded pension liabilities, obligations to dealers, and warranty obligations to customers.

Just six weeks later, on June 11, the bankruptcy was resolved when all of Chrysler's assets and operations were sold to a new corporation for $2 billion. The $2 billion gave secured creditors 29 cents on the dollar. Fiat agreed to take over management of New Chrysler and received a 35% equity stake. New Chrysler received $6 billion in fresh loans from the U.S. Treasury and the Canadian government, in addition to $9.5 billion lent earlier. The Treasury and Canadian government also got 8% and 2% equity stakes, respectively.

---

[35]For a discussion of these changes see S. T. Bharath, V. Panchapagesan, and I. M. Werner, "The Changing Nature of Chapter 11," working paper, Ohio State University, November 2010. Available at SSRN: https://ssrn.com/abstract=1102366 or http://dx.doi.org/10.2139/ssrn.1102366.

[36]The numbers refer to bankruptcies that were not prepackaged. See http://lopucki.law.ucla.edu.

The secured bondholders were, of course, unhappy. The court and government did not pause to see if Chrysler was really worth only $2 billion or if a higher value could have been achieved by breaking up the company. But the unsecured creditors must have been unhappier still, right? The sale for $2 billion left nothing to them.

Wrong! The trade creditors got a $5.3 billion debt claim on New Chrysler, 100 cents on the dollar. The unfunded pension liabilities and dealer and warranty obligations were likewise carried over dollar-for-dollar to New Chrysler. The VEBA trust got a $4.6 billion claim and a 55% equity stake.

We noted that junior creditors and stockholders sometimes get small slices of reorganized companies that emerge from bankruptcy. These consolation prizes are referred to as *violations of absolute priority* because absolute priority pays senior creditors in full before junior creditors or stockholders get anything. But the Chrysler bankruptcy was resolved with *reverse* priority: Junior claims were honored and senior claims mostly wiped out.

What this means for U.S. bankruptcy law and practice is not clear. Perhaps Chrysler's 42-day bankruptcy was a one-off deal never to be repeated, except by GM. But now secured investors worry that "junior creditors might leapfrog them if things don't work out."[37]

● ● ● ● ●

33.5 Self-Test

True or false? Assume a proceeding under Chapter 11 of the U.S. bankruptcy law.
   a. When a company becomes bankrupt, it is usually in the interests of the equityholders to seek a liquidation rather than a reorganization.

   b. A reorganization plan must be presented for approval by each class of creditors.

   c. In a reorganization, creditors may be paid with a mixture of cash and securities.

   d. Debtor-in-possession debt refers to debts that the company owed before filing for bankruptcy.

   e. Chapter 11 reorganizations are inefficient when they prolong the operating life of a business that is worth more in liquidation than alive.

Workouts

If Chapter 11 reorganizations are not efficient, why don't firms bypass the bankruptcy courts and get together with their creditors to work out a solution? Many firms that are in distress *do* first seek a negotiated settlement, or *workout*. For example, they can seek to delay payment of the debt or negotiate an interest rate holiday. However, shareholders and junior creditors know that senior creditors are anxious to avoid formal bankruptcy proceedings. So they are likely to be tough negotiators, and senior creditors generally need to make concessions to reach agreement.[38] The larger the firm, and the more complicated its capital structure, the less likely it is that everyone will agree to any proposal.

---

[37]George J. Schultze, quoted in M. Roe and D. Skeel, "Assessing the Chrysler Bankruptcy," *Michigan Law Review* 108 (2010), pp. 728–772. This article reviews the legal issues created by the reverse priority of creditors in the sale to New Chrysler. See also A. D. Goolsbee, and A. B. Krueger, "A Retrospective Look at Rescuing and Restructuring General Motors and Chrysler," *Journal of Economic Perspectives* 29 (2015), pp. 3–24.

[38]Franks and Torous show that creditors make even greater concessions to junior creditors in informal workouts than in Chapter 11. See J. R. Franks and W. N. Torous, "A Comparison of Financial Recontracting in Distressed Exchanges and Chapter 11 Reorganizations," *Journal of Financial Economics* 35 (1994), pp. 349–370.

Sometimes the firm does agree to an informal workout with its creditors and then files under Chapter 11 to obtain the approval of the bankruptcy court. Such *prepackaged* or *prenegotiated bankruptcies* reduce the likelihood of subsequent litigation and allow the firm to gain the special tax advantages of Chapter 11.[39] For example, in 2020 Neiman Marcus arranged a *prepack* after reaching agreement with its creditors. Since 1980, about 30% of U.S. bankruptcies have been prepackaged or prenegotiated.[40]

BEYOND THE PAGE

International bankruptcy procedures

mhhe.com/brealey14e

Alternative Bankruptcy Procedures

The U.S. bankruptcy system is often described as a debtor-friendly system. Its principal focus is on rescuing firms in distress. But this comes at a cost because there are many instances in which the firm's assets would be better deployed in other uses. Michael Jensen, a critic of Chapter 11, has argued that "the U.S. bankruptcy code is fundamentally flawed. It is expensive, it exacerbates conflicts of interest among different classes of creditors, and it often takes years to resolve individual cases." Jensen's proposed solution is to require that any bankrupt company be put immediately on the auction block and the proceeds distributed to claimants in accordance with the priority of their claims.[41]

In some countries, the bankruptcy system is even more friendly to debtors. For example, in France the primary duties of the bankruptcy court are to keep the firm in business and preserve employment. Only once these duties have been performed does the court have a responsibility to creditors. Creditors have minimal control over the process, and it is the court that decides whether the firm should be liquidated or preserved. If the court chooses liquidation, it may select a bidder who offers a lower price but better prospects for employment.

The UK is often cited as at the other end of the scale. When a British firm is unable to pay its debts, the control rights pass to the creditors. Most commonly, a designated secured creditor appoints a *receiver,* who assumes direction of the firm, sells sufficient assets to repay the secured creditors, and ensures that any excess funds are used to pay off the other creditors according to the priority of their claims.

Davydenko and Franks, who have examined alternative bankruptcy systems, found that banks responded to these differences in the bankruptcy code by adjusting their lending practices. Nevertheless, as you would expect, lenders recover a smaller proportion of their money in those countries that have a debtor-friendly bankruptcy system. For example, in debtor-friendly France the banks recover on average only 47% of the money owed by bankrupt firms, while in the UK, the corresponding figure is 69%.[42]

Of course, the grass is always greener elsewhere. In the United States and France, critics complain about the costs of trying to save businesses that are no longer viable. By contrast, in countries such as the UK, bankruptcy laws are blamed for the demise of healthy businesses and Chapter 11 is held up as a model of an efficient bankruptcy system.

---

[39]In a prepackaged bankruptcy, the debtor gains agreement to the reorganization plan before the filing. In a prenegotiated bankruptcy, the debtor negotiates the terms of the plan only with the principal creditors.

[40]Data from Lynn LoPucki's Bankruptcy Research Database at http://lopucki.law.ucla.edu.

[41]M. C. Jensen, "Corporate Control and the Politics of Finance," *Journal of Applied Corporate Finance* 4 (Summer 1991), pp. 13–33. An ingenious alternative set of bankruptcy procedures is proposed in L. Bebchuk, "A New Approach to Corporate Reorganizations," *Harvard Law Review* 101 (1988), pp. 775–804; and P. Aghion, O. Hart, and J. Moore, "The Economics of Bankruptcy Reform," *Journal of Law, Economics and Organization* 8 (1992), pp. 523–546.

[42]S. A. Davydenko and J. R. Franks, "Do Bankruptcy Codes Matter? A Study of Defaults in France, Germany and the U.K.," *Journal of Finance* 63 (2008), pp. 565–608. For descriptions of bankruptcy in Sweden and Finland, see P. Stromberg, "Conflicts of Interest and Market Illiquidity in Bankruptcy Auctions: Theory and Tests," *Journal of Finance* 55 (2000), pp. 2641–2692; and S. A. Ravid and S. Sundgren, "The Comparative Efficiency of Small-Firm Bankruptcies: A Study of the U.S. and Finnish Bankruptcy Codes," *Financial Management* 27 (Winter 1998), pp. 28–40.

KEY
TAKEAWAYS

- **Leveraged buyouts (LBOs)** In an LBO, a company is bought out and taken private by an investment partnership. The LBO transaction is financed largely by debt. Most LBOs are diet deals; the cash requirements for debt service force managers to shed unneeded assets, improve operating efficiency, and forego wasteful expenditure. The managers and employees are given a significant stake in the business, so they have strong incentives to make these improvements.

- **Leveraged restructurings** In a leveraged restructuring, the company puts *itself* on a diet. Large amounts of debt are added, and the proceeds are paid out to shareholders. The company is forced to generate cash to service the debt, but there is no change in control and the company stays public.

- **Private equity** Most investments in LBOs are made by private-equity partnerships. The limited partners, who put up the bulk of the money, are mostly institutional investors, including pension funds, endowments, and insurance companies. The general partners, who organize and manage the funds, receive a management fee and get a carried interest in the fund's profits.

- **Diversification in private-equity funds** We called these private-equity partnerships "temporary conglomerates." They are conglomerates because they assemble a portfolio of companies in unrelated industries. They are temporary because the partnership has a limited life, usually about 10 years. At the end of this period, the partnership's investments must be sold or taken public again in IPOs. Private-equity funds do not buy and hold; they buy, fix, and sell. Investors in the partnership therefore do not have to worry about wasteful reinvestment of free cash flow.

- **Conglomerates** Public conglomerates have been declining in the United States. There are two possible reasons for this. First, since the market values of divisions can't be observed separately, it is harder to set incentives for divisional managers. Second, conglomerates' internal capital markets are inefficient. It is difficult for management to appreciate investment opportunities in many different industries. Internal capital markets are prone to overinvestment and cross-subsidies.

- **Divestment** Assets may be divested by spin-offs, carve-outs, or asset sales. In a spin-off, the parent firm splits off part of its business into a separate public company and gives its shareholders stock in the company. In a carve-out, the parent raises cash by separating part of its business and selling shares through an IPO. These divestitures are generally good news to investors; it appears that the businesses are moving to better homes, where they can be well managed and more profitable. Similar improvements in efficiency and profitability are observed in privatizations, which are spin-offs or carve-outs of businesses owned by governments.

- **Bankruptcy and distress** Companies in distress may reorganize by getting together with their creditors to arrange a workout. If a workout proves impossible, the company must file for bankruptcy. Chapter 11 of the Bankruptcy Act, which is used by most large public companies, seeks to reorganize the company and put it back on its feet again. However, the goal of paying off the company's creditors often conflicts with the aim of keeping the business going. As a result, Chapter 11 sometimes allows a firm to continue to operate when its assets could be better used elsewhere and the proceeds used to pay off creditors.

FURTHER
READING

Eckbo and Thorburn provide a general overview of corporate restructuring:

B. E. Eckbo and K. S. Thorburn, "Corporate Restructurings: Breakups and LBOs," in B. E. Eckbo (ed.), *Handbook of Empirical Corporate Finance* (Amsterdam: Elsevier/North-Holland, 2007), Chapter 16.

The paper by Renneboog and Vansteenkiste provides a broad survey of the literature on LBOs. Papers by Kaplan and Stein and by Kaplan and Stromberg provide evidence on the evolution and performance of LBOs. Jensen, the chief proponent of the free-cash-flow theory of takeovers, gives a spirited and controversial defense of LBOs:

L. Renneboog and C. Vansteenkiste, "Leveraged Buyouts: Motives and Sources of Value," *Annals of Corporate Governance* 2 (2017), pp. 291–389.

S. N. Kaplan and J. C. Stein, "The Evolution of Buyout Pricing and Financial Structure (Or What Went Wrong) in the 1980s," *Journal of Applied Corporate Finance* 6 (Spring 1993), pp. 72–88.

S. N. Kaplan and P. Stromberg, "Leveraged Buyouts and Private Equity," *Journal of Economic Perspectives* 23 (2009), pp. 121–146.

M. C. Jensen, "The Eclipse of the Public Corporation," *Harvard Business Review* 67 (September/October 1989), pp. 61–74.

The Summer 2006, Fall 2011, and Winter 2014 issues of the Journal of Applied Corporate Finance *include several articles on private equity. Privatization is surveyed in:*

W. L. Megginson, *The Financial Economics of Privatization* (Oxford, UK: Oxford University Press, 2005).

The following books and articles survey the bankruptcy process. Bris, Welch, and Zhu give a detailed comparison of bankrupt firms' experience in Chapter 7 versus Chapter 11:

E. I. Altman, E.S. Hotchkiss, and W. Wang, *Corporate Financial Distress, Restructuring, and Bankruptcy,* 4th ed. (New York: John Wiley & Sons, 2019).

E. S. Hotchkiss, K. John, R. M. Mooradian, and K. S. Thorburn, "Bankruptcy and the Resolution of Financial Distress," in B. E. Eckbo (ed.), *Handbook of Empirical Corporate Finance* (Amsterdam: Elsevier/North-Holland, 2007), Chapter 14.

L. Senbet and J. Seward, "Financial Distress, Bankruptcy and Reorganization," in R. A. Jarrow, V. Maksimovic, and W. T. Ziemba (eds.), *North-Holland Handbooks of Operations Research and Management Science: Finance,* vol. 9 (New York: Elsevier, 1995), pp. 921–961.

J. S. Bhandari, L. A. Weiss, and B. E. Adler (eds.), *Corporate Bankruptcy: Economic and Legal Perspectives* (Cambridge, UK: Cambridge University Press, 2008).

A. Bris, I. Welch, and N. Zhu, "The Costs of Bankruptcy: Chapter 7 Liquidation versus Chapter 11 Reorganization," *Journal of Finance* 61 (2006), pp. 1253–1303.

Here are several good case studies on topics covered in this chapter:

B. Burrough and J. Helyar, *Barbarians at the Gate: The Fall of RJR Nabisco* (New York: Harper & Row, 1990).

G. P. Baker, "Beatrice: A Study in the Creation and Destruction of Value," *Journal of Finance* 47 (1992), pp. 1081–1120.

K. H. Wruck, "Financial Policy as a Catalyst for Organizational Change: Sealed Air's Leveraged Special Dividend," *Journal of Applied Corporate Finance* 7 (Winter 1995), pp. 20–37.

J. Allen, "Reinventing the Corporation: The Satellite Structure of Thermo Electron," *Journal of Applied Corporate Finance* 11 (Summer 1998), pp. 38–47.

R. Parrino, "Spinoffs and Wealth Transfers: The Marriott Case," *Journal of Financial Economics* 43 (1997), pp. 241–274.

C. Eckel, D. Eckel, and V. Singal, "Privatization and Efficiency: Industry Effects of the Sale of British Airways," *Journal of Financial Economics* 43 (1997), pp. 275–298.

L. A. Weiss and K. H. Wruck, "Information Problems, Conflicts of Interest, and Asset Stripping: Chapter 11's Failure in the Case of Eastern Airlines," *Journal of Financial Economics* 48 (1998), pp. 55–97.

W. Megginson and D. Scannapieco, "The Financial and Economic Lessons of Italy's Privatization Program," *Journal of Applied Corporate Finance* 18 (Summer 2006), pp. 56–65.

● ● ● ● ●

PROBLEM SETS      **Select problems are available in McGraw Hill's** *Connect.* **Please see the preface for more information.**

1. **Vocabulary (S33.1–S33.4)** Define the following terms:

   a. LBO.

   b. MBO.

   c. Spin-off.

   d. Carve-out.

   e. Asset sale.

   f. Privatization.

   g. Leveraged restructuring.

2. **Leveraged buyouts (S33.1)** True or false?

   a. One of the first tasks of an LBO's financial manager is to pay down debt.

   b. Once an LBO or MBO goes private, it almost always stays private.

   c. Many early MBOs were arranged for unwanted divisions of large diversified companies.

   d. "Carried interest" refers to the deferral of interest payments on LBO debt.

   e. Private-equity partnerships have limited lives. The main purpose is to force the general partners to seek out quick-payback investments.

   f. Managers of private-equity partnerships have an incentive to make risky investments.

3. **Leveraged buyouts (S33.1)** Read *Barbarians at the Gate* (Further Reading). What agency costs can you identify? (*Hint:* See Chapter 19.) Do you think the LBO was well-designed to reduce these costs?

4. **Leveraged buyouts (S33.1)** For what kinds of firm would an LBO or MBO transaction *not* be productive?

5. **Private-equity partnerships (S33.2)** Private-equity partnerships have a limited term. What are the advantages of this arrangement?

6. **Private-equity partnerships (S33.2)** Explain the structure of a private-equity partnership. Pay particular attention to incentives and compensation. What types of investment were such partnerships designed to make?

7. **Private-equity partnerships (S33.2)** We described carried interest as an option. What kind of option? How does this option change incentives in a private-equity partnership? Can you think of circumstances where these incentive changes would be perverse—that is, potentially value-destroying? Explain.

8. **Conglomerates (S33.2)** What advantages have been claimed for public conglomerates?

9. **Conglomerates (S33.2)** List the disadvantages of traditional U.S. conglomerates. Can private-equity firms overcome these disadvantages?

10. **Restructuring (S33.3)** True or false?

   a. Carve-out or spin-off of a division improves incentives for the division's managers.

   b. The announcement of a spin-off is generally followed by a sharp fall in the stock price.

   c. Privatizations are generally followed by massive layoffs.

   d. On average, privatization seems to improve efficiency and add value.

11. **Divestitures (S33.3)** Examine some recent examples of divestitures. What do you think were the underlying reasons for them? How did investors react to the news?

12. **Privatization (S33.3)** "Privatization appears to bring efficiency gains because public companies are better able to reduce agency costs." Why do you think this may (or may not) be true?

13. **Privatization (S33.3)** What are the government's motives in a privatization?

14. **Bankruptcy (S33.4)** What is the difference between Chapter 7 and Chapter 11 bankruptcies?

15. **Bankruptcy (S33.4)** True or false?

   a. When a company becomes bankrupt, it is usually in the interests of stockholders to seek a liquidation rather than a reorganization.

   b. In Chapter 11, a reorganization plan must be presented for approval by each class of creditor.

c. In a reorganization, creditors may be paid off with a mixture of cash and securities.

d. When a company is liquidated, one of the most valuable assets to be sold off is the tax-loss carry-forward.

16. **Bankruptcy (S33.4)** We described several problems with Chapter 11 bankruptcy. Which of these problems could be mitigated by negotiating a prepackaged bankruptcy?

17. **Bankruptcy (S33.4)** Explain why equity can sometimes have a positive value even when companies file for bankruptcy.

● ● ● ● ●

SOLUTIONS TO SELF-TEST QUESTIONS

33.1 LBOs are usually diet deals, where high debt forces companies to improve efficiency and conserve cash. This would not be appropriate for a growth company with profitable investment opportunities and high cash needs.

33.2 Carried interest provides the general partners with zero payoff until the limited partners have been repaid and then with a proportion of the profits above this level. This is identical to a call option on a proportion of the profits with an exercise price equal to the limited partners' investment.

33.3 Managers cannot observe the market values of divisions and therefore face difficulties in deciding on value-maximizing investment. This difficulty increases in conglomerates, where managers must evaluate investments in many different industries. In addition, decisions when there are internal capital markets can be influenced by administrative frictions, lobbying and internal politics.

33.4 In a spin-off, shareholders are given equity in the division that is divested. There are no direct cash consequences. In a carve-out, the division is sold in an IPO and, therefore, the parent company receives the cash raised.

33.5 a. False (it is in shareholders' interest to attempt to rehabilitate the business).
   b. True.
   c. True.
   d. False (DIP debt refers to money that the company may be permitted to borrow while in Chapter 11).
   e. True.

CHAPTER

34

Conclusion: What We Do and Do Not Know about Finance

It is time to sign off. We will finish by thinking about some of the things that we do and do not know about finance.

34-1   What We Do Know: The Seven Most Important Ideas in Finance

What would you say if you were asked to name the seven most important ideas in finance? Here is our list.

1. Net Present Value

When you wish to know the value of a used car, you look at prices in the secondhand car market. Similarly, when you wish to know the value of a future cash flow, you look at prices quoted in the capital markets, where claims to future cash flows are traded (remember, those highly paid investment bankers are just secondhand cash-flow dealers). If you can buy cash flows for your shareholders at a cheaper price than they would have to pay in the capital market, you have increased the value of their investment.

This is the simple idea behind *net present value* (NPV). When we calculate an investment project's NPV, we are asking whether the project is worth more than it costs. We are estimating its value by calculating what its cash flows would be worth if a claim on them were offered separately to investors and traded in the capital markets.

That is why we calculate NPV by discounting future cash flows at the opportunity cost of capital—that is, at the expected rate of return offered by securities having the same degree of risk as the project. In well-functioning capital markets, all equivalent-risk assets are priced to offer the same expected return. By discounting at the opportunity cost of capital, we calculate the price at which investors in the project could expect to earn that rate of return.

Notice what an important idea it is. The NPV rule allows thousands of shareholders, who may have vastly different levels of wealth and attitudes toward risk, to participate in the same enterprise and to delegate its operation to a professional manager. They give the manager one simple instruction: "Maximize net present value."

2. The Capital Asset Pricing Model

Some people say that modern finance is all about the capital asset pricing model. That's non-sense. If the capital asset pricing model had never been invented, our advice to financial managers would be essentially the same. The attraction of the model is that it gives us a manageable way of thinking about the required return on a risky investment.

Again, it is an attractively simple idea. There are two kinds of risk: risks that you can diversify away and those that you can't. You can measure the *nondiversifiable,* or *market,* risk of an investment by the extent to which the value of the investment is affected by a change in the *aggregate* value of all the assets in the economy. This is called the *beta* of the investment. The only risks that people care about are the ones that they can't get rid of—the nondiversifiable ones. This is why the required return on an asset increases in line with its beta.

Many people are worried by some of the rather strong assumptions behind the capital asset pricing model, or they are concerned about the difficulties of estimating a project's beta. They are right to be worried about these things. In 10 or 20 years' time, we may have much better theories than we do now.[1] But we will be extremely surprised if those future theories do not still insist on the crucial distinction between diversifiable and nondiversifiable risks—and that, after all, is the main idea underlying the capital asset pricing model.

3. Efficient Capital Markets

The third fundamental idea is that security prices accurately reflect available information and respond rapidly to new information as soon as it becomes available. This *efficient-market theory* comes in three flavors, corresponding to different definitions of "available information." The weak form (or random-walk theory) says that prices reflect all the information in past prices. The semistrong form says that prices reflect all publicly available information, and the strong form holds that prices reflect all acquirable information.

Don't misunderstand the efficient-market idea. It doesn't say that there are no taxes or costs; it doesn't say that there aren't some clever people and some stupid ones. It merely implies that competition in capital markets is very tough—there are no money machines or arbitrage opportunities, and security prices reflect the true underlying values of assets.

Extensive empirical testing of the efficient-market hypothesis began around 1970. By 2018, after more than 40 years of work, the tests have uncovered dozens of statistically significant anomalies. Sorry, but this work does *not* translate into dozens of ways to make easy money. Superior returns are elusive. For example, only a few mutual fund managers can generate superior returns for a few years in a row, and then only in small amounts.[2] Statisticians can beat the market, but real investors have a much harder time of it. And on that essential matter there is now widespread agreement.[3]

4. Value Additivity and the Law of the Conservation of Value

The principle of *value additivity* states that the value of the whole is equal to the sum of the values of the parts. It is sometimes called the *law of the conservation of value.*

When we appraise a project that produces a succession of cash flows, we always assume that values add up. In other words, we assume

$$PV(\text{project}) = PV(C_1) + PV(C_2) + \cdots + PV(C_t)$$

$$= \frac{C_1}{1+r} + \frac{C_2}{(1+r)^2} + \cdots + \frac{C_t}{(1+r)^t}$$

---

[1]We must confess that we made this prediction 35 years ago in the first edition of this book. Sooner or later we will be right.

[2]See, for example, R. Kosowski, A. Timmerman, R. Wermers, and H. White, "Can Mutual Fund 'Stars' Really Pick Stocks? New Evidence from a Bootstrap Analysis," *Journal of Finance* 61 (2006), pp. 2551–2595.

[3]Some years ago, a young, upwardly mobile investment manager boasted to one of the authors that if he could not beat the market by 25% every year, he would shoot himself. Few people today would say that with a straight face.

We similarly assume that the sum of the present values of projects A and B equals the present value of a composite project AB.[4] But value additivity also means that you can't increase value by putting two whole companies together unless you thereby increase the total cash flow. In other words, there are no benefits to mergers solely for diversification.

5. Capital Structure Theory

If the law of the conservation of value works when you add up cash flows, it must also work when you subtract them.[5] Therefore, financing decisions that simply divide up operating cash flows don't increase overall firm value. This is the basic idea behind Modigliani and Miller's famous proposition 1: In perfect markets changes in capital structure do not affect value. As long as the *total* cash flow generated by the firm's assets is unchanged by capital structure, value is independent of capital structure. The value of the whole pie does not depend on how it is sliced.

Of course, MM's proposition is not The Answer, but it does tell us where to look for reasons why capital structure decisions may matter. Taxes are one possibility. Debt provides a corporate interest tax shield, and this tax shield may more than compensate for any extra personal tax that the investor has to pay on debt interest. Also, high debt levels may spur managers to work harder and to run a tighter ship. But debt has its drawbacks if it leads to costly financial distress.

6. Option Theory

In everyday conversation, we often use the word "option" as synonymous with "choice" or "alternative"; thus, we speak of someone as "having a number of options." In finance, *option* refers specifically to the opportunity to trade in the future on terms that are fixed today. Smart managers know that it is often worth paying today for the option to buy or sell an asset tomorrow.

Since options are so important, the financial manager needs to know how to value them. Finance experts always knew the relevant variables—the exercise price and the exercise date of the option, the risk of the underlying asset, and the rate of interest. But it was Black and Scholes who first showed how these can be put together in a usable formula.

The Black–Scholes formula was developed for simple call options and does not directly apply to the more complicated options often encountered in corporate finance. But Black and Scholes's most basic ideas—for example, the risk-neutral valuation method implied by their formula—work even where the formula doesn't. Valuing the real options described in Chapter 23 may require extra number crunching but no extra concepts.

7. Agency Theory

A modern corporation is a team effort involving a number of players, such as managers, employees, shareholders, and bondholders. For a long time, economists used to assume without question that all these players acted for the common good, but in the last 30 years, they have had a lot more to say about the possible conflicts of interest and how companies attempt to overcome such conflicts. These ideas are known collectively as *agency theory.*

---

[4]That is, if

$$PV(A) = PV[C_1(A)] + PV[C_2(A)] + \cdots + PV[C_t(A)]$$
$$PV(B) = PV[C_1(B)] + PV[C_2(B)] + \cdots + PV[C_t(B)]$$

and if for each period t, $C_t(AB) = C_t(A) + C_t(B)$, then

$$PV(AB) = PV(A) + PV(B)$$

[5]If you start with the cash flow $C_t(AB)$ and split it into two pieces, $C_t(A)$ and $C_t(B)$, then total value is unchanged. In other words, $PV[C_t(A)] + PV[C_t(B)] = PV[C_t(AB)]$. See Footnote 4.

Consider, for example, the relationship between the shareholders and the managers. The shareholders (the *principals*) want managers (their *agents*) to maximize firm value. In the United States, the ownership of many major corporations is widely dispersed, and no single shareholder can check on the managers or reprimand those who are slacking. So, to encourage managers to pull their weight, firms seek to tie the managers' compensation to the value that they have added. For those managers who persistently neglect shareholders' interests, there is the threat that their firm will be taken over and they will be turfed out.

Some corporations are owned by a few major shareholders, and therefore, there is less distance between ownership and control. For example, the families, companies, and banks that hold or control large stakes in many German companies can review top management's plans and decisions as insiders. In most cases, they have the power to force changes as necessary. However, hostile takeovers in Germany are rare.

We discussed the problems of management incentives and corporate control in Chapter 19, but this was not the only place in the book where agency issues arose. For example, in Chapters 17 and 25, we looked at some of the conflicts that arise between shareholders and bondholders, and we described how loan agreements try to anticipate and minimize these conflicts.

These ideas are basic to the financial manager's job. If, by reading this book, you really understand these ideas and know how to apply them, you have learned a great deal.

34-2   What We Do Not Know: 10 Unsolved Problems in Finance

Since the unknown is never exhausted, the list of what we do not know about finance could go on forever. We list and briefly discuss 10 unsolved problems that seem ripe for productive research.

1. What Determines Project Risk and Present Value?

A good capital investment is one that has a positive NPV. We have talked at some length about how to calculate NPV, but we have given you very little guidance about how to find positive-NPV projects, except to say in Section 11-3 that projects have positive NPVs when the firm can earn economic rents. But why do some companies earn economic rents while others in the same industry do not? Are the rents merely windfall gains, or can they be anticipated and planned for? What is their source, and how long do they persist before competition destroys them? Very little is known about any of these important questions.

Here is a related question: Why are some real assets risky and others relatively safe? In Section 9-3, we suggested a few reasons for differences in project betas—differences in operating leverage, for example, or in the extent to which a project's cash flows respond to the performance of the national economy. These are useful clues, but we have, as yet, no general procedure for estimating project betas. Assessing project risk is therefore still largely a seat-of-the-pants matter.

2. Risk and Return—What Have We Missed?

In 1848, John Stuart Mill wrote, "Happily there is nothing in the laws of value which remains for the present or any future writer to clear up; the theory is complete." Economists today are not so sure about that. For example, the capital asset pricing model is an enormous step toward understanding the effect of risk on the value of an asset, but there are many puzzles left, some statistical and some theoretical.

The statistical problems arise because the capital asset pricing model is hard to prove or disprove conclusively. It appears that average returns from low-beta stocks are too high (that is, higher than the capital asset pricing model predicts) and that those from high-beta stocks are too low; but this could be a problem with the way that the tests are conducted and not with the model itself.[6] We also described the puzzling discovery by Fama and French that expected returns appear to be related to the firm's size and to the ratio of the book value of the stock to its market value. Nobody understands why this should be so; perhaps these variables are related to variable x, that mysterious second risk variable that investors may rationally take into account in pricing shares.[7]

Meanwhile, scholars toil on the theoretical front. We discussed some of their work in Section 8-4. But just for fun, here is another example: Suppose that you love fine wine. It may make sense for you to buy shares in a grand cru chateau, even if doing so soaks up a large fraction of your personal wealth and leaves you with a relatively undiversified portfolio. However, you are *hedged* against a rise in the price of fine wine: Your hobby will cost you more in a bull market for wine, but your stake in the chateau will make you correspondingly richer. Thus, you are holding a relatively undiversified portfolio for a good reason. We would not expect you to demand a premium for bearing that portfolio's undiversifiable risk.

In general, if two people have different tastes, it may make sense for them to hold different portfolios. You may hedge your consumption needs with an investment in wine making, whereas somebody else may do better to invest in a chain of ice cream parlors. The capital asset pricing model isn't rich enough to deal with such a world. It assumes that all investors have similar tastes: The hedging motive does not enter, and therefore they hold the same portfolio of risky assets.

Merton has extended the capital asset pricing model to accommodate the hedging motive.[8] If enough investors are attempting to hedge against the same thing, the model implies a more complicated risk–return relationship. However, it is not yet clear who is hedging against what, and so the model remains difficult to test.

So, the capital asset pricing model survives not from a lack of competition but from a surfeit. There are too many plausible alternative risk measures, and so far, no consensus exists on the right course to plot if we abandon beta.

In the meantime, we must recognize the capital asset pricing model for what it is: an incomplete but extremely useful way of linking risk and return. Recognize too that the model's most basic message, that diversifiable risk doesn't matter, is accepted by nearly everyone.

3. How Important Are the Exceptions to the Efficient-Market Theory?

The efficient-market theory is one of the most important ideas in finance, but how well does it stand up? We have already come across a number of possible exceptions. Some of these could simply be coincidences because the more researchers study stock performance, the more strange coincidences they are likely to find. For example, there is evidence that daily returns around new moons have been roughly double those around full moons.[9] It seems difficult to believe that this is anything other than a chance relationship—fun to read about but not a concern for serious investors or financial managers. But not all exceptions can be dismissed so easily. For example, we saw in Chapter 12 that shares seem to exhibit momentum so that past winners continue to be winners. This seems to suggest that investors initially tend to

---

[6]See R. Roll, "A Critique of the Asset Pricing Theory's Tests: Part 1: On Past and Potential Testability of the Theory," *Journal of Financial Economics* 4 (March 1977), pp. 129–176; and, for a critique of the critique, see D. Mayers and E. M. Rice, "Measuring Portfolio Performance and the Empirical Content of Asset Pricing Models," *Journal of Financial Economics* 7 (March 1979), pp. 3–28.

[7]Fama and French point out that small firms, and firms with high book-to-market ratios, are also low-profitability firms. Such firms may suffer more in downturns in the economy. Thus, size and book-to-market measures may be proxies for exposure to business-cycle risk. See E. F. Fama and K. R. French, "Size and Book-to-Market Factors in Earnings and Returns," *Journal of Finance* 50 (1995), pp. 131–155.

[8]See R. Merton, "An Intertemporal Capital Asset Pricing Model," *Econometrica* 41 (1973), pp. 867–887.

[9]K. Yuan, L. Zheng, and Q. Zhu, "Are Investors Moonstruck? Lunar Phases and Stock Returns," *Journal of Empirical Finance* 13 (2006), pp. 1–23.

underreact to news. Of course, we can't expect investors never to make mistakes. If they have been slow to react in the past, perhaps they will learn from this mistake and price the stocks more efficiently in the future.

Some researchers believe that the efficient-market hypothesis ignores important aspects of human behavior. For example, psychologists find that people tend to place too much emphasis on recent events when they are predicting the future. If so, we may find that investors are liable to overreact to new information. It will be interesting to see how far such behavioral observations can help us to understand apparent anomalies.

During the dot-com boom of the late 1990s, stock prices rose to astronomic levels. The Nasdaq Composite Index rose 580% from the beginning of 1995 to its peak in March 2000 and then fell by nearly 80%. Such gyrations were not confined to the United States. For example, stock prices on Germany's Neuer Markt rose 1,600% in the three years from its foundation in 1997, before falling by 95% by October 2002.

This is not the only occasion that asset prices have reached unsustainable levels. In the late 1980s, there was a surge in the prices of Japanese stock and real estate. In 1989, at the peak of the real estate boom, choice properties in Tokyo's Ginza district were selling for about $1 million a square foot. Over the next 17 years, Japanese real estate prices fell by 70%.[10]

Maybe such extreme price movements can be explained by standard valuation techniques. However, others argue that stock prices are liable to speculative bubbles, where investors are caught up in a scatty whirl of irrational exuberance.[11] Now that may be true of your Uncle Harry or Aunt Hetty, but why don't hard-headed professional investors bail out of the overpriced stocks? Perhaps they would do so if it was their money at stake, but maybe there is an agency problem that stems from the way that their performance is measured and rewarded that encourages them to run with the herd.[12] (Remember the remark by the CEO of Citigroup: "As long as the music is playing, you've got to get up and dance.")

These are important questions. Much more research is needed before we have a full understanding of why asset prices sometimes get so out of line with what appears to be their discounted future payoffs.

4. Is Management an Off-Balance-Sheet Liability?

Closed-end funds are firms whose only asset is a portfolio of common stocks. One might think that if you knew the value of these common stocks, you would also know the value of the firm. However, this is not the case. The stock of the closed-end fund often sells for substantially less than the value of the fund's portfolio.[13]

All this might not matter much except that it could be just the tip of the iceberg. For example, real estate stocks appear to sell for less than the market values of the firms' net assets. In the late 1970s and early 1980s, the market values of many large oil companies were less than the market values of their oil reserves. Analysts joked that you could buy oil cheaper on Wall Street than in West Texas.

All these are special cases in which it was possible to compare the market value of the whole firm with the values of its separate assets. But perhaps if we could observe the values of other firms' separate parts, we might find that the value of the whole was often less than the sum of the values of the parts.

---

[10]See W. Ziemba and S. Schwartz, *Invest Japan* (Chicago, IL: Probus, 1992), p. 109.

[11]See C. Kindleberger, *Manias, Panics, and Crashes: A History of Financial Crises,* 4th ed. (New York: Wiley, 2000); and R. Shiller, *Irrational Exuberance* (Princeton, NJ: Princeton University Press, 2000).

[12]Investment managers may reason that if the stocks continue to do well, they will benefit from increased business in the future; on the other hand, if the stocks do badly, it is the customers who incur the losses and the worst that can happen to the managers is that they have to find new jobs. See F. Allen, "Do Financial Institutions Matter?" *Journal of Finance* 56 (2001), pp. 1165–1174.

[13]There are relatively few closed-end funds. Most mutual funds are *open-end.* This means that they stand ready to buy or sell additional shares at a price equal to the fund's net asset value per share. Therefore, the share price of an open-end fund always equals net asset value.

Whenever firms calculate the net present value of a project, they implicitly assume that the value of the whole project is simply the sum of the values of all the years' cash flows. We referred to this earlier as the law of the conservation of value. If we cannot rely on that law, the tip of the iceberg could turn out to be a hot potato.

We don't understand why closed-end investment companies or any of the other firms sell at a discount on the market values of their assets. One explanation is that the value added by the firm's management is less than the cost of the management. That is why we suggest that management may be an off-balance-sheet liability. For example, the discount of oil company shares from oil-in-the-ground value can be explained if investors expected the profits from oil production to be frittered away in negative-NPV investments and bureaucratic excess. The present value of growth opportunities (PVGO) was negative!

We do not mean to portray managers as leeches soaking up cash flows meant for investors. Managers commit their human capital to the firm and rightfully expect a reasonable cash return on these personal investments. If investors extract too great a share of the firm's cash flow, the personal investments are discouraged, and the long-run health and growth of the firm can be damaged.

In most firms, managers and employees co-invest with stockholders and creditors—human capital from the insiders and financial capital from outside investors. So far we know very little about how this co-investment works.

5. How Can We Explain the Success of New Securities and New Markets?

In the last 50 years, companies and the securities exchanges have created an enormous number of new securities: options, futures, options on futures; zero-coupon bonds, floating-rate bonds; bonds with collars and caps, asset-backed bonds; catastrophe bonds; . . . the list is endless. In some cases, it is easy to explain the success of new markets or securities; perhaps they allow investors to insure themselves against new risks, or they result from a change in tax or in regulation. Sometimes a market develops because of a change in the costs of issuing or trading different securities. But there are many successful innovations that cannot be explained so easily. Why do investment bankers continue to invent, and successfully sell, complex new securities that outstrip our ability to value them? The truth is we don't understand why some innovations in markets succeed and others never get off the ground.

And then there are the innovations that do get off the ground but crash later, including many of the complex and overrated securities backed by subprime mortgages. Subprime mortgages are not intrinsically bad, of course: They may be the only route to home ownership for some worthy people. But subprime loans also put many homeowners in nasty traps when house prices fell and jobs were lost. Securities based on subprime mortgages caused enormous losses in the banking industry. A number of new securities and derivatives went out of favor during the crisis. It will be interesting to see which will remain permanently consigned to the dustbin and which will be dusted off and recover their usefulness.

6. How Can We Resolve the Payout Controversy?

We spent all of Chapter 15 on payout policy without being able to resolve the payout controversy. Many people believe dividends are good; others point out that dividends attract more tax, and therefore, it is better for firms to repurchase stock; and still others believe that as long as the firm's investment decisions are unaffected, the payout decision is irrelevant.

Perhaps the problem is that we are asking the wrong question. Instead of inquiring whether dividends are good or bad, perhaps we should be asking *when* it makes sense to pay high or low dividends. For example, investors in mature firms with few investment opportunities may welcome the financial discipline imposed by a high dividend payout. For younger firms or firms with a temporary cash surplus, the tax advantage of stock repurchase may be more influential. But we don't know enough yet about how payout policy should vary from firm to firm.

The way that companies distribute cash has been changing. An increasing number of companies do not pay any dividends, while the volume of stock repurchases has mushroomed. This may partly reflect the growth in the proportion of small high-growth firms with lots of investment opportunities, but this does not appear to be the complete explanation. Understanding these shifts in company payout policy may also help us to understand how that policy affects firm value.

7. What Risks Should a Firm Take?

Firms need to manage risk. In many cases, this simply means having contingency plans in case there is a threat to the supply of raw materials or the loss of an important market. But in other cases, there are different actions that the firm can take to protect itself. For example,

- When a firm expands production, managers often reduce the cost of failure by building in the option to alter the product mix or to bail out of the project altogether.
- By reducing the firm's borrowing, managers can spread operating risks over a larger equity base.
- Most businesses take out insurance against a variety of specific hazards.
- Managers often use futures or other derivatives to protect against adverse movements in commodity prices, interest rates, and exchange rates.

All these actions reduce risk. But less risk can't always be better. The point of risk management is not to reduce risk but to add value. We wish we could give general guidance on what bets the firm should place and what the *appropriate* level of risk is.

In practice, risk management decisions interact in complicated ways. For example, firms that are hedged against commodity price fluctuations may be able to afford more debt than those that are not hedged. Hedging can make sense if it allows the firm to take greater advantage of interest tax shields, provided the costs of hedging are sufficiently low.

How can a company set a risk management strategy that adds up to a sensible whole?

8. What Is the Value of Liquidity?

Unlike Treasury bills, cash pays no interest. On the other hand, cash provides more liquidity than Treasury bills. People who hold cash must believe that this additional liquidity offsets the loss of interest. In equilibrium, the marginal value of the additional liquidity must equal the interest rate on bills.

Now what can we say about corporate holdings of cash? It is wrong to ignore the liquidity gain and to say that the cost of holding cash is the lost interest. This would imply that cash always has a *negative* NPV. It is equally foolish to say that because the marginal value of liquidity is equal to the loss of interest, it doesn't matter how much cash the firm holds. This would imply that cash always has a *zero* NPV. We know that the marginal value of cash to a holder declines with the size of the cash holding, but we don't really understand how to value the liquidity service of cash, and therefore, we can't say how much cash is enough or how readily the firm should be able to raise it. To complicate matters further, we note that cash can be raised on short notice by borrowing or by issuing other new securities, as well as by selling assets. The financial manager with a $100 million unused line of credit may sleep just as soundly as one whose firm holds $100 million in marketable securities. In our chapters on working capital management, we largely finessed these questions by presenting models that are really too simple or by speaking vaguely of the need to ensure an "adequate" liquidity reserve.

Here is another problem. You are a partner in a private-equity firm contemplating a major new investment. You have a forecast of the future cash flows and an estimate of the return that investors would require from the business *if it were a publicly traded company*. But how much extra return do you need to compensate for the fact that the stock cannot be traded? An addition of 1 or 2 percentage points to the discount rate can make a huge difference to the estimated value.

The crisis of 2007–2009 demonstrated that investors seem to value liquidity much more highly at some times than at others. Despite massive injections of liquidity by central banks, many financial markets effectively dried up. For example, banks became increasingly reluctant to lend to one another on an unsecured basis and would do so only at a large premium. Financial markets work well most of the time, but we don't understand well why they sometimes shut down or clog up, and we can offer relatively little advice to managers as to how to respond.

9. How Can We Explain Merger Waves?

Of course, there are many plausible motives for merging. If you single out a *particular* merger, it is usually possible to think up a reason that merger could make sense. But that leaves us with a special hypothesis for each merger. What we need is a general hypothesis to explain merger waves. For example, everybody seemed to be merging in 1998–2000 and again in 2006–2007, but in the intervening years, mergers went out of fashion.

There are other instances of apparent financial fashions. For example, from time to time, there are hot new-issue periods when there seem to be an insatiable supply of speculative new issues and an equally insatiable demand for them. We don't understand why hard-headed businessmen sometimes seem to behave like a flock of sheep, but the following story may contain the seeds of an explanation.

It is early evening and George is trying to decide between two restaurants, the Hungry Horse and the Golden Trough. Both are empty and, because there seems to be little reason to prefer one to the other, George tosses a coin and opts for the Hungry Horse. Shortly afterward, Georgina pauses outside the two restaurants. She somewhat prefers the Golden Trough, but observing George inside the Hungry Horse while the other restaurant is empty, she decides that George may know something that she doesn't, and therefore, the rational decision is to copy George. Fred is the third person to arrive. He sees that George and Georgina have both chosen the Hungry Horse and, putting aside his own judgment, decides to go with the flow. And so it is with subsequent diners, who simply look at the packed tables in the one restaurant and the empty tables elsewhere and draw the obvious conclusions. Each diner behaves fully rationally in balancing his or her own views with the revealed preferences of the other diners. Yet the popularity of the Hungry Horse owed much to the toss of George's coin. If Georgina had been the first to arrive or if all diners could have pooled their information before coming to a decision, the Hungry Horse might not have scooped the jackpot.

Economists refer to this imitative behavior as a *cascade*.[14] It remains to be seen how far cascades or some alternative theory can help to explain financial fashions.

10. Why Are Financial Systems So Prone to Crisis?

The crisis that started in 2007 was an unwelcome reminder of the fragility of financial systems. One moment, everything seems to be going fine; the next moment, markets crash, banks fail; and before long, the economy is in recession. Carmen Reinhart and Kenneth Rogoff have documented the effects of banking crises in many countries.[15] They find that systemic banking crises are typically preceded by credit booms and asset price bubbles. When the bubbles burst, housing prices drop, on average, by 35% and stock prices fall by 55%. Output falls by

---

[14]For an introduction to cascades, see S. Bikhchandani, D. Hirshleifer, and I. Welch, "Learning from the Behavior of Others: Conformity, Fads, and Informational Cascades," *Journal of Economic Perspectives* 12 (Summer 1998), pp. 151–170.

[15]See C. Reinhart and K. Rogoff, "The Aftermath of Financial Crises," *American Economic Review* 99 (May 2009), pp. 466–472.

9% over the following two years, and unemployment rises by 7% over a period of four years. Central government debt nearly doubles compared with its pre-crisis level.

At the start of 2010, the increased government debt in Greece and a number of other periphery eurozone countries caused the financial crisis to change into a sovereign debt crisis. First Greece, and later Ireland and Portugal, required a bailout from the IMF and other eurozone countries. Spain and Italy also needed to arrange government bailouts for their banks. In 2012, Greece finally defaulted on its government debt, and continued to lurch from one crisis to the next.

Our understanding of these financial crises is limited. We need to know what causes them, how they can be prevented, and how they can be managed when they do occur. We reviewed the roots of the Crisis of 2007-09 in Chapter 13. But crisis prevention will have to incorporate principles and practices that we discussed in other chapters, such as the importance of good governance systems, well-constructed compensation schemes, and efficient risk management. The interaction of politics and economics at such times is particularly important but poorly appreciated. Understanding financial crises will occupy economists and financial regulators for many years to come.[16] Let's hope they figure out the last one before the next one knocks on the door.

34-3   A Final Word

That concludes our list of unsolved problems. We have given you the 10 uppermost in our minds. If there are others that you find more interesting and challenging, by all means construct your own list and start thinking about it.

It will take years for our 10 problems to be finally solved and replaced with a fresh list. In the meantime, we invite you to go on to study further what we *already* know about finance. We also invite you to apply what you have learned from reading this book.

Now that the book is done, we sympathize with Huckleberry Finn. At the end of his book he says:

> So there ain't nothing more to write, and I am rotten glad of it, because if I'd a' knowed what a trouble it was to make a book I wouldn't a' tackled it, and I ain't a' going to no more.

---

[16]For a review of the current literature on financial crises, see F. Allen, A. Babus, and E. Carletti, "Financial Crises: Theory and Evidence," *Annual Review of Financial Economics* 1 (2009), pp. 97–116.

Glossary

A

Adjusted present value (APV) *Net present value* of an asset if financed solely by equity plus the *present value* of any financing side effects.

Agency costs Costs that arise when an agent (e.g., a manager) does not act solely in the interests of the principal (e.g., the shareholder).

Agency problem An agency problem occurs when the interests of the principal are not the same as the agent acting on their behalf.

Annuity Investment that produces a level stream of cash flows for a limited number of periods.

Annuity factor *Present value* of $1 paid for each of t periods.

APT *Arbitrage pricing theory.*

APV *Adjusted present value.*

Arbitrage Purchase of one security and simultaneous sale of another to give a risk-free profit. Often used loosely to describe the taking of offsetting positions in related securities—for example, at the time of a takeover bid.

Arbitrage pricing theory (APT) Model in which expected returns increase linearly with an asset's sensitivity to a small number of pervasive factors.

Ask price (offer price) Price at which a dealer is willing to sell (cf. *bid price*).

Automated Clearing House (ACH) Private electronic system run by banks for high-volume, low-value payments.

B

Basis point One-hundredth of 1 percent.

Basis risk Residual risk that results when the two sides of a hedge do not move exactly together.

Benefit corporation A type of corporation that states specific public benefits in its articles of incorporation, such as protecting the environment.

Beta Measure of *market risk*.

Binomial method Method for valuing *options* that assumes there are only two possible changes in the asset price in any one period.

Break-even analysis Break-even analysis involves calculating the level of output or revenue such that the firm just breaks even.

Bridge loan Short-term loan to provide temporary financing until more permanent financing is arranged.

C

Call option Option to buy an asset at a specified exercise price on or before a specified exercise date (cf. *put option*).

CAPEX Capital expenditure.

Capital asset pricing model (CAPM) Model in which expected returns increase linearly with an asset's *beta*.

Capital budget List of planned investment projects, usually prepared annually.

Capital budgeting The process of deciding which investments to undertake and which to turn down.

Capital lease *Financial lease.*

Capital structure Mix of different securities issued by a firm.

CAPM *Capital asset pricing model.*

Carve-out Public offering of shares in a subsidiary.

Certainty equivalent A certain cash flow that has the same present value as a specified risky cash flow.

Closed-end fund A closed-end fund is a company whose assets consist of investments in a number of industrial and commercial companies. The fund has a fixed number of shares that they issue that are traded on an exchange.

Commercial paper (CP) Unsecured *notes* issued by companies and maturing within nine months.

Common stock Shares of ownership in a company, which entitle the owner to dividends and voting rights.

Company cost of capital The opportunity cost of capital for an investment in all the firm's assets and the correct discount rate for its average-risk projects.

Compound interest Reinvestment of each interest payment on money invested to earn more interest (cf. *simple interest*).

Concentration account If the firm's customers make payments to a regional collection center, the deposits can be automatically transferred to a centralized concentration account.

Conglomerate merger *Merger* between two companies in unrelated businesses (cf. *horizontal merger, vertical merger*).

Consumer credit Bills awaiting payment from final customer to a company.

Conversion price *Par value* of a *convertible bond* divided by the number of shares into which it may be exchanged.

Conversion ratio Number of shares for which a *convertible bond* may be exchanged.

Convertible bond *Bond* that may be converted into another security at the holder's option. Similarly convertible *preferred stock*.

Corporation   A business that is legally separate from its owners.

Correlation coefficient   Normalized measure of the co-movement between two variables taking values between −1 and +1.

Cost of equity   Expected rate of return demanded by investors in the firm's shares.

Covariance   Measure of the co-movement between two variables.

Credit default swap (CDS)   An agreement where the seller of the CDS will compensate the buyer in case of default of the asset being insured.

D

DCF   *Discounted cash flow.*

Debenture   Unsecured *bond*.

Debt capacity   Firm's optimal amount of debt.

Degree of operating leverage (DOL)   The percentage change in profits for a 1% change in sales.

Direct lease   *Lease* in which the *lessor* purchases new equipment from the manufacturer and leases it to the *lessee* (cf. *sale and lease-back*).

Discount factor   *Present value* of $1 received at a stated future date.

Discounted cash flow (DCF)   Future cash flows multiplied by *discount factors* to obtain *present value*.

Dividend discount model   Model showing that the value of a share is equal to the discounted value of future *dividends*.

Dividend yield   Annual *dividend* divided by share price.

DuPont formula   Formula expressing relationship between return on assets, sales-to-assets, profit margin, and measures of leverage.

Duration   The average number of years to an asset's *discounted cash flows.*

E

EAR   *Effective annual rate.*

Economic depreciation   Decline in *present value* of an asset.

Economic income   Cash flow plus change in *present value.*

Economic rent   Any payment in excess of the costs needed for the good or service to be produced.

Effective annual rate (EAR)   The interest rate, compounded once per year, that is equivalent to an annual percentage rate compounded multiple times per year.

Efficient frontier   Consists of the set of efficient portfolios.

Efficient portfolio   Portfolio that offers the lowest risk *(standard deviation)* for its *expected return* and the highest expected return for its level of risk.

Equipment trust certificate (ETC)   Form of *secured debt* generally used to finance railroad equipment. The trustee retains ownership of the equipment until the debt is repaid.

ETF   *Exchange-traded fund.*

Eurobond   (1) Bond that is denominated in one country's currency but marketed internationally outside that country. (2) Also used to refer to suggested sovereign bond issues that would be guaranteed by all eurozone governments.

Evergreen credit   *Revolving credit* without maturity.

Ex-dividend   If a stock is traded on or after its ex-dividend date, it is said to trade ex-dividend and the seller rather than the buyer receives the dividend.

Exchange-traded fund (ETF)   A stock designed to track a stock market index.

Expectations theory   Theory that *forward interest rate (forward exchange rate)* equals expected *spot rate.*

Expected yield   The expected return on a bond taking into account the possibility of default and reduced payments in this case.

F

Face value   The amount of debt that must be repaid, also called *principal* or *par value.*

Factor   (1) A common influence on security prices (e.g., the level of interest rates or oil prices); (2) a business providing *factoring.*

Financial assets   Claims on *real assets.*

Financial engineering   Combining or dividing existing instruments to create new financial products.

Financial intermediary   An organization that raises money from many investors and provides financing to individuals, corporations, and other organizations.

Financial lease (capital lease, full-payout lease)   Long-term, noncancelable lease (cf. *operating lease).*

Financial leverage (gearing)   Use of debt to increase the *expected return* on *equity.* Financial leverage is measured by the ratio of debt to debt plus equity (cf. *operating leverage).*

Financial markets   Markets in which securities are issued and traded.

Flow-to-equity method   Discounts cash flows to equity after interest and taxes at the equity cost of capital.

Forward contract   Agreement to buy or sell an asset in the future at an agreed-upon price.

Forward exchange rate   Exchange rate fixed today for exchanging currency at some future date (cf. *spot exchange rate).*

forward interest rate Interest rate fixed today on a loan to be made at some future date (cf. spot interest rate).

Forward price Agreed-upon price for a *forward contract*.

Free cash flow (FCF) Cash not required for operations or for reinvestment.

Fudge factors A fudge factor is a figure included in a calculation to account for an unquantified influence.

Full-payout lease *Financial lease*.

Full-service lease (rental lease) *Lease* in which the *lessor* promises to maintain and insure the equipment (cf. *net lease*).

Futures contract A contract to buy a commodity or security on a future date at a price that is fixed today. Unlike forward contracts, futures are traded on organized exchanges and are *marked to market* daily.

Futures exchange Exchange where *futures contracts* are traded.

G

generally accepted accounting principles (GAAP) Procedures for preparing financial statements.

H

Hedge fund An investment fund charging a performance fee and open to a limited range of investors. Funds often follow complex strategies including *short sales*.

Hedge ratio (delta, option delta) The number of shares to buy for each *option* sold to create a safe position; more generally, the number of units of an asset that should be bought to hedge one unit of a liability.

High-yield bond *Junk bond*.

Horizontal merger *Merger* between two companies that manufacture similar products (cf. *vertical merger, conglomerate merger*).

I

Indenture Formal agreement, that is, establishing the terms of a *bond* issue.

Initial public offering (IPO) A company's first public issue of *common stock*.

Intangible assets Assets that have no physical substance, such as patents, brands, and corporate culture.

Internal rate of return (IRR) *Discount rate* at which investment has zero *net present value*.

Investment opportunity set The possible combinations of expected return and risk that an investor can achieve by combining the available assets into a portfolio.

IPO *Initial public offering*.

J

Junk bond (high-yield bond) Debt that is rated below an *investment-grade bond*.

K

Keiretsu A network of Japanese companies organized around a major bank.

L

Lease Long-term rental agreement.

Lessee User of a leased asset (cf. *lessor*).

Lessor Owner of a leased asset (cf. *lessee*).

Leveraged buyout (LBO) Acquisition in which (1) a large part of the purchase price is debt-financed and (2) the remaining *equity* is privately held by a small group of investors.

Leveraged lease *Lease* in which the *lessor* finances part of the cost of the asset by an issue of debt secured by the asset and the lease payments.

Limited liability Limitation of a shareholder's losses to the amount invested.

Liquidity Ability to sell an asset on short notice at close to the market price.

Lockbox system Form of *concentration banking*. Customers send payments to a post office box. A local bank collects and processes the checks and transfers surplus funds to the company's principal bank.

M

Management buyout (MBO) *Leveraged buyout* whereby the acquiring group is led by the firm's management.

Margin Cash or securities set aside by an investor as evidence that he or she can honor a commitment.

Marked to market An arrangement whereby the profits or losses on a *futures* contract are settled up each day.

Market capitalization Market value of outstanding share capital.

Market portfolio The portfolio of all stocks in the economy, where the weights correspond to the fraction of the overall market that each stock represents.

Market risk (systematic risk) Risk that cannot be diversified away.

Market value added Difference between market value and book value of firm's equity.

Market-to-book ratio Ratio of market value to book value of firm's *equity*.

MBO *Management buyout*.

Medium-term note (MTN)   Debt with a typical maturity of 1 to 10 years offered regularly by a company using the same procedure as *commercial paper*.

Mezzanine financing   A form of finance that is senior only to common equity. It can be either debt or preferred stock.

Money market   Market for short-term safe investments.

Monoline insurer   A monoline insurance company is one that insures only one kind of insurance.

Monte Carlo simulation   Method for calculating the probability distribution of possible outcomes, that is, from a project.

Mortgage bond   *Bond* secured against property.

Mutual fund   Managed investment fund whose shares are sold to investors.

Mutually exclusive projects   Two projects that cannot both be undertaken.

N

Negotiable certificate of deposit (CD)   A certificate for a time deposit of $1 million or more that can be sold before maturity.

Net lease   *Lease* in which the *lessee* promises to maintain and insure the equipment (cf. *full-service lease*).

Net present value (NPV)   A project's net contribution to wealth—*present value* minus initial investment.

Net working capital   *Current assets* minus *current liabilities*.

Note   Unsecured debt with a maturity of up to 10 years.

Notional value   Face value of an instrument on which the calculation of payments are based.

O

Open-end fund   A company whose assets consist of investments in a number of companies. Investors can purchase from the fund or redeem shares with it at any time and the number of shares adjusts to reflect these purchases and redemptions.

Operating lease   Short-term, cancelable *lease* (cf. *financial lease*).

Operating profit margin   After-tax operating income as a percentage of sales.

Opportunity cost of capital (hurdle rate, cost of capital)   *Expected return* that is foregone by investing in a project rather than in comparable financial securities.

P

Par value   Face value of a bond.

Payback period   Time until the cumulative cash flow equals the initial investment.

Payback rule   Requirement that project should recover its initial investment within a specified time.

Payout ratio   *Dividend* as a proportion of earnings per share.

Pension fund   Investment plan set up by an employer to provide for employees' retirement.

Perpetuity   Investment offering a level stream of cash flows in perpetuity (cf. *consol*).

Perpetuity due   *Perpetuity* whose payments occur at the start of each period.

Perquisites   Special benefits that accrue as a result of a person's job.

Preferred stock   Stock that takes priority over common stock in regard to *dividends*. Dividends may not be paid on *common stock* unless the dividend is paid on all preferred stock (cf. *cumulative preferred stock*). The dividend rate on preferred is usually fixed at time of issue.

Present value (PV)   Discounted value of future cash flows.

Privatization   Sale of a government-owned company to private investors.

Profitability index   Ratio of a project's *NPV* to the initial investment.

Project finance   Debt that is a claim against the cash flows from a particular project rather than against the firm as a whole.

Promised yield   The yield promised by a bond issuer if there is no default.

Prospectus   Summary of the *registration statement* providing information on an issue of securities.

Put option   *Option* to sell an asset at a specified *exercise price* on or before a specified exercise date (cf. *call option*).

Put–call parity   The relationship between the prices of European *put* and *call options*.

PVGO   *Present value of growth opportunities.*

R

Rate of return   Total income and capital appreciation per period per dollar invested.

Real assets   *Tangible assets* and *intangible assets* used to carry on business (cf. *financial assets*).

Real option   The flexibility to modify, postpone, expand, or abandon a project.

Registration statement   A detailed document prepared for the Securities and Exchange Commission that presents information about a firm's proposed financing and the firm's history, existing business, and plans for the future.

Rental lease   *Full-service lease.*

Replicating portfolio   Package of assets whose returns exactly replicate those of an *option*.

Responsible business   A business that seeks to create value for shareholders through creating value for society.

Return on assets (ROA)   After-tax operating income as a percentage of total assets.

Return on capital (ROC)   After-tax operating income as a percentage of long-term capital.

Return on equity (ROE)   Net income as a percentage of the book value of equity.

Revolving credit   Legally assured *line of credit* with a bank.

ROE   *Return on equity.*

S

Sale and lease-back   Sale of an existing asset to a financial institution that then *leases* it back to the user (cf. *direct lease*).

Scenario analysis   Analysis of the profitability of a project under alternative economic scenarios.

Securities   Claims on *real assets.*

Security market line (SML)   Line representing the relationship between *expected return* and *market risk.*

Self-liquidating loan   Loan to finance *current assets.* The sale of the current assets provides the cash to repay the loan.

Sensitivity analysis   Considers how different uncertain inputs to a model affect the output.

Shareholder capitalism   A form of capitalism in which managers' sole objective is to act in shareholders' interests.

Specific risk (idiosyncratic risk, residual risk, unique risk, unsystematic risk)   Risk that can be eliminated by diversification.

Spin-off   Distribution of shares in a subsidiary to the company's shareholders so that they hold shares separately in the two firms.

Spot exchange rate   Exchange rate on currency for immediate delivery (cf. *forward exchange rate).*

Spot price   Price of asset for immediate delivery (in contrast to *forward* or *futures* price).

Spot rate   Interest rate fixed today on a loan that is made today (cf. *forward interest rate).*

Stakeholder capitalism   A form of capitalism in which managers act in the interest of employees, customers, suppliers, communities, the government, and the environment, as well as shareholders.

Standard deviation   Square root of the *variance*—a measure of variability.

Stripped bond (strip)   *Bond* that is subdivided into a series of *zero-coupon bonds.*

T

Tangible assets   Physical assets such as oil fields, factories, and machines—assets you can touch.

Term loan   Medium-term, privately placed loan, usually made by a bank.

Term structure of interest rates   Relationship between interest rates on loans of different maturities (cf. *yield curve).*

Trade credit   *Accounts receivable.*

Trust deed   Agreement between trustee and borrower setting out terms of a *bond.*

V

Variance   Mean squared deviation from the expected value; a measure of variability.

Vertical merger   *Merger* between a supplier and its customer (cf. *horizontal merger, conglomerate merger).*

W

Warrant   Long-term *call option* issued by a company.

Working capital   *Current assets* less *current liabilities.* The term is commonly used as synonymous with *net working capital.*

Y

Yield to maturity   *Internal rate of return* on a bond.

Index